SUMMARY OF SELECTED FINANCIAL RATIOS

RATIO NAME	FORMULA	PAGE REFERENCE*
Liquidity Analysis		
Working capital	Current Assets − Current Liabilities	67, 667
Current ratio	$\frac{\text{Current Assets}}{\text{Current Liabilities}}$	68, **79,** 668
Acid-test ratio (quick ratio)	$\frac{\text{Cash + Marketable Securities + Current Receivables}}{\text{Current Liabilities}}$	668
Cash flow from operations to current liabilities ratio	$\frac{\text{Net Cash Provided by Operating Activities}}{\text{Average Current Liabilities}}$	669
Accounts receivable turnover ratio	$\frac{\text{Net Credit Sales}}{\text{Average Accounts Receivable}}$	**344,** 669
Number of days' sales in receivables	$\frac{\text{Number of Days in the Period}}{\text{Accounts Receivable Turnover}}$	670
Inventory turnover ratio	$\frac{\text{Cost of Goods Sold}}{\text{Average Inventory}}$	254, **255,** 671
Number of days' sales in inventory	$\frac{\text{Number of Days in the Period}}{\text{Inventory Turnover}}$	671
Cash-to-cash operating cycle	Number of Days' Sales in Inventory + Number of Days' Sales in Receivables	671
Solvency Analysis		
Debt-to-equity ratio	$\frac{\text{Total Liabilities}}{\text{Total Stockholders' Equity}}$	672
Times interest earned ratio	$\frac{\text{Net Income + Interest Expense + Income Tax Expense}}{\text{Interest Expense}}$	673
Debt service coverage ratio	$\frac{\text{Cash Flow from Operations before Interest and Tax Payments}}{\text{Interest and Principal Payments}}$	673
Cash flow from operations to capital expenditures ratio	$\frac{\text{Cash Flow from Operations} - \text{Total Dividends Paid}}{\text{Cash Paid for Acquisitions}}$	674
Profitability Analysis		
Gross profit ratio	$\frac{\text{Gross Profit}}{\text{Net Sales}}$	**233,** 666
Profit margin ratio	$\frac{\text{Net Income}}{\text{Net Sales}}$	**81,** 666
Return on assets ratio	$\frac{\text{Net Income + Interest Expense, Net of Tax}}{\text{Average Total Assets}}$	676
Return on sales ratio	$\frac{\text{Net Income + Interest Expense, Net of Tax}}{\text{Net Sales}}$	676
Asset turnover ratio	$\frac{\text{Net Sales}}{\text{Average Total Assets}}$	401, 676
Return on common stockholders' equity ratio	$\frac{\text{Net Income} - \text{Preferred Dividends}}{\text{Average Common Stockholders' Equity}}$	677
Earnings per share	$\frac{\text{Net Income} - \text{Preferred Dividends}}{\text{Weighted Average Number of Common Shares Outstanding}}$	679
Price/earnings ratio	$\frac{\text{Current Market Price}}{\text{Earnings per Share}}$	679
Dividend payout ratio	$\frac{\text{Common Dividends per Share}}{\text{Earnings per Share}}$	536, 680
Dividend yield ratio	$\frac{\text{Common Dividends per Share}}{\text{Market Price per Share}}$	680
Cash flow adequacy	$\frac{\text{Cash Flow from Operating Activities} - \text{Capital Expenditures}}{\text{Average Amount of Debt Maturing over Next Five Years}}$	619, **620–621**

***boldface = Ratio Decision Model**

6E

Financial Accounting

The Impact on Decision Makers

Gary A. Porter
Senior Lecturer
University of Minnesota

•

Curtis L. Norton
Arizona State University

SOUTH-WESTERN
CENGAGE Learning™

Australia • Brazil • Canada • Mexico • Singapore • Spain • United Kingdom • United States

SOUTH-WESTERN
CENGAGE Learning™

Financial Accounting: The Impact on Decision Makers, 6th Edition
Gary A. Porter, Curtis L. Norton

VP/Editorial Director: Jack W. Calhoun

Editor-in-Chief: Rob Dewey

Acquisitions Editor: Matthew Filimonov

Sr. Developmental Editor: Craig Avery

Editorial Assistant: Heather McAuliffe

Marketing Manager: Steven E. Joos

Marketing Coordinator: Gretchen Wildauer

Marketing Communications Manager: Elizabeth Shipp

Sr. Content Project Manager: Kim Kusnerak

Technology Project Manager: Robin Browning

Manufacturing Coordinator: Doug Wilke

Production Service: LEAP Publishing Services, Inc.

Composition: International Typesetting and Composition

Copyeditor: Marianne Miller

Art Directors: Linda Helcher/Stacy Jenkins Shirley

Internal Designer: Chris A. Miller Design

Cover Designer: Beckmeyer Design

Cover Image: Michael Grimm/Digital Vision/© Getty Images

Photography Manager: John Hill

Photo Researcher: Sam Marshall

Library of Congress Control Number: 2007940877
Student Edition ISBN 13: 978-0-324-65523-0
Student Edition ISBN 10: 0-324-65523-1
Instructor's Edition ISBN 13: 978-0-324-65849-1
Instructor's Edition ISBN 10: 0-324-65849-4
Instructor's Edition Book Only ISBN 13: 978-0-324-65848-4
Instructor's Edition Book Only ISBN 10: 0-324-65848-6

South-Western Cengage Learning
5191 Natorp Boulevard
Mason, OH 45040
USA

Cengage Learning products are represented in Canada by Nelson Education, Ltd.

For your course and learning solutions, visit **academic.cengage.com**
Purchase any of our products at your local college store or at our preferred online store **www.ichapters.com**

Printed in Canada
1 2 3 4 5 10 09 08 07

To those who really "count":
Melissa
Kathy, Amy, Andrew

PREFA

Start Them Of with Porter/Norto

OUR GOAL has been consistent from day one: A stud financial accounting course needs to understand how to re comprehend a simple annual report. Even more, that student needs to be able to discern what information is needed to make sound business decisions. This is why, from the very first edition, we have pursued a careful balance between a preparer perspective and a user focus. From our experience, students need to understand both how transactions are recorded and statements are prepared, and also how accounting information is used and why it is important to decision-making.

What is new for the sixth edition is our increased emphasis on study materials written and focused on how students actually learn and prefer to study. Extensive feedback from both students and educators reveals the need to keep students motivated by offering a number of opportunities to review and test their knowledge. Frequent reinforcement and instant feedback builds confidence and success.

> "If I need help and there is no professor around, the instant feedback from the textbook is like your own personal tutor."
>
> —Tia Pinkelton, Northern Kentucky University

From our balanced perspective to our focus on how students actually learn, we invite you to discover why Porter/Norton will Start Your Students Off Right!

REVISI

89.2°
imm

goals by focusing our innovation on how we

and Focus Students. The sixth edition continues our streamlined approach that emphasizes key points. Extensive rveys on student learning behavior reveal that a majority of stu- ave their book broken up into readily mastered segments. That's why ent in-text opportunities for review and feedback in the form of our inno- w **Portable On-Demand (POD) Reviews**.

"Instant feedback helps me understand where I went wrong before finishing it and having to start over."

—Karalyn Schierberg,
Northern Kentucky University

POD REVIEW 1.2

LO2 *Distinguish among the forms of organization.*

- Some entities are organized to earn a profit while others are organized to serve various segments of society.
- The three forms of business entities are sole proprietorships, partnerships, and corporations.

QUESTIONS

1. *Kellogg's is organized as which of the following business entities?*
   a. sole proprietorship
   b. partnership
   c. corporation
   d. none of the above

2. *One of the advantages of the corporate form of organization is*
   a. the ease of transfer of ownership.
   b. the limited liability of the stockholder.
   c. the ability to raise large amounts of capital in a relatively brief period of time.
   d. all of the above are advantages of the corporate form of organization.

"Introductory accounting students are often overwhelmed and need assistance in understanding major topics of importance. POD Reviews help students understand what is most vital in the chapter information."

—Dori Danko,
Grand Valley State University

"POD Reviews will help students with test preparation. Quizzing at regular intervals should lead to better exam performance."

—Christopher Denstel,
Louisiana State University

Students Succeed When They Know Why Accounting Is Important. Using real-world, relevant flagship companies like Nike, Apple, Starbucks, and Coca-Cola helps show why accounting is important to a business. Experience has shown that knowing the why helps students succeed.

Getting an 'A' in Accounting Is Still About Homework. Experience shows that student success is still largely a measure of doing homework. That is why this book contains a range of problems and exercises—including A & B problems, review problems, warm-up exercises, and more—that are designed to motivate and build skills in a systematic, step-by-step manner. The addition of **Brief Exercises** enhances this important success tool.

BRIEF EXERCISES

LO1 **Brief Exercise 4-1** Measurement in Financial Statements

What are two possible attributes to be measured when an item is to be included in financial statements? What unit of money is used to measure items in the United States?

LO2 **Brief Exercise 4-2** Accrual Basis of Accounting

For the following situations, indicate the date on which revenue would be recognized, assuming the accrual basis of accounting.

______ a. On June 10, a customer orders a product over the phone. The product is shipped to the customer on June 14, and the customer pays the amount owed on July 10.

______ b. On March 15, a law firm agrees to draft a legal document for a client. The document is completed and delivered to the client on April 5, and the client pays the amount owed on May 2.

______ c. A homeowner signs a contract on August 6 to have a company install a central air conditioning system. The work is completed on August 30, and the homeowner pays the amount owed on September 25.

LO3 **Brief Exercise 4-3** Revenue Recognition

Explain whether a company must have an inflow of an asset to be able to recognize revenue. Also give two examples of situations in which revenue is earned continuously over a period of time.

Solutions to brief exercises appear in the solutions manual.

93% of instructors consider completing homework to be either very or critically important to student success in accounting

47% of students consider completing homework to be either very or critically important to success in accounting

KEY FEATURES IN THIS EDITION

START THEM OFF RIGHT!

NEW! Portable On-Demand (POD) Reviews provide opportunities to review and test students' knowledge after each learning outcome. The POD Reviews, consisting of learning outcome, key points for the section just read, and two or three short multiple-choice questions, give instant feedback to students to help them master key concepts. Found after each chapter outcome, the POD Reviews combine a conceptual overview with a quick quiz to engage students in the content.

"The POD Reviews are an excellent idea. Placing them after every learning objective creates immediate feedback and affirmation of their understanding."

—Benjamin W. Bean, Utah Valley State College

POD REVIEW 3.1

LO1 *Explain the difference between an external and internal event.*

- Both of these different types of events affect an entity and are usually recorded in the accounting system as a transaction.
  - External events are interactions between an entity and its environment.
  - Internal events are interactions entirely within an entity.

QUESTIONS

1. *Which of the following events is not an external event?*
   a. a sale to a customer
   b. a purchase of inventory from a supplier
   c. payment to the newspaper for advertising
   d. recognition of the use of equipment by the recording of depreciation

2. *Which of the following is necessary to recognize an event as a transaction?*
   a. It must be subject to measurement.
   b. It must be an external event.
   c. It must be an internal event.
   d. It must be an event that recurs regularly.

Answers to POD Reviews appear at the end of the chapter.

Enhanced Journal Entry Model. Students need to understand how transactions affect the financial statements. The sixth edition, like previous editions, supplements nearly all journal entries with the accounting equation. The sixth edition enhances this feature to include a **transaction-effects equation** that reflects how each transaction affects the income statement and balance sheet. This more conceptual approach helps students see both the preparation of journal entries and debits and credits and the impact of decisions on the balance sheet and income statement.

The adjusting entry for the month of March is as follows:

Mar. 31	Interest Expense	150	
	Interest Payable		150
	To record interest for one month on a 9%, $20,000 loan.		

		Balance Sheet				Income Statement
ASSETS	=	**LIABILITIES**	+	**STOCKHOLDERS' EQUITY**	+	**REVENUES − EXPENSES**
		Interest Payable 150				Interest Expense (150)

The same adjusting entry is made at the end of April.

Apr. 30	Interest Expense	150	
	Interest Payable		150
	To record interest for one month on a 9%, $20,000 loan.		

		Balance Sheet				Income Statement
ASSETS	=	**LIABILITIES**	+	**STOCKHOLDERS' EQUITY**	+	**REVENUES − EXPENSES**
		Interest Payable 150				Interest Expense (150)

The entry on Granger's books on May 30 when it repays the principal and interest is as follows:

May 30	Interest Payable	300	
	Interest Expense	150	
	Notes Payable	20,000	
	Cash		20,450
	To record payment of a 9%, 90-day, $20,000 loan with interest.		

Balance Sheet								Income Statement	
ASSETS		=	LIABILITIES		+	STOCKHOLDERS' EQUITY	+	REVENUES − EXPENSES	
Cash	(20,450)		Interest Payable	(300)				Interest Expense	(150)
			Notes Payable	(20,000)					

Learning Outcomes Approach. The use of Learning Outcomes throughout the book and supplements, rather than Learning Objectives, reflects a fundamental shift in our philosophy about how instructors should be able to access and use quizzing and testing for pre-testing, post-testing, and assessment.

MAKE SOUND BUSINESS DECISIONS

Financial Decision Framework. Chapter 1 introduces a framework for financial decision making as a process that illustrates how to use financial information to make business and investment decisions.

1. **Formulate the Question**
2. **Gather Information**
3. **Read the Financials**
4. **Analyze the Financials**
5. **Make the Decision**
6. **Assess the Decision**

Using this model, students learn not only what accounting is and who uses financial information, but also how that information is the basis for decision making.

Enhanced Ratio Decision Model. Each time a ratio is introduced, the Ratio Decision Model walks students step-by-step through developing and using a financial ratio from financial statement excerpts that highlight ratio terms. To encourage critical thinking, the model depicts the financial statement line items that actually make up the ratio to help students understand where the numbers come from. Most importantly, the model highlights the interrelationship of the statements and the numbers and emphasizes the importance of comparing the results with both prior performance and industry competitors.

New in the sixth edition, the Ratio Decision Model includes two years of ratios for both the focus company and one of its competitors to allow better comparisons.

USING THE RATIO DECISION MODEL: ANALYZING THE CURRENT RATIO

Use the following Ratio Decision Model to evaluate the current ratio for General Mills or any other public company.

1. Formulate the Question
Managers, investors, and creditors are all interested in a company's liquidity. They must be able to answer the following question:

Is the company liquid enough to pay its obligations as they come due?

2. Gather the Information from the Financial Statements
The current ratio measures liquidity. To calculate the ratio, it is essential to know a company's current assets and liabilities. Current assets are the most liquid of all assets. Current liabilities are the debts that will be paid the soonest.

- Current assets: From the balance sheet
- Current liabilities: From the balance sheet

3. Calculate the Ratio

$$\text{Current Ratio} = \frac{\text{Current Assets}}{\text{Current Liabilities}}$$

General Mills
Partial Balance Sheet

	May 28, 2006
Assets	
Total current assets	$3,176
Liabilities and Stockholders' Equity	
Total current liabilities	$6,138

$$\text{Current Ratio} = \frac{\$3{,}176}{\$6{,}138} = 0.52 \text{ to } 1$$

4. Compare the Ratio with Others
Ratios are of no use in a vacuum. It is necessary to compare them with prior years and with competitors.

General Mills		Kellogg's	
May 28, 2006	May 29, 2005	December 30, 2006	December 31, 2005
0.52 to 1	0.73 to 1	0.60 to 1	0.69 to 1

5. Interpret the Results
In general, the higher the current ratio, the more liquid the company. However, earlier in the chapter you learned that rules of thumb do not always apply. It is necessary to take into account the nature of a company's business when evaluating ratios and other measures of performance. Also, ratios should be compared with those of prior years and with the same ratios of competitors. However, it should be noted that in making comparisons, the year-end is different for General Mills (end of May) and Kellogg's (end of December). Both companies operate with a relatively low current ratio compared to companies in other industries.

Ethical Decision Model. In the wake of accounting and business scandals of the last few years, the sixth edition provides a step-by-step ethical analysis and decision tool that students can rely on to help them base their business decisions on ethical and social principles throughout their careers.

ENGAGE RELEVANT FINANCIAL INFORMATION

NEW Flagship Companies provide relevance and promote critical thinking. Excerpts from both the Kellogg's and General Mills annual reports are included to provide relevance to the role of accounting in business. Also, the inclusion of two reports from companies in the same field allow for comparisons that encourage critical thinking.

REVISED Concentration on Fewer Real-World Financial Statements. Examples are generated from the chapter-opening company to reinforce concepts with clear, easy-to-follow examples. A focus on fewer companies and examples minimizes distracting and complicated alternative financial formats and numbers. Students can concentrate on learning one business or one industry and one set of financial statements that apply to the company example within the chapter.

Coverage of the PCAOB, Sarbanes-Oxley, Auditing Standards for Internal Control, and International Accounting Issues. In response to the accounting and reporting scandals that have occurred in the last few years, the sixth edition introduces the role of Sarbanes-Oxley and the PCAOB in Chapter 1. Chapter 6 devotes an entire section to Sarbanes-Oxley in the context of internal control. Students are exposed to Section 404 of SOX and the new management report on internal control required by this monumental legislation.

The text has provided coverage of international accounting issues where appropriate, and the book's Web site (www.academic.cengage.com/accounting/porter) will be used to update adopters as further developments occur relating to the use of international accounting standards.

CHAPTER-BY-CHAPTER CHANGES

Chapter 1: Accounting as a Form of Communication

- Integrated the "Getting Started in Business" module with Chapter 1 to provide a seamless introduction to the role of accounting in a business.
- Added Kellogg's as the new focus company for Chapter 1. Chosen for its straightforward financial statements and high brand recognition, Kellogg's provides an ideal opportunity to introduce students to the relevance of financial accounting. A portion of Kellogg's 10-K is reproduced in the appendix, allowing for a comparison case with General Mills, Chapter 2's focus company.
- Included the statement of cash flows in Exhibit 1-10 showing the relationships among the financial statements.
- Moved "The Accounting Profession" from Chapter 1 to Appendix A at the end of the book. Based on reviewer feedback, this change allows students to better focus on essential material.
- Added a brief section on the role of auditors in determining whether accounting standards are being followed ahead of the discussion of ethics and the introduction of an ethical decision model.
- Added a fuller discussion of the harmonization of accounting standards, as this convergence of U.S. and international accounting standards and practices is an issue that future business students will likely face.
- Within the section on ethics, added a Hot Topics feature illustrating why Kellogg's was named one of the most ethical companies for 2007.
- In addition to the new Brief Exercises, the following end-of-chapter material is new or updated: New: DC1-3; Updated: E1-13, P1-8, P1-8A, P1-9A, DC1-1, DC1-2.

Chapter 2: Financial Statements and the Annual Report

- Added General Mills as the focus company for Chapter 2. General Mills is a well-known industry competitor to Chapter 1's Kellogg's and is used as a comparison company in the Ratio Decision Model on the current ratio and profit margin in this chapter. Like Kellogg's, General Mills's financial statements are very straightforward.
- Changed the chapter company examples to focus on a hypothetical retail business from the service company used in the fifth edition. Based on reviewer feedback, this chapter employs Dixon Sporting Goods to introduce the financial statements. Instructors indicated that they prefer to cover inventories and cost of goods sold early in the book.
- Reinstated coverage of the operating cycle in connection with a return to a focus on product companies rather than service companies. This key coverage was suggested by reviewers' desire for early treatment of inventories and cost of goods sold.
- Included General Mills's complete balance sheet to give students a full picture of this statement. (In the fifth edition, the balance sheet for the chapter focus company was a condensed version.)
- Added a Hot Topics feature on Kraft Foods' search for a buyer for its Post® cereals: Would the buyer General Mills or Kellogg's?
- In addition to the new Brief Exercises, the following end-of-chapter material is new or updated: New: DC2-1; Updated: P2-10, P2-10A, DC2-2.

Chapter 3: Processing Accounting Information

- Added Southwest Airlines as the focus company for Chapter 3. The operation of an airline is easy for students to understand, and they can easily relate to how an airline generates revenue and the types of expenses it incurs.
- Introduced a new transaction format at the end of the chapter, which is used in the remainder of the text. The new format includes both the journal entry and a **transaction-effects equation** showing the effect of the entry on the financial statements.
- Replaced the term *owner's equity* with *stockholders' equity* to reflect the public-corporation focus of the book, starting in the transaction analysis equation and carried through elsewhere in the chapter.
- Added a Hot Topics feature on Southwest Airlines teaming up with PayPal to make buying its tickets online safer. This allows instructors to link online purchases with revenues on Southwest's income statement featured in the chapter.
- In addition to the new Brief Exercises, the following end-of-chapter material is new or updated: New: DC3-1; Updated: DC3-2, DC3-3.

Chapter 4: Income Measurement and Accrual Accounting

- Added Nordstrom, Inc. as the focus company for Chapter 4. Students buy products from retailers such as Nordstrom and can easily understand the nature of their business. For example, a new section was added to illustrate how Nordstrom recognizes revenue and reports liabilities arising from the use of gift cards.
- Began using the new transaction-effects equation as an element with all journal entries to provide a conceptual basis for recording transactions.
- Added a Hot Topics feature on Nordstrom's announced return of $1.5 billion to stockholders. Generation of excess cash comes in the context of the chapter opener's discussion of accruals, deferrals, and accounts receivable for the company, introduced in this chapter.
- Added explanation of the receivables that arise from two different forms of credit Nordstrom extends to customers. One is from the company's own private label card and the other from its co-branded VISA® credit card.
- In addition to the new Brief Exercises, the following end-of-chapter material is new or updated: New: DC4-1; Updated: E4-23, DC4-2, DC4-3.

Chapter 5: Inventories and Cost of Goods Sold

- Added Gap Inc. as the focus company for Chapter 5. Gap's brands are highly recognized, particularly with college students.
- Moved the operating cycle coverage to Chapter 2 for better and earlier integration of a business that sells a product.
- Added a Hot Topics feature on Gap Inc.'s closing of its Forth & Towne stores and the accounting implications shown in the 2007 financial statements.
- In addition to the new Brief Exercises, the following end-of-chapter material is new or updated: New: DC5-1, DC5-3; Updated: E5-16, P5-2, P5-6, P5-9, P5-15, P5-16, P5-2A, P5-6A, P5-9A, P5-15A, DC5-2.

Chapter 6: Cash and Internal Control

- Added Sears Holdings Corp. as the focus company for Chapter 6. Focusing on cash and cash equivalents is graphically illustrated in the opener using the first line of Sears' balance sheet.
- Added a Hot Topics feature on the merger of Sears and K-Mart that focuses on cash flows and the management of excess cash as a key to the success of the combined companies.
- Revised the Sarbanes-Oxley coverage around Sears' management report on its internal controls and on its auditors' report on internal control.
- In addition to the new Brief Exercises, the following end-of-chapter material is new: DC6-1.

Chapter 7: Receivables and Investments

- Updated the Apple chapter opener with the most current information available and replaced the financial statements for Apple, Inc. as the focus company for Chapter 7. Apple has high name recognition among students, and the company has been in the spotlight recently with the introduction of its new iPhone.
- Chapter 7 has undergone significant revision and reorganization:
  - Receivables is placed at the start of the chapter, prior to investments. This order is more logical, as companies often invest excess cash from the collection of their receivables. Thus, investments follow receivables.
  - Coverage of investments has been consolidated into the body of the chapter with the elimination of the appendix in the fifth edition. In doing so, the coverage has been streamlined considerably, with the elimination of any discussion of the distinction between trading securities and available-for-sale securities.
- Added a Hot Topics feature covering Apple's record-setting third-quarter 2007 revenues.
- In addition to the new Brief Exercises, the following end-of-chapter material is new or updated: New: DC7-3; Updated: E7-3, P7-3, P7-3A, DC7-1, DC7-2.

Chapter 8: Operating Assets: Property, Plant, and Equipment, and Intangibles

- Updated the Nike chapter opener with the most current information available and replaced the financial statements for Nike as the focus company for Chapter 8.
- Eliminated coverage of natural resources as a result of reviewer comments.
- Added a Hot Topics feature on Nike's introduction of it ZOOM footwear, depending on Nike's brand identity as a valuable intangible asset.
- In addition to the new Brief Exercises, the following end-of-chapter material is new or updated: New: DC8-1, DC8-2; Updated: P8-11, P8-11A.

Chapter 9: Current Liabilities, Contingencies, and the Time Value of Money

- Added Starbucks as the focus company for Chapter 9.
- Included new information on Starbucks and its competitors to allow for clean industry-specific comparisons. Also new is supporting end-of-chapter material to engage students.
- Deleted material on the use of the calculator for time value of money. This allows the instructor to focus on the two preferred methods: use of time value tables and the use of Excel®. Both of these methods appear at the end of the chapter.
- Updated Exhibit 9-1 on current and quick ratios to focus only on Starbucks and its industry competitors, based on reviewer comments.
- Added a Hot Topics feature that focuses on a possible contingent liability: lawsuits targeting Starbucks' use of milk having artificial growth hormone.
- Deleted the appendix on payroll accounting as a result of reviewer feedback.
- In addition to the new Brief Exercises, the following end-of-chapter material is new: P9-2, P9-3, P9-2A, P9-3A, DC9-1, DC9-2, DC9-3, DC9-4.

Chapter 10: Long-Term Liabilities

- Updated the Coca-Cola chapter opener with the most current information available and replaced the financial statements as the focus company for Chapter 10. Focuses on Coke's long-term growth plans needing long-term investments to support that growth.
- Deleted material on the use of the calculator to calculate present value of bonds. This change was made for consistency with the elimination of calculators for time value in Chapter 9.
- Deleted the appendix on pensions, as reviewers indicated that it was beyond the scope of the introductory financial accounting course.
- Added a separate Learning Outcome (and related Brief Exercise) to support the chapter's ratio coverage.

- Added a Hot Topics feature comparing Coca-Cola and PepsiCo for product introductions and how much these companies depend on long-term financing.
- In addition to the new Brief Exercises, the following end-of-chapter material is new or updated: New: DC10-1, DC10-2; Updated: P10-10, P10-10A, DC10-3.

Chapter 11: Stockholders' Equity

- Added Southwest Airlines as the focus company for Chapter 11. Southwest's performance is key to building shareholder value, shown by its stockholders' equity section.
- All exhibits that include actual company information were replaced with new companies for continued relevance.
- Shortened and made more concise the section on preferred stock for easier review by students.
- Added a Hot Topics feature on Southwest's 124th consecutive dividend in the face of a number of future challenges found in its 2006 annual report.
- In addition to the new Brief Exercises, the following end-of-chapter material is new or updated: New: DC11-1, DC11-2; Updated: P11-7, 11-7A.

Chapter 12: The Statement of Cash Flows

- Updated the chapter opener with the most current information available and replaced the financial statements from Best Buy as the focus company for Chapter 12. Best Buy increased its cash and cash equivalents by 60% in 2006, and an updated cash flows analysis is continued in the chapter.
- Updated Exhibit 12-1 comparing cash flows of various companies to include Best Buy competitor Circuit City.
- Added a Hot Topics feature on Best Buy's 2007 statement of cash flows that reported expenditure of $733 million on additions to property and equipment.
- In addition to the new Brief Exercises, the following end-of-chapter material is new: DC12-1, DC12-2, DC12-3.

Chapter 13: Financial Statement Analysis

- Updated the chapter opener with the most current information available and replaced the financial statements from Wm. Wrigley Jr. Co. as the focus company for Chapter 13.
- Added a Hot Topics feature on how Wrigley's financed its purchase of a Russian premium chocolate maker.
- In addition to the new Brief Exercises, the following end-of-chapter material is new or updated: New: DC13-3; Updated: E13-3, E13-4, E13-5, E13-6, DC13-1, DC13-2, DC13-4.

Appendix A: The Accounting Profession

- Based on reviewer feedback, this topic was moved from Chapter 1.

Appendix B: Excerpts from Kellogg's Form 10-K for 2006

- New for this edition is Kellogg's, the focus company used in Chapter 1.

Appendix C: Excerpts from General Mills's Form 10-K for 2006

- New for this edition is General Mills, the focus company used in Chapter 2.

SUPPLEMENTS

CengageNOW™ for Porter/Norton, *Financial Accounting: The Impact on Decision Makers* is an **online teaching and learning resource** that gives you **more control in less time** and **delivers better outcomes**—NOW. CengageNOW offers all of your teaching and learning resources in one place to help teach an accounting course. CengageNOW satisfies students who prefer to use digital resources to study. CengageNOW includes:

- Homework
- Interactive Course Assignments
- Personalized Study Plans
- Integrated eBook
- Assessment Options
- Course Management Tools, including Grade Book

Flexible Assignment Options. With CengageNOW's flexible homework and gradebook options, you can automatically grade all end-of-chapter assignments, weigh grades, choose points or percentages, and set the number of attempts and due dates per problem to best suit your overall course plan. Furthermore, all end-of-chapter exercises and problems are included, and select activities can be algorithmically modified to create unlimited versions for testing and practice.

Measure Course Outcomes. CengageNOW can not only help improve student performance, but also provides information you can use. Students can master key concepts and prepare for exams with CengageNOW's Personalized Study—a diagnostic program plus study plan—preloaded with an Integrated eBook and other text-specific material. In addition, CengageNOW identifies and reports content and results as it relates to accounting course outcomes (AACSB, AICPA, and ACBSP) through quizzing, assessment options, homework exercises, problems, and tutorials.

Instructors, contact your Cengage sales representative about the CengageNOW version that's right for you.

HELPING STUDENTS SUCCEED

Excel® Templates. Many problems in each chapter may be solved on a Microsoft Excel spreadsheet to increase student awareness of basic software applications. Those selected assignments that may be solved using the Excel spreadsheets are identified by icons in the text. Downloadable from the Student Resources page of the product Web site.

Web Resources. Many helpful Web resources, including quizzes, topical discussions, POD Review audio downloads, and more, are available for students to access. These items help reinforce and shed light on text topics. We invite you to discover more by logging into the text Web site.

"POD Reviews keep students alert and break the chapter up into manageable learning objectives. Great idea!"

—Paul Copley, James Madison University

HELPING INSTRUCTORS SHINE

Beyond the extraordinary advantages of using **CengageNOW™**, an unsurpassed package of supplementary resources helps you plan, manage, and teach your course. Additionally, special resources are available to help assess the progress of your students.

Instructor's Resource CD-ROM (ISBN 0-324-65843-5). This all-in-one resource contains all of the key instructor ancillaries. The Instructor's Manual, by Catherine Lumbattis (Southern Illinois University), contains detailed lecture outlines, lecture topics, and suggestions for classroom activities. The Solutions Manual, by the text authors, consists of solutions to all the end-of-chapter material keyed to learning outcomes and using the new transaction-effects equation notation for journal entries. The Test Bank, by Andrew Morgret (University of Memphis), contains a comprehensive set of test items to meet every assessment need from brief exercises to problems and decision cases. The Test Bank in ExamView® is an easy-to-use test-creation program making it simple to customize tests to your specific class needs as you edit or create questions and store customized exams. An ideal tool for online testing on its own, ExamView is also included within CengageNOW. Instructor PowerPoint slides are also included on the Instructor's Resource CD-ROM as well as downloadable from the instructor resource page of the text's Web site (www.academic.cengage.com/accounting/porter), which contains the solutions manual, instructor's manual, PowerPoint® and presentation slides, giving instructors the ultimate tool for customizing lectures and presentations.

Instructor's PowerPoint® Slides. Located on the Instructor's Resource CD-ROM and on the text's Web site, these colorful slides, by Catherine Lumbattis (Southern Illinois University), reinforce chapter content and provide a rich tool for in-class lectures and out-of-class reviewing.

Assessment Tools. The testing materials accompanying the sixth edition were revised to accommodate your need to accurately assess student performance outcomes and measure progress towards achieving departmental and college objectives.

ACKNOWLEDGMENTS

REVIEWERS

Throughout the course of our writing, we are indebted to those individuals who provided valuable guidance to our ongoing efforts. These include:

Sheryl J. Alley, Ball State University
Monica Banyi, Oregon State University
Benjamin W. Bean, Utah Valley State College
Paul Copley, James Madison University
Marcia Croteau, University of Maryland, Baltimore County
Dori Danko, Grand Valley State University
Christopher E. Denstel, Louisiana State University
Robert Derstine, Villanova University
Cathy Duffy, Carthage College
Carolyn Galantine, Pepperdine University
Abo Habib, Minnesota State University, Mankato
Shelley Kane, Wake Technical Community College
Howard Keller, Indiana University, Indianapolis
Yaw M. Mensah, Rutgers University
Charles J. Russo, Bloomsburg University of Pennsylvania
Gary Schader, Keane University
Albert Schepanski, University of Iowa
Richard Schroeder, University of North Carolina, Charlotte
L. Murphy Smith, Texas A&M University
Pamela S. Stuerke, University of Missouri, St. Louis
Bill Talbot, Montgomery College
Manjuri Talukdar, Northern Illinois University
Christian Wurst, Temple University

We also wish to thank participants in a financial accounting survey whose findings helped guide us in our revision.

Throughout the first five editions, many other individuals have contributed helpful suggestions that have resulted in many positive changes. Although they are not cited here, we remain grateful for their assistance.

We also wish to thank several individuals whose help with supplements and verification have aided us in the revision: Philip Babin (University of Memphis), Chris Jonick (Gainesville State College), Leslie Kauffman (LEAP Publishing), Cathy Lumbattis (Southern Illinois University, Carbondale), Andy Morgret (University of Memphis), Janice Stoudemire (Midlands Technical College), Sara Wilson (Cats Publishing), Jeff Wong (University of Nevada, Reno), and Gail Wright (Bryant College). We are grateful to Malvine Litten and her staff at LEAP Publishing for their invaluable production assistance. Finally, we are grateful to the editorial and marketing staff at Cengage, primarily Matt Filimonov, Craig Avery, Steve Joos, Robin Browning, and Kim Kusnerak for their extensive help with the sixth edition.

Gary A. Porter
Curtis L. Norton
November 2007

MEET THE AUTHORS

Gary A. Porter earned Ph.D. and M.B.A. degrees from the University of Colorado and his B.S.B.A. from Drake University. Recently retired as Professor of Accounting, Dr. Porter served as Department Chair and taught at numerous universities. He is currently a Senior Lecturer at the University of Minnesota. Dr. Porter has published in the *Journal of Accounting Education, Journal of Accounting, Auditing & Finance,* and *Journal of Accountancy*, among others, and has conducted numerous workshops on the subjects of introductory accounting education and corporate financial reporting.

Dr. Porter's professional activities include experience as a staff accountant with Deloitte & Touche in Denver, a participant in KPMG Peat Marwick Foundation's Faculty Development program, and a leader in numerous bank training programs. He has won an Excellence in Teaching Award from the University of Colorado and Outstanding Professor Awards from both San Diego State University and the University of Montana. He served on the Illinois CPA Society's Innovations in Accounting Education Grants Committee, the steering committee of the Midwest region of the American Accounting Association, and the board of directors of the Chicago chapter of Financial Executives International.

Curtis L. Norton is a Professor Emeritus at Northern Illinois University in DeKalb, Illinois, where he has taught since 1976. He currently is teaching in NIU's highly acclaimed CPA Review program. He is also a Visiting Professor at Arizona State University at the West Campus. He earned his Ph.D. from Arizona State University, his M.B.A. from the University of South Dakota, and his B.S. from Jamestown College, North Dakota. His extensive list of publications include articles in *Accounting Horizons, The Journal of Accounting Education, Journal of Accountancy, Journal of Corporate Accounting, Journal of the American Taxation Association, Real Estate Review, The Accounting Review, CPA Journal*, and many others. In 1988–1989, Dr. Norton received the University Excellence in Teaching Award, the highest university-wide teaching recognition at NIU. He is also a consultant and has conducted training programs for governmental authorities, bank, utilities, and other entities.

Dr. Norton is a member of the American Accounting Association and a member and officer of Financial Executives International.

BRIEF CONTENTS

CONTENTS

© Getty Images

Each chapter contains some or all of the following end-of-chapter material:

• Ratio Review • Accounts Highlighted • Key Terms Quiz • Alternate Terms • Warmup Exercises & Solutions • Review Problem & Solution • Appendix Review Problem & Solution • Questions • Brief Exercises • Exercises • Multiconcept Exercises • Problems • Multiconcept Problems • Alternate Problems • Alternate Multiconcept Problems • Decision Cases • Solutions to Key Terms Quiz • Answers to POD Review

© James F. Quinn/MCT/Landov

© AP Photo/Mark Lennihan

© Amy Etra/PhotoEdit. All rights reserved.

© AP Photo/Paul Sakuma

© Justin Sullivan/Getty Images

© Justin Sullivan/Getty Images

CHAPTER 7 Receivables and Investments 334

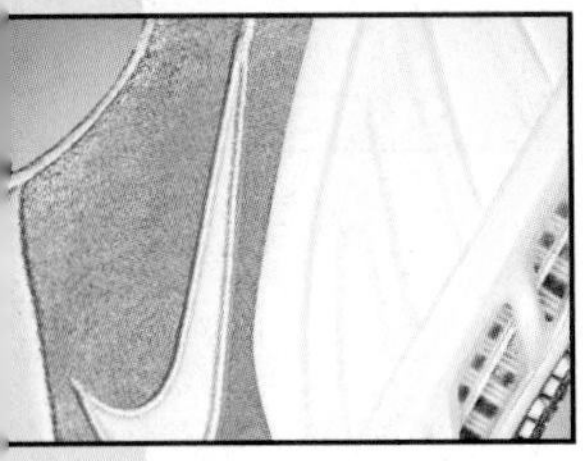

© PRNewsFoto/NIKE

CHAPTER 8 Operating Assets: Property, Plant, and Equipment, and Intangibles 376

© Bob Pardue/Alamy

CHAPTER 9 Current Liabilities, Contingencies, and the Time Value of Money 424

© Christian Veron/Reuters/Landov

© AP Photo/Mark Lennihan

CHAPTER 1

Accounting as a Form of Communication

Learning Outcomes

After studying this chapter, you should be able to:

LO1 Explain what business is about.

LO2 Distinguish among the forms of organization.

LO3 Describe the various types of business activities.

LO4 Define accounting and identify the primary users of accounting information and their needs.

LO5 Explain the purpose of each of the financial statements and the relationships among them and prepare a set of simple statements.

LO6 Identify and explain the primary assumptions made in preparing financial statements.

LO7 Identify the various groups involved in setting accounting standards and the role of auditors in determining whether the standards are followed.

LO8 Explain the critical role that ethics play in providing useful financial information.

Study Links...

A Look at This Chapter

Business is the foundation upon which accounting rests. After a brief introduction to business, we begin the study of accounting by considering what accounting is and who uses the information it provides. We will see that accounting is an important form of communication and that financial statements are the medium that accountants use to communicate with those who have some interest in the financial affairs of a company.

A Look at Upcoming Chapters

Chapter 1 introduces accounting and financial statements. Chapter 2 looks in more detail at the composition of the statements and the conceptual framework that supports the work of an accountant. Chapter 3 steps back from financial statements and examines how companies process economic events as a basis for preparing the statements. Chapter 4 completes the introduction to the accounting model by considering the importance of accrual accounting in this communication process.

Kellogg Company

MAKING BUSINESS DECISIONS

Pick your favorite company. Maybe it is Abercrombie & Fitch because you buy all of your clothes there. Or maybe it is Google because you use its search engine nearly every day. Or is it Coca-Cola because you like its commercials? At any rate, have you ever considered how the company got started? Consider Kellogg Company. The Battle Creek, Michigan–based cereal company got its start over one hundred years ago when two brothers by sheer chance discovered toasted flakes. W. K. Kellogg and his brother, Dr. John Harvey Kellogg, were cooking wheat for a type of granola, left for a while, and came back to find that the wheat had become stale. They put the wheat through the rollers anyway, and what came out was a thin flake. From this came the formation of the Battle Creek Toasted Corn Flake Company, the forerunner of Kellogg Company.

From this modest start, Kellogg Company has grown to the point that it employs 25,000 people around the globe, manufactures its products in 17 countries, and markets those products in more than 180 countries. The company's brand names are among the most recognizable in the world, including such heavyweights as Kellogg's®, Keebler®, Rice Krispies®, and Special K®.

As you will see throughout your study of business, all companies must make decisions and all decisions inherently involve risks. When the Kellogg brothers made the decision to form their company in 1906, they risked some of their own money to start a business that eventually revolutionized the way people eat breakfast. Over the course of one hundred years, Kellogg Company has faced any number of other critical decisions. One of the most far-reaching of these decisions was made in 2001 when it finalized the acquisition of Keebler Foods Company. At one time in its history, cereal was Kellogg Company's only business. The company's product mix changed dramatically in 2001 when it acquired Keebler, a leading producer of cookies and crackers, for over $4 billion.

How does management of a company, its stockholders, and others interested in the financial well-being of a company know if the company is making good business decisions? Was Keebler "worth" the $4 billion that Kellogg Company paid for it? Although questions such as these have no clear-cut answers, the numbers produced by an accounting system go a long way in assessing a company's financial performance. Consider the Financial Highlights shown here as they appeared in Kellogg Company's 2006 annual report. The first chart shows that sales have increased for six consecutive years, not coincidentally the length of time since the company acquired Keebler. Net sales in 2006 reached nearly $11 billion. Operating profit, a measure that gives an indication as to how well a company is controlling the costs necessary to generate sales, has also risen steadily over this period, as shown in the second chart.

© Getty Images

Of course, it isn't just companies that use financial information in making decisions. For example, when you were deciding whether to enroll at your present school, you needed information about the tuition and other costs at the different schools you were considering. When a stockbroker decides whether to recommend to a client the purchase of stock in a company, the broker needs information about the company's profits and needs to know whether it pays dividends. When trying to decide whether to loan money to a company, a banker must consider the company's current debts.

This book explores how accounting can help everyone make informed decisions. Before turning to the role of

(*continued*)

accounting in decision making, we need to explore business in more detail. Then we turn to the measures that accountants use to assess a company's performance:

- What is business? (See pp. 4–5.)
- What forms of organization carry on business activities? (See pp. 6–8.)
- In what types of business activities do those organizations engage? (See pp. 8–10.)
- What is revenue? How is it measured? (See pp. 16–17.)
- What is net income? How is it measured? (See pp. 16–17.)
- How do revenue and net income relate to a company's assets? (See pp. 15–17.)
- Where do the various items appear on a company's financial statements? (See pp. 15–18.)

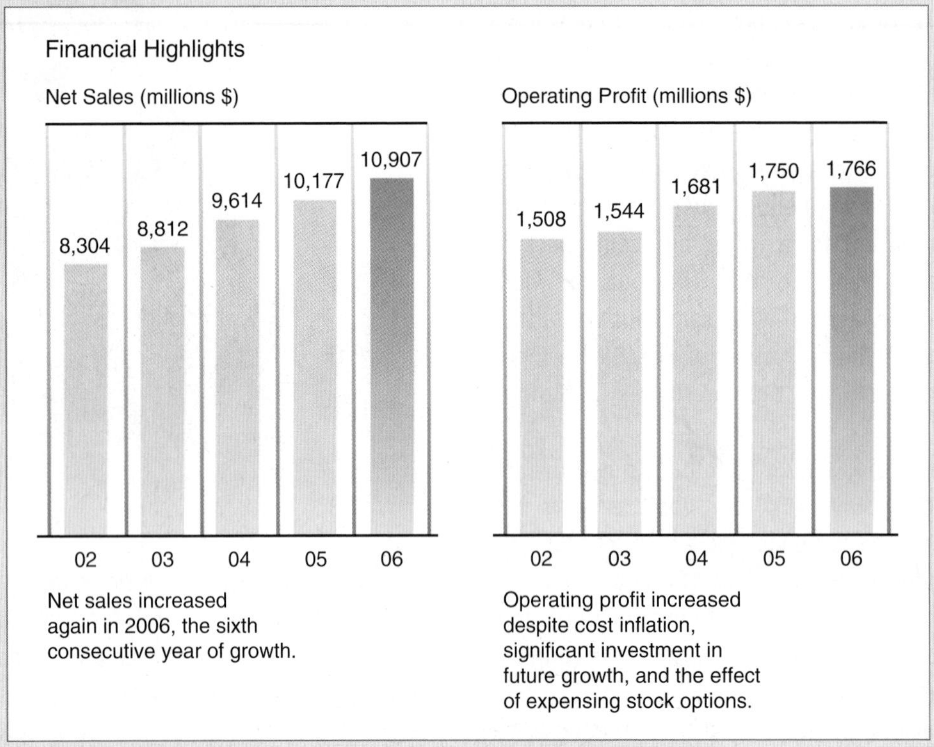

Source: Kellogg Company's web site and its 2006 annual report.

What Is Business?

LO1 Explain what business is about.

Business
All of the activities necessary to provide the members of an economic system with goods and services.

Just as Kellogg's got its start over one hundred years ago in Battle Creek, Michigan, your study of accounting has to start somewhere. All disciplines have a foundation on which they rest. For accounting, that foundation is business.

Broadly defined, **business** consists of all activities necessary to provide the members of an economic system with goods and services. Certain business activities focus on the providing of goods or products, such as ice cream, automobiles, and computers. Some of these companies, such as Kellogg's, produce or manufacture the products. Other companies are involved in the distribution of the goods, either as wholesalers (who sell to retail outlets) or retailers (who sell to consumers). Other business activities, by their nature, are service-oriented. Corporate giants such as **Citicorp**, **Walt Disney**, **Time Warner**, and **United Airlines** remind us of the prominence of service activities in the world today. The relatively recent phenomenon of various "service providers," such as health-care organizations and Internet companies, is a testimony to the growing importance of the service sector in the U.S. economy.

To appreciate the kinds of business enterprises in our economy, consider the various types of companies that have a stake in the delivery of a box of cereal to the grocery store.

First, Kellogg's must contract with various suppliers of the raw materials, such as grains that are needed to produce cereal. For example, assume that Kellogg's buys grains from Wholesome Wheat. As a *manufacturer* or *producer,* Kellogg's takes the grain and other various raw materials and transforms them into a finished product. At this stage, a *distributor* or *wholesaler* gets involved. For example, assume that Kellogg's sells cereal to Duffy's Distributors. Duffy's Distributors, in turn, sells the products to many different *retailers,* such as **Albertson's** and **Safeway**. Although maybe less obvious, any number of *service* companies are also involved in the process. For example, ABC Transport hauls the grains to Kellogg's for production, and others move the cereal along to Duffy's Distributors. Still others get the cereal to supermarkets and other retail outlets. Exhibit 1-1 summarizes the process.

EXHIBIT 1-1 **Types of Businesses**

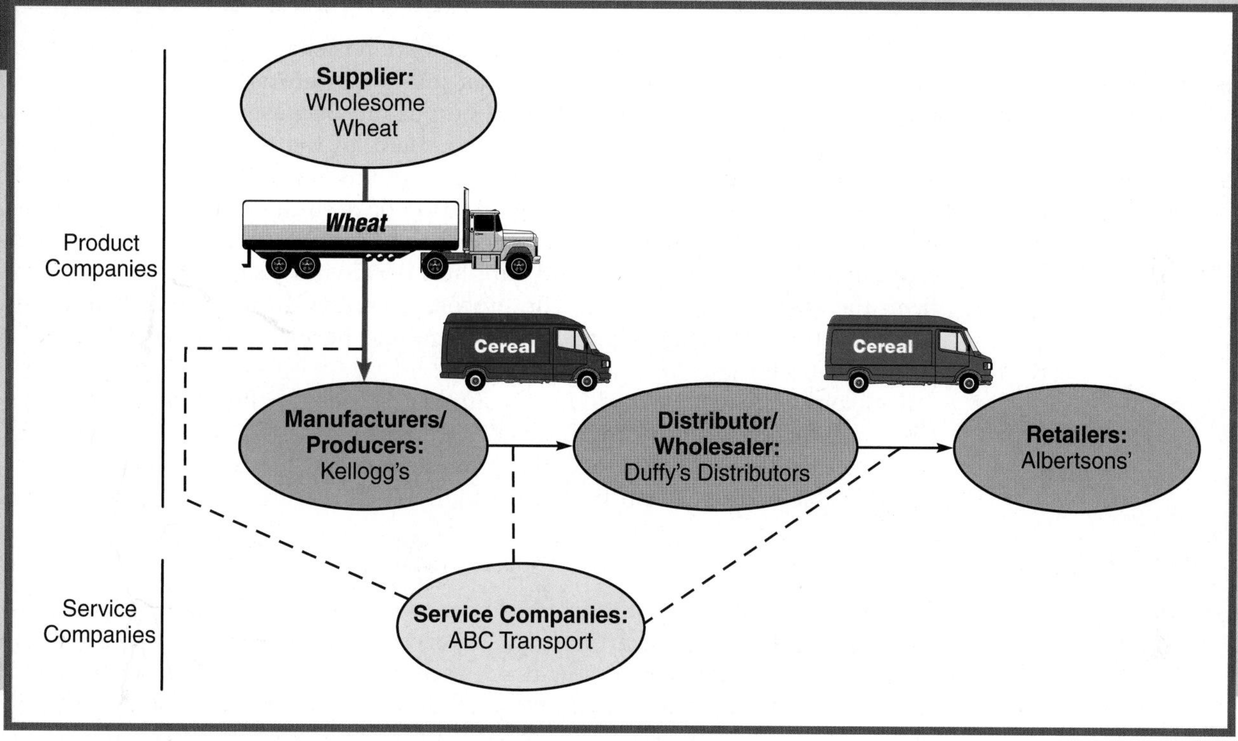

POD REVIEW 1.1

LO1 *Explain what business is about.*

- Business consists of all activities necessary to provide members of an economic system with goods and services. Suppliers, manufacturers, wholesalers, and retailers are examples of product companies.

QUESTIONS

1. *A department store is an example of a*
   a. wholesaler.
   b. manufacturer.
   c. retailer.
   d. supplier.

2. *An airline is an example of a*
   a. service provider.
   b. retailer.
   c. supplier.
   d. producer.

Forms of Organization

LO2 Distinguish among the forms of organization.

There are many different types of organizations in our society. One convenient way to categorize the myriad types is to distinguish between those that are organized to earn money and those that exist for some other purpose. Although the lines can become blurred, *business entities* such as Kellogg's generally are organized to earn a profit, whereas *nonbusiness entities* generally exist to serve various segments of society. Both types are summarized in Exhibit 1-2.

BUSINESS ENTITIES

Business entity
An organization operated to earn a profit.

Business entities are organized to earn a profit. Legally, a profit-oriented company is one of three types: a sole proprietorship, a partnership, or a corporation.

Sole proprietorship
A form of organization with a single owner.

Economic entity concept
The assumption that a single, identifiable unit must be accounted for in all situations.

Sole Proprietorships This form of organization is characterized by a single owner. Many small businesses are organized as **sole proprietorships**. Very often the business is owned and operated by the same person. Because of the close relationship between the owner and the business, the affairs of the two must be kept separate. This is one example in accounting of the **economic entity concept**, which requires that a single, identifiable unit of organization be accounted for in all situations. For example, assume that Bernie Berg owns a neighborhood grocery store. In paying the monthly bills, such as utilities and supplies, Bernie must separate his personal costs from the costs associated with the grocery business. In turn, financial statements prepared for the business must not intermingle Bernie's personal affairs with the company affairs.

Unlike the distinction made for accounting purposes between an individual's personal and business affairs, the Internal Revenue Service (IRS) does not recognize the separate existence of a proprietorship from its owner. That is, a sole proprietorship is not a taxable entity; any profits earned by the business are taxed on the return of the individual.

Partnership
A business owned by two or more individuals; the organization form often used by accounting firms and law firms.

Partnerships A **partnership** is a business owned by two or more individuals. Many small businesses begin as partnerships. When two or more partners start out, they need some sort of agreement as to how much each will contribute to the business and how they will divide any profits. In many small partnerships, the agreement is often just an oral understanding between the partners. In large businesses, the partnership agreement is formalized in a written document.

Although a partnership may involve just two owners, some have thousands of partners. Public accounting firms, law firms, and other types of service companies are often

EXHIBIT 1-2 **Forms of Organization**

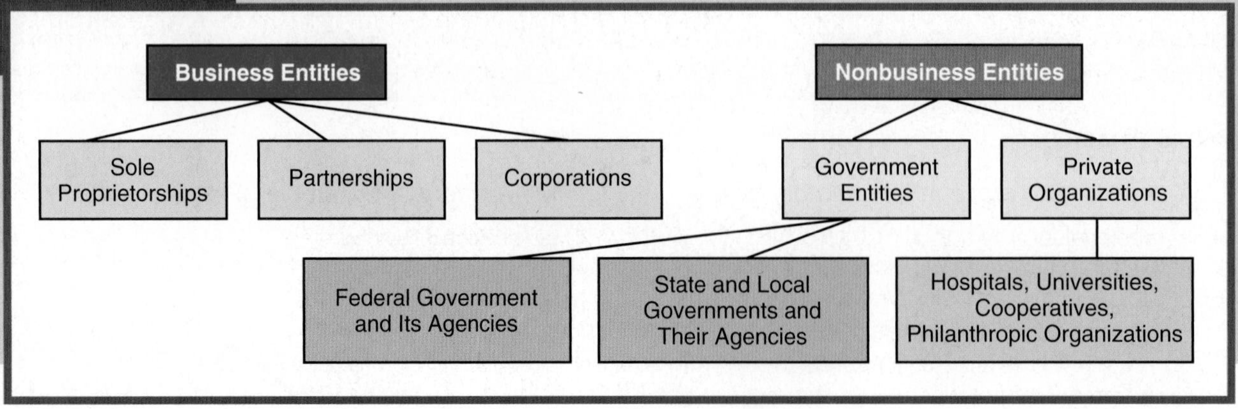

organized as partnerships. Like a sole proprietorship, a partnership is not a taxable entity. The individual partners pay taxes on their proportionate shares of the profits of the business.

Corporations Although sole proprietorships and partnerships dominate in sheer number, corporations control an overwhelming majority of the private resources in this country. A **corporation** is an entity organized under the laws of a particular state. Each of the 50 states is empowered to regulate the creation and operation of businesses organized as corporations in it. Even though Kellogg's is headquartered in Michigan, for legal reasons, it is incorporated under the laws of the state of Delaware.

Corporation
A form of entity organized under the laws of a particular state; ownership evidenced by shares of stock.

To start a corporation, one must file articles of incorporation with the state. If the articles are approved by the state, a corporate charter is issued, and the corporation can begin to issue stock. A **share of stock** is a certificate that acts as evidence of ownership in a corporation. Although not always the case, stocks of many corporations are traded on organized stock exchanges, such as the New York and American Stock Exchanges. Kellogg Company stock is traded on the New York Stock Exchange.

Share of stock
A certificate that acts as evidence of ownership in a corporation.

Advantages of Incorporation What are the advantages of running a business as a corporation?

- **One of the primary advantages of the corporate form of organization is the ability to raise large amounts of money in a relatively brief period of time.** This is what prompted Kellogg Company to eventually "go public." To raise money, the company sold a specific type of security: stock. As stated earlier, a share of stock is simply a certificate that evidences ownership in a corporation. Sometimes corporations issue another type of security called a bond. A **bond** is similar in that it is a certificate or piece of paper issued to someone. However, it is different from a share of stock in that a bond represents a promise by the company to repay a certain amount of money at a future date. In other words, if you were to buy a bond from a company, you would be lending it money. Interest on the bond is usually paid semiannually. You will learn more about stocks and bonds later.

Bond
A certificate that represents a corporation's promise to repay a certain amount of money and interest in the future.

- **The ease of transfer of ownership in a corporation is another advantage of this form of organization.** If you hold shares of stock in a corporation whose stock is actively traded and you decide that you want out, you simply call your broker and put in an order to sell. Another distinct advantage is the limited liability of the stockholder. Generally speaking, a stockholder is liable only for the amount contributed to the business. That is, if a company goes out of business, the most the stockholder stands to lose is the amount invested. On the other hand, both proprietors and general partners usually can be held personally liable for the debts of the business.

NONBUSINESS ENTITIES

Most **nonbusiness entities** are organized for a purpose other than to earn a profit. They exist to serve the needs of various segments of society. For example, a hospital is organized to provide health care to its patients. A municipal government is operated for the benefit of its citizens. A local school district exists to meet the educational needs of the youth in the community.

Nonbusiness entity
An organization operated for some purpose other than to earn a profit.

All of these entities are distinguished by the lack of an identifiable owner. The lack of an identifiable owner and of the profit motive changes to some extent the type of accounting used by nonbusiness entities. This type, called *fund accounting,* is discussed in advanced accounting courses. Regardless of the lack of a profit motive in nonbusiness entities, there is still a demand for the information provided by an accounting system. For example, a local government needs detailed cost breakdowns in order to levy taxes. A hospital may want to borrow money and will need financial statements to present to the prospective lender.

ORGANIZATIONS AND SOCIAL RESPONSIBILITY

Although nonbusiness entities are organized specifically to serve members of society, U.S. business entities also have become more sensitive to their broader social responsibilities. Because they touch the lives of so many members of society, most large corporations recognize the societal aspects of their overall mission and have established programs to meet their social responsibilities. Some companies focus their efforts on local charities, while others donate to national or international causes. All of the companies showcased in the chapter openers of this book have programs in place to meet their corporate giving objectives.

POD REVIEW 1.2

LO2 *Distinguish among the forms of organization.*

- Some entities are organized to earn a profit while others are organized to serve various segments of society.
- The three forms of business entities are sole proprietorships, partnerships, and corporations.

QUESTIONS

1. *Kellogg's is organized as which of the following business entities?*
   a. sole proprietorship
   b. partnership
   c. corporation
   d. none of the above

2. *One of the advantages of the corporate form of organization is*
   a. the ease of transfer of ownership.
   b. the limited liability of the stockholder.
   c. the ability to raise large amounts of capital in a relatively brief period of time.
   d. all of the above are advantages of the corporate form of organization.

The Nature of Business Activity

LO3 Describe the various types of business activities.

Because corporations dominate business activity in the United States, this book will focus on this form of organization. Corporations engage in a multitude of different types of activities. It is possible to categorize all of them into one of three types, however: financing, investing, and operating.

FINANCING ACTIVITIES

All businesses must start with financing. Simply put, money is needed to start a business. W. K. Kellogg needed money in 1906 to start his new company. The company found itself in need of additional financing later and thus eventually made the decision to sell stock to the public. Most companies not only sell stock to raise money but also borrow from various sources to finance their operations.

Liability
An obligation of a business.

Capital stock
Indicates the owners' contributions to a corporation.

Accounting has its own unique terminology. In fact, accounting is often referred to as *the language of business*. The discussion of financing activities brings up two important accounting terms: *liabilities* and *capital stock*. A **liability** is an obligation of a business; it can take many different forms. When a company borrows money at a bank, the liability is called a *note payable*. When a company sells bonds, the obligation is termed *bonds payable*. Amounts owed to the government for taxes are called *taxes payable*. Assume that Kellogg's buys corn to be used to produce Corn Flakes®. Assume that the supplier gives Kellogg's 30 days to pay the amount owed. During this 30-day period, Kellogg's has an obligation called *accounts payable*.

Capital stock is the term used by accountants to indicate the dollar amount of stock sold to the public. Capital stock differs from liabilities in one very important respect.

Those who buy stock in a corporation are not lending money to the business, as are those who buy bonds in the company or make a loan in some other form to the company. Someone who buys stock in a company is called a **stockholder**, and that person is providing a permanent form of financing to the business. In other words, there is not a due date at which time the stockholder will be repaid. Normally, the only way for a stockholder to get back his or her original investment from buying stock is to sell it to someone else. Someone who buys bonds in a company or in some other way makes a loan to it is called a **creditor**. A creditor does *not* provide a permanent form of financing to the business. That is, the creditor expects repayment of the amount loaned and, in many instances, payment of interest for the use of the money.

Stockholder
One of the owners of a corporation. ***Alternate term:*** *Shareholder.*

Creditor
Someone to whom a company or person has a debt. ***Alternate term:*** *Lender.*

INVESTING ACTIVITIES

There is a natural progression in a business from financing activities to investing activities. That is, once funds are generated from creditors and stockholders, money is available to invest.

An **asset** is a future economic benefit to a business. For example, cash is an asset to a company. To Kellogg's, its buildings and the equipment that it uses to make cereal are assets. At any time, Kellogg's has on hand raw materials and products in various stages of production. These materials and products are called *inventories* and are another valuable asset of the company.

Asset
A future economic benefit.

An asset represents the right to receive some sort of benefit in the future. The point is that not all assets are tangible in nature, as are inventories and buildings and equipment. For example, assume that Kellogg's sells cereal to one of its customers and allows the company to pay at the end of 30 days. At the time of the sale, Kellogg's doesn't have cash yet, but it has another valuable asset. The right to collect the amount due from the customer in 30 days is an asset called an *account receivable.* As a second example, assume that a company acquires from an inventor a patent that will allow the company the exclusive right to manufacture a certain product. The right to the future economic benefits from the patent is an asset. In summary, an asset is a valuable resource to the company that controls it.

At this point, you should notice the inherent tie between assets and liabilities. How does a company satisfy its liabilities, that is, its obligations? Although there are some exceptions, most liabilities are settled by transferring assets. The asset most often used to settle a liability is cash.

OPERATING ACTIVITIES

Once funds are obtained from financing activities and investments are made in productive assets, a business is ready to begin operations. Every business is organized with a purpose in mind. The purpose of some businesses is to sell a *product.* For example, Kellogg's was organized to produce and sell cereal. Other companies provide *services.* Service-oriented businesses are becoming an increasingly important sector of the U.S. economy. Some of the largest corporations in this country, such as banks and airlines, sell services rather than products.

Accountants have a name for the sale of products and services. **Revenue** is the inflow of assets resulting from the sale of products and services. When a company makes a cash sale, the asset it receives is cash. When a sale is made on credit, the asset received is an account receivable. Revenue represents the dollar amount of sales of products and services for a specific period of time.

Revenue
An inflow of assets resulting from the sale of goods and services.

We have thus far identified one important operating activity: the sale of products and services. However, costs must be incurred to operate a business. Kellogg's must pay its employees salaries and wages. Suppliers must be paid for purchases of inventory, and the utility company has to be paid for heat and electricity. The government must be paid the taxes owed it. All of these are examples of important operating activities of a business. Accountants use a specific name for the costs incurred in operating a business. An **expense** is the outflow of assets resulting from the sale of goods and services.

Expense
An outflow of assets resulting from the sale of goods and services.

Exhibit 1-3 summarizes the three types of activities conducted by a business. The discussion and the exhibit present a simplification of business activity; but actual businesses

EXHIBIT 1-3 A Model of Business Activities

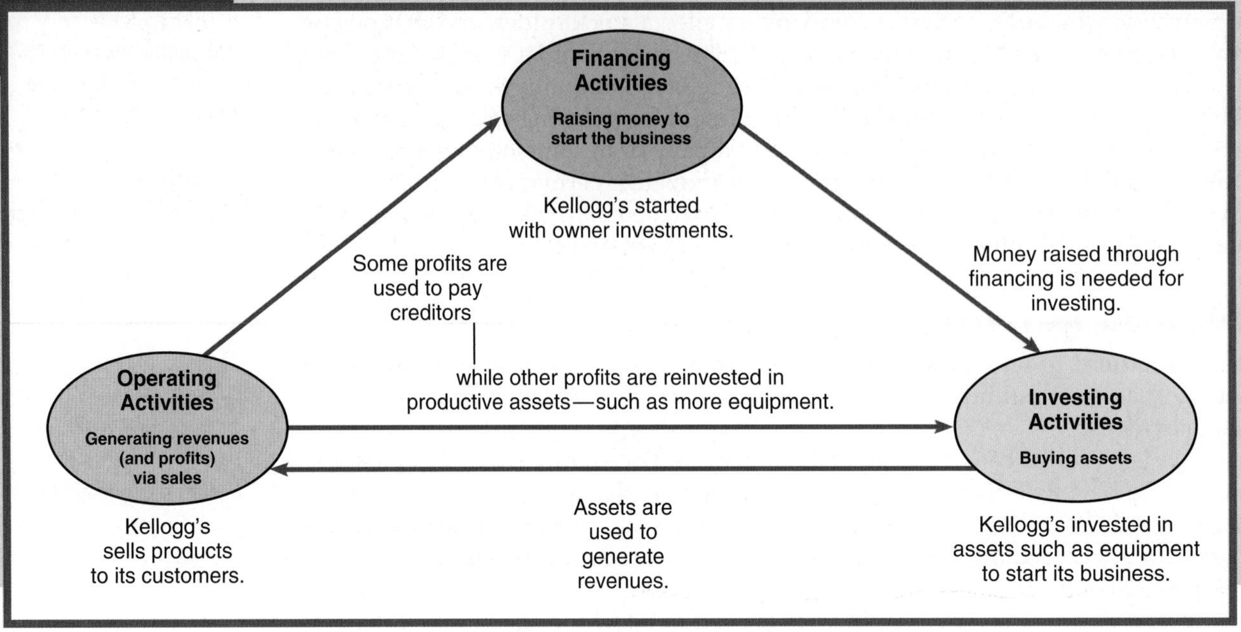

are in a constant state of motion with many different financing, investing, and operating activities going on at any one time. Still, the model as portrayed in Exhibit 1-3 should be helpful as you begin the study of accounting. To summarize, a company obtains money from various types of financing activities, uses the money raised to invest in productive assets, and then provides goods and services to its customers.

POD REVIEW 1.3

LO3 *Describe the various types of business activities.*

- All business activities can be categorized as being operating, investing, or financing activities.
- Financing activities involve raising money from contributions made by the owners of a business as well as obtaining loans from outsiders.
- Companies invest the amounts raised from financing activities in various types of assets, such as inventories, buildings, and equipment.
- Once funds are obtained and investments are made in productive assets, a business can begin operations. Operating activities involve providing goods and services to customers.

QUESTIONS

1. *Capital stock as a form of financing differs from borrowing because*
   a. stock has a due date.
   b. stock does not have a due date.
   c. borrowing is a permanent form of financing.
   d. there are no significant differences between the two forms of financing.

2. *Which of the following is* not *an asset?*
   a. accounts payable
   b. cash
   c. accounts receivable
   d. building

3. *The inflow of assets resulting from the sale of products and services is called a(n)*
   a. expense.
   b. asset.
   c. revenue.
   d. liability.

What Is Accounting and What Information Do Users of Accounting Reports Need?

LO4 Define accounting and identify the primary users of accounting information and their needs.

Accounting is not just a procedural record-keeping activity done by people who are "good at math." In fact, **accounting** is "the process of identifying, measuring, and communicating economic information to permit informed judgments and decisions by users of the information.[1]

Each of the three activities in this definition—*identifying, measuring,* and *communicating*—requires the judgment of a trained professional. Note that the definition refers to the users of economic information and the decisions they make. Who *are* the users of accounting information? We turn now to this important question.

Accounting
The process of identifying, measuring, and communicating economic information to various users.

USERS OF ACCOUNTING INFORMATION AND THEIR NEEDS

It is helpful to categorize users of accounting information on the basis of their relationship to the organization. Internal users, primarily the managers of a company, are involved in the daily affairs of the business. All other groups are external users.

INTERNAL USERS

The management of a company is in a position to obtain financial information in a way that best suits its needs. For example, if management of a Kellogg's production facility center needs to know whether the plant's revenues are enough to cover its operating costs, this information exists in the accounting system and can be reported. If the manager wants to find out if the monthly payroll is more or less than the budgeted amount, a report can be generated to provide the answer. **Management accounting** is the branch of accounting concerned with providing internal users (management) with information to facilitate planning and control. The ability to produce management accounting reports is limited only by the extent of the data available and the cost involved in generating the relevant information.

Management accounting
The branch of accounting concerned with providing management with information to facilitate planning and control.

EXTERNAL USERS

External users, those not directly involved in the operations of a business, need information that differs from that needed by internal users. In addition, the ability of external users to obtain the information is more limited. Without the day-to-day contact with the affairs of the business, outsiders must rely on the information presented to them by the management of the company.

Certain external users such as the IRS require that information be presented in a very specific manner, and they have the authority of the law to ensure that they get the required information. Stockholders, bondholders, and other creditors must rely on *financial statements* for their information.[2] **Financial accounting** is the branch of accounting concerned with communication with outsiders through financial statements.

Financial accounting
The branch of accounting concerned with the preparation of financial statements for outsider use.

1 American Accounting Association, *A Statement of Basic Accounting Theory* (Evanston, Ill.: American Accounting Association, 1966), p. 1.

2 Technically, stockholders are insiders because they own stock in the business. In most large corporations, however, it is not practical for stockholders to be involved in the daily affairs of the business. Thus, they are better categorized here as external users because they normally rely on general-purpose financial statements, as do creditors.

Stockholders and Potential Stockholders Both existing and potential stockholders need financial information about a business. If you currently own stock in Kellogg's, you need information that will aid in your decision either to continue to hold the stock or to sell it. If you are considering buying stock, you need financial information that will help in choosing among competing alternative investments. What has been the recent performance of the company in the stock market? What were its profits for the most recent year? How do these profits compare with those of the prior year? Did the company pay any dividends? One source for much of this information is the company's financial statements.

Bondholders, Bankers, and Other Creditors Before buying a bond in a company (remember you are lending money to the company), you need to feel comfortable that the company will be able to pay you the amount owed at maturity and the periodic interest payments. Financial statements can help you to decide whether to purchase a bond. Similarly, before lending money, a bank needs information that will help it determine the company's ability to repay both the amount of the loan and interest. Therefore, a set of financial statements is a key ingredient in a loan proposal.

Government Agencies Numerous government agencies have information needs specified by law. For example, the IRS is empowered to collect a tax on income from both individuals and corporations. Every year a company prepares a tax return to report to the IRS the amount of income it earned. Another government agency, the Securities and Exchange Commission (SEC), was created in the aftermath of the Great Depression. This regulatory agency sets the rules under which financial statements must be prepared for corporations that sell their stock to the public on organized stock exchanges. Similar to the IRS, the SEC prescribes the manner in which financial information is presented to it. Companies operating in specialized industries submit financial reports to other regulatory agencies, such as the Interstate Commerce Commission (ICC) and the Federal Trade Commission (FTC).

Other External Users Many other individuals and groups rely on financial information given to them by businesses. A supplier of raw material needs to know the creditworthiness of a company before selling it a product on credit. To promote its industry, a trade association must gather financial information on the various companies in the industry. Other important users are stockbrokers and financial analysts. They use financial reports in advising their clients on investment decisions. In reaching their decisions, all of these users rely to a large extent on accounting information provided by management. Exhibit 1-4 summarizes the various users of financial information and the types of decisions they must make.

USING FINANCIAL ACCOUNTING INFORMATION

As stated earlier, financial accounting is concerned with communication with external users. One of the primary external users of accounting information is a stockholder. The box on page 14 contains a Financial Decision Framework that can be used to help make investment decisions using financial accounting information. Here you'll consider whether to buy a company's stock.

For example, for the last few months, you have been eagerly awaiting an earnings announcement from Kellogg's. You have bought the company's products for a few years but never gave much thought to the financial side of its business.

You log on to Kellogg's web site; and after clicking on the Investor Relations link, you begin to wonder . . . should I or shouldn't I buy stock in the company? Use the Financial Decision Framework on page 14 to help you make a decision.

EXHIBIT 1-4 Users of Accounting Information

Categories of Users	Examples of Users	Common Decision	Relevant Question
Internal	Management	Should we build another plant?	How much will it cost to build the new plant?
External	Stockholder	Should I buy shares of Kellogg's stock?	How much did the company earn last year?
	Banker	Should I lend money to Kellogg's?	What debts or liabilities does the company have?
	Employee	Should I ask for a raise?	How much are the company's revenues, and how much is it paying out in salaries and wages? Is the compensation it is paying reasonable compared to its revenues?
	Supplier	Should I allow Kellogg's to buy grain from me and pay me later?	What is the current amount of the company's accounts payable?

POD REVIEW 1.4

LO4 *Define accounting and identify the primary users of accounting information and their needs.*

- The primary users of financial statements are those who depend on the economic information conveyed in those statements to make decisions. Primary users may be broadly classified as internal users and users external to the company.
  - Internal users are usually managers of a company.
  - External users include stockholders, investors, creditors, and government agencies.

QUESTIONS

1. *Which of the following groups is* not *an external user of accounting information?*
   a. stockholders
   b. bankers
   c. management
   d. all of the above are external users

2. *The branch of accounting that is concerned with communication with outsiders through financial statements is*
   a. management accounting.
   b. financial accounting.
   c. income tax accounting.
   d. none of the above.

FINANCIAL DECISION FRAMEWORK

Use the following decision process to help you make an investment decision about Kellogg's or any other public company.

1. Formulate the Question
For about the same amount I pay in a year for the company's products ($100) I could buy 2 shares of Kellogg's stock at $50 per share.

- Should I invest $100 in Kellogg's?

2. Gather Information from the Financial Statements and Other Sources
The information needed will come from a variety of sources:

- My personal finances at the present time
- Alternative uses for the $100
- The outlook for the industry
- Publicly available information about Kellogg's, including its financial statements

3. Analyze the Financials
The information in the financial statements can be used to perform:

- Ratio analysis (looking at relationships among financial statement items).
- Horizontal analysis (looking at trends over time).
- Vertical analysis (comparing financial statement items in a single period).
- Comparisons with competitors.
- Comparisons with industry averages.

4. Make the Decision
Taking into account all of the various sources of information, you decide either to:

- Use the $100 for something else.
- Invest the $100 in Kellogg's.

5. Interpret the Results
If you do decide to invest, you will want to monitor your investment periodically. Whether you made a good decision will be based on the answers to these two questions:

- Have I received any dividends on my shares?
- Has the price of the stock increased above the $50 per share that I paid?

A critical step in this framework is gathering information from the financial statements, the means by which an accountant communicates information about a company to those interested in it. We explore these statements in the next section.

Financial Statements: How Accountants Communicate

LO5 Explain the purpose of each of the financial statements and the relationships among them and prepare a set of simple statements.

The primary focus of this book is financial accounting. This branch of accounting is concerned with informing management and outsiders about a company through financial statements. We turn now to the composition of the four major statements: the balance sheet, the income statement, the statement of retained earnings, and the statement of cash flows.

THE ACCOUNTING EQUATION

The accounting equation is the foundation for the entire accounting system:

Assets = Liabilities + Owners' Equity

- **The *left side* of the accounting equation refers to the *assets* of the company.** Those items that are valuable economic resources and that will provide future benefit to the company should appear on the left side of the equation.

- **The *right side* of the equation indicates who provided, or has a claim to, those assets.** Some of the assets were provided by creditors, and they have a claim to them. For example, if a company has a delivery truck, the dealer that provided the truck to the company has a claim to the assets until the dealer is paid. The delivery truck would appear on the left side of the equation as an asset to the company; the company's *liability* to the dealer would appear on the right side of the equation. Other assets are provided by the owners of the business. Their claims to these assets are represented by the portion of the right side of the equation called **owners' equity**.

The term *stockholders' equity* is used to refer to the owners' equity of a corporation. **Stockholders' equity** is the mathematical difference between a corporation's assets and its obligations or liabilities. That is, after the amounts owed to bondholders, banks, suppliers, and other creditors are subtracted from the assets, the amount remaining is the stockholders' equity, the amount of interest or claim that the owners have on the assets of the business.

Stockholders' equity arises in two distinct ways. First, it is created when a company issues stock to an investor. As noted earlier, capital stock reflects ownership in a corporation in the form of a certificate. It represents the amounts contributed by the owners to the company. Second, as owners of shares in a corporation, stockholders have a claim on the assets of a business when it is profitable. **Retained earnings** represents the owners' claims to the company's assets that result from its earnings that have not been paid out in dividends. It is the earnings accumulated or retained by the company.

Study Tip

The accounting equation and the financial statements are at the heart of this course. Memorize the accounting equation, and make sure you study this introduction to how the financial statements should look, how to read them, and what they say about a company.

Owners' equity
The owners' claims on the assets of an entity.

Stockholders' equity
The owners' equity in a corporation.

Retained earnings
The part of owners' equity that represents the income earned less dividends paid over the life of an entity.

THE BALANCE SHEET

The balance sheet (sometimes called the *statement of financial position*) is the financial statement that summarizes the assets, liabilities, and owners' equity of a company. It is a snapshot of the business at a certain date. A balance sheet can be prepared on any day of the year, although it is most commonly prepared on the last day of a month, quarter, or year. At any point in time, the balance sheet must be "in balance." That is, assets must equal liabilities and owners' equity.

For a company such as Kellogg's, real financial statements can be quite complex, especially this early in your study of accounting. Therefore, before we attempt to read Kellogg's statements, we will start with a hypothetical company. Top of the World owns and operates a ski resort in the Rockies. The company's balance sheet on June 30, 2008, the end of its first year of business, is presented in Exhibit 1-5. As you study the exhibit, note the description for each item to help you understand it better.

Balance sheet
The financial statement that summarizes the assets, liabilities, and owners' equity at a specific point in time.
Alternate term: *Statement of financial position.*

EXHIBIT 1-5 **Top of the World's Balance Sheet**

Top of the World
Balance Sheet
June 30, 2008
(in thousands of dollars)

Assets		**Liabilities and Stockholders' Equity**	
Cash	$ 200	Accounts payable	$ 700
Accounts receivable	600	Salaries and wages payable	400
Land	4,000	Notes payable	3,000
Lodge, lifts, and equipment	2,500	Capital stock	2,000
		Retained earnings	1,200
Total assets	$7,300	Total liabilities and stockholders' equity	$7,300

Cash: Cash on hand as well as in checking and savings accounts
Accounts receivable: Amounts owed by customers
Land: The ski mountain owned by the company
Lodge, lifts, and equipment: The building, ski lifts, and ski equipment owned by the company
Accounts payable: Amounts owed to suppliers
Salaries and wages payable: Amounts owed to employees
Notes payable: Amounts owed to the bank
Capital stock: Owners' contributions to the corporation
Retained earnings: Income earned less dividends paid over life of corporation

EXHIBIT 1-6 The Relationship between the Accounting Equation and the Balance Sheet

Assets	=	Liabilities	+	Owners' Equity
Economic resources Examples: • Cash • Accounts receivable • Land		**Creditors' claims to the assets** Examples: • Accounts payable • Notes payable		**Owners' claims to the assets** Examples: • Capital stock • Retained earnings

Terminology Note: Exhibit 1-6 refers to Owners' Equity, while Exhibit 1-5 refers to Stockholders' Equity. Remember, both are correct! *Owners' equity* is the general term by which we refer to ownership. "Stockholders' equity" refers only to ownership of a corporation by shareholders. Because we emphasize corporations in this book, we will use the term *Stockholders' equity*.

Two items should be noted in the heading of the statement. First, the company chose a date other than December 31, the calendar year-end, to finish its accounting or fiscal year. Although December 31 is the most common year-end, some companies choose a date other than this to conclude their year. Often this choice is based on when a company's peak selling season is over. For example, **Gap Inc.**, ends its accounting year on the Saturday closest to January 31, after the busy holiday season. By June 30, Top of the World's ski season has ended and the company can devote its attention to preparing its financial statements. The second item to note in the heading of the statements is the last line: "in thousands of dollars." This means, for example, that rather than cash being \$200, the amount is actually 1,000 × \$200, or \$200,000.

Exhibit 1-6 summarizes the relationship between the accounting equation and the items that appear on a balance sheet.

Income statement
A statement that summarizes revenues and expenses.
Alternate term: *Statement of income.*

THE INCOME STATEMENT

An income statement, or statement of income as it is sometimes called, summarizes the revenues and expenses of a company for a period of time. An income statement for Top of the World for its first year in business is shown in Exhibit 1-7. **Unlike the**

EXHIBIT 1-7 Top of the World's Income Statement

Top of the World
Income Statement
For the Year Ended June 30, 2008
(in thousands of dollars)

	Revenues:		
Two types of revenue	Lift tickets	\$5,800	
	Equipment rentals	2,200	
	Total revenues		\$8,000
	Expenses:		
All costs of running a ski resort	Salaries and wages	\$2,000	
	Depreciation	100	
	Water, gas, and electricity	1,500	
	Insurance	1,100	
	Interest	300	
	Income taxes	1,000	
	Total expenses		6,000
	Net income		\$2,000

balance sheet, an income statement is a *flow* statement. That is, it summarizes the flow of revenues and expenses for the year. The top portion of Exhibit 1-7 makes it clear that the ski company has two distinct types of revenues: those from selling lift tickets and those from renting ski equipment. For example, if you paid the company $50 for a one-day lift ticket and another $30 to rent your equipment for the day, each of those amounts would be included in Top of the World's revenues for the year. The expenses reported on the income statement represent all of the various costs necessary to run a ski resort. For example, a significant cost for such an operation is its payroll, as represented by salaries and wages on the income statement. Note that the amount reported for salaries and wages expense on the income statement is not the same amount that appeared as salaries and wages payable on the balance sheet. The expense of $2,000 on the income statement represents the total cost for the year, while the payable of $400 on the balance sheet is the amount owed to employees on June 30, 2008. We will have much more to say in later chapters about differences between balance sheet and income statement items. Finally, note that the excess of revenues over expenses, or **net income**, appears as the bottom line on the income statement. A company's net income is sometimes referred to as its profits or earnings.

Net income
The excess of revenues over expenses. ***Alternate term:*** *Profits or earnings.*

THE STATEMENT OF RETAINED EARNINGS

As discussed earlier, Retained Earnings represents the accumulated earnings of a corporation less the amount paid in dividends to stockholders. **Dividends** are distributions of the net income or profits of a business to its stockholders. Not all businesses pay cash dividends. Among those companies that do pay dividends, the frequency with which they pay differs. For example, most companies that pay dividends do so four times a year.

Dividends
A distribution of the net income of a business to its owners.

A statement of retained earnings explains the change in retained earnings during the period. The basic format for the statement is as follows:

Statement of retained earnings
The statement that summarizes the income earned and dividends paid over the life of a business.

Beginning balance	$xxx,xxx
Add: Net income for the period	xxx,xxx
Deduct: Dividends for the period	xxx,xxx
Ending balance	$xxx,xxx

A statement of retained earnings for Top of the World is shown in Exhibit 1-8. Revenues minus expenses, or net income, is an increase in retained earnings; and dividends are a decrease in the balance. Why are dividends shown on a statement of retained earnings instead of on an income statement? Dividends are not an expense and thus are not a component of net income, as are expenses. Instead, they are a *distribution* of the income of the business to its stockholders.

Recall that stockholders' equity consists of two parts: capital stock and retained earnings. In lieu of a separate statement of retained earnings, many corporations prepare a comprehensive statement to explain the changes both in the various capital stock accounts and in retained earnings during the period. Kellogg's, for example, presents the more comprehensive statement of shareholders' equity.

EXHIBIT 1-8 **Top of the World's Statement of Retained Earnings**

Top of the World
Statement of Retained Earnings
For the Year Ended June 30, 2008
(in thousands of dollars)

Retained earnings, beginning of the year	$ 0
Add: Net income for the year	2,000
Deduct: Dividends for the year	(800)
Retained earnings, end of the year	$1,200

THE STATEMENT OF CASH FLOWS

Statement of cash flows The financial statement that summarizes a company's cash receipts and cash payments during the period from operating, investing, and financing activities.

The statement of cash flows summarizes the cash flow effects of a company's operating, investing, and financing activities for the period. In essence, it shows the reader where a company got cash during the year and how it used that cash. (We will have more to say about this in Chapter 2.)

A statement of cash flows for Top of the World is shown in Exhibit 1-9. Note the three categories of cash flow: operating, investing, and financing. The major source of cash to the company from its operations was the cash it collected from its customers. After deducting cash payments for operating activities, the ski company generated $2,600 from its operations. During the period, the company spent $6,600 on various assets. The last category shows that the issuance of a note generated $3,000 of cash and the issuance of stock produced another $2,000. Finally, the company paid dividends of $800. The net increase in cash from these three categories is $200; and since the company was new this year, this number is also its ending cash balance.

RELATIONSHIPS AMONG THE FINANCIAL STATEMENTS

Note the natural progression in the items from one statement to another. Normally, a company starts the period with balances in each of the items on its balance sheet. Because Top of the World is a new company, Exhibit 1-10 shows zero balances on July 1, 2007, the beginning of its first year in business. Next, the company operated during the year, the result was net income of $2,000 as shown on the income statement at the top of the exhibit. The net income naturally flows ❶ onto the statement of retained earnings. Again, because the ski company is new, its beginning retained earnings balance is zero. After the distribution of $800 to the owners in cash dividends ❷, ending retained earnings amounts to $1,200. The ending retained earnings

EXHIBIT 1-9 **Top of the World's Statement of Cash Flows**

Top of the World
Statement of Cash Flows
For the Year Ended June 30, 2008
(in thousands of dollars)

Cash flows from operating activities:		
Cash collected from customers		$ 7,400
Cash payments for:		
Salaries and wages	$ 1,600	
Water, gas, and electricity	1,500	
Insurance	400	
Interest	300	
Income taxes	1,000	
Total cash payments		4,800
Net cash provided by operating activities		$ 2,600
Cash flows from investing activities:		
Purchase of land	$(4,000)	
Purchase of lodge, lifts, and equipment	(2,600)	
Net cash used by investing activities		(6,600)
Cash flows from financing activities:		
Proceeds from issuance of long-term note	$ 3,000	
Proceeds from issuance of capital stock	2,000	
Dividends declared and paid	(800)	
Net cash provided by financing activities		4,200
Net increase in cash		$ 200
Cash at beginning of year		0
Cash at end of year		$ 200

EXHIBIT 1-10 Relationships among the Financial Statements

Top of the World
Income Statement
For Year Ended June 30, 2008

Revenues	$8,000
Less: Expenses	6,000
Net income	**$2,000** ❶

Top of the World
Statement of Retained Earnings
For Year Ended June 30, 2008

Beginning balance, retained earnings	$ 0
Add: Net income	**2,000** ❶
Deduct: Cash dividends	**(800)** ❷
Ending balance, retained earnings	**$1,200** ❸

Top of the World
Balance Sheets

	JUNE 30, 2008	JULY 1, 2007
Assets:		
Cash	$ 200 ❹	$0
Accounts receivable	600	0
Land	4,000	0
Lodge, lifts, and equipment	2,500	0
Total assets	$7,300	$0
Liabilities	$4,100	$0
Capital stock	2,000	0
Retained earnings	1,200 ❸	0
Total liabilities and stockholders' equity	$7,300	$0

Top of the World
Statement of Cash Flows
For Year Ended June 30, 2008

Net cash provided by operating activities	$ 2,600
Net cash used by investing activities	(6,600)
Net cash provided by financing activities	4,200
Net increase in cash	$ 200
Cash at beginning of year	0
Cash at end of year	**$ 200** ❹

number flows ❸ onto the ending balance sheet along with the other June 30, 2008, balance sheet items. Finally, the net increase in cash at the bottom of the statement of cash flows equals ❹ the amount shown on the June 30, 2008, balance sheet.

LOOKING AT FINANCIAL STATEMENTS FOR A REAL COMPANY: KELLOGG'S

You would certainly expect the financial statements of companies in the real world to be more complex than those for a hypothetical company such as Top of the World. Still, even this early in your study of accounting, there are certain fundamental points about all financial statements, real-world or otherwise, that you can appreciate.

Real World Practice

1-1 Reading Kellogg's Balance Sheet

State Kellogg's financial position on December 30, 2006, in terms of the accounting equation. What amount do Kellogg's customers owe on December 30, 2006? What amount does Kellogg's owe its suppliers on this same date?

KELLOGG'S BALANCE SHEET

Balance sheets for Kellogg's at the end of two recent years are shown in Exhibit 1-11. For comparative purposes, the company reports its financial position not only at the end of the most recent year, December 30, 2006, but also on December 31, 2005. Also note the statement across from the headings for the two years that the amounts are in millions of dollars. For example, this means that Kellogg's had $10,714 × 1,000,000, or $10,714,000,000, of total assets at the end of 2006.

TOTAL ASSETS: $10,714 × 1,000,000 = 10,714,000,000 = Approximately 10.7 billion dollars!

A quick comparison of Kellogg's assets with those of Top of the World reveals one significant difference. Because the ski company is a service company, it does not have an inventory account on its balance sheet. Conversely, "Inventories" of $823.9 million at the end of 2006 is a significant asset for Kellogg's. This account includes the various raw materials and products in various stages of production that have not yet been sold to customers.

Various types of liabilities are reported on Kellogg's balance sheets, and we will return to look more closely at many of these in later chapters. For now, it is worth

EXHIBIT 1-11 Kellogg's Balance Sheet

Consolidated Balance Sheet

(millions, except share data)	2006	2005
Current assets **[A]**		
Cash and cash equivalents	$ 410.6	$ 219.1
Accounts receivable, net	944.8	879.1
Inventories	823.9	717.0
Other current assets	247.7	381.3
Total current assets	$ 2,427.0	$ 2,196.5
Property, net	2,815.6	2,648.4
Other assets	5,471.4	5,729.6
Total assets	$10,714.0	$10,574.5
=		
Current liabilities **[L]**		
Current maturities of long-term debt	$ 723.3	$ 83.6
Notes payable	1,268.0	1,111.1
Accounts payable	910.4	883.3
Other current liabilities	1,118.5	1,084.8
Total current liabilities	$ 4,020.2	$ 3,162.8
Long-term debt	3,053.0	3,702.6
Other liabilities	1,571.8	1,425.4
+		
Shareholders' equity **[SE]**		
Common stock, $.25 par value, 1,000,000,000 shares authorized		
Issued: 418,515,339 shares in 2006 and 418,451,198 shares in 2005	104.6	104.6
Capital in excess of par value	292.3	58.9
Retained earnings	3,630.4	3,266.1
Treasury stock at cost: 20,817,930 shares in 2006 and 13,121,446 shares in 2005	(912.1)	(569.8)
Accumulated other comprehensive income (loss)	(1,046.2)	(576.1)
Total shareholders' equity	$ 2,069.0	$ 2,283.7
Total liabilities and shareholders' equity	$10,714.0	$10,574.5

Materials and goods in various stages of production account for over $800 million of the assets.

Total assets of almost $11 billion

Creditors' claims are about $8.6 billion.

Creditors' claims and shareholders' equity is the same as total assets.

noting that total liabilities amount to $8,645 million at the end of 2006. Total shareholders' equity amounts to $2,069 million, of which the balance in retained earnings is $3,630.4 million.

KELLOGG'S INCOME STATEMENT

Comparative income statements for three recent years are shown in Exhibit 1-12. As was the case for the balance sheet, you are not expected at this point to understand fully all of the complexities involved on the income statement of a real company. However, note the two largest items on the income statement: Net sales and Cost of goods sold. For now, it is sufficient for you to understand that the former is the revenue Kellogg's earned from selling its various products and the latter is the cost of these products. Net sales for the most recent year amounted to nearly $11 billion, and Kellogg's cost to produce the goods sold was just over $6 billion. Net income for the year amounted to just over $1 billion after selling, general, and administrative expense; interest expense; income taxes; and two other minor items are taken into account.

Real World Practice

1-2 Reading Kellogg's Income Statement

Compute the percentage increase in Net sales and Cost of goods sold from 2005 to 2006. Which of these two items on the income statement increased by the larger percentage? What does this mean to the management of Kellogg's?

POD REVIEW 1.5

LO5 *Explain the purpose of each of the financial statements and the relationships among them and prepare a set of simple statements.*

- Four major financial statements are covered in this chapter: balance sheet, income statement, statement of retained earnings, and statement of cash flows.
  - The balance sheet is a snapshot of a company's financial position at the end of the period. It reflects the assets, liabilities, and stockholders' equity accounts.
  - The income statement summarizes the financial activity for a period of time. Items of revenues, expenses, gains, and losses are reflected in the income statement.
  - Ultimately, all net income (loss) and dividends are reflected in retained earnings on the balance sheet. The statement of retained earnings links the income statement to the balance sheet by showing how net income (loss) and dividends affect the retained earnings account.
  - The statement of cash flows summarizes the cash flow effects of a company's operating, investing and financing activities.

QUESTIONS

1. *Which of the following financial statements summarizes the financial position of a company at a point in time?*
   a. income statement
   b. balance sheet
   c. statement of retained earnings
   d. statement of cash flows

2. *On a statement of retained earnings, how are net income and dividends treated?*
   a. Net income is added and dividends are deducted.
   b. Both net income and dividends are added.
   c. Both net income and dividends are deducted.
   d. Net income is deducted, and dividends are added.

3. *Revenues are reported on which of the following financial statements?*
   a. balance sheet only
   b. income statement only
   c. both the balance sheet and the income statement
   d. neither the balance sheet nor the income statement

EXHIBIT 1-12 Kellogg's Income Statement

Consolidated Statement of Earnings

(millions, except per share data)	2006	2005	2004
Net sales	$10,906.7	$10,177.2	$9,613.9
Cost of goods sold	6,081.5	5,611.6	5,298.7
Selling, general, and administrative expense	3,059.4	2,815.3	2,634.1
Operating profit	$ 1,765.8	$ 1,750.3	$1,681.1
Interest expense	307.4	300.3	308.6
Other income (expense), net	13.2	(24.9)	(6.6)
Earnings before income taxes	1,471.6	1,425.1	1,365.9
Income taxes	466.5	444.7	475.3
Earnings (loss) from joint venture	(1.0)	—	—
Net earnings	$ 1,004.1	$ 980.4	$ 890.6
Per share amounts:			
Basic	$ 2.53	$ 2.38	$ 2.16
Diluted	2.51	2.36	2.14

Net sales reached nearly $11 billion.

Costs of products sold were over $6 billion.

Net income for the year was over $1 billion.

The Conceptual Framework: Foundation for Financial Statements

LO6 Identify and explain the primary assumptions made in preparing financial statements.

Many people perceive the work of an accountant as being routine. In reality, accounting is anything but routine and requires a great deal of judgment on the part of the accountant. The record-keeping aspect of accounting—what we normally think of as bookkeeping—is the routine part of the accountant's work and is only a small part of it. Most of the job deals with communicating relevant information to financial statement users.

CONCEPTUAL FRAMEWORK FOR ACCOUNTING

Study Tip

The concepts in this section underlie everything you will learn throughout the course. You'll encounter them later in the context of specific topics.

The accounting profession has developed a *conceptual framework for accounting* that aids accountants in their role as interpreters and communicators of relevant information. The purpose of the framework is to act as a foundation for the specific principles and standards needed by the profession. An important part of the conceptual framework is a set of assumptions accountants make in preparing financial statements. We will briefly consider these assumptions, returning to a more detailed discussion of them in later chapters.

ECONOMIC ENTITY CONCEPT

The *economic entity concept* was discussed earlier in this chapter when we explored the different types of business entities. **This assumption requires that an identifiable, specific entity be the subject of a set of financial statements.** For example, even though some of Kellogg's employees are stockholders and therefore own part of Kellogg's, their personal affairs must be kept separate from the business affairs. When we look at a balance sheet for the company, we need assurance that it shows the financial position of that entity only and does not intermingle the personal assets and liabilities of the employees or any of the other stockholders.

COST PRINCIPLE

Cost principle
Assets are recorded at the cost to acquire them. ***Alternate term:*** *Original cost or historical cost.*

The **cost principle** requires that **accountants record assets at the cost paid to acquire them and continue to show this amount on all balance sheets until the company disposes of them.** With a few exceptions, companies do not carry assets at their market value (how much they could sell the asset for today), but at original cost. Accountants use the term *historical cost* to refer to the original cost of an asset. Why not show an asset such as land at market value? The *subjectivity* inherent in determining market values supports the practice of carrying assets at their historical cost. The cost of an asset is verifiable by an independent observer and is more *objective* than market value.

GOING CONCERN

Accountants assume that the entity being accounted for is a **going concern**. That is, they assume that Kellogg's is **not in the process of liquidation and that it will continue indefinitely into the future.** Another important reason for using historical cost rather than market value to report assets is the going concern assumption. When we assume that a business is *not* a going concern, we assume that it is in the process of liquidation. If this is the case, market value might be more relevant than cost as a basis for recognizing the assets. But if we are able to assume that a business will continue indefinitely, cost can be more easily justified as a basis for valuation. The **monetary unit** used in preparing the statements of Kellogg's is the dollar. The reason for using the dollar as the monetary unit is that it is the recognized medium of exchange in the United States. It provides a convenient yardstick to measure the position and earnings of the business. As a yardstick, however, the dollar, like the currencies of all other countries, is subject to instability. We are all well aware that a dollar will not buy as much today as it did 10 years ago.

Going concern
The assumption that an entity is not in the process of liquidation and that it will continue indefinitely.

Monetary unit
The yardstick used to measure amounts in financial statements; the dollar in the United States.

Inflation is evidenced by a general rise in the level of prices in an economy. Its effect on the measuring unit used in preparing financial statements is an important concern to the accounting profession. Although accountants have experimented with financial statements adjusted for the changing value of the measuring unit, the financial statements now prepared by corporations are prepared under the assumption that the monetary unit is relatively stable. At various times in the past, this has been a reasonable assumption and at other times not so reasonable.

TIME PERIOD ASSUMPTION

Under the **time period** assumption, **accountants assume that it is possible to prepare an income statement that accurately reflects net income or earnings for a specific time period.** In the case of Kellogg's, this time period is one year. It is somewhat artificial to measure the earnings of a business for a period of time indicated on a calendar, whether it be a month, a quarter, or a year. Of course, the most accurate point in time to measure the earnings of a business is at the end of its life. Accountants prepare periodic statements, however, because the users of the statements demand information about the entity on a regular basis.

Time period
An artificial segment on the calendar used as the basis for preparing financial statements.

GENERALLY ACCEPTED ACCOUNTING PRINCIPLES

Financial statements prepared by accountants must conform to **generally accepted accounting principles (GAAP)**. This term refers to the various methods, rules, practices, and other procedures that have evolved over time in response to the need for some form of regulation over the preparation of financial statements. As changes have taken place in the business environment over time, GAAP have developed in response to these changes.

Generally accepted accounting principles (GAAP)
The various methods, rules, practices, and other procedures that have evolved over time in response to the need to regulate the preparation of financial statements.

ACCOUNTING AS A SOCIAL SCIENCE

Accounting is a service activity. As we have seen, its purpose is to provide financial information to decision makers. Thus, accounting is a *social* science. Accounting principles are much different from the rules that govern the *physical* sciences. For example, it is a rule of nature that an object dropped from your hand will eventually hit the ground rather than be suspended in air. There are no rules comparable to this in accounting. The principles that govern financial reporting are not governed by nature, instead, they develop in response to changing business conditions. For example, consider the lease of an office building. Leasing has developed in response to the need to have access to valuable assets, such as office space, without spending the large sum necessary to buy the asset. As leasing has increased in popularity, the accounting profession has been left to develop guidelines, some of which are quite complex, to be followed in accounting for leases. Those guidelines are now part of GAAP.

POD REVIEW 1.6

LO6 *Identify and explain the primary assumptions made in preparing financial statements.*

- The usefulness of accounting information is enhanced through the various assumptions set forth in the conceptual framework developed by the accounting profession. This conceptual framework is the foundation for the methods, rules, and practices that make up generally accepted accounting principles (GAAP).
- Important assumptions in the conceptual framework are as follows:
  - Economic entity concept
  - Cost principle
  - Going concern
  - Monetary unit
  - Time period

QUESTIONS

1. *You decide to form a partnership with a friend. Which accounting concept requires that you separate your personal affairs from those of the partnership?*
   a. cost principle
   b. going concern
   c. time period
   d. economic entity

2. *How do accountants justify reporting assets on a balance sheet at their historical cost?*
   a. Cost is more objective than market value.
   b. Cost is more subjective than market value.
   c. Cost is an indication of what assets are worth.
   d. Cost is never used to report assets on a balance sheet.

Setting Accounting Standards

LO7 Identify the various groups involved in setting accounting standards and the role of auditors in determining whether the standards are followed.

Management of a company is responsible for preparation of the financial statements. So how can a stockholder feel comfortable that the statements are an accurate picture of the company's financial health? This section looks at who determines the rules that must be followed in preparing financial statements and what the role of auditors is in making sure the rules are followed.

WHO DETERMINES THE RULES OF THE GAME?

No one group is totally responsible for setting the standards or principles to be followed in preparing financial statements. The process is a joint effort among the following groups.

The federal government, through the **Securities and Exchange Commission (SEC)**, has the ultimate authority to determine the rules for preparing financial statements by companies whose securities are sold to the general public. However, for the most part, the SEC has allowed the accounting profession to establish its own rules.

Securities and Exchange Commission (SEC) The federal agency with ultimate authority to determine the rules for preparing statements for companies whose stock is sold to the public.

The **Financial Accounting Standards Board (FASB)** sets these accounting standards in the United States. A small independent group with a large staff, the board has issued more than 150 financial accounting standards and seven statements of financial accounting concepts since its creation in the early 1970s. These standards deal with a variety of financial reporting issues, such as the proper accounting for lease arrangements and pension plans; and the concepts are used to guide the board in setting accounting standards.

Financial Accounting Standards Board (FASB)
The group in the private sector with authority to set accounting standards.

The **American Institute of Certified Public Accountants (AICPA)** is the professional organization of **certified public accountants (CPAs)**. The CPA is the designation for an individual who has passed a uniform exam administered by the AICPA and met other requirements as determined by individual states. AICPA advises the FASB and in the past was involved in setting the auditing standards to be followed by public accounting firms. However, the **Public Company Accounting Oversight Board (PCAOB)** was created by an Act of Congress in 2002, and this five-member body now has the authority to set the standards for conducting audits.

American Institute of Certified Public Accountants (AICPA)
The professional organization of certified public accountants.

Certified Public Accountant (CPA)
The designation for an individual who has passed a uniform exam administered by the AICPA and has met other requirements as determined by individual states.

Public Company Accounting Oversight Board (PCAOB)
A five-member body created by an act of Congress in 2002 to set auditing standards.

Finally, if you are considering buying stock in **Porsche**, the German-based car manufacturer, you'll want to be sure that the rules Porsche follows in preparing its statements are similar to those the FASB requires for U.S. companies. Unfortunately, accounting standards can differ considerably from one country to another. The **International Accounting Standards Board (IASB)** was created in 2001. Prior to that time, the organization was known as the International Accounting Standards Committee (IASC), which was formed in 1973 to develop worldwide accounting standards. Organizations from many different countries, including the FASB in this country, participate in the IASB's efforts to develop international reporting standards. Although the group has made considerable progress, compliance with the standards of the IASB is strictly voluntary and much work remains to be done in developing international accounting standards.

International Accounting Standards Board (IASB)
The organization formed to develop worldwide accounting standards.

The FASB currently has a project on its agenda to work with the IASB toward convergence of accounting standards. Earlier in this chapter we saw that the cost principle requires that assets such as property and equipment be reported on the balance sheet at their historical cost, that is, at the amount paid to acquire them. However, under international accounting standards, it is permissible to report certain types of assets on the balance sheet at their market value. With significant differences such as this between U.S. and international standards, it may be some time before all differences are eliminated.

A recent development by the SEC is an indication that standard setters in the U.S. continue to work closely with those in the international community. In the past, foreign companies who filed their financial statements with the SEC were required to adjust those statements to conform to U.S. accounting standards. As long as foreign companies follow the standards of the IASB, they are no longer required to make these adjustments.

THE AUDIT OF FINANCIAL STATEMENTS

Financial statements are prepared by a company's accountants and are the responsibility of the company's management. Because most stockholders are not actively involved in the daily affairs of the business, they must rely on someone else to ensure that management is fairly presenting the financial statements of the business. The primary objective of an audit is to assure stockholders and other users that the statements are fairly presented. In this respect, **auditing** is the process of examining the financial statements and the underlying records of a company to render an opinion as to whether the statements are fairly presented.

Auditing
The process of examining the financial statements and the underlying records of a company to render an opinion as to whether the statements are fairly presented.

The external auditor performs various tests and procedures to be able to render an opinion. The next chapter will examine the auditors' report, which is essentially the auditors' opinion concerning the fairness of the presentation of the financial statements. Note that the auditors' report is an *opinion*, not a statement of fact. The firms that provide external audits for their clients are called public accounting firms. These firms range in size from those with a single owner to others with thousands of partners.

POD REVIEW 1.7

LO7 *Identify the various groups involved in setting accounting standards and the role of auditors in determining whether the standards are followed.*

- Financial statements are the responsibility of management. Various groups are involved in setting the standards that are used in preparing the statements. Although the SEC has the ultimate authority to determine the rules, the FASB currently sets the standards in the United States.
- The role of the external auditor is to perform various tests and procedures to render an opinion as to whether the financial statements of a company are fairly presented.

QUESTIONS

1. *Which of the following groups is currently responsible for setting accounting standards in the United States?*
   a. American Institute of Certified Public Accountants
   b. Financial Accounting Standards Board
   c. Public Company Accounting Oversight Board
   d. International Accounting Standards Board

2. *Who ultimately has responsibility for a company's financial statements?*
   a. stockholders
   b. management
   c. external auditors
   d. Securities and Exchange Commission

Introduction to Ethics in Accounting

LO8 Explain the critical role that ethics play in providing useful financial information.

WHY SHOULD ACCOUNTANTS BE CONCERNED WITH ETHICS?

In the modern business world, rapidly changing markets, technological improvements, and business innovation all affect financial decisions. Decision makers consider information received from many sources, such as other investors in the marketplace, analysts' forecasts, and companies whose corporate officers and executives may be encouraging "aggressive" accounting and reporting practices.

Business Ethics Takes a Hit In recent years, the news has been filled with reports of questionable accounting practices by some companies.

- **As a decision maker outside a company, you should be aware of the potential for ethical conflicts that arise within organizations. Ask questions, do research, and don't just accept everything as fact.**
- **If you are a decision maker within a company, you should stay alert for potential pressures on you or others to make choices that are not in the best interest of the company, its owners, and its employees as a whole.**

Companies may use aggressive accounting practices to misrepresent their earnings; executives may misuse their companies' funds. You may encounter a corporate board of directors that undermines the goals of its own company or a public accounting firm that fails its auditing duty to watch for and disclose wrongdoing.

As a decision maker, you may analyze business information to project capital expansion, to open markets for new products, or to anticipate tax liabilities. You may be responsible for making financial reporting decisions that will affect others inside or outside the organization. Knowledge of the professional standards of accounting procedures will be critical for your decision-making process. It will also help you recognize when information is not consistent with the standards and needs to be questioned.

Applying Different Rules for Different Circumstances: Ethical Dilemmas in Accounting It is important to note that you may encounter circumstances when it appears as if GAAP may not have been used to resolve particular accounting issues. This may occur because there are several conflicting rules, because no specific GAAP rules seem applicable, or because of fraud. In such situations, an ethical dilemma is likely to exist. Resolving the dilemma may involve one or more decision makers. In most instances, an accountant plays a significant role in the process.

As accountants analyze and attempt to solve the ethical dilemmas posed by certain financial transactions and complex business reporting decisions, they can turn to their profession's conceptual framework. (You will learn more about this framework in Chapter 2.) According to the profession, "Financial reporting should provide information that is useful to present and potential investors and creditors and other users in making rational investment, credit, and similar decisions."[3]

Is the Information Relevant and Reliable? When the accountant asks if the quality of the information that is disclosed is good or if it needs to be improved, the answer (which shapes all accounting decisions that follow) is this: If the information is *both* relevant and reliable, its quality is good.

Relevant information is information that is useful to the decision-making process. Relevant information may provide clear information about past financial events that is helpful for predicting the future. To be relevant, the information must also be timely; that is, it must be available at the time the decision is being made.

Accounting information should also be reliable; it should accurately represent what it claims to represent. Reliability includes *verifiability;* thus, there is documentation from one or more independent parties that supports the accuracy of the information. Reliability also includes *neutrality,* which means the presentation of information is free from bias toward a particular result. Neutral information can be used by anyone, and it does not try to influence the decision in one direction. Basically, accounting information that is reliable will report economic activity that accurately represents the situation without trying to influence behavior in any particular direction.[4]

Normally, the uncertainties of business transactions and reporting decisions must be resolved in accordance with GAAP following the FASB statements. However, the appropriate application of accounting principles may not be easy to determine. You must be alert to pressures on the decision-making process that may be due to the self-interests of one or more of the decision makers. Bias, deception, and even fraud may distort the disclosed information. Whatever the circumstances, the dilemmas should be resolved by questioning and analyzing the situation.

Moral and Social Context of Ethical Behavior All decision makers should consider the moral and social implications of their decisions. How will the decisions affect others, such as shareholders, creditors, employees, suppliers, customers, and the local community? The process of determining the most ethical choice involves identifying the most significant facts of the situation. For financial reporting, this includes identifying who may be affected and how, the relevant GAAP principles, and a realistic appraisal of the possible consequences of the decision. To assist your decision making for the cases and assignments, we offer an ethical decision model, shown in Exhibit 1-13 and explained here.

IDENTIFICATION

1. Recognize the ethical dilemma. A dilemma occurs when this awareness is combined with the inability to clearly apply accounting principles to represent the situation accurately.

---

3 *Original Pronouncements: Accounting Standards* (New York: John Wiley and Sons, Inc. 2001–2002 edition), III, Concept One, paragraph 34, p. 1014.

4 *Original Pronouncements: Accounting Standards* (New York: John Wiley and Sons, Inc. 2001–2002 edition), III, p. 1022; FASB, paragraphs 46, 47, 48, 56, 63, 77, 81; pp. 48–49, 51–53, 56–59.

EXHIBIT 1-13 **Ethics and Accounting: A Decision-Making Model**

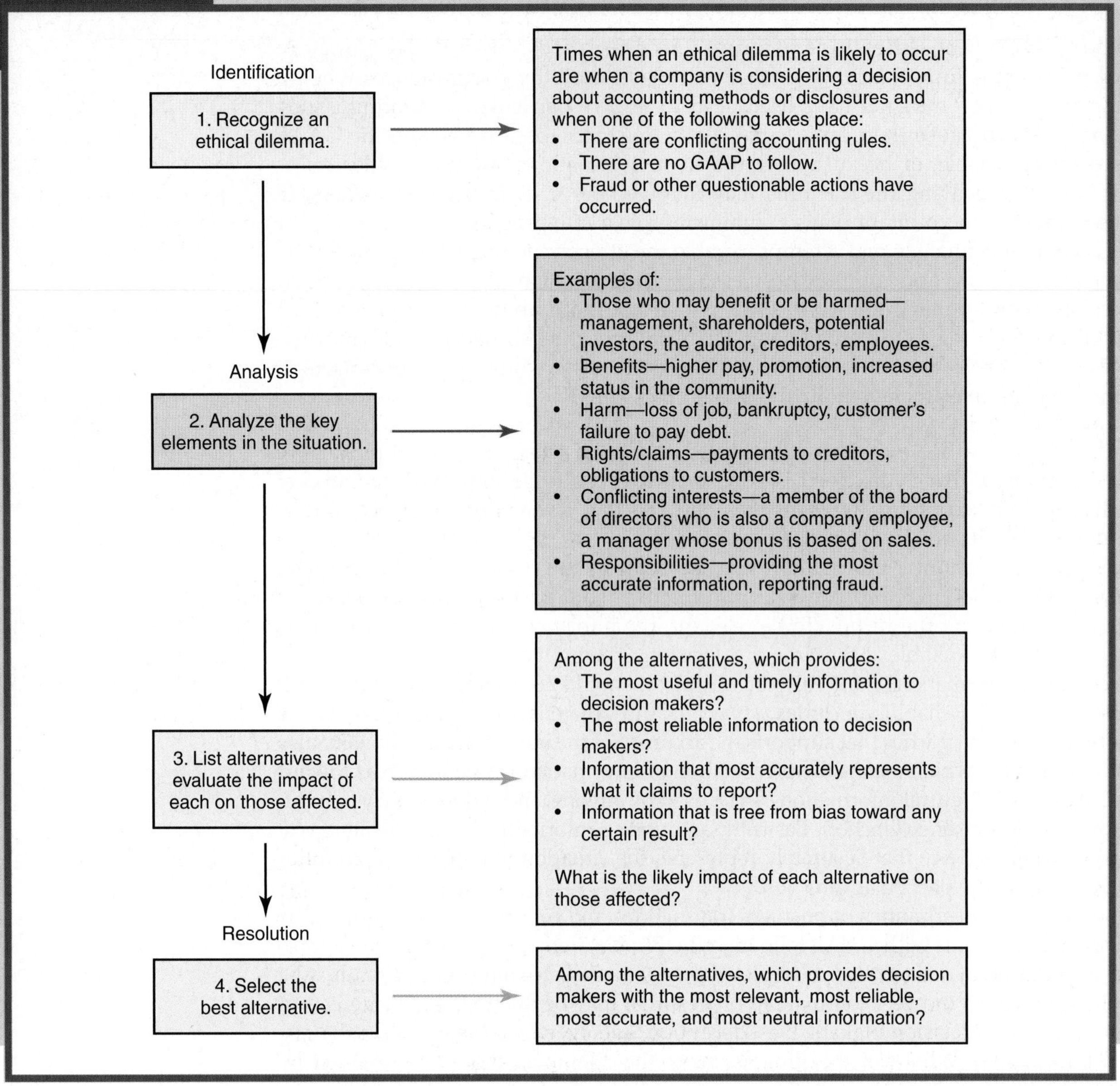

ANALYSIS

2. Analyze the key elements in the situation by answering these questions in sequence:
   a. Who may benefit or be harmed?
   b. How are they likely to benefit or be harmed?
   c. What rights or claims may be violated?
   d. What specific interests are in conflict?
   e. What are my responsibilities and obligations?
3. Determine what alternative methods are available to report the transaction, situation, or event. Answer the following questions:
   a. How relevant and reliable are the alternatives? Timeliness should be considered; potential bias must be identified.
   b. Does the report accurately represent the situation it claims to describe?
   c. Is the information free from bias?

RESOLUTION

4. Select the best or most ethical alternative, considering all of the circumstances and consequences.

© Getty Images

Hot Topics

Kellogg's—One of the World's Most Ethical Companies

Ethisphere magazine placed Kellogg's on its 2007 list of most ethical companies. Given the inherent judgments necessary in making ethical decisions, you can imagine the challenge presented in trying to determine the World's Most Ethical Companies™. However, this is just what *Ethisphere* magazine does. For its 2007 list, *Ethisphere* looked at more than 5,000 companies across 30 separate industries and eventually came up with fewer than 100 companies for this honor. *Ethisphere* compares companies in the same industry, and Kellogg's was chosen in the Food and Beverage category. The cereal maker's efforts are focused on its ethics and compliance program known within the company as its "K values." Today Kellogg's uses 100% recycled packaging; and more than one hundred years ago, the company introduced boxes that could be recycled.

Other well-known companies that made this prestigious list in 2007 included McDonald's, General Electric, John Deere, and Google. Undoubtedly, the firms named as one of the World's Most Ethical Companies™ are proud of this designation. Whether or not they make the list in future years, the challenge is to seek continuous improvement in their ethical business practices, including ways in which they present accounting information to external users.

Sources: http://www2.kelloggs.com and http://ethisphere.com.

ACCOUNTANTS AND ETHICAL JUDGMENTS

Remember the primary goal of accounting: to provide useful information to aid in the decision-making process. As discussed, the work of the accountant in providing useful information is anything but routine and requires the accountant to make subjective judgments about what information to present and how to present it. The latitude given accountants in this respect is one of the major reasons accounting is a profession and its members are considered professionals. Along with this designation as a professional, however, comes a serious responsibility. As we noted, financial statements are prepared for external parties who must rely on these statements to provide information on which to base important decisions.

At the end of each chapter are cases titled "Ethical Decision Making." The cases require you to evaluate difficult issues and make a decision. Judgment is needed in deciding which accounting method to select or how to report a certain item in the statements. As you are faced with these decisions, keep in mind the trust that various financial statement users place in the accountant.

THE CHANGING FACE OF THE ACCOUNTING PROFESSION

Probably no time in the history of the accounting profession in the United States has seen more turmoil and change than the period since the start of the new millennium. Corporate scandals have led to some of the largest bankruptcies in the history of business. The involvement of the auditors in one of these scandals resulted in the demise of one of the oldest and most respected public accounting firms in the world. Many have referred to the "financial reporting crisis" that grew out of this time period.

Although the issues involved in the financial reporting crisis are complex, the accounting questions in these cases were often very basic. For example, the most fundamental accounting issue involved in the **Enron** case revolved around the entity concept that was explained earlier in this chapter. Specifically, should various entities under the control of Enron have been included in the company's financial statements? Similarly, the major question in the **WorldCom** case was whether certain costs should have been treated as expenses when incurred rather than accounted for as assets.

Earlier in the chapter we described the various services that accounting firms provide to their clients. The scandals of the last few years have resulted in a major focus on the nonaudit services provided by these firms and the issue of auditor independence. For example, is it possible for an accounting firm to remain independent in rendering an opinion on a company's financial statements while simultaneously advising the company on other matters?

Sarbanes-Oxley Act
An act of Congress in 2002 intended to bring reform to corporate accountability and stewardship in the wake of a number of major corporate scandals.

In 2002, Congress passed the **Sarbanes-Oxley Act**. The act was a direct response to the corporate scandals mentioned earlier and was an attempt to bring about major reforms in corporate accountability and stewardship, given the vast numbers of stockholders, creditors, employees, and others affected in one way or another by these scandals. Among the most important provisions in the act are the following:

1. **The establishment of a new Public Company Accounting Oversight Board**
2. **A requirement that the external auditors report directly to the company's audit committee**
3. **A clause to prohibit public accounting firms who audit a company from providing any other services that could impair their ability to act independently in the course of their audit**

Events of the last few years have placed accountants and the work they do in the spotlight more than ever before. More than ever, accountants realize the burden of responsibility they have to communicate openly and honestly with the public concerning the financial well-being of businesses. Whether you will someday be an accountant or simply a user of the information an accountant provides, it is important to appreciate the critical role accounting plays in the smooth functioning of the free enterprise system.

POD REVIEW 1.8

LO8 *Explain the critical role that ethics play in providing useful financial information.*

- All decision makers must consider the moral and social implications of their decisions.
- Recent news of questionable accounting practices has placed increased scrutiny on the accounting profession. Professional judgment is often needed to arrive at appropriate decisions when some question arises about the application of GAAP.

QUESTIONS

1. *For accounting information to be useful in making informed decisions it must be*
   a. relevant.
   b. reliable.
   c. both relevant and reliable.
   d. neither of these qualities is important.

2. *The first step in the ethical decision-making model presented in this section is to*
   a. list the alternatives and evaluate the impact of each on those who may be affected.
   b. recognize an ethical dilemma.
   c. analyze the key elements in the situation.
   d. select the best alternative.

KEY TERMS QUIZ

Note to the student: We conclude each chapter with a quiz on the key terms, which are shown in bold in the chapter. Because of the large number of terms introduced in this chapter, there are two quizzes on key terms.

Read each definition below and write the number of the definition in the blank beside the appropriate term. The first one has been done for you. The quiz solutions appear at the end of the chapter. When reviewing terminology, come back to your completed key terms quiz. Study tip: Also check the glossary in the margin or at the end of the book.

Quiz 1: Introduction to Business

_______ **Business**
_______ **Business entity**
_______ **Sole proprietorship**
_______ **Economic entity concept**
_______ **Partnership**
_______ **Corporation**
_______ **Share of stock**
_______ **Bond**
_______ **Nonbusiness entity**
_______ **Liability**
_______ **Capital stock**
_______ **Stockholder**
_______ **Creditor**
___1___ **Asset**
_______ **Revenue**
_______ **Expense**

1. A future economic benefit.
2. A business owned by two or more individuals; the organization form often used by accounting firms and law firms.
3. An inflow of assets resulting from the sale of goods and services.
4. A form of entity organized under the laws of a particular state; ownership evidenced by shares of stock.
5. An organization operated for some purpose other than to earn a profit.
6. An outflow of assets resulting from the sale of goods and services.
7. An obligation of a business.
8. A certificate that acts as evidence of ownership in a corporation.
9. A certificate that represents a corporation's promise to repay a certain amount of money and interest in the future.
10. One of the owners of a corporation.
11. Someone to whom a company or person has a debt.
12. The assumption that a single, identifiable unit must be accounted for in all situations.
13. A form of organization with a single owner.
14. Indicates the owners' contributions to a corporation.
15. All of the activities necessary to provide the members of an economic system with goods and services.
16. An organization operated to earn a profit.

Quiz 2: Introduction to Accounting

_______ **Accounting**
_______ **Management accounting**
_______ **Financial accounting**
_______ **Owners' equity**
_______ **Stockholders' equity**
_______ **Retained earnings**
_______ **Balance sheet**
_______ **Income statement**
_______ **Net income**
_______ **Dividends**
_______ **Statement of retained earnings**
_______ **Statement of cash flows**
_______ **Cost principle**
_______ **Going concern**
_______ **Monetary unit**
_______ **Time period**
_______ **Generally accepted accounting principles (GAAP)**
_______ **Securities and Exchange Commission (SEC)**
_______ **Financial Accounting Standards Board (FASB)**
_______ **American Institute of Certified Public Accountants (AICPA)**
_______ **Certified Public Accountant (CPA)**
_______ **Public Company Accounting Oversight Board (PCAOB)**
_______ **International Accounting Standards Board (IASB)**
_______ **Auditing**
_______ **Sarbanes-Oxley Act**

1. A statement that summarizes revenues and expenses for a period of time.
2. The statement that summarizes the income earned and dividends paid over the life of a business.
3. The owners' equity of a corporation.
4. The process of identifying, measuring, and communicating economic information to various users.
5. The branch of accounting concerned with communication with outsiders through financial statements.
6. The owners' claims to the assets of an entity.
7. The financial statement that summarizes the assets, liabilities, and owners' equity at a specific point in time.
8. The part of owners' equity that represents the income earned less dividends paid over the life of an entity.
9. The branch of accounting concerned with providing management with information to facilitate the planning and control functions.
10. A distribution of the net income of a business to its stockholders.
11. The various methods, rules, practices, and other procedures that have evolved over time in response to the need to regulate the preparation of financial statements.
12. Assets are recorded and reported at the cost paid to acquire them.
13. The federal agency with ultimate authority to determine the rules for preparing statements for companies whose stock is sold to the public.
14. The assumption that an entity is not in the process of liquidation and that it will continue indefinitely.
15. The group in the private sector with authority to set accounting standards.
16. The yardstick used to measure amounts in financial statements; the dollar in the United States.
17. The professional organization for certified public accountants.
18. A length of time on the calendar used as the basis for preparing financial statements.
19. The process of examining the financial statements and the underlying records of a company to render an opinion as to whether the statements are fairly presented.
20. The organization formed to develop worldwide accounting standards.
21. An act of Congress in 2002 intended to bring reform to corporate accountability and stewardship in the wake of a number of major corporate scandals.
22. The excess of revenues over expenses.
23. The designation for an individual who has passed a uniform exam administered by the AICPA and has met other requirements as determined by individual states.
24. A five-member body created by an act of Congress in 2002 to set auditing standards.
25. The financial statement that summarizes a company's cash receipts and cash payments during the period from operating, investing, and financing activities.

ALTERNATE TERMS

Balance sheet Statement of financial position

Cost principle Original cost; historical cost

Creditor Lender

Income statement Statement of income or statement of operations

Net income Profits or earnings

Stockholder Shareholder

Stockholders' equity Shareholders' equity

WARMUP EXERCISES & SOLUTIONS

LO2 **Warmup Exercise 1-1** Your Assets and Liabilities

Consider your own situation in terms of assets and liabilities.

Required

1. Name three of your financial assets.
2. Name three of your financial liabilities.

Key to the Solution Refer to Exhibit 1-6 for definitions of assets and liabilities.

Study Tip

Use these exercises to become accustomed to the assignments that follow.

REVIEW

LO2 **Warmup Exercise 1-2** Kellogg's Assets and Liabilities

Think about **Kellogg's** business in balance sheet terms.

Required
1. Name three of Kellogg's assets.
2. Name three of Kellogg's liabilities.

Key to the Solution Refer to Exhibit 1-11 if you need to see Kellogg's balance sheet.

LO2 **Warmup Exercise 1-3** Kellogg's and the Accounting Equation

Place **Kellogg's** total assets, total liabilities, and total stockholders' equity in the form of the accounting equation. (Use the December 30, 2006, amounts.)

Key to the Solution Refer to Exhibit 1-11.

SOLUTIONS TO WARMUP EXERCISES

Warmup Exercise 1-1

1. Possible personal financial assets might include checking accounts, savings accounts, certificates of deposit, money market accounts, stocks, bonds, and mutual funds.
2. Possible personal financial liabilities might include student loans, car loans, home mortgages, and amounts borrowed from relatives.

Warmup Exercise 1-2

1. Kellogg's assets are Cash and cash equivalents, Accounts receivable, Inventories, Other current assets, Property, and Other assets.
2. Kellogg's liabilities are Current maturities of long-term debt, Notes payable, Accounts payable, Other current liabilities, Long-term debt, and Other liabilities.

Warmup Exercise 1-3

$$\text{Assets} = \text{Liabilities} + \text{Stockholders' Equity}$$
$$\$10{,}714{,}000{,}000 = \$8{,}645{,}000{,}000 + \$2{,}069{,}000{,}000$$

REVIEW PROBLEM & SOLUTION

Greenway Corporation is organized on June 1, 2008. The company will provide lawn-care and tree-trimming services on a contract basis. Following is an alphabetical list of the items that should appear on its income statement for the first month and on its balance sheet at the end of the first month. (You will need to determine on which statement each should appear.)

Accounts payable	$ 800
Accounts receivable	500
Building	2,000
Capital stock	5,000
Cash	3,300
Gas, utilities, and other expenses	300
Land	4,000
Lawn-care revenue	1,500
Notes payable	6,000
Retained earnings (beginning balance)	0
Salaries and wages expense	900
Tools	800
Tree-trimming revenue	500
Truck	2,000

Study Tip

At the end of each chapter is a problem to test your understanding of some of the major ideas presented in the chapter. Try to solve the problem before turning to the solution that follows it.

Required
1. Prepare an income statement for the month of June.
2. Prepare a balance sheet at June 30, 2008. *Note:* You will need to determine the balance in Retained Earnings at the end of the month.

3. The financial statements you have just prepared are helpful; but in many ways, they are a starting point. Assuming that this is your business, what additional questions do the financial statements raise that you need to consider?

SOLUTION TO REVIEW PROBLEM

1.

Greenway Corporation
Income Statement
For the Month Ended June 30, 2008

Revenues:		
Lawn care	$1,500	
Tree trimming	500	$2,000
Expenses:		
Salaries and wages	$ 900	
Gas, utilities, and other expenses	300	1,200
Net income		$ 800

2.

Greenway Corporation
Balance Sheet
June 30, 2008

Assets		Liabilities and Stockholders' Equity	
Cash	$ 3,300	Accounts payable	$ 800
Accounts receivable	500	Notes payable	6,000
Truck	2,000	Capital stock	5,000
Tools	800	Retained earnings	800
Building	2,000		
Land	4,000		
Total assets	$12,600	Total liabilities and stockholders' equity	$12,600

3. Following are examples of questions that the financial statements raise:
   - During June, 75% of the revenue was from lawn care and the other 25% was from trimming trees. Will this relationship hold in future months?
   - Are the expenses representative of those that will be incurred in the future? Will any other expenses arise, such as advertising and income taxes?
   - When can we expect to collect the accounts receivable? Is there a chance that not all will be collected?
   - How soon will the accounts payable need to be paid?
   - What is the interest rate on the note payable? When is interest paid? When is the note itself due?

HOMEWORK

QUESTIONS

1. What is business about? What do all businesses have in common?
2. What is an asset? Give three examples.
3. What is a liability? How does the definition of *liability* relate to the definition of *asset?*
4. Business entities are organized as one of three distinct forms. What are these three forms?
5. What are the three distinct types of business activity in which companies engage? Assume that you start your own company to rent bicycles in the summer and skis in the winter. Give an example of at least one of each of the three types of business activities in which you would engage.
6. What is accounting? Define it in terms understandable to someone without a business background.
7. How do financial accounting and management accounting differ?
8. What are five different groups of users of accounting information? Briefly describe the types of decisions each group must make.
9. How does owners' equity fit into the accounting equation?
10. What are the two distinct elements of owners' equity in a corporation? Define each element.
11. What is the purpose of a balance sheet?

12. How should a balance sheet be dated: as of a particular day or for a particular period of time? Explain your answer.
13. What does the term *cost principle* mean?
14. What is the purpose of an income statement?
15. How should an income statement be dated: as of a particular day or for a particular period of time? Explain your answer.
16. Rogers Corporation starts the year with a Retained Earnings balance of $55,000. Net income for the year is $27,000. The ending balance in Retained Earnings is $70,000. What was the amount of dividends for the year?
17. How do the duties of the controller of a corporation typically differ from those of the treasurer?
18. What are the three basic types of services performed by public accounting firms?
19. Evaluate the following statement: The auditors are in the best position to evaluate a company because they have prepared the financial statements.
20. What is the relationship between the cost principle and the going concern assumption?
21. Why does inflation present a challenge to the accountant? Relate your answer to the monetary unit assumption.
22. What is meant by the term *generally accepted accounting principles?*
23. What role has the Securities and Exchange Commission played in setting accounting standards? Contrast its role with that played by the Financial Accounting Standards Board.

BRIEF EXERCISES

LO1 **Brief Exercise 1-1** Types of Businesses

List the names of three companies with which you are familiar that are manufacturers or producers. Also list the names of three companies that are retailers. Finally, provide the names of three service providers.

LO2 **Brief Exercise 1-2** Forms of Organization

What does it mean when you own a share of stock in a company rather than one of its bonds?

LO3 **Brief Exercise 1-3** Business Activities

Assume that you are starting a new business. In which type of business activity will you engage first? Identify the order in which the remaining two activities will occur.

LO4 **Brief Exercise 1-4** Users of Accounting Information

List three examples of external users of accounting information.

LO5 **Brief Exercise 1-5** The Accounting Equation and the Balance Sheet

State the accounting equation. What two distinct parts make up stockholders' equity?

LO6 **Brief Exercise 1-6** Monetary Unit

What monetary unit is used to prepare financial statements for companies in the United States? for companies in Japan?

LO7 **Brief Exercise 1-7** The Role of Auditors

Do a company's external auditors prepare the company's financial statements? Explain.

LO8 **Brief Exercise 1-8** Making Ethical Decisions

List the four steps that can help a person make ethical decisions.

EXERCISES

LO4

Exercise 1-1 Users of Accounting Information and Their Needs

Listed below are a number of the important users of accounting information. Following the list are descriptions of a major need of each of these various users. Fill in each blank with the one user group that is most likely to have the need described.

Company management	**Banker**
Stockholder	**Supplier**
Securities and Exchange Commission	**Labor union**
Internal Revenue Service	

User Group	Needs Information About
____________	1. The profitability of each division in the company
____________	2. The prospects for future dividend payments
____________	3. The profitability of the company since the last contract with the workforce was signed
____________	4. The financial status of a company issuing securities to the public for the first time
____________	5. The prospects that a company will be able to meet its interest payments on time
____________	6. The prospects that a company will be able to pay for its purchases on time
____________	7. The profitability of the company based on the tax code

LO5

Exercise 1-2 The Accounting Equation

For each of the following independent cases, fill in the blank with the appropriate dollar amount.

	Assets	=	Liabilities	+	Owners' Equity
Case 1	$125,000		$ 75,000		$ ______
Case 2	400,000		______		100,000
Case 3	______		320,000		95,000

LO5

Exercise 1-3 The Accounting Equation

Ginger Enterprises began the year with total assets of $500,000 and total liabilities of $250,000. Using this information and the accounting equation, answer each of the following independent questions.

1. What was the amount of Ginger's owners' equity at the beginning of the year?
2. If Ginger's total assets increased by $100,000 and its total liabilities increased by $77,000 during the year, what was the amount of Ginger's owners' equity at the end of the year?
3. If Ginger's total liabilities increased by $33,000 and its owners' equity decreased by $58,000 during the year, what was the amount of its total assets at the end of the year?
4. If Ginger's total assets doubled to $1,000,000 and its owners' equity remained the same during the year, what was the amount of its total liabilities at the end of the year?

LO5

Exercise 1-4 The Accounting Equation

Using the accounting equation, answer each of the following independent questions.

1. Burlin Company starts the year with $100,000 in assets and $80,000 in liabilities. Net income for the year is $25,000, and no dividends are paid. How much is owners' equity at the end of the year?
2. Chapman Inc. doubles the amount of its assets from the beginning to the end of the year. Liabilities at the end of the year amount to $40,000, and owners' equity is $20,000. What is the amount of Chapman's assets at the beginning of the year?

3. During the year, the liabilities of Dixon Enterprises triple in amount. Assets at the beginning of the year amount to $30,000, and owners' equity is $10,000. What is the amount of liabilities at the end of the year?

LO5

Exercise 1-5 Changes in Owner's Equity

The following amounts are available from the records of Coaches and Carriages Inc. at the end of the years indicated:

December 31	Total Assets	Total Liabilities
2006	$ 25,000	$ 12,000
2007	79,000	67,000
2008	184,000	137,000

Required

1. Compute the changes in Coaches and Carriages' owners' equity during 2007 and 2008.
2. Compute the amount of Coaches and Carriages' net income (or loss) for 2007 assuming that no dividends were paid during the year.
3. Compute the amount of Coaches and Carriages' net income (or loss) for 2008 assuming that dividends paid during the year amounted to $10,000.

LO5

Exercise 1-6 The Accounting Equation

For each of the following cases, fill in the blank with the appropriate dollar amount.

	Case 1	Case 2	Case 3	Case 4
Total assets, end of period	$40,000	$____	$75,000	$50,000
Total liabilities, end of period	____	15,000	25,000	10,000
Capital stock, end of period	10,000	5,000	20,000	15,000
Retained earnings, beginning of period	15,000	8,000	10,000	20,000
Net income for the period	8,000	7,000	____	9,000
Dividends for the period	2,000	1,000	3,000	____

LO5

Exercise 1-7 Classification of Financial Statement Items

Classify each of the following items according to (1) whether it belongs on the income statement (IS) or balance sheet (BS) and (2) whether it is a revenue (R), expense (E), asset (A), liability (L), or stockholders' equity (SE) item.

Item	Appears on the	Classified as
Example: Cash	BS	A
1. Salaries expense	____	____
2. Equipment	____	____
3. Accounts payable	____	____
4. Membership fees earned	____	____
5. Capital stock	____	____
6. Accounts receivable	____	____
7. Buildings	____	____
8. Advertising expense	____	____
9. Retained earnings	____	____

LO5

Exercise 1-8 Net Income (or Loss) and Retained Earnings

The following information is available from the records of Prestige Landscape Design Inc. at the end of the 2008 calendar year:

Accounts payable	$ 5,000	Landscaping revenues	$25,000
Accounts receivable	4,500	Office equipment	7,500
Capital stock	8,000	Rent expense	6,500
Cash	13,000	Retained earnings, beginning of year	8,500
Dividends paid during the year	3,000	Salary and wage expense	12,000

Required
Use the previous information to answer the following questions.

1. What is Prestige's net income for the year ended December 31, 2008?
2. What is Prestige's retained earnings balance at the end of the year?
3. What is the total amount of Prestige's assets at the end of the year?
4. What is the total amount of Prestige's liabilities at the end of the year?
5. How much owners' equity does Prestige have at the end of the year?
6. What is Prestige's accounting equation at December 31, 2008?

LO5

Exercise 1-9 Statement of Retained Earnings

Ace Corporation has been in business for many years. Retained earnings on January 1, 2008, is $235,800. The following information is available for the first two months of 2008:

	January	February
Revenues	$83,000	$96,000
Expenses	89,000	82,000
Dividends paid	0	5,000

Required
Prepare a statement of retained earnings for the month ended February 29, 2008.

LO6

Exercise 1-10 Accounting Principles and Assumptions

The following basic accounting principles and assumptions were discussed in the chapter:

Economic entity
Monetary unit
Cost principle
Going concern
Time period

Fill in each of the blanks with the accounting principle or assumption that is relevant to the situation described.

_______________ 1. Genesis Corporation is now in its 30th year of business. The founder of the company is planning to retire at the end of the year and turn the business over to his daughter.

_______________ 2. Nordic Company purchased a 20-acre parcel of property on which to build a new factory. The company recorded the property on the records at the amount of cash given to acquire it.

_______________ 3. Jim Bailey enters into an agreement to operate a new law firm in partnership with a friend. Each partner will make an initial cash investment of $10,000. Jim opens a checking account in the name of the partnership and transfers $10,000 from his personal account into the new account.

_______________ 4. Multinational Corp. has a division in Japan. Prior to preparing the financial statements for the company and all of its foreign divisions, Multinational translates the financial statements of its Japanese division from yen to U.S. dollars.

_______________ 5. Camden Company has always prepared financial statements annually, with a year-end of June 30. Because the company is going to sell its stock to the public for the first time, quarterly financial reports will also be required by the Securities and Exchange Commission.

LO7 **Exercise 1-11** Organizations and Accounting

Match each of the organizations listed below with the statement that most adequately describes the role of the group.

Securities and Exchange Commission
International Accounting Standards Board
Financial Accounting Standards Board
American Institute of Certified Public Accountants

______________________ 1. The federal agency with ultimate authority to determine rules used for preparing financial statements for companies whose stock is sold to the public

______________________ 2. The group in the private sector with authority to set accounting standards

______________________ 3. The professional organization for certified public accountants

______________________ 4. The organization formed to develop worldwide accounting standards

MULTICONCEPT EXERCISES

LO4,5 **Exercise 1-12** Users of Accounting Information and the Financial Statements

Following are a number of users of accounting information and examples of questions they need answered before making decisions. Fill in each blank to indicate whether the user is most likely to find the answer by looking at the income statement (IS), the balance sheet (BS), or the statement of retained earnings (RE).

User	Question	Financial Statement
Stockholder	How did this year's sales compare to last year's?	______________
Banker	How much debt does the company already have on its books?	______________
Supplier	How much does the company currently owe to its suppliers?	______________
Stockholder	How much did the company pay in dividends this past year?	______________
Advertising account manager	How much did the company spend this past year to generate sales?	______________
Banker	What collateral or security can the company provide to ensure that any loan I make will be repaid?	______________

LO5,6 **Exercise 1-13** Kellogg's Land

Refer to **Kellogg's** balance sheet reproduced in the chapter.

Required
In which of the assets would you expect Kellogg's land to be included? What does this amount represent (i.e., cost, market value)? Why does Kellogg's carry its land at one or the other values?

PROBLEMS

LO4

Problem 1-1 You Won the Lottery

You have won a lottery! You will receive $200,000, after taxes, each year for the next five years.

Required

Describe the process you will go through in determining how to invest your winnings. Consider at least two options and make a choice. You may consider the stock of a certain company, bonds, real estate investments, bank deposits, and so on. Be specific. What information do you need to make a final decision? How will your decision be affected by the fact that you will receive the winnings over a five-year period rather than in one lump sum? Would you prefer one payment? Explain.

LO4

Problem 1-2 Users of Accounting Information and Their Needs

Havre Company would like to buy a building and equipment to produce a new product line. Some information about Havre is more useful to some people involved in the project than to others.

Required

Complete the following chart by identifying the information listed on the left with the user's need to know the information. Identify the information as one of the following:

a. *Need* to know
b. *Helpful* to know
c. *Not necessary* to know

	User of the Information		
Information	**Management**	**Stockholders**	**Banker**
1. Amount of current debt, repayment schedule, and interest rate	_____	_____	_____
2. Fair market value of the building	_____	_____	_____
3. Condition of the roof and heating and cooling, electrical, and plumbing systems	_____	_____	_____
4. Total cost of the building, improvements, and equipment to set up production	_____	_____	_____
5. Expected sales from the new product, variable production costs, and related selling costs	_____	_____	_____

LO5

Problem 1-3 Balance Sheet

The following items are available from records of Freescia Corporation at the end of the 2008 calendar year:

Accounts payable	$12,550	Notes payable	$50,000
Accounts receivable	23,920	Office equipment	12,000
Advertising expense	2,100	Retained earnings, end of year	37,590
Buildings	85,000	Salary and wage expense	8,230
Capital stock	25,000	Sales revenue	14,220
Cash	4,220		

Required

Prepare a balance sheet. *Hint:* Not all of the items listed should appear on a balance sheet. For each non-balance-sheet item, indicate where it should appear.

LO5

Problem 1-4 Corrected Balance Sheet

Dave is the president of Avon Consulting Inc. Avon began business on January 1, 2008. The company's controller is out of the country on business. Dave needs a copy of the company's balance sheet for a meeting tomorrow and asks his assistant to obtain the required information from the company's records. She presents Dave with the following balance sheet. He asks you to review it for accuracy.

HOMEWORK

Avon Consulting Inc.
Balance Sheet
For the Year Ended December 31, 2008

Assets		Liabilities and Stockholders' Equity	
Accounts payable	$13,000	Accounts receivable	$16,000
Cash	21,000	Capital stock	20,000
Cash dividends paid	16,000	Net income for 2008	72,000
Furniture and equipment	43,000	Supplies	9,000

Required

1. Prepare a corrected balance sheet.
2. Draft a memo explaining the major differences between the balance sheet Dave's assistant prepared and the one you prepared.

LO5

Problem 1-5 Income Statement, Statement of Retained Earnings, and Balance Sheet

The following list, in alphabetical order, shows the various items that regularly appear on the financial statements of Maple Park Theatres Corp. The amounts shown for balance sheet items are balances as of September 30, 2008 (with the exception of retained earnings, which is the balance on September 1, 2008); and the amounts shown for income statement items are balances for the month ended September 30, 2008.

Accounts payable	$17,600	Furniture and fixtures	$34,000
Accounts receivable	6,410	Land	26,000
Advertising expense	14,500	Notes payable	20,000
Buildings	60,000	Projection equipment	25,000
Capital stock	50,000	Rent expense—movies	50,600
Cash	15,230	Retained earnings	73,780
Concessions revenue	60,300	Salaries and wages expense	46,490
Cost of concessions sold	23,450	Ticket sales	95,100
Dividends paid during the month	8,400	Water, gas, and electricity	6,700

Required

1. Prepare an income statement for the month ended September 30, 2008.
2. Prepare a statement of retained earnings for the month ended September 30, 2008.
3. Prepare a balance sheet at September 30, 2008.
4. You have $1,000 to invest. On the basis of the statements you prepared, would you use it to buy stock in Maple Park? Explain. What other information would you want before making a final decision?

LO5

Problem 1-6 Income Statement and Balance Sheet

Green Bay Corporation began business in July 2008 as a commercial fishing operation and a passenger service between islands. Shares of stock were issued to the owners in exchange for cash. Boats were purchased by making a down payment in cash and signing a note payable for the balance. Fish are sold to local restaurants on open account, and customers are given 15 days to pay their account. Cash fares are collected for all passenger traffic. Rent for the dock facilities is paid at the beginning of each month. Salaries and wages are paid at the end of the month. The following amounts are from the records of Green Bay Corporation at the end of its first month of operations:

Accounts receivable	$18,500	Notes payable	$60,000
Boats	80,000	Passenger service revenue	12,560
Capital stock	40,000	Rent expense	4,000
Cash	7,730	Retained earnings	???
Dividends	5,400	Salary and wage expense	18,230
Fishing revenue	21,300		

Required

1. Prepare an income statement for the month ended July 31, 2008.
2. Prepare a balance sheet at July 31, 2008.
3. What information would you need about Notes Payable to fully assess Green Bay's long-term viability? Explain your answer.

LO5

Problem 1-7 Corrected Financial Statements

Hometown Cleaners Inc. operates a small dry-cleaning business. The company has always maintained a complete and accurate set of records. Unfortunately, the company's accountant left in a dispute with the president and took the 2008 financial statements with him. The following income statement and balance sheet were prepared by the company's president:

Hometown Cleaners Inc.
Income Statement
For the Year Ended December 31, 2008

Revenues:		
Accounts receivable	$15,200	
Cleaning revenue—cash sales	32,500	$47,700
Expenses:		
Dividends	$ 4,000	
Accounts payable	4,500	
Utilities	12,200	
Salaries and wages	17,100	37,800
Net income		$ 9,900

Hometown Cleaners Inc.
Balance Sheet
December 31, 2008

Assets		Liabilities and Stockholders' Equity	
Cash	$ 7,400	Cleaning revenue—credit sales	$26,200
Building and equipment	80,000	Capital stock	20,000
Less: Notes payable	(50,000)	Net income	9,900
Land	40,000	Retained earnings	21,300
Total assets	$77,400	Total liabilities and stockholders' equity	$77,400

The president is very disappointed with the net income for the year because it has averaged $25,000 over the last 10 years. She has asked for your help in determining whether the reported net income accurately reflects the profitability of the company and whether the balance sheet is prepared correctly.

Required

1. Prepare a corrected income statement for the year ended December 31, 2008.
2. Prepare a statement of retained earnings for the year ended December 31, 2008. (The actual balance of retained earnings on January 1, 2008, was $42,700. Note that the December 31, 2008, retained earnings balance shown is incorrect. The president simply "plugged in" this amount to make the balance sheet balance.)
3. Prepare a corrected balance sheet at December 31, 2008.
4. Draft a memo to the president explaining the major differences between the income statement she prepared and the one you prepared.

LO5

Problem 1-8 Statement of Retained Earnings for The Walt Disney Company

The Walt Disney Company reported the following amounts in various statements included in its 2006 annual report. (All amounts are stated in millions of dollars.)

Net income for 2006	$ 3,374
Dividends declared and paid in 2006	519
Retained earnings, October 1, 2005	17,775
Retained earnings, September 30, 2006	20,630

Required

1. Prepare a statement of retained earnings for The Walt Disney Company for the year ended September 30, 2006.
2. The Walt Disney Company does not actually present a statement of retained earnings in its annual report. Instead, it presents a broader statement of shareholders' equity. Describe the information that would be included on this statement and that is not included on a statement of retained earnings.

LO4 **Problem 1-9** Information Needs and Setting Accounting Standards

The Financial Accounting Standards Board requires companies to supplement their consolidated financial statements with disclosures about segments of their businesses. To comply with this standard, **Time Warner Inc.**'s 2006 annual report provides various disclosures for the five segments in which it operates: AOL, Cable, Filmed Entertainment, Networks, and Publishing.

Required

Which users of accounting information do you think the Financial Accounting Standards Board had in mind when it set this standard? What types of disclosures do you think these users would find helpful?

MULTICONCEPT PROBLEM

LO5,6 **Problem 1-10** Primary Assumptions Made in Preparing Financial Statements

Joe Hale opened a machine repair business in leased retail space, paying the first month's rent of $300 and a $1,000 security deposit with a check on his personal account. He took the tools, worth about $7,500, from his garage to the shop. He also bought some equipment to get started. The new equipment had a list price of $5,000, but Joe was able to purchase it on sale at **Sears** for only $4,200. He charged the new equipment on his personal Sears charge card. Joe's first customer paid $400 for services rendered, so Joe opened a checking account for the company. He completed a second job, but the customer has not paid Joe the $2,500 for his work. At the end of the first month, Joe prepared the following balance sheet and income statement:

Joe's Machine Repair Shop
Balance Sheet
July 31, 2008

Cash	$ 400		
Equipment	5,000	Equity	$5,400
Total	$5,400	Total	$5,400

Joe's Machine Repair Shop
Income Statement
For the Month Ended July 31, 2008

Sales		$ 2,900
Rent	$ 300	
Tools	4,200	4,500
Net loss		$(1,600)

Joe believes that he should show a greater profit next month because he won't have large expenses for items such as tools.

Required

Identify the assumptions that Joe has violated and explain how each event should have been handled. Prepare a corrected balance sheet and income statement.

ALTERNATE PROBLEMS

LO4 **Problem 1-1A** What to Do with a Million Dollars?

You have inherited $1 million!

Required

Describe the process you will go through in determining how to invest your inheritance. Consider at least two options and choose one. You may consider the stock of a certain company, bonds, real estate investments, bank deposits, and so on. Be specific. What information do you need to make a final decision? Where do you find the information you need? What additional information will you need to consider if you want to make a change in your investment?

LO4

Problem 1-2A Users of Accounting Information and Their Needs

Billings Inc. would like to buy a franchise to provide a specialized service. Some information about Billings is more useful to some people involved in the project than to others.

Required

Complete the following chart by identifying the information listed on the left with the user's need to know the information. Identify the information as one of the following:

a. *Need* to know
b. *Helpful* to know
c. *Not necessary* to know

	User of the Information		
Information	**Manager**	**Stockholders**	**Franchisor**
1. Expected revenue from the new service.	______	______	______
2. Cost of the franchise fee and recurring fees to be paid to the franchisor.	______	______	______
3. Cash available to Billings, the franchisee, to operate the business after the franchise is purchased.	______	______	______
4. Expected overhead costs of the service outlet.	______	______	______
5. Billings' required return on its investment.	______	______	______

LO5

Problem 1-3A Balance Sheet

The following items are available from the records of Victor Corporation at the end of its fiscal year, July 31, 2008:

Accounts payable	$16,900	Delivery expense	$ 4,600
Accounts receivable	5,700	Notes payable	50,000
Buildings	35,000	Office equipment	12,000
Butter and cheese inventory	12,100	Retained earnings, end of year	26,300
Capital stock	25,000	Salary and wage expense	8,230
Cash	21,800	Sales revenue	14,220
Computerized mixers	25,800	Tools	5,800

Required

Prepare a balance sheet. *Hint:* Not all of the items listed should appear on a balance sheet. For each non-balance-sheet item, indicate where it should appear.

LO5

Problem 1-4A Corrected Balance Sheet

Pete is the president of Island Enterprises. Island Enterprises began business on January 1, 2008. The company's controller is out of the country on business. Pete needs a copy of the company's balance sheet for a meeting tomorrow and asks his assistant to obtain the required information from the company's records. She presents Pete with the following balance sheet. He asks you to review it for accuracy.

Island Enterprises
Balance Sheet
For the Year Ended December 31, 2008

Assets		**Liabilities and Stockholders' Equity**	
Accounts payable	$ 29,600	Accounts receivable	$ 23,200
Building and equipment	177,300	Supplies	12,200
Cash	14,750	Capital stock	100,000
Cash dividends paid	16,000	Net income for 2008	113,850

Required

1. Prepare a corrected balance sheet.
2. Draft a memo explaining the major differences between the balance sheet Pete's assistant prepared and the one you prepared.

HOMEWORK

LO5

Problem 1-5A Income Statement, Statement of Retained Earnings, and Balance Sheet

The following list, in alphabetical order, shows the various items that regularly appear on the financial statements of Sterns Audio Book Rental Corp. The amounts shown for balance sheet items are balances as of December 31, 2008 (with the exception of retained earnings, which is the balance on January 1, 2008); and the amounts shown for income statement items are balances for the year ended December 31, 2008.

Accounts payable	$ 4,500	Dividends paid during the year	$ 12,000
Accounts receivable	300	Notes payable	10,000
Advertising expense	14,500	Rental revenue	125,900
Audiotape inventory	70,000	Rent paid on building	60,000
Capital stock	50,000	Retained earnings	35,390
Cash	2,490	Salaries and wages expense	17,900
Display fixtures	45,000	Water, gas, and electricity	3,600

Required

1. Prepare an income statement for the year ended December 31, 2008.
2. Prepare a statement of retained earnings for the year ended December 31, 2008.
3. Prepare a balance sheet at December 31, 2008.
4. You have $1,000 to invest. On the basis of the statements you prepared, would you use it to buy stock in this company? Explain. What other information would you want before deciding?

LO5

Problem 1-6A Income Statement and Balance Sheet

Fort Worth Corporation began business in January 2008 as a commercial carpet-cleaning and drying service. Shares of stock were issued to the owners in exchange for cash. Equipment was purchased by making a down payment in cash and signing a note payable for the balance. Services are performed for local restaurants and office buildings on open account, and customers are given 15 days to pay their accounts. Rent for office and storage facilities is paid at the beginning of each month. Salaries and wages are paid at the end of the month. The following amounts are from the records of Fort Worth Corporation at the end of its first month of operations:

Accounts receivable	$24,750	Equipment	$62,000
Capital stock	80,000	Notes payable	30,000
Cash	51,650	Rent expense	3,600
Cleaning revenue	45,900	Retained earnings	???
Dividends	5,500	Salary and wage expense	8,400

Required

1. Prepare an income statement for the month ended January 31, 2008.
2. Prepare a balance sheet at January 31, 2008.
3. What information would you need about Notes Payable to fully assess Fort Worth's long-term viability? Explain your answer.

LO5

Problem 1-7A Corrected Financial Statements

Heidi's Bakery Inc. operates a small pastry business. The company has always maintained a complete and accurate set of records. Unfortunately, the company's accountant left in a dispute with the president and took the 2008 financial statements with her. The following balance sheet and income statement were prepared by the company's president:

Heidi's Bakery Inc.
Income Statement
For the Year Ended December 31, 2008

Revenues:		
Accounts receivable	$15,500	
Pastry revenue—cash sales	23,700	$39,200
Expenses:		
Dividends	$ 5,600	
Accounts payable	6,800	
Utilities	9,500	
Salaries and wages	18,200	40,100
Net loss		$ (900)

Heidi's Bakery Inc.
Balance Sheet
December 31, 2008

Assets		**Liabilities and Stockholders' Equity**	
Cash	$ 3,700	Pastry revenue—	
Building and equipment	60,000	credit sales	$22,100
Less: Notes payable	(40,000)	Capital stock	30,000
Land	50,000	Net loss	(900)
		Retained earnings	22,500
		Total liabilities and	
Total assets	$73,700	stockholders' equity	$73,700

The president is very disappointed with the net loss for the year because net income has averaged $21,000 over the last 10 years. He has asked for your help in determining whether the reported net loss accurately reflects the profitability of the company and whether the balance sheet is prepared correctly.

Required

1. Prepare a corrected income statement for the year ended December 31, 2008.
2. Prepare a statement of retained earnings for the year ended December 31, 2008. (The actual amount of retained earnings on January 1, 2008, was $39,900. The December 31, 2008, retained earnings balance shown is incorrect. The president simply "plugged in" this amount to make the balance sheet balance.)
3. Prepare a corrected balance sheet at December 31, 2008.
4. Draft a memo to the president explaining the major differences between the income statement he prepared and the one you prepared.

LO5

Problem 1-8A Statement of Retained Earnings for Brunswick Corporation

Brunswick Corporation reported the following amounts in various statements included in its 2006 annual report. (All amounts are stated in millions of dollars.)

Net earnings for 2006	$ 133.9
Cash dividends declared and paid in 2006	55.0
Retained earnings, December 31, 2005	1,741.8
Retained earnings, December 31, 2006	1,820.7

Required

1. Prepare a statement of retained earnings for Brunswick Corporation for the year ended December 31, 2006.
2. Brunswick does not actually present a statement of retained earnings in its annual report. Instead, it presents a broader statement of shareholders' equity. Describe the information that would be included on this statement and that is not included on a statement of retained earnings.

LO4

Problem 1-9A Information Needs and Setting Accounting Standards

The Financial Accounting Standards Board requires companies to supplement their consolidated financial statements with disclosures about segments of their businesses. To comply with this standard, **Marriott International**'s 2006 annual report provides various disclosures for the six segments in which it operates: North American Full-Service Lodging, North American Limited-Service Lodging, International Lodging, Luxury Lodging, Timeshare, and Synthetic Fuel.

Required

Which users of accounting information do you think the Financial Accounting Standards Board had in mind when it set this standard? What types of disclosures do you think these users would find helpful?

ALTERNATE MULTICONCEPT PROBLEM

LO5,6

Problem 1-10A Primary Assumptions Made in Preparing Financial Statements

Millie Abrams opened a ceramic studio in leased retail space, paying the first month's rent of $300 and a $1,000 security deposit with a check on her personal account. She took molds and paint, worth about $7,500, from her home to the studio. She also bought a new firing kiln to start the business.

The new kiln had a list price of $5,000; but Millie was able to trade in her old kiln, worth $500 at the time of trade, on the new kiln. Therefore, she paid only $4,500 cash. She wrote a check on her personal account. Millie's first customers paid a total of $1,400 to attend classes for the next two months. Millie opened a checking account in the company's name with the $1,400. She has conducted classes for one month and has sold $3,000 of unfinished ceramic pieces called *greenware.* All greenware sales are cash. Millie incurred $1,000 of personal cost in making the greenware. At the end of the first month, Millie prepared the following balance sheet and income statement:

Millie's Ceramic Studio
Balance Sheet
July 31, 2008

Cash	$1,400		
Kiln	5,000	Equity	$6,400
Total	$6,400	Total	$6,400

Millie's Ceramic Studio
Income Statement
For the Month Ended July 31, 2008

Sales		$4,400
Rent	$300	
Supplies	600	900
Net income		$3,500

Millie needs to earn at least $3,000 each month for the business to be worth her time. She is pleased with the results.

Required
Identify the assumptions that Millie has violated and explain how each event should have been handled. Prepare a corrected balance sheet and income statement.

DECISION CASES

READING AND INTERPRETING FINANCIAL STATEMENTS

LO4,5 **Decision Case 1-1** An Annual Report as Ready Reference

Refer to the excerpts from **Kellogg's** annual report reprinted at the back of the book and identify where each of the following users of accounting information would first look to answer their respective questions about Kellogg's.

1. Investors: How much did the company earn for each share of stock that I own? Were any dividends paid, and how much was reinvested in the company?
2. Potential investors: What amount of earnings can I expect to see from Kellogg's in the near future?
3. Suppliers: Should I extend credit to Kellogg's? Does it have sufficient cash or cashlike assets to repay accounts payable?
4. IRS: How much does Kellogg's owe for taxes?
5. Bankers: What is Kellogg's long-term debt? Should I make a new loan to the company?

LO5 **Decision Case 1-2** Reading and Interpreting Kellogg's Financial Statements

Refer to the financial statements for **Kellogg's** reproduced in the chapter and answer the following questions.

1. What was the company's net income for 2006?
2. State Kellogg's financial position on December 30, 2006, in terms of the accounting equation.
3. By what amount did Property, net, increase during 2006? Explain what would cause an increase in this item.

LO5 **Decision Case 1-3** Comparing Two Companies in the Same Industry: Kellogg's and General Mills

Refer to the financial information for **Kellogg's** and **General Mills** reproduced at the end of the book and answer the following questions.

1. What was the net sales amount for each company for the most recent year? Did each company's net sales increase or decrease from its total amount in the prior year?

2. What was each company's net income for the most recent year? Did each company's net income increase or decrease from its net income for the prior year?
3. What was the total asset balance for each company at the end of its most recent year? Among its assets, what was the largest asset each company reported on its year-end balance sheet?
4. Did either company pay its stockholders any dividents during the most recent year? Explain how you can tell.

MAKING FINANCIAL DECISIONS

LO4

Decision Case 1-4 An Investment Opportunity

You have saved enough money to pay for your college tuition for the next three years when a high school friend comes to you with a deal. He is an artist who has spent most of the past two years drawing on the walls of old buildings. The buildings are about to be demolished, and your friend thinks you should buy the walls before the buildings are demolished and open a gallery featuring his work. Of course, you are levelheaded and would normally say no. Recently, however, your friend has been featured on several local radio and television shows and is talking to some national networks about doing a feature on a well-known news show. To set up the gallery would take all of your savings, but your friend thinks that you will be able to sell his artwork for 10 times the cost of your investment. What kinds of information about the business do you need before deciding to invest all of your savings? What kind of profit split would you suggest to your friend if you decided to open the gallery?

LO5

Decision Case 1-5 Preparation of Projected Statements for a New Business

Upon graduation from MegaState University, you and your roommate decide to start your respective careers in accounting and salmon fishing in Remote, Alaska. Your career as a CPA in Remote is going well, as is your roommate's job as a commercial fisherman. After one year in Remote, he approaches you with a business opportunity.

> As we are well aware, the DVD rental business has yet to reach Remote and the nearest rental facility is 250 miles away. We each put up our first year's savings of $5,000 and file for articles of incorporation with the state of Alaska to do business as Remote DVD World. In return for our investment of $5,000, we will each receive equal shares of capital stock in the corporation. Then we go to the Corner National Bank and apply for a $10,000 loan. We take the total cash of $20,000 we have now raised and buy 2,000 DVDs at $10 each from a mail-order supplier. We rent the movies for $3 per title and sell monthly memberships for $25, allowing a member to check out an unlimited number of movies during the month. Individual rentals would be a cash-and-carry business, but we would give customers until the 10th of the following month to pay for a monthly membership. My most conservative estimate is that during the first month alone, we will rent 800 movies and sell 200 memberships. As I see it, we will have only two expenses. First, we will hire four high school students to run the store for 15 hours each per week and pay them $5 per hour. Second, the landlord of a vacant store in town will rent us space in the building for $1,000 per month.

Required
1. Prepare a projected income statement for the first month of operations.
2. Prepare a balance sheet as it would appear at the end of the first month of operations.
3. Assume that the bank is willing to make the $10,000 loan. Would you be willing to join your roommate in this business? Explain your response. Also indicate any information other than what he has provided that you would like to have before making a final decision.

ETHICAL DECISION MAKING

LO4,5,8

Decision Case 1-6 Identification of Errors in Financial Statements and Preparation of Revised Statements

Lakeside Slammers Inc. is a minor league baseball organization that has just completed its first season. You and three other investors organized the corporation; each put up $10,000 in cash for shares of capital stock. Because you live out of state, you have not been actively involved in the daily affairs of the club. However, you are thrilled to receive a dividend check for $10,000 at the end of the season—an amount equal to your original investment. Included with the check are the following financial statements, along with supporting explanations:

Lakeside Slammers Inc.
Income Statement
For the Year Ended December 31, 2008

Revenues:		
Single-game ticket revenue	$420,000	
Season ticket revenue	140,000	
Concessions revenue	280,000	
Advertising revenue	100,000	$940,000
Expenses:		
Cost of concessions sold	$110,000	
Salary expense—players	225,000	
Salary and wage expense—staff	150,000	
Rent expense	210,000	695,000
Net income		$245,000

Lakeside Slammers Inc.
Statement of Retained Earnings
For the Year Ended December 31, 2008

Beginning balance, January 1, 2008	$ 0
Add: Net income for 2008	245,000
Deduct: Cash dividends paid in 2008	(40,000)
Ending balance, December 31, 2008	$205,000

Lakeside Slammers Inc.
Balance Sheet
December 31, 2008

Assets		**Liabilities and Stockholders' Equity**	
Cash	$ 5,000	Notes payable	$ 50,000
Accounts receivable:		Capital stock	40,000
Season tickets	140,000	Additional owners' capital	80,000
Advertisers	100,000	Parent club's equity	125,000
Auxiliary assets	80,000	Retained earnings	205,000
Equipment	50,000		
Player contracts	125,000		
Total assets	$500,000	Total liabilities and stockholders' equity	$500,000

Additional information:

a. Single-game tickets sold for $4 per game. The team averaged 1,500 fans per game. With 70 home games × $4 per game × 1,500 fans, single-game ticket revenue amounted to $420,000.

b. No season tickets were sold during the first season. During the last three months of 2008, however, an aggressive sales campaign resulted in the sale of 500 season tickets for the 2009 season. Therefore, the controller (who is also one of the owners) chose to record an Account Receivable—Season Tickets and corresponding revenue for 500 tickets × $4 per game × 70 games, or $140,000.

c. Advertising revenue of $100,000 resulted from the sale of the 40 signs on the outfield wall at $2,500 each for the season. However, none of the advertisers have paid their bills yet (thus, an account receivable of $100,000 on the balance sheet) because the contract with Lakeside required payment only if the team averaged 2,000 fans per game during the 2008 season. The controller believes that the advertisers will be sympathetic to the difficulties of starting a new franchise and will be willing to overlook the slight deficiency in the attendance requirement.

d. Lakeside has a working agreement with one of the major league franchises. The minor league team is required to pay $5,000 *every* year to the major league team for each of the 25 players on its roster. The controller believes that each of the players is an asset to the organization and has therefore recorded $5,000 × 25, or $125,000, as an asset called Player Contracts. The item on the right side of the balance sheet entitled Parent Club's Equity is the amount owed to the major league team by February 1, 2009, as payment for the players for the 2008 season.

e. In addition to the cost described in (d), Lakeside directly pays each of its 25 players a $9,000 salary for the season. This amount—$225,000—has already been paid for the 2008 season and is reported on the income statement.

f. The items on the balance sheet entitled Auxiliary Assets on the left side and Additional Owners' Capital on the right side represent the value of the controller's personal residence. She has a mortgage with the bank for the full value of the house.

g. The $50,000 note payable resulted from a loan that was taken out at the beginning of the year to finance the purchase of bats, balls, uniforms, lawn mowers, and other miscellaneous supplies needed to operate the team. (Equipment is reported as an asset for the same amount.) The loan, with interest, is due on April 15, 2009. Even though the team had a very successful first year, Lakeside is a little short of cash at the end of 2008 and has asked the bank for a three-month extension of the loan. The controller reasons, "By the due date of April 15, 2009, the cash due from the new season ticket holders will be available, things will be cleared up with the advertisers, and the loan can be easily repaid."

Required

1. Identify any errors you think the controller has made in preparing the financial statements.
2. On the basis of your answer in (1), prepare a revised income statement, statement of retained earnings, and balance sheet.
3. On the basis of your revised financial statements, identify any ethical dilemma you now face. Does the information regarding the season ticket revenue provide reliable information to an outsider? Does the $100,000 advertising revenue on the income statement represent the underlying economic reality of the transaction? Do you have a responsibility to share these revisions with the other three owners? What is your responsibility to the bank?
4. Using Exhibit 1-13 and the related text as your guide, analyze the key elements in the situation and answer the following questions. Support your answers by explaining your reasoning.
   a. Who may benefit or be harmed?
   b. How are they likely to benefit or be harmed?
   c. What rights or claims may be violated?
   d. What specific interests are in conflict?
   e. What are your responsibilities and obligations?
   f. Do you believe the information provided by the organization is relevant, is reliable, accurately represents what it claims to report, and is unbiased?

LO8

Decision Case 1-7 Responsibility for Financial Statements and the Role of the Auditor

Financial statements are the means by which accountants communicate to external users. Recent financial reporting scandals have focused attention on the accounting profession and its role in the preparation of these statements and the audits performed on the statements.

1. Who is responsible for the preparation of the financial statements that are included in a company's annual report?
2. Who performs an audit of the financial statements referred to in (1) above?
3. Why is it important for those who are responsible for an audit of the financial statements to be independent of those who prepare the statements? Explain your answer.

SOLUTIONS TO KEY TERMS QUIZ

Quiz 1: Introduction to Business

15	**Business**	5	**Nonbusiness entity**
16	**Business entity**	7	**Liability**
13	**Sole proprietorship**	14	**Capital stock**
12	**Economic entity concept**	10	**Stockholder**
2	**Partnership**	11	**Creditor**
4	**Corporation**	1	**Asset**
8	**Share of stock**	3	**Revenue**
9	**Bond**	6	**Expense**

Quiz 2: Introduction to Accounting

4	**Accounting**	8	**Retained earnings**
9	**Management accounting**	7	**Balance sheet**
5	**Financial accounting**	1	**Income statement**
6	**Stockholder's equity**	22	**Net income**
3	**Stockholders' equity**	10	**Dividends**

2 Statement of retained earnings
25 Statement of cash flows
12 Cost principle
14 Going concern
16 Monetary unit
18 Time period
11 Generally accepted accounting principles (GAAP)
13 Securities and Exchange Commission (SEC)
15 Financial Accounting Standards Board (FASB)
17 American Institute of Certified Public Accountants (AICPA)
23 Certified Public Accountant (CPA)
24 Public Company Accounting Oversight Board (PCAOB)
20 International Accounting Standards Board (IASB)
19 Auditing
21 Sarbanes-Oxley Act

ANSWERS TO POD REVIEW

LO1	1. c	2. a	
LO2	1. c	2. d	
LO3	1. b	2. a	3. c
LO4	1. c	2. b	
LO5	1. b	2. a	3. b
LO6	1. d	2. a	
LO7	1. b	2. b	
LO8	1. c	2. b	

CHAPTER

2

Financial Statements and the Annual Report

Learning Outcomes

After studying this chapter, you should be able to:

LO1 Describe the objectives of financial reporting.

LO2 Describe the qualitative characteristics of accounting information.

LO3 Explain the concept and purpose of a classified balance sheet and prepare the statement.

LO4 Use a classified balance sheet to analyze a company's financial position.

LO5 Explain the difference between a single-step and a multiple-step income statement and prepare each type of income statement.

LO6 Use a multiple-step income statement to analyze a company's operations.

LO7 Identify the components of the statement of retained earnings and prepare the statement.

LO8 Identify the components of the statement of cash flows and prepare the statement.

LO9 Read and use the financial statements and other elements in the annual report of a publicly held company.

Study Links...

A Look at the Previous Chapter
Chapter 1 introduced how investors, creditors, and others use accounting and the outputs of the accounting system—financial statements—in making business decisions. Chapter 1 introduced the Financial Decision Model and the Ethical Decision Framework—two of the three key decision tools needed for informed and ethical decision making.

A Look at This Chapter
Chapter 2 takes a closer look at the financial statements as well as other elements that make up an annual report. It also introduces the third decision model needed for making financial decisions, the Ratio Decision Model. Here you'll learn how to use financial statement numbers to develop ratios that reflect the financial trends of a business.

A Look at the Upcoming Chapter
Chapter 3 steps back from a firm's financial statements to discuss how business transactions and the resulting accounting information are handled. The chapter begins by looking at transactions—what they are; how they are analyzed; and how accounting procedures facilitate turning them into journal entries, ledger accounts, and trial balances on which financial statements are based.

General Mills

MAKING BUSINESS DECISIONS

Brand names are the lifeblood of any consumer product company, and General Mills boasts some of the most recognizable names in the world. Who cannot identify with Cheerios® and Wheaties® in General Mills's Big G division? Or is there anyone who is not familiar with the name Betty Crocker®? Finally, the company leads the U.S. yogurt market with products such as Yoplait® and Colombo®.

As you will see throughout your study of accounting, financial statements and their numbers tell a story about a company's performance. The first chart included here shows how General Mills has increased its net sales in each of the last four years. While there has been a steady growth in sales for the last three years, note the big jump in 2003 from $7.9 billion to $10.5 billion, an increase of 32%. The answer as to why sales increased so dramatically in 2003 is because this was the first full year of operations after General Mills acquired Pillsbury® from Diageo plc. To its already impressive list of brands, General Mills added names such as Green Giant®, Old El Paso®, and Häagen-Dazs®.

Adding new products to a consumer foods company helps to grow sales, but it is not a guarantee that a company's bottom line will improve. With the acquisition of another company comes additional recurring costs of running those businesses. What measures are available to indicate whether a company has been successful in controlling its costs? The accompanying table shows that the measure "Segment Operating Profit" increased by 5% during 2006. On the other hand, the next line indicates that "Net Earnings" actually decreased by 12% during 2006. What would cause one measure of a company's performance to increase and another to decrease?

As you continue your study of accounting, you should look for answers to that question as well as to a number of key questions, as follows:

© James F. Quinn/MCT/Landov

- What makes a set of financial statements understandable? (See p. 57.)
- What distinguishes a current asset from a long-term asset? a current liability from a long-term liability? (See pp. 62–65.)
- How can the numbers on a classified balance sheet be used to measure a company's liquidity? (See p. 79.)
- How can the numbers on an income statement be used to measure a company's profitability? (See pp. 80–81.)
- What useful nonfinancial information can be found in a company's annual report? (See pp. 82–83.)

(*continued*)

2006 Financial Highlights

In Millions, Except per Share Data

Fiscal Year Ended	May 28, 2006	May 29, 2005	Change
Net Sales	$ 11,640	$ 11,244	4%
Segment Operating Profit	2,119	2,024	5
Net Earnings	1,090	1,240	−12
Diluted Earnings per Share	2.90	3.08	−6
Average Diluted Common Shares Outstanding	379	409	−7
Dividends per Share	$ 1.34	$ 1.24	8

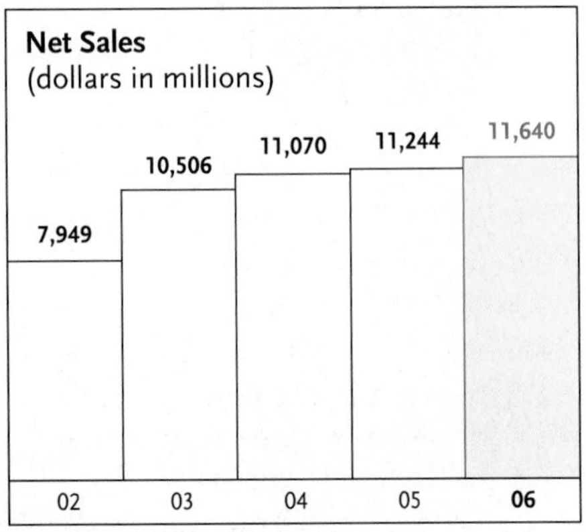

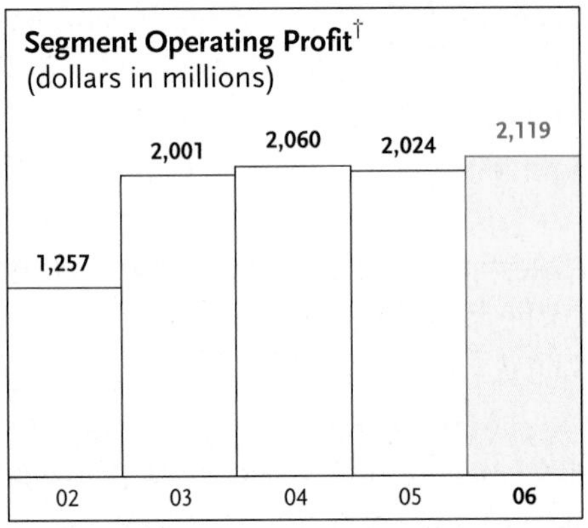

Fiscal 2004 included 53 weeks. All other fiscal periods shown included 52 weeks.
†See page 24 of the 2006 Annual Report on Form 10-K for discussion of these non-GAAP measures.
Source: General Mills's 2006 annual report.

Objectives of Financial Reporting

LO1 Describe the objectives of financial reporting.

As was discussed in Chapter 1, a variety of external users need information to make sound business decisions. These users include stockholders; bondholders; bankers; and other types of creditors, such as suppliers. All of these users must make an initial decision about investing in a company, regardless of whether it is in the form of a stock, a bond, or a note. The balance sheet, the income statement, and the statement of cash flows, along with the supporting notes and other information found in an annual report, are the key sources of information needed to make sound decisions.

- **The *balance sheet* tells what obligations will be due in the near future and what assets will be available to satisfy them.**
- **The *income statement* tells the revenues and expenses for a period of time.**
- **The *statement of cash flows* tells where cash came from and how it was used during the period.**
- **The *notes* provide essential details about the company's accounting policies and other key factors that affect its financial condition and performance.**

To use the basic information that is found, decision makers must understand the underlying accounting principles that have been applied to create the reported information in the statements. In preparing financial statements, accountants consider:

- **The objectives of financial reporting.**
- **The characteristics that make accounting information useful.**
- **The most useful way to display the information found in the balance sheet, the income statement, and the statement of cash flows.**

The users of financial information are the main reason financial statements are prepared. After all, it is the investors, creditors, and other groups and individuals outside and inside the company who must make economic decisions based on these statements. Therefore, as you learned in Chapter 1, financial statements must be based on agreed-upon assumptions such as time period, going concern, and other GAAP.

Moreover, when the accountants for companies such as **General Mills** prepare their financial statements, they must keep in mind financial reporting objectives that are focused on providing the most understandable and useful information possible. **Financial reporting has one overall objective and a set of related objectives, all of them concerned with how the information may be most useful to the readers.**

THE PRIMARY OBJECTIVE OF FINANCIAL REPORTING

The primary objective of financial reporting is to provide economic information to permit users of the information to make informed decisions. Users include both the management of a company (internal users) and others not involved in the daily operations of the business (external users). The external users usually do not have access to the detailed records of the business and don't have the benefit of daily involvement in the affairs of the company. They make their decisions based on *financial statements* prepared by management. According to the FASB, "Financial reporting should provide information that is useful to present and potential investors and creditors and other users in making rational investment, credit, and similar decisions."[1]

You can see from that statement how closely the objective of financial reporting is tied to decision making. **The purpose of financial reporting is to help the users reach their decisions in an informed manner.**

SECONDARY OBJECTIVES OF FINANCIAL REPORTING

Three secondary objectives follow from the primary objective of financial reporting. They are as follows:

- **Reflect Prospective Cash Receipts to Investors and Creditors**

  Investor: If I buy stock in this company, how much cash will I receive:

  - In dividends?
  - From the sale of the stock?

  Banker: If I lend money to this company, how much cash will I receive:

  - In interest on the loan?
  - When and if the loan is repaid?

- **Reflect Prospective Cash Flows to the Company**

  Investors, bankers, and other users ultimately care about their cash receipts; but this depends to some extent on the company's skills in managing its *own* cash flows.

1 *Statement of Financial Accounting Concepts [SFAC] No. 1*, "Objectives of Financial Reporting by Business Enterprises" (Stamford, Conn.: Financial Accounting Standards Board, November 1978), par. 34.

- **Reflect the Company's Resources and Claims to its Resources**

  A company's cash flows are inherently tied to the information on the:
  - Balance sheet (assets, liabilities, and owners' equity).
  - Income statement (revenues and expenses).

Exhibit 2-1 summarizes the objectives of financial reporting as they pertain to someone considering whether to buy stock in General Mills. The exhibit should help you understand how something as abstract as a set of financial reporting objectives can be applied to a decision-making situation.

EXHIBIT 2-1 The Application of Financial Reporting Objectives

Financial Reporting Objective	Potential Investor's Questions
1. The primary objective: Provide information for decision making.	Based on the financial information, should I buy shares of stock in General Mills?
2. Secondary objective: Reflect prospective cash receipts to investors and creditors.	How much cash, if any, will I receive in dividends each year and how much from the sale of the stock of General Mills in the future?
3. Secondary objective: Reflect prospective cash flows to an enterprise.	After paying its suppliers and employees and meeting all of its obligations, how much cash will General Mills take in during the time I own the stock?
4. Secondary objective: Reflect resources and claims to resources.	How much has General Mills invested in new stores?

POD REVIEW 2.1

LO1 *Describe the objectives of financial reporting.*

- The main objective of financial statements is to convey useful and timely information to parties for making economic decisions.
  - Decision makers include investors, creditors, and other individuals or groups inside and outside the firm.
- Secondary objectives include providing information to evaluate cash flows, resources of the company, and claims to those resources.

QUESTIONS

1. *The primary purpose of financial reporting is to*
   a. help users reach decisions in an informed manner.
   b. provide the information necessary to prepare a tax return.
   c. provide a historical record of a company's performance.
   d. none of the above.

2. *All of the following are secondary objectives of financial reporting* except
   a. reflect prospective cash receipts to investors and creditors.
   b. reflect prospective cash flows to the company.
   c. reflect the company's resources and claims to its resources.
   d. All of the above are secondary objectives of financial reporting.

What Makes Accounting Information Useful? Qualitative Characteristics

LO2 Describe the qualitative characteristics of accounting information.

Since accounting information must be useful for decision making, what makes this information useful? This section focuses on the qualities that accountants strive for in their financial reporting and on some of the challenges that accountants face in making reporting judgments. It also reveals what users of financial information expect from financial statements.

Quantitative considerations such as tuition costs certainly were a concern when you chose your current school. In addition, your decision required you to make subjective judgments about the *qualitative* characteristics you were looking for in a college. Similarly, there are certain qualities that make accounting information useful.

UNDERSTANDABILITY

For anything to be useful, it must be understandable.

Usefulness and understandability go hand in hand. However, **understandability** of financial information varies considerably depending on the background of the user. For example, should financial statements be prepared so that they are understandable by anyone with a college education? Or should it be assumed that all readers of financial statements have completed at least one accounting course? Is a background in business necessary for a good understanding of financial reports, regardless of one's formal training? As you might expect, there are no simple answers to those questions. However, the FASB believes that **financial information should be comprehensible to *those who are willing to spend the time to understand it*:**

Understandability The quality of accounting information that makes it comprehensible to those willing to spend the necessary time.

> *Financial information is a tool and, like most tools, cannot be of much direct help to those who are unable or unwilling to use it or who misuse it. Its use can be learned, however, and financial reporting should provide information that can be used by all—nonprofessionals as well as professionals—who are willing to learn to use it properly.*[2]

RELEVANCE

Understandability alone is certainly not enough to render information useful.

To be useful, information must be relevant.

Relevance is the capacity of information to make a difference in a decision.[3] For example, assume that you are a banker evaluating the financial statements of a company that has come to you for a loan. All of the financial statements point to a strong and profitable company. However, today's newspaper revealed that the company has been named in a multimillion-dollar lawsuit. Undoubtedly, this information would be relevant to your talks with the company, and disclosure of the lawsuit in the financial statements would make them even more relevant to your lending decision.

Relevance The capacity of information to make a difference in a decision.

RELIABILITY

What makes accounting information reliable? According to the FASB, "Accounting information is reliable to the extent that users can depend on it to represent the economic conditions or events that it purports to represent."[4]

2 *SFAC No. 1*, par. 36.
3 *Statement of Financial Accounting Concepts [SFAC] No. 2*, "Qualitative Characteristics of Accounting Information" (Stamford, Conn.: Financial Accounting Standards Board, May 1980), par. 47.
4 *SFAC No. 2*, par. 62.

Reliability
The quality that makes accounting information dependable in representing the events that it purports to represent.

Reliability has three basic characteristics:

1. *Verifiability* Information is verifiable when we can make sure that it is free from error—for example, by looking up the cost paid for an asset in a contract or an invoice.
2. *Representational faithfulness* Information is representationally faithful when it corresponds to an actual event—such as when the purchase of land corresponds to a transaction in the company's records.
3. *Neutrality* Information is neutral when it is not slanted to portray a company's position in a better or worse light than the actual circumstances would dictate—such as when the probable losses from a major lawsuit are disclosed accurately in the notes to the financial statements, with all potential effects on the company, rather than minimized as a very remote possible loss.

COMPARABILITY AND CONSISTENCY

Comparability
For accounting information, the quality that allows a user to analyze two or more companies and look for similarities and differences.

Comparability allows comparisons to be made *between or among companies*.

GAAP allow a certain amount of freedom in choosing among competing alternative treatments for certain transactions.

Depreciation
The process of allocating the cost of a long-term tangible asset over its useful life.

For example, under GAAP, companies may choose from a number of methods of accounting for the depreciation of certain long-term assets. **Depreciation** is the *process of allocating* the cost of a long-term tangible asset, such as a building or equipment, over its useful life. Each method may affect the value of the assets differently. How does this freedom of choice affect the ability of investors to make comparisons between companies?

Assume that you are considering buying stock in one of three companies. As their annual reports indicate, one of the companies uses what is called the "accelerated" depreciation method and the other two companies use what is called the "straight-line" depreciation method. (We'll learn about these methods in Chapter 8.) Does this lack of a common depreciation method make it impossible for you to compare the performance of the three companies?

Obviously, comparisons among the companies would be easier and more meaningful if all three used the same depreciation method. However, comparisons are not impossible just because companies use different methods. Certainly, the more alike—that is, uniform—statements are in terms of the principles used to prepare them, the more comparable they will be. However, the profession allows a certain freedom of choice in selecting from alternative GAAP.

To render statements of companies using different methods more meaningful, *disclosure* assumes a very important role. For example, as we will see later in this chapter, the first note in the annual report of a publicly traded company is the disclosure of its accounting policies. The reader of this note for each of the three companies is made aware that the companies do not use the same depreciation method. Disclosure of accounting policies allows the reader to make some sort of subjective adjustment to the statements of one or more of the companies and thus to compensate for the different depreciation method being used.

Consistency
For accounting information, the quality that allows a user to compare two or more accounting periods for a single company.

Consistency means that financial statements can be compared *within a single company from one accounting period to the next.* Consistency is closely related to the concept of comparability. Both involve the relationship between two numbers—comparability between numbers of different companies (usually for the same period) and comparability between the numbers of a single company for different periods. However, whereas financial statements are comparable when they can be compared between one company and another, statements are consistent when they can be compared within a single company from one accounting period to the next.

Occasionally, companies decide to change from one accounting method to another. Will it be possible to compare a company's earnings in a period in which it switches methods with its earnings in prior years if the methods differ? Like the different methods used by different companies, changes in accounting methods from one period to the next do not make comparisons impossible, only more difficult. When a company makes an accounting change, accounting standards require various disclosures to help the reader evaluate the impact of the change.

MATERIALITY

For accounting information to be useful, it must be relevant to a decision.

The concept of **materiality** is closely related to relevance and deals with the size of an error in accounting information. The issue is whether the error is large enough to affect the judgment of someone relying on the information. Consider the following example. A company pays cash for two separate purchases: one for a $5 pencil sharpener and the other for a $50,000 computer. Theoretically, each expenditure results in the acquisition of an asset that should be depreciated over its useful life. However, what if the company decides to account for the $5 paid for the pencil sharpener as an expense of the period rather than treat it in the theoretically correct manner by depreciating it over the life of the pencil sharpener? *Will this error in any way affect the judgment of someone relying on the financial statements?* Because such a slight error will *not* affect any decisions, minor expenditures of this nature are considered *immaterial* and are accounted for as an expense of the period.

Materiality
The magnitude of an accounting information omission or misstatement that will affect the judgment of someone relying on the information.

The *threshold* for determining materiality will vary from one company to the next depending to a large extent on the size of the company. Many companies establish policies that *any* expenditure under a certain dollar amount should be accounted for as an expense of the period. The threshold might be $50 for the corner grocery store but $1,000 for a large corporation. Finally, in some instances, the amount of a transaction may be immaterial by company standards but may still be considered significant by financial statement users. For example, a transaction involving illegal or unethical behavior by a company officer would be of concern, regardless of the dollar amounts involved.

CONSERVATISM

Conservatism is the practice of using the least optimistic estimate when two estimates of amounts are about equally likely. It is a holdover from earlier days when the primary financial statement was the balance sheet and the primary user of this statement was the banker. It was customary to deliberately understate assets on the balance sheet because this resulted in an even larger margin of safety that the assets being provided as collateral for a loan were sufficient.

Conservatism
The practice of using the least optimistic estimate when two estimates of amounts are about equally likely.

Today the balance sheet is not the only financial statement, and deliberate understatement of assets is no longer considered desirable. The practice of conservatism is reserved for those situations in which there is *uncertainty* about how to account for a particular item or transaction: "Thus, if two estimates of amounts to be received or paid in the future are about equally likely, conservatism dictates using the less optimistic estimate; however, if two amounts are not equally likely, conservatism does not necessarily dictate using the more pessimistic amount rather than the more likely one."[5]

Various accounting rules are based on the concept of conservatism. For example, inventory held for resale is reported on the balance sheet at *the lower-of-cost-or-market value*. This rule requires a company to compare the cost of its inventory with the market price, or current cost to replace that inventory, and report the lower of the two amounts on the balance sheet at the end of the year. Chapter 5 will more fully explore the lower-of-cost-or-market rule as it pertains to inventory.

Exhibit 2-2 summarizes the qualities that make accounting information useful.

EXHIBIT 2-2 What Characteristics Make Information Useful?

Characteristic	Why Important?
Understandability	Must understand information to use it
Relevance	Must be information that could affect a decision
Reliability	Must be able to rely on the information
Comparability	Must be able to compare with other companies
Consistency	Must be able to compare with prior years
Materiality	Must be an amount large enough to affect a decision
Conservatism	If any doubt, use the least optimistic estimate

5 *SFAC No. 2*, par. 95.

AN INTERNATIONAL PERSPECTIVE ON QUALITATIVE CHARACTERISTICS

Chapter 1 introduced the IASB and its efforts to improve the development of accounting standards around the world. Interestingly, four of the most influential members of this group, representing the standard-setting bodies in the United States, the United Kingdom, Canada, and Australia, agree on the primary objective of financial reporting. All recognize that the primary objective is to provide information useful in making economic decisions.

The standard-setting body in the United Kingdom distinguishes between qualitative characteristics that relate to *content* of the information presented and those that relate to *presentation*. Similar to the FASB, this group recognizes relevance and reliability as the primary characteristics related to content. Comparability and understandability are the primary qualities related to the presentation of the information.

The concept of conservatism is also recognized in other countries. For example, both the IASB and the standard-setting body in the United Kingdom list "prudence" among their qualitative characteristics. Prudence requires the use of caution in making the various estimates required in accounting. Like the U.S. standard-setting body, these groups recognize that prudence does not justify the deliberate understatement of assets or revenues or the deliberate overstatement of liabilities or expenses.

POD REVIEW 2.2

LO2 *Describe the qualitative characteristics of accounting information.*

- Qualitative characteristics of accounting information are those attributes that make the information useful to users of the financial statements and include:
  - Understandability—this pertains to those who are willing to spend the time to understand the information.
  - Relevance—this is the capacity of information to make a difference in a decision.
  - Reliability—information that investors can depend on must be verifiable, neutral (not biased), and faithful in what it represents.
  - Comparable and consistent—GAAP provides guidelines that help standardize accounting practices and make information from one company to another or from one period to the next period for the same company comparable.
  - Conservatism—where uncertainty about how to account for economic activity exists, accounting choices that result in the least optimistic amount should be employed.

QUESTIONS

1. *The accounting characteristic that allows for comparisons to be made within a single company from one period to the next is*
   a. comparability.
   b. consistency.
   c. reliability.
   d. materiality.

2. *All of the following are characteristics that make accounting information useful* except
   a. relevance.
   b. materiality.
   c. reliability.
   d. All of the above are characteristics of useful accounting information.

The Classified Balance Sheet

LO3 Explain the concept and purpose of a classified balance sheet and prepare the statement.

Now that we have learned about the conceptual framework of accounting, we turn to the outputs of the system: the financial statements. First, using a hypothetical company, Dixon Sporting Goods, we will consider the significance of a *classified balance sheet*. We will then examine the *income statement*, the *statement of retained earnings*, and the *statement of cash flows* for this company. The chapter concludes with a brief look at the financial statements of a real company, General Mills, and at the other elements in an annual report.[6]

WHAT ARE THE PARTS OF THE BALANCE SHEET? UNDERSTANDING THE OPERATING CYCLE

The first part of this chapter stressed the importance of *cash flow*. For a company that sells a product, the **operating cycle** begins when cash is invested in inventory and ends when cash is collected by the enterprise from its customers.

Operating cycle
The period of time between the purchase of inventory and the collection of any receivable from the sale of the inventory.

Consider the typical operating cycle for a bike shop. Assume that on August 1, the shop buys a bike from the manufacturer for $400. At this point, the shop has merely substituted one asset, cash, for another, inventory. Assume that on August 20, 20 days after buying the bike, the shop sells it to a customer for $500. If the customer pays cash for the bike, the bike shop will have completed its cash-to-cash operating cycle in a total of 20 days, as shown in Exhibit 2-3.

Consider how the shop's operating cycle is extended if it sells the same bike to a customer on August 20 and allows the customer to pay for it in 30 days. Instead of an operating cycle of 20 days, a total of 50 days has passed between the use of cash to buy the bike from the manufacturer and the collection of cash from the customer, as shown in Exhibit 2-4.

EXHIBIT 2-3 **Operating Cycle: Cash Sale**

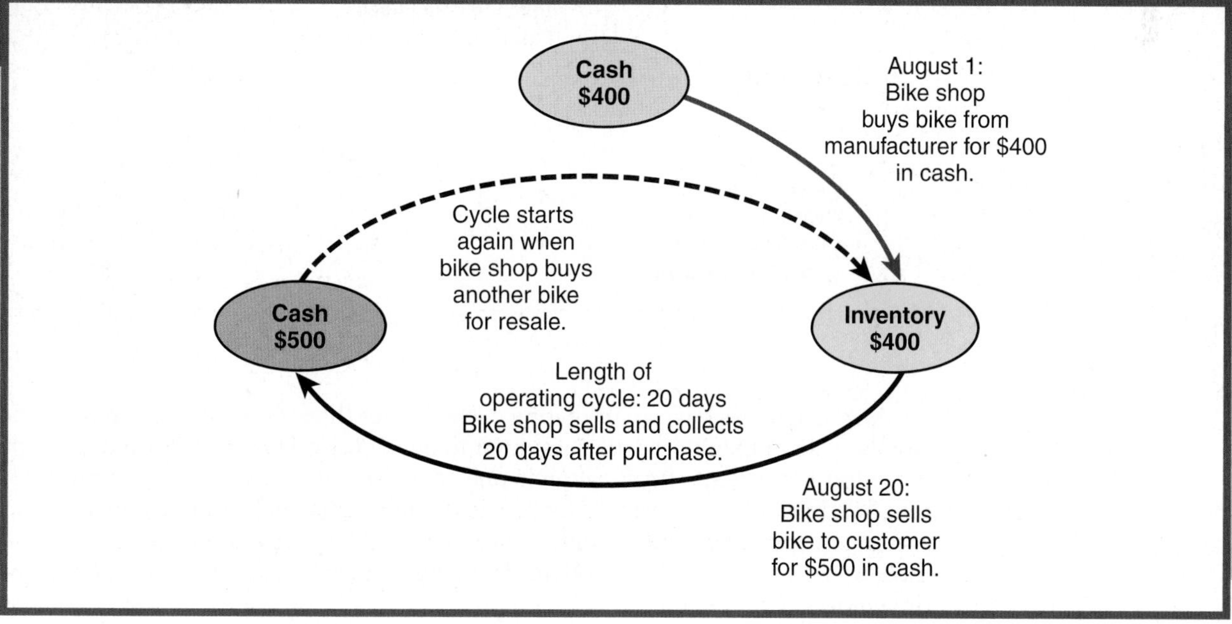

6 FASB is currently considering a number of changes in the format and presentation of the financial statements. Because any proposed changes are in the preliminary stages, we will not consider them further in this textbook.

EXHIBIT 2-4 Operating Cycle: Sale on Credit

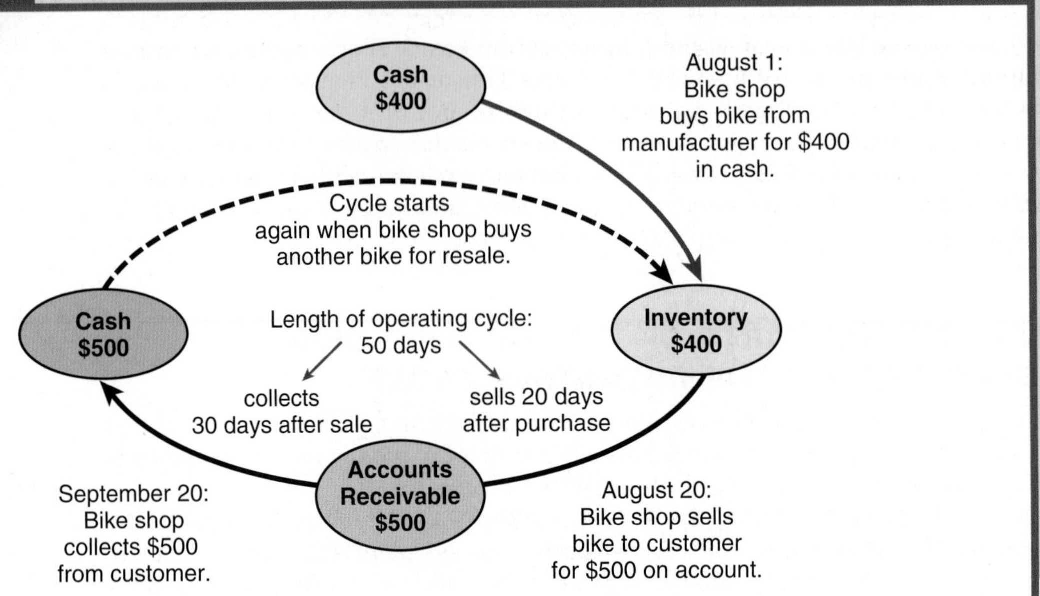

CURRENT ASSETS

Current asset
An asset that is expected to be realized in cash or sold or consumed during the operating cycle or within one year if the cycle is shorter than one year.

The basic distinction on a classified balance sheet is between current and noncurrent items. **Current assets** are "cash and other assets that are reasonably expected to be realized in cash or sold or consumed during the normal operating cycle of a business or within one year if the operating cycle is shorter than one year."[7]

The current assets section of Dixon Sporting Goods' balance sheet appears as follows:

Dixon Sporting Goods
Partial Balance Sheet

Current assets		
Cash	$ 5,000	
Marketable securities	11,000	
Accounts receivable	23,000	
Merchandise inventory	73,500	
Prepaid insurance	4,800	
Store supplies	700	
Total current assets		$ 118,000

Most businesses have an operating cycle shorter than one year. For example, the bike shop's cycle in Exhibit 2-4 was assumed to be 50 days. Therefore, for most companies, the cutoff for current classification is one year. We will use the one-year cutoff for current classification in the remainder of this chapter. Thus, on Dixon's balance sheet, cash, accounts receivable, and inventory are classified as current assets because they *are* cash or will be *realized* in (converted to) cash (accounts receivable) or will be *sold* (inventory) within one year.

7 Accounting Principles Board, *Statement of the Accounting Principles Board, No. 4*, "Basic Concepts and Accounting Principles Underlying Financial Statements of Business Enterprises" (New York: American Institute of Certified Public Accountants, 1970), par. 198.

In addition to cash, accounts receivable, and inventory, the two other most common types of current assets are marketable securities and prepaid expenses. Excess cash is often invested in the stocks and bonds of other companies as well as in various government instruments. If the investments are made for the short term, they are classified as current and are typically called *short-term investments* or *marketable securities.* (Alternatively, some investments are made for the purpose of exercising influence over another company and thus are made for the long term. These investments are classified as noncurrent assets.) Various prepayments, such as office supplies, rent, and insurance, are classified as *prepaid expenses* and thus are current assets. These assets qualify as current because they are usually *consumed* within one year.

NONCURRENT ASSETS

Any asset not meeting the definition of a current asset is classified as *long-term* or *noncurrent*. Three common categories of long-term assets are investments; property, plant, and equipment; and intangibles. For Dixon, these are as follows:

Dixon Sporting Goods
Partial Balance Sheet

Investments			
Land held for future office site			$150,000
Property, plant, and equipment			
Land		$100,000	
Buildings	$150,000		
Less: Accumulated depreciation	60,000	90,000	
Store furniture and fixtures	$ 42,000		
Less: Accumulated depreciation	12,600	29,400	
Total property, plant, and equipment			219,400
Intangible assets			
Franchise agreement			55,000

Investments Recall from the discussion of current assets, that stocks and bonds expected to be sold within the next year are classified as current assets. Securities not expected to be sold within the next year are classified as *investments.* In many cases, the investment is in the common stock of another company. Sometimes companies invest in another company either to exercise some influence over it or actually to control its operations. Other types of assets classified as investments are land held for future use and buildings and equipment not currently used in operations. For example, Dixon classifies as an investment some land it holds for a future office site. A special fund held for the retirement of debt or for the construction of new facilities is also classified as an investment.

Property, Plant, and Equipment This category consists of the various *tangible, productive assets* used in the operation of a business. Land, buildings, equipment, machinery, furniture and fixtures, trucks, and tools are all examples of assets held for use in the *operation* of a business rather than for *resale.* The distinction between inventory and equipment, for instance, depends on the company's *intent* in acquiring the asset. For example, **IBM** classifies a computer system as inventory because IBM's intent in manufacturing the asset is to offer it for resale. However, this same computer in the hands of a law firm would be classified as equipment because the firm's intent in buying the asset from IBM is to use it in the long-term operation of the business.

The relative size of property, plant, and equipment depends largely on a company's business. Consider **Xcel Energy**, a utility company with nearly $22 billion in total assets at the end of 2006. Over 70% of the total assets was invested in property, plant, and equipment. On the other hand, property and equipment represented less than 5% of the total assets of **Microsoft**, the highly successful software company.

Regardless of the relative size of property, plant, and equipment, all assets in this category are subject to depreciation with the exception of land. A separate accumulated depreciation account is used to account for the depreciation recorded on each of these assets over its life.

Intangibles Intangible assets are similar to property, plant, and equipment in that they provide benefits to the firm over the long term. The distinction, however, is in the *form* of the asset. *Intangible assets lack physical substance.* Trademarks, copyrights, franchise rights, patents, and goodwill are examples of intangible assets. The cost principle governs the accounting for intangibles, just as it does for tangible assets. For example, the amount paid to an inventor for the patent rights to a new project is recorded as an intangible asset. Similarly, the amount paid to purchase a franchise for a fast-food restaurant for the exclusive right to operate in a certain geographic area is recorded as an intangible asset. With a few exceptions, intangibles are written off to expense over their useful lives. *Depreciation* is the name given to the process of writing off tangible assets; the same process for intangible assets is called *amortization*. Depreciation and amortization are both explained more fully in Chapter 8.

CURRENT LIABILITIES

Current liability
An obligation that will be satisfied within the next operating cycle or within one year if the cycle is shorter than one year.

The definition of a current liability is closely tied to that of a current asset. A **current liability** is an obligation that will be satisfied within the next operating cycle or within one year if the cycle (as is normally the case) is shorter than one year. For example, the classification of a note payable on the balance sheet depends on its maturity date. If the note will be paid within the next year, it is classified as current; otherwise, it is classified as a long-term liability. On the other hand, accounts payable, wages payable, and income taxes payable are all short-term or current liabilities, as on Dixon's balance sheet:

Dixon Sporting Goods
Partial Balance Sheet

Current liabilities		
Accounts payable	$15,700	
Salaries and wages payable	9,500	
Income taxes payable	7,200	
Interest payable	2,500	
Bank loan payable	25,000	
Total current liabilities		$ 59,900

Most liabilities are satisfied by the payment of cash. However, certain liabilities are eliminated from the balance sheet when the company performs services. For example, the liability Subscriptions Received in Advance, which would appear on the balance sheet of a magazine publisher, is satisfied not by the payment of any cash, but by delivery of the magazine to the customers. Finally, it is possible to satisfy one liability by substituting another in its place. For example, a supplier might ask a customer to sign a written promissory note to replace an existing account payable if the customer is unable to pay at the present time.

LONG-TERM LIABILITIES

Any obligation that will not be paid or otherwise satisfied within the next year or the operating cycle, whichever is longer, is classified as a long-term liability, or long-term debt. Notes payable and bonds payable, both promises to pay money in the future, are two common forms of long-term debt. Some bonds have a life as long as 25 or 30 years.

Dixon's notes payable for $120,000 is classified as a long-term liability because it is not due in the next year:

Dixon Sporting Goods **Partial Balance Sheet**	
Long-term debt	
Notes payable, due December 31, 2018	$120,000

STOCKHOLDERS' EQUITY

Recall that stockholders' equity represents the owners' claims on the assets of the business. These claims arise from two sources: *contributed capital* and *earned capital*. The stockholders' equity section of Dixon's balance sheet reports the following:

Dixon Sporting Goods **Partial Balance Sheet**		
Contributed capital		
Capital stock, $10 par, 5,000 shares issued and outstanding	$ 50,000	
Paid-in capital in excess of par value	25,000	
Total contributed capital	$ 75,000	
Retained earnings	287,500	
Total stockholders' equity		$362,500

Contributed capital appears on the balance sheet in the form of capital stock, and earned capital takes the form of retained earnings. *Capital stock* indicates the owners' investment in the business. *Retained earnings* represents the accumulated earnings, or net income, of the business since its inception less all dividends paid during that time.

Most companies have a single class of capital stock called *common stock*. This is the most basic form of ownership in a business. All other claims against the company, such as those of *creditors* and *preferred stockholders*, take priority. *Preferred stock* is a form of capital stock that, as the name implies, carries with it certain preferences. For example, the company must pay dividends on preferred stock before it makes any distribution of dividends on common stock. In the event of liquidation, preferred stockholders have priority over common stockholders in the distribution of the entity's assets.

Capital stock may appear as two separate items on the balance sheet: *Par Value* and *Paid-in Capital in Excess of Par Value*. The total of these two items tells us the amount that has been paid by the owners for the stock. We will take a closer look at these items in Chapter 11.

Exhibit 2-5 shows a complete classified balance sheet for Dixon Sporting Goods.

Study Tip

Do not try to memorize each of the items listed on the balance sheet in Exhibit 2-5 or any of the other exhibits shown in the chapter. Instead, read each account title and try to understand what would be included in the account. Account titles vary from one company to the next, and the names used by a company should give you an indication of what is included in the account.

EXHIBIT 2-5 **Classified Balance Sheet for Dixon Sporting Goods**

DIXON SPORTING GOODS INC.
BALANCE SHEET
AT DECEMBER 31, 2008

ASSETS

Current assets				
Cash			$ 5,000	
Marketable securities			11,000	
Accounts receivable			23,000	
Merchandise inventory			73,500	
Prepaid insurance			4,800	
Store supplies			700	
Total current assets				$118,000
Investments				
Land held for future office site				150,000
Property, plant, and equipment				
Land			$100,000	
Buildings		$150,000		
Less: Accumulated depreciation		60,000	90,000	
Store furniture and fixtures		$ 42,000		
Less: Accumulated depreciation		12,600	29,400	
Total property, plant, and equipment				219,400
Intangible assets				
Franchise agreement				55,000
Total assets				$542,400

Callouts: "These assets are cash now, will be collected in cash, or will be consumed in one year." (current assets); "These assets will not be sold or used up within one year." (investments, property, plant, and equipment, intangible assets)

LIABILITIES

Current liabilities			
Accounts payable		$ 15,700	
Salaries and wages payable		9,500	
Income taxes payable		7,200	
Interest payable		2,500	
Bank loan payable		25,000	
Total current liabilities			$ 59,900
Long-term debt			
Notes payable, due December 31, 2018			120,000
Total liabilities			$179,900

Callouts: "These are liabilities that will be satisfied within one year." (current liabilities); "These are liabilities that will not be satisfied within one year." (long-term debt)

STOCKHOLDERS' EQUITY

Contributed capital			
Capital stock, $10 par, 5,000 shares issued and outstanding		$ 50,000	
Paid-in capital in excess of par value		25,000	
Total contributed capital		$ 75,000	
Retained earnings		287,500	
Total stockholders' equity			362,500
Total liabilities and stockholders' equity			$542,400

Callout: "These are owners' claims on assets."

POD REVIEW 2.3

LO3 *Explain the concept and purpose of a classified balance sheet and prepare the statement.*

- The classified balance sheet classifies items of assets, liabilities, and stockholders' equity in a way that makes them useful to users of this financial statement.
  - Assets and liabilities are classified according to the length of time they will serve the company or require its resources.
    - Current assets or liabilities are those whose expected lives are one year or one operating cycle, whichever is longer. Noncurrent assets or liabilities are expected to last beyond this period of time.
    - Within current or noncurrent classifications, assets and liabilities are further subclassified into categories that describe the nature of these assets and liabilities; for example, "Property, Plant, and Equipment."

QUESTIONS

1. *All of the following are examples of current assets* except
   a. cash.
   b. prepaid insurance.
   c. land.
   d. accounts receivable.

2. *A company has an obligation due in 2012. On a balance sheet prepared at the end of 2008, the obligation should be classified as*
   a. a current asset.
   b. a current liability.
   c. a long-term debt.
   d. none of the above.

Using a Classified Balance Sheet: Introduction to Ratios

LO4 Use a classified balance sheet to analyze a company's financial position.

A classified balance sheet separates assets and liabilities into those that are current and those that are noncurrent. This distinction is very useful in any analysis of a company's financial position.

WORKING CAPITAL

Investors, bankers, and other interested readers use the balance sheet to evaluate the liquidity of a business. **Liquidity** is a relative term and deals with the ability of a company to pay its debts as they come due. As you might expect, bankers and other creditors are particularly interested in the liquidity of businesses to which they have lent money. A comparison of current assets and current liabilities is a starting point in evaluating the ability of a company to meet its obligations. **Working capital** is the difference between current assets and current liabilities at a point in time. Referring to Exhibit 2-5, you can see that the working capital for Dixon Sporting Goods on December 31, 2008, is as follows:

Liquidity
The ability of a company to pay its debts as they come due.

Working capital
Current assets minus current liabilities.

Working Capital

Formula	For Dixon Sporting Goods
Current Assets − Current Liabilities	\$118,000 − \$59,900 = \$58,100

The management of working capital is an important task for any business. A company must continually strive for a *balance* in managing its working capital. For example, too little working capital—or in the extreme, negative working capital—may signal the inability to pay creditors on a timely basis. However, an overabundance of working capital could indicate that the company is not investing enough of its available funds in productive resources, such as new machinery and equipment.

CURRENT RATIO

Current ratio
Current assets divided by current liabilities.

Because it is an absolute dollar amount, working capital is limited in its informational value. For example, $1 million may be an inadequate amount of working capital for a large corporation but far too much for a smaller company. In addition, a certain dollar amount of working capital may have been adequate for a company earlier in its life but is inadequate now. However, a related measure of liquidity, the **current ratio**, allows us to *compare* the liquidity of companies of different sizes and of a single company over time. The ratio is computed by dividing current assets by current liabilities. The following formula shows that Dixon Sporting Goods has a current ratio of just under 2 to 1:

Current Ratio

Formula	For Dixon Sporting Goods	
Current Assets / Current Liabilities	$118,000 / $ 59,900	= 1.97 to 1

Dixon Sporting Goods
Partial Balance Sheet

Current assets		
Cash	$ 5,000	
Marketable securities	11,000	
Accounts receivable	23,000	
Merchandise inventory	73,500	
Prepaid insurance	4,800	
Store supplies	700	
Total current assets		$118,000

Current liabilities		
Accounts payable	$15,700	
Salaries and wages payable	9,500	
Income taxes payable	7,200	
Interest payable	2,500	
Bank loan payable	25,000	
Total current liabilities		$59,900

In general, the higher the current ratio, the more liquid the company. Some analysts use a rule of thumb of 2 to 1 for the current ratio as a sign of short-term financial health. However, rules of thumb can be dangerous. Historically, companies in certain industries have operated quite efficiently with a current ratio of less than 2 to 1, whereas a ratio much higher than that is necessary to survive in other industries. Consider **Gap Inc.**, the popular clothing company. On February 3, 2007, it had a current ratio of 2.21 to 1. On the other hand, companies in the telephone communication business routinely have current ratios from well under 1 to 1. **AT&T**'s current ratio at the end of 2006 was only 0.63 to 1.

Unfortunately, neither the amount of working capital nor the current ratio tells us anything about the *composition* of current assets and current liabilities. For example, assume that two companies have total current assets equal to $100,000. Company A has cash of $10,000, accounts receivable of $50,000, and inventory of $40,000. Company B also has cash of $10,000 but accounts receivable of $20,000 and inventory of $70,000. All other things being equal, Company A is more liquid than Company B because more of its total current assets are in receivables than inventory. Receivables are only one step away from being cash, whereas inventory must be sold and then the receivable collected. Note that Dixon's inventory of $73,500 makes up a large portion of its total current assets of $118,000. An examination of the *relative* size of the various current assets for a company may reveal certain strengths and weaknesses not evident in the current ratio.

In addition to the composition of the current assets, the *frequency* with which they are "turned over" is important. For instance, how long does it take to sell an item of inventory? How long is required to collect an account receivable? Many companies could not exist with the current ratio of 0.90 reported by **Southwest Airlines** at the end of 2006. However, think about the nature of the airline business. Without large amounts in inventories or accounts receivable, an airline can operate with a lower current ratio than a manufacturing company can for example.

POD REVIEW 2.4

LO4 *Use a classified balance sheet to analyze a company's financial position.*

- Classifications within the balance sheet allow users to analyze various aspects of a company's financial position; for example, its liquidity.
  - Liquidity relates to the ability of a company to pay its obligations as they come due.
  - Working capital and the current ratio are two measures of liquidity.

QUESTIONS

1. *Working capital is computed by*
   a. dividing current assets by current liabilities.
   b. dividing current liabilities by current assets.
   c. deducting current liabilities from current assets.
   d. deducting current assets from current liabilities.

2. *A company reports current assets of $50,000 and current liabilities of $20,000. Its current ratio is*
   a. 0.40.
   b. 2.50.
   c. 1.00.
   d. none of the above.

The Income Statement

LO5 Explain the difference between a single-step and a multiple-step income statement and prepare each type of income statement.

The income statement summarizes the results of operations of an entity for a *period of time*. At a minimum, all companies prepare income statements at least once a year. Companies that must report to the SEC prepare financial statements, including an income statement, every three months. Monthly income statements are usually prepared for internal use by management.

WHAT APPEARS ON THE INCOME STATEMENT?

From an accounting perspective, it is important to understand what transactions of an entity should appear on the income statement. In general, the income statement reports the excess of revenue over expense—that is, the *net income* (or in the event of an excess of expense over revenue, the net loss of the period). As a reference to the "bottom line" on an income statement, it is common to use the term *profits* or *earnings* as synonyms for *net income*.

As discussed in Chapter 1, *revenue* is the inflow of assets resulting from the sale of products and services. It represents the dollar amount of sales of products and services for a period of time. An *expense* is the outflow of assets resulting from the sale of goods and services for a period of time. Wages and salaries, utilities, and taxes are examples of expenses.

Certain special types of revenues, called *gains*, are sometimes reported on the income statement, as are certain special types of expenses, called *losses*. For example, assume that Sanders Company holds a parcel of land for a future building site. The company paid $50,000 for the land ten years ago. The state pays Sanders $60,000 for the property to use in a new highway project. Sanders has a special type of revenue from the condemnation of its property. It will recognize a *gain* of $10,000: the excess of the cash received from the state, $60,000, over the cost of the land, $50,000.

FORMAT OF THE INCOME STATEMENT

Different formats are used by corporations to present their results. The major choice a company makes is whether to prepare the income statement in a single-step or a multiple-step form. Both forms are generally accepted although more companies use the multiple-step form. Next, we'll explain the differences between the two forms and their variations.

Single-step income statement
An income statement in which all expenses are added together and subtracted from all revenues.

Single-Step Format for the Income Statement In a **single-step income statement**, all expenses and losses are added together and then deducted *in a single step* from all revenues and gains to arrive at net income. A single-step format for the income statement of Dixon Sporting Goods is presented in Exhibit 2-6. The primary advantage of the single-step form is its simplicity. No attempt is made to classify revenues or expenses or to associate any of the expenses with any of the revenues.

Multiple-step income statement
An income statement that shows classifications of revenues and expenses as well as important subtotals.

Gross profit
Sales less cost of goods sold.

Multiple-Step Format for the Income Statement The purpose of the **multiple-step income statement** is to subdivide the income statement into specific sections and provide the reader with important subtotals. This format is illustrated for Dixon Sporting Goods in Exhibit 2-7.

The multiple-step income statement for Dixon indicates three important subtotals. First, ❶ cost of goods sold is deducted from sales to arrive at **gross profit**:

Gross Profit = Sales − Cost of Goods Sold	
Sales	$357,500
Cost of goods sold	218,300
Gross profit	$139,200

EXHIBIT 2-6 Income Statement (Single-Step Format) for Dixon Sporting Goods

DIXON SPORTING GOODS INC.
INCOME STATEMENT (SINGLE-STEP FORMAT)
FOR THE YEAR ENDED DECEMBER 31, 2008

Revenues		
Sales	$357,500	
Interest	1,500	
Total revenues		$359,000
Expenses		
Cost of goods sold	$218,300	
Depreciation on store furniture and fixtures	4,200	
Advertising	13,750	
Salaries and wages for sales staff	22,000	
Depreciation on buildings and amortization of trademark	6,000	
Salaries and wages for office staff	15,000	
Insurance	3,600	
Supplies	1,050	
Interest	16,900	
Income taxes	17,200	
Total expenses		318,000
Net income		$ 41,000

In a **single-step** income statement, expenses are deducted from revenues in one step.

EXHIBIT 2-7 Income Statement (Multiple-Step Format) for Dixon Sporting Goods

In a **multiple-step** income statement:

- ❶ Sales and the **costs** of sales are compared.
- Expenses of the business are detailed.
- Isolating expenses and revenues by type is useful in analyzing a business.
- ❷ Operating income is highlighted.
- ❸ "Nonoperating" revenues and expenses are included here.
- ❹

DIXON SPORTING GOODS INC.
INCOME STATEMENT (MULTIPLE-STEP FORMAT)
FOR THE YEAR ENDED DECEMBER 31, 2008

Sales		$357,500	
Cost of goods sold		218,300	
Gross profit			$139,200
Operating expenses			
Selling expenses			
Depreciation on store furniture and fixtures	$ 4,200		
Advertising	13,750		
Salaries and wages	22,000		
Total selling expenses		$ 39,950	
General and administrative expenses			
Depreciation on buildings and amortization of trademark	$ 6,000		
Salaries and wages	15,000		
Insurance	3,600		
Supplies	1,050		
Total general and administrative expenses		25,650	
Total operating expenses			65,600
Income from operations			$ 73,600
Other revenues and expenses			
Interest revenue		$ 1,500	
Interest expense		16,900	
Excess of other expenses over other revenue			15,400
Income before income taxes			$ 58,200
Income tax expense			17,200
Net income			$ 41,000

Cost of goods sold, as the name implies, is the cost of the units of inventory sold during the year. It is logical to associate cost of goods sold with the sales revenue for the year because the latter represents the *selling price* of the inventory sold during the period.

The second important subtotal on Dixon's income statement is ❷ *income from operations* of $73,600. This is found by subtracting *total operating expenses* of $65,600 from the gross profit of $139,200. Operating expenses are further subdivided between *selling expenses* and *general and administrative expenses.* For example, note that two depreciation amounts are included in operating expenses. Depreciation on store furniture and fixtures is classified as a selling expense because the store is where sales take place. On the other hand, we will assume that the buildings are offices for the administrative staff; thus, depreciation on the buildings is classified as a general and administrative expense.

The third important subtotal on the income statement is ❸ *income before income taxes* of $58,200. Interest revenue and interest expense, neither of which is an operating item, are included in *other revenues and expenses.* The excess of interest expense of $16,900 over interest revenue of $1,500, which equals $15,400, is subtracted from income from operations to arrive at income before income taxes. Finally, ❹ *income tax expense* of $17,200 is deducted to arrive at *net income* of $41,000.

POD REVIEW 2.5

LO5 ***Explain the difference between a single-step and a multiple-step income statement and prepare each type of income statement.***

- The multiple-step income statement classifies revenues and expenses in a manner that makes the statement more useful than the simple single-step income statement. Important subtotals are presented in the multiple-step income statement, including the following:
  - Gross profit
  - Income from operations
  - Income before income taxes

QUESTIONS

1. *The income statement summarizes the results of operations*
   a. at a given point in time.
   b. for a period of time.
   c. since a company began in business.
   d. none of the above.

2. *Which of the following descriptions would appear on a multiple-step income statement but not on a single-step income statement?*
   a. total revenues
   b. total expenses
   c. income before income taxes
   d. net income

Using an Income Statement

LO6 Use a multiple-step income statement to analyze a company's operations.

Profit margin
Net income divided by sales. ***Alternate term:*** *Return on sales.*

An important use of the income statement is to evaluate the *profitability* of a business. For example, a company's **profit margin** is the ratio of its net income to its sales or revenues. Some analysts refer to a company's profit margin as its *return on sales*. If the profit margin is high, this generally means that the company is generating revenue but that it is also controlling its costs. Dixon Sporting Goods would compute its profit margin by dividing its net income by its total sales as follows:

Profit Margin

Formula	For Dixon Sporting Goods
$\frac{\text{Net Income}}{\text{Sales}}$	$\frac{\$41{,}000}{\$357{,}500} = 11\%$

Dixon Sporting Goods
Partial Income Statement

Sales	$357,500
Net income	$ 41,000

A profit margin of 11% tells you that for every dollar of sales, Dixon has $0.11 in net income.

Keep two key factors in mind when evaluating any financial statement ratio.

- **How does this year's ratio differ from ratios of prior years?** For example, a decrease in the profit margin may indicate that the company is having trouble this year controlling certain costs.
- **How does the ratio compare with industry norms?** For example, in some industries, the profit margin is considerably lower than in many other industries, such as in mass merchandising. (**Wal-Mart**'s profit margin was only 3.3% for the year ended January 31, 2007.) It is helpful to compare key ratios, such as the profit margin, with an industry average or with the same ratio for a close competitor of the company.

POD REVIEW 2.6

LO6 *Use a multiple-step income statement to analyze a company's operations.*

- The multiple-step income statement can be used to evaluate different aspects of a company's profitability.
- Profit margin is one useful ratio used to evaluate the relative profitability.

QUESTIONS

1. *Profit margin is computed by*
   a. dividing net income by operating revenues.
   b. dividing operating revenues by net income.
   c. deducting net income from operating revenues.
   d. none of the above.

2. *In evaluating a company's profit margin, it is important to compare it with*
   a. prior years.
   b. industry norms.
   c. both prior years and industry norms.
   d. neither prior years nor industry norms.

The Statement of Retained Earnings

LO7 Identify the components of the statement of retained earnings and prepare the statement.

The purpose of a statement of stockholders' equity is to explain the changes in the components of owners' equity during the period. Retained earnings and capital stock are the two primary components of stockholders' equity. If during the period no changes occur in a company's capital stock, the company may choose to present a statement of retained earnings instead of a statement of stockholders' equity. A statement of retained earnings for Dixon Sporting Goods is shown in Exhibit 2-8.

The statement of retained earnings provides an important link between the income statement and the balance sheet. Dixon's net income of $41,000, as detailed on the income statement, is an *addition* to retained earnings. Note that the dividends declared and paid of $25,000 do not appear on the income statement because they are a payout, or *distribution*, of net income to stockholders rather than one of the expenses deducted to arrive at net income. Accordingly, they appear as a direct deduction on the statement of retained earnings. The beginning balance in retained earnings is carried forward from last year's statement of retained earnings.

EXHIBIT 2-8 **Statement of Retained Earnings for Dixon Sporting Goods**

Dixon Sporting Goods
Statement of Retained Earnings
For the Year Ended December 31, 2008

Retained earnings, January 1, 2008	$271,500
Add: Net income for 2008	41,000
	$312,500
Less: Dividends declared and paid in 2008	(25,000)
Retained earnings, December 31, 2008	$287,500

POD REVIEW 2.7

LO7 *Identify the components of the statement of retained earnings and prepare the statement.*

- The statement of retained earnings provides a link between the income statement and the balance sheet.
- It explains the changes in retained earnings during the period, of which net income (loss) is an important component.

QUESTIONS

1. *Which of the following indicates the proper treatment of net income and dividends on a statement of retained earnings?*
   a. Net income is added and dividends are deducted.
   b. Net income is deducted and dividends are added.
   c. Net income is added and dividends are added.
   d. Net income is deducted and dividends are deducted.

2. *Dividends are reported on*
   a. the income statement and the statement of retained earnings.
   b. the income statement but not the statement of retained earnings.
   c. the statement of retained earnings but not the income statement.
   d. neither the income statement nor the statement of retained earnings.

The Statement of Cash Flows

LO8 Identify the components of the statement of cash flows and prepare the statement.

All publicly held corporations are required to present a statement of cash flows in their annual reports. **The purpose of the statement is to summarize the cash flow effects of a company's operating, investing, and financing activities for the period.** The statement of cash flows for Dixon Sporting Goods consists of three categories:

Operating activities
Investing activities
Financing activities

Each of the three categories can result in a net inflow or a net outflow of cash.

- Dixon's **operating activities** generated $56,100 of cash during the period. Operating activities concern the purchase and sale of a product—in this case, the acquisition of sporting goods from distributors and the subsequent sale of those goods. As you can readily see, Dixon had one major source of cash, the collection from its customers of $362,500. Similarly, Dixon's largest use of cash was the $217,200 it paid for inventory. Chapter 12 will discuss the statement of cash flows in detail and the preparation of this section of the statement.

Dixon Sporting Goods
Partial Statement of Cash Flows

CASH FLOWS FROM OPERATING ACTIVITIES		
Cash collected from customers	$362,500	
Cash collected in interest	1,500	
Total cash collections		$364,000
Cash payments for:		
Inventory	$217,200	
Salaries and wages	38,500	
Interest	16,900	
Store supplies	850	
Insurance	4,800	
Advertising	13,750	
Income taxes	15,900	
Total cash payments		307,900
Net cash provided by operating activities		$ 56,100

Investing and financing activities were described in Chapter 1.

- **Investing activities** involve the acquisition and sale of long-term or noncurrent assets, such as long-term investments, property, plant, and equipment, and intangible assets.

Dixon Sporting Goods
Partial Statement of Cash Flows

CASH FLOWS FROM INVESTING ACTIVITIES	
Purchase of land for future office site	$(150,000)

Dixon spent $150,000 for land for a future office site. This is an investing activity.

- **Financing activities** result from the issuance and repayment, or retirement, of long-term liabilities and capital stock and the payment of dividends.

Dixon Sporting Goods
Partial Statement of Cash Flows

CASH FLOWS FROM FINANCING ACTIVITIES		
Dividends declared and paid	$(25,000)	
Proceeds from issuance of long-term note	120,000	
Net cash provided by financing activities		$95,000

The company had two financing activities: dividends of $25,000 required the use of cash, and the issuance of a long-term note generated cash of $120,000.

The complete cash flow statement for Dixon Sporting Goods is shown in Exhibit 2-9. The balance of cash on the bottom of the statement of $5,000 must agree with the balance for cash shown on the balance sheet in Exhibit 2-5.

EXHIBIT 2-9 Statement of Cash Flows for Dixon Sporting Goods Inc.

DIXON SPORTING GOODS INC.
STATEMENT OF CASH FLOWS
FOR THE YEAR ENDED DECEMBER 31, 2008

CASH FLOWS FROM OPERATING ACTIVITIES		
Cash collected from customers	$362,500	
Cash collected in interest	1,500	
Total cash collections		$364,000
Cash payments for:		
Inventory	$217,200	
Salaries and wages	38,500	
Interest	16,900	
Store supplies	850	
Insurance	4,800	
Advertising	13,750	
Income taxes	15,900	
Total cash payments		307,900
Net cash provided by operating activities		$ 56,100
CASH FLOWS FROM INVESTING ACTIVITIES		
Purchase of land for future office site		(150,000)
CASH FLOWS FROM FINANCING ACTIVITIES		
Dividends declared and paid	$ (25,000)	
Proceeds from issuance of long-term note	120,000	
Net cash provided by financing activities		95,000
Net increase in cash		$ 1,100
Cash at beginning of year		3,900
Cash at end of year		$ 5,000

Operating activities involve the purchase and sale of products or services.

Investing activities involve the acquisition and sale of long-term assets.

Financing activities involve the issuance and repayment of long-term liabilities and stock and the payment of dividends.

POD REVIEW 2.8

LO8 *Identify the components of the statement of cash flows and prepare the statement.*

- The statement of cash flows classifies cash inflows and outflows as originating from three activities: operating, investing, and financing.
  - Operating activities are related to the primary purpose of a business.
  - Investing activities are those generally involved with the acquisition and sale of noncurrent assets.
  - Financing activities are related to the acquisition and repayment of capital that ultimately funds the operations of a business; for example, borrowing or the issuance of stock.

QUESTIONS

1. *The three categories of activities reported on a statement of cash flows are*
   a. operating, investing, and producing.
   b. operating, investing, and financing.
   c. investing, financing, and selling.
   d. none of the above.

2. *The purchase of new equipment would be reported on a statement of cash flows as*
   a. an operating activity.
   b. a financing activity.
   c. an investing activity.
   d. none of the above.

Looking at Financial Statements for a Real Company: General Mills, Inc.

LO9 Read and use the financial statements and other elements in the annual report of a publicly held company.

The financial statements for the sporting goods company introduced the major categories on each of the statements. We now turn to these categories on the financial statements of an actual company, General Mills. The statements for a real company are more complex and require additional analysis and a better understanding of accounting to fully appreciate them. Therefore, we will concentrate on certain elements of the statements.

GENERAL MILLS'S BALANCE SHEET

Balance sheets for General Mills at the end of each of two years are shown in Exhibit 2-10, on page 78. General Mills releases what are called *consolidated financial statements*, which reflect the position and results of all operations that are controlled by a single entity. Like most other large corporations, General Mills owns other companies. Often these companies are legally separate and are called *subsidiaries*. How a company accounts for its investment in a subsidiary is covered in advanced accounting courses.

General Mills presents comparative balance sheets to indicate its financial position at the end of each of the last two years. As a minimum standard, the SEC requires that the annual report include balance sheets as of the two most recent year ends and income statements for each of the three most recent years. Note that all amounts on the balance sheet are stated in millions of dollars. This type of rounding is a common practice in the financial statements of large corporations and is justified under the materiality concept. Knowing the exact dollar amount of each asset would not change a decision made by an investor.

The current ratio was introduced earlier in the chapter. We will use the information on General Mills's balance sheet to analyze its current ratio (see page 79).

Real World Practice

2-1 Reading General Mills's Balance Sheet

What was the amount of working capital at May 28, 2006? at May 29, 2005? Did the company's total assets increase or decrease during the year?

GENERAL MILLS'S INCOME STATEMENT

We have examined two basic formats for the income statement: the single-step format and the multiple-step format. In practice, numerous variations on these two basic formats exist, depending to a large extent on the nature of a company's business.

Multiple-step income statements for General Mills for a three-year period are presented in Exhibit 2-11, on page 80. The inclusion of three years allows the reader to note certain general trends during this period. For example, note the steady increase in net sales during this period. In fact, the increase in net sales from the first year, 2004, to the third year, 2006, can be calculated as:

$$\frac{\text{Increase in net sales from 2004 to 2006:}}{\text{Net sales in 2004}} \quad \frac{\$11{,}640 - \$11{,}070}{\$11{,}070} = \frac{\$570}{\$11{,}070} = 5.1\%$$

Real World Practice

2-2 Reading General Mills's Income Statements

Compute the percentage increase in General Mills's net income over the three years. That is, by what percent did it increase from 2004 to 2006? Compare the percentage increase in net income to the percentage increase in net sales. What does a comparison of the two tell you?

EXHIBIT 2-10 Comparative Balance Sheets for General Mills, Inc.

General Mills, Inc., and Subsidiaries
Consolidated Balance Sheets

In Millions	May 28, 2006	May 29, 2005
ASSETS		
Current Assets:		
Cash and cash equivalents	$ 647	$ 573
Receivables	1,076	1,034
Inventories	1,055	1,037
Prepaid expenses and other current assets	216	203
Deferred income taxes	182	208
Total Current Assets	3,176	3,055
Land, Buildings and Equipment	2,997	3,111
Goodwill	6,652	6,684
Other Intangible Assets	3,607	3,532
Other Assets	1,775	1,684
Total Assets	$18,207	$18,066
LIABILITIES AND EQUITY		
Current Liabilities:		
Accounts payable	$ 1,151	$ 1,136
Current portion of long-term debt	2,131	1,638
Notes payable	1,503	299
Other current liabilities	1,353	1,111
Total Current Liabilities	6,138	4,184
Long-term Debt	2,415	4,255
Deferred Income Taxes	1,822	1,851
Other Liabilities	924	967
Total Liabilities	11,299	11,257
Minority Interests	1,136	1,133
Stockholders' Equity:		
Cumulative preference stock, none issued	—	—
Common stock, 502 shares issued	50	50
Additional paid-in capital	5,737	5,691
Retained earnings	5,107	4,501
Common stock in treasury, at cost, shares of 146 in 2006 and 133 in 2005	(5,163)	(4,460)
Unearned compensation	(84)	(114)
Accumulated other comprehensive income	125	8
Total Stockholders' Equity	5,772	5,676
Total Liabilities and Equity	$18,207	$18,066

See accompanying notes to consolidated financial statements.

Look at the headings on comparative balance sheets to see whether the most recent year-end is placed before or after the prior year's year-end. General Mills places the latest year on the left, which is the most common technique.

USING THE RATIO DECISION MODEL: ANALYZING THE CURRENT RATIO

Use the following Ratio Decision Model to evaluate the current ratio for General Mills or any other public company.

1. Formulate the Question

Managers, investors, and creditors are all interested in a company's liquidity. They must be able to answer the following question:

Is the company liquid enough to pay its obligations as they come due?

2. Gather the Information from the Financial Statements

The current ratio measures liquidity. To calculate the ratio, it is essential to know a company's current assets and liabilities. Current assets are the most liquid of all assets. Current liabilities are the debts that will be paid the soonest.

- Current assets: From the balance sheet
- Current liabilities: From the balance sheet

3. Calculate the Ratio

$$\textbf{Current Ratio} = \frac{\textbf{Current Assets}}{\textbf{Current Liabilities}}$$

General Mills
Partial Balance Sheet

	May 28, 2006
Assets	
Total current assets	$3,176
Liabilities and Stockholders' Equity	
Total current liabilities	$6,138

$$\text{Current Ratio} = \frac{\$3{,}176}{\$6{,}138} = 0.52 \text{ to } 1$$

4. Compare the Ratio with Others

Ratios are of no use in a vacuum. It is necessary to compare them with prior years and with competitors.

General Mills		Kellogg's	
May 28, 2006	May 29, 2005	December 30, 2006	December 31, 2005
0.52 to 1	0.73 to 1	0.60 to 1	0.69 to 1

5. Interpret the Results

In general, the higher the current ratio, the more liquid the company. However, earlier in the chapter you learned that rules of thumb do not always apply. It is necessary to take into account the nature of a company's business when evaluating ratios and other measures of performance. Also, ratios should be compared with those of prior years and with the same ratios of competitors. However, it should be noted that in making comparisons, the year-end is different for General Mills (end of May) and Kellogg's (end of December). Both companies operate with a relatively low current ratio compared to companies in other industries.

EXHIBIT 2-11 Comparative Income Statements for General Mills, Inc.

General Mills, Inc., and Subsidiaries
Consolidated Statements of Earnings

In Millions, Except per Share Data Fiscal Year Ended	May 28, 2006	May 29, 2005	May 30, 2004
Net Sales	$11,640	$11,244	$11,070
Costs and Expenses:			
Cost of sales	6,966	6,834	6,584
Selling, general and administrative	2,678	2,418	2,443
Interest, net	399	455	508
Restructuring and other exit costs	30	84	26
Divestitures (gain)	—	(499)	—
Debt repurchase costs		–137	—
Total Costs and Expenses	10,073	9,429	9,561
Earnings before Income Taxes and After-tax Earnings from Joint Ventures	1,567	1,815	1,509
Income Taxes	541	664	528
After-tax Earnings from Joint Ventures	64	89	74
Net Earnings	$ 1,090	$ 1,240	$ 1,055
Earnings per Share—Basic	$ 3.05	$ 3.34	$ 2.82
Earnings per Share—Diluted	$ 2.90	$ 3.08	$ 2.60
Dividends per Share	$ 1.34	$ 1.24	$ 1.10

See accompanying notes to consolidated financial statements.

We now turn our attention to how to calculate General Mills's profit margin and what it can tell us about the company's profitability.

USING THE RATIO DECISION MODEL: ANALYZING THE PROFIT MARGIN

Use the following Ratio Decision Model to evaluate the profit margin for General Mills or any other public company.

1. Formulate the Question
Managers, investors, and creditors are all interested in a company's profitability. They must be able to answer the following question:

How profitable has the company been in recent years?

2. Gather the Information from the Financial Statements
The profit margin is a measure of a company's profitability. To calculate the ratio, it is essential to know a company's sales and expenses and the difference between the two, net income.

- Net income—from the income statement
- Net sales—from the income statement

3. Calculate the Ratio

$$\text{Profit Margin} = \frac{\text{Net Income}}{\text{Net Sales}}$$

General Mills
Partial Income Statement

For the year ending May 28, 2006

Net sales	$11,640
Net income (earnings)	1,090

$$\text{Profit Margin} = \frac{\$1{,}090}{\$11{,}640} = 9.4\%$$

4. Compare the Ratio with Others

A comparison with prior performance helps determine whether profitability is increasing or decreasing.

General Mills		Kellogg's	
Year Ended May 28, 2006	**Year Ended May 29, 2005**	**Year Ended December 30, 2006**	**Year Ended December 31, 2005**
9.4%	11.0%	9.2%	9.6%

5. Interpret the Results

A high profit margin indicates that the company is controlling its expenses. This is because sales minus expenses equals net income; if the ratio of net income to sales is high, the company is not only generating revenue but also minimizing expenses. Also, ratios should be compared with those of prior years and with the same ratios for competitors. Both companies' profit margins indicate that the companies are able to control their expenses while increasing their sales.

The decline in General Mills's profit margin from 2005 to 2006 is a prime example of why ratios alone do not tell the whole story. Note the line item on the company's 2005 income statement titled "Divestitures (gain)," amounting to $499 million. This is a gain that would not be expected to recur; and without it, the profit margin in 2005 would not have been as high and would have been more in line with the ratio for 2006.

© James F. Quinn/MCT/Landov

Hot Topics

Who Will Reign Supreme over the Breakfast Table?

The food industry was all abuzz recently when *The Wall Street Journal* reported that Kraft Foods was looking for a buyer for its Post® cereals. Two obvious candidates to buy Post® are the two cereal powerhouses Kellogg's and General Mills. According to *Bloomberg News*, Kellogg's and General Mills currently hold shares of the U.S. cereal market of about 34% and 30%, respectively. Post®, with popular brands such as Shredded Wheat and Fruity Pebbles, comes in with a market share of about 14%. The watchful eye of the government's antitrust division is only one of the concerns that potential suitors such as Kellogg's and General Mills must consider. They also must wrestle with whether now is the time to expand further into a segment of the business that has seen relatively flat sales. And with all of this comes a price tag likely to be in the $2 to $3 billion range. Stay tuned for the latest developments in the battle for supremacy at the breakfast table.

Source: Pioneer Press, August 16, 2006; http://www.TwinCities.com

OTHER ELEMENTS OF AN ANNUAL REPORT

No two annual reports look the same. The appearance of an annual report depends not only on the size of a company but also on the budget devoted to the preparation of the report. Some companies publish bare-bones annual reports, whereas others issue a glossy report complete with pictures of company products and employees. In recent years, many companies, as a cost-cutting measure, have scaled back the amount spent on the annual report.

Privately held companies tend to distribute only financial statements, without the additional information normally included in the annual reports of public companies. For the annual reports of public companies, however, certain basic elements are considered standard:

- A letter to the stockholders from either the president or the chair of the board of directors appears in the first few pages of most annual reports.
- A section describing the company's products and markets is usually included.
- At the heart of any annual report is the financial report or review, which consists of the financial statements accompanied by notes to explain various items on the statements. We will now consider these other elements as presented in the 2006 annual report of General Mills.

Report of Independent Accountants (Auditors' Report) As you can see in Exhibit 2-12, General Mills is audited by **KPMG LLP**, one of the largest international

EXHIBIT 2-12 Report of Independent Accountants for General Mills, Inc.

Report of Independent Registered Public Accounting Firm on the Consolidated Financial Statements and Related Financial Statement Schedule

The Board of Directors and Stockholders General Mills, Inc.:

We have audited the accompanying consolidated balance sheets of General Mills, Inc. and subsidiaries as of May 28, 2006 and May 29, 2005, and the related consolidated statements of earnings, stockholders' equity and comprehensive income, and cash flows for each of the fiscal years in the three-year period ended May 28, 2006. In connection with our audits of the consolidated financial statements we also have audited the accompanying financial statement schedule.These consolidated financial statements and financial statement schedule are the responsibility of the Company's management. Our responsibility is to express an opinion on these consolidated financial statements and financial statement schedule based on our audits.

We conducted our audits in accordance with the standards of the Public Company Accounting Oversight Board (United States). Those standards require that we plan and perform the audit to obtain reasonable assurance about whether the financial statements are free of material misstatement. An audit includes examining, on a test basis, evidence supporting the amounts and disclosures in the financial statements. An audit also includes assessing the accounting principles used and significant estimates made by management, as well as evaluating the overall financial statement presentation. We believe that our audits provide a reasonable basis for our opinion.

In our opinion, the consolidated financial statements referred to above present fairly, in all material respects, the financial position of General Mills, Inc. and subsidiaries as of May 28, 2006 and May 29, 2005, and the results of their operations and their cash flows for each of the fiscal years in the three-year period ended May 28, 2006 in conformity with U.S. generally accepted accounting principles. Also, in our opinion, the accompanying financial statement schedule, when considered in relation to the basic consolidated financial statements taken as a whole, presents fairly, in all material respects, the information set forth therein.

We also have audited, in accordance with the standards of the Public Company Accounting Oversight Board (United States), the effectiveness of General Mills' internal control over financial reporting as of May 28, 2006, based on criteria established in Internal Control—Integrated Framework issued by the Committee of Sponsoring Organizations of the Treadway Commission (COSO), and our report dated July 27, 2006 expressed an unqualified opinion on management's assessment of, and the effective operation of, internal control over financial reporting.

KPMG LLP

Minneapolis, Minnesota
July 27, 2006

accounting firms in the world. Two key phrases should be noted in the first sentence of the third paragraph of the independent accountants' report (also called the **auditors' report**): *in our opinion* and *present fairly*. The report indicates that responsibility for the statements rests with General Mills and that the auditors' job is to *express an opinion* on the statements based on certain tests. It would be impossible for an auditing firm to spend the time or money to retrace and verify every single transaction that General Mills entered into during the year. Instead, the auditing firm performs various tests of the accounting records to be able to assure itself that the statements are free of *material misstatement*. Auditors do not "certify" the total accuracy of a set of financial statements but render an opinion as to the reasonableness of those statements.

Auditors' report
The opinion rendered by a public accounting firm concerning the fairness of the presentation of the financial statements. ***Alternate term:*** *Report of independent accountants.*

The Ethical Responsibility of Management and the Auditors The management of a company and its auditors share a common purpose: to protect the interests of stockholders. In large corporations, the stockholders are normally removed from the daily affairs of the business. The need for a professional management team to run the business is a practical necessity, as is the need for a periodic audit of the company's records. Because stockholders cannot run the business themselves, they need assurances that the business is being operated effectively and efficiently and that the financial statements presented by management are a fair representation of the company's operations and financial position. The management and the auditors have a very important ethical responsibility to their constituents: the stockholders of the company.

Management Discussion and Analysis Preceding the financial statements is a section of General Mills's annual report titled "Management's Discussion and Analysis of Financial Condition and Results of Operations." This report gives management the opportunity to discuss the financial statements and provide the stockholders with explanations for certain amounts reported in the statements. For example, management explains the change in its selling, general, and administrative expenses as follows:

> *Selling, general and administrative (SG&A) expense increased by $260 million in fiscal 2006 versus fiscal 2005. SG&A as a percent of net sales increased from 21.5 percent in fiscal 2005 to 23.0 percent in fiscal 2006. The increase in SG&A from fiscal 2005 was largely the result of a $97 million increase in domestic employee benefit costs, including incentives; an $86 million increase in customer freight expense, primarily due to increased fuel costs; a $46 million increase in consumer marketing spending; and $23 million of increases in our environmental reserves.*[8]

Notes to Consolidated Financial Statements The sentence "See accompanying notes to consolidated financial statements" appears at the bottom of each of General Mills's four financial statements. These comments, or *notes*, as they are commonly called, are necessary to satisfy the need for *full disclosure* of all facts relevant to a company's results and financial position. Note 1 is a summary of *significant accounting policies*. The company's policies for depreciating assets and recognizing revenue are among the important items contained in this note. For example, General Mills describes its policy for depreciating its buildings and equipment as follows:

> *Buildings and equipment are recorded at historical cost and depreciated over estimated useful lives, primarily using the straight-line method. Ordinary maintenance and repairs are charged to operating costs. Buildings are usually depreciated over 40 to 50 years, and equipment is usually depreciated over three to 15 years.*[9]

In addition to the summary of significant accounting policies, other notes discuss such topics as income taxes and stock option plans.

This completes discussion of the makeup of the annual report. By now, you should appreciate the flexibility that companies have in assembling the report, aside from the need to follow GAAP in preparing the statements. The accounting standards followed in preparing the statements, as well as the appearance of the annual report itself, differ in other countries. As has been noted elsewhere, although many corporations operate internationally, accounting principles are far from being standardized.

---

8 General Mills, Inc., 2006 10K, pp. 32–33.
9 General Mills, Inc., 2006 10K, p. 70.

POD REVIEW 2.9

LO9 ***Read and use the financial statements and other elements in the annual report of a publicly held company.***

- The classified balance sheet and multiple-step income statement are more complex than simpler versions of these financial statements and yield more useful information to decision makers.
- Annual reports contain more information than just the financial statements. This information can be used alone or in conjunction with the financial statements to gain a more complete financial picture of a company.
    - Management's Discussion and Analysis provides explanatory comments about certain results reflected in the financial statements and sometimes forward-looking commentary.
    - The Report of Independent Accountants is provided by the company's auditor, whose job is to express an opinion on whether the financial statements fairly represent the accounting treatment of a company's economic activity for the year.
    - Notes to the Consolidated Financial Statements are generally supplementary disclosures required by GAAP that help explain detail behind the accounting treatment of certain items in the financial statements.

QUESTIONS

1. *The SEC requires that the annual report include*
    a. balance sheets for the two most recent year-ends and income statements for each of the three most recent years.
    b. balance sheets for the three most recent year-ends and income statements for each of the three most recent years.
    c. balance sheets for the two most recent year-ends and income statements for each of the two most recent years.
    d. balance sheets for the three most recent year-ends and income statements for each of the two most recent years.

2. *Which of the following is usually not included in a company's annual report?*
    a. management discussion and analysis
    b. notes to the consolidated financial statements
    c. report of independent accountants
    d. All of the following are included in an annual report.

REVIEW

RATIO REVIEW

Working Capital = Current Assets (balance sheet) − Current Liabilities (balance sheet)

$$\text{Current Ratio} = \frac{\text{Current Assets (balance sheet)}}{\text{Current Liabilities (balance sheet)}}$$

$$\text{Profit Margin} = \frac{\text{Net Income (income statement)}}{\text{Sales or Revenues (income statement)}}$$

KEY TERMS QUIZ

Read each definition below and write the number of the definition in the blank beside the appropriate term. The quiz solutions appear at the end of the chapter.

_______ **Understandability**
_______ **Relevance**
_______ **Reliability**
_______ **Comparability**
_______ **Depreciation**
_______ **Consistency**
_______ **Materiality**
_______ **Conservatism**
_______ **Operating cycle**
_______ **Current asset**
_______ **Current liability**
_______ **Liquidity**
_______ **Working capital**
_______ **Current ratio**
_______ **Single-step income statement**
_______ **Multiple-step income statement**
_______ **Gross profit**
_______ **Profit margin**
_______ **Auditors' report**

1. An income statement in which all expenses are added together and subtracted from all revenues.
2. The magnitude of an omission or a misstatement in accounting information that will affect the judgment of someone relying on the information.
3. The capacity of information to make a difference in a decision.
4. An income statement that provides the reader with classifications of revenues and expenses as well as with important subtotals.
5. The practice of using the least optimistic estimate when two estimates of amounts are about equally likely.
6. The quality of accounting information that makes it comprehensible to those willing to spend the necessary time.
7. Current assets divided by current liabilities.
8. The quality of accounting information that makes it dependable in representing the events that it purports to represent.
9. An obligation that will be satisfied within the next operating cycle or within one year if the cycle is shorter than one year.
10. Current assets minus current liabilities.
11. Net income divided by sales.
12. The quality of accounting information that allows a user to analyze two or more companies and look for similarities and differences.
13. An asset that is expected to be realized in cash or sold or consumed during the operating cycle or within one year if the cycle is shorter than one year.
14. The ability of a company to pay its debts as they come due.
15. The quality of accounting information that allows a user to compare two or more accounting periods for a single company.
16. The allocation of the cost of a long-term tangible asset over its useful life.
17. The period of time between the purchase of inventory and the collection of any receivable from the sale of the inventory.
18. Sales less cost of goods sold.
19. The opinion rendered by a public accounting firm concerning the fairness of the presentation of the financial statements.

ALTERNATE TERMS

Auditors' report Report of independent accountants

Balance sheet Statement of financial position or condition

Capital stock Contributed capital

Income statement Statement of income

Income tax expense Provision for income taxes

Long-term assets Noncurrent assets

Long-term liability Long-term debt

Net income Profits or earnings

Profit margin Return on sales

Retained earnings Earned capital

Stockholders' equity Shareholders' equity

WARMUP EXERCISES & SOLUTIONS

Warmup Exercise 2-1 Identifying Ratios

State the equation for each of the following:

1. Working capital
2. Current ratio
3. Profit margin

Key to the Solution Review the various ratios discussed in the chapter.

Warmup Exercise 2-2 Calculating Ratios

Bridger reported net income of $150,000 and sales of $1,000,000 for the year. Its current assets were $300,000 and its current liabilities were $200,000 at year-end.

Required
Compute each of the following ratios for Bridger:

1. Current ratio
2. Profit margin

Key to the Solution Recall the equation for each of these ratios as presented in the chapter.

Warmup Exercise 2-3 Determining Liquidity

Big has current assets of $500,000 and current liabilities of $400,000. Small reports current assets of $80,000 and current liabilities of $20,000.

Required
Which company is more liquid? Why?

Key to the Solution Calculate the current ratio for each company and compare them.

SOLUTIONS TO WARMUP EXERCISES

Warmup Exercise 2-1

1. Working Capital = Current Assets − Current Liabilities

2. $\text{Current Ratio} = \dfrac{\text{Current Assets}}{\text{Current Liabilities}}$

3. $\text{Profit Margin} = \dfrac{\text{Net Income}}{\text{Sales or Revenues}}$

Warmup Exercise 2-2

1. $\dfrac{\$300{,}000}{\$200{,}000} = \underline{\underline{1.5 \text{ to } 1}}$

2. $\dfrac{\$150{,}000}{\$1{,}000{,}000} = \underline{\underline{15\%}}$

Warmup Exercise 2-3

On the surface, Small Company appears to be more liquid. Its current ratio of $80,000/$20,000, or 4 to 1, is significantly higher than Big's current ratio of $500,000/$400,000, or 1.25 to 1.

REVIEW

REVIEW PROBLEM & SOLUTION

The following review problem will give you the opportunity to apply what you have learned by preparing both an income statement and a balance sheet.

The following items, listed in alphabetical order, are taken from the records of Grizzly Inc., a chain of outdoor recreational stores in the Northwest. Use the items to prepare two statements. First, prepare an income statement for the year ended December 31, 2008. The income statement should be in multiple-step form. Second, prepare a classified balance sheet at December 31, 2008. All amounts are in thousands of dollars.

Accounts payable	$ 6,500
Accounts receivable	8,200
Accumulated depreciation—buildings	25,000
Accumulated depreciation—furniture and fixtures	15,000
Advertising expense	3,100
Buildings	80,000
Capital stock, $1 par, 10,000 shares issued and outstanding	10,000
Cash	2,400
Commissions expense	8,600
Cost of goods sold	110,000
Depreciation on buildings	2,500
Depreciation on furniture and fixtures	1,200
Furniture and fixtures	68,000
Income taxes payable	2,200
Income tax expense	13,000
Insurance expense	2,000
Interest expense	12,000
Interest payable	1,000
Interest revenue	2,000
Land	100,000
Long-term notes payable, due December 31, 2016	120,000
Merchandise inventories	6,000
Office supplies	900
Paid-in capital in excess of par value	40,000
Prepaid rent	3,000
Rent expense for salespeople's autos	9,000
Retained earnings	48,800
Salaries and wages for office staff	11,000
Sales revenue	190,000

SOLUTION TO REVIEW PROBLEM

1. Multiple-step income statement:

Grizzly Inc.
Income Statement
For the Year Ended December 31, 2008
(In thousands of dollars)

Sales revenue		$190,000	
Cost of goods sold		110,000	
Gross profit			$ 80,000
Operating expenses:			
Selling expenses:			
Advertising expense	$ 3,100		
Depreciation on furniture and fixtures	1,200		
Rent expense for salespeople's autos	9,000		
Commissions expense	8,600		
Total selling expenses		$ 21,900	
General and administrative expenses:			
Depreciation on buildings	$ 2,500		
Insurance expense	2,000		
Salaries and wages for office staff	11,000		
Total general and administrative expenses		15,500	
Total operating expenses			37,400
Income from operations			$ 42,600

(continued)

REVIEW

Other revenues and expenses:		
Interest revenue	$ 2,000	
Interest expense	12,000	
Excess of other expenses over other revenue		10,000
Income before income taxes		$ 32,600
Income tax expense		13,000
Net income		$ 19,600

2. Classified balance sheet:

Grizzly Inc.
Balance Sheet
At December 31, 2008
(In thousands of dollars)

Assets			
Current assets:			
Cash		$ 2,400	
Accounts receivable		8,200	
Merchandise inventories		6,000	
Office supplies		900	
Prepaid rent		3,000	
Total current assets			$ 20,500
Property, plant, and equipment:			
Land		$100,000	
Buildings	$ 80,000		
Less: Accumulated depreciation	25,000	55,000	
Furniture and fixtures	$ 68,000		
Less: Accumulated depreciation	15,000	53,000	
Total property, plant, and equipment			208,000
Total assets			$228,500
Liabilities			
Current liabilities:			
Accounts payable		$ 6,500	
Income taxes payable		2,200	
Interest payable		1,000	
Total current liabilities			$ 9,700
Long-term notes payable, due December 31, 2016			120,000
Total liabilities			$129,700
Stockholders' Equity			
Contributed capital:			
Capital stock, $1 par, 10,000 shares issued and outstanding		$ 10,000	
Paid-in capital in excess of par value		40,000	
Total contributed capital		$ 50,000	
Retained earnings		48,800	
Total stockholders' equity			98,800
Total liabilities and stockholders' equity			$228,500

QUESTIONS

1. How would you evaluate the following statement: The cash flows to a company are irrelevant to an investor; all the investor cares about is the potential for receiving dividends on the investment?

2. A key characteristic of useful financial information is understandability. How does this qualitative characteristic relate to the background of the user of the information?

3. What does *relevance* mean with regard to the use of accounting information?

4. What is the qualitative characteristic of comparability? Why is it important in preparing financial statements?

5. What is the difference between comparability and consistency as they relate to the use of accounting information?

6. How does the concept of materiality relate to the size of a company?

7. How does the concept of the operating cycle relate to the definition of a current asset?

8. How would you evaluate the following statement: A note payable with an original maturity of five years will be classified on the balance sheet as a long-term liability until it matures?

9. How do the two basic forms of owners' equity items for a corporation—capital stock and retained earnings—differ?

10. What are the limitations of working capital as a measure of the liquidity of a business as opposed to the current ratio?

11. What is meant by a company's capital structure?

12. What is the major weakness of the single-step form for the income statement?

13. How does a statement of retained earnings act as a link between an income statement and a balance sheet?

14. In auditing the financial statements of a company, does the auditor *certify* that the statements are totally accurate and without errors of any size or variety? Explain.

15. What is the first note in the annual report of all publicly held companies? What is its purpose?

BRIEF EXERCISES

LO1 **Brief Exercise 2-1** Objectives of Financial Reporting

State the primary objective of financial reporting.

LO2 **Brief Exercise 2-2** Qualitative Characteristics of Accounting Information

List four qualities that make accounting information useful.

LO3 **Brief Exercise 2-3** Classification of Assets

For each of the following assets, indicate whether it is a current asset (CA) or a noncurrent asset (NCA).

__________ Accounts receivable
__________ Land
__________ Inventories
__________ Cash
__________ Furniture and fixtures
__________ Office supplies
__________ Buildings

LO4 **Brief Exercise 2-4** Working Capital and Current Ratio

A company reported current assets of $80,000 and current liabilities of $60,000. Compute the amount of working capital and the current ratio.

LO5 **Brief Exercise 2-5** Multiple-Step versus Single-Step Income Statement

A retailer is considering whether to prepare a multiple-step or a single-step income statement. Provide three lines that appear on a multiple-step statement that do not appear on a single-step statement.

LO6 **Brief Exercise 2-6** Profit Margin

A company reported sales of $100,000; cost of goods sold of $60,000; selling, general, and administrative expenses of $15,000; and income tax expense of $10,000. Compute the company's profit margin.

LO7 **Brief Exercise 2-7** Retained Earnings

A company started the year with retained earnings of $200,000. During the year, it reported net income of $80,000 and paid dividends of $50,000. Compute the company's ending retained earnings.

LO8 **Brief Exercise 2-8** Investing and Financing Activities

A company borrowed $100,000 from its bank and the next day used $80,000 of the cash from the loan to buy a new piece of equipment for its plant. Explain how each of those activities are reported on a statement of cash flows.

LO9 **Brief Exercise 2-9** Elements of an Annual Report

List three examples of the types of information that normally appear in a company's annual report.

EXERCISES

LO2

Exercise 2-1 Characteristics of Useful Accounting Information

Fill in the blank with the qualitative characteristic for each of the following descriptions.

_______________ 1. Information that users can depend on to represent the events that it purports to represent

_______________ 2. Information that has the capacity to make a difference in a decision

_______________ 3. Information that is valid, that indicates an agreement between the underlying data and the events represented

_______________ 4. Information that allows for comparisons to be made from one accounting period to the next

_______________ 5. Information that is free from error

_______________ 6. Information that is meaningful to those who are willing to learn to use it properly

_______________ 7. Information that is not slanted to portray a company's position any better or worse than the circumstances warrant

_______________ 8. Information that allows for comparisons to be made between or among companies

LO3

Exercise 2-2 Classification of Assets and Liabilities

Indicate the appropriate classification of each of the following as a current asset (CA), noncurrent asset (NCA), current liability (CL), or long-term liability (LTL).

______ 1. Inventory
______ 2. Accounts payable
______ 3. Cash
______ 4. Patents
______ 5. Notes payable, due in six months
______ 6. Taxes payable
______ 7. Prepaid rent (for the next nine months)
______ 8. Bonds payable, due in 10 years
______ 9. Machinery

LO5

Exercise 2-3 Selling Expenses and General and Administrative Expenses

Operating expenses are subdivided between selling expenses and general and administrative expenses when a multiple-step income statement is prepared. Identify each of the following items as a selling expense (S) or general and administrative expense (G&A).

______ 1. Advertising expense
______ 2. Depreciation expense—store furniture and fixtures
______ 3. Office rent expense
______ 4. Office salaries expense
______ 5. Store rent expense
______ 6. Store salaries expense
______ 7. Insurance expense
______ 8. Supplies expense
______ 9. Utilities expense

LO5

Exercise 2-4 Missing Income Statement Amounts

For each of the following cases, fill in the blank with the appropriate dollar amount.

	Sara's Coffee Shop	Amy's Deli	Jane's Bagels
Net sales	$35,000	$ ______	$78,000
Cost of goods sold	______	45,000	______
Gross profit	7,000	18,000	______
Selling expenses	3,000	______	9,000
General and administrative expenses	1,500	2,800	______
Total operating expenses	______	8,800	13,600
Net income	$ 2,500	$ 9,200	$25,400

LO6

Exercise 2-5 Income Statement Ratio

The 2008 income statement of Holly Enterprises shows operating revenues of $134,800, selling expenses of $38,310, general and administrative expenses of $36,990, interest expense of $580, and income tax expense of $13,920. Holly's stockholders' equity was $280,000 at the beginning of the year and $320,000 at the end of the year. The company has 20,000 shares of stock outstanding at December 31, 2008.

Required
Compute Holly's profit margin. What other information would you need in order to comment on whether this ratio is favorable?

LO7

Exercise 2-6 Statement of Retained Earnings

Landon Corporation was organized on January 2, 2006, with the investment of $100,000 by each of its two stockholders. Net income for its first year of business was $85,200. Net income increased during 2007 to $125,320 and to $145,480 during 2008. Landon paid $20,000 in dividends to each of the two stockholders in each of the three years.

Required
Prepare a statement of retained earnings for the year ended December 31, 2008.

LO8

Exercise 2-7 Components of the Statement of Cash Flows

Identify each of the following items as operating (O), investing (I), financing (F), or not on the statement of cash flows (N).

______ 1. Paid for supplies
______ 2. Collected cash from customers
______ 3. Purchased land (held for resale)
______ 4. Purchased land (for construction of new building)
______ 5. Paid dividend
______ 6. Issued stock
______ 7. Purchased computers (for use in the business)
______ 8. Sold old equipment

LO9

Exercise 2-8 Basic Elements of Financial Reports

Most financial reports contain the following list of basic elements. For each element, identify the person(s) who prepared the element and describe the information a user would expect to find in each element. Some information is verifiable; other information is subjectively chosen by management. Comment on the verifiability of information in each element.

1. Management discussion and analysis
2. Product/markets of company
3. Financial statements
4. Notes to financial statements
5. Independent accountants' report

MULTICONCEPT EXERCISES

LO3,5,7

Exercise 2-9 Financial Statement Classification

Potential stockholders and lenders are interested in a company's financial statements. Identify the statement—balance sheet (BS), income statement (IS), or retained earnings statement (RE)—on which each of the following items would appear.

_______ 1. Accounts payable
_______ 2. Accounts receivable
_______ 3. Advertising expense
_______ 4. Bad debt expense
_______ 5. Bonds payable
_______ 6. Buildings
_______ 7. Cash
_______ 8. Common stock
_______ 9. Depreciation expense
_______ 10. Dividends
_______ 11. Land held for future expansion
_______ 12. Loan payable
_______ 13. Office supplies
_______ 14. Patent
_______ 15. Patent amortization expense
_______ 16. Prepaid insurance
_______ 17. Retained earnings
_______ 18. Sales
_______ 19. Utilities expense
_______ 20. Wages payable

LO5,6

Exercise 2-10 Single- and Multiple-Step Income Statement

Some headings and/or items are used on either the single-step or the multiple-step income statement. Some are used on both. Identify each of the following items as single-step (S), multiple-step (M), both formats (B), or not used on either income statement (N).

_______ 1. Sales
_______ 2. Cost of goods sold
_______ 3. Selling expenses
_______ 4. Total revenues
_______ 5. Utilities expense
_______ 6. Administrative expense
_______ 7. Net income
_______ 8. Supplies on hand
_______ 9. Accumulated depreciation
_______ 10. Income before income taxes
_______ 11. Gross profit

LO5,6

Exercise 2-11 Multiple-Step Income Statement

Gaynor Corporation's partial income statement is as follows:

Sales	$1,200,000
Cost of sales	450,000
Selling expenses	60,800
General and administrative expenses	75,000

Required

Determine the profit margin. Would you consider investing in Gaynor Corporation? Explain your answer.

PROBLEMS

LO2

Problem 2-1 Materiality

Joseph Knapp, a newly hired accountant wanting to impress his boss, stayed late one night to analyze the office supplies expense. He determined the cost by month for the previous 12 months of each of the following: computer paper, copy paper, fax paper, pencils and pens, notepads, postage, stationery, and miscellaneous items.

Required

1. What did Joseph think his boss would learn from this information? What action might be taken as a result of knowing it?
2. Would this information be more relevant if Joseph worked for a hardware store or for a real estate company? Discuss.

HOMEWORK

LO2

Problem 2-2 Costs and Expenses

The following costs are incurred by a retailer:

1. Display fixtures in a retail store
2. Advertising
3. Merchandise for sale
4. Incorporation (i.e., legal costs, stock issue costs)
5. Cost of a franchise
6. Office supplies
7. Wages and salaries
8. Computer software
9. Computer hardware

Required

For each cost, explain whether all of the cost or only a portion of the cost would appear as an expense on the income statement for the period in which the cost was incurred. If not all of the cost would appear on the income statement for that period, explain why not.

LO3

Problem 2-3 Classified Balance Sheet

The following balance sheet items, listed in alphabetical order, are available from the records of Ruth Corporation at December 31, 2008:

Accounts payable	$ 18,255
Accounts receivable	23,450
Accumulated depreciation—automobiles	22,500
Accumulated depreciation—buildings	40,000
Automobiles	112,500
Bonds payable, due December 31, 2012	160,000
Buildings	200,000
Capital stock, $10 par value	150,000
Cash	13,230
Income taxes payable	6,200
Interest payable	1,500
Inventory	45,730
Land	250,000
Long-term investments	85,000
Notes payable, due June 30, 2009	10,000
Office supplies	2,340
Paid-in capital in excess of par value	50,000
Patents	40,000
Prepaid rent	1,500
Retained earnings	311,095
Salaries and wages payable	4,200

Required

1. Prepare in good form a classified balance sheet as of December 31, 2008.
2. Compute Ruth's current ratio.
3. On the basis of your answer to (2), does Ruth appear to be liquid? What other information do you need to fully answer that question?

LO4

Problem 2-4 Financial Statement Ratios

The following items, in alphabetical order, are available from the records of Walker Corporation as of December 31, 2008 and 2007:

	December 31, 2008	December 31, 2007
Accounts payable	$ 8,400	$ 5,200
Accounts receivable	27,830	35,770
Cash	20,200	19,450
Cleaning supplies	450	700
Interest payable	–0–	1,200
Inventory	24,600	26,200
Marketable securities	6,250	5,020
Note payable, due in six months	–0–	12,000
Prepaid rent	3,600	4,800
Taxes payable	1,450	1,230
Wages payable	1,200	1,600

HOMEWORK

Required

1. Calculate the following as of December 31, 2008 and December 31, 2007:
   a. Working capital
   b. Current ratio
2. On the basis of your answers to (1), comment on the relative liquidity of the company at the beginning and the end of the year. As part of your answer, explain the change in the company's liquidity from the beginning to the end of 2008.

LO4

Problem 2-5 Working Capital and Current Ratio

The balance sheet of Stevenson Inc. includes the following items:

Cash	$ 23,000
Accounts receivable	13,000
Inventory	45,000
Prepaid insurance	800
Land	80,000
Accounts payable	54,900
Salaries payable	1,200
Capital stock	100,000
Retained earnings	5,700

Required

1. Determine the current ratio and working capital.
2. Beyond the information provided in your answers to (1), what does the composition of the current assets tell you about Stevenson's liquidity?
3. What other information do you need to fully assess Stevenson's liquidity?

LO5

Problem 2-6 Single-Step Income Statement

The following income statement items, arranged in alphabetical order, are taken from the records of Shaw Corporation for the year ended December 31, 2008:

Advertising expense	$ 1,500
Commissions expense	2,415
Cost of goods sold	29,200
Depreciation expense—office building	2,900
Income tax expense	1,540
Insurance expense—salesperson's auto	2,250
Interest expense	1,400
Interest revenue	1,340
Rent revenue	6,700
Salaries and wages expense—office	12,560
Sales revenue	48,300
Supplies expense—office	890

Required

1. Prepare a single-step income statement for the year ended December 31, 2008.
2. What weaknesses do you see in this form for the income statement?

LO5

Problem 2-7 Multiple-Step Income Statement and Profit Margin

Refer to the list of income statement items in Problem 2-6. Assume that Shaw Corporation classifies all operating expenses into two categories: (1) selling and (2) general and administrative.

Required

1. Prepare a multiple-step income statement for the year ended December 31, 2008.
2. What advantages do you see in this form for the income statement?
3. Compute Shaw's profit margin.
4. Comment on Shaw's profitability. What other factors need to be taken into account to assess Shaw's profitability?

LO8

Problem 2-8 Statement of Cash Flows

Colorado Corporation was organized on January 1, 2008, with the investment of $250,000 in cash by its stockholders. The company immediately purchased an office building for $300,000, paying

HOMEWORK

$210,000 in cash and signing a three-year promissory note for the balance. Colorado signed a five-year, $60,000 promissory note at a local bank during 2008 and received cash in the same amount. During its first year, Colorado collected $93,970 from its customers. It paid $65,600 for inventory, $20,400 in salaries and wages, and another $3,100 in taxes. Colorado paid $5,600 in cash dividends.

Required

1. Prepare a statement of cash flows for the year ended December 31, 2008.
2. What does this statement tell you that an income statement does not?

LO9

Problem 2-9 Basic Elements of Financial Reports

Comparative income statements for Grammar Inc. are as follows:

	2008	2007
Sales	$1,000,000	$500,000
Cost of sales	500,000	300,000
Gross profit	$ 500,000	$200,000
Operating expenses	120,000	100,000
Operating income	$ 380,000	$100,000
Loss on sale of subsidiary	(400,000)	—
Net income (loss)	$ (20,000)	$100,000

Required

The president and management believe that the company performed better in 2008 than it did in 2007. Write the president's letter to be included in the 2008 annual report. Explain why the company is financially sound and why shareholders should not be alarmed by the $20,000 loss in a year when operating revenues increased significantly.

MULTICONCEPT PROBLEMS

LO2,4

Problem 2-10 Comparing Coca-Cola and PepsiCo

The current items, listed in alphabetical order, are taken from the consolidated balance sheets of **Coca-Cola** and **PepsiCo** as of December 31, 2006. (All amounts are in millions of dollars.)

Coca-Cola	
Accounts payable and accrued expenses	$5,055
Accrued income taxes	567
Cash and cash equivalents	2,440
Current maturities of long-term debt	33
Inventories	1,641
Loans and notes payable	3,235
Marketable securities	150
Prepaid expenses and other assets	1,623
Trade accounts receivable, less allowance of $63	2,587
PepsiCo	
Accounts and notes receivable, net	$3,725
Accounts payable and other current liabilities	6,496
Cash and cash equivalents	1,651
Income taxes payable	90
Inventories	1,926
Prepaid expenses and other current assets	657
Short-term investments	1,171
Short-term obligations	274

Required

1. Compute working capital and the current ratio for both companies.
2. On the basis of your answers to (1), which company appears to be more liquid?
3. As you know, other factors affect a company's liquidity in addition to its working capital and current ratio. Comment on the *composition* of each company's current assets and ways this composition affects the company's liquidity.

LO2,5

Problem 2-11 Comparability and Consistency in Income Statements

The following income statements were provided by Gleeson Company, a retailer:

2008 Income Statement		2007 Income Statement	
Sales	$1,700,000	Sales	$1,500,000
Cost of sales	520,000	Cost of sales	$ 450,000
Gross profit	$1,180,000	Sales salaries	398,000
Selling expense	$ 702,000	Advertising	175,000
Administrative expense	95,000	Office supplies	54,000
Total selling and administrative expense	$ 797,000	Depreciation—building	40,000
		Delivery expense	20,000
		Total expenses	$1,137,000
Net income	$ 383,000	Net income	$ 363,000

Required

1. Identify each income statement as either single-step or multiple-step format.
2. Convert the 2007 income statement to the same format as the 2008 income statement.

LO1,4,8

Problem 2-12 Cash Flow

Franklin Co., a specialty retailer, has a history of paying quarterly dividends of $0.50 per share. Management is trying to determine whether the company will have adequate cash on December 31, 2009, to pay a dividend if one is declared by the board of directors. The following additional information is available:

- All sales are on account, and accounts receivable are collected one month after the sale. Sales volume has been increasing 5% each month.
- All purchases of merchandise are on account, and accounts payable are paid one month after the purchase. Cost of sales is 40% of the sales price. Inventory levels are maintained at $75,000.
- Operating expenses in addition to the mortgage are paid in cash. They amount to $3,000 per month and are paid as they are incurred.

Franklin Co.
Balance Sheet
September 30, 2009

Cash	$ 5,000	Accounts payable	$ 5,000
Accounts receivable	12,500	Mortgage note**	150,000
Inventory	75,000	Common stock—$1 par	50,000
Note receivable*	10,000	Retained earnings	66,500
Building/Land	169,000	Total liabilities and	
Total assets	$271,500	stockholders' equity	$271,500

*Note receivable represents a one-year, 5% interest-bearing note, due November 1, 2009.
**Mortgage note is a 30-year, 7% note due in monthly installments of $1,200.

Required

Determine the cash that Franklin will have available to pay a dividend on December 31, 2009. Round all amounts to the nearest dollar. What can Franklin's management do to increase the cash available? Should management recommend that the board of directors declare a dividend? Explain.

ALTERNATE PROBLEMS

LO2

Problem 2-1A Materiality

Jane Erving, a newly hired accountant wanting to impress her boss, stayed late one night to analyze the long-distance calls by area code and time of day placed. She determined the monthly cost for the previous 12 months by hour and area code called.

Required

1. What did Jane think her boss would learn from this information? What action might be taken as a result of knowing it?
2. Would this information be more relevant if Jane worked for a hardware store or for a real estate company? Discuss.

LO2 **Problem 2-2A** Costs and Expenses

The following costs are incurred by a retailer:

1. Point of sale systems in a retail store
2. An ad in the yellow pages
3. An inventory-control computer software system
4. Shipping merchandise for resale to chain outlets

Required

For each cost, explain whether all of the cost or only a portion of the cost would appear as an expense on the income statement for the period in which the cost was incurred. If not all of the cost would appear on the income statement for that period, explain why not.

LO3 **Problem 2-3A** Classified Balance Sheet

The following balance sheet items, listed in alphabetical order, are available from the records of Singer Company at December 31, 2008:

Accounts payable	$ 34,280	Land	$250,000
Accounts receivable	26,700	Marketable securities	15,000
Accumulated depreciation—buildings	40,000	Merchandise inventory	112,900
Accumulated depreciation—equipment	12,500	Notes payable, due April 15, 2009	6,500
Bonds payable, due December 31, 2014	250,000	Office supplies	400
Buildings	150,000	Paid-in capital in excess of par value	75,000
Capital stock, $1 par value	200,000	Patents	45,000
Cash	60,790	Prepaid rent	3,600
Equipment	84,500	Retained earnings	113,510
Income taxes payable	7,500	Salaries payable	7,400
Interest payable	2,200		

Required

1. Prepare a classified balance sheet as of December 31, 2008.
2. Compute Singer's current ratio.
3. On the basis of your answer to (2), does Singer appear to be liquid? What other information do you need to fully answer that question?

LO4 **Problem 2-4A** Financial Statement Ratios

The following items, in alphabetical order, are available from the records of Quinn Corporation as of December 31, 2008 and 2007:

	December 31, 2008	December 31, 2007
Accounts payable	$10,500	$ 6,500
Accounts receivable	16,500	26,000
Cash	12,750	11,800
Interest receivable	200	–0–
Note receivable, due 12/31/2010	12,000	12,000
Office supplies	900	1,100
Prepaid insurance	400	250
Salaries payable	1,800	800
Taxes payable	10,000	5,800

Required

1. Calculate the following as of December 31, 2008 and December 31, 2007:
   a. Working capital
   b. Current ratio
2. On the basis of your answers to (1), comment on the relative liquidity of the company at the beginning and the end of the year. As part of your answer, explain the change in the company's liquidity from the beginning to the end of 2008.

LO4

Problem 2-5A Working Capital and Current Ratio

The balance sheet of Kapinski Inc. includes the following items:

Cash	$ 23,000
Accounts receivable	43,000
Inventory	75,000
Prepaid insurance	2,800
Land	80,000
Accounts payable	84,900
Salaries payable	3,200
Capital stock	100,000
Retained earnings	35,700

Required

1. Determine the current ratio and working capital.
2. Kapinski appears to have a positive current ratio and a large net working capital. Why would it have trouble paying bills as they come due?
3. Suggest three things that Kapinski can do to help pay its bills on time.

LO5

Problem 2-6A Single-Step Income Statement

The following income statement items, arranged in alphabetical order, are taken from the records of Corbin Enterprises for the year ended December 31, 2008:

Advertising expense	$ 9,000
Cost of goods sold	150,000
Depreciation expense—computer	4,500
Dividend revenue	2,700
Income tax expense	30,700
Interest expense	1,900
Rent expense—office	26,400
Rent expense—salesperson's car	18,000
Sales revenue	350,000
Supplies expense—office	1,300
Utilities expense	6,750
Wages expense—office	45,600

Required

1. Prepare a single-step income statement for the year ended December 31, 2008.
2. What weaknesses do you see in this form for the income statement?

LO5

Problem 2-7A Multiple-Step Income Statement and Profit Margin

Refer to the list of income statement items in Problem 2-6A. Assume that Corbin Enterprises classifies all operating expenses into two categories: (1) selling and (2) general and administrative.

Required

1. Prepare a multiple-step income statement for the year ended December 31, 2008.
2. What advantages do you see in this form for the income statement?
3. Compute Corbin's profit margin.
4. Comment on Corbin's profitability. What other factors need to be taken into account to assess Corbin's profitability?

LO8

Problem 2-8A Statement of Cash Flows

Wisconsin Corporation was organized on January 1, 2008, with the investment of $400,000 in cash by its stockholders. The company immediately purchased a manufacturing facility for $300,000, paying $150,000 in cash and signing a five-year promissory note for the balance. Wisconsin signed another five-year note at the bank for $50,000 during 2008 and received cash in the same amount. During its first year, Wisconsin collected $310,000 from its customers. It paid $185,000 for inventory, $30,100 in salaries and wages, and another $40,000 in taxes. Wisconsin paid $4,000 in cash dividends.

Required

1. Prepare a statement of cash flows for the year ended December 31, 2008.
2. What does this statement tell you that an income statement does not?

LO9 **Problem 2-9A** Basic Elements of Financial Reports

Comparative income statements for Thesaurus Inc. are as follows:

	2008	2007
Operating revenues	$500,000	$200,000
Operating expenses	120,000	100,000
Operating income	$380,000	$100,000
Gain on the sale of subsidiary	—	400,000
Net income	$380,000	$500,000

Required

The president and management believe that the company performed better in 2008 than it did in 2007. Write the president's letter to be included in the 2008 annual report. Explain why the company is financially sound and why shareholders should not be alarmed by the reduction in income in a year when operating revenues increased significantly.

ALTERNATE MULTICONCEPT PROBLEMS

LO2,4 **Problem 2-10A** Comparing Starwood Hotels & Resorts and Hilton Hotels

The following current items, listed in alphabetical order, are taken from the consolidated balance sheets of **Starwood Hotels & Resorts** and **Hilton Hotels** as of December 31, 2006. (All amounts are in millions of dollars.) Any assets or liabilities with which you may not be familiar are noted parenthetically.

Starwood Hotels & Resorts	
Accounts payable	$179
Accounts receivables, net of allowance for doubtful accounts of $49	593
Accrued expenses (liability)	955
Accrued salaries, wages, and benefits	383
Accrued taxes and other	139
Cash and cash equivalents	183
Inventories	566
Prepaid expenses and other	139
Restricted cash	329
Short-term borrowings and current maturities of long-term debt	805

Hilton Hotels	
Accounts payable and accrued expenses	$ 772
Accounts receivable, net	312
Cash and cash equivalents	1,154
Current maturities of long-term debt	47
Current portion of notes receivable, net	40
Deferred income taxes (asset)	85
Income taxes payable	45
Inventories	219
Prepaid expenses and other	97
Restricted cash	182

Required

1. Compute working capital and the current ratio for both companies.
2. On the basis of your answers to (1), which company appears to be more liquid?
3. As you know, other factors affect a company's liquidity in addition to its working capital and current ratio. Comment on the *composition* of each company's current assets and ways this composition affects the company's liquidity.

LO2,5

Problem 2-11A Comparability and Consistency in Income Statements

The following income statements were provided by Chisholm Company, a wholesale food distributor:

	2008	2007
Sales	$1,700,000	$1,500,000
Cost of sales	$ 612,000	$ 450,000
Sales salaries	427,000	398,000
Delivery expense	180,000	175,000
Office supplies	55,000	54,000
Depreciation—truck	40,000	40,000
Computer line expense	23,000	20,000
Total expenses	$1,337,000	$1,137,000
Net income	$ 363,000	$ 363,000

Required

1. Identify each income statement as either single-step or multiple-step format.
2. Restate each item in the income statements as a percentage of sales. Why did net income remain unchanged when sales increased in 2008?

LO1,4,8

Problem 2-12A Cash Flow

Roosevelt Inc., a consulting service, has a history of paying annual dividends of $1 per share. Management is trying to determine whether the company will have adequate cash on December 31, 2009, to pay a dividend if one is declared by the board of directors. The following additional information is available:

- All sales are on account, and accounts receivable are collected one month after the sale. Sales volume has been decreasing 5% each month.
- Operating expenses are paid in cash in the month incurred. Average monthly expenses are $10,000 (excluding the biweekly payroll).
- Biweekly payroll is $4,500, and it will be paid December 15 and December 31.
- Unearned revenue is expected to be earned in December. This amount was taken into consideration in the expected sales volume.

Roosevelt Inc.
Balance Sheet
December 1, 2009

Cash	$ 15,000	Unearned revenue	$ 2,000
Accounts receivable	40,000	Note payable*	30,000
Computer equipment	120,000	Common stock—$2 par	50,000
		Retained earnings	93,000
Total assets	$175,000	Total liabilities and stockholders' equity	$175,000

*The note payable plus 3% interest for six months is due January 15, 2010.

Required

Determine the cash that Roosevelt will have available to pay a dividend on December 31, 2009. Round all amounts to the nearest dollar. Should management recommend that the board of directors declare a dividend? Explain.

DECISION CASES

READING AND INTERPRETING FINANCIAL STATEMENTS

LO4

Decision Case 2-1 Comparing Two Companies in the Same Industry: General Mills and Kellogg's

Refer to the financial information for **General Mills** and **Kellogg's** reproduced at the back of the book for the information needed to answer the following questions.

Required

1. Compute each company's working capital at the end of the two most recent years. Also, for each company, compute the change in working capital during the most recent year.
2. Compute each company's current ratio at the end of the two most recent years. Compute the percentage change in the ratio during the most recent year.
3. How do the two companies differ in terms of the accounts that made up their current assets at the end of the most recent year? What is the largest current asset each company reports on the balance sheet at the end of the most recent year?
4. On the basis of your answers to (2) and (3), comment on each company's liquidity.

LO4

Decision Case 2-2 Reading General Mills's Balance Sheet

Refer to **General Mills**'s balance sheet reproduced at the back of the book to answer the following questions.

Required

1. Which is the largest of General Mills's current assets on May 28, 2006? What percentage of total current assets does it represent? Is it favorable or unfavorable that this is the company's largest current asset? Explain your answer.
2. Which is the second largest of General Mills's current assets on May 28, 2006? What percentage of total current assets does it represent? Explain what this asset represents and why it is such a significant asset for a company such as General Mills.
3. Explain what events would cause each of those accounts to both increase and decrease during the year.

MAKING FINANCIAL DECISIONS

LO8

Decision Case 2-3 Analysis of Cash Flow for a Small Business

Charles, a financial consultant, has been self-employed for two years. His list of clients has grown, and he is earning a reputation as a shrewd investor. Charles rents a small office, uses the pool secretarial services, and has purchased a car that he is depreciating over three years. The following income statements cover Charles's first two years of business:

	Year 1	Year 2
Commissions revenue	$ 25,000	$65,000
Rent	$ 12,000	$12,000
Secretarial services	3,000	9,000
Car expenses, gas, insurance	6,000	6,500
Depreciation	15,000	15,000
Net income	$(11,000)	$22,500

Charles believes that he should earn more than $11,500 for working very hard for two years. He is thinking about going to work for an investment firm where he can earn $40,000 per year. What would you advise Charles to do?

LO9

Decision Case 2-4 Factors Involved in an Investment Decision

As an investor, you are considering purchasing stock in a chain of theaters. The annual reports of several companies are available for comparison.

Required

Prepare an outline of the steps you would follow to make your comparison. Start by listing the first section that you would read in the financial reports. What would you expect to find there? Why did you choose that section to read first? Continue with the other sections of the financial report.

ETHICAL DECISION MAKING

LO2

Decision Case 2-5 The Expenditure Approval Process

Roberto is the plant superintendent of a small manufacturing company that is owned by a large corporation. The corporation has a policy that any expenditure over $1,000 must be approved by the chief financial officer in the corporate headquarters. The approval process takes a minimum of three weeks. Roberto would like to order a new labeling machine that is expected to reduce costs and pay for itself in six months. The machine costs $2,200, but Roberto can buy the sales rep's demo for $1,800. Roberto has asked the sales rep to send two separate bills for $900 each.

What would you do if you were the sales rep? Do you agree or disagree with Roberto's actions? What do you think about the corporate policy?

LO4,6

Decision Case 2-6 Susan Applies for a Loan

Susan Spiffy, owner of Spiffy Cleaners, a drive-through dry cleaners, would like to expand her business from its current location to a chain of cleaners. Revenues at the one location have been increasing an average of 8% each quarter. Profits have been increasing accordingly. Susan is conservative in spending and is a very hard worker. She has an appointment with a banker to apply for a loan to expand the business. To prepare for the appointment, she instructs you, as chief financial officer and payroll clerk, to copy the quarterly income statements for the past two years but not to include a balance sheet. Susan already has a substantial loan from another bank. In fact, she has very little of her own money invested in the business.

Required

Before answering the following questions, you may want to refer to Exhibit 1-13 and the related text on pages 27–29. Support each answer with your reasoning.

1. What is the ethical dilemma in this case? Who would be affected and how would they be affected if you follow Susan's instructions? (Would they benefit? Would they be harmed?) What responsibility do you have in this situation?
2. If the banker does not receive the balance sheet, will he have all of the relevant and reliable information needed for his decision-making process? Why or why not? Will the information provided by Susan be free from bias?
3. What should you do? Might anyone be harmed by Susan's accounting decision? Explain.

SOLUTIONS TO KEY TERMS QUIZ

6	**Understandability**
3	**Relevance**
8	**Reliability**
12	**Comparability**
16	**Depreciation**
15	**Consistency**
2	**Materiality**
5	**Conservatism**
17	**Operating cycle**
13	**Current asset**
9	**Current liability**
14	**Liquidity**
10	**Working capital**
7	**Current ratio**
1	**Single-step income statement**
4	**Multiple-step income statement**
18	**Gross profit**
11	**Profit margin**
19	**Auditors' report**

ANSWERS TO POD REVIEW

LO1	1. a	2. d
LO2	1. b	2. d
LO3	1. c	2. c
LO4	1. c	2. b
LO5	1. b	2. c
LO6	1. a	2. c
LO7	1. a	2. c
LO8	1. b	2. c
LO9	1. a	2. d

CHAPTER

3

Processing Accounting Information

Learning Outcomes

After studying this chapter, you should be able to:

LO1 Explain the difference between an external and internal event.

LO2 Explain the role of source documents in an accounting system.

LO3 Analyze the effects of transactions on the accounting equation and understand how these transactions affect the balance sheet and the income statement.

LO4 Define the concept of a general ledger and understand the use of the T account as a method for analyzing transactions.

LO5 Explain the rules of debits and credits.

LO6 Explain the purposes of a journal and the posting process.

LO7 Explain the purpose of a trial balance.

Study Links...

A Look at Previous Chapters
Up to this point, we have focused on the role of accounting in decision making and the way accountants use financial statements to communicate useful information to various users of the statements.

A Look at This Chapter
This chapter considers how accounting information is processed. We begin by considering the *inputs* to an accounting system, that is, the transactions entered into by a business. We look at how transactions are analyzed, and then we turn to a number of accounting tools and procedures designed to facilitate the preparation of the *outputs* of the system, the financial statements. Ledger accounts, journal entries, and trial balances are tools that allow a company to process vast amounts of data efficiently.

A Look at the Upcoming Chapter
Chapter 4 concludes our overview of the accounting model. We examine the accrual basis of accounting and its effect on the measurement of income. Adjusting entries, which are the focus of the accrual basis are discussed in detail in Chapter 4, along with the other steps in the accounting cycle.

Southwest Airlines

MAKING BUSINESS DECISIONS

Try to think of an industry with which you are familiar that has routinely suffered financial losses in recent years. For many people, one of the first to come to mind is the airline industry. Many of the major carriers have not only reported large losses but also have filed for bankruptcy.

Southwest Airlines is one of very few carriers that did not contribute to the dismal record posted by the airline industry as a whole. According to the company's web site, the Dallas-based carrier is the lone profitable airline throughout the worst five-year period in the history of the industry. In fact, 2006 marked the 34th consecutive year that Southwest Airlines was profitable, a record few companies in any industry can claim. As shown on the accompanying comparative income statements, bottom-line net income reached nearly $500 million in 2006.

How has the company been able to post a record that is the envy of its peers? By now, you know that in its simplest form, earnings (or net income) is the result of deducting expenses from revenues. The first line on the comparative income statements begins to tell the story of the company's success. The company has historically offered some of the lowest fares in the industry, and customers have responded by regularly filling the seats on its flights. Passenger revenue has grown steadily over the three years reported, reaching $8.75 billion in 2006. However, as many companies can attest, the other part of the equation to achieving profitability is to control costs. While passenger revenues increased by 20% in 2006, the company's largest expense—salaries, wages, and benefits—rose by only 10%. However, fuel and oil, a significant cost of doing business for airlines, rose steeply in 2006. Southwest continues to look for ways to control this expense, entering into hedging agreements to lock in its cost for fuel.

In our study of accounting, we have not yet given any thought to how the numbers on an income statement

© AP Photo/Mark Lennihan

(or on any of the other statements) got where they did. After all, before the information on the statements can be used for decision making, someone must decide how to record the various transactions that underlie the amounts reported. As you study this chapter, look for answers to these key questions:

- What source documents are used as the necessary evidence to record transactions? (See pp. 107–108.)
- What is the double-entry system of accounting? What is its role in the recording process? (See pp. 115–117.)
- What are some of the tools that accountants use to effectively and efficiently process the information that appears on financial statements? (See pp. 121–125.)

(*continued*)

Southwest Airlines Co.
Consolidated Statement of Income

Passenger revenue grew by 20% in 2006.

While salaries, wages, and benefits increased by only 10%.

However, rising fuel costs continue to present a challenge.

The bottom line increased by 3% during 2006 to nearly $500 million.

	Years Ended December 31,		
	2006	2005	2004
	(In millions, except per share amounts)		
OPERATING REVENUES:			
Passenger	$8,750	$7,279	$6,280
Freight	134	133	117
Other	202	172	133
Total operating revenues	9,086	7,584	6,530
OPERATING EXPENSES			
Salaries, wages, and benefits	3,052	2,782	2,578
Fuel and oil	2,138	1,341	1,000
Maintenance materials and repairs	468	446	472
Aircraft rentals	158	163	179
Landing fees and other rentals	495	454	408
Depreciation and amortization	515	469	431
Other operating expenses	1,326	1,204	1,058
Total operating expenses	8,152	6,859	6,126
OPERATING INCOME	934	725	404
OTHER EXPENSES (INCOME):			
Interest expense	128	122	88
Capitalized interest	(51)	(39)	(39)
Interest income	(84)	(47)	(21)
Other (gains) losses, net	151	(90)	37
Total other expenses (income)	144	(54)	65
INCOME BEFORE INCOME TAXES	790	779	339
PROVISION FOR INCOME TAXES	291	295	124
NET INCOME	$ 499	$ 484	$ 215
NET INCOME PER SHARE, BASIC	$ .63	$ .61	$ .27
NET INCOME PER SHARE, DILUTED	$ .61	$ .60	$ .27

See accompanying notes.

Source: Southwest Airlines web site and 2006 annual report.

Economic Events: The Basis for Recording Transactions

LO1 Explain the difference between an external and internal event.

Many different types of economic events affect an entity during the year. A sale is made to a customer. Supplies are purchased from a vendor. A loan is taken out at the bank. A fire destroys a warehouse. A new contract is signed with the union. In short, "An **event** is a happening of consequence to an entity."[1]

Event
A happening of consequence to an entity.

External event
An event involving interaction between an entity and its environment.

Internal event
An event occurring entirely within an entity.

EXTERNAL AND INTERNAL EVENTS

Two types of events affect an entity: internal and external.

- An **external event** "involves interaction between the entity and its environment."[2] For example, the *payment* of wages to an employee is an external event, as is a *sale* to a customer.
- An **internal event** occurs entirely within the entity. The use of a piece of equipment is an internal event.

1 *Statement of Financial Accounting Concepts (SFAC) No. 3*, "Elements of Financial Statements of Business Enterprises" (Stamford, Conn.: Financial Accounting Standards Board, 1982), par. 65.
2 *SFAC No. 3*.

We will use the term **transaction** to refer to any event, external or internal, that is recognized in a set of financial statements.[3]

What is necessary to recognize an event in the records? Are all economic events recognized as transactions by the accountant? The answers to those questions involve the concept of *measurement*. An event must be measured to be recognized. Certain events are relatively easy to measure: the payroll for the week, the amount of equipment destroyed by an earthquake, or the sales for the day. Not all events that affect an entity can be measured *reliably*, however. For example, how does a manufacturer of breakfast cereal measure the effect of a drought on the price of wheat? A company hires a new chief executive. How can it reliably measure the value of the new officer to the company? There is no definitive answer to the measurement problem in accounting. It is a continuing challenge to the accounting profession and something we will return to throughout the text.

Transaction
Any event that is recognized in a set of financial statements.

Real World Practice

3-1 Reading Southwest Airlines' Financial Statements

Is the purchase of a new airplane an internal or external event? The company subsequently recognizes the use of the plane by recording depreciation. Is this an internal or external event?

POD REVIEW 3.1

LO1 *Explain the difference between an external and internal event.*

- Both of these different types of events affect an entity and are usually recorded in the accounting system as a transaction.
  - External events are interactions between an entity and its environment.
  - Internal events are interactions entirely within an entity.

QUESTIONS

1. *Which of the following events is* not *an external event?*
   a. a sale to a customer
   b. a purchase of inventory from a supplier
   c. payment to the newspaper for advertising
   d. recognition of the use of equipment by the recording of depreciation

2. *Which of the following is necessary to recognize an event as a transaction?*
   a. It must be subject to measurement.
   b. It must be an external event.
   c. It must be an internal event.
   d. It must be an event that recurs regularly.

The Role of Source Documents in Recording Transactions

LO2 Explain the role of source documents in an accounting system.

The first step in the recording process is *identification*. A business needs a systematic method for recognizing events as transactions. A **source document** provides the evidence needed in an accounting system to record a transaction. Source documents take many different forms. An invoice received from a supplier is the source document for a purchase of inventory on credit. A cash register tape is the source document used by a retailer to recognize a cash sale. The payroll department sends the accountant the time cards for the week as the necessary documentation to record wages.

Not all recognizable events are supported by a standard source document. For certain events, some form of documentation must be generated. For example, no standard

Source document
A piece of paper that is used as evidence to record a transaction.

3 Technically, a *transaction* is defined by the FASB as a special kind of external event in which the entity exchanges something of value with an outsider. Because the term *transaction* is used in practice to refer to any event that is recognized in the statements, we will use this broader definition.

source document exists to recognize the financial consequences from a fire or the settlement of a lawsuit. Documentation is just as important for those types of events as it is for standard, recurring transactions.

POD REVIEW 3.2

LO2 *Explain the role of source documents in an accounting system.*

- Source documents provide the evidence needed to begin the procedures for recording and processing a transaction.
- These documents need not be in hard copy form and can come from parties that are either internal or external to the company.

QUESTIONS

1. *A source document is*
   a. the same form for all transactions.
   b. the evidence needed to record a transaction.
   c. not used in a computerized accounting system.
   d. none of the above.

2. *Which of the following is an example of a source document?*
   a. a cash register tape
   b. an invoice from a customer's purchase
   c. an employee's time card
   d. All of the above are examples of source documents.

Analyzing the Effects of Transactions on the Accounting Equation

LO3 Analyze the effects of transactions on the accounting equation and understand how these transactions affect the balance sheet and the income statement.

Economic events are the basis for recording transactions in an accounting system. For every transaction, it is essential to analyze its effect on the accounting equation:

Assets = Liabilities + Stockholders' Equity

We will now consider a series of events and their recognition as transactions for a hypothetical corporation, Glengarry Health Club. The transactions are for the month of January 2008, the first month of operations for the new business.

(1) Issuance of capital stock. The company is started when Karen Bradley and Kathy Drake file articles of incorporation with the state to obtain a charter. Each invests $50,000 in the business. In return, each receives 5,000 shares of capital stock. Thus, at this point, each of them owns 50% of the outstanding stock of the company and has a claim to 50% of its assets. The effect of this transaction on the accounting equation is to increase both assets and stockholders' equity:

	Assets					=	Liabilities		+	Stockholders' Equity	
Transaction Number	Cash	Accounts Receivable	Equipment	Building	Land		Accounts Payable	Notes Payable		Capital Stock	Retained Earnings
1	$100,000									$100,000	
Totals			$100,000							$100,000	

As you can see, each side of the accounting equation increases by $100,000. Cash is increased; and because the owners contributed this amount, their claim to the assets is increased in the form of Capital Stock.

(2) Acquisition of property in exchange for a note. The company buys a piece of property for $200,000. The seller agrees to accept a five-year promissory note. The note is given by the health club to the seller and is a written promise to repay the principal amount of the loan at the end of five years. To the company, the promissory note is a liability. The property consists of land valued at $50,000 and a newly constructed building valued at $150,000. The effect of this transaction on the accounting equation is to increase both assets and liabilities by $200,000:

	Assets					=	Liabilities		+	Stockholders' Equity	
Transaction Number	Cash	Accounts Receivable	Equipment	Building	Land		Accounts Payable	Notes Payable		Capital Stock	Retained Earnings
Bal.	$100,000									$100,000	
2				$150,000	$50,000			$200,000			
Bal.	$100,000			$150,000	$50,000			$200,000		$100,000	
Totals			$300,000					$300,000			

(3) Acquisition of equipment on an open account. Karen and Kathy contact an equipment supplier and buy $20,000 of exercise equipment: treadmills, barbells, and stationary bicycles. The supplier agrees to accept payment in full in 30 days. The health club has acquired an asset and at the same time incurred a liability:

	Assets					=	Liabilities		+	Stockholders' Equity	
Transaction Number	Cash	Accounts Receivable	Equipment	Building	Land		Accounts Payable	Notes Payable		Capital Stock	Retained Earnings
Bal.	$100,000			$150,000	$50,000			$200,000		$100,000	
3			$20,000				$20,000				
Bal.	$100,000		$20,000	$150,000	$50,000		$20,000	$200,000		$100,000	
Totals			$320,000					$320,000			

(4) Sale of monthly memberships on account. The owners open their doors for business. During January, they sell 300 monthly club memberships for $50 each, or a total of $15,000. The members have until the 10th of the following month to pay. Glengarry does not have cash from the new members; instead, it has a promise from each member to pay cash in the future. The promise from a customer to pay an amount owed is an asset called an *account receivable.* The other side of this transaction is an increase in the stockholders' equity (specifically, Retained Earnings) in the business. In other words, the assets have increased by $15,000 without any increase in a liability or any decrease in another asset. The increase in stockholders' equity indicates that the owners' residual interest in the assets of the business has increased by this amount. More specifically, an inflow of assets resulting from the sale of goods and services by a business is called *revenue.* The change in the accounting equation is as follows:

	Assets					=	Liabilities		+	Stockholders' Equity	
Transaction Number	Cash	Accounts Receivable	Equipment	Building	Land		Accounts Payable	Notes Payable		Capital Stock	Retained Earnings
Bal.	$100,000		$20,000	$150,000	$50,000		$20,000	$200,000		$100,000	
4		$15,000									$15,000
Bal.	$100,000	$15,000	$20,000	$150,000	$50,000		$20,000	$200,000		$100,000	$15,000
Totals			$335,000					$335,000			

(5) Sale of court time for cash. In addition to memberships, Glengarry sells court time. Court fees are paid at the time of use and amount to $5,000 for the first month:

	Assets					= Liabilities		+ Stockholders' Equity	
Transaction Number	Cash	Accounts Receivable	Equipment	Building	Land	Accounts Payable	Notes Payable	Capital Stock	Retained Earnings
Bal.	$100,000	$15,000	$20,000	$150,000	$50,000	$20,000	$200,000	$100,000	$15,000
5	5,000								5,000
Bal.	$105,000	$15,000	$20,000	$150,000	$50,000	$20,000	$200,000	$100,000	$20,000
Totals			$340,000				$340,000		

The only difference between this transaction and that of (4) is that cash is received rather than a promise being made to pay at a later date. Both transactions result in an increase in an asset and an increase in the owners' claim to the assets. In both cases, there is an inflow of assets in the form of Accounts Receivable or Cash. Thus, in both cases, the company has earned revenue.

(6) Payment of wages and salaries. The wages and salaries for the first month amount to $10,000. The payment of this amount results in a decrease in Cash and a decrease in the owners' claim on the assets, that is, a decrease in Retained Earnings. More specifically, an outflow of assets resulting from the sale of goods or services is called an *expense*. The effect of this transaction is to decrease both sides of the accounting equation:

	Assets					= Liabilities		+ Stockholders' Equity	
Transaction Number	Cash	Accounts Receivable	Equipment	Building	Land	Accounts Payable	Notes Payable	Capital Stock	Retained Earnings
Bal.	$105,000	$15,000	$20,000	$150,000	$50,000	$20,000	$200,000	$100,000	$20,000
6	−10,000								−10,000
Bal.	$ 95,000	$15,000	$20,000	$150,000	$50,000	$20,000	$200,000	$100,000	$10,000
Totals			$330,000				$330,000		

(7) Payment of utilities. The cost of utilities for the first month is $3,000. Glengarry pays this amount in cash. Both the utilities and the salaries and wages are expenses, and they have the same effect on the accounting equation. Cash is decreased, accompanied by a corresponding decrease in the owners' claim on the assets of the business:

	Assets					= Liabilities		+ Stockholders' Equity	
Transaction Number	Cash	Accounts Receivable	Equipment	Building	Land	Accounts Payable	Notes Payable	Capital Stock	Retained Earnings
Bal.	$95,000	$15,000	$20,000	$150,000	$50,000	$20,000	$200,000	$100,000	$10,000
7	−3,000								−3,000
Bal.	$92,000	$15,000	$20,000	$150,000	$50,000	$20,000	$200,000	$100,000	$ 7,000
Totals			$327,000				$327,000		

(8) Collection of accounts receivable. Even though the January monthly memberships are not due until the 10th of the following month, some of the members pay their bills by the end of January. The amount received from members in payment of their accounts is $4,000. The effect of the collection of an open account is to increase Cash and decrease Accounts Receivable:

	Assets					= Liabilities		+ Stockholders' Equity	
Transaction Number	Cash	Accounts Receivable	Equipment	Building	Land	Accounts Payable	Notes Payable	Capital Stock	Retained Earnings
Bal.	$92,000	$15,000	$20,000	$150,000	$50,000	$20,000	$200,000	$100,000	$7,000
8	4,000	−4,000							
Bal.	$96,000	$11,000	$20,000	$150,000	$50,000	$20,000	$200,000	$100,000	$7,000
Totals			$327,000				$327,000		

This is the first transaction we have seen that affects only one side of the accounting equation. In fact, the company simply traded assets: Accounts Receivable for Cash. Thus, note that the totals for the accounting equation remain at $327,000. Also note that Retained Earnings is not affected by this transaction because revenue was recognized earlier, in **(4)**, when Accounts Receivable was increased.

(9) Payment of dividends. At the end of the month, Karen and Kathy, acting on behalf of Glengarry Health Club, decide to pay a dividend of $1,000 on the shares of stock that each of them owns, or $2,000 in total. The effect of this dividend is to decrease both Cash and Retained Earnings. That is, the company is returning cash to the owners based on the profitable operations of the business for the first month. The transaction not only reduces Cash but also decreases the owners' claims on the assets of the company. Dividends are not an expense but rather a direct reduction of Retained Earnings. The effect on the accounting equation is as follows:

	Assets					=	Liabilities		+	Stockholders' Equity	
Transaction Number	Cash	Accounts Receivable	Equipment	Building	Land		Accounts Payable	Notes Payable		Capital Stock	Retained Earnings
Bal.	$96,000	$11,000	$20,000	$150,000	$50,000		$20,000	$200,000		$100,000	$7,000
9	−2,000										−2,000
Bal.	$94,000	$11,000	$20,000	$150,000	$50,000		$20,000	$200,000		$100,000	$5,000
Totals			$325,000							$325,000	

The Cost Principle An important principle governs the accounting for both the exercise equipment in **(3)** and the building and land in **(2)**. **The *cost principle* requires that we record an asset at the cost to acquire it and continue to show this amount on all balance sheets until we dispose of the asset.** With a few exceptions, an asset is not carried at its market value but at its original cost. *Why not show the land on future balance sheets at its market value?* Although this might seem more appropriate in certain instances, the subjectivity inherent in determining market values is a major reason behind the practice of carrying assets at their historical cost. The cost of an asset can be verified by an independent observer and is more *objective* than market value.

To summarize, Exhibit 3-1 indicates the effect of each transaction on the accounting equation, specifically the individual items increased or decreased by each transaction. Note the *dual* effect of each transaction. At least two items were involved in each transaction. For example, the initial investment by the owners resulted in an increase in an asset and an increase in Capital Stock. The payment of the utility bill caused a decrease in an asset and a decrease in Retained Earnings.

You can now see the central idea behind the accounting equation: Even though individual transactions may change the amount and composition of the assets and liabilities, the *equation* must always balance *for* each transaction, and the *balance sheet* must balance *after* each transaction.

BALANCE SHEET AND INCOME STATEMENT FOR GLENGARRY HEALTH CLUB

A balance sheet for Glengarry Health Club appears in Exhibit 3-2. All of the information needed to prepare this statement is available in Exhibit 3-1. The balances at the bottom of this exhibit are entered on the balance sheet, with assets on the left side and liabilities and stockholders' equity on the right side.

An income statement for Glengarry is shown in Exhibit 3-3. An income statement summarizes the revenues and expenses of a company for a period of time. In the example, the statement is for the month of January, as indicated on the third line of the heading of the statement. Glengarry earned revenues from two sources: (1) memberships and (2) court fees. Two types of expenses were incurred: (1) salaries and wages and (2) utilities. The difference between the total revenues of $20,000 and the total expenses of $13,000 is the net income for the month of $7,000. Finally, remember that dividends appear on a statement of retained earnings rather than on the income statement. They are a *distribution* of net income of the period, not a *determinant* of net income as are expenses.

EXHIBIT 3-1 Glengarry Health Club Transactions for the Month of January

	Assets					=	Liabilities		+	Stockholders' Equity	
Trans. No.	Cash	Accounts Receivable	Equipment	Building	Land		Accounts Payable	Notes Payable		Capital Stock	Retained Earnings
1	$100,000									$100,000	
2				$150,000	$50,000			$200,000			
Bal.	$100,000			$150,000	$50,000			$200,000		$100,000	
3			$20,000				$20,000				
Bal.	$100,000		$20,000	$150,000	$50,000		$20,000	$200,000		$100,000	
4		$15,000									$ 15,000
Bal.	$100,000	$15,000	$20,000	$150,000	$50,000		$20,000	$200,000		$100,000	$ 15,000
5	5,000										5,000
Bal.	$105,000	$15,000	$20,000	$150,000	$50,000		$20,000	$200,000		$100,000	$ 20,000
6	−10,000										−10,000
Bal.	$ 95,000	$15,000	$20,000	$150,000	$50,000		$20,000	$200,000		$100,000	$ 10,000
7	−3,000										−3,000
Bal.	$ 92,000	$15,000	$20,000	$150,000	$50,000		$20,000	$200,000		$100,000	$ 7,000
8	4,000	−4,000									
Bal.	$ 96,000	$11,000	$20,000	$150,000	$50,000		$20,000	$200,000		$100,000	$ 7,000
9	−2,000										−2,000
Bal.	$ 94,000	$11,000	$20,000	$150,000	$50,000		$20,000	$200,000		$100,000	$ 5,000

Total assets: $325,000

Total liabilities and stockholders' equity: $325,000

EXHIBIT 3-2 Balance Sheet for Glengarry Health Club

Glengarry Health Club
Balance Sheet
January 31, 2008

Assets		Liabilities and Stockholders' Equity	
Cash	$ 94,000	Accounts payable	$ 20,000
Accounts receivable	11,000	Notes payable	200,000
Equipment	20,000	Capital stock	100,000
Building	150,000	Retained earnings	5,000
Land	50,000	Total liabilities and stockholders' equity	$325,000
Total assets	$325,000		

EXHIBIT 3-3 Income Statement for Glengarry Health Club

Glengarry Health Club
Income Statement
For the Month Ended January 31, 2008

Revenues:		
Memberships	$15,000	
Court fees	5,000	$20,000
Expenses:		
Salaries and wages	$10,000	
Utilities	3,000	13,000
Net income		$ 7,000

We have seen how transactions are analyzed and how they affect the accounting equation and ultimately the financial statements. While the approach we took in analyzing the nine transactions of the Glengarry Health Club was manageable, can you imagine using this type of analysis for a company with *thousands* of transactions in any one month? We now turn to various *tools* that the accountant uses to process a large volume of transactions effectively and efficiently.

POD REVIEW 3.3

LO3 ***Analyze the effects of transactions on the accounting equation and understand how these transactions affect the balance sheet and the income statement.***

- The accounting equation illustrates the relationship between assets, liabilities, and stockholders' equity accounts. Understanding these relationships helps to see the logic behind the double-entry system in recording transactions.
  - The accounting equation: Assets = Liabilities + Stockholders' Equity
  - This equality must always be maintained. The equation can be expanded to show the linkage between the balance sheet and the income statement through the Retained Earnings account:

    Assets = Liabilities + Capital Stock + Retained Earnings

QUESTIONS

1. *A company borrows $5,000 at a local bank. This transaction would result in*
   a. an increase in Cash and a decrease in Retained Earnings.
   b. an increase in Cash and an increase in Accounts Payable.
   c. an increase in Cash and an increase in Notes Payable.
   d. none of the above.

2. *The collection of the amount owed by a customer on account would result in*
   a. an increase in Cash and an increase in Accounts Receivable.
   b. an increase in Cash and a decrease in Accounts Receivable.
   c. an increase in Cash and an increase in Retained Earnings.
   d. none of the above.

What Is an Account?

LO4 Define the concept of a general ledger and understand the use of the T account as a method for analyzing transactions.

An account is the basic unit for recording transactions. It is the record used to accumulate monetary amounts for each asset, liability, and component of stockholders' equity, such as Capital Stock, Retained Earnings, and Dividends. It is the basic recording unit for each element in the financial statements. Each revenue and expense has its own account. In the Glengarry Health Club example, nine accounts were used: Cash, Accounts Receivable, Equipment, Building, Land, Accounts Payable, Notes Payable, Capital Stock, and Retained Earnings. (Recall that revenues, expenses, and dividends were recorded directly in the Retained Earnings account. Later in the chapter we will see that each revenue and expense usually is recorded in a separate account.) In the real world, a company might have hundreds, even thousands, of individual accounts.

Account
A record used to accumulate amounts for each individual asset, liability, revenue, expense, and component of stockholders' equity.

No two entities have exactly the same set of accounts. To a certain extent, the accounts used by a company depend on its business. For example, a manufacturer normally has three inventory accounts: Raw Materials, Work in Process, and Finished Goods. A retailer uses just one account for inventory, a Merchandise Inventory account. A service business has no need for an inventory account.

Chart of accounts
A numerical list of all accounts used by a company.

Real World Practice

3-2 **Reading Southwest Airlines' Balance Sheet**

How many operating expenses does the company report on its income statement? What is the dollar amount of the largest of these?

CHART OF ACCOUNTS

Companies need a way to organize the large number of accounts they use to record transactions. A **chart of accounts** is a numerical list of all of the accounts an entity uses. The numbering system is a convenient way to identify accounts. For example, all asset accounts might be numbered from 100 to 199; liability accounts, from 200 to 299; equity accounts, from 300 to 399; revenues, from 400 to 499; and expenses, from 500 to 599. A chart of accounts for a hypothetical company, Widescreen Theaters Corporation, is shown in Exhibit 3-4. Note the division of account numbers within each of the financial statement categories. Within the asset category, the various cash accounts are numbered from 100 to 109; receivables, from 110 to 119; and so on. Not all of the numbers are assigned. For example, only three of the available nine numbers are currently utilized for cash accounts. This allows the company to add accounts as needed.

General ledger
A book, a file, a hard drive, or another device containing all of the accounts. ***Alternate term:*** *Set of accounts.*

THE GENERAL LEDGER

Companies store their accounts in different ways depending on their accounting system. In a manual system, a separate card or sheet is used to record the activity in each account. A **general ledger** is simply the file or book that contains the accounts.[4] For example, the general ledger for Widescreen Theaters Corporation might consist of a file of cards in a cabinet, with a card for each of the accounts listed in the chart of accounts.

In today's business world, most companies have an automated accounting system. The computer is ideally suited for the job of processing vast amounts of data rapidly. **All of the tools discussed in this chapter are as applicable to computerized systems as they are to manual systems. It is merely the appearance of the tools that differs between manual**

EXHIBIT 3-4 **Chart of Accounts for a Theater**

100–199:	ASSETS	300–399:	STOCKHOLDERS' EQUITY
100–109:	Cash	301:	Preferred Stock
101:	Cash, Checking, Second National Bank	302:	Common Stock
102:	Cash, Savings, Third State Bank	303:	Retained Earnings
103:	Cash, Change, or Petty Cash Fund (coin and currency)	400–499:	REVENUES
		401:	Tickets
110–119:	Receivables	402:	Video Rentals
111:	Accounts Receivable	403:	Concessions
112:	Due from Employees	404:	Interest
113:	Notes Receivable	500–599:	EXPENSES
120–129:	Prepaid Assets	500–509:	Rentals
121:	Cleaning Supplies	501:	Films
122:	Prepaid Insurance	502:	Videos
130–139:	Property, Plant, and Equipment	510–519:	Concessions
131:	Land	511:	Candy
132:	Theater Buildings	512:	Soda
133:	Projection Equipment	513:	Popcorn
134:	Furniture and Fixtures	520–529:	Wages and Salaries
200–299:	LIABILITIES	521:	Hourly Employees
200–209:	Short-Term Liabilities	522:	Salaries
201:	Accounts Payable	530–539:	Utilities
202:	Wages and Salaries Payable	531:	Heat
203:	Taxes Payable	532:	Electric
203.1:	Income Taxes Payable	533:	Water
203.2:	Sales Taxes Payable	540–549:	Advertising
203.3:	Unemployment Taxes Payable	541:	Newspaper
204:	Short-Term Notes Payable	542:	Radio
204.1:	Six-Month Note Payable to First State Bank	550–559:	Taxes
210–219:	Long-Term Liabilities	551:	Income Taxes
211:	Bonds Payable, due in 2013	552:	Unemployment Taxes

4 In addition to a general ledger, many companies maintain subsidiary ledgers. For example, an accounts receivable subsidiary ledger contains a separate account for each customer. The use of a subsidiary ledger for Accounts Receivable is discussed further in Chapter 7.

and computerized systems. For example, the ledger in an automated system might be contained on a computer file server rather than stored in a file cabinet. Throughout the book, a manual system will be used to explain the various tools, such as ledger accounts. The reason is that it is easier to illustrate and visualize the tools in a manual system. However, all of the ideas apply just as well to a computerized system of accounting.

THE DOUBLE-ENTRY SYSTEM

The origin of the double-entry system of accounting can be traced to Venice, Italy, in 1494. In that year, Fra Luca Pacioli, a Franciscan monk, wrote a mathematical treatise. Included in his book was the concept of debits and credits that is still used almost universally today.

THE T ACCOUNT

The form for a general ledger account will be illustrated later in the chapter. However, the form of account often used to analyze transactions is called the *T account,* so named because it resembles the capital letter *T*. The name of the account appears across the horizontal line. One side is used to record increases; the other side, decreases. But as you will see, the same side is not used for increases for every account. As a matter of convention, the *left* side of an *asset* account is used to record *increases;* the *right* side, to record *decreases.* To illustrate a T account, we will look at the Cash account for Glengarry Health Club. The transactions recorded in the account can be traced to Exhibit 3-1.

Left side of an asset account shows increases.

Shows the account name

Right side of an asset account shows decreases.

Cash

Increases		Decreases	
Investment by owners	100,000	Wages and salaries	10,000
Court fees collected	5,000	Utilities	3,000
Accounts collected	4,000	Dividends	2,000
	109,000		15,000
Bal.	94,000		

The amounts $109,000 and $15,000 are called *footings.* They represent the totals of the amounts on each side of the account. Neither these amounts nor the balance of $94,000 represents transactions. They are simply shown to indicate the totals and the balance in the account.

POD REVIEW 3.4

LO4 ***Define the concept of a general ledger and understand the use of the T account as a method for analyzing transactions.***

- The general ledger is a crucial part of the accounting system that lists all accounts and their balances. Financial statements may be prepared from current account balances in the general ledger.
- T accounts are a convenient way to analyze the activity in any particular account. The left side of a T account represents debits made to an account, and the right side represents credits made to an account.

QUESTIONS

1. *As an accounting convention, the left side of an asset account is used to record*
   a. increases.
   b. decreases.
   c. both increases and decreases.
   d. none of the above.

2. *The file or book that contains all of a company's accounts is called*
   a. a journal.
   b. a general ledger.
   c. a balance sheet.
   d. none of the above.

Debits and Credits

LO5 Explain the rules of debits and credits.

Rather than refer to the left or right side of an account, accountants use specific labels for each side. The *left* side of any account is the **debit** side, and the *right* side of any account is the **credit** side.

Debit
An entry on the left side of an account.

Credit
An entry on the right side of an account.

Account Name	
Left Side Debits	Right Side Credits

We will also use the terms *debit* and *credit* as verbs. If we *debit* the Cash account, we enter an amount on the left side. Similarly, if we want to enter an amount on the right side of an account, we *credit* the account. To *charge* an account has the same meaning as to *debit* it. No such synonym exists for the act of crediting an account.

Note that *debit* and *credit* are *locational* terms. They simply refer to the left or right side of a T account. They do *not* represent increases or decreases. As you will see, when one type of account is increased (for example, the Cash account), the increase is on the left, or *debit*, side. When certain other types of accounts are increased, however, the entry will be on the right, or *credit*, side.

Study Tip

Once you know the rule to increase an asset with a debit, the rules for the other increases and decreases follow logically. For example, because a liability is the opposite of an asset, it is increased with a credit. And it follows logically that it would be decreased with a debit.

As you would expect from your understanding of the accounting equation, the conventions for using T accounts for assets and liabilities are opposite. Assets are future economic benefits, and liabilities are obligations to transfer economic benefits in the future. If an asset is *increased* with a *debit*, how do you think a liability would be increased? **Because assets and liabilities are opposites, if an asset is increased with a debit, a liability is increased with a credit.** Thus, the right side, or credit side, of a liability account is used to record an increase. Like liabilities, stockholders' equity accounts are on the opposite side of the accounting equation from assets. **Thus, like a liability, a stockholders' equity account is increased with a credit.** We can summarize the logic of debits and credits, increases and decreases, and the accounting equation in the following way:

Assets		=	Liabilities		+	Stockholders' Equity	
Debits Increases +	Credits Decreases −		Debits Decreases −	Credits Increases +		Debits Decreases −	Credits Increases +

Note again that debits and credits are location-oriented. Debits are always on the left side of an account, credits, always on the right side.

DEBITS AND CREDITS FOR REVENUES, EXPENSES, AND DIVIDENDS

Revenues In the Glengarry Health Club example, revenues recognized in **(4)** and **(5)** were an increase in Retained Earnings. The sale of memberships was not only an increase in the asset Accounts Receivable but also an increase in the stockholders' equity account Retained Earnings. The transaction resulted in an increase in the owners' claim on the assets of the business. Rather than being recorded directly in Retained Earnings, however, each revenue item is maintained in a separate account. The following logic is used to arrive at the rules for increasing and decreasing revenues:[5]

Retained Earnings	
− Debit	+ Credit

Revenues	
− Debit	+ Credit

1. **Retained Earnings is increased with a credit.**
2. **Revenue is an increase in Retained Earnings.**
3. **Revenue is increased with a credit.**
4. **Because revenue is increased with a credit, it is decreased with a debit.**

5 We normally think of revenues and expenses as being increased, not decreased. Because we will need to decrease them as part of the closing procedure, it is important to know how to reduce as well as increase these accounts.

Expenses The same logic is applied to the expenses recognized in **(6)** and **(7)**. The rules for increasing and decreasing expense accounts are as follows:

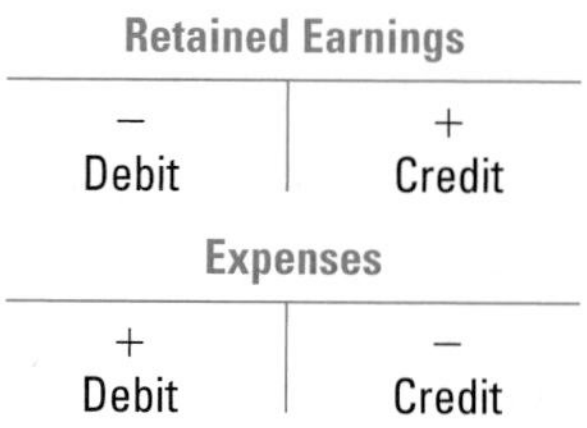

1. **Retained Earnings is decreased with a debit.**
2. **Expense is a decrease in Retained Earnings.**
3. **Expense is increased with a debit.**
4. **Because expense is increased with a debit, it is decreased with a credit.**

Dividends Recall that the dividend in **(9)** reduced cash. But dividends also reduce the owners' claim on the assets of the business. Earlier we recognized this decrease in the owners' claim as a reduction of Retained Earnings. As we do for revenue and expense accounts, we will use a separate Dividends account.

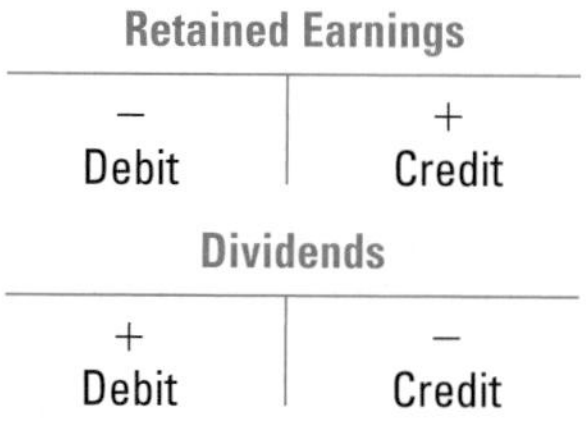

1. **Retained Earnings is decreased with a debit.**
2. **Dividends are a decrease in Retained Earnings.**
3. **Dividends are increased with a debit.**
4. **Because dividends are increased with a debit, they are decreased with a credit.**

SUMMARY OF THE RULES FOR INCREASING AND DECREASING ACCOUNTS

Using the accounting equation, the rules for increasing and decreasing the various types of accounts can be summarized as follows:

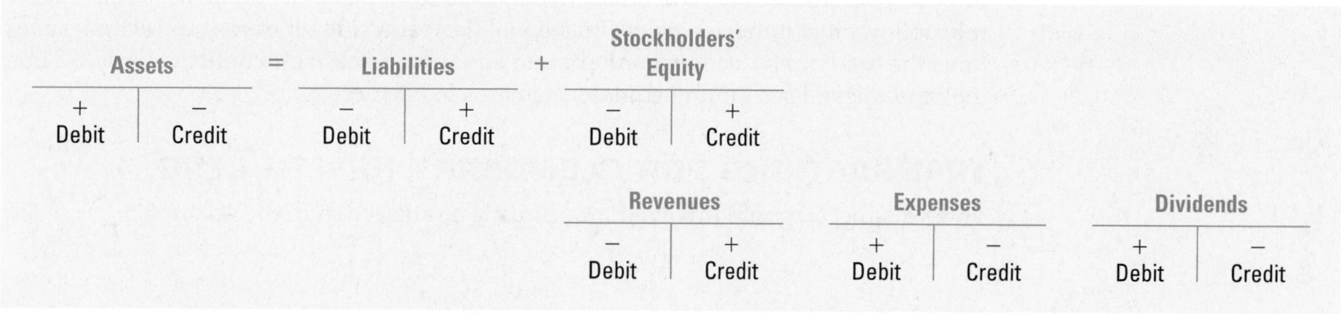

NORMAL ACCOUNT BALANCES

Each account has a "normal" balance. For example, assets normally have debit balances. Would it be possible for an asset such as Cash to have a credit balance? Assume that a company has a checking account with a bank. A credit balance in the account would indicate that the decreases in the account, from checks written and other bank charges, were more than the deposits into the account. If this were the case, however, the company would no longer have an asset, Cash, but instead would have a liability to the bank. The normal balances for the accounts we have looked at are as follows:

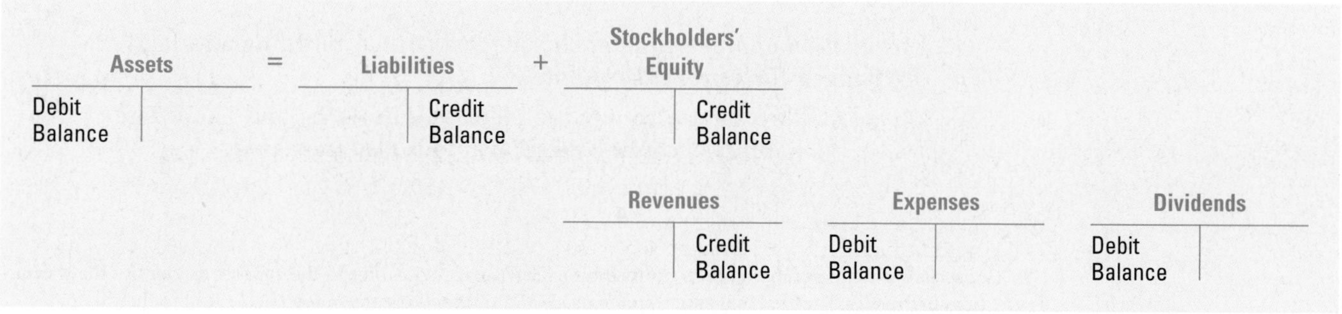

DEBITS AREN'T BAD, AND CREDITS AREN'T GOOD

Students often approach their first encounter with debits and credits with preconceived notions. The use of the terms *debit* and *credit* in everyday language leads to many of these notions: Joe is a real credit to his team. Nancy should be credited with saving Mary's career. They both appear to be positive statements. You must resist the temptation to associate the term *credit* with something good or positive and the term *debit* with something bad or negative. **In accounting, debit means one thing: an entry made on the left side of an account. A credit means an entry made on the right side of an account.**

DEBITS AND CREDITS APPLIED TO TRANSACTIONS

Recall the first transaction recorded by Glengarry Health Club earlier in the chapter: the owners invested $100,000 cash in the business. The transaction resulted in an increase in the Cash account and an increase in the Capital Stock account. Applying the rules of debits and credits, we would *debit* the Cash account for $100,000 and *credit* the Capital Stock account for the same amount.[6]

Cash	
100,000	

Capital Stock	
	100,000

Double-entry system
A system of accounting in which every transaction is recorded with equal debits and credits and the accounting equation is kept in balance.

You now can see why we refer to the **double-entry system** of accounting. Every transaction is recorded so that the equality of debits and credits is maintained, and in the process, the accounting equation is kept in balance. **Every transaction is entered in at least two accounts on opposite sides of T accounts. The first transaction resulted in an increase in an asset account and an increase in a stockholders' equity account. For every transaction, the debit side must equal the credit side. The debit of $100,000 to the Cash account equals the credit of $100,000 to the Capital Stock account.** It naturally follows that if the debit side must equal the credit side for every transaction, at any time, the total of all debits recorded must equal the total of all credits recorded. Thus, the fundamental accounting equation remains in balance.

TRANSACTIONS FOR GLENGARRY HEALTH CLUB

Three distinct steps are involved in recording a transaction in the accounts:

1. ***Analyze* the transaction.** That is, decide what accounts are increased or decreased and by how much.
2. ***Recall* the rules of debits and credits** as they apply to the transaction being analyzed.
3. ***Record* the transaction** using the rules of debits and credits.

We have already explained the logic for the debit to the Cash account and the credit to the Capital Stock account for the initial investment by the health club owners. We now analyze the remaining eight transactions for the month. Refer to Exhibit 3-1 for a summary of the transactions.

(2) *Acquisition of property in exchange for a note.* A building and land are exchanged for a promissory note.

Analyze: **Two asset accounts are increased: Building and Land. The liability account Notes Payable is also increased.**

6 We will use the number of each transaction as it was labeled earlier in the chapter to identify the transaction. In practice, a formal ledger account is used, and transactions are entered according to their date.

Recall: An asset is increased with a debit, and a liability is increased with a credit.

Record:

Building	
(2) 150,000	

Notes Payable	
	200,000 (2)

Land	
(2) 50,000	

(3) *Acquisition of equipment on an open account.* Exercise equipment is purchased from a supplier on open account. The purchase price is $20,000.

Analyze: An asset account, Equipment, is increased. A liability account, Accounts Payable, is also increased. Thus, the transaction is identical to the last transaction in that an asset or assets are increased and a liability is increased.

Recall: An asset is increased with a debit, and a liability is increased with a credit.

Record:

Equipment	
(3) 20,000	

Accounts Payable	
	20,000 (3)

(4) *Sale of monthly memberships on account.* Three hundred club memberships are sold for $50 each. The members have until the 10th of the following month to pay.

Analyze: The asset account Accounts Receivable is increased by $15,000. This amount is an asset because the company has the right to collect it in the future. The owners' claim to the assets is increased by the same amount. Recall, however, that we do not record these claims—revenues—directly in a stockholders' equity account but instead use a separate revenue account. We will call the account Membership Revenue.

Recall: An asset is increased with a debit. Stockholders' equity is increased with a credit. Because revenue is an increase in stockholders' equity, it is increased with a credit.

Record:

Accounts Receivable	
(4) 15,000	

Membership Revenue	
	15,000 (4)

(5) *Sale of court time for cash.* Court fees are paid at the time of use and amount to $5,000 for the first month.

Analyze: The asset account Cash is increased by $5,000. The stockholders' claim to the assets is increased by the same amount. The account used to record the increase in the stockholders' claim is Court Fee Revenue.

Recall: An asset is increased with a debit. Stockholders' equity is increased with a credit. Because revenue is an increase in stockholders' equity, it is increased with a credit.

Record:

Cash	
(1) 100,000	
(5) 5,000	

Court Fee Revenue	
	5,000 (5)

(6) *Payment of wages and salaries.* Wages and salaries amount to $10,000, and they are paid in cash.

Analyze: The asset account Cash is decreased by $10,000. At the same time, the owners' claim to the assets is decreased by this amount. However, rather than record a decrease directly to Retained Earnings, we set up an expense account, Wage and Salary Expense.

Recall: An asset is decreased with a credit. Stockholders' equity is decreased with a debit. Because expense is a decrease in stockholders' equity, it is increased with a debit.

Record:

Cash	
(1) 100,000	**10,000 (6)**
(5) 5,000	

Wage and Salary Espense	
(6) 10,000	

(7) *Payment of utilities.* The utility bill of $3,000 for the first month is paid in cash.

Analyze: The asset account Cash is decreased by $3,000. At the same time, the owners' claim to the assets is decreased by this amount. However, rather than record a decrease directly to Retained Earnings, we set up an expense account, Utilities Expense.

Recall: An asset is decreased with a credit. Stockholders' equity is decreased with a debit. Because expense is a decrease in stockholders' equity, it is increased with a debit.

Record:

Cash	
(1) 100,000	10,000 (6)
(5) 5,000	**3,000 (7)**

Utilities Expense	
(7) 3,000	

(8) *Collection of accounts receivable.* Cash of $4,000 is collected from members for their January dues.

Analyze: Cash is increased by the amount collected from the members. Another asset, Accounts Receivable, is decreased by the same amount. Glengarry has simply traded one asset for another.

Recall: An asset is increased with a debit and decreased with a credit. Thus, one asset is debited, and another is credited.

Record:

Cash	
(1) 100,000	10,000 (6)
(5) 5,000	3,000 (7)
(8) 4,000	

Accounts Receivable	
(4) 15,000	**4,000 (8)**

(9) *Payment of dividends.* Dividends of $2,000 are distributed to the owners.

Analyze: The asset account Cash is decreased by $2,000. At the same time, the owners' claim to the assets is decreased by this amount. Earlier in the chapter we decreased Retained Earnings for dividends paid to the owners. Now we will use a separate account, Dividends, to record these distributions.

Recall: **An asset is decreased with a credit. Retained earnings is decreased with a debit. Because dividends are a decrease in retained earnings, they are increased with a debit.**

Record:

Cash	
(1) 100,000	10,000 (6)
(5) 5,000	3,000 (7)
(8) 4,000	**2,000 (9)**

Dividends	
(9) 2,000	

POD REVIEW 3.5

LO5 *Explain the rules of debits and credits.*

- Debits and credits represent the left and right sides of a T account, respectively. They take on meaning only when associated with the recording of transactions involving asset, liability, and equity accounts.
  - In general, debits increase asset accounts, and credits increase liability and equity accounts.
  - The double-entry system requires that total debits equal total credits for any transaction recorded in the accounting system.

QUESTIONS

1. *The payment of the amount owed to a supplier on account would be recorded as*
   a. a debit to Cash and a credit to Accounts Payable.
   b. a debit to Accounts Payable and a credit to Cash.
   c. a debit to Accounts Receivable and a credit to Cash.
   d. none of the above.

2. *A theater sells a movie ticket for cash. This would be recorded as*
   a. a debit to Sales Revenue and a credit to Cash.
   b. a debit to Cash and a credit to Accounts Receivable.
   c. a debit to Cash and a credit to Sales Revenue.
   d. none of the above.

The Journal: The Firm's Chronological Record of Transactions

LO6 Explain the purposes of a journal and the posting process.

Each of the nine transactions was entered directly in the ledger accounts. By looking at the Cash account, we see that it increased by $5,000 in **(5)**. But what was the other side of this transaction? That is, what account was credited? To have a record of *each entry,* transactions are recorded first in a journal. A **journal** is a chronological record of transactions entered into by a business. Because a journal lists transactions in the order in which they took place, it is called the *book of original entry.* Transactions are recorded first in a journal and then are posted to the ledger accounts. **Posting** is the process of transferring a journal entry to the ledger accounts:

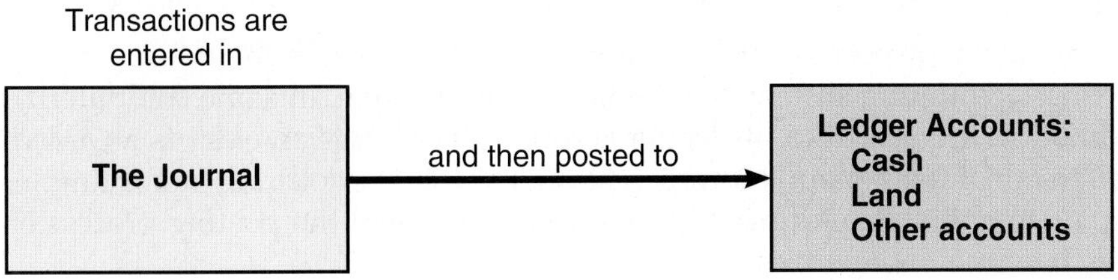

Journal
A chronological record of transactions. ***Alternate term:*** *Book of original entry.*

Posting
The process of transferring amounts from a journal to the ledger accounts.

Note that posting does not result in any change in the amounts recorded. It is simply a process of re-sorting the transactions from a chronological order to a topical arrangement.

Journalizing
The act of recording journal entries.

A journal entry is recorded for each transaction. **Journalizing** is the process of recording entries in a journal. A standard format is normally used for recording journal entries. Consider the original investment (see **(1)**, Issuance of capital stock, on page 108) by the owners of Glengarry Health Club. The format of the journal entry is as follows:

		Debit	Credit
Jan. xx	Cash	100,000	
	Capital Stock		100,000
	To record the issuance of 10,000 shares of stock for cash.		

Each journal entry contains a date with columns for the amounts debited and credited. Accounts credited are indented to distinguish them from accounts debited. A brief explanation normally appears on the line below the entry.

General journal
The journal used in place of a specialized journal.

Transactions are normally recorded in a **general journal**. Specialized journals may be used to record repetitive transactions. For example, a cash receipts journal may be used to record all transactions in which cash is received. Special journals accomplish the same purpose as a general journal, but they save time in recording similar transactions. This chapter will use a general journal to record all transactions.

An excerpt from Glengarry Health Club's general journal appears in the top portion of Exhibit 3-5. One column needs further explanation. *Post. Ref.* is an abbreviation for *Posting Reference.* As part of the posting process, which is explained later in this section, the debit and credit amounts are posted to the appropriate accounts and this column is filled in with the number assigned to the account.

Journal entries and ledger accounts are *tools* used by the accountant. The end result, a set of financial statements, is the most important part of the process. Journalizing provides a chronological record of each transaction. So why not just prepare financial statements directly from the journal entries? Isn't it extra work to *post* the entries to the ledger accounts? In the simple example of Glengarry Health Club, it would be possible to prepare the statements directly from the journal entries. In real-world situations, however, the number of transactions in any given period is so large that it would be virtually impossible, if not very inefficient, to bypass the accounts. Accounts provide a convenient summary of the activity as well as the balance for a specific financial statement item.

The posting process for Glengarry Health Club is illustrated in Exhibit 3-5 for the health club's fifth transaction, in which cash is collected for court fees. Rather than a T-account format for the general ledger accounts, the *running balance form* is illustrated. A separate column indicates the balance in the ledger account after each transaction. The use of the explanation column in a ledger account is optional. Because an explanation of the entry in the account can be found by referring to the journal, this column is often left blank.

Note the cross-referencing between the journal and the ledger. As amounts are entered in the ledger accounts, the Posting Reference column is filled in with the page number of the journal. For example, GJ1 indicates page 1 from the general journal. At the same time, the Posting Reference column of the journal is filled in with the appropriate account number.

The frequency of posting differs among companies, partly based on the degree to which their accounting system is automated. For example, in some computerized systems, amounts are posted to the ledger accounts at the time an entry is recorded in the journal. In a manual system, posting is normally done periodically; for example, daily, weekly, or monthly. Regardless of when it is performed, the posting process changes nothing. It simply reorganizes the transactions by account.

EXHIBIT 3-5 Posting from the Journal to the Ledger

General Journal — **Page No. 1**

Date		Account Titles and Explanation	Post. Ref.	Debit	Credit
2008 Jan.	XX	Accounts Receivable	5	15,000	
		Membership Revenue	40		15,000
		Sold 300 memberships at $50 each.			
	XX	Cash	1	5,000	
		Court Fee Revenue	44		5,000
		Collected court fees.			

General Ledger
Cash — **Account No. 1**

Date		Explanation	Post. Ref.	Debit	Credit	Balance
2008 Jan.	XX		GJ1	100,000		100,000
	XX		GJ1	5,000		105,000

Court Fee Revenue — **Account No. 44**

Date		Explanation	Post. Ref.	Debit	Credit	Balance
2008 Jan.	XX		GJ1		5,000	5,000

POD REVIEW 3.6

LO6 *Explain the purposes of a journal and the posting process.*

- A journal documents the details of transactions by date. Entries are made to a journal every time a transaction occurs.
  - Similar transactions that occur regularly may be recorded in special journals.
- Ultimately, information is posted from the journal to the ledgers for each individual account.

QUESTIONS

1. *The posting reference column in a general journal is used*
   a. to indicate the page number of the journal.
   b. to indicate the account number for the account being debited or credited.
   c. to indicate the date of the transaction.
   d. This column is normally left blank.

2. *Entries are posted from*
   a. the journal to the ledger.
   b. the ledger to the journal.
   c. the journal directly to the financial statements.
   d. order differs depending on the type of company.

© AP Photo/Mark Lennihan

Hot Topics

Southwest Airlines and PayPal Team Up

Southwest Airlines has always prided itself on its low fares and the ease of flying with the airline. Now the company has teamed up with PayPal to make it even easier and more secure to buy tickets online. PayPal, a company owned by eBay, allows its subscribers to pay over the Internet without sharing financial information. Besides using credit cards, customers have even more payment options from which to choose, including debit cards, bank accounts, and stored balances. For Southwest Airlines, an obvious motivation for its new alliance with PayPal is the potential for increased business from customers looking for a safe way to purchase tickets online. Whether the partnership puts more people in Southwest's seats and increases its revenue even further remains to be seen.

Source: Southwest Airlines news release, July 10, 2007; http://www.southwest.com.

The Trial Balance

LO7 Explain the purpose of a trial balance.

Trial balance
A list of each account and its balance; used to prove equality of debits and credits.

Accountants use one other tool to facilitate the preparation of a set of financial statements. A **trial balance** is a list of each account and its balance at a specific point in time. The trial balance is *not* a financial statement but merely a convenient device to prove the equality of the debit and credit balances in the accounts. It can be as informal as an adding machine tape with the account titles penciled in next to the debit and credit amounts. A trial balance for Glengarry Health Club as of January 31, 2008, is shown in Exhibit 3-6. The balance in each account was determined by adding the increases and subtracting the decreases for the account for the transactions detailed earlier.

Certain types of errors are detectable from a trial balance. For example, if the balance of an account is incorrectly computed, the total of the debits and credits in the trial balance will not equal. If a debit is posted to an account as a credit, or vice versa, the trial balance will be out of balance. The omission of part of a journal entry in the posting process will also be detected by the preparation of a trial balance.

EXHIBIT 3-6 Trial Balance for Glengarry Health Club

"unadjusted" trial Balance

Glengarry Health Club
Trial Balance
January 31, 2008

Account Titles	Debits	Credits
Cash	$ 94,000	
Accounts Receivable	11,000	
Equipment	20,000	
Building	150,000	
Land	50,000	
Accounts Payable		$ 20,000
Notes Payable		200,000
Capital Stock		100,000
Membership Revenue		15,000
Court Fee Revenue		5,000
Wage and Salary Expense	10,000	
Utility Expense	3,000	
Dividends	2,000	
Totals	$340,000	$340,000

Do not attribute more significance to a trial balance, however, than is warranted. It does provide a convenient summary of account balances for preparing financial statements. It also assures us that the balances of all of the debit accounts equal the balances of all of the credit accounts. But an equality of debits and credits does not necessarily mean that the *correct* accounts were debited and credited in an entry. For example, the entry to record the purchase of land by signing a promissory note *should* result in a debit to Land and a credit to Notes Payable. If the accountant incorrectly debited Cash instead of Land, the trial balance would still show an equality of debits and credits. A trial balance can be prepared at any time; it is usually prepared before the release of a set of financial statements.

Study Tip

Remember from p. 117 that every account has a normal balance, either debit or credit. Note the normal balance for each account on this trial balance.

POD REVIEW 3.7

LO7 *Explain the purpose of a trial balance.*

- At the end of a period, a trial balance may be prepared that lists all of the accounts in the general ledger along with their debit or credit balances.
- The purpose of the trial balance is to see whether total debits equals total credits. This provides some assurance that the accounting equation was adhered to in the processing of transactions but is no guarantee that transactions have been recorded properly.

QUESTIONS

1. *A trial balance*
   a. is one of the primary financial statements.
   b. will not balance if the wrong account is debited.
   c. is a list of each account and its balance.
   d. none of the above.

2. *Which of the following errors would* not *be detected by the preparation of a trial balance?*
   a. Cash was debited when the debit should have been to Accounts Receivable.
   b. An entry was recorded with a debit to Cash for $500 and a credit to Accounts Receivable for $5,000.
   c. The balance in one of the accounts was computed incorrectly.
   d. All of the above errors would be detected by the preparation of a trial balance.

A FINAL NOTE: PROCESSING ACCOUNTING INFORMATION

This chapter analyzed the effects of the transactions of Glengarry Health Club on the accounting equation and showed how those transactions were recorded as journal entries with the use of debits and credits. In addition to understanding how transactions are recorded in debit and credit form, it is important to know the effect of these transactions on the financial statements. **To emphasize this point, whenever a journal entry is shown in future chapters, we will also show how the transaction affects the financial statements.** For example, the sale of memberships would appear as follows:

Jan. xx	Accounts Receivable	15,000	
	Membership Revenue		15,000
	To record sale of 300 memberships at $50 each.		

Balance Sheet							Income Statement
ASSETS		=	**LIABILITIES**	+	**STOCKHOLDERS' EQUITY**	+	**REVENUES − EXPENSES**
Accounts Receivable	15,000						Membership Revenue 15,000

Note that both ways of illustrating the transaction show the two accounts involved, Accounts Receivable and Membership Revenue. The journal entry presents the changes in these accounts in debit and credit form, and the transactions effect equation indicates the impact on the balance sheet and the income statement. Note in this version of the equation that the income statement is viewed as an extension of the balance sheet. As you learned earlier in the chapter, revenues do result in an increase in retained earnings and thus stockholders' equity; but first, they must be recorded on the income statement.

To illustrate one additional transaction with this new format, recall **(6)** for Glengarry in which $10,000 was paid in wages and salaries. The journal entry and effect on the accounting equation are as follows:

Jan. xx	Wage and Salary Expense	10,000	
	Cash		10,000
	To record payment of wages and salaries.		

			Balance Sheet				Income Statement
ASSETS		=	**LIABILITIES**	+	**STOCKHOLDERS' EQUITY**	+	**REVENUES − EXPENSES**
Cash	(10,000)						Wage and Salary Expense (10,000)

Note the logic for bracketing both amounts in the transactions effect form. Because the asset account Cash decreased, the amount of decrease is in brackets in the transaction effect form. Wage and Salary Expense increased by $10,000. But because an expense reduces net income on the income statement, the amount is bracketed.

REVIEW

KEY TERMS QUIZ

Read each definition below and write the number of the definition in the blank beside the appropriate term. The quiz solutions appear at the end of the chapter.

_______	**Event**	_______	**Debit**
_______	**External event**	_______	**Credit**
_______	**Internal event**	_______	**Double-entry system**
_______	**Transaction**	_______	**Journal**
_______	**Source document**	_______	**Posting**
_______	**Account**	_______	**Journalizing**
_______	**Chart of accounts**	_______	**General journal**
_______	**General ledger**	_______	**Trial balance**

1. A numerical list of all accounts used by a company.
2. A list of each account and its balance at a specific point in time; used to prove the equality of debits and credits.
3. A happening of consequence to an entity.
4. An entry on the right side of an account.
5. An event occurring entirely within an entity.
6. A piece of paper, such as a sales invoice, that is used as the evidence to record a transaction.
7. The act of recording journal entries.
8. An entry on the left side of an account.
9. The process of transferring amounts from a journal to the appropriate ledger accounts.
10. An event involving interaction between an entity and its environment.
11. The record used to accumulate monetary amounts for each individual asset, liability, revenue, expense, and component of stockholders' equity.
12. A book, a file, a hard drive, or another device containing all of a company's accounts.
13. A chronological record of transactions.

14. Any event, external or internal, that is recognized in a set of financial statements.
15. The journal used in place of a specialized journal.
16. A system of accounting in which every transaction is recorded with equal debits and credits and the accounting equation is kept in balance.

ALTERNATE TERMS

Credit side of an account Right side of an account

Debit an account Charge an account

Debit side of an account Left side of an account

General ledger Set of accounts

Journal Book of original entry

Journalize an entry Record an entry

Posting an account Transferring an amount from the journal to the ledger

WARMUP EXERCISES & SOLUTIONS

LO3,5 **Warmup Exercise 3-1** Your Debits and Credits

Assume that you borrow $1,000 from your roommate by signing an agreement to repay the amount borrowed in six months.

Required

1. What is the effect of this transaction on your own accounting equation?
2. Prepare the journal entry to record this transaction in your own records.

Key to the Solution Recall Exhibit 3-1 for the effects of transactions on the accounting equation and refer to the summary of the rules for increasing and decreasing accounts on p. 117.

LO3,5 **Warmup Exercise 3-2** A Bank's Debits and Credits

The Third State Bank loans a customer $5,000 in exchange for a promissory note.

Required

1. What is the effect of this transaction on the bank's accounting equation?
2. Prepare the journal entry to record this transaction in the bank's records.

Key to the Solution Recall Exhibit 3-1 for the effects of the transaction on the accounting equation and refer to the summary of the rules for increasing and decreasing accounts on p. 117.

LO3,5,8 **Warmup Exercise 3-3** Debits and Credits for Southwest Airlines

Assume that Southwest Airlines borrows $25 million by signing a promissory note. The next day the company uses the money to buy a new airplane.

Required

1. What is the effect of each of these transactions on Southwest Airlines' accounting equation?
2. Prepare the journal entries to record both transactions in Southwest Airlines' records.

Key to the Solution Recall Exhibit 3-1 for the effects of transactions on the accounting equation and refer to the summary of the rules for increasing and decreasing accounts on p. 117.

SOLUTIONS TO WARMUP EXERCISES

Warmup Exercise 3-1

1. If you borrow $1,000 from your roommate, assets in the form of cash increase $1,000 and liabilities in the form of a note payable increase $1,000.
2. Cash 1,000

2. Cash	1,000	
Notes Payable		1,000

Warmup Exercise 3-2

1. If a bank loans a customer $5,000, the bank's assets in the form of a note receivable increase $5,000 and its assets in the form of cash decrease $5,000.

2. Notes Receivable	5,000	
Cash		5,000

Warmup Exercise 3-3

1. If Southwest Airlines borrows $25 million, assets in the form of cash increase $25 million and liabilities in the form of a note payable increase $25 million. If the company uses the money to buy an airplane, assets in the form of flight equipment increase 25 million and assets in the form of cash decrease $25 million.
2.

Cash	25,000,000	
Notes Payable		25,000,000
Flight Equipment	25,000,000	
Cash		25,000,000

REVIEW PROBLEM & SOLUTION

The following transactions are entered into by Sparkle Car Wash during its first month of operations:

a. Articles of incorporation are filed with the state, and 20,000 shares of capital stock are issued. Cash of $40,000 is received from the new owners for the shares.
b. A five-year promissory note is signed at the local bank. The cash received from the loan is $120,000.
c. An existing car wash is purchased for $150,000 in cash. The values assigned to the land, building, and equipment are $25,000, $75,000, and $50,000, respectively.
d. Cleaning supplies are purchased on account for $2,500 from a distributor. None of the supplies are used in the first month.
e. During the first month, $1,500 is paid to the distributor for the cleaning supplies. The remaining $1,000 will be paid next month.
f. Gross receipts from car washes during the first month of operations amount to $7,000.
g. Wages and salaries paid in the first month amount to $2,000.
h. The utility bill of $800 for the month is paid.
i. A total of $1,000 in dividends is paid to the owners.

Required

1. Prepare a table to summarize the preceding transactions as they affect the accounting equation. Use the format in Exhibit 3-1. Identify each transaction by letter.
2. Prepare an income statement for the month.
3. Prepare a balance sheet at the end of the month.

SOLUTION TO REVIEW PROBLEM

1.

Sparkle Car Wash
Transactions for the Month

	Assets					=	Liabilities		+	Stockholders' Equity	
Trans.	**Cash**	**Cleaning Supplies**	**Land**	**Building**	**Equipment**		**Accounts Payable**	**Notes Payable**		**Capital Stock**	**Retained Earnings**
a.	$ 40,000									$40,000	
b.	120,000							$120,000			
Bal.	$160,000							$120,000		$40,000	
c.	−150,000		$25,000	$75,000	$50,000						
Bal.	$ 10,000		$25,000	$75,000	$50,000			$120,000		$40,000	
d.		$2,500					$2,500				
Bal.	$ 10,000	$2,500	$25,000	$75,000	$50,000		$2,500	$120,000		$40,000	
e.	−1,500						−1,500				
Bal.	$ 8,500	$2,500	$25,000	$75,000	$50,000		$1,000	$120,000		$40,000	
f.	7,000										7,000
Bal.	$ 15,500	$2,500	$25,000	$75,000	$50,000		$1,000	$120,000		$40,000	$ 7,000
g.	−2,000										−2,000
Bal.	$ 13,500	$2,500	$25,000	$75,000	$50,000		$1,000	$120,000		$40,000	$ 5,000
h.	−800										−800
Bal.	$ 12,700	$2,500	$25,000	$75,000	$50,000		$1,000	$120,000		$40,000	$ 4,200
i.	−1,000										−1,000
Bal.	$ 11,700	$2,500	$25,000	$75,000	$50,000		$1,000	$120,000		$40,000	$ 3,200

Total assets: $164,200

Total liabilities and stockholders' equity: $164,200

2.

Sparkle Car Wash
Income Statement
For the Month Ended XX/XX/XX

Car wash revenue		$7,000
Expenses:		
Wages and salaries	$2,000	
Utilities	800	2,800
Net income		$4,200

3.

Sparkle Car Wash
Balance Sheet
XX/XX/XX

Assets		Liabilities and Stockholders' Equity	
Cash	$ 11,700	Accounts payable	$ 1,000
Supplies	2,500	Notes payable	120,000
Land	25,000	Capital stock	40,000
Building	75,000	Retained earnings	3,200
Equipment	50,000	Total liabilities	
Total assets	$164,200	and stockholders' equity	$164,200

QUESTIONS

1. What are the two types of events that affect an entity? Describe each.
2. What is the significance of source documents to the recording process? Give two examples of source documents.
3. What are four different forms of cash?
4. How does an account receivable differ from a note receivable?
5. What is meant by this statement: One company's account receivable is another company's account payable?
6. What do accountants mean when they refer to the double-entry system of accounting?
7. Stockholders' equity represents the claim of the owners on the assets of the business. What is the distinction relative to the owners' claim between the Capital Stock account and the Retained Earnings account?
8. If an asset account is increased with a debit, what is the logic for increasing a liability account with a credit?
9. A friend comes to you with the following plight: "I'm confused. An asset is something positive, and it is increased with a debit. However, an expense is something negative, and it is also increased with a debit. I don't get it." How can you "straighten out" your friend?
10. The payment of dividends reduces cash. If the Cash account is reduced with a credit, why is the Dividends account debited when dividends are paid?
11. If Cash is increased with a debit, why does the bank credit your account when you make a deposit?
12. Your friend presents the following criticism of the accounting system: "Accounting involves so much duplication of effort. First, entries are recorded in a journal; then the same information is recorded in a ledger. No wonder accountants work such long hours!" Do you agree with this criticism? Explain.
13. How does the T account differ from the running balance form for an account? How are they similar?
14. What is the benefit of using a cross-referencing system between a ledger and a journal?
15. How often should a company post entries from the journal to the ledger?
16. What is the purpose of a trial balance?

BRIEF EXERCISES

LO1 **Brief Exercise 3-1** External and Internal Events

Explain how an external event differs from an internal event.

LO2 **Brief Exercise 3-2** Source Documents

Provide three examples of source documents and the event for which each would provide the evidence to record.

LO3

Brief Exercise 3-3 Effects of Transactions on the Accounting Equation

List the three elements in the accounting equation. How is the third element expanded to show the linkage between the balance sheet and the income statement?

LO4

Brief Exercise 3-4 Types of Accounts

For each of the following accounts, indicate whether it is a balance sheet (BS) account or an income statement (IS) account.

_______ **Prepaid insurance**
_______ **Sales revenue**
_______ **Income taxes payable**
_______ **Accounts receivable**
_______ **Utilities expense**
_______ **Furniture and fixtures**
_______ **Retained earnings**

LO5

Brief Exercise 3-5 Debits and Credits

For each of the following accounts, indicate whether it would be increased with a debit or a credit.

_______ **Accounts payable**
_______ **Office supplies**
_______ **Interest revenue**
_______ **Income tax expense**
_______ **Income tax payable**
_______ **Cash**
_______ **Common stock**
_______ **Land**

LO6

Brief Exercise 3-6 Journalizing Transactions

Prepare in good form the journal entry to record each of the following transactions on the books of ABC.

January 10, 2007: ABC is incorporated by issuing $50,000 of common stock to each of the three owners.
January 12, 2007: ABC borrows $100,000 at the local bank.
January 15, 2007: ABC pays $200,000 cash to buy 10 acres of land.

LO7

Brief Exercise 3-7 Trial Balance

For each of the following errors, indicate with a *Y* for yes or an *N* for no whether it would be detected by preparation of a trial balance.

_______ a. Cash is debited instead of Accounts Receivable for a sale on account.
_______ b. A sale on account for $500 is recorded with a debit to Accounts Receivable for $500 and a credit to Sales for $5,000.
_______ c. A cash sale is recorded by debiting Cash and Sales for the same amount.

EXERCISES

LO1

Exercise 3-1 Types of Events

For each of the following events, identify whether it is an external event that would be recorded as a transaction (E), an internal event that would be recorded as a transaction (I), or not recorded (NR).

_______ 1. A vendor for a company's supplies is paid an amount owed on account.
_______ 2. A customer pays its open account.
_______ 3. A new chief executive officer is hired.
_______ 4. The biweekly payroll is paid.
_______ 5. Depreciation on equipment is recognized.
_______ 6. A new advertising agency is hired to develop a series of newspaper ads for the company.
_______ 7. The advertising bill for the first month is paid.
_______ 8. The accountant determines the federal income taxes owed based on the income earned during the period.

LO2

Exercise 3-2 Source Documents Matched with Transactions

Following are a list of source documents and a list of transactions. Indicate by letter next to each transaction the source document that would serve as evidence for the recording of the transaction.

Source Documents

a. Purchase invoice
b. Sales invoice
c. Cash register tape
d. Time cards
e. Promissory note
f. Stock certificates
g. Monthly statement from utility company
h. No standard source document would normally be available

Transactions

_______ 1. Utilities expense for the month is recorded.
_______ 2. A cash settlement is received from a pending lawsuit.
_______ 3. Owners contribute cash to start a new corporation.
_______ 4. The biweekly payroll is paid.
_______ 5. Services are provided in exchange for cash.
_______ 6. Equipment is acquired on a 30-day open account.
_______ 7. Service is provided to a customer.
_______ 8. A building is acquired by signing an agreement to repay a stated amount plus interest in six months.

LO3

Exercise 3-3 The Effect of Transactions on the Accounting Equation

For each of the following transactions, indicate whether it increases (I), decreases (D), or has no effect (NE) on the total dollar amount of each of the elements of the accounting equation.

Transactions	Assets	= Liabilities	+ Stockholders' Equity
Example: Common stock is issued in exchange for cash.	I	NE	I
1. Equipment is purchased for cash.			
2. Services are provided to customers on account.			
3. Services are provided to customers in exchange for cash.			
4. An account payable is paid off.			
5. Cash is collected on an account receivable.			
6. Buildings are purchased in exchange for a three-year note payable.			
7. Advertising bill for the month is paid.			
8. Dividends are paid to stockholders.			
9. Land is acquired by issuing shares of stock to the owner of the land.			

LO3

Exercise 3-4 Types of Transactions

There are three elements to the accounting equation: assets, liabilities, and stockholders' equity. Although other possibilities exist, five types of transactions are described here. For *each* of these five types, write descriptions of two transactions that illustrate these types of transactions.

Type of Transaction	Assets	= Liabilities	+ Stockholders' Equity
1.	Increase	Increase	
2.	Increase		Increase
3.	Decrease	Decrease	
4.	Decrease		Decrease
5.	Increase Decrease		

HOMEWORK

LO4

Exercise 3-5 Balance Sheet Accounts and Their Use

Choose from the following list of account titles the one that most accurately fits the description of that account or is an example of that account. An account title may be used more than once or not at all.

Cash	**Accounts Receivable**	**Notes Receivable**
Prepaid Asset	**Land**	**Buildings**
Investments	**Accounts Payable**	**Notes Payable**
Taxes Payable	**Retained Earnings**	**Common Stock**
Preferred Stock		

______________ 1. A written obligation to repay a fixed amount, with interest, at some time in the future

______________ 2. Twenty acres of land held for speculation

______________ 3. An amount owed by a customer

______________ 4. Corporate income taxes owed to the federal government

______________ 5. Ownership in a company that allows the owner to receive dividends before common shareholders receive any distributions

______________ 6. Five acres of land used as the site for a factory

______________ 7. Amounts owed on an open account to a vendor, due in 90 days

______________ 8. A checking account at a bank

______________ 9. A warehouse used to store equipment

______________ 10. Claims by the owners on the undistributed net income of a business

______________ 11. Rent paid on an office building in advance of use of the facility

LO5

Exercise 3-6 Normal Account Balances

Each account has a normal balance. For the following list of accounts, indicate whether the normal balance of each is a debit or a credit.

Account	Normal Balance
1. Cash	________
2. Prepaid Insurance	________
3. Retained Earnings	________
4. Bonds Payable	________
5. Investments	________
6. Capital Stock	________
7. Advertising Fees Earned	________
8. Wages and Salaries Expense	________
9. Wages and Salaries Payable	________
10. Office Supplies	________
11. Dividends	________

LO5

Exercise 3-7 Debits and Credits

The new bookkeeper for Darby Corporation is getting ready to mail the daily cash receipts to the bank for deposit. Because his previous job was at a bank, he is aware that the bank "credits" an account for all deposits and "debits" an account for all checks written. Therefore, he makes the following entry before sending the daily receipts to the bank:

June 5	Accounts Receivable	10,000	
	Sales Revenue	2,450	
	Cash		12,450
	To record cash received on June 5: $10,000 collections on account and $2,450 in cash sales.		

Required

Explain why that entry is wrong and prepare the correct journal entry. Why does the bank refer to cash received from a customer as a *credit* to that customer's account?

LO7 **Exercise 3-8** Trial Balance

The following list of accounts was taken from the general ledger of Spencer Corporation on December 31, 2008. The bookkeeper thought it would be helpful if the accounts were arranged in alphabetical order. Each account contains the balance that is normal for that type of account; for example, Cash normally has a debit balance. Prepare a trial balance as of this date with the accounts arranged in the following order: (1) assets, (2) liabilities, (3) stockholders' equity, (4) revenues, (5) expenses, and (6) dividends.

Account	Balance
Accounts Payable	$ 7,650
Accounts Receivable	5,325
Automobiles	9,200
Buildings	150,000
Capital Stock	100,000
Cash	10,500
Commissions Expense	2,600
Commissions Revenue	12,750
Dividends	2,000
Equipment	85,000
Heat, Light, and Water Expense	1,400
Income Tax Expense	1,700
Income Taxes Payable	2,500
Interest Revenue	1,300
Land	50,000
Notes Payable	90,000
Office Salaries Expense	6,000
Office Supplies	500
Retained Earnings	110,025

MULTICONCEPT EXERCISES

LO3,4,5 **Exercise 3-9** Journal Entries Recorded Directly in T Accounts

Record each of the following transactions directly in T accounts using the numbers preceding the transactions to identify them in the accounts. Each account needs a separate T account.

1. Received contribution of $6,500 from each of the three principal owners of the We-Go Delivery Service in exchange for shares of stock.
2. Purchased office supplies for cash of $130.
3. Purchased a van for $15,000 on an open account. The company has 25 days to pay for the van.
4. Provided delivery services to residential customers for cash of $125.
5. Billed a local business $200 for delivery services. The customer is to pay the bill within 15 days.
6. Paid the amount due on the van.
7. Received the amount due from the local business billed in (5).

LO4,7 **Exercise 3-10** Trial Balance

Refer to the transactions recorded directly in T accounts for the We-Go Delivery Service in Exercise 3-9. Assume that all of the transactions took place during December 2008. Prepare a trial balance at December 31, 2008.

LO3,4,5 **Exercise 3-11** Determining an Ending Account Balance

Jessie's Accounting Services was organized on June 1, 2008. The company received a contribution of $1,000 from each of the two principal owners. During the month, Jessie's Accounting Services provided services for cash of $1,400 and services on account for $450, received $250 from customers in payment of their accounts, purchased supplies on account for $600 and equipment on account for $1,350, received a utility bill for $250 that will not be paid until July, and paid the full amount due on the equipment. Use a T account to determine the company's Cash balance on June 30, 2008.

LO3,4,5

Exercise 3-12 Reconstructing a Beginning Account Balance

During the month, services performed for customers on account amounted to $7,500 and collections from customers in payment of their accounts totaled $6,000. At the end of the month, the Accounts Receivable account had a balance of $2,500. What was the Accounts Receivable balance at the beginning of the month?

LO3,5,6

Exercise 3-13 Journal Entries

Prepare the journal entry to record each of the following independent transactions. (Use the number of the transaction in lieu of a date for identification purposes.)

1. Services provided on account of $1,530
2. Purchases of supplies on account for $1,365
3. Services provided for cash of $750
4. Purchase of equipment for cash of $4,240
5. Issuance of a promissory note for $2,500
6. Collections on account for $890
7. Sale of capital stock in exchange for a parcel of land; the land is appraised at $50,000
8. Payment of $4,000 in salaries and wages
9. Payment of open account in the amount of $500

LO3,5,6

Exercise 3-14 Journal Entries

Following is a list of transactions entered into during the first month of operations of Gardener Corporation, a new landscape service. Prepare in journal form the entry to record each transaction.

April 1: Articles of incorporation are filed with the state, and 100,000 shares of common stock are issued for $100,000 in cash.
April 4: A six-month promissory note is signed at the bank. Interest at 9% per annum will be repaid in six months along with the principal amount of the loan of $50,000.
April 8: Land and a storage shed are acquired for a lump sum of $80,000. On the basis of an appraisal, 25% of the value is assigned to the land and the remainder to the building.
April 10: Mowing equipment is purchased from a supplier at a total cost of $25,000. A down payment of $10,000 is made, with the remainder due by the end of the month.
April 18: Customers are billed for services provided during the first half of the month. The total amount billed of $5,500 is due within ten days.
April 27: The remaining balance due on the mowing equipment is paid to the supplier.
April 28: The total amount of $5,500 due from customers is received.
April 30: Customers are billed for services provided during the second half of the month. The total amount billed is $9,850.
April 30: Salaries and wages of $4,650 for the month of April are paid.

LO5,6

Exercise 3-15 The Process of Posting Journal Entries to General Ledger Accounts

On June 1, Campbell Corporation purchased 10 acres of land in exchange for a promissory note in the amount of $50,000. Using the formats shown in Exhibit 3-5, prepare the journal entry to record this transaction in a general journal and post it to the appropriate general ledger accounts. The entry will be recorded on page 7 of the general journal. Use whatever account numbers you like in the general ledger. Assume that none of the accounts to be debited or credited currently contain a balance.

If at a later date you wanted to review this transaction, would you examine the general ledger or the general journal? Explain your answer.

PROBLEMS

LO1

Problem 3-1 Events to Be Recorded in Accounts

The following events take place at Dillon's Delivery Service:

1. Supplies are ordered from vendors who will deliver the supplies within the week.
2. Vendors deliver supplies on account, payment due in 30 days.
3. Customers' deliveries are made, and the customers are billed.
4. Trash is taken to dumpsters, and the floors are cleaned.
5. Cash is received from customers billed in (3).

6. Cash is deposited in the bank night depository.
7. Employees are paid weekly paychecks.
8. Vendors noted in (2) are paid for the supplies delivered.

Required

Identify each event as internal (I) or external (E) and indicate whether each event would or would not be recorded in the *accounts* of the company. For each event that is to be recorded, identify the names of at least two accounts that would be affected.

LO3

Problem 3-2 Transaction Analysis and Financial Statements

Just Rolling Along Inc. was organized on May 1, 2008, by two college students who recognized an opportunity to make money while spending their days at a beach along Lake Michigan. The two entrepreneurs plan to rent bicycles and in-line skates to weekend visitors to the lakefront. The following transactions occurred during the first month of operations:

May 1: Received contribution of $9,000 from each of the two principal owners of the new business in exchange for shares of stock.
May 1: Purchased ten bicycles for $300 each on an open account. The company has 30 days to pay for the bicycles.
May 5: Registered as a vendor with the city and paid the $15 monthly fee.
May 9: Purchased 20 pairs of in-line skates at $125 per pair, 20 helmets at $50 each, and 20 sets of protective gear (knee and elbow pads and wrist guards) at $45 per set for cash.
May 10: Purchased $100 in miscellaneous supplies on account. The company has 30 days to pay for the supplies.
May 15: Paid $125 bill from local radio station for advertising for the last two weeks of May.
May 17: Customers rented in-line skates and bicycles for cash of $1,800.
May 24: Billed the local park district $1,200 for in-line skating lessons provided to neighborhood children. The park district is to pay one-half of the bill within 5 working days and the rest within 30 days.
May 29: Received 50% of the amount billed to the park district.
May 30: Customers rented in-line skates and bicycles for cash of $3,000.
May 30: Paid wages of $160 to a friend who helped over the weekend.
May 31: Paid the balance due on the bicycles.

Required

1. Prepare a table to summarize the preceding transactions as they affect the accounting equation. Use the format in Exhibit 3-1. Identify each transaction with the date.
2. Prepare an income statement for the month ended May 31, 2008.
3. Prepare a classified balance sheet at May 31, 2008.
4. Why do you think the two college students decided to incorporate their business rather than operate it as a partnership?

LO3

Problem 3-3 Transaction Analysis and Financial Statements

Expert Consulting Services Inc. was organized on March 1, 2008, by two former college roommates. The corporation provides computer consulting services to small businesses. The following transactions occurred during the first month of operations:

March 2: Received contributions of $20,000 from each of the two principal owners of the new business in exchange for shares of stock.
March 7: Signed a two-year promissory note at the bank and received cash of $15,000. Interest, along with the $15,000, will be repaid at the end of the two years.
March 12: Purchased $700 in miscellaneous supplies on account. The company has 30 days to pay for the supplies.
March 19: Billed a client $4,000 for services rendered by Expert in helping to install a new computer system. The client is to pay 25% of the bill upon its receipt and the remaining balance within 30 days.
March 20: Paid $1,300 bill from the local newspaper for advertising for the month of March.
March 22: Received 25% of the amount billed to the client on March 19.
March 26: Received cash of $2,800 for services provided in assisting a client in selecting software for its computer.
March 29: Purchased a computer system for $8,000 in cash.
March 30: Paid $3,300 of salaries and wages for March.
March 31: Received and paid $1,400 in gas, electric, and water bills.

Required

1. Prepare a table to summarize the preceding transactions as they affect the accounting equation. Use the format in Exhibit 3-1. Identify each transaction with the date.
2. Prepare an income statement for the month ended March 31, 2008.
3. Prepare a classified balance sheet at March 31, 2008.
4. From reading the balance sheet you prepared in (3), what events would you expect to take place in April? Explain your answer.

LO3

Problem 3-4 Transactions Reconstructed from Financial Statements

The following financial statements are available for Elm Corporation for its first month of operations:

Elm Corporation
Income Statement
For the Month Ended June 30, 2008

Service revenue		$93,600
Expenses:		
Rent	$ 9,000	
Salaries and wages	27,900	
Utilities	13,800	50,700
Net income		$42,900

Elm Corporation
Balance Sheet
June 30, 2008

Assets		Liabilities and Stockholders' Equity	
Cash	$ 22,800	Accounts payable	$ 18,000
Accounts receivable	21,600	Notes payable	90,000
Equipment	18,000	Capital stock	30,000
Building	90,000	Retained earnings	38,400
Land	24,000	Total liabilities and	
Total assets	$176,400	stockholders' equity	$176,400

Required

Using the format illustrated in Exhibit 3-1, prepare a table to summarize the transactions entered into by Elm Corporation during its first month of business. State any assumptions you believe are necessary in reconstructing the transactions.

MULTICONCEPT PROBLEMS

LO1,2

Problem 3-5 Identification of Events with Source Documents

Many events are linked to a source document. The following is a list of events that occurred in an entity:

a. Paid a one-year insurance policy.
b. Paid employee payroll.
c. Provided services to a customer on account.
d. Identified supplies in the storeroom destroyed by fire.
e. Received payment of bills from customers.
f. Purchased land for future expansion.
g. Calculated taxes due.
h. Entered into a car lease agreement and paid the tax, title, and license.

Required

For each item (a) through (h), indicate whether the event should or should not be recorded in the entity's accounts. For each item that should be recorded in the entity's books:

1. Identify one or more source documents that are generated from the event.
2. Identify which source document would be used to record an event when it produces more than one source document.
3. For each document, identify the information that is most useful in recording the event in the accounts.

LO3,5 **Problem 3-6** Accounts Used to Record Transactions

A list of accounts, with an identifying number for each, is provided. Following the list of accounts is a series of transactions entered into by a company during its first year of operations.

Required

For each transaction, indicate the account or accounts that should be debited and credited.

1. Cash
2. Accounts Receivable
3. Office Supplies
4. Buildings
5. Automobiles
6. Land
7. Accounts Payable
8. Income Tax Payable
9. Notes Payable
10. Capital Stock
11. Retained Earnings
12. Service Revenue
13. Wage and Salaries Expense
14. Selling Expense
15. Utilities Expense
16. Income Tax Expense

Transactions	Accounts Debited	Accounts Credited
Example: Purchased land and building in exchange for a three-year promissory note.	4, 6	9
a. Issued capital stock for cash.		
b. Purchased ten automobiles; paid part in cash and signed a 60-day note for the balance.		
c. Purchased land in exchange for a note due in six months.		
d. Purchased office supplies; agreed to pay total bill by the 10th of the following month.		
e. Billed clients for services performed during the month and gave them until the 15th of the following month to pay.		
f. Received cash on account from clients for services rendered to them in past months.		
g. Paid employees salaries and wages earned during the month.		
h. Paid newspaper for company ads appearing during the month.		
i. Received monthly gas and electric bill from the utility company; payment is due anytime within the first ten days of the following month.		
j. Computed amount of taxes due based on the income of the period; amount will be paid in the following month.		

LO3,4,5 **Problem 3-7** Transaction Analysis and Journal Entries Recorded Directly in T Accounts

Four brothers organized Beverly Entertainment Enterprises on October 1, 2008. The following transactions occurred during the first month of operations:

October 1: Received contributions of $10,000 from each of the four principal owners of the new business in exchange for shares of stock.

October 2: Purchased the Arcada Theater for $125,000. The seller agreed to accept a down payment of $12,500 and a seven-year promissory note for the balance. The Arcada property consists of land valued at $35,000 and a building valued at $90,000.

October 3: Purchased new seats for the theater at a cost of $5,000, paying $2,500 down and agreeing to pay the remainder in 60 days.

October 12: Purchased candy, popcorn, cups, and napkins for $3,700 on an open account. The company has 30 days to pay for the concession supplies.

October 13: Sold tickets for the opening-night movie for cash of $1,800 and took in $2,400 at the concession stand.

October 17: Rented out the theater to a local community group for $1,500. The community group is to pay one-half of the bill within 5 working days and has 30 days to pay the remainder.

October 23: Received 50% of the amount billed to the community group.

October 24: Sold movie tickets for cash of $2,000 and took in $2,800 at the concession stand.

October 26: The four brothers, acting on behalf of Beverly Entertainment, paid a dividend of $750 on the shares of stock owned by each of them, or $3,000 in total.

October 27: Paid $500 for utilities.
October 30: Paid wages and salaries of $2,400 total to the ushers, projectionist, concession stand workers, and maintenance crew.
October 31: Sold movie tickets for cash of $1,800 and took in $2,500 at the concession stand.

Required

1. Prepare a table to summarize the preceding transactions as they affect the accounting equation. Use the format in Exhibit 3-1. Identify each transaction with a date.
2. Record each transaction directly in T accounts using the dates preceding the transactions to identify them in the accounts. Each account involved in the problem needs a separate T account.

LO4,7

Problem 3-8 Trial Balance and Financial Statements

Refer to the table for Beverly Entertainment Enterprises in (1) of Problem 3-7.

Required

1. Prepare a trial balance at October 31, 2008.
2. Prepare an income statement for the month ended October 31, 2008.
3. Prepare a statement of retained earnings for the month ended October 31, 2008.
4. Prepare a classified balance sheet at October 31, 2008.

LO3,5,6

Problem 3-9 Journal Entries

Atkins Advertising Agency began business on January 2, 2008. The transactions entered into by Atkins during its first month of operations are as follows:

a. Acquired its articles of incorporation from the state and issued 100,000 shares of capital stock in exchange for $200,000 in cash.
b. Purchased an office building for $150,000 in cash. The building is valued at $110,000, and the remainder of the value is assigned to the land.
c. Signed a three-year promissory note at the bank for $125,000.
d. Purchased office equipment at a cost of $50,000, paying $10,000 down and agreeing to pay the remainder in ten days.
e. Paid wages and salaries of $13,000 for the first half of the month. Office employees are paid twice a month.
f. Paid the balance due on the office equipment.
g. Sold $24,000 of advertising during the first month. Customers have until the 15th of the following month to pay their bills.
h. Paid wages and salaries of $15,000 for the second half of the month.
i. Recorded $3,500 in commissions earned by the salespeople during the month. They will be paid on the fifth of the following month.

Required

Prepare in journal form the entry to record each transaction.

LO3,4,5

Problem 3-10 Journal Entries Recorded Directly in T Accounts

Refer to the transactions for Atkins Advertising Agency in Problem 3-9.

Required

1. Record each transaction directly in T accounts using the letters preceding the transactions to identify them in the accounts. Each account involved in the problem needs a separate T account.
2. Prepare a trial balance at January 31, 2008.

LO3,5,7

Problem 3-11 The Detection of Errors in a Trial Balance and Preparation of a Corrected Trial Balance

Malcolm Inc. was incorporated on January 1, 2008, with the issuance of capital stock in return for $90,000 of cash contributed by the owners. The only other transaction entered into prior to beginning operations was the issuance of a $75,300 note payable in exchange for building and equipment. The following trial balance was prepared at the end of the first month by the bookkeeper for Malcolm Inc:

Malcolm Inc.
Trial Balance
January 31, 2008

Account Titles	Debits	Credits
Cash	$ 9,980	
Accounts Receivable	8,640	
Land	80,000	
Building	50,000	
Equipment	23,500	
Notes Payable		$ 75,300
Capital Stock		90,000
Service Revenue		50,340
Wage and Salary Expense	23,700	
Advertising Expense	4,600	
Utilities Expense	8,420	
Dividends		5,000
Totals	$208,840	$220,640

Required

1. Identify the *two* errors in the trial balance. Ignore depreciation expense and interest expense.
2. Prepare a corrected trial balance.

LO3,5, 6,7

Problem 3-12 Journal Entries, Trial Balance, and Financial Statements

Blue Jay Delivery Service is incorporated on January 2, 2008, and enters into the following transactions during its first month of operations:

January 2: Filed articles of incorporation with the state and issued 100,000 shares of capital stock. Cash of $100,000 is received from the new owners for the shares.
January 3: Purchased a warehouse and land for $80,000 in cash. An appraiser values the land at $20,000 and the warehouse at $60,000.
January 4: Signed a three-year promissory note at the Third State Bank in the amount of $50,000.
January 6: Purchased five new delivery trucks for a total of $45,000 in cash.
January 31: Performed services on account that amounted to $15,900 during the month. Cash amounting to $7,490 was received from customers on account during the month.
January 31: Established an open account at a local service station at the beginning of the month. Purchases of gas and oil during January amounted to $3,230. Blue Jay has until the 10th of the following month to pay its bill.

Required

1. Prepare journal entries on the books of Blue Jay to record the transactions entered into during the month.
2. Prepare a trial balance at January 31, 2008.
3. Prepare an income statement for the month ended January 31, 2008.
4. Prepare a classified balance sheet at January 31, 2008.
5. Assume that you are considering buying stock in this company. Beginning with the transaction to record the purchase of the property on January 3, list any additional information you would like to have about each of the transactions during the remainder of the month.

LO3,5, 6,7

Problem 3-13 Journal Entries, Trial Balance, and Financial Statements

Neveranerror Inc. was organized on June 2, 2008, by a group of accountants to provide accounting and tax services to small businesses. The following transactions occurred during the first month of business:

June 2: Received contributions of $10,000 from each of the three owners of the business in exchange for shares of stock.
June 5: Purchased a computer system for $12,000. The agreement with the vendor requires a down payment of $2,500 with the balance due in 60 days.
June 8: Signed a two-year promissory note at the bank and received cash of $20,000.
June 15: Billed $12,350 to clients for the first half of June. Clients are billed twice a month for services performed during the month, and the bills are payable within ten days.
June 17: Paid a $900 bill from the local newspaper for advertising for the month of June.

June 23: Received the amounts billed to clients for services performed during the first half of the month.
June 28: Received and paid gas, electric, and water bills. The total amount is $2,700.
June 29: Received the landlord's bill for $2,200 for rent on the office space that Neveranerror leases. The bill is payable by the 10th of the following month.
June 30: Paid salaries and wages for June. The total amount is $5,670.
June 30: Billed $18,400 to clients for the second half of June.
June 30: Declared and paid dividends in the amount of $6,000.

Required

1. Prepare journal entries on the books of Neveranerror Inc. to record the transactions entered into during the month. Ignore depreciation expense and interest expense.
2. Prepare a trial balance at June 30, 2008.
3. Prepare the following financial statements:
   a. Income statement for the month ended June 30, 2008
   b. Statement of retained earnings for the month ended June 30, 2008
   c. Classified balance sheet at June 30, 2008
4. Assume that you have just graduated from college and have been approached to join this company as an accountant. From your reading of the financial statements for the first month, would you consider joining the company? Explain your answer. Limit your answer to financial considerations only.

ALTERNATE PROBLEMS

LO1

Problem 3-1A Events to Be Recorded in Accounts

The following events take place at Anaconda Accountants Inc.:

1. Supplies are ordered from vendors, who will deliver the supplies within the week.
2. Vendors deliver supplies on account, payment due in 30 days.
3. New computer system is ordered.
4. Old computer system is sold for cash.
5. Services are rendered to customers on account. The invoices are mailed and due in 30 days.
6. Cash received from customer payments is deposited in the bank night depository.
7. Employees are paid weekly paychecks.
8. Vendors noted in (2) are paid for the supplies delivered.

Required

Identify each event as internal (I) or external (E) and indicate whether each event would or would not be recorded in the *accounts* of the company. For each event that is to be recorded, identify the names of at least two accounts that would be affected.

LO3

Problem 3-2A Transaction Analysis and Financial Statements

Beachway Enterprises was organized on June 1, 2008, by two college students who recognized an opportunity to make money while spending their days at a beach in Florida. The two entrepreneurs plan to rent beach umbrellas. The following transactions occurred during the first month of operations:

June 1: Received contributions of $2,000 from each of the two principal owners of the new business in exchange for shares of stock.
June 1: Purchased 25 beach umbrellas for $250 each on account. The company has 30 days to pay for the beach umbrellas.
June 5: Registered as a vendor with the city and paid the $35 monthly fee.
June 10: Purchased $50 in miscellaneous supplies on an open account. The company has 30 days to pay for the supplies.
June 15: Paid $70 bill from a local radio station for advertising for the last two weeks of June.
June 17: Customers rented beach umbrellas for cash of $1,000.
June 24: Billed a local hotel $2,000 for beach umbrellas provided for use during a convention being held at the hotel. The hotel is to pay one-half of the bill in 5 days and the rest within 30 days.
June 29: Received 50% of the amount billed to the hotel.
June 30: Customers rented beach umbrellas for cash of $1,500.
June 30: Paid wages of $90 to a friend who helped over the weekend.
June 30: Paid the balance due on the beach umbrellas.

Required

1. Prepare a table to summarize the preceding transactions as they affect the accounting equation. Use the format in Exhibit 3-1. Identify each transaction with a date.
2. Prepare an income statement for the month ended June 30, 2008.
3. Prepare a classified balance sheet at June 30, 2008.

LO3

Problem 3-3A Transaction Analysis and Financial Statements

Dynamic Services Inc. was organized on March 1, 2008, by two former college roommates. The corporation will provide computer tax services to small businesses. The following transactions occurred during the first month of operations:

March 2: Received contributions of $10,000 from each of the two principal owners in exchange for shares of stock.
March 7: Signed a two-year promissory note at the bank and received cash of $7,500. Interest, along with the $7,500, will be repaid at the end of the two years.
March 12: Purchased miscellaneous supplies on account for $350, payment due in 30 days.
March 19: Billed a client $2,000 for tax preparation services. According to an agreement between the two companies, the client is to pay 25% of the bill upon its receipt and the remaining balance within 30 days.
March 20: Paid a $650 bill from the local newspaper for advertising for the month of March.
March 22: Received 25% of the amount billed the client on March 19.
March 26: Received cash of $1,400 for services provided in assisting a client in preparing its tax return.
March 29: Purchased a computer system for $4,000 in cash.
March 30: Paid $1,650 in salaries and wages for March.
March 31: Received and paid $700 of gas, electric, and water bills.

Required

1. Prepare a table to summarize the preceding transactions as they affect the accounting equation. Use the format in Exhibit 3-1. Identify each transaction with the date.
2. Prepare an income statement for the month ended March 31, 2008.
3. Prepare a classified balance sheet at March 31, 2008.
4. From reading the balance sheet you prepared in (3), what events would you expect to take place in April? Explain your answer.

LO3

Problem 3-4A Transactions Reconstructed from Financial Statements

The following financial statements are available for Oak Corporation for its first month of operations:

Oak Corporation
Income Statement
For the Month Ended July 31, 2008

Service revenue		$75,400
Expenses:		
Rent	$ 6,000	
Salaries and wages	24,600	
Utilities	12,700	43,300
Net income		$32,100

Oak Corporation
Balance Sheet
July 31, 2008

Assets		Liabilities and Stockholders' Equity	
Cash	$13,700	Wages payable	$ 6,000
Accounts receivable	25,700	Notes payable	50,000
Equipment	32,000	Unearned service revenue	4,500
Furniture	14,700	Capital stock	30,000
Land	24,000	Retained earnings	19,600
Total assets	$110,100	Total liabilities and stockholders' equity	$110,100

Required

Describe as many transactions as you can that were entered into by Oak Corporation during the first month of business.

ALTERNATE MULTICONCEPT PROBLEMS

LO1,2

Problem 3-5A Identification of Events with Source Documents

Many events are linked to a source document. The following is a list of events that occurred in an entity:

a. Paid a security deposit and six months' rent on a building.
b. Hired three employees and agreed to pay them $400 per week.
c. Provided services to a customer for cash.
d. Reported a fire that destroyed a billboard that is on the entity's property and that is owned and maintained by another entity.
e. Received payment of bills from customers.
f. Purchased stock in another entity to gain some control over it.
g. Signed a note at the bank and received cash.
h. Contracted with a cleaning service to maintain the interior of the building in good repair. No money is paid at this time.

Required

For each item (a) through (h), indicate whether the event should or should not be recorded in the entity's accounts. For each item that should be recorded in the entity's books:

1. Identify one or more source documents that are generated from the event.
2. Identify which source document would be used to record an event when it produces more than one source document.
3. For each document, identify the information that is most useful in recording the event in the accounts.

LO3,5

Problem 3-6A Accounts Used to Record Transactions

A list of accounts, with an identifying number for each, is provided. Following the list of accounts is a series of transactions entered into by a company during its first year of operations.

Required

For each transaction, indicate the account or accounts that should be debited and credited.

1. Cash
2. Accounts Receivable
3. Prepaid Insurance
4. Office Supplies
5. Automobiles
6. Land
7. Accounts Payable
8. Income Tax Payable
9. Notes Payable
10. Capital Stock
11. Retained Earnings
12. Service Revenue
13. Wage and Salary Expense
14. Utilities Expense
15. Income Tax Expense

Transactions	Accounts Debited	Accounts Credited
Example: Purchased office supplies for cash.	4	1
a. Issued capital stock for cash.		
b. Purchased an automobile and signed a 60-day note for the total amount.		
c. Acquired land in exchange for capital stock.		
d. Received cash from clients for services performed during the month.		
e. Paid employees salaries and wages earned during the month.		
f. Purchased flyers and signs from a printer, payment due in ten days.		
g. Paid for the flyers and signs purchased in (f).		
h. Received monthly telephone bill; payment is due within ten days of receipt.		
i. Paid for a six-month liability insurance policy.		
j. Paid monthly telephone bill.		
k. Computed amount of taxes due based on the income of the period and paid the amount.		

LO3,4,5 **Problem 3-7A** Transaction Analysis and Journal Entries Recorded Directly in T Accounts

Three friends organized Rapid City Roller Rink on October 1, 2008. The following transactions occurred during the first month of operations:

October 1: Received contribution of $22,000 from each of the three principal owners of the new business in exchange for shares of stock.
October 2: Purchased land valued at $15,000 and a building valued at $75,000. The seller agreed to accept a down payment of $9,000 and a five-year promissory note for the balance.
October 3: Purchased new tables and chairs for the lounge at the roller rink at a cost of $25,000, paying $5,000 down and agreeing to pay for the remainder in 60 days.
October 9: Purchased 100 pairs of roller skates for cash at $35 per pair.
October 12: Purchased food and drinks for $2,500 on an open account. The company has 30 days to pay for the concession supplies.
October 13: Sold tickets for cash of $400 and took in $750 at the concession stand.
October 17: Rented out the roller rink to a local community group for $750. The community group is to pay one-half of the bill within 5 working days and has 30 days to pay the remainder.
October 23: Received 50% of the amount billed to the community group.
October 24: Sold tickets for cash of $500 and took in $1,200 at the concession stand.
October 26: The three friends, acting on behalf of Rapid City Roller Rink, paid a dividend of $250 on the shares of stock owned by each of them, or $750 in total.
October 27: Paid $1,275 for utilities.
October 30: Paid wages and salaries of $2,250.
October 31: Sold tickets for cash of $700 and took in $1,300 at the concession stand.

Required

1. Prepare a table to summarize the preceding transactions as they affect the accounting equation. Use the format in Exhibit 3-1. Identify each transaction with a date.
2. Record each transaction directly in T accounts using the dates preceding the transactions to identify them in the accounts. Each account involved in the problem needs a separate T account.

LO4,7 **Problem 3-8A** Trial Balance and Financial Statements

Refer to the table for Rapid City Roller Rink in (1) of Problem 3-7A.

Required

1. Prepare a trial balance at October 31, 2008.
2. Prepare an income statement for the month ended October 31, 2008.
3. Prepare a statement of retained earnings for the month ended October 31, 2008.
4. Prepare a classified balance sheet at October 31, 2008.

LO3,5,6 **Problem 3-9A** Journal Entries

Castle Consulting Agency began business in February 2008. The transactions entered into by Castle during its first month of operations are as follows:

a. Acquired articles of incorporation from the state and issued 10,000 shares of capital stock in exchange for $150,000 in cash.
b. Paid monthly rent of $400.
c. Signed a five-year promissory note for $100,000 at the bank.
d. Received $5,000 cash from a customer for services to be performed over the next two months.
e. Purchased software to be used on future jobs. The software costs $950 and is expected to be used on five to eight jobs over the next two years.
f. Billed customers $12,500 for work performed during the month.
g. Paid office personnel $3,000 for the month of February.
h. Received a utility bill of $100. The total amount is due in 30 days.

Required

Prepare in journal form the entry to record each transaction.

LO3,4,5,7

Problem 3-10A Journal Entries Recorded Directly in T Accounts

Refer to the transactions for Castle Consulting Agency in Problem 3-9A.

Required

1. Record each transaction directly in T accounts using the letters preceding the transactions to identify them in the accounts. Each account involved in the problem needs a separate T account.
2. Prepare a trial balance at February 28, 2008.

LO3,4,5,7

Problem 3-11A Entries Prepared from a Trial Balance and Proof of the Cash Balance

Russell Company was incorporated on January 1, 2008, with the issuance of capital stock in return for $120,000 of cash contributed by the owners. The only other transaction entered into prior to beginning operations was the issuance of a $50,000 note payable in exchange for equipment and fixtures. The following trial balance was prepared at the end of the first month by the bookkeeper for Russell Company:

Russell Company
Trial Balance
January 31, 2008

Account Titles	Debits	Credits
Cash	$???	
Accounts Receivable	30,500	
Equipment and Fixtures	50,000	
Wages Payable		$ 10,000
Notes Payable		50,000
Capital Stock		120,000
Service Revenue		60,500
Wage and Salary Expense	24,600	
Advertising Expense	12,500	
Rent Expense	5,200	

Required

1. Determine the balance in the Cash account.
2. Identify all of the transactions that affected the Cash account during the month. Use a T account to prove what the balance in Cash will be after all transactions are recorded.

LO3,5,6

Problem 3-12A Journal Entries

Overnight Delivery Inc. is incorporated on January 2, 2008, and enters into the following transactions during its second month of operations:

February 2: Paid $400 for wages earned by employees for the week ending January 31.
February 3: Paid $3,230 for gas and oil billed on an open account in January.
February 4: Declared and paid $2,000 cash dividends to stockholders.
February 15: Received $8,000 cash from customer accounts.
February 26: Provided $16,800 of services on account during the month.
February 27: Received a $3,400 bill from the local service station for gas and oil used during February.

Required

1. Prepare journal entries on the books of Overnight to record the transactions entered into during February.
2. For the transactions on February 2, 3, 4, and 27, indicate whether the amount is an expense of operating in the month of January or February or is not an expense in either month.

LO3,5,6

Problem 3-13A Journal Entries and a Balance Sheet

Krittersbegone Inc. was organized on July 1, 2008, by a group of technicians to provide termite inspections and treatment to homeowners and small businesses. The following transactions occurred during the first month of business:

July 2: Received contributions of $3,000 from each of the six owners in exchange for shares of stock.
July 3: Paid $1,000 rent for the month of July.
July 5: Purchased flashlights, tools, spray equipment, and ladders for $18,000, with a down payment of $5,000 and the balance due in 30 days.

July 17: Paid a $200 bill for the distribution of door-to-door advertising.
July 28: Paid August rent and July utilities to the landlord in the amounts of $1,000 and $450, respectively.
July 30: Received $8,000 in cash from homeowners for services performed during the month. In addition, billed $7,500 to other customers for services performed during the month. Billings are due in 30 days.
July 30: Paid commissions of $9,500 to the technicians for July.
July 31: Received $600 from a business client to perform services over the next two months.

Required

1. Prepare journal entries on the books of Krittersbegone to record the transactions entered into during the month. Ignore depreciation expense.
2. Prepare a classified balance sheet dated July 31, 2008. From the balance sheet, what cash inflow and what cash outflow can you predict in the month of August? Who would be interested in the cash flow information? Why?

DECISION CASES

READING AND INTERPRETING FINANCIAL STATEMENTS

LO4 **Decision Case 3-1** Comparing Two Companies in the Same Industry: Kellogg's and General Mills

Refer to the income statements for **Kellogg's** and **General Mills** reproduced at the end of the book.

Required

1. Which is the largest expense for each company in the most recent year? What is its dollar amount? Is it logical that this would be the largest expense given the nature of each company's business? Explain your answer.
2. One of the accounts on each company's income statement is "Selling, general and administrative expense." For each of the two most recent years, compute the ratio of this expense to net sales for each company. Did this ratio increase or decrease from one year to the next? Which company has the lower ratio in each of the two years?
3. Compute the ratio of income taxes to income (earnings) before taxes (use "Earnings before Income Taxes and After-tax Earnings from Joint Ventures" for General Mills) for the two most recent years for each company. Is the ratio the same for Kellogg's for both years? Is the ratio the same for General Mills for both years? Which company has the higher ratio for each of the two years?

LO3,5,6 **Decision Case 3-2** Reading and Interpreting General Mills's Statement of Cash Flows

Refer to **General Mills**'s statement of cash flows for the year ended May 28, 2006, as reproduced at the end of the book.

Required

1. What amount did the company spend on purchases of land, buildings, and equipment during the year? Prepare the journal entry to record these purchases.
2. What amount did the company pay to retire long-term debt during the year? Prepare the journal entry to record the payment.

LO1,3,5,6 **Decision Case 3-3** Reading and Interpreting Southwest Airlines' Balance Sheet

The following item appears in the current liabilities section of **Southwest Airlines**' balance sheet at December 31, 2006.

Air traffic liability	$799 million

In addition, one of Southwest Airlines' notes reads as follows: "Tickets sold are initially deferred as 'air traffic liability.' Passenger revenue is recognized when transportation is provided. 'Air traffic liability' primarily represents tickets sold for future travel dates and estimated refunds and exchanges of tickets sold for past travel dates."

Required

1. What economic event caused Southwest Airlines to incur this liability? Was it an external or internal event?
2. Describe the effect on the accounting equation from the transaction to record the air traffic liability.
3. Assume that one customer purchases a $500 ticket in advance. Prepare the journal entry on Southwest Airlines' books to record this transaction.
4. What economic event will cause Southwest Airlines to reduce its air traffic liability? Is this an external or internal event?

MAKING FINANCIAL DECISIONS

LO2,3

Decision Case 3-4 Cash Flow versus Net Income

Shelia Young started a real estate business at the beginning of January. After approval by the state for a charter to incorporate, she issued 1,000 shares of stock to herself and deposited $20,000 in a bank account under the name Young Properties. Because business was booming, she spent all of her time during the first month selling properties rather than keeping financial records.

At the end of January, Shelia comes to you with the following plight:

> I put $20,000 in to start this business at the beginning of the month. My January 31 bank statement shows a balance of $17,000. After all of my efforts, it appears as if I'm "in the hole" already! On the other hand, that seems impossible—we sold five properties for clients during the month. The total sales value of these properties was $600,000, and I received a commission of 5% on each sale. Granted, one of the five sellers still owes me an $8,000 commission, but the other four have been collected in full. Three of the sales, totaling $400,000, were actually made by my assistants. I pay them 4% of the sales value of a property. Sure, I have a few office expenses for my car, utilities, and a secretary; but that's about it. How can I have possibly lost $3,000 this month?

You agree to help Shelia figure out how she did this month. The bank statement is helpful. The total deposits during the month amount to $22,000. Shelia explains that this amount represents the commissions on the four sales collected so far. The canceled checks reveal the following expenditures:

Check No.	Payee—Memo at Bottom of Check	Amount
101	Stevens Office Supply	$ 2,000
102	Why Walk, Let's Talk Motor Co.—new car	3,000
103	City of Westbrook—heat and lights	500
104	Alice Hill—secretary	2,200
105	Ace Property Management—office rent for month	1,200
106	Jerry Hayes (sales assistant)	10,000
107	Joan Harper (sales assistant)	6,000
108	Don's Fillitup—gas and oil for car	100

According to Shelia, the $2,000 check to Stevens Office Supply represents the down payment on a word processor and a copier for the office. The remaining balance is $3,000 that must be paid to Stevens by February 15. Similarly, the $3,000 check is the down payment on a car for the business. A $12,000 note was given to the car dealer and is due along with interest in one year.

1. Prepare an income statement for the month of January for Young Properties.
2. Prepare a statement of cash flows for the month of January for Young Properties.
3. Draft a memo to Shelia Young explaining as simply and clearly as possible why she *did* in fact have a profitable first month in business but experienced a decrease in her cash account. Support your explanation with any necessary figures.
4. The down payments on the car and the office equipment are reflected on the statement of cash flows. They are assets that will benefit the business for a number of years. Do you think that any of the cost associated with the acquisition of these assets should be recognized in some way on the income statement? Explain your answer.

LO3,5,6,7

Decision Case 3-5 Loan Request

Simon Fraser started a landscaping and lawn-care business in April 2008 by investing $20,000 cash in the business in exchange for capital stock. Because his business is in the Midwest, the

HOMEWORK

season begins in April and concludes in September. He prepared the following trial balance (with accounts in alphabetical order) at the end of the first season in business:

Fraser Landscaping
Trial Balance
September 30, 2008

	Debits	Credits
Accounts Payable	—	$13,000
Accounts Receivable	$23,000	
Capital Stock		20,000
Cash	1,200	
Gas and Oil Expense	15,700	
Insurance Expense	2,500	
Landscaping Revenue		33,400
Lawn Care Revenue		24,000
Mowing Equipment	5,000	
Rent Expense	6,000	
Salaries Expense	22,000	
Truck	15,000	
Totals	$90,400	$90,400

Simon is pleased with his first year in business. "I paid myself a salary of $22,000 during the year and still have $1,200 in the bank. Sure, I have a few bills outstanding, but my accounts receivable will more than cover those." In fact, Simon is so happy with the first year that he has come to you in your role as a lending officer at the local bank to ask for a $20,000 loan to allow him to add another truck and mowing equipment for the second season.

Required

1. From your reading of the trial balance, what do you believe Simon did with the $20,000 in cash he originally contributed to the business? Reconstruct the journal entry to record the transaction that you think took place.
2. Prepare an income statement for the six months ended September 30, 2008.
3. The mowing equipment and truck are assets that will benefit the business for a number of years. Do you think that any of the costs associated with the purchase of these assets should have been recognized as expenses in the first year? How would this have affected the income statement?
4. Prepare a classified balance sheet as of September 30, 2008. As a banker, what two items on the balance sheet concern you the most? Explain your answer.
5. As a banker, would you loan Simon $20,000 to expand his business during the second year? Draft a memo to respond to Simon's request for the loan, indicating whether you will make the loan.

ETHICAL DECISION MAKING

LO3,5,6 Decision Case 3-6 Delay in the Posting of a Journal Entry

As assistant controller for a small consulting firm, you are responsible for recording and posting the daily cash receipts and disbursements to the ledger accounts. After you have posted the entries, your boss, the controller, prepares a trial balance and the financial statements. You make the following entries on June 30, 2008:

2008			
June 30	Cash	1,430	
	Accounts Receivable	1,950	
	Service Revenue		3,380
	To record daily cash receipts.		
June 30	Advertising Expense	12,500	
	Utilities Expense	22,600	
	Rent Expense	24,000	
	Salary and Wage Expense	17,400	
	Cash		76,500
	To record daily cash disbursements.		

The daily cash disbursements are much larger on June 30 than on any other day because many of the company's major bills are paid on the last day of the month. After you have recorded these two transactions and *before* you have posted them to the ledger accounts, your boss comes to you with the following request:

> As you are aware, the first half of the year has been a tough one for the consulting industry and for our business in particular. With first-half bonuses based on net income, I am wondering whether you or I will get a bonus this time around. However, I have a suggestion that should allow us to receive something for our hard work and at the same time not hurt anyone. Go ahead and post the June 30 cash receipts to the ledger, but don't bother to post that day's cash disbursements. Even though the treasurer writes the checks on the last day of the month and you normally journalize the transaction on the same day, it is silly to bother posting the entry to the ledger since it takes at least a week for the checks to clear the bank.

Required

1. Explain why the controller's request will result in an increase in net income.
2. Do you agree with the controller that the omission of the entry on June 30 "will not hurt anyone"? Whom could it hurt? Does omitting the entry provide information that is free from bias? Explain your answer.
3. What would you do if the controller told you to do this? To whom should you talk about this issue? Is this situation an ethical issue? Why or why not?

LO5,6

Decision Case 3-7 Debits and Credits

You are controller for an architectural firm whose accounting year ends on December 31. As part of the management team, you receive a year-end bonus directly related to the firm's earnings for the year. One of your duties is to review the journal entries recorded by the bookkeepers. A new bookkeeper prepared the following journal entry:

Dec. 3	Cash	10,000	
	Service Revenue		10,000
	To record deposit from client.		

You notice that the explanation for the journal entry refers to the amount as a deposit, and the bookkeeper explains to you that the firm plans to provide the services to the client in March of the following year.

1. Did the bookkeeper prepare the correct journal entry to account for the client's deposit? Explain your answer.
2. What would you do as controller for the firm? Do you have a responsibility to do anything to correct the books? Explain your answer.

SOLUTIONS TO KEY TERMS QUIZ

3	**Event**	8	**Debit**
10	**External event**	4	**Credit**
5	**Internal event**	16	**Double-entry system**
14	**Transaction**	13	**Journal**
6	**Source document**	9	**Posting**
11	**Account**	7	**Journalizing**
1	**Chart of accounts**	15	**General journal**
12	**General ledger**	2	**Trial balance**

ANSWERS TO POD REVIEW

LO1	1. d	2. a
LO2	1. b	2. d
LO3	1. c	2. b
LO4	1. a	2. b
LO5	1. b	2. c
LO6	1. b	2. a
LO7	1. c	2. a

CHAPTER

4

Income Measurement and Accrual Accounting

Learning Outcomes

After studying this chapter, you should be able to:

LO1 Explain the significance of recognition and measurement in the preparation and use of financial statements.

LO2 Explain the differences between the cash and accrual bases of accounting.

LO3 Describe the revenue recognition principle and explain its application in various situations.

LO4 Describe the matching principle and the various methods for recognizing expenses.

LO5 Identify the four major types of adjusting entries and prepare them for a variety of situations.

LO6 Explain the steps in the accounting cycle and the significance of each step.

LO7 Explain why and how closing entries are made at the end of an accounting period.

LO8 Understand how to use a work sheet as a basis for preparing financial statements (Appendix).

Study Links...

A Look at the Previous Chapter
Chapter 3 looked at how information is processed. Various tools, such as journal entries, accounts, and trial balances, were introduced as convenient aids in the preparation of periodic financial statements.

A Look at This Chapter
This chapter begins by considering the roles of recognition and measurement in the process of preparing financial statements. The accrual basis of accounting is examined, and we see how this basis affects the measurement of income. We look at how revenues and expenses are recognized in an accrual system and at what role adjusting entries have in this process.

A Look at the Upcoming Chapter
Chapter 4 completes our overview of the accounting model. In the next section, we examine accounting for the various assets of a business. Chapter 5 begins by looking at how companies that sell products account for their inventory.

Nordstrom, Inc.

MAKING BUSINESS DECISIONS

From a single shoe store in Seattle, Washington, in 1901, Nordstrom, Inc., has grown to become one of the most highly respected fashion retailers in the country. With its reputation for superior customer service, the company has seen its sales climb steadily to a record of over $8.5 billion in its fiscal year 2006.

Because Nordstrom uses the accrual basis of accounting, certain accounts appear on its balance sheet that would not appear if it used the simpler cash basis. These accounts are important not just to ensure that debits equal credits in an accounting system but also to provide information to stockholders, bankers, and other users of the statements. Consider the four accounts highlighted in the Current assets and Current liabilities sections of Nordstrom's partial balance sheet shown on the next page.

Accounts receivable come about when a company sells a product or service and give the customer a certain period of time to pay the amount due. For Nordstrom, these receivables arise when its customers use the company's private label card or a cobranded Nordstrom VISA® credit card. As shown in the Current assets section of the partial balance sheets, accounts receivable is second only to merchandise inventories in size.

Prepaid expenses represent amounts Nordstrom has paid in advance for items such as insurance and other operating costs. For example, when the company prepays its insurance bill, an asset is created. Over time, the asset expires and is replaced by an expense. Users of the statements understand that prepaid expenses are different from accounts receivable in that prepayments will not be converted into cash as will receivables.

Accrued salaries, wages and related benefits appear on the liabilities side of Nordstrom's balance sheet. For a retailer such as Nordstrom, payroll is one of its largest costs. This account represents amounts owed to employees but have not yet been paid at the balance sheet date. Accrued salaries and wages is one example of what this chapter will refer to as **accrued expenses**. They represent amounts owed to employees in wages and salaries, to the government in taxes, and to a variety of other short-term creditors. The amount of outstanding accrued expenses provides important information to users of the balance sheet. For example, a banker knows that within the next year, the amount of accrued expenses will need to be satisfied, usually by the payment of cash.

Finally, note the line for Other current liabilities on the partial balance sheet. A note to the financial statements explains that this account includes the company's gift card liabilities. These liabilities arise when the company receives cash from someone who purchases a gift card to be used at a later date. Up until the time the card is used, Nordstrom has a liability. As you will see later in the chapter, gift card liabilities are one example of what accountants call **deferred revenue**. This term is used for situations in which a company receives cash in advance of providing products or services to its customers.

This chapter will explore in more detail these four types of accounts that arise in an accrual accounting system.

(*continued*)

The chapter will help you answer important questions about the accrual process, such as:

- What important information does the accrual basis of accounting provide to users of the statements that a cash basis does not? (See pp. 155–156.)
- What is meant by the revenue recognition principle. Why is it important? (See pp. 159–160.)
- What is meant by the matching principle? How is it applied? (See pp. 160–161.)
- What are the various types of adjustments that companies make? How are the adjustments recorded in an accounting system? (See pp. 162–176.)

Nordstrom, Inc.
Consolidated Balance Sheets (Partial)
Amounts in thousands

	February 3, 2007	January 28, 2006
ASSETS		
Current assets:		
Cash and cash equivalents	$402,559	$462,656
Short-term investments	—	54,000
Accounts receivable, net	684,376	639,558
Investments in asset backed securities	428,175	561,136
Merchandise inventories	997,289	955,978
Current deferred tax assets, net	169,320	145,470
Prepaid expenses and other	60,474	55,359
Total current assets	2,742,193	2,874,157
LIABILITIES AND SHAREHOLDERS' EQUITY		
Current liabilities:		
Accounts payable	$576,796	$540,019
Accrued salaries, wages and related benefits	339,965	285,982
Other current liabilities	433,487	409,076
Income taxes payable	76,095	81,617
Current portion of long-term debt	6,800	306,618
Total current liabilities	1,433,143	1,623,312

The accompanying Notes to Consolidated Financial Statements are an integral part of these financial statements.

Recognition and Measurement in Financial Statements

LO1 Explain the significance of recognition and measurement in the preparation and use of financial statements.

Accounting is a communication process. To successfully communicate information to the users of financial statements, accountants and managers must answer two questions:

1. **What economic events should be communicated, or *recognized,* in the statements?**
2. **How should the effects of these events be *measured* in the statements?**

The dual concepts of recognition and measurement are crucial to the success of accounting as a form of communication.

Recognition
The process of recording an item in the financial statements as an asset, a liability, a revenue, an expense, or the like.

RECOGNITION

"**Recognition is the process of formally recording or incorporating an item into the financial statements of an entity as an asset, a liability, a revenue, an expense, or the like.** Recognition includes depiction of an item in both words and numbers, with the amount included in the totals of the financial statements."[1] We see in this definition the central idea behind general purpose financial statements. They are a form of communication between the entity and external users. Stockholders, bankers, and other creditors have limited access to relevant information about a company. They depend on the periodic financial statements that management issues to provide the necessary information to make decisions. Acting on behalf of management, accountants have a moral and ethical responsibility to provide users with financial information that will be useful in making their decisions. The process by which the accountant depicts, or describes, the effects of economic events on the entity is called *recognition*.

Items such as assets, liabilities, revenues, and expenses depicted in financial statements are *representations*. Simply stated, the accountant cannot show a stockholder or another user the company's assets, such as cash and buildings. What the user sees in a set of financial statements is a depiction of the real thing. That is, the accountant describes, with words and numbers, the various items in a set of financial statements. The system is imperfect at best and, for that reason, is always in the process of change. As society and the business environment have become more complex, the accounting profession has strove for ways to improve financial statements as a means of communicating with statement users.

MEASUREMENT

Accountants depict a financial statement item in both words and *numbers*. The accountant must *quantify* the effects of economic events on the entity. It is not enough to decide that an event is important and thus warrants recognition in the financial statements. To be able to recognize an event, the statement preparer must measure the event's financial effects on the company.

Measurement of an item in financial statements requires that two choices be made:

- First, the accountant must decide on the *attribute* to be measured.
- Second, a scale of measurement, or *unit of measure*, must be chosen.

Choice 1: The Attribute to Be Measured Assume that a company holds a parcel of real estate as an investment. What attribute—that is, *characteristic*—of the property should be used to measure and thus recognize it as an asset on the balance sheet? The cost of the asset at the time it is acquired is the most logical choice. *Cost* is the amount of cash or its equivalent paid to acquire the asset. But how do we report the property on a balance sheet a year from now?

- The simplest approach is to show the property on the balance sheet at its original cost, thus the designation **historical cost**. The use of historical cost is not only simple but also *verifiable*. Assume that two accountants are asked to independently measure the cost of the asset. After examining the sales contract for the land, they should arrive at the same amount.
- An alternative to historical cost as the attribute to be measured is **current value**. Current value is the amount of cash or its equivalent that could be received currently from the sale of the asset. For the company's piece of property, current value is the *estimated* selling price of the land, reduced by any commissions or other fees involved in making the sale. But the amount is only an estimate, not an actual amount. If the company has not yet sold the property, how can we know for certain its selling price? We have to compare it to similar properties that have sold recently.

Historical cost
The amount paid for an asset and used as a basis for recognizing it on the balance sheet and carrying it on later balance sheets.

Current value
The amount of cash or its equivalent that could be received by selling an asset currently.

The choice between current value and historical cost as the attribute to be measured is a good example of the trade-off between *relevance* and *reliability*. As indicated

1 *Statement of Financial Accounting Concepts No. 5,* "Recognition and Measurement in Financial Statements of Business Enterprises" (Stamford, Conn.: Financial Accounting Standards Board, December 1984), par. 6.

earlier, historical cost is verifiable and is thus, to a large extent, a reliable measure. But is it as relevant to the needs of the decision makers as current value? Put yourself in the position of a banker trying to decide whether to lend money to the company. In evaluating the company's assets as collateral for the loan, is it more relevant to your decision to know what the firm paid for a piece of land 20 years ago or what it could be sold for today? But what *could* the property be sold for today? Two accountants might not arrive at the same current value for the land. Whereas value or selling price may be more relevant to your decision on the loan, the reliability of this amount is often questionable.

Because of its objective nature, historical cost is the attribute used to measure many of the assets recognized on the balance sheet. However, certain other attributes, such as current value, have increased in popularity in recent years. Other chapters of the book will discuss some of the alternatives to historical cost.

Choice 2: The Unit of Measure Regardless of the attribute of an item to be measured, it is still neccessary to choose a yardstick, or unit of measure. The yardstick currently used is units of money. *Money* is something accepted as a medium of exchange or as a means of payment. The unit of money in the United States is the dollar. In Japan, the medium of exchange is the yen; and in Great Britain, it is the pound.

The use of the dollar as a unit of measure for financial transactions is widely accepted. The *stability* of the dollar as a yardstick is subject to considerable debate, however. Consider an example. You are thinking about buying a certain parcel of land. As part of your decision process, you measure the dimensions of the property and determine that the lot is 80 feet wide and 120 feet deep. Thus, the unit of measure used to determine the lot's size is the square foot. The company that owns the land offers to sell it for $10,000. Although the offer sounds attractive, you decide against the purchase today.

You return in one year to take a second look at the lot. You measure the lot again and, not surprisingly, find the width still to be 80 feet and the depth 120 feet. The owner is still willing to sell the lot for $10,000. This may appear to be the same price as last year. But the *purchasing power* of the unit of measure, the dollar, may very possibly have changed since last year. Even though the foot is a stable measuring unit, the dollar often is not. A *decline* in the purchasing power of the dollar is evidenced by a continuing *rise* in the general level of prices in an economy. For example, rather than paying $10,000 last year to buy the lot, you could have spent the $10,000 on other goods or services. However, a year later the same $10,000 may very well not buy the same amount of goods and services.

Inflation, or a rise in the general level of prices in the economy, results in a decrease in purchasing power. In the past, the accounting profession has experimented with financial statements adjusted for the changing value of the dollar. As inflation has declined in recent years in the United States, the debate over the use of the dollar as a stable measuring unit has somewhat subsided.[2] It is still important to recognize the inherent weakness in the use of a measuring unit that is subject to change, however.

SUMMARY OF RECOGNITION AND MEASUREMENT IN FINANCIAL STATEMENTS

The purpose of financial statements is to communicate various types of economic information about a company. The job of the accountant is to decide which information should be recognized in the financial statements and how the effects of that information on the entity should be measured. Exhibit 4-1 summarizes the role of recognition and measurement in the preparation of financial statements.

2 The rate of inflation in some countries, most noticeably those in South America, has far exceeded the rate in the United States. Companies operating in some of these countries with hyperinflationary economies are required to make adjustments to their statements.

EXHIBIT 4-1 **Recognition and Measurement in Financial Statements**

ECONOMIC EVENTS	are	RECOGNIZED with	MEASURED with
Such as: **Purchase of supplies** **Sale of products** **Payment of wages** **Warehouse fire** **Many other events**	→	*Words:* Cash Land *Numbers:* $3 million $13,927	*Attribute:* Historical cost *Unit of Measure:* The dollar

POD REVIEW 4.1

LO1 *Explain the significance of recognition and measurement in the preparation and use of financial statements.*

- Determining which economic events should be recognized and how they should be measured is critical for accounting information to be useful.
  - Recognition drives how and when the effects of economic events are described in the financial statements.
  - Measurement involves deciding on the attribute of an economic event that must be measured and the appropriate unit of measure.

QUESTIONS

1. *The process of recording an item in the financial statements is called*
   a. measurement.
   b. recognition.
   c. posting.
   d. none of the above.

2. *The amount of cash that could be received by selling an asset currently is called*
   a. current value.
   b. historical cost.
   c. depreciated cost.
   d. none of the above.

The Accrual Basis of Accounting

LO2 Explain the differences between the cash and accrual bases of accounting.

The accrual basis of accounting is the foundation for the measurement of income in our modern system of accounting. The best way to understand the accrual basis is to compare it with the simpler cash approach.

COMPARING THE CASH AND ACCRUAL BASES OF ACCOUNTING

The cash and accrual bases of accounting differ with respect to the *timing* of the recognition of revenues and expenses. For example, assume that on July 24, Barbara White, a salesperson for Spiffy House Painters, contracts with a homeowner to repaint a house for $1,000. A large crew comes in and paints the house the next day, July 25. The customer has 30 days from the day of completion of the job to pay and does, in fact, pay Spiffy on August 25. When should Spiffy recognize the $1,000 as revenue—as soon as the contract is signed on July 24; on July 25, when the work is done; or on August 25, when the customer pays the bill?

When Is Revenue Recognized?

July 24	July 25	August 25
Contract is signed.	House is painted.	Customer pays for job.

No Revenue Yet	Accrual Basis:	Cash Basis:
	When house is painted	When cash is received

Cash basis
A system of accounting in which revenues are recognized when cash is received and expenses are recognized when cash is paid.

Accrual basis
A system of accounting in which revenues are recognized when earned and expenses are recognized when incurred.

- In an income statement prepared on a **cash basis**, revenues are recognized when cash is *received*. Thus, on a cash basis, the $1,000 would not be recognized as revenue until the cash is collected, on August 25.
- In an income statement prepared on an **accrual basis**, revenue is recognized when it is *earned*. On this basis, the $1,000 would be recognized as revenue on July 25, when the house is painted. This is the point at which the revenue is earned.

Recall from Chapter 3 the journal entry to recognize revenue before cash is received. Although cash has not yet been received, another account, Accounts Receivable, is recognized as an asset. This asset represents the right to receive cash in the future. The entry on completion of the job is as follows:

July 25	Accounts Receivable	1,000	
	Service Revenue		1,000
	To recognize revenue from house painting.		

The accounting equation must balance after each transaction is recorded. Throughout the remainder of the book, each time a journal entry is recorded, the effect of the entry on the equation is illustrated. The effect of the preceding entry on the equation is as follows:

		Balance Sheet				Income Statement
ASSETS	=	**LIABILITIES**	+	**STOCKHOLDERS' EQUITY**	+	**REVENUES − EXPENSES**
Accounts Receivable 1,000						Service Revenue 1,000

At the time cash is collected, accounts receivable is reduced and cash is increased:

Aug. 25	Cash	1,000	
	Accounts Receivable		1,000
	To record cash received from house painting.		

Balance Sheet							Income Statement
ASSETS		=	LIABILITIES	+	STOCKHOLDERS' EQUITY	+	REVENUES − EXPENSES
Cash	1,000						
Accounts Receivable	(1,000)						

Assume that Barbara White is paid a 10% commission for all contracts and is paid on the 15th of the month following the month a house is painted. Thus, for this job, she will receive a $100 commission check on August 15. When should Spiffy recognize her commission of $100 as an expense? On July 24, when White gets the homeowner to sign a contract? When the work is completed, on July 25? Or on August 15, when she receives the commission check? Again, on a cash basis, commission expense would be recognized on August 15, when cash is *paid* to the salesperson. But on an accrual basis, expenses are recognized when they are *incurred.* In the example, the commission expense is incurred when the house is painted, on July 25.

Exhibit 4-2 summarizes the essential differences between recognition of revenues and expenses on a cash basis and recognition on an accrual basis.

EXHIBIT 4-2 **Comparing the Cash and Accrual Bases of Accounting**

	Cash Basis	Accrual Basis
Revenue is recognized	**When Received**	**When Earned**
Expense is recognized	**When Paid**	**When Incurred**

WHAT THE INCOME STATEMENT AND THE STATEMENT OF CASH FLOWS REVEAL

Most business entities, other than the very smallest, use the accrual basis of accounting. Thus, the income statement reflects the accrual basis. Revenues are recognized when they are earned; expenses, when they are incurred. At the same time, however, stockholders and creditors are also interested in information concerning the cash flows of an entity. The purpose of a statement of cash flows is to provide this information. Keep in mind that even though a statement of cash flows is presented in a complete set of financial statements, the accrual basis is used for recording transactions and for preparing a balance sheet and an income statement.

Recall the example of Glengarry Health Club in Chapter 3. The club earned revenue from two sources—memberships and court fees. Both forms of revenue were recognized on the income statement presented in that chapter and are reproduced in the top portion of Exhibit 4-3. Recall, however, that members have 30 days to pay and that at the end of the first month of operation, only $4,000 of the membership fees of $15,000 had been collected.

Now consider the statement of cash flows for the first month of operation, partially reproduced in the bottom portion of Exhibit 4-3. Because we want to compare the income statement to the statement of cash flows, only the Operating Activities section of the statement is shown. (The Investing and Financing Activities sections have been omitted from the statement.) Why is net income for the month a *positive* $7,000 but cash from operating activities is a *negative* $4,000? Of the membership revenue of $15,000 reflected on the income statement, only $4,000 was collected in cash. Glengarry has

EXHIBIT 4-3 Comparing the Income Statement and the Statement of Cash Flows

Membership revenue is $15,000, but only $4,000 was collected in cash. This $11,000 difference explains why net income is different from cash used by operating activities.

The **income statement** for Glengarry Health Club shows the following:

Revenues:		
Memberships	$15,000	
Court fees	5,000	$ 20,000
Expenses:		
Salaries and wages	$10,000	
Utilities	3,000	(13,000)
Net income		$ 7,000

Net income and cash used by operating activities differ by $11,000.

A **partial statement of cash flows** for Glengarry Health Club shows the following:

Cash received from:		
Membership fees	$ 4,000	
Court fees	5,000	$ 9,000
Cash paid for:		
Salaries and wages	$10,000	
Utilities	3,000	(13,000)
Cash used by operating activities		$ (4,000)

accounts receivable for the other $11,000. Thus, cash from operating activities, as reflected on a statement of cash flows, is $11,000 *less* than net income of $7,000, or a negative $4,000.

Each of these two financial statements serves a useful purpose:

- The income statement reflects the revenues actually earned by the business, regardless of whether cash has been collected.
- The statement of cash flows tells the reader about the actual cash inflows during a period of time.

ACCRUAL ACCOUNTING AND TIME PERIODS

The time period assumption was introduced in Chapter 1. We assume that it is possible to prepare an income statement that fairly reflects the earnings of a business for a specific period of time, such as a month or a year. It is somewhat artificial to divide the operations of a business into periods of time as indicated on a calendar. The conflict arises because earning income is a *process* that takes place over a period of time rather than at any one point in time.

Consider an alternative to our present system of reporting the operations of a business on a periodic basis. A new business begins operations with an investment of $50,000. The business operates for ten years, during which time no records are kept other than a checkbook for the cash on deposit at the bank. At the end of the ten years, the owners decide to go their separate ways and convert all of their assets to cash. They divide among them the balance of $80,000 in the bank account. What is the profit of the business for the ten-year period? The answer is $30,000, the difference between the original cash of $50,000 contributed and the cash of $80,000 available at liquidation.

The point of this simple example is that we could be very precise and accurate in measuring the income of a business if it were not necessary to artificially divide operations according to a calendar. Stockholders, bankers, and other interested parties cannot wait until a business liquidates to make decisions, however. They need information on a periodic basis. Thus, the justification for the accrual basis of accounting lies in the needs of financial statement users for periodic information on the financial position and the profitability of the entity.

POD REVIEW 4.2

LO2 *Explain the differences between the cash and accrual bases of accounting.*

- Cash and accrual bases are two alternatives used to account for transactions or economic events. They differ in the timing of when revenues and expenses are recognized.
  - Under the accrual method, which is the focus of this text, revenues are recognized when earned and expenses are recognized when incurred.
  - By contrast, under the cash method, revenues are recognized when cash is received and expenses are recognized when cash is paid.

QUESTIONS

1. *Under the accrual method, expenses are recognized*
   a. when cash is paid.
   b. at the end of the accounting period.
   c. when they are incurred.
   d. when revenue is earned.

2. *A landscaping business signs a contract with a new customer on April 1. New trees are planted for the customer on May 1, and the bill for the services is paid on June 1. Under the accrual basis, the business should recognize revenue on*
   a. April 1.
   b. May 1.
   c. June 1.
   d. December 31.

The Revenue Recognition Principle

LO3 Describe the revenue recognition principle and explain its application in various situations.

"**Revenues** are inflows or other enhancements of assets of an entity or settlements of its liabilities (or a combination of both) from delivering or producing goods, rendering services, or other activities that constitute the entity's ongoing major or central operations."[3] Two points should be noted about this formal definition of revenues. First, an asset is not always involved when revenue is recognized. The recognition of revenue may result from the settlement of a liability rather than from the acquisition of an asset. Second, entities generate revenue in different ways: some companies produce goods, others distribute or deliver the goods to users, and still others provide some type of service.

On the accrual basis, revenues are recognized when earned. However, the **revenue recognition principle** involves two factors. Revenues are recognized in the income statement when they are both *realized* and *earned*. Revenues are realized when goods or services are exchanged for cash or claims to cash, usually at the time of sale. This is normally interpreted to mean at the time the product or service is delivered to the customer. However, in certain situations, it may be necessary to modify or interpret the meaning of the revenue recognition principle. The application of the principle to long-term contracts, franchises, commodities, and installment sales are covered in intermediate accounting courses.

Revenues
Inflows of assets or settlements of liabilities from delivering or producing goods, rendering services, or conducting other activities.

Revenue recognition principle
Revenues are recognized in the income statement when they are realized, or realizable, and earned.

In some cases, revenue is earned continuously over time. In these cases, a product or service is not delivered at a specific point in time; instead, the earnings process takes place with the passage of time. Rent and interest are two examples. Interest is the cost associated with the use of someone else's money. When should a bank recognize the

3 *Statement of Financial Accounting Concepts No. 6,* "Elements of Financial Statements" (Stamford, Conn.: Financial Accounting Standards Board, December 1985), par. 78.

interest earned from granting a 90-day loan? Even though the interest may not be received until the loan is repaid, interest is earned every day the loan is outstanding. Later in the chapter we will look at the process for recognizing interest earned but not yet received. The same procedure is used to recognize revenue from rent that is earned but uncollected.

POD REVIEW 4.3

LO3 ***Describe the revenue recognition principle and explain its application in various situations.***

- Revenues are inflows of assets (or reductions of liabilities), generally from providing goods or services to customers.
  - Revenues must be realized and earned to be recognized on the income statement.

QUESTIONS

1. *Under the revenue recognition principle, revenues are recognized*
   a. when they are realized, or realizable, and earned.
   b. when cash is received.
   c. when expenses are incurred.
   d. at the end of the accounting period.

2. *Which of the following would result in the recognition of revenue?*
   a. A manufacturer delivers a component to a supplier.
   b. A retailer sells a product to a consumer.
   c. A bank provides a service to a customer.
   d. All of the above would result in the recognition of revenue.

Expense Recognition and the Matching Principle

LO4 Describe the matching principle and the various methods for recognizing expenses.

Companies incur a variety of costs. A new office building is constructed. Supplies are purchased. Employees perform services. The electric meter is read. In each of those situations, the company incurs a cost regardless of when it pays cash. Conceptually, **any time a cost is incurred, an asset is acquired.** However, according to the definition in Chapter 1, an asset represents a future economic benefit. An asset ceases being an asset and becomes an expense when the economic benefits from having incurred the cost have expired. Assets are unexpired costs, and expenses are expired costs.

At what point do costs expire and become expenses? The expense recognition principle requires that expenses be recognized in different ways depending on the nature of the cost. The ideal approach to recognizing expenses is to match them with revenues. Under the **matching principle**, the accountant attempts to associate revenues of a period with the costs necessary to generate those revenues. For certain types of expenses, a direct form of matching is possible; for others, it is necessary to associate costs with a particular period. The classic example of direct matching is cost of goods sold expense with sales revenue. Cost of goods sold is the cost of the inventory associated with a particular sale. A cost is incurred and an asset is recorded when the inventory is purchased. The asset, inventory, becomes an expense when it is sold. Another example of a cost that can be matched directly with revenue is commissions. The commission paid to a salesperson can be matched directly with the sale.

Matching principle
The association of revenue of a period with all of the costs necessary to generate that revenue.

An indirect form of matching is used to recognize the benefits associated with certain types of costs, most noticeably long-term assets such as buildings and equipment. These costs benefit many periods, but it is not usually possible to match them directly with a specific sale of a product. Instead, they are matched with the periods during which they will provide benefits. For example, an office building may be useful to a company for 30 years. *Depreciation* is the process of allocating the cost of a tangible long-term asset to its useful life. Depreciation Expense is the account used to recognize this type of expense.

The benefits associated with the incurrence of certain other costs are treated in accounting as expiring simultaneously with the acquisition of the costs. The justification for this treatment is that no future benefits from the incurrence of the cost are discernible. This is true of most selling and administrative costs. For example, the costs of heat and light in a building benefit only the current period and therefore are recognized as expenses as soon as the costs are incurred. Likewise, income taxes incurred during the period do not benefit any period other than the current period; thus, they are written off as an expense in the period incurred.

The relationships among costs, assets, and expenses are depicted in Exhibit 4-4 using three examples. First, costs incurred for purchases of merchandise result in an asset, Merchandise Inventory, and are eventually matched with revenue at the time the product is sold. Second, costs incurred for office space result in an asset, Office Building, which is recognized as Depreciation Expense over the useful life of the building. Third, the cost of heating and lighting benefits only the current period and thus is recognized immediately as Utilities Expense.

According to the FASB, **expenses** are "outflows or other using up of assets or incurrences of liabilities (or a combination of both) from delivering or producing goods, rendering services, or carrying out other activities that constitute the entity's ongoing major or central operations."[4] The key point to note about expenses is that they come about in two different ways:

Expenses
Outflows of assets or incurrences of liabilities resulting from delivering goods, rendering services, or carrying out other activities.

- From the use of an asset
- From the recognition of a liability

For example, when a retailer sells a product, the asset sacrificed is Inventory. Cost of Goods Sold is the expense account that is debited when the Inventory account is credited. As you will see in the next section, the incurrence of an expense also may result in a liability.

EXHIBIT 4-4 **Relationships among Costs, Assets, and Expenses**

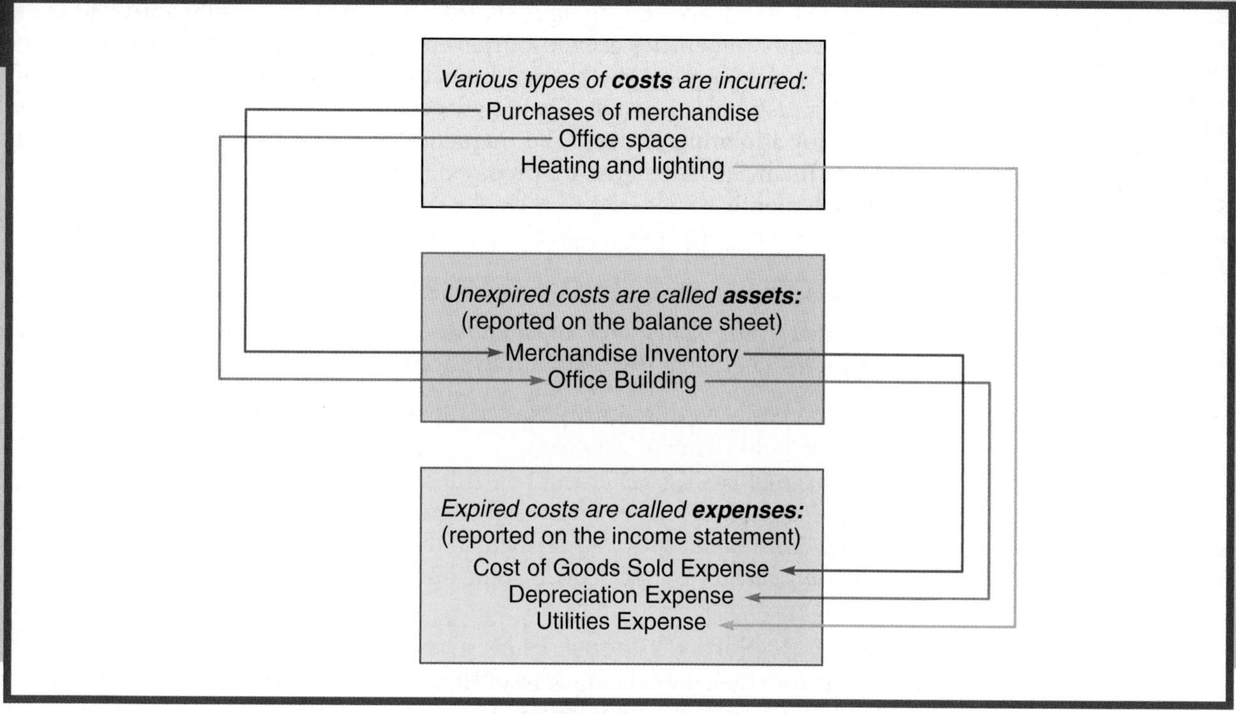

4 SFAC No. 6, par. 80.

POD REVIEW 4.4

LO4 Describe the matching principle and the various methods for recognizing expenses.

- The matching principle attempts to associate expenses with the time periods in which the expenditures help generate revenues.
- This principle is particularly important with expenditures for items that last for more than one accounting period. An example is the depreciation of a building.

QUESTIONS

1. *The association of revenue of a period with all of the costs necessary to generate that revenue is called*
   a. the revenue recognition principle.
   b. the matching principle.
   c. the income recognition principle.
   d. none of the above.

2. *The matching principle requires that the cost of a new piece of equipment be recognized as an expense*
   a. in the period the equipment is purchased.
   b. in the period cash is paid for the equipment.
   c. over the estimated useful life of the equipment.
   d. Never; the cost of equipment is not recognized as an expense.

Accrual Accounting and Adjusting Entries

LO5 Identify the four major types of adjusting entries and prepare them for a variety of situations.

Adjusting entries Journal entries made at the end of a period by a company using the accrual basis of accounting.

The accrual basis of accounting necessitates a number of adjusting entries at the end of a period. **Adjusting entries** are the journal entries the accountant makes at the end of a period for a company on the accrual basis of accounting. **Adjusting entries are not needed if a cash basis is used. It is the very nature of the accrual basis that results in the need for adjusting entries.** The frequency of the adjustment process depends on how often financial statements are prepared. Most businesses make adjustments at the end of each month.

TYPES OF ADJUSTING ENTRIES

Why are there four basic types, or categories, of adjusting entries? The answer lies in the distinction between the cash and the accrual bases of accounting:

- On a cash basis, no differences exist in the timing of revenue and the receipt of cash. The same holds true for expenses.
- On an accrual basis, *revenue* can be earned before or after cash is received. *Expenses* can be incurred before or after cash is paid. Each of these four distinct situations requires a different type of adjustment at the end of the period. We will consider each of the four categories and look at some examples of each.

(1) Cash Paid Before Expense Is Incurred (Deferred Expense) Assets are often acquired before their actual use in the business. Insurance policies typically are prepaid, as is rent. Office supplies are purchased in advance of their use, as are all types of property and equipment. Recall that unexpired costs are assets. As the costs expire and the benefits are used up, the asset must be written off and replaced with an expense.

Assume that on September 1, Nordstrom prepays $2,400 for an insurance policy for the next 12 months. The entry to record the prepayment is as follows:

Sept. 1	Prepaid Insurance	2,400	
	Cash		2,400
	To prepay insurance policy for 12 months.		

Balance Sheet							Income Statement
ASSETS		=	**LIABILITIES**	+	**STOCKHOLDERS' EQUITY**	+	**REVENUES − EXPENSES**
Prepaid Insurance	2,400						
Cash	(2,400)						

An asset account, Prepaid Insurance, is recorded because the company will receive benefits over the next 12 months. Because the insurance is for a 12-month period, $200 of benefits from the asset expires at the end of each month. The adjusting entry at the end of September to record this expiration accomplishes two purposes: (1) it recognizes the reduction in the asset Prepaid Insurance, and (2) it recognizes the expense associated with using up the benefits for one month. From the last chapter, you should recall that an asset is decreased with a credit and that an expense is increased with a debit, as follows:

Sept. 30	Insurance Expense	200	
	Prepaid Insurance		200
	To recognize $200 of insurance expense for the month.		

Balance Sheet							Income Statement	
ASSETS		=	**LIABILITIES**	+	**STOCKHOLDERS' EQUITY**	+	**REVENUES − EXPENSES**	
Prepaid Insurance	(200)						Insurance Expense	(200)

T accounts are an invaluable aid in understanding adjusting entries. They allow you to focus on the transactions and balances that will be included in the more formal general ledger accounts. The T accounts for Prepaid Insurance and Insurance Expense appear as follows after posting the original entry on September 1 and the adjusting entry on September 30:

Prepaid Insurance

	Debit	Credit	
9/1	2,400		
		200	9/30
Bal.	2,200		

Insurance Expense

	Debit	Credit
9/30	200	

The balance in Prepaid Insurance represents the unexpired benefits from the prepayment of insurance for the remaining 11 months: $\$200 \times 11 = \$2{,}200$. The Insurance Expense account reflects the expiration of benefits during the month of September.

Recall that depreciation is the process of allocating the cost of a long-term tangible asset over its estimated useful life. The accountant does not attempt to measure the decline in *value* of the asset, but tries to allocate the cost of the asset over its useful life. Thus, the adjustment for depreciation is similar to the one made for insurance expense. Assume that on January 1, Nordstrom buys new store fixtures, for which it pays $5,000. The entry to record the purchase is as follows:

Jan. 1	Store Fixtures	5,000	
	Cash		5,000
	To record purchase of store fixtures for cash.		

Balance Sheet							Income Statement
ASSETS		=	**LIABILITIES**	+	**STOCKHOLDERS' EQUITY**	+	**REVENUES − EXPENSES**
Store Fixtures	5,000						
Cash	(5,000)						

Two estimates must be made in depreciating the fixtures: (1) the useful life of the asset and (2) the salvage value of the fixtures at the end of their useful lives. Estimated salvage value is the amount a company expects to receive when it sells an asset at the end of its estimated useful life. According to the notes to its financial statements, Nordstrom uses an estimated useful life for its store fixtures and equipment of 3 to 15 years. Although it is not stated, assume that Nordstrom uses an estimated useful life of five years and an estimated salvage value of $500 at the end of that time for these particular fixtures. Thus, the *depreciable cost* of the fixtures is $5,000 − $500, or $4,500. A later chapter will consider alternative methods for allocating the depreciable cost over the useful life of an asset. For now, we will use the simplest approach (and the one that Nordstrom uses), called the **straight-line method**, which assigns an equal amount of depreciation to each period. The monthly depreciation is found by dividing the depreciable cost of $4,500 over the estimated useful life of 60 months (5 years = 60 months), which equals $75 per month.

Straight-line method The assignment of an equal amount of depreciation to each period.

The adjustment to recognize depreciation is conceptually the same as the adjustment to write off Prepaid Insurance. That is, the asset account is reduced and an expense is recognized. However, accountants normally use a contra account to reduce the total amount of long-term tangible assets by the amount of depreciation. A **contra account** has a balance that is opposite the balance in its related account. For example, Accumulated Depreciation is used to record the decrease in a long-term asset for depreciation; thus, it carries a credit balance. An *increase* in Accumulated Depreciation is recorded with a *credit* because we want to *decrease* the amount of assets and assets are *decreased* by a *credit*. The entry to record depreciation at the end of January is as follows:

Contra account An account with a balance that is opposite that of a related account.

Jan. 31	Depreciation Expense	75	
	Accumulated Depreciation		75
	To record depreciation on store fixtures.		

Balance Sheet						Income Statement
ASSETS	=	**LIABILITIES**	+	**STOCKHOLDERS' EQUITY**	+	**REVENUES − EXPENSES**
Accumulated Depreciation (75)						Depreciation Expense (75)

Study Tip

Think of the Accumulated Depreciation account as an extension of the related asset account, in this case, the Store Fixtures account. Therefore, although the Store Fixtures account is not directly reduced for depreciation, a credit to its companion account, Accumulated Depreciation, has the effect of reducing the asset.

Why do companies use a contra account for depreciation rather than simply reduce the long-term asset directly? If the asset account were reduced each time depreciation was recorded, its original cost would not be readily determinable from the accounting records. For various reasons, businesses need to know the original cost of each asset. One of the most important reasons is the need to know historical cost for computation of depreciation for tax purposes.

The T accounts for Store Fixtures, Accumulated Depreciation, and Depreciation Expense show the following balances at the end of the first month:

Store Fixtures

	Debit	Credit	
1/1	5,000		

Accumulated Depreciation

	Debit	Credit	
		75	1/31

Depreciation Expense

	Debit	Credit	
1/31	75		

On a balance sheet prepared on January 31, the contra account is shown as a reduction in the carrying value of the store fixtures:

Store Fixtures	$5,000	
Less: Accumulated Depreciation	75	4,925

(2) Cash Received Before Revenue Is Earned (Deferred Revenue) Recognizing accounting's symmetry will be a great help in your studies. Note that one company's asset is another company's liability. In the earlier example involving the purchase of an insurance policy, a second company, the insurance company, received the cash paid by the first company, Nordstrom. At the time cash is received, the insurance company has a liability because it has taken cash from Nordstrom but has not yet performed the service to earn the revenue. The revenue will be earned with the passage of time. This is the entry on the books of the insurance company on September 1:

Sept. 1	Cash	2,400	
	Insurance Collected in Advance		2,400
	To record receipt of cash on insurance policy for 12 months.		

Balance Sheet							Income Statement
ASSETS		=	LIABILITIES		+	STOCKHOLDERS' EQUITY	+	REVENUES − EXPENSES
Cash	2,400		Insurance Collected in Advance	2,400				

The account Insurance Collected in Advance is a liability. The insurance company is obligated to provide Nordstrom protection for the next 12 months. With the passage of time, the liability is satisfied. The adjusting entry at the end of each month accomplishes two purposes: it recognizes (1) the reduction in the liability and (2) the revenue earned each month. Recall that we decrease a liability with a debit and increase revenue with a credit:

Sept. 30	Insurance Collected in Advance	200	
	Insurance Revenue		200
	To recognize insurance revenue earned for the month.		

Balance Sheet							Income Statement	
ASSETS		=	LIABILITIES		+	STOCKHOLDERS' EQUITY	+	REVENUES − EXPENSES	
			Insurance Collected in Advance	(200)				Insurance Revenue	200

The balance in Insurance Collected in Advance reflects the remaining liability, and the balance in the Insurance Revenue account indicates the amount earned for the month:

Insurance Collected in Advance

		2,400	9/1
9/30	200		
		2,200	Bal.

Insurance Revenue

		200	9/30

As another example of deferred revenue, consider the following sentence from the note on revenue recognition in Nordstrom's 2006 annual report (page 33): "We recognize revenue associated with our gift cards upon redemption of the card."

To illustrate how this works, assume that on March 1, a generous friend gives you a $100 Nordstrom gift card. At the time the friend buys the card, Nordstrom has an

Hot Topics

What to Do with an Extra $1.5 Billion?

What does a company do when it finds itself in the enviable position of generating excess cash—more than is needed to fund future operations? Recently, Nordstrom announced two uses for its idle cash, both of which will return money to stockholders. One was approval of the company's quarterly dividend, a move that will pay out $0.135 per share and signal to stockholders that the company is operating profitably. The other use is on a much larger scale, one that will require $1.5 billion of cash. Over a period that could stretch to 24 months, Nordstrom will buy back shares of stock from its stockholders.

Companies have different motives in repurchasing shares of their stock, including the desire to have shares available to distribute to employees for bonuses and benefit plans. Also, buying back shares can help boost the market price of the company's stock. Regardless of intent, returning $1.5 billion of cash to stockholders is a sign that a company is optimistic about its future and about the industry in which it operates.

Source: Nordstrom news release, August 21, 2007; http://www.nordstrom.com.

increase in cash of $100 but has yet to earn any revenue. As the above note explains, Nordstrom does not recognize any revenue until you redeem the card. This will be the point at which Nordstrom gives you merchandise and earns revenue. Until the card is redeemed, Nordstrom has a liability; that is, it is obligated to deliver merchandise in the future. That liability is mentioned in another note on page 37 of Nordstrom's annual report (amounts are in thousands of dollars): "Included in other current liabilities were gift card liabilities of $171,631 and $154,683 at the end of 2006 and 2005."

The entry that Nordstrom would make upon receipt of $100 from your friend is as follows:

Mar. 1	Cash	100	
	Deferred Revenue (gift card liability)		100
	To record receipt of cash from gift card.		

Balance Sheet									Income Statement	
ASSETS		=	LIABILITIES		+	STOCKHOLDERS' EQUITY		+	REVENUES − EXPENSES	
Cash	100		Deferred Revenue	100						

Like Insurance Collected in Advance in the earlier example, Deferred Revenue is a liability. Assume that you redeem your card at a Nordstrom store on March 31. The entry on Nordstrom's books on this date would be as follows:

Mar. 31	Deferred Revenue (gift card liability)	100	
	Sales Revenue		100
	To record receipt of cash from gift card.		

Balance Sheet									Income Statement	
ASSETS		=	LIABILITIES		+	STOCKHOLDERS' EQUITY		+	REVENUES − EXPENSES	
			Deferred Revenue	(100)					Sales Revenue	100

4-1 Real World Practice

Reading Nordstrom's Balance Sheet

As described in this section, the note from page 37 of Nordstrom's annual report explains that gift card liabilities are included in other current liabilities. Refer to Nordstrom's partial balance sheet shown in the chapter opener. Where do other current liabilities appear on the balance sheet? What percentage of this account is made up of gift card liabilities at the end of 2006 and 2005?

(3) Expense Incurred Before Cash Is Paid (Accrued Liability) This situation is the opposite of **(1)**. That is, cash is paid *after* an expense is actually incurred rather than *before* its incurrence, as was the case in **(1)**. Many normal operating costs, such as payroll, various types of taxes, and utilities, fit this situation.

Refer to Nordstrom's partial balance sheet in the chapter opener. The second line under current liabilities represents the company's accrued liabilities for salaries, wages and related benefits, amounting to nearly $340 million on February 3, 2007.

Assume that at one of its stores, Nordstrom pays a total of $280,000 in wages on every other Friday. Assume that the last payday was Friday, May 31. The next two paydays will be Friday, June 14, and Friday, June 28. The journal entry will be the same on each of these paydays:

June 14	Wages Expense	280,000	
(and	Cash		280,000
June 28)	To pay the biweekly payroll.		

Balance Sheet							Income Statement	
ASSETS		=	**LIABILITIES**	+	**STOCKHOLDERS' EQUITY**	+	**REVENUES − EXPENSES**	
Cash	(280,000)						Wages Expense	(280,000)

On a balance sheet prepared as of June 30, a liability must be recognized. Even though the next payment is not until July 12, Nordstrom owes employees wages for the last two days of June and must recognize an expense for the wages earned by employees for those two days. We will assume that the store is open seven days a week and that the daily cost is 1/14th of the biweekly amount of $280,000, or $20,000. In addition to recognizing a liability on June 30, Nordstrom must adjust the records to reflect an expense associated with the cost of wages for the last two days of the month:

June 30	Wages Expense	40,000	
	Wages Payable		40,000
	To record wages for last two days of the month.		

Balance Sheet							Income Statement	
ASSETS	=	**LIABILITIES**		+	**STOCKHOLDERS' EQUITY**	+	**REVENUES − EXPENSES**	
		Wages Payable	40,000				Wages Expense	(40,000)

What entry will be made on the next payday, July 12? Nordstrom will need to eliminate the liability of $40,000 for the last two days of wages recorded on June 30 because the amount has now been paid. An additional $240,000 of expense has been incurred for the $20,000 cost per day associated with the first 12 days in July. Finally, cash is reduced by $280,000, which represents the biweekly payroll. The entry recorded is as follows:

July 12	Wages Payable	40,000	
	Wages Expense	240,000	
	Cash		280,000
	To pay the biweekly payroll.		

4-2 Real World Practice

Reading Nordstrom's Balance Sheet

Refer to Nordstrom's balance sheet shown in the chapter opener. What is the amount of Accrued Salaries, Wages and Related Benefits at the end of each of the two years shown? Compute the ratio of this liability to total current liabilities at the end of each of the two years.

Balance Sheet								Income Statement	
ASSETS		=	LIABILITIES		+	STOCKHOLDERS' EQUITY	+	REVENUES − EXPENSES	
Cash	(280,000)		Wages Payable	(40,000)				Wages Expense	(240,000)

The following time line illustrates the amount of expense incurred in each of the two months, June and July, for the biweekly payroll:

2 days' expense in June: $40,000 — 12 days' expense in July: $240,000

Friday, June 28: Last payday — Sunday, June 30: End of accounting period — Friday, July 12: Next payday

Another typical expense incurred before the payment of cash is interest. In many cases, the interest on a short-term loan is repaid with the amount of the loan, called the *principal*, on the maturity date. For example, assume that Granger Company takes out a 9%, 90-day, $20,000 loan with its bank on March 1. The principal and interest will be repaid on May 30. The entry on Granger's books on March 1 follows:

Mar. 1	Cash	20,000	
	Notes Payable		20,000
	To record issuance of 9%, 90-day, $20,000 note.		

Balance Sheet								Income Statement
ASSETS		=	LIABILITIES		+	STOCKHOLDERS' EQUITY	+	REVENUES − EXPENSES
Cash	20,000		Notes Payable	20,000				

The basic formula for computing interest follows:

$$I = P \times R \times T$$

where I = the dollar amount of interest
P = the principal amount of the loan
R = the annual rate of interest as a percentage
T = time in years (often stated as a fraction of a year).

The total interest on Granger's loan is as follows:

$$\$20{,}000 \times 0.09 \times 3/12 = \underline{\underline{\$450}}$$

Therefore, the amount of interest that must be recognized as expense at the end of March is one-third of $450 because one month of a total of three has passed. Alternatively, the formula for finding the total interest on the loan can be modified to compute the interest for one month.[5]

$$\$20{,}000 \times 0.09 \times 1/12 = \underline{\underline{\$150}}$$

The adjusting entry for the month of March is as follows:

Mar. 31	Interest Expense	150	
	Interest Payable		150
	To record interest for one month on a 9%, $20,000 loan.		

Balance Sheet								Income Statement	
ASSETS		=	LIABILITIES		+	STOCKHOLDERS' EQUITY	+	REVENUES − EXPENSES	
			Interest Payable	150				Interest Expense	(150)

The same adjusting entry is made at the end of April.

Apr. 30	Interest Expense	150	
	Interest Payable		150
	To record interest for one month on a 9%, $20,000 loan.		

Balance Sheet								Income Statement	
ASSETS		=	LIABILITIES		+	STOCKHOLDERS' EQUITY	+	REVENUES − EXPENSES	
			Interest Payable	150				Interest Expense	(150)

The entry on Granger's books on May 30 when it repays the principal and interest is as follows:

May 30	Interest Payable	300	
	Interest Expense	150	
	Notes Payable	20,000	
	Cash		20,450
	To record payment of a 9%, 90-day, $20,000 loan with interest.		

Balance Sheet								Income Statement	
ASSETS		=	LIABILITIES		+	STOCKHOLDERS' EQUITY	+	REVENUES − EXPENSES	
Cash	(20,450)		Interest Payable	(300)				Interest Expense	(150)
			Notes Payable	(20,000)					

The reduction in Interest Payable eliminates the liability recorded at the end of March and April. The recognition of $150 in Interest Expense is the cost associated with the month of May.[6] The reduction in Cash represents the $20,000 of principal and the total interest of $450 for three months.

---

5 In practice, interest is calculated on the basis of days rather than months. For example, the interest for March would be $\$20{,}000 \times .09 \times 30/365$, or $147.95, to reflect 30 days in the month out of a total of 365 days in the year. The reason the number of days in March is 30 rather than 31 is because in computing interest, businesses normally count the day a note matures but not the day it is signed. To simplify the calculations, we will use months, even though the result is slightly inaccurate.

6 This assumes that Granger did not make a separate entry prior to this to recognize interest expense for the month of May. If a separate entry had been made, a debit of $450 would be made to Interest Payable.

(4) Revenue Earned Before Cash Is Received (Accrued Asset) Revenue is sometimes earned before the receipt of cash. Rent and interest are earned with the passage of time and require an adjustment if cash has not yet been received. For example, assume that Grand Management Company rents warehouse space to a number of tenants. Most of its contracts call for prepayment of rent for six months at a time. Its agreement with one tenant, however, allows the tenant to pay Grand $2,500 in monthly rent anytime within the first ten days of the following month. The adjusting entry on Grand's books at the end of April, the first month of the agreement, is as follows:

Apr. 30	Rent Receivable	2,500	
	Rent Revenue		2,500
	To record rent earned for the month of April.		

Balance Sheet							Income Statement	
ASSETS		=	**LIABILITIES**	+	**STOCKHOLDERS' EQUITY**	+	**REVENUES − EXPENSES**	
Rent Receivable	2,500						Rent Revenue	2,500

When the tenant pays its rent on May 7, the effect on Grand's books is as follows:

May 7	Cash	2,500	
	Rent Receivable		2,500
	To record rent collected for the month of April.		

Balance Sheet							Income Statement
ASSETS		=	**LIABILITIES**	+	**STOCKHOLDERS' EQUITY**	+	**REVENUES − EXPENSES**
Cash	2,500						
Rent Receivable	(2,500)						

Study Tip

Now that you have seen examples of all four types of adjusting entries, think about a key difference between deferrals (the first two categories) and accruals (the last two categories). When you make adjusting entries involving deferrals, you must consider any existing balance in a deferred balance sheet account. Conversely, there is no existing account when an accrual is made.

Although the example of rent was used to illustrate this category, the membership revenue of Glengarry Health Club in Chapter 3 also could be used as an example. Whenever a company records revenue before cash is received, some type of receivable is increased and revenue is also increased. In that chapter, the health club earned membership revenue even though members had until the following month to pay their dues.

The same principle would apply to any amounts that customers owed to Nordstrom at the end of a period. As shown in the chapter opener, Nordstrom reported Accounts Receivable, Net of approximately $684 million on February 3, 2007. A note to the financial statements explains that these receivables arise from two forms of credit that the company offers customers. First, Nordstrom has its own private label card. Second, the company offers a cobranded Nordstrom VISA® credit card.

ACCRUALS AND DEFERRALS

One of the challenges in learning accounting concepts is to gain an understanding of the terminology. Part of the difficulty stems from the alternative terms used by different accountants to mean the same thing. For example, the asset created when insurance is paid for in advance is termed a *prepaid asset* by some and a *prepaid expense* by others. Someone else might refer to it as a *deferred expense.*

Deferral
Cash has been paid or received but expense or revenue has not yet been recognized.

Deferred expense
An asset resulting from the payment of cash before the incurrence of expense.

The term **deferral** will be used here to refer to a situation in which cash has been paid or received but the expense or revenue has been deferred to a later time. A **deferred expense** indicates that cash has been paid but the recognition of expense has been deferred. Because a deferred expense represents a *future benefit* to a company, it is an asset. An alternative name for deferred expense is *prepaid expense.* Prepaid insurance and office supplies are deferred expenses. An adjusting entry is made periodically to record the portion of the deferred expense that has expired. A **deferred revenue** means that cash has been received but the recognition of any revenue has been deferred until a later time. Because a deferred revenue represents an *obligation* to a company, it is a liability. An alternative name for deferred revenue is *unearned revenue*. Rent collected in advance is deferred revenue. The periodic adjusting entry recognizes the portion of the deferred revenue that is earned in that period.

This chapter has discussed in detail the accrual basis of accounting, which involves recognizing changes in resources and obligations as they occur, not simply when cash changes hands. More specifically, the term **accrual** will be used to refer to a situation in which no cash has been paid or received yet but it is necessary to recognize, or accrue, an expense or a revenue. An **accrued liability** is recognized at the end of the period in cases in which an expense has been incurred but cash has not yet been paid. Wages payable and interest payable are examples of accrued liabilities. An **accrued asset** is recorded when revenue has been earned but cash has not yet been collected. Rent receivable is an accrued asset.

Deferred revenue
A liability resulting from the receipt of cash before the recognition of revenue.

Accrual
Cash has not yet been paid or received but expense has been incurred or revenue earned.

Accrued liability
A liability resulting from the recognition of an expense before the payment of cash.

Accrued asset
An asset resulting from the recognition of a revenue before the receipt of cash.

SUMMARY OF ADJUSTING ENTRIES

The four types of adjusting entries are summarized in Exhibit 4-5. Common examples of each are shown, along with the structure of the entries associated with the four categories. Finally, the following generalizations should help you gain a better understanding of adjusting entries and how they are used:

1. **An adjusting entry is an internal transaction. It does not involve another entity.**
2. **Because it is an internal transaction, an adjusting entry does not involve an increase or decrease in Cash.**
3. **At least one balance sheet account and one income statement account are involved in an adjusting entry. It is the nature of the adjustment process that an asset or liability account is adjusted with a corresponding change in a revenue or an expense account.**

COMPREHENSIVE EXAMPLE OF ADJUSTING ENTRIES

We will now consider a comprehensive example involving the transactions for the first month of operations and the end-of-period adjusting entries for a hypothetical business, Duffy Transit Company. The trial balance in Exhibit 4-6 was prepared after

EXHIBIT 4-5 Accruals and Deferrals

Type	Situation	Examples	Entry during Period	Entry at End of Period

Deferred expense	Cash paid before expense is incurred	Insurance policy
		Supplies
		Rent
		Buildings, equipment
			Asset
			  Cash
				Expense
				  Asset

Deferred revenue	Cash received before revenue is earned	Deposits, rent
		Subscriptions
		Gift certificates
			Cash
			  Liability
				Liability
				  Revenue

Accrued liability	Expense incurred before cash is paid	Salaries, wages Interest Taxes Rent	No Entry	Expense Liability
Accrued asset	Revenue earned before cash is received	Interest Rent	No Entry	Asset Revenue

EXHIBIT 4-6 Unadjusted Trial Balance

Duffy Transit Company
Unadjusted Trial Balance
January 31

	Debit	Credit
Cash	$ 50,000	
Prepaid Insurance	48,000	
Land	20,000	
Buildings—Garage	160,000	
Equipment—Buses	300,000	
Discount Tickets Sold in Advance		$ 25,000
Notes Payable		150,000
Capital Stock		400,000
Daily Ticket Revenue		30,000
Gas, Oil, and Maintenance Expense	12,000	
Wage and Salary Expense	10,000	
Dividends	5,000	
Totals	$605,000	$605,000

posting to the accounts the transactions entered into during the first month of business. As discussed in Chapter 3, a trial balance can be prepared at any point in time. Because the trial balance is prepared *before* taking into account adjusting entries, it is called an *unadjusted* trial balance. This is the first month of operations for Duffy. Thus, the Retained Earnings account does not yet appear on the trial balance. After the first month, this account will have a balance and will appear on subsequent trial balances.

Duffy wants to prepare a balance sheet at the end of January and an income statement for its first month of operations. Use of the accrual basis necessitates a number of adjusting entries to update certain asset and liability accounts and to recognize the correct amounts for the various revenues and expenses.

USING A TRIAL BALANCE TO PREPARE ADJUSTING ENTRIES

A trial balance is an important tool to use in preparing adjusting entries. The deferred expenses on Duffy's trial balance, such as Prepaid Insurance, must be reduced with a corresponding increase in expense. Similarly, any deferred revenues, such as Discount Tickets Sold in Advance, must be adjusted and a corresponding amount of revenue recognized. In addition, any accrued assets, such as Rent Receivable, and accrued liabilities, such as Interest Payable, which do not currently appear on the trial balance, must be recognized.

ADJUSTING ENTRIES AT THE END OF JANUARY

At the beginning of January, Duffy issued an 18-month, 12%, $150,000 promissory note for cash. Although interest will not be repaid until the loan's maturity date, Duffy must accrue interest for the first month. The calculation of interest for one month is $\$150{,}000 \times 0.12 \times 1/12$. The adjusting entry is as follows:

		Debit	Credit
(a)	Interest Expense	1,500	
	Interest Payable		1,500
	To record interest for one month on 12%, $150,000 promissory note.		

Balance Sheet							Income Statement	
ASSETS	=	LIABILITIES		+	STOCKHOLDERS' EQUITY	+	REVENUES − EXPENSES	
		Interest Payable	1,500				Interest Expense	(1,500)

The wages and salaries on the trial balance were paid in cash. At the end of the month, Duffy owes employees an additional $2,800 in salaries and wages:

(b)	Wage and Salary Expense	2,800	
	Wages and Salaries Payable		2,800
	To record wages and salaries owed.		

Balance Sheet							Income Statement	
ASSETS	=	LIABILITIES		+	STOCKHOLDERS' EQUITY	+	REVENUES − EXPENSES	
		Wages and Salaries Payable	2,800				Wage and Salary Expense	(2,800)

At the beginning of January, Duffy acquired a garage to house the buses at a cost of $160,000. Land is not subject to depreciation. The cost of the land acquired in connection with the purchase of the building will remain on the books until the property is sold. The garage has an estimated useful life of 20 years and an estimated salvage value of $16,000 at the end of its life. The monthly depreciation is found by dividing the depreciable cost of $144,000 by the useful life of 240 months:

$$\frac{\$160{,}000 - \$16{,}000}{20 \text{ years} \times 12 \text{ months}} = \frac{\$144{,}000}{240 \text{ months}} = \underline{\underline{\$600}} \text{ per month}$$

The entry to record the depreciation on the garage for January for a full month is as follows:

(c)	Depreciation Expense—Garage	600	
	Accumulated Depreciation—Garage		600
	To record depreciation for the month.		

Balance Sheet						Income Statement	
ASSETS		=	LIABILITIES	+	STOCKHOLDERS' EQUITY +	REVENUES − EXPENSES	
Accumulated Depreciation—Garage	(600)					Depreciation Expense—Garage	(600)

Duffy purchased ten buses for $30,000 each at the beginning of January. The buses have an estimated useful life of five years, at which time the company plans to sell them for $6,000 each. The monthly depreciation on the ten buses is as follows:

$$10 \times \frac{\$30{,}000 - \$6{,}000}{5 \text{ years} \times 12 \text{ months}} = 10 \times \frac{\$24{,}000}{60 \text{ months}} = \underline{\underline{\$4{,}000}} \text{ per month}$$

The entry to recognize the depreciation on the buses for the first month is as follows:

(d)	Depreciation Expense—Buses	4,000	
	Accumulated Depreciation—Buses		4,000
	To record depreciation for the month.		

Balance Sheet						Income Statement	
ASSETS		=	LIABILITIES	+	STOCKHOLDERS' EQUITY +	REVENUES − EXPENSES	
Accumulated Depreciation—Buses	(4,000)					Depreciation Expense—Buses	(4,000)

Prepaid Insurance on the trial balance represents an insurance policy purchased for $48,000 on January 1. The policy provides property and liability protection for a 24-month period. The adjusting entry to allocate the cost to expense for the first month is as follows:

(e)	Insurance Expense	2,000	
	Prepaid Insurance		2,000
	To record expiration of insurance benefits.		

Balance Sheet							Income Statement	
ASSETS		=	LIABILITIES		+	STOCKHOLDERS' EQUITY	+	REVENUES − EXPENSES
Prepaid Insurance	(2,000)							Insurance Expense (2,000)

In addition to selling tickets on the bus, Duffy sells discount tickets at the terminal. The tickets are good for a ride anytime within 12 months of purchase. Thus, as these tickets are sold, Duffy debits Cash and credits a liability account, Discount Tickets Sold in Advance. The sale of $25,000 worth of these tickets was recorded during January and thus is reflected on the trial balance. At the end of the first month, Duffy counts the number of tickets that has been redeemed. Because $20,400 worth of tickets has been turned in, this is the amount by which the company reduces its liability and recognizes revenue for the month:

(f)	Discount Tickets Sold in Advance	20,400	
	Discount Ticket Revenue		20,400
	To record redemption of discount tickets.		

Balance Sheet							Income Statement	
ASSETS		=	LIABILITIES		+	STOCKHOLDERS' EQUITY	+	REVENUES − EXPENSES
			Discount Tickets Sold in Advance	(20,400)				Discount Ticket Revenue 20,400

Duffy does not need all of the space in its garage and rents a section of it to another company for $2,500 per month. The tenant has until the 10th day of the following month to pay its rent. The adjusting entry on Duffy's books on the last day of the month is as follows:

(g)	Rent Receivable	2,500	
	Rent Revenue		2,500
	To record rent earned but not yet received.		

Balance Sheet							Income Statement	
ASSETS		=	LIABILITIES		+	STOCKHOLDERS' EQUITY	+	REVENUES − EXPENSES
Rent Receivable	2,500							Rent Revenue 2,500

Corporations pay estimated taxes on a quarterly basis. Because Duffy is preparing an income statement for the month of January, it must estimate its taxes for the month. We will assume a corporate tax rate of 34% on income before tax. The computation of Income Tax Expense is as follows. (The amounts shown for the revenues and expenses reflect the effect of the adjusting entries).

Revenues:		
Daily Ticket Revenue	$30,000	
Discount Ticket Revenue	20,400	
Rent Revenue	2,500	$52,900
Expenses:		
Gas, Oil, and Maintenance Expense	$12,000	
Wage and Salary Expense	12,800	
Depreciation Expense	4,600	
Insurance Expense	2,000	
Interest Expense	1,500	32,900
Net Income before Tax		$20,000
Times the Corporate Tax Rate		× 0.34
Income Tax Expense		$ 6,800

Based on this estimate of taxes, the final adjusting entry recorded on Duffy's books for the month is as follows:

(h)	Income Tax Expense	6,800	
	Income Tax Payable		6,800
	To record estimated income taxes for the month.		

Balance Sheet					Income Statement
ASSETS	=	LIABILITIES	+	STOCKHOLDERS' EQUITY	+	REVENUES − EXPENSES
		Income Tax Payable 6,800				Income Tax Expense (6,800)

An adjusted trial balance, shown in Exhibit 4-7, indicates the equality of debits and credits after the adjusting entries have been recorded. Note the addition of a number of new

EXHIBIT 4-7 **Adjusted Trial Balance**

Duffy Transit Company
Adjusted Trial Balance
January 31

	Debit	Credit
Cash	$ 50,000	
Prepaid Insurance	46,000	
Land	20,000	
Buildings—Garage	160,000	
Accumulated Depreciation—Garage		$ 600
Equipment—Buses	300,000	
Accumulated Depreciation—Buses		4,000
Gas, Oil, and Maintenance Expense	12,000	
Wage and Salary Expense	12,800	
Dividends	5,000	
Discount Tickets Sold in Advance		4,600
Notes Payable		150,000
Capital Stock		400,000
Daily Ticket Revenue		30,000
Rent Receivable	2,500	
Interest Expense	1,500	
Income Tax Expense	6,800	
Depreciation Expense—Garage	600	
Depreciation Expense—Buses	4,000	
Insurance Expense	2,000	
Interest Payable		1,500
Wages and Salaries Payable		2,800
Income Tax Payable		6,800
Discount Ticket Revenue		20,400
Rent Revenue		2,500
Totals	$623,200	$623,200

accounts that did not appear on the unadjusted trial balance in Exhibit 4-6. The new trial balance includes the accounts that were added when adjusting entries were recorded.

ETHICAL CONSIDERATIONS FOR A COMPANY ON THE ACCRUAL BASIS

The accrual basis requires the recognition of revenues when earned and expenses when incurred regardless of when cash is received or paid. Adjusting entries are *internal* transactions in that they do not involve an exchange with an outside entity. Because adjustments do not involve another company, accountants may at times feel pressure from others within the organization either to speed or delay the recognition of certain adjustments.

Consider the following two examples for a landscaping company that is concerned about its bottom line, that is, its net income. A number of jobs are in progress; but because of inclement weather, none of them are very far along. Management asks the accountant to recognize all of the revenue from a job in progress even though no significant work has been done on the job. Further, the accountant has been asked to delay the recognition of various short-term accrued liabilities (and, of course, the accompanying expenses) until the beginning of the new year.

The "correct" response of the accountant to each of those requests may seem obvious: no revenue on the one job should be recognized, and all accrued liabilities should be expensed at year-end. The pressures of the daily work environment make these decisions difficult for the accountant, however. The accountant must remember that his or her primary responsibility in preparing financial statements is to portray the affairs of the company accurately to the various outside users. Bankers, stockholders, and others rely on the accountant to serve their best interests.

POD REVIEW 4.5

LO5 *Identify the four major types of adjusting entries and prepare them for a variety of situations.*

- Adjusting entries are made at the end of an accounting period to update revenue or expense accounts in accordance with the revenue recognition and matching principles.
- There are four basic categories of adjusting entries:
  - Adjustments where cash is paid before expenses are incurred—deferred expenses
  - Adjustments where cash is received before revenues are earned—deferred revenue
  - Adjustments where expenses are incurred before cash is paid—accrued liabilities
  - Adjustments where revenues are recognized before cash is received—accrued assets

QUESTIONS

1. *A company owes its employees wages not yet paid at the end of an accounting period. The adjusting entry needed at the end of the period will be a*
   a. debit to an expense and a credit to a liability.
   b. debit to an expense and a credit to an asset.
   c. debit to an expense and a credit to cash.
   d. debit to a liability and a credit to an expense.

2. *A magazine publisher makes the appropriate entry when it receives cash in advance of providing magazines to its subscribers. When the magazines are delivered, the publisher will make an entry that includes*
   a. a debit to cash and a credit to revenue.
   b. a debit to accounts receivable and a credit to revenue.
   c. a debit to a liability and a credit to revenue.
   d. none of the above.

The Accounting Cycle

LO6 Explain the steps in the accounting cycle and the significance of each step.

This chapter has focused on accrual accounting and the adjusting entries it necessitates. Adjusting entries are one key component in the **accounting cycle**. The accountant for a business follows a series of steps each period. The objective is always the same: **collect the necessary information to prepare a set of financial statements.** Together these steps make up the accounting cycle. The name comes from the fact that the steps are repeated each period.

Accounting cycle A series of steps performed each period and culminating with the preparation of a set of financial statements.

The steps in the accounting cycle are shown in Exhibit 4-8. Note that Step 1 involves not only *collecting* information but also *analyzing* it. Transaction analysis is probably the most challenging of all of the steps in the accounting cycle. It requires the ability to think logically about an event and its effect on the financial position of the entity. Once the transaction is analyzed, it is recorded in the journal, as indicated by the second step in the exhibit. The first two steps in the cycle take place continuously.

Journal entries are posted to the accounts on a periodic basis. The frequency of posting to the accounts depends on two factors: the type of accounting system used by a company and the volume of transactions. In a manual system, entries might be posted daily, weekly, or even monthly depending on the amount of activity. The larger the number of transactions a company records, the more often it posts. In an automated accounting system, posting is likely done automatically by the computer each time a transaction is recorded.

THE USE OF A WORK SHEET

Step 4 in Exhibit 4-8 calls for the preparation of a work sheet. The end of an accounting period is a busy time. In addition to recording daily recurring transactions, the accountant

EXHIBIT 4-8 Steps in the Accounting Cycle

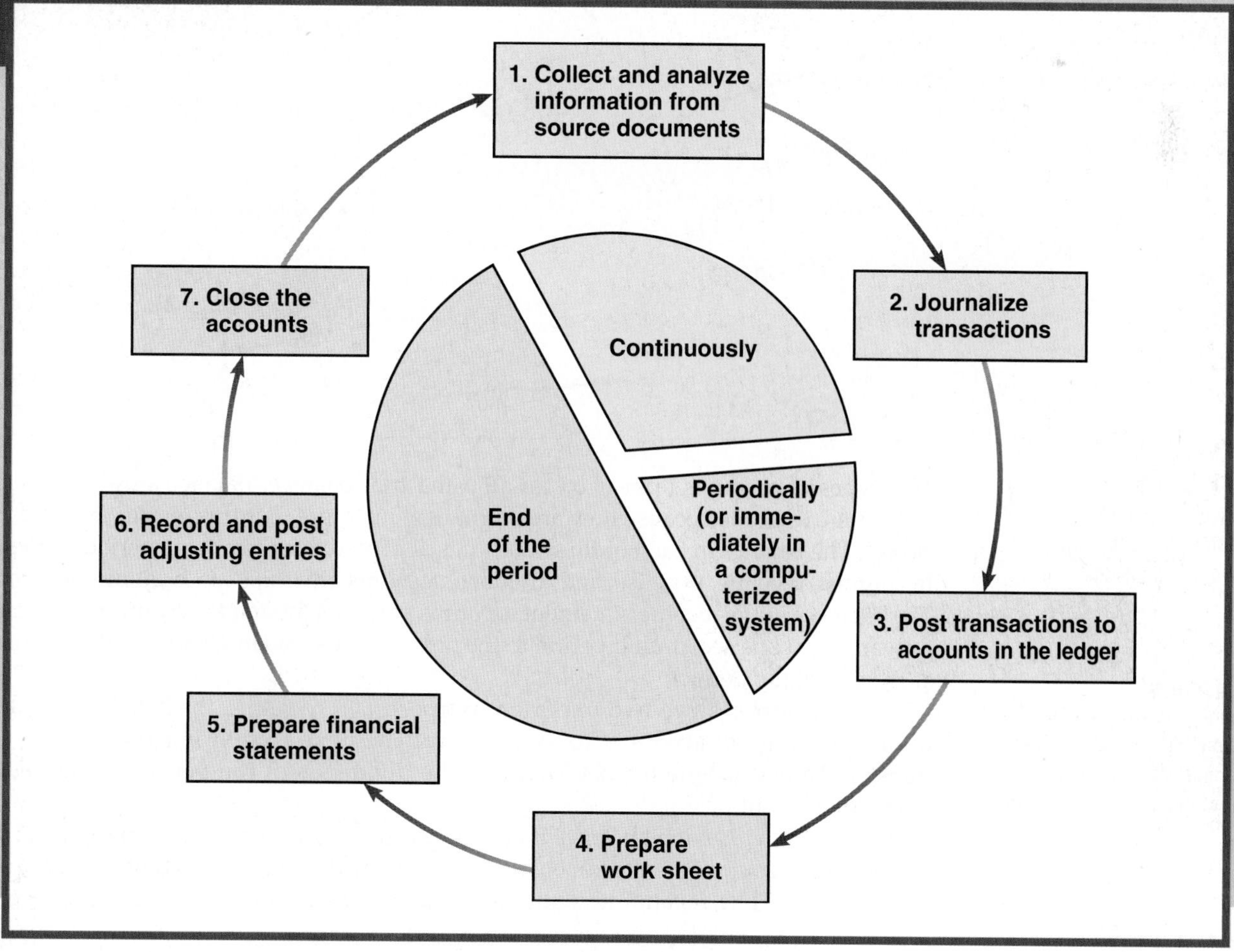

Work sheet
A device used at the end of the period to gather the information needed to prepare financial statements without actually recording and posting adjusting entries.

must record adjusting entries as the basis for preparing financial statements. The time available to prepare the statements is usually very limited. The use of a **work sheet** allows the accountant to gather and organize the information required to adjust the accounts without actually recording and posting the adjusting entries to the accounts. Recording adjusting entries and posting them to the accounts can be done after the financial statements are prepared. **The work sheet itself is not a financial statement.** Instead, it is a useful device to organize the information needed to prepare the financial statements at the end of the period.

It is not essential that a work sheet be used before financial statements are prepared. If it is not used, Step 6, recording and posting adjusting entries, comes before Step 5, preparing the financial statements. This chapter's appendix illustrates how a work sheet is used to facilitate the preparation of financial statements.

POD REVIEW 4.6

LO6 *Explain the steps in the accounting cycle and the significance of each step.*

- The accounting cycle involves seven steps that are repeated each period. (See Exhibit 4-8.)
  - Collecting and analyzing data and journalizing transactions occur on a continuous basis.
  - Periodically, transactions are posted to accounts in the ledger.
  - At the end of the period, a work sheet is prepared, financial statements are prepared, adjusting entries are recorded and posted, and accounts are closed.

QUESTIONS

1. *Which of the following steps in the accounting cycle is* not *in the correct order?*
   a. Journalize transactions and post them to accounts in the ledger.
   b. Prepare a work sheet and prepare financial statements.
   c. Close the accounts and record and post adjusting entries.
   d. All of the above are in the correct order.

2. *Which of the following steps in the accounting cycle is* not *performed at the end of the accounting period?*
   a. Collect and analyze information from source documents.
   b. Prepare a work sheet.
   c. Record and post adjusting entries.
   d. Close the accounts.

The Closing Process

LO7 Explain why and how closing entries are made at the end of an accounting period.

Real accounts
The name given to balance sheet accounts because they are permanent and are not closed at the end of the period.

Two types of accounts appear on an adjusted trial balance. Balance sheet accounts are called **real accounts** because they are permanent in nature. For this reason, they are never closed. The balance in each of these accounts is carried over from one period to the next. In contrast, revenue, expense, and dividend accounts are *temporary* or **nominal accounts**. The balances in the income statement accounts and the Dividends account are *not* carried forward from one accounting period to the next. For this reason, these accounts are closed at the end of the period.

Closing entries serve two important purposes: (1) to return the balances in all temporary or nominal accounts to zero to start the next accounting period and (2) to transfer the net income (or net loss) and the dividends of the period to the Retained Earnings account.

An account with a debit balance is closed by crediting the account for the amount of the balance. An account with a credit balance is closed by debiting the account for the amount of the balance. Thus, revenue accounts are debited in the closing process. Expense accounts are credited to close them. In this way, the balance of each income statement account is restored to zero to start the next accounting period.

Various approaches are used to accomplish the same two purposes: restore the temporary accounts to zero and update the Retained Earnings account. We will use a holding account called Income Summary to facilitate the closing process. A single entry is made to close all of the revenue accounts. The total amount debited to the revenue accounts is credited to Income Summary. Similarly, a single entry is made to close all of the expense accounts, and the offsetting debit is made to Income Summary. This account acts as a temporary storage account. After closing the revenue and expense accounts, Income Summary has a *credit* balance *if revenues exceed expenses.* Finally, the credit balance in Income Summary is closed by debiting the account and crediting Retained Earnings for the same amount. The net result of the process is that all of the revenues less expenses (i.e., net income) have been transferred to Retained Earnings.

The Dividends account is closed directly to Retained Earnings. Because dividends are *not* an expense, the Dividends account is not closed first to the Income Summary account, as are expense accounts. A credit is made to close the Dividends account with an offsetting debit to Retained Earnings.

The closing process for Duffy Transit Company is illustrated with the use of T accounts in Exhibit 4-9. Rather than show each individual revenue and expense account, a single revenue account and a single expense account are used in the exhibit to illustrate the flow in the closing process.

The first closing entry ❶ results in a zero balance in each of the three revenue accounts; and the total of the three amounts, $52,900, which represents all of the revenue of the period, is transferred to the Income Summary account. The second entry ❷ closes each of the seven expense accounts and transfers the total expenses of $39,700 as a debit to the Income Summary account. At this point, the Income Summary account has a credit balance of $13,200, which represents the net income of the period. The third entry ❸ closes this temporary holding account and transfers the net income to the Retained Earnings account. Finally, the fourth entry ❹ closes the Dividends account and transfers the $5,000 to the debit side of the Retained Earnings account. The Retained Earnings account is now updated to its correct ending balance of $8,200.

Nominal accounts
The name given to revenue, expense, and dividend accounts because they are temporary and are closed at the end of the period.

Closing entries
Journal entries made at the end of the period to return the balance in all nominal accounts to zero and transfer the net income or loss and the dividends to Retained Earnings.

EXHIBIT 4-9 **The Closing Process**

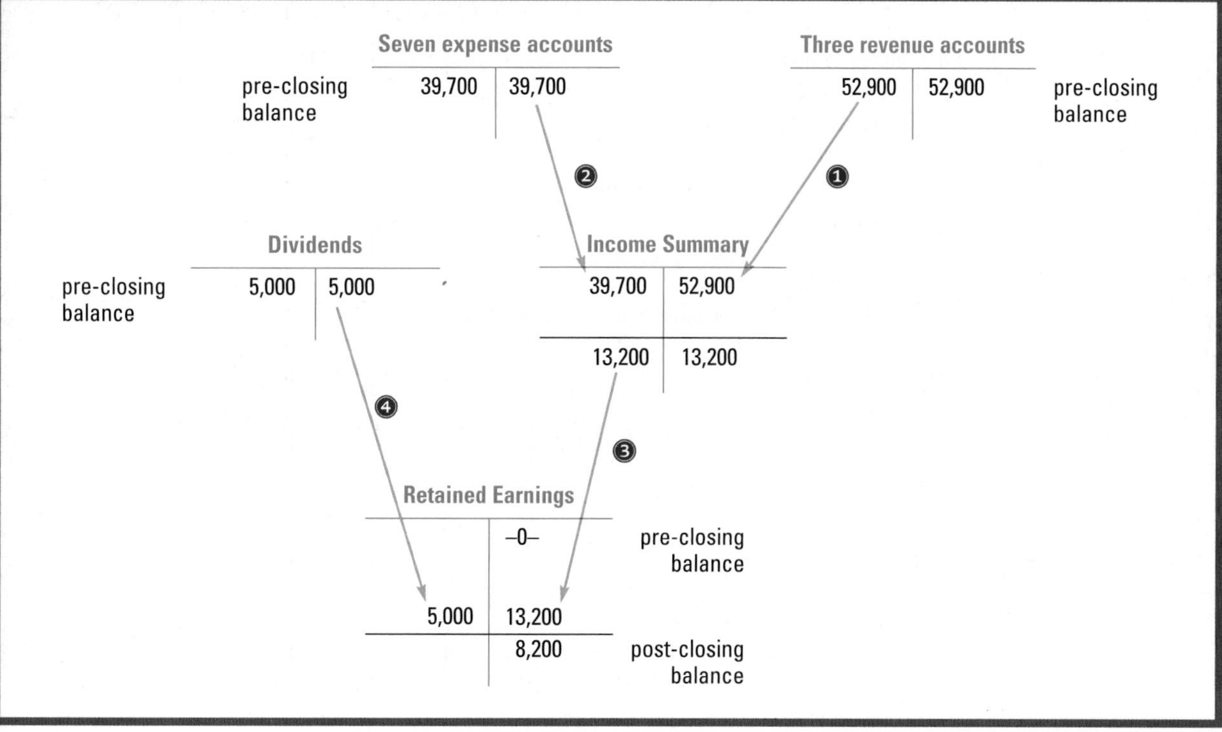

The four closing entries in journal form are shown in Exhibit 4-10. Note that each individual revenue and expense account is closed. Keep in mind that the Post. Ref. column will be filled in with the appropriate account numbers when the entries are posted to the ledger accounts.

INTERIM FINANCIAL STATEMENTS

Recall that certain steps in the accounting cycle are sometimes carried out only once a year rather than each month, as in our example. For ease of illustration, we assumed a monthly accounting cycle. Many companies adjust and close the accounts only once a year, however. They use a work sheet more frequently than that as the basis for preparing interim statements. Statements prepared monthly, quarterly, or at other intervals less than a year in duration are called **interim statements**. Many companies prepare monthly financial statements for their own internal use. Similarly, corporations whose shares are publicly traded on one of the stock exchanges are required to file quarterly financial statements with the SEC.

Interim statements Financial statements prepared monthly, quarterly, or at other intervals less than a year in duration.

Suppose that a company prepares monthly financial statements for internal use and completes the accounting cycle in its entirety only once a year. In this case, a work sheet is prepared each month as the basis for interim financial statements. Formal adjusting and closing entries are prepared only at the end of each year. The adjusting entries that appear on the monthly work sheet are not posted to the accounts. They are entered on the work sheet simply as a basis for preparing the monthly financial statements.

EXHIBIT 4-10 Closing Entries Recorded in the Journal

DATE		ACCOUNT TITLES AND EXPLANATION	POST. REF.	DEBIT	CREDIT
Jan.	31	Daily Ticket Revenue		30,000	
		Discount Ticket Revenue		20,400	
		Rent Revenue		2,500	
		Income Summary			52,900
		To close revenue accounts to Income Summary.			
	31	Income Summary		39,700	
		Gas, Oil, and Maintenance Expense			12,000
		Wage and Salary Expense			12,800
		Interest Expense			1,500
		Depreciation Expense—Garage			600
		Depreciation Expense—Buses			4,000
		Insurance Expense			2,000
		Income Tax Expense			6,800
		To close expense accounts to Income Summary.			
	31	Income Summary		13,200	
		Retained Earnings			13,200
		To close Income Summary to Retained Earnings.			
	31	Retained Earnings		5,000	
		Dividends			5,000
		To close Dividends to Retained Earnings.			

POD REVIEW 4.7

LO7 *Explain why and how closing entries are made at the end of an accounting period.*

- Journal entries that close the nominal (temporary) accounts achieve two important objectives:
  - They return the balance of all nominal accounts to zero so that the accounts are ready to record activity for the next accounting period.
  - They transfer net income (loss) and dividends to retained earnings.

QUESTIONS

1. *Which types of accounts are closed at the end of an accounting period?*
   a. real accounts only
   b. nominal accounts only
   c. both real and nominal accounts
   d. Neither real nor nominal accounts are closed.

2. *Which of the following accounts would never be credited in a closing entry?*
   a. Revenue
   b. Expense
   c. Dividends
   d. Retained Earnings

APPENDIX

Accounting Tools: Work Sheets

Work sheets were introduced in the chapter as useful tools to aid the accountant. This appendix presents a detailed discussion of work sheets.

Work Sheets

LO8 Understand how to use a work sheet as a basis for preparing financial statements.

A work sheet is used to organize the information needed to prepare financial statements without recording and posting formal adjusting entries. There is no one single format for a work sheet. We will illustrate a ten-column work sheet by using the information in the chapter for the Duffy Transit Company. The format for a ten-column work sheet appears in Exhibit 4-11. We will concentrate on the steps to complete the work sheet, which has already been completed.

EXHIBIT 4-11 The Work Sheet

Duffy Transit Company
Work Sheet
For the Month Ended January 31

Account Titles	Unadjusted Trial Balance		Adjusting Entries		Adjusted Trial Balance		Income Statement		Balance Sheet	
	Debit	Credit	Debit	Credit	Debit	Credit	Debit	Credit	Debit	Credit
Cash	50,000				50,000				50,000	
Prepaid Insurance	48,000			(e) 2,000	46,000				46,000	
Land	20,000				20,000				20,000	
Buildings—Garage	160,000				160,000				160,000	
Accumulated Depreciation—Garage		–0–		(c) 600		600				600
Equipment—Buses	300,000				300,000				300,000	
Accumulated Depreciation—Buses		–0–		(d) 4,000		4,000				4,000
Discount Tickets Sold in Advance		25,000	(f) 20,400			4,600				4,600
Notes Payable		150,000				150,000				150,000
Capital Stock		400,000				400,000				400,000
Retained Earnings		–0–				–0–				–0–
Daily Ticket Revenue		30,000				30,000		30,000		
Gas, Oil, and Maintenance Expense	12,000				12,000		12,000			
Wage and Salary Expense	10,000		(b) 2,800		12,800		12,800			
Dividends	5,000				5,000				5,000	
	605,000	605,000								
Interest Expense			(a) 1,500		1,500		1,500			
Depreciation Expense—Garage			(c) 600		600		600			
Depreciation Expense—Buses			(d) 4,000		4,000		4,000			
Insurance Expense			(e) 2,000		2,000		2,000			
Discount Ticket Revenue				(f) 20,400		20,400		20,400		
Rent Receivable			(g) 2,500		2,500				2,500	
Rent Revenue				(g) 2,500		2,500		2,500		
Interest Payable				(a) 1,500		1,500				1,500
Wages and Salaries Payable				(b) 2,800		2,800				2,800
Income Tax Expense			(h) 6,800		6,800		6,800			
Income Tax Payable				(h) 6,800		6,800				6,800
			40,600	40,600	623,200	623,200	39,700	52,900	583,500	570,300
Net Income							13,200			13,200
							52,900	52,900	583,500	583,500

STEP 1: THE UNADJUSTED TRIAL BALANCE COLUMNS

The starting point for the work sheet is the first two columns, which must be filled in with the appropriate amounts from the unadjusted trial balance of Duffy Transit Company shown in Exhibit 4-6 on p. 172. The trial balance is labeled *unadjusted* because it does not reflect the adjusting entries at the end of the period.

At this point, only the accounts used during the period are entered on the work sheet. Any accounts that are used for the first time during the period because of the adjusting entries will be added in the next step. All but the first two columns of the work sheet should be ignored at this time. Three accounts are included on the work sheet even though they do not have a balance: (1) Accumulated Depreciation—Garage, (2) Accumulated Depreciation—Buses, and (3) Retained Earnings. After this first month of operations, these accounts will have a balance and will appear on an unadjusted trial balance.

STEP 2: THE ADJUSTING ENTRIES COLUMNS

The third and fourth columns of the work sheet have been completed in Exhibit 4-11. Rather than take the time now to prepare adjusting entries and post them to their respective accounts, the accountant makes the entries in these two columns of the work sheet. Formal entries can be made after the financial statements have been prepared. The addition of these two columns to the work sheet requires that the accounts used for the first time in the period be added because of the adjustment process. Letters, which are typically used on a work sheet to identify the adjusting entries, are used here. In practice, the work sheet can be many pages long, and the use of identifying letters makes it easier to locate and match the debit and credit sides of each adjusting entry.

The two columns are totaled to ensure the equality of debits and credits for the adjusting entries. Keep in mind that the entries made in these two columns of the work sheet are *not* the actual adjusting entries; those will be recorded in the journal at a later time, after the financial statements have been prepared.

STEP 3: THE ADJUSTED TRIAL BALANCE COLUMNS

Columns 5 and 6 of the work sheet represent an adjusted trial balance. The amounts entered in these two columns are found by adding or subtracting any debits or credits in the adjusting entries columns to or from the unadjusted balances. For example, Cash is not adjusted; thus the $50,000 unadjusted amount is carried over to the Debit column of the adjusted trial balance. The $2,000 credit adjustment to Prepaid Insurance is subtracted from the unadjusted debit balance of $48,000, resulting in a debit balance of $46,000 on the adjusted trial balance. Finally, note the equality of the debits and credits on the new trial balance, $623,200.

STEP 4: THE INCOME STATEMENT COLUMNS

An adjusted trial balance is the basis for preparing the financial statements. The purpose of the last four columns of the work sheet is to separate the accounts into those that will appear on the income statement and those that will appear on the balance sheet. The income statement columns are completed next.

The three revenue accounts appear in the credit column, and the seven expense accounts appear in the debit column. These amounts are simply carried over, or extended, from the adjusted trial balance. Because Duffy's revenues exceed its expenses, the total of the credit column, $52,900, exceeds the total of the debit column, $39,700. The difference between the two columns, the net income of the period of $13,200, is entered in the debit column. One purpose for showing the net income in this column is to balance the two columns. In addition, the entry in the debit column will be matched with an entry in the balance sheet credit column to represent the transfer of net income to retained earnings. If revenues were *less* than expenses, the *net loss* would be entered in the income statement *credit* column.

STEP 5: THE BALANCE SHEET COLUMNS

Why do the income statement columns appear before the balance sheet columns on the work sheet? The income statement is in fact a *subset* of the balance sheet, and information from the income statement columns flows into the balance sheet columns. Recall that net income causes an increase in the owners' claim to the assets (i.e., an increase in stockholders' equity) through the Retained Earnings account and, thus, is entered in the balance sheet credit column of the work sheet. In Exhibit 4-11, the amount of *net income*, $13,200, is carried over from the debit column of the income statement to the credit column of the balance sheet. If a company experiences a *net loss* for the period, the amount of the loss is entered in the credit column of the income statement and in the debit column of the balance sheet.

You will note that the Retained Earnings account has a zero balance in the last column of the work sheet because this is the first month of operations for Duffy Transit Company. On future work sheets, the account will reflect the balance from the end of the previous month. Dividends appear in the debit column, and net income appears in the credit column. Thus, the ending balance of Retained Earnings can be found by taking its beginning balance, adding the net income of the period, and deducting the dividends. The completed work sheet provides all of the information necessary to prepare an income statement, a statement of retained earnings, and a balance sheet.

Note: A review problem based on this appendix appears on page 189.

POD REVIEW 4.8

LO8 *Understand how to use a work sheet as a basis for preparing financial statements.*

- A work sheet is a useful device for organizing the information necessary to prepare financial statements without going through the formal process of recording and posting adjusting entries.
  - The format for a work sheet includes two columns each (debits and credits) for the unadjusted trial balance, the adjustments, the adjusted trial balance, the income statement, and the balance sheet.

QUESTIONS

1. *A work sheet*
   a. is not one of the financial statements.
   b. is one of the four basic financial statements.
   c. should be prepared at the beginning of each accounting period.
   d. none of the above.

2. *Which of the following sets of columns on a work sheet is* not *in the correct order?*
   a. Unadjusted trial balance and Adjusting entries
   b. Balance sheet and Income statement
   c. Adjusted trial balance and Income statement
   d. All of the above are in the correct order.

ACCOUNTS HIGHLIGHTED

Account Titles	Where It Appears	In What Section	Page Number
Prepaid Insurance	Balance Sheet	Current Assets	163
Accumulated Depreciation	Balance Sheet	Noncurrent Assets (contra)	164
Deferred Revenue	Balance Sheet	Current Liabilities*	166
Wages Payable	Balance Sheet	Current Liabilities	167
Interest Payable	Balance Sheet	Current Liabilities	169
Rent Receivable	Balance Sheet	Current Assets	170

**If any part of deferred revenue will not be earned within the next year, it should be classified as a noncurrent liability.*

KEY TERMS QUIZ

Read each definition below and write the number of the definition in the blank beside the appropriate term. The quiz solutions appear at the end of the chapter.

_______ **Recognition**
_______ **Historical cost**
_______ **Current value**
_______ **Cash basis**
_______ **Accrual basis**
_______ **Revenues**
_______ **Revenue recognition principle**
_______ **Matching principle**
_______ **Expenses**
_______ **Adjusting entries**
_______ **Straight-line method**
_______ **Contra account**
_______ **Deferral**
_______ **Deferred expense**
_______ **Deferred revenue**
_______ **Accrual**
_______ **Accrued liability**
_______ **Accrued asset**
_______ **Accounting cycle**
_______ **Work sheet**
_______ **Real accounts**
_______ **Nominal accounts**
_______ **Closing entries**
_______ **Interim statements**

1. A device used at the end of the period to gather the information needed to prepare financial statements without actually recording and posting adjusting entries.
2. Inflows or other enhancements of assets or settlements of liabilities from delivering or producing goods, rendering services, or conducting other activities.
3. Journal entries made at the end of a period by a company using the accrual basis of accounting.
4. Journal entries made at the end of the period to return the balance in all nominal accounts to zero and transfer the net income or loss and the dividends of the period to Retained Earnings.
5. A liability resulting from the receipt of cash before the recognition of revenue.
6. The name given to balance sheet accounts because they are permanent and are not closed at the end of the period.
7. An asset resulting from the recognition of a revenue before the receipt of cash.
8. The amount of cash or its equivalent that could be received by selling an asset currently.
9. The assignment of an equal amount of depreciation to each period.
10. Cash has been paid or received but expense or revenue has not yet been recognized.
11. A system of accounting in which revenues are recognized when earned and expenses are recognized when incurred.
12. Cash has not yet been paid or received but expense has been incurred or revenue earned.
13. Financial statements prepared monthly, quarterly, or at other intervals less than a year in duration.

14. Revenues are recognized in the income statement when they are realized, or realizable, and earned.
15. The process of recording an item in the financial statements as an asset, a liability, a revenue, an expense, or the like.
16. An asset resulting from the payment of cash before the incurrence of expense.
17. The name given to revenue, expense, and dividend accounts because they are temporary and are closed at the end of the period.
18. A system of accounting in which revenues are recognized when cash is received and expenses are recognized when cash is paid.
19. A liability resulting from the recognition of an expense before the payment of cash.
20. The association of revenue of a period with all of the costs necessary to generate that revenue.
21. An account with a balance that is opposite that of a related account.
22. The amount that is paid for an asset and that is used as a basis for recognizing it on the balance sheet and carrying it on later balance sheets.
23. Outflows or other using up of assets or incurrences of liabilities resulting from delivering goods, rendering services, or carrying out other activities.
24. A series of steps performed each period and culminating with the preparation of a set of financial statements.

ALTERNATE TERMS

Historical cost Original cost

Asset Unexpired cost

Deferred expense Prepaid expense, prepaid asset

Deferred revenue Unearned revenue

Expense Expired cost

Nominal account Temporary account

Real account Permanent account

WARMUP EXERCISES & SOLUTIONS

LO5

Warmup Exercise 4-1 Prepaid Insurance

ABC Corp. purchases a 24-month fire insurance policy on January 1, 2008, for $5,400.

Required

Prepare the necessary adjusting journal entry on January 31, 2008.

Key to the Solution Determine what proportion and therefore what dollar amount of the policy has expired after one month.

LO5

Warmup Exercise 4-2 Depreciation

DEF Corp. purchased a new car for one of its salespeople on March 1, 2008, for $25,000. The estimated useful life of the car is four years with an estimated salvage value of $1,000.

Required

Prepare the necessary adjusting journal entry on March 31, 2008.

Key to the Solution Determine what dollar amount of the cost of the car should be depreciated and what amount should be depreciated each month.

LO5

Warmup Exercise 4-3 Interest on a Note

On April 1, 2008, GHI Corp. took out a 12%, 120-day, $10,000 loan at its bank.

Required

Prepare the necessary adjusting journal entry on April 30, 2008.

Key to the Solution Determine the monthly interest cost on a loan that accrues interest at the rate of 12% per year.

SOLUTIONS TO WARMUP EXERCISES

Warmup Exercise 4-1

Jan. 31	Insurance Expense	225	
	Prepaid Insurance		225
	To recognize $225 of insurance expense for the month.		

Balance Sheet						Income Statement
ASSETS	=	LIABILITIES	+	STOCKHOLDERS' EQUITY	+	REVENUES – EXPENSES
Prepaid Insurance (225)						Insurance Expense (225)

Warmup Exercise 4-2

Mar. 31	Depreciation Expense	500	
	Accumulated Depreciation		500
	To recognize depreciation on car.		

Balance Sheet						Income Statement
ASSETS	=	LIABILITIES	+	STOCKHOLDERS' EQUITY	+	REVENUES – EXPENSES
Accumulated Depreciation (500)						Depreciation Expense (500)

Warmup Exercise 4-3

Apr. 30	Interest Expense	100	
	Interest Payable		100
	To record interest for one month on a 12%, $10,000 loan.		

Balance Sheet						Income Statement
ASSETS	=	LIABILITIES	+	STOCKHOLDERS' EQUITY	+	REVENUES – EXPENSES
		Interest Payable 100				Interest Expense (100)

REVIEW PROBLEM & SOLUTION

The trial balance of Northern Airlines at January 31 is shown. It was prepared after posting the recurring transactions for the month of January, but it does not reflect any month-end adjustments.

Northern Airlines
Unadjusted Trial Balance
January 31

Cash	$ 75,000	
Parts Inventory	45,000	
Land	80,000	
Buildings—Hangars	250,000	
Accumulated Depreciation—Hangars		$ 24,000
Equipment—Aircraft	650,000	
Accumulated Depreciation—Aircraft		120,000
Tickets Sold in Advance		85,000
Capital Stock		500,000
Retained Earnings		368,000
Ticket Revenue		52,000
Maintenance Expense	19,000	
Wage and Salary Expense	30,000	
Totals	$1,149,000	$1,149,000

The following additional information is available:

a. Airplane parts needed for repairs and maintenance are purchased regularly, and the amounts paid are added to the asset account Parts Inventory. At the end of each month, the inventory is counted. At the end of January, the amount of parts on hand is $36,100. *Hint:* What adjusting entry is needed to reduce the asset account to its proper carrying value? Any expense involved should be included in Maintenance Expense.
b. The estimated useful life of the hangar is 20 years with an estimated salvage value of $10,000 at the end of its life. The original cost of the hangar was $250,000.
c. The estimated useful life of the aircraft is ten years with an estimated salvage value of $50,000. The original cost of the aircraft was $650,000.
d. As tickets are sold in advance, the amounts are added to Cash and to the liability account Tickets Sold in Advance. A count of the redeemed tickets reveals that $47,000 worth of tickets were used during January.
e. Wages and salaries owed but unpaid to employees at the end of January total $7,600.
f. Northern rents excess hangar space to other companies. The amount owed but unpaid to Northern at the end of January is $2,500.
g. Assume a corporate income tax rate of 34%.

Required

1. Set up T accounts for each of the accounts listed on the trial balance. Set up any other T accounts that will be needed to prepare adjusting entries.
2. Post the month-end adjusting entries directly to the T accounts; do not take time to put the entries in journal format first. Use the letters (a) through (g) from the additional information to identify each entry.
3. Prepare a trial balance to prove the equality of debits and credits after posting the adjusting entries.

SOLUTION TO REVIEW PROBLEM

1. and 2.

Cash

Bal.	75,000		

Parts Inventory

Bal.	45,000		
		8,900	(a)
Bal.	36,100		

Land

Bal.	80,000		

Buildings—Hangars

Bal.	250,000		

Accumulated Depreciation—Hangars

		24,000	Bal.
		1,000	(b)
		25,000	Bal.

Equipment—Aircraft

Bal.	650,000		

Accumulated Depreciation—Aircraft

		120,000	Bal.
		5,000	(c)
		125,000	Bal.

Tickets Sold in Advance

		85,000	Bal.
(d)	47,000		
		38,000	Bal.

Capital Stock

		500,000	Bal.

Retained Earnings

		368,000	Bal.

Ticket Revenue

		52,000	Bal.
		47,000	(d)
		99,000	Bal.

Maintenance Expense

Bal.	19,000		
(a)	8,900		
Bal.	27,900		

Wage and Salary Expense			
Bal.	30,000		
(e)	7,600		
Bal.	37,600		

Depreciation Expense—Hangars			
(b)	1,000		

Depreciation Expense—Aircraft			
(c)	5,000		

Rent Receivable			
(f)	2,500		

Rent Revenue			
		2,500	(f)

Wages and Salaries Payable			
		7,600	(e)

Income Tax Expense			
(g)	10,200		

Income Taxes Payable			
		10,200	(g)

3.

Northern Airlines
Adjusted Trial Balance
January 31

Cash	$ 75,000	
Parts Inventory	36,100	
Land	80,000	
Buildings—Hangars	250,000	
Accumulated Depreciation—Hangars		$ 25,000
Equipment—Aircraft	650,000	
Accumulated Depreciation—Aircraft		125,000
Tickets Sold in Advance		38,000
Capital Stock		500,000
Retained Earnings		368,000
Ticket Revenue		99,000
Maintenance Expense	27,900	
Wage and Salary Expense	37,600	
Depreciation Expense—Hangars	1,000	
Depreciation Expense—Aircraft	5,000	
Rent Receivable	2,500	
Rent Revenue		2,500
Wages and Salaries Payable		7,600
Income Tax Expense	10,200	
Income Taxes Payable		10,200
Totals	$1,175,300	$1,175,300

APPENDIX REVIEW PROBLEM

Note to the Student: The following problem is based on the information for the Northern Airlines review problem you just completed. Try to prepare the work sheet without referring to the adjusting entries you prepared in solving that problem.

Required

Refer to the unadjusted trial balance and the additional information for Northern Airlines. Prepare a ten-column work sheet for the month of January.

REVIEW

SOLUTION TO REVIEW PROBLEM

Northern Airlines
Work Sheet
For the Month Ended January 31

Account Titles	Unadjusted Trial Balance Debit	Unadjusted Trial Balance Credit	Adjusting Entries Debit	Adjusting Entries Credit	Adjusted Trial Balance Debit	Adjusted Trial Balance Credit	Income Statement Debit	Income Statement Credit	Balance Sheet Debit	Balance Sheet Credit
Cash	75,000				75,000				75,000	
Parts Inventory	45,000			(a) 8,900	36,100				36,100	
Land	80,000				80,000				80,000	
Buildings—Hangars	250,000				250,000				250,000	
Accumulated Depreciation—Hangars		24,000		(b) 1,000		25,000				25,000
Equipment—Aircraft	650,000				650,000				650,000	
Accumulated Depreciation—Aircraft		120,000		(c) 5,000		125,000				125,000
Tickets Sold in Advance		85,000	(d) 47,000			38,000				38,000
Capital Stock		500,000				500,000				500,000
Retained Earnings		368,000				368,000				368,000
Ticket Revenue		52,000		(d) 47,000		99,000		99,000		
Maintenance Expense	19,000		(a) 8,900		27,900		27,900			
Wage and Salary Expense	30,000		(e) 7,600		37,600		37,600			
	1,149,000	1,149,000								
Depreciation Expense—Hangars			(b) 1,000		1,000		1,000			
Depreciation Expense—Aircraft			(c) 5,000		5,000		5,000			
Rent Receivable			(f) 2,500		2,500				2,500	
Income Tax Expense			(g) 10,200		10,200		10,200			
Wages and Salaries Payable				(e) 7,600		7,600				7,600
Rent Revenue				(f) 2,500		2,500		2,500		
Income Taxes Payable				(g) 10,200		10,200				10,200
			82,200	82,200	1,175,300	1,175,300	81,700	101,500	1,093,600	1,073,800
Net Income							19,800			19,800
							101,500	101,500	1,093,600	1,093,600

QUESTIONS

1. What is meant by the following statement? The items depicted in financial statements are merely *representations* of the real thing.
2. What is the meaning of the following statement? The choice between historical cost and current value is a good example of the trade-off in accounting between relevance and reliability.
3. A realtor earns a 10% commission on the sale of a $150,000 home. The realtor lists the home on June 5, the sale occurs on June 12, and the seller pays the realtor the $15,000 commission on July 8. When should the realtor recognize revenue from the sale assuming (a) the cash basis of accounting and (b) the accrual basis of accounting?
4. What does the following statement mean? If I want to assess the cash flow prospects for a company "down the road," I look at the company's most recent statement of cash flows. An income statement prepared under the accrual basis of accounting is useless for this purpose.
5. What is the relationship between the time period assumption and accrual accounting?
6. Is it necessary for an asset to be acquired when revenue is recognized? Explain your answer.
7. A friend says to you: "I just don't get it. Assets cost money. Expenses reduce income. There must be some relationship among assets, costs, and expenses—I'm just not sure what it is!" What is the relationship? Can you give an example of it?
8. What is the meaning of *depreciation* to the accountant?
9. What are the four basic types of adjusting entries? Give an example of each.
10. What are the rules of debit and credit as they apply to the contra asset account Accumulated Depreciation?
11. Which of the following steps in the accounting cycle requires the most thought and judgment by the accountant: (a) preparing a trial balance, (b) posting adjusting and closing entries, or (c) analyzing and recording transactions? Explain your answer.
12. What is the difference between a real account and a nominal account?
13. What two purposes are served in making closing entries?
14. Why is the Dividends account closed directly to Retained Earnings rather than to the Income Summary account?
15. Assuming the use of a work sheet, are the formal adjusting entries recorded and posted to the accounts before or after the financial statements are prepared? Explain your answer. Would your answer change if a work sheet was not prepared? Explain. (Appendix)
16. Some companies use an eight-column work sheet rather than the ten-column format illustrated in the chapter. Which two columns are not used in the eight-column format? Why could these two columns be eliminated? (Appendix)
17. Why do the income statement columns appear before the balance sheet columns on a work sheet? (Appendix)
18. Does the Retained Earnings account that appears in the balance sheet credit column of a work sheet reflect the beginning or the ending balance in the account? Explain your answer. (Appendix)
19. One asset account will always be carried over from the unadjusted trial balance columns of a work sheet to the balance sheet columns of the work sheet without any adjustment. What account is this? (Appendix)

BRIEF EXERCISES

LO1 **Brief Exercise 4-1** Measurement in Financial Statements

What are two possible attributes to be measured when an item is to be included in financial statements? What unit of money is used to measure items in the United States?

LO2 **Brief Exercise 4-2** Accrual Basis of Accounting

For the following situations, indicate the date on which revenue would be recognized, assuming the accrual basis of accounting.

_______ a. On June 10, a customer orders a product over the phone. The product is shipped to the customer on June 14, and the customer pays the amount owed on July 10.

_______ b. On March 15, a law firm agrees to draft a legal document for a client. The document is completed and delivered to the client on April 5, and the client pays the amount owed on May 2.

_______ c. A homeowner signs a contract on August 6 to have a company install a central air conditioning system. The work is completed on August 30, and the homeowner pays the amount owed on September 25.

LO3 **Brief Exercise 4-3** Revenue Recognition

Explain whether a company must have an inflow of an asset to be able to recognize revenue. Also give two examples of situations in which revenue is earned continuously over a period of time.

LO4

Brief Exercise 4-4 Matching Principle

Assume that a company purchases merchandise for resale on December 20, 2008. The merchandise is still on hand on December 31, the company's year-end. On January 12, 2009, the merchandise is sold to a customer. Explain how the merchandise will be treated on any of the financial statements at year-end. In which year will revenue from the sale be recorded? In which year will cost of goods sold expense be recorded?

LO5

Brief Exercise 4-5 Adjusting Entries

For the following situations, indicate the type of account to be debited and credited in a year-end adjusting entry. Use the following legend: A = Asset; L = Liability; R = Revenue; E = Expense.

Debit	Credit	Situation
_____	_____	1. A company owes employees for wages earned but not yet paid.
_____	_____	2. Rent is earned for the month, and the tenant is given until the 10th of the following month to pay.
_____	_____	3. A portion of an insurance policy paid for in advance has expired.
_____	_____	4. A gift card is redeemed by its recipient.

LO6

Brief Exercise 4-6 Steps in the Accounting Cycle

Recall the steps in the accounting cycle shown in Exhibit 4-8. Assume that a company does not prepare a work sheet. Which of the two remaining steps in the accounting cycle are performed in a different order than they would be if a work sheet were prepared? Explain your answer.

LO7

Brief Exercise 4-7 Closing Entries

For the following accounts, indicate whether each would be (Yes) or would not be (No) closed at the end of the accounting period.

_____	1. Prepaid insurance	_____	5. Depreciation expense
_____	2. Supplies expense	_____	6. Accumulated depreciation
_____	3. Capital stock	_____	7. Cash
_____	4. Sales revenue	_____	8. Income tax expense

LO8

Brief Exercise 4-8 Work Sheet

Explain why the income statement columns come before the balance sheet columns on a work sheet.

EXERCISES

LO3

Exercise 4-1 Revenue Recognition

The highway department contracted with a private company to collect tolls and maintain facilities on a turnpike. Users of the turnpike can pay cash as they approach the toll booth, or they can purchase a pass. The pass is equipped with an electronic sensor that subtracts the toll fee from the pass balance as the motorist slowly approaches a special toll booth. The passes are issued in $10 increments. Refunds are available to motorists who do not use the pass balance, but they are issued very infrequently. Last year $3,000,000 was collected at the traditional toll booths, $2,000,000 of passes were issued, and $1,700,000 of passes were used at the special toll booth. How much should the company recognize as revenue for the year? Explain how the revenue recognition rule should be applied in this case.

LO4

Exercise 4-2 The Matching Principle

Three methods of matching costs with revenue were described in the chapter: (a) directly match a specific form of revenue with a cost incurred in generating that revenue, (b) indirectly match a cost with the periods during which it will provide benefits or revenue, and (c) immediately recognize a cost incurred as an expense because no future benefits are expected. For each of the following costs, indicate how it is normally recognized as expense by indicating either (a), (b), or (c). If you think that more than one answer is possible for any of the situations, explain why.

1. New office copier
2. Monthly bill from the utility company for electricity
3. Office supplies
4. Biweekly payroll for office employees
5. Commissions earned by salespeople
6. Interest incurred on a six-month loan from the bank
7. Cost of inventory sold during the current period
8. Taxes owed on income earned during current period
9. Cost of three-year insurance policy

LO5

Exercise 4-3 Accruals and Deferrals

For the following situations, indicate whether each involves a deferred expense (DE), a deferred revenue (DR), an accrued liability (AL), or an accrued asset (AA).

Example: __DE__ Office supplies purchased in advance of their use

______ 1. Wages earned by employees but not yet paid

______ 2. Cash collected from subscriptions in advance of publishing a magazine

______ 3. Interest earned on a customer loan for which principal and interest have not yet been collected

______ 4. One year's premium on life insurance policy paid in advance

______ 5. Office building purchased for cash

______ 6. Rent collected in advance from a tenant

______ 7. State income taxes owed at the end of the year

______ 8. Rent owed by a tenant but not yet collected

LO5

Exercise 4-4 Office Supplies

Somerville Corp. purchases office supplies once a month and prepares monthly financial statements. The asset account Office Supplies on Hand has a balance of $1,450 on May 1. Purchases of supplies during May amount to $1,100. Supplies on hand at May 31 amount to $920. Prepare the necessary adjusting entry on Somerville's books on May 31. What will be the effect on net income for May if this entry is *not* recorded?

LO5

Exercise 4-5 Prepaid Rent—Quarterly Adjustments

On September 1, Northhampton Industries signed a six-month lease for office space, which is effective September 1. Northhampton agreed to prepay the rent and mailed a check for $12,000 to the landlord on September 1. Assume that Northhampton prepares adjusting entries only four times a year: on March 31, June 30, September 30, and December 31.

Required

1. Compute the rental cost for each full month.
2. Prepare the journal entry to record the payment of rent on September 1.
3. Prepare the adjusting entry on September 30.
4. Assume that the accountant prepares the adjusting entry on September 30 but forgets to record an adjusting entry on December 31. Will net income for the year be understated or overstated? by what amount?

LO5

Exercise 4-6 Depreciation

On July 1, 2008, Red Gate Farm buys a combine for $100,000 in cash. Assume that the combine is expected to have a seven-year life and an estimated salvage value of $16,000 at the end of that time.

Required

1. Prepare the journal entry to record the purchase of the combine on July 1, 2008.
2. Compute the depreciable cost of the combine.
3. Using the straight-line method, compute the monthly depreciation.
4. Prepare the adjusting entry to record depreciation at the end of July 2008.
5. Compute the combine's carrying value that will be shown on Red Gate's balance sheet prepared on December 31, 2008.

LO5

Exercise 4-7 Prepaid Insurance—Annual Adjustments

On April 1, 2008, Briggs Corp. purchases a 24-month property insurance policy for $72,000. The policy is effective immediately. Assume that Briggs prepares adjusting entries only once a year, on December 31.

Required

1. Compute the monthly cost of the insurance policy.
2. Prepare the journal entry to record the purchase of the policy on April 1, 2008.
3. Prepare the adjusting entry on December 31, 2008.
4. Assume that the accountant forgets to record an adjusting entry on December 31, 2008. Will net income for the year ended December 31, 2008, be understated or overstated? Explain your answer.

LO5

Exercise 4-8 Subscriptions

Horse Country Living publishes a monthly magazine for which a 12-month subscription costs $30. All subscriptions require payment of the full $30 in advance. On August 1, 2008, the balance in the Subscriptions Received in Advance account was $40,500. During the month of August, the company sold 900 yearly subscriptions. After the adjusting entry at the end of August, the balance in the Subscriptions Received in Advance account is $60,000.

Required

1. Prepare the journal entry to record the sale of the 900 yearly subscriptions during the month of August.
2. Prepare the adjusting journal entry on August 31.
3. Assume that the accountant made the correct entry during August to record the sale of the 900 subscriptions but forgot to make the adjusting entry on August 31. Would net income for August be overstated or understated? Explain your answer.

LO5

Exercise 4-9 Customer Deposits

Wolfe & Wolfe collected $9,000 from a customer on April 1 and agreed to provide legal services during the next three months. Wolfe & Wolfe expects to provide an equal amount of services each month.

Required

1. Prepare the journal entry for the receipt of the customer deposit on April 1.
2. Prepare the adjusting entry on April 30.
3. What will be the effect on net income for April if the entry in (2) is not recorded?

LO5

Exercise 4-10 Wages Payable

Denton Corporation employs 50 workers in its plant. Each employee is paid $10 per hour and works seven hours per day, Monday through Friday. Employees are paid every Friday. The last payday was Friday, October 20.

Required

1. Compute the dollar amount of the weekly payroll.
2. Prepare the journal entry on Friday, October 27, for the payment of the weekly payroll.
3. Denton prepares monthly financial statements. Prepare the adjusting journal entry on Tuesday, October 31, the last day of the month.
4. Prepare the journal entry on Friday, November 3, for the payment of the weekly payroll.
5. Will net income for the month of October be understated or overstated if Denton doesn't bother with an adjusting entry on October 31? Explain your answer.

LO5

Exercise 4-11 Interest Payable

Billings Company takes out a 12%, 90-day, $100,000 loan with First National Bank on March 1, 2008.

Required

1. Prepare the journal entry on March 1, 2008.
2. Prepare the adjusting entries for the months of March and April 2008.
3. Prepare the entry on May 30, 2008, when Billings repays the principal and interest to First National.

LO5

Exercise 4-12 Property Taxes Payable—Annual Adjustments

Lexington Builders owns property in Kaneland County. Lexington's 2007 property taxes amounted to $50,000. Kaneland County will send out the 2008 property tax bills to property owners during April 2009. Taxes must be paid by June 1, 2009. Assume that Lexington prepares adjusting entries only once a year, on December 31, and that property taxes for 2008 are expected to increase by 5% over those for 2007.

Required

1. Prepare the adjusting entry required to record the property taxes payable on December 31, 2008.
2. Prepare the journal entry to record the payment of the 2008 property taxes on June 1, 2009.

LO5

Exercise 4-13 Interest Receivable

On June 1, 2008, MicroTel Enterprises lends $60,000 to MaxiDriver Inc. The loan will be repaid in 60 days with interest at 10%.

Required

1. Prepare the journal entry on MicroTel's books on June 1, 2008.
2. Prepare the adjusting entry on MicroTel's books on June 30, 2008.
3. Prepare the entry on MicroTel's books on July 31, 2008, when MaxiDriver repays the principal and interest.

LO5

Exercise 4-14 Unbilled Accounts Receivable

Mike and Cary repair computers for small local businesses. Heavy thunderstorms during the last week of June resulted in a record number of service calls. Eager to review the results of operations for the month of June, Mike prepared an income statement and was puzzled by the lower-than-expected amount of revenues. Cary explained that he had not yet billed the company's customers for $40,000 of work performed during the last week of the month.

Required

1. Should revenue be recorded when services are performed or when customers are billed? Explain your answer.
2. Prepare the adjusting entry required on June 30.

LO5

Exercise 4-15 The Effect of Ignoring Adjusting Entries on Net Income

For each of the following independent situations, determine whether the effect of ignoring the required adjusting entry will result in an understatement (U), will result in an overstatement (O), or will have no effect (NE) on net income for the period.

Situation	Effect on Net Income
Example: Taxes owed but not yet paid are ignored.	O
1. A company fails to record depreciation on equipment.	______
2. Sales made during the last week of the period are not recorded.	______
3. A company neglects to record the expired portion of a prepaid insurance policy. (Its cost was originally debited to an asset account.)	______
4. Interest due but not yet paid on a long-term note payable is ignored.	______
5. Commissions earned by salespeople but not payable until the 10th of the following month are ignored.	______
6. A landlord receives cash on the date a lease is signed for the rent for the first six months and credits Unearned Rent Revenue. The landlord fails to make any adjustment at the end of the first month.	______

LO5

Exercise 4-16 The Effect of Adjusting Entries on the Accounting Equation

Determine whether recording each of the following adjusting entries will increase (I), decrease (D), or have no effect (NE) on each of the three elements of the accounting equation.

	Assets	= Liabilities	+ Stock. Equity
Example: Wages earned during the period but not yet paid are accrued.	NE	I	D
1. Prepaid insurance is reduced for the portion of the policy that has expired during the period.	____	____	____
2. Interest incurred during the period but not yet paid is accrued.	____	____	____
3. Depreciation for the period is recorded.	____	____	____
4. Revenue is recorded for the earned portion of a liability for amounts collected in advance from customers.	____	____	____
5. Rent revenue is recorded for amounts owed by a tenant but not yet received.	____	____	____
6. Income taxes owed but not yet paid are accrued.	____	____	____

LO5

Exercise 4-17 Reconstruction of Adjusting Entries from Unadjusted and Adjusted Trial Balances

Following are the unadjusted and adjusted trial balances for Power Corp. on May 31, 2008:

	Unadjusted Trial Balance		Adjusted Trial Balance	
	Debit	**Credit**	**Debit**	**Credit**
Cash	$ 3,160		$ 3,160	
Accounts Receivable	7,300		9,650	
Supplies on Hand	400		160	
Prepaid Rent	2,400		2,200	
Equipment	9,000		9,000	
Accumulated Depreciation		$ 2,800		$ 3,200
Accounts Payable		2,600		2,600
Capital Stock		5,000		5,000
Retained Earnings		8,990		8,990
Service Revenue		6,170		8,520
Promotions Expense	2,050		2,050	
Wage Expense	1,250		2,350	
Wages Payable				1,100
Supplies Expense			240	
Depreciation Expense			400	
Rent Expense			200	
Totals	$25,560	$25,560	$29,410	$29,410

Required

1. Reconstruct the adjusting entries that were made on Power's books at the end of May.
2. By how much would Power's net income for May have been overstated or understated (indicate which) if these adjusting entries had not been recorded?

LO6

Exercise 4-18 The Accounting Cycle

The steps in the accounting cycle are listed in random order. Fill in the blank next to each step to indicate its order in the cycle. The first step in the cycle is filled in as an example.

Order	Procedure
____	Prepare a work sheet.
____	Close the accounts.
1	Collect and analyze information from source documents.
____	Prepare financial statements.
____	Post transactions to accounts in the ledger.
____	Record and post adjusting entries.
____	Journalize daily transactions.

LO6

Exercise 4-19 Trial Balance

The following account titles, arranged in alphabetical order, are from the records of Hadley Realty Corporation. The balance in each account is the normal balance for that account. The balances are as of December 31, after adjusting entries have been made. Prepare an adjusted trial balance, listing the accounts in the following order: (1) assets; (2) liabilities; (3) stockholders' equity accounts, including dividends; (4) revenues; and (5) expenses.

Accounts Payable	$12,300	Interest Expense	$ 200
Accounts Receivable	21,230	Interest Payable	200
Accumulated Depreciation—Automobiles	12,000	Land	40,000
Accumulated Depreciation—Buildings	15,000	Notes Payable	20,000
Automobiles	48,000	Office Supplies	1,680
Buildings	60,000	Office Supplies Expense	5,320
Capital Stock	25,000	Prepaid Insurance	1,200
Cash	2,460	Rent Expense	2,400
Commissions Earned	17,420	Retained Earnings	85,445
Commissions Expense	2,300	Wages and Salaries Expense	1,245
Dividends	1,500	Wages and Salaries Payable	470
Insurance Expense	300		

LO7

Exercise 4-20 Closing Entries

At the end of the year, the adjusted trial balance for Devonshire Corporation contains the following amounts for the income statement accounts. (The balance in each account is the normal balance for that type of account.)

Account	Balance
Advertising Fees Earned	$58,500
Interest Revenue	2,700
Wage and Salary Expense	14,300
Utilities Expense	12,500
Insurance Expense	7,300
Depreciation Expense	16,250
Interest Expense	2,600
Income Tax Expense	3,300
Dividends	2,000

Required

1. Prepare all necessary journal entries to close Devonshire Corporation's accounts at the end of the year.
2. Assume that the accountant for Devonshire forgets to record the closing entries. What will be the effect on net income for the *following* year? Explain your answer.

LO7

Exercise 4-21 Preparation of a Statement of Retained Earnings from Closing Entries

Fisher Corporation reported a Retained Earnings balance of $125,780 on January 1, 2008. Fisher Corporation made the following three closing entries on December 31, 2008. (The entry to transfer net income to Retained Earnings was intentionally omitted.) Prepare a statement of retained earnings for Fisher for the year.

Dec. 31	Service Revenue	65,400	
	Interest Revenue	20,270	
	Income Summary		85,670
31	Income Summary	62,345	
	Salary and Wage Expense		23,450
	Rent Expense		20,120
	Interest Expense		4,500
	Utilities Expense		10,900
	Insurance Expense		3,375
31	Retained Earnings	6,400	
	Dividends		6,400

LO7

Exercise 4-22 Reconstruction of Closing Entries

The following T accounts summarize entries made to selected general ledger accounts of Cooper & Company. Certain entries, dated December 31, are closing entries. Prepare the closing entries that were made on December 31.

Maintenance Revenue

12/31	90,000	64,000	12/1 bal.
		13,000	12/15
		13,000	12/30

Wages Expense

12/1 bal.	11,000	12,000	12/31
12/15	500		
12/30	500		

Supplies Expense

12/1 bal.	2,500	2,750	12/31
12/31	250		

Retained Earnings

12/31	5,000	45,600	12/1 bal.
		75,250	12/31

Dividends

12/1 bal.	5,000	5,000	12/31

Income Summary

12/31	14,750	90,000	12/31
12/31	75,250		

LO7

Exercise 4-23 Closing Entries for Nordstrom

The following accounts appear on **Nordstrom**'s 2006 financial statements. The accounts are listed in alphabetical order, and the balance in each account is the normal balance for that account. All amounts are in thousands of dollars. Prepare closing entries for Nordstrom for 2006.

Cash dividends paid	$ 110,158
Cost of sales and related buying and occupancy costs	5,353,949
Income tax expense	427,654
Interest expense, net	42,758
Other income including finance charges, net	238,525
Net sales	8,560,698
Selling, general and administrative expenses	2,296,863

LO7

Exercise 4-24 Closing Entries

Royston Realty reported the following accounts on its income statement:

Commissions Earned	$54,000	Travel and Entertainment	$4,500
Real Estate Board Fees Paid	5,000	Insurance Expired	780
Computer Line Charge	864	Advertising Expense	1,460
Depreciation on Computer	450	Office Supplies Used	940
Car Expenses	2,200		

Required

1. Prepare the necessary entries to close the temporary accounts.
2. Explain why the closing entries are necessary and when they should be recorded.

LO8

Exercise 4-25 The Difference between a Financial Statement and a Work Sheet (Appendix)

The balance sheet columns of the work sheet for Jones Corporation show total debits and total credits of $255,000 each. Dividends for the period are $3,000. Accumulated depreciation is $14,000 at the end of the period. Compute the amount that should appear on the balance sheet (i.e., the formal financial statement) for *total assets*. How do you explain the difference between this amount and the amount that appears as the total debits and total credits on the work sheet?

LO8

Exercise 4-26 Ten-Column Work Sheet (Appendix)

Indicate whether the amount in each of the following accounts should be carried over from the adjusted trial balance column of the work sheet to the income statement (IS) column or to the balance sheet (BS) column. Also indicate whether the account normally has a debit (D) balance or a credit (C) balance.

BS-D **Example:** Cash

______ 1. Accumulated Depreciation—Trucks
______ 2. Subscriptions Sold in Advance
______ 3. Accounts Receivable
______ 4. Dividends
______ 5. Capital Stock
______ 6. Prepaid Insurance
______ 7. Depreciation Expense—Trucks
______ 8. Office Supplies
______ 9. Office Supplies Expense
______ 10. Subscription Revenue
______ 11. Interest Receivable
______ 12. Interest Revenue
______ 13. Interest Expense
______ 14. Interest Payable
______ 15. Retained Earnings

MULTICONCEPT EXERCISES

LO1,2,3 Exercise 4-27 Revenue Recognition, Cash and Accrual Basis

Hathaway Health Club sold three-year memberships at a reduced rate during its opening promotion. It sold 1,000 three-year nonrefundable memberships for $366 each. The club expects to sell 100 additional three-year memberships for $900 each over each of the next two years. Membership fees are paid when clients sign up. The club's bookkeeper has prepared the following income statement for the first year of business and projected income statements for Years 2 and 3.

Cash-basis income statements:

	Year 1	Year 2	Year 3
Sales	$366,000	$ 90,000	$ 90,000
Equipment*	$100,000	$ 0	$ 0
Salaries and Wages	50,000	50,000	50,000
Advertising	5,000	5,000	5,000
Rent and Utilities	36,000	36,000	36,000
Net income (loss)	$175,000	$ (1,000)	$ (1,000)

**Equipment was purchased at the beginning of Year 1 for $100,000 and is expected to last for three years and then to be worth $1,000.*

Required

1. Convert the income statements for each of the three years to the accrual basis.
2. Describe how the revenue recognition principle applies. Do you believe that the cash-basis or the accrual-basis income statements are more useful to management? to investors? Why?

LO4,5 Exercise 4-28 Depreciation Expense

During 2008, Carter Company acquired three assets with the following costs, estimated useful lives, and estimated salvage values:

Date	Asset	Cost	Estimated Useful Life	Estimated Salvage Value
March 28	Truck	$ 18,000	5 years	$ 3,000
June 22	Computer	55,000	10 years	5,000
October 3	Building	250,000	30 years	10,000

The company uses the straight-line method to depreciate all assets and computes depreciation to the nearest month. For example, the computer system will be depreciated for six months in 2008.

Required

1. Compute the depreciation expense that Carter will record on each of the three assets for 2008.
2. Comment on the following statement: Accountants could save time and money by simply expensing the cost of long-term assets when they are purchased. In addition, this would be more accurate because depreciation requires estimates of useful life and salvage value.

LO4,5 Exercise 4-29 Accrual of Interest on a Loan

On July 1, 2008, Paxson Corporation takes out a 12%, two-month, $50,000 loan at Friendly National Bank. Principal and interest are to be repaid on August 31.

Required

1. Prepare the journal entries for July 1 to record the borrowing, for July 31 to record the accrual of interest, and for August 31 to record repayment of the principal and interest.
2. Evaluate the following statement: It would be much easier not to bother with an adjusting entry on July 31 and simply record interest expense on August 31 when the loan is repaid.

PROBLEMS

LO5

Problem 4-1 Adjusting Entries

Kretz Corporation prepares monthly financial statements and therefore adjusts its accounts at the end of every month. The following information is available for March 2008:

a. Kretz Corporation takes out a 90-day, 8%, $15,000 note on March 1, 2008, with interest and principal to be paid at maturity.
b. The asset account Office Supplies on Hand has a balance of $1,280 on March 1, 2008. During March, Kretz adds $750 to the account for purchases during the period. A count of the supplies on hand at the end of March indicates a balance of $1,370.
c. The company purchased office equipment last year for $62,600. The equipment has an estimated useful life of six years and an estimated salvage value of $5,000.
d. The company's plant operates seven days per week with a daily payroll of $950. Wage earners are paid every Sunday. The last day of the month is Saturday, March 31.
e. The company rented an idle warehouse to a neighboring business on February 1, 2008, at a rate of $2,500 per month. On this date, Kretz Corporation credited Rent Collected in Advance for six months' rent received in advance.
f. On March 1, 2008, Kretz Corporation credited a liability account, Customer Deposits, for $4,800. This sum represents an amount that a customer paid in advance and that Kretz will earn evenly over a four-month period.
g. Based on its income for the month, Kretz Corporation estimates that federal income taxes for March amount to $3,900.

Required

For each of the preceding situations, prepare in general journal form the appropriate adjusting entry to be recorded on March 31, 2008.

LO5

Problem 4-2 Effects of Adjusting Entries on the Accounting Equation

Refer to the information provided for Kretz Corporation in Problem 4-1.

Required

1. Prepare a table to summarize the required adjusting entries as they affect the accounting equation. Use the format in Exhibit 3-1 on page 112. Identify each adjustment by letter.
2. Assume that Kretz reports income of $23,000 before any of the adjusting entries. What net income will Kretz report for March?

LO5

Problem 4-3 Adjusting Entries—Annual Adjustments

Palmer Industries prepares annual financial statements and adjusts its accounts only at the end of the year. The following information is available for the year ended December 31, 2008:

a. Palmer purchased computer equipment two years ago for $15,000. The equipment has an estimated useful life of five years and an estimated salvage value of $250.
b. The Office Supplies account had a balance of $3,600 on January 1, 2008. During 2008, Palmer added $17,600 to the account for purchases of office supplies during the year. A count of the supplies on hand at the end of December 2008 indicates a balance of $1,850.
c. On August 1, 2008, Palmer credited a liability account, Customer Deposits, for $24,000. This sum represents an amount that a customer paid in advance and that will be earned evenly by Palmer over a six-month period.
d. Palmer rented some office space on November 1, 2008, at a rate of $2,700 per month. On that date, Palmer debited Prepaid Rent for three months' rent paid in advance.
e. Palmer took out a 120-day, 9%, $200,000 note on November 1, 2008, with interest and principal to be paid at maturity.
f. Palmer operates five days per week with an average daily payroll of $500. Palmer pays its employees every Thursday. December 31, 2008, is a Wednesday.

Required

1. For each of the preceding situations, prepare in general journal form the appropriate adjusting entry to be recorded on December 31, 2008.
2. Assume that Palmer's accountant forgets to record the adjusting entries on December 31, 2008. Will net income for the year be understated or overstated? by what amount? (Ignore the effect of income taxes.)

LO5

Problem 4-4 Recurring and Adjusting Entries

Following are Butler Realty Corporation's accounts, identified by number. The company has been in the real estate business for ten years and prepares financial statements monthly. Following the list of accounts is a series of transactions entered into by Butler. For each transaction, enter the number(s) of the account(s) to be debited and credited.

Accounts

1. Cash
2. Accounts Receivable
3. Prepaid Rent
4. Office Supplies
5. Automobiles
6. Accumulated Depreciation
7. Land
8. Accounts Payable
9. Salaries and Wages Payable
10. Income Tax Payable
11. Notes Payable
12. Capital Stock, $10 par
13. Paid-In Capital in Excess of Par
14. Commissions Revenue
15. Office Supply Expense
16. Rent Expense
17. Salaries and Wages Expense
18. Depreciation Expense
19. Interest Expense
20. Income Tax Expense

Transaction	Debit	Credit
a. Example: Issued additional shares of stock to owners at amount in excess of par.	1	12, 13
b. Purchased automobiles for cash.	______	______
c. Purchased land; made cash down payment and signed a promissory note for the balance.	______	______
d. Paid cash to landlord for rent for next 12 months.	______	______
e. Purchased office supplies on account.	______	______
f. Collected cash for commissions from clients for properties sold during the month.	______	______
g. Collected cash for commissions from clients for properties sold the prior month.	______	______
h. During the month, sold properties for which cash for commissions will be collected from clients next month.	______	______
i. Paid for office supplies purchased on account in an earlier month.	______	______
j. Recorded an adjustment to recognize wages and salaries incurred but not yet paid.	______	______
k. Recorded an adjustment for office supplies used during the month.	______	______
l. Recorded an adjusting entry for the portion of prepaid rent that expired during the month.	______	______
m. Made required month-end payment on note taken out in (c); payment is part principal and part interest.	______	______
n. Recorded adjusting entry for monthly depreciation on the autos.	______	______
o. Recorded adjusting entry for income taxes.	______	______

LO5

Problem 4-5 Use of Account Balances as a Basis for Adjusting Entries—Annual Adjustments

The following account balances are taken from the records of Chauncey Company at December 31, 2008. The Prepaid Insurance account represents the cost of a three-year policy purchased on August 1, 2008. The Rent Collected in Advance account represents the cash received from a tenant on June 1, 2008, for 12 months' rent beginning on that date. The Note Receivable represents a nine-month promissory note received from a customer on September 1, 2008. Principal and interest at an annual rate of 9% will be received on June 1, 2009.

Prepaid Insurance	$ 7,200 debit	
Rent Collected in Advance		$6,000 credit
Note Receivable	50,000 debit	

Required

1. Prepare the three necessary adjusting entries on the books of Chauncey on December 31, 2008. Assume that Chauncey prepares adjusting entries only once a year, on December 31.
2. Assume that adjusting entries are made at the end of each month rather than only at the end of the year. What would be the balance in Prepaid Insurance *before* the December adjusting entry was made? Explain your answer.

HOMEWORK

LO5

Problem 4-6 Use of a Trial Balance as a Basis for Adjusting Entries

Bob Reynolds operates a real estate business. A trial balance on April 30, 2008, *before* any adjusting entries are recorded, appears as follows:

Reynolds Realty Company
Unadjusted Trial Balance
April 30, 2008

	Debit	Credit
Cash	$15,700	
Prepaid Insurance	450	
Office Supplies	250	
Office Equipment	50,000	
Accumulated Depreciation—Office Equipment		$ 5,000
Automobile	12,000	
Accumulated Depreciation—Automobile		1,400
Accounts Payable		6,500
Unearned Commissions		9,500
Notes Payable		2,000
Capital Stock		10,000
Retained Earnings		40,000
Dividends	2,500	
Commissions Earned		17,650
Utilities Expense	2,300	
Salaries Expense	7,400	
Advertising Expense	1,450	
Totals	$92,050	$92,050

Other Data

a. The monthly insurance cost is $50.
b. Office supplies on hand on April 30, 2008, amount to $180.
c. The office equipment was purchased on April 1, 2007. On that date, it had an estimated useful life of ten years.
d. On September 1, 2007, the automobile was purchased; it had an estimated useful life of five years.
e. A deposit is received in advance of providing any services for first-time customers. Amounts received in advance are recorded initially in the account Unearned Commissions. Based on services provided to these first-time customers, the balance in this account at the end of April should be $5,000.
f. Repeat customers are allowed to pay for services one month after the date of the sale of their property. Services rendered during the month but not yet collected or billed to these customers amount to $1,500.
g. Interest owed on the note payable but not yet paid amounts to $20.
h. Salaries owed but unpaid to employees at the end of the month amount to $2,500.

Required

1. Prepare in general journal form the necessary adjusting entries at April 30, 2008. Label the entries (a) through (h) to correspond to the other data.
2. Note that the unadjusted trial balance reports a credit balance in Accumulated Depreciation—Office Equipment of $5,000. Explain why the account contains a balance of $5,000 on April 30, 2008.

LO5

Problem 4-7 Effects of Adjusting Entries on the Accounting Equation

Refer to the information provided for Reynolds Realty Company in Problem 4-6.

Required

1. Prepare a table to summarize the required adjusting entries as they affect the accounting equation. Use the format in Exhibit 3-1 on page 112. Identify each adjustment by letter.
2. Compute the net increase or decrease in net income for the month from the recognition of the adjusting entries you prepared in (1). (Ignore income taxes.)

LO5

Problem 4-8 Reconstruction of Adjusting Entries from Account Balances

Taggart Corp. records adjusting entries each month before preparing monthly financial statements. The following selected account balances are taken from its trial balances on June 30, 2008. The "unadjusted" columns set forth the general ledger balances before the adjusting entries were posted. The "adjusted" columns reflect the month-end adjusting entries.

	Unadjusted		Adjusted	
Account Title	**Debit**	**Credit**	**Debit**	**Credit**
Prepaid Insurance	$3,600		$3,450	
Equipment	9,600		9,600	
Accumulated Depreciation		$1,280		$1,360
Notes Payable		9,600		9,600
Interest Payable		2,304		2,448

Required

1. The company purchased a 36-month insurance policy on June 1, 2007 . Reconstruct the adjusting journal entry for insurance on June 30, 2008.
2. What was the original cost of the insurance policy? Explain your answer.
3. The equipment was purchased on February 1, 2007, for $9,600. Taggart uses straight-line depreciation and estimates that the equipment will have no salvage value. Reconstruct the adjusting journal entry for depreciation on June 30, 2008.
4. What is the equipment's estimated useful life in months? Explain your answer.
5. Taggart signed a two-year note payable on February 1, 2007, for the purchase of the equipment. Interest on the note accrues on a monthly basis and will be paid at maturity along with the principal amount of $9,600. Reconstruct the adjusting journal entry for interest on June 30, 2008.
6. What is the monthly interest rate on the loan? Explain your answer.

LO5

Problem 4-9 Use of a Trial Balance to Record Adjusting Entries in T Accounts

Four Star Video has been in the video rental business for five years. An unadjusted trial balance at May 31, 2008, follows.

Four Star Video
Unadjusted Trial Balance
May 31, 2008

	Debit	Credit
Cash	$ 4,000	
Prepaid Rent	6,600	
Video Inventory	25,600	
Display Stands	8,900	
Accumulated Depreciation		$ 5,180
Accounts Payable		3,260
Customer Subscriptions		4,450
Capital Stock		5,000
Retained Earnings		22,170
Rental Revenue		9,200
Wage and Salary Expense	2,320	
Utilities Expense	1,240	
Advertising Expense	600	
Totals	$49,260	$49,260

The following additional information is available:

a. Four Star rents a store in a shopping mall and prepays the annual rent of $7,200 on April 1 of each year.

b. The asset account Video Inventory represents the cost of videos purchased from suppliers. When a new title is purchased from a supplier, its cost is debited to this account. When a title has served its useful life and can no longer be rented (even at a reduced price), it is removed from the inventory in the store. Based on the monthly count, the cost of titles on hand at the end of May is $23,140.

c. The display stands have an estimated useful life of five years and an estimated salvage value of $500.
d. Wages and salaries owed but unpaid to employees at the end of May amount to $1,450.
e. In addition to individual rentals, Four Star operates a popular discount subscription program. Customers pay an annual fee of $120 for an unlimited number of rentals. Based on the $10 per month earned on each of these subscriptions, the amount earned for the month of May is $2,440.
f. Four Star accrues income taxes using an estimated tax rate equal to 30% of the income for the month.

Required

1. Set up T accounts for each of the accounts listed in the trial balance. Based on the additional information given, set up any other T accounts that will be needed to prepare adjusting entries.
2. Post the month-end adjusting entries directly to the T accounts but do not bother to put the entries in journal format first. Use the letters (a) through (f) from the additional information to identify the entries.
3. Prepare a trial balance to prove the equality of debits and credits after posting the adjusting entries.
4. On the basis of the information you have, does Four Star appear to be a profitable business? Explain your answer.

LO5

Problem 4-10 Effects of Adjusting Entries on the Accounting Equation

Refer to the information provided for Four Star Video in Problem 4-9.

Required

Prepare a table to summarize the required adjusting entries as they affect the accounting equation. Use the format in Exhibit 3-1 on page 112. Identify each adjustment by letter.

MULTICONCEPT PROBLEMS

LO3,4,7

Problem 4-11 Revenue and Expense Recognition and Closing Entries

Two years ago Darlene Darby opened a delivery service. Darby reports the following accounts on her income statement:

Sales	$69,000
Advertising expense	3,500
Salaries expense	39,000
Rent expense	10,000

These amounts represent two years of revenue and expenses. Darby asks you how she can tell how much of the income is from the first year of business and how much is from the second year. She provides the following additional data:

a. Sales in the second year are double those of the first year.
b. Advertising expense is for a $500 opening promotion and weekly ads in the newspaper.
c. Salaries represent one employee for the first nine months and two employees for the remainder of the time. Each is paid the same salary. No raises have been granted.
d. Rent has not changed since the business opened.

Required

1. Prepare income statements for Years 1 and 2.
2. Prepare the closing entries for each year. Prepare a short explanation for Darby about the purpose of closing temporary accounts.

LO5,6,8

Problem 4-12 Ten-Column Work Sheet (Appendix)

The following unadjusted trial balance is available for Ace Consulting Inc. on June 30, 2008:

Ace Consulting Inc.
Unadjusted Trial Balance
June 30, 2008

Cash	$ 6,320	
Accounts Receivable	14,600	
Supplies on Hand	800	
Prepaid Rent	4,800	
Furniture and Fixtures	18,000	
Accumulated Depreciation		$ 5,625
Accounts Payable		5,200
Capital Stock		10,000
Retained Earnings		17,955
Consulting Revenue		12,340
Utilities Expense	4,100	
Wage and Salary Expense	2,500	
Totals	$51,120	$51,120

Required

1. Enter the unadjusted trial balance in the first two columns of a ten-column work sheet.
2. Enter the necessary adjustments in the appropriate columns of the work sheet for each of the following:
   a. Wages and salaries earned by employees at the end of June but not yet paid amount to $2,380.
   b. Supplies on hand at the end of June amount to $550.
   c. Depreciation on furniture and fixtures for June is $375.
   d. Ace prepays the rent on its office space on June 1 of each year. The rent amounts to $400 per month.
   e. Consulting services rendered and billed for which cash has not yet been received amount to $4,600.
3. Complete the remaining columns of the work sheet.

LO5,6,8 **Problem 4-13** Monthly Transactions, Ten-Column Work Sheet, and Financial Statements (Appendix)

Moonlight Bay Inn is incorporated on January 2, 2008, by its three owners, each of whom contributes $20,000 in cash in exchange for shares of stock in the business. In addition to the sale of stock, the following transactions are entered into during the month of January:

January 2: A Victorian inn is purchased for $50,000 in cash. An appraisal performed on this date indicates that the land is worth $15,000, and the remaining balance of the purchase price is attributable to the house. The owners estimate that the house will have an estimated useful life of 25 years and an estimated salvage value of $5,000.

January 3: A two-year, 12%, $30,000 promissory note was signed at the Second State Bank. Interest and principal will be repaid on the maturity date of January 3, 2010.

January 4: New furniture for the inn is purchased at a cost of $15,000 in cash. The furniture has an estimated useful life of 10 years and no salvage value.

January 5: A 24-month property insurance policy is purchased for $6,000 in cash.

January 6: An advertisement for the inn is placed in the local newspaper. Moonlight Bay pays $450 cash for the ad, which will run in the paper throughout January.

January 7: Cleaning supplies are purchased on account for $950. The bill is payable within 30 days.

January 15: Wages of $4,230 for the first half of the month are paid in cash.

January 16: A guest mails the business $980 in cash as a deposit for a room to be rented for two weeks. The guest plans to stay at the inn during the last week of January and the first week of February.

January 31: Cash receipts from rentals of rooms for the month amount to $8,300.

January 31: Cash receipts from operation of the restaurant for the month amount to $6,600.

January 31: Each stockholder is paid $200 in cash dividends.

Required

1. Prepare journal entries to record each of the preceding transactions.
2. Post each of the journal entries to T accounts.

3. Place the balance in each of the T accounts in the unadjusted trial balance columns of a ten-column work sheet.
4. Enter the appropriate adjustments in the next two columns of the work sheet for each of the following:
   a. Depreciation of the house
   b. Depreciation of the furniture
   c. Interest on the promissory note
   d. Recognition of the expired portion of the insurance
   e. Recognition of the earned portion of the guest's deposit
   f. Wages earned during the second half of January amount to $5,120 and will be paid on February 3.
   g. Cleaning supplies on hand on January 31 amount to $230.
   h. A gas and electric bill that is received from the city amounts to $740 and is payable by February 5.
   i. Income taxes are to be accrued at a rate of 30% of income before taxes.
5. Complete the remaining columns of the work sheet.
6. Prepare in good form the following financial statements:
   a. Income statement for the month ended January 31, 2008
   b. Statement of retained earnings for the month ended January 31, 2008
   c. Balance sheet at January 31, 2008
7. Assume that you are the loan officer at Second State Bank. (Refer to the transaction on January 3.) What are your reactions to Moonlight's first month of operations? Are you comfortable with the loan you made? Explain your answer.

ALTERNATE PROBLEMS

LO5

Problem 4-1A Adjusting Entries

Flood Relief Inc. prepares monthly financial statements and therefore adjusts its accounts at the end of every month. The following information is available for June 2008:

a. Flood received a $10,000, 4%, two-year note receivable from a customer for services rendered. The principal and interest are due on June 1, 2010. Flood expects to be able to collect the note and interest in full at that time.
b. Office supplies totaling $5,600 were purchased during the month. The asset account Supplies is debited whenever a purchase is made. A count in the storeroom on June 30, 2008, indicates that supplies on hand amount to $507. The supplies on hand at the beginning of the month total $475.
c. The company purchased machines last year for $170,000. The machines are expected to be used for four years and have an estimated salvage value of $2,000.
d. On June 1, the company paid $4,650 for rent for June, July, and August. The asset Prepaid Rent was debited; it did not have a balance on June 1.
e. The company operates seven days per week with a weekly payroll of $7,000. Wage earners are paid every Sunday. The last day of the month is Saturday, June 30.
f. Based on its income for the month, Flood estimates that federal income taxes for June amount to $2,900.

Required
For each of the preceding situations, prepare in general journal form the appropriate adjusting entry to be recorded on June 30, 2008.

LO5

Problem 4-2A Effects of Adjusting Entries on the Accounting Equation

Refer to the information provided for Flood Relief Inc. in Problem 4-1A.

Required
1. Prepare a table to summarize the required adjusting entries as they affect the accounting equation. Use the format in Exhibit 3-1 on page 112. Identify each adjustment by letter.
2. Assume that Flood Relief reports income of $35,000 before any of the adjusting entries. What net income will Flood Relief report for June?

LO5

Problem 4-3A Adjusting Entries—Annual Adjustments

Ogonquit Enterprises prepares annual financial statements and adjusts its accounts only at the end of the year. The following information is available for the year ended December 31, 2008:

a. Ogonquit purchased office furniture last year for $25,000. The furniture has an estimated useful life of seven years and an estimated salvage value of $4,000.
b. The Supplies account had a balance of $1,200 on January 1, 2008. During 2008, Ogonquit added $12,900 to the account for purchases of supplies during the year. A count of the supplies on hand at the end of December 2008 indicates a balance of $900.
c. On July 1, 2008, Ogonquit credited a liability account, Customer Deposits, for $8,800. This sum represents an amount that a customer paid in advance and that will be earned evenly by Ogonquit over an eight-month period.
d. Ogonquit rented some warehouse space on September 1, 2008, at a rate of $4,000 per month. On that date, Ogonquit debited Prepaid Rent for six months' rent paid in advance.
e. Ogonquit took out a 90-day, 6%, $30,000 note on November 1, 2008, with interest and principal to be paid at maturity.
f. Ogonquit operates five days per week with an average weekly payroll of $4,150. Ogonquit pays its employees every Thursday. December 31, 2008, is a Wednesday.

Required

1. For each of the preceding situations, prepare in general journal form the appropriate adjusting entry to be recorded on December 31, 2008.
2. Assume that Ogonquit's accountant forgets to record the adjusting entries on December 31, 2008. Will net income for the year be understated or overstated? by what amount? (Ignore the effect of income taxes.)

LO5

Problem 4-4A Recurring and Adjusting Entries

Following are the accounts of Dominique Inc., an interior decorator. The company has been in the decorating business for ten years and prepares quarterly financial statements. Following the list of accounts is a series of transactions entered into by Dominique. For each transaction, enter the number(s) of the account(s) to be debited and credited.

Accounts

1. Cash
2. Accounts Receivable
3. Prepaid Rent
4. Office Supplies
5. Office Equipment
6. Accumulated Depreciation
7. Accounts Payable
8. Salaries and Wages Payable
9. Income Tax Payable
10. Interim Financing Notes Payable
11. Capital Stock, $1 par
12. Paid-In Capital in Excess of Par
13. Consulting Revenue
14. Office Supply Expense
15. Rent Expense
16. Salaries and Wages Expense
17. Depreciation Expense
18. Interest Expense
19. Income Tax Expense

Transaction	Debit	Credit
a. Example: Issued additional shares of stock to owners; shares issued at greater than par.	1	12, 13
b. Purchased office equipment for cash.	____	____
c. Collected open accounts receivable from customer.	____	____
d. Purchased office supplies on account.	____	____
e. Paid office rent for the next six months.	____	____
f. Paid interest on an interim financing note.	____	____
g. Paid salaries and wages.	____	____
h. Purchased office equipment; made a down payment in cash and signed an interim financing note.	____	____
i. Provided services on account.	____	____
j. Recorded depreciation on equipment.	____	____
k. Recorded income taxes due next month.	____	____
l. Recorded the used office supplies.	____	____
m. Recorded the used portion of prepaid rent.	____	____

LO5

Problem 4-5A Use of Account Balances as a Basis for Adjusting Entries—Annual Adjustments

The following account balances are taken from the records of Laugherty Inc. at December 31, 2008. The Supplies account represents the cost of supplies on hand at the beginning of the year plus all purchases. A physical count on December 31, 2008, shows only $1,520 of supplies on hand. The Unearned Revenue account represents the cash received from a customer on May 1, 2008, for 12 months of service beginning on that date. The Note Payable represents a six-month promissory note signed with a supplier on September 1, 2008. Principal and interest at an annual rate of 10% will be paid on March 1, 2009.

Supplies	$5,790 debit	
Unearned Revenue		$ 1,800 credit
Note Payable		60,000 credit

Required

1. Prepare the three necessary adjusting entries on the books of Laugherty on December 31, 2008. Assume that Laugherty prepares adjusting entries only once a year, on December 31.
2. Assume that adjusting entries are made at the end of each month rather than only at the end of the year. What would be the balance in Unearned Revenue *before* the December adjusting entry was made? Explain your answer.

LO5

Problem 4-6A Use of a Trial Balance as a Basis for Adjusting Entries

Lori Matlock operates a graphic arts business. A trial balance on June 30, 2008, *before* recording any adjusting entries, appears as follows:

Matlock Graphic Arts Studio
Unadjusted Trial Balance
June 30, 2008

	Debit	Credit
Cash	$ 7,000	
Prepaid Rent	18,000	
Supplies	15,210	
Office Equipment	46,120	
Accumulated Depreciation—Equipment		$ 4,000
Accounts Payable		1,800
Notes Payable		2,000
Capital Stock		50,000
Retained Earnings		24,350
Dividends	8,400	
Revenue		46,850
Utilities Expense	2,850	
Salaries Expense	19,420	
Advertising Expense	12,000	
Totals	$129,000	$129,000

Other Data

a. The monthly rent is $600.
b. Supplies on hand on June 30, 2008, amount to $1,290.
c. The office equipment was purchased on June 1, 2007. On that date, it had an estimated useful life of ten years and a salvage value of $6,120.
d. Interest owed on the note payable but not yet paid amounts to $50.
e. Salaries of $620 are owed but unpaid to employees at the end of the month.

Required

1. Prepare in general journal form the necessary adjusting entries at June 30, 2008. Label the entries (a) through (e) to correspond to the other data.
2. Note that the unadjusted trial balance reports a credit balance in Accumulated Depreciation—Equipment of $4,000. Explain why the account contains a balance of $4,000 on June 30, 2008.

LO5

Problem 4-7A Effects of Adjusting Entries on the Accounting Equation

Refer to the information provided for Matlock Graphic Arts Studio in Problem 4-6A.

Required

1. Prepare a table to summarize the required adjusting entries as they affect the accounting equation. Use the format in Exhibit 3-1 on page 112. Identify each adjustment by letter.
2. Compute the net increase or decrease in net income for the month from the recognition of the adjusting entries you prepared in (1). (Ignore income taxes.)

LO5

Problem 4-8A Reconstruction of Adjusting Entries from Account Balances

Zola Corporation records adjusting entries each month before preparing monthly financial statements. The following selected account balances are taken from its trial balances on June 30, 2008. The "unadjusted" columns set forth the general ledger balances before the adjusting entries were posted. The "adjusted" columns reflect the month-end adjusting entries.

	Unadjusted		Adjusted	
Account Title	**Debit**	**Credit**	**Debit**	**Credit**
Prepaid Rent	$4,000		$3,000	
Equipment	9,600		9,600	
Accumulated Depreciation		$ 800		$ 900
Notes Payable		9,600		9,600
Interest Payable		768		864

Required

1. The company paid for a six-month lease on April 1, 2008. Reconstruct the adjusting journal entry for rent on June 30, 2008.
2. What amount was prepaid on April 1, 2008? Explain your answer.
3. The equipment was purchased on September 30, 2007, for $9,600. Zola uses straight-line depreciation and estimates that the equipment will have no salvage value. Reconstruct the adjusting journal entry for depreciation on June 30, 2008.
4. What is the equipment's estimated useful life in months? Explain your answer.
5. Zola signed a two-year note on September 30, 2007, for the purchase of the equipment. Interest on the note accrues on a monthly basis and will be paid at maturity along with the principal amount of $9,600. Reconstruct the adjusting journal entry for interest expense on June 30, 2008.
6. What is the monthly interest rate on the loan? Explain your answer.

LO5

Problem 4-9A Use of a Trial Balance to Record Adjusting Entries in T Accounts

Lewis and Associates has been in the termite inspection and treatment business for five years. An unadjusted trial balance at June 30, 2008, follows.

Lewis and Associates
Unadjusted Trial Balance
June 30, 2008

	Debit	**Credit**
Cash	$ 6,200	
Accounts Receivable	10,400	
Prepaid Rent	4,400	
Chemical Inventory	9,400	
Equipment	18,200	
Accumulated Depreciation		$ 1,050
Accounts Payable		1,180
Capital Stock		5,000
Retained Earnings		25,370
Treatment Revenue		40,600
Wages and Salary Expense	22,500	
Utilities Expense	1,240	
Advertising Expense	860	
Totals	$73,200	$73,200

The following additional information is available:

a. Lewis rents a warehouse with office space and prepays the annual rent of $4,800 on May 1 of each year.
b. The asset account Equipment represents the cost of treatment equipment, which has an estimated useful life of ten years and an estimated salvage value of $200.
c. Chemical inventory on hand equals $1,300.
d. Wages and salaries owed but unpaid to employees at the end of the month amount to $1,080.
e. Lewis accrues income taxes using an estimated tax rate equal to 30% of the income for the month.

Required

1. Set up T accounts for each of the accounts listed in the trial balance. Based on the additional information given, set up any other T accounts that will be needed to prepare adjusting entries.
2. Post the month-end adjusting entries directly to the T accounts but do not bother to put the entries in journal format first. Use the letters (a) through (e) from the additional information to identify the entries.
3. Prepare a trial balance to prove the equality of debits and credits after posting the adjusting entries.
4. On the basis of the information you have, does Lewis appear to be a profitable business? Explain your answer.

LO5

Problem 4-10A Effects of Adjusting Entries on the Accounting Equation

Refer to the information provided for Lewis and Associates in Problem 4-9A.

Required

Prepare a table to summarize the required adjusting entries as they affect the accounting equation. Use the format in Exhibit 3-1 on page 112. Identify each adjustment by letter.

ALTERNATE MULTICONCEPT PROBLEMS

LO3,4,7

Problem 4-11A Revenue and Expense Recognition and Closing Entries

Two years ago Sue Stern opened an audio book rental shop. Sue reports the following accounts on her income statement:

Sales	$84,000
Advertising expense	10,500
Salaries expense	12,000
Depreciation on tapes	5,000
Rent expense	18,000

These amounts represent two years of revenue and expenses. Sue asks you how she can tell how much of the income is from the first year and how much is from the second year of business. She provides the following additional data:

a. Sales in the second year are triple those of the first year.
b. Advertising expense is for a $1,500 opening promotion and weekly ads in the newspaper.
c. Salaries represent one employee who was hired eight months ago. No raises have been granted.
d. Rent has not changed since the shop opened.

Required

1. Prepare income statements for Years 1 and 2.
2. Prepare the closing entries for each year. Prepare a short explanation for Sue about the purpose of closing temporary accounts.

LO5,7,8

Problem 4-12A Ten-Column Work Sheet and Closing Entries (Appendix)

The unadjusted trial balance for Forever Green Landscaping on August 31, 2008, follows.

HOMEWORK

Forever Green Landscaping
Unadjusted Trial Balance
August 31, 2008

Cash	$ 6,460	
Accounts Receivable	23,400	
Supplies on Hand	1,260	
Prepaid Insurance	3,675	
Equipment	28,800	
Accumulated Depreciation—Equipment		$ 9,200
Buildings	72,000	
Accumulated Depreciation—Buildings		16,800
Accounts Payable		10,500
Notes Payable		10,000
Capital Stock		40,000
Retained Earnings		42,100
Service Revenue		14,200
Advertising Expense	1,200	
Gasoline and Oil Expense	1,775	
Wage and Salary Expense	4,230	
Totals	$142,800	$142,800

Required

1. Enter the unadjusted trial balance in the first two columns of a ten-column work sheet.
2. Enter the necessary adjustments in the appropriate columns of the work sheet for each of the following:
   a. A count of the supplies on hand at the end of August reveals a balance of $730.
   b. The company paid $4,200 in cash on May 1, 2008, for a two-year insurance policy.
   c. The equipment has a four-year estimated useful life and no salvage value.
   d. The buildings have an estimated useful life of 30 years and no salvage value.
   e. The company leases space in its building to another company. The agreement requires the tenant to pay Forever Green $700 on the 10th of each month for the previous month's rent.
   f. Wages and salaries earned by employees at the end of August but not yet paid amount to $3,320.
   g. The company signed a six-month promissory note on August 1, 2008. Interest at an annual rate of 12% and the principal amount of $10,000 are due on February 1, 2009.
3. Complete the remaining columns of the work sheet.
4. Assume that Forever Green closes its books at the end of each month before preparing financial statements. Prepare the necessary closing entries at August 31, 2008.

LO5,6,8 Problem 4-13A Ten-Column Work Sheet and Financial Statements (Appendix)

The following unadjusted trial balance is available for Tenfour Trucking Company on January 31, 2008:

Tenfour Trucking Company
Unadjusted Trial Balance
January 31, 2008

Cash	$ 27,340	
Accounts Receivable	41,500	
Prepaid Insurance	18,000	
Warehouse	40,000	
Accumulated Depreciation—Warehouse		$ 21,600
Truck Fleet	240,000	
Accumulated Depreciation—Truck Fleet		112,500
Land	20,000	
Accounts Payable		32,880
Notes Payable		50,000
Interest Payable		4,500
Customer Deposits		6,000
Capital Stock		100,000
Retained Earnings		40,470
Freight Revenue		165,670
Gas and Oil Expense	57,330	
Maintenance Expense	26,400	
Wage and Salary Expense	43,050	
Dividends	20,000	
Totals	$533,620	$533,620

Required

1. Enter the unadjusted trial balance in the first two columns of a ten-column work sheet.
2. Enter the necessary adjustments in the appropriate columns of the work sheet for each of the following:
   a. Prepaid insurance represents the cost of a 24-month policy purchased on January 1, 2008.
   b. The warehouse has an estimated useful life of 20 years and an estimated salvage value of $4,000.
   c. The truck fleet has an estimated useful life of six years and an estimated salvage value of $15,000.
   d. The promissory note was signed on January 1, 2007. Interest at an annual rate of 9% and the principal of $50,000 are due on December 31, 2008.
   e. The customer deposits represent amounts paid in advance by new customers. A total of $4,500 of the balance in Customer Deposits was earned during January 2008.
   f. Wages and salaries earned by employees at the end of January but not yet paid amount to $8,200.
   g. Income taxes are accrued at a rate of 30% at the end of each month.
3. Complete the remaining columns of the work sheet.
4. Prepare in good form the following financial statements:
   a. Income statement for the month ended January 31, 2008
   b. Statement of retained earnings for the month ended January 31, 2008
   c. Balance sheet at January 31, 2008
5. Compute Tenfour's current ratio. What does this ratio tell you about the company's liquidity?
6. Compute Tenfour's profit margin. What does this ratio tell you about the company's profitability?

DECISION CASES

READING AND INTERPRETING FINANCIAL STATEMENTS

LO3

Decision Case 4-1 Comparing Two Companies in the Same Industry: Kellogg's and General Mills

Refer to the financial information for **Kellogg's** and **General Mills** reproduced at the end of the book for the information needed to answer the following questions.

Required

1. Locate the note in each company's annual report in which it discusses revenue recognition. How does each company describe the point at which it recognizes revenue from customers? Are there any significant differences in the organizations' revenue recognition policies?
2. What dollar amount does Kellogg's report for accounts receivable on its most recent balance sheet? What percent of the company's total current assets are comprised of accounts receivable? What is the dollar amount of General Mills's receivables on its most recent balance sheet? What percent of total current assets is comprised of receivables? For which company does its receivables constitute a higher percentage of its total current assets?

LO3

Decision Case 4-2 Reading and Interpreting Nordstrom's Notes—Revenue Recognition

The following excerpt is taken from Note 1 on page 33 of Nordstrom's 2006 annual report:

Revenue Recognition

We record revenues net of estimated returns and we exclude sales taxes. Our retail stores record revenue at the point of sale. Our catalog and online sales include shipping revenue and are recorded upon estimated delivery to the customer. We recognize revenue associated with our gift cards upon redemption of the gift card. As part of the normal sales cycle, we receive customer merchandise returns. To recognize the financial impact of sales returns, we estimate the amount of goods that will be returned and reduce sales and cost of sales accordingly. We utilize historical return patterns to estimate our expected returns. Our sales return reserves were $54,546 and $51,172 at the end of 2006 and 2005.

Required

1. According to the note, when does Nordstrom recognize revenue from sales in its retail stores? How does this differ from the way the company recognizes revenue from its catalog and online sales? Why would the way in which revenue from these two types of sales differ?

2. According to the note, how does Nordstrom recognize revenue associated with its gift cards? Assume that you buy a gift card for a friend. What entry does Nordstrom make at the time you buy the card? What entry does Nordstrom make when your friend redeems the card?

LO3 **Decision Case 4-3** Reading and Interpreting Sears Holdings Corporation's Notes—Revenue Recognition

The following excerpt is taken from page 65 of the **Sears Holdings Corporation** (parent company of Kmart and Sears) 2006 annual report: "Revenues from the sale of service contracts are deferred and amortized over the lives of the associated contracts, while the associated service costs are expensed as incurred."

Required

1. Assume that you buy a wide-screen television from Sears for $2,500, including a $180 service contract that will cover three years. Why does Sears recognize the revenue associated with the service contract over its life even though cash is received at the time of the sale?
2. How much revenue will Sears recognize from your purchase of the television and the service contract in Years 1, 2, and 3? (Assume a straight-line approach.) What corresponding account can you look for in the financial statements to determine the amount of service contract revenue that will be recognized in the future?

MAKING FINANCIAL DECISIONS

LO2,3,4 **Decision Case 4-4** The Use of Net Income and Cash Flow to Evaluate a Company

After you have gained five years of experience with a large CPA firm, one of your clients, Duke Inc., asks you to take over as chief financial officer for the business. Duke advises its clients on the purchase of software products and assists them in installing the programs on their computer systems. Because the business is relatively new (it began servicing clients in January 2008), its accounting records are somewhat limited. In fact, the only statement available is the following income statement for the first year:

Duke Inc.
Statement of Income
For the Year Ended December 31, 2008

Revenues		$1,250,000
Expenses:		
Salaries and wages	$480,000	
Supplies	65,000	
Utilities	30,000	
Rent	120,000	
Depreciation	345,000	
Interest	138,000	
Total expenses		1,178,000
Net income		$ 72,000

Based on its relatively modest profit margin of 5.76% (net income of $72,000 divided by revenues of $1,250,000), you are concerned about joining the new business. To alleviate your concerns, the president of the company is able to give you the following additional information:

a. Clients are given 90 days to pay their bills for consulting services provided by Duke. On December 31, 2008, $230,000 of the revenues is yet to be collected in cash.
b. Employees are paid on a monthly basis. Salaries and wages of $480,000 include the December payroll of $40,000, which will be paid on January 5, 2009.
c. The company purchased $100,000 of operating supplies when it began operations in January. The balance of supplies on hand at December 31 amounts to $35,000.
d. Office space is rented in a downtown high-rise building at a monthly cost of $10,000. When the company moved into the office in January, it prepaid its rent for the next 18 months beginning January 1, 2008.
e. On January 1, 2008, Duke purchased a computer system and related accessories at a cost of $1,725,000. The estimated useful life of the system is five years.
f. The computer system was purchased by signing a three-year, 8% note payable for $1,725,000 on the date of purchase. The principal amount of the note and interest for the three years are due on January 1, 2011.

Required

1. Based on the income statement and the additional information given, prepare a statement of cash flows for Duke for 2008. (*Hint:* Simply list all of the cash inflows and outflows that relate to operations.)
2. On the basis of the income statement given and the statement of cash flows prepared in (1), do you think it would be a wise decision to join the company as its chief financial officer? Include in your response any additional questions that you believe are appropriate to ask before joining the company.

LO4

Decision Case 4-5 Depreciation

Jenner Inc., a graphic arts studio, is considering the purchase of computer equipment and software for a total cost of $18,000. Jenner can pay for the equipment and software over three years at the rate of $6,000 per year. The equipment is expected to last 10 to 20 years; but because of changing technology, Jenner believes it may need to replace the system in as soon as three to five years. A three-year lease of similar equipment and software is available for $6,000 per year. Jenner's accountant has asked you to recommend whether the company should purchase or lease the equipment and software and to suggest the length of time over which to depreciate the software and equipment if the company makes the purchase.

Required

Ignoring the effect of taxes, would you recommend the purchase or the lease? Why or why not? Referring to the definition of *depreciation*, what appropriate useful life should be used for the equipment and software?

ETHICAL DECISION MAKING

LO2,3,4,5

Decision Case 4-6 Revenue Recognition and the Matching Principle

Listum & Sellum Inc. is a medium-sized midwestern real estate company. It was founded five years ago by its two principal stockholders, Willie Listum and Dewey Sellum. Willie is president of the company, and Dewey is vice president of sales. Listum & Sellum has enjoyed tremendous growth since its inception by aggressively seeking out listings for residential real estate and paying a generous commission to the selling agent.

The company receives a 6% commission for selling a client's property and gives two-thirds of this, or 4% of the selling price, to the selling agent. For example, if a house sells for $100,000, Listum & Sellum receives $6,000 and pays $4,000 of this to the selling agent. At the time of the sale, the company records a debit of $6,000 to Accounts Receivable and a credit of $6,000 to Sales Revenue. The accounts receivable is normally collected within 30 days. Also at the time of sale, the company debits $4,000 to Commissions Expense and credits Commissions Payable for the same amount. Sales agents are paid by the 15th of the month following the month of the sale. In addition to the commissions expense, Listum & Sellum's other two major expenses are advertising of listings in local newspapers and depreciation of the company's fleet of Cadillacs (Dewey believes that all of the sales agents should drive Cadillacs). The newspaper ads will run for one month, and the company has until the 10th of the following month to pay that month's bill. The automobiles are depreciated over four years (Dewey doesn't believe that any salesperson should drive a car that is more than four years old).

Due to a downturn in the economy in the Midwest, sales have been sluggish for the first 11 months of the current year, which ends on June 30. Willie is very disturbed by the slow sales this particular year because a large note payable to the local bank is due in July and the company plans to ask the bank to renew the note for another three years. Dewey seems less concerned by the unfortunate timing of the recession and has some suggestions as to how he and Willie can "paint the rosiest possible picture for the banker" when they go for the loan extension in July. In fact, Dewey has some very specific recommendations for you as to how to account for transactions during June, the last month in the fiscal year.

You are the controller for Listum & Sellum and have been treated very well by Willie and Dewey since joining the company two years ago. In fact, Dewey insists that you drive the top-of-the-line Cadillac. Following are his suggestions:

> First, for any sales made in June, we can record the 6% commission revenue immediately but delay recording the 4% commission expense until July, when the sales agent is paid. We record the sales at the same time we always have, the sales agents get paid when they always have, the bank sees how profitable we have been, we get our loan, and everybody is happy!

HOMEWORK

Second, since we won't be paying our advertising bills for the month of June until July 10, we can wait until then to record the expense. The timing seems perfect since we are meeting with the bank for the loan extension on July 8.

Third, since we will be depreciating the fleet of "Caddys" for the year ending June 30, how about changing the estimated useful life on them to eight years instead of four years? We won't say anything to the sales agents; no need to rile them up about having to drive their cars for eight years. Anyhow, the change to eight years would just be for accounting purposes. In fact, we could even switch back to four years for accounting purposes next year. Likewise, the changes in recognizing commission expense and advertising expense don't need to be permanent either; these are just slight bookkeeping changes to help us get over the hump!

Required

1. Explain why each of the three proposed changes in accounting will result in an increase in net income for the year ending June 30.
2. Identify any concerns you have with each of the three proposed changes in accounting from the perspective of GAAP. If these changes are made, do the financial statements faithfully represent what they claim to represent? Are these changes merely bookkeeping changes? Explain your answer.
3. From an ethical perspective, identify any concerns you have with each of the three proposed changes in accounting. Do the proposed changes provide information that is free from bias? Explain your answer.
4. Does the controller benefit by making the proposed changes? Are outsiders harmed? Explain your answer.

LO4

Decision Case 4-7 Advice to a Potential Investor

Century Company was organized 15 months ago as a management consulting firm. At that time, the owners invested a total of $50,000 cash in exchange for stock. Century purchased equipment for $35,000 cash and supplies to be used in the business. The equipment is expected to last seven years with no salvage value. Supplies are purchased on account and paid for in the month after the purchase. Century normally has about $1,000 of supplies on hand. Its client base has increased so dramatically that the president and chief financial officer have approached an investor to provide additional cash for expansion. The balance sheet and income statement for the first year of business are as follows:

Century Company
Balance Sheet
December 31, 2008

Assets		Liabilities and Stockholders' Equity	
Cash	$10,100	Accounts payable	$ 2,300
Accounts receivable	1,200	Common stock	50,000
Supplies	16,500	Retained earnings	10,500
Equipment	35,000		
Total	$62,800	Total	$62,800

Century Company
Income Statement
For the Year Ended December 31, 2008

Revenues		$82,500
Wages and salaries	$60,000	
Utilities	12,000	72,000
Net income		$10,500

Required

The investor has asked you to look at these financial statements and give an opinion about Century's future profitability. Are the statements prepared in accordance with GAAP? Why or why not? Based on these two statements, what would you advise? What additional information would you need to give an educated opinion?

SOLUTIONS TO KEY TERMS QUIZ

15	**Recognition**	10	**Deferral**
22	**Historical cost**	16	**Deferred expense**
8	**Current value**	5	**Deferred revenue**
18	**Cash basis**	12	**Accrual**
11	**Accrual basis**	19	**Accrued liability**
2	**Revenues**	7	**Accrued asset**
14	**Revenue recognition principle**	24	**Accounting cycle**
20	**Matching principle**	1	**Work sheet**
23	**Expenses**	6	**Real accounts**
3	**Adjusting entries**	17	**Nominal accounts**
9	**Straight-line method**	4	**Closing entries**
21	**Contra account**	13	**Interim statements**

INTEGRATIVE PROBLEM

Completing Financial Statements, Computing Ratios, Comparing Accrual versus Cash Income, and Evaluating the Company's Cash Needs

Mountain Home Health Inc. provides home nursing services in the Great Smoky Mountains of Tennessee. When contacted by a client or referred by a physician, nurses visit the patient and discuss needed services with the physician.

Mountain Home Health earns revenue from patient services. Most of the revenue comes from billing insurance companies, the state of Tennessee, or the Medicare program. Amounts billed are recorded in the Billings Receivable account. Insurance companies, states, and the federal government do not fully fund all procedures. For example, the state of Tennessee pays an average 78% of billed amounts. Mountain Home Health has already removed the uncollectible amounts from the Billings Receivable account and reports it and Medical Services Revenue at the net amount. Services provided but not yet recorded totaled $16,000, net of allowances for uncollectible amounts. The firm earns a minor portion of its total revenue directly from patients in the form of cash.

Employee salaries, medical supplies, depreciation, and gasoline are the major expenses. Employees are paid every Friday for work performed during the Saturday-to-Friday pay period. Salaries amount to $800 per day. In 2008, December 31 falls on a Wednesday. Medical supplies (average use of $1,500 per week) are purchased periodically to support health-care coverage. The inventory of supplies on hand on December 31 amounted to $8,653.

The firm owns five automobiles (all purchased at the same time) that average 50,000 miles per year and are replaced every three years. They typically have no residual value. The building has an expected life of 20 years with no residual value. Straight-line depreciation is used on all of the firm's assets. Gasoline costs, which are a cash expenditure, average $375 per day. The firm purchases a three-year extended warranty contract to cover maintenance costs. The contract costs $9,000. (Assume equal use each year.)

On December 29, 2008, Mountain Home Health declared a dividend of $10,000, payable on January 15, 2009. The firm makes annual mortgage payments of principal and interest each June 30. The interest rate on the mortgage is 6%.

The following unadjusted trial balance is available for Mountain Home Health on December 31, 2008:

Mountain Home Health, Inc.
Unadjusted Trial Balance
December 31, 2008

	Debit	Credit
Cash	$ 77,400	
Billings Receivable (net)	151,000	
Medical Supplies	73,000	
Extended Warranty	3,000	
Automobiles	90,000	
Accumulated Depreciation—Automobiles		$ 60,000
Building	200,000	
Accumulated Depreciation—Building		50,000
Accounts Payable		22,000
Dividend Payable		10,000
Mortgage Payable		100,000
Capital Stock		100,000
Additional Paid-In Capital		50,000
Retained Earnings		99,900
Medical Services Revenue		550,000
Salary and Wages Expense	$ 288,000	
Gasoline Expense	137,500	
Utilities Expense	12,000	
Dividends	10,000	
Totals	$1,041,900	$1,041,900

Required

1. Set up T accounts for each of the accounts listed on the trial balance. Based on the information provided, set up any other T accounts that will be needed to prepare adjusting entries.
2. Post the year-end adjusting entries directly to the T accounts but do not bother to put the entries in journal format first.
3. Prepare a statement of income and a statement of retained earnings for Mountain Home Health for the year ended December 31, 2008.
4. Prepare a balance sheet for Mountain Home Health as of December 31, 2008.
5. Compute the following as of December 31, 2008: (a) Working capital and (b) Current ratio.
6. Which adjusting entries could cause a difference between cash- and accrual-based income?
7. Mary Francis, controller of Mountain Home, became concerned about the company's cash flow after talking to a local bank loan officer. The firm tries to maintain a seven-week supply of cash to meet the demands of payroll, medical supply purchases, and gasoline. Determine the amount of cash Mountain Home needs to meet the seven-week supply.

ANSWERS TO POD REVIEWS

LO1	1. b	2. a
LO2	1. c	2. b
LO3	1. a	2. d
LO4	1. b	2. c
LO5	1. a	2. c
LO6	1. c	2. a
LO7	1. b	2. a
LO8	1. a	2. b

CHAPTER 5

Inventories and Cost of Goods Sold

Learning Outcomes

After studying this chapter, you should be able to:

- **LO1** Identify the forms of inventory held by different types of businesses and the types of costs incurred.
- **LO2** Show that you understand how wholesalers and retailers account for sales of merchandise.
- **LO3** Show that you understand how wholesalers and retailers account for cost of goods sold.
- **LO4** Use the gross profit ratio to analyze a company's ability to cover its operating expenses and earn a profit.
- **LO5** Explain the relationship between the valuation of inventory and the measurement of income.
- **LO6** Apply the inventory costing methods of specific identification, weighted average, FIFO, and LIFO by using a periodic system.
- **LO7** Analyze the effects of the different costing methods on inventory, net income, income taxes, and cash flow.
- **LO8** Analyze the effects of an inventory error on various financial statement items.
- **LO9** Apply the lower-of-cost-or-market rule to the valuation of inventory.
- **LO10** Explain why and how the cost of inventory is estimated in certain situations.
- **LO11** Analyze the management of inventory.
- **LO12** Explain the effects that inventory transactions have on the statement of cash flows.
- **LO13** Explain the differences in the accounting for periodic and perpetual inventory systems and apply the inventory costing methods using a perpetual system (Appendix).

Study Links...

A Look at the Previous Chapter
Chapter 4 completed our introduction to the accounting model. That chapter examined the role of adjusting entries in an accrual accounting system.

A Look at This Chapter
Starting in this chapter, we move beyond the basic accounting model to consider the accounting for the various elements in the financial statements. We start by looking at how companies that sell a product account for their inventories and the eventual sale of them.

A Look at the Upcoming Chapter
Each of the remaining chapters in this section of the book examine other assets of a company. Chapter 6 considers the most liquid of all assets, cash, and looks at the ways in which companies maintain control over it and other valuable assets.

Gap Inc. MAKING BUSINESS DECISIONS

Billing itself as one of the world's largest specialty retailers, Gap Inc. had its humble beginning when Doris and Don Fisher opened their first store in San Francisco in 1969. From that single store, the company has grown to operate more than 3,100 stores and to generate revenue that exceeded $15.9 billion in fiscal 2006. It counts among its brands some of the most recognizable in the world of apparel: Gap, Banana Republic, Old Navy, and Piperlime.

As a retailer, Gap Inc. measures success in terms of what it earns from buying and selling jeans and other clothing apparel. The statements of income shown here provide an accounting of the company's success in this regard. Net sales have remained relatively steady in each of the last three years, amounting to about $16 billion annually. As is evident from the income statements, the cost that a retailer pays for the merchandise that it sells is the most important factor in determining whether the company is profitable. For Gap Inc., "Cost of goods sold and occupancy expenses" amounted to approximately $10 billion in each year. One of the biggest challenges a retailer faces is controlling the cost of its inventory while at the same time ensuring the quality of its merchandise.

© AP Photo/Paul Sakuma

Besides being important for retailers to control the cost of what they sell, it is also imperative that they minimize the amount of stock they carry at any one time. The cost of carrying inventory, including storage and insurance, can be significant. Gap Inc. must minimize the amount of inventory on hand, but at the same time make sure it has enough merchandise to meet customers' demands. The significance of inventory as an asset to Gap Inc. is indicated by the partial balance sheet shown here.

This chapter looks at the accounting for inventories and cost of goods sold and shows how closely connected they are. We will answer the following important questions:

- How does Gap Inc. keep track of the cost of its inventory? (See pp. 227–228.)
- When the company makes a sale, how does it determine the amount to assign to the cost of the product sold? (See pp. 236–244.)
- How can the relationship between the company's sales and the cost of those sales be used to help assess the company's performance? (See pp. 233–234.)
- How can the relationship between Gap Inc.'s sales on its income statement and its inventory on the balance sheet be used to assess how well it is managing its inventory? (See pp. 254–256.)

(*continued*)

Gap, Inc.
Consolidated Statements of Income

($ in millions except per share amounts, shares in thousands)	53 Weeks Ended February 3, 2007	52 Weeks Ended January 28, 2006	52 Weeks Ended January 29, 2005
Net sales	$ 15,943	$ 16,023	$ 16,267
Cost of goods sold and occupancy expenses	10,294	10,154	9,886
Gross profit	5,649	5,869	6,381
Operating expenses	4,475	4,124	4,296
Loss on early retirement of debt	—	—	105
Interest expense	41	45	167
Interest income	(131)	(93)	(59)
Earnings before income taxes	1,264	1,793	1,872
Income taxes	486	680	722
Net earnings	$ 778	$ 1,113	$ 1,150
Weighted average number of shares—basic	831,087	881,058	893,357
Weighted average number of shares—diluted	835,973	902,306	991,122
Earnings per share—basic	$ 0.94	$ 1.26	$ 1.29
Earnings per share—diluted	$ 0.93	$ 1.24	$ 1.21

Net sales have amounted to about $16 billion in each of the last three years.

Cost of sales and occupancy expenses have been about $10 billion.

See Notes to the Consolidated Financial Statements

Gap, Inc.
Consolidated Balance Sheets (Partial)

($ In millions, except per value, shares in thousands)	February 3, 2007	January 28, 2006
Assets		
Current assets:		
Cash and cash equivalents	$ 2,030	$ 2,035
Short-term investments	570	952
Restricted cash	44	55
Merchandise inventory	1,796	1,696
Other current assets	589	501
Total current assets	5,029	5,239

The company's inventory on hand increased during the year and represents over one third of the current assets.

Source: Gap Inc's. 2006 annual report.

The Nature of Inventory

LO1 Identify the forms of inventory held by different types of businesses and the types of costs incurred.

This chapter discusses accounting by companies that sell products, or what accountants call inventory. Companies that sell inventory can be broadly categorized into two types:

- Retailers and wholesalers purchase inventory in finished form and hold it for resale. For example, as a retailer **Gap Inc.** buys clothes directly from other companies and then offers them for sale to consumers.
- In contrast, manufacturers transform raw materials into a finished product prior to sale. A good example of a manufacturing company is **IBM**. It buys all of the various materials that are needed to make computers and then sells the finished product to its customers.

Whether a company is a wholesaler, retailer, or manufacturer, its inventory is an asset that is held for *resale* in the normal course of business. The distinction between inventory and an operating asset is the *intent* of the owner. For example, some of the computers that IBM owns are operating assets because they are used in various activities of the business, such as the payroll and accounting functions. Many more of the computers IBM owns are inventory, however, because the company makes them and intends to sell them. This chapter is concerned with the proper valuation of inventory and the related effect on cost of goods sold.

THREE TYPES OF INVENTORY COST AND THREE FORMS OF INVENTORY

It is important to distinguish between the *types* of inventory costs incurred and the *form* the inventory takes. Wholesalers and retailers incur a single type of cost, the *purchase price,* of the inventory they sell. On the balance sheet, they use a single account for inventory, titled **Merchandise Inventory**. Wholesalers and retailers buy merchandise in finished form and offer it for resale without transforming the product in any way. Merchandise companies typically have a relatively large dollar amount in inventory. For example, on its February 3, 2007, balance sheet, Gap Inc. reported merchandise inventory of $1,796 million and total assets of $8,544 million. It is not unusual for inventories to account for half the total assets of a merchandise company.

Merchandise Inventory
The account wholesalers and retailers use to report inventory held for resale.

The cost of inventory to a *merchandiser* is limited to the product's purchase price, which may include other costs mentioned soon. Conversely, three distinct *types* of costs are incurred by a *manufacturer*—direct materials, direct labor, and manufacturing overhead. Each is explained here.

1. Direct materials, also called **raw materials**, are the ingredients used in making a product. The costs of direct materials used in making a pair of shoes include the costs of fabric, plastic, and rubber.
2. Direct labor consists of the amounts paid to workers to manufacture the product. The hourly wage paid to an assembly line worker is a primary ingredient in the cost to make the shoes.
3. Manufacturing overhead includes all other costs that are related to the manufacturing process but cannot be directly matched to specific units of output. Depreciation of a factory building and the salary of a supervisor are two examples of overhead costs. Accountants have developed various techniques to assign, or allocate, these manufacturing overhead costs to specific products.

Raw materials
The inventory of a manufacturer before the addition of any direct labor or manufacturing overhead. ***Alternate term:*** *Direct materials.*

In addition to the three types of costs incurred in a production process, the inventory of a manufacturer takes three distinct *forms.* The three forms or stages in the development of inventory—raw materials, work in process, and finished goods—are discussed next.

1. Direct materials or raw materials enter a production process in which they are transformed into a finished product by the addition of direct labor and manufacturing overhead.
2. At any time, including the end of an accounting period, some of the materials have entered the process and some labor costs have been incurred but the product is not finished. The cost of unfinished products is appropriately called **work in process** or *work in progress.*
3. Inventory that has completed the production process and is available for sale is called **finished goods**. Finished goods are the equivalent of merchandise inventory for a retailer or wholesaler in that both represent the inventory of goods held for sale.

Work in process
The cost of unfinished products in a manufacturing company. ***Alternate term:*** *Work in progress.*

Finished goods
A manufacturer's inventory that is complete and ready for sale.

Many manufacturers disclose the dollar amounts of the various forms of inventory in their annual report. For example, **IBM** disclosed on p. 79 of its 2006 annual report the following amounts, stated in millions of dollars:

Inventories: at December 31	Millions
Finished goods	$ 506
Work in process and raw materials	2,304
	$2,810

As you can see, finished goods make up less than 20% of IBM's total inventories. However, this may not be the case for other types of businesses, where finished goods are more significant. For example, consider the following excerpt from Caterpillar Inc.'s 2006 annual report:

December 31	(In millions)
Raw materials	$2,182
Work in process	977
Finished goods	2,915
Supplies	277
Total inventories	$6,351

As the company that makes construction machinery and other related products, Caterpillar has nearly one-half of its inventory in finished products.

Exhibit 5-1 summarizes the relationships between the types of costs incurred and the forms of inventory for different types of businesses.

POD REVIEW 5.1

LO1 *Identify the forms of inventory held by different types of businesses and the types of costs incurred.*

- Inventory is a current asset held for resale in the normal course of business. The nature of inventory held depends on whether a business is a reseller of goods (wholesaler or retailer) or a manufacturer.
  - Resellers incur a single cost to purchase inventory held for sale.
  - Manufacturers incur costs that can be classified as raw materials, direct labor, and manufacturing overhead.

QUESTIONS

1. *The inventory of a retailer is limited to a single type of cost, the purchase price of the inventory it sells. The three distinct types of cost to a manufacturer are*
   a. direct materials, direct labor, and work in process.
   b. direct materials, direct labor, and manufacturing overhead.
   c. direct labor, manufacturing overhead, and finished goods.
   d. none of the above.

2. *The three forms or states in the development of inventory for a manufacturer are*
   a. direct materials, direct labor, and finished goods.
   b. direct materials, direct labor, and manufacturing overhead.
   c. direct materials, work in process, and finished goods.
   d. none of the above.

EXHIBIT 5-1 **Relationships between Types of Businesses and Inventory Costs**

Type of Business	Inventory	Costs Included in Inventory
Retailer/Wholesaler →	Merchandise inventory	Cost to purchase
Manufacturer →	Raw materials	Cost of materials before entered into production
Manufacturer →	Work in process	Costs of direct materials used, direct labor, and overhead in unfinished items
Manufacturer →	Finished goods	Cost of completed but unsold items

Net Sales of Merchandise

LO2 Show that you understand how wholesalers and retailers account for sales of merchandise.

A *condensed* multiple-step income statement for Daisy's Running Depot is presented in Exhibit 5-2. First note the period covered by the statement: for the year ended December 31, 2008. Daisy's ends its fiscal year on December 31; however, many merchandisers end their fiscal year on a date other than December 31. Retailers often choose a date toward the end of January because the busy holiday shopping season is over and time can be devoted to closing the records and preparing financial statements. For example, **Gap Inc.** ends its fiscal year on the Saturday closest to the end of January.

We will concentrate on the first two items on Daisy's statement: net sales and cost of goods sold. The major difference between this income statement and one for a service company is the inclusion of cost of goods sold. Because a service company does not sell a product, it does not report cost of goods sold. On the income statement of a merchandising company, cost of goods sold is deducted from net sales to arrive at **gross profit** or gross margin.

The first section of Daisy's income statement is presented in Exhibit 5-2. Two deductions—for sales returns and allowances and sales discounts—are made from sales revenue to arrive at **net sales**. **Sales revenue**, or sales, is a *representation of the inflow of assets*, either cash or accounts receivable, from the sale of a product during the period.

Gross profit
Net sales less cost of goods sold. ***Alternate term:*** *Gross margin.*

Net sales
Sales revenue less sales returns and allowances and sales discounts.

Sales revenue
A representation of the inflow of assets. ***Alternate term:*** *Sales.*

EXHIBIT 5-2 **Condensed Income Statement for a Merchandiser**

Daisy's Running Depot
Income Statement
For the Year Ended December 31, 2008

Net sales	$100,000
Cost of goods sold	60,000
Gross profit	$ 40,000
Selling and administrative expenses	29,300
Net income before tax	$ 10,700
Income tax expense	4,280
Net income	$ 6,420

SALES RETURNS AND ALLOWANCES

The cornerstone of marketing is to satisfy the customer. Most companies have standard policies that allow the customer to return merchandise within a stipulated period of time. **Nordstrom**, the Seattle-based retailer, has a very liberal policy regarding returns. That policy has, in large measure, fueled its growth. A company's policy might be that a customer who is not completely satisfied can return the merchandise anytime within 30 days of purchase for a full refund. Alternatively, the customer may be given an *allowance* for spoiled or damaged merchandise—that is, the customer keeps the merchandise but receives a credit for a certain amount in the account balance. Typically, a single account, **Sales Returns and Allowances**, is used to account for both returns and allowances. If the customer has already paid for the merchandise, either a cash refund is given or the credit amount is applied to future purchases.

Sales Returns and Allowances
Contra-revenue account used to record refunds to customers and reductions of their accounts.

CREDIT TERMS AND SALES DISCOUNTS

Most companies have a standard credit policy. Special notation is normally used to indicate a particular firm's policy for granting credit. For example, credit terms of n/30 mean that the net amount of the selling price (i.e., the amount determined after deducting any returns or allowances) is due within 30 days of the date of the invoice. Net, 10 EOM means that the net amount is due anytime within ten days after the end of the month in which the sale took place.

Study Tip

Recall Accumulated Depreciation, a contra account introduced in Chapter 4. It reduces a long-term asset. In other cases, such as this one involving sales, a contra account reduces an income statement account.

Another common element of the credit terms offered to customers is sales discounts, a reduction from the selling price given for early payment. For example, assume that Daisy's offers a customer credit terms of 1/10, n/30. This means that the customer can deduct 1% from the selling price if the bill is paid within ten days of the date of the invoice. Normally the discount period begins the day *after* the invoice date. If the customer does not pay within the first 10 days, the full invoice amount is due within 30 days. Finally, note that the use of *n* for *net* in this notation is a misnomer. Although the amount due is net of any returns and allowances, it is the *gross* amount that is due within 30 days. That is, no discount is given if the customer does not pay early.

How valuable to the customer is a 1% discount for payment within the first ten days? Assume that a $1,000 sale is made. If the customer pays at the end of ten days, the cash paid will be $990 rather than $1,000, a net savings of $10. The customer has saved $10 by paying 20 days earlier than required by the 30-day term. If we assume 360 days in a year, there are 360/20, or 18, periods of 20 days each in a year. Thus, a savings of $10 for 20 days is equivalent to a savings of $10 times 18, or $180 for the year. An annual return of $180/$990, or 18.2%, would be difficult to match with any other type of investment. In fact, a customer might want to consider borrowing the money to pay off the account early.

The **Sales Discounts** account is a contra-revenue account and thus reduces sales as shown on the income statement in Exhibit 5-3.

Sales Discounts
A contra-revenue account used to record discounts given to customers for early payment of their accounts.

EXHIBIT 5-3 Net Sales Section of the Income Statement

Daisy's Running Depot
Partial Income Statement
For the Year Ended December 31, 2008

Sales revenue	$103,500	
Less: Sales returns and allowances	2,000	
Sales discounts	1,500	
Net sales		$100,000

© AP Photo/Paul Sakuma

Hot Topics

Some Work and Some Don't

Not every marketing idea pans out for companies—and certainly not in the fashion-conscious retail sector. Gap Inc. discovered this recently when it decided to close its 19 Forth & Towne stores. The marketing concept was started as a pilot program in 2005 but did not sustain the type of growth necessary to become a full-fledged member of the family, which includes the well-known Gap, Banana Republic, and Old Navy brand names. The brunt of the accounting implications for closure of the Forth & Towne stores was felt during the 2007 fiscal year. The loss for the first half of 2007 amounted to approximately $54 million. In the end, Gap made a difficult business decision to cut its losses and to invest in its existing brands as well as to provide support for other projects with the potential to be around for the "long haul."

Source: http://www.gapinc.com

POD REVIEW 5.2

LO2 *Show that you understand how wholesalers and retailers account for sales of merchandise.*

- Net sales represents sales less deductions for discounts and merchandise returned (returns and allowances) and is a key figure on the income statement.
  - Sales discounts are given to customers who pay their bills promptly.
  - Returns and allowances have the same effect on sales that sales discounts do; that is, they reduce sales.

QUESTIONS

1. *Net sales is equal to*
   a. sales revenue less sales returns and allowances and sales discounts.
   b. sales revenue less cost of goods sold.
   c. sales revenue less selling and administrative expenses.
   d. none of the above.

2. *What type of account is Sales Discounts?*
   a. contra-asset
   b. revenue
   c. contra-revenue
   d. expense

The Cost of Goods Sold

LO3 Show that you understand how wholesalers and retailers account for cost of goods sold.

The cost of goods sold section of the income statement for Daisy's is shown in Exhibit 5-4. Let's take a look at the basic model for cost of goods sold.

THE COST OF GOODS SOLD MODEL

The recognition of cost of goods sold as an expense is an excellent example of the *matching principle.* Sales revenue represents the *inflow* of assets, in the form of cash and

EXHIBIT 5-4 **Cost of Goods Sold Section of the Income Statement**

Daisy's Running Depot
Partial Income Statement
For the Year Ended December 31, 2008

Cost of goods sold:			
Inventory, January 1, 2008		$15,000	
Purchases	$65,000		
Less: Purchase returns and allowances	1,800		
Purchase discounts	3,700		
Net purchases	$59,500		
Add: Transportation-in	3,500		
Cost of goods purchased		63,000	
Cost of goods available for sale		$78,000	
Less: Inventory, December 31, 2008		18,000	
Cost of goods sold			$60,000

accounts receivable, from the sale of products during the period. Likewise, cost of goods sold represents the *outflow* of an asset, inventory, from the sale of those same products. The company needs to match the revenue of the period with one of the most important costs necessary to generate the revenue, the cost of the merchandise sold.

It may be helpful in understanding cost of goods sold to realize what it is not. *Cost of goods sold is not necessarily equal to the cost of purchases of merchandise during the period.* Except in the case of a new business, a merchandiser starts the year with a certain stock of inventory on hand, called *beginning inventory.* For Daisy's, beginning inventory is the dollar cost of merchandise on hand on January 1, 2008. During the year, Daisy's purchases merchandise. When the cost of goods purchased is added to beginning inventory, the result is **cost of goods available for sale**. Just as the merchandiser starts the period with an inventory of merchandise on hand, a certain amount of ending inventory is usually on hand at the end of the year. For Daisy's, this is its inventory on December 31, 2008.

Cost of goods available for sale
Beginning inventory plus cost of goods purchased.

As shown in Exhibit 5-5, think of cost of goods available for sale as a "pool" of costs to be distributed between what was sold and what was not sold. If we subtract from the pool the cost of what did not sell, the *ending inventory*, we will have the amount that did

EXHIBIT 5-5 **The Cost of Goods Sold Model**

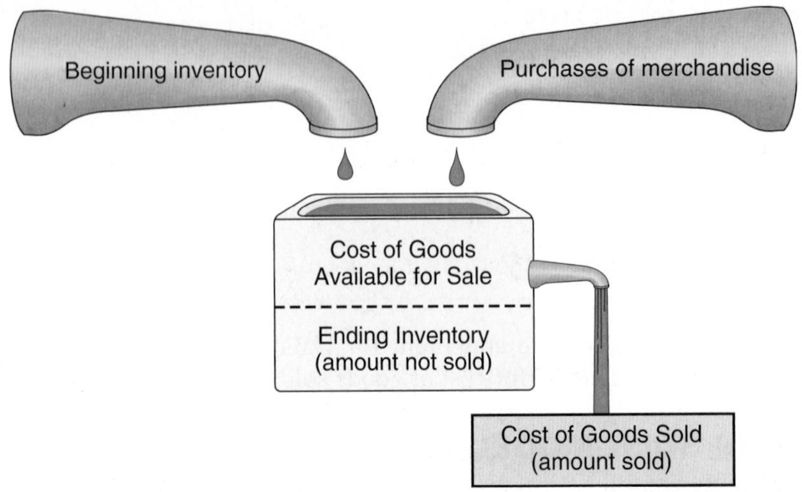

sell, the **cost of goods sold**. Cost of goods sold is simply the difference between the cost of goods available for sale and the ending inventory.

Cost of goods sold
Cost of goods available for sale minus ending inventory.

Beginning inventory	What is on hand to start the period
+ Cost of goods purchased	What was acquired for resale during the period
= Cost of goods available for sale	The "pool" of costs to be distributed
− Ending inventory	What was not sold during the period and therefore is on hand to start the next period
= Cost of goods sold	What was sold during the period

The cost of goods sold model for a merchandiser is illustrated in Exhibit 5-6. The amounts used for the illustration are taken from the cost of goods sold section of Daisy's income statement as shown in Exhibit 5-4. Notice that ending inventory exceeds beginning inventory by $3,000. That means that the cost of goods purchased exceeds cost of goods sold by that same amount. Indeed, a key point for stockholders, bankers, and other users is whether inventory is building up, that is, whether a company is not selling as much inventory during the period as it is buying. A buildup may indicate that the company's products are becoming less desirable or that prices are becoming uncompetitive.

INVENTORY SYSTEMS: PERPETUAL AND PERIODIC

Before looking more closely at the accounting for cost of goods sold, you need to understand the difference between the periodic and the perpetual inventory systems. All businesses use one of these two distinct approaches to account for inventory. With the **perpetual system**, the Inventory account is updated perpetually, or after each sale or purchase of merchandise. Conversely, with the **periodic system**, the Inventory account is updated only at the end of the period.

Perpetual system
A system in which the Inventory account is increased at the time of each purchase and decreased at the time of each sale.

In a perpetual system, every time goods are purchased, the Inventory account is increased with a debit, with a corresponding credit for an increase in Accounts Payable for a credit purchase or a credit for a decrease in the Cash account for a cash purchase. In addition to recognizing the increases in Accounts Receivable or Cash and in Sales Revenue when goods are sold, the accountant also records an entry to recognize the cost of the goods sold and the decrease in the cost of inventory on hand.

Periodic system
A system in which the Inventory account is updated only at the end of the period.

EXHIBIT 5-6 The Cost of Goods Sold Model: Example for a Merchandiser

Description	Item	Amount
Merchandise on hand to start the period	Beginning inventory	$15,000
Acquisitions of merchandise during the period	+Cost of goods purchased	63,000
Pool of merchandise available for sale during the period	=Cost of goods available for sale	$78,000
Merchandise on hand at end of period	−Ending inventory	(18,000)
Expense recognized on the income statement	=Cost of goods sold	$60,000

A $3,000 excess of ending inventory over beginning inventory means that the company bought $3,000 more than it sold ($63,000 bought versus $60,000 sold).

Assume for example that Daisy's sells a pair of running shoes that costs the company $70. In addition to the entry to record the sale, Daisy's would also record this entry:

Cost of Goods Sold	70	
Inventory		70
To record the sale of inventory under perpetual system.		

Balance Sheet								Income Statement	
ASSETS		=	LIABILITIES	+	STOCKHOLDERS' EQUITY		+	REVENUES − EXPENSES	
Inventory	(70)							Cost of Goods Sold	(70)

Thus, at any point during the period, the inventory account is up to date. It has been increased for the cost of purchases during the period and reduced for the cost of the sales.

Why don't all companies use the procedure just described, the perpetual system? Depending on the volume of inventory transactions (i.e., purchases and sales of merchandise), a perpetual system can be extremely costly to maintain. Historically, businesses with a relatively small volume of sales at a high unit price have used perpetual systems. For example, dealers in automobiles, furniture, appliances, and jewelry normally use a perpetual system. Each purchase of a unit of merchandise, such as an automobile, can be easily identified and an increase recorded in the Inventory account. For instance, when an auto is sold, the dealer can determine the cost of the particular car sold by looking at a perpetual inventory record.

However, can you imagine a similar system for a supermarket or a hardware store? Consider a checkout stand in a grocery store. Through the use of a cash register tape, the sales revenue for that particular stand is recorded at the end of the day. Because of the tremendous volume of sales of various items of inventory, from cans of vegetables to boxes of soap, it may not be feasible to record the cost of goods sold every time a sale takes place. This illustrates a key point in financial information: **the cost of the information should never exceed its benefit**. If a store manager had to stop and update the records each time a can of **Campbell's** soup was sold, the retailer's business would be disrupted.

Real World Practice

5-1 Understanding Gap Inc.'s Inventory System

Given the nature of its products, would you expect that **Gap Inc.** uses a perpetual or a periodic inventory system? Explain your answer.

To a certain extent, the ability of mass merchandisers to maintain perpetual inventory records has improved with the advent of point-of-sale terminals. When a cashier runs a can of corn over the sensing glass at the checkout stand and the bar code is read, the company's computer receives a message that a can of corn has been sold. In some companies, however, an update of the inventory record is in units only and is used as a means to determine when a product needs to be reordered. The company still relies on a periodic system to maintain the *dollar* amount of inventory. The remainder of this chapter limits its discussion to the periodic system. The perpetual system is discussed in more detail in the appendix to this chapter.

BEGINNING AND ENDING INVENTORIES IN A PERIODIC SYSTEM

In a periodic system, the Inventory account is *not* updated each time a sale or purchase is made. Throughout the year, the Inventory account contains the amount of merchandise on hand at the beginning of the year. The account is adjusted only at the end of the year. A company using the periodic system must physically count the units of inventory on hand at the end of the period. The number of units of each product is then multiplied by the cost per unit to determine the dollar amount of ending inventory. Refer to Exhibit 5-4 for Daisy's Running Depot. The procedure just described was used to determine its ending inventory of $18,000. Because one period's ending inventory is the next period's beginning inventory, the beginning inventory of $15,000 was based on the count at the end of the prior year.

In summary, the ending inventory in a periodic system is determined by counting the merchandise, not by looking at the Inventory account at the end of the period. The periodic system results in a trade-off. Use of the periodic system reduces record keeping but at the expense of a certain degree of control. Losses of merchandise due to theft, breakage, spoilage, or other reasons may go undetected in a periodic system because management may assume that all merchandise not on hand at the end of the year was sold. In a retail

EXHIBIT 5-7 **Cost of Goods Purchased**

Daisy's Running Depot
Partial Income Statement
For the Year Ended December 31, 2008

Purchases	$65,000	
Less: Purchase returns and allowances	1,800	
Purchase discounts	3,700	
Net purchases	$59,500	
Add: Transportation-in	3,500	
Cost of goods purchased		$63,000

store, some of the merchandise may have been shoplifted rather than sold. In contrast, with a perpetual inventory system, a count of inventory at the end of the period serves as a control device. For example, if the Inventory account shows a balance of $45,000 at the end of the year but only $42,000 of merchandise is counted, management is able to investigate the discrepancy. No such control feature exists in a periodic system.

In addition to the loss of control, the use of a periodic system presents a dilemma when a company wants to prepare *interim* financial statements. Because most companies that use a periodic system find it cost-prohibitive to count the entire inventory more than once a year, they use estimation techniques to determine inventory for monthly or quarterly statements. These techniques are discussed later in this chapter.

THE COST OF GOODS PURCHASED

The cost of goods purchased section of Daisy's income statement is shown in Exhibit 5-7. The company purchased $65,000 of merchandise during the period. Two amounts are deducted from purchases to arrive at net purchases: purchase returns and allowances of $1,800 and purchase discounts of $3,700. The cost of $3,500 incurred by Daisy's to ship the goods to its place of business is called **transportation-in** and is added to net purchases of $59,500 to arrive at the cost of goods purchased of $63,000. Another name for transportation-in is *freight-in*.

Transportation-in
An adjunct account used to record freight costs paid by the buyer. ***Alternate term:*** *Freight-in.*

Purchases Assume that Daisy's buys shoes on account from Nike at a cost of $4,000. **Purchases** is the temporary account used in a periodic inventory system to record acquisitions of merchandise. The journal entry to record the purchase is as follows:

Feb. 8	Purchases	4,000	
	Accounts Payable		4,000
	To record the purchase of merchandise on account.		

Balance Sheet						Income Statement
ASSETS	=	**LIABILITIES**	+	**STOCKHOLDERS' EQUITY**	+	**REVENUES − EXPENSES**
		Accounts Payable 4,000				Purchases (4,000)

It is important to understand that Purchases is *not* an asset account. It is included in the income statement as an integral part of the calculation of cost of goods sold and is therefore shown as a reduction of owners' equity in the accounting equation. Because Purchases is a temporary account, it is closed at the end of the period.

Purchases
An account used in a periodic inventory system to record acquisitions of merchandise.

Purchase Returns and Allowances Returns and allowances were discussed earlier in the chapter from the seller's point of view. From the standpoint of the buyer, purchase returns and allowances are reductions in the cost to purchase merchandise. Rather than record these reductions directly in the Purchases account, the accountant uses a separate account. The account, **Purchase Returns and Allowances**, is a contra account to Purchases. Because Purchases has a normal debit balance, the normal balance in Purchase Returns and Allowances is a credit balance. The use of a contra

Purchase Returns and Allowances
A contra-purchases account used in a periodic inventory system when a refund is received from a supplier or a reduction is given in the balance owed to a supplier.

account allows management to monitor the amount of returns and allowances. For example, a large number of returns during the period relative to the amount purchased may signal that the purchasing department is not buying from reputable sources.

Suppose that Daisy's returns $850 of merchandise to Nike for credit on Daisy's account. The return decreases both liabilities and purchases. Note that because a return reduces purchases, it actually increases net income and thus also increases owners' equity. The journal entry is as follows:

Sept. 6	Accounts Payable	850	
	Purchase Returns and Allowances		850
	To record the return of merchandise for credit to account.		

		Balance Sheet				Income Statement
ASSETS	=	**LIABILITIES**	+	**STOCKHOLDERS' EQUITY**	+	**REVENUES − EXPENSES**
		Accounts Payable (850)				Purchases Returns and Allowances 850

The entry to record an allowance for merchandise retained rather than returned is the same as the entry for a return.

Purchase Discounts Discounts were discussed earlier in the chapter from the seller's viewpoint. Merchandising companies often purchase inventory on terms that allow for a cash discount for early payment, such as 2/10, net 30. To the buyer, a cash discount is called a *purchase discount* and results in a reduction of the cost to purchase merchandise. Management must monitor the amount of purchase discounts taken as well as those opportunities missed by not taking advantage of the discounts for early payment.

Assume a purchase of merchandise on March 13 for $500, with credit terms of 1/10, net 30. The entry at the time of the purchase is as follows:

Mar. 13	Purchases	500	
	Accounts Payable		500
	To record purchase on account, terms 1/10, net 30.		

		Balance Sheet				Income Statement
ASSETS	=	**LIABILITIES**	+	**STOCKHOLDERS' EQUITY**	+	**REVENUES − EXPENSES**
		Accounts Payable 500				Purchases (500)

If the company does not pay within the discount period, the accountant simply makes an entry to record the payment of $500 cash and the reduction of accounts payable. However, assume that the company does pay its account on March 23, within the discount period. The following entry would be made:

Mar. 23	Accounts Payable	500	
	Cash		495
	Purchase Discounts		5
	To record payment on account.		

		Balance Sheet				Income Statement
ASSETS	=	**LIABILITIES**	+	**STOCKHOLDERS' EQUITY**	+	**REVENUES − EXPENSES**
Cash (495)		Accounts Payable (500)				Purchases Discounts 5

Purchase Discounts
A contra-purchases account used to record reductions in purchase price for early payment to a supplier.

The **Purchase Discounts** account is contra to the Purchases account and thus increases owners' equity, as shown in the previous accounting equation. Also note in Exhibit 5-7 that purchase discounts are deducted from purchases on the income statement. Finally, note that the effect on the income statement is the same as illustrated earlier for a purchase return: because purchases are reduced, net income is increased.

Shipping Terms and Transportation Costs The *cost principle* governs the recording of all assets. All costs necessary to prepare an asset for its intended use should be included in its cost. The cost of an item to a merchandising company is not necessarily limited to its invoice price. For example, any sales tax paid should be included in computing total cost. Any transportation costs incurred by the buyer should likewise be included in the cost of the merchandise.

The buyer does not always pay to ship the merchandise. This depends on the terms of shipment. Goods are normally shipped either **FOB destination point** or **FOB shipping point**; *FOB* stands for "free on board." When merchandise is shipped FOB destination point, it is the responsibility of the seller to deliver the products to the buyer. Thus, the seller either delivers the product to the customer or pays a trucking firm, the railroad, or another carrier to transport it. Alternatively, the agreement between the buyer and the seller may provide for the goods to be shipped FOB shipping point. In this case, the merchandise is the responsibility of the buyer as soon as it leaves the seller's premises. When the terms of shipment are FOB shipping point, the buyer incurs transportation costs.

FOB destination point
Terms that require the seller to pay for the cost of shipping the merchandise to the buyer.

FOB shipping point
Terms that require the buyer to pay for the shipping costs.

Refer to Exhibit 5-7. Transportation-in represents the freight costs Daisy's paid for inbound merchandise. These costs are added to net purchases, as shown in the exhibit, and increase the cost of goods purchased. Assume that on delivery of a shipment of goods, Daisy's pays an invoice for $300 from Rocky Mountain Railroad. The terms of shipment are FOB shipping point. The entry on the books of Daisy's follows.

May 10	Transportation-in	300	
	Cash		300
	To record the payment of freight costs.		

Balance Sheet						Income Statement	
ASSETS		=	**LIABILITIES**	+	**STOCKHOLDERS' EQUITY**	+	**REVENUES – EXPENSES**
Cash	(300)						Transportation-in (300)

The total of net purchases and transportation-in is called the *cost of goods purchased*. Transportation-in will be closed at the end of the period. In summary, cost of goods purchased consists of the following:

> Purchases
> Less: Purchase returns and allowances
> Purchase discounts
> Equals: Net purchases
> Add: Transportation-in
> Equals: Cost of goods purchased

How should the seller account for the freight costs it pays when the goods are shipped FOB destination point? This cost, sometimes called *transportation-out*, is not an addition to the cost of purchases of the seller; instead, it is one of the costs necessary to *sell* the merchandise. Transportation-out is classified as a *selling expense* on the income statement.

Shipping Terms and Transfer of Title to Inventory Terms of shipment take on additional significance at the end of an accounting period. It is essential that a company establish a proper cutoff at year-end. For example, what if Daisy's purchases merchandise that is in transit at the end of the year? To whom does the inventory belong, Daisy's or the seller? The answer depends on the terms of shipment. If goods are shipped FOB destination point, they remain the legal property of the seller until they reach their destination. Alternatively, legal title to goods shipped FOB shipping point passes to the buyer as soon as the seller turns the goods over to the carrier.

The example in Exhibit 5-8 is intended to summarize the discussion about shipping terms and ownership of merchandise. Assume that Nike sells running shoes to Daisy's toward the end of the year and that the merchandise is in transit at the end of the year. Nike, the seller of the goods, pays the transportation charges only if the terms are FOB destination point. However, Nike records a sale for goods in transit at year-end only if

EXHIBIT 5-8 Shipping Terms and Transfer of Title to Inventory

FACTS **Assume that on December 28, 2008, Nike ships running shoes to Daisy's Running Depot. The trucking company delivers the merchandise to Daisy's on January 2, 2009. Daisy's fiscal year-end is December 31.**

		If Merchandise Is Shipped FOB	
Company		**Destination Point**	**Shipping Point**
Nike (seller)	Pay freight costs?	Yes	No
	Record sale in 2008?	No	Yes
	Include inventory on balance sheet at December 31, 2008?	Yes	No
Daisy's (buyer)	Pay freight costs?	No	Yes
	Record purchase in 2008?	No	Yes
	Include inventory on balance sheet at December 31, 2008?	No	Yes

the terms of shipment are FOB shipping point. If Nike does not record a sale because the goods are shipped FOB destination point, the inventory appears on its December 31 balance sheet. Daisy's, the buyer, pays freight costs only if the goods are shipped FOB shipping point. Only in this situation does Daisy's record a purchase of the merchandise and include it as an asset on its December 31 balance sheet.

POD REVIEW 5.3

LO3 *Show that you understand how wholesalers and retailers account for cost of goods sold.*

- The cost of goods sold represents goods sold, as opposed to the inventory purchased during the year. Cost of goods sold is matched with the sales of the period.
  - The cost of goods sold in any one period is equal to: Beginning inventory + Purchases − Ending inventory.
  - Under the perpetual method, the inventory account is updated after each sale or purchase of merchandise.
  - In contrast, under the periodic method, the inventory account is updated only at the end of the period.
- The cost of goods purchased includes any costs necessary to acquire the goods less any purchase discounts, returns, and allowances.
  - Transportation-in is the cost to ship goods to a company and is typically classified as part of cost of goods purchased.

QUESTIONS

1. *Cost of goods available for sale is equal to*
   a. cost of goods sold less beginning inventory.
   b. beginning inventory less ending inventory.
   c. beginning inventory less cost of goods sold.
   d. none of the above.

2. *The type of inventory system in which the Inventory account is updated at the time of each sale is called*
   a. a periodic system.
   b. a perpetual system.
   c. an accrual system.
   d. none of the above.

The Gross Profit Ratio

The first three lines on Daisy's income statement in Exhibit 5-2 are as follows:

Net sales	$100,000
Cost of goods sold	60,000
Gross profit	$ 40,000

LO4 Use the gross profit ratio to analyze a company's ability to cover its operating expenses and earn a profit.

Gross profit ratio Gross profit divided by net sales.

The relationship between gross profit and net sales—as measured by the **gross profit ratio**—is one of the most important measures used by managers, investors, and creditors to assess the performance of a company.

Gross Profit Ratio

Formula	For Daisy Sporting Goods
$\frac{\text{Gross Profit}}{\text{Net Sales}}$	$\frac{\$40,000}{\$100,000} = 40\%$

A 40% gross profit ratio says that for every dollar of sales, Daisy has a gross profit of 40 cents. In other words, after deducting 60 cents for the cost of the product, the company has 40 cents on the dollar to cover its operating costs and to earn a profit. We will now apply the ratio decision model to analyze this ratio for Gap Inc.

USING THE RATIO DECISION MODEL: ANALYZING THE GROSS PROFIT RATIO

Use the following Ratio Decision Model to evaluate the gross profit ratio for Gap Inc. or any other public company.

1. Formulate the Question
The gross profit ratio tells us how many cents on every dollar are available to cover expenses other than cost of goods sold and to earn a profit.

How much of the sales revenue is used for the cost of the products? Thus, how much is left to cover other expenses and to earn net income?

2. Gather the Information from the Financial Statements
Both gross profit and net sales are reported on Gap Inc.'s income statement for its 2006 fiscal year:

- Net sales: From the Income Statement for the Year
- Gross profit: From the Income Statement for the Year

3. Calculate the Ratio

$$\text{Gross Profit Ratio} = \frac{\text{Gross Profit}}{\text{Net Sales}}$$

(continued)

Gap Inc.
Partial Consolidated Statements of Income
(in millions)

	Year Ended		
	February 3, 2007	January 28, 2006	January 29, 2005
Net sales	$15,943	$16,023	$16,267
Cost of goods sold and occupancy expenses	10,294	10,154	9,886
Gross profit	5,649	5,869	6,381

$$\text{Gross Profit Ratio} = \frac{\$5{,}649}{\$15{,}943} = 35.4\%$$

4. Compare the Ratio with Others

Management and other users compare the gross profit ratio with that of prior years to see if it has increased, decreased, or remained relatively steady. It is also important to compare the ratio with those of other companies in the same industry.

Gap Inc.		American Eagle Outfitters, Inc.	
Year Ended February 3, 2007	Year Ended January 28, 2006	Year Ended February 3, 2007	Year Ended January 28, 2006
35.4%	36.6%	48.0%	46.4%

5. Interpret the Results

For every dollar of sales, Gap Inc. has approximately 35 cents available after deducting the cost of its products. The ratio was slightly higher in the prior year. Note the higher gross profit ratios for one of Gap's competitors. American Eagle Outfitters. Of course, the gross profit ratio alone is not enough to determine a company's profitability. Only if all of the expenses other than cost of goods sold are less than a company's gross profit will it report net income on the bottom line of the income statement.

POD REVIEW 5.4

LO4 *Use the gross profit ratio to analyze a company's ability to cover its operating expenses and earn a profit.*

- The gross profit ratio is the relationship between gross profit and net sales. Managers, investors, and creditors use this important ratio to measure one aspect of profitability.
  - The ratio is calculated as follows: $\dfrac{\text{Gross profit}}{\text{Net sales}}$

QUESTIONS

1. *The gross profit ratio is computed by*
   a. dividing gross profit by net sales.
   b. dividing net sales by gross profit.
   c. dividing gross profit by cost of goods sold.
   d. none of the above.

2. *To evaluate a company's gross profit ratio,*
   a. the ratio should be compared with those of prior years.
   b. the ratio should be compared with those of competitors.
   c. the ratio should be compared with those of both prior years and competitors.
   d. the ratio should be evaluated without any comparisons made to those of prior years or competitors.

Inventory Valuation and the Measurement of Income

LO5 Explain the relationship between the valuation of inventory and the measurement of income.

One of the most fundamental concepts in accounting is the relationship between *asset valuation* and the *measurement of income*. Recall a point made in Chapter 4:

Assets are unexpired costs, and expenses are expired costs.

Thus, **the value assigned to an asset on the balance sheet determines the amount eventually recognized as an expense on the income statement.** For example, the amount recorded as the cost of an item of plant and equipment will dictate the amount of depreciation expense recognized on the income statement over the life of the asset. Similarly, the amount recorded as the cost of inventory determines the amount recognized as cost of goods sold on the income statement when the asset is sold. An error in assigning the proper amount to inventory on the balance sheet will affect the amount recognized as cost of goods sold on the income statement. You can understand the relationship between inventory as an asset and cost of goods sold by recalling the cost of goods sold section of the income statement. Assume the following example:

Beginning inventory	$ 500
Add: Purchases	1,200
Cost of goods available for sale	$1,700
Less: Ending inventory	(600)
Cost of goods sold	$1,100

The amount assigned to ending inventory is deducted from cost of goods available for sale to determine cost of goods sold. **If the ending inventory amount is incorrect, cost of goods sold will be wrong; thus, the net income of the period will be in error as well.** (Inventory errors will be discussed later in the chapter.)

INVENTORY COSTS: WHAT SHOULD BE INCLUDED?

All assets, including inventory, are initially recorded at cost. Cost is defined as "the price paid or consideration given to acquire an asset. As applied to inventories, cost means in principle the sum of the applicable expenditures and charges directly or indirectly incurred in bringing an article to its existing condition and location."[1]

Note the reference to the existing *condition* and *location*. This means that certain costs may also be included in the "price paid." Here are examples:

- As you saw earlier in the chapter, any freight costs incurred by the buyer in shipping inventory to its place of business should be included in the cost of the inventory.
- The cost of insurance taken out during the time that inventory is in transit should be added to the cost of the inventory.
- The cost of storing inventory before it is ready to be sold should be included in cost.
- Various types of taxes paid, such as excise and sales taxes, are other examples of costs necessary to put the inventory into a position to be able to sell it.

However, it is often difficult to allocate many of these incidental costs among the various items of inventory purchased. For example, consider a $500 freight bill that a supermarket paid on a merchandise shipment that included 100 different items of inventory. To address the practical difficulty in assigning this type of cost to the different products, many companies have a policy by which transportation costs are charged to expense of the period when they are immaterial in amount. Thus, shipments of merchandise are recorded at the net invoice price, that is, after taking any cash discounts for early payment. It is a practical solution to a difficult allocation problem. Once again, the company must apply the cost/benefit test to accounting information.

1 *Accounting Research Bulletin No. 43,* "Inventory Pricing" (New York: American Institute of Certified Public Accountants, June 1953), Ch. 4, statement 3.

POD REVIEW 5.5

LO5 *Explain the relationship between the valuation of inventory and the measurement of income.*

- Inventory costs ultimately become the cost of goods sold reflected in the income statement.
  - Since inventory is not expensed as the cost of goods sold until merchandise is sold, determining which costs belong in inventory affects the timing of when these expenses are reflected in net income.

QUESTIONS

1. *Why is it important that the proper amount be assigned to inventory?*
   a. Because the amount assigned to inventory will affect the amount eventually recorded as cost of goods sold.
   b. Because the amount assigned to inventory will affect the amount eventually recorded as selling and administrative expenses.
   c. Because the amount assigned to inventory will affect the amount eventually recorded as net sales.
   d. none of the above

2. *Which of the following should not be included in the cost of inventory?*
   a. freight cost incurred to buy inventory
   b. cost of insurance taken out during the time inventory is in transit
   c. cost to store inventory before it is ready to be sold
   d. freight cost incurred to ship inventory to a customer

Inventory Costing Methods with a Periodic System

LO6 Apply the inventory costing methods of specific identification, weighted average, FIFO, and LIFO by using a periodic system.

To this point, we have assumed that the cost to purchase an item of inventory is constant. For most merchandisers, however, the unit cost of inventory changes frequently. Consider a simple example. Everett Company purchases merchandise twice during the first year of business. The dates, the number of units purchased, and the costs are as follows:

February 4	200 units purchased at \$1.00 per unit = \$200
October 13	200 units purchased at \$1.50 per unit = \$300

Everett sells 200 units during the first year. Individual sales of the units take place relatively evenly throughout the year. The question is, *which* 200 units did the company sell— the \$1.00 units or the \$1.50 units or some combination of each? Recall the earlier discussion of the relationship between asset valuation and income measurement. The question is important because the answer determines not only the value assigned to the 200 units of ending inventory but also the amount allocated to cost of goods sold for the 200 units sold.

One possible method of assigning amounts to ending inventory and cost of goods sold is to specifically identify which 200 units were sold and which 200 units are on hand. This method is feasible for a few types of businesses in which units can be identified by serial numbers, but it is totally impractical in most situations. As an alternative to specific identification, we could make an assumption as to which units were sold and which are on hand. Three different answers are possible, as follows:

1. 200 units sold at \$1.00 each = \$200 cost of goods sold
and 200 units on hand at \$1.50 each = \$300 ending inventory
or

2. 200 units sold at \$1.50 each = \$300 cost of goods sold
and 200 units on hand at \$1.00 each = \$200 ending inventory

or

3. 200 units sold at $1.25 each = $250 cost of goods sold
and 200 units on hand at $1.25 each = $250 ending inventory

The third alternative assumes an *average cost* for the 200 units on hand and the 200 units sold. The average cost is the cost of the two purchases of $200 and $300, or $500, divided by the 400 units available to sell, or $1.25 per unit.

If we are concerned with the actual physical flow of the units of inventory, all three methods illustrated may be incorrect. The only approach that will yield a "correct" answer in terms of the actual flow of *units* of inventory is the specific identification method. In the absence of a specific identification approach, it is impossible to say which particular units were actually sold. In fact, there may have been sales from each of the two purchases; that is, some of the $1.00 units may have been sold and some of the $1.50 units may have been sold. To solve the problem of assigning costs to identical units, accountants have developed inventory costing assumptions or methods. Each of these methods makes a specific assumption about the flow of costs rather than the physical flow of units. The only approach that uses the actual flow of the units in assigning costs is the specific identification method.

To take a closer look at specific identification as well as three alternative approaches to valuing inventory, we will use the following example:

	Units	Unit Cost	Total Cost
Beginning inventory			
January 1	500	$10	$ 5,000*
Purchases			
January 20	300	11	$ 3,300
April 8	400	12	4,800
September 5	200	13	2,600
December 12	100	14	1,400
Total purchases	1,000 units		$12,100
Available for sale	1,500 units		$17,100
Units sold	900 units		?
Units in ending inventory	600 units		?

**Beginning inventory of $5,000 is carried over as the ending inventory from the prior period. It is highly unlikely that each of the four methods we will illustrate would result in the same dollar amount of inventory at any point in time. It is helpful when first learning the methods, however, to assume the same amount of beginning inventory.*

The question marks indicate the dilemma. What portion of the cost of goods available for sale of $17,100 should be assigned to the 900 units sold? What portion should be assigned to the 600 units remaining in ending inventory? The purpose of an inventory costing method is to provide a reasonable answer to those two questions.

SPECIFIC IDENTIFICATION METHOD

It is not always necessary to make an assumption about the flow of costs. In certain situations, it may be possible to specifically identify which units are sold and which units are on hand. A serial number on an automobile allows a dealer to identify a car on hand and thus its unit cost. An appliance dealer with 15 refrigerators on hand at the end of the year can identify the unit cost of each by matching a tag number with the purchase records. To illustrate the use of the **specific identification method** for the example, assume that the merchandiser is able to identify the specific units in the inventory at the end of the year and their costs as follows:

Specific identification method
An inventory costing method that relies on matching unit costs with the actual units sold.

Units on Hand

Date Purchased	Units	Cost	Total Cost
January 20	100	$11	$1,100
April 8	300	12	3,600
September 5	200	13	2,600
Ending inventory	600		$7,300

One of two techniques can be used to find cost of goods sold. We can deduct ending inventory from the cost of goods available for sale, as follows:

Cost of goods available for sale	$17,100
Less: Ending inventory	7,300
Equals: Cost of goods sold	$ 9,800

Or we can calculate cost of goods sold independently by matching the units sold with their respective unit costs. By eliminating the units in ending inventory from the original acquisition schedule, the units sold and their costs are as follows:

Units Sold

Date purchased	Units	Cost	Total Cost
Beginning Inventory	500	$10	$5,000
January 20	200	11	2,200
April 8	100	12	1,200
December 12	100	14	1,400
Cost of goods sold	900		$9,800

The practical difficulty of keeping track of individual items of inventory sold is not the only problem with the use of this method. The method also allows management to manipulate income. For example, assume that a company is not having a particularly good year. Management may be tempted to do whatever it can to boost net income. One way it can do this is by selectively selling units with the lowest-possible unit cost. By doing so, the company can keep cost of goods sold down and net income up. Because of the potential for manipulation with the specific identification method, coupled with the practical difficulty of applying it in most situations, it is not widely used.

WEIGHTED AVERAGE COST METHOD

Weighted average cost method
An inventory costing method that assigns the same unit cost to all units available for sale during the period.

The **weighted average cost method** is a relatively easy approach to costing inventory. It assigns the same unit cost to all units available for sale during the period. The weighted average cost is calculated as follows for the example:

$$\frac{\text{Cost of Goods Available for Sale}}{\text{Units Available for Sale}} = \text{Weighted Average Cost}$$

$$\frac{\$17{,}100}{1{,}500} = \$11.40$$

Ending inventory is found by multiplying the weighted average unit cost by the number of units on hand:

$$\text{Weighted Average Cost} \times \text{Number of Units in Ending Inventory} = \text{Ending Inventory}$$

$$\$11.40 \times 600 = \$6{,}840$$

Cost of goods sold can be calculated in one of two ways:

Cost of goods available for sale	$17,100
Less: Ending inventory	6,840
Equals: Cost of goods sold	$10,260

or

$$\text{Weighted Average Cost} \times \text{Number of Units Sold} = \text{Cost of Goods Sold}$$

$$\$11.40 \times 900 = \$10{,}260$$

Note that the computation of the weighted average cost is based on the cost of all units available for sale during the period, not just the beginning inventory or purchases. Also note that the method is called the *weighted* average cost method. As the name indicates, each of the individual unit costs is multiplied by the number of units acquired at each price. The simple arithmetic average of the unit costs for the beginning inventory and the four purchases is ($10 + $11 + $12 + $13 + $14)/5 = $12. The weighted average cost is slightly less than $12 ($11.40), however, because more units were acquired at the lower prices than at the higher prices.

FIRST-IN, FIRST-OUT METHOD (FIFO)

The **FIFO method** assumes that the first units in, or purchased, are the first units out, or sold. The first units sold during the period are assumed to come from the beginning inventory. After the beginning inventory is sold, the next units sold are assumed to come from the first purchase during the period and so on. Thus, ending inventory consists of the most recent purchases of the period. In many businesses, this cost-flow assumption is a fairly accurate reflection of the physical flow of products. For example, to maintain a fresh stock of products, the physical flow in a grocery store is first-in, first-out.

FIFO method
An inventory costing method that assigns the most recent costs to ending inventory.

To calculate ending inventory, we start with the most recent inventory acquired and work backward:

Units on Hand

Date Purchased	Units	Cost	Total Cost
December 12	100	$14	$1,400
September 5	200	13	2,600
April 8	300	12	3,600
Ending inventory	600		$7,600

Cost of goods sold can then be found as follows:

Cost of goods available for sale	$17,100
Less: Ending inventory	7,600
Equals: Cost of goods sold	$ 9,500

Or because the FIFO method assumes that the first units in are the first ones sold, cost of goods sold can be calculated by starting with the beginning inventory and working forward:

Units Sold

Date Purchased	Units	Cost	Total Cost
Beginning Inventory	500	$10	$5,000
January 20	300	11	3,300
April 8	100	12	1,200
Units sold	900	Cost of goods sold	$9,500

LAST-IN, FIRST-OUT METHOD (LIFO)

The **LIFO method** assumes that the last units in, or purchased, are the first units out, or sold. The first units sold during the period are assumed to come from the latest purchase made during the period and so on. Can you think of any businesses where the physical flow of products is last-in, first-out? Although this situation is not as common as a FIFO physical flow, a stockpiling operation, such as in a rock quarry, operates on this basis.

LIFO method
An inventory method that assigns the most recent costs to cost of goods sold.

Study Tip

There may be cases, such as this illustration of LIFO, in which it is easier to determine ending inventory and then deduct it from cost of goods available for sale to find cost of goods sold. This approach is easier in this example because there are fewer layers in ending inventory than in cost of goods sold. In other cases, it may be quicker to determine cost of goods sold first and then plug in ending inventory.

To calculate ending inventory using LIFO, we start with the beginning inventory and work forward:

Units on Hand

Date Purchased	Units	Cost	Total Cost
Beginning inventory	500	$10	$5,000
January 20	100	11	1,100
Ending inventory	600		$6,100

Cost of goods sold can then be found as follows:

Cost of goods available for sale	$17,100
Less: Ending inventory	6,100
Equals: Cost of goods sold	$11,000

Or because the LIFO method assumes that the last units in are the first ones sold, cost of goods sold can be calculated by starting with the most recent inventory acquired and working backward:

Units Sold

Date Purchased	Units	Cost	Total Cost
December 12	100	$14	$ 1,400
September 5	200	13	2,600
April 8	400	12	4,800
January 20	200	11	2,200
Units sold	900	Cost of goods sold	$11,000

POD REVIEW 5.6

LO6 *Apply the inventory costing methods of specific identification, weighted average, FIFO, and LIFO by using a periodic system.*

- The purchase price of inventory items may change frequently, and several alternatives are available to assign costs to the goods sold and those that remain in ending inventory.
  - Specific identification assigns the actual costs of acquisition to items of inventory. In some circumstances, it is not practical to do this.
  - Three other methods involve making assumptions about the cost of inventory:
    - Weighted average assigns the same unit cost to all units available for sale during the period.
    - The FIFO method assumes that the first units purchased are the first units sold.
    - The LIFO method assumes that the last units purchased are the first units sold.

QUESTIONS

1. *For which of the following products is a company most likely to use the specific identification method?*
   a. boxes of soap in a grocery store
   b. automobiles at a car dealer
   c. car batteries at an auto parts store
   d. The specific identification cannot be used by any companies.

2. *Which inventory method assigns the most recent costs to ending inventory?*
   a. FIFO
   b. LIFO
   c. weighted average
   d. specific identification

Selecting an Inventory Costing Method

LO7 Analyze the effects of the different costing methods on inventory, net income, income taxes, and cash flow.

The mechanics of each of the inventory costing methods are straightforward. But how does a company decide on the best method to use to value its inventory? According to the accounting profession, **the primary determinant in selecting an inventory costing method should be the ability of the method to accurately reflect the net income of the period.** But how and why does a particular costing method accurately reflect the net income of the period? Because there is no easy answer to this question, accountants have raised a number of arguments to justify the use of one method over the others. We turn now to some of those arguments.

COSTING METHODS AND CASH FLOW

Comparative income statements for the example are presented in Exhibit 5-9. Note that with the use of the weighted average method, net income is between the amounts for FIFO and LIFO. Because the weighted average method normally yields results between the other two methods, we concentrate on the two extremes, LIFO and FIFO. The major advantage of using the weighted average method is its simplicity.

The original data for the example involved a situation in which prices were rising throughout the period: beginning inventory cost $10 per unit, and the last purchase during the year was at $14. With LIFO, the most recent costs are assigned to cost of goods sold; with FIFO, the older costs are assigned to expense. Thus, in a period of rising prices, the assignment of the higher prices to cost of goods sold under LIFO results in a lower gross profit under LIFO than under FIFO ($7,000 for LIFO and $8,500 for FIFO). Because operating expenses are not affected by the choice of inventory method, the lower gross profit under LIFO results in lower income before tax, which in turn leads to lower taxes. If we assume a 40% tax rate, income tax expense under LIFO is only $2,000, compared with $2,600 under FIFO, a savings of $600 in taxes. Another way to look at the taxes saved by using LIFO is to focus on the difference in the expense under each method, as follows:

LIFO cost of goods sold	$11,000
− FIFO cost of goods sold	9,500
Additional expense from use of LIFO	$ 1,500
× Tax rate	0.40
Tax savings from the use of LIFO	$ 600

Study Tip

During a period of falling prices, all of the effects shown here would be just the opposite. For example, cost of goods sold would be lower under LIFO than under FIFO.

EXHIBIT 5-9 Income Statements for the Inventory Costing Methods

	Weighted Average	FIFO	LIFO
Sales revenue—$20 each	$18,000	$18,000	$18,000
Beginning inventory	$ 5,000	$ 5,000	$ 5,000
Purchases	12,100	12,100	12,100
Cost of goods available for sale	$17,100	$17,100	$17,100
Ending inventory	**6,840**	**7,600**	**6,100**
Cost of goods sold	**$10,260**	**$ 9,500**	**$11,000**
Gross profit	**$ 7,740**	**$ 8,500**	**$ 7,000**
Operating expenses	2,000	2,000	2,000
Net income before tax	**$ 5,740**	**$ 6,500**	**$ 5,000**
Income tax expense (40%)	**2,296**	**2,600**	**2,000**
Net income	**$ 3,444**	**$ 3,900**	**$ 3,000**

NOTE: Figures that differ among the three methods are in bold.

To summarize, during a period of rising prices, the two methods result in the following:

Item	LIFO	Relative To	FIFO
Cost of goods sold	Higher		Lower
Gross profit	Lower		Higher
Income before taxes	Lower		Higher
Taxes	Lower		Higher

In conclusion, lower taxes with the use of LIFO result in cash savings.

The tax savings available from the use of LIFO during a period of rising prices is largely responsible for its popularity. Keep in mind, however, that the cash saved from a lower tax bill with LIFO is only a temporary savings, or what is normally called a *tax deferral.* At some point in the life of the business, the inventory that is carried at the older, lower-priced amounts will be sold. This will result in a tax bill higher than that under FIFO. Yet even a tax deferral is beneficial; given the opportunity, it is better to pay less tax today and more in the future because today's tax savings can be invested.

LIFO LIQUIDATION

Recall the assumption made about which costs remain in inventory when LIFO is used. The costs of the oldest units remain in inventory; and if prices are rising, the costs of these units will be lower than the costs of more recent purchases. Now assume that the company sells more units than it buys during the period. When a company using LIFO experiences a liquidation, some of the units assumed to be sold come from the older layers, with a relatively low unit cost. This situation, called a **LIFO liquidation**, presents a dilemma for the company.

LIFO liquidation
The result of selling more units than are purchased during the period, which can have negative tax consequences if a company is using LIFO.

A partial or complete liquidation of the older, lower-priced units will result in a low cost of goods sold figure and a correspondingly high gross profit for the period. In turn, the company faces a large tax bill because of the relatively high gross profit. In fact, a liquidation causes the tax advantages of using LIFO to reverse on the company, which is faced with paying off some of the taxes that were deferred in earlier periods. Should a company facing this situation buy inventory at the end of the year to avoid the consequences of a liquidation? That is a difficult question to answer and depends on many factors, including the company's cash position. The accountant must at least be aware of the potential for a large tax bill if a liquidation occurs.

Of course, a LIFO liquidation also benefits—and may even distort—reported earnings if the liquidation is large enough. For this reason and the tax problem, many companies are reluctant to liquidate their LIFO inventory. The problem often festers, and companies find themselves with inventory costed at decade-old price levels.

THE LIFO CONFORMITY RULE

Would it be possible for a company to have the best of both worlds? That is, could it use FIFO to report its income to stockholders, thus maximizing the amount of net income reported to this group, and use LIFO to report to the IRS, minimizing its taxable income and the amount paid to the government? Unfortunately, the IRS says that if a company chooses LIFO for reporting cost of goods sold on its tax return, it must also use LIFO on its books, that is, in preparing its income statement. This is called the **LIFO conformity rule**. Note that the rule applies only to the use of LIFO on the tax return. A company is free to use different methods in preparing its tax return and its income statement as long as the method used for the tax return is *not* LIFO.

LIFO conformity rule
The IRS requirement that when LIFO is used on a tax return, it must also be used in reporting income to stockholders.

THE LIFO RESERVE: ESTIMATING LIFO'S EFFECT ON INCOME AND ON TAXES PAID FOR WINNEBAGO INDUSTRIES

If a company decides to use LIFO, an investor can still determine how much more income the company would have reported had it used FIFO. In addition, he or she can approximate the tax savings to the company from the use of LIFO. Consider Note 3 from the 2006 annual report for **Winnebago Industries**, the RV maker.

Note 3: Inventories

Inventories consist of the following: (dollars in thousands)	**August 26, 2006**	**August 27, 2005**
Finished goods	$ 33,420	$ 67,998
Work-in-process	35,166	45,657
Raw materials	40,080	38,461
	108,666	152,116
LIFO reserve	(31,585)	(31,461)
	$ 77,081	$120,655

The above value of inventories, before reduction for the LIFO reserve, approximates replacement cost at the respective dates.

The following steps explain the logic for using the information in the inventory note to estimate LIFO's effect on income and on taxes:

1. **The excess of the value of a company's inventory stated at FIFO over the value stated at LIFO is called the LIFO reserve. The *cumulative* excess of the value of Winnebago Industries' inventory on a FIFO basis over the value on a LIFO basis is $31,585,000 at the end of 2006.**
2. **Because Winnebago Industries reports inventory at a lower value on its balance sheet using LIFO, it will report a higher cost of goods sold amount on the income statement. Thus, the LIFO reserve not only represents the excess of the inventory balance on a FIFO basis over that on a LIFO basis but also represents the cumulative amount by which cost of goods sold on a LIFO basis exceeds cost of goods sold on a FIFO basis.**
3. **The increase in Winnebago Industries' LIFO reserve in 2006 was $124,000 ($31,585,000 − $31,461,000). This means that the increase in cost of goods sold for 2006 from using LIFO instead of FIFO was also this amount. Thus, income before tax for 2006 was $124,000 lower because the company used LIFO.**
4. **If we assume a corporate tax rate of 35%, the tax savings from using LIFO amounted to $124,000 × 0.35, or $43,400.**

LIFO reserve
The excess of the value of a company's inventory stated at FIFO over the value stated at LIFO.

COSTING METHODS AND INVENTORY PROFITS

FIFO, LIFO, and weighted average are all cost-based methods to value inventory. They vary in terms of which costs are assigned to inventory and which are assigned to cost of goods sold, but all three assign *historical costs* to inventory. In the previous example, the unit cost for inventory purchases gradually increased during the year from $10 for the beginning inventory to a high of $14 on the date of the last purchase.

An alternative to assigning any of the historical costs incurred during the year to ending inventory and cost of goods sold is to use **replacement cost** to value each of these. Assume that the cost to replace a unit of inventory at the end of the year is $15. Use of a replacement cost system results in the following:

Replacement cost
The current cost of a unit of inventory.

Ending inventory = 600 units × $15 per unit = $ 9,000

Cost of goods sold = 900 units × $15 per unit = $13,500

A replacement cost approach is not acceptable under the profession's current standards, but many believe that it provides more relevant information to users.

Inventory profit
The portion of the gross profit that results from holding inventory during a period of rising prices.

Inventory must be replaced if a company is to remain in business. Many accountants argue that the use of historical cost in valuing inventory leads to what is called **inventory profit**, particularly when FIFO is used in a period of rising prices. For example, cost of goods sold in the illustration was only $9,500 on a FIFO basis, compared with $13,500 when the replacement cost of $15 per unit was used. The $4,000 difference between the two cost of goods sold figures is a profit from holding the inventory during a period of rising prices and is called *inventory profit*. To look at this another way, assume that the units are sold for $20 each. The following analysis reconciles the difference between gross profit on a FIFO basis and on a replacement cost basis:

Sales revenue (900 units × $20)		$18,000
Cost of goods sold—FIFO basis		9,500
Gross profit—FIFO basis		$ 8,500
Cost of goods sold—replacement cost basis	$13,500	
Cost of goods sold—FIFO basis	9,500	
Profit from holding inventory during a period of inflation		4,000
Gross profit on a replacement cost basis		$ 4,500

Those who argue in favor of a replacement cost approach would report only $4,500 of gross profit. They believe that the additional $4,000 of profit reported on a FIFO basis is simply due to holding the inventory during a period of rising prices. According to this viewpoint, if the 900 units sold during the period are to be replaced, a necessity if the company is to continue operating, the use of replacement cost in calculating cost of goods sold results in a better measure of gross profit than if it is calculated using FIFO.

Given that our current standards require the use of historical costs rather than replacement costs, does any one of the costing methods result in a better approximation of replacement cost of goods sold than the others? Because LIFO assigns the cost of the most recent purchases to cost of goods sold, it most nearly approximates the results with a replacement cost system. The other side of the argument, however, is that whereas LIFO results in the best approximation of replacement cost of goods sold on the income statement, FIFO most nearly approximates replacement cost of the inventory on the balance sheet. A comparison of the amounts from the example verifies this:

	Ending Inventory	Cost of Goods Sold
Weighted average	$6,840	$10,260
FIFO	7,600	9,500
LIFO	6,100	11,000
Replacement cost	9,000	13,500

CHANGING INVENTORY METHODS

The purpose of each of the inventory costing methods is to match costs with revenues. If a company believes that a different method will result in a better matching than that being provided by the method currently being used, the company should change methods. A company must be able to justify a change in methods, however. Taking advantage of the tax breaks offered by LIFO is *not* a valid justification for a change in methods.

INVENTORY VALUATION IN OTHER COUNTRIES

The acceptable methods of valuing inventory differ considerably around the world. Although FIFO is the most popular method in the United States, LIFO continues to be widely used, as is the average cost method. Many countries prohibit the use of LIFO for tax or financial reporting purposes. Chapter 1 mentioned the attempts by the IASB to develop worldwide accounting standards. This group does not allow the use of LIFO by companies that follow its standards.

POD REVIEW 5.7

LO7 ***Analyze the effects of the different costing methods on inventory, net income, income taxes, and cash flow.***

- The ability to measure net income accurately for a period should be the driving force behind selecting an inventory costing method.
  - Inventory costing methods impact the cost of goods sold and, therefore, net income.
  - When a company uses LIFO for tax purposes, it must use it for financial reporting purposes as well.

QUESTIONS

1. *Which inventory method results in the least amount of income before taxes, assuming a period of rising prices?*
   a. FIFO
   b. LIFO
   c. weighted average cost
   d. none of the above

2. *The LIFO conformity rule requires that if a company*
   a. uses LIFO in reporting income to stockholders, it also must use LIFO on its tax return.
   b. uses LIFO on its tax return, it also must use LIFO in reporting income to stockholders.
   c. uses LIFO on its tax return, it must use FIFO in reporting income to stockholders.
   d. none of the above.

Inventory Errors

LO8 Analyze the effects of an inventory error on various financial statement items.

Earlier in the chapter we considered the inherent tie between the valuation of assets, such as inventory, and the measurement of income, such as cost of goods sold. The importance of inventory valuation to the measurement of income can be illustrated by considering inventory errors. Many different types of inventory errors exist. Some errors are mathematical; for example, a bookkeeper may incorrectly add a column total. Other errors relate specifically to the physical count of inventory at year-end. For example, the count might inadvertently omit one section of a warehouse. Other errors arise from cutoff problems at year-end.

For example, assume that merchandise in transit at the end of the year is shipped FOB (free on board) shipping point. Under these shipment terms, the inventory belongs to the buyer at the time it is shipped. Because the shipment has not arrived at the end of the year, however, it cannot be included in the physical count. Unless some type of control is in place, the amount in transit may be erroneously omitted from the valuation of inventory at year-end.

To demonstrate the effect of an inventory error on the income statement, consider the following example. Through a scheduling error, two different inventory teams were assigned to count the inventory in the same warehouse on December 31, 2008. The correct amount of ending inventory is $250,000; but because two different teams counted the same inventory in one warehouse, the amount recorded is $300,000. The effect of this error on net income is analyzed in the left half of Exhibit 5-10.

The overstatement of ending inventory in 2008 leads to an understatement of the 2008 cost of goods sold expense. Because cost of goods sold is understated, gross profit for the year is overstated. Operating expenses are unaffected by an inventory error. Thus, net income is overstated by the same amount of overstatement of gross profit.[2]

2 An overstatement of gross profit also results in an overstatement of income tax expense. Thus, because tax expense is overstated, the overstatement of net income is not as large as the overstatement of gross profit. For now, we will ignore the effect of taxes.

EXHIBIT 5-10 Effects of Inventory Error on the Income Statement

	2007			2008		
	Reported	Corrected	Effect of Error	Reported	Corrected	Effect of Error
Sales	$1,000*	$1,000		$1,500	$1,500	
Cost of goods sold:						
Beginning inventory	$ 200	$ 200		**$ 300**	**$ 250**	$50 OS
Add: Purchases	700	700		1,100	1,100	
Cost of goods available for sale	$ 900	$ 900		**$1,400**	**$1,350**	50 OS
Less: Ending inventory	**300**	**250**	$50 OS†	350	350	
Cost of goods sold	**$ 600**	**$ 650**	50 US‡	**$1,050**	**$1,000**	50 OS
Gross profit	**$ 400**	**$ 350**	50 OS	**$ 450**	**$ 500**	50 US
Operating expenses	100	100		120	120	
Net income	**$ 300**	**$ 250**	50 OS	**$ 330**	**$ 380**	50 US

NOTE: Figures that differ as a result of the error are in bold.
**All amounts are in thousands of dollars.*
†OS = Overstatement
‡US = Understatement

The most important conclusion from the exhibit is that an overstatement of ending inventory leads to a corresponding overstatement of net income.

Unfortunately, the effect of a misstatement of the year-end inventory is not limited to the net income for that year. As indicated in the right-hand portion of Exhibit 5-10, the error also affects the income statement for the following year. This happens simply because the ending inventory of one period is the beginning inventory of the following period. The overstatement of the 2009 beginning inventory leads to an overstatement of cost of goods available for sale. Because cost of goods available for sale is overstated, cost of goods sold is also overstated. The overstatement of cost of goods sold expense results in an understatement of gross profit and thus an understatement of net income.

Exhibit 5-10 illustrates the nature of a *counterbalancing error.* The effect of the overstatement of net income in the first year, 2008, is offset or counterbalanced by the understatement of net income by the same dollar amount in the following year. If the net incomes of two successive years are misstated in the opposite direction by the same amount, what is the effect on retained earnings? Assume that retained earnings at the beginning of 2008 is correctly stated at $300,000. The counterbalancing nature of the error is seen by analyzing retained earnings. For 2008, the analysis would indicate the following (OS = overstated and US = understated):

	2008 Reported	2008 Corrected	Effect of Error
Beginning retained earnings	$300,000	$300,000	Correct
Add: Net income	300,000	250,000	$50,000 OS
Ending retained earnings	$600,000	$550,000	$50,000 OS

An analysis for 2009 would show the following:

	2009 Reported	2009 Corrected	Effect of Error
Beginning retained earnings	$600,000	$550,000	$50,000 OS
Add: Net income	330,000	380,000	$50,000 US
Ending retained earnings	$930,000	$930,000	Correct

Thus, even though retained earnings is overstated at the end of the first year, it is correctly stated at the end of the second year. This is the nature of a counterbalancing error.

The effect of the error on the balance sheet is shown in Exhibit 5-11. The only accounts affected by the error are Inventory and Retained Earnings. The overstatement

EXHIBIT 5-11 **Effects of Inventory Error on the Balance Sheet**

	2008		2009	
	Reported	**Corrected**	**Reported**	**Corrected**
Inventory	**$ 300***	**$ 250**	$ 350	$ 350
All other assets	1,700	1,700	2,080	2,080
Total assets	**$2,000**	**$1,950**	$2,430	$2,430
Total liabilities	$ 400	$ 400	$ 500	$ 500
Capital stock	1,000	1,000	1,000	1,000
Retained earnings	**600**	**550**	930	930
Total liabilities and stockholders' equity	**$2,000**	**$1,950**	$2,430	$2,430

NOTE: Figures that differ as a result of the error are in bold.
**All amounts are in thousands of dollars.*

of the 2008 ending inventory results in an overstatement of total assets at the end of the first year. Similarly, as the earlier analysis indicates, the overstatement of 2008 net income leads to an overstatement of retained earnings by the same amount. Because the error is counterbalancing, the 2009 year-end balance sheet is correct. That is, ending inventory is not affected by the error; thus, the amount for total assets at the end of 2009 is also correct. The effect of the error on retained earnings is limited to the first year because of the counterbalancing nature of the error.

The effects of inventory errors on various financial statement items are summarized in Exhibit 5-12. The analysis focused on the effects of an overstatement of inventory. The effects of an understatement are just the opposite and are summarized in the bottom portion of the exhibit.

Not all errors are counterbalancing. For example, if a section of a warehouse continues to be omitted from the physical count every year, both beginning and ending inventories will be incorrect each year and the error will not counterbalance.

Part of the auditor's job is to perform the necessary tests to obtain reasonable assurance that inventory has not been overstated or understated. If there is an error and

Study Tip

Note the logic behind the notion that an overstatement of ending inventory leads to overstatements of total assets and retained earnings at the end of the year. This is logical because a balance sheet must balance; that is, the left side must equal the right side. If the left side (inventory) is overstated the right side (retained earnings) will also be overstated.

EXHIBIT 5-12 **Summary of the Effects of Inventory Errors**

	Effect of Overstatement of Ending Inventory on	
	Current Year	**Following Year**
Cost of goods sold	Understated	Overstated
Gross profit	Overstated	Understated
Net income	Overstated	Understated
Retained earnings, end of year	Overstated	Correctly stated
Total assets, end of year	Overstated	Correctly stated

	Effect of Understatement of Ending Inventory on	
	Current Year	**Following Year**
Cost of goods sold	Overstated	Understated
Gross profit	Understated	Overstated
Net income	Understated	Overstated
Retained earnings, end of year	Understated	Correctly stated
Total assets, end of year	Understated	Correctly stated

inventory is wrong, however, both the balance sheet and the income statement will be distorted. For example, if ending inventory is overstated, inflating total assets, cost of goods sold will be understated, boosting profits. Thus, such an error overstates the financial health of the organization in two ways. A lender or an investor must make a decision based on the current year's statement and cannot wait until the next accounting cycle, when this error is reversed. This is one reason that investors and creditors insist on audited financial statements.

POD REVIEW 5.8

LO8 *Analyze the effects of an inventory error on various financial statement items.*

- The link between the balance sheet and the income statement can be seen through the effect of errors in inventory valuation.
    - Overstatement of ending inventory results in an understatement of the cost of goods sold and therefore an overstatement of net income.
    - The effects of errors in inventory may offset themselves over time. These are known as counterbalancing errors.

QUESTIONS

1. *A company erroneously omits one section of its warehouse in the year-end inventory. The error will result in*
    a. an overstatement of cost of goods sold for the current year.
    b. an understatement of cost of goods sold for the current year.
    c. an overstatement of inventory on the year-end balance sheet.
    d. none of the above.

2. *A company erroneously counts the same section of its warehouse twice in the year-end inventory. Assuming no error is made in the year-end count the following year, the error will result in*
    a. an overstatement of cost of goods sold in the following year.
    b. an understatement of cost of goods sold in the following year.
    c. an overstatement of ending inventory on the year-end balance sheet of the following year.
    d. none of the above.

Valuing Inventory at Lower of Cost or Market

LO9 Apply the lower-of-cost-or-market rule to the valuation of inventory.

Lower-of-cost-or-market (LCM) rule
A conservative inventory valuation approach that is an attempt to anticipate declines in the value of inventory before its actual sale.

One of the components sold by an electronics firm has become economically obsolete. A particular style of suit sold by a retailer is outdated and can no longer be sold at regular price. In both instances, it is likely that the retailer will have to sell the merchandise for less than the normal selling price. In these situations, a departure from the cost basis of accounting may be necessary because the market value of the inventory may be less than its cost to the company. The departure is called the **lower-of-cost-or-market (LCM) rule.**

At the end of each accounting period, the original cost, as determined using one of the costing methods such as FIFO, is compared with the market price of the inventory. If market is less than cost, the inventory is written down to the lower amount.

For example, if cost is $100,000 and market value is $85,000, the accountant makes the following entry:

Dec. 31	Loss on Decline in Value of Inventory	15,000	
	Inventory		15,000
	To record decline in value of inventory.		

Balance Sheet							Income Statement
ASSETS		=	**LIABILITIES**	+	**STOCKHOLDERS' EQUITY**	+	**REVENUES – EXPENSES**
Inventory	(15,000)						Loss on Decline in Value of Inventory (15,000)

Note that the entry reduces assets in the form of inventory and net income. The reduction in net income is the result of reporting the Loss on Decline in Value of Inventory on the income statement as an item of Other Expense.

WHY REPLACEMENT COST IS USED AS A MEASURE OF MARKET

A better name for the lower-of-cost-or-market rule would be the lower-of-cost-or-replacement-cost rule because accountants define *market* as "replacement cost."[3] To understand why replacement cost is used as a basis to compare with original cost, consider the following example. Assume that The Finish Line pays $75 for a pair of running shoes and normally sells them for $100. Thus, the normal markup on selling price is $25/$100, or 25%, as indicated in the column Before Price Change in Exhibit 5-13. Now assume that this style of running shoes becomes less popular. The retailer checks with Nike and finds that because of the style change, the cost to the retailer to replace the pair of running shoes is now only $60. The retailer realizes that if the shoes are to be sold at all, they will have to be offered at a reduced price. The selling price is dropped from $100 to $80. If the retailer now buys a pair of shoes for $60 and sells them for $80, the gross profit will be $20 and the gross profit percentage will be maintained at 25%, as indicated in the right-hand column of Exhibit 5-13.

To compare the results with and without the use of the LCM rule, assume that the facts are the same as before and that the retailer has ten pairs of those shoes in inventory

EXHIBIT 5-13 Gross Profit Percentage Before and After Price Change

	Before Price Change	After Price Change
Selling price	$100	$80
Cost	75	60
Gross profit	$ 25	$20
Gross profit percentage	25%	25%

3 Technically, the use of replacement cost as a measure of market value is subject to two constraints. First, market cannot be more than the net realizable value of the inventory. Second, inventory should not be recorded at less than net realizable value less a normal profit margin. The rationale for these two constraints is covered in intermediate accounting texts. For our purposes, we assume that replacement cost falls between the two constraints.

on December 31, 2008. In addition, assume that all ten pair are sold at a clearance sale in January 2009 at the reduced price of $80 each. If the lower-of-cost-or-market rule is not used, the results for the two years will be as follows:

LCM Rule Not Used	2008	2009	Total
Sales revenue ($80 per unit)	$ 0	$800	$800
Cost of goods sold			
(original cost of $75 per unit)	0	(750)	(750)
Gross profit	$ 0	$ 50	$ 50

If the LCM rule is not applied, the gross profit is distorted. Instead of the normal 25%, a gross profit percentage of $50/$800, or 6.25%, is reported in 2009 when the ten pairs of shoes are sold. If the LCM rule is applied, however, the results for the two years are as follows:

LCM Rule Used	2008	2009	Total
Sales revenue ($80 per unit)	$ 0	$800	$800
Cost of goods sold			
(replacement cost of $60 per unit)	0	(600)	(600)
Loss on decline in value of inventory:			
10 units × ($75 − $60)	(150)	0	(150)
Gross profit	$(150)	$200	$ 50

The use of the LCM rule serves two important functions: (1) to report the loss in value of the inventory, $15 per pair of running shoes, or $150 total, in the year the loss occurs and (2) to report in the year the shoes are actually sold the normal gross profit of $200/$800, or 25%, which is not affected by a change in the selling price.

CONSERVATISM IS THE BASIS FOR THE LOWER-OF-COST-OR-MARKET RULE

The departure from the cost basis is normally justified on the basis of *conservatism*. According to the accounting profession, conservatism is "a prudent reaction to uncertainties to try to insure that uncertainties and risks inherent in business situations are adequately considered."[4] In the example, the future selling price of a pair of shoes is uncertain because of style changes. The use of the LCM rule serves two purposes. First, the inventory of shoes is written down from $75 to $60 for each pair. Second, the decline in value of the inventory is recognized at the time it is first observed rather than after the shoes are sold. An investor in a company with deteriorating inventory has good reason to be alarmed. Merchandisers who do not make the proper adjustments to their product lines go out of business as they compete with the lower prices of warehouse clubs and the lower overhead of e-business and home shopping networks.

You should realize that the write-down of the shoes violates the historical cost principle, which says that assets should be carried on the balance sheet at their original cost. But the LCM rule is considered a valid exception to the principle because it is a prudent reaction to the uncertainty involved and thus an application of conservatism in accounting.

Real World Practice

5-2 Reading Kellogg's Financial Statements

A note to Kellogg's financial statements states that "[i]nventories are valued at the lower of cost (principally average) or market." Why do you think the application of the lower-of-cost-or-market rule would be important to a business such as Kellogg's? In applying the rule, how does the company define "cost"?

APPLICATION OF THE LCM RULE

We have yet to consider how the LCM rule is applied to the entire inventory of a company. Three different interpretations of the rule are possible:

4 *Statement of Financial Accounting Concepts No. 2*, "Qualitative Characteristics of Accounting Information" (Stamford, Conn.: Financial Accounting Standards Board, May 1980), par. 95.

1. **The lower of total cost or total market value for the entire inventory could be reported.**
2. **The lower of cost or market value for each individual product or item could be reported.**
3. **The lower of cost or market value for groups of items could be reported. A company is free to choose any one of these approaches in applying the lower-of-cost-or-market rule. Three different answers are possible depending on the approach selected.**

The item-by-item approach (Number 2) is the most popular of the three approaches for two reasons. First, it produces the most conservative result. The reason is that with either a group-by-group or a total approach, increases in the values of some items of inventory offset declines in the values of other items. The item-by-item approach, however, ignores increases in value and recognizes all declines in value. Second, the item-by-item approach is the method required for tax purposes, although unlike LIFO, it is not required for book purposes merely because it is used for tax computations.

Consistency is important in deciding which approach to use in applying the LCM rule. As is the case with the selection of one of the inventory costing methods discussed earlier in the chapter, the approach chosen to apply the rule should be used consistently from one period to the next.

POD REVIEW 5.9

LO9 *Apply the lower-of-cost-or-market rule to the valuation of inventory.*

- The principle of conservatism in accounting may warrant a departure from historical cost. This departure is known as the lower-of-cost-or-market rule (LCM).
  - Under LCM, the historical cost of inventory is compared with its replacement cost. If the replacement cost is lower, the inventory account is reduced and a loss is recognized.

QUESTIONS

1. *The use of the lower-of-cost-or-market rule to value inventory is justified on the basis of what principle?*
   a. cost
   b. materiality
   c. conservatism
   d. reliability

2. *The journal entry to write down inventory to its market value results in a(n)*
   a. gain on the income statement.
   b. loss on the income statement.
   c. direct charge (debit) to retained earnings.
   d. increase in a liability.

Methods for Estimating Inventory Value

LO10 Explain why and how the cost of inventory is estimated in certain situations.

Situations arise in which it may not be practicable or even possible to measure inventory at cost. At times it may be necessary to *estimate* the amount of inventory. Two similar methods are used for very different purposes to estimate the amount of inventory. They are the gross profit method and the retail inventory method.

EXHIBIT 5-14 **The Gross Profit Method for Estimating Inventory**

Income Statement Model	Gross Profit Method Model
Beginning Inventory	Beginning Inventory
+ Purchases	+ Purchases
= Cost of Goods Available for Sale	= Cost of Goods Available for Sale
− Ending Inventory (per count)	− Estimated Cost of Goods Sold
= Cost of Goods Sold	= Estimated Inventory

GROSS PROFIT METHOD

Gross profit method A technique used to establish an estimate of the cost of inventory stolen, destroyed, or otherwise damaged or of the amount of inventory on hand at an interim date.

A company that uses a periodic inventory system may experience a problem if inventory is stolen or destroyed by fire, flooding, or some other type of catastrophe. Without a perpetual inventory record, what is the cost of the inventory stolen or destroyed? The **gross profit method** is a useful technique to estimate the cost of inventory lost in these situations. The method relies entirely on the ability to reliably estimate the ratio of gross profit to sales.

Exhibit 5-14 illustrates how the normal income statement model used to find cost of goods sold can be rearranged to estimate inventory. The model on the left shows the components of cost of goods sold as they appear on the income statement. Assuming a periodic system, the inventory on hand at the end of the period is counted and is subtracted from cost of goods available for sale to determine cost of goods sold. The model is rearranged on the right as a basis for estimating inventory under the gross profit method. The only difference in the two models is in the reversal of the last two components: ending inventory and cost of goods sold. Rather than attempting to estimate ending inventory, we are trying to estimate the amount of inventory that should be on hand at a specific date, such as the date of a fire or flood. The estimate of cost of goods sold is found by estimating gross profit and deducting this estimate from sales revenue.

To understand this method, assume that on March 12, 2008, a portion of Hardluck Company's inventory is destroyed in a fire. The company determines, by a physical count, that the cost of merchandise not destroyed is $200. Hardluck needs to estimate the cost of the inventory lost for purposes of insurance reimbursement. If the insurance company pays Hardluck an amount equivalent to the cost of the inventory destroyed, no loss will be recognized. If the cost of the inventory destroyed exceeds the amount reimbursed by the insurance company, a loss will be recorded for the excess amount.

Assume that the insurance company agrees to pay Hardluck $250 as full settlement for the inventory lost in the fire. From its records, Hardluck is able to determine the following amounts for the period from January 1 to the date of the fire, March 12:

Net sales from January 1 to March 12	$6,000
Beginning inventory—January 1	1,200
Purchases from January 1 to March 12	3,500

Assume that based on recent years' experience, Hardluck estimates its gross profit ratio as 30% of net sales. The steps it will take to estimate the lost inventory are as follow:

1. Determine gross profit:

Net Sales	×	Gross Profit Ratio	=	Gross Profit
$6,000	×	30%	=	$1,800

2. Determine cost of goods sold:

Net Sales	−	Gross Profit	=	Cost of Goods Sold
$6,000	−	$1,800	=	$4,200

3. Determine cost of goods available for sale at time of fire:

Beginning Inventory	+	Purchases	=	Cost of Goods Available for Sale
$1,200	+	$3,500	=	$4,700

4. Determine inventory at time of fire:

Cost of Goods Available for Sale	−	Cost of Goods Sold	=	Inventory
$4,700	−	$4,200	=	$500

5. Determine amount of inventory destroyed:

Inventory at Time of Fire	−	Inventory Not Destroyed	=	Inventory Destroyed
$500	−	$200	=	$300

Hardluck would make the following entry to recognize a loss for the excess of the cost of the lost inventory over the amount of reimbursement from the insurance company:

Mar. 12	Loss on Insurance Settlement	50	
	Cash (from insurance company)	250	
	Inventory		300
	To record the insurance settlement from fire.		

Balance Sheet						Income Statement	
ASSETS		=	**LIABILITIES**	+	**STOCKHOLDERS' EQUITY**	+	**REVENUES − EXPENSES**
Cash	250					Loss on Insurance Settlement	(50)
Inventory	(300)						

Another situation in which the gross profit method is used is for *interim financial statements.* Most companies prepare financial statements at least once every three months. In fact, the **SEC** requires a quarterly report from corporations whose stock is publicly traded. However, companies using the periodic inventory system find it cost prohibitive to count the inventory every three months. The gross profit method is used to estimate the cost of the inventory at these interim dates. A company is allowed to use the method only in interim reports. Inventory reported in the annual report must be based on actual, not estimated, cost.

RETAIL INVENTORY METHOD

The counting of inventory in most retail businesses is an enormous undertaking. Imagine the time involved to count all of the various items stocked in a hardware store. Because of the time and cost involved in counting inventory, most retail businesses take a physical inventory only once a year. The **retail inventory method** is used to estimate inventory for interim statements, typically prepared monthly.

Retail inventory method
A technique used by retailers to convert the retail value of inventory to a cost basis.

The retail inventory method has another important use. Consider the year-end inventory count in a large supermarket. One employee counts the number of tubes of toothpaste on the shelf and relays the relevant information to another employee or to a tape-recording device: "16 tubes of 8-ounce ABC brand toothpaste at $1.69." The key is that the price recorded is the *selling price* or *retail price* of the product, not its cost. It is much quicker to count the inventory at retail than to trace the cost of each item to purchase invoices. The retail method can then be used to convert the inventory from retail to cost. The methodology used with the retail inventory method, whether for interim statements or at year-end, is similar to the approach used with the gross profit method and is covered in detail in intermediate accounting textbooks.

POD REVIEW 5.10

LO10 *Explain why and how the cost of inventory is estimated in certain situations.*

- Certain circumstances arise that prohibit an accurate accounting of inventory, such as floods or fires that destroy merchandise.
  - Under these circumstances, the gross profit method may be used to estimate the cost of inventory.

QUESTIONS

1. *The gross profit method can be used*
   a. to estimate the amount of inventory destroyed in a flood when the periodic system is used.
   b. to estimate the amount of inventory on hand at an interim date, such as the end of a quarter.
   c. to estimate the amount of inventory on hand at the end of the year.
   d. both (a) and (b).

2. *A company's entire inventory is destroyed in a fire. Beginning inventory was $25,000. Net sales and purchases up to the date of the fire were $70,000 and $40,000, respectively. The company estimates its gross profit ratio as 20% of net sales. Using the gross profit method, the estimated inventory lost in the fire is*
   a. $9,000.
   b. $11,000.
   c. $41,000.
   d. none of the above.

Analyzing the Management of Inventory

LO11 Analyze the management of inventory.

Inventory turnover ratio A measure of the number of times inventory is sold during the period.

Inventory is the lifeblood of a company that sells a product. Gap Inc. must strike a balance between maintaining a sufficient variety of products to meet customers' needs and incurring the high cost of carrying inventory. The cost of storage and the lost income from the money tied up in inventory make inventory very expensive to keep on hand. Thus, the more quickly a company can sell—that is, turn over—its inventory, the better. The **inventory turnover ratio** is calculated as follows:

$$\text{Inventory Turnover Ratio} = \frac{\text{Cost of Goods Sold}}{\text{Average Inventory}}$$

It is a measure of the number of times inventory is sold during the period.

Use the Ratio Decision Model on pages 255–256 to compute and analyze the inventory turnover ratio for Gap Inc.

USING THE RATIO DECISION MODEL: ANALYZING THE MANAGEMENT OF INVENTORY

Use the following Ratio Decision Model to analyze the inventory of Gap Inc. or any other public company.

1. Formulate the Question

Managers, investors, and creditors are all interested in how well a company manages its inventory. The quicker inventory can be sold, the sooner the money will be available to invest in more inventory or to use for other purposes. Those interested must be able to answer the following question:

How many times a year does a company turn over its inventory?

2. Gather the Information from the Financial Statements

Cost of goods sold is reported on the income statement, representing a flow for a period of time. On the other hand, inventory is an asset, representing a balance at a point in time. Thus, a comparison of the two requires the cost of goods sold for the year and an average of the balance in inventory:

- Cost of goods sold: From the income statement for the year
- Average inventory: From the balance sheets at the end of the two most recent years

3. Calculate the Ratio

$$\text{Inventory Turnover Ratio} = \frac{\text{Cost of Goods Sold}}{\text{Average Inventory}}$$

Gap Inc.
Partial Consolidated Statements of Income
(in millions)

	Year Ended		
	February 3, 2007	January 28, 2006	January 29, 2005
Net sales	$15,943	$16,023	$16,267
Cost of goods sold and occupancy costs	10,294	10,154	9,886

Gap Inc.
Partial Consolidated Balance Sheets
(in millions)

	February 3, 2007	Januray 28, 2006
Assets		
Current Assets:		
Merchandise inventory	$1,796	$1,696

Average merchandise inventory = ($1,796 + $1,696)/2 = **$1,746**

$$\text{Inventory Turnover} = \frac{\$10,294}{\$1,746} = 5.9 \text{ times}$$

4. Compare the Ratio with Others

Management compares the current year's turnover rate with prior years to see if the company is experiencing slower or faster turns of its inventory. It is also important to compare the rate with that of other companies in the same industry:

Gap Inc.		American Eagle Outfitters Inc.	
Year Ended February 3, 2007	Year Ended January 28, 2006	Year Ended February 3, 2007	Year Ended January 28, 2006
5.9 times	5.8 times	6.1 times	6.5 times

(*continued*)

Number of days' sales in inventory
A measure of how long it takes to sell inventory.

5. Interpret the Results

This ratio tells us that in fiscal year 2006, Gap Inc. turned over its inventory an average of 5.9 times. This is slightly higher than in the prior year and slightly slower than its competitor American Eagle Outfitters Inc. An alternative way to look at a company's efficiency in managing its inventory is to calculate the number of days, on average, that inventory is on hand before it is sold. This measure is called the **number of days' sales in inventory** and is calculated as follows for Gap Inc. in 2006, assuming 360 days in a year:

$$\text{Number of Days' Sales in Inventory} = \frac{\text{Number of Days in the Period}}{\text{Inventory Turnover Ratio}}$$

$$= \frac{360}{5.9}$$

$$= 61 \text{ days}$$

This measure tells us that it took Gap Inc. 61 days, or two months, on average to sell its inventory.

POD REVIEW 5.11

LO11 *Analyze the management of inventory.*

- Inventory turnover is a measure of how efficiently inventory is managed. The ratio measures how quickly inventory is sold and is calculated as follows:

$$\frac{\text{Cost of goods sold}}{\text{Average inventory}}$$

The higher the ratio, the less time inventory resides in storage (i.e., the more quickly it turns over).

- The average length of time that it takes to sell inventory can be derived from the inventory turnover ratio:

$$\text{Number of days' sales in inventory} = \frac{\text{Number of days in the period}}{\text{Inventory turnover ratio}}$$

QUESTIONS

1. *Which of the following strategies should a company pursue concerning its inventory?*
   a. Maintain an inventory stock much higher than anticipated demand so that there is virtually no risk of running out of inventory.
   b. Maintain an inventory stock lower than anticipated demand so as to avoid the high costs of carrying it.
   c. Attempt to strike a balance between maintaining a sufficient amount of inventory to meet demand and incurring the high cost of carrying it.
   d. none of the above

2. *A company began the year with $50,000 in inventory and ended the year with $70,000 in inventory. Cost of goods sold for the year amounted to $720,000. Assuming 360 days in a year, how long, on average, does it take the company to sell its inventory?*
   a. 12 days
   b. 30 days
   c. 60 days
   d. none of the above

How Inventories Affect the Cash Flows Statement

LO12 Explain the effects that inventory transactions have on the statement of cash flows.

The effects on the income statement and the statement of cash flows from inventory-related transactions differ significantly. This chapter has focused on how the purchase and sale of inventory are reported on the income statement. We found that the cost of the inventory sold during the period is deducted on the income statement as cost of goods sold.

The appropriate reporting on a statement of cash flows for inventory transactions depends on whether the direct or indirect method is used. If the direct method is used to prepare the Operating Activities category of the statement, the amount of cash paid to suppliers of inventory is shown as a deduction in this section of the statement.

If the more popular indirect method is used, it is necessary to make adjustments to net income for the changes in two accounts: Inventories and Accounts Payable. These adjustments are summarized in Exhibit 5-15. An increase in inventory is deducted because it indicates that the company is building up its stock of inventory and thus expending cash. A decrease in inventory is added to net income. An increase in accounts payable is added because it indicates that during the period, the company increased the amount it owes suppliers and therefore conserved its cash. A decrease in accounts payable is deducted because the company actually reduced the amount owed suppliers during the period.

The Operating Activities category of the statement of cash flows for Gap Inc. is presented in Exhibit 5-16. The increase in inventory is deducted because the increase in this asset uses the company's cash. A decrease in accounts payable also uses Gap Inc. cash. Thus, the decrease in this item in 2006 is deducted from net income.

EXHIBIT 5-15 **Inventories and the Statement of Cash Flows**

Item	**Cash Flow Statement**	
	Operating Activities	
	Net income	xxx
Increase in inventory	→	−
Decrease in inventory	→	+
Increase in accounts payable	→	+
Decrease in accounts payable	→	−
	Investing Activities	
	Financing Activities	

EXHIBIT 5-16 Partial Consolidated Statement of Cash Flows for Gap Inc.

GAP INC.
CONSOLIDATED STATEMENTS OF CASH FLOWS

($ in millions)	53 Weeks Ended February 3, 2007	52 Weeks Ended January 28, 2006	52 Weeks Ended January 29, 2005
Cash Flows from Operating Activities:			
Net earnings	$ 778	$1.113	$1.150
Adjustments to reconcile net earnings to net cash provided by operating activities:			
Depreciation and amortization (a)	530	625	615
Share-based compensation	54	22	5
Tax benefit from exercise of stock options and vesting of service awards	25	19	31
Excess tax benefit from exercise of stock options	(23)	—	—
Other non-cash items	11	(69)	21
Deferred income taxes	(41)	(46)	(80)
Change in operating assets and liabilities:			
Merchandise inventory	(97)	114	(90)
Other assets	12	(104)	(18)
Accounts payable	(25)	(102)	39
Accrued expenses and other current liabilities	75	(121)	(23)
Income taxes payable, net	(102)	(19)	(112)
Lease incentives and other liabilities	53	119	59
Net cash provided by operating activities	1.250	1.551	1.597

Increase here *uses* cash and thus is deducted. (Merchandise inventory)

Decrease here *uses* cash and thus is deducted. (Accounts payable)

(a) Depreciation and amortization includes the amortization of lease incentives of $84 million, $82 million, and $92 million for fiscal 2005, 2006, and 2004, respectively.

See Notes to the Consolidated Financial Statements

POD REVIEW 5.12

LO12 *Explain the effects that inventory transactions have on the statement of cash flows.*

- Under the indirect method of calculating cash flows from operating activities, both the changes in the inventory account and the accounts payable account must be taken into consideration.

QUESTIONS

1. *On a statement of cash flows prepared using the indirect method, a decrease in inventory is*
   a. deducted from net income.
   b. added to net income.
   c. ignored.
   d. deducted from net income or added to net income depending on the size of the decrease.

2. *A company's change in accounts payable was added back to net income on the statement of cash flows prepared using the indirect method. This is an indication that the amount owed to suppliers during the period*
   a. increased.
   b. decreased.
   c. was unchanged.
   d. none of the above.

APPENDIX

Accounting Tools: Inventory Costing Methods with the Use of a Perpetual Inventory System

LO13 Explain the differences in the accounting for periodic and perpetual inventory systems and apply the inventory costing methods using a perpetual system (Appendix).

The illustrations of the inventory costing methods in the chapter assumed the use of a periodic inventory system. This appendix will show how the methods are applied when a company maintains a perpetual inventory system. It is important to understand the difference between inventory *costing systems* and inventory *methods*. The two inventory systems differ in terms of how often the inventory account is updated: periodically or perpetually. However, when a company sells identical units of product and the cost to purchase each unit is subject to change, the company also must choose an inventory costing method such as FIFO, LIFO, or weighted average.

Earlier, the chapter provided illustrations of the various costing methods with a periodic system. The same data is now used to illustrate how the methods differ when a perpetual system is used. Keep in mind that if a company uses specific identification, the results will be the same regardless of whether it uses the periodic or perpetual system. To compare the periodic and perpetual systems for the other methods, we must add one important piece of information: the date of each of the sales. The original data as well as number of units sold on the various dates are summarized as follows:

Date	Purchases	Sales	Balance
Beginning inventory			500 units @ $10
January 20	300 units @ $11		800 units
February 18		450 units	350 units
April 8	400 units @ $12		750 units
June 19		300 units	450 units
September 5	200 units @ $13		650 units
October 20		150 units	500 units
December 12	100 units @ $14		600 units

FIFO Costing with a Perpetual System

Exhibit 5-17 illustrates the FIFO method on a perpetual basis. The basic premise of FIFO applies whether a periodic or a perpetual system is used: the first units purchased are assumed to be the first units sold. With a perpetual system, however, this concept is applied *at the time of each sale*. For example, note in the exhibit which 450 units are assumed to be sold on February 18. The 450 units sold are taken from the beginning inventory of 500 units with a unit cost of $10. Thus, the inventory or balance after this sale as shown in the last three columns is 50 units at $10 and 300 units at $11, for a total of $3,800. The purchase on April 8 of 400 units at $12 is added to the running balance. On a FIFO basis, the sale of 300 units on June 19 comes from the remainder of the beginning inventory of 50 units and another 250 units from the first purchase at $11 on January 20. The balance after this sale is 50 units at $11 and 400 units at $12. You should follow through the last three transactions in the exhibit to make sure you understand

EXHIBIT 5-17 **Perpetual System: FIFO Cost-Flow Assumption**

	Purchases			**Sales**			**Balance**		
Date	**Units**	**Unit Cost**	**Total Cost**	**Units**	**Unit Cost**	**Total Cost**	**Units**	**Unit Cost**	**Balance**
1/1							500	$10	$5,000
1/20	300	$11	$3,300				500	10	
							300	11	8,300
2/18				450	$10	$4,500	50	10	
							300	11	3,800
4/8	400	12	4,800				50	10	
							300	11	
							400	12	8,600
6/19				50	10	500	50	11	
				250	11	2,750	400	12	5,350
9/5	200	13	2,600				50	11	
							400	12	
							200	13	7,950
10/20				50	11	550	300	12	
				100	12	1,200	200	13	6,200
12/12	100	14	1,400				300	12	
							200	13	
							100	14	7,600

the application of FIFO on a perpetual basis. An important point to note about the ending inventory of $7,600 is that it is the same amount calculated for FIFO periodic earlier in the chapter:

FIFO periodic (Exhibit 5-9)	$7,600
FIFO perpetual (Exhibit 5-17)	$7,600

Whether the method is applied each time a sale is made or only at the end of the period, the earliest units in are the first units out, and the two systems will yield the same ending inventory under FIFO.

LIFO Costing with a Perpetual System

A LIFO cost flow with the use of a perpetual system is illustrated in Exhibit 5-18. First, note which 450 units are assumed to be sold on February 18. The sale consists of the most recent units acquired, 300 units at $11, and then 150 units from the beginning inventory at $10. Thus, the balance after this sale is simply the remaining 350 units from the beginning inventory priced at $10. The purchase on April 8 results in a balance of 350 units at $10 and 400 units at $12.

Note what happens with LIFO when it is applied on a perpetual basis. In essence, a gap is created. Units acquired at the earliest price of $10 and units acquired at the most recent price of $12 are on hand, but none of those at the middle price of $11 remain. This situation arises because LIFO is applied every time a sale is made rather than only at the end of the year. Because of this difference, the amount of ending inventory differs depending on which system is used:

LIFO periodic (Exhibit 5-9)	$6,100
LIFO perpetual (Exhibit 5-18)	$6,750

EXHIBIT 5-18 **Perpetual System: LIFO Cost-Flow Assumption**

	Purchases			Sales			Balance		
Date	Units	Unit Cost	Total Cost	Units	Unit Cost	Total Cost	Units	Unit Cost	Balance
1/1							500	$10	$5,000
1/20	300	$11	$3,300				500	10	
							300	11	8,300
2/18				300	$11	$3,300			
				150	10	1,500	350	10	3,500
4/8	400	12	4,800				350	10	
							400	12	8,300
6/19				300	12	3,600	350	10	
							100	12	4,700
9/5	200	13	2,600				350	10	
							100	12	
							200	13	7,300
10/20				150	13	1,950	350	10	
							100	12	
							50	13	5,350
12/12	100	14	1,400				350	10	
							100	12	
							50	13	
							100	14	6,750

Moving Average with a Perpetual System

When a weighted average cost assumption is applied with a perpetual system, it is sometimes called a **moving average**. As indicated in Exhibit 5-19, each time a purchase is made, a new weighted average cost must be computed, thus the name *moving average*. For example, the goods available for sale after the January 20 purchase consist of 500 units at $10 and 300 units at $11, which results in an average cost of $10.38. This is

Moving average
The name given to an average cost method when a weighted average cost assumption is used with a perpetual inventory system.

EXHIBIT 5-19 **Perpetual System: Moving Average Cost-Flow Assumption**

	Purchases			Sales			Balance		
Date	Units	Unit Cost	Total Cost	Units	Unit Cost	Total Cost	Units	Unit Cost	Balance
1/1							500	$10.00	$5,000
1/20	300	$11	$3,300				800	10.38*	8,304
2/18				450	$10.38	$4,671	350	10.38	3,633
4/8	400	12	4,800				750	11.24†	8,430
6/19				300	11.24	3,372	450	11.24	5,058
9/5	200	13	2,600				650	11.78‡	7,657
10/20				150	11.78	1,767	500	11.78	5,890
12/12	100	14	1,400				600	12.15§	7,290

The moving average prices per unit are calculated as follows:
**($5,000 + $3,300)/800 units = $10.38 (rounded to nearest cent)*
†($3,633 + $4,800)/750 units = $11.24
‡($5,058 + $2,600)/650 units = $11.78
§($5,890 + $1,400)/600 units = $12.15

the unit cost applied to the 450 units sold on February 18. The 400 units purchased on April 8 require the computation of a new unit cost, as indicated in the second footnote to the exhibit. As you might have suspected, the ending inventory with an average cost flow differs depending on whether a periodic or a perpetual system is used:

Weighted average periodic (Exhibit 5-9)	$6,840
Moving average perpetual (Exhibit 5-19)	$7,290

POD REVIEW 5.13

LO13 *Explain the differences in the accounting for periodic and perpetual inventory systems and apply the inventory costing methods using a perpetual system.*

- The three inventory costing methods—FIFO, LIFO, and weighted average—may be used in combination with a perpetual inventory system.
    - The inventory costing method is applied after each sale of merchandise to update the Inventory account.
    - The results from using LIFO differ depending on whether a periodic or perpetual system is used. The same is true with weighted average, which is called moving average in a perpetual system.

QUESTIONS

1. *For which inventory method does the dollar amount of inventory on hand at the end of the period* not *differ regardless of whether a company uses a periodic or a perpetual inventory system?*
    a. weighted average cost
    b. FIFO
    c. LIFO
    d. The results always differ depending on the system used.

2. *Moving average is the name given to the use of*
    a. the specific identification method used with a perpetual inventory system.
    b. an average cost method used with a periodic inventory system.
    c. an average cost method used with a perpetual inventory system.
    d. none of the above.

RATIO REVIEW

$$\text{Gross Profit Ratio} = \frac{\text{Gross Profit (Income Statement)}}{\text{Net Sales (Income Statement)}}$$

$$\text{Inventory Turnover Ratio} = \frac{\text{Cost of Goods Sold (Income Statement)}}{\text{Average Inventory* (Balance Sheet)}}$$

**Average inventory can be estimated using the following calculation:*

$$\frac{\text{Beginning Inventory} + \text{Ending Inventory}}{2}$$

$$\text{Number of Days' Sales in Inventory} = \frac{\text{Number of Days in the Period**}}{\text{Inventory Turnover Ratio}}$$

***Usually assume 360 days unless some other number is a better estimate of the number of days in the period.*

ACCOUNTS HIGHLIGHTED

Account Titles	Where It Appears	In What Section	Page Number
Merchandise Inventory	Balance Sheet	Current Assets	221
Sales Revenue	Income Statement	Sales	223
Sales Returns and Allowances	Income Statement	Contra to Sales Revenue	224
Sales Discounts	Income Statement	Contra to Sales Revenue	224
Cost of Goods Sold	Income Statement	Expenses	227
Purchases	Income Statement	Cost of Goods Sold	229
Purchase Returns and Allowances	Income Statement	Contra to Purchases	229
Purchase Discounts	Income Statement	Contra to Purchases	230
Transportation-in	Income Statement	Added to Purchases	229
Transportation-out	Income Statement	Selling Expense	231
Loss on Decline in Value of Inventory	Income Statement	Other Expenses	249

KEY TERMS QUIZ

Because of the large number of terms introduced in this chapter, there are two quizzes on key terms. Read each definition below and write the number of the definition in the blank beside the appropriate term. The quiz solutions appear at the end of the chapter.

Quiz 1: Merchandise Accounting

_______ **Merchandise Inventory**
_______ **Raw materials**
_______ **Work in process**
_______ **Finished goods**
_______ **Gross profit**
_______ **Net sales**
_______ **Sales revenue**
_______ **Sales Returns and Allowances**
_______ **Sales Discounts**
_______ **Cost of goods available for sale**
_______ **Cost of goods sold**
_______ **Perpetual system**
_______ **Periodic system**
_______ **Transportation-in**
_______ **Purchases**
_______ **Purchase Returns and Allowances**
_______ **Purchase Discounts**
_______ **FOB destination point**
_______ **FOB shipping point**
_______ **Gross profit ratio**

1. The contra-revenue account used to record refunds to customers and reductions of their accounts.
2. The adjunct account used to record freight costs paid by the buyer.
3. The system in which the Inventory account is increased at the time of each purchase of merchandise and decreased at the time of each sale.
4. The contra-purchases account used in a periodic inventory system when a refund is received from a supplier or a reduction is given in the balance owed to the supplier.
5. The contra-revenue account used to record discounts given to customers for early payment of their accounts.
6. Terms that require the seller to pay for the cost of shipping the merchandise to the buyer.
7. Terms that require the buyer to pay the shipping costs.
8. The system in which the Inventory account is updated only at the end of the period.
9. Beginning inventory plus cost of goods purchased.
10. The contra-purchases account used to record reductions in purchase price for early payment to the supplier.
11. The account used in a periodic inventory system to record acquisitions of merchandise.

12. Sales revenue less sales returns and allowances and sales discounts.
13. Cost of goods available for sale minus ending inventory.
14. Gross profit divided by net sales.
15. Sales less cost of goods sold.
16. The cost of unfinished products in a manufacturing company.
17. The account that wholesalers and retailers use to report inventory held for sale.
18. The inventory of a manufacturer before the addition of any direct labor or manufacturing overhead.
19. A manufacturer's inventory that is complete and ready for sale.
20. A representation of the inflow of assets from the sale of a product.

Quiz 2: Inventory Valuation

_______ **Specific identification method**
_______ **Weighted average cost method**
_______ **FIFO method**
_______ **LIFO method**
_______ **LIFO liquidation**
_______ **LIFO conformity rule**
_______ **LIFO reserve**
_______ **Replacement cost**
_______ **Inventory profit**
_______ **Lower-of-cost-or-market (LCM) rule**
_______ **Gross profit method**
_______ **Retail inventory method**
_______ **Inventory turnover ratio**
_______ **Number of days' sales in inventory**
_______ **Moving average (Appendix)**

1. The name given to an average cost method when a weighted average cost assumption is used with a perpetual inventory system.
2. An inventory costing method that assigns the same unit cost to all units available for sale during the period.
3. A conservative inventory valuation approach that is an attempt to anticipate declines in the value of inventory before its actual sale.
4. An inventory costing method that assigns the most recent costs to ending inventory.
5. The current cost of a unit of inventory.
6. An inventory costing method that assigns the most recent costs to cost of goods sold.
7. A measure of how long it takes to sell inventory.
8. A technique used to establish an estimate of the cost of inventory stolen, destroyed, or otherwise damaged or of the amount of inventory on hand at an interim date.
9. A technique used by retailers to convert the retail value of inventory to a cost basis.
10. The IRS requirement that when LIFO is used on a tax return, it must also be used in reporting income to stockholders.
11. An inventory costing method that relies on matching unit costs with the actual units sold.
12. The portion of the gross profit that results from holding inventory during a period of rising prices.
13. The result of selling more units than are purchased during the period, which can have negative tax consequences if a company is using LIFO.
14. The excess of the value of a company's inventory stated at FIFO over the value stated at LIFO.
15. A measure of the number of times inventory is sold during a period.

ALTERNATE TERMS

Gross profit Gross margin

Interim statements Quarterly or monthly statements

Market (value for inventory) Replacement cost

Merchandiser Wholesaler, retailer

Raw materials Direct materials

Retail price Selling price

Sales revenue Sales

Transportation-in Freight-in

Work in process Work in progress

WARMUP EXERCISES & SOLUTIONS

LO2

Warmup Exercise 5-1 Net Sales

McDowell Merchandising reported sales revenue, sales returns and allowances, and sales discounts of $57,000, $1500, and $900, respectively, in 2008.

Required
Prepare the net sales section of McDowell's 2008 income statement.

Key to the Solution Refer to Exhibit 5-3.

LO3

Warmup Exercise 5-2 Cost of Goods Sold

The following amounts are taken from White Wholesaler's records. (All amounts are for 2008.)

Inventory, January 1	$14,200
Inventory, December 31	10,300
Purchases	87,500
Purchase Discounts	4,200
Purchase Returns and Allowances	1,800
Transportation-in	4,500

Required
Prepare the cost of goods sold section of White's 2008 income statement.

Key to the Solution Refer to Exhibit 5-4.

LO6

Warmup Exercise 5-3 Inventory Valuation

Busby Corp. began the year with 75 units of inventory that it paid $2 each to acquire. During the year, it purchased an additional 100 units for $3 each. Busby sold 150 units during the year.

Required
1. Compute cost of goods sold and ending inventory assuming Busby uses FIFO.
2. Compute cost of goods sold and ending inventory assuming Busby uses LIFO.

Key to the Solution Review the mechanics of the methods beginning on page 238.

LO9

Warmup Exercise 5-4 Lower of Cost or Market

Glendive reports its inventory on a FIFO basis and has inventory with a cost of $78,000 on December 31. The cost to replace the inventory on this date would be only $71,000.

Required
Prepare the appropriate journal entry on December 31.

Key to the Solution Recall the need to write down inventory when market is less than cost.

LO11

Warmup Exercise 5-5 Inventory Turnover

Sidney began the year with $130,000 in merchandise inventory and ended the year with $190,000. Sales and cost of goods sold for the year were $900,000 and $640,000, respectively.

Required
1. Compute Sidney's inventory turnover ratio.
2. Compute the number of days' sales in inventory.

Key to the Solution Review how these two statistics are computed on pages 255–256.

SOLUTIONS TO WARMUP EXERCISES

Warmup Exercise 5-1

McDowell Merchandising
Partial Income Statement
For the Year Ended December 31, 2008

Sales revenue	$57,000	
Less: Sales returns and allowances	1,500	
Sales discounts	900	
Net sales		$54,600

Warmup Exercise 5-2

White Wholesalers
Partial Income Statement
For the Year Ended December 31, 2008

Inventory, January 1, 2008		$ 14,200	
Purchases	$87,500		
Less: Purchase returns and allowances	1,800		
Purchase discounts	4,200		
Net purchases	$81,500		
Add: Transportation-in	4,500		
Cost of goods purchased		86,000	
Cost of goods available for sale		$100,200	
Less: Inventory, December 31, 2008		10,300	
Cost of goods sold			$89,900

Warmup Exercise 5-3

1. Cost of goods sold: (75 × $2) + (75 × $3) = $375

   Ending inventory: 25 × $3 = $ 75

2. Cost of goods sold: (100 × $3) + (50 × $2) = $400

   Ending inventory: 25 × $2 = $ 50

Warmup Exercise 5-4

Dec. 31	Loss on Decline in Value of Inventory	7,000	
	Inventory		7,000
	To record decline in value of inventory.		

Balance Sheet							Income Statement	
ASSETS		=	LIABILITIES	+	STOCKHOLDERS' EQUITY	+	REVENUES − EXPENSES	
Inventory	(7,000)						Loss on Decline in Value of Inventory	(7,000)

Warmup Exercise 5-5

1. $$\text{Inventory Turnover Ratio} = \frac{\text{Cost of Goods Sold}}{\text{Average Inventory}}$$

$$= \frac{\$640{,}000}{(\$130{,}000 + \$190{,}000)/2}$$

$$= \frac{\$640{,}000}{\$160{,}000} = 4 \text{ times}$$

2. $$\text{Number of Days' Sales in Inventory} = \frac{\text{Number of Days in the Period}}{\text{Inventory Turnover Ratio}}$$

$$= \frac{360}{4} = 90 \text{ days}$$

REVIEW

REVIEW PROBLEM & SOLUTION

Stewart Distributing Company sells a single product for $2 per unit and uses a periodic inventory system. The following data are available for the year:

Date	Transaction	Number of Units	Unit Cost	Total
1/1	Beginning inventory	500	$1.00	$500.00
2/5	Purchase	350	1.10	385.00
4/12	Sale	(550)		
7/17	Sale	(200)		
9/23	Purchase	400	1.30	520.00
11/5	Sale	(300)		

Required

1. Compute cost of goods sold assuming the use of the weighted average costing method.
2. Compute the dollar amount of ending inventory assuming the FIFO costing method.
3. Compute gross profit assuming the LIFO costing method.
4. Assume a 40% tax rate. Compute the amount of taxes saved if Stewart uses the LIFO method rather than the FIFO method.

SOLUTION TO REVIEW PROBLEM

1. Cost of goods sold, weighted average cost method:

Cost of goods available for sale	
$500 + $385 + $520 =	$1,405
Divided by:	
Units available for sale:	
500 + 350 + 400 =	÷ 1,250 units
Weighted average cost	$1.124 per unit
× Number of units sold:	
550 + 200 + 300 =	× 1,050 units
Cost of goods sold	$1,180.20

2. Ending inventory, FIFO cost method:

Units available for sale	1,250
− Units sold	− 1,050
= Units in ending inventory	200
× Most recent purchase price of	× $ 1.30
= Ending inventory	$ 260

3. Gross profit, LIFO cost method:

Sales revenue: 1,050 units × $2 each		$2,100
Cost of goods sold		
400 units × $1.30 =	$520	
350 units × $1.10 =	385	
300 units × $1.00 =	300	− 1,205
Gross profit		$ 895

4. Taxes saved from using LIFO instead of FIFO:

LIFO Cost of goods sold		$1,205
− FIFO Cost of goods sold:		
Cost of goods available for sale	$1,405	
Ending inventory from part (2)	260	
Cost of goods sold		− 1,145
Additional expense from use of LIFO		$ 60
× Tax rate		× 0.40
Tax savings from the use of LIFO		$ 24

QUESTIONS

1. What are three distinct types of costs that manufacturers incur? Describe each of them.
2. When a company gives a cash refund on returned merchandise, why doesn't it just reduce Sales Revenue instead of using a contra-revenue account?
3. What do credit terms 3/20, n/60 mean? How valuable to the customer is the discount offered in these terms?
4. What is the difference between a periodic inventory system and a perpetual inventory system?
5. How have point-of-sale terminals improved the ability of mass merchandisers to use a perpetual inventory system?
6. In a periodic inventory system, what kind of account is Purchases? Is it an asset or an expense or neither?
7. Why are shipping terms such as FOB shipping point or FOB destination point important in deciding ownership of inventory at the end of the year?
8. How and why are transportation-in and transportation-out recorded differently?
9. How is a company's gross profit determined? What does the gross profit ratio tell you about a company's performance during the year?
10. What is the relationship between the valuation of inventory as an asset on the balance sheet and the measurement of income?
11. What is the justification for including freight costs incurred in acquiring incoming goods in the cost of the inventory rather than simply treating the cost as an expense of the period? What is the significance of this decision for accounting purposes?
12. What are the inventory characteristics that would allow a company to use the specific identification method? Give at least two examples of inventory for which the method is appropriate.
13. How can the specific identification method allow management to manipulate income?
14. What is the significance of the adjective *weighted* in the weighted average cost method? Use an example to illustrate your answer.
15. Which inventory method, FIFO or LIFO, more nearly approximates the physical flow of products in most businesses? Explain your answer.
16. York Inc. manufactures notebook computers and has experienced noticeable declines in the purchase price of many of the components it uses, including computer chips. Which inventory costing method should York use if it wants to maximize net income? Explain your answer.
17. Which inventory costing method should a company use when it wants to minimize taxes? Does your response depend on whether prices are rising or falling? Explain your answers.
18. The president of Ace Retail is commenting on the company's new controller: "The woman is brilliant! She has shown us how we can maximize our income and at the same time minimize the amount of taxes we have to pay the government. Because the cost to purchase our inventory constantly goes up, we will use FIFO to calculate cost of goods sold on the income statement to minimize the amount charged to cost of goods sold and thus maximize net income. For tax purposes, however, we will use LIFO because this will minimize taxable income and thus minimize the amount we have to pay in taxes." Should the president be enthralled with the new controller? Explain your answer.
19. What does the term *LIFO liquidation* mean? How can it lead to poor buying habits?
20. Historical-based costing methods are sometimes criticized for leading to inventory profits. In a period of rising prices, which inventory costing method will lead to the most "inventory profit"? Explain your answer.
21. Is it acceptable for a company to disclose in its annual report that it is switching from some other inventory costing method to LIFO to save on taxes? Explain.
22. Delevan Corp. uses a periodic inventory system and is counting its year-end inventory. Due to a lack of communication, two different teams count the same section of the warehouse. What effect will this error have on net income?
23. What is the rationale for valuing inventory at the lower of cost or market?
24. Why is it likely that the result from applying the lower-of-cost-or-market rule using a total approach (i.e., by comparing total cost to total market value) and the result from applying the rule on an item-by-item basis will differ?
25. Patterson's controller makes the following suggestion: "I have a brilliant way to save us money. Because we are already using the gross profit method for our quarterly statements, we start using it to estimate the year-end inventory for the annual report and save the money normally spent to have the inventory counted on December 31." What do you think of his suggestion?
26. Why does a company save time and money by using the retail inventory method at the end of the year?
27. Ralston Corp.'s cost of sales has remained steady over the last two years. During this same time period, however, its inventory has increased considerably. What does this information tell you about the company's inventory turnover? Explain your answer.
28. Why is the weighted average cost method called a moving average when a company uses a perpetual inventory system? (Appendix)

BRIEF EXERCISES

LO1 **Brief Exercise 5-1** Types and Forms of Inventory Costs for a Manufacturer

What are the three types of costs incurred by a manufacturer? What are the three forms that inventory can take for a manufacturer?

LO2 **Brief Exercise 5-2** Net Sales

During the current period, Boston Corp. sold products to customers for a total of $85,000. Due to defective products, customers were given $2,000 in refunds for products that were returned and another $4,500 in reductions to their account balances. Discounts in the amount of $6,500 were given for early payment of account balances. Prepare the net sales section of Boston's income statement.

LO3 **Brief Exercise 5-3** Cost of Goods Sold

For each of the following items, indicate whether it increases (I) or decreases (D) cost of goods sold.

______ Purchases
______ Beginning inventory
______ Purchase discounts
______ Transportation-in
______ Ending inventory
______ Purchase returns and allowances

LO4 **Brief Exercise 5-4** Gross Profit Ratio

Dexter Inc. recorded net sales of $50,000 during the period, and its cost of goods sold amounted to $30,000. Compute the company's gross profit ratio.

LO5 **Brief Exercise 5-5** Valuation of Inventory and Measurement of Income

Baxter operates a chain of electronics stores and buys its products from a number of different manufacturers around the world. Give at least three examples of costs that Baxter might incur that should be added to the purchase price of its inventory.

LO6 **Brief Exercise 5-6** Inventory Costing Methods

Belden started the year with 1,000 units of inventory with a unit cost of $5. During the year, it bought 3,000 units at a cost of $6 per unit. A year-end count revealed 500 units on hand. Compute ending inventory assuming both FIFO and LIFO.

LO7 **Brief Exercise 5-7** Selecting an Inventory Costing Method

A company currently uses the LIFO method to value its inventory. For each of the following items, indicate whether it would be higher (H) or lower (L) if the company changed to the FIFO method. Assume a period of rising prices.

______ Cost of goods sold
______ Gross profit
______ Income before taxes
______ Income taxes
______ Cash outflow

LO8 **Brief Exercise 5-8** Inventory Error

Due to a clerical error, a company overstated by $50,000 the amount of inventory on hand at the end of the year. Will net income for the year be overstated or understated? Identify the two accounts on the year-end balance sheet that will be in error and indicate whether they will be understated or overstated.

LO9

Brief Exercise 5-9 Lower-of-Cost-or-Market Rule

The cost of Wright Corp.'s inventory at the end of the year was $75,000; however, due to obsolescence, the cost to replace the inventory was only $55,000. Prepare the journal entry needed at the end of the year.

LO10

Brief Exercise 5-10 Gross Profit Method

A company's entire inventory is destroyed in a fire. Beginning inventory in the year of the fire amounted to $20,000. Net sales and purchases up to the date of the fire were $100,000 and $70,000, respectively. The estimated gross profit ratio is 25%. Using the gross profit method, estimate the amount of inventory destroyed.

LO11

Brief Exercise 5-11 Inventory Turnover

Two companies each recorded $10 million in cost of goods sold for the year. Company A had average inventory of $100,000 on hand during the year. Company B's average inventory was $1 million. One company is a car dealer, and the other is a wholesaler of fresh fruits and vegetables. Which company sells cars, and which company sells fruits and vegetables? Explain your answer.

LO12

Brief Exercise 5-12 Cash Flow Effects

Grogan's inventory increased by $50,000 during the year, and its accounts payable increased by $35,000. Indicate how each of those changes would be reflected on a statement of cash flows prepared using the indirect method.

LO13

Brief Exercise 5-13 Inventory Methods Using a Perpetual System

Will the dollar amount assigned to inventory differ when a company uses the weighted average cost method depending on whether a periodic or perpetual inventory system is used? Explain your answer.

EXERCISES

LO1

Exercise 5-1 Classification of Inventory Costs

Put an *X* in the appropriate column next to the inventory item to indicate its most likely classification on the books of a company that manufactures furniture and then sells it in retail company stores.

	Classification			
Inventory Item	**Raw Material**	**Work in Process**	**Finished Goods**	**Merchandise Inventory**
Fabric				
Lumber				
Unvarnished tables				
Chairs on the showroom floor				
Cushions				
Decorative knobs				
Drawers				
Sofa frames				
Chairs in the plant warehouse				
Chairs in the retail storeroom				

LO1

Exercise 5-2 Inventoriable Costs

During the first month of operations, ABC Company incurred the following costs in ordering and receiving merchandise for resale. No inventory was sold.

List price, $100, 200 units purchased
Volume discount, 10% off list price
Paid freight costs, $56
Insurance cost while goods were in transit, $32
Long-distance phone charge to place orders, $4.35
Purchasing department salary, $1,000
Supplies used to label goods at retail price, $9.75
Interest paid to supplier, $46

Required
What amount do you recommend the company record as merchandise inventory on its balance sheet? Explain your answer. For any items not to be included in inventory, indicate their appropriate treatment in the financial statements.

LO2 **Exercise 5-3** Perpetual and Periodic Inventory Systems

Following is a partial list of account balances for two different merchandising companies. The amounts in the accounts represent the balances at the end of the year *before* any adjustments are made or the books are closed.

Company A		**Company B**	
Sales Revenue	$50,000	Sales Revenue	$85,000
Sales Discounts	3,000	Sales Discounts	2,000
Merchandise Inventory	12,000	Merchandise Inventory	9,000
Cost of Goods Sold	38,000	Purchases	41,000
		Purchase Discounts	4,000
		Purchases Returns and Allowances	1,000

Required
1. Identify which inventory system, perpetual or periodic, each of the two companies uses. Explain how you know which system each company uses by looking at the types of accounts on its books.
2. How much inventory does Company A have on hand at the end of the year? What is its cost of goods sold for the year?
3. Explain why you cannot determine Company B's cost of goods sold for the year from the information available.

LO2 **Exercise 5-4** Perpetual and Periodic Inventory Systems

From the following list, identify whether the merchandisers described would most likely use a perpetual or a periodic inventory system.

______ Appliance store
______ Car dealership
______ Drugstore
______ Furniture store
______ Grocery store
______ Hardware store
______ Jewelry store

How might changes in technology affect the ability of merchandisers to use perpetual inventory systems?

LO3 **Exercise 5-5** Missing Amounts in Cost of Goods Sold Model

For each of the following independent cases, fill in the missing amounts.

	Case 1	**Case 2**	**Case 3**
Beginning inventory	$ (a)	$2,350	$1,890
Purchases (gross)	6,230	5,720	(e)
Purchase returns and allowances	470	800	550
Purchase discounts	200	(c)	310
Transportation-in	150	500	420
Cost of goods available for sale	7,110	(d)	8,790
Ending inventory	(b)	1,750	1,200
Cost of goods sold	5,220	5,570	(f)

LO3

Exercise 5-6 Purchase Discounts

For each of the following transactions of Buckeye Corporation, prepare the appropriate journal entry. (All purchases on credit are made with terms of 1/10, net 30; and Buckeye uses the periodic system of inventory.)

July 3: Purchased merchandise on credit from Wildcat Corp. for $3,500.
July 6: Purchased merchandise on credit from Cyclone Company for $7,000.
July 12: Paid amount owed to Wildcat Corp.
August 5: Paid amount owed to Cyclone Company.

LO3

Exercise 5-7 Purchases—Periodic System

For each of the following transactions of Wolverine Corporation, prepare the appropriate journal entry. The company uses the periodic system.

March 3: Purchased merchandise from Spartan Corp. for $2,500 with terms of 2/10, net/30. Shipping costs of $250 were paid to Neverlate Transit Company.
March 7: Purchased merchandise from Boilermaker Company for $1,400 with terms of net/30.
March 12: Paid amount owed to Spartan Corp.
March 15: Received a credit of $500 on defective merchandise purchased from Boilermaker Company. The merchandise was kept.
March 18: Purchased merchandise from Gopher Corp. for $1,600 with terms of 2/10, net 30.
March 22: Received a credit of $400 from Gopher Corp. for spoiled merchandise returned to Gopher. This is the amount of credit exclusive of any discount.
April 6: Paid amount owed to Boilermaker Company.
April 18: Paid amount owed to Gopher Corp.

LO3

Exercise 5-8 Shipping Terms and Transfer of Title

On December 23, 2008, Miller Wholesalers ships merchandise to Michael Retailers with terms of FOB destination point. The merchandise arrives at Michael's warehouse on January 3, 2009.

Required

1. Identify who pays to ship the merchandise.
2. Determine whether the inventory should be included as an asset on Michael's December 31, 2008, balance sheet. Should the sale be included on Miller's 2008 income statement? Explain.
3. Explain how your answers to (2) would have been different if the terms of shipment had been FOB shipping point.

LO3

Exercise 5-9 Transfer of Title to Inventory

Identify whether the transactions described should be recorded by Cameron Companies during December 2008 (fill in the blank with a D) or January 2009 (fill in the blank with a J).

Purchases of merchandise that are in transit from vendors to Cameron Companies on December 31, 2008.

______ Shipped FOB shipping point
______ Shipped FOB destination point

Sales of merchandise that are in transit to customers of Cameron Companies on December 31, 2008.

______ Shipped FOB shipping point
______ Shipped FOB destination point

LO5

Exercise 5-10 Inventory and Income Manipulation

The president of SOS Inc. is concerned that the net income at year-end will not reach the expected figure. When the sales manager receives a large order on the last day of the fiscal year, the president tells the accountant to record the sale but to ignore any inventory adjustment because the physical inventory has already been taken. How will this affect the current year's net income? next year's income? What would you do if you were the accountant? Assume that SOS uses a periodic inventory system.

LO6

Exercise 5-11 Inventory Costing Methods

VanderMeer Inc. reported the following information for the month of February:

Inventory, February 1	65 units @ $20
Purchases:	
February 7	50 units @ $22
February 18	60 units @ $23
February 27	45 units @ $24

During February, VanderMeer sold 140 units. The company uses a periodic inventory system.

Required

What is the value of ending inventory and cost of goods sold for February under the following assumptions:

1. Of the 140 units sold, 55 cost $20, 35 cost $22, 45 cost $23, and 5 cost $24.
2. FIFO
3. LIFO
4. Weighted average

LO7

Exercise 5-12 Evaluation of Inventory Costing Methods

Write the letter of the method that is most applicable to each statement.

a. Specific identification
b. Average cost
c. First-in, first-out (FIFO)
d. Last-in, first-out (LIFO)

_______ 1. Is the most realistic ending inventory
_______ 2. Results in cost of goods sold being closest to current product costs
_______ 3. Results in highest income during periods of inflation
_______ 4. Results in highest ending inventory during periods of inflation
_______ 5. Smooths out costs during periods of inflation
_______ 6. Is not practical for most businesses
_______ 7. Puts more weight on the cost of the larger number of units purchased
_______ 8. Is an assumption that most closely reflects the physical flow of goods for most businesses

LO8

Exercise 5-13 Inventory Errors

For each of the following independent situations, fill in the blanks to indicate the effect of the error on each of the various financial statement items. Indicate an understatement (U), an overstatement (O), or no effect (NE). Assume that each of the companies uses a periodic inventory system.

	Balance Sheet		Income Statement	
Error	**Inventory**	**Retained Earnings**	**Cost of Goods Sold**	**Net Income**
1. Goods in transit at year-end are not included in the physical count; they were shipped FOB shipping point.	_______	_______	_______	_______
2. One section of a warehouse is counted twice during the year-end count of inventory.	_______	_______	_______	_______
3. During the count at year-end, the inventory sheets for one of the stores of a discount retailer are lost.	_______	_______	_______	_______

LO8

Exercise 5-14 Transfer of Title to Inventory

For each of the following transactions, indicate which company should include the inventory on its December 31, 2008 balance sheet:

1. Michelson Supplies Inc. shipped merchandise to PJ Sales on December 28, 2008, terms FOB destination. The merchandise arrives at PJ's on January 4, 2009.
2. Quarton Inc. shipped merchandise to Filbrandt on December 25, 2008, FOB destination. Filbrandt received the merchandise on December 31, 2008.
3. James Bros. Inc. shipped merchandise to Randall Company on December 27, 2008, FOB shipping point. Randall Company received the merchandise on January 3, 2009.
4. Hinz Company shipped merchandise to Barner Inc. on December 24, 2008, FOB shipping point. The merchandise arrived at Barner's on December 29, 2008.

LO10

Exercise 5-15 Gross Profit Method

On February 12, a hurricane destroys the entire inventory of Suncoast Corporation. An estimate of the amount of inventory lost is needed for insurance purposes. The following information is available:

Inventory on January 1	$ 15,400
Net sales from January 1 to February 12	105,300
Purchases from January 1 to February 12	84,230

Suncoast estimates its gross profit ratio as 25% of net sales. The insurance company has agreed to pay Suncoast $10,000 as a settlement for the inventory destroyed.

Required
Determine the effect on the accounting equation of the adjustment to recognize the inventory lost and the insurance reimbursement.

LO11

Exercise 5-16 Inventory Turnover for Best Buy

The following amounts are available from the 2007 annual report of **Best Buy Co., Inc.** (All amounts are in millions of dollars.)

Cost of goods sold (for year ended March 3, 2007)	$27,165
Merchandise inventories, March 3, 2007	4,028
Merchandise inventories, February 25, 2006	3,338

Required
1. Compute Best Buy's inventory turnover ratio for 2007.
2. What is the average length of time it takes to sell an item of inventory? Explain your answer.
3. Do you think the average length of time it took Best Buy to sell inventory in 2007 is reasonable? What other information do you need to fully answer that question?

LO12

Exercise 5-17 Impact of Transactions Involving Inventories on Statement of Cash Flows

From the following list, identify whether the change in the account balance during the year is added to (A) or deducted from (D) net income when the indirect method is used to determine cash flows from operating activities.

______	Increase in accounts payable	______	Increase in inventories
______	Decrease in accounts payable	______	Decrease in inventories

LO12

Exercise 5-18 Effects of Transactions Involving Inventories on the Statement of Cash Flows—Direct Method

Masthead Company's comparative balance sheets included inventory of $180,400 at December 31, 2007, and $241,200 at December 31, 2008. Masthead's comparative balance sheets also included accounts payable of $85,400 at December 31, 2007, and $78,400 at December 31, 2008. Masthead's accounts payable balances are composed solely of amounts due to suppliers for purchases of inventory on account. Cost of goods sold, as reported by Masthead on its 2008 income statement, amounted to $1,200,000.

Required
What is the amount of cash payments for inventory that Masthead will report in the Operating Activities category of its 2008 statement of cash flows assuming that the direct method is used?

LO12 **Exercise 5-19** Effects of Transactions Involving Inventories on the Statement of Cash Flows—Indirect Method

Refer to all of the facts in Exercise 5-18.

Required

Assume instead that Masthead uses the indirect method to prepare its statement of cash flows. Indicate how each item will be reflected as an adjustment to net income in the Operating Activities category of the statement of cash flows.

MULTICONCEPT EXERCISES

LO2,3 **Exercise 5-20** Income Statement for a Merchandiser

Fill in the missing amounts in the following income statement for Carpenters Department Store Inc.

Sales revenue		$125,600	
Less: Sales returns and allowances		(a)	
Net sales			$122,040
Cost of goods sold:			
Beginning inventory		$ 23,400	
Purchases	$ (b)		
Less: Purchase discounts	1,300		
Net purchases	$ (c)		
Add: Transportation-in	6,550		
Cost of goods purchased		81,150	
Cost of goods available for sale		$104,550	
Less: Ending inventory		(e)	
Cost of goods sold			(d)
Gross profit			$ 38,600
Operating expenses			(f)
Income before tax			$ 26,300
Income tax expense			10,300
Net income			$ (g)

LO2,3 **Exercise 5-21** Partial Income Statement—Periodic System

LaPine Company has the following account balances as of December 31, 2008:

Purchase returns and allowances	$ 400
Inventory, January 1	4,000
Sales	80,000
Transportation-in	1,000
Sales returns and allowances	500
Purchase discounts	800
Inventory, December 31	3,800
Purchases	30,000
Sales discounts	1,200

Required

Prepare a partial income statement for LaPine Company for 2008 through gross profit. Calculate LaPine's gross profit ratio for 2008.

LO6,7 **Exercise 5-22** Inventory Costing Methods—Periodic System

The following information is available concerning the inventory of Carter Inc.:

	Units	Unit Cost
Beginning inventory	200	$10
Purchases:		
March 5	300	11
June 12	400	12
August 23	250	13
October 2	150	15

During the year, Carter sold 1,000 units. It uses a periodic inventory system.

Required

1. Calculate ending inventory and cost of goods sold for each of the following three methods:
   a. Weighted average
   b. FIFO
   c. LIFO
2. Assume an estimated tax rate of 30%. How much more or less (indicate which) will Carter pay in taxes by using FIFO instead of LIFO? Explain your answer.

LO5,9

Exercise 5-23 Lower-of-Cost-or-Market Rule

Awards Etc. carries an inventory of trophies and ribbons for local sports teams and school clubs. The cost of trophies has dropped in the past year, which pleases the company except for the fact that it has on hand considerable inventory that was purchased at the higher prices. The president is not pleased with the lower profit margin the company is earning. "The lower profit margin will continue until we sell all of this old inventory," he grumbled to the new staff accountant. "Not really," replied the accountant. "Let's write down the inventory to the replacement cost this year, and then next year our profit margin will be in line with the competition."

Required

Explain why the inventory can be carried at an amount less than its cost. Which accounts will be affected by the write-down? What will be the effect on income in the current year and future years?

LO7,13

Exercise 5-24 Inventory Costing Methods—Perpetual System (Appendix)

The following information is available concerning Stillwater Inc.:

	Units	Unit Cost
Beginning inventory	200	$10
Purchases:		
March 5	300	11
June 12	400	12
August 23	250	13
October 2	150	15

Stillwater, which uses a perpetual system, sold 1,000 units for $22 each during the year. Sales occurred on the following dates:

	Units
February 12	150
April 30	200
July 7	200
September 6	300
December 3	150

Required

1. Calculate ending inventory and cost of goods sold for each of the following three methods:
   a. Moving average
   b. FIFO
   c. LIFO
2. For each of the three methods, compare the results with those of Carter in Exercise 5-22. Which method gives a different answer depending on whether a company uses a periodic or a perpetual inventory system?
3. Assume the use of the perpetual system and an estimated tax rate of 30%. How much more or less (indicate which) will Stillwater pay in taxes by using LIFO instead of FIFO? Explain your answer.

PROBLEMS

LO1 **Problem 5-1** Inventory Costs in Various Businesses

Businesses incur various costs in selling goods and services. Each business must decide which costs are expenses of the period and which should be included in the cost of the inventory: The following table lists various types of businesses along with certain types of costs they incur:

		Accounting Treatment		
Business	**Types of Costs**	**Expense of the Period**	**Inventory Cost**	**Other Treatment**
Retail shoe store	Shoes for sale			
	Shoe boxes			
	Advertising signs			
Grocery store	Canned goods on the shelves			
	Produce			
	Cleaning supplies			
	Cash registers			
Frame shop	Wooden frame supplies			
	Nails			
	Glass			
Walk-in print shop	Paper			
	Copy machines			
	Toner cartridges			
Restaurant	Frozen food			
	China and silverware			
	Prepared food			
	Spices			

Required
Fill in the table to indicate the correct accounting for each type of cost by placing an *X* in the appropriate column. For any costs that receive other treatment, explain what the appropriate treatment is for accounting purposes.

LO4 **Problem 5-2** Calculation of Gross Profit for Wal-Mart and Target

The following information was summarized from the consolidated statements of income of **Wal-Mart Stores, Inc. and Subsidiaries** for the years ended January 31, 2007 and 2006, and the consolidated statements of operations of **Target Corporation** for the years ended February 3, 2007, and January 28, 2006. (For each company, years are labeled as 2006 and 2005, respectively, although Wal-Mart labels these as the 2007 and 2006 fiscal years.)

	2006		2005	
(in Millions)	**Sales***	**Cost of Sales**	**Sales***	**Cost of Sales**
Wal-Mart	$344,992	$264,152	$308,945	$237,649
Target	57,878	39,399	51,271	34,927

**Described as net sales by Wal-Mart.*

Required
1. Calculate the gross profit ratios for Wal-Mart and Target for 2006 and 2005.
2. Which company appears to be performing better? What factors might cause the difference in the gross profit ratios of the two companies? What other information should you consider to determine how these companies are performing in this regard?

LO7 **Problem 5-3** Evaluation of Inventory Costing Methods

Users of financial statements rely on the information available to them to decide whether to invest in a company or lend it money. As an investor, you are comparing three companies in the same industry. The cost to purchase inventory is rising in the industry. Assume that all expenses

HOMEWORK

incurred by the three companies are the same except for cost of goods sold. The companies use the following methods to value ending inventory:

Company A—weighted average cost
Company B—first-in, first-out (FIFO)
Company C—last-in, first-out (LIFO)

Required

1. Which of the three companies will report the highest net income? Explain your answer.
2. Which of the three companies will pay the least in income taxes? Explain your answer.
3. Which method of inventory costing do you believe is superior to the others in providing information to potential investors? Explain.
4. Explain how your answers to (1), (2), and (3) would change if the costs to purchase inventory had been falling instead of rising.

LO8

Problem 5-4 Inventory Error

The following highly condensed income statements and balance sheets are available for Budget Stores for a two-year period. (All amounts are stated in thousands of dollars.)

Income Statements	2008	2007
Revenues	$20,000	$15,000
Cost of goods sold	13,000	10,000
Gross profit	$ 7,000	$ 5,000
Operating expenses	3,000	2,000
Net income	$ 4,000	$ 3,000

Balance Sheets	December 31, 2008	December 31, 2007
Cash	$ 1,700	$ 1,500
Inventory	4,200	3,500
Other current assets	2,500	2,000
Long-term assets	15,000	14,000
Total assets	$23,400	$21,000
Liabilities	$ 8,500	$ 7,000
Capital stock	5,000	5,000
Retained earnings	9,900	9,000
Total liabilities and stockholders' equity	$23,400	$21,000

Before releasing the 2008 annual report, Budget's controller learns that the inventory of one of the stores (amounting to $600,000) was inadvertently omitted from the count on December 31, 2007. The inventory of the store was correctly included in the December 31, 2008, count.

Required

1. Prepare revised income statements and balance sheets for Budget Stores for each of the two years. Ignore the effect of income taxes.
2. If Budget did not prepare revised statements before releasing the 2008 annual report, what would be the amount of overstatement or understatement of net income for the two-year period? What would be the overstatement or understatement of retained earnings at December 31, 2008, if revised statements were not prepared?
3. Given your answers in (2), does it matter if Budget bothers to restate the financial statements of the two years to rectify the error? Explain your answer.

LO10

Problem 5-5 Gross Profit Method of Estimating Inventory Losses

On August 1, an office supply store was destroyed by an explosion in its basement. A small amount of inventory valued at $4,500 was saved. An estimate of the amount of inventory lost is needed for insurance purposes. The following information is available:

Inventory, January 1	$ 3,200
Purchases, January–July	164,000
Sales, January–July	113,500

HOMEWORK

The normal gross profit ratio is 40%. The insurance company will pay the store $65,000.

Required

1. Using the gross profit method, estimate the amount of inventory lost in the explosion.
2. Prepare the appropriate journal entry to recognize the inventory loss and the insurance reimbursement.

LO11

Problem 5-6 Inventory Turnover for Apple Computer and Hewlett-Packard

The following information was summarized from the 2006 annual report of **Apple Computer, Inc.**:

	(in millions)
Cost of sales for the year ended:	
September 30, 2006	$13,717
September 24, 2005 (as restated)	9,889
Inventories:	
September 30, 2006	$ 270
September 24, 2005 (as restated)	165
Net sales for the year ended:	
September 30, 2006	19,315
September 24, 2005 (as restated)	13,931

The following information was summarized from the fiscal year 2006 annual report of **Hewlett-Packard Company**:

	(in millions)
Cost of sales* for the year ended:	
October 31, 2006	$55,248
October 31, 2005	52,550
Inventory:	
October 31, 2006	7,750
October 31, 2005	6,877
Net revenue for the year ended:	
October 31, 2006	91,658
October 31, 2005	86,696

**Described as "cost of products" by Hewlett-Packard:*

Required

1. Calculate the gross profit ratios for Apple Computer and Hewlett-Packard for each of the two years presented.
2. Calculate the inventory turnover ratios for both companies for the most recent year.
3. Which company appears to be performing better? What other information should you consider to determine how these companies are performing in this regard?

LO12

Problem 5-7 Effects of Changes in Inventory and Accounts Payable Balances on Statement of Cash Flows

Copeland Antiques reported a net loss of $33,200 for the year ended December 31, 2008. The following items were included on Copeland's balance sheets at December 31, 2008 and 2007:

	12/31/08	12/31/07
Cash	$ 65,300	$ 46,100
Trade accounts payable	123,900	93,700
Inventories	192,600	214,800

Copeland uses the indirect method to prepare its statement of cash flows. Copeland does not have any other current assets or current liabilities and did not enter into any investing or financing activities during 2008.

Required

1. Prepare Copeland's 2008 statement of cash flows.
2. Draft a brief memo to the president explaining why cash increased during such an unprofitable year.

MULTICONCEPT PROBLEMS

LO2,3,12

Problem 5-8 Purchases and Sales of Merchandise, Cash Flows

Two Wheeler, a bike shop, opened for business on April 1. It uses a periodic inventory system. The following transactions occurred during the first month of business:

April 1: Purchased five units from Duhan Co. for $500 total, with terms 3/10, net 30, FOB destination.
April 10: Paid for the April 1 purchase.
April 15: Sold one unit for $200 cash.
April 18: Purchased ten units from Clinton Inc. for $900 total, with terms 3/10, net/30, FOB destination.
April 25: Sold three units for $200 each, cash.
April 28: Paid for the April 18 purchase.

Required

1. For each of the preceding transactions of Two Wheeler, prepare the appropriate journal entry.
2. Determine net income for the month of April. Two Wheeler incurred and paid $100 for rent and $50 for miscellaneous expenses during April. Ending inventory is $967. (Ignore income taxes.)
3. Assuming that these are the only transactions during April (including rent and miscellaneous expenses), compute net cash flow from operating activities.
4. Explain why cash outflow is so much larger than expenses on the income statement.

LO2,3,4

Problem 5-9 Gap Inc.'s Sales, Cost of Goods Sold, and Gross Profit

The consolidated balance sheets of **Gap Inc.** included merchandise inventory in the amount of $1,796,000,000 as of February 3, 2007 (the end of fiscal year 2006) and $1,696,000,000 as of January 28, 2006 (the end of fiscal year 2005). Net sales were $15,943,000,000 and $16,023,000,000 at the end of fiscal years 2006 and 2005, respectively. Cost of goods sold and occupancy expenses were $10,294,000,000 and $10,154,000,000 at the end of fiscal years 2006 and 2005, respectively.

Required

1. Unlike most other merchandisers, Gap Inc. doesn't include accounts receivable on its balance sheet. Why doesn't Gap Inc.'s balance sheet include this account?
2. Prepare the appropriate journal entry to record sales during the year ended February 3, 2007.
3. Gap Inc. sets forth net sales but not gross sales on its income statement. What type(s) of deduction(s) would be made from gross sales to arrive at the amount of net sales reported? Why might the company decide not to report the amount(s) of the deduction(s) separately?
4. Reconstruct the cost of goods sold section of Gap Inc.'s 2006 income statement.
5. Calculate the gross profit ratios for Gap Inc. for 2006 and 2005 and comment on any change noted. Is the company's performance improving? Explain. What factors might have caused the change in the gross profit ratio?

LO2,3

Problem 5-10 Financial Statements

A list of accounts for Maple Inc. at 12/31/08 follows.

Accounts Receivable	$ 2,359	Land	$20,000
Advertising Expense	4,510	Purchase Discounts	800
Buildings and Equipment, Net	55,550	Purchases	40,200
Capital Stock	50,000	Retained Earnings, January 1, 2008	32,550
Cash	590	Salaries Expense	25,600
Depreciation Expense	2,300	Salaries Payable	650
Dividends	6,000	Sales	84,364
Income Tax Expense	3,200	Sales Returns	780
Income Tax Payable	3,200	Transportation-in	375
Interest Receivable	100	Utilities Expense	3,600
Inventory:			
January 1, 2008	6,400		
December 31, 2008	7,500		

Required

1. Determine cost of goods sold for 2008.
2. Determine net income for 2008.
3. Prepare a balance sheet dated December 31, 2008.

LO5,6,7

Problem 5-11 Comparison of Inventory Costing Methods—Periodic System

Bitten Company's inventory records show 600 units on hand on October 1 with a unit cost of $5 each. The following transactions occurred during the month of October:

Date	Unit Purchases	Unit Sales
October 4		500 @ $10.00
8	800 @ $5.40	
9		700 @ $10.00
18	700 @ $5.76	
20		800 @ $11.00
29	800 @ $5.90	

All expenses other than cost of goods sold amount to $3,000 for the month. The company uses an estimated tax rate of 30% to accrue monthly income taxes.

Required

1. Prepare a chart comparing cost of goods sold and ending inventory using the periodic system and the following costing methods:

	Cost of Goods Sold	Ending Inventory	Total
Weighted average			
FIFO			
LIFO			

2. What does the Total column represent?
3. Prepare income statements for each of the three methods.
4. Will the company pay more or less tax if it uses FIFO rather than LIFO? How much more or less?

LO5,7, 13

Problem 5-12 Comparison of Inventory Costing Methods—Perpetual System (Appendix)

Repeat Problem 5-11 using the perpetual system.

LO5,6,7

Problem 5-13 Inventory Costing Methods—Periodic System

Oxendine Company's inventory records for the month of November reveal the following:

Inventory, November 1	200 units @ $18.00
November 4, purchase	250 units @ $18.50
November 7, sale	300 units @ $42.00
November 13, purchase	220 units @ $18.90
November 18, purchase	150 units @ $19.00
November 22, sale	380 units @ $42.50
November 24, purchase	200 units @ $19.20
November 28, sale	110 units @ $43.00

Selling and administrative expenses for the month were $10,800. Depreciation expense was $4,000. Oxendine's tax rate is 35%.

Required

1. Calculate the cost of goods sold and ending inventory under each of the following three methods assuming a periodic inventory system: (a) FIFO, (b) LIFO, and (c) weighted average.
2. Calculate the gross profit and net income under each costing assumption.
3. Under which costing method will Oxendine pay the least taxes? Explain your answer.

LO5,6,7

Problem 5-14 Inventory Costing Methods—Periodic System

Following is an inventory acquisition schedule for Weaver Corp. for 2008:

	Units	Unit Cost
Beginning inventory	5,000	$10
Purchases:		
February 4	3,000	9
April 12	4,000	8
September 10	2,000	7
December 5	1,000	6

During the year, Weaver sold 12,500 units at $12 each. All expenses except cost of goods sold and taxes amounted to $20,000. The tax rate is 30%.

Required

1. Compute cost of goods sold and ending inventory under each of the following three methods assuming a periodic inventory system: (a) weighted average, (b) FIFO, and (c) LIFO.
2. Prepare income statements under each of the three methods.
3. Which method do you recommend so that Weaver pays the least amount of taxes during 2008? Explain your answer.
4. Weaver anticipates that unit costs for inventory will increase throughout 2009. Will Weaver be able to switch from the method you recommended that it use in 2008 to another method to take advantage of the increase in prices for tax purposes? Explain your answer.

LO1,7,9

Problem 5-15 Interpreting Gannett Co.'s Inventory Accounting Policy

The 2006 annual report of **Gannett Co., Inc.** (publisher of *USA Today* and many other newspapers) includes the following in the note that summarizes its accounting policies:

> **Inventories** Inventories, consisting principally of newsprint, printing ink, plate material and production film for the company's newspaper publishing operations, are valued primarily at the lower of cost (first-in, first-out) or market. At certain U.S. newspapers, however, newsprint inventory is carried on a last-in, first-out basis.

Required

1. What *types* of inventory cost does Gannett carry? What about newspapers? Are newspapers considered inventory?
2. Why would the company choose two different methods to value its inventory?

LO7,9

Problem 5-16 Interpreting Sears' Inventory Accounting Policy

The 2006 annual report of **Sears Holdings Corporation** (the parent of Kmart and Sears) includes the following information in the note that describes its accounting policies relating to merchandise inventories:

> Merchandise inventories are valued at the lower of cost or market. For Kmart and Sears Domestic, cost is primarily determined using the retail inventory method ("RIM"). Kmart merchandise inventories are valued under the RIM using primarily a first-in, first-out (FIFO) cost flow assumption. Sears Domestic merchandise inventories are valued under the RIM using primarily a last-in, first-out (LIFO) cost flow assumption. For Sears Canada, cost is determined using the average cost method, based on individual items.

Your grandfather knows that you are studying accounting and asks you what this information means.

Required

1. Sears uses the LIFO cost flow assumption for some of its inventories. Does this mean that it sells its newest merchandise first? Explain your answer.
2. Does Sears report merchandise inventories on its balance sheet at their retail value? Explain your answer.

ALTERNATE PROBLEMS

LO1 **Problem 5-1A** Inventory Costs in Various Businesses

Sound Traxs Inc. sells and rents DVDs to retail customers. The accountant is aware that at the end of the year, she must account for inventory but is unsure what DVDs are considered inventory and how to value them. DVDs purchased by the company are placed on the shelf for rental. Every three weeks the company performs a detailed analysis of the rental income from each DVD and decides whether to keep it as a rental or to offer it for sale in the resale section of the store. Resale DVDs sell for $10 each regardless of the price Sound Traxs paid for the tape.

Required

1. How should Sound Traxs account for each of the two types of DVDs—rentals and resales—on its balance sheet?
2. How would you suggest Sound Traxs account for the DVDs as they are transferred from one department to another?

LO4 **Problem 5-2A** Calculation of Gross Profit for Best Buy and Circuit City

The following information was summarized from the 2007 and 2006 consolidated statements of income of **Best Buy, Inc.** (for the years ended March 3, 2007 and February 25, 2006) and **Circuit City** (for the years ended February 28, 2007 and February 28, 2006). For each company, years are labeled as 2007 and 2006, respectively.

	2007		2006	
(in Millions)	Sales*	Cost of Goods Sold**	Sales*	Cost of Goods Sold**
Best Buy	$35,934	$27,165	$30,848	$23,122
Circuit City	$12,430	$ 9,501	11,514	8,704

**Described as "Revenue" by Best Buy and as "Net Sales" by Circuit City.*
***Described as "cost of sales, buying and warehousing" by Circuit City.*

Required

1. Calculate the gross profit ratios for Best Buy and Circuit City for 2007 and 2006.
2. Which company appears to be performing better? What factors might cause the difference in the gross profit ratios of the two companies? What other information should you consider to determine how these companies are performing in this regard?

LO7 **Problem 5-3A** Evaluation of Inventory Costing Methods

Three large mass merchandisers use the following methods to value ending inventory:

Company X—weighted average cost
Company Y—first-in, first-out (FIFO)
Company Z—last-in, first-out (LIFO)

The cost of inventory has steadily increased over the past ten years of the product life. Recently, however, prices have started to decline slightly due to foreign competition.

Required

1. Will the effect on net income of the decline in cost of goods sold be the same for all three companies? Explain your answer.
2. Company Z would like to change its inventory costing method from LIFO to FIFO. Write an acceptable note for its annual report to justify the change.

LO8 **Problem 5-4A** Inventory Error

The following condensed income statements and balance sheets are available for Planter Stores for a two-year period. (All amounts are stated in thousands of dollars.)

Income Statements	2008	2007
Revenues	$35,982	$26,890
Cost of goods sold	12,594	9,912
Gross profit	$23,388	$16,978
Operating expenses	13,488	10,578
Net income	$ 9,900	$ 6,400

Balance Sheets	December 31, 2008	December 31, 2007
Cash	$ 9,400	$ 4,100
Inventory	4,500	5,400
Other current assets	1,600	1,250
Long-term assets, net	24,500	24,600
Total assets	$40,000	$35,350
Current liabilities	$ 9,380	$10,600
Capital stock	18,000	18,000
Retained earnings	12,620	6,750
Total liabilities and stockholders' equity	$40,000	$35,350

Before releasing the 2008 annual report, Planter's controller learns that the inventory of one of the stores (amounting to $500,000) was counted twice in the December 31, 2007, inventory. The inventory was correctly counted in the December 31, 2008, inventory.

Required

1. Prepare revised income statements and balance sheets for Planter Stores for each of the two years. Ignore the effect of income taxes.
2. Compute the current ratio at December 31, 2007, before the statements are revised and compute the current ratio at the same date after the statements are revised. If Planter applied for a loan in early 2008 and the lender required a current ratio of at least 1 to 1, would the error have affected the loan? Explain your answer.
3. If Planter did not prepare revised statements before releasing the 2008 annual report, what would be the amount of overstatement or understatement of net income for the two-year period? What would be the overstatement or understatement of retained earnings at December 31, 2008, if revised statements were not prepared?
4. Given your answers to (2) and (3), does it matter if Planter bothers to restate the financial statements of the two years to correct the error? Explain your answer.

LO10

Problem 5-5A Gross Profit Method of Estimating Inventory Losses

On July 1, an explosion destroyed a fireworks supply company. A small amount of inventory valued at $4,500 was saved. An estimate of the amount of inventory lost is needed for insurance purposes. The following information is available:

Inventory, January 1	$14,200
Purchases, January–June	77,000
Sales, January–June	93,500

The normal gross profit ratio is 70%. The insurance company will pay the supply company $50,000.

Required

1. Using the gross profit method, estimate the amount of inventory lost in the explosion.
2. Prepare the appropriate journal entry to recognize the inventory loss and the insurance reimbursement.

LO11

Problem 5-6A Inventory Turnover for Wal-Mart and Target

The following information was summarized from the 2007 annual report of **Wal-Mart Stores, Inc.**:

	(in millions)
Cost of sales for the year ended January 31:	
2007	$264,152
2006	237,649
Inventories, January 31:	
2007	33,685
2006	31,910

The following information was summarized from the 2006 annual report of **Target Corporation**:

	(in millions)
Cost of sales for the year ended:	
February 3, 2007	$39,399
January 28, 2006	34,927
Inventory:	
February 3, 2007	6,254
January 28, 2006	5,838

Required

1. Calculate the inventory turnover ratios for Wal-Mart for the year ending January 31, 2007, and Target for the year ending February 3, 2007.
2. Which company appears to be performing better? What other information should you consider to determine how these companies are performing in this regard?

LO12 **Problem 5-7A** Effects of Changes in Inventory and Accounts Payable Balances on Statement of Cash Flows

Carpetland City reported net income of $78,500 for the year ended December 31, 2008. The following items were included on Carpetland's balance sheet at December 31, 2008 and 2007:

	12/31/08	12/31/07
Cash	$ 14,400	$26,300
Trade accounts payable	23,900	93,700
Inventories	105,500	84,900

Carpetland uses the indirect method to prepare its statement of cash flows. Carpetland does not have any other current assets or current liabilities and did not enter into any investing or financing activities during 2008.

Required

1. Prepare Carpetland's 2008 statement of cash flows.
2. Draft a brief memo to the president to explain why cash decreased during a profitable year.

ALTERNATE MULTICONCEPT PROBLEMS

LO2,3, 12 **Problem 5-8A** Purchases and Sales of Merchandise, Cash Flows

Chestnut Corp., a ski shop, opened for business on October 1. It uses a periodic inventory system. The following transactions occurred during the first month of business:

October 1: Purchased three units from Elm Inc. for $249 total, terms 2/10, net 30, FOB destination.
October 10: Paid for the October 1 purchase.
October 15: Sold one unit for $200 cash.
October 18: Purchased ten units from Wausau Company for $800 total, with terms 2/10, net/30, FOB destination.
October 25: Sold three units for $200 each, cash.
October 30: Paid for the October 18 purchase.

Required

1. For each of the preceding transactions of Chestnut, prepare the appropriate journal entry.
2. Determine the number of units on hand on October 31.
3. If Chestnut started the month with $2,000, determine its balance in cash at the end of the month assuming that these are the only transactions that occurred during October. Why has the cash balance decreased when the company reported net income?

LO2,3,4 **Problem 5-9A** Walgreen's Sales, Cost of Goods Sold, and Gross Profit

The following information was summarized from the consolidated balance sheets of **Walgreen Co. and Subsidiaries** as of August 31, 2006 and August 31, 2005 and the consolidated statements of income for the years ended August 31, 2006 and August 31, 2005.

(in millions)	2006	2005
Accounts receivable, net	$ 2,062.7	$ 1,396.3
Cost of sales	34,240.4	30,413.8
Inventories	6,050.4	5,592.7
Net sales	47,409.0	42,201.6

Required

1. Prepare the appropriate journal entry related to the collection of accounts receivable and sales during 2006. Assume that all of Walgreen's sales are on account.
2. Walgreen Co. sets forth net sales but not gross sales on its income statement. What type(s) of deduction(s) would be made from gross sales to arrive at the amount of net sales reported? Why might the company decide not to report the amount(s) of the deduction(s) separately?
3. Reconstruct the cost of goods sold section of Walgreen's 2006 income statement.
4. Calculate the gross profit ratios for Walgreen Co. for 2006 and 2005 and comment on the change noted, if any. Is the company's performance improving? What factors might have caused the change in the gross profit ratio?

LO2,3

Problem 5-10A Financial Statements

A list of accounts for Lloyd Inc. at December 31, 2008, follows.

Accounts Receivable	$ 56,359
Advertising Expense	12,900
Capital Stock	50,000
Cash	22,340
Dividends	6,000
Income Tax Expense	1,450
Income Tax Payable	1,450
Inventory	
January 1, 2008	6,400
December 31, 2008	5,900
Purchase Discounts	1,237
Purchases	62,845
Retained Earnings, January 1, 2008	28,252
Salaries Payable	650
Sales	112,768
Sales Returns	1,008
Transportation-in	375
Utilities Expense	1,800
Wages and Salaries Expense	23,000
Wages Payable	120

Required

1. Determine cost of goods sold for 2008.
2. Determine net income for 2008.
3. Prepare a balance sheet dated December 31, 2008.

LO5,6,7

Problem 5-11A Comparison of Inventory Costing Methods—Periodic System

Stellar Inc.'s inventory records show 300 units on hand on November 1 with a unit cost of $4 each. The following transactions occurred during the month of November:

Date	Unit Purchases	Unit Sales
November 4		200 @ $9.00
8	500 @ $4.50	
9		500 @ $9.00
18	700 @ $4.75	
20		400 @ $9.50
29	600 @ $5.00	

All expenses other than cost of goods sold amount to $2,000 for the month. The company uses an estimated tax rate of 25% to accrue monthly income taxes.

Required

1. Prepare a chart comparing cost of goods sold and ending inventory using the periodic system and the following costing methods:

	Cost of Goods Sold	Ending Inventory	Total
Weighted average			
FIFO			
LIFO			

2. What does the Total column represent?
3. Prepare income statements for each of the three methods.
4. Will the company pay more or less tax if it uses FIFO rather than LIFO? How much more or less?

LO5,7, 13

Problem 5-12A Comparison of Inventory Costing Methods—Perpetual System (Appendix)

Repeat Problem 5-11A using the perpetual system.

LO5,6,7

Problem 5-13A Inventory Costing Methods—Periodic System

Story Company's inventory records for the month of November reveal the following:

Inventory, November 1	300 units @ \$27.00
November 4, purchase	375 units @ \$26.50
November 7, sale	450 units @ \$63.00
November 13, purchase	330 units @ \$26.00
November 18, purchase	225 units @ \$25.40
November 22, sale	570 units @ \$63.75
November 24, purchase	300 units @ \$25.00
November 28, sale	165 units @ \$64.50

Selling and administrative expenses for the month were \$16,200. Depreciation expense was \$6,000. Story's tax rate is 35%.

Required

1. Calculate the cost of goods sold and ending inventory under each of the following three methods assuming a periodic inventory system: (a) FIFO, (b) LIFO, and (c) weighted average.
2. Calculate the gross profit and net income under each costing assumption.
3. Under which costing method will Story pay the least taxes? Explain your answer.

LO5,6,7

Problem 5-14A Inventory Costing Methods—Periodic System

Following is an inventory acquisition schedule for Fees Corp. for 2008:

	Units	Unit Cost
Beginning inventory	4,000	\$20
Purchases:		
February 4	2,000	18
April 12	3,000	16
September 10	1,000	14
December 5	2,500	12

During the year, Fees sold 11,000 units at \$30 each. All expenses except cost of goods sold and taxes amounted to \$60,000. The tax rate is 30%.

Required

1. Compute cost of goods sold and ending inventory under each of the following three methods assuming a periodic inventory system: (a) weighted average, (b) FIFO, and (c) LIFO.
2. Prepare income statements under each of the three methods.
3. Which method do you recommend so that Fees pays the least amount of taxes during 2008? Explain your answer.
4. Fees anticipates that unit costs for inventory will increase throughout 2009. Will Fees be able to switch from the method you recommended that it use in 2008 to another method to take advantage of the increase in prices for tax purposes? Explain your answer.

LO1,7,9

Problem 5-15A Interpreting The New York Times Company's Financial Statements

The 2006 annual report of **The New York Times Company** includes the following note:

6. Inventories
Inventories as shown in the accompanying Consolidated Balance Sheets were as follows:

	December	
(In thousands)	**2006**	**2005**
Newsprint and magazine paper	$32,594	$28,190
Other inventory	4,102	3,910
Total	$36,696	$32,100

Inventories are stated at the lower of cost or current market value. Cost was determined utilizing the LIFO method for 78% of inventory in 2006 and 77% of inventory in 2005. The replacement cost of inventory was approximately $45 million as of December 2006 and $40 million as of December 2005.

Required
1. What *types* of inventory costs does The New York Times Company carry? What about newspapers? Are newspapers considered inventory?
2. Why would the company choose more than one method to value its inventory?

LO7,9

Problem 5-16A Interpreting Home Depot's Financial Statements

The 2006 annual report for **Home Depot** includes the following information in the note that summarizes its accounting policies:

> Merchandise Inventories. The majority of the Company's Merchandise Inventories are stated at the lower of cost (first-in, first-out) or market, as determined by the retail inventory method.

A friend knows that you are studying accounting and asks you what this note means.

Required
1. Home Depot uses the first-in, first-out method. Does this mean that it always sells its oldest merchandise first? Explain your answer.
2. Does Home Depot report inventories on its balance sheet at their retail value? Explain your answer.

DECISION CASES

READING AND INTERPRETING FINANCIAL STATEMENTS

LO1,3

Decision Case 5-1 Comparing Two Companies in the Same Industry: Kellogg's and General Mills

Refer to the financial information for **Kellogg's** and **General Mills** reproduced at the end of this book and answer the following questions.

Required
1. Are Kellogg's and General Mills merchandisers, manufacturers, or service providers?
2. What is the dollar amount of inventories that each company reports on its balance sheet at the end of the most recent year? What percentage of total assets do inventories represent for each company?
3. Refer to Note 1 in Kellogg's annual report. What inventory valuation method does the company use? What is the advantage to the company of using this method?
4. Refer to Note 1 in General Mills's annual report. What inventory valuation method, or methods, does the company use? Does the fact that Kellogg's and General Mills use different methods make it difficult to compare the two companies?
5. Given the nature of their businesses, which inventory system, periodic or perpetual, would you expect both Kellogg's and General Mills to use? Explain your answer.

LO7 **Decision Case 5-2** Reading and Interpreting J.C.Penney's Financial Statements

JCPenney reports merchandise inventory in the Current Assets section of the balance sheet in its 2006 annual report as follows (amounts in millions of dollars):

	2006	2005
Merchandise inventory (net of LIFO reserves of $8 and $24)	$3,400	$3,210

Required
1. What method does JCPenney use to report the value of its inventory?
2. What is the amount of the LIFO reserve at the end of each of the two years?
3. Explain the meaning of the increase or decrease in the LIFO reserve during 2006. What does this tell you about inventory costs for the company? Are they rising or falling? Explain your answer.

LO7,9 **Decision Case 5-3** Reading and Interpreting Gap Inc.'s Inventory Note

The 2006 annual report for Gap Inc. includes the following information in the note that summarizes its accounting policies:

Merchandise Inventory

In fiscal 2005, we implemented a new inventory system and effective January 29, 2006 (the beginning of fiscal 2006), we changed our inventory flow assumption from the first-in, first-out ("FIFO") method to the weighted average cost method ("WAC"). The change in inventory accounting method did not have a material impact on the fiscal 2006 financial statements and, because the effect on prior periods presented is not material, they have not been restated as would be required by SFAS 154.

We review our inventory levels in order to identify slow-moving merchandise and broken assortments (items no longer in stock in a sufficient range of sizes) and use markdowns to clear merchandise. We value inventory at the lower of cost or market and record a reserve when future estimated selling price is less than cost. In addition, we estimate and accrue shortage for the period between the last physical count and the balance sheet date. Our shortage estimate can be affected by changes in merchandise mix and changes in actual shortage trends. We estimate and accrue shortage for the period between the last physical count and the balance sheet date. Our shortage estimate can be affected by changes in merchandise mix and changes in actual shortage trends.

Required
1. What inventory costing method did Gap Inc. use prior to the 2006 fiscal year?
2. What inventory costing method did Gap Inc. change to beginning with the 2006 fiscal year? Why would a company decide to change its inventory method?
3. Gap Inc. values its inventory at the lower of cost or market. How does the company define *market*? What factors does it take into account in deciding whether to write down its inventory?

MAKING FINANCIAL DECISIONS

LO2,3,4 **Decision Case 5-4** Gross Profit for a Merchandiser

Emblems For You sells specialty sweatshirts. The purchase price is $10 per unit, plus 10% tax and a shipping cost of 50¢ per unit. When the units arrive, they must be labeled, at an additional cost of 75¢ per unit. Emblems purchased, received, and labeled 1,500 units, of which 750 units were sold during the month for $20 each. The controller has prepared the following income statement:

Sales	$15,000
Cost of sales ($11 × 750)	8,250
Gross profit	$ 6,750
Shipping expense	750
Labeling expense	1,125
Net income	$ 4,875

Emblems is aware that a gross profit of 40% is standard for the industry. The marketing manager believes that Emblems should lower the price because the gross profit is higher than the industry average.

Required
1. Calculate Emblems' gross profit ratio.
2. Explain why Emblems should or should not lower its selling price.

HOMEWORK

LO2,3,4

Decision Case 5-5 Pricing Decision

Caroline's Candy Corner sells gourmet chocolates. The company buys chocolates in bulk for $5 per pound plus 5% sales tax. Credit terms are 2/10, net 25; and the company always pays promptly to take advantage of the discount. The chocolates are shipped to Caroline FOB shipping point. Shipping costs are $0.05 per pound. When the chocolates arrive at the shop, Caroline's Candy repackages them into one-pound boxes labeled with the store name. Boxes cost $0.70 each. The company pays its employees an hourly wage of $5.25 plus a commission of $0.10 per pound.

Required

1. What is the cost per one-pound box of chocolates?
2. What price must Caroline's Candy charge in order to have a 40% gross profit?
3. Do you believe this is a sufficient gross profit for this kind of business? Explain. What other costs might the company still incur?

LO3

Decision Case 5-6 Use of a Perpetual Inventory System

Darrell Keith is starting a new business. He plans to keep a tight control over it. Therefore, he wants to know *exactly* how much gross profit he earns on each unit that he sells. Darrell sets up an elaborate numbering system to identify each item as it is purchased and to match the item with a sales price. Each unit is assigned a number as follows:

0000-000-00-000

a. The first four numbers represent the month and day an item was received.
b. The second set of numbers is the last three numbers of the purchase order that authorized the purchase of the item.
c. The third set of numbers is the two-number department code assigned to different types of products.
d. The last three numbers are a chronological code assigned to units as they are received during a given day.

Required

1. Write a short memo to Darrell explaining the benefits and costs involved in a perpetual inventory system in conjunction with his quest to know exactly how much he will earn on each unit.
2. Comment on Darrell's inventory system assuming that he is selling (a) automobiles or (b)trees, shrubs, and plants.

LO6,7

Decision Case 5-7 Inventory Costing Methods

You are the controller for Georgetown Company. At the end of its first year of operations, the company is experiencing cash flow problems. The following information has been accumulated during the year:

Purchases	
January	1,000 units @ $8
March	1,200 units @ 8
October	1,500 units @ 9

During the year, Georgetown sold 3,000 units at $15 each. The expected tax rate is 35%. The president doesn't understand how to report inventory in the financial statements because no record of the cost of the units sold was kept as each sale was made.

Required

1. What inventory system must Georgetown use?
2. Determine the number of units on hand at the end of the year.
3. Explain cost-flow assumptions to the president and the method you recommend. Prepare income statements to justify your position, comparing your recommended method with at least one other method.

LO8

Decision Case 5-8 Inventory Errors

You are the controller of a rapidly growing mass merchandiser. The company uses a periodic inventory system. As the company has grown and accounting systems have developed, errors have occurred in both the physical count of inventory and the valuation of inventory on the balance sheet. You have been able to identify the following errors as of December 2008:

- In 2006, one section of the warehouse was counted twice. The error resulted in inventory overstated on December 31, 2006, by approximately $45,600.
- In 2007, the replacement cost of some inventory was less than the FIFO value used on the balance sheet. The inventory would have been $6,000 less on the balance sheet dated December 31, 2007.
- In 2008, the company used the gross profit method to estimate inventory for its quarterly financial statements. At the end of the second quarter, the controller made a math error and understated the inventory by $20,000 on the quarterly report. The error was not discovered until the end of the year.

Required
What, if anything, should you do to correct each of these errors? Explain your answers.

ETHICAL DECISION MAKING

LO2

Decision Case 5-9 Sales Returns and Allowances

You are the controller for a large chain of discount merchandise stores. You receive a memo from the sales manager for the midwestern region. He raises an issue regarding the proper treatment of sales returns. The manager urges you to discontinue the "silly practice" of recording Sales Returns and Allowances each time a customer returns a product. In the manager's mind, this is a waste of time and unduly complicates the financial statements. The manager recommends, "Things could be kept a lot simpler by just reducing Sales Revenue when a product is returned."

Required
1. What might the sales manager's motivation have been for writing the memo? Might he believe that the present practice is a waste of time that unduly complicates the financial statements? Explain.
2. Do you agree with the sales manager's recommendation? Explain why you agree or disagree.
3. Write a brief memo to the sales manager outlining your position on this matter.

LO7

Decision Case 5-10 Selection of an Inventory Method

As controller of a widely held public company, you are concerned with making the best decisions for the stockholders. At the end of its first year of operations, you are faced with the choice of method to value inventory. Specific identification is out of the question because the company sells a large quantity of diversified products. You are trying to decide between FIFO and LIFO. Inventory costs have increased 33% over the year. The chief executive officer has instructed you to do whatever it takes in all areas to report the highest income possible.

Required
1. Which method will satisfy the chief executive officer?
2. Which method is in the best interest of the stockholders? Explain your answer.
3. Write a brief memo to the chief executive officer to convince him that reporting the highest income is not always the best approach for the shareholders.

LO9

Decision Case 5-11 Write-Down of Obsolete Inventory

As a newly hired staff accountant, you are assigned the responsibility of physically counting inventory at the end of the year. The inventory count proceeds in a timely fashion. The inventory is outdated, however. You suggest that the inventory cannot be sold for the cost at which it is carried and that the inventory should be written down to a much lower level. The controller replies that experience has taught her how the market changes and she knows that the units in the warehouse will be more marketable again. The company plans to keep the goods until they are back in style.

Required
1. What effect will writing off the inventory have on the current year's income?
2. What effect does not writing off the inventory have on the year-end balance sheet?
3. What factors should you consider in deciding whether to persist in your argument that the inventory should be written down?
4. If you fail to write down the inventory, do outside readers of the statements have reliable information? Explain your answer.

SOLUTIONS TO KEY TERMS QUIZ

Quiz 1: Merchandise Accounting

17	Merchandise Inventory	13	Cost of goods sold
18	Raw materials	3	Perpetual system
16	Work in process	8	Periodic system
19	Finished goods	2	Transportation-in
15	Gross profit	11	Purchases
12	Net sales	4	Purchase Returns and Allowances
20	Sales revenue	10	Purchase Discounts
1	Sales Returns and Allowances	6	FOB destination point
5	Sales Discounts	7	FOB shipping point
9	Cost of goods available for sale	14	Gross profit ratio

Quiz 2: Inventory Valuation

11	Specific identification method	12	Inventory profit
2	Weighted average cost method	3	Lower-of-cost-or-market (LCM) rule
4	FIFO method	8	Gross profit method
6	LIFO method	9	Retail inventory method
13	LIFO liquidation	15	Inventory turnover ratio
10	LIFO conformity rule	7	Number of days' sales in inventory
14	LIFO reserve	1	Moving average (Appendix)
5	Replacement cost		

ANSWERS TO POD REVIEW

LO1	1. b	2. c
LO2	1. a	2. c
LO3	1. d	2. b
LO4	1. a	2. c
LO5	1. a	2. d
LO6	1. b	2. a
LO7	1. b	2. b
LO8	1. a	2. a
LO9	1. c	2. b
LO10	1. d	2. a
LO11	1. c	2. b
LO12	1. b	2. a
LO13	1. b	2. c

CHAPTER 6

Cash and Internal Control

Learning Outcomes

After studying this chapter, you should be able to:

LO1 Identify and describe the various forms of cash reported on a balance sheet.

LO2 Show that you understand various techniques that companies use to control cash.

LO3 Explain the importance of internal control to a business and the significance of the Sarbanes-Oxley Act of 2002.

LO4 Describe the basic internal control procedures.

LO5 Describe the various documents used in recording purchases and their role in controlling cash disbursements.

Study Links...

A Look at the Previous Chapter
Chapter 5 introduced companies that sell a product and examined how they account for purchases and sales of their merchandise. The chapter also considered how the companies track their product costs and value their inventory according to one of the cost flow methods.

A Look at This Chapter
Sale of merchandise results in the collection of cash at some point from the customer. Chapter 6 considers this most liquid of all assets and the ways in which companies try to maintain control over cash as well as other valuable assets.

A Look at the Upcoming Chapter
Two other liquid assets appear toward the top of a balance sheet. Chapter 7 considers how companies account for the receivables that result from sales on credit as well as how they account for investments that are made with available cash.

Sears Holdings Corporation

MAKING BUSINESS DECISIONS

Sears Holdings Corporation is the parent company of Kmart and Sears, Roebuck and Co. As its name implies, the parent's business purpose is to "hold" two of the oldest and most recognizable retailers in the country. The merger of Kmart and Sears was finalized in 2005 and resulted in the creation of the third-largest broadline retailer in the United States, with total revenues in the 2006 fiscal year of over $53 billion. Between its Kmart and Sears locations in this country and its Sears Canada outlets, the company operates nearly 3,800 full-line and specialty retail stores.

Sears Holding Corporation, like all businesses, relies on a steady flow of cash to run smoothly. Cash is needed to continually supply Kmart and Sears stores with the merchandise that they stock—from home appliances to clothing apparel. As the most liquid of all assets, cash is needed for many other uses as well, including acquisition of other businesses, purchase of property and equipment, and repayment of long-term debt. The accompanying balance sheet shows that cash and cash equivalents actually decreased during the 2006 fiscal year but still amounted to nearly $4 billion at year-end and accounted for over 13% of total assets.

© Justin Sullivan/Getty Images

Because cash is such a liquid asset, control over cash is crucial to a company's long-term success. And with so many locations, retailers such as Sears Holdings must pay particular attention to the flow of cash and merchandise into and out of all of its stores. This chapter will look closely at the accounting for cash and cash equivalents and at the ways companies maintain effective control over all valuable assets, including cash. Following are some important questions we will answer:

- What does the first line on Sears Holdings' balance sheet represent; that is, what is included in cash and cash equivalents? (See pp. 296–298.)
- What are some of the techniques that companies use to control cash? (See pp. 299–306.)
- Why is it essential for a company to maintain an effective internal control system? What are some of the basic procedures that help make a system effective? (See pp. 307–313.)
- How can the use of business documents add to the effectiveness of an internal control system? (See pp. 314–321.)

(continued)

SEARS HOLDINGS CORPORATION
CONSOLIDATED BALANCE SHEETS (PARTIAL)

millions, except per share data	February 3, 2007	January 28, 2006
ASSETS		
Current assets		
Cash and cash equivalents	$ 3,968	$ 4,440
Accounts receivable	847	811
Merchandise inventories	9,907	9,068
Prepaid expenses and other current assets	372	372
Deferred income taxes	312	516
Total current assets	15,406	15,207
Property and equipment		
Land	2,105	2,146
Buildings and improvements	5,981	5,920
Furniture, fixtures, and equipment	2,408	2,268
Capital leases	352	367
Gross property and equipment	10,846	10,701
Less accumulated depreciation	(1,714)	(878)
Total property and equipment, net	9,132	9,823
Goodwill	1,692	1,684
Tradenames and other intangible assets	3,437	3,448
Other assets	399	411
Total Assets	$ 30,066	$ 30,573

Most liquid of all assets; decreased by $472 million

Is still over 13% of total assets

See accompanying Notes to Consolidated Financial Statements.

Source: Sears Holdings Corporation 2006 annual report.

What Constitutes Cash?

LO1 Identify and describe the various forms of cash reported on a balance sheet.

Cash takes many different forms. Coin and currency on hand and cash on deposit in the form of checking, savings, and money market accounts are the most obvious forms of cash. Also included in cash are various forms of checks, including undeposited checks from customers, cashier's checks, and certified checks. The proliferation of different types of financial instruments on the market today makes it very difficult to decide on the appropriate classification of these various items. The key to the classification of an amount as cash is that it be *readily available to pay debts*. Technically, a bank has the legal right to demand that a customer notify it before making withdrawals from savings accounts, or time deposits, as they are often called. Because this right is rarely exercised, however, savings accounts are normally classified as cash. In contrast, a certificate of deposit has a specific maturity date and carries a penalty for early withdrawal and therefore is not included in cash.

Real World Practice

6-1 Reading General Mills's Statement of Cash Flows

According to the company's statement of cash flows, did its cash and cash equivalents increase or decrease during the most recent year? Summarize the changes in cash and cash equivalents for the year using the framework shown at the top of the next page.

CASH EQUIVALENTS AND THE STATEMENT OF CASH FLOWS

Note that the first item on Sears Holidings' balance sheet in the chapter opener is Cash and cash equivalents. Examples of items normally classified as cash equivalents are commercial paper issued by corporations, Treasury bills issued by the federal government, and money market funds offered by financial institutions. According to current accounting standards, classification as a **cash equivalent** is limited to those investments that are readily convertible to known amounts of cash and that have an original maturity to the investor of three months or less. Note that according to that definition, a six-month bank certificate of deposit would *not* be classified as a cash equivalent.

The statement of cash flows that accompanies Sears Holdings' balance sheet is shown in Exhibit 6-1. Note the direct tie between this statement and the balance sheet. (Refer to the Current Assets section of the company's balance sheet shown in the chapter opener.)

Cash equivalent
An investment that is readily convertible to a known amount of cash and has an original maturity to the investor of three months or less.

(Amounts in millions)

Beginning balance in cash and cash equivalents		$ 4,440	1/28/06 balance sheet
Add: Cash provided by operating activities	$ 1,444		Statement of cash flows
Deduct: Cash used in investing activities	(663)		
Deduct: Cash used in financing activities	(1,252)		
Deduct: Effect of exchange rate changes	(1)		
Net decrease in cash and cash equivalents		(472)	
Ending balance in cash and cash equivalents		$3,968	2/3/07 balance sheet

POD REVIEW 6.1

LO1 *Identify and describe the various forms of cash reported on a balance sheet.*

- Cash can take many forms; however, the key attribute is that the asset is readily available to pay debts.
- Cash equivalents are those investments that are readily convertible to a known amount of cash. "Readily" has been interpreted to be three months or less.

QUESTIONS

1. *Which of the following items should* not *be included in cash on the balance sheet?*
   a. coin and currency on hand
   b. customer's undeposited check
   c. money market account
   d. All of the above should be included in cash on the balance sheet.

2. *A cash equivalent is*
   a. an investment in the stock of another company that can be sold on demand.
   b. an investment that is readily convertible to a known amount of cash and has an original maturity to the investor of three months or less.
   c. coin and currency on hand, checking and savings accounts, and money market accounts.
   d. none of the above.

© Justin Sullivan/Getty Images

Hot Topics

A $53 Billion Start-Up

In his message to stockholders in March 2007, the chair of Sears Holdings, Ed Lampert, described the business as a start-up. Not too many companies finish their first year with sales in excess of $53 billion and cash of nearly $4 billion. Of course, not many companies start out as a result of the merger of two of the most highly recognized corporations in the world. Lampert acknowledges that the parent company for Sears, Roebuck and Co. and Kmart is not your traditional start-up operation. He points out that what makes the company different from most new businesses is its ability to generate cash flow. And Lampert proudly points to the fact that Sears Holdings ended the 2007 fiscal year with $1.2 billion more in cash than in debt. What the company does with its excess cash is central to its ability to be successful in the highly competitive retail sector—and in the process, move beyond being a $53 billion start-up business.

Source: http://www.searsholdings.com/invest.

EXHIBIT 6-1 **Sears Holdings' Statement of Cash Flows**

SEARS HOLDINGS CORPORATION
CONSOLIDATED STATEMENTS OF CASH FLOWS

millions	2006	2005	2004
Cash Flows From Operating Activities			
Net income	$ 1,490	$ 858	$1,106
Adjustments to reconcile net income to net cash provided by operating activities:			
Depreciation and amortization	1,142	932	27
Cumulative effect of change in accounting principle, net of tax	—	90	—
Provision for uncollectible credit card accounts	—	49	—
Gain on total return swaps, net	(74)	—	—
Gain on sales of assets	(82)	(39)	(946)
Gain on sale of investments	(18)	(38)	—
Change in operating assets and liabilities (net of acquisitions and dispositions):			
Deferred income taxes	258	58	597
Credit card receivables	—	(380)	—
Merchandise inventories	(841)	208	(43)
Merchandise payables	(145)	(71)	251
Income and other taxes	(173)	(53)	66
Other operating assets	193	318	100
Other operating liabilities	(306)	366	(90)
Net cash provided by operating activities	1.444	2.298	1,068
Cash Flows From Investing Activities			
Acquisitions of businesses, net of cash acquired	(283)	(1,020)	—
Proceeds from sale of business	—	2,044	—
Proceeds from sales of property and investments	143	157	562
Purchases of property and equipment	(513)	(546)	(230)
Change in collateral on total return swaps, net	(80)	—	—
Cash settlements on total return swaps, net	70	—	—
Net cash (used in) provided by investing activities	(663)	635	332
Cash Flows From Financing Activities			
Proceeds from debt issuances	524	176	—
Repayments of long-term debt	(875)	(577)	(53)
Decrease in short-term borrowings, primarily 90 days or less	(83)	(414)	—
Proceeds from termination of interest rate swaps	—	60	—
Sears Canada dividend paid to minority shareholders	—	(794)	—
Issuance of subsidiary stock	—	59	—
Purchase of treasury stock	(816)	(590)	—
Debt issue costs	(2)	(27)	—
Income tax benefit on exercise of nonqualified stock options	—	53	—
Proceeds from the exercise of stock options	—	102	—
Net cash used in financing activities	(1,252)	(1,952)	(53)
Effect of exchange rate changes on cash and cash equivalents	(1)	24	—
NET (DECREASE) INCREASE IN CASH AND CASH EQUIVALENTS	(472)	1,005	1,347
CASH AND CASH EQUIVALENTS, BEGINNING OF YEAR	4,440	3,435	2,088
CASH AND CASH EQUIVALENTS, END OF YEAR	$ 3,968	$ 4,440	$3,435
Supplemental Disclosure About Noncash Investing and Financing Activities:			
Bankruptcy related settlements resulting in the receipt of treasury stock	$ 3	$ 25	$ 88
Sale of owned and assignment of leased properties	—	—	403
Conversion of 9% convertible note	—	63	—
Capital lease obligation incurred	61	65	49
Supplemental Cash Flow Data:			
Income taxes paid	574	114	6
Cash interest paid	282	255	52

See accompanying Notes to Consolidated Financial Statements.

Control Over Cash

LO2 Show that you understand various techniques that companies use to control cash.

Because cash is universally accepted as a medium of exchange, control over it is critical to the smooth functioning of any business, no matter how large or small.

CASH MANAGEMENT

In addition to the need to guard against theft and other abuses related to the physical custody of cash, management of this asset is also important. Cash management is necessary to ensure that at any time, Sears Holdings has neither too little nor too much cash on hand. The need to have enough cash on hand is obvious: suppliers, employees, taxing agencies, banks, and all other creditors must be paid on time if an entity is to remain in business. It is equally important that a company not maintain cash on hand and on deposit in checking accounts beyond a minimal amount that is necessary to support ongoing operations since cash is essentially a nonearning asset. Granted, some checking accounts pay a very meager rate of interest. However, the superior return that could be earned by investing idle cash in various forms of marketable securities dictates that companies carefully monitor the amount of cash on hand at all times.

An important tool in the management of cash, the cash flows statement, is discussed in detail in Chapter 12. Cash budgets, which are also critical to the management of cash, are discussed in management accounting and business finance texts. Cash management is just one important aspect of control over cash. Beyond cash management, companies often use two other cash control features: bank reconciliations and petty cash funds. Before turning to those control devices, we need to review the basic features of a bank statement.

READING A BANK STATEMENT

Two fundamental principles of internal control are applicable to cash. First, all cash receipts should be deposited intact daily; and second, all cash payments should be made by check. Checking accounts at banks are critical in this regard. These accounts allow a company to carefully monitor and control cash receipts and cash payments. Control is aided further by the monthly **bank statement**. Most banks mail their customers a monthly bank statement for each account. The statement provides a detailed list of all activity for a particular account during the month. An example of a typical bank statement is shown in Exhibit 6-2. Note that the bank statement indicates the activity in one of the cash accounts maintained by Mickey's Marathon Sports at the Mt. Etna State Bank.

Bank statement
A detailed list, provided by the bank, of all activity for a particular account during the month.

Before you look at the various items that appear on a bank statement, it is important to understand the route a check takes after it is written. Assume that Mickey's writes a check on its account at the Mt. Etna State Bank. Mickey's mails the check to one of its suppliers, Keese Corp., which deposits the check in its account at the Second City Bank. At this point, Second City presents the check to Mt. Etna for payment, and Mt. Etna reduces the balance in Mickey's account accordingly. The canceled check has now "cleared" the banking system. Either the canceled check itself or a copy of it is returned with Mickey's next bank statement.

The following types of items appear on Mickey's bank statement:

Canceled checks—Mickey's checks that cleared the bank during the month of June are listed with the corresponding check number and the date paid. Keep in mind that some of these checks may have been written by Mickey's in a previous month but were not presented for payment to the bank until June. You also should realize that during June, Mickey's may have written some checks that do not yet appear on the bank statement because they have not been presented for payment. A check written by a company but not yet presented to the bank for payment is called an **outstanding check**.

Outstanding check
A check written by a company but not yet presented to the bank for payment.

Deposits—In keeping with the internal control principle calling for the deposit of all cash receipts intact, most companies deposit all checks, coin, and currency on a daily basis. For the sake of brevity, we have limited to four the number of deposits that Mickey's made during the month. Keep in mind that Mickey's also may have made a deposit on the last day or two of the month and that this deposit may not yet be reflected on the bank statement. This type of deposit is called a **deposit in transit**.

Deposit in transit
A deposit recorded on the books but not yet reflected on the bank statement.

EXHIBIT 6-2 Bank Statement

Mt. Etna State Bank
Chicago, Illinois
Statement of Account

Mickey's Marathon Sports
502 Dodge St.
Chicago, IL 66666

FOR THE MONTH ENDING **June 30, 2008**
ACCOUNT **0371-22-514**

Date	Description	Subtractions	Additions	Balance
6-01	Previous balance			3,236.41
6-01	Check 497	723.40		2,513.01
6-02	Check 495	125.60		2,387.41
6-06	Check 491	500.00		1,887.41
6-07	Deposit		1,423.16	3,310.57
6-10	Check 494	185.16		3,125.41
6-13	NSF check	245.72		2,879.69
6-15	Deposit		755.50	3,635.19
6-18	Check 499	623.17		3,012.02
6-20	Check 492	125.00		2,887.02
6-22	Deposit		1,875.62	4,762.64
6-23	Service charge	20.00		4,742.64
6-24	Check 493	875.75		3,866.89
6-24	Check 503	402.10		3,464.79
6-26	Customer note, interest		550.00	4,014.79
6-26	Service fee on note	16.50		3,998.29
6-27	Check 500	1,235.40		2,762.89
6-28	Deposit		947.50	3,710.39
6-30	Check 498	417.25		3,293.14
6-30	Interest earned		15.45	3,308.59
6-30	Statement Totals	5,495.05	5,567.23	

Study Tip

Review your own bank statement to see the similarities and differences between it and the one illustrated here. Also look on the reverse side of your statement for the form of a reconciliation the bank provides. It may or may not be the same format illustrated in Exhibit 6-3.

NSF check—NSF is an abbreviation for "not sufficient funds." The NSF check listed on the bank statement on June 13 is a customer's check that Mickey's recorded on its books, deposited, and thus included in its cash account. When Mt. Etna State Bank learned that the check was not good because the customer did not have sufficient funds on hand in its bank account to cover the check, the bank deducted the amount from Mickey's account. Mickey's needs to contact its customer to collect the amount due; ideally, the customer will issue a new check once it has sufficient funds in its account.

Service charge—Banks charge for various services that they provide to customers. Among the most common bank service charges are monthly activity fees and fees charged for new checks, for the rental of a lockbox at the bank in which to store valuable company documents, and for the collection of customer notes by the bank.

Customer note and interest—It is often convenient to have customers pay amounts owed to a company directly to that company's bank. The bank simply acts as a collection agency for the company.

Interest earned—Most checking accounts pay interest on the average daily balance in the account. Rates paid on checking accounts are usually significantly less than could be earned on most other forms of investment.

Bank reconciliation
A form used by the accountant to reconcile or resolve any differences between the balance shown on the bank statement for a particular account with the balance shown in the accounting records.

THE BANK RECONCILIATION

For a company such as Sears Holdings with approximately 3,800 retail stores, you can imagine the large number of bank accounts that it maintains. A **bank reconciliation** should be prepared for each individual bank account as soon as the bank statement is received. Ideally, the reconciliation should be performed or, at a minimum, thoroughly reviewed by someone independent of custody, record-keeping, and authorization responsibilities relating to cash. As the name implies, the purpose of a bank reconciliation is to *reconcile*, or resolve, any differences between the balance that the bank shows for an account with the balance that appears on the company's books. Differences between the two amounts are investigated; and if necessary, adjustments are made. The following steps are used in preparing a bank reconciliation:

1. Trace deposits listed on the bank statement to the books. Any deposits recorded on the books but not yet shown on the bank statement are deposits in transit. Prepare a list of the deposits in transit.
2. Arrange the canceled checks in numerical order and trace each of them to the books. Any checks recorded on the books but not yet listed on the bank statement are outstanding. Prepare a list of the outstanding checks.
3. List all items, other than deposits, shown as additions on the bank statement, such as interest paid by the bank for the month and amounts collected by the bank from one of the company's customers. When the bank pays interest or collects an amount owed to a company by one of the company's customers, the bank increases, or *credits*, its liability to the company on its own books. For that reason, these items are called **credit memoranda**. Prepare a list of credit memoranda.
4. List all amounts, other than canceled checks, shown as subtractions on the bank statement, such as any NSF checks and the various service charges mentioned earlier. When a company deposits money in a bank, a liability is created on the books of the bank. Therefore, when the bank reduces the amount of its liability for these various items, it ***debits*** the liability on its own books. For this reason, these items are called **debit memoranda**. Prepare a list of debit memoranda.
5. Identify any errors made by the bank or by the company in recording the various cash transactions.
6. Use the information collected in Steps 1 through 5 to prepare a bank reconciliation.

Credit memoranda
Additions on a bank statement for such items as interest paid on the account and notes collected by the bank for the customer.

Debit memoranda
Deductions on a bank statement for items such as NSF checks and various service charges.

Companies use a number of different *formats* in preparing bank reconciliations. For example, some companies take the balance shown on the bank statement and reconcile this amount to the balance shown on the books. Another approach, which will be illustrated for Mickey's, involves reconciling the bank balance and the book balance to an adjusted balance, rather than one to the other. As you will see, the advantage of this approach is that it yields the correct balance and makes it easy for the company to make any necessary adjustments to its books. A bank reconciliation for Mickey's Marathon Sports is shown in Exhibit 6-3.

The following are explanations for the various items on the reconciliation:

1. The balance per bank statement of $3,308.59 is taken from the June statement as shown in Exhibit 6-2.
2. Mickey's records showed a deposit for $642.30 made on June 30 that is not reflected on the bank statement. The deposit in transit is listed as an addition to the bank statement balance.
3. The accounting records indicate three checks written but not yet reflected on the bank statement. The three outstanding checks are as follows:

496	$ 79.89
501	$213.20
502	$424.75

Outstanding checks are the opposite of deposits in transit and therefore are deducted from the bank statement balance.

4. The adjusted balance of $3,233.05 is found by adding the deposit in transit and deducting the outstanding checks from the bank statement balance.
5. The $2,895.82 book balance on June 30 is taken from the company's records as of that date.
6. According to the bank statement, $550 was added to the account on June 26 for the collection of a note with interest. We assume that the repayment of the note

EXHIBIT 6-3 Bank Reconciliation

Mickey's Marathon Sports
Bank Reconciliation
June 30, 2007

Balance per bank statement, June 30			$3,308.59
Add:	Deposit in transit		642.30
Deduct:	Outstanding checks:		
	No. 496	$ 79.89	
	No. 501	213.20	
	No. 502	424.75	(717.84)
Adjusted balance, June 30			$3,233.05
Balance per books, June 30			$2,895.82
Add:	Customer note collected	$500.00	
	Interest on customer note	50.00	
	Interest earned during June	15.45	
	Error in recording check 498	54.00	619.45
Deduct:	NSF check	$245.72	
	Collection fee on note	16.50	
	Service charge for lockbox	20.00	(282.22)
Adjusted balance, June 30			$3,233.05

accounted for $500 of this amount and that the other $50 was for interest. The bank statement notifies Mickey's that the note with interest has been collected. Therefore, Mickey's must add $550 to the book balance.

7. An entry on June 30 on the bank statement shows an increase of $15.45 for interest earned on the bank account during June. This amount is added to the book balance.
8. A review of the canceled checks returned with the bank statement detected an error that Mickey's made. The company records indicated that check 498 was recorded incorrectly as $471.25; the check was actually written for $417.25 and reflected as such on the bank statement. This error, referred to as a *transposition error,* resulted from transposing the 7 and the 1 in recording the check in the books. The error is the difference between the amount of $471.25 recorded and the amount of $417.25 that should have been recorded, or $54.00. Because Mickey's recorded the cash payment at too large an amount, $54.00 must be added back to the book balance.
9. In addition to canceled checks, three other deductions appear on the bank statement. Each of these must be deducted from the book balance:
   a. A customer's NSF check for $245.72 (see June 13 entry on bank statement)
   b. A $16.50 fee charged by the bank to collect the customer's note discussed in (6) (see June 26 entry on bank statement)
   c. A service fee of $20.00 charged by the bank for rental of a lockbox (see June 23 entry on bank statement)
10. The additions of $619.45 and deductions of $282.22 resulted in an adjusted cash balance of $3,233.05. Note that this adjusted balance agrees with the adjusted bank statement balance on the bank reconciliation [see (4)]. Thus, all differences between the two balances have been explained.

THE BANK RECONCILIATION AND THE NEED FOR ADJUSTMENTS TO THE RECORDS

After it completes the bank reconciliation, Mickey's must prepare a number of adjustments in the form of journal entries on its records. In fact, all of the information for these adjustments will be from one section of the bank reconciliation. Do you think that the additions and deductions made to the bank balance or the ones made to the book balance are the basis for the adjustments? It is logical that the additions and deductions to the Cash account *on the books* should be the basis for the adjustments because these are items that Mickey's was unaware of before receiving the bank statement. Conversely, the additions and deductions to the bank's balance, (i.e., the deposits in transit and the outstanding checks) are items that Mickey's has already recorded on its books.

The first journal entry recognizes the bank's collection of a customer's note, with interest:

June 30	Cash	550.00	
	Notes Receivable		500.00
	Interest Revenue		50.00
	To record the collection of note and interest.		

Balance Sheet							Income Statement	
ASSETS		=	**LIABILITIES**	+	**STOCKHOLDERS' EQUITY**	+	**REVENUES – EXPENSES**	
Cash	550.00						Interest Revenue	50.00
Notes Receivable	(500.00)							

The next entry is needed to record interest earned and paid by the bank on the average daily balance maintained in the checking account during June:

June 30	Cash	15.45	
	Interest Revenue		15.45
	To record interest earned on checking account.		

Balance Sheet							Income Statement	
ASSETS		=	**LIABILITIES**	+	**STOCKHOLDERS' EQUITY**	+	**REVENUES – EXPENSES**	
Cash	15.45						Interest Revenue	15.45

Recall the error in recording check 498: it was actually written for $417.25, the amount paid by the bank. Mickey's recorded the cash disbursement on its books as $471.25, however. If we assume that the purpose of the cash payment was to buy supplies, the Cash account is understated and the Supplies account is overstated by the amount of the error. The entry needed to correct both accounts is as follows:

June 30	Cash	54.00	
	Supplies		54.00
	To correct for error in recording purchase of supplies.		

Balance Sheet							Income Statement
ASSETS		=	**LIABILITIES**	+	**STOCKHOLDERS' EQUITY**	+	**REVENUES – EXPENSES**
Cash	54.00						
Supplies	(54.00)						

The customer's NSF check is handled by reducing the Cash account and reinstating the Account Receivable:

June 30	Accounts Receivable	245.72	
	Cash		245.72
	To record customer's NSF check.		

		Balance Sheet				Income Statement	
ASSETS		= LIABILITIES	+	STOCKHOLDERS' EQUITY	+	REVENUES – EXPENSES	
Accounts Receivable	245.72						
Cash	(245.72)						

Finally, two entries are needed to recognize the expenses incurred in connection with the fees charged by the bank for collecting the customer's note and for renting the lockbox:

June 30	Collection Fee Expense	16.50	
	Cash		16.50
	To record collection fee on note.		

		Balance Sheet				Income Statement	
ASSETS		= LIABILITIES	+	STOCKHOLDERS' EQUITY	+	REVENUES – EXPENSES	
Cash	(16.50)					Collection Fee Expense	(16.50)

June 30	Rent Expense—Lockbox	20.00	
	Cash		20.00
	To record rental charge on lockbox.		

		Balance Sheet				Income Statement	
ASSETS		= LIABILITIES	+	STOCKHOLDERS' EQUITY	+	REVENUES – EXPENSES	
Cash	(20.00)					Rent Expense—Lockbox	(20.00)

Note that a separate entry was made to record each of the increases and decreases in the Cash account. Some companies combine all of the increases in Cash in a single journal entry and all of the decreases in a second entry. Finally note that supervisory review and approval should take place before any of these entries are posted.

ESTABLISHING A PETTY CASH FUND

Petty cash fund
Money kept on hand for making minor disbursements in coin and currency rather than by writing checks.

Recall one of the fundamental rules in controlling cash: all disbursements should be made by check. Most businesses make an exception to this rule in the case of minor expenditures, for which they use a **petty cash fund**. This fund consists of coin and currency kept on hand to make minor disbursements. The necessary steps in setting up and maintaining a petty cash fund are as follows:

1. A check is written for a lump-sum amount, such as $100 or $500. The check is cashed, and the coin and currency are entrusted to a petty cash custodian.
2. A journal entry is made to record the establishment of the fund.
3. Upon presentation of the necessary documentation, employees receive minor disbursements from the fund. In essence, cash is traded from the fund in exchange for a receipt.
4. Periodically, the fund is replenished by writing and cashing a check in the amount necessary to bring the fund back to its original balance.
5. At the time the fund is replenished, an adjustment is made to record its replenishment and to recognize the various expenses incurred.

The use of this fund is normally warranted on the basis of cost versus benefits. That is, the benefits in time saved in making minor disbursements from cash are thought to outweigh the cost associated with the risk of loss from decreased control over cash disbursements. The fund also serves a practical purpose for certain expenditures, such as taxi fares and messengers, that often must be paid in cash.

AN EXAMPLE OF A PETTY CASH FUND

Assume that on August 1, the treasurer of Mickey's Marathon Sports cashes a check for $200 and remits the cash to the newly appointed petty cash custodian. On this date, the following journal entry is made:

Aug. 1	Petty Cash Fund	200.00	
	Cash		200.00
	To record establishment of petty cash fund.		

Balance Sheet							Income Statement
ASSETS		=	LIABILITIES	+	STOCKHOLDERS' EQUITY	+	REVENUES − EXPENSES
Petty Cash Fund	200.00						
Cash	(200.00)						

During August, the custodian disburses coin and currency to various individuals who present receipts to the custodian for the following:

U.S. Post Office	$ 55.00
Overnight Delivery Service	69.50
Office Supply Express	45.30
Total expenditures	$169.80

At the end of August, the custodian counts the coin and currency on hand and determines the balance to be $26.50. Next, the treasurer writes and cashes a check in the amount of $173.50, which is the amount needed to return the balance in the account to $200.00.

The treasurer remits the cash to the custodian. The following entry is made:

Aug. 31	Postage Expense	55.00	
	Delivery Expense	69.50	
	Office Expense	45.30	
	Cash Over and Short	3.70	
	Cash		173.50
	To record replenishment of petty cash fund.		

Balance Sheet							Income Statement	
ASSETS		=	LIABILITIES	+	STOCKHOLDERS' EQUITY	+	REVENUES − EXPENSES	
Cash	(173.50)						Postage Expense	(55.00)
							Delivery Expense	(69.50)
							Office Expense	(45.30)
							Cash Over and Short	(3.70)

The Cash Over and Short account is necessary because the total expenditures for the month were only $169.80, but a check in the amount of $173.50 was necessary to restore the fund balance to $200.00. The discrepancy of $3.70 could be due to any number of factors, such as an error in making change. Any large discrepancies would be investigated, particularly if they recur. Assuming that the discrepancy is immaterial, a debit balance in the Cash Over and Short account is normally closed to Miscellaneous Expense. A credit balance in the account is closed to Other Income. The use of a petty cash fund is summarized in Exhibit 6-4.

Now that we have considered the importance of control over cash, we turn to the broader topic of internal control systems.

EXHIBIT 6-4 Use of a Petty Cash Fund

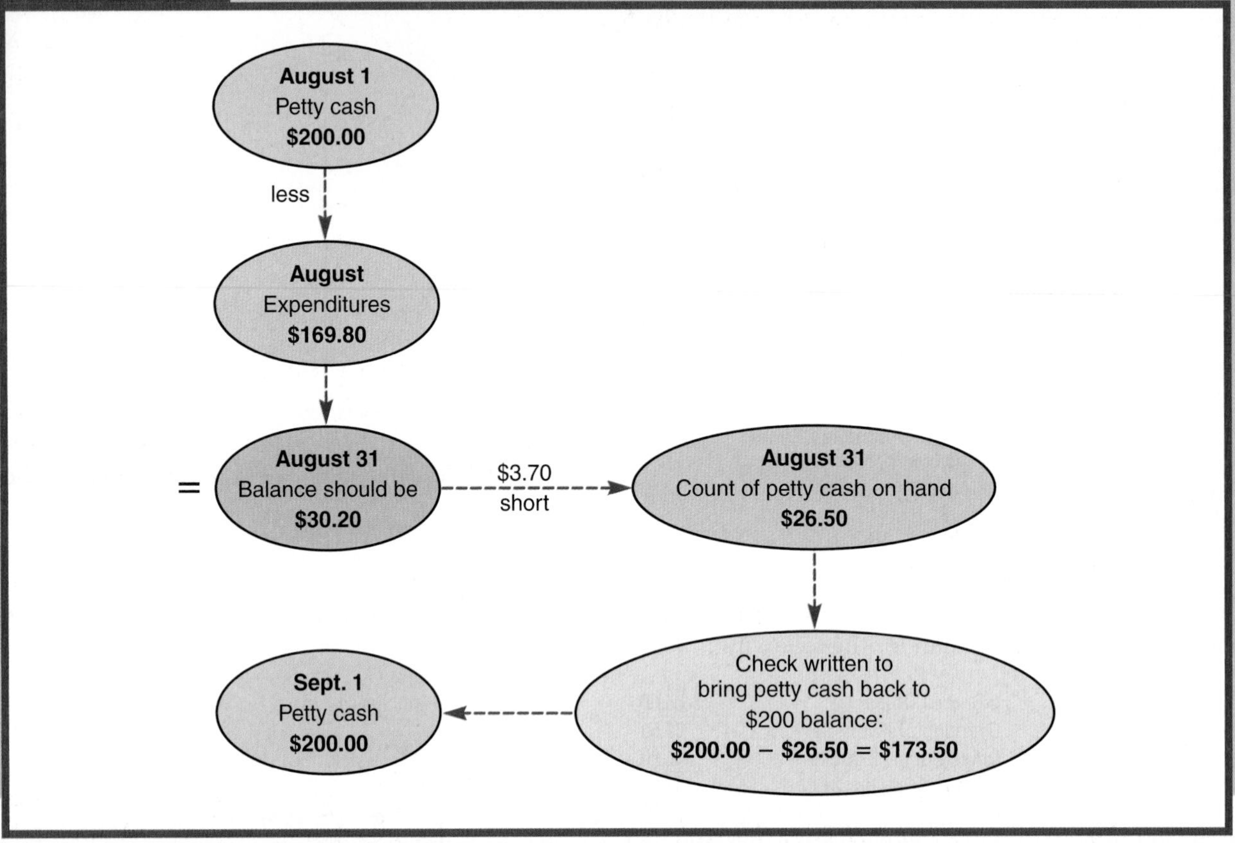

POD REVIEW 6.2

LO2 ***Show that you understand various techniques that companies use to control cash.***

- The liquidity of cash makes controls over it very important to have in place.
  - Cash management means managing the need to have enough cash on hand to ensure cash flow needs but not so much that excess funds earn little return and may be vulnerable to misappropriation.
  - Bank reconciliations use third-party documents (bank statement) to reconcile differences between the amount in the bank and on the books. Done by an independent party, bank reconciliations are effective control procedures.
  - Petty cash funds are an effective way to minimize access to large cash accounts to pay for relatively small expenditures.

QUESTIONS

1. *Which of the following is* not *an addition to the balance per the books on a bank reconciliation that adjusts both the bank statement and balance per the books to the adjusted balance?*
   a. interest earned on the bank account
   b. deposits in transit
   c. collection by the bank on a customer's note
   d. All of the above are additions.

2. *Which of the following is the correct entry when a petty cash fund is established?*
   a. Cash is debited, and Petty Cash Fund is credited.
   b. Petty Cash Fund is debited, and Cash is credited.
   c. Expense accounts are debited, and Petty Cash Fund is credited.
   d. Expense accounts are debited, and Cash is credited.

An Introduction to Internal Control

LO3 Explain the importance of internal control to a business and the significance of the Sarbanes-Oxley Act of 2002.

An employee of a large auto parts warehouse routinely takes spare parts home for personal use. A payroll clerk writes and signs two checks for an employee and then splits the amount of the second check with the worker. Through human error, an invoice is paid for merchandise never received from the supplier. These cases sound quite different from one another, but they share one important characteristic. They all point to a deficiency in a company's internal control system. An **internal control system** consists of the policies and procedures necessary to ensure the safeguarding of an entity's assets, the reliability of its accounting records, and the accomplishment of its overall objectives.

Internal control system Policies and procedures necessary to ensure the safeguarding of an entity's assets, the reliability of its accounting records, and the accomplishment of overall company objectives.

Three assets are especially critical to the operation of a merchandising company such as Sears Holdings: cash, accounts receivable, and inventory. Activities related to those three assets compose the operating cycle of a business. Cash is used to buy inventory; the inventory is eventually sold; and assuming a sale on credit, the account receivable from the customer is collected. After considering an important Congressional act, we turn to the ways in which a company attempts to *control* the assets at its disposal, a subject that is explored further at appropriate points in the book.

THE SARBANES-OXLEY ACT OF 2002

As briefly described in Chapter 1, the **Sarbanes-Oxley Act** of 2002 (commonly referred to as SOX) was a direct response by Congress to the numerous corporate scandals that surfaced in the first few years of the new millennium. High-profile cases involving questionable accounting practices by companies such as **Enron** and **WorldCom** caused the federal government to step in and attempt to restore the public's confidence in the financial reporting system. The various provisions of SOX are far-reaching, including provisions designed to ensure the independence of a company's auditors. For example, external auditors can no longer provide bookkeeping, human resource, information system design, and brokerage services for clients that they audit.

Sarbanes-Oxley Act An act of Congress in 2002 intended to bring reform to corporate accountability and stewardship in the wake of a number of major corporate scandals.

Another major part of SOX, specifically Section 404, deals directly with a company's internal control system. Among the more important provisions in Section 404 is the one that requires the annual report to include an **internal control report**. In the report, management is required to:

Internal control report A report required by Section 404 of the Sarbanes-Oxley Act to be included in a company's annual report in which management assesses the effectiveness of the internal control structure.

1. **State its responsibility to establish and maintain an adequate internal control structure and procedures for financial reporting.**
2. **Assess the effectiveness of its internal control structure and procedures for financial reporting.**

Sears Holdings' Report on Internal Control over Financial Reporting is shown in Exhibit 6-5. The first paragraph states management's responsibility for its system of internal control, and the fourth paragraph indicates that management believes internal control over financial reporting is effective.

Also note the last paragraph in Exhibit 6-5. Another important provision in SOX is that a company's outside auditors must issue a report on their assessment of the company's internal control. The statement in the last paragraph calls attention to this report. **Deloitte & Touche** is Sears Holdings' independent auditor, and its report is shown in Exhibit 6-6. Note the reference in the second paragraph to the **Public Company Accounting Oversight Board (PCAOB)**. The PCAOB is the five-member body created by SOX that is given authority to set auditing standards in the United States.

Public Company Accounting Oversight Board The five-member body created by the Sarbanes-Oxley Act that was given the authority to set auditing standards in the United States.

The last paragraph in Deloitte & Touche's report also contains two important statements, namely, that in their opinion:

1. **Management's assessment that the company maintained effective internal control over financial reporting is fairly stated.**
2. **Sears Holdings has maintained effective internal control over financial reporting.**

EXHIBIT 6-5 Management Report on Internal Control—Sears Holdings

Management's Annual Report on Internal Control Over Financial Reporting

March 27, 2007

Management states its responsibility for the internal control system. →

The management of Sears Holdings Corporation is responsible for establishing and maintaining adequate internal control over financial reporting. Internal control over financial reporting is a process designed by, or under the supervision of, the Company's principal executive and principal financial officers and effected by the Company's board of directors, management and other personnel to provide reasonable assurance regarding the reliability of financial reporting and the preparation of financial statements for external purposes in accordance with generally accepted accounting principles and includes those policies and procedures that:

- pertain to the maintenance of records that in reasonable detail accurately and fairly reflect the transactions and dispositions of the assets of the Company;
- provide reasonable assurance that transactions are recorded as necessary to permit preparation of financial statements in accordance with generally accepted accounting principles, and that receipts and expenditures of the Company are being made only in accordance with authorizations of management and directors of the Company; and
- provide reasonable assurance regarding prevention or timely detection of unauthorized acquisition, use or disposition of the Company's assets that could have a material effect on the financial statements.

Because of inherent limitations, internal control over financial reporting may not prevent or detect misstatements. Projections of any evaluation of effectiveness to future periods are subject to the risks that controls may become inadequate because of changes in conditions, or that the degree of compliance with the policies or procedures may deteriorate.

Management assessed the effectiveness of the Company's internal control over financial reporting as of February 3, 2007. In making its assessment, management used the criteria set forth in the Internal Control—Integrated Framework issued by the Committee of Sponsoring Organizations of the Treadway Commission (COSO). The assessment included the documentation and understanding of the Company's internal control over financial reporting. Management evaluated the design effectiveness and tested the operating effectiveness of internal controls over financial reporting to form its conclusion.

Management assesses the effectiveness of the internal control system. →

Based on this evaluation, management concluded that, as of February 3, 2007, the Company's internal control over financial reporting is effective to provide reasonable assurance that the Company's financial statements are fairly presented in conformity with generally accepted accounting principles.

Auditors have issued a report on management's assessment. →

Deloitte & Touche LLP, independent registered public accounting firm, has reported on management's assertion with respect to the effectiveness of the Company's internal control over financial reporting as of February 3, 2007, as stated in their report included herein.

Board of directors
A group composed of key officers of a corporation and outside members responsible for general oversight of the affairs of the entity.

Audit committee
A board of directors subset that acts as a direct contact between the stockholders and the independent accounting firm.

Note at the top of the independent auditors' report in Exhibit 6-6 that it is directed to the board of directors and stockholders of Sears Holdings. The **board of directors** usually consists of key officers of the corporation as well as a number of directors whom it does not directly employ. For example, Sears Holdings' board of eight directors consists of two insiders and six outsiders. Another key provision in SOX was one requiring that the audit committee be made up entirely of outside directors. The **audit committee** is a subset of the board of directors that provides direct contact between stockholders and the independent accounting firm.

One of the most frequently debated issues in many of the high-profile cases involving financial reporting scandals was the behavior of the key officers of the companies. Many stockholders and others affected by these scandals thought that top management should have taken more responsibility for the accuracy of the information presented in the financial statements. Another provision in SOX directly addressed this issue. For the first time ever, the chief executive officer (CEO) and the chief financial officer (CFO) for a company must sign a statement certifying that the information in the financial statements fairly presents the financial condition and results of operations of the company.

EXHIBIT 6-6 **Auditor's Report on Internal Control**

REPORT OF INDEPENDENT REGISTERED PUBLIC ACCOUNTING FIRM

To the Board of Directors and Stockholders of Sears Holdings Corporation

We have audited the accompanying consolidated balance sheet of Sears Holdings Corporation and subsidiaries (the "Company") as of February 3, 2007 and January 28, 2006 and the related consolidated statements of income, shareholders' equity and cash flows for the fiscal years then ended. Our audits also included the financial statement schedule, listed in the Index at Item 8, for the years ended February 3, 2007 and January 28, 2006. We also have audited management's assessment, included in the accompanying Management's Annual Report on Internal Control over Financial Reporting, that the Company maintained effective internal control over financial reporting as of February 3, 2007, based on criteria established in *Internal Control—Integrated Framework* issued by the Committee of Sponsoring Organizations of the Treadway Commission (COSO). The Company's management is responsible for these financial statements and financial statement schedule, for maintaining effective internal control over financial reporting, and for its assessment of the effectiveness of internal control over financial reporting. Our responsibility is to express an opinion on these financial statements and financial statement schedule, an opinion on management's assessment, and an opinion on the effectiveness of the Company's internal control over financial reporting based on our audits.

Audit followed the standards of the Public Company Accounting Oversight Board. →

We conducted our audits in accordance with the standards of the Public Company Accounting Oversight Board (United States). Those standards require that we plan and perform the audit to obtain reasonable assurance about whether the financial statements are free of material misstatement and whether effective internal control over financial reporting was maintained in all material respects. Our audit of the financial statements included examining, on a test basis, evidence supporting the amounts and disclosures in the financial statements, assessing the accounting principles used and significant estimates made by management, and evaluating the overall financial statement presentation. Our audit of internal control over financial reporting included obtaining an understanding of internal control over financial reporting, evaluating management's assessment, testing and evaluating the design and operating effectiveness of internal control, and performing such other procedures as we considered necessary in the circumstances. We believe that our audits provide a reasonable basis for our opinion.

A company's internal control over financial reporting is a process designed by, or under the supervision of, the company's principal executive and principal financial officers, or persons performing similar functions, and effected by the company's board of directors, management, and other personnel to provide reasonable assurance regarding the reliability of financial reporting and the preparation of financial statements of external purposes in accordance with generally accepted accounting principles. A company's internal control over financial reporting includes those policies and procedures that (1) pertain to the maintenance of records that, in reasonable detail, accurately and fairly reflect the transactions and dispositions of the assets of the company; (2) provide reasonable assurance that transactions are recorded as necessary to permit preparation of financial statements in accordance with generally accepted accounting principles and that receipts and expenditures of the company are being made only in accordance with authorizations of management and directors of the company; and (3) provide reasonable assurance regarding prevention or timely detection of unauthorized acquisition, use, or disposition of the company's assets that could have a material effect on the financial statements.

Because of the inherent limitations of internal control over financial reporting, including the possibility of collusion or improper management override of controls, material misstatements due to error or fraud may not be prevented or detected on a timely basis. Also, projections of any evaluation of the effectiveness of the internal control over financial reporting to future periods are subject to the risk that the controls may become inadequate because of changes in conditions, or that the degree of compliance with the policies or procedures may deteriorate.

Auditors' opinions →

In our opinion, the consolidated financial statements referred to above present fairly, in all material respects, the financial position of the Company as of February 3, 2007 and January 28, 2006, and the results of its operations and its cash flows for the fiscal years then ended, in conformity with accounting principles generally accepted in the United States of America. Also, in our opinion, such financial statement schedule, when considered in relation to the basic consolidated financial statements taken as a whole, presents fairly, in all material respects, the information for the fiscal years ended February 3, 2007 and January 28, 2006 set forth therein. Also in our opinion, management's assessment that the Company maintained effective internal control over financial reporting as of February 3, 2007, is fairly stated in all material respects, based on the criteria

Continued

EXHIBIT 6-6 Auditor's Report on Internal Control (continued)

established in *Internal Control—Integrated Framework* issued by the Committee of Sponsoring Organizations of the Treadway Commission. Furthermore, in our opinion, the Company maintained, in all material respects, effective internal control over financial reporting as of February 3, 2007, based on the criteria established in *Internal Control—Integrated Framework* issued by the Committee of Sponsoring Organizations of the Treadway Commission.

As discussed in Notes 3 and 10 to the consolidated financial statements, the Company changed its method of accounting for pension and other postretirement benefits in both fiscal 2006 and fiscal 2005, and its method of accounting for certain indirect buying, warehousing and distribution costs in fiscal 2005.

/s/ DELOITTE & TOUCHE LLP

Deloitte & Touche LLP

Chicago, Illinois
March 27, 2007

This provision places the responsibility for the information in the financial statements directly in the hands of the company's CEO and CFO.

THE CONTROL ENVIRONMENT

The success of an internal control system begins with the competence of the people in charge of it. Management's operating style will have a determinable impact on the effectiveness of various policies. An autocratic style in which a few key officers tightly control operations will result in an environment different from that of a decentralized organization in which departments have more freedom to make decisions. Personnel policies and practices form another factor in the internal control of a business. An appropriate system for hiring competent employees and firing incompetent ones is crucial to an efficient operation. After all, no internal control system will work very well if employees who are dishonest or poorly trained are on the payroll. On the other hand, too few people doing too many tasks defeats the purpose of an internal control system. Finally, the effectiveness of internal control in a business is influenced by the board of directors, particularly its audit committee.

THE ACCOUNTING SYSTEM

Accounting system
Methods and records used to accurately report an entity's transactions and to maintain accountability for its assets and liabilities.

An **accounting system** consists of all of the methods and records used to report an entity's transactions accurately and to maintain accountability for its assets and liabilities. Regardless of the degree of computer automation, the use of a journal to record transactions is an integral part of all accounting systems. Refinements may be made to the basic components of the system depending on the company's needs. For example, most companies use specialized journals to record recurring transactions, such as sales of merchandise on credit.

An accounting system can be completely manual; fully computerized; or as is often the case, a mixture of the two. Internal controls are important to all businesses regardless of the degree of automation of the accounting system. The system must be capable of handling the volume and the complexity of transactions entered into by a business. Most businesses use computers because of the sheer volume of transactions. The computer is ideally suited to the task of processing large numbers of repetitive transactions efficiently and quickly.

The cost of computing has dropped so substantially that virtually every business can now afford a system. Today some computer software that is designed for home-based businesses costs under $100 and is meant to run on machines that cost less than $1,000. Inexpensive software that categorizes expenses and prints checks, produces financial statements, and analyzes financial ratios is available.

POD REVIEW 6.3

LO3 ***Explain the importance of internal control to a business and the significance of the Sarbanes-Oxley Act of 2002.***

- The Sarbanes-Oxley Act of 2002 required publicly traded companies to improve the documentation and functioning of their internal controls.
  - Management must now render an opinion on the efficiency of the internal control system in place at its company. A strong control environment is a must for companies.
  - Auditors also must increase their documentation and understanding of the internal controls of their clients.
  - Significant amounts of resources have been devoted to comply with the provisions of Sarbanes-Oxley.

QUESTIONS

1. *What is the five-member body created by the Sarbanes-Oxley Act that was given authority to set auditing standards in the United States?*
   a. Securities and Exchange Commission
   b. Financial Accounting Standards Board
   c. International Accounting Standards Board
   d. none of the above

2. *The composition of a company's audit committee*
   a. must consist of a majority of directors who are key officers of the company.
   b. must consist of a majority of directors who are outsiders.
   c. must consist entirely of directors who are outsiders.
   d. none of the above.

Internal Control Procedures

LO4 Describe the basic internal control procedures.

Management establishes policies and procedures on a number of different levels to ensure that corporate objectives will be met. Some procedures are formalized in writing. Others may not be written but are just as important. Certain **administrative controls** within a company are more concerned with the efficient operation of the business and adherence to managerial policies than with the accurate reporting of financial information. For example, a company policy that requires all prospective employees to be interviewed by the personnel department is an administrative control. Other **accounting controls** primarily concern safeguarding assets and ensuring the reliability of the financial statements. We now turn to a discussion of some of the most important internal control procedures:

- Proper authorizations
- Segregation of duties
- Independent verification
- Safeguarding of assets and records
- Independent review and appraisal
- Design and use of business documents

Administrative controls Procedures concerned with efficient operation of the business and adherence to managerial policies.

Accounting controls Procedures concerned with safeguarding the assets or the reliability of the financial statements.

Proper Authorizations Management grants specific departments the authority to perform various activities. Along with the *authority* comes *responsibility*. Most large organizations give the authority to hire new employees to the personnel department. Management authorizes the purchasing department to order goods and services for the company and the credit department to establish specific policies for granting credit to customers. By specifically authorizing certain individuals to carry out specific tasks for the business, management is able to hold those same people accountable for the outcome of their actions.

The authorizations for some transactions are general in nature; others are specific. For example, a cashier authorizes the sale of a book in a bookstore by ringing up the transaction (a general authorization). However, the bookstore manager's approval may be required before a book can be returned (a specific authorization).

Segregation of Duties What might happen if one employee is given the authority to prepare checks and to sign them? What might happen if a single employee is allowed to order inventory and receive it from the shipper? Or what if the cashier at a checkout stand records the daily receipts in the journal? If the employee in each of those situations is honest and never makes mistakes, nothing bad will happen. However, if the employee is dishonest or makes errors, the company can experience losses. All of those situations point to the need for the segregation of duties, which is one of the most fundamental of all internal control procedures. Without segregation of duties, an employee is able not only to perpetrate a fraud but also to conceal it. A good system of internal control requires that the *physical custody* of assets be separated from the *accounting* for those same assets.

Like most internal control principles, the concept of segregation of duties is an ideal that is not always attainable. For example, many smaller businesses do not have adequate personnel to achieve complete segregation of key functions. In certain instances, these businesses need to rely on the direct involvement of the owners in the business and on independent verification.

Independent Verification Related to the principle of segregation of duties is the idea of independent verification. The work of one department should act as a check on the work of another. For example, the physical count of the inventory in a perpetual inventory system provides such a check. The accounting department maintains the general ledger card for inventory and updates it as sales and purchases are made. The physical count of the inventory by an independent department acts as the check on the work of the accounting department. As another example, consider the bank reconciliation shown earlier in the chapter (Exhibit 6-3) as a control device. The reconciliation of a company's bank account with the bank statement by someone not responsible for either the physical custody of cash or the cash records acts as an independent check on the work of these parties.

Safeguarding of Assets and Records Adequate safeguards must be in place to protect assets and the accounting records from losses of various kinds. Cash registers, safes, and lockboxes are important safeguards for cash. Secured storage areas with limited access are essential for the safekeeping of inventory. Protection of the accounting records against misuse is equally important. For example, access to a computerized accounting record should be limited to those employees authorized to prepare journal entries. This can be done with the use of a personal identification number and a password to access the system.

Independent Review and Appraisal A well-designed system of internal control provides for periodic review and appraisal of the accounting system as well as the people operating it. The group primarily responsible for review and appraisal of the system is the **internal audit staff**. Most large corporations have a full-time staff of internal auditors. They provide management with periodic reports on the effectiveness of the control system and the efficiency of operations.

Internal audit staff
The department responsible for monitoring and evaluating the internal control system.

The primary concern of the independent public accountants (or external auditors) is whether the financial statements have been presented fairly. Internal auditors focus more on the efficiency with which the organization is run. They are responsible for periodically reviewing both accounting and administrative controls. The internal audit staff also helps to ensure that the company's policies and procedures are followed.

Design and Use of Business Documents *Business documents* are the crucial link between economic transactions entered into by an entity and the accounting record of those events. They are often called *source documents.* Many of them are generated by computer, but a few may be completed manually. The source document for the recognition of the expense of an employee's wages is the time card. The source documents for a sale include the sales order, the sales invoice, and the related shipping document. Business documents must be designed so that they capture all relevant information about an economic event. They are also designed to ensure that related transactions are properly classified.

Business documents must be properly controlled. For example, a key feature for documents is a *sequential numbering system* just like you have for your personal checks. This system results in a complete accounting for all documents in the series and negates the opportunity for an employee to misdirect one. Another key feature of well-designed business documents is the use of *multiple copies.* The various departments involved in a particular activity, such as sales or purchasing, are kept informed of the status of outstanding orders through the use of copies of documents.

LIMITATIONS ON INTERNAL CONTROL

Internal control is a relative term. No system of internal control is totally foolproof. An entity's size affects the degree of control that it can obtain. In general, large organizations are able to devote a substantial amount of resources to safeguarding assets and records because these companies have the assets to justify the cost. Because the installation and maintenance of controls can be costly, an internal audit staff is a luxury that many small businesses cannot afford. The mere segregation of duties can result in added costs if two employees must be involved in a task previously performed by only one.

Segregation of duties can be effective in preventing collusion, but no system of internal control can ensure that it will not happen. It does no good to have one employee count the cash at the end of the day and another to record it if the two act in concert to steal from the company. Rotation of duties can help lessen the likelihood of problems of this sort. An employee is less likely to collude with someone to steal if the assignment is a temporary one. Another control feature, a system of authorizations, is meaningless if management continually overrides it. Management must have enough faith in a system of internal control to support it.

Intentional acts to misappropriate company assets are not the only problem. All sorts of human errors can weaken a system of internal control. Misunderstood instructions, carelessness, fatigue, and distraction can all lead to errors. A well-designed system of internal control should result in the best possible people being hired to perform the various tasks, but no one is perfect.

Real World Practice

6-2 Reading Sears' Holdings Management's Report

Refer to Exhibit 6-5 for Management's Annual Report on Internal Control Over Financial Reporting for Sears Holdings. Where in this report does management discuss limitations on internal control? According to the report, why are there risks in making any projections about the effectiveness of controls in the future?

POD REVIEW 6.4

LO4 *Describe the basic internal control procedures.*

- Control procedures are actions that company personnel take to make sure policies set forth by management are followed.
- Important accounting controls are concerned with safeguarding assets and producing accurate and timely financial statements. They include:
  - Proper authorizations—only certain personnel may authorize transactions.
  - Segregation of duties—physical custody of assets must not be combined with the ability to account for those assets.
  - Independent verification—for example, an inventory count.
  - Safeguarding assets and records—both must be adequately protected.
  - Independent review and appraisal—done primarily by internal audit.
  - Design and use of business documents—source document control.

QUESTIONS

1. *Controls that a company establishes to safeguard assets and ensure the reliability of the financial statements are called*
   a. administrative controls.
   b. accounting controls.
   c. fiscal controls.
   d. none of the above.

2. *The group within an organization that is responsible for monitoring and evaluating the internal control system is called the*
   a. internal audit staff.
   b. accounting staff.
   c. board of directors.
   d. audit committee.

Computerized Business Documents and Internal Control

LO5 Describe the various documents used in recording purchases and their role in controlling cash disbursements.

Specific internal controls are necessary to control cash receipts and cash disbursements for all of the stores owned by Sears Holdings. In addition to the separation of the custodianship of cash from the recording of it in the accounts, two other fundamental principles apply to its control. First, all cash receipts should be deposited *intact* in the bank on a *daily* basis. *Intact* means that no disbursements should be made from the cash received from customers. The second basic principle is related to the first: all cash disbursements should be made by check. The use of sequentially numbered checks results in a clear record of all disbursements. The only exception to this rule is the use of a petty cash fund to make cash disbursements for minor expenditures such as postage stamps and repairs.

CONTROL OVER CASH RECEIPTS

Most merchandisers receive checks and currency from customers in two ways: (1) cash received over the counter, that is, from cash sales and (2) cash received in the mail, that is, cash collections from credit sales. Each type of cash receipt poses its own control problems.

Cash Received Over the Counter Several control mechanisms are used to handle these cash payments. First, cash registers allow the customer to see the display, which deters the salesclerk from ringing up a sale for less than the amount received from the customer and pocketing the difference. A locked-in cash register tape is another control feature. At various times during the day, an employee other than the clerk unlocks the register, removes the tape, and forwards it to the accounting department. At the end of the shift, the salesclerk remits the coin and currency from the register to a central cashier. Any difference between the amount of cash remitted to the cashier and the amount on the tape submitted to the accounting department is investigated.

Finally, prenumbered customer receipts, prepared in duplicate, are a useful control mechanism. The customer is given a copy, and the salesclerk retains another. The salesclerk is accountable for all numbers in a specific series of receipts and must be able to explain any differences between the amount of cash remitted to the cashier and the amount collected per the receipts.

Cash Received in the Mail Most customers send checks rather than currency through the mail. Any form of cash received in the mail from customers should be applied to their account balances. The customer wants assurance that the account is appropriately reduced for the amount of the payment. The company must be assured that all cash received is deposited in the bank and that the account receivable is reduced accordingly.

To achieve a reasonable degree of control, two employees should be present when the mail is opened.[1] The first employee opens the mail in the presence of the second employee, counts the money received, and prepares a control list of the amount received on that particular day. The list, often called a *prelist*, is prepared in triplicate. The second employee takes the original to the cashier along with the total cash received on that day. The cashier is the person who makes the bank deposit. One copy of the prelist is forwarded to the accounting department to be used as the basis for recording the increase in Cash and the decrease in Accounts Receivable. The other copy is retained by one of the two people who opens the mail. A comparison of the prelist to the bank deposit slip is a timely way to detect receipts that do not make it to the bank. Because the two employees acting in concert could circumvent the control process, rotation of duties is important.

1 In some companies, this control procedure may be omitted because of the cost of having two employees present when the mail is opened.

Monthly customer statements act as an additional control device for customer payments received in the mail. Assume that the two employees responsible for opening the mail and remitting checks to the cashier decide to pocket a check received from a customer. Checks made payable to a company can be stolen and cashed. The customer provides the control element. Because the check is not remitted to the cashier, the accounting department will not be notified to reduce the customer's account for the payment. The monthly statement, however, should alert the customer to the problem. The amount the customer thought was owed will be smaller than the balance due on the statement. At this point, the customer should ask the company to investigate the discrepancy. As evidence of its payment on account, the customer will be able to point to a canceled check—which was cashed by the unscrupulous employees.

Finally, keep in mind that the use of customer statements as a control device will be effective only if the employees responsible for the custody of cash received through the mail, for record keeping, and for authorization of adjustments to customers' accounts are not allowed to prepare and mail statements to customers. Employees allowed to do so are in a position to alter customers' statements.

Cash Discrepancies Discrepancies occur occasionally due to theft by dishonest employees and to human error. For example, if a salesclerk intentionally or unintentionally gives the wrong amount of change, the amount remitted to the cashier will not agree with the cash register tape. Any material differences should be investigated. Of particular significance are *recurring* differences between the amount remitted by any one cashier and the amount on the cash register tape.

THE ROLE OF COMPUTERIZED BUSINESS DOCUMENTS IN CONTROLLING CASH DISBURSEMENTS

A company makes cash payments for a variety of reasons; for example, to purchase merchandise, supplies, plants, and equipment; to pay operating expenditures; and to cover payroll expenses. We will concentrate on the disbursement of cash to purchase goods for resale, focusing particularly on the role of business documents in the process. Merchandising companies rely on a smooth and orderly inflow of quality goods for resale to customers. Suppliers must be paid on time so that the companies can continue to make goods available.

Business documents play a vital role in the purchasing function. The example that follows begins with a requisition for merchandise by the shoe department of Mickey's Marathon Sports. The example continues through the receipt of the goods and the eventual payment to the supplier. The entire process is summarized in Exhibit 6-7. You will want to refer to this exhibit throughout the remainder of this section.

Purchase Requisition The shoe department at Mickey's Marathon Sports reviews its stock weekly to determine if any items need replenishing. On the basis of its needs, the supervisor of the shoe department fills out the **purchase requisition form** shown in Exhibit 6-8 on page 317. The form indicates the supplier or vendor, Fleet Foot.

Purchase requisition form
Form a department uses to initiate a request to order merchandise.

The purchasing department has the responsibility for making the final decision on a vendor. Giving the purchasing department this responsibility means that it is held accountable for acquiring the goods at the lowest price, given certain standards for merchandise quality. Mickey's assigns a separate item number to each of the thousands of individual items of merchandise it stocks. Note that the requisition also indicates the vendor's number for each item. The unit of measure for each item is indicated in the quantity column. For example, "24 PR" means 24 pairs of shoes. The original and a copy of the purchase requisition are sent to the purchasing department. The shoe department keeps one copy for its records.

Purchase Order Like many other businesses, Mickey's uses a computerized purchasing system. Most companies have purchased software or have developed software internally to perform such functions as purchasing, sales, and payroll. The software is

EXHIBIT 6-7 Document Flow for the Purchasing Function

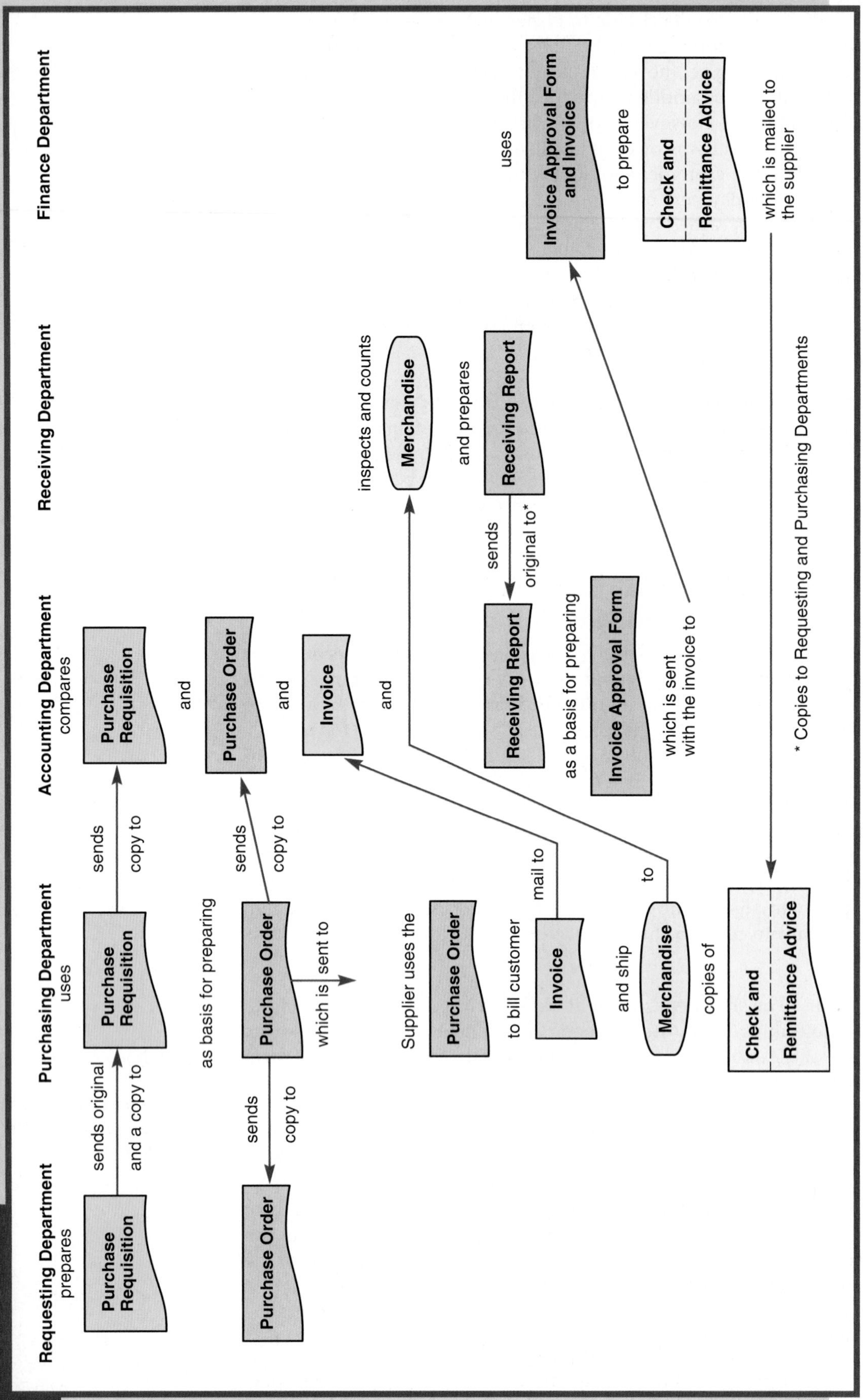

EXHIBIT 6-8 Purchase Requisition

Mickey's Marathon Sports
502 Dodge St.
Chicago, IL 66666

PURCHASE REQUISITION

Date 5/28/08 **PR 75638**

Preferred vendor Fleet Foot

Date needed by 6/5/08

The following items are requested for weekly dept. order

Item No.	Quantity	Description/Vendor No.
314627	24 PR	Sprinter/5265
323515	12 PR	Blazer/7512
323682	6 PR	Enduros/1580

Requested by Joe Smith **Department** Shoe department

capable not only of increasing the speed and accuracy of the process but also of generating the necessary documents.

A computer-generated **purchase order** is shown in Exhibit 6-9. Purchase orders are usually prenumbered; a company should periodically investigate any missing numbers.

Purchase order
A form sent by the purchasing department to the supplier.

EXHIBIT 6-9 Computer-Generated Purchase Order

Mickey's Marathon Sports
502 Dodge St.
Chicago, IL 66666

PURCHASE ORDER

TO: **PO 54296**
Fleet Feet
590 West St.
Milwaukee, WI 77777

Date 5/30/08 **Ship by** Best Express **Instructions** FOB destination point
Terms 2/10, net 30 **Date required** 6/5/08

Item No.	Quantity	Description/Vendor No.	Unit price	Amount
314627	24 PR	Sprinter/5265	$60.50	$1,452.00
323515	12 PR	Blazer/7512	53.70	644.40
323682	6 PR	Enduros/1580	75.40	452.40
				$2,548.80

Approved by Mary Jones

The purchasing department uses its copy of the purchase requisition as a basis for preparing the purchase order. An employee in the purchasing department keys in the relevant information from the purchase requisition and adds the unit cost for each item gathered from the vendor's price guide. The software program generates a purchase order, as shown in Exhibit 6-9. You should trace all of the information for at least one of the three items ordered from the purchase requisition to the purchase order.

The system generates the original purchase order and three copies. As indicated in Exhibit 6-7, the original is sent to the supplier after a supervisor in the purchasing department approves it. One copy is sent to the accounting department, where it will be matched with the original requisition. A second copy is sent to the shoe department as confirmation that its request for the items has been attended to by the purchasing department. The purchasing department keeps the third copy for its records.

A purchase order is not the basis for recording a purchase and a liability. Legally, the order is merely an offer by the company to purchase goods from the supplier. Technically, the receipt of goods from the supplier is the basis for the purchaser's recognition of a liability. As a matter of practice, however, most companies record the payable upon receipt of the invoice.

Invoice When Fleet Foot ships the merchandise, it also mails an invoice to Mickey's, requesting payment according to the agreed-upon terms, in this case 2/10, net 30. Recall from Chapter 5 that this means that the customer (Mickey's) receives a 2% discount by paying within 10 days of purchase; if not, the full amount is due within 30 days of purchase. The **invoice** may be mailed separately or included with the shipment of merchandise. Fleet Foot, the seller, calls this document a *sales invoice;* it is the basis for recording a sale and an account receivable. Mickey's, the buyer, calls the same document a *purchase invoice,* which is the basis for recording a purchase and an account payable. The invoice that Fleet Foot sent to Mickey's accounting department is shown in Exhibit 6-10.

Invoice
A form sent by the seller to the buyer as evidence of a sale.

EXHIBIT 6-10 Invoice

NO. 427953

Fleet Foot
590 West St.
Milwaukee, WI 77777

INVOICE

Sold to Mickey's Marathon Sports
502 Dodge St.
Chicago, IL 66666
Ship to Same
Terms 2/10, net 30

Date 6/2/08
Order No. 54296
Shipped via Best Express
Date shipped 6/2/08
Ship terms FOB destination

Quantity	Description/No.	Price	Amount
24 PR	Sprinter/5265	$60.50	$1,452.00
12 PR	Blazer/7512	53.70	644.40
6 PR	Enduros/1589	75.40	452.40
			$2,548.80

EXHIBIT 6-11 **Computer-Generated Receiving Report**

Mickey's Marathon Sports
502 Dodge St.
Chicago, Il 66666

Receiving Report

RR 23637

Purchase Order No. 54296 — **Date ordered** 5/30/08
Vendor Fleet Foot — **Date required** 6/5/08
Ship via Best Express
Terms 2/10, net 30

Quantity Received	Our Item No.	Description/Item No.	Remarks
24 PR	314627	Sprinter/5265	Box damaged but merchandise ok
12 PR	323515	Blazer/7512	
6 PR	323682	Enduros/1589	

Received by Bob Reed **Date** 6/4/08

Receiving Report The accounting department receives the invoice for the three items ordered. Within a few days before or after the receipt of the invoice, the merchandise arrives at Mickey's warehouse. As soon as the items are unpacked, the receiving department inspects and counts them. The same software used to generate the purchase order also generates a receiving report, as shown in Exhibit 6-11.

Mickey's uses a **blind receiving report**. The column for the quantity received is left blank and is filled in by the receiving department. Rather than simply being able to indicate that the number ordered was received, an employee must count the pairs of shoes to determine that the number ordered is actually received. You should trace all of the relevant information for one of the three items ordered from the purchase order to the receiving report. The accounting system generates an original receiving report and three copies. The receiving department keeps one copy for its records and sends the original to the accounting department. One copy is sent to the purchasing department to be matched with the purchase order, and the other copy is sent to the shoe department as verification that the items it originally requested have been received.

Blind receiving report
A form used by the receiving department to account for the quantity and condition of merchandise received from a supplier.

Invoice Approval Form At this point, Mickey's accounting department has copies of the purchase requisition from the shoe department, the purchase order from the purchasing department, the invoice from the supplier, and the receiving report from the warehouse. The accounting department uses an **invoice approval form** to document the accuracy of the information on each of these other forms. The invoice approval form for Mickey's Marathon Sports is shown in Exhibit 6-12.

Invoice approval form
A form the accounting department uses before making payment to document the accuracy of all information about a purchase. ***Alternate term:*** *Voucher.*

The invoice is compared to the purchase requisition to ensure that the company is billed for goods that it requested. A comparison of the invoice with the purchase order ensures that the goods were in fact ordered. Finally, the receiving report is compared with the invoice to verify that all goods for which the company is being billed were received. An accounting department employee must also verify the mathematical accuracy of the amounts that appear on the invoice. The date the invoice must be paid to

EXHIBIT 6-12 Invoice Approval Form

Mickey's Marathon Sports
502 Dodge St.
Chicago, IL 66666

Invoice Approval Form

	No.	Check
Purchase Requisition	PR 75638	✓
Purchase Order	PO 54296	✓
Receiving Report	RR 23637	✓

Invoice:

No. 427953
Date 6/2/08
Price ✓
Extensions ✓
Footings ✓

Last Day to Pay for Discount 6/12/08

Approved for Payment by Alice Johnson

take advantage of the discount is noted so that the finance department will be sure to send the check by this date. At this point, the accounting department prepares the journal entry to increase the inventory and accounts payable accounts. The invoice approval form and the invoice are then sent to the finance department. Some businesses call the invoice approval form a *voucher;* it is used for all expenditures, not just for purchases of merchandise. Finally, it is worth noting that some businesses do not use a separate invoice approval form; they simply note approval directly on the invoice.

Check with Remittance Advice Mickey's finance department is responsible for issuing checks. This results from the need to segregate custody of cash (the signed check) from record keeping (the updating of the ledger). On receipt of the invoice approval form from the accounting department, a clerk in the finance department processes a check with a remittance advice attached, as shown in Exhibit 6-13.[2]

Before the check is signed, the documents referred to on the invoice approval form are reviewed and canceled to prevent reuse. The clerk then forwards the check to one of the company officers authorized to sign checks. According to one of Mickey's internal control policies, only the treasurer and the assistant treasurer are authorized to sign checks. Both officers must sign check amounts above a specified dollar limit. To maintain separation of duties, the finance department should mail the check. The remittance advice informs the supplier as to the nature of the payment and is torn off by the supplier before cashing the check.

2 In some companies, an employee in the accounting department prepares checks and sends them to the finance department for review and signature. Most companies use computer-generated checks rather than manually typed ones.

EXHIBIT 6-13 **Check with Remittance Advice**

3690

Mickey's Marathon Sports
502 Dodge St.
Chicago, IL 66666

June 12 20 08

PAY TO THE
ORDER OF Fleet Foot $2,497.82

Two thousand four hundred ninety seven and 82/100 DOLLARS

Second National Bank
Missoula, MT

3690 035932 9321

John B. Martin

Purchase Order No.	**Invoice No.**	**Invoice Date**	**Description**	**Amount**
PO 54296	427953	6/2/07	24 PR Sprinter	$1,452.00
			12 PR Blazer	644.40
			6 PR Enduros	452.40
			Total	$2,548.80
			Less: 2% discount	50.98
			Net remitted	$2,497.82

POD REVIEW 6.5

LO5 ***Describe the various documents used in recording purchases and their role in controlling cash disbursement.***

- The documents used to record purchase transactions are instrumental in controlling both cash and inventory.
- The document flow diagram in Exhibit 6-7 provides an excellent summary of documents in the purchasing process. Some of the key documents are as follows:
  - Purchase order
  - Receiving report
  - Vendor invoice
  - Check

QUESTIONS

1. *The form sent by the seller to the buyer as evidence of a sale is called a(n)*
   a. purchase requisition form.
   b. purchase order.
   c. invoice.
   d. invoice approval form.

2. *Which of the following departments in an organization is responsible for preparing the invoice approval form to document all of the information about a particular purchase?*
   a. the department making a purchase request
   b. the purchasing department
   c. the accounting department
   d. the receiving department

ACCOUNTS HIGHLIGHTED

Account Titles	Where It Appears	In What Section	Page Number
Cash and Cash Equivalents	Balance Sheet	Current Assets	296
Petty Cash Fund	Balance Sheet	Current Assets	304
Cash Over and Short	Income Statement	Other Income/Expense	305

KEY TERMS QUIZ

Read each definition below and write the number of the definition in the blank beside the appropriate term. The quiz solutions appear at the end of the chapter.

_______ **Cash equivalent**
_______ **Bank statement**
_______ **Outstanding check**
_______ **Deposit in transit**
_______ **Bank reconciliation**
_______ **Credit memoranda**
_______ **Debit memoranda**
_______ **Petty cash fund**
_______ **Internal control system**
_______ **Sarbanes-Oxley Act**
_______ **Internal control report**
_______ **Public Company Accounting Oversight Board**
_______ **Board of directors**
_______ **Audit committee**
_______ **Accounting system**
_______ **Administrative controls**
_______ **Accounting controls**
_______ **Internal audit staff**
_______ **Purchase requisition form**
_______ **Purchase order**
_______ **Invoice**
_______ **Blind receiving report**
_______ **Invoice approval form**

1. The form sent by the seller to the buyer as evidence of a sale.
2. The group composed of key officers of a corporation and outside members responsible for the general oversight of the affairs of the entity.
3. Policies and procedures necessary to ensure the safeguarding of an entity's assets, the reliability of its accounting records, and the accomplishment of overall company objectives.
4. Procedures concerned with safeguarding the assets or the reliability of the financial statements.
5. The form a department uses to initiate a request to order merchandise.
6. A form the accounting department uses before making payment to document the accuracy of all information about a purchase.
7. A form used by the accountant to reconcile or resolve any differences between the balance shown on the bank statement for a particular account with the balance shown in the accounting records.
8. An investment that is readily convertible to a known amount of cash and has an original maturity to the investor of three months or less.
9. Deductions on a bank statement for items such as NSF checks and various service charges.
10. A check written by a company but not yet presented to the bank for payment.
11. A detailed list, prepared by the bank, of all activity for a particular account during the month.
12. A report required by Section 404 of SOX to be included in a company's annual report in which management assesses the effectiveness of the internal control structure.
13. A deposit recorded on the books but not yet reflected on the bank statement.
14. The methods and records used to accurately report an entity's transactions and to maintain accountability for its assets and liabilities.
15. Additions on a bank statement for such items as interest paid on the account and notes collected by the bank.
16. The board of directors subset that acts as a direct contact between the stockholders and the independent accounting firm.

17. Money kept on hand for making minor disbursements in coin and currency rather than by writing checks.
18. The five-member body created by the Sarbanes-Oxley Act that was given the authority to set auditing standards in the United States.
19. A form used by the receiving department to account for the quantity and condition of merchandise received from a supplier.
20. Procedures concerned with efficient operation of the business and adherence to managerial policies.
21. The form sent by the purchasing department to the supplier.
22. An act of Congress in 2002 intended to bring reform to corporate accountability and stewardship in the wake of a number of major corporate scandals.
23. The department responsible for monitoring and evaluating the internal control system.

ALTERNATE TERMS

Invoice Purchase invoice, sales invoice

Invoice approval form Voucher

WARMUP EXERCISES & SOLUTIONS

LO1

Warmup Exercise 6-1 Composition of Cash

For the following items, indicate whether each should be included (I) or excluded (E) from the line item titled Cash and cash equivalents on the balance sheet.

______ 1. Certificate of deposit maturing in 60 days
______ 2. Checking account
______ 3. Certificate of deposit maturing in six months
______ 4. Savings account
______ 5. Shares of GM stock
______ 6. Petty cash
______ 7. Corporate bonds maturing in 30 days
______ 8. Certified check

Key to the Solution Recall the key to classification as part of cash: the amount must be readily available to pay debts, and cash equivalents must have an original maturity to the investor of three months or less.

LO4

Warmup Exercise 6-2 Internal Control

List the internal control procedures discussed in the text.

Key to the Solution Refer to the section in the chapter that discusses internal control procedures.

SOLUTIONS TO WARMUP EXERCISES

Warmup Exercise 6-1

1. I 2. I 3. E 4. I 5. E 6. I 7. E 8. I

Warmup Exercise 6-2

1. Proper authorizations
2. Segregation of duties
3. Independent verification
4. Safeguarding of assets and records
5. Independent review and appraisal
6. Design and use of business documents

REVIEW

REVIEW PROBLEM & SOLUTION

The following information is available for McCarthy Corp. on June 30, 2008:

a. The balance in cash as reported on the June 30, 2008, bank statement is $5,654.98.
b. McCarthy made a deposit of $865 on June 30 that is not included on the bank statement.
c. A comparison between the canceled checks returned with the bank statement and McCarthy's records indicated that two checks had not yet been returned to the bank for payment. The amounts of the two checks were $236.77 and $116.80.
d. The Cash account on the company's books reported a balance on June 30 of $4,165.66.
e. McCarthy rents some excess storage space in one of its warehouses, and the tenant pays its monthly rent directly to the bank for deposit in McCarthy's account. The bank statement indicates that a deposit of $1,500.00 was made during the month of June.
f. Interest earned on the checking account and added to McCarthy's account during June was $11.75.
g. Bank service charges were $15 for the month of June as reported on the bank statement.
h. A comparison between the checks returned with the bank statement and the company's records revealed that a check written by the company in the amount of $56 was recorded by the company erroneously as a check for $560.

Required
Prepare a bank reconciliation for the month of June in good form.

SOLUTION TO REVIEW PROBLEM

McCarthy Corp.
Bank Reconciliation
June 30, 2008

Balance per bank statement, June 30		$5,654.98
Add: Deposit in transit		865.00
Deduct: Outstanding checks:		
	$ 236.77	
	116.80	(353.57)
Adjusted balance, June 30		$6,166.41
Balance per books, June 30		$4,165.66
Add: Tenant's rent collected by bank	$1,500.00	
Interest earned on checking account	11.75	
Error in recording check	504.00	2,015.75
Deduct: Bank service charges		(15.00)
Adjusted balance, June 30		$6,166.41

QUESTIONS

1. What is a cash equivalent? Why is it included with cash on the balance sheet?
2. Why does the purchase of an item classified as a cash equivalent *not* appear on the statement of cash flows as an investing activity?
3. A friend says to you: "I understand why it is important to deposit all receipts intact and not keep coin and currency sitting around the business. Beyond this control feature, however, I believe that a company should strive to keep the maximum amount possible in checking accounts to be able to pay bills on time." How would you evaluate your friend's statement?
4. A friend says to you: "I'm confused. I have a memo included with my bank statement indicating a $20 service charge for printing new checks. If the bank is deducting this amount from my account, why do they call it a 'debit memorandum'? I thought a decrease in a cash account would be a credit, not a debit." How can you explain this?
5. Different formats for bank reconciliations are possible. What is the format for a bank reconciliation in which a service charge for a lockbox is *added* to the balance per the bank statement? Explain your answer.
6. What circumstances led to the passage of the Sarbanes-Oxley Act in 2002?

7. What is the typical composition of a board of directors of a publicly held corporation?

8. An order clerk fills out a purchase requisition for an expensive item of inventory and the receiving report when the merchandise arrives. The clerk takes the inventory home, then sends the invoice to the accounting department so that the supplier will be paid. What basic internal control procedure could have prevented this misuse of company assets?

9. What are some of the limitations on a company's effective system of internal control?

10. What two basic procedures are essential to an effective system of internal control over cash?

11. How would you evaluate the following statement? The only reason a company positions its cash register so that customers can see the display is so customers feel comfortable knowing they are being charged the correct amount for the purchase.

12. Which document, a purchase order or an invoice, is the basis for recording a purchase and a corresponding liability? Explain your answer.

13. What is a blind receiving report? How does it act as a control device?

14. What is the purpose of comparing a purchase invoice with a purchase order? of comparing a receiving report with a purchase invoice?

BRIEF EXERCISES

LO1 **Brief Exercise 6-1** Composition of Cash

Using Y for yes and N for no, indicate whether each of the following items should or should not be included with cash and cash equivalents on the balance sheet.

_______ Cash in a checking account
_______ Coin and currency in a cash register drawer
_______ A six-month certificate of deposit
_______ Postage stamps
_______ An amount owed by an employee for a travel advance
_______ A three-month Treasury bill
_______ Cash in a money market account

LO2 **Brief Exercise 6-2** Bank Reconciliation

Indicate whether each of the following items is an adjustment to the balance per books (BK) or to the balance per bank statement (BS) on a reconciliation that adjusts the bank balance and the bank statement to the correct balance.

_______ Customer's NSF check
_______ Service charge for a lockbox
_______ Outstanding checks
_______ Interest earned on an account for the month
_______ Check written on the account but recorded on the books at the wrong amount
_______ Deposits in transit

LO3 **Brief Exercise 6-3** Sarbanes-Oxley Act

Provide answers to each of the following questions.

1. Who is responsible for establishing and maintaining an adequate internal control structure for a company?
2. Who provides an independent opinion as to whether management has maintained effective internal control over financial reporting?
3. To whom should the independent auditors' report be directed?
4. Which committee of the board of directors provides direct contact between stockholders and the independent accounting firm?

LO4 **Brief Exercise 6-4** Internal Control Procedures

List the names of at least four important internal control procedures.

LO5

Brief Exercise 6-5 Business Documents

Number each of the following documents to indicate the order in which each document would be used.

_______ Purchase order
_______ Invoice approval form
_______ Check and remittance advice
_______ Purchase requisition
_______ Invoice
_______ Receiving report

EXERCISES

LO1

Exercise 6-1 Cash Equivalents

Systematic Enterprises invested its excess cash in the following instruments during December 2008:

Certificate of deposit, due January 31, 2011	$ 75,000
Certificate of deposit, due March 30, 2009	150,000
Commercial paper, original maturity date February 28, 2009	125,000
Deposit into a money market fund	25,000
Investment in stock	65,000
90-day Treasury bills	100,000
Treasury note, due December 1, 2038	500,000

Required
Determine the amount of cash equivalents that should be combined with cash on the company's balance sheet at December 31, 2008, and for purposes of preparing a statement of cash flows for the year ended December 31, 2008.

LO2

Exercise 6-2 Items on a Bank Reconciliation

Assume that a company is preparing a bank reconciliation for the month of June. It reconciles the bank balance and the book balance to the correct balance. For each of the following items, indicate whether the item is an addition to the bank balance (A-Bank), an addition to the book balance (A-Book), a deduction from the bank balance (D-Bank), or a deduction from the book balance (D-Book) or would not appear on the June reconciliation (NA).

_______ 1. Check written in June but not yet returned to the bank for payment
_______ 2. Customer's NSF check
_______ 3. Customer's check written in the amount of $54 but recorded on the books in the amount of $45*
_______ 4. Service charge for new checks
_______ 5. Principal and interest on a customer's note collected for the company by the bank
_______ 6. Customer's check deposited on June 30 but not reflected on the bank statement
_______ 7. Check written on the company's account, paid by the bank, and returned with the bank statement
_______ 8. Check written on the company's account for $123 but recorded on the books as $132*
_______ 9. Interest on the checking account for the month of June

*Answer in terms of the adjustment needed to correct for the error.

LO2

Exercise 6-3 Petty Cash Fund

On January 2, 2008, Cleaver Video Stores decided to set up a petty cash fund. The treasurer established the fund by writing and cashing a $300 check and placing the coin and currency in a locked petty cash drawer. Edward Haskell was designated as the custodian for the fund. During January, the following receipts were given to Haskell in exchange for cash from the fund:

U.S. Post Office (stamps)	$76.00
Speedy Delivery Service	45.30
Cake N Cookies (party for retiring employee)	65.40
Office Supply Superstore (paper, pencils)	36.00

A count of the cash in the drawer on January 31 revealed a balance of $74.10. The treasurer wrote and cashed a check on the same day to restore the fund to its original balance of $300. Prepare the necessary journal entries, with explanations, for January. Assume that all stamps and office supplies were used during the month.

LO4

Exercise 6-4 Internal Control

The university drama club is planning a raffle. The president overheard you talking about internal control to another accounting student, so she asked you to set up some guidelines to "make sure" that all money collected for the raffle is accounted for by the club.

Required

1. Describe guidelines that the club should follow to achieve an acceptable level of internal control.
2. Comment on the president's request that she "be sure" all money is collected and recorded.

LO4

Exercise 6-5 Segregation of Duties

The following tasks are performed by three employees, each of whom is capable of performing all of the tasks. Do not concern yourself with the time required to perform the tasks, but with the need to provide for segregation of duties. Assign the duties by using a check mark to indicate which employee should perform each task. Remember that you can assign any one of the tasks to any of the employees.

	Employee		
Task	**Mary**	**Sue**	**John**
Prepare invoices			
Mail invoices			
Pick up mail from post office			
Open mail, separate checks			
List checks on deposit slip in triplicate			
Post payment to customer's account			
Deposit checks			
Prepare monthly schedule of accounts receivable			
Reconcile bank statements			

MULTICONCEPT EXERCISE

LO1,2

Exercise 6-6 Composition of Cash

Using Y for yes and N for no, indicate whether each of the following items should be included in cash and cash equivalents on the balance sheet. If an item should not be included in cash and cash equivalents, indicate where it should appear on the balance sheet.

_______ 1. Checking account at Third County Bank
_______ 2. Petty cash fund
_______ 3. Coin and currency
_______ 4. Postage stamps
_______ 5. An IOU from an employee
_______ 6. Savings account at the Ft. Worth Savings & Loan
_______ 7. A six-month CD
_______ 8. Undeposited customer checks
_______ 9. A customer's check returned by the bank and marked NSF
_______ 10. Sixty-day U.S. Treasury bills
_______ 11. A cashier's check

PROBLEMS

LO2

Problem 6-1 Bank Reconciliation

The following information is available to assist you in preparing a bank reconciliation for Calico Corners on May 31, 2008:

a. The balance on the May 31, 2008, bank statement is $8,432.11.
b. Not included on the bank statement is a $1,250 deposit made by Calico Corners late on May 31.
c. A comparison between the canceled checks returned with the bank statement and the company records indicated that the following checks are outstanding at May 31:

No. 123	$ 23.40
No. 127	145.00
No. 128	210.80
No. 130	67.32

d. The Cash account on the company's books shows a balance of $9,965.34.
e. The bank acts as a collection agency for interest earned on some municipal bonds held by Calico Corners. The May bank statement indicates interest of $465.00 earned during the month.
f. Interest earned on the checking account and added to Calico Corners' account during May was $54.60. Miscellaneous bank service charges amounted to $50.00.
g. A customer's NSF check in the amount of $166.00 was returned with the May bank statement.
h. A comparison between the deposits listed on the bank statement and the company's books revealed that a customer's check in the amount of $123.45 was recorded on the books during May but was never added to the company's account. The bank erroneously added the check to the account of Calico Closet, which has an account at the same bank.
i. The comparison of deposits per the bank statement with those per the books revealed that another customer's check in the amount of $101.10 was correctly added to the company's account. In recording the check on the company's books, however, the accountant erroneously increased the Cash account to $1,011.00.

Required

1. Prepare a bank reconciliation in good form.
2. A friend says to you: "I don't know why companies bother to prepare bank reconciliations—it seems a waste of time. Why don't they just do like I do and adjust the cash account for any difference between what the bank shows as a balance and what shows up in the books?" Explain to your friend why a bank reconciliation should be prepared as soon as a bank statement is received.

LO4

Problem 6-2 Internal Control Procedures

You are opening a summer business, a chain of three drive-through snow-cone stands. You have hired other college students to work and have purchased a cash register with locked-in tapes. You retain one key, and the other is available to the lead person on each shift.

Required

1. Write a list of the procedures for all employees to follow when ringing up sales and giving change.
2. Write a list of the procedures for the lead person to follow in closing out at the end of the day. Be specific so that employees will have few if any questions.
3. What is your main concern in the design of internal control for the snow-cone stands? How did you address that concern? Be specific.

LO5

Problem 6-3 The Design of Internal Control Documents

Motel $49.99 has purchased a large warehouse to store all supplies used by housekeeping departments in the company's expanding chain of motels. In the past, each motel bought supplies from local distributors and paid for the supplies from cash receipts.

Required

1. Name some potential problems with the old system.
2. Design a purchase requisition form and a receiving report to be used by the housekeeping departments and the warehouse. Indicate how many copies of each form should be used and who should receive each copy.

MULTICONCEPT PROBLEMS

LO1,2 **Problem 6-4** Cash and Liquid Assets on the Balance Sheet

The following accounts are listed in a company's general ledger. The accountant wants to place the items in order of liquidity on the balance sheet.

Accounts receivable
Certificates of deposit (six months)
Investment in stock
Prepaid rent
Money market fund
Petty cash fund

Required
Rank the accounts in terms of liquidity. Identify items to be included in the total of cash and explain why the items not included in cash on the balance sheet are not as liquid as cash. Explain how these items should be classified.

LO3,4 **Problem 6-5** Internal Control

At Morris Mart Inc., all sales are on account. Mary Morris-Manning is responsible for mailing invoices to customers, recording the amount billed, opening mail, and recording the payment. Mary is very devoted to the family business and never takes off more than one or two days for a long weekend. The customers know Mary and sometimes send personal notes with their payments. Another clerk handles all aspects of accounts payable. Mary's brother, who is president of Morris Mart, has hired an accountant to help with expansion.

Required
1. List some problems with the current accounts receivable system.
2. What suggestions would you make to improve internal control?
3. How would you explain to Mary that she personally is not the problem?

ALTERNATE PROBLEMS

LO2 **Problem 6-1A** Bank Reconciliation

The following information is available to assist you in preparing a bank reconciliation for Karen's Catering on March 31, 2008:

a. The balance on the March 31, 2008, bank statement is $6,506.10.
b. Not included on the bank statement is a $423 deposit made by Karen's late on March 31.
c. A comparison between the canceled checks listed on the bank statement and the company records indicated that the following checks are outstanding at March 31:

No. 112	$ 42.92
No. 117	307.00
No. 120	10.58
No. 122	75.67

d. The bank acts as a collection agency for checks returned for insufficient funds. The March bank statement indicates that one such check in the amount of $45.00 was collected and deposited and a collection fee of $4.50 was charged.
e. Interest earned on the checking account and added to Karen's account during March was $4.30. Miscellaneous bank service charges amounted to $22.
f. A comparison between the deposits listed on the bank statement and the company's books revealed that a customer's check in the amount of $1,250 appears on the bank statement in March but was never added to the customer's account on the company's books.
g. The comparison of checks cleared per the bank statement with those per the books revealed that the wrong amount was charged to the company's account for a check. The amount of the check was $990. The proof machine encoded the check in the amount of $909, the amount charged against the company's account.

Required

1. Determine the balance on the books before any adjustments as well as the corrected balance to be reported on the balance sheet.
2. What would you recommend Karen do as a result of the bank error in (g)? Why?

LO4

Problem 6-2A Internal Control Procedures

The loan department in a bank is subject to regulation. Internal auditors work for the bank to ensure that the loan department complies with requirements. The internal auditors must verify that each car loan file has a note signed by the maker, verification of insurance, and a title issued by the state that names the bank as co-owner.

Required

1. Explain why the bank and the regulatory agency are concerned with these documents.
2. Describe the internal control procedures that should be in place to ensure that these documents are obtained and safeguarded.

LO5

Problem 6-3A The Design of Internal Control Documents

Tiger's Group is a newly formed company that produces and sells children's movies about an imaginary character. The movies are in such great demand that they are shipped to retail outlets as soon as they are produced. The company must pay a royalty to several actors for each movie that it sells to retail outlets.

Required

1. Describe some internal control features that should be in place to ensure that all royalties are paid to the actors.
2. Design the shipping form that Tiger's Group should use for the movies. Make sure you include authorizations and indicate the number of copies and the routing of the copies.

ALTERNATE MULTICONCEPT PROBLEMS

LO1,2

Problem 6-4A Cash and Liquid Assets on the Balance Sheet

The following accounts are listed in a company's general ledger:

	December 31, 2008	December 31, 2007
Accounts receivable	$12,300	$10,000
Certificates of deposit (three months)	10,000	10,000
Marketable securities	4,500	4,000
Petty cash fund	1,200	1,500
Money market fund	25,800	28,000
Cash in checking account	6,000	6,000

Required

1. Which items are cash equivalents?
2. Explain where items that are not cash equivalents should be classified on the balance sheet.
3. What are the amount and the direction of change in cash and cash equivalents for 2008? Is the company as liquid at the end of 2008 as it was at the end of 2007? Explain your answer.

LO3,4

Problem 6-5A Internal Control

Abbott Inc. is expanding and needs to hire more personnel in the accounting office. Barbara Barker, the chief accounting clerk, knew that her cousin Cheryl was looking for a job. Barbara and Cheryl are also roommates. Barbara offered Cheryl a job as her assistant. Barbara will be responsible for Cheryl's performance reviews and training.

Required

1. List some problems with the proposed personnel situations in the accounting department.
2. Explain why accountants are concerned with the hiring of personnel. What suggestions would you make to improve internal control at Abbott?
3. How would you explain to Barbara and Cheryl that they personally are not the problem?

DECISION CASES

READING AND INTERPRETING FINANCIAL STATEMENTS

LO1 **Decision Case 6-1** Comparing Two Companies in the Same Industry: Kellogg's and General Mills

Refer to the financial information for **Kellogg's** and **General Mills** reproduced at the end of this book.

Required:

1. What is the balance in Cash and cash equivalents on the balance sheet of each company at the end of the most recent year? What is the amount of increase or decrease in this balance from the end of the prior year?
2. On what other statement in each company's annual report does the increase or decrease in cash and cash equivalents appear? Explain why it appears on this statement.
3. According to the notes to their financial statements, how does each company define "Cash and cash equivalents"? Are there any differences in their definitions?

LO3 **Decision Case 6-2** Reading and Interpreting IBM's Report of Management

IBM's 2006 annual report includes the following selected paragraphs from its Report of Management found on page 54:

> IBM maintains an effective internal control structure. It consists, in part, of organizational arrangements with clearly defined lines of responsibility and delegation of authority, and comprehensive systems and control procedures. An important element of the control environment is an ongoing internal audit program. Our system also contains self-monitoring mechanisms, and actions are taken to correct deficiencies as they are identified. . . .
>
> PricewaterhouseCoopers LLP, an independent registered public accounting firm, is retained to audit IBM's consolidated financial statements and management's assessment of the effectiveness of the company's internal control over financial reporting. Its accompanying report is based on audits conducted in accordance with the standards of the Public Company Accounting Oversight Board (United States). . . .
>
> The Audit Committee of the Board of Directors is composed solely of independent, nonmanagement directors, and is responsible for recommending to the Board the independent registered public accounting firm to be retained for the coming year, subject to stockholder ratification. The Audit Committee meets periodically and privately with the independent registered public accounting firm, with the company's internal auditors, as well as with IBM management, to review accounting, auditing, internal control structure and financial reporting matters.

Required:

1. Describe the main components of IBM's internal control structure.
2. Who is IBM's external auditor? In addition to auditing IBM's financial statements, what else does this firm audit? What body's standards does the firm follow in conducting its audit?
3. What is the composition of IBM's Audit Committee? Describe its role.

MAKING FINANCIAL DECISIONS

LO1 **Decision Case 6-3** Liquidity

R Montague and J Capulet distribute films to movie theaters. Following are the current assets for each distributor at the end of the year. (All amounts are in millions of dollars.)

	R Montague	J Capulet
Cash	$10	$ 5
Six-month certificates of deposit	9	0
Short-term investments in stock	0	6
Accounts receivable	15	23
Allowance for doubtful accounts	(1)	(1)
Total current assets	$33	$33

HOMEWORK

Required
As a loan officer for the First National Bank of Verona Heights, assume that both companies have come to you asking for a $10 million six-month loan. If you could lend money to only one of the two, which one would it be? Justify your answer by writing a brief memo to the president of the bank.

ETHICAL DECISION MAKING

LO3,4 **Decision Case 6-4** Cash Receipts in a Bookstore

You were recently hired by a large retail bookstore chain. Your training involved spending a week at the largest and most profitable store in the district. The store manager assigned the head cashier to train you on the cash register and closing procedures required by the company's home office. In the process, the head cashier instructed you to keep an envelope for cash over and short that would include cash or IOUs equal to the net amount of overages or shortages in the cash drawer. "It is impossible to balance exactly, so just put extra cash in this envelope and use the cash when you are short." You studied accounting for one semester in college and remembered your professor saying that "all deposits should be made intact daily."

Required
Draft a memo to the store manager detailing any problems you see with the current system. This memo should address the issue of the reliability of the cash receipts number. It should also answer the following question: Does this method provide information to the company that would enable someone to detect whether theft has occurred during the particular day in question? Your memo should suggest an alternative method of internal control for cash receipts.

SOLUTIONS TO KEY TERMS QUIZ

8	Cash equivalent	2	Board of directors
11	Bank statement	16	Audit committee
10	Outstanding check	14	Accounting system
13	Deposit in transit	20	Administrative controls
7	Bank reconciliation	4	Accounting controls
15	Credit memoranda	23	Internal audit staff
9	Debit memoranda	5	Purchase requisition form
17	Petty cash fund	21	Purchase order
3	Internal control system	1	Invoice
22	Sarbanes-Oxley Act	19	Blind receiving report
12	Internal control report	6	Invoice approval form
18	Public Company Accounting Oversight Board		

ANSWERS TO POD REVIEW

LO1	1. d	2. b
LO2	1. b	2. b
LO3	1. d	2. c
LO4	1. b	2. a
LO5	1. c	2. c

CHAPTER 7

Receivables and Investments

Learning Outcomes

After studying this chapter, you should be able to:

LO1 Show that you understand how to account for accounts receivable, including bad debts.

LO2 Explain how information about sales and receivables can be combined to evaluate how efficient a company is in collecting its receivables.

LO3 Show that you understand how to account for interest-bearing notes receivable.

LO4 Explain various techniques that companies use to accelerate the inflow of cash from sales.

LO5 Show that you understand the accounting for and disclosure of various types of investments that companies make.

LO6 Explain the effects of transactions involving liquid assets on the statement of cash flows.

Study Links...

A Look at the Previous Chapter
Chapter 6 looked at the various forms that cash can take and the importance of cash control to a business.

A Look at This Chapter
As you learned in earlier chapters, receivables result from the sale of products and services on account. This chapter examines the accounting for accounts and notes receivable, including how to account for bad debts. Many companies invest the cash they collect from customers in various types of financial instruments as well as in the stocks and bonds of other companies. This chapter also illustrates the accounting and reporting for these investments.

A Look at the Upcoming Chapters
This chapter concludes our look at a company's most liquid assets, that is, its current assets. Chapter 8 focuses on the long-term operational assets, such as property, plant, and equipment and intangibles, necessary to run a business. Chapters 9 and 10 explore the use of liabilities to finance the purchase of assets.

Apple Inc. MAKING BUSINESS DECISIONS

For years, the names **Apple Inc.** and Macintosh have been synonymous. Incorporated in the state of California in 1977, the company made a name for itself by carving out a niche in the personal computer (PC) market and developing its own operating system to run its Mac desktops and laptops.

A few years ago, however, Apple broadened its horizons and in the process, revolutionized the music business by introducing the iPod. To provide synergies between its Mac PCs and the new iPods, Apple developed its iTunes Music Store, allowing customers to download songs from the iTunes Music Store, which is available on either a Mac or Windows PC.

Apple's innovations did not stop with the iPod. In early 2007, looking to capitalize on the success of the iPod, the company announced its new iPhone. This feature-packed unit is three products in one: a mobile phone, an iPod, and an Internet communications device. The revolutionary phone allows the user to make a call by just pointing at a name or number. The iPod built into the product has a $3\frac{1}{2}$-inch wide-screen display that allows the music lover to view the album cover artwork when selecting songs to play. The features in the communications device include e-mail, web browsing, searching, and even Google maps.

Have Apple's key product innovations paid off for it and its stockholders? The tools learned in previous chapters, as well as those presented in this chapter, will help you answer that question. Recall that a company's comparative income statements show the reader whether sales have increased and, if so, whether that increase has translated to an improved bottom line, that is, an increase in net income. As reported in its 2006 annual report, Apple's sales more than doubled from $8.3 billion in 2004 to $19.3 billion in 2006. Even more dramatic was the improvement of the bottom line: from a meager $266 million in net income in 2004 to $2.0 billion in 2006.

What company wouldn't be envious of Apple's steady sales climb over recent years? Keep in mind, though, that sales and cash are not the same. As with most companies, Apple makes many of its sales on credit; and it must collect the resulting accounts receivable to add

cash to its balance sheet. And as you know from personal experience, idle cash does not earn a very good return—most bank accounts these days pay barely 2% interest. So it becomes equally important to understand what Apple does with its cash. Investments on the balance sheet indicate what the company does with idle cash, cash that is not immediately needed to buy more inventory or plant and equipment or to repay loans.

The accompanying partial balance sheet gives you an idea of the importance of Apple's three most liquid assets: cash and cash equivalents, short-term investments, and accounts receivable. But beyond the absolute dollar amounts and their relative size, what else would you want to know about each of those assets? The last chapter looked at cash and cash equivalents. This chapter will answer some important questions about receivables and investments, such as:

- How does a company report accounts receivable on its balance sheet? (See pp. 336–337.)

(continued)

- What is the purpose of subtracting an allowance from the balance of accounts receivable? (See p. 338.)
- Can the relationship between sales on the income statement and accounts receivable on the balance sheet be of any value in assessing a company's performance? (See pp. 343–345.)
- How does a company report short-term investments on its balance sheet? (See p. 356.)
- What types of investments do companies make? (See pp. 353–354.)
- How does a company earn income from these investments? (See pp. 355–356.)

Answers to those questions are found in the text. They can help you decide whether Apple's forays into the digital music business and mobile phones were wise business decisions.

Consolidated Balance Sheets (Partial)
(In millions, except share amounts)

Apple's three most important liquid assets → Cash and cash equivalents, Short-term investments, Accounts receivable

	September 30, 2006	September 24, 2005
ASSETS:		**As Restated(1)**
Current assets:		
Cash and cash equivalents	$ 6,392	$ 3,491
Short-term investments	3,718	4,770
Accounts receivable, less allowances of $52 and $46, respectively	1,252	895
Inventories	270	165
Deferred tax assets	607	331
Other current assets	2,270	648
Total current assets	$14,509	$10,300

(1) See Note 2, "Restatement of Consolidated Financial Statements," in Notes to Consolidated Financial Statements.
See accompanying Notes to Consolidated Financial Statements.
Source: Apple Computer Company's 2006 annual report.

Accounts Receivable

LO1 Show that you understand how to account for accounts receivable, including bad debts.

Account receivable
A receivable arising from the sale of goods or services with a verbal promise to pay.

Receivables can result from a variety of transactions. The most common type of receivable is the one that arises from the sale of goods or services to customers with a verbal promise to pay within a specified period of time. This type of receivable is called an **account receivable**. Accounts receivable do not bear interest. Apple or any other company would rather not sell on credit, preferring to make all sales for cash. Selling on credit causes two problems: it slows down the inflow of cash to the company, and it raises the possibility that the customer may not pay its bill on time or possibly ever. To remain competitive, however, Apple and most other businesses must sell their products and services on credit.

THE USE OF A SUBSIDIARY LEDGER

Apple states on page 7 of its 2006 annual report that it "sells to education, consumer, creative professional, business, and government customers." Accounts receivable is the asset that arises from a sale on credit to any of those customers. For example, assume

Apple sells $25,000 of hardware to a school. The journal entry to record the sale would be as follows:

Accounts Receivable	25,000	
Sales Revenue		25,000
To record sale on open account.		

Balance Sheet						Income Statement
ASSETS	=	LIABILITIES	+	STOCKHOLDERS' EQUITY	+	REVENUES − EXPENSES
Accounts Receivable 25,000						Sales Revenue 25,000

It is important for control purposes that Apple keep a record of to whom the sale was made and include that amount on a periodic statement or bill sent to the customer (in this case, a school). What if a company has a hundred or a thousand different customers? Some mechanism is needed to track the balance owed by each of these customers. The mechanism that companies use is called a **subsidiary ledger**.

A subsidiary ledger contains the necessary detail on each of a number of items that collectively make up a single general ledger account, called the **control account**. This detail is shown in the following example for accounts receivable:

Subsidiary ledger
The detail for a number of individual items that collectively make up a single general ledger account.

Control account
The general ledger account that is supported by a subsidiary ledger.

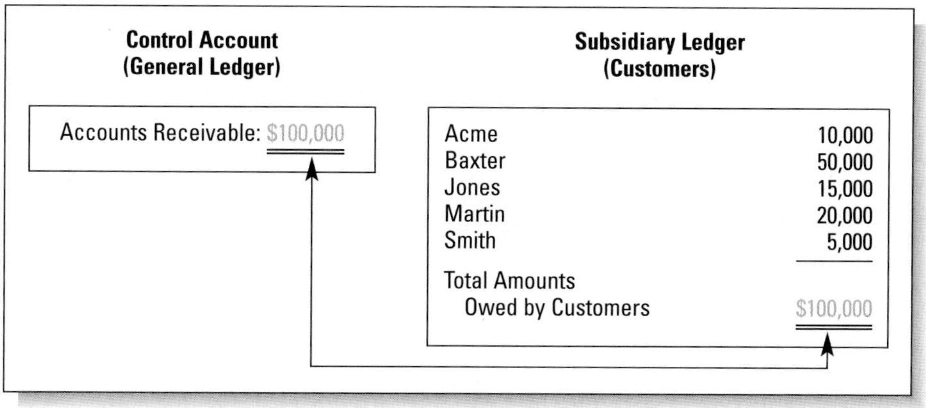

In theory, any one of the accounts in the general ledger could be supported by a subsidiary ledger. In addition to Accounts Receivable, two other common accounts supported by subsidiary ledgers are Plant and Equipment and Accounts Payable. An accounts payable subsidiary ledger contains a separate account for each of the suppliers or vendors from which a company purchases inventory. A plant and equipment subsidiary ledger consists of individual accounts, along with their balances, for each of the various long-term tangible assets the company owns.

It is important to understand that a subsidiary ledger does not take the place of the control account in the general ledger. Instead, at any point in time, the balances of the accounts that make up the subsidiary ledger should total to the single balance in the related control account. The remainder of this chapter will illustrate the use of only the control account. However, whenever a specific customer's account is increased or decreased, the name of the customer will be noted next to the control account in the journal entry.

Real World Practice

7-1 Reading Apple's Balance Sheet

Refer to **Apple**'s partial balance sheet as presented in the chapter opener. By what amount did accounts receivable increase or decrease during 2006? How significant are accounts receivable to the amount of total current assets at the end of 2006?

THE VALUATION OF ACCOUNTS RECEIVABLE

Apple's 2006 annual report revealed the following receivables on the balance sheet:

(amounts in millions)	September 30, 2006	September 24, 2005
Accounts receivable, less allowances of $52 and $46, respectively	$1,252	$895

Apple does not sell its products under the assumption that any particular customer will not pay its bill. In fact, the credit department of a business is responsible for performing a credit check on all potential customers before granting them credit. Management of Apple is not naive enough, however, to believe that all customers will be able to pay their accounts when due. This would be the case only if (1) all customers were completely trustworthy and (2) customers never experienced unforeseen financial difficulties that made it impossible to pay on time.

The reduction in Apple's receivables for an allowance is how most companies deal with bad debts in their accounting records. Bad debts are unpaid customer accounts that a company gives up trying to collect. Some companies describe the allowance more fully as the allowance for doubtful accounts or the allowance for uncollectible accounts. Using the end of 2006 as an example, Apple believes that the net recoverable amount of its receivables is $1,252 million even though the gross amount of receivables is $52 million higher than this amount. The company has reduced the gross receivables for an amount it believes is necessary to reflect the asset on the books at the net recoverable amount or net realizable value. We now take a closer look at how a company accounts for bad debts.

TWO METHODS TO ACCOUNT FOR BAD DEBTS

Assume that Roberts Corp. makes a $500 sale to Dexter Inc. on November 10, 2008, with credit terms of 2/10, net 60. (Credit terms were explained in Chapter 5.) Roberts makes the following entry on its books on this date:

2008			
Nov. 10	Accounts Receivable—Dexter	500	
	Sales Revenue		500
	To record sale on credit, terms of 2/10, net 60.		

Balance Sheet						Income Statement
ASSETS	=	**LIABILITIES**	+	**STOCKHOLDERS' EQUITY**	+	**REVENUES − EXPENSES**
Accounts Receivable—Dexter 500						Sales Revenue 500

Assume further that Dexter not only misses taking advantage of the discount for early payment but also is unable to pay within 60 days. After pursuing the account for four months into 2009, the credit department of Roberts informs the accounting department that it has given up on collecting the $500 from Dexter and advises that the account be written off. To do so, the accounting department makes the following entry:

2009			
May 1	Bed Debts Expense	500	
	Accounts Receivable—Dexter		500
	To write off Dexter account.		

Balance Sheet						Income Statement
ASSETS	=	**LIABILITIES**	+	**STOCKHOLDERS' EQUITY**	+	**REVENUES − EXPENSES**
Accounts Receivable—Dexter (500)						Bad Debts Expense (500)

Direct write-off method The recognition of bad debts expense at the point an account is written off as uncollectible.

This approach to accounting for bad debts is called the **direct write-off method**. Do you see any problems with its use?

- What about Roberts' balance sheet at the end of 2008? By ignoring the possibility that not all of its outstanding accounts receivable will be collected, Roberts is overstating the value of this asset at December 31, 2008.
- What about the income statement for 2008? By ignoring the possibility of bad debts on sales made during 2008, Roberts has violated the matching principle. This principle requires that all costs associated with making sales in a period be matched with the sales of that period. Roberts has overstated net income for 2008 by ignoring bad debts as expense. The problem is one of timing: even though any one particular

account may not prove to be uncollectible until a later period (e.g., the Dexter account), the cost associated with making sales on credit (bad debts) should be recognized in the period of sale.

Accountants use the **allowance method** to overcome the deficiencies of the direct write-off method. They estimate the amount of bad debts before these debts actually occur. For example, assume that Roberts' total sales during 2008 amount to $600,000 and that at the end of the year, the outstanding accounts receivable total $250,000. Also assume that Roberts estimates from past experience that 1% of the sales of the period, or $6,000, will prove to be uncollectible. Under the allowance method, Roberts makes the following adjusting entry at the end of 2008.

Allowance method
A method of estimating bad debts on the basis of either the net credit sales of the period or the accounts receivable at the end of the period.

2008			
Dec. 31	Bad Debts Expense	6,000	
	Allowance for Doubtful Accounts		6,000
	To record estimated bad debts for the year.		

Balance Sheet							Income Statement
ASSETS	=	LIABILITIES	+	STOCKHOLDERS' EQUITY	+		REVENUES − EXPENSES
Allowance for Doubtful Accounts (6,000)							Bad Debts Expense (6,000)

The debit recognizes the cost associated with the reduction in value of the asset Accounts Receivable. The cost is charged to the income statement in the form of Bad Debts Expense. A contra-asset account is used to reduce the asset to its net realizable value. This is accomplished by crediting an allowance account, **Allowance for Doubtful Accounts.** Roberts presents accounts receivable on its December 31, 2008, balance sheet as follows:

Allowance for doubtful accounts
A contra-asset account used to reduce accounts receivable to its net realizable value.
Alternate Term: *Allowance for uncollectible accounts*

Accounts receivable	$250,000
Less: Allowance for doubtful accounts	(6,000)
Net accounts receivable	$244,000

WRITE-OFFS OF UNCOLLECTIBLE ACCOUNTS WITH THE ALLOWANCE METHOD

Like the direct write-off method, the allowance method reduces Accounts Receivable to write off a specific customer's account. If the account receivable no longer exists, there is no need for the related allowance account; thus, this account is reduced as well. For example, assume, as we did earlier, that Dexter's $500 account is written off on May 1, 2009. Under the allowance method, the following entry is recorded:

Study Tip

Note the similarities between the Allowance for Doubtful Accounts contra account and another contra account, Accumulated Depreciation. Both are used to reduce an asset account to a lower carrying or book value.

2009			
May 1	Allowance for Doubtful Accounts	500	
	Accounts Receivable—Dexter		500
	To record the write-off of Dexter account.		

Balance Sheet							Income Statement
ASSETS	=	LIABILITIES	+	STOCKHOLDERS' EQUITY	+		REVENUES − EXPENSES
Allowance for Doubtful Accounts 500							
Accounts Receivable—Dexter (500)							

To summarize, whether the direct write-off method or the allowance method is used, the entry to write off a specific customer's account reduces Accounts Receivable. It is the debit that differs between the two methods:

- Under the direct write-off method, an *expense* is increased.
- Under the allowance method, the *allowance* account is reduced.

TWO APPROACHES TO THE ALLOWANCE METHOD OF ACCOUNTING FOR BAD DEBTS

Because the allowance method results in a better matching, accounting standards require the use of it rather than the direct write-off method unless bad debts are immaterial in amount. Accountants use one of two different variations of the allowance method to estimate bad debts. One approach emphasizes matching bad debts expense with revenue on the income statement and bases bad debts on a percentage of the sales of the period. This was the method illustrated earlier for Roberts Corp. The other approach emphasizes the net realizable amount (value) of accounts receivable on the balance sheet and bases bad debts on a percentage of the accounts receivable balance at the end of the period.

Percentage of Net Credit Sales Approach If a company has been in business for enough years, it may be able to use the past relationship between bad debts and net credit sales to predict bad debt amounts. *Net* means that credit sales have been adjusted for sales discounts and returns and allowances. Assume that the accounting records for Bosco Corp. reveal the following:

Year	Net Credit Sales	Bad Debts
2002	$1,250,000	$ 26,400
2003	1,340,000	29,350
2004	1,200,000	23,100
2005	1,650,000	32,150
2006	2,120,000	42,700
	$7,560,000	$153,700

Although the exact percentage varied slightly over the five-year period, the average percentage of bad debts to net credit sales is very close to 2% ($153,700/$7,560,000 = 0.02033). Bosco needs to determine whether this estimate is realistic for the current period. For example, are current economic conditions considerably different from those in prior years? Has the company made sales to any new customers with significantly different credit terms? If the answers to these types of questions are yes, Bosco should consider adjusting the 2% experience rate to estimate future bad debts. Otherwise, it should proceed with this estimate. Assuming that it uses the 2% rate and that its net credit sales during 2007 are $2,340,000, Bosco makes the following entry:

2008			
Dec. 31	Bad Debts Expense	46,800	
	Allowance for Doubtful Accounts		46,800
	To record estimated bad debts: 0.02 × $2,340,000.		

Balance Sheet						Income Statement
ASSETS	=	LIABILITIES	+	STOCKHOLDERS' EQUITY	+	REVENUES − EXPENSES
Allowance for Doubtful Accounts (46,800)						Bad Debts Expense (46,800)

Thus, Bosco matches bad debt expense of $46,800 with sales revenue of $2,340,000.

Percentage of Accounts Receivable Approach Some companies believe that they can more accurately estimate bad debts by relating them to the balance in the Accounts Receivable account at the end of the period rather than to the sales of the period. The objective with both approaches is the same, however: to use past experience with bad debts to predict future amounts. Assume that the records for Cougar Corp. reveal the following:

Year	Balance in Accounts Receivable December 31	Bad Debts
2003	$ 650,000	$ 5,250
2004	785,000	6,230
2005	854,000	6,950
2006	824,000	6,450
2007	925,000	7,450
	$4,038,000	$32,330

The ratio of bad debts to the ending balance in Accounts Receivable over the past five years is $32,330/$4,038,000, or approximately 0.008 (0.8%). Assuming balances in Accounts Receivable and the Allowance for Doubtful Accounts on December 31, 2008, of $865,000 and $2,100, respectively, Cougar records the following entry:

2008			
Dec. 31	Bad Debts Expense	4,820	
	Allowance for Doubtful Accounts		4,820
	To record estimated bad debts.		
	Credit balance required in allowance account after adjustment ($865,000 × 0.8%)	$6,920	
	Less: Credit balance in allowance account before adjustment	2,100	
	Amount for bad debt expense entry	$4,820	

Balance Sheet					Income Statement
ASSETS	=	LIABILITIES	+	STOCKHOLDERS' EQUITY	+ REVENUES − EXPENSES
Allowance for Doubtful Accounts (4,820)					Bad Debts Expense (4,820)

Note the one major difference between this approach and the percentage of sales approach:

- Under the percentage of net credit sales approach, the balance in the allowance account is ignored and the bad debts expense is simply a percentage of the sales of the period.
- Under the percentage of accounts receivable approach, however, the balance in the allowance account must be considered.

The following T account for Allowance for Doubtful Accounts reflects the balance before and after adjustment:

Allowance for Doubtful Accounts	
	2,100 Bal. before adjustment
	4,820 Adjusting entry
	6,920 Bal. after adjustment

In other words, making an adjustment for $4,820 results in a balance in the account of $6,920, which is 0.8% of the Accounts Receivable balance of $865,000. The net realizable value of Accounts Receivable is determined as follows:

Accounts receivable	$865,000
Less: Allowance for doubtful accounts	(6,920)
Net realizable value	$858,080

Aging of Accounts Receivable Some companies use a variation of the percentage of accounts receivable approach to estimate bad debts. This variation is actually a refinement of the approach because it considers the length of time that the receivables have been outstanding. It stands to reason that the older an account receivable is, the less likely it is to be collected. An **aging schedule** categorizes the various accounts by length of time outstanding. An example of an aging schedule is shown in Exhibit 7-1. We assume that the company's policy is to allow 30 days for payment of an outstanding account. After that time, the account is past due. An alphabetical list of customers appears in the first column, with the balance in each account shown in the appropriate column to the right. The dotted lines after A. Matt's account indicate that many more accounts appear in the records; only a few have been included to show the format of the schedule. The totals on the aging schedule are used as the basis for estimating bad debts, as shown in Exhibit 7-2.

Note that the estimated percentage of uncollectibles increases as the period of time the accounts have been outstanding lengthens. If we assume that the Allowance for

Real World Practice

7-2 Reading Apple's Balance Sheet

Refer to the excerpt from **Apple**'s balance sheet in the chapter opener. Compute for each of the two year-ends the amount of accounts receivable before deducting the balance in the allowance account. Did this amount increase or decrease during 2006? Did the allowance account increase or decrease during 2006? What would cause the allowance account to increase or decrease in any one year?

Aging schedule
A form used to categorize the various individual accounts receivable according to the length of time each has been outstanding.

EXHIBIT 7-1 **Aging Schedule**

		Number of Days Past Due			
Customer	**Current**	**1–30**	**31–60**	**61–90**	**Over 90**
L. Ash	$ 4,400				
B. Budd	3,200				
C. Cox		$ 6,500			
E. Fudd					$6,300
G. Hoff			$ 900		
A. Matt	5,500				
......					
......					
......					
T. West		3,100			
M. Young				$ 4,200	
Totals*	$85,600	$31,200	$24,500	$18,000	$9,200

**Only a few of the customer accounts are illustrated; thus, the column totals are higher than the amounts for the accounts illustrated.*

Doubtful Accounts has a balance of $1,230 before adjustment, the adjusting entry is as follows:

2008			
Dec. 31	Bad Debts Expense	13,324	
	Allowance for Doubtful Accounts		13,324
	To record estimated bad debts.		

Credit balance required in allowance account after adjustment	$14,554
Less: Credit balance in allowance account before adjustment	1,230
Amount for bad debt expense entry	$13,324

Balance Sheet					Income Statement
ASSETS	=	**LIABILITIES**	+	**STOCKHOLDERS' EQUITY**	+ **REVENUES – EXPENSES**
Allowance for Doubtful Accounts (13,324)					Bad Debts Expense (13,324)

The net realizable value of accounts receivable would be determined as follows:

Accounts receivable	$168,500
Less: Allowance for doubtful accounts	14,554
Net realizable value	$153,946

EXHIBIT 7-2 **Use of an Aging Schedule to Estimate Bad Debts**

Category	Amount	Estimated Percent Uncollectible	Estimated Amount Uncollectible
Current	$ 85,600	1%	$ 856
Past due:			
1–30 days	31,200	4%	1,248
31–60 days	24,500	10%	2,450
61–60 days	18,000	30%	5,400
Over 90 days	9,200	50%	4,600
Totals	$168,500		$14,554

POD REVIEW 7.1

LO1 ***Show that you understand how to account for accounts receivable, including bad debts.***

- Accounts receivable arise from sales on credit. Companies with many customers may keep detailed records of accounts receivable in a separate subsidiary ledger.
- Because not all customers pay their accounts receivable, an estimate of the accounts receivable less any doubtful accounts must be presented on the balance sheet.
- Bad debts are estimated under the allowance method by one of two approaches:
  - Percentage of net credit sales
  - Percentage of net receivables

QUESTIONS

1. *Why is the allowance method of recognizing bad debts used?*
   a. It results in recognizing the expense of granting credit in the period in which the account is written off.
   b. It results in matching expense with the revenue of the period in which the sale took place.
   c. It results in recognizing the maximum amount of write-off in each period.
   d. The allowance method cannot be justified and therefore is not allowed.
2. *What accounts are debited and credited at the end of the period to recognize bad debts under the allowance method?*
   a. Bad Debts expense is debited, and Accounts Receivable is credited.
   b. Allowance for Doubtful Accounts is debited, and Bad Debts Expense is credited.
   c. Bad Debts Expense is debited, and Allowance for Doubtful Accounts is credited.
   d. None of the above is the correct entry.
3. *Which of the two approaches to recognizing bad debts considers any existing balance in the Allowance for Doubtful Accounts account?*
   a. percentage of sales approach
   b. percentage of accounts receivable approach
   c. both the percentage of sales approach and the percentage of accounts receivable approach
   d. Neither method takes into account any existing balance in the Allowance for Doubtful Accounts account.

The Accounts Receivable Turnover Ratio

LO2 Explain how information about sales and receivables can be combined to evaluate how efficient a company is in collecting its receivables.

Managers, investors, and creditors are keenly interested in how well a company manages its accounts receivable. One simple measure is to compare a company's sales to its accounts receivable. The result is the accounts receivable turnover ratio:

$$\text{Accounts Receivable Turnover} = \frac{\text{Net Credit Sales}}{\text{Average Accounts Receivable}}$$

Typically, the faster the turnover is, the better. For example, if a company has sales of $10 million and an average accounts receivable of $1 million, it turns over its accounts receivable ten times per year. If we assume 360 days in a year, that is once every 36 days. An observer would compare that figure with historical figures to see if the company is experiencing slower or faster collections. A comparison also could be made to other companies in the same industry. If receivables are turning over too slowly, the company's credit department may not be operating effectively; therefore, the company is missing opportunities with the cash that isn't available. On the other hand, a turnover rate that is too fast might mean that the company's credit policies are too stringent and that sales are being lost as a result.

USING THE RATIO DECISION MODEL: ANALYZING THE ACCOUNTS RECEIVABLE RATE OF COLLECTION

Use the following Ratio Decision Model to evaluate the accounts receivable rate of collection of Apple or any public company:

1. Formulate the Question

Managers, investors, and creditors are interested in how well a company manages its accounts receivable. Each dollar of sales on credit produces a dollar of accounts receivable. And the quicker each dollar of accounts receivable can be collected, the sooner the money will be available for other purposes. *So how quickly is a company such as Apple able to collect its accounts receivable?*

2. Gather the Information from the Financial Statements

Recall from earlier chapters that sales are recorded on an income statement, representing a *flow* for a period of time. Accounts receivable, an asset, represents a *balance* at a point in time. Thus, a comparison of the two requires the amount of net credit sales for the year and an average of the balance in accounts receivable:

- Net credit sales: From the income statement for the year
- Average accounts receivable: From the beginning and ending balance sheets

3. Calculate the Ratio

$$\textbf{Accounts Receivable Turnover} = \frac{\textbf{Net Credit Sales}}{\textbf{Average Accounts Receivable}}$$

Apple's Consolidated Statements of Operations (Partial)
(In millions, except share and per share amounts)

Three fiscal years ended September 30, 2006	2006	2005 (As Restated)	2004 (As Restated)
Net sales	$19,315	$13,931	$8,279
Cost of sales	13,717	9,889	6,022
Gross margin	$ 5,598	$ 4,042	$2,257

Apple's Consolidated Balance Sheets (Partial)
(in millions)

	September 30, 2006	September 24, 2005 (As Restated)
ASSETS		
Current assets:		
Cash and cash equivalents	$6,392	$3,491
Short-term investments	3,718	4,770
Accounts receivable, less allowances of $52 and $46, respectively	1,252	895

$$\text{Accounts Receivable Turnover} = \frac{\$19{,}315^*}{\$1{,}073.5} = 18.0 \text{ times}$$

**Assuming all sales are on credit.*

Average accounts receivable less allowances = ($1,252 + $895)/2 = $1,073.5

4. Compare the Ratio with Others

Management compares the current year's turnover rate with that of prior years to see if the company is experiencing slower or faster collections. It is also important to compare the rate with that of other companies in the same industry:

Apple Computer		Hewlett-Packard	
Year Ended September 30, 2006	**Year Ended September 24, 2005**	**Year Ended October 31, 2006**	**Year Ended October 31, 2005**
18.0 times	19.1 times	8.8 times	8.6 times

5. Interpret the Results

Typically, the more times a company turns over its receivables each year, the better. Apple's turnover decreased slightly, from 19.1 times in 2005 to 18.0 times in 2006. If we assume 360 days in a year, a turnover of 18 times means receivables are collected on average every 20 days (360/18). Apple's turnover is faster than Hewlett Packard's, resulting in fewer days to collect receivables.

POD REVIEW 7.2

LO2 *Explain how information about sales and receivables can be combined to evaluate how efficient a company is in collecting its receivables.*

- Information about net credit sales and the average accounts receivable balance may be combined to calculate the accounts receivables turnover to see how well a company is managing its collections on account.

QUESTIONS

1. *The amounts needed to compute the accounts receivable turnover ratio can be found on*
   a. the balance sheet only.
   b. the income statement only.
   c. both the balance sheet and the income statement.
   d. the statement of cash flows.

2. *Oak Corp. had sales during the year of $10,000,000 and an average accounts receivable of $2,000,000. Its accounts receivable turnover ratio is*
   a. 5 times.
   b. 0.2 times.
   c. 10 times.
   d. none of the above.

© Justin Sullivan/Getty Images

Hot Topics

A Record-Setting Quarter

For Apple, the three months ending on June 30, 2007, set a record for the third quarter of its fiscal year. The company reported revenues of $5.41 billion compared to $4.37 billion for the quarter ending on June 30, 2006. Similarly, net income for the most recent three months was $818 million, well above the $472 million reported in the same quarter of the prior year. And to what did Apple attribute these results? For starters, the company shipped more Macs in the quarter than it had in any other three-month period in its history. Sales of its popular iPods remained strong. And to add to the buzz, the iPhone made its long-awaited debut in late June 2007. Macs, iPods, and iPhones—they all did their part to make the third quarter of 2007 a memorable one for Apple.

Source: http://www.apple.com.

Notes Receivable

LO3 Show that you understand how to account for interest-bearing notes receivable.

Promissory note
A written promise to repay a definite sum of money on demand or at a fixed or determinable date in the future.

Maker
The party that agrees to repay the money for a promissory note at some future date.

Payee
The party that will receive the money from a promissory note at some future date.

Note receivable
An asset resulting from the acceptance of a promissory note from another company.

Note payable
A liability resulting from the signing of a promissory note.

A promissory note is a written promise to repay a definite sum of money on demand or at a fixed or determinable date in the future. Promissory notes normally require the payment of interest for the use of someone else's money. The party that agrees to repay money is the **maker** of the note, and the party that receives money in the future is the **payee**. A company that holds a promissory note received from another company has an asset, called a **note receivable**; the company that makes or gives a promissory note to another company has a liability, a **note payable**. Over the life of the note, the maker incurs interest expense on its note payable and the payee earns interest revenue on its note receivable. The following summarizes this relationship:

Party	Recognizes on Balance Sheet	Recognizes on Income Statement
Maker	Note payable	Interest expense
Payee	Note receivable	Interest revenue

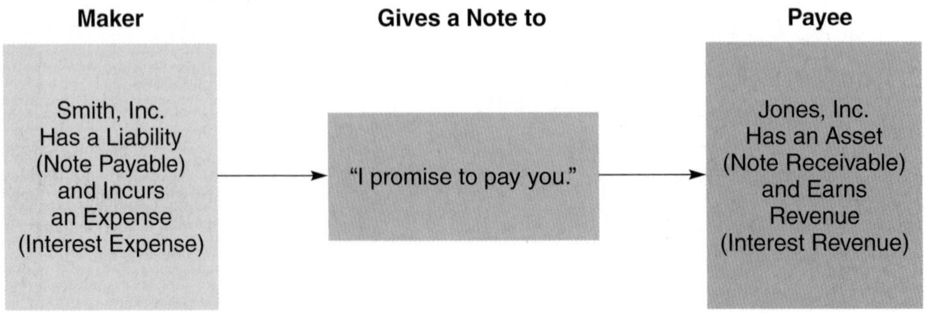

Promissory notes are used for a variety of purposes. Banks normally require a company to sign a promissory note to borrow money. Promissory notes are often used in the sale of consumer durables with relatively high purchase prices, such as appliances and automobiles. At times, a promissory note is issued to replace an existing overdue account receivable.

IMPORTANT TERMS CONNECTED WITH PROMISSORY NOTES

It is important to understand the following terms when dealing with promissory notes:

Principal—the amount of cash received, or the fair value of the products or services received, by the maker when a promissory note is issued.

Maturity date—the date the promissory note is due.

Term—the length of time a note is outstanding, that is, the period of time between the date it is issued and the date it matures.

Maturity value—the amount of cash the maker is to pay the payee on the maturity date of the note.

Interest—the difference between the principal amount of the note and its maturity value.

Key terms for promissory notes
These terms, with their definitions in the text, are important for your understanding.

Assume that on December 13, 2008, HighTec sells a computer to Baker Corp. at an invoice price of $15,000. Because Baker is short of cash, it gives HighTec a 90-day, 12% promissory note. The total amount of interest due on the maturity date is determined as follows:

$$\$15{,}000 \times 0.12 \times 90/360 = \underline{\underline{\$450}}$$

The entry to record receipt of the note by HighTec is as follows:

2008			
Dec. 13	Notes Receivable	15,000	
	Sales Revenue		15,000
	To record sale of computer in exchange for promissory note.		

Balance Sheet						Income Statement
ASSETS	=	**LIABILITIES**	+	**STOCKHOLDERS' EQUITY**	+	**REVENUES − EXPENSES**
Notes Receivable 15,000						Sales Revenue 15,000

If we assume that December 31 is the end of HighTec's accounting year, an adjustment is needed to recognize interest earned but not yet received. It is required when a company uses the accrual basis of accounting. The question is, how many days of interest have been earned during December? It is normal practice to count the day a note matures but not the day it is signed in computing interest. Thus, in the example, interest would be earned for 18 days (December 14 to December 31) during 2008 and for 72 days in 2009:

Month	Number of Days Outstanding
December 2008	18 days
January 2009	31 days
February 2009	28 days
March 2009	13 days (matures on March 13, 2009)
Total days	90 days

Thus, the amount of interest earned during 2008 is $\$15{,}000 \times 0.12 \times 18/360$, or $90. An adjusting entry is made on December 31 to record interest earned during 2008:

2008			
Dec. 31	Interest Receivable	90	
	Interest Revenue		90
	To record interest earned: $\$15{,}000 \times 0.12 \times 18/360$.		

Balance Sheet						Income Statement
ASSETS	=	**LIABILITIES**	+	**STOCKHOLDERS' EQUITY**	+	**REVENUES − EXPENSES**
Interest Receivable 90						Interest Revenue 90

On March 13, 2009, HighTec collects the principal amount of the note and interest from Baker and records this entry:

2009			
Mar. 13	Cash	15,450	
	Notes Receivable		15,000
	Interest Revenue		360
	Interest Receivable		90
	To record collection of promissory note.		

Balance Sheet: ASSETS		=	LIABILITIES	+	STOCKHOLDERS' EQUITY	+	Income Statement: REVENUES − EXPENSES	
Cash	15,450						Interest Revenue	360
Notes Receivable	(15,000)							
Interest Receivable	(90)							

This entry accomplishes a number of purposes. First, it removes the amount of $15,000 originally recorded in the Notes Receivable account. Second, it increases Interest Revenue for the interest earned during the 72 days in 2009 that the note was outstanding. The calculation of interest earned during 2009 is as follows:

$$\$15,000 \times 0.12 \times 72/360 = \$360$$

Third, the entry decreases Interest Receivable by $90 to remove this account from the records now that the note has been collected. Finally, it increases Cash by $15,450, which represents the principal amount of the note, $15,000, plus interest of $450 for 90 days.

POD REVIEW 7.3

LO3 *Show that you understand how to account for interest-bearing notes receivable.*

- Notes receivable ultimately result in the receipt of both interest and principal to the holder of the notes.
- Because interest receipts may not coincide with the end of the period, adjusting entries may need to be made to accrue interest receivable and interest revenue.

QUESTIONS

1. *Maple Corp. borrows $10,000 at a local bank. Maple will recognize the following accounts:*
   a. notes payable and interest revenue
   b. notes receivable and interest revenue
   c. notes payable and interest expense
   d. notes receivable and interest expense

2. *Elm Inc. borrows $50,000 on a 120-day, 12% promissory note. The total interest that Elm will repay at maturity is*
   a. $500.
   b. $2,000.
   c. $6,000.
   d. none of the above.

Accelerating the Inflow of Cash from Sales

LO4 Explain various techniques that companies use to accelerate the inflow of cash from sales.

Earlier in the chapter we pointed out why cash sales are preferable to credit sales: credit sales slow down the inflow of cash to the company and create the potential for bad debts. To remain competitive, most businesses find it necessary to grant credit to customers. That is, if one company won't grant credit to a customer, the customer may find another company that will. Companies have found it possible, however, to circumvent the problems inherent in credit sales. We now consider some approaches that companies use to speed up the flow of cash from sales.

CREDIT CARD SALES

Most retail establishments as well as many service businesses accept one or more major credit cards. Among the most common cards are MasterCard®, VISA®, American Express®, Carte Blanche®, Discover Card®, and Diners Club®. Most merchants find that they must honor at least one or more of these credit cards to remain competitive. In return for a fee, the merchant passes the responsibility for collection on to the credit card company. Thus, the credit card issuer assumes the risk of nonpayment. The basic relationships among the three parties—the customer, the merchant, and the credit company—are illustrated in Exhibit 7-3. Assume that Joe Smith buys an iPod in an Apple store and charges the $200 cost to his VISA credit card. When Joe is presented with his bill, he is asked to sign a multiple-copy **credit card draft**, or invoice. Joe keeps one copy of the draft and leaves the other two copies at the Apple store. The store keeps one copy as the basis for recording its sales of the day and sends the other copy to VISA for payment. VISA uses the copy of the draft it gets for two purposes: to reimburse Apple $190 (keeping $10, or 5% of the original sale, as a collection fee) and to include Joe Smith's $200 purchase on the monthly bill it mails him.

Credit card draft
A multiple-copy document used by a company that accepts a credit card for a sale. ***Alternate term:*** *Invoice.*

Assume that total credit card sales on June 5 amount to $8,000. The entry on Apple's books on that day is as follows:

June 5	Accounts Receivable—VISA	8,000	
	Sales Revenue		8,000
	To record daily credit card sales.		

Balance Sheet							Income Statement	
ASSETS		=	LIABILITIES	+	STOCKHOLDERS' EQUITY	+	REVENUES − EXPENSES	
Accounts Receivable—VISA	8,000						Sales Revenue	8,000

EXHIBIT 7-3 Basic Relationships among Parties with Credit Card Sales

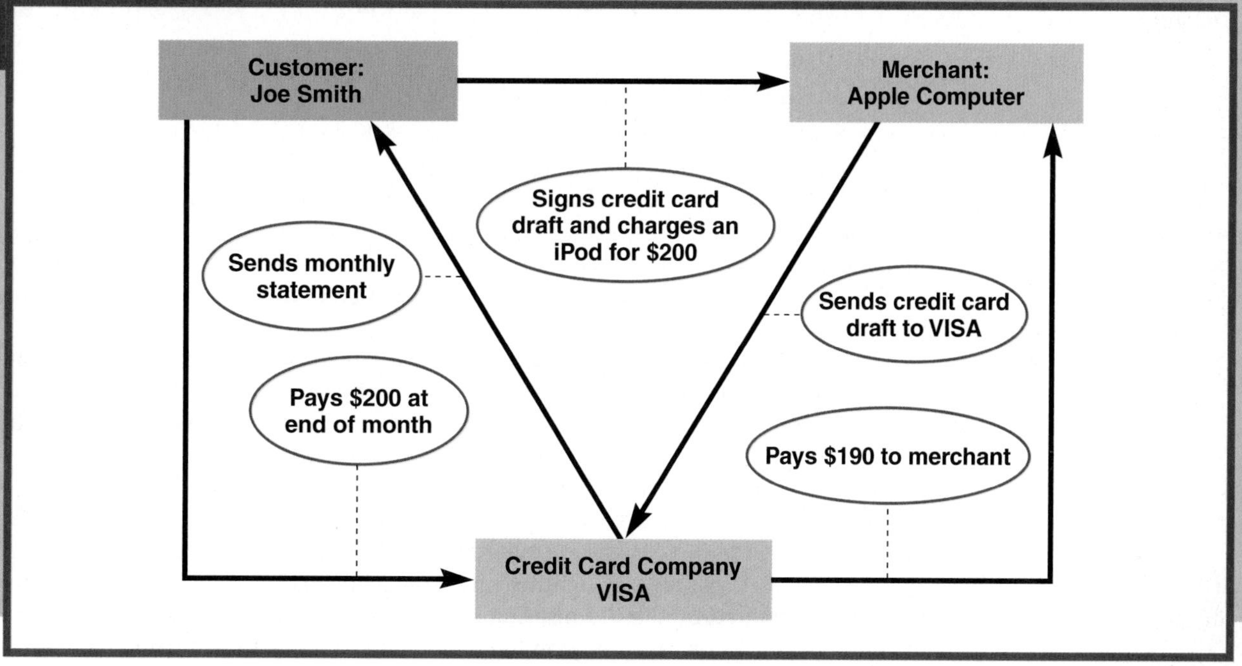

Assume that Apple remits the credit card draft to VISA once a week and that the total sales for the week ending June 11 amount to $50,000. Further assume that on June 13, VISA pays the amount due to Apple after deducting a 5% collection fee. The entry on Apple's books is as follows:

June 13	Cash	47,500	
	Collection Fee Expense	2,500	
	Accounts Receivable—VISA		50,000
	To record weekly receipts from credit card company.		

Balance Sheet							Income Statement	
ASSETS		=	**LIABILITIES**	+	**STOCKHOLDERS' EQUITY**	+	**REVENUES − EXPENSES**	
Cash	47,500						Collection Fee Expense	(2,500)
Accounts Receivable—VISA	(50,000)							

Some credit cards, such as MasterCard and VISA, allow a merchant to present a credit card draft directly for deposit in a bank account, in much the same way the merchant deposits checks, coins, and currency. Obviously, this type of arrangement is even more advantageous for the merchant because the funds are available as soon as the drafts are credited to the bank account. Assume that on July 9, Apple presents VISA credit card drafts to its bank for payment in the amount of $20,000 and that the collection charge is 4%. The entry on its books on the date of deposit is as follows:

July 9	Cash	19,200	
	Collection Fee Expense	800	
	Sales Revenue		20,000
	To record credit card sales.		

Balance Sheet							Income Statement	
ASSETS		=	**LIABILITIES**	+	**STOCKHOLDERS' EQUITY**	+	**REVENUES − EXPENSES**	
Cash	19,200						Collection Fee Expense	(800)
							Sales Revenue	20,000

DISCOUNTING NOTES RECEIVABLE

Discounting
The process of selling a promissory note.

Promissory notes are negotiable, which means that they can be endorsed and given to someone else for collection. In other words, a company can sign the back of a note (just as it would a check), sell it to a bank, and receive cash before the note's maturity date. This process, called **discounting**, is another way for companies to speed the collection of cash from receivables. A note can be sold immediately to a bank on the date it is issued, or it can be sold after it has been outstanding but before the due date.

When a note is discounted at a bank, it is normally done "with recourse." This means that if the original customer fails to pay the bank the total amount due on the maturity date of the note, the company that transferred the note to the bank is liable for the full amount. Because there is uncertainty as to whether the company will have to make good on any particular note that it discounts at the bank, a contingent liability exists from the time the note is discounted until its maturity date. The accounting profession has adopted guidelines to decide whether a particular uncertainty requires that the company record a contingent liability on its balance sheet. Under these guidelines, the contingency created by the discounting of a note with recourse is not recorded as a liability. However, a note in the financial statements is used to inform the reader of the existing uncertainty.

POD REVIEW 7.4

LO4 *Explain various techniques that companies use to accelerate the inflow of cash from sales.*

- To be competitive, companies must make sales on credit to customers.
- One way to avoid bad debts associated with extending credit directly to the customer and to accelerate cash collections from sales is to accept credit cards for payment of goods and services.

QUESTIONS

1. *Boston makes $20,000 of credit card sales during the week and is charged 5% by the credit card company. Boston will record sales revenue of*
   a. $10,000.
   b. $19,000.
   c. $20,000.
   d. none of the above.

2. *When a company discounts a promissory note at the bank*
   a. it receives cash later than it would if it held the note to maturity.
   b. it receives cash sooner than it would if it held the note to maturity.
   c. it receives cash at the same time it would if it held the note to maturity.
   d. Discounting is not allowed as a standard practice.

Accounting for Investments

LO5 Show that you understand the accounting for and disclosure of various types of investments that companies make.

The investments that companies make take a variety of forms and are made for various reasons. Some corporations find themselves with excess cash during certain times of the year and invest this idle cash in various highly liquid financial instruments, such as certificates of deposit and money market funds. Chapter 6 pointed out that these investments are included with cash and are called cash equivalents when they have an original maturity to the investor of three months or less. Otherwise, they are accounted for as short-term investments.

In addition to investments in highly liquid financial instruments, some companies invest in the stocks and bonds of other corporations as well as bonds issued by various government agencies. Securities issued by corporations as a form of ownership in the business, such as common stock and preferred stock, are called **equity securities**. Because these securities are a form of ownership, they do not have a maturity date. As we will see later, investments in equity securities can be classified as either current or long-term depending on the company's intent. Alternatively, securities issued by corporations and governmental bodies as a form of borrowing are called **debt securities** and often take the form of bonds. The term of a bond can be relatively short, such as five years, or much longer, such as 20 or 30 years. Regardless of the term, classification as a current or noncurrent asset by the investor depends on whether it plans to sell or redeem the debt securities within the next year.

Equity securities Securities issued by corporations as a form of ownership in the business. ***Alternate term:*** *Stocks.*

Debt securities Securities issued by corporations and governmental bodies as a form of borrowing. ***Alternate term:*** *Bonds.*

INVESTMENTS IN HIGHLY LIQUID FINANCIAL INSTRUMENTS

We now turn to the appropriate accounting for these various types of investments. We begin by considering the accounting for highly liquid financial instruments such as certificates of deposit and then turn to the accounting for investments in the stocks and bonds of other companies.

Investing Idle Cash The seasonal nature of most businesses leads to a potential cash shortage during certain times of the year and an excess of cash during other times. Companies typically deal with cash shortages by borrowing on a short-term basis either from a bank in the form of notes or from other entities in the form of commercial paper. The maturities of the bank notes or the commercial paper generally range anywhere from 30 days to six months. These same companies use various financial instruments as a way to invest excess cash during other times of the year. We will present the accounting for the most common type of highly liquid financial instrument, a certificate of deposit (CD).

Accounting for an Investment in a Certificate of Deposit (CD) Assume that on October 2, 2008, Creston Corp. invests $100,000 of excess cash in a 120-day CD. The CD matures on January 30, 2009, at which time Creston receives the $100,000 invested and interest at an annual rate of 6%. The entry to record the purchase of the CD is as follows:

2008			
Oct. 2	Short-Term Investments—CD	100,000	
	Cash		100,000
	To record purchase of 6%, 120-day CD.		

Balance Sheet							Income Statement
ASSETS		=	**LIABILITIES**	+	**STOCKHOLDERS' EQUITY**	+	**REVENUES − EXPENSES**
Short-Term Investments—CD	100,000						
Cash	(100,000)						

Assuming December 31 is the end of Creston's fiscal year, an entry is needed on this date to record interest earned during 2008 even though no cash will be received until the CD matures in 2009:

2008			
Dec. 31	Interest Receivable	1,500	
	Interest Revenue		1,500
	To record interest earned: $100,000 × 0.06 × 90/360.		

Balance Sheet							Income Statement	
ASSETS		=	**LIABILITIES**	+	**STOCKHOLDERS' EQUITY**	+	**REVENUES − EXPENSES**	
Interest Receivable	1,500						Interest Revenue	1,500

The basic formula to compute interest is as follows:

$$\text{Interest (I)} = \text{Principal (P)} \times \text{Interest Rate (R)} \times \text{Time (T)}$$

Because interest rates are normally stated on an annual basis, time is interpreted to mean the fraction of a year that the investment is outstanding. The amount of interest is based on the principal or amount invested ($100,000) times the rate of interest (6%) times the fraction of a year the CD was outstanding in 2008 (29 days in October + 30 days in November + 31 days in December = 90 days). To simplify interest calculations, it is easiest to assume 360 days in a year. With the availability of computers to do the work, however, most businesses now use 365 days in a year to calculate interest. Throughout this book, we assume 360 days in a year to allow us to focus on concepts rather than detailed calculations. Thus, in the example, the fraction of a year that the CD is outstanding during 2008 is 90/360.

The entry on January 30 to record the receipt of the principal amount of the CD of $100,000 and interest for 120 days is as follows:

2009			
Jan. 30	Cash	102,000	
	Short-Term Investments—CD		100,000
	Interest Receivable		1,500
	Interest Revenue		500
	To record the maturity of the $100,000 CD.		

Balance Sheet							Income Statement	
ASSETS		=	**LIABILITIES**	+	**STOCKHOLDERS' EQUITY**	+	**REVENUES − EXPENSES**	
Cash	102,000						Interest Revenue	500
Short-Term Investment—CD	(100,000)							
Interest Receivable	(1,500)							

This combination journal entry removes both the CD and the interest receivable from the records and recognizes $500 in interest earned during the first 30 days of 2009: $\$100{,}000 \times 0.06 \times 30/360 = \$500$. Exhibit 7-4 summarizes the calculation of interest in each of the two accounting periods.

INVESTMENTS IN STOCKS AND BONDS

Corporations frequently invest in the securities of other businesses. As mentioned earlier, these investments take two forms: debt securities (bonds) and equity securities (stocks).

No Significant Influence Corporations have varying motivations for investing in the stocks and bonds of other companies. We will refer to the company that invests as the *investor* and the company whose stocks or bonds are purchased as the *investee*.

EXHIBIT 7-4 Interest Calculation

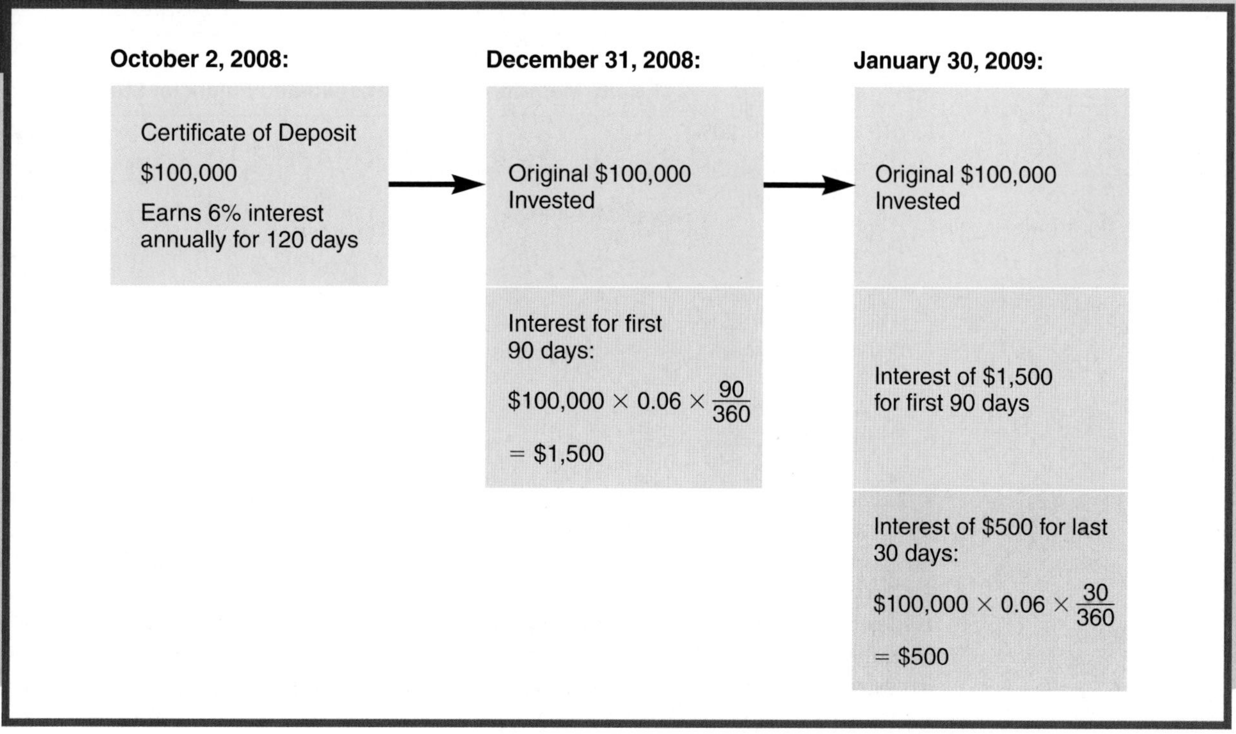

In addition to buying certificates of deposit and other financial instruments, companies invest excess funds in stocks and bonds over the short run. For example, Apple invests primarily in bonds of other companies. The seasonality of certain businesses may result in otherwise idle cash being available during certain times of the year. In other cases, stocks and bonds are purchased as a way to invest cash over the long run. Often these types of investments are made in anticipation of a need for cash at some distant point in the future. For example, a company may invest today in a combination of stocks and bonds because it will need cash 10 years from now to build a new plant. The investor may be interested primarily in periodic income in the form of interest and dividends, in appreciation in the value of the securities, or in some combination of the two.

Significant Influence Sometimes shares of stock in another company are bought with a different purpose in mind. If a company buys a relatively large percentage of the common stock of the investee, it may be able to secure significant influence over the policies of this company. For example, a company might buy 30% of the common stock of a supplier of its raw materials to ensure a steady source of inventory. When an investor is able to secure influence over the investee, the equity method of accounting is used. According to current accounting standards, this method is appropriate when an investor owns at least 20% of the common stock of the investee.

Control Finally, a corporation may buy stock in another company with the purpose of obtaining control over that other entity. Normally, this requires an investment in excess of 50% of the common stock of the investee. When an investor owns more than half the stock of another company, accountants normally prepare a set of consolidated financial statements. This involves combining the financial statements of the individual entities into a single set of statements. An investor with an interest of more than 50% in another company is called the parent, and the investee in these situations is called the subsidiary.

The remainder of this section will discuss how companies account for investments that do not give them any significant influence over the other company. (Accounting for investments in which there is either significant influence or control is covered in advanced accounting textbooks.) The following chart summarizes the accounting by an investor for investments in the common stock of another company:

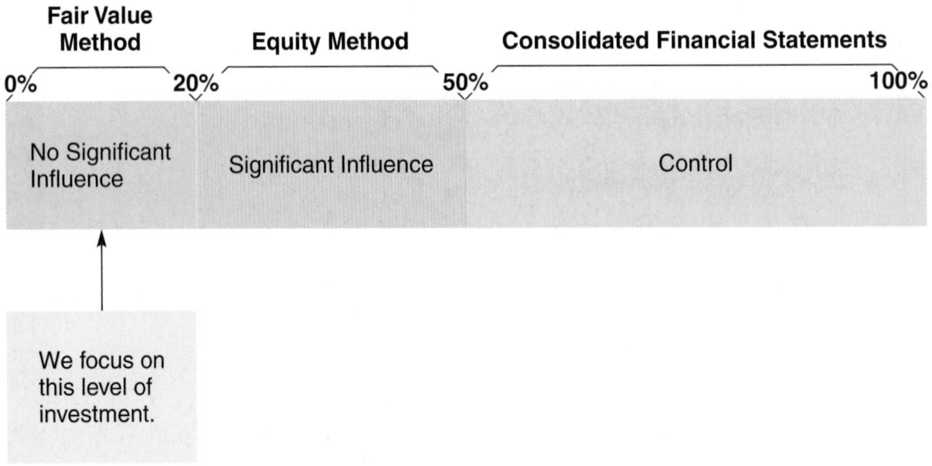

Investments in Bonds Consider the following example. On January 1, 2008, ABC issues $10,000,000 of bonds that will mature in ten years. Assume that Atlantic buys $100,000 of these bonds at face value, which is the amount that will be repaid to the investor when the bonds mature. In many instances, bonds are purchased at an amount more or less than face value. However, the discussion here will be limited to the simpler case in which bonds are purchased for face value. The bonds pay 10% interest semiannually on June 30 and December 31. This means that Atlantic will receive 5% of $100,000, or $5,000, on each of those dates. The entry on Atlantic's books to record the purchase is as follows:

2008			
Jan. 1	Investment in Bonds	100,000	
	Cash		100,000
	To record purchase of ABC bonds.		

Balance Sheet					Income Statement	
ASSETS		= **LIABILITIES**	+ **STOCKHOLDERS' EQUITY**	+	**REVENUES – EXPENSES**	
Investment in Bonds	100,000					
Cash	(100,000)					

On June 30, Atlantic must record the receipt of semiannual interest. The entry on this date is as follows:

2008			
June 30	Cash	5,000	
	Interest Revenue		5,000
	To record interest income on ABC bonds.		

Balance Sheet					Income Statement	
ASSETS		= **LIABILITIES**	+ **STOCKHOLDERS' EQUITY**	+	**REVENUES – EXPENSES**	
Cash	5,000				Interest Revenue	5,000

Note that income was recognized when interest was received. If interest is not received at the end of an accounting period, a company should accrue interest earned but not yet received.

Assume that before the maturity date, Atlantic needs cash and decides to sell the bonds. Any difference between the proceeds received from the sale of the bonds and the amount paid for the bonds is recognized as either a gain or a loss. For example, assume that on July 1, 2008, Atlantic sells all of its ABC bonds at 99. This means that the amount of cash received is $0.99 \times \$100,000$, or $99,000. The entry on July 1, 2008, is as follows:

2008			
July 1	Cash	99,000	
	Loss on Sale of Bonds	1,000	
	Investment in Bonds		100,000
	To record sale of ABC bonds.		

Balance Sheet					Income Statement	
ASSETS		= **LIABILITIES**	+ **STOCKHOLDERS' EQUITY**	+	**REVENUES – EXPENSES**	
Cash	99,000				Loss on Sale of Bonds	(1,000)
Investment in Bonds	(100,000)					

The $1,000 loss on the sale of the bonds is the excess of the amount paid for the purchase of the bonds of $100,000 over the cash proceeds from the sale of $99,000. The loss is reported in the Other Income and Expenses section on the 2008 income statement.

Investments in Stocks All investments in stock are recorded initially at cost, including any brokerage fees, commissions, or other fees paid to acquire the shares. Assume that on February 1, 2008, Dexter Corp. pays $50,000 for shares of Stuart common stock and another $1,000 in commissions.

The entry on Dexter's books on the date of purchase is as follows:

2008			
Feb. 1	Investment in Stuart Common Stock	51,000	
	Cash		51,000
	To record purchase of common stock for cash.		

Balance Sheet							Income Statement
ASSETS		=	**LIABILITIES**	+	**STOCKHOLDERS' EQUITY**	+	**REVENUES – EXPENSES**
Investment in Stuart Common Stock	51,000						
Cash	(51,000)						

Many companies attempt to pay dividends every year as a signal of overall financial strength and profitability.[1] Assume that on March 31, 2008, Dexter received dividends of $500 from Stuart. The dividends received are recognized as income, as shown in the following entry on Dexter's books:

2008			
March 31	Cash	500	
	Dividend Income		500
	To record receipt of dividends on common stock.		

Balance Sheet							Income Statement	
ASSETS		=	**LIABILITIES**	+	**STOCKHOLDERS' EQUITY**	+	**REVENUES – EXPENSES**	
Cash	500						Dividend Income	500

Unlike interest on a bond or note, dividends do not accrue over time. In fact, a company has no legal obligation to pay dividends until its board of directors declares them. Up to that point, the investor has no guarantee that dividends will ever be paid.

Assume that Dexter sells the Stuart stock on May 20, 2008, for $53,000. In this case, Dexter recognizes a gain for the excess of the cash proceeds, $53,000, over the amount recorded on the books, $51,000.

2008			
May 20	Cash	53,000	
	Investment in Stuart Common Stock		51,000
	Gain on Sale of Stock		2,000
	To record sale of Stuart common stock.		

Balance Sheet							Income Statement	
ASSETS		=	**LIABILITIES**	+	**STOCKHOLDERS' EQUITY**	+	**REVENUES – EXPENSES**	
Cash	53,000						Gain on Sale of Stock	2,000
Investment in Stuart Common Stock	(51,000)							

The gain is classified on the income statement as other income.

VALUATION AND REPORTING FOR INVESTMENTS ON THE FINANCIAL STATEMENTS

Investments in the bonds and stocks of other companies are reported on a company's balance sheet as assets. Whether the investments are reported as current assets or noncurrent assets depends on the company's intent. That is, if the company intends to sell the investments within the next year, they are normally classified as current assets. All other investments are classified on the balance sheet as noncurrent.

1 IBM's September 2007 dividend continued a string of consecutive quarterly dividends that started in 1916.

In addition to the question of where investments are reported at the end of the period, another issue is their valuation. For example, you know that accounts receivable are reported at net realizable value. How should an investment in the bonds or stock of another company be reported on a year-end balance sheet? Two possibilities exist. First, investments could be reported at their cost. Or because most investments in the bonds and stocks of other companies are actively traded, they could be reported at their market, or fair, value. As a general rule, investments are reported on the balance sheet at their fair value. However, the question still remains as to when any gains or losses from recognizing the changes in the fair value of investments should be recorded on the income statement. The accounting rules in this area are somewhat complex; and for that reason, they are usually covered in advanced accounting courses.

POD REVIEW 7.5

LO5 *Show that you understand the accounting for and disclosure of various types of investments that companies make.*

- Typically, excess cash expected to last for short periods of time is invested in highly liquid financial instruments, such as CDs.
- Sometimes cash is invested in securities of other corporations:
  - Equity securities—securities issued by corporations as a form of ownership in the business.
  - Debt securities—securities issued by corporation as a form of borrowing.
- At times, a company may want to purchase a relatively large portion of another firm's stock to acquire influence over that firm.

QUESTIONS

1. *A company invests excess cash in a certificate of deposit. At the end of an accounting period before the CD matures, the company will recognize*
   a. interest expense.
   b. interest revenue.
   c. the receipt of cash.
   d. none of the above.

2. *Baxter pays $15,000 to buy stock in another company and an additional $400 in commissions. Three months later Baxter sells the stock for $16,000. At the time of sale, Baxter will recognize a*
   a. gain of $1,000.
   b. loss of $1,000.
   c. gain of $600.
   d. loss of $600.

How Liquid Assets Affect the Statement of Cash Flows

LO6 Explain the effects of transactions involving liquid assets on the statement of cash flows.

As was discussed in Chapter 6, cash equivalents are combined with cash on the balance sheet. These items are very near maturity and do not present any significant risk of collectibility. Because of this, any purchases or redemptions of cash equivalents are not considered significant activities to be reported on a statement of cash flows.

The purchase and sale of investments are considered significant activities and therefore are reported on the statement of cash flows. Cash flows from purchases, sales, and maturities of investments are usually classified as investing activities. The following excerpt from **Apple**'s 2006 statement of cash flows illustrates the reporting for these activities (all amounts in millions of dollars):

Investing Activities	2006	2005 (Restated)	2004 (Restated)
Purchases of short-term investments	(7,255)	(11,470)	(3,270)
Proceeds from maturities of short-term investments	7,226	8,609	1,141
Proceeds from sales of investments	1,086	586	806
Purchases of long-term investments	(25)	—	—

The collection of either accounts receivable or notes receivable generates cash for a business and affects the operating activities section of the statement of cash flows. Most companies use the indirect method of reporting cash flows and begin the statement of cash flows with the net income of the period. Net income includes the sales revenue for the period. Therefore, a decrease in accounts receivable or notes receivable during the period indicates that the company collected more cash than it recorded in sales revenue. Thus, a decrease in accounts receivable or notes receivable must be added back to net income because more cash was collected than is reflected in the sales revenue number. Alternatively, an increase in accounts receivable or notes receivable indicates that the company recorded more sales revenue than cash collected during the period. Therefore, an increase in accounts receivable or notes receivable requires deduction from the net income of the period to arrive at cash flow from operating activities. The following excerpt from Apple's 2006 statement of cash flows illustrates how it reports the change in accounts receivable on its statement of cash flows (all amounts in millions of dollars):

Operating Activities	2006	2005 (Restated)	2004 (Restated)
Changes in operating assets and liabilities:			
Accounts receivable	(357)	(121)	(8)

These adjustments as well as the cash flows from buying and selling investments are summarized in Exhibit 7-5. A complete discussion of the statement of cash flows, including the reporting of investments, will be presented in Chapter 12.

EXHIBIT 7-5 **How Investments and Receivables Affect the Statement of Cash Flows**

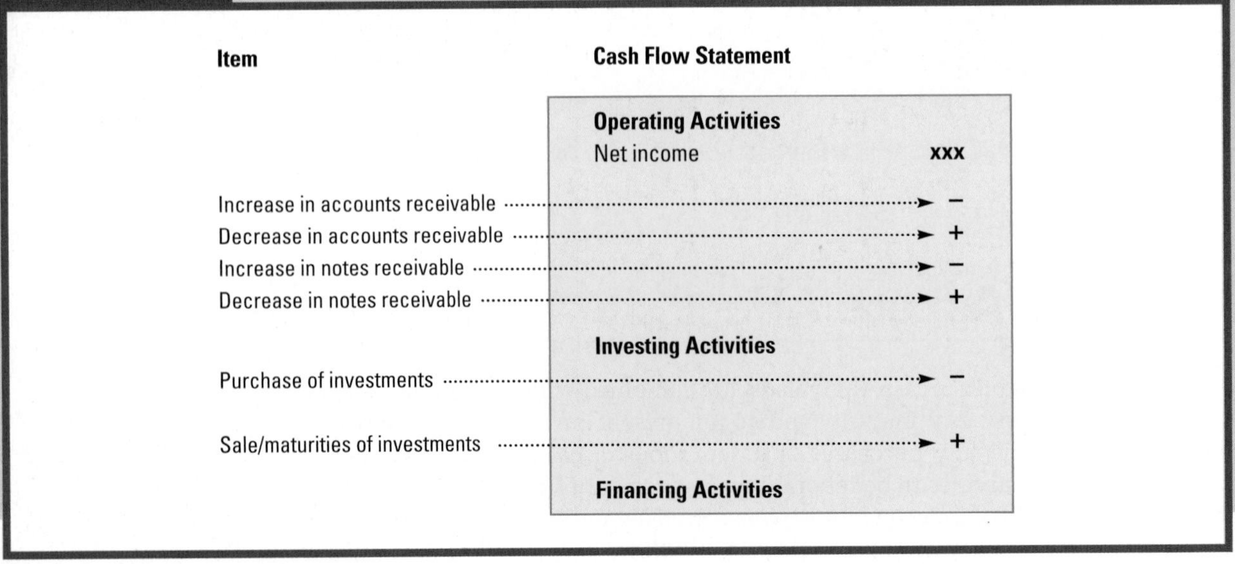

POD REVIEW 7.6

LO6 *Explain the effects of transactions involving liquid assets on the statement of cash flows.*

- Changes in cash equivalents are not shown on the statement.
- Cash flows related to the purchase and sale of investments are classified as Investing Activities in the statement of cash flows.
- Under the indirect method, increases in accounts and notes receivable are deducted and decreases in these accounts are added back in the Operating Activities section of the statement.

QUESTIONS

1. *How should an increase in accounts receivable be reported on the statement of cash flows using the indirect method?*
   a. as an addition
   b. as a deduction
   c. It depends on the amount of the increase.
   d. Changes in accounts receivable balances are not reported on the statement of cash flows.

2. *How should a decrease in notes receivable be reported on the statement of cash flows using the indirect method?*
   a. as an addition
   b. as a deduction
   c. It depends on the amount of the increase.
   d. Changes in notes receivable balances are not reported on the statement of cash flows.

RATIO REVIEW

$$\text{Accounts Receivable Turnover} = \frac{\text{Net Credit Sales (Income Statement)}}{\text{Average Accounts Receivable (Balance Sheet)}}$$

ACCOUNTS HIGHLIGHTED

Account Titles	Where It Appears	In What Section	Page Number
Accounts receivable	Balance Sheet	Current Assets	336
Allowance for doubtful accounts	Balance Sheet	Current Assets	339
Bad debts expense	Income Statement	Operating Expenses	338
Notes receivable	Balance Sheet	Current or Noncurrent Assets	346
Interest receivable	Balance Sheet	Current Assets	352
Interest revenue	Income Statement	Other Income	352
Short-term investments	Balance Sheet	Current Assets	352

KEY TERMS QUIZ

Read each definition and write the number of the definition in the blank beside the appropriate term. The quiz solutions appear at the end of the chapter.

_______ **Account receivable**
_______ **Subsidiary ledger**
_______ **Control account**
_______ **Direct write-off method**
_______ **Allowance method**
_______ **Allowance for doubtful accounts**
_______ **Aging schedule**
_______ **Promissory note**
_______ **Maker**
_______ **Payee**
_______ **Note receivable**
_______ **Note payable**
_______ **Principal**
_______ **Maturity date**
_______ **Term**
_______ **Maturity value**
_______ **Interest**
_______ **Credit card draft**
_______ **Discounting**
_______ **Equity securities**
_______ **Debt securities**

1. Securities issued by corporations as a form of ownership in the business.
2. Securities issued by corporations and governmental bodies as a form of borrowing.
3. A method of estimating bad debts on the basis of either the net credit sales of the period or the accounts receivable at the end of the period.
4. The party that will receive the money from a promissory note at some future date.
5. A written promise to repay a definite sum of money on demand or at a fixed or determinable date in the future.
6. A liability resulting from the signing of a promissory note.
7. A multiple-copy document used by a company that accepts a credit card for a sale.
8. An asset resulting from the acceptance of a promissory note from another company.
9. The process of selling a promissory note.
10. The party that agrees to repay the money for a promissory note at some future date.
11. A form used to categorize the various individual accounts receivable according to the length of time each has been outstanding.
12. The detail for a number of individual items that collectively make up a single general ledger account.
13. The recognition of bad debts expense at the point an account is written off as uncollectible.
14. The general ledger account that is supported by a subsidiary ledger.
15. The difference between the principal amount of the note and its maturity value.
16. The amount of cash received, or the fair value of the products or services received, by the maker when a promissory note is issued.
17. The amount of cash the maker is to pay the payee on the maturity date of the note.
18. The length of time a note is outstanding, that is, the period of time between the date it is issued and the date it matures.
19. The date the promissory note is due.
20. A contra-asset account used to reduce accounts receivable to its net realizable value.
21. A receivable arising from the sale of goods or services with a verbal promise to pay.

ALTERNATE TERMS

Allowance for doubtful accounts Allowance for uncollectible accounts

Credit card draft Invoice

Debt securities Bonds

Equity securities Stocks

Net realizable value Net recoverable amount

Short-term investments Marketable securities

WARMUP EXERCISES

Warmup Exercise 7-1 Accounting for Bad Debts

Brown Corp. ended the year with balances in Accounts Receivable of $60,000 and in Allowance for Doubtful Accounts of $800 (credit balance before adjustment). Net sales for the year amounted to

$200,000. Prepare the necessary journal entry on its books at the end of the year assuming the following:

1. Estimated percentage of net sales uncollectible is 1%.
2. Estimated percentage of year-end accounts receivable uncollectible is 4%.

Key to the Solution Recall that the percentage of net sales approach does not take into account any existing balance in the allowance account, but the percentage of receivables approach does.

Warmup Exercise 7-2 Investments

Indicate whether each of the following events will result in an increase (I), will result in a decrease (D), or will have no effect (NE) on net income for the period.

1. Stock hold as an investment is sold for more than its carrying value.
2. An interest check is received for bonds held as an investment.
3. Stock hold as an investment is sold for less than its carrying value.
4. Bonds held as an investment are redeemed on their maturity date at face value.
5. Stock is purchased and a commission is paid to a broker.

Key to the Solution Recall from earlier in the chapter the accounting for the various types of investments.

SOLUTIONS TO WARMUP EXERCISES

Warmup Exercise 7-1

1.	Bad Debts Expense	2,000	
	Allowance for Doubtful Accounts		2,000
	To record estimated bad debts.		

Balance Sheet							Income Statement
ASSETS	=	LIABILITIES	+	STOCKHOLDERS' EQUITY	+	REVENUES − EXPENSES	
Allowance for Doubtful Accounts (2,000)						Bad Debts Expense	(2,000)

2.	Bad Debts Expense	1,600	
	Allowance for Doubtful Accounts		1,600
	To record estimated bad debts.		

Balance Sheet							Income Statement
ASSETS	=	LIABILITIES	+	STOCKHOLDERS' EQUITY	+	REVENUES − EXPENSES	
Allowance for Doubtful Accounts (1,600)						Bad Debts Expense	(1,600)

Warmup Exercise 7-2

1. I 2. I 3. D 4. NE 5. NE

REVIEW PROBLEM

The following items pertain to the current assets section of the balance sheet for Jackson Corp. at the end of its accounting year, December 31, 2008. Each item must be considered and any necessary adjustment recognized. Additionally, the accountant for Jackson wants to develop the current assets section of the balance sheet as of the end of 2008.

a. Cash and cash equivalents amount to $19,375.
b. A 9%, 120-day certificate of deposit was purchased on December 1, 2008, for $10,000.
c. Gross accounts receivable at December 31, 2008, amount to $44,000. Before adjustment, the balance in the Allowance for Doubtful Accounts is $340. Based on past experience, the accountant estimates that 3% of the gross accounts receivable outstanding at December 31, 2008, will prove to be uncollectible.
d. A customer's 12%, 90-day promissory note in the amount of $6,000 is held at the end of the year. The note has been held for 45 days during 2008.

Required

1. Record the accounting entries required in (b), (c), and (d).
2. Prepare the current assets section of Jackson's balance sheet as of December 31, 2008. In addition to the information in the preceding items, the balances in Inventory and Prepaid Insurance on this date are $65,000 and $4,800, respectively.

SOLUTION TO REVIEW PROBLEM

1. The following entries are recorded at December 31, 2008:
   b. Jackson needs an adjusting entry to record interest earned on the certificate of deposit at the Second State Bank. The CD has been outstanding for 30 days during 2008; therefore, the amount of interest earned is calculated as follows:

$$\$10,000 \times 0.09 \times 30/360 = \$75$$

The adjusting entry follows:

2008			
Dec. 31	Interest Receivable	75	
	Interest Revenue		75
	To record interest earned during 2007.		

Balance Sheet							Income Statement	
ASSETS		=	**LIABILITIES**	+	**STOCKHOLDERS' EQUITY**	+	**REVENUES – EXPENSES**	
Interest Receivable	75						Interest Revenue	75

c. Based on gross accounts receivable of $44,000 at year-end and an estimate that 3% of this amount will be uncollectible, the balance in the Allowance for Doubtful Accounts should be $1,320 ($44,000 × 3%). Given a current balance of $340, an adusting entry for $980 ($1,320 − $340) is needed to bring the balance to the desired amount of $1,320:

2008			
Dec. 31	Bad Debts Expense	980	
	Allowance for Doubtful Accounts		980
	To record estimated bad debts for the year.		

Balance Sheet							Income Statement	
ASSETS		=	**LIABILITIES**	+	**STOCKHOLDERS' EQUITY**	+	**REVENUES – EXPENSES**	
Allowance for Doubtful Accounts	(980)						Bad Debts Expense	(980)

d. An adjusting entry is needed to accrue interest on the promissory note ($6,000 × 0.12 × 45/360 = $90):

2008			
Dec. 31	Interest Receivable	90	
	Interest Revenue		90
	To record interest earned on promissory note.		

Balance Sheet							Income Statement	
ASSETS		=	**LIABILITIES**	+	**STOCKHOLDERS' EQUITY**	+	**REVENUES – EXPENSES**	
Interest Receivable	90						Interest Revenue	90

2. The current assets section of Jackson's balance sheet appears as follows:

Jackson Corp.
Partial Balance Sheet
December 31, 2008

Current assets:		
Cash and cash equivalents		$ 19,375
Certificate of deposit		10,000
Accounts receivable	$44,000	
Less: Allowance for doubtful accounts	1,320	42,680
Notes receivable		6,000
Interest receivable		165*
Inventory		65,000
Prepaid insurance		4,800
Total current assets		$148,020

**$75 from CD and $90 from promissory note*

QUESTIONS

1. What is the theoretical justification for the allowance method of accounting for bad debts?
2. When bad debts are estimated, why is the balance in Allowance for Doubtful Accounts considered when the percentage of accounts receivable approach is used but not when the percentage of net credit sales approach is used?
3. When estimating bad debts on the basis of a percentage of accounts receivable, what is the advantage of using an aging schedule?
4. What is the distinction between an account receivable and a note receivable?
5. Why does the discounting of a note receivable with recourse result in a contingent liability? Should the liability be reported on the balance sheet? Explain.
6. On December 31, Stockton Inc. invests idle cash in two different certificates of deposit. The first is an 8%, 90-day CD; and the second has an interest rate of 9% and matures in 120 days. How is each of these CDs classified on the December 31 balance sheet?
7. Stanzel Corp. purchased 1,000 shares of IBM common stock. What will determine whether the shares are classified as current assets or noncurrent assets?
8. What is the appropriate treatment of any fees or commissions paid to purchase stock in another company?

BRIEF EXERCISES

LO1 **Brief Exercise 7-1** Accounting for Bad Debts

Badger recorded $500,000 of net sales for the year of which 2% is estimated to be uncollectible.

Prepare the journal entry at the end of the year to record bad debts.

LO2 **Brief Exercise 7-2** Accounts Receivable Turnover

Hawkeye recorded sales of $240,000 for the year. Accounts receivable amounted to $40,000 at the beginning of the year and $20,000 at the end of the year.

Compute the company's accounts receivable turnover for the year.

LO3 **Brief Exercise 7-3** Accounting for Notes Receivable

On November 1, 2008, Gopher borrowed $50,000 on a 6%, 90-day promissory note.

Prepare any necessary journal entry on December 31, the end of the company's fiscal year.

LO4

Brief Exercise 7-4 Accounting for Credit Card Sales

On July 20, Wolverine presents credit card drafts to its bank in the amount of $10,000; the collection charge is 4%.

Prepare the journal entry on Wolverine's books on July 20, the date of deposit.

LO5

Brief Exercise 7-5 Accounting for Sale of Stock

On March 5, Spartan sold stock in another company for $12,300. Spartan bought the stock on February 14 for $10,100.

Prepare the journal entry on Spartan's books on March 5.

LO6

Brief Exercise 7-6 Accounts Receivable on the Statement of Cash Flows

Wildcat started the year with $25,000 in accounts receivable and ended the year with $40,000 in the account.

Describe how information regarding the company's accounts receivable should be reflected on its statement of cash flows, assuming use of the indirect method.

EXERCISES

LO1

Exercise 7-1 Comparison of the Direct Write-Off and Allowance Methods of Accounting for Bad Debts

In its first year of business, Rideaway Bikes has net income of $145,000, exclusive of any adjustment for bad debt expense. The president of the company has asked you to calculate net income under each of two alternatives of accounting for bad debts: the direct write-off method and the allowance method. The president would like to use the method that will result in the higher net income. So far, no adjustments have been made to write off uncollectible accounts or to estimate bad debts. The relevant data are as follows:

Write-offs of uncollectible accounts during the year	$10,500
Net credit sales	$650,000
Estimated percentage of net credit sales that will be uncollectible	2%

Required

Compute net income under each of the two alternatives. Does Rideaway have a choice as to which method to use? If so, should it base its choice on which method will result in the higher net income? (Ignore income taxes.) Explain.

LO1

Exercise 7-2 Allowance Method of Accounting for Bad Debts—Comparison of the Two Approaches

Kandel Company had the following data available for 2008 (before making any adjustments):

Accounts receivable, 12/31/08	$320,100 (dr.)
Allowance for doubtful accounts	2,600 (cr.)
Net credit sales, 2008	834,000 (cr.)

Required

1. Prepare the journal entry to recognize bad debts under the following assumptions: (a) bad debts expense is expected to be 2% of net credit sales for the year and (b) Kandel expects it will not be able to collect 6% of the balance in accounts receivable at year-end.
2. Assume instead that the balance in the allowance account is a $2,600 debit. How will this affect your answers to (1)?

HOMEWORK

LO2

Exercise 7-3 Accounts Receivable Turnover for General Mills

The 2006 annual report of **General Mills** (the maker of Cheerios® and Wheaties®) reported the following amounts (in millions of dollars):

Net Sales, for the year ended May 28, 2006	$11,640
Receivables, May 28, 2006	1,076
Receivable, May 29, 2005	1,034

Required

1. Compute General Mills's accounts receivable turnover ratio for 2006. (Assume that all sales are on credit.)
2. What is the average collection period in days for an account receivable? Explain your answer.
3. Give some examples of the types of customers you would expect General Mills to have. Do you think the average collection period for sales to these customers is reasonable? What other information do you need to fully answer that question?

LO3

Exercise 7-4 Notes Receivable

On September 1, 2008, Dougherty Corp. accepted a six-month, 7%, $45,000 interest-bearing note from Rozelle Company in payment of an accounts receivable. Dougherty's year-end is December 31. Rozelle paid the note and interest on the due date.

Required

1. Who is the maker and who is the payee of the note?
2. What is the maturity date of the note?
3. Prepare all necessary journal entries that Dougherty needs to make in connection with this note.

LO4

Exercise 7-5 Credit Card Sales

Darlene's Diner accepts American Express® credit cards from its customers. Darlene's is closed on Sundays and on that day records the weekly sales and remits the credit card drafts to American Express. For the week ending on Sunday, June 12, cash sales totaled $2,430 and credit card sales amounted to $3,500. On June 15, Darlene's received $3,360 from American Express as payment for the credit card drafts. Prepare the necessary journal entries on June 12 and June 15. As a percentage, what collection fee is American Express charging Darlene?

LO5

Exercise 7-6 Certificate of Deposit

On May 31, 2008, Elmer Corp. purchased a 120-day, 9% certificate of deposit for $50,000. The CD was redeemed on September 28, 2008. Prepare the journal entries on Elmer's books to account for:

a. The purchase of the CD.
b. The accrual of interest adjustment for interest earned through June 30, the end of the company's fiscal year.
c. The redemption of the CD.

Assume 360 days in a year.

LO5

Exercise 7-7 Classification of Cash Equivalents and Investments on a Balance Sheet

Classify each of the following items as a cash equivalent (CE), a short-term investment (STI), or a long-term investment (LTI).

1. A 120-day certificate of deposit.
2. Three hundred shares of GM common stock. The company plans on selling the stock in six months.
3. A six-month U.S Treasury bill.
4. A 60-day certificate of deposit.
5. Ford Motor Co. bonds maturing in 15 years. The company intends to hold the bonds until maturity.
6. Commercial paper issued by ABC Corp., maturing in four months.
7. Five hundred shares of Chrysler common stock. The company plans to sell the stock in 60 days to help pay for a note due at that time at the bank.
8. Two hundred shares of GE preferred stock. The company intends to hold the stock for ten years and then sell it to help finance construction of a new factory.
9. Ten-year U.S. Treasury bonds. The company plans to sell the bonds on the open market in six months.
10. A 90-day U.S. Treasury bill.

LO5

Exercise 7-8 Purchase and Sale of Bonds

Starship Enterprises enters into the following transactions during 2008 and 2009:

2008

Jan. 1: Purchased $100,000 face value of Northern Lights Inc. bonds at face value. The newly issued bonds have an inerest rate of 8% paid semiannually on June 30 and December 31. The bonds mature in five years.

June 30: Received interest on the Northern Lights bonds.

Dec. 31: Received interest on the Northern Lights bonds.

2009

Jan. 1: Sold the Northern Lights Inc. bonds for $102,000.

Required

1. Prepare all necessary journal entries on Starship's records to account for its investment in the Northern Lights bonds.
2. Why was Starship able to sell its Northern Lights bonds for $102,000?

LO5

Exercise 7-9 Investment in Stock

On October 1, 2008, Chicago Corp. purchases 1,000 shares of the preferred stock of Denver Corp. for $40 per share. Chicago pays another $1,000 in commissions. On October 20, 2008, Denver declares and pays a dividend of $1 per share. Chicago sells the stock on November 5, 2008, at a price of $45 per share.

Required

Prepare all necessary journal entries on Chicago's books in connection with its investment, beginning with the purchase of the preferred stock on October 1, 2008; the dividend received on October 20, 2008; and the sale on November 5, 2008.

LO5

Exercise 7-10 Investment in Stock

On August 15, 2008, Cubs Corp. purchases 5,000 shares of common stock in Sox Inc. at a market price of $15 per share. In addition, Cubs pays brokerage fees of $1,000. On October 20, 2008, Cubs sells the Sox stock for $10 per share.

Required

Prepare all necessary entries on Cubs's books in connection with the investment beginning with the purchase of the common stock on August 15, 2008 and the sale on October 20, 2008.

LO6

Exercise 7-11 Impact of Transactions Involving Receivables on Statement of Cash Flows

From the following list, identify whether the change in the account balance during the year would be added to or deducted from net income when the indirect method is used to determine cash flows from operating activities:

Increase in accounts receivable
Decrease in accounts receivable
Increase in notes receivable
Decrease in notes receivable

LO6

Exercise 7-12 Cash Collections—Direct Method

Emily Enterprises' comparative balance sheets included accounts receivable of $224,600 at December 31, 2007, and $205,700 at December 31, 2008. Sales reported on Emily's 2008 income statement amounted to $2,250,000. What is the amount of cash collections that Emily will report in the operating activities category of its 2008 statement of cash flows assuming that the direct method is used?

MULTICONCEPT EXERCISE

LO1,5,6 **Exercise 7-13** Impact of Transactions Involving Cash, Securities, and Receivables on Statement of Cash Flows

From the following list, identify each item as operating (O), investing (I), financing (F), or not separately reported on the statement of cash flows (N). Assume that the indirect method is used to determine the cash flows from operating activities.

Purchase of cash equivalents
Redemption of cash equivalents
Purchase of investments
Sale of investments
Write-off of customer account (under the allowance method)

PROBLEMS

LO1 **Problem 7-1** Allowance Method for Accounting for Bad Debts

At the beginning of 2008, EZ Tech Company's accounts receivable balance was $140,000 and the balance in Allowance for Doubtful Accounts was $2,350 (cr.). EZ Tech's sales in 2008 were $1,050,000, 80% of which were on credit. Collections on account during the year were $670,000. The company wrote off $4,000 of uncollectible accounts during the year.

Required

1. Prepare summary journal entries related to the sale, collections, and write-offs of accounts receivable during 2008.
2. Prepare journal entries to recognize bad debts assuming (a) bad debt expense is 3% of credit sales and (b) amounts expected to be uncollectible are 6% of the year-end accounts receivable.
3. What is the net realizable value of accounts receivable on December 31, 2008, under each assumption in (2)?
4. What effect does the recognition of bad debt expense have on the net realizable value? What effect does the write-off of accounts have on the net realizable value?

LO1 **Problem 7-2** Aging Schedule to Account for Bad Debts

Sparkle Jewels distributes fine stones. It sells on credit to retail jewelry stores and extends terms that require the stores to pay in 60 days. For accounts that are not overdue, Sparkle has found that there is a 95% probability of collection. For accounts up to one month past due, the likelihood of collection decreases to 80%. If accounts are between one and two months past due, the probability of collection is 60%; and if an account is over two months past due, Sparkle Jewels estimates only a 40% chance of collecting the receivable.

On December 31, 2008, the balance in Allowance for Doubtful Accounts is $12,300. The amounts of gross receivables by age on this date are as follows:

Category	Amount
Current	$200,000
Past due:	
Less than one month	45,000
One to two months	25,000
Over two months	10,000

Required

1. Prepare a schedule to estimate the amount of uncollectible accounts at December 31, 2008.
2. On the basis of the schedule in (1), prepare the journal entry on December 31, 2008, to estimate bad debts.

LO2

Problem 7-3 Accounts Receivable Turnover for Coca-Cola and PepsiCo

The following information was summarized from the 2006 annual report of **The Coca-Cola Company**:

	(In millions)
Trade accounts receivable, less allowances of $63 and $72, respectively	
December 31, 2006	$ 2,587
December 31, 2005	2,281
Net operating revenues for the year ended December 31:	
2006	24,088
2005	23,104

The following information was summarized from the 2006 annual report of **PepsiCo**:

	(In millions)
Accounts and notes, receivable, net	
December 30, 2006	$ 3,725
December 31, 2005	3,261
Net revenue for the year ended:	
December 30, 2006	35,137
December 31, 2005	32,562

Required

1. Calculate the accounts receivable turnover ratios for Coca-Cola and PepsiCo for 2006.
2. Calculate the average collection period, in days, for both companies for 2006. Comment on the reasonableness of the collection periods for these companies considering the nature of their business.
3. Which company appears to be performing better? What other information should you consider in determining how these companies are performing?

LO4

Problem 7-4 Credit Card Sales

Gas stations sometimes sell gasoline at a lower price to customers who pay cash than to customers who use a credit card. A local gas station owner pays 2% of the sales price to the credit card company when customers pay with a credit card. The owner pays $0.75 per gallon of gasoline and must earn at least $0.25 per gallon of gross margin to stay competitive.

Required

1. Determine the price the owner must charge credit card customers to maintain the station's gross margin.
2. How much discount could the owner offer to cash customers and still maintain the same gross margin?

LO5

Problem 7-5 Investments in Bonds and Stock

Swartz Inc. enters into the following transactions during 2008:

July 1:	Paid $10,000 to acquire on the open market $10,000 face value of Gallatin bonds. The bonds have a stated annual interest rate of 6% with interest paid semiannually on June 30 and December 31. The bonds mature in $5\frac{1}{2}$ years.
Oct. 23:	Purchased 600 shares of Eagle Rock common stock at $20 per share.
Nov. 21:	Purchased 200 shares of Montana preferred stock at $30 per share.
Dec. 10:	Received dividends of $1.50 per share on the Eagle Rock stock and $2.00 per share on the Montana stock.
Dec. 28:	Sold 400 shares of Eagle Rock common stock at $25 per share.
Dec. 31:	Received interest from the Gallatin bonds.

Required

Prepare all necessary journal entries on Swartz's records to account for its investments during 2008.

LO5 **Problem 7-6** Investments in Stock

Atlas Superstores occasionally finds itself with excess cash to invest and consequently entered into the following transactions during 2008:

Jan. 15: Purchased 200 shares of Sears common stock at $50 per share, plus $500 in commissions.
May 23: Received dividends of $2 per share on the Sears stock.
June 1: Purchased 100 shares of Ford Motor Co. stock at $74 per share, plus $300 in commissions.
Oct. 20: Sold all of the Sears stock at $42 per share, less commissions of $400.
Dec. 15: Received notification from Ford Motor Co. that a $1.50 per share dividend had been declared. The checks will be mailed to stockholders on January 10, 2009.

Required
Prepare journal entries on the books of Atlas Superstores during 2008 to record these transactions, including any necessary entry on December 15 when the dividend was declared.

LO6 **Problem 7-7** Effects of Changes in Receivable Balances on Statement of Cash Flows

Stegner Inc. reported net income of $130,000 for the year ended December 31, 2008. The following items were included on Stegner's balance sheets at December 31, 2008 and 2007:

	12/31/08	12/31/07
Cash	$105,000	$110,000
Accounts receivable	223,000	83,000
Notes receivable	95,000	100,000

Stegner uses the indirect method to prepare its statement of cash flows. Stegner does not have any other current assets or current liabilities and did not enter into any investing or financing activities during 2008.

Required
1. Prepare Stegner's 2008 statement of cash flows.
2. Draft a brief memo to the owner to explain why cash decreased during a profitable year.

MULTICONCEPT PROBLEM

LO1,3 **Problem 7-8** Accounts and Notes Receivable

Linus Corp. sold merchandise for $5,000 to C. Brown on May 15, 2008, with payment due in 30 days. Subsequent to this, Brown experienced cash flow problems and was unable to pay its debt. On August 10, 2008, Linus stopped trying to collect the outstanding receivable from Brown and wrote off the account as uncollectible. On December 1, 2008, Brown sent Linus a check for $1,000 and offered to sign a two-month, 9%, $4,000 promissory note to satisfy the remaining obligation. Brown paid the entire amount due Linus, with interest, on January 31, 2009. Linus ends its accounting year on December 31 each year and uses the allowance method to account for bad debts.

Required
1. Prepare all of the necessary journal entries on the books of Linus Corp. from May 15, 2008 to January 31, 2009.
2. Why would Brown bother to send Linus a check for $1,000 on December 1 and agree to sign a note for the balance, given that such a long period of time had passed since the original purchase?

ALTERNATE PROBLEMS

LO1 **Problem 7-1A** Allowance Method for Accounting for Bad Debts

At the beginning of 2008, Miyazaki Company's accounts receivable balance was $105,000 and the balance in Allowance for Doubtful Accounts was $1,950. Miyazaki's sales in 2008 were $787,500, 80% of which were on credit. Collections on account during the year were $502,500. The company wrote off $3,000 of uncollectible accounts during the year.

Required

1. Prepare summary journal entries related to the sales, collections, and write-offs of accounts receivable during 2008.
2. Prepare journal entries to recognize bad debts assuming (a) bad debt expense is 3% of credit sales and (b) amounts expected to be uncollectible are 6% of the year-end accounts receivable.
3. What is the net realizable value of accounts receivable on December 31, 2008, under each assumption in (2)?
4. What effect does the recognition of bad debt expense have on the net realizable value? What effect does the write-off of accounts have on the net realizable value?

LO1 **Problem 7-2A** Aging Schedule to Account for Bad Debts

Rough Stuff is a distributor of large rocks. It sells on credit to commercial landscaping companies and extends terms that require customers to pay in 60 days. For accounts that are not overdue, Rough Stuff has found that there is a 90% probability of collection. For accounts up to one month past due, the likelihood of collection decreases to 75%. If accounts are between one and two months past due, the probability of collection is 65%; and if an account is over two months past due, Rough Stuff estimates only a 25% chance of collecting the receivable.

On December 31, 2008, the credit balance in Allowance for Doubtful Accounts is $34,590. The amounts of gross receivables, by age, on this date are as follows:

Category	Amount
Current	$200,000
Past due:	
Less than one month	60,300
One to two months	35,000
Over two months	45,000

Required

1. Prepare a schedule to estimate the amount of uncollectible accounts at December 31, 2008.
2. Rough Stuff knows that $40,000 of the $45,000 amount that is more than two months overdue is due from one customer that is in severe financial trouble. It is rumored that the customer will be filing for bankruptcy in the near future. As controller for Rough Stuff, how would you handle this situation?
3. Show how accounts receivable would be presented on the December 31, 2007, balance sheet.

LO2 **Problem 7-3A** Accounts Receivable Turnover for Best Buy and Circuit City

The following information was summarized from a recent annual report of **Best Buy Co. Inc.**:

	(In millions)
Receivables:	
March 3, 2007	$ 548
February 25, 2006	449
Revenues for the year ended:	
March 3, 2007	35,934
February 25, 2006	30,848

The following information was summarized from a recent annual report of **Circuit City Stores, Inc.** (Receivables are net of allowances.)

	(In thousands)
Accounts receivable, net of allowance for doubtful accounts	
February 28, 2007	$ 382,555
February 28, 2006	220,869
Net sales for the year ended:	
February 28, 2007	12,429,754
February 28, 2006	11,514,151

Required

1. Calculate the accounts receivable turnover ratios for Best Buy and Circuit City for 2007.
2. Calculate the average collection period, in days, for both companies for 2007. Comment on the reasonableness of the collection periods for these companies considering the nature of their business.
3. Which company appears to be performing better? What other information should you consider in determining how these companies are performing?

LO4

Problem 7-4A Credit Card Sales

A local fast-food store is considering accepting major credit cards in its outlets. Current annual sales are $800,000 per outlet. The company can purchase the equipment needed to handle credit cards and have an additional phone line installed in each outlet for approximately $800 per outlet. The equipment will be an expense in the year it is installed. The employee training time is minimal. The credit card company will charge a fee equal to 1.5% of sales for the use of credit cards. The company is unable to determine by how much, if any, sales will increase and whether cash customers will use a credit card rather than cash. No other fast-food stores in the local area accept credit cards for sales payment.

Required

1. Assuming only 5% of existing cash customers will use a credit card, what increase in sales is necessary to pay for the credit card equipment in the first year?
2. What other factors might the company consider in addition to an increase in sales dollars?

LO5

Problem 7-5A Investments in Bonds and Stock

Vermont Corp. enters into the following transactions during 2008:

July 1: Paid $10,000 to acquire on the open market $10,000 face value of Maine bonds. The bonds have a stated annual interest rate of 8% with interest paid semiannually on June 30 and December 31. The remaining life of the bonds on the date of purchase is $3\frac{1}{2}$ years.
Oct. 23: Purchased 1,000 shares of Virginia common stock at $15 per share.
Nov. 21: Purchased 600 shares of Carolina preferred stock at $8 per share.
Dec. 10: Received dividends of $0.50 per share on the Virginia stock and $1.00 per share on the Carolina stock.
Dec. 28: Sold 700 shares of Virginia common stock at $19 per share.
Dec. 31: Received interest from the Maine bonds.

Required

Prepare all necessary journal entries on Vermont's records to account for its investments during 2008.

LO5

Problem 7-6A Investments in Stock

Trendy Supercenter occasionally finds itself with excess cash to invest and consequently entered into the following transactions during 2008:

Jan. 15: Purchased 100 shares of IBM common stock at $130 per share, plus $250 in commissions.
May 23: Received dividends of $1 per share on the IBM stock.
June 1: Purchased 200 shares of General Motors stock at $60 per share, plus $300 in commissions.
Oct. 20: Sold all of the IBM stock at $140 per share, less commissions of $400.
Dec. 15: Received notification from General Motors that a $0.75 per share dividend had been declared. The checks will be mailed to stockholders on January 10, 2009.

Required

Prepare journal entries on the books of Trendy Supercenter during 2008 to record these transactions, including any necessary entry on December 15 when the dividend was declared.

LO6

Problem 7-7A Effects of Changes in Receivable Balances on Statement of Cash Flows

St. Charles Antique Market reported a net loss of $6,000 for the year ended December 31, 2008. The following items were included on St. Charles Antique Market's balance sheets at December 31, 2008 and 2007:

	12/31/08	12/31/07
Cash	$ 36,300	$ 3,100
Accounts receivable	79,000	126,000
Notes receivable	112,600	104,800

St. Charles Antique Market uses the indirect method to prepare its statement of cash flows. It does not have any other current assets or current liabilities and did not enter into any investing or financing activities during 2008.

Required

1. Prepare St. Charles Antique Market's 2008 statement of cash flows.
2. Draft a brief memo to the owner to explain why cash increased during such an unprofitable year.

ALTERNATE MULTICONCEPT PROBLEM

LO1,3

Problem 7-8A Accounts and Notes Receivable

Tweety Inc. sold merchandise for $6,000 to P.D. Cat on July 31, 2008, with payment due in 30 days. Subsequent to this, Cat experienced cash flow problems and was unable to pay its debt. On December 24, 2008, Tweety stopped trying to collect the outstanding receivable from Cat and wrote off the account as uncollectible. On January 15, 2009, Cat sent Tweety a check for $1,500 and offered to sign a two-month, 8%, $4,500 promissory note to satisfy the remaining obligation. Cat paid the entire amount due Tweety, with interest, on March 15, 2009. Tweety ends its accounting year on December 31 each year.

Required

1. Prepare all of the necessary journal entries on the books of Tweety Inc. from July 31, 2008, to March 15, 2009.
2. Why would Cat bother to send Tweety a check for $1,500 on January 15 and agree to sign a note for the balance, given that such a long period of time had passed since the original purchase?

DECISION CASES

READING AND INTERPRETING FINANCIAL STATEMENTS

LO1

Decision Case 7-1 Reading Apple's Balance Sheet and Notes to the Statements

Following is information available in **Apple Computer**'s 2006 annual report in Note 3 to the financial statements:

The following table summarizes the activity in the allowance for doubtful accounts (in millions):

	September 30, 2006	September 24, 2005	September 25, 2004
Beginning allowance balance	$ 46	$ 47	$ 49
Charged to costs and expenses	17	8	3
Deductions (a)	(11)	(9)	(5)
Ending allowance balance	$ 52	$ 46	$ 47

(a) Represents amounts written off against the allowance, net recoveries.

Use this information and that provided in the chapter opener to answer the following questions.

Required

1. What is the balance in Apple's Allowance for Doubtful Accounts at the end of 2006 and 2005?
2. What is the net realizable value of accounts receivable at the end of each of these two years?
3. What was the amount of bad debts expense for 2006 and 2005?
4. What was the amount of accounts receivable written off in 2006 and 2005?
5. Compare the amounts of accounts written off in 2006 and 2005 to the amounts written off in 2004. Why do you think the amounts written off have increased significantly in the two most recent years?

LO1,6

Decision Case 7-2 Reading Apple Computer's Statement of Cash Flows

The following items appeared in the Investing Activities section of **Apple Computer**'s 2006 statement of cash flows. (All amounts are in millions of dollars.)

	2006	2005 (Restated)	2004 (Restated)
Purchases of short-term investments	$(7,255)	$(11,470)	$(3,270)
Proceeds from maturities of short-term investments	7,226	8,609	1,141
Proceeds from sales of investments	1,086	586	806
Purchases of long-term investments	(25)	—	—

Required

1. What amount did Apple spend in 2006 to purchase short-term investments? How does this amount compare to the amounts spent in the two prior years?
2. What amount did Apple receive from investments that matured in 2006? How does this amount compare to the amounts received in the two prior years?
3. The third line in the preceding excerpt reports proceeds from sales, rather than maturities, of investments. Why would certain types of investments mature while others would be sold?

LO3

Decision Case 7-3 Comparing Two Companies in the Same Industry: Kellogg's and General Mills

Refer to the financial statement information of **Kellogg's** and **General Mills** reproduced at the end of this book.

1. Calculate the account receivables turnover ratios for both companies for the most recent year.
2. Calculate the average length of time it takes each company to collect its accounts receivable.
3. Compare the two companies on the basis of your calculations in (1) and (2).

MAKING FINANCIAL DECISIONS

LO1,5

Decision Case 7-4 Liquidity

Oak and Maple both provide computer consulting services to their clients. The following are the current assets for each company at the end of the year. (All amounts are in millions of dollars.)

	Oak	Maple
Cash	$10	$ 5
Six-month certificates of deposit	9	0
Short-term investments in stock	0	6
Accounts receivable	15	23
Allowance for doubtful accounts	(1)	(1)
Total current assets	$33	$33

Required

As a loan officer for the First National Bank of Verona Heights, assume that both companies have come to you asking for a $10 million, six-month loan. If you could lend money to only one of the two, which one would it be? Justify your answer by writing a brief memo to the president of the bank.

ETHICAL DECISION MAKING

LO4 **Decision Case 7-5** Notes Receivable

Patterson Company is a large diversified business with a unit that sells commercial real estate. As a company, Patterson has been profitable in recent years with the exception of the real estate business, where economic conditions have resulted in weak sales. The vice president of the real estate division is aware of the poor performance of his group and needs to find ways to "show a profit."

During the current year, the division is successful in selling a 100-acre tract of land for a new shopping center. The original cost of the property to Patterson was $4 million. The buyer has agreed to sign a $10 million note with payments of $2 million due at the end of each of the next five years. The property was appraised late last year at a market value of $7.5 million. The vice president has come to you, the controller, asking that you record a sale for $10 million with a corresponding increase in Notes Receivable for $10 million.

Required

1. Does the suggestion by the vice president as to how to record the sale violate any accounting principle? If so, explain the principle it violates.
2. What would you do? Write a brief memo to the vice president explaining the proper accounting for the sale.

SOLUTIONS TO KEY TERMS QUIZ

21	**Account receivable**	6	**Note payable**
12	**Subsidiary ledger**	16	**Principal**
14	**Control account**	19	**Maturity date**
13	**Direct write-off method**	18	**Term**
3	**Allowance method**	17	**Maturity value**
20	**Allowance for doubtful accounts**	15	**Interest**
11	**Aging schedule**	7	**Credit card draft**
5	**Promissory note**	9	**Discounting**
10	**Maker**	1	**Equity securities**
4	**Payee**	2	**Debt securities**
8	**Note receivable**		

ANSWERS TO POD REVIEW

LO1	1. b	2. c	3. b
LO2	1. c	2. a	
LO3	1. c	2. b	
LO4	1. c	2. b	
LO5	1. b	2. a	
LO6	1. a	2. c	

CHAPTER 8

Operating Assets: Property, Plant, and Equipment, and Intangibles

Learning Outcomes

After studying this chapter, you should be able to:

LO1 Understand balance sheet disclosures for operating assets.

LO2 Determine the acquisition cost of an operating asset.

LO3 Explain how to calculate the acquisition cost of assets purchased for a lump sum.

LO4 Describe the impact of capitalizing interest as part of the acquisition cost of an asset.

LO5 Compare depreciation methods and understand the factors affecting the choice of method.

LO6 Understand the impact of a change in the estimate of the asset life or residual value.

LO7 Determine which expenditures should be capitalized as asset costs and which should be treated as expenses.

LO8 Analyze the effect of the disposal of an asset at a gain or loss.

LO9 Understand the balance sheet presentation of intangible assets.

LO10 Understand the proper amortization of intangible assets.

LO11 Explain the impact that long-term assets have on the statement of cash flows.

LO12 Understand how investors can analyze a company's operating assets.

Study Links...

A Look at Previous Chapters
Chapter 7 presented the accounting for a company's current assets of accounts receivable, notes receivable, and investments. These assets are important aspects of short-term liquidity.

A Look at This Chapter
This chapter examines a company's operating assets of property, plant, and equipment as well as natural resources and intangibles. These assets are an important indicator of a company's ability to produce revenue in the long term.

A Look at Upcoming Chapters
Later chapters discuss the financing of long-term assets. Chapter 10 presents long-term liabilities as a source of financing. Chapter 11 describes the use of stock as a source of funds for financing long-term assets.

Nike MAKING BUSINESS DECISIONS

Nike is the largest seller of athletic footwear, athletic apparel, equipment, and accessories in the world. To achieve this position of dominance requires a large investment in property, plant, and equipment. The Nike World Campus, owned by Nike and located in Beaverton, Oregon, is a 176-acre facility of 16 buildings that functions as the world headquarters and is occupied by almost 6,000 employees. The company has distribution and customer service facilities in Tennessee, Oregon, and New Hampshire as well as in Japan and Europe. At May 31, 2006, the company's balance sheet indicates over $1.6 billion of property, plant, and equipment. The company's decisions to continually invest in new plant and equipment are very important and a key to the company's future. Investors and others who read Nike's financial statements must analyze the company's tangible assets in order to gauge the company's ability to generate profits in future periods.

But Nike's intangible assets are equally important. The Nike brand name and company logo are some of the most recognizable in the world. During the second quarter ended November 30, 2003, Nike completed the acquisition of Converse Inc. The purchase price was $310 million, and the majority of the purchase represented identifiable intangible assets such as trademarks and copyrights. Nearly all of the remainder represented the intangible asset known as goodwill. The acquisition of Converse further strengthened Nike and granted it an even more dominant position in the athletic footwear business.

Accountants have had to consider carefully the accounting for all long-lived assets but especially for intangible assets. Investors must be able to read Nike's financial statements and understand how their assets influence the value of the company. The stock price should accurately reflect the value of those assets and the company's ability to use the assets wisely.

The accompanying partial balance sheet presents Nike's property, plant, and equipment and its intangible assets. This chapter will consider the following:

- What financial statement disclosures are available for a company's operating assets? (See pp. 378–379.)
- How should a company depreciate or amortize such assets? (See pp. 396–398.)
- How can an investor analyze the operating assets portion of the balance sheet when evaluating a company? (See pp. 401–403.)

Answers to those questions are found in the text. They can help you evaluate Nike's assets using its financial statements.

(*continued*)

NIKE, INC.
CONSOLIDATED BALANCE SHEETS

	May 31,	
	2006	2005
	(In millions)	
ASSETS		
Current assets:		
Cash and equivalents	$ 954.2	$1,388.1
Short-term investments	1,348.8	436.6
Accounts receivable, less allowance for doubtful accounts of $67.6 and $80.4	2,395.9	2,262.1
Inventories (Note 2)	2,076.7	1,811.1
Deferred income taxes (Note 8)	203.3	110.2
Prepaid expenses and other current assets	380.1	343.0
Total current assets	7,359.0	6,351.1
Property, plant, and equipment, net (Note 3)	1,657.7	1,605.8
Identifiable intangible assets, net (Note 4)	405.5	406.1
Goodwill (Note 4)	130.8	135.4
Deferred income taxes and other assets (Note 8)	316.6	295.2
Total assets	$9,869.6	$8,793.6

Operating Assets: Property, Plant, and Equipment

LO1 Understand balance sheet disclosures for operating assets.

BALANCE SHEET PRESENTATION

Operating assets constitute the major productive assets of many companies. Current assets are important to a company's short-term liquidity, but operating assets are absolutely essential to its long-term future. These assets must be used to produce the goods or services the company sells to customers. The dollar amount invested in operating assets may be very large, as is the case with most manufacturing companies. On the other hand, operating assets on the balance sheet may be insignificant to a company's value, as is the case with a computer software firm or many of the so-called Internet firms. Users of financial statements must assess the operating assets to make important decisions. For example, lenders are interested in the value of the operating assets as collateral when they are making lending decisions. Investors must evaluate whether the operating assets indicate long-term potential and can provide a return to the stockholders.

The terms used to describe the operating assets and the balance sheet presentation of those assets vary somewhat by company. Some firms refer to this category of assets as *fixed* or *plant assets*. Other firms prefer to present operating assets in two categories: *tangible assets* and *intangible assets*. The balance sheet of **Nike, Inc.**, uses one line item for *property, plant, and equipment* and presents the details in the notes. Because the latter term can encompass a variety of items, we will use the more descriptive term *intangible assets* for the second category. We begin by examining the accounting issues concerned with the first category: property, plant, and equipment.

The May 31, 2006, notes of Nike, Inc., present property, plant, and equipment shown at the top of the page (in millions). Note that the acquisition costs of the land, buildings, machinery and equipment, leasehold improvements, and construction in process are stated and that the amount of accumulated depreciation is deducted to determine the net amount. The accumulated depreciation is related to the last four assets, since land is not a depreciable item.

Note 3—Property, Plant, and Equipment
Property, plant, and equipment includes the following:

	May 31,	
	2006	**2005**
	(In millions)	
Land	$ 195.9	$ 185.4
Buildings	842.6	823.9
Machinery and equipment	1,661.7	1,528.4
Leasehold improvements	626.7	568.4
Construction in process	81.4	73.1
	3,408.3	3,179.2
Less accumulated depreciation	1,750.6	1,573.4
	$1,657.7	$1,605.8

POD REVIEW 8.1

LO1 *Understand balance sheet disclosures for operating assets.*

- Operating assets are the major productive assets of many companies, and investors must be able to evaluate the long-term potential of these assets for a return on their investments.
  - Operating assets may be classified as being either tangible or intangible assets.
  - Tangible assets are referred to as property, plant, and equipment (or fixed assets).
  - Intangible assets include goodwill, patents, copyrights, and various types of intellectual property.

QUESTIONS

1. *The Property, Plant, and Equipment category should include all of the following except*
   a. land.
   b. buildings.
   c. equipment.
   d. long-term investments.

2. *What is the effect of accumulated depreciation in the Property, Plant, and Equipment category?*
   a. It decreases some accounts.
   b. It increases some accounts.
   c. There is no effect since accumulated depreciation is not part of the category.
   d. Accumulated depreciation is deducted from all accounts in the category.

ACQUISITION OF PROPERTY, PLANT, AND EQUIPMENT

LO2 Determine the acquisition cost of an operating asset.

Assets classified as property, plant, and equipment are initially recorded at acquisition cost (also referred to as *historical cost*). As indicated in Nike's notes, these assets are normally presented on the balance sheet at original acquisition cost minus accumulated depreciation. It is important, however, to define the term acquisition cost (also known as original cost) in a more exact manner. What items should be included as part of the original acquisition? **Acquisition cost** should include all of the costs that are normal and necessary to acquire the asset and prepare it for its intended use. Items included in acquisition cost generally include the following:

Acquisition cost
The amount that includes all of the cost normally necessary to acquire an asset and prepare it for its intended use.
Alternate terms: *Historical cost or original cost.*

- Purchase price
- Taxes paid at time of purchase (for example, sales tax)
- Transportation charges
- Installation costs

An accountant must exercise careful judgment to determine which costs are "normal" and "necessary" and should be included in the calculation of the acquisition cost of operating assets. Acquisition cost should not include expenditures unrelated to the acquisition (for example, repair costs if an asset is damaged during installation) or costs incurred after the asset was installed and use begun.

POD REVIEW 8.2

LO2 Determine the acquisition cost of an operating asset.

- Assets classified as property, plant, and equipment (or fixed assets) are initially recorded at the cost to acquire the assets, also referred to as historical cost.
  - Acquisition costs include those costs that are normal and necessary to acquire the asset and prepare it for its intended use. Generally, acquisition costs include purchase price, taxes paid at time of purchase, transportation charges, and installation costs.

QUESTIONS

1. *Which of the following should not be included in the acquisition cost of property, plant, and equipment?*
   a. installation costs
   b. repair costs if an asset is damaged after purchase
   c. taxes paid at time of purchase
   d. transportation costs

2. *Another term for* acquisition cost *is*
   a. fair market value.
   b. replacement cost.
   c. historical cost.
   d. net realizable value.

LO3 Explain how to calculate the acquisition cost of assets purchased for a lump sum.

Group Purchase Quite often a firm purchases several assets as a group and pays a lump-sum amount. This is most common when a company purchases land and a building situated on it and pays a lump-sum amount for both. It is important to measure the acquisition cost of the land and the building separately. Land is not a depreciable asset, but the amount allocated to the building is subject to depreciation. In cases such as this, the purchase price should be allocated between land and building on the basis of the proportion of the *fair market value* of each.

For example, assume that on January 1, ExerCo purchased a building and the land on which it is situated for $100,000. The accountant was able to establish that the fair market value of the two assets on January 1 were as follows:

Land	$ 30,000
Building	90,000
Total	$120,000

On the basis of the estimated market values, the purchase price should be allocated as follows:

To land	$100,000 × $30,000/$120,000 = $25,000
To building	$100,000 × $90,000/$120,000 = $75,000

The journal entry to record the purchase would be as follows:

Jan. 1	Land	25,000	
	Building	75,000	
	Cash		100,000
	To record the purchase of land and building for a lump-sum amount.		

Balance Sheet							Income Statement
ASSETS		=	LIABILITIES	+	STOCKHOLDERS' EQUITY	+	REVENUES − EXPENSES
Land	25,000						
Building	75,000						
Cash	(100,000)						

Market value is best established by an independent appraisal of the property. If such appraisal is not possible, the accountant must rely on the market value of other similar assets, on the value of the assets in tax records, or on other available evidence.

These efforts to allocate dollars between land and buildings will permit the appropriate allocation for depreciation. But when an investor or a lender views the balance sheet, he or she is often more interested in the current market value. The best things that can be said about historical cost are that it is a verifiable number and that it is conservative. But it is still up to the lender or the investor to determine the appropriate value for these assets.

POD REVIEW 8.3

LO3 *Explain how to calculate the acquisition cost of assets purchased for a lump sum.*

- If more than one asset is purchased for a single sum of money, the acquisition costs must be allocated between the assets.
  - In these cases, the purchase price should be allocated between the assets acquired based on the proportion of the fair market value each asset represents of the total purchase price.

QUESTIONS

1. *When land and building are acquired for a lump sum,*
   a. the entire amount should be considered cost of the land.
   b. the entire amount should be considered cost of the building.
   c. the purchase amount should be allocated on the basis of the historical cost of the two assets.
   d. the purchase amount should be allocated on the basis of the market values of the two assets.

2. *It is important to allocate the lump sum purchase price between land and building because*
   a. land is not depreciable.
   b. building is not depreciable.
   c. neither land nor building is depreciable.
   d. both land and building are depreciable.

LO4 Describe the impact of capitalizing interest as part of the acquisition cost of an asset.

Capitalization of Interest We have seen that acquisition cost may include several items. But should the acquisition cost of an asset include the interest cost necessary to finance the asset? That is, should interest be treated as an asset, or should it be treated as an expense of the period?

Generally, the interest on borrowed money should be treated as an expense of the period. If a company buys an asset and borrows money to finance the purchase, the interest on the borrowed money is not considered part of the asset's cost. Financial statements generally treat investing and financing as separate decisions. Purchase of an asset, an investing activity, is treated as a business decision that is separate from the decision concerning the financing of the asset. Therefore, interest is treated as a period cost and should appear on the income statement as interest expense in the period incurred.

Capitalization of interest
Interest on constructed assets is added to the asset account.

There is one exception to this general guideline, however. If a company constructs an asset over a period of time and borrows money to finance the construction, the amount of interest incurred during the construction period is not treated as interest expense. Instead, the interest must be included as part of the acquisition cost of the asset. This is referred to as **capitalization of interest**. The amount of interest that is capitalized (treated as an asset) is based on the *average accumulated expenditures*. The logic of using the average accumulated expenditure is that this number represents an average amount of money tied up in the project over a year. If it takes $400,000 to construct a building, the interest should not be figured on the full $400,000 because there were times during the year when less than the full amount was being used.

When the cost of building an asset is $400,000 and the amount of interest to be capitalized is $10,000, the acquisition cost of the asset is $410,000. The asset should appear on the balance sheet at that amount. Depreciation of the asset should be based on $410,000, less any residual value.

Study Tip

Land improvements represent a depreciable asset with a limited life. Land itself is not depreciable.

Land improvements
Costs that are related to land but that have a limited life.

Land Improvements It is important to distinguish between land and other costs associated with it. The acquisition cost of land should be kept in a separate account because land has an unlimited life and is not subject to depreciation. Other costs associated with land should be recorded in an account such as Land Improvements. For example, the costs of paving a parking lot are properly treated as **land improvements**, which have a limited life. Some landscaping costs also have a limited life. Therefore, the acquisition costs of land improvements should be depreciated over their useful lives.

POD REVIEW 8.4

LO4 *Describe the impact of capitalizing interest as a part of the acquisition cost of an asset.*

- Generally, the interest on borrowed money used to acquire assets should not be capitalized; instead, it should be treated as an expense of the period.
- One important exception to this general guideline exists for interest incurred from money borrowed to construct assets. This interest must be capitalized as part of the acquisition cost of the asset.

QUESTIONS

1. *Interest should be capitalized on which of the following?*
   a. all assets
   b. all purchased assets
   c. all assets constructed by the company
   d. assets that have a cost exceeding $1 million

2. *The amount of interest capitalized should be based on*
   a. the expenditures that exist at the end of the period.
   b. the expenditures that exist at the beginning of the period.
   c. the average accumulated expenditures.
   d. an amount specified by the company's auditors.

LO5 Compare depreciation methods and understand the factors affecting the choice of method.

USE AND DEPRECIATION OF PROPERTY, PLANT, AND EQUIPMENT

All property, plant, and equipment, except land, have a limited life and decline in usefulness over time. The accrual accounting process requires a proper *matching* of expenses and revenue to measure income accurately. Therefore, the accountant must estimate the decline in usefulness of operating assets and allocate the acquisition cost in a manner consistent with the decline in usefulness. This allocation is the process generally referred to as **depreciation**.

Depreciation
The allocation of the original cost of an asset to the periods benefited by its use.

Unfortunately, proper matching for operating assets is not easy because of the many factors involved. An asset's decline in usefulness is related to *physical deterioration* factors such as wear and tear. In some cases, the physical deterioration results from heavy use of the asset in the production process, but it also may result from the passage of time or exposure to the elements.

The decline in an asset's usefulness is also related to *obsolescence* factors. Some operating assets, such as computers, decline in usefulness simply because they have been surpassed by a newer model or newer technology. Finally, the decline in an asset's usefulness is related to a company's *repair and maintenance* policy. A company with an aggressive and extensive repair and maintenance program will not experience a decline in usefulness of operating assets as rapidly as one without such a policy.

Because the decline in an asset's usefulness is related to a variety of factors, several depreciation methods have been developed. In theory, a company should use a depreciation method that allocates the original cost of the asset to the periods benefited and that allows the company to accurately match the expense to the revenue generated by the asset. We will present three methods of depreciation: *straight line*, *units of production*, and *double declining balance*.

All depreciation methods are based on the asset's original acquisition cost. In addition, all methods require an estimate of two additional factors: the asset's *life* and its *residual value*. The residual value (also referred to as *salvage value*) should represent the amount that could be obtained from selling or disposing of the asset at the end of its useful life. Often this may be a small amount or even zero.

Real World Practice

8-1 Reading Nike's Balance Sheet

What amount did Nike present for operating assets for 2006? Why did the company not show depreciation on the balance sheet?

Straight-Line Method The **straight-line method** of depreciation allocates the cost of the asset evenly over time. This method calculates the annual depreciation as follows:

Straight-line method
A method by which the same dollar amount of depreciation is recorded in each year of asset use.

Depreciation = (Acquisition Cost − Residual Value)/Life

For example, assume that on January 1, 2008, ExerCo, a manufacturer of exercise equipment, purchased a machine for $20,000. The company estimated that the machine's life would be five years and its residual value at the end of 2012 would be $2,000. The annual depreciation should be calculated as follows:

Depreciation = (Acquisition Cost − Residual Value)/Life
Depreciation = ($20,000 − $2,000)/5
= $3,600

An asset's **book value** is defined as its acquisition cost minus its total amount of accumulated depreciation. Thus, the book value of the machine in this example is $16,400 at the end of 2008.

Book value
The original cost of an asset minus the amount of accumulated depreciation.

Book Value = Acquisition Cost − Accumulated Depreciation
Book Value = $20,000 − $3,600
= $16,400

The book value at the end of 2009 is $12,800.

Book Value = Acquisition Cost − Accumulated Depreciation
Book Value = $20,000 − (2 × $3,600)
= $12,800

The most attractive features of the straight-line method are its ease and its simplicity. It is the most popular method for presenting depreciation in the annual report to stockholders.

Units-of-Production Method In some cases, the decline in an asset's usefulness is directly related to wear and tear as a result of the number of units it produces. In those cases, depreciation should be calculated by the **units-of-production method**. With this method, the asset's life is expressed in terms of the number of units that the asset can produce. The depreciation *per unit* can be calculated as follows:

Units-of-production method
Depreciation is determined as a function of the number of units the asset produces.

Depreciation per Unit = (Acquisition Cost − Residual Value)/ Total Number of Units in Asset's Life

The annual depreciation for a given year can be calculated based on the number of units produced during that year, as follows:

Annual Depreciation = Depreciation per Unit × Units Produced in Current Year

For example, assume that ExerCo in the previous example wanted to use the units-of-production method for 2008. Also assume that ExerCo has been able to estimate that the total number of units that will be produced during the asset's five-year life is 18,000. During 2008, ExerCo produced 4,000 units. The depreciation per unit for ExerCo's machine can be calculated as follows:

Depreciation per Unit = (Acquisition Cost − Residual Value)/Life in Units
Depreciation per Unit = ($20,000 − $2,000)/18,000
= $1 per Unit

The amount of depreciation that should be recorded as an expense for 2008 is $4,000:

Annual Depreciation = Depreciation per Unit × Units Produced in 2008
Annual Depreciation = $1 per Unit × 4,000 Units
= $4,000

Depreciation will be recorded until the asset produces 18,000 units. The machine cannot be depreciated below its residual value of $2,000.

The units-of-production method is most appropriate when the accountant is able to estimate the total number of units that will be produced over the asset's life. For example, if a factory machine is used to produce a particular item, the life of the asset may be expressed in terms of the number of units produced. Further, the units produced must be related to particular time periods so that depreciation expense can be matched accurately with the related revenue. A variation of the units-of-production method can be used when the life of the asset is expensed in other factors, such as miles driven or hours of use.

Accelerated depreciation
A higher amount of depreciation is recorded in the early years and a lower amount in the later years. ***Alternate term:*** *Allowance for depreciation.*

Double-declining-balance method
Depreciation is recorded at twice the straight-line rate, but the balance is reduced each period.

Accelerated Depreciation Methods In some cases, more cost should be allocated to the early years of an asset's use and less to the later years. For those assets, an accelerated method of depreciation is appropriate. The term **accelerated depreciation** refers to several depreciation methods by which a higher amount of depreciation is recorded in the early years than in later years.

One form of accelerated depreciation is the **double-declining-balance method**. Under this method, depreciation is calculated at double the straight-line rate but on a declining amount. The first step is to calculate the straight-line rate as a percentage. The straight-line rate for the ExerCo asset with a five-year life is as follows:

100%/5 Years = 20%

The second step is to double the straight-line rate, as follows:

2 × 20% = 40%

This rate will be applied in all years to the asset's book value at the beginning of each year. As depreciation is recorded, the book value declines. Thus, a constant rate is applied to a declining amount. This constant rate is applied to the full cost or initial book value, not to cost minus residual value as in the other methods. However, the machine cannot be depreciated below its residual value.

Study Tip

Residual value is deducted for all depreciation methods except for the declining-balance methods.

The amount of depreciation for 2008 would be calculated as follows:

Depreciation = Beginning Book Value × Rate
Depreciation = $20,000 × 40%
= $8,000

The amount of depreciation for 2008 would be calculated as follows:

Depreciation = Beginning Book Value × Rate
Depreciation = ($20,000 − $8,000) × 40%
= $4,800

The complete depreciation schedule for ExerCo for all five years of the machine's life would be as follows:

Year	Rate	Book Value at Beginning of Year	Depreciation	Book Value at End of Year
2008	40%	$20,000	$ 8,000	$12,000
2009	40	12,000	4,800	7,200
2010	40	7,200	2,880	4,320
2011	40	4,320	1,728	2,592
2012	40	2,592	592	2,000
Total			$18,000	

In the ExerCo example, the depreciation for 2012 cannot be calculated as $2,592 × 40% because this would result in an accumulated depreciation amount of more than $18,000. The total amount of depreciation recorded in Years 1 through 4 is $17,408. The accountant should record only $592 depreciation ($18,000 − $17,408) in 2012 so that the remaining value of the machine is $2,000 at the end of 2012.

The double-declining-balance method of depreciation results in an accelerated depreciation pattern. It is most appropriate for assets subject to a rapid decline in usefulness as a result of technical or obsolescence factors. Double-declining-balance depreciation is not widely used for financial statement purposes but may be appropriate for certain assets. As discussed earlier, most companies use straight-line depreciation for financial statement purposes because it generally produces the highest net income, especially in growing companies that have a stable or expanding base of assets.

Comparison of Depreciation Methods In this section, you have learned about several methods of depreciating operating assets. Exhibit 8-1 presents a comparison of the depreciation and book values of the ExerCo asset for 2008–2012 using the straight-line and double-declining-balance methods. (We have excluded the units-of-production method.) Note that both methods result in a depreciation total of $18,000 over the five-year period. The amount of depreciation per year depends, however, on the method of depreciation chosen.

Nonaccountants often misunderstand the accountant's concept of depreciation. Accountants do not consider depreciation to be a process of *valuing* the asset. That is, depreciation does not describe the increase or decrease in the market value of the asset. Accountants consider depreciation to be a process of *cost allocation*. The purpose is to allocate the original acquisition cost to the periods benefited by the asset. The depreciation method chosen should be based on the decline in the asset's usefulness. A company can choose a different depreciation method for each individual fixed asset or for each class or category of fixed assets.

The choice of depreciation method can have a significant impact on the bottom line. If two companies are essentially identical in every other respect, a different depreciation method for fixed assets can make one company look more profitable than another. Or a company that uses accelerated depreciation for one year can find that its otherwise

EXHIBIT 8-1 **Comparison of Depreciation and Book Values of Straight-Line and Double-Declining-Balance Methods**

	Straight-Line		Double-Declining-Balance	
Year	Depreciation	Book Value	Depreciation	Book Value
2008	$ 3,600	$16,400	$ 8,000	$12,000
2009	3,600	12,800	4,800	7,200
2010	3,600	9,200	2,880	4,320
2011	3,600	5,600	1,728	2,592
2012	3,600	2,000	592	2,000
Totals	$18,000		$18,000	

declining earnings are no longer declining if it switches to straight-line depreciation. Investors should pay some attention to depreciation methods when comparing companies. Statement users must be aware of the different depreciation methods to understand the calculation of income and to compare companies that may not use the same methods.

Some investors ignore depreciation altogether when evaluating a company, not because they do not know that assets depreciate but because they want to focus on cash flow instead of earnings. Depreciation is a "noncash" charge that reduces net income.

Depreciation and Income Taxes Financial accounting involves the presentation of financial statements to external users of accounting information, users such as investors and creditors. When depreciating an asset for financial accounting purposes, the accountant should choose a depreciation method that is consistent with the asset's decline in usefulness and that properly allocates its cost to the periods that benefit from its use.

Depreciation is also deducted for income tax purposes. Sometimes depreciation is referred to as a *tax shield* because it reduces (as do other expenses) the amount of income tax that would otherwise have to be paid. When depreciating an asset for tax purposes, a company should generally choose a depreciation method that reduces the present value of its tax burden to the lowest possible amount over the life of the asset. Normally, this is best accomplished with an accelerated depreciation method, which allows a company to save more income tax in the early years of the asset. This happens because the higher depreciation charges reduce taxable income more than the straight-line method does. The method allowed for tax purposes is referred to as MACRS, which stands for Modified Accelerated Cost Recovery System. As a form of accelerated depreciation, it results in a larger amount of depreciation in the early years of asset life and a smaller amount in later years.

Choice of Depreciation Method As stated, in theory, a company should choose the depreciation method that best allocates the original cost of the asset to the periods benefited by the use of the asset. Theory aside, it is important to examine the other factors that affect a company's decision in choosing a depreciation method or methods. Exhibit 8-2 presents the factors that affect this decision and the likely choice that arises

EXHIBIT 8-2 Management's Choice of Depreciation Method

Factor	Likely Choice
Simplicity	The straight-line method is easiest to compute and record.
Reporting to stockholders	Usually firms want to maximize net income in reporting to stockholders and will use the straight-line method.
Comparability	Usually firms use the same depreciation method as other firms in the same industry or line of business.
Management bonus plans	If management is paid a bonus based on net income, it will likely use the straight-line method.
Technological competitiveness	If technology is changing rapidly, a firm should consider an accelerated method of depreciation.
Reporting to the Internal Revenue Service	Firms will usually use an accelerated method of depreciation to minimize taxable income in reporting to the IRS.

from each factor. Usually, the factor that is most important is whether depreciation is calculated for presentation on the financial statements to stockholders or whether it is calculated for income tax purposes.

When depreciation is calculated for financial statement purposes, a company generally wants to present the most favorable impression (the highest income) possible. Therefore, most companies choose the straight-line method of depreciation. In fact, more than 90% of large companies use the straight-line method for financial statement purposes.

If the objective of the company's management is to minimize its income tax liability, the company will generally not choose the straight-line method for tax purposes. As discussed in the preceding section, accelerated depreciation allows the company to save more on income taxes because depreciation is a tax shield.

Therefore, it is not unusual for a company to use *two* depreciation methods for the same asset, one for financial reporting purposes and another for tax purposes. This may seem somewhat confusing, but it is the direct result of the differing goals of financial and tax accounting. See Chapter 10 for more about this issue.

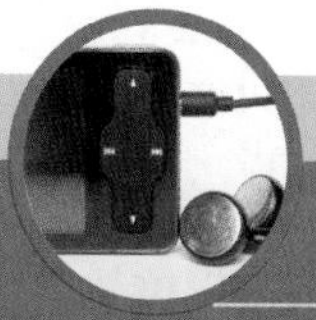

POD REVIEW 8.5

LO5 *Compare depreciation methods and understand the factors affecting the choice of method.*

- All property, plant, and equipment (except land) have a limited life; and a proper matching of expenses through depreciation is required. Several depreciation methods are available, including straight-line, units-of-production, and accelerated depreciation methods.
- In theory, the depreciation method that best allocates the original cost of the asset to the periods benefited by the use of the asset should be chosen. However, depreciation method choices are often influenced by tax and shareholder perceptions.

QUESTIONS

1. *Which of the following assets is not depreciated, depleted, or amortized over its life?*
   a. land
   b. natural resources
   c. buildings
   d. equipment

2. *Which of the following statements about the accumulated depreciation account is true?*
   a. It is a long-term liability.
   b. It provides a contra account to intangible assets.
   c. It provides a contra account to tangible assets so that their net book value approximates their market value.
   d. It represents the total depreciation charged over the life of the asset to which it relates and reduces the book value of the asset.

LO6 Understand the impact of a change in the estimate of the asset life or residual value.

Change in Depreciation Estimate An asset's acquisition cost is known at the time it is purchased, but its life and its residual value must be estimated. These estimates are then used as the basis for depreciating it. Occasionally, an estimate of the asset's life or residual value must be altered after the depreciation process has begun. This is an example of an accounting change that is referred to as a **change in estimate**.

Change in estimate A change in the life of the asset or in its residual value.

Assume the same facts as in the ExerCo example. The company purchased a machine on January 1, 2008, for $20,000. ExerCo estimated that the machine's life would be five years and its residual value at the end of five years would be $2,000.

Assume that ExerCo has depreciated the machine using the straight-line method for two years. At the beginning of 2010, ExerCo believes that the total machine life will be seven years, or another five years beyond the two years the machine has been used. Thus, depreciation must be adjusted to reflect the new estimate of the asset's life.

A change in estimate should be recorded *prospectively*, meaning that the depreciation recorded in prior years is not corrected or restated. Instead, the new estimate should affect the current year and future years. ExerCo should depreciate the remaining depreciable amount during 2010 through 2014. The amount to be depreciated over that time period should be calculated as follows:

Acquisition Cost, January 1, 2008	$20,000
Less: Accumulated Depreciation	
(2 years at $3,600 per year)	7,200
Book Value, January 1, 2010	$12,800
Less: Residual Value	2,000
Remaining Depreciable Amount	$10,800

The remaining depreciable amount should be recorded as depreciation over the remaining life of the machine. In the ExerCo case, the depreciation amount for 2010 and the following four years would be $2,160:

Depreciation = Remaining Depreciable Amount/Remaining Life
Depreciation = $10,800/5 Years
= $2,160

The journal entry to record depreciation for the year 2010 is as follows:

2010			
Dec. 31	Depreciation Expense	2,160	
	Accumulated Depreciation		2,160
	To record depreciation for 2010.		

Balance Sheet							Income Statement
ASSETS		=	**LIABILITIES**	+	**STOCKHOLDERS' EQUITY**	+	**REVENUES – EXPENSES**
Accumulated Depreciation	(2,160)						Depreciation Expense (2,160)

If the change in estimate is a material amount, the company should disclose in the footnotes to the 2010 financial statements that depreciation has changed as a result of a change in estimate. The company's auditors have to be very careful that management's decision to change its estimate of the depreciable life of the asset is not an attempt to manipulate earnings. Particularly in capital-intensive manufacturing concerns, lengthening the useful life of equipment can have a material impact on earnings.

A change in estimate of an asset's residual value is treated in a manner similar to a change in an asset's life. There should be no attempt to correct or restate the income statements of past periods that were based on the original estimate. Instead, the accountant should use the new estimate of residual value to calculate depreciation for the current and future years.

POD REVIEW 8.6

LO6 ***Understand the impact of a change in the estimate of the asset life or residual value.***

- Occasionally, an estimate of the asset's life or residual value must be modified after the depreciation process has begun. This is an example of an accounting change that is referred to as *a change in estimate.*

QUESTIONS

1. *An example of a change in estimate is*
   a. a change in the estimated life of a depreciable asset.
   b. a change in the salvage value of an asset.
   c. Both (a) and (b) are changes in estimate.
   d. Neither (a) nor (b) is a change in estimate.

2. *When a change in estimate occurs*
   a. the company should restate the statements of past periods because of the change.
   b. the company should show a line on its income statement titled Change in Estimate.
   c. the change should not be recorded by the company.
   d. the change should affect the current period and future periods.

CAPITAL VERSUS REVENUE EXPENDITURES

Accountants often must decide whether certain expenditures related to operating assets should be treated as an addition to the cost of the asset or as an expense. One of the most common examples involving this decision concerns repairs to an asset. Should the repairs constitute capital expenditures or revenue expenditures?

LO7 Determine which expenditures should be capitalized as asset costs and which should be treated as expenses.

- A **capital expenditure** is a cost that is added to the acquisition cost of an asset.
- A **revenue expenditure** is not treated as part of the cost of the asset but as an expense on the income statement.

Thus, the company must decide whether to treat an item as an asset (balance sheet) and depreciate its cost over its life or to treat it as an expense (income statement) of a single period.

The distinction between capital and revenue expenditures is a matter of judgment. Generally, the following guidelines should be followed:

- When an expenditure *increases the life of the asset or its productivity*, it should be treated as a capital expenditure and added to the asset account.
- When an expenditure *simply maintains an asset in its normal operating condition*, however, it should be treated as an expense.

The *materiality* of the expenditure must also be considered. Most companies establish a policy of treating an expenditure that is smaller than a specified amount as a revenue expenditure (an expense on the income statement).

It is very important that a company not improperly capitalize a material expenditure that should have been written off right away. The capitalization policies of companies are closely watched by Wall Street analysts who try to assess the value of these companies. When a company is capitalizing rather than expensing certain items to artificially boost earnings, that revelation can be very damaging to the stock price.

Capital expenditure
A cost that improves the asset and is added to the asset account. ***Alternate term:*** *Item treated as asset.*

Revenue expenditure
A cost that keeps an asset in its normal operating condition and is treated as an expense. ***Alternate term:*** *Item treated as an expense of the period.*

Expenditures related to operating assets may be classified in several categories. For each type of expenditure, its treatment as capital or revenue should be as follows:

Category	Example	Asset or Expense
Normal maintenance	Repaint	Expense
Minor repair	Replace spark plugs	Expense
Major repair	Replace a vehicle's engine	Asset if life or productivity is enhanced
Addition	Add a wing to a building	Asset

An item treated as a capital expenditure affects the amount of depreciation that should be recorded over the asset's remaining life. We return to the ExerCo example to illustrate. Assume again that ExerCo purchased a machine on January 1, 2008, for $20,000. ExerCo estimated that its residual value at the end of five years would be $2,000 and has depreciated the machine using the straight-line method for 2008 and 2009. At the beginning of 2010, ExerCo made a $3,000 overhaul to the machine, extending its life by three years. Because the expenditure qualifies as a capital expenditure, the cost of overhauling the machine should be added to the asset account. The journal entry to record the overhaul is as follows:

2010			
Jan. 1	Machine	3,000	
	Cash		3,000
	To record the overhaul of an operating asset.		

Balance Sheet						Income Statement
ASSETS		=	**LIABILITIES** +	**STOCKHOLDERS' EQUITY**	+	**REVENUES − EXPENSES**
Machine	3,000					
Cash	(3,000)					

For the years 2008 and 2009, ExerCo recorded depreciation of $3,600 per year:

Depreciation = (Acquisition Cost − Residual Value)/Life
Depreciation = ($20,000 − $2,000)/5
= $3,600

Beginning in 2010, the company should record depreciation of $2,300 per year, computed as follows:

Original Cost, January 1, 2008	$20,000
Less: Accumulated Depreciation (2 years × $3,600)	7,200
Book Value, January 1, 2010	$12,800
Plus: Major Overhaul	3,000
Less: Residual Value	(2,000)
Remaining Depreciable Amount	$13,800

Depreciation = Remaining Depreciable Amount/Remaining Life
Depreciation per year = $13,800/6 Years
= $2,300

The entry to record depreciation for the year 2010 is as follows:

2010			
Dec. 31	Depreciation Expense	2,300	
	Accumulated Depreciation—Asset		2,300
	To record annual depreciation on operating asset.		

Balance Sheet						Income Statement	
ASSETS		=	**LIABILITIES** +	**STOCKHOLDERS' EQUITY**	+	**REVENUES − EXPENSES**	
Accumulated Depreciation—Asset	(2,300)					Depreciation Expense	(2,300)

ENVIRONMENTAL ASPECTS OF OPERATING ASSETS

As the number of the government's environmental regulations has increased, businesses have been required to expend more money complying with them. A common example involves costs to comply with federal requirements to clean up contaminated soil surrounding plant facilities. In some cases, the costs are very large and may exceed the value of the property. Should such costs be considered an expense and recorded entirely in one accounting period, or should they be treated as a capital expenditure and added to the cost of the asset? If there is a legal obligation to clean up the property or to restore the property to its original condition, companies are required to record the cost of asset retirement obligations as part of the cost of the asset. For example, if a company owns a factory and has made a binding promise to restore to its original condition the property used by the factory, the costs of restoring the property must be added to the asset account. Of course, it is sometimes difficult to determine whether a legal obligation exists. It is important, however, for companies at least to conduct a thorough investigation to determine the potential environmental considerations that may affect the value of operating assets and to ponder carefully the accounting implications of new environmental regulations.

POD REVIEW 8.7

LO7 *Determine which expenditures should be capitalized as asset costs and which should be treated as expenses.*

- The nature of some expenditures related to a capital asset, such as repairs and replacement parts, must be determined for the proper financial accounting treatment.
  - Capital expenditures are added to the acquisition cost of an asset and are depreciated over time.
  - Revenue expenditures are not treated as part of the cost of the asset, but as an expense on the income statement in the period incurred.

QUESTIONS

1. *A capital expenditure is*
   a. added to the cost of the asset.
   b. treated as an expense of the period.
   c. an expenditure that maintains the asset in its normal operating condition.
   d. deducted from the cost of the asset.

2. *A revenue expenditure is*
   a. added to the cost of the asset.
   b. treated as an expense of the period.
   c. an expenditure that improves the asset.
   d. deducted from the cost of the asset.

DISPOSAL OF PROPERTY, PLANT, AND EQUIPMENT

LO8 Analyze the effect of the disposal of an asset at a gain or loss.

An asset may be disposed of in any of several different ways. One common method is to sell the asset for cash. Sale of an asset involves two important considerations. First, depreciation must be recorded up to the date of sale. If the sale does not occur at the fiscal year-end, usually December 31, depreciation must be recorded for a partial period from the beginning of the year to the date of sale. Second, the company selling the asset must calculate and record the gain or loss on its sale.

Gain on Sale of Assets Refer again to the ExerCo example. Assume that ExerCo purchased a machine on January 1, 2008, for $20,000, estimating its life to be five years and the residual value to be $2,000. ExerCo used the straight-line method of depreciation. Assume that ExerCo sold the machine on July 1, 2010, for $12,400. Depreciation for the six-month time period from January 1 to July 1, 2010, is $1,800 ($3,600 per year × 1/2 year = $1,800) and should be recorded as follows:

2010			
July 1	Depreciation Expense	1,800	
	Accumulated Depreciation—Machine		1,800
	To record depreciation for a six-month time period.		

Balance Sheet						Income Statement
ASSETS	=	**LIABILITIES**	+	**STOCKHOLDERS' EQUITY**	+	**REVENUES – EXPENSES**
Accumulated Depreciation—Machine (1,800)						Depreciation Expense (1,800)

After the July 1 entry, the balance of the Acumulated Depreciation—Machine account is $9,000, which reflects depreciation for the $2\frac{1}{2}$ years from the date of purchase to the date of sale. The entry to record the sale is as follows:

2010			
July 1	Accumulated Depreciation—Machine	9,000	
	Cash	12,400	
	Machine		20,000
	Gain on Sale of Asset		1,400
	To record the sale of the machine.		

Balance Sheet						Income Statement
ASSETS	=	**LIABILITIES**	+	**STOCKHOLDERS' EQUITY**	+	**REVENUES – EXPENSES**
Accumulated Depreciation—Machine 9,000						Gain on Sale of Asset 1,400
Cash 12,400						
Machine (20,000)						

Gain on Sale of Asset
The excess of the selling price over the asset's book value.

When an asset is sold, all accounts related to it must be removed. In the preceding entry, the Machine account is reduced (credited) to eliminate the account and the Accumulated Depreciation—Machine account is reduced (debited) to eliminate it. The **Gain on Sale of Asset** indicates the amount by which the sale price of the machine *exceeds* the book value. Thus, the gain can be calculated as follows:

Asset cost	$20,000
Less: Accumulated depreciation	9,000
Book value	$11,000
Sale price	12,400
Gain on sale of asset	$ 1,400

The account **Gain on Sale of Asset is an income statement account** and should appear in the Other Income/Expense category of the statement. The Gain on Sale of Asset account is not treated as revenue because it does not constitute the company's ongoing or central activity. Instead, it appears as income but in a separate category to denote its incidental nature.

Loss on Sale of Assets The calculation of a loss on the sale of an asset is similar to that of a gain. Assume in the previous example that ExerCo had sold the machine on July 1, 2010, for $10,000 cash. As in the example, depreciation must be recorded to the date of sale, July 1. Following is the entry to record the sale of the asset:

2010			
July 1	Accumulated Depreciation—Machine	9,000	
	Cash	10,000	
	Loss on Sale of Asset	1,000	
	Machine		20,000
	To record the sale of the machine.		

Balance Sheet							Income Statement	
ASSETS		=	LIABILITIES	+	STOCKHOLDERS' EQUITY	+	REVENUES − EXPENSES	
Accumulated Depreciation—Machine	9,000						Loss on Sale of Asset	(1,000)
Cash	10,000							
Machine	(20,000)							

The **Loss on Sale of Asset** indicates the amount by which the asset's sales price is *less than* its book value. Thus, the loss could be calculated as follows:

Loss on Sale of Asset
The amount by which selling price is less than book value.

Asset cost	$20,000
Less: Accumulated depreciation	9,000
Book value	$11,000
Sale price	10,000
Loss on sale of asset	$ 1,000

The **Loss on Sale of Asset account is an income statement account** and should appear in the Other Income/Expense category of the income statement.

POD REVIEW 8.8

LO8 *Analyze the effect of the disposal of an asset at a gain or loss.*

- Assets are usually disposed of through sales, which are exchange transactions that result in a gain or loss.
  - The gain or loss on an asset is the difference between the sales (or exchange) price and the book value of the asset, where book value is the acquisition cost less any accumulated depreciation on the asset.

QUESTIONS

1. *A gain on sale of asset occurs when the sale price of the asset is*
   a. less than its book value.
   b. less than accumulated depreciation.
   c. more than its book value.
   d. more than accumulated depreciation.

2. *A loss on sale of asset occurs when the sale price of the asset is*
   a. less than its book value.
   b. less than accumulated depreciation.
   c. more than its book value.
   d. more than accumulated depreciation.

Operating Assets: Intangible Assets

LO9 Understand the balance sheet presentation of intangible assets.

Intangible assets are long-term assets with no physical properties. Because one cannot see or touch most intangible assets, it is easy to overlook their importance. Intangibles are recorded as assets, however, because they provide future economic benefits to the company. In fact, an intangible asset may be the most important asset a company owns or controls. For example, a pharmaceutical company may own some property, plant, and equipment, but its most important asset may be its patent for a particular drug or process. Likewise, the company that publishes this textbook may consider the copyrights to textbooks to be among its most important revenue-producing assets.

Intangible assets
Assets with no physical properties.

The balance sheet includes the intangible assets that meet the accounting definition of assets. Patents, copyrights, and brand names are included because they are owned by the company and will produce a future benefit that can be identified and measured.

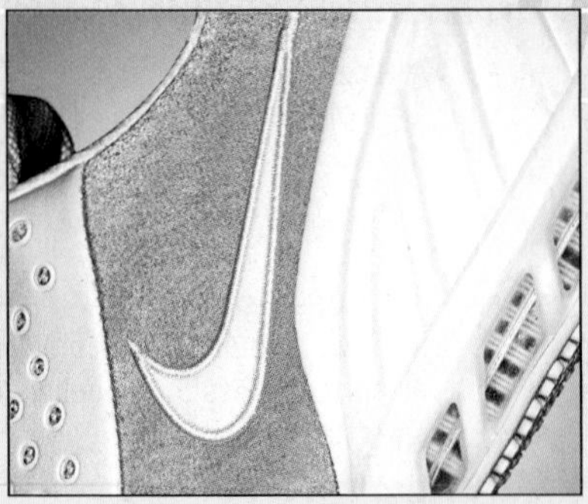

© PRNewsFoto/Nike

Hot Topics

The Nike Brand: Intangible? Yes. Valuable? Absolutely!

Nike's brand name and company logo are among the most recognizable in the world. They may be intangible assets, but they are some of the company's most valuable assets. How does Nike use these assets to create sales? By having great-looking and great-performing products that sport the brand name using recognizable athletes and effective marketing and advertising campaigns. In 2007, Nike announced its ZOOM footwear line, bearing the tag "quick is deadly." The shoes are designed for athletes who demand a lower and more responsive cushioning system and feature top-name athletes such as football player LaDainian Tomlinson, basketball player Steve Nash, runner Lauren Fleshman, and Olympic sprinters Asafa Powell and Sanya Richards. The ad campaign features print, broadcast, and digital advertising and public relations applications. But all of it is based on the brand name and identity that Nike has established for many years.

The balance sheet, however, would indicate only the acquisition cost of those assets, not the value of the assets to the company or the sales value of the assets.

Of course, the balance sheet does not include all of the items that may produce future benefit to the company. A company's employees, its management team, its location, or the intellectual capital of a few key researchers may well provide important future benefits and value. They are not recorded on the balance sheet, however, because they do not meet the accountant's definition of *assets* and cannot be easily identified or measured.

BALANCE SHEET PRESENTATION

Intangible assets are long-term assets and should be shown separately from property, plant, and equipment. Exhibit 8-3 contains a list of the most common intangible assets. Some companies develop a separate category, Intangible Assets, for the various types of intangibles. Nike presents only two lines for intangible assets: one for Identifiable Intangible Assets and another for Goodwill. Exhibit 8-4 presents the note that indicates that the company's intangible assets consist of patents, trademarks, and goodwill. The presentation of intangible assets varies widely, however.

Goodwill
The excess of the purchase price to acquire a business over the value of the individual net assets acquired. ***Alternate term:*** *Purchase price in excess of the market value of the assets.*

The nature of many intangibles is fairly evident, but goodwill is not so easily understood. **Goodwill** represents the amount of the purchase price paid in excess of the market value of the individual net assets when a business is purchased. Goodwill is recorded only when a business is purchased. It is not recorded when a company engages in activities that do not involve the purchase of another business entity. For example, customer loyalty or a good management team may represent goodwill, but neither meets the accountants' criteria to be recorded as an asset on a firm's financial statements.

EXHIBIT 8-3 Most Common Intangible Assets

Intangible Asset	Description
Patent	Right to use, manufacture, or sell a product; granted by the U.S. Patent Office. Patents have a legal life of 20 years.
Copyright	Right to reproduce or sell a published work. Copyrights are granted for 50 years plus the life of the creator.
Trademark	A symbol or name that allows a product or service to be identified; provides legal protection for 20 years in addition to an indefinite number of renewal periods.
Goodwill	The excess of the purchase price to acquire a business over the value of the individual net assets acquired.

EXHIBIT 8-4 The Nike, Inc., Consolidated Assets Section and Intangibles Notes

The following table summarizes the Company's identifiable intangible assets balances as of May 31, 2006:

	May 31, 2006		
(In millions)	**Gross Carrying Amount**	**Accumulated Amortization**	**Net Carrying Amount**
Amortized intangible assets:			
Patents	$ 34.1	$ (10.5)	$ 23.6
Trademarks	46.4	(11.8)	34.6
Other	21.5	(15.7)	5.8
Total	$102.0	$ (38.0)	$ 64.0
Unamortized intangible assets:			
Trademarks			$341.5
Total			$405.5
Goodwill			$130.8

International accounting standards allow firms *either* to present goodwill separately as an asset or to deduct it from stockholders' equity at the time of purchase. The result is that the presentation of goodwill on the financial statements of non-U.S. companies can look much different from that for U.S. companies. Similarly, some investors in U.S. companies believe that goodwill is not an asset because it is difficult to determine the factors that caused this asset. They prefer to focus their attention on a company's tangible assets. These investors simply reduce the amount shown on the balance sheet by the amount of goodwill, deducting it from total assets and reducing stockholders' equity by the same amount.

ACQUISITION COST OF INTANGIBLE ASSETS

As was the case with property, plant, and equipment, **the acquisition cost of an intangible asset includes all of the costs to acquire the asset and prepare it for its intended use.** This should include all necessary costs, such as legal costs incurred at the time of acquisition. Acquisition cost also should include those costs that are incurred after acquisition and that are necessary to the existence of the asset. For example, if a firm must pay legal fees to protect a patent from infringement, the costs should be considered part of the acquisition cost and should be included in the patent account.

Research and Development Costs You should also be aware of one item that is similar to intangible assets but is *not* on the balance sheet. **Research and development costs** are expenditures incurred in the discovery of new knowledge and the translation of research into a design or plan for a new product or service or in a significant improvement to an existing product or service. Firms that engage in research and development do so because they believe such activities provide future benefit to the company. In fact, many firms have become leaders in an industry by engaging in research and development and the discovery of new products or technology. It is often very difficult, however, to identify the amount of future benefits of research and development and to associate those benefits with specific time periods. Because of the difficulty in predicting future benefits, the FASB has ruled that firms are not allowed to treat research and development costs as assets; all such expenditures must be treated as expenses in the period incurred. Many firms, especially high-technology ones, argue that this accounting rule results in seriously understated balance sheets. In their view, an important "asset"

Research and development costs
Costs incurred in the discovery of new knowledge.

is not portrayed on their balance sheet. They also argue that they are at a competitive disadvantage when compared with foreign companies that are allowed to treat at least a portion of research and development as an asset. Users of financial statements somehow need to be aware of those "hidden assets" when analyzing the balance sheets of companies that must expense research and development costs.

It is important to distinguish between patent costs and research and development costs. Patent costs include legal and filing fees necessary to acquire a patent. Such costs are capitalized as an intangible asset, Patent. However, the Patent account should not include the costs of research and development of a new product. Those costs are not capitalized but are treated as an expense, Research and Development.

POD REVIEW 8.9

LO9 *Understand the balance sheet presentation of intangible assets.*

- Intangible assets are long-term assets that should be shown separately from property, plant, and equipment on the balance sheet.

QUESTIONS

1. *Which of the following is not an intangible asset?*
   a. patents
   b. improvements to a building that the company already owns
   c. trademarks
   d. goodwill arising as a result of an acquisition

2. *Research and development costs should be*
   a. presented as an intangible asset.
   b. presented as property, plant, and equipment.
   c. presented as an intangible asset if the research was conducted internally.
   d. treated as an expense.

LO10 Understand the proper amortization of intangible assets.

AMORTIZATION OF INTANGIBLES

There has been considerable discussion over the past few years about whether intangible assets should be amortized and, if so, over what period of time. The term *amortization* is very similar to depreciation of property, plant, and equipment. Amortization involves allocating the acquistion cost of an intangible asset to the periods benefited by the use of the asset. When an intangible asset is amortized, most companies use the straight-line method of amortization. We will use that method for illustration purposes. Occasionally, however, you may see instances of an accelerated form of amortization if the decline in usefulness of the intangible asset does not occur evenly over time.

Intangibles with Finite Life **If an intangible asset has a finite life, amortization must be recognized.** A finite life exists when an intangible asset is legally valid for only a certain length of time. For example, a patent is granted for a time period of 20 years and gives the patent holder the legal right to exclusive use of the patented design or invention. A copyright is likewise granted for a specified legal life. A finite life also exists when there is no legal life but the management of the company knows for certain that it will be able to use the intangible asset only for a specified period of time. For example, a company may have purchased the right to use a list of names and addresses of customers for a two-year time period. In that case, the intangible asset can be used only for two years and has a finite life.

When an intangible asset with a finite life is amortized, the time period over which amortization should be recorded must be considered carefully. The general guideline that should be followed is this: **amortization should be recorded over the legal life or the**

useful life, whichever is shorter. For example, patents may have a legal life of 20 years, but many are not useful for that long because new products and technology make the patent obsolete. The patent should be amortized over the number of years in which the firm receives benefits, which may be a period shorter than the legal life.

Assume that Nike developed a patent for a new shoe product on January 1, 2008. The costs involved with patent approval were $10,000, and the company wants to record amortization on the straight-line basis over a five-year life with no residual value. The accounting entry to record the amortization for 2008 is as follows:

2008			
Dec. 31	Patent Amortization Expense	2,000	
	Accumulated Amortization—Patent		2,000
	To record amortization of patent for one year.		

Balance Sheet							Income Statement
ASSETS		=	**LIABILITIES**	+	**STOCKHOLDERS' EQUITY**	+	**REVENUES − EXPENSES**
Accumulated Amortization—Patent	(2,000)						Patent Amortization Expense (2,000)

Rather than use an accumulated amortization account, some companies decrease (credit) the intangible asset account directly. In that case, the preceding transaction is recorded as follows:

2008			
Dec. 31	Patent Amortization Expense	2,000	
	Patent		2,000
	To record amortization of patent for one year.		

Balance Sheet							Income Statement
ASSETS		=	**LIABILITIES**	+	**STOCKHOLDERS' EQUITY**	+	**REVENUES − EXPENSES**
Patent	(2,000)						Patent Amortization Expense (2,000)

No matter which of the two preceding entries is used, the asset should be reported on the balance sheet at acquisition cost ($10,000) less accumulated amortization ($2,000), or $8,000, as of December 31, 2008.

Intangibles with Indefinite Life While intangibles such as patents and copyrights have a finite life, many others do not. **If an intangible asset has an indefinite life, amortization should not be recognized.** For example, a television or radio station may have paid to acquire a broadcast license. A broadcast license is usually for a certain time period but can be renewed at the end of that time period. In that case, the life of the asset is indefinite and amortization of the intangible asset representing the broadcast rights should not be recognized. A second example would be a trademark. For many companies, such as **Nike** and **Coca-Cola**, a trademark is a valuable asset that provides name recognition and enhances sales. A trademark is granted for a certain time period but can be renewed at the end of that period, so the life may be quite indefinite. The value of some trademarks may continue for a long time. If the life of an intangible asset represented by trademarks is indefinite, amortization should not be recorded. Note in Exhibit 8-4 that Nike has considered some trademarks to have an indefinite life and has not amortized them. Others have been amortized because they have a limited life.

Goodwill Goodwill is an important intangible asset on the balance sheet of many companies. Until 2001, accounting rules had required companies to record amortization of goodwill over a time period not to exceed 40 years. However, in 2001, the FASB ruled that goodwill should be treated as an intangible asset with an *indefinite* life and that companies should no longer record amortization expense related to goodwill. Companies have generally favored the new accounting stance. The hope is that it will allow companies to more accurately inform statement users of their true value.

While companies should not record amortization of intangible assets with an indefinite life, they are required each year to determine whether the asset has been *impaired*. A discussion of asset impairment is beyond the scope of this text; but generally, it means that a loss should be recorded when the value of the asset has declined. For example, some trademarks, such as Xerox and Polaroid, that were quite powerful in the past have declined in value over time. When an impairment of the asset is recognized, the loss is recorded in the time period that the value declines rather than the date the asset is sold. It requires a great deal of judgment to determine when intangible assets have been impaired because the true value of an intangible asset is often difficult to determine. A rather drastic example of impairment occurs when a company realizes that an intangible asset has become completely worthless and should be written off.

Assume that Nike learns on January 1, 2009, when accumulated amortization is $2,000 (or the book value of the patent is $8,000), that a competing company has developed a new product that renders Nike's patent worthless. Nike has a loss of $8,000 and should record an entry to write off the asset as follows:

2009			
Jan. 1	Loss on Patent	8,000	
	Accumulated Amortization—Patent	2,000	
	Patent		10,000
	To record the write-off of patent.		

Balance Sheet							Income Statement	
ASSETS		=	**LIABILITIES**	+	**STOCKHOLDERS' EQUITY**	+	**REVENUES – EXPENSES**	
Accumulated Amortization	2,000						Loss on Patent	(8,000)
Patent	(10,000)							

POD REVIEW 8.10

LO10 *Understand the proper amortization of intangible assets.*

- The amortization of intangibles is a process similar to that of depreciating capital assets.
- If an intangible asset has a finite useful life, amortization expense must be taken on the asset over the legal life or useful life, whichever is shorter.

QUESTIONS

1. *Regarding amortization of intangible assets,*
   a. all intangible assets should be amortized.
   b. no intangible assets should be amortized.
   c. intangible assets with an infinite life should be amortized.
   d. intangible assets with a finite life should be amortized.

2. *Intangibles that have a finite life*
   a. should not be amortized.
   b. should be treated in the same manner as those that have an infinite life.
   c. should be amortized over the legal life or useful life, whichever is shorter.
   d. should be amortized over the legal life or useful life, whichever is longer.

How Long-Term Assets Affect the Statement of Cash Flows

LO11 Explain the impact that long-term assets have on the statement of cash flows.

Determining the impact that acquisition, depreciation, and sale of long-term assets have on the statement of cash flows is important. Each of these business activities influences the statement of cash flows. Exhibit 8-5 illustrates the items discussed in this chapter and their effect on the statement of cash flows.

The acquisition of a long-term asset is an investing activity and should be reflected in the Investing Activities category of the statement of cash flows. The acquisition should appear as a deduction, or negative item, in that section because it requires the use of cash to purchase the asset. This applies whether the long-term asset is property, plant, and equipment or an intangible asset.

The depreciation or amortization of a long-term asset is not a cash item. It was referred to earlier as a noncash charge to earnings. Nevertheless, it must be presented on the statement of cash flows (if the indirect method is used for the statement). The reason is that it was deducted from earnings in calculating the net income figure. Therefore, it must be eliminated or "added back" if the net income amount is used to indicate the amount of cash generated from operations. **Thus, depreciation and amortization should be presented in the Operating Activities category of the statement of cash flows as an addition to net income.**

The sale or disposition of long-term assets is an investing activity. When an asset is sold, the amount of cash received should be reflected as an addition or plus amount in the Investing Activities category of the statement of cash flows. If the asset was sold at a gain or loss, however, one additional aspect should be reflected. Because the gain or loss was reflected on the income statement, it should be eliminated from the net income amount presented in the Operating Activities category (if the indirect method is used). A sale of an asset is not an activity related to normal ongoing operations, and all amounts involved with the sale should be removed from the Operating Activities category. Exhibit 8-6 indicates the Operating and Investing categories of the 2006 statement of cash flows of **Nike, Inc.** The company had a net income of $1,392.0 million during 2006. Nike's performance is an excellent example of the difference between net income and actual cash flow. Note that the company generated a positive cash flow from operating activities of $1,667.9 million. One of the primary reasons was that depreciation of $282.0 million and amortization of $8.9 million affected the income statement but did not involve a cash outflow and therefore are added back on the statement of cash flows. Also note that the Investing Activities category indicates major outlays of cash for new property, plant, and equipment of $333.7 million. These cash outflows are indications of Nike's need for cash that must be generated from its operating activities.

EXHIBIT 8-5 **Long-Term Assets and the Statement of Cash Flows**

Item	Cash Flow Statement	
	Operating Activities	
	Net income	XXX
Depreciation and Amortization	→	+
Gain on sale of asset	→	−
Loss on sale of asset	→	+
	Investing Activities	
Purchase of asset	→	−
Sale of asset	→	+
	Financing Activities	

EXHIBIT 8-6 **Nike, Inc.'s Consolidated Partial Statement of Cash Flows**

Year ended May 31, (millions)	2006
Cash provided (used) by operations:	
Net income	$ 1,392.0
Income charges not affecting cash:	
Depreciation	282.0
Deferred income taxes	(26.0)
Amortization and other	8.9
Income tax benefit from exercise of stock options	54.2
Changes in certain working capital components:	
Decrease (increase) in accounts receivable	(85.1)
(Increase) decrease in inventories	(200.3)
(Increase) decrease in prepaids and other current assets	(37.2)
Increase in accounts payable, accrued liabilities and income taxes payable	279.4
Cash provided by operations	1,667.9
Cash provided (used) by investing activities:	
Purchases of short-term investments	(2,619.7)
Maturities of short-term investments	1,709.8
Additions to property, plant and equipment and other	(333.7)
Disposals of property, plant and equipment	1.6
Increase in other assets	(30.3)
(Decrease) increase in other liabilities	4.3
Acquisition of subsidiary, net of cash acquired	—
Cash used by investing activities	(1,268.0)

POD REVIEW 8.11

LO11 *Explain the impact that long-term assets have on the statement of cash flows.*

- Long-term assets impact the statement of cash flows when they are acquired, depreciated, and sold.
  - Cash used to acquire long-term assets or cash received on the sale of long-term assets is reflected in the Investing Activities section of the statement of cash flows.
  - Depreciation and amortization are noncash expenses recorded on the accrual income statement. Accordingly, net income on a cash basis must be arrived at by adding depreciation and amortization back to accrual net income.

QUESTIONS

1. *On the statement of cash flows (indirect method), the amount for depreciation should be presented in which category?*
   a. Operating
   b. Investing
   c. Financing
   d. Should not be presented

2. *When a company purchases property, plant, and equipment, an amount should appear in which category of the statement of cash flows?*
   a. Operating
   b. Investing
   c. Financing
   d. Should not be presented

Analyzing Long-Term Assets for Average Life and Asset Turnover

LO12 Understand how investors can analyze a company's operating assets.

Because long-term assets constitute the major productive assets of most companies, it is important to analyze the age and composition of these assets. Analysis of the age of the assets can be accomplished fairly easily for those companies that use the straight-line method of depreciation. A rough measure of the average life of the assets can be calculated as follows:

$$\text{Average Life} = \frac{\text{Property, Plant, and Equipment}}{\text{Depreciation Expense}}$$

The average age of the assets can be calculated as follows:

$$\text{Average Age} = \frac{\text{Accumulated Depreciation}}{\text{Depreciation Expense}}$$

The asset category of the balance sheet is also important in analyzing a company's profitability. The asset turnover is a measure of the productivity of the assets and is measured as follows:

$$\text{Asset Turnover} = \frac{\text{Net Sales}}{\text{Average Total Assets}}$$

This ratio is a measure of how many dollars of assets are necessary for every dollar of sales. That is, the ratio is a measure of how productive the assets are in generating sales. If a company is using its assets efficiently, each dollar of assets will create a high amount of sales. A company with less productive assets will generate fewer sales from its dollar of assets. Technically, a ratio is based on average total assets, but long-term assets often constitue the largest portion of a company's total assets.

For more on these measures of the age, life, and performance of the assets of Nike, Inc., and the way they are used, see the Ratio Decision Model on pages 402–403.

POD REVIEW 8.12

LO12 *Understand how investors can analyze a company's operating assets.*

- Investors are interested in how productive a company's operating assets are.
- The Ratio Decision Model is a valuable tool that can be used to examine the productivity of operating assets with the asset turnover ratio.

QUESTIONS

1. *Which of the following sets of ratios can be used to gain insight into a company's management of its fixed assets?*
   a. current ratio, quick ratio
   b. inventory turnover ratio, accounts receivable turnover
   c. debt-to-equity ratio times interest earned
   d. average age, asset turnover

2. *What does it mean when the asset turnover ratio increases for a company?*
   a. It is a favorable indication.
   b. It is an unfavorable indication.
   c. It means that less sales were created for each dollar of assets.
   d. It means that the average life of the assets has increased.

USING THE RATIO DECISION MODEL: ANALYZING AVERAGE LIFE AND ASSET TURNOVER

Use the following Ratio Decision Model to evaluate the average life and asset turnover for Nike or any other public company.

1. Formulate the Question

Long-term assets constitute the major productive assets of most companies. Investors and others who read financial statements must determine the age and composition of the operating assets. Two important questions are:

What is the average *life* of the assets?
What is the average *age* of the assets?

The operating asset category is also important in analyzing whether the operating assets will allow the company to be profitable in future periods. Therefore, a third question is:

How *productive* are the operating assets?

The productivity of assets can be calculated using the Asset Turnover ratio.

2. Gather the Information from the Financial Statements

Average Life and Average Age

For companies that use the straight-line method of depreciation:

- Total property, plant, and equipment: From the balance sheet (see Nike's Note 3)
- Total accumulated depreciation: From the balance sheet (see Nike's Note 3)
- Annual depreciation expense: From the statement of cash flows

Asset Turnover

- Average total assets: From the income statement

3. Calculate the ratio

$$\text{Average Life} = \frac{\text{Property, Plant, and Equipment}}{\text{Depreciation Expense}}$$

Nike, Inc.
Note 3—Property, Plant, and Equipment

	May 31, 2006	May 31, 2005
	(in millions)	
Land	$ 195.9	$ 185.4
Buildings	842.6	823.9
Machinery and equipment	1,661.7	1,528.4
Leasehold improvements	626.7	568.4
Construction in process	81.4	73.1
	3,408.3	3,179.2
Less accumulated depreciation	1,750.6	1,573.4
	$1,657.7	$1,605.8

Nike, Inc.
Partial Consolidated Statements of Cash Flows

	Year Ended May 31, 2006	Year Ended May 31, 2005
	(in millions)	
Depreciation	$282.0	$257.2

$$\text{Average Life} = \frac{\$3{,}408.3}{\$282.0} = 12.1 \text{ years}$$

$$\text{Average Age} = \frac{\text{Accumulated Depreciation}}{\text{Depreciation Expense}}$$

$$\text{Average Age} = \frac{\$1{,}750.6}{\$282.0} = 6.2 \text{ years}$$

$$\text{Asset Turnover} = \frac{\text{Net Sales}}{\text{Average Total Assets}}$$

Nike, Inc.
Partial Consolidated Statements of Income

	Year Ended May 31,		
	2006	2005	2004
		(in millions)	
Revenues	$14,954.9	$13,739.7	$12,253.1

Nike, Inc.
Partial Consolidated Balance Sheets

	May 31,	
	2006	2005
	(in millions)	
ASSETS		
Total assets	$9,869.6	$8,793.6

Average total assets = ($9,869.6 + $8,793.6)/2 = **$9,331.6**

$$\text{Asset Turnover} = \frac{\$14{,}954.9}{\$9{,}331.6} = 1.60$$

4. Compare the Ratio with Others
Nike's age, composition, and productivity of operating assets should be compared to those of prior years and to those of companies in the same industry.

	Nike 2006	Nike 2005	Foot Locker 06	Foot Locker 05
Average life of assets	12.10	12.40	5.67	5.93
Average age of assets	6.20	6.10	1.93	1.98
Asset turnover	1.60	1.65	1.75	1.72

5. Interpret the Results
The average life and age of Nike's assets has been consistent from year to year and is in line with other companies in the industry. The asset turnover ratio is a measure of how many dollars of assets are necessary for every dollar of sales. If a company uses its assets efficiently, each dollar of asset will create a high amount of sales. Technically, this ratio is based on average *total* assets, but operating assets constitute the largest portion of a company's total assets. Nike's asset turnover ratio indicates that each dollar of assets in 2006 produced $1.60 of sales. It is an indication that the assets are currently productive and will be able to provide a profit in future periods.

RATIO REVIEW

$$\text{Average Life} = \frac{\text{Property, Plant, and Equipment}}{\text{Depreciation Expense}}$$

$$\text{Average Age} = \frac{\text{Accumulated Depreciation}}{\text{Depreciation Expense}}$$

$$\text{Asset Turnover} = \frac{\text{Net Sales}}{\text{Average Total Assets}}$$

ACCOUNTS HIGHLIGHTED

Account Title	Appears on the	In the Section of	Page Number
Land	Balance Sheet	Operating Assets	380
Buildings	Balance Sheet	Operating Assets	380
Machinery	Balance Sheet	Operating Assets	390
Accumulated depreciation (a contra account)	Balance Sheet	Operating Assets	388
Depreciation expense	Income Statement	Operating Expenses	388
Gain on sale of asset	Income Statement	Other Income	392
Loss on sale of asset	Income Statement	Other Expense	392
Copyright	Balance Sheet	Intangible Assets	394
Trademark	Balance Sheet	Intangible Assets	394
Goodwill	Balance Sheet	Intangible Assets	394
Amortization expense	Income Statement	Operating Expenses	397
Accumulated amortization (a contra account)	Balance Sheet	Intangible Assets	397

KEY TERMS QUIZ

Read each definition below and write the number of the definition in the blank beside the appropriate term. The quiz solutions appear at the end of the chapter.

_______ **Acquisition cost**

_______ **Capitalization of interest**

_______ **Land improvements**

_______ **Depreciation**

_______ **Straight-line method**

_______ **Book value**

_______ **Units-of-production method**

_______ **Accelerated depreciation**

_______ **Double-declining-balance method**

_______ **Change in estimate**

_______ **Capital expenditure**

_______ **Revenue expenditure**

_______ **Gain on Sale of Asset**

_______ **Loss on Sale of Asset**

_______ **Intangible assets**

_______ **Goodwill**

_______ **Research and development costs**

1. This amount includes all of the costs normally necessary to acquire an asset and prepare it for its intended use.
2. Additions made to a piece of property, such as paving or landscaping a parking lot. The costs are treated separately from land for purposes of recording depreciation.
3. A method by which the same dollar amount of depreciation is recorded in each year of asset use.
4. A method by which depreciation is determined as a function of the number of units the asset produces.

5. The process of treating the cost of interest on constructed assets as a part of the asset cost rather than an expense.
6. A change in the life of an asset or in its expected residual value.
7. The allocation of the original acquisition cost of an asset to the periods benefited by its use.
8. A cost that improves an operating asset and is added to the asset account.
9. The original acquisition cost of an asset minus the amount of accumulated depreciation.
10. A cost that keeps an operating asset in its normal operating condition and is treated as an expense of the period.
11. An account whose amount indicates that the selling price received on an asset's disposal exceeds its book value.
12. An account whose amount indicates that the book value of an asset exceeds the selling price received on its disposal.
13. A term that refers to several methods by which a higher amount of depreciation is recorded in the early years of an asset's life and a lower amount is recorded in the later years.
14. Long-term assets that have no physical properties; for example, patents, copyrights, and goodwill.
15. A method by which depreciation is recorded at twice the straight-line rate but the depreciable balance is reduced in each period.
16. The amount indicating that the purchase price of a business exceeded the total fair market value of the identifiable net assets at the time the business was acquired.
17. Expenditures incurred in the discovery of new knowledge and the translation of research into a design or plan for a new product.

ALTERNATE TERMS

Accumulated depreciation Allowance for depreciation

Acquisition cost Historical cost or original cost

Capitalize expenditure Item treated as asset

Construction in progress Construction in process

Goodwill Purchase price in excess of the market value of assets

Hidden assets Unrecorded or off–balance-sheet assets

Property, Plant, and Equipment Fixed assets

Prospective Current and future years

Residual value Salvage value

Revenue expenditure An expense of the period

WARMUP EXERCISES

LO5

Warmup Exercise 8-1 Depreciation Methods

Assume that a company purchases a depreciable asset on January 1 for $10,000. The asset has a four-year life and will have zero residual value at the end of the fourth year.

Required
Calculate depreciation expense for each of the four years using the straight-line method and the double-declining-balance method.

LO5

Warmup Exercise 8-2 Depreciation and Cash Flow

Use the information from Exercise 8-1. Assume that the double-declining-balance method will be used for tax purposes and the straight-line method will be used for the financial statement to be given to the stockholders. Also assume that the tax rate is 40%.

Required
How much will the tax savings be in the first year as a result of using the accelerated method of depreciation?

SOLUTIONS TO WARMUP EXERCISES

Warmup Exercise 8-1

Year	Straight-Line	Double-Declining-Balance
1	$2,500*	$10,000 × 0.50** = $5,000
2	2,500	($10,000 − $5,000) × 0.50 = $2,500
3	2,500	($10,000 − $7,500) × 0.50 = $1,250
4	2,500	($10,000 − $8,750) × 0.50 = $625

**$10,000/4 years*

***Straight-line rate as a percentage is 1 year/4 years, or 25%. Double the rate is 25% × 2, or 50%.*

Warmup Exercise 8-2

The tax savings is equal to the difference in depreciation between the two methods times the tax rate. Therefore, the tax savings is ($5,000 − $2,500) × 0.40 = $1,000.

REVIEW PROBLEM

The accountant for Becker Company wants to develop a balance sheet as of December 31, 2008. A review of the asset records has revealed the following information:

a. Asset A was purchased on July 1, 2006, for $40,000 and has been depreciated on the straight-line basis using an estimated life of six years and a residual value of $4,000.
b. Asset B was purchased on January 1, 2007, for $66,000. The straight-line method has been used for depreciation purposes. Originally, the estimated life of the asset was projected to be six years with a residual value of $6,000; however, at the beginning of 2008, the accountant learned that the remaining life of the asset was only three years with a residual value of $2,000.
c. Asset C was purchased on January 1, 2007, for $50,000. The double-declining-balance method has been used for depreciation purposes, with a four-year life and a residual value estimate of $5,000.

Required

1. Assume that these assets represent pieces of equipment. Calculate the acquisition cost, accumulated depreciation, and book value of each asset as of December 31, 2008.
2. How would the assets appear on the balance sheet on December 31, 2008?
3. Assume that Becker Company sold Asset B on January 2, 2009, for $25,000. Calculate the amount of the resulting gain or loss and prepare the journal entry for the sale. Where would the gain or loss appear on the income statement?

SOLUTION TO REVIEW PROBLEM

1.

Asset A

2006	Depreciation	($40,000 − $4,000)/6 × 1/2 Year	= $ 3,000
2007		($40,000 − $4,000)/6	= 6,000
2008		($40,000 − $4,000)/6	= 6,000
Accumulated Depreciation			$15,000

Asset B

2007	Depreciation	($66,000 − $6,000)/6	= $10,000
2008		($66,000 − $10,000 − $2,000)/3	= 18,000
Accumulated Depreciation			$28,000

Note the impact of the change in estimate on 2007 depreciation.

Asset C

2007	Depreciation	$50,000 × 25% × 2	= $25,000
2008		($50,000 − $25,000) × (25% × 2)	= 12,500
Accumulated Depreciation			$37,500

REVIEW

Becker Company
Summary of Asset Cost and Accumulated Depreciation
As of December 31, 2008

Asset	Acquisition Cost	Accumulated Depreciation	Book Value
A	$ 40,000	$15,000	$25,000
B	66,000	28,000	38,000
C	50,000	37,500	12,500
Totals	$156,000	$80,500	$75,500

2. The assets would appear in the Long-Term Assets category of the balance sheet as follows:

Equipment	$156,000	
Less: Accumulated depreciation	80,500	
Equipment (net)		$75,500

3.

Asset B book value	$ 38,000
Selling price	25,000
Loss on sale of asset	$ 13,000

The journal entry to record the sale is as follows:

2009			
Jan. 2	Cash	25,000	
	Accumulated Depreciation	28,000	
	Loss on Sale of Asset	13,000	
	Asset B		66,000
	To record the sale of Asset B.		

		Balance Sheet				Income Statement	
ASSETS		= LIABILITIES	+	STOCKHOLDERS' EQUITY	+	REVENUES − EXPENSES	
Cash	25,000					Loss on Sale of Asset	(13,000)
Accumulated Depreciation	28,000						
Asset B	(66,000)						

The Loss on Sale of Asset account should appear in the Other Income/Other Expense category of the income statement. It is similar to an expense but is not the company's major activity.

QUESTIONS

1. What are several examples of operating assets? Why are operating assets essential to a company's long-term future?
2. What is the meaning of the term *acquisition cost of operating assets*? Give some examples of costs that should be included in the acquisition cost.
3. When assets are purchased as a group, how should the acquisition cost of the individual assets be determined?
4. Why is it important to account separately for the cost of land and building even when the two assets are purchased together?
5. Under what circumstances should interest be capitalized as part of the cost of an asset?
6. What factors may contribute to the decline in usefulness of operating assets? Should the choice of depreciation method be related to these factors? Must a company choose just one method of depreciation for all assets?
7. Why do you think most companies use the straight-line method of depreciation?
8. How should the residual value of an operating asset be treated when the straight-line method is used? How should it be treated when the double-declining-balance method is used?
9. Why do many companies use one method to calculate depreciation for the income statement developed for stockholders and another method for income tax purposes?

10. What should a company do if it finds that the original estimate of the life of an asset or the residual value of the asset must be changed?

11. What are the meanings of the terms *capital expenditures* and *revenue expenditures*? What determines whether an item is a capital or revenue expenditure?

12. How is the gain or loss on the sale of an operating asset calculated? Where would the Gain on Sale of Asset account appear on the financial statements?

13. What are several examples of items that constitute intangible assets? In what category of the balance sheet should intangible assets appear?

14. What is the meaning of the term *goodwill*? Give an example of a transaction that would result in the recording of goodwill on the balance sheet.

15. Do you agree with the FASB's ruling that all research and development costs should be treated as an expense on the income statement? Explain.

16. Do you agree with some accountants who argue that intangible assets have an indefinite life and therefore should not be subject to amortization? Explain.

17. When an intangible asset is amortized, should the asset's amortization occur over its legal life or over its useful life? Give an example in which the legal life exceeds the useful life.

18. Suppose that an intangible asset is being amortized over a ten-year time period but a competitor has just introduced a new product that will have a serious negative impact on the asset's value. Should the company continue to amortize the intangible asset over the ten-year life?

BRIEF EXERCISES

LO1

Brief Exercise 8-1 Property, Plant, and Equipment Classification

Which of the following would be in the Property, Plant, and Equipment category on the balance sheet?

Land
Buildings
Accumulated depreciation
Patent
Leasehold improvements
Construction in process

LO2

Brief Exercise 8-2 Determine Acquisition Cost

Which of the following would be considered part of the acquisition cost of an asset?

Transportation costs
Installation costs
Repair costs incurred at the time of purchase
Repair costs incurred after the asset has been installed and used
Interest on loan to purchase the asset

LO3

Brief Exercise 8-3 Lump-Sum Purchase

On December 1, 2007, Company X bought from Company Y land and an accompanying warehouse for $800,000. The fair market values of the land and the building at the time of purchase were $700,000 and $300,000, respectively. How much of the purchase price should Company X allocate to land? how much to the building?

LO4

Brief Exercise 8-4 Capitalization of Interest

A company begins construction of an asset on January 1, 2007, and completes construction on December 1, 2007. The company pays the following amounts related to construction:

$1,000,000	January 1
$2,000,000	July 1
$1,000,000	December 31

Calculate the average accumulated expenditures for the purpose of capitalizing interest.

LO5 **Brief Exercise 8-5** Depreciation Methods

A company uses the double-declining-balance method of depreciation. The company purchases an asset for $40,000, which is expected to have a ten-year life and a $4,000 residual value.

What depreciation rate will be applied each year?
What amount will be charged for depreciation in the first and second years?
What amount will be treated as depreciation over the ten-year life?

LO6 **Brief Exercise 8-6** Change in Depreciation Estimate

A company purchased an asset on January 1, 2006, for $10,000. The asset was expected to have a ten-year life and a $1,000 salvage value. The company uses the straight-line method of depreciation. On January 1, 2008, the company determines that the asset will last only five more years.

Calculate the amount of depreciation for 2008.

LO7 **Brief Exercise 8-7** Capital Expenditure

A company purchased an asset on January 1, 2006, for $10,000. The asset was expected to have a ten-year life and a $1,000 salvage value. The company uses the straight-line method of depreciation. On January 1, 2008, the company made a major repair to the asset of $5,000, extending its life. The asset is expected to last ten years from January 1, 2008.

Calculate the amount of depreciation for 2008.

LO8 **Brief Exercise 8-8** Sale of Asset

A machine with a cost of $100,000 and accumulated depreciation of $80,000 was sold at a loss of $6,000. What amount of cash was received from the sale?

LO9 **Brief Exercise 8-9** Classification of Intangible Assets

Which of the following would be considered intangible assets on the balance sheet? Which intangibles should be amortized?

Patents
Copyrights
Research and Development
Goodwill
The company's advantageous location
Broadcast rights

LO10 **Brief Exercise 8-10** Amortization of Intangible

A company develops a patent on January 1, 2006; and the costs involved with patent approval are $12,000. The legal life of the patent is 20 years, but the company projects that it will provide useful benefits for only 12 years. At January 1, 2008, the company discovers that a competitor will introduce a new product, making this patent useless in five years. How much amortization should be recorded in 2006, 2007, and 2008?

LO11 **Brief Exercise 8-11** Operating Assets and Cash Flows

In which category of the statement of cash flows (indirect method) should the following items appear?

Depreciation of an operating asset
Gain on the sale of an asset
Amortization of an intangible
Loss on the sale of an asset
Amount paid to purchase an asset
Amount received upon sale of an asset

LO12

Brief Exercise 8-12 Analysis of Operating Assets

At December 31, 2008, a company has the following amounts on its financial statements:

Property, plant, and equipment	$10,000
Accumulated depreciation	5,000
Total Assets at January 1, 2008	30,000
Total Assets at December 31, 2008	40,000
Net sales	62,000
Depreciation expense	1,000

Calculate the following ratios:

Average life of the assets
Average age of the assets
Asset turnover

EXERCISES

LO2

Exercise 8-1 Acquisition Cost

On January 1, 2008, Ruby Company purchased a piece of equipment with a list price of $60,000. The following amounts were related to the equipment purchase:

- Terms of the purchase were 2/10, net 30. Ruby paid for the purchase on January 8.
- Freight costs of $1,000 were incurred.
- A state agency required that a pollution-control device be installed on the equipment at a cost of $2,500.
- During installation, the equipment was damaged and repair costs of $4,000 were incurred.
- Architect's fees of $6,000 were paid to redesign the work space to accommodate the new equipment.
- Ruby purchased liability insurance to cover possible damage to the asset. The three-year policy cost $8,000.
- Ruby financed the purchase with a bank loan. Interest of $3,000 was paid on the loan during 2008.

Required

Determine the acquisition cost of the equipment.

LO3

Exercise 8-2 Lump-Sum Purchase

To add to his growing chain of grocery stores, on January 1, 2008, Danny Marks bought a grocery store of a small competitor for $520,000. An appraiser, hired to assess the value of the assets acquired, determined that the land had a market value of $200,000, the building a market value of $150,000, and the equipment a market value of $250,000.

Required

1. What is the acquisition cost of each asset? Prepare a journal entry to record the acquisition.
2. Danny plans to depreciate the operating assets on a straight-line basis for 20 years. Determine the amount of depreciation expense for 2008 on these newly acquired assets. You can assume zero residual value for all assets.
3. How would the assets appear on the balance sheet as of December 31, 2008?

LO5

Exercise 8-3 Straight-Line and Units-of-Production Methods

Assume that Sample Company purchased factory equipment on January 1, 2008, for $60,000. The equipment has an estimated life of five years and an estimated residual value of $6,000. Sample's accountant is considering whether to use the straight-line or the units-of-production method to depreciate the asset. Because the company is beginning a new production process, the equipment will be used to produce 10,000 units in 2008; but production subsequent to 2008 will increase by 10,000 units each year.

Required

Calculate the depreciation expense, the accumulated depreciation, and the book value of the equipment under both methods for each of the five years of the asset's life. Do you think that the units-of-production method yields reasonable results in this situation? Explain.

LO5

Exercise 8-4 Accelerated Depreciation

Koffman's Warehouse purchased a forklift on January 1, 2008, for $6,000. The forklift is expected to last for five years and have a residual value of $600. Koffman's uses the double-declining-balance method for depreciation.

Required

1. Calculate the depreciation expense, the accumulated depreciation, and the book value for each year of the forklift's life.
2. Prepare the journal entry to record depreciation expense for 2008.
3. Refer to Exhibit 8-2. What factors may have influenced Koffman to use the double-declining-balance method?

LO6

Exercise 8-5 Change in Estimate

Assume that Bloomer Company purchased a new machine on January 1, 2008, for $80,000. The machine has an estimated useful life of nine years and a residual value of $8,000. Bloomer has chosen to use the straight-line method of depreciation. On January 1, 2010, Bloomer discovered that the machine would not be useful beyond December 31, 2013, and estimated its value at that time to be $2,000.

Required

1. Calculate the depreciation expense, the accumulated depreciation, and the book value of the asset for each year 2008 to 2013.
2. Was the depreciation recorded in 2008 and 2009 wrong? If so, why was it not corrected?

LO8

Exercise 8-6 Asset Disposal

Assume that Gonzalez Company purchased an asset on January 1, 2006, for $60,000. The asset had an estimated life of six years and an estimated residual value of $6,000. The company used the straight-line method to depreciate the asset. On July 1, 2008, the asset was sold for $40,000 cash.

Required

1. Make the journal entry to record depreciation for 2008. Also record all transactions necessary for the sale of the asset.
2. How should the gain or loss on the sale of the asset be presented on the income statement?

LO8

Exercise 8-7 Asset Disposal

Refer to Exercise 8-6. Assume that Gonzalez Company sold the asset on July 1, 2008, and received $15,000 cash and a note for an additional $15,000.

Required

1. Make the journal entry to record depreciation for 2008. Also record all transactions necessary for the sale of the asset.
2. How should the gain or loss on the sale of the asset be presented on the income statement?

LO10

Exercise 8-8 Amortization of Intangibles

For each of the following intangible assets, indicate the amount of amortization expense that should be recorded for the year 2008 and the amount of accumulated amortization on the balance sheet as of December 31, 2008.

	Trademark	Patent	Copyright
Cost	$40,000	$50,000	$80,000
Date of purchase	1/1/01	1/1/03	1/1/06
Useful life	indefinite	10 yrs.	20 yrs.
Legal life	undefined	20 yrs.	50 yrs.
Method	SL*	SL	SL

**Represents the straight-line method.*

LO11

Exercise 8-9 Impact of Transactions Involving Operating Assets on Statement of Cash Flows

From the following list, identify each item as operating (O), investing (I), financing (F), or not separately reported on the statement of cash flows (N).

______ Purchase of land
______ Proceeds from sale of land
______ Gain on sale of land
______ Purchase of equipment
______ Depreciation expense
______ Proceeds from sale of equipment
______ Loss on sale of equipment

LO11

Exercise 8-10 Impact of Transactions Involving Intangible Assets on Statement of Cash Flows

From the following list, identify each item as operating (O), investing (I), financing (F), or not separately reported on the statement of cash flows (N).

______ Cost incurred to acquire copyright
______ Proceeds from sale of patent
______ Gain on sale of patent
______ Research and development costs
______ Amortization of patent

MULTICONCEPT EXERCISES

LO1,7

Exercise 8-11 Capital versus Revenue Expenditures

On January 1, 2006, Jose Company purchased a building for $200,000 and a delivery truck for $20,000. The following expenditures related to the building and the truck have been incurred during 2008:

- The building was painted at a cost of $5,000.
- To prevent leaking, new windows were installed in the building at a cost of $10,000.
- To allow an improved flow of production, a new conveyor system was installed at a cost of $40,000.
- The delivery truck was repainted with a new company logo at a cost of $1,000.
- To allow better handling of large loads, a hydraulic lift system was installed on the truck at a cost of $5,000.
- The truck's engine was overhauled at a cost of $4,000.

Required

1. Determine which of those costs should be capitalized. Also record the journal entry for the capitalized costs. Assume that all costs were incurred on January 1, 2008.
2. Determine the amount of depreciation for the year 2008. The company uses the straight-line method and depreciates the building over 25 years and the truck over 6 years. Assume zero residual value for all assets.
3. How would the assets appear on the balance sheet of December 31, 2008?

LO4,5

Exercise 8-12 Capitalization of Interest and Depreciation

During 2008, Mercator Company borrowed $80,000 from a local bank. In addition, Mercator used $120,000 of cash to construct a new corporate office building. Based on average accumulated expenditures, the amount of interest capitalized during 2008 was $8,000. Construction was completed and the building was occupied on January 1, 2009.

Required

1. Determine the acquisition cost of the new building.
2. The building has an estimated useful life of 20 years and a $5,000 salvage value. Assuming that Mercator uses the straight-line basis to depreciate its operating assets, determine the amount of depreciation expense for 2008 and 2009.

LO9,10 **Exercise 8-13** Research and Development and Patents

Erin Company incurred the following costs during 2008 and 2009.

a. Research and development costs of $20,000 were incurred. The research was conducted to discover a new product to sell to customers in future years. A product was successfully developed, and a patent for the new product was granted during 2008. Erin is unsure of the period benefited by the research but believes the product will result in increased sales over the next five years.
b. Legal costs and application fees of $10,000 for the patent were incurred on January 1, 2008. The patent was granted for a life of 20 years.
c. A patent infringement suit was successfully defended at a cost of $8,000. Assume that all costs were incurred on January 1, 2009.

Required
Determine how the costs in (a) and (b) should be presented on Erin's financial statements as of December 31, 2008. Also determine the amount of amortization of intangible assets that Erin should record in 2008 and 2009.

PROBLEMS

LO3 **Problem 8-1** Lump-Sum Purchase of Assets and Subsequent Events

Carter Development Company purchased, for cash, a large tract of land that was immediately platted and deeded into the following smaller sections:

Section 1, retail development with highway frontage
Section 2, multifamily apartment development
Section 3, single-family homes in the largest section

Based on recent sales of similar property, the fair market values of the three sections are as follows:

Section 1, $630,000
Section 2, $378,000
Section 3, $252,000

Required
1. What value is assigned to each section of land if the tract was purchased for (a) $1,260,000, (b) $1,560,000, and (c) $1,000,000?
2. How does the purchase of the tract affect the balance sheet?
3. Why would Carter be concerned with the value assigned to each section? Would Carter be more concerned with the values assigned if instead of purchasing three sections of land, it purchased land with buildings? Explain.

LO5 **Problem 8-2** Depreciation as a Tax Shield

The term *tax shield* refers to the amount of income tax saved by deducting depreciation for income tax purposes. Assume that Supreme Company is considering the purchase of an asset as of January 1, 2008. The cost of the asset with a five-year life and zero residual value is $100,000. The company will use the straight-line method of depreciation.

Supreme's income for tax purposes before recording depreciation on the asset will be $50,000 per year for the next five years. The corporation is currently in the 35% tax bracket.

Required
Calculate the amount of income tax that Supreme must pay each year if the asset is not purchased. Calculate the amount of income tax that Supreme must pay each year if the asset is purchased. What is the amount of the depreciation tax shield?

LO5 **Problem 8-3** Book versus Tax Depreciation

Griffith Delivery Service purchased a delivery truck for $33,600. The truck has an estimated useful life of six years and no salvage value. For purposes of preparing financial statements, Griffith is planning to use straight-line depreciation. For tax purposes, Griffith follows MACRS. Depreciation expense using MACRS is $6,720 in Year 1, $10,750 in Year 2, $6,450 in Year 3, $3,870 in each of Years 4 and 5, and $1,940 in Year 6.

Required

1. What is the difference between straight-line and MACRS depreciation expense for each of the six years?
2. Griffith's president has asked why you use one method for the books and another for tax calculations. "Can you do this? Is it legal? Don't we take the same total depreciation either way?" he asked. Write a brief memo answering his questions and explaining the benefits of using two methods for depreciation.

LO11

Problem 8-4 Depreciation and Cash Flow

O'hare Company's only asset as of January 1, 2008, was a limousine. During 2008, only the following three transactions occurred:

Services of $100,000 were provided on account.

All accounts receivable were collected.

Depreciation on the limousine was $15,000.

Required

1. Develop an income statement for O'hare for 2008.
2. Determine the amount of the net cash inflow for O'hare for 2008.
3. Explain in one or more sentences why the amount of the net income on O'hare's income statement does not equal the amount of the net cash inflow.
4. If O'hare developed a cash flow statement for 2008 using the indirect method, what amount would appear in the category titled Cash Flow from Operating Activities?

LO11

Problem 8-5 Reconstruct Net Book Values Using Statement of Cash Flows

Centralia Stores Inc. had property, plant, and equipment, net of accumulated depreciation of $4,459,000 and intangible assets, net of accumulated amortization, of $673,000 at December 31, 2008. The company's 2008 statement of cash flows, prepared using the indirect method, included the following items:

The Cash Flows from Operating Activities section included three additions to net income: (1) depreciation expense in the amount of $672,000, (2) amortization expense in the amount of $33,000, and (3) loss on the sale of equipment in the amount of $35,000. The Cash Flows from Operating Activities section also included a subtraction from net income for the gain on the sale of a copyright of $55,000. The Cash Flows from Investing Activities section included outflows for the purchase of a building in the amount of $292,000 and $15,000 for the payment of legal fees to protect a patent from infringement. The Cash Flows from Investing Activities section also included inflows from the sale of equipment in the amount of $315,000 and the sale of a copyright in the amount of $75,000.

Required

1. Determine the book values of the assets that were sold during 2008.
2. Reconstruct the amount of property, plant, and equipment, net of accumulated depreciation, that was reported on the company's balance sheet at December 31, 2007.
3. Reconstruct the amount of intangibles, net of accumulated amortization, that was reported on the company's balance sheet at December 31, 2007.

MULTICONCEPT PROBLEMS

LO1,3,5,7,8

Problem 8-6 Cost of Assets, Subsequent Book Values, and Balance Sheet Presentation

The following events took place at Pete's Painting Company during 2008:

a. On January 1, Pete bought a used truck for $14,000. He added a tool chest and side racks for ladders for $4,800. The truck is expected to last four years and then be sold for $800. Pete uses straight-line depreciation.
b. On January 1, he purchased several items at an auction for $2,400. These items had fair market values as follows:

10 cases of paint trays and roller covers	$ 200
Storage cabinets	600
Ladders and scaffolding	2,400

Pete will use all of the paint trays and roller covers this year. The storage cabinets are expected to last nine years; the ladders and scaffolding, four years.

c. On February 1, Pete paid the city $1,500 for a three-year license to operate the business.
d. On September 1, Pete sold an old truck for $4,800. The truck had cost $12,000 when it was purchased on September 1, 2003. It had been expected to last eight years and have a salvage value of $800.

Required

1. For each situation, explain the value assigned to the asset when it is purchased [or for (d), the book value when sold].
2. Determine the amount of depreciation or other expense to be recorded for each asset for 2008.
3. How would these assets appear on the balance sheet as of December 31, 2008?

LO2,5

Problem 8-7 Cost of Assets and the Effect on Depreciation

Early in its first year of business, Toner Company, a fitness and training center, purchased new workout equipment. The acquisition included the following costs:

Purchase price	$150,000
Tax	15,000
Transportation	4,000
Setup*	25,000
Painting*	3,000

**The equipment was adjusted to Toner's specific needs and painted to match the other equipment in the gym.*

The bookkeeper recorded an asset, Equipment, $165,000 (purchase price and tax). The remaining costs were expensed for the year. Toner used straight-line depreciation. The equipment was expected to last ten years with zero salvage value.

Required

1. How much depreciation did Toner report on its income statement related to this equipment in Year 1? What do you believe is the correct amount of depreciation to report in Year 1?
2. Income is $100,000 before costs related to the equipment are reported. How much income will Toner report in Year 1? What amount of income should it report? You can ignore income tax.
3. Using the equipment as an example, explain the difference between a cost and an expense.

LO5,7,8

Problem 8-8 Capital Expenditures, Depreciation, and Disposal

Merton Company purchased a building on January 1, 2007, at a cost of $364,000. Merton estimated that the building's life would be 25 years and the residual value at the end of 25 years would be $14,000.

On January 1, 2008, the company made several expenditures related to the building. The entire building was painted and floors were refinished at a cost of $21,000. A federal agency required Merton to install additional pollution control devices in the building at a cost of $42,000. With the new devices, Merton believed it was possible to extend the life of the building by an additional six years.

In 2009, Merton altered its corporate strategy dramatically. The company sold the building on April 1, 2009, for $392,000 in cash and relocated all operations to another state.

Required

1. Determine the amount of depreciation that should be reflected on the income statement for 2007 and 2008.
2. Explain why the cost of the pollution control equipment was not expensed in 2008. What conditions would have allowed Merton to expense the equipment? If Merton has a choice, would it prefer to expense or capitalize the equipment?
3. What amount of gain or loss did Merton record when it sold the building? What amount of gain or loss would have been reported if the pollution control equipment had been expensed in 2008?

LO6,10

Problem 8-9 Amortization of Intangible, Revision of Rate

During 2003, Reynosa Inc.'s research and development department developed a new manufacturing process. Research and development costs were $85,000. The process was patented on October 1, 2003. Legal costs to acquire the patent were $11,900. Reynosa decided to expense the patent over a 20-year time period. Reynosa's fiscal year ends on September 30.

On October 1, 2008, Reynosa's competition announced that it had obtained a patent on a new process that would make Reynosa's patent completely worthless.

Required

1. How should Reynosa record the $85,000 and $11,900 costs?
2. How much amortization expense should Reynosa report in each year through the year ended September 30, 2008?
3. What amount of loss should Reynosa report in the year ended September 30, 2009?

LO8,11

Problem 8-10 Purchase and Disposal of Operating Asset and Effects on Statement of Cash Flows

On January 1, 2008, Castlewood Company purchased some machinery for its production line for $104,000. Using an estimated useful life of eight years and a residual value of $8,000, the annual straight-line depreciation of the machinery was calculated to be $12,000. Castlewood used the machinery during 2008 and 2009 but then decided to automate its production process. On December 31, 2009, Castlewood sold the machinery at a loss of $5,000 and purchased new, fully automated machinery for $205,000.

Required

1. How would the previous transactions be presented on Castlewood's statements of cash flows for the years ended December 31, 2008 and 2009?
2. Why would Castlewood sell at a loss machinery that had a remaining useful life of six years and purchase new machinery with a cost almost twice that of the old?

LO9,10,11

Problem 8-11 Amortization of Intangibles and Effects on Statement of Cash Flows

Tableleaf Inc. purchased a patent a number of years ago. The patent is being amortized on a straight-line basis over its estimated useful life. The company's comparative balance sheets as of December 31, 2008 and 2007, included the following line item:

	12/31/08	12/31/07
Patent, less accumulated amortization of $119,000 (2008) and $102,000 (2007)	$170,000	$187,000

Required

1. How much amortization expense was recorded during 2008?
2. What was the patent's acquisition cost? When was it acquired? What is its estimated useful life? How was the acquisition of the patent reported on that year's statement of cash flows?
3. Assume that Tableleaf uses the indirect method to prepare its statement of cash flows. How is the amortization of the patent reported annually on the statement of cash flows?
4. How would the sale of the patent on January 1, 2009, for $200,000 be reported on the 2009 statement of cash flows?

ALTERNATE PROBLEMS

LO3

Problem 8-1A Lump-Sum Purchase of Assets and Subsequent Events

Dixon Manufacturing purchased, for cash, three large pieces of equipment. Based on recent sales of similar equipment, the fair market values are as follows:

Piece 1	$200,000
Piece 2	$200,000
Piece 3	$440,000

Required

1. What value is assigned to each piece of equipment if the equipment was purchased for (a) $480,000, (b) $680,000, and (c) $800,000?
2. How does the purchase of the equipment affect total assets?

LO5

Problem 8-2A Depreciation as a Tax Shield

The term *tax shield* refers to the amount of income tax saved by deducting depreciation for income tax purposes. Assume that Rummy Company is considering the purchase of an asset as of

January 1, 2008. The cost of the asset with a five-year life and zero residual value is $60,000. The company will use the double-declining-balance method of depreciation.

Rummy's income for tax purposes before recording depreciation on the asset will be $62,000 per year for the next five years. The corporation is currently in the 30% tax bracket.

Required

Calculate the amount of income tax that Rummy must pay each year if the asset is not purchased and the amount of income tax that Rummy must pay each year if the asset is purchased. What is the amount of tax shield over the life of the asset? What is the amount of tax shield for Rummy if it uses the straight-line method over the life of the asset? Why would Rummy choose to use the accelerated method?

LO5

Problem 8-3A Book versus Tax Depreciation

Payton Delivery Service purchased a delivery truck for $28,200. The truck will have a useful life of six years and zero salvage value. For the purposes of preparing financial statements, Payton is planning to use straight-line depreciation. For tax purposes, Payton follows MACRS. Depreciation expense using MACRS is $5,650 in Year 1, $9,025 in Year 2, $5,400 in Year 3, $3,250 in each of Years 4 and 5, and $1,625 in Year 6.

Required

1. What is the difference between straight-line and MACRS depreciation expense for each of the six years?
2. Payton's president has asked why you use one method for the books and another for tax calculations. "Can you do this? Is it legal? Don't we take the same total depreciation either way?" he asked. Write a brief memo answering his questions and explaining the benefits of using two methods for depreciation.

LO11

Problem 8-4A Amortization and Cash Flow

Book Company's only asset as of January 1, 2008, was a copyright. During 2008, only the following three transactions occurred:

Royalties earned from copyright use, $500,000 in cash
Cash paid for advertising and salaries, $62,500
Amortization, $50,000

Required

1. What amount of income will Book report in 2008?
2. What is the amount of cash on hand at December 31, 2008?
3. Explain how the cash balance increased from zero at the beginning of the year to its end-of-year balance. Why does the increase in cash not equal the income?

LO11

Problem 8-5A Reconstruct Net Book Values Using Statement of Cash Flows

E-Gen Enterprises Inc. had property, plant, and equipment, net of accumulated depreciation, of $1,555,000 and intangible assets, net of accumulated amortization, of $34,000 at December 31, 2008. The company's 2008 statement of cash flows, prepared using the indirect method, included the following items:

The Cash Flows from Operating Activities section included three additions to net income: (1) depreciation expense in the amount of $205,000, (2) amortization expense in the amount of $3,000, and (3) loss on the sale of land in the amount of $17,000. The Cash Flows from Operating Activities section also included a subtraction from net income for the gain on the sale of a trademark of $7,000. The Cash Flows from Investing Activities section included outflows for the purchase of equipment in the amount of $277,000 and $6,000 for the payment of legal fees to protect a copyright from infringement. The Cash Flows from Investing Activities section also included inflows from the sale of land in the amount of $187,000 and the sale of a trademark in the amount of $121,000.

Required

1. Determine the book values of the assets that were sold during 2008.
2. Reconstruct the amount of property, plant, and equipment, net of accumulated depreciation, that was reported on the company's balance sheet at December 31, 2007.
3. Reconstruct the amount of intangibles, net of accumulated amortization, that was reported on the company's balance sheet at December 31, 2007.

ALTERNATE MULTICONCEPT PROBLEMS

LO1,5,8,9,10

Problem 8-6A Cost of Assets, Subsequent Book Values, and Balance Sheet Presentation

The following events took place at Tasty-Toppins Inc., a pizza shop that specializes in home delivery, during 2008:

a January 1, purchased a truck for $16,000 and added a cab and oven at a cost of $10,900. The truck is expected to last five years and be sold for $300 at the end of that time. The company uses straight-line depreciation for its trucks.

b. January 1, purchased equipment for $2,700 from a competitor who was retiring. The equipment is expected to last three years with zero salvage value. The company uses the double-declining-balance method to depreciate its equipment.

c. April 1, sold a truck for $1,500. The truck had been purchased for $8,000 exactly five years earlier, had an expected salvage value of $1,000, and was depreciated over an eight-year life using the straight-line method.

d. July 1, purchased a $14,000 patent for a unique baking process to produce a new product. The patent is valid for 15 more years; however, the company expects to produce and market the product for only four years. The patent's value at the end of the four years will be zero.

Required

For each situation, explain the amount of depreciation or amortization recorded for each asset in the current year and the book value of each asset at the end of the year. For (c), indicate the accumulated depreciation and book value at the time of sale.

LO2,5

Problem 8-7A Cost of Assets and the Effect on Depreciation

Early in its first year of business, Key Inc., a locksmith and security consultant, purchased new equipment. The acquisition included the following costs:

Purchase price	$168,000
Tax	16,500
Transportation	4,400
Setup*	1,100
Operating Cost for First Year	26,400

**The equipment was adjusted to Key's specific needs.*

The bookkeeper recorded the asset Equipment at $216,400. Key used straight-line depreciation. The equipment was expected to last ten years with zero residual value.

Required

1. Was $216,400 the proper amount to record for the acquisition cost? If not, explain how each expenditure should be recorded.
2. How much depreciation did Key report on its income statement related to this equipment in Year 1? How much should have been reported?
3. If Key's income before the costs associated with the equipment is $55,000, what amount of income did Key report? What amount should it have reported? You can ignore income tax.
4. Explain how Key should determine the amount to capitalize when recording an asset. What is the effect on the income statement and balance sheet of Key's error?

LO7,8

Problem 8-8A Capital Expenditures, Depreciation, and Disposal

Wagner Company purchased a retail shopping center on January 1, 2007, at a cost of $612,000. Wagner estimated that the life of the building would be 25 years and the residual value at the end of 25 years would be $12,000.

On January 1, 2008, the company made several expenditures related to the building. The entire building was painted and floors were refinished at a cost of $115,200. A local zoning agency required Wagner to install additional fire protection equipment, including sprinklers and built-in alarms, at a cost of $87,600. With the new protection, Wagner believed it was possible to increase the residual value of the building to $30,000.

In 2009, Wagner altered its corporate strategy dramatically. The company sold the retail shopping center on January 1, 2009, for $360,000 cash.

Required

1. Determine the amount of depreciation that should be reflected on the income statement for 2007 and 2008.
2. Explain why the cost of the fire protection equipment was not expensed in 2008. What conditions would have allowed Wagner to expense it? If Wagner has a choice, would it prefer to expense or capitalize the equipment?
3. What amount of gain or loss did Wagner record when it sold the building? What amount of gain or loss would have been reported if the fire protection equipment had been expensed in 2008?

LO6,10 **Problem 8-9A** Amortization of Intangible, Revision of Rate

During 2003, Maciel Inc.'s research and development department developed a new manufacturing process. Research and development costs were $350,000. The process was patented on October 1, 2003. Legal costs to acquire the patent were $23,800. Maciel decided to expense the patent over a 20-year time period using the straight-line method. Maciel's fiscal year ends on September 30.

On October 1, 2008, Maciel's competition announced that it had obtained a patent on a new process that would make Maciel's patent completely worthless.

Required

1. How should Maciel record the $350,000 and $23,800 costs?
2. How much amortization expense should Maciel report in each year through the year ended September 30, 2008?
3. What amount of loss should Maciel report in the year ended September 30, 2009?

LO8,11 **Problem 8-10A** Purchase and Disposal of Operating Asset and Effects on Statement of Cash Flows

On January 1, 2008, Mansfield Inc. purchased a medium-sized delivery truck for $45,000. Using an estimated useful life of five years and a residual value of $5,000, the annual straight-line depreciation of the trucks was calculated to be $8,000. Mansfield used the truck during 2008 and 2009 but then decided to purchase a larger delivery truck. On December 31, 2009, Mansfield sold the delivery truck at a loss of $12,000 and purchased a new, larger delivery truck for $80,000.

Required

1. How would the previous transactions be presented on Mansfield's statements of cash flows for the years ended December 31, 2008 and 2009?
2. Why would Mansfield sell at a loss a truck that had a remaining useful life of three years and purchase a new truck with a cost almost twice that of the old?

LO9,10 11 **Problem 8-11A** Amortization of Intangibles and Effects on Statement of Cash Flows

Quickster Inc. acquired a patent a number of years ago. The patent is being amortized on a straight-line basis over its estimated useful life. The company's comparative balance sheets as of December 31, 2008 and 2007, included the following line item:

	12/31/08	12/31/07
Patent, less accumulated amortization of $1,661,000 (2008) and $1,510,000 (2007)	$1,357,000	$1,508,000

Required

1. How much amortization expense was recorded during 2008?
2. What was the patent's acquisition cost? When was it acquired? What is its estimated useful life? How was the acquisition of the patent reported on that year's statement of cash flows?
3. Assume that Quickster uses the indirect method to prepare its statement of cash flows. How is the amortization of the patent reported annually on the statement of cash flows?
4. How would the sale of the patent on January 1, 2009, for $1,700,000 be reported on the 2009 statement of cash flows?

DECISION CASES

READING AND INTERPRETING FINANCIAL STATEMENTS

LO1,9

Decision Case 8-1 General Mills

Refer to the financial statements and notes for **General Mills** included at the back of the book.

Required

1. What items does the company list in the Property and Equipment category?
2. What method is used to depreciate the operating assets?
3. What is the estimated useful life of the operating assets?
4. What are the accumulated depreciation and book values of property and equipment for the most recent fiscal year?
5. Were any assets purchased or sold during the most recent fiscal year? Explain.

LO1,9

Decision Case 8-2 Comparing Two Companies in the Same Industry: General Mills and Kellogg's

Refer to the financial information for **General Mills** and **Kellogg's** included at the back of the book.

Required

1. Compare the list of property, plant, and equipment for General Mills to the list on the Kellogg's balance sheet. How are the lists similar? Note the differences between the lists and provide a logical reason for the differences.
2. What method is used by each company to depreciate the assets? Why do you think each company has chosen the method it uses?
3. What are the accumulated depreciation and book values of the property and equipment for each company? What does this information tell you about these competitors?
4. What is the estimated life of General Mills's assets? How does this compare to the estimated life of Kellogg's assets?
5. Refer to the Investing Activities portion of the cash flow statements of the two companies. Were any assets purchased or sold by either company during the year? This section of the statements does not tell whether there was a gain or loss on the sale of long-term assets. Where would you find that information?

MAKING FINANCIAL DECISIONS

LO1,5

Decision Case 8-3 Comparing Companies

Assume that you are a financial analyst attempting to compare the financial results of two companies. The 2008 income statement of Straight Company is as follows:

Sales		$720,000
Cost of goods sold		360,000
Gross profit		$360,000
Administrative costs	$ 96,000	
Depreciation expense	120,000	216,000
Income before tax		$144,000
Tax expense (40%)		57,600
Net income		$ 86,400

Straight Company depreciates all operating assets using the straight-line method for tax purposes and for the annual report provided to stockholders. All operating assets were purchased on the same date, and all assets had an estimated life of five years when purchased. Straight Company's balance sheet reveals that on December 31, 2008, the balance of the Accumulated Depreciation account was $240,000.

You want to compare the annual report of Straight Company to that of Accelerated Company. Both companies are in the same industry; and both have the same assets, sales, and expenses except that Accelerated uses the double-declining-balance method for depreciation for income tax purposes and for the annual report provided to stockholders.

Required

Develop Accelerated Company's 2008 income statement. As a financial analyst interested in investing in one of the companies, do you find Straight or Accelerated to be more attractive? Because depreciation is a "noncash" expense, should you be indifferent in deciding between the two companies? Explain your answer.

LO5 **Decision Case 8-4** Depreciation Alternatives

Medsupply Inc. produces supplies used in hospitals and nursing homes. Its sales, production, and costs to produce are expected to remain constant over the next five years. The corporate income tax rate is expected to increase over the next three years. The current rate, 15%, is expected to increase to 20% next year, then to 25%, continuing at that rate indefinitely.

Medsupply is considering the purchase of new equipment that is expected to last five years and to cost $150,000 with zero salvage value. As the controller, you are aware that the company can use one method of depreciation for accounting purposes and another method for tax purposes. You are trying to decide between the straight-line and the double-declining-balance methods.

Required

Recommend which method to use for accounting purposes and which to use for tax purposes. Be able to justify your answer on both a numerical and a theoretical basis. How does a noncash adjustment to income, such as depreciation, affect cash flow?

ETHICAL DECISION MAKING

LO3 **Decision Case 8-5** Valuing Assets

Denver Company recently hired Terry Davis as an accountant. He was given responsibility for all accounting functions related to fixed asset accounting. Tammy Sharp, Terry's boss, asked him to review all transactions involving the current year's acquisition of fixed assets and to take necessary action to ensure that acquired assets were recorded at proper values. Terry is satisfied that all transactions are proper except for an April 15 purchase of an office building and the land on which it is situated. The purchase price of the acquisition was $200,000. However, Denver Company has not reported the land and building separately.

Terry hired an appraiser to determine the market values of the land and the building. The appraiser reported that his best estimates of the values were $150,000 for the building and $70,000 for the land. When Terry proposed that these values be used to determine the acquisition cost of the assets, Tammy disagreed. She told Terry to request another appraisal of the property and asked him to stress to the appraiser that the land component of the acquisition could not be depreciated for tax purposes. The second appraiser estimated that the values were $180,000 for the building and $40,000 for the land. Terry and Tammy agreed that the second appraisal should be used to determine the acquisition cost of the assets.

Required

Did Terry and Tammy act ethically in this situation? Explain your answer.

LO5 **Decision Case 8-6** Depreciation Estimates

Langsom's Mfg. is planning for a new project. Usually, Langsom's depreciates long-term equipment for ten years. The equipment for this project is specialized and will have no further use at the end of the project in three years. The manager of the project wants to depreciate the equipment over the usual ten years and plans on writing off the remaining book value at the end of Year 3 as a loss. You believe that the equipment should be depreciated over the three-year life.

Required

Which method do you think is conceptually better? What should you do if the manager insists on depreciating the equipment over ten years?

SOLUTIONS TO KEY TERMS QUIZ

1	**Acquisition cost**	6	**Change in estimate**
5	**Capitalization of interest**	8	**Capital expenditure**
2	**Land improvements**	10	**Revenue expenditure**
7	**Depreciation**	11	**Gain on Sale of Asset**
3	**Straight-line method**	12	**Loss on Sale of Asset**
9	**Book value**	14	**Intangible assets**
4	**Units-of-production method**	16	**Goodwill**
13	**Accelerated depreciation**	17	**Research and development costs**
15	**Double-declining-balance method**		

INTEGRATIVE PROBLEM

Correct an income statement and statement of cash flows and assess the impact of a change in inventory method; compute the effect of a bad-debt recognition.

The following income statement, statement of cash flows, and additional information are available for PEK Company:

PEK Company
Income Statement
For the Year Ended December 31, 2008

Sales revenue		$1,250,000
Cost of goods sold		636,500
Gross profit		$ 613,500
Depreciation on plant equipment	$58,400	
Depreciation on buildings	12,000	
Interest expense	33,800	
Other expenses	83,800	188,000
Income before taxes		$ 425,500
Income tax expense (30% rate)		127,650
Net income		$ 297,850

PEK Company
Statement of Cash Flows
For the Year Ended December 31, 2008

Cash flows from operating activities:	
Net income	$297,850
Adjustments to reconcile net income to net cash provided by operating activities (includes depreciation expense)	83,200
Net cash provided by operating activities	$381,050
Cash flows from financing activities:	
Dividends	(35,000)
Net increase in cash	$346,050

Additional information:

a. Beginning inventory and purchases for the one product the company sells are as follows:

	Units	Unit Cost
Beginning inventory	50,000	$2.00
Purchases:		
February 5	25,000	2.10
March 10	30,000	2.20
April 15	40,000	2.50
June 16	75,000	3.00
September 5	60,000	3.10
October 3	40,000	3.25

b. During the year, the company sold 250,000 units at $5 each.
c. PEK uses the periodic FIFO method to value its inventory and the straight-line method to depreciate all of its long-term assets.
d. During the year-end audit, it was discovered that a January 3, 2008, transaction for the lump-sum purchase of a mixing machine and a boiler was not recorded. The fair market values of the mixing machine and the boiler were $200,000 and $100,000, respectively. Each asset has an estimated useful life of ten years with no residual value expected. The purchase of the assets was financed by issuing a $270,000 five-year promissory note directly to the seller. Interest of 8% is paid annually on December 31.

Required

1. Prepare a revised income statement and a revised statement of cash flows to take into account the omission of the entry to record the purchase of the two assets. (Hint: You will need to take into account any change in income taxes as a result of changes in any income statement items. Assume that income taxes are paid on December 31 of each year.)
2. Assume the same facts as in (1), except that the company is considering the use of an accelerated method rather than the straight-line method for the assets purchased on January 3, 2008. All other assets would continue to be depreciated on a straight-line basis. Prepare a revised income statement and a revised statement of cash flows assuming the company decides to use the accelerated method for these two assets rather than the straight-line method, resulting in depreciation of $49,091 for 2008.

Treat the answers in requirements (3) and (4) as independent of the other parts.

3. Assume PEK decides to use the LIFO method rather than the FIFO method to value its inventory and recognize cost of goods sold for 2008. Compute the effect (amount of increase or decrease) this would have on cost of goods sold, income tax expense, and net income.
4. Assume PEK failed to record an estimate of bad debts for 2008. (Bad debt expense is normally included in "other expenses.") Before any adjustment, the balance in Allowance for Doubtful Accounts is $8,200. The credit manager estimates that 3% of the $800,000 of sales on account will prove to be uncollectible. Based on this information, compute the effect (amount of increase or decrease) of recognition of the bad debt estimate on other expenses, income tax expense, and net income.

ANSWERS TO POD REVIEW

LO1	1. d	2. a
LO2	1. b	2. c
LO3	1. d	2. a
LO4	1. c	2. c
LO5	1. a	2. d
LO6	1. c	2. d
LO7	1. a	2. b
LO8	1. c	2. a
LO9	1. b	2. d
LO10	1. d	2. c
LO11	1. a	2. b
LO12	1. d	2. a

CHAPTER 9

Current Liabilities, Contingencies, and the Time Value of Money

Learning Outcomes

After studying this chapter, you should be able to:

LO1 Identify the components of the current liability category of the balance sheet.

LO2 Examine how accruals affect the current liability category.

LO3 Show that you understand how changes in current liabilities affect the statement of cash flows.

LO4 Determine when contingent liabilities should be presented on the balance sheet or disclosed in notes and how to calculate their amounts.

LO5 Explain the difference between simple and compound interest.

LO6 Calculate amounts using the future value and present value concepts.

LO7 Apply the compound interest concepts to some common accounting situations.

Study Links...

A Look at Previous Chapters

The previous chapters were concerned with the asset portion of the balance sheet. We examined the accounting for current assets, such as inventory, as well as long-term assets such as property, plant, and equipment.

A Look at This Chapter

This chapter examines the accounting for current liabilities that are an important aspect of a company's liquidity. Chapter 9 also discusses how contingent liabilities should be treated on the financial statement. Finally, the chapter introduces the concept of the time value of money. This important concept will be used extensively in future chapters.

A Look at the Upcoming Chapter

Chapter 10 presents the accounting for long-term liabilities. The time value of money concept developed in Chapter 9 is applied to several long-term liability issues in Chapter 10.

Starbucks Corporation

MAKING BUSINESS DECISIONS

When you think of coffee, Starbucks Corporation may come to mind. The company's objective is to establish itself as one of the most recognized and respected brands in the world. It took only a few years for the company to be well on its way to achieving that goal. The company offers brewed coffees, espresso beverages, cold blended beverages, various complementary food items, coffee-related accessories and equipment, a selection of premium teas, and a line of compact discs through its retail stores. For several years, the company experienced a very high growth rate and its stock skyrocketed. Part of its growth was the result of expansion; and in 2006, it had more than 12,000 retail outlets. But during 2006, the growth began to slow and the company faced increased competition from other outlets such as Caribou Coffee and Green Mountain Coffee. Still, the company reported net earnings of $117.3 million, or 15 cents a share, for the quarter ended October 1, 2006.

A look at the company's balance sheet reveals that Starbucks must monitor its liquidity carefully. A significant portion of the company's assets are current assets because most of its sales involve cash, credit card, and debit card. But the company also has a significant amount of current liabilities. The company realizes the importance of maintaining its current liabilities at a level that will allow them to be paid when they are due. In short, the company's long-term profitability goals are directly linked to its ability to effectively manage its current liabilities and liquidity.

The accompanying partial balance sheet presents Starbucks Corporation's current assets and liabilities. This chapter will consider the following questions:

- What accounts should be presented in the current liabilities section of the balance sheet? (See pp. 426–432.)

- How are changes in the current liability accounts related to the amount of cash available to the company? (See pp. 432–434.)
- What is the proper recording and disclosure of liabilities that are contingent on future events? (See pp. 434–437.)

Answers to those questions and additional information related to current liabilities are found in this text. All of that information can help you evaluate the current liabilities section of the balance sheet of Starbucks.

(*continued*)

Starbucks Corporation
Partial Consolidated Balance Sheets
In thousands, except share data

FISCAL YEAR ENDED	October 1, 2006	October 2, 2005
ASSETS		
Current assets:		
Cash and cash equivalents	$ 312,606	$ 173,809
Short-term investments-available-for-sale securities	87,542	95,379
Short-term investments-trading securities	53,496	37,848
Accounts receivable, net of allowances of $3,827 and $3,079, respectively	224,271	190,762
Inventories	636,222	546,299
Prepaid expenses and other current assets	126,874	94,429
Deferred income taxes, net	88,777	70,808
Total current assets	$1,529,788	$1,209,334
Current liabilities:		
Accounts payable	$ 340,937	$ 220,975
Accrued compensation and related costs	288,963	232,354
Accrued occupancy costs	54,868	44,496
Accrued taxes	94,010	78,293
Short-term borrowings	700,000	277,000
Other accrued expenses	224,154	198,082
Deferred revenue	231,926	175,048
Current portion of long-term debt	762	748
Total current liabilities	$1,935,620	$1,226,996

Current Liabilities

LO1 Identify the components of the current liability category of the balance sheet.

A classified balance sheet presents financial statement items by category to provide more information to financial statement users. The balance sheet generally presents two categories of liabilities: current and long-term.

Current liabilities finance the working capital of the company. At any given time during the year, current liabilities may fluctuate substantially. The company must generate sufficient cash flow to retire these debts as they come due. As long as the company's ratio of current assets to current liabilities stays fairly constant from quarter to quarter or year to year, financial statement users will not be too concerned.

The current liability portion of the 2006 balance sheet of **Starbucks Corporation** is presented in the chapter opener. Some companies list the accounts in the current liability category in the order of payment due date. That is, the account that requires payment first is listed first, the account requiring payment next is listed second, and so on. This allows users of the statement to assess the cash flow implications of each account. Starbucks presents the Accounts Payable account as the first current liability, but it is difficult to tell if the other current liabilities are presented in the order that they will require payment.

Current liability
Accounts that will be satisfied within one year or the current operating cycle. ***Alternate term:*** *Short-term liability.*

Current liabilities were first introduced in Chapter 2. In general, a **current liability** is an obligation that will be satisfied within one year. Although current liabilities are not due immediately, they are still recorded at face value, that is, the time until payment is not taken into account. If it were taken into account, current liabilities would be recorded at a slight discount to reflect interest earned between now and the due date. The face value amount is generally used for all current liabilities because the time period involved is short enough that it is not necessary to record or calculate an interest factor. In addition, when interest rates are low, there is no need to worry about the interest that could be earned in this short period of time. Chapter 10 shows that many long-term liabilities must be stated at their present value on the balance sheet.

The current liability classification is important because it is closely tied to the concept of *liquidity*. Management of a firm must be prepared to pay current liabilities within a short time period. Therefore, management must have access to liquid assets, cash, or other assets that can be converted to cash in amounts sufficient to pay the current liabilities. Firms that do not have sufficient resources to pay their current liabilities are often said to have a liquidity problem.

A handy ratio to help creditors or potential creditors determine a company's liquidity is the current ratio. (See Chapter 2 for an introduction to the current ratio.) A current ratio of current assets to current liabilities of 2 to 1 is usually a comfortable margin. If the firm has a large amount of inventory, it is sometimes useful to exclude inventory (prepayments are also excluded) when computing the ratio. That provides the "quick" ratio. Usually, a quick ratio of at least 1.5 to 1 would be preferred so that the company could pay its bills on time. Of course, the guidelines given for the current ratio 2 to 1 and the quick ratio 1.5 to 1 are only rules of thumb. The actual current and quick ratios of companies vary widely and depend on the company, the management policies, and the type of industry. Exhibit 9-1 presents the current and quick ratios for Starbucks and two of its competitors. The ratios vary from company to company, yet all are solid companies without liquidity problems. Note especially that the current ratio for Starbucks is considerably less than 2 to 1 because of the nature of its business and because of the efficient use of its current assets.

Accounting for current liabilities is an area in which U.S. accounting standards are similar to those of most other countries. Nearly all countries encourage firms to provide a breakdown of liabilities into current and long-term to allow users to evaluate liquidity.

Real World Practice

9-1 Reading Starbucks Balance Sheet

Refer to Starbucks' October 1, 2006, balance sheet in the chapter opener. What accounts are listed as current liabilities? How much did Accounts Payable change from 2005 to 2006?

ACCOUNTS PAYABLE

Accounts payable represent amounts owed for the purchase of inventory, goods, or services acquired in the normal course of business. Often Accounts Payable is the first account listed in the current liability category because it requires the payment of cash before other current liabilities.

Accounts payable Amounts owed for inventory, goods, or services acquired in the normal course of business.

Normally, a firm has an established relationship with several suppliers, and formal contractual arrangements with those suppliers are unnecessary. Accounts payable usually do not require the payment of interest, but terms may be given to encourage early payment. For example, terms may be stated as 2/10, n30, which means that a 2% discount is available if payment occurs within the first ten days and that if payment is not made within ten days, the full amount must be paid within 30 days.

Timely payment of accounts payable is an important aspect of the management of cash flow. Generally, it is to the company's benefit to take advantage of discounts when they are available. After all, if your supplier is going to give you a 2% discount for paying on Day 10 instead of Day 30, that means you are earning 2% on your money over 20/360 of a year. If you took the 2% discount throughout the year, you would be getting a 36% annual return on your money, since there are 18 periods of 20 days each in a year. It is essential, therefore, that the accounts payable system be established in a manner that alerts management to take advantage of discounts offered.

NOTES PAYABLE

Many companies have an account in the current liability category designated as Notes Payable. **How is a note payable different from an account payable?** The most important difference is that an account payable is not a formal contractual arrangement,

EXHIBIT 9-1 Current and Quick Ratios of Selected Companies for 2006

Company	Industry	Current Ratio	Quick Ratio
Starbucks	Food	.79	.39
Caribou Coffee	Food	.92	.56
Green Mountain	Food	1.74	.89

Notes payable
Amounts owed that are represented by a formal contract.

whereas a **note payable** is represented by a formal agreement or note signed by the parties to the transaction. Notes payable may arise from dealing with a supplier or from acquiring a cash loan from a bank or creditor. Those notes that are expected to be paid within one year of the balance sheet date should be classified as current liabilities.

The accounting for notes payable depends on whether the interest is paid on the note's due date or is deducted before the borrower receives the loan proceeds. With the first type of note, the terms stipulate that the borrower receives a short-term loan and agrees to repay the principal and interest at the note's due date. For example, assume that Hot Coffee Inc. receives a one-year loan from First National Bank on January 1. The face amount of the note of $1,000 must be repaid on December 31 along with interest at the rate of 12%. Hot Coffee would make the following entries to record the loan and its repayment:

Jan. 1	Cash	1,000	
	Notes Payable		1,000
	To record the loan of $1,000.		

Balance Sheet							Income Statement
ASSETS		=	LIABILITIES		+ STOCKHOLDERS' EQUITY	+	REVENUES − EXPENSES
Cash	1,000		Notes Payable	1,000			

Dec. 31	Notes Payable	1,000	
	Interest Expense	120	
	Cash		1,120
	To record the repayment of loan with interest.		

Balance Sheet							Income Statement	
ASSETS		=	LIABILITIES		+ STOCKHOLDERS' EQUITY	+	REVENUES − EXPENSES	
Cash	(1,120)		Notes Payable	(1,000)			Interest Expense	(120)

Banks also use another form of note, one in which the interest is deducted in advance. Suppose that on January 1, 2008, First National Bank granted to Hot Coffee a $1,000 loan, due on December 31, 2008, but deducted the interest in advance and gave Hot Coffee the remaining amount of $880 ($1,000 face amount of the note less interest of $120). This is sometimes referred to as *discounting a note* because a Discount on Notes Payable account is established when the loan is recorded. On January 1, Hot Coffee must make the following entry:

Jan. 1	Cash	880	
	Discount on Notes Payable	120	
	Notes Payable		1,000
	To record the loan of $1,000 less interest deducted in advance.		

Balance Sheet							Income Statement
ASSETS		=	LIABILITIES		+ STOCKHOLDERS' EQUITY	+	REVENUES − EXPENSES
Cash	880		Notes Payable	1,000			
			Discount on Notes Payable	(120)			

Discount on notes payable
A contra liability that represents interest deducted from a loan in advance.

The **Discount on Notes Payable** account should be treated as a reduction of Notes Payable (and should have a debit balance). If a balance sheet was developed immediately after the January 1 loan, the note would appear in the current liability category as follows:

Notes Payable	$1,000
Less: Discount on Notes Payable	120
Net Liability	$ 880

The original balance in the Discount on Notes Payable account represents interest that must be transferred to interest expense over the life of the note. Before Hot Coffee presents its year-end financial statements, it must make an adjustment to transfer the discount to interest expense. The effect of the adjustment on December 31 is as follows:

Study Tip

Discount on Notes Payable is a contra-liability account and will have a debit balance.

Dec. 31	Interest Expense	120	
	Discount on Notes Payable		120
	To record the interest on note payable.		

Balance Sheet							Income Statement
ASSETS	=	**LIABILITIES**		+	**STOCKHOLDERS' EQUITY**	+	**REVENUES – EXPENSES**
		Discount on Notes Payable	120				Interest Expense (120)

Thus, the balance of the Discount on Notes Payable account is zero and $120 has been transferred to interest expense. When the note is repaid on December 31, 2008, Hot Coffee must repay the full amount of the note as follows:

Dec. 31	Notes Payable	1,000	
	Cash		1,000
	To record payment of the note on its due date.		

Balance Sheet								Income Statement
ASSETS		=	**LIABILITIES**		+	**STOCKHOLDERS' EQUITY**	+	**REVENUES – EXPENSES**
Cash	(1,000)		Notes Payable	(1,000)				

It is important to compare the two types of notes payable. In the previous two examples, the stated interest rate on each note was 12%. The dollar amount of interest incurred in each case was $120. However, the interest *rate* on a discounted note, the second example, is always higher than it appears. Hot Coffee received the use of only $880, yet it was required to repay $1,000. Therefore, the interest rate incurred on the note was actually $120/$880, or approximately 13.6%.

CURRENT MATURITIES OF LONG-TERM DEBT

Another account that appears in the current liability category of Starbucks' balance sheet is **Current Portion of Long-Term Debt.** On other companies' balance sheets, this item may appear as Current Maturities of Long-Term Debt. This account should appear when a firm has a liability and must make periodic payments. For example, assume that on January 1, 2008, your firm obtained a $10,000 loan from the bank. The terms of the loan require you to make payments in the amount of $1,000 per year for ten years payable each January 1 beginning January 1, 2009. On December 31, 2008, an entry should be made to classify a portion of the balance as a current liability as follows:

Current maturities of long-term debt
The portion of a long-term liability that will be paid within one year. ***Alternate terms:*** *Long-term debt, current portion.*

2008			
Dec. 31	Long-Term Liability	1,000	
	Current Portion of Liability		1,000
	To record the current portion of bank loan.		

Balance Sheet							Income Statement
ASSETS	=	**LIABILITIES**		+	**STOCKHOLDERS' EQUITY**	+	**REVENUES – EXPENSES**
		Current Portion of Liability	1,000				
		Long-Term Liability	(1,000)				

The December 31, 2008, balance sheet should indicate that the liability for the note payable is classified into two portions: a $1,000 current liability that must be repaid within one year and a $9,000 long-term liability.

On January 1, 2009, the company must pay $1,000; the entry should be recorded as follows:

2009			
Jan. 1	Current Portion of Liability	1,000	
	Cash		1,000
	To record payment of $1,000 on bank loan.		

Balance Sheet								Income Statement
ASSETS		=	**LIABILITIES**		+	**STOCKHOLDERS' EQUITY**	+	**REVENUES − EXPENSES**
Cash	(1,000)		Current Portion of Liability	(1,000)				

On December 31, 2009, the company should again record the current portion of the liability. Therefore, the 2009 year-end balance sheet should indicate that the liability is classified into two portions: a $1,000 current liability and an $8,000 long-term liability. The process should be repeated each year until the bank loan has been fully paid. When an investor or a creditor reads a balance sheet, he or she wants to distinguish between debt that is long-term and debt that is short-term. Therefore, it is important to segregate the portion of the debt that becomes due within one year.

The balance sheet account labeled Current Portion of Long-Term Debt should include only the amount of principal to be paid. The amount of interest that has been incurred but is unpaid should be listed separately in an account such as Interest Payable.

POD REVIEW 9.1

LO1 *Identify the components of the current liability category of the balance sheet.*

- Current liabilities are obligations of a company that generally must be satisfied within one year. Some companies list them in the balance sheet in order of the account that requires payment first.
- Current liability accounts include accounts payable, notes payable, the current portion of long-term debt, taxes payable, and accrued liabilities.

QUESTIONS

1. *For users of financial statements, the current liability classification in the balance sheet is important because it is closely tied to the concept of*
   a. materiality.
   b. liquidity.
   c. profitability.
   d. leverage.

2. *Alpha Company has current assets of $100,000 and current liabilities of $40,000. How much inventory could it purchase on account and achieve its minimum desired current ratio of 2 to 1?*
   a. $10,000
   b. $20,000
   c. $40,000
   d. It cannot purchase any inventory on account and achieve its minimum desired current ratio.

LO2 Examine how accruals affect the current liability category.

TAXES PAYABLE

Starbucks has an amount of $94,010,000 in the current liability category designated as Accrued Taxes. Other companies may label the account as Taxes Payable. Corporations pay a variety of taxes, including federal and state income taxes, property taxes, and other taxes. Usually, the largest dollar amount is incurred for state and federal income taxes. Taxes are an expense of the business and should be accrued in the same manner as any other business expense. A company that ends its accounting year on December 31 is not required to calculate the amount of tax owed to the government until the following March 15 or April 15, depending on the type of business. Therefore, the business must make an accounting entry, usually as one of the year-end adjusting entries, to record the amount of tax that has been incurred but is unpaid. Normally, the entry is recorded as follows:

Dec. 31	Tax Expense	xxx	
	Tax Payable		xxx
	To accrue income tax for the year.		

Balance Sheet							Income Statement	
ASSETS	=	**LIABILITIES**		+	**STOCKHOLDERS' EQUITY**	+	**REVENUES − EXPENSES**	
		Tax Payable	xxx				Tax Expense	(xxx)

The calculation of the amount of tax a business owes is very complex. For now, the important point is that taxes are an expense when incurred (not when paid) and must be recorded as a liability as incurred.

Some analysts prefer to measure a company's profits before it pays taxes for several reasons. For one thing, tax rates change from year to year. A small change in the tax rate may drastically change a firm's profitability. Also, investors should realize that taxes occur every year but that tax changes are not a recurring element of a business. Additionally, taxes are somewhat beyond the control of a company's management. For these reasons, **it is important to consider a firm's operations *before* taxes to better evaluate management's ability to control operations**.

OTHER ACCRUED LIABILITIES

Starbucks' 2006 balance sheet listed an amount of $224,154,000 as current liability under the category of Other Accrued Expenses. What items might be included in this category?

Previous chapters, especially Chapter 4, provided many examples of accrued liabilities. **Accrued liabilities** include any amount that has been incurred due to the passage of time but has not been paid as of the balance sheet date. A common example is salary or wages payable. Suppose that your firm has a payroll of $1,000 per day Monday through Friday and that employees are paid at the close of work each Friday. Also suppose that December 31 is the end of your accounting year and that it falls on a Tuesday. Your firm will have to record the following entry as of December 31:

Accrued liability
A liability that has been incurred but has not yet been paid.

Dec. 31	Salary Expense	2,000	
	Salary Payable		2,000
	To record two days' salary as expense.		

Balance Sheet							Income Statement	
ASSETS	=	**LIABILITIES**		+	**STOCKHOLDERS' EQUITY**	+	**REVENUES − EXPENSES**	
		Salary Payable	2,000				Salary Expense	(2,000)

The amount of the salary payable would be classified as a current liability and could appear in a category such as Other Accrued Expenses.

Interest is another item that often must be accrued at year-end. Assume that you received a one-year loan of $10,000 on December 1. The loan carries a 12% interest rate.

On December 31, an accounting entry must be made to record interest even though the money may not actually be due:

Dec. 31	Interest Expense	100	
	Interest Payable		100
	To record one month's interest as expense.		

Balance Sheet									Income Statement	
ASSETS	=	**LIABILITIES**		+	**STOCKHOLDERS' EQUITY**		+	**REVENUES − EXPENSES**	
		Interest Payable	100					Interest Expense	(100)

The Interest Payable account should be classified as a current liability, assuming that it is to be paid within one year of the December 31 date.

POD REVIEW 9.2

LO2 *Examine how accruals affect the current liability category.*

- Accrued liabilities result from expenses that are incurred but have not yet been paid.
- Common accrued liabilities include taxes payable, salaries payable, and interest payable.

QUESTIONS

1. *An invoice received from a supplier for $5,000 on January 1 with terms 3/15, net 30 means that the company should pay*
   a. $5,000 between January 4 and January 16.
   b. $4,850 before the end of January.
   c. $4,250 before January 4.
   d. either $4,850 before January 16 or $5,000 before the end of the month.

2. *When a liability is accrued, the account debited in the transaction is*
   a. an asset.
   b. an expense.
   c. another liability account.
   d. a stockholders' equity account.

LO3 Show that you understand how changes in current liabilities affect the statement of cash flows.

READING THE STATEMENT OF CASH FLOWS FOR CHANGES IN CURRENT LIABILITIES

It is important to understand the impact that current liabilities have on a company's cash flows. Exhibit 9-2 illustrates the placement of current liabilities on the statement of cash flows (using the indirect method) and their effect. Most current liabilities are directly related to a firm's ongoing operations. Therefore, the change in the balance of each current liability account should be reflected in the Operating Activities category of the statement of cash flows. A decrease in a current liability account indicates that cash has been used to pay the liability and should appear as a deduction on the cash flow statement. An increase in a current liability account indicates a recognized expense that has not yet been paid. Look for it as an increase in the Operating Activities category of the cash flow statement.

A partial statement of cash flows of **Starbucks Corporation** is presented in Exhibit 9-3. Note that for 2006, the company has a positive amount on the statement of cash flows of $104,966,000 for Accounts Payable and $132,725,000 for Accrued Taxes. That is an indication that those two accounts increased, resulting in a positive cash flow for the company.

EXHIBIT 9-2 Current Liabilities on the Statement of Cash Flows

Item	Cash Flow Statement	
	Operating Activities	
	Net income	xxx
Increase in current liability	→	+
Decrease in current liability	→	−
	Investing Activities	
	Financing Activities	
Increase in notes payable	→	+
Decrease in notes payable	→	−

Almost all current liabilities appear in the Operating Activities category of the statement of cash flows, but there are exceptions. If a current liability is not directly related to operating activities, it should not appear in that category. For example, if Starbucks uses some notes payable as a means of financing, distinct from operating activities, those borrowings and repayments are reflected in the Financing Activities rather than the Operating Activities category. Perhaps that is the reason the rather large increase in short-term borrowings does not appear in the Operating Activities portion of the statement of cash flows.

EXHIBIT 9-3 Starbucks Corporation Partial Consolidated Statement of Cash Flows (In thousands)

FISCAL YEAR ENDED	October 1, 2006	October 2, 2005
OPERATING ACTIVITIES		
Net earnings	$ 564,259	$ 494,370
Adjustments to reconcile net earnings to net cash provided by operating activities:		
Cumulative effect of accounting change for FIN 47, net of taxes	17,214	—
Depreciation and amortization	412,625	367,207
Provision for impairments and asset disposals	19,622	19,464
Deferred income taxes, net	(84,324)	(31,253)
Equity in income of investees	(60,570)	(49,537)
Distributions of income from equity investees	49,238	30,919
Stock-based compensation	105,664	—
Tax benefit from exercise of stock options	1,318	109,978
Excess tax benefit from exercise of stock options	(117,368)	—
Net amortization of premium on securities	2,013	10,097
Cash provided/(used) by changes in operating assets and liabilities:		
Inventories	(85,527)	(121,618)
Accounts payable	104,966	9,717
Accrued compensation and related costs	54,424	22,711
Accrued taxes	132,725	14,435
Deferred revenue	56,547	53,276
Other operating assets and liabilities	(41,193)	(6,851)
Net cash provided by operating activities	1,131,633	922,915

POD REVIEW 9.3

LO3 *Show that you understand how changes in current liabilities affect the statement of cash flows.*

- Most current liabilities are directly related to the ongoing operations of a company.
  - Decreases in current liabilities indicate that cash has been used to satisfy obligations and are cash outflows not represented by some expenses in the income statement.
  - Increases in current liabilities indicate that some expenses in the income statement have not been paid in cash and are not cash outflows represented by some expenses on the income statement.

QUESTIONS

1. *In the statement of cash flows, a decrease in accounts payable would be shown as a(n)*
   a. increase in the Operating Activities category.
   b. decrease in the Operating Activities category.
   c. increase in the Financing category.
   d. decrease in the Financing category.

2. *In the statement of cash flows, an increase in a current liability will appear as a(n)*
   a. increase in the Operating Activities category.
   b. decrease in the Operating Activities category.
   c. increase in the Financing category.
   d. decrease in the Financing category.

Contingent Liabilities

LO4 Determine when contingent liabilities should be presented on the balance sheet or disclosed in notes and how to calculate their amounts.

You have seen that accountants must exercise a great deal of expertise and judgment in deciding what to record and in determining the amount to record. This is certainly true regarding contingent liabilities. A **contingent liability** is an obligation that involves an existing condition for which the outcome is not known with certainty and depends on some event that will occur in the future. The actual amount of the liability must be estimated because we cannot clearly predict the future. The important accounting issues are whether contingent liabilities should be recorded and, if so, in what amounts.

Contingent liability An existing condition for which the outcome is not known but depends on some future event. ***Alternate term:*** *Contingent loss.*

This is a judgment call that is normally resolved through discussions among the company's management and its outside auditors. Management usually would rather not disclose contingent liabilities until they come due. The reason is that investors' and creditors' judgment of management is based on the company's earnings, and the recording of a contingent liability must be accompanied by a charge to (reduction in) earnings. Auditors, on the other hand, want management to disclose as much information as possible because the auditors are essentially representing the interests of investors and creditors who want to know as much as possible.

Study Tip

Contingent liabilities are recorded only if they are probable and if the amount can be reasonably estimated.

CONTINGENT LIABILITIES THAT ARE RECORDED

A contingent liability should be accrued and presented on the balance sheet if it is probable and if the amount can be reasonably estimated. But when is an event *probable,* and what does *reasonably estimated* mean? The terms must be defined based on the facts of each situation. A financial statement user would want the company to err on the side of full disclosure. On the other hand, the company should not be required to disclose every remote possibility.

Product Warranties and Guarantees: Common Contingent Liabilities That Are Recorded A common contingent liability that must be presented as a liability by firms involves product warranties and guarantees. Many firms sell products for which they provide the customer a warranty against defects that may develop in the products. If a product becomes defective within the warranty period, the selling firm ensures that it will repair or replace the item. This is an example of a contingent liability because the expense of fixing a product depends on some of the products becoming defective—an uncertain, although likely, event.

At the end of each period, the selling firm must estimate how many of the products sold in the current year will become defective in the future and the cost of repair or replacement. This type of contingent liability is often referred to as an **estimated liability** to emphasize that the costs are not known at year-end and must be estimated.

Estimated liability
A contingent liability that is accrued and reflected on the balance sheet.

As an example, assume that Quickkey Computer sells a computer product for $5,000. When the customer buys the product, Quickkey provides a one-year warranty in case the product must be repaired. Assume that in 2008, Quickkey sold 100 computers for a total sales revenue of $500,000. At the end of 2008, Quickkey must record an estimate of the warranty costs that will occur on 2008 sales. Using an analysis of past warranty records, Quickkey estimates that repairs will average 2% of total sales. Therefore, Quickkey should record the following transaction at the end of 2008:

Dec. 31	Warranty Expense	10,000	
	Estimated Liability		10,000
	To record estimated liability at 2% of sales.		

Balance Sheet						Income Statement
ASSETS	=	**LIABILITIES**	+	**STOCKHOLDERS' EQUITY**	+	**REVENUES − EXPENSES**
		Estimated Liability 10,000				Warranty Expense (10,000)

The amount of warranty costs that a company presents as an expense is of interest to investors and potential creditors. If the expense as a percentage of sales begins to rise, a logical conclusion is that the product is becoming less reliable.

Warranties are an excellent example of the matching principle. In the Quickkey example, the warranty costs related to 2008 sales were estimated and recorded in 2008. This was done to match the 2008 sales with the expenses related to those sales. When actual repairs of the computers occur in 2009, they do not result in an expense. The repair costs incurred in 2009 should be treated as a reduction in the liability that had been estimated previously.

Because items such as warranties involve estimation, you may wonder what happens if the amount estimated is not accurate. The company must analyze past warranty records carefully and incorporate any changes in customer buying habits, usage, technological changes, and other changes. Still, even with careful analysis, the actual amount of the expense is not likely to equal the estimated amount. Generally, firms do not change the amount of the expense recorded in past periods for such differences. They may adjust the amount recorded in future periods, however.

Premiums or Coupons: Other Contingent Liabilities That Are Recorded Warranties provide an example of a contingent liability that must be estimated and recorded. Another example is premium or coupon offers that accompany many products. Cereal boxes are an everyday example of premium offers. The boxes often allow customers to purchase a toy or game at a reduced price if the purchase is accompanied by cereal box tops or proof of purchase. The offer given to cereal customers represents a contingent liability. At the end of each year, the cereal company must estimate the number of premium offers that will be redeemed and the cost involved and must report a contingent liability for that amount.

Some Lawsuits and Legal Claims Are Contingent Liabilities That Must Be Recorded Legal claims that have been filed against a firm are also examples of contingent liabilities. In today's business environment, lawsuits and legal claims are a fact of life. They represent a contingent liability because an event has occurred but the outcome of that event, the resolution of the lawsuit, is not known. The defendant in the lawsuit must make a judgment about the lawsuit's outcome to decide whether the item should be recorded on the balance sheet or should be disclosed in the notes. When it is probable that the legal claim's outcome will be unfavorable, an amount should be recorded as a contingent liability on the balance sheet.

As you might imagine, firms are not very eager to record contingent lawsuits as liabilities because the amount of loss is often difficult to estimate. Also, some may view the accountant's decision as an admission of guilt when a lawsuit is recorded as a liability before the courts have finalized a decision. Accountants often must consult with lawyers or other legal experts to determine the probability of the loss of a lawsuit. In cases involving contingencies, it is especially important that the accountant make an independent judgment based on the facts and not be swayed by the desires of other parties.

CONTINGENT LIABILITIES THAT ARE DISCLOSED

Any contingent liability that is probable and that can be reasonably estimated must be reported as a liability. We now must consider contingent liabilities that do not meet the probable criterion or cannot be reasonably estimated. In either case, **a contingent liability must be disclosed in the financial statement notes but not reported on the balance sheet if the contingent liability is at least reasonably possible.**

Although information in the notes to the financial statements contains important data on which investors base decisions, some accountants believe that note disclosure does not have the same impact as does recording a contingent liability on the balance sheet. For one thing, note disclosure does not affect the important financial ratios that investors use to make decisions.

The previous section discussed the treatment of a contingent liability that was probable and therefore was recorded on the balance sheet as a liability. Most lawsuits, however, are not recorded as liabilities because the risk of loss is not considered probable or the amount of the loss cannot be reasonably estimated. If a company does not record a lawsuit as a liability, it still must consider whether the lawsuit should be disclosed in the notes to the financial statements. When the risk of loss is at least *reasonably possible,* the company should provide note disclosure. This is the course of action taken for most contingent liabilities involving lawsuits.

© Bob Pardue/Alamy

Hot Topics

Starbuck's Liability for Products

Companies have a liability for the products they produce. Sometimes the liability can occur in unexpected ways. In 2006, Starbucks announced that it was taking steps to make the milk and other dairy products that it serves free of an artificial growth hormone. The hormone is used in dairies to increase milk production but was targeted by consumer groups as being a potential health hazard. Starbucks began to use alternative dairy products in all of its company-owned stores and encouraged a similar move in the other licensed operations. No legal claims have been filed against Starbucks because of its dairy products.

Does Starbucks have a contingent liability? If so, how should it be treated in the financial statements?

Exhibit 9-4 contains excerpts from the notes to the 2006 financial statements of Starbucks Corporation. The note indicates that Starbucks is subject to a variety of lawsuits. The note also indicates that the company does not believe the lawsuits will have a "material adverse effect" on the company's condition. The excerpt in Exhibit 9-4 is an example of contingent liabilities that have been disclosed in the notes to the financial statements *but have not been recorded as liabilities on the balance sheet.* Readers of the financial statements and analysts must read the notes carefully to determine the impact of such contingent liabilities.

The amount and the timing of the cash outlays associated with contingent liabilities are especially difficult to determine. Lawsuits, for example, may extend several years into the future, and the dollar amount of possible loss may be subject to great uncertainty.

EXHIBIT 9-4 **Note Disclosure of Contingencies for Starbucks Corporation**

Legal Proceedings

On October 8, 2004, a former hourly employee of the Company filed a lawsuit in San Diego County Superior Court entitled Jou Chau v. Starbucks Coffee Company. The lawsuit alleges that the Company violated the California Labor Code by allowing shift supervisors to receive tips. . . . In addition to recovery of an unspecified amount of tips distributed to shift supervisors, the lawsuit seeks penalties under California Labor Code Section 203 for willful failure to pay wages due. Plaintiff also seeks attorneys fees and costs. On March 30, 2006, the Court issued an order certifying the case as a class action, with the plaintiff representing a class of all persons employed as baristas in the state of California since October 8, 2000. The size of the class has yet to be determined. The Company cannot estimate the possible loss to the Company, if any. The Company believes its practices comply with California law, and the Company intends to vigorously defend the lawsuit. Trial is currently set for May 2007.

The Company is party to various other legal proceedings arising in the ordinary course of its business, but it is not currently a party to any legal proceeding that management believes would have a material adverse effect on the consolidated financial position or results of operations of the Company.

CONTINGENT LIABILITIES VERSUS CONTINGENT ASSETS

Contingent liabilities that are probable and can be reasonably estimated must be presented on the balance sheet before the outcome of the future events is known. This accounting rule applies only to contingent losses or liabilities. It does not apply to contingencies by which the firm may gain. Generally, contingent gains or **contingent assets** are not reported until the gain actually occurs. **That is, contingent liabilities may be accrued but contingent assets are not accrued.** This may seem inconsistent—it is. Remember that accounting is a discipline based on a conservative set of principles. It is prudent and conservative to delay the recording of a gain until an asset is actually received but to record contingent liabilities in advance.

Contingent asset
An existing condition for which the outcome is not known but by which the company stands to gain. ***Alternate term:*** *Contingent gain.*

Of course, even though the contingent assets are not reported, the information still may be important to investors. Wall Street analysts make their living trying to place a value on contingent assets that they believe will result in future benefits. By buying stock of a company that has unrecorded assets (or advising their clients to do so), investment analysts hope to make money when those assets become a reality.

POD REVIEW 9.4

LO4 *Determine when contingent liabilities should be presented on the balance sheet or disclosed in notes and how to calculate their amounts.*

- Contingent liabilities should be accrued and disclosed only when the event they depend on is probable and the amount can be reasonably estimated.
- The amount of a contingent liability is often an estimate made by experts both inside the firm (managers for amounts of warranty expenses) and outside the firm (e.g., attorneys for amounts in a lawsuit).

QUESTIONS

1. *Omega Company is involved in two unrelated lawsuits, one as the plaintiff and one as the defendant. As a result of the two lawsuits, the company has a contingent asset and a contingent liability. How should Omega record these on its balance sheet?*
   a. Omega should record the contingent liability and the contingent asset separately on the balance sheet.
   b. Omega should record the contingent liability and the contingent asset on the balance sheet by offsetting the liability against the asset.
   c. Omega must record the contingent asset if the realization of the asset is probable and the amount can be reasonably estimated, but Omega must not record the contingent liability on the balance sheet.
   d. Omega must not record the contingent asset, but Omega must record the contingent liability on the balance sheet if the liability is probable and the amount can be reasonably estimated.
2. *A contingent liability that is probable and where the amount can reasonably be estimated should*
   a. be recorded as a liability.
   b. not be recorded as a liability but disclosed in the notes.
   c. be neither recorded as a liability nor disclosed in the notes.
   d. be recorded in the same manner as a contingent asset.

Time Value of Money Concepts

Time value of money An immediate amount should be preferred over an amount in the future.

This section will discuss the impact that interest has on decision making because of the time value of money. The **time value of money** concept means that people prefer a payment at the present time rather than in the future because of the interest factor. If an amount is received at the present time, it can be invested; and the resulting accumulation will be larger than if the same amount is received in the future. Thus, there is a *time value* to cash receipts and payments. This time value concept is important to you for two reasons: it affects your personal financial decisions, and it affects accounting valuation decisions.

Exhibit 9-5 indicates some of the personal and accounting decisions affected by the time value of money concept. In your personal life, you make decisions based on the time value of money concept nearly every day. When you invest money, you are interested in how much will be accumulated and you must determine the *future value* based on the amount of interest that will be compounded. When you borrow money, you must determine the amount of the loan payments. You may not always realize it, but the amount of the loan payment is based on the *present value* of the loan, another time value of money concept.

Time value of money is also important because of its implications for accounting valuations. Chapter 10 explains that the issue price of a bond is based on the present value of the cash flows that the bond will produce. The valuation of the bond and the recording of the bond on the balance sheet are based on this concept. Further, the amount that is considered interest expense on the financial statements is also based on

EXHIBIT 9-5 Importance of the Time Value of Money

Personal Financial Decision	Action
■ How much money will accumulate if you invest in a CD or money market account? →	Calculate the future value based on compound interest.
■ If you take out an auto loan, what will be the monthly loan payments? →	Calculate the payments based on the present value of the loan.
■ If you invest in the bond market, what should you pay for a bond? →	Calculate the present value of the bond based on compound interest.
■ If you win the lottery, should you take an immediate payment or payment over time? →	Calculate the present value of the alternatives based on compound interest.

Valuation Decisions on the Financial Statements	Valuation
■ Long-term assets →	Historical cost, but not higher than present value of the cash flows
■ Notes receivable →	Present value of the cash flows
■ Loan payments →	Based on the present value of the loan
■ Bond issue price →	Present value of the cash flows
■ Leases →	Present value of the cash flows

time value of money concepts. The bottom portion of Exhibit 9-5 indicates that the valuations of many other accounts, including Notes Receivable and Leases, are based on compound interest calculations.

The time value of money concept is used in almost every advanced business course. Investment courses, marketing courses, and many other business courses use the time value of money concept. **In fact, it is probably the most important decision-making tool to master in preparation for the business world.** This section of the text begins with an explanation of how simple interest and compound interest differ and proceeds to the concepts of present values and future values.

SIMPLE INTEREST

LO5 Explain the difference between simple and compound interest.

Simple interest is interest earned on the principal amount. If the amount of principal is unchanged from year to year, the interest per year will remain the same. Interest can be calculated using the following formula:

Simple interest Interest is calculated on the principal amount only.

$$I = P \times R \times T$$

where

I = Dollar amount of interest per year
P = Principal
R = Interest rate as a percentage
T = Time in years

For example, assume that a firm has signed a two-year note payable for $3,000. Interest and principal are to be paid at the due date with simple interest at the rate of 10% per year. The amount of interest on the note would be $600, calculated as $3,000 × 0.10 × 2. The firm would be required to pay $3,600 on the due date: $3,000 principal and $600 interest.

COMPOUND INTEREST

Compound interest
Interest calculated on the principal plus previous amounts of interest. ***Alternate term:*** *Interest on interest.*

Compound interest means that interest is calculated on the principal plus previous amounts of accumulated interest. Thus, interest is compounded, or there is interest on interest. For example, assume a $3,000 note payable for which interest and principal are due in two years with interest compounded annually at 10% per year. Interest would be calculated as follows:

Year	Principal Amount at Beginning of Year	Interest at 10%	Accumulated at Year-End
1	$3,000	$300	$3,300
2	3,300	330	3,630

We would be required to pay $3,630 at the end of two years, $3,000 principal and $630 interest. A comparison of the note payable with 10% simple interest in the first example with the note payable with 10% compound interest in the second example clearly indicates that the amount accumulated with compound interest is a higher amount because of the interest-on-interest feature.

POD REVIEW 9.5

LO5 *Explain the difference between simple and compound interest.*

- Simple interest is earned only on the principal amount, whereas compound interest is earned on the principal plus previous amounts of accumulated interest.

QUESTIONS

1. *If you invest money for five years, which will be larger?*
   a. an investment that earns simple interest
   b. an investment that earns compound interest
   c. The investments will be the same.
   d. It depends on how frequently compounding occurs.

2. *If you invest money for five years, which will be larger?*
   a. an investment where interest is compounded annually
   b. an investment where interest is compounded semiannually
   c. an investment where interest is compounded daily
   d. The investments will be the same.

LO6 Calculate amounts using the future value and present value concepts.

INTEREST COMPOUNDING

For most accounting problems, we will assume that compound interest is compounded annually. In actual business practice, compounding usually occurs over much shorter intervals. This can be confusing because the interest rate is often stated as an annual rate even though it is compounded over a shorter period. If compounding is not done annually, you must adjust the interest rate by dividing the annual rate by the number of compounding periods per year.

For example, assume that the note payable from the previous example carried a 10% interest rate compounded semiannually for two years. The 10% annual rate should be converted to 5% per period for four semiannual periods. The amount of interest would be compounded, as in the previous example, but for four periods instead of two. The compounding process is as follows:

Period	Principal Amount at Beginning of Year	Interest at 5% per Period	Accumulated at End of Period
1	$3,000	$150	$3,150
2	3,150	158	3,308
3	3,308	165	3,473
4	3,473	174	3,647

The example illustrates that compounding more frequently results in a larger amount accumulated. In fact, many banks and financial institutions now compound interest on savings accounts on a daily basis.

In the remainder of this section, we will assume that compound interest is applicable. Four compound interest calculations must be understood:

1. **Future value of a single amount**
2. **Present value of a single amount**
3. **Future value of an annuity**
4. **Present value of an annuity**

FUTURE VALUE OF A SINGLE AMOUNT

We are often interested in the amount of interest plus principal that will be accumulated at a future time. This is called a *future amount* or *future value*. The future amount is always larger than the principal amount (payment) because of the interest that accumulates. The formula to calculate the **future value of a single amount** is as follows:

Future value of a single amount
Amount accumulated at a future time from a single payment or investment.

$$FV = p(1 + i)^n$$

where

FV = Future value to be calculated
p = Present value or principal amount
i = Interest rate
n = Number of periods of compounding

Example 1: Your three-year-old son Robert inherits $50,000 in cash and securities from his grandfather. If the funds are left in the bank and in the stock market and receive an annual return of 10%, how much will be available in 15 years when Robert starts college?

Solution:

$$\begin{aligned} FV &= \$50{,}000(1 + 0.10)^{15} \\ &= \$50{,}000(4.177) \\ &= \$208{,}850 \end{aligned}$$

In some cases, we will use time diagrams to illustrate the relationships. A time diagram to illustrate a future value would be of the following form:

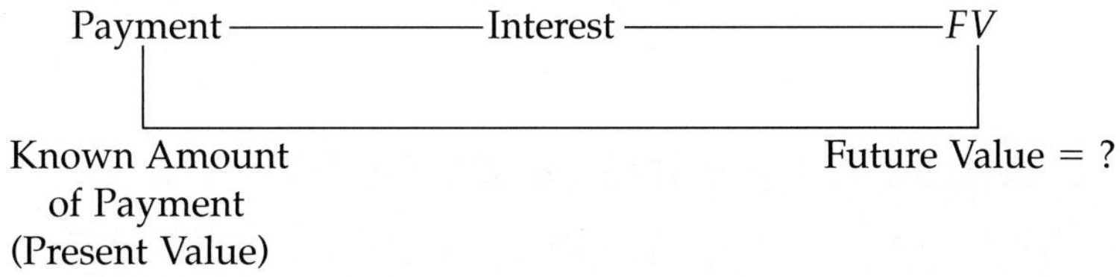

Example 2: Consider a $2,000 note payable that carries interest at the rate of 10% compounded annually. The note is due in two years, and the principal and interest must be paid at that time. The amount that must be paid in two years is the future value. The future value can be calculated in the manner used in the previous examples:

Year	Principal Amount at Beginning of Year	Interest at 10%	Accumulated at Year-End
1	$2,000	$200	$2,200
2	2,200	220	2,420

The future value can also be calculated by using the following formula:

$$
\begin{aligned}
FV &= \$2{,}000(1 + 0.10)^2 \\
&= \$2{,}000(1.21) \\
&= \$2{,}420
\end{aligned}
$$

Instead of a formula, other methods can be used to calculate future value. Tables can be constructed to assist in the calculations. Table 9-1 on page 448 indicates the future value of $1 at various interest rates for various time periods. To find the future value of a two-year note at 10% compounded annually, you read across the line for two periods and down the 10% column, which gives you an interest rate factor of 1.210. Because the table has been constructed for future values of $1, we would determine the future value of $2,000 as follows:

$$
\begin{aligned}
FV &= \$2{,}000 \times 1.210 \\
&= \$2{,}420
\end{aligned}
$$

A second method used to perform the calculations is to use the built-in functions of a computerized spreadsheet. Appendix A will illustrate how to use a common spreadsheet, Microsoft® Excel®, to perform the same calculations. *Note that the numbers produced by each method may differ by a few dollars because of rounding differences. You should ignore those small differences and concentrate on the methods used to perform the interest rate calculations.*

Remember that compounding does not always occur annually. How does this affect the calculation of future value amounts?

Example 3: Suppose that we want to find the future value of a $2,000 note payable due in two years. The note payable requires interest to be compounded quarterly at the rate of 12% per year. To calculate the future value, we must adjust the interest rate to a quarterly basis by dividing the 12% rate by the number of compounding periods per year, which in the case of quarterly compounding is four:

$$12\%/4 \text{ quarters} = 3\% \text{ per quarter}$$

Also, the number of compounding periods is eight—four per year times two years.

The future value of the note can be found in two ways. First, we can insert the proper values into the future value formula:

$$
\begin{aligned}
FV &= \$2{,}000(1 + 0.03)^8 \\
&= \$2{,}000(1.267) \\
&= \$2{,}534
\end{aligned}
$$

We can arrive at the same future value amount with the use of Table 9-1. Refer to the interest factor in the table indicated for eight periods and 3%. The future value would be calculated as follows:

$$
\begin{aligned}
FV &= \$2{,}000(\text{interest factor}) \\
&= \$2{,}000(1.267) \\
&= \$2{,}534
\end{aligned}
$$

PRESENT VALUE OF A SINGLE AMOUNT

Present value of a single amount
The amount at a present time that is equivalent to a payment or an investment at a future time.

In many situations, we do not want to calculate how much will be accumulated at a future time. Rather, we want to determine the present amount that is equivalent to an amount at a future time. This is the present value concept. The **present value of a single amount** represents the value today of a single amount to be received or paid at a future time. This can be portrayed in a time diagram as follows:

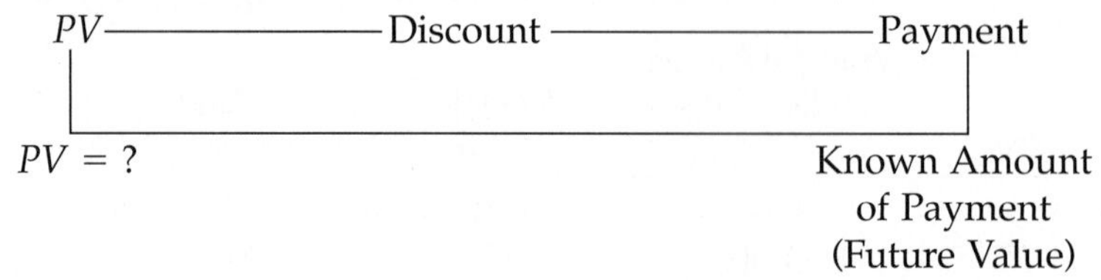

The time diagram portrays discount rather than interest because we often speak of "discounting" the future payment back to the present time.

Example 4: Suppose that you know that you will receive $2,000 in two years. You also know that if you had the money now, you could invest it at 10% compounded annually. What is the present value of the $2,000? Another way to ask the same question is, what amount must be invested today at 10% compounded annually to have $2,000 accumulated in two years?

The formula used to calculate present value is as follows:

$$PV = \text{Future value} \times (1 + i)^{-n}$$

where

$$\begin{aligned} PV &= \text{Present value amount in dollars} \\ \text{Future value} &= \text{Amount to be received in the future} \\ i &= \text{Interest rate or discount rate} \\ n &= \text{Number of periods} \end{aligned}$$

Study Tip

When interest rates *increase*, present values *decrease*. This is called an *inverse relationship*.

We can use the present value formula to solve for the present value of the $2,000 note as follows:

$$\begin{aligned} PV &= \$2{,}000 \times (1 + 0.10)^{-2} \\ &= \$2{,}000 \times (0.826) \\ &= \$1{,}652 \end{aligned}$$

Example 5: A recent magazine article projects that it will cost $120,000 to attend a four-year college ten years from now. If that is true, how much money would you have to put into an account today to fund that education, assuming a 5% rate of return?

$$\begin{aligned} PV &= \$120{,}000(1 + 0.05)^{-10} \\ &= \$120{,}000(0.614) \\ &= \$73{,}680 \end{aligned}$$

Tables have also been developed to determine the present value of $1 at various interest rates and number of periods. Table 9-2 on page 449 presents the present value or discount factors for an amount of $1 to be received at a future time. To use the table for the two-year note example, you must read across the line for two periods and down the 10% column to the discount factor of 0.826. The present value of $2,000 would be calculated as follows:

$$\begin{aligned} PV &= \$2{,}000(\text{discount factor}) \\ &= \$2{,}000(0.826) \\ &= \$1{,}652 \end{aligned}$$

Two other points are important. First, the example illustrates that the present value amount is always less than the future payment. This happens because of the discount factor. In other words, if we had a smaller amount at the present (the present value), we could invest it and earn interest that would accumulate to an amount equal to the larger amount (the future payment). Second, study of the present value and future value formulas indicates that each is the reciprocal of the other. When we want to calculate a present value amount, we normally use Table 9-2 and multiply a discount factor times the payment. However, we could also use Table 9-1 and divide by the interest factor. Thus, the present value of the $2,000 to be received in the future could also be calculated as follows:

$$\begin{aligned} PV &= \$2{,}000/1.210 \\ &= \$1{,}652 \end{aligned}$$

FUTURE VALUE OF AN ANNUITY

The present value and future value amounts are useful when a single amount is involved. Many accounting situations involve an annuity, however. **Annuity** means a series of payments of equal amounts. Consider the calculation of the future value when a series of payments is involved.

Annuity
A series of payments of equal amounts.

Example 6: Suppose that you are to receive $3,000 per year at the end of each of the next four years. Also assume that each payment could be invested at an interest rate of 10% compounded annually. How much would be accumulated in principal and interest by the end of the fourth year? This is an example of an annuity of payments of equal amounts. A time diagram would portray the payments as follows:

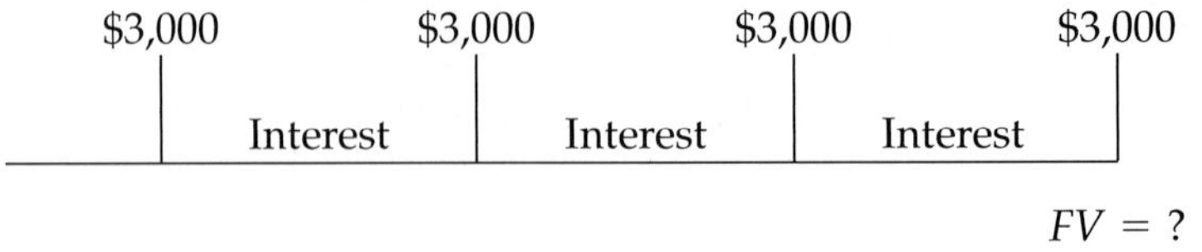

Because we are interested in calculating the future value, we could use the future value of $1 concept and calculate the future value of each $3,000 payment using Table 9-1 as follows:

$3,000 × 1.331 Interest for 3 Periods	$ 3,993
3,000 × 1.210 Interest for 2 Periods	3,630
3,000 × 1.100 Interest for 1 Period	3,300
3,000 × 1.000 Interest for 0 Periods	3,000
Total Future Value	$13,923

Note that four payments would be received but that only three of them would draw interest because the payments are received at the end of each period.

Future value of an annuity
The amount accumulated in the future when a series of payments is invested and accrues interest. ***Alternate term:*** *Amount of an annuity.*

Fortunately, there is an easier method to calculate the **future value of an annuity**. Table 9-3 on page 450 has been constructed to indicate the future value of a series of payments of $1 per period at various interest rates and number of periods. The table can be used for the previous example by reading across the four-period line and down the 10% column to a table factor of 4.641. The future value of an annuity of $3,000 per year can be calculated as follows:

$$\begin{aligned} FV &= \$3{,}000(\text{table factor}) \\ &= \$3{,}000(4.641) \\ &= \$13{,}923 \end{aligned}$$

Example 7: Your cousin had a baby girl two weeks ago and is already thinking about sending her to college. When the girl is 15, how much money would be in her college account if your cousin deposited $2,000 into it on each of her 15 birthdays? The interest rate is 10%.

$$\begin{aligned} FV &= \$2{,}000(\text{table factor}) \\ &= \$2{,}000(31.772) \end{aligned}$$

When compounding occurs more frequently than annually, adjustments must be made to the interest rate and number of periods, adjustments similar to those discussed previously for single amounts.

Example 8: How would the future value be calculated if the previous example was modified so that $1,000 was deposited semiannually and the interest rate was 10% compounded semiannually (or 5% per period) for 15 years? Table 9-3 could be used by reading across the line for 30 periods and down the column for 5% to obtain a table factor of 66.439. The future value would be calculated as follows:

$$\begin{aligned} FV &= \$1{,}000(\text{table factor}) \\ &= \$1{,}000(66.439) \\ &= \$66{,}439 \end{aligned}$$

Comparing the two examples illustrates once again that more frequent compounding results in larger accumulated amounts.

PRESENT VALUE OF AN ANNUITY

Many accounting applications of the time value of money concept concern situations for which we want to know the present value of a series of payments that will occur in the future. This involves calculating the present value of an annuity. An annuity is a series of payments of equal amounts.

Example 9: Suppose that you will receive an annuity of $4,000 per year for four years, with the first received one year from today. The amounts received can be invested at a rate of 10% compounded annually. What amount would you need at the present time to have an amount equivalent to the series of payments and interest in the future? To answer that question, you must calculate the **present value of an annuity**. A time diagram of the series of payments would appear as follows:

Present value of an annuity
The amount at a present time that is equivalent to a series of payments and interest in the future.

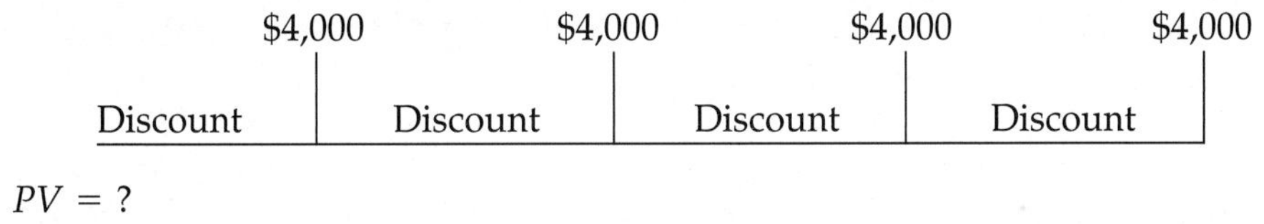

Because you are interested in calculating the present value, you could refer to the present value of $1 concept and discount each of the $4,000 payments individually using table factors from Table 9-2 as follows:

$4,000 × 0.683 Factor for 4 Periods	$ 2,732
4,000 × 0.751 Factor for 3 Periods	3,004
4,000 × 0.826 Factor for 2 Periods	3,304
4,000 × 0.909 Factor for 1 Period	3,636
Total Present Value	$12,676

For a problem of any size, it is very cumbersome to calculate the present value of each payment individually. Therefore, tables have been constructed to ease the computational burden. Table 9-4 on page 451 provides table factors to calculate the present value of an annuity of $1 per year at various interest rates and number of periods. The previous example can be solved by reading across the four-year line and down the 10% column to obtain a table factor of 3.170. The present value would then be calculated as follows:

$$\begin{aligned} PV &= \$4{,}000(\text{table factor}) \\ &= \$4{,}000(3.170) \\ &= \$12{,}680 \end{aligned}$$

Note that there is a $4 difference in the present value calculated by the first and second methods. This difference is caused by a small amount of rounding in the table factors.

Example 10: You just won the lottery. You can take your $1 million in a lump sum today, or you can receive $100,000 per year over the next 12 years. Assuming a 5% interest rate, which would you prefer, ignoring tax considerations?

Solution:

$$\begin{aligned} PV &= \$100{,}000(\text{table factor}) \\ &= \$100{,}000(8.863) \\ &= \$886{,}300 \end{aligned}$$

Because the present value of the payments over 12 years is less than the $1 million immediate payment, you should take the immediate payment.

POD REVIEW 9.6

LO6 *Calculate amounts using the future value and present value concepts.*

- Present and future value calculations are made for four different scenarios:
  - Future value of a single amount
  - Present value of a single amount
  - Future value of an annuity
  - Present value of an annuity

QUESTIONS

1. *You plan to invest $1,000 and want to determine how much will be accumulated in five years if you earn interest at 8% per year. This is an example of*
   a. future value of a single amount.
   b. future value of an annuity.
   c. present value of a single amount.
   d. present value of an annuity.

2. *You plan to invest $1,000 per year and want to determine how much will be accumulated in five years if you earn interest at 8% per year compounded annually. This is an example of*
   a. future value of a single amount.
   b. future value of an annuity.
   c. present value of a single amount.
   d. present value of an annuity.

LO7 Apply the compound interest concepts to some common accounting situations.

SOLVING FOR UNKNOWNS

In some cases, the present value or future value amounts will be known but the interest rate or the number of payments must be calculated. The formulas presented thus far can be used for such calculations, but you must be careful to analyze each problem to make sure you have chosen the correct relationship. Two examples will be used to illustrate the power of the time value of money concepts.

Assume that you have just purchased an automobile for $14,420 and must decide how to pay for it. Your local bank has graciously granted you a five-year loan. Because you are a good credit risk, the bank will allow you to make annual payments on the loan at the end of each year. The amount of the loan payments, which include principal and interest, is $4,000 per year. You are concerned that your total payments will be $20,000 ($4,000 per year for five years) and want to calculate the interest rate that is being charged on the loan.

Because the market or present value of the car, as well as the loan, is $14,420, a time diagram of the example would appear as follows:

$4,000	$4,000	$4,000	$4,000	$4,000
Discount	Discount	Discount	Discount	Discount

$PV = \$14,420$

The interest rate we must solve for represents the discount rate that was applied to the $4,000 payments to result in a present value of $14,420. Therefore, the applicable formula is the following:

$$PV = \$4,000(\text{table factor})$$

In this case, PV is known, so the formula can be rearranged as follows:

$$\begin{aligned}\text{Table factor} &= PV/\$4,000\\ &= \$14,420/\$4,000\\ &= 3.605\end{aligned}$$

The value of 3.605 represents a table factor in Table 9-4. You must read across the five-year line until you find a table factor of 3.605. In this case, that table factor is found in the 12% column. Therefore, the rate of interest being paid on the auto loan is 12%.

The second example involves solving for the number of interest periods. Assume that you want to accumulate $12,000 as a down payment on a home. You believe that you can save $1,000 per semiannual period; and your bank will pay interest of 8% per year, or 4% per semiannual period. How long will it take you to accumulate the desired amount?

The accumulated amount of $12,000 represents the future value of an annuity of $1,000 per semiannual period. Therefore, we can use the interest factors of Table 9-3 to assist in the solution. The applicable formula in this case is the following:

$$FV = \$1{,}000(\text{table factor})$$

The future value is known to be $12,000, and we must solve for the interest factor or table factor. Therefore, we can rearrange the formula as follows:

$$\begin{aligned}\text{Table factor} &= FV/\$1{,}000\\ &= \$12{,}000/\$1{,}000\\ &= 12.00\end{aligned}$$

Using Table 9-3, you must scan down the 4% column until you find a table value that is near 12.00. The closest table value you find is 12.006. That table value corresponds to ten periods. Therefore, if $1,000 is deposited per semiannual period and the money is invested at 4% per semiannual period, it will take ten semiannual periods (five years) to accumulate $12,000.

POD REVIEW 9.7

LO7 ***Apply the compound interest concepts to some common accounting situations.***

- Often all of the variables necessary to calculate amounts related to present and future value concepts will be available except for one unknown amount that can be solved for.
- Financial calculators allow for these situations and easily solve for unknown values such as present or future value, payments, and interest rate.

QUESTIONS

1. *You want to buy a car costing $20,000 and make loan payments over five years at 10% interest per year. You must solve for the amount of the payments. In doing so, the amount of $20,000 represents*

   a. an annuity.
   b. a future value.
   c. a present value.
   d. the payment amount.

2. *You want to accumulate $20,000 by your 25th birthday and will invest money in the bank each year where it will earn interest at 10% compounded annually. You must solve for the amount to invest each year. In doing so, the $20,000 amount represents*

   a. an annuity.
   b. a future value.
   c. a present value.
   d. the amount to invest.

TABLE 9-1 Future Value of $1

(N) PERIODS	Rate of Interest in % 2	3	4	5	6	7	8	9	10	11	12	15
1	1.020	1.030	1.040	1.050	1.060	1.070	1.080	1.090	1.100	1.110	1.120	1.150
2	1.040	1.061	1.082	1.103	1.124	1.145	1.166	1.188	1.210	1.232	1.254	1.323
3	1.061	1.093	1.125	1.158	1.191	1.225	1.260	1.295	1.331	1.368	1.405	1.521
4	1.082	1.126	1.170	1.216	1.262	1.311	1.360	1.412	1.464	1.518	1.574	1.749
5	1.104	1.159	1.217	1.276	1.338	1.403	1.469	1.539	1.611	1.685	1.762	2.011
6	1.126	1.194	1.265	1.340	1.419	1.501	1.587	1.677	1.772	1.870	1.974	2.313
7	1.149	1.230	1.316	1.407	1.504	1.606	1.714	1.828	1.949	2.076	2.211	2.660
8	1.172	1.267	1.369	1.477	1.594	1.718	1.851	1.993	2.144	2.305	2.476	3.059
9	1.195	1.305	1.423	1.551	1.689	1.838	1.999	2.172	2.358	2.558	2.773	3.518
10	1.219	1.344	1.480	1.629	1.791	1.967	2.159	2.367	2.594	2.839	3.106	4.046
11	1.243	1.384	1.539	1.710	1.898	2.105	2.332	2.580	2.853	3.152	3.479	4.652
12	1.268	1.426	1.601	1.796	2.012	2.252	2.518	2.813	3.138	3.498	3.896	5.350
13	1.294	1.469	1.665	1.886	2.133	2.410	2.720	3.066	3.452	3.883	4.363	6.153
14	1.319	1.513	1.732	1.980	2.261	2.579	2.937	3.342	3.797	4.310	4.887	7.076
15	1.346	1.558	1.801	2.079	2.397	2.759	3.172	3.642	4.177	4.785	5.474	8.137
16	1.373	1.605	1.873	2.183	2.540	2.952	3.426	3.970	4.595	5.311	6.130	9.358
17	1.400	1.653	1.948	2.292	2.693	3.159	3.700	4.328	5.054	5.895	6.866	10.761
18	1.428	1.702	2.026	2.407	2.854	3.380	3.996	4.717	5.560	6.544	7.690	12.375
19	1.457	1.754	2.07	2.527	3.026	3.617	4.316	5.142	6.116	7.263	8.613	14.232
20	1.486	1.806	2.191	2.653	3.207	3.870	4.661	5.604	6.727	8.062	9.646	16.367
21	1.516	1.860	2.279	2.786	3.400	4.141	5.034	6.109	7.40	8.949	10.804	18.822
22	1.546	1.916	2.370	2.925	3.604	4.430	5.437	6.659	8.140	9.934	12.100	21.645
23	1.577	1.974	2.465	3.072	3.820	4.741	5.871	7.258	8.954	11.026	13.552	24.891
24	1.608	2.033	2.563	3.225	4.049	5.072	6.341	7.911	9.850	12.239	15.179	28.625
25	1.641	2.094	2.666	3.386	4.292	5.427	6.848	8.623	10.835	13.585	17.000	32.919
26	1.673	2.157	2.772	3.556	4.549	5.807	7.396	9.399	11.918	15.080	19.040	37.857
27	1.707	2.221	2.883	3.733	4.822	6.214	7.988	10.245	13.110	16.739	21.325	43.535
28	1.741	2.288	2.999	3.920	5.112	6.649	8.627	11.167	14.421	18.580	23.884	50.066
29	1.776	2.357	3.119	4.116	5.418	7.114	9.317	12.172	15.863	20.624	26.750	57.575
30	1.811	2.427	3.243	4.322	5.743	7.612	10.063	13.268	17.449	22.892	29.960	66.212

TABLE 9-2 Present Value of $1

(N) PERIODS	Rate of Interest in %											
	2	3	4	5	6	7	8	9	10	11	12	15
1	0.980	0.971	0.962	0.952	0.943	0.935	0.926	0.917	0.909	0.901	0.893	0.870
2	0.961	0.943	0.925	0.907	0.890	0.873	0.857	0.842	0.826	0.812	0.797	0.756
3	0.942	0.915	0.889	0.864	0.840	0.816	0.794	0.772	0.751	0.731	0.712	0.658
4	0.924	0.888	0.855	0.823	0.792	0.763	0.735	0.708	0.683	0.659	0.636	0.572
5	0.906	0.863	0.822	0.784	0.747	0.713	0.681	0.650	0.621	0.593	0.567	0.497
6	0.888	0.837	0.790	0.746	0.705	0.666	0.630	0.596	0.564	0.535	0.507	0.432
7	0.871	0.813	0.760	0.711	0.665	0.623	0.583	0.547	0.513	0.482	0.452	0.376
8	0.853	0.789	0.731	0.677	0.627	0.582	0.540	0.502	0.467	0.434	0.404	0.327
9	0.837	0.766	0.703	0.645	0.592	0.544	0.500	0.460	0.424	0.391	0.361	0.284
10	0.820	0.744	0.676	0.614	0.558	0.508	0.463	0.422	0.386	0.352	0.322	0.247
11	0.804	0.722	0.650	0.585	0.527	0.475	0.429	0.388	0.350	0.317	0.287	0.215
12	0.788	0.701	0.625	0.557	0.497	0.444	0.397	0.356	0.319	0.286	0.257	0.187
13	0.773	0.681	0.601	0.530	0.469	0.415	0.368	0.326	0.290	0.258	0.229	0.163
14	0.758	0.661	0.577	0.505	0.442	0.388	0.340	0.299	0.263	0.232	0.205	0.141
15	0.743	0.642	0.555	0.481	0.417	0.362	0.315	0.275	0.239	0.209	0.183	0.123
16	0.728	0.623	0.534	0.458	0.394	0.339	0.292	0.252	0.218	0.188	0.163	0.107
17	0.714	0.605	0.513	0.436	0.371	0.317	0.270	0.231	0.198	0.170	0.146	0.093
18	0.700	0.587	0.494	0.416	0.350	0.296	0.250	0.212	0.180	0.153	0.130	0.081
19	0.686	0.570	0.475	0.396	0.331	0.277	0.232	0.194	0.164	0.138	0.116	0.070
20	0.673	0.554	0.456	0.377	0.312	0.258	0.215	0.178	0.149	0.124	0.104	0.061
21	0.660	0.538	0.439	0.359	0.294	0.242	0.199	0.164	0.135	0.112	0.093	0.053
22	0.647	0.522	0.422	0.342	0.278	0.226	0.184	0.150	0.123	0.101	0.083	0.046
23	0.634	0.507	0.406	0.326	0.262	0.211	0.170	0.138	0.112	0.091	0.074	0.040
24	0.622	0.492	0.390	0.310	0.247	0.197	0.158	0.126	0.102	0.082	0.066	0.035
25	0.610	0.478	0.375	0.295	0.233	0.184	0.146	0.116	0.092	0.074	0.059	0.030
26	0.598	0.464	0.361	0.281	0.220	0.172	0.135	0.106	0.084	0.066	0.053	0.026
27	0.586	0.450	0.347	0.268	0.207	0.161	0.125	0.098	0.076	0.060	0.047	0.023
28	0.574	0.437	0.333	0.255	0.196	0.150	0.116	0.090	0.069	0.054	0.042	0.020
29	0.563	0.424	0.321	0.243	0.185	0.141	0.107	0.082	0.063	0.048	0.037	0.017
30	0.552	0.412	0.308	0.231	0.174	0.131	0.099	0.075	0.057	0.044	0.033	0.015

TABLE 9-3 **Future Value of Annuity of $1**

(N) PERIODS	Rate of Interest in % 2	3	4	5	6	7	8	9	10	11	12	15
1	1.000	1.000	1.000	1.000	1.000	1.000	1.000	1.000	1.000	1.000	1.000	1.000
2	2.020	2.030	2.040	2.050	2.060	2.070	2.080	2.090	2.100	2.110	2.120	2.150
3	3.060	3.091	3.122	3.153	3.184	3.215	3.246	3.278	3.310	3.342	3.374	3.473
4	4.122	4.184	4.246	4.310	4.375	4.440	4.506	4.573	4.641	4.710	4.779	4.993
5	5.204	5.309	5.416	5.526	5.637	5.751	5.867	5.985	6.105	6.228	6.353	6.742
6	6.308	6.468	6.633	6.802	6.975	7.153	7.336	7.523	7.716	7.913	8.115	8.754
7	7.434	7.662	7.898	8.142	8.394	8.654	8.923	9.200	9.487	9.783	10.089	11.067
8	8.583	8.892	9.214	9.549	9.897	10.260	10.637	11.028	11.436	11.859	12.300	13.727
9	9.755	10.159	10.583	11.027	11.491	11.978	12.488	13.021	13.579	14.164	14.776	16.786
10	10.950	11.464	12.006	12.578	13.181	13.816	14.487	15.193	15.937	16.722	17.549	20.304
11	12.169	12.808	13.486	14.207	14.972	15.784	16.645	17.560	18.531	19.561	20.655	24.349
12	13.412	14.192	15.026	15.917	16.870	17.888	18.977	20.141	21.384	22.713	24.133	29.002
13	14.680	15.618	16.627	17.713	18.882	20.141	21.495	22.953	24.523	26.212	28.029	34.352
14	15.974	17.086	18.292	19.599	21.015	22.550	24.215	26.019	27.975	30.095	32.393	40.505
15	17.293	18.599	20.024	21.579	23.276	25.129	27.152	29.361	31.772	34.405	37.280	47.580
16	18.639	20.157	21.825	23.657	25.673	27.888	30.324	33.003	35.950	39.190	42.753	55.717
17	20.012	21.762	23.698	25.840	28.213	30.840	33.750	36.974	40.545	44.501	48.884	65.075
18	21.412	23.414	25.645	28.132	30.906	33.999	37.450	41.301	45.599	50.396	55.750	75.836
19	22.841	25.117	27.671	30.539	33.760	37.379	41.446	46.018	51.159	56.939	63.440	88.212
20	24.297	26.870	29.778	33.066	36.786	40.995	45.762	51.160	57.275	64.203	72.052	102.444
21	25.783	28.676	31.969	35.719	39.993	44.865	50.423	56.765	64.002	72.265	81.699	118.810
22	27.299	30.537	34.248	38.505	43.392	49.006	55.457	62.873	71.403	81.214	92.503	137.632
23	28.845	32.453	36.618	41.430	46.996	53.436	60.893	69.532	79.543	91.148	104.603	159.276
24	30.422	34.426	39.083	44.502	50.816	58.177	66.765	76.790	88.497	102.174	118.155	184.168
25	32.030	36.459	41.646	47.727	54.865	63.249	73.106	84.701	98.347	114.413	133.334	212.793
26	33.671	38.553	44.312	51.113	59.156	68.676	79.954	93.324	109.182	127.999	150.334	245.712
27	35.344	40.710	47.084	54.669	63.706	74.484	87.351	102.723	121.100	143.079	169.374	283.569
28	37.051	42.931	49.968	58.403	68.528	80.698	95.339	112.968	134.210	159.817	190.699	327.104
29	38.792	45.219	52.966	62.323	73.640	87.347	103.966	124.135	148.631	178.397	214.583	377.170
30	40.568	47.575	56.085	66.439	79.058	94.461	113.283	136.308	164.494	199.021	241.333	434.745

TABLE 9-4 Present Value of Annuity of $1

(N) PERIODS	Rate of Interest in % 2	3	4	5	6	7	8	9	10	11	12	15
1	0.980	0.971	0.962	0.952	0.943	0.935	0.926	0.917	0.909	0.901	0.893	0.870
2	1.942	1.913	1.886	1.859	1.833	1.808	1.783	1.759	1.736	1.713	1.690	1.626
3	2.884	2.829	2.775	2.723	2.673	2.624	2.577	2.531	2.487	2.444	2.402	2.283
4	3.808	3.717	3.630	3.546	3.465	3.387	3.312	3.240	3.170	3.102	3.037	2.855
5	4.713	4.580	4.452	4.329	4.212	4.100	3.993	3.890	3.791	3.696	3.605	3.352
6	5.601	5.417	5.242	5.076	4.917	4.767	4.623	4.486	4.355	4.231	4.111	3.784
7	6.472	6.230	6.002	5.786	5.582	5.389	5.206	5.033	4.868	4.712	4.564	4.160
8	7.325	7.020	6.733	6.463	6.210	5.971	5.747	5.535	5.335	5.146	4.968	4.487
9	8.162	7.786	7.435	7.108	6.802	6.515	6.247	5.995	5.759	5.537	5.328	4.772
10	8.983	8.530	8.111	7.722	7.360	7.024	6.710	6.418	6.145	5.889	5.650	5.019
11	9.787	9.253	8.760	8.306	7.887	7.499	7.139	6.805	6.495	6.207	5.938	5.234
12	10.575	9.954	9.385	8.863	8.384	7.943	7.536	7.161	6.814	6.492	6.194	5.421
13	11.348	10.635	9.986	9.394	8.853	8.358	7.904	7.487	7.103	6.750	6.424	5.583
14	12.106	11.296	10.563	9.899	9.295	8.745	8.244	7.786	7.367	6.982	6.628	5.724
15	12.849	11.938	11.118	10.380	9.712	9.108	8.559	8.061	7.606	7.191	6.811	5.847
16	13.578	12.561	11.652	10.838	10.106	9.447	8.851	8.313	7.824	7.379	6.974	5.954
17	14.292	13.166	12.166	11.274	10.477	9.763	9.122	8.544	8.022	7.549	7.120	6.047
18	14.992	13.754	12.659	11.690	10.828	10.059	9.372	8.756	8.201	7.702	7.250	6.128
19	15.678	14.324	13.134	12.085	11.158	10.336	9.604	8.950	8.365	7.839	7.366	6.198
20	16.351	14.877	13.590	12.462	11.470	10.594	9.818	9.129	8.514	7.963	7.469	6.259
21	17.011	15.415	14.029	12.821	11.764	10.836	10.017	9.292	8.649	8.075	7.562	6.312
22	17.658	15.937	14.451	13.163	12.042	11.061	10.201	9.442	8.772	8.176	7.645	6.359
23	18.292	16.444	14.857	13.489	12.303	11.272	10.371	9.580	8.883	8.266	7.718	6.399
24	18.914	16.936	15.247	13.799	12.550	11.469	10.529	9.707	8.985	8.348	7.784	6.434
25	19.523	17.413	15.622	14.094	12.783	11.654	10.675	9.823	9.077	8.422	7.843	6.464
26	20.121	17.877	15.983	14.375	13.003	11.826	10.810	9.929	9.161	8.488	7.896	6.491
27	20.707	18.327	16.330	14.643	13.211	11.987	10.935	10.027	9.237	8.548	7.943	6.514
28	21.281	18.764	16.663	14.898	13.406	12.137	11.051	10.116	9.307	8.602	7.984	6.534
29	21.844	19.188	16.984	15.141	13.591	12.278	11.158	10.198	9.370	8.650	8.022	6.551
30	22.396	19.600	17.292	15.372	13.765	12.409	11.258	10.274	9.427	8.694	8.055	6.566

Accounting Tools: Using Excel® for Problems Involving Interest Calculations

APPENDIX

The purpose of this appendix is to illustrate how the functions built in to the Excel® spreadsheet can be used to calculate future value and present value amounts. The use of Excel® will be illustrated with the same examples that are used in this chapter.

To view the Excel® functions, click on the PASTE function of the Excel® toolbar (the paste function is on the top of the Excel® toolbar and is noted by the symbol *fx*); then choose the FINANCIAL option. Several different calculations are available. We will illustrate two of them: FV and PV.

Example 1: Your three-year-old son Robert inherits $50,000 in cash and securities from his grandfather. If the funds are left in the bank and in the stock market and receive an annual return of 10%, how much will be available in 15 years when Robert starts college?

Solution: In Excel®, use the FV function and enter the values as follows:

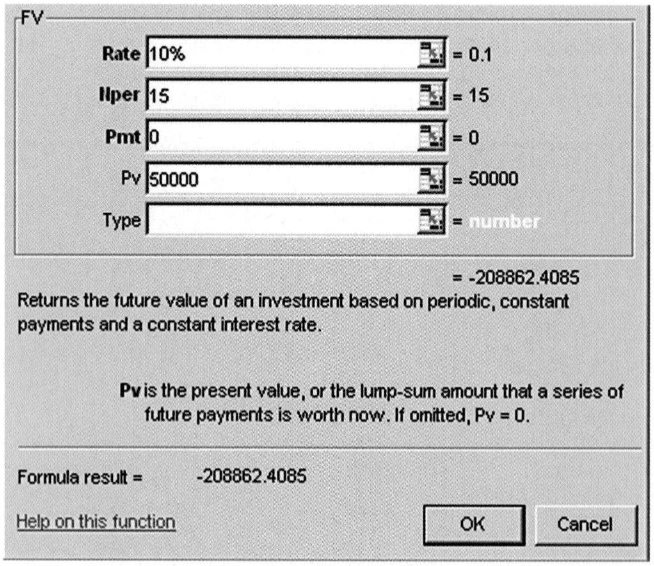

Note that the future value of $208,862 is slightly different from that given in the body of the text because of rounding when using the table factors.

Example 2: Consider a $2,000 note payable that carries interest at the rate of 10% compounded annually. The note is due in two years, and the principal and interest must be paid at that time. What amount must be paid in two years?

Solution: In Excel®, use the FV function and enter the values as follows:

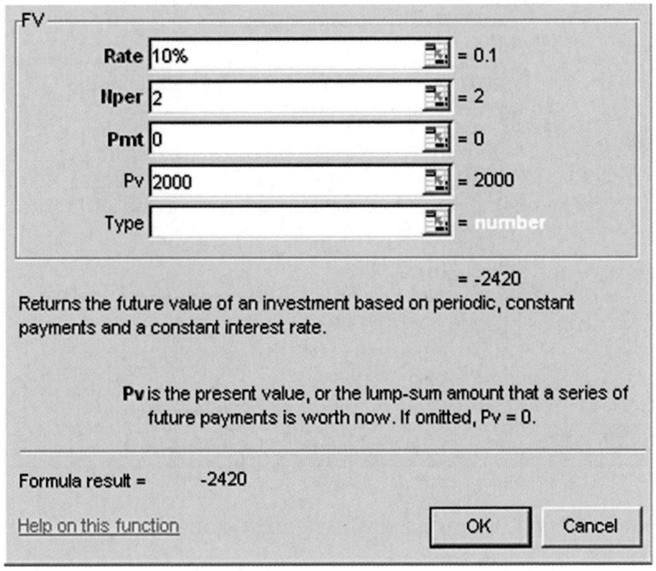

The future value is $2,420.

Example 3: Suppose that we want to find the future value of a $2,000 note payable due in two years. The note payable requires interest to be compounded quarterly at the rate of 12% per year. What future amount must be paid in two years?

Solution: In Excel®, use the FV function and enter the values as follows:
The future value is $2,534 (rounded to the nearest dollar).

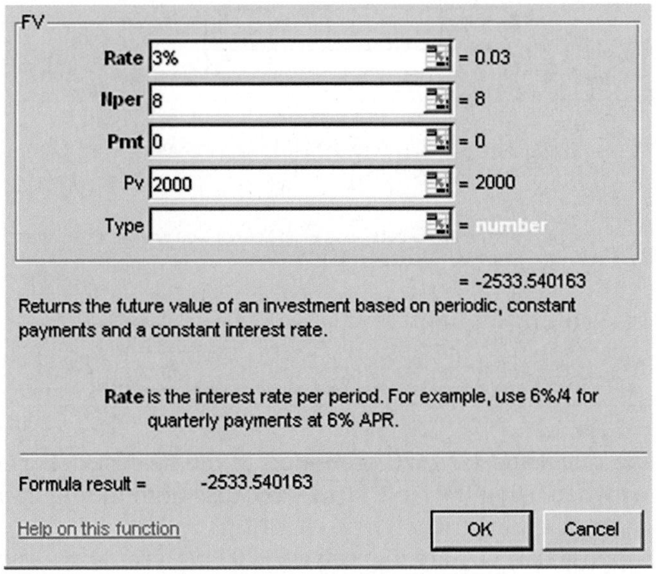

Example 4: Suppose that you know that you will receive $2,000 in two years. You also know that if you had the money now, you could invest it at 10% compounded annually. What is the present value of the $2,000?

Solution: Since this problem requires the calculation of a present value, the PV function of Excel® should be chosen and used as follows:

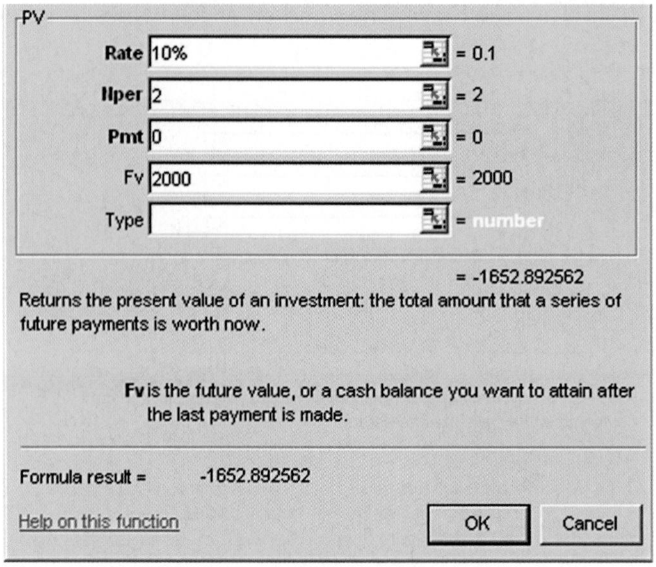

The present value is $1,653 (rounded to the nearest dollar).

Example 5: A recent magazine article projects that it will cost $120,000 to attend a four-year college ten years from now. If that is true, how much money would you have to put into an account today to fund that education, assuming a 5% rate of return?

Solution: The PV function of Excel® should again be used as follows:

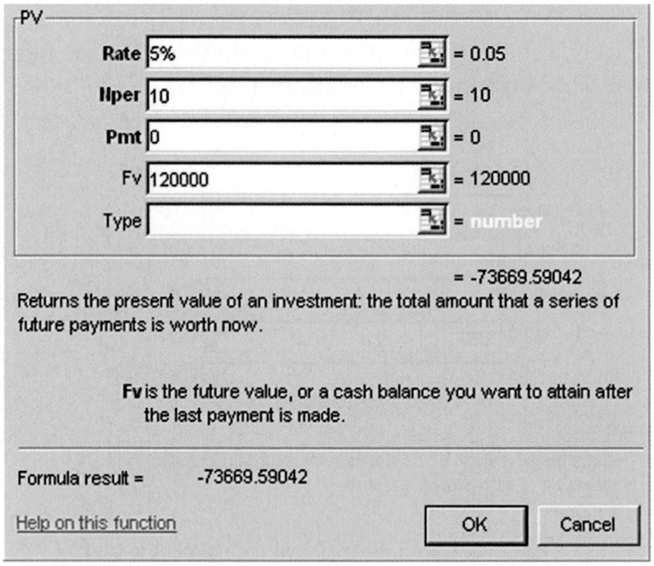

The present value calculated ($73,670—rounded to the nearest dollar) differs slightly from that derived when using the table factors because of rounding in the tables.

Example 6: Suppose that you are to receive $3,000 per year at the end of each of the next four years. Also assume that each payment could be invested at an interest rate of 10% compounded annually. How much would be accumulated in principal and interest by the end of the fourth year?

Solution: This problem involves the calculation of the future value of an annuity; you should use the FV function of Excel® as follows:

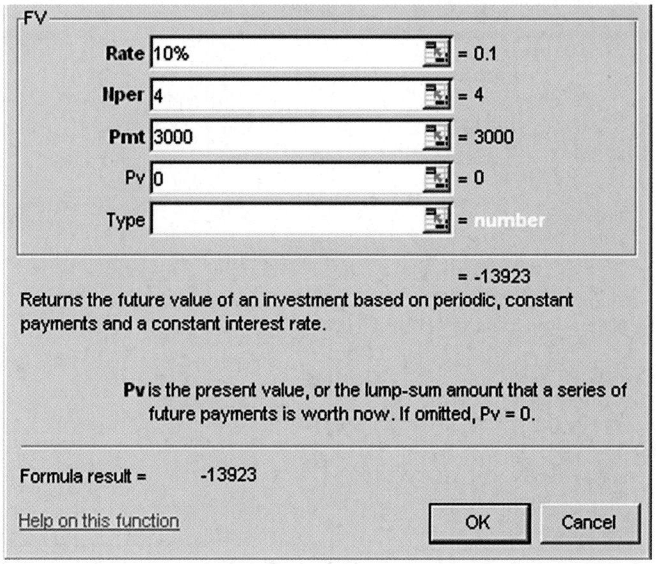

The future value of the series of payments is $13,923. Note that the payments are simply entered as the Pmt variable in the spreadsheet.

Example 7: Your cousin had a baby girl two weeks ago and is already thinking about sending her to college. When the girl is 15, how much money would be in her college account if your cousin deposited $2,000 into it on each of her 15 birthdays? The interest rate is 10%.

Solution: Use the Excel® FV function as follows:

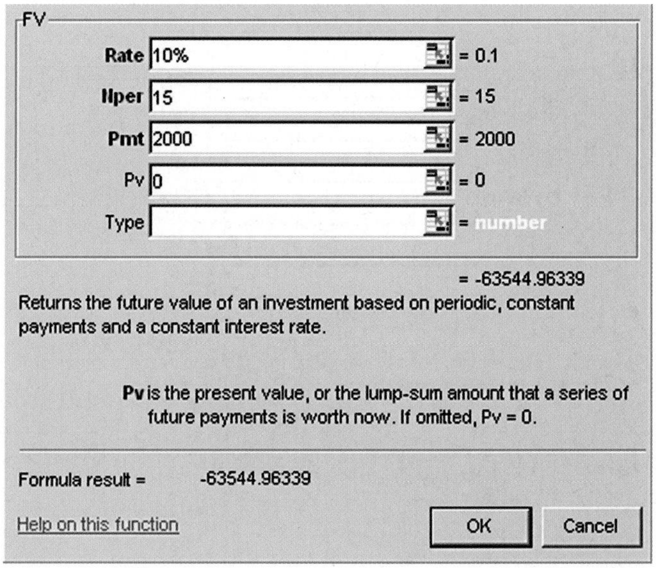

The future value amount is $63,545 (rounded to the nearest dollar).

Example 8: How would the future value be calculated if the previous example was modified so that $1,000 was deposited semiannually and the interest rate was 10% compounded semiannually (or 5% per period) for 15 years?

Solution: Because the compounding is semiannual, use the FV function of Excel as follows:

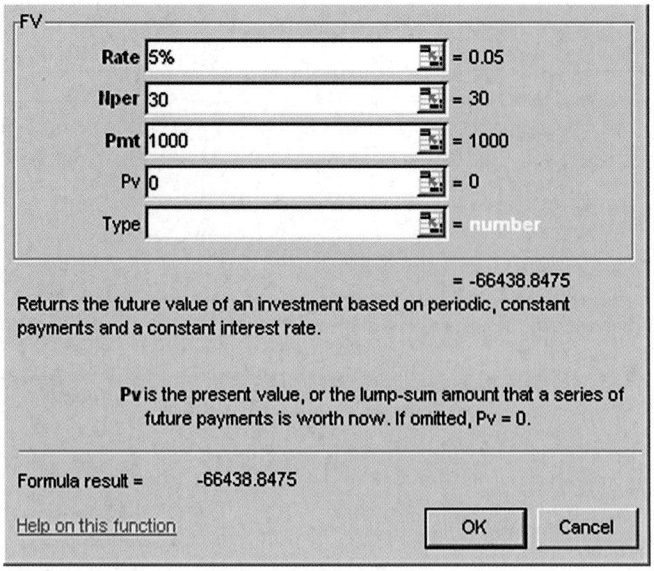

The future value is $66,439 (rounded to the nearest dollar).

Example 9: Suppose that you will receive an annuity of $4,000 per year for four years, with the first received one year from today. The amounts received can be invested at a rate of 10% compounded annually. What amount would you need at the present time to have an amount equivalent to the series of payments and interest in the future?

Solution: This problem involves the calculation of the present value of an annuity, so use the PV function of Excel® as follows:

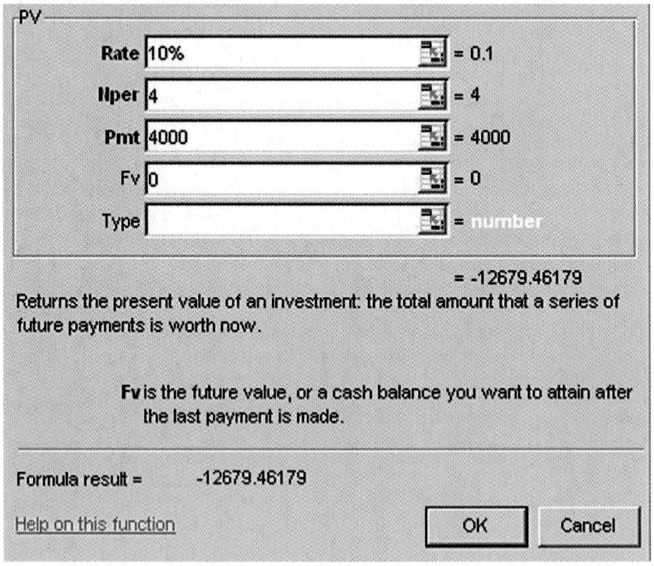

The present value of $12,679 (rounded to the nearest dollar) differs slightly from that derived from the tables because of rounding in the table factors.

Example 10: You just won the lottery. You can take your $1 million in a lump sum today, or you can receive $100,000 per year over the next 12 years. Assuming a 5% interest rate, which would you prefer, ignoring tax considerations?

Solution: Use the PV function of Excel® as follows:

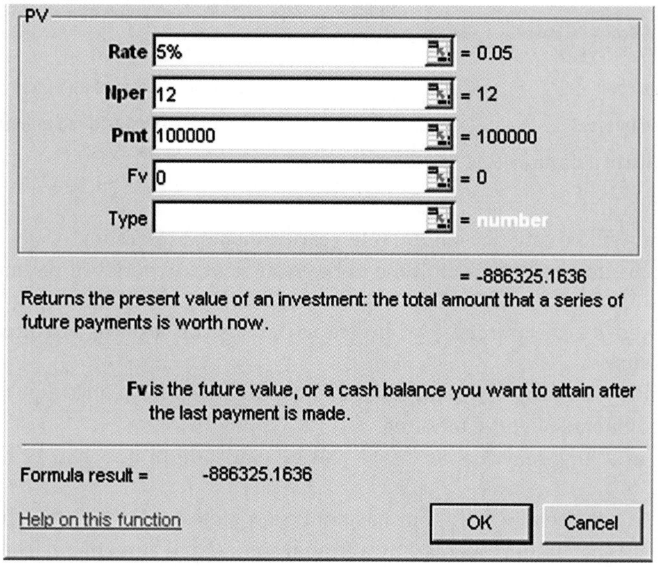

Because the present value of the payments over 12 years is $886,325 (rounded to the nearest dollar) and is less than the $1 million available immediately, you should choose the immediate payment.

RATIO REVIEW

Working Capital* = Current Assets − Current Liabilities
Current Ratio = Current Assets/Current Liabilities
Quick Ratio = Quick Assets/Current Liabilities**

**Working capital is defined and discussed in Chapter 2.*
***Quick assets are those assets that can be converted into cash quickly. They may be measured differently by different companies but generally are measured as Total Current Assets − Inventory − Prepaid Expenses.*

ACCOUNTS HIGHLIGHTED

Account Titles	Where It Appears	In What Section	Page Number
Accounts Payable	Balance Sheet	Current Liabilities	427
Notes Payable	Balance Sheet	Current Liabilities	428
Current Maturities of Long-Term Debt	Balance Sheet	Current Liabilities	429
Taxes Payable	Balance Sheet	Current Liabilities	430
Accrued Liabilities	Balance Sheet	Current Liabilities	431
Contingent Liabilities	Balance Sheet	Current Liabilities or Long-term (depending upon when it will be paid)	434

KEY TERMS QUIZ

Read each definition below and write the number of the definition in the blank beside the appropriate term. The quiz solutions appear at the end of the chapter.

_______ **Current liability**
_______ **Accounts payable**
_______ **Notes payable**
_______ **Discount on notes payable**
_______ **Current maturities of long-term debt**
_______ **Accrued liability**
_______ **Contingent liability**
_______ **Estimated liability**

______ **Contingent asset**
______ **Time value of money**
______ **Simple interest**
______ **Compound interest**
______ **Future value of a single amount**
______ **Present value of a single amount**
______ **Annuity**
______ **Future value of an annuity**
______ **Present value of an annuity**

1. Accounts that will be satisfied within one year or the next operating cycle.
2. The amount needed at the present time to be equivalent to a series of payments and interest in the future.
3. Amounts owed for the purchase of inventory, goods, or services acquired in the normal course of business.
4. A contra-liability account that represents interest deducted from a loan or note in advance.
5. A series of payments of equal amount.
6. The portion of a long-term liability that will be paid within one year of the balance sheet date.
7. A liability that has been incurred but has not been paid as of the balance sheet date.
8. Amounts owed that are represented by a formal contractual agreement. These amounts usually require the payment of interest.
9. A liability that involves an existing condition for which the outcome is not known with certainty and depends on some future event.
10. Interest that is earned or paid on the principal amount only.
11. A contingent liability that is accrued and is reflected on the balance sheet. Common examples are warranties, guarantees, and premium offers.
12. An amount that involves an existing condition dependent upon some future event by which the company stands to gain. These amounts are not normally reported.
13. Interest calculated on the principal plus previous amounts of interest accumulated.
14. The concept that indicates that people should prefer to receive an immediate amount at the present time over an equal amount in the future.
15. The amount that will be accumulated in the future when one amount is invested at the present time and accrues interest until the future time.
16. The amount that will be accumulated in the future when a series of payments is invested and accrues interest until the future time.
17. The present amount that is equivalent to an amount at a future time.

ALTERNATE TERMS

Accrued interest Interest payable

Compound interest Interest on interest

Contingent asset Contingent gain

Contingent liability Contingent loss

Current liability Short-term liability

Current maturities of long-term debt Long-term debt, current portion

Discounting a note Interest in advance

Future value of an annuity Amount of an annuity

Income tax liability Income tax payable

Warranties Guarantees

WARMUP EXERCISES

LO1 **Warmup Exercise 9-1**

A company has the following current assets: Cash, $10,000; Accounts Receivable, $70,000; and Inventory, $20,000. The company also has current liabilities of $40,000. Calculate the company's current ratio and quick ratio.

REVIEW

LO3 **Warmup Exercise 9-2**

A company has the following current liabilities at the beginning of the period: Accounts Payable, $30,000; Taxes Payable $10,000. At the end of the period, the balances of the account are as follows: Accounts Payable, $20,000; Taxes Payable, $15,000. What amounts will appear in the cash flow statement? In what category of the statement will they appear?

LO6 **Warmup Exercise 9-3**

A. You invest $1,000 at the beginning of the year. How much will be accumulated in five years if you earn 10% interest compounded annually?
B. You invest $1,000 *per year* at the end of each year for five years. How much will be accumulated in five years if you earn 10% interest compounded annually?
C. You will receive $1,000 in five years. What is the present value of that amount if you earn 10% interest compounded annually?
D. You will receive $1,000 *per year* at the end of each year for five years. What is the present value of that amount if you earn 10% interest compounded annually?

SOLUTIONS TO WARMUP EXERCISES

Warmup Exercise 9-1

Current Ratio: Current Assets/Current Liabilities
Cash ($10,000) + Accounts Receivable ($70,000) + Inventory ($20,000) = $100,000
$100,000/$40,000 = 2.5 Current Ratio

Quick Ratio: Quick Assets/Current Liabilities
Cash ($10,000) + Accounts Receivable ($70,000) = $80,000
$80,000/$40,000 = 2.0 Quick Ratio

Warmup Exercise 9-2

The amounts appearing in the cash flow statement should be in the Operating Activities category of the statement. The amounts shown should be the *changes* in the balances of the accounts.

Accounts Payable decreased by $10,000 and should appear as a decrease in the cash flow statement.

Taxes Payable increased by $5,000 and should appear as an increase in the cash flow statement.

Warmup Exercise 9-3

A. FV = $1,000(table factor) — using Table 9-1
= $1,000(1.611) — where $i = 10\%$, $n = 5$
= $1,611

B. FV = $1,000(table factor) — using Table 9-3
= $1,000(6.105) — where $i = 10\%$, $n = 5$
= $6,105

C. PV = $1,000(table factor) — using Table 9-2
= $1,000(0.621) — where $i = 10\%$, $n = 5$
= $621

D. PV = $1,000(table factor) — using Table 9-4
= $1,000(3.791) — where $i = 10\%$, $n = 5$
= $3,791

REVIEW PROBLEM

Part A

The accountant for Lunn Express wants to develop a balance sheet as of December 31, 2008. The following items pertain to the liability category and must be considered to determine the items that should be reported in the Current Liabilities section of the balance sheet. You may assume that Lunn began business on January 1, 2008; therefore, the beginning balance of all accounts was zero.

a. During 2008, Lunn purchased $100,000 of inventory on account from suppliers. By year-end, $40,000 of the balance had been eliminated as a result of payments. All items were purchased on terms of 2/10, n/30. Lunn uses the gross method of recording payables.
b. On April 1, 2008, Lunn borrowed $10,000 on a one-year note payable from Philips Bank. Terms of the loan indicate that Lunn must repay the principal and 12% interest at the due date of the note.
c. On October 1, 2008, Lunn also borrowed $8,000 from Dove Bank on a one-year note payable. Dove Bank deducted 10% interest in advance and gave to Lunn the net amount. At the due date, Lunn must repay the principal of $8,000.
d. On January 1, 2008, Lunn borrowed $20,000 from Owens Bank by signing a ten-year note payable. Terms of the note indicate that Lunn must make annual payments of principal each January 1 beginning in 2009 and must pay interest each January 1 in the amount of 8% of the outstanding balance of the loan.
e. The accountant for Lunn has completed an income statement for 2008 that indicates that income before taxes was $10,000. Lunn must pay tax at the rate of 40% and must remit the tax to the Internal Revenue Service by April 15, 2009.
f. As of December 31, 2008, Lunn owes its employees salaries of $3,000 for work performed in 2008. The employees will be paid on the first payday of 2009.
g. During 2008, two lawsuits were filed against Lunn. In the first lawsuit, a customer sued for damages because of an injury that occurred on Lunn's premises. Lunn's legal counsel advised that it is probable that the lawsuit will be settled in 2009 at an amount of $7,000. The second lawsuit involves a patent infringement suit of $14,000 filed against Lunn by a competitor. The legal counsel has advised that Lunn may be at fault but that a loss does not appear probable at this time.

Part B

a. What amount will be accumulated by January 1, 2012, if $5,000 is invested on January 1, 2008, at 10% interest compounded semiannually?
b. Assume that $5,000 is to be received on January 1, 2012. What amount at January 1, 2008, is equivalent to the $5,000 that is to be received in 2012? Assume that interest is compounded annually at 10%.
c. What amount will be accumulated by January 1, 2012, if $5,000 is invested each semiannual period for eight periods beginning June 30, 2008, and ending December 31, 2011? Interest will accumulate at 10% compounded semiannually.
d. Assume that $5,000 is to be received each semiannual period for eight periods beginning on June 30, 2008. What amount at January 1, 2012, is equivalent to the future series of payments? Assume that interest will accrue at 10% compounded semiannually.
e. Assume that a new bank has begun a promotional campaign to attract savings accounts. The bank advertisement indicates that customers who invest $1,000 will double their money in ten years. Assuming annual compounding of interest, what rate of interest is the bank offering?

Required

1. Consider all items in Part A. Develop the Current Liabilities section of Lunn's balance sheet as of December 31, 2008. To make investment decisions about this company, what additional data would you need? You do not need to consider the notes that accompany the balance sheet.
2. Answer the five questions in Part B.

SOLUTION TO REVIEW PROBLEM PART A

The accountant's decisions for items (a) through (g) of Part A should be as follows:

a. The balance of the Accounts Payable account should be $60,000. The payables should be reported at the gross amount, and discounts would not be reported until the time of payment.

b. The note payable to Philips Bank of $10,000 should be included as a current liability. Also, interest payable of $900 ($10,000 × 12% × 9/12) should be considered a current liability.
c. The note payable to Dove Bank should be considered a current liability and listed at $8,000 minus the contra account Discount on Note Payable of $600 ($8,000 × 10% × 9/12 remaining).
d. The debt to Owens Bank should be split between current liability and long-term liability with the current portion shown as $2,000. Also, interest payable of $1,600 ($20,000 × 8% × 1 year) should be considered a current liability.
e. Income taxes payable of $4,000 ($10,000 × 40%) is a current liability.
f. Salaries payable of $3,000 represent a current liability.
g. The lawsuit involving the customer must be reported as a current liability of $7,000 because the possibility of loss is probable. The second lawsuit should not be reported but should be disclosed as a note to the balance sheet.

Lunn Express
Partial Balance Sheet
As of December 31, 2008

Current Liabilities		
Accounts payable		$60,000
Interest payable ($900 + $1,600)		2,500
Salaries payable		3,000
Taxes payable		4,000
Note payable to Philips Bank		10,000
Note payable to Dove Bank	$8,000	
Less: Discount on note payable	(600)	7,400
Current maturity of long-term debt		2,000
Contingent liability for pending lawsuit		7,000
Total Current Liabilities		$95,900

Other data necessary to make an investment decision might include current assets and total assets as of December 31, 2008. If current assets are significantly larger than current liabilities, you can be assured that the company is capable of paying its short-term debt. The dollar amount of current assets and liabilities must be evaluated with regard to the size of the company. The larger the company, the less significant $95,900 in current liabilities would be.

SOLUTION TO PART B

a. $FV = \$5{,}000(\text{table factor})$ using Table 9-1
$= \$5{,}000(1.477)$ where $i = 5\%, n = 8$
$= \$7{,}385$

b. $PV = \$5{,}000(\text{table factor})$ using Table 9-2
$= \$5{,}000(0.683)$ where $i = 10\%, n = 4$
$= \$3{,}415$

c. FV annuity $= \$5{,}000(\text{table factor})$ using Table 9-3
$= \$5{,}000(9.549)$ where $i = 5\%, n = 8$
$= \$47{,}745$

d. PV annuity $= \$5{,}000(\text{table factor})$ using Table 9-4
$= \$5{,}000(6.463)$ where $i = 5\%, n = 8$
$= \$32{,}315$

REVIEW

e. $FV = \$1{,}000(\text{table factor})$ using Table 9-1

Because the future value is known to be $2,000, the formula can be written as

$$\$2{,}000 = \$1{,}000(\text{table factor})$$

and rearranged as

Table factor = $2,000/$1,000 = 2.0.

In Table 9-1, the table factor of 2.0 and ten years corresponds with an interest rate of between 7% and 8%.

QUESTIONS

1. What is the definition of *current liabilities*? Why is it important to distinguish between current and long-term liabilities?
2. Most firms attempt to pay their accounts payable within the discount period to take advantage of the discount. Why is that normally a sound financial move?
3. Assume that your local bank gives you a $1,000 loan at 10% per year but deducts the interest in advance. Is 10% the "real" rate of interest that you will pay? How can the true interest rate be calculated?
4. Is the account Discount on Notes Payable an income statement or balance sheet account? Does it have a debit or credit balance?
5. A firm's year ends on December 31. Its tax is computed and submitted to the U.S. Treasury on March 15 of the following year. When should the taxes be reported as a liability?
6. What is a contingent liability? Why are contingent liabilities accounted for differently than contingent assets?
7. Many firms believe that it is very difficult to estimate the amount of a possible future contingency. Should a contingent liability be reported even when the dollar amount of the loss is not known? Should it be disclosed in the notes to financial statements?
8. Assume that a lawsuit has been filed against your firm. Your legal counsel has assured you that a loss is not probable. How should the lawsuit be disclosed on the financial statements?
9. What is the difference between simple interest and compound interest? Is the amount of interest higher or lower when the interest is simple rather than compound?
10. What is the effect when interest is compounded quarterly versus annually?
11. What is the meaning of the terms *present value* and *future value*? How can you determine whether to calculate the present value or the future value of an amount?
12. What is the meaning of the word *annuity*? Can the present value of an annuity be calculated as a series of single amounts? If so, how?
13. Assume that you know the total dollar amount of a loan and the amount of the monthly payments. How can you determine the interest rate as a percentage of the loan?
14. The present value and future value concepts are applied to measure the amount of several accounts common in accounting. What are some accounts that are valued in this manner?

BRIEF EXERCISES

LO1

Brief Exercise 9-1 Liquidity

Beta Company has current assets of $80,000 and current liabilities of $60,000. How much of its short-term notes payable could it pay in cash and achieve its minimum desired current ratio of 2 to 1?

LO2

Brief Exercise 9-2 Credit Terms

You receive an invoice from a supplier for $5,000 on January 1 with terms 3/15, net 30. If you pay between January 1 and January 16, how much must you pay? If you pay after January 16, how much must you pay?

LO3

Brief Exercise 9-3 Current Liabilities and Cash Flows

In the statement of cash flows, how should the following appear:

A decrease in a current liability account
An increase in a current liability account

Should changes in current liability accounts always appear in the Operating Activities category? Give an example of a current liability account that may not appear in the Operating Activities category.

LO4 **Brief Exercise 9-4** Contingent Liabilities

Omega Company is involved in two unrelated lawsuits, one as the plaintiff and one as the defendant. As a result of these two lawsuits, the company has a contingent asset and a contingent liability. How should Omega record these on its balance sheet?

LO5 **Brief Exercise 9-5** Simple and Compound Interest

You invest $1,000 for five years at 5% simple interest at Bank 1
You invest $1,000 for five years at Bank 2 where interest at 5% is compounded annually.
Compute the amounts that will be accumulated.

LO6 **Brief Exercise 9-6** Present Value and Future Value

You are required to pay $5,000 for college fees for each for the next four years, and a generous uncle has offered to give you enough money now to cover these future payments. How much must he give you now if you can invest at 10% per year compounded? annually?

LO7 **Brief Exercise 9-7** Solving for an Interest Rate

You are required to pay $5,000 for college fees for each of the next four years, and a not-quite-as-generous uncle offers to give you $14,275 toward your college fees. What is the annual interest rate that you need to earn to allow you to invest the money and meet the four payments?

EXERCISES

LO1 **Exercise 9-1** Current Liabilities

The following items are accounts on Smith's balance sheet of December 31, 2007:

Taxes Payable
Accounts Receivable
Notes Payable, 9%, due in 90 days
Investment in Bonds
Capital Stock
Accounts Payable
Estimated Warranty Payable in 2008
Retained Earnings
Trademark
Mortgage Payable ($10,000 due every year until 2024)

Required
Identify which of the accounts should be classified as a current liability on Smith's balance sheet. For each item that is not a current liability, indicate the category of the balance sheet in which it would be classified.

LO1 **Exercise 9-2** Current Liabilities

The following items represent liabilities on a firm's balance sheet:

a. An amount of money owed to a supplier based on the terms 2/20, net 40, for which no note was executed.
b. An amount of money owed to a creditor on a note due April 30, 2009.
c. An amount of money owed to a creditor on a note due August 15, 2010.
d. An amount of money owed to employees for work performed during the last week in December.
e. An amount of money owed to a bank for the use of borrowed funds due on March 1, 2009.
f. An amount of money owed to a creditor as an annual installment payment on a ten-year note.
g. An amount of money owed to the federal government based on the company's annual income.

Required

1. For each item, state whether it should be classified as a current liability on the December 31, 2008, balance sheet. Assume that the operating cycle is shorter than one year. If the item should not be classified as a current liability, indicate where on the balance sheet it should be presented.
2. For each item identified as a current liability in (1), state the account title that is normally used to report the item on the balance sheet.
3. Why would an investor or creditor be interested in whether an item is a current or a long-term liability?

LO1

Exercise 9-3 Current Liabilities Section

Jackie Company had the following accounts and balances on December 31, 2008:

Income Taxes Payable	$61,250	Notes Payable, 10%, due June 2, 2009	$ 1,000
Allowance for Doubtful Accounts	17,800	Accounts Receivable	67,500
Accounts Payable	24,400	Discount on Notes Payable	150
Interest Receivable	5,000	Current Maturities of Long-Term Debt	6,900
Unearned Revenue	4,320	Interest Payable	3,010
Wages Payable	6,000		

Required

Prepare the Current Liabilities section of Jackie Company's balance sheet as of December 31, 2008.

LO2

Exercise 9-4 Transaction Analysis

Polly's Cards & Gifts Shop had the following transactions during the year:

a. Polly's purchased inventory on account from a supplier for $8,000. Assume that Polly's uses a periodic inventory system.
b. On May 1, land was purchased for $44,500. A 20% down payment was made; and an 18-month, 8% note was signed for the remainder.
c. Polly's returned $450 worth of inventory purchased in (a), which was found broken when the inventory was received.
d. Polly's paid the balance due on the purchase of inventory.
e. On June 1, Polly signed a one-year, $15,000 note to First State Bank and received $13,800.
f. Polly's sold 200 gift certificates for $25 each for cash. Sales of gift certificates are recorded as a liability. At year-end, 35% of the gift certificates had been redeemed.
g. Sales for the year were $120,000, of which 90% were for cash. State sales tax of 6% applied to all sales must be remitted to the state by January 31.

Required

1. Record all necessary journal entries relating to these transactions.
2. Assume that Polly's accounting year ends on December 31. Prepare any necessary adjusting journal entries.
3. What is the total of the current liabilities at the end of the year?

LO2

Exercise 9-5 Current Liabilities and Ratios

Several accounts that appeared on Kruse's 2008 balance sheet are as follows:

Accounts Payable	$ 55,000	Equipment	$950,000
Marketable Securities	40,000	Taxes Payable	15,000
Accounts Receivable	180,000	Retained Earnings	250,000
Notes Payable, 12%, due in 60 days	20,000	Inventory	85,000
Capital Stock	1,150,000	Allowance for Doubtful Accounts	20,000
Salaries Payable	10,000	Land	600,000
Cash	15,000		

Required

1. Prepare the Current Liabilities section of Kruse's 2008 balance sheet.
2. Compute Kruse's working capital.
3. Compute Kruse's current ratio. What does this ratio indicate about Kruse's condition?

LO2

Exercise 9-6 Discounts

Each of the following situations involves the use of discounts.

1. How much discount may Seals Inc. take in each of the following transactions? What was the annualized interest rate?
   a. Seals purchases inventory costing $450, 2/10, n/40.
   b. Seals purchases new office furniture costing $1,500, terms 1/10, n/30.
2. Calculate the discount rate that Croft Co. received in each of these transactions.
   a. Croft purchased office supplies costing $200 and paid within the discount period with a check for $196.
   b. Croft purchased merchandise for $2,800. It paid within the discount period with a check for $2,674.

LO2

Exercise 9-7 Notes Payable and Interest

On July 1, 2008, Jo's Flower Shop borrowed $25,000 from the bank. Jo signed a ten-month, 8% promissory note for the entire amount. Jo's uses a calendar year-end.

Required

1. Prepare the journal entry on July 1 to record the issuance of the promissory note.
2. Prepare any adjusting entries needed at year-end.
3. Prepare the journal entry on May 1 to record the payment of principal and interest.

LO2

Exercise 9-8 Non-Interest-Bearing Notes Payable

On October 1, 2008, Ratkowski Inc. borrowed $18,000 from Second National Bank by issuing a 12-month note. The bank discounted the note at 9%.

Required

1. Prepare the journal entry needed to record the issuance of the note.
2. Prepare the journal entry needed at December 31, 2008, to accrue interest.
3. Prepare the journal entry to record the payment of the note on October 1, 2009.
4. What effective rate of interest did Ratkowski pay?

LO3

Exercise 9-9 Impact of Transactions Involving Current Liabilities on Statement of Cash Flows

From the following list, identify whether the change in the account balance during the year would be reported as an operating (O), investing (I), or financing (F) activity or not separately reported on the statement of cash flows (N). Assume that the indirect method is used to determine the cash flows from operating activities.

_______ Accounts payable
_______ Current maturities of long-term debt
_______ Notes payable
_______ Other accrued liabilities
_______ Salaries and wages payable
_______ Taxes payable

LO3

Exercise 9-10 Impact of Transactions Involving Contingent Liabilities on Statement of Cash Flows

From the following list, identify whether the change in the account balance during the year would be reported as an operating (O), investing (I), or financing (F) activity or not separately reported on the statement of cash flows (N). Assume that the indirect method is used to determine the cash flows from operating activities.

_______ Estimated liability for warranties
_______ Estimated liability for product premiums
_______ Estimated liability for probable loss relating to litigation

LO4

Exercise 9-11 Warranties

Clean Corporation manufactures and sells dishwashers. Clean provides all customers with a two-year warranty guaranteeing to repair, free of charge, any defects reported during this time period. During the year, it sold 100,000 dishwashers for $325 each. Analysis of past warranty records indicates that 12% of all sales will be returned for repair within the warranty period. Clean expects to incur expenditures of $14 to repair each dishwasher. The account Estimated Liability for Warranties had a balance of $120,000 on January 1. Clean incurred $150,000 in actual expenditures during the year.

Required

Prepare all journal entries necessary to record the events related to the warranty transactions during the year. Determine the adjusted ending balance in the Estimated Liability for Warranties account.

LO5

Exercise 9-12 Simple Versus Compound Interest

For each of the following notes, calculate the simple interest due at the end of the term.

Note	Face Value (Principal)	Rate	Term
1	$20,000	4%	6 years
2	20,000	6%	4 years
3	20,000	8%	3 years

Now assume that the interest on the notes is compounded annually. Calculate the amount of interest due at the end of the term for each note.

Finally assume that the interest on the notes is compounded semiannually. Calculate the amount of interest due at the end of the term for each note.

What conclusion can you draw from a comparison of your results of each of the three scenarios?

LO5

Exercise 9-13 Present Value, Future Value

Brian Inc. estimates that it will need $150,000 in ten years to expand its manufacturing facilities. A bank has agreed to pay Brian 5% interest compounded annually if the company deposits the entire amount now needed to accumulate $150,000 in ten years. How much money does Brian need to deposit?

LO6

Exercise 9-14 Effect of Compounding Period

Kern Company deposited $1,000 in the bank on January 1, 2008, earning 8% interest. Kern Company withdraws the deposit plus accumulated interest on January 1, 2010. Compute the amount of money Kern withdraws from the bank assuming that interest is compounded (a) annually, (b) semiannually, and (c) quarterly.

LO6

Exercise 9-15 Present Value, Future Value

The following situations involve time value of money calculations.

1. A deposit of $7,000 is made on January 1, 2008. The deposit will earn interest at a rate of 8%. How much will be accumulated on January 1, 2013, assuming that interest is compounded (a) annually, (b) semiannually, and (c) quarterly?
2. A deposit is made on January 1, 2008, to earn interest at an annual rate of 8%. The deposit will accumulate to $15,000 by January 1, 2013. How much money was originally deposited assuming that interest is compounded (a) annually, (b) semiannually, and (c) quarterly?

LO6

Exercise 9-16 Present Value, Future Value

The following situations require the application of the time value of money.

1. On January 1, 2008, $16,000 is deposited. Assuming an 8% interest rate, calculate the amount accumulated on January 1, 2013, if interest is compounded (a) annually, (b) semiannually, and (c) quarterly.
2. Assume that a deposit made on January 1, 2008, earns 8% interest. The deposit plus interest accumulated to $20,000 on January 1, 2013. How much was invested on January 1, 2008, if interest was compounded (a) annually, (b) semiannually, and (c) quarterly?

LO7

Exercise 9-17 Annuity

Steve Jones has decided to start saving for his son's college education by depositing $2,000 at the end of every year for 15 years. A bank has agreed to pay interest at the rate of 4% compounded annually. How much will Steve have in the bank immediately after his 15th deposit?

LO7 **Exercise 9-18** Calculation of Years

Kelly Seaver has decided to start saving for her daughter's college education. Kelly wants to accumulate $41,000. The bank will pay interest at the rate of 4% compounded annually. If Kelly plans to make payments of $1,600 at the end of each year, how long will it take her to accumulate $41,000?

LO7 **Exercise 9-19** Value of Payments

Upon graduation from college, Susana Lopez signed an agreement to buy a used car. Her annual payments, which are due at the end of each year for two years, are $1,480. The car dealer used a 12% rate compounded annually to determine the amount of the payments.

Required

1. What should Susana consider the value of the car to be?
2. If she had wanted to make quarterly payments, what would her payments have been based on the value of the car as determined in (1)? How much less interest would she have paid if she had been making quarterly payments instead of annual payments? What would have happened to the payment amount and the interest if she had asked for monthly payments?

MULTICONCEPT EXERCISES

LO6,7 **Exercise 9-20** Compare Alternatives

Jane Bauer has won the lottery and has four options for receiving her winnings:

1. Receive $100,000 at the beginning of the current year
2. Receive $108,000 at the end of the year
3. Receive $20,000 at the end of each year for eight years
4. Receive $10,000 at the end of each year for 30 years

Jane can invest her winnings at an interest rate of 8% compounded annually at a major bank. Which of the payment options should Jane choose?

LO6,7 **Exercise 9-21** Two Situations

The following situations involve the application of the time value of money concepts.

1. Sampson Company just purchased a piece of equipment with a value of $53,300. Sampson financed this purchase with a loan from the bank and must make annual loan payments of $13,000 at the end of each year for the next five years. Interest is compounded annually on the loan. What is the interest rate on the bank loan?
2. Simon Company needs to accumulate $200,000 to repay bonds due in six years. Simon estimates it can save $13,300 at the end of each semiannual period at a local bank offering an annual interest rate of 8% compounded semiannually. Will Simon have enough money saved at the end of six years to repay the bonds?

PROBLEMS

LO2 **Problem 9-1** Notes and Interest

Glencoe Inc. operates with a June 30 year-end. During 2008, the following transactions occurred:

a. January 1: Signed a one-year, 10% loan for $25,000. Interest and principal are to be paid at maturity.
b. January 10: Signed a line of credit with the Little Local Bank to establish a $400,000 line of credit. Interest of 9% will be charged on all borrowed funds.
c. February 1: Issued a $20,000 non-interest-bearing, six-month note to pay for a new machine. Interest on the note, at 12%, was deducted in advance.
d. March 1: Borrowed $150,000 on the line of credit.
e. June 1: Repaid $100,000 on the line of credit, plus accrued interest.
f. June 30: Made all necessary adjusting entries.
g. August 1: Repaid the non-interest-bearing note.
h. September 1: Borrowed $200,000 on the line of credit.
i. November 1: Issued a three-month, 8%, $12,000 note in payment of an overdue open account.
j. December 31: Repaid the one-year loan [from (a)] plus accrued interest.

Required

1. Record all journal entries necessary to report these transactions.
2. As of December 31, which notes are outstanding? How much interest is due on each?

LO3

Problem 9-2 Effects of Panera Bread's Current Liabilities on Its Statement of Cash Flows

The following items are classified as current liabilities on **Panera Bread Company**'s consolidated balance sheet at December 27, 2006 and December 27, 2005:

(In thousands)	December 26, 2006	December 27, 2005
Current liabilities:		
Accounts payable	$ 5,800	$ 4,422
Accrued expenses	102,718	81,559
Deferred revenue	1,092	884
Total current liabilities	109,610	86,865

Required

1. Panera Bread uses the indirect method to prepare its statement of cash flows. Prepare the Operating Activities section of the cash flow statement, which indicates how each item will be reflected as an adjustment to net income. If you did not include any of the preceding items, explain why.
2. How would you decide if Panera Bread has the ability to pay these liabilities as they become due?

LO3

Problem 9-3 Effects of Wendy's International's Changes in Current Assets and Liabilities on Its Statement of Cash Flows

The following items, listed in alphabetical order, are included in the Current Assets and Current Liabilities categories on the consolidated balance sheet of **Wendy's International, Inc.**, at December 31, 2006 and January 1, 2006:

(In thousands)	December 31, 2006	January 1, 2006
Current liabilities		
Accounts payable	$ 93,465	$ 92,340
Accrued expenses		
Salaries and wages	47,329	34,871
Taxes	46,138	60,984
Insurance	57,353	58,147
Other	32,199	34,079
Advertising fund restricted liabilities	28,568	35,651
Current portion of long-term obligations	87,396	2,497
Total current liabilities	2,218	264,783
Current liabilities of discontinued operations	394,666	583,352

Required

1. Wendy's uses the indirect method to prepare its statement of cash flows. Prepare the Operating Activities section of the cash flow statement, which indicates how each item will be reflected as an adjustment to net income.
2. If you did not include any of the preceding items in your answer to (1), explain how these items would be reported on the statement of cash flows.

LO4

Problem 9-4 Warranties

Clearview Company manufactures and sells high-quality television sets. The most popular line sells for $1,000 each and is accompanied by a three-year warranty to repair, free of charge, any defective unit. Average costs to repair each defective unit will be $90 for replacement parts and $60 for labor. Clearview estimates that warranty costs of $12,600 will be incurred during 2008. The company actually sold 600 television sets and incurred replacement part costs of $3,600 and labor costs of $5,400 during the year. The adjusted 2008 ending balance in the Estimated Liability for Warranties account is $10,200.

Required

1. How many defective units from this year's sales does Clearview Company estimate will be returned for repair?
2. What percentage of sales does Clearview Company estimate will be returned for repair?
3. What steps should Clearview take if actual warranty costs incurred during 2009 are significantly higher than the estimated liability recorded at the end of 2008?

LO4 **Problem 9-5** Warranties

Bombeck Company sells a product for $1,500. When the customer buys it, Bombeck provides a one-year warranty. Bombeck sold 120 products during 2008. Based on analysis of past warranty records, Bombeck estimates that repairs will average 3% of total sales.

Required

1. Prepare the journal entry to record the estimated liability.
2. Assume that during 2008, products under warranty must be repaired using repair parts from inventory costing $4,950. Prepare the journal entry to record the repair of products.

LO5 **Problem 9-6** Comparison of Simple and Compound Interest

On June 30, 2008, Rolf Inc. borrowed $25,000 from its bank, signing an 8%, two-year note.

Required

1. Assuming that the bank charges simple interest on the note, prepare the journal entry Rolf will record on each of the following dates:

   December 31, 2008
   December 31, 2009
   June 30, 2010

2. Assume instead that the bank charges 8% on the note, which is compounded semiannually. Prepare the necessary journal entries on the dates in (1).
3. How much additional interest expense will Rolf have in (2) than in (1)?

LO6 **Problem 9-7** Investment with Varying Interest Rate

Shari Thompson invested $1,000 in a financial institution on January 1, 2008. She leaves her investment in the institution until December 31, 2012. How much money does Shari accumulate if she earns interest, compounded annually, at the following rates?

2008	4%
2009	5
2010	6
2011	7
2012	8

LO6 **Problem 9-8** Comparison of Alternatives

On January 1, 2008, Chen Yu's Office Supply Store plans to remodel the store and install new display cases. Chen has the following options of payment. Chen's interest rate is 8%.

a. Pay $180,000 on January 1, 2008.
b. Pay $196,200 on January 1, 2009.
c. Pay $220,500 on January 1, 2010.
d. Make four annual payments of $55,000 beginning on December 31, 2008.

Required

Which option should he choose? (*Hint:* Calculate the present value of each option as of January 1, 2008.)

MULTICONCEPT PROBLEMS

LO2,5 **Problem 9-9** Interest in Advance versus Interest Paid When Loan Is Due

On July 1, 2008, Leach Company needs exactly $103,200 in cash to pay an existing obligation. Leach has decided to borrow from State Bank, which charges 14% interest on loans. The loan will be due in one year. Leach is unsure, however, whether to ask the bank for (a) an interest-bearing loan with interest and principal payable at the end of the year or (b) a loan due in one year but with interest deducted in advance.

Required

1. What will be the face value of the note assuming that:
   a. Interest is paid when the loan is due?
   b. Interest is deducted in advance?

2. Calculate the effective interest rate on the note assuming that:
   a. Interest is paid when the loan is due.
   b. Interest is deducted in advance.
3. Assume that Leach negotiates and signs the one-year note with the bank on July 1, 2008. Also assume that Leach's accounting year ends December 31. Prepare all of the journal entries necessary to record the issuance of the note and the interest on the note assuming that:
   a. Interest is paid when the loan is due.
   b. Interest is deducted in advance.
4. Prepare the appropriate balance sheet presentation for July 1, 2008, immediately after the note has been issued assuming that:
   a. Interest is paid when the loan is due.
   b. Interest is deducted in advance.

LO1,4

Problem 9-10 Contingent Liabilities

Several items are listed for which the outcome of events is unknown at year-end.

a. A company offers a two-year warranty on sales of new computers. It believes that 4% of the computers will require repairs.
b. The company is involved in a trademark infringement suit. The company's legal experts believe that an award of $500,000 in the company's favor will be made.
c. A company is involved in an environmental cleanup lawsuit. The company's legal counsel believes that the outcome may be unfavorable but has not been able to estimate the costs of the possible loss.
d. A soap manufacturer has included a coupon offer in the Sunday newspaper supplements. The manufacturer estimates that 25% of the 50-cent coupons will be redeemed.
e. A company has been sued by the federal government for price fixing. The company's legal counsel believes that there will be an unfavorable verdict and has made an estimate of the probable loss.

Required
1. Identify which of the items (a) through (e) should be recorded at year-end.
2. Identify which of the items (a) through (e) should not be recorded but should be disclosed in the year-end financial statements.

LO6,7

Problem 9-11 Time Value of Money Concepts

The following situations involve the application of the time value of money concept.

1. Janelle Carter deposited $9,750 in the bank on January 1, 1991, at an interest rate of 11% compounded annually. How much has accumulated in the account by January 1, 2008?
2. Mike Smith deposited $21,600 in the bank on January 1, 1998. On January 2, 2008, this deposit has accumulated to $42,487. Interest is compounded annually on the account. What rate of interest did Mike earn on the deposit?
3. Lee Spony made a deposit in the bank on January 1, 2001. The bank pays interest at the rate of 8% compounded annually. On January 1, 2008, the deposit has accumulated to $15,000. How much money did Lee originally deposit on January 1, 2001?
4. Nancy Holmes deposited $5,800 in the bank on January 1 a few years ago. The bank pays an interest rate of 10% compounded annually, and the deposit is now worth $15,026. How many years has the deposit been invested?

LO6,7

Problem 9-12 Comparison of Alternatives

Brian Imhoff's grandparents want to give him some money when he graduates from high school. They have offered Brian three choices:

a. Receive $15,000 immediately. Assume that interest is compounded annually.
b. Receive $2,250 at the end of each six months for four years. Brian will receive the first check in six months.
c. Receive $4,350 at the end of each year for four years. Assume that interest is compounded annually.

Required
Brian wants to have money for a new car when he graduates from college in four years. Assuming an interest rate of 8%, what option should he choose to have the most money in four years?

ALTERNATE PROBLEMS

LO2 **Problem 9-1A** Notes and Interest

McLaughlin Inc. operates with a June 30 year-end. During 2008, the following transactions occurred:

a. January 1: Signed a one-year, 10% loan for $35,000. Interest and principal are to be paid at maturity.
b. January 10: Signed a line of credit with the Little Local Bank to establish a $560,000 line of credit. Interest of 9% will be charged on all borrowed funds.
c. February 1: Issued a $28,000 non-interest-bearing, six-month note to pay for a new machine. Interest on the note, at 12%, was deducted in advance.
d. March 1: Borrowed $210,000 on the line of credit.
e. June 1: Repaid $140,000 on the line of credit, plus accrued interest.
f. June 30: Made all necessary adjusting entries.
g. August 1: Repaid the non-interest-bearing note.
h. September 1: Borrowed $280,000 on the line of credit.
i. November 1: Issued a three-month, 8%, $16,800 note in payment of an overdue open account.
j. December 31: Repaid the one-year loan [from (a)] plus accrued interest.

Required

1. Record all journal entries necessary to report these transactions.
2. As of December 31, which notes are outstanding? How much interest is due on each?

LO3 **Problem 9-2A** Effects of McDonald's Current Liabilities on Its Statement of Cash Flows

The following items are classified as current liabilities on **McDonald's** consolidated statements of financial condition (or balance sheet) at December 31 (in millions):

	December 31,	
	2006	**2005**
Notes payable	$ —	$ 544.0
Accounts payable	834.1	678.0
Income taxes	250.9	569.6
Other taxes	251.4	233.1
Accrued interest	135.1	158.5
Accrued payroll and other liabilities	1,518.9	1,158.1
Current maturities of long-term debt	17.7	658.5
Discontinued operations	—	107.9
Total current liabilities	$3,008.1	$4,107.7

Required

1. McDonald's uses the indirect method to prepare its statement of cash flows. Prepare the Operating Activities section of the cash flow statement, which indicates how each item will be reflected as an adjustment to net income. If you did not include any of the preceding items, explain why.
2. How would you decide if McDonald's has the ability to pay these liabilities as they become due?

LO3 **Problem 9-3A** Effects of Darden Restaurants' Changes in Current Assets and Liabilities on Its Statement of Cash Flows

The following items, listed in alphabetical order, are included in the Current Liabilities category on the consolidated balance sheet of **Darden Restaurants** at May 27, 2007 and May 28, 2006:

(In millions)	May 27, 2007	May 28, 2006
Current liabilities:		
Accounts payable	$ 178.0	$ 213.2
Short-term debt	211.4	44.0
Accrued payroll	108.5	123.2
Accrued income taxes	75.9	64.8
Other accrued taxes	43.4	46.9
Unearned revenues	109.9	100.8
Current portion of long-term debt	—	149.9
Other current liabilities	305.0	283.3
Liabilities associated with assets held for sale	42.3	—
Total current liabilities	$1,074.4	$1,026.1

Required

1. Darden Restaurants uses the indirect method to prepare its statement of cash flows. Prepare the Operating Activities section of the cash flow statement, which indicates how each item will be reflected as an adjustment to net income.
2. If you did not include any of the preceding items in your answer to (1), explain how these items would be reported on the statement of cash flows.

LO4

Problem 9-4A Warranties

Sound Company manufactures and sells high-quality stereos. The most popular line sells for $2,000 each and is accompanied by a three-year warranty to repair, free of charge, any defective unit. Average costs to repair each defective unit will be $180 for replacement parts and $120 for labor. Sound estimates that warranty costs of $25,200 will be incurred during 2008. The company actually sold 600 sets and incurred replacement part costs of $7,200 and labor costs of $10,800 during the year. The adjusted 2008 ending balance in the Estimated Liability for Warranties account is $20,400.

Required

1. How many defective units from this year's sales does Sound Company estimate will be returned for repair?
2. What percentage of sales does Sound Company estimate will be returned for repair?

LO4

Problem 9-5A Warranties

Beck Company sells a product for $3,200. When the customer buys it, Beck provides a one-year warranty. Beck sold 120 products during 2008. Based on analysis of past warranty records, Beck estimates that repairs will average 4% of total sales.

Required

1. Prepare the journal entry to record the estimated liability.
2. Assume that during 2008, products under warranty must be repaired using repair parts from inventory costing $10,200. Prepare the journal entry to record the repair of products.
3. Assume that the balance of the Estimated Liabilities for Warranties accounts as of the beginning of 2008 was $1,100. Calculate the balance of the account as of the end of 2008.

LO5

Problem 9-6A Comparison of Simple and Compound Interest

On June 30, 2008, Rolloff Inc. borrowed $25,000 from its bank, signing a 6% note. Principal and interest are due at the end of two years.

Required

1. Assuming that the note earns simple interest for the bank, calculate the amount of interest accrued on each of the following dates:

   December 31, 2008
   December 31, 2009
   June 30, 2010

2. Assume instead that the note earns 6% for the bank but is compounded semiannually. Calculate the amount of interest accrued on the same dates as in (1).
3. How much additional interest expense will Rolloff have to pay with semiannual interest?

LO6

Problem 9-7A Investment with Varying Interest Rate

Trena Thompson invested $2,000 in a financial institution on January 1, 2008. She leaves her investment in the institution until December 31, 2012. How much money does Trena accumulate if she earns interest, compounded annually, at the following rates?

2008	4%
2009	5
2010	6
2011	7
2012	8

LO6

Problem 9-8A Comparison of Alternatives

On January 1, 2008, Chen Yu's Office Supply Store plans to remodel the store and install new display cases. Chen has the following options of payment. Chen's interest rate is 8%.

HOMEWORK

a. Pay $270,000 on January 1, 2008.
b. Pay $294,300 on January 1, 2009.
c. Pay $334,750 on January 1, 2010.
d. Make four annual payments of $82,500 beginning on December 31, 2008.

Required
Which option should he choose? (*Hint:* Calculate the present value of each option as of January 1, 2008.)

ALTERNATE MULTICONCEPT PROBLEMS

LO2,5 **Problem 9-9A** Interest in Advance versus Interest Paid When Loan Is Due

On July 1, 2008, Moton Company needs exactly $206,400 in cash to pay an existing obligation. Moton has decided to borrow from State Bank, which charges 14% interest on loans. The loan will be due in one year. Moton is unsure, however, whether to ask the bank for (a) an interest-bearing loan with interest and principal payable at the end of the year or (b) a non-interest-bearing loan due in one year but with interest deducted in advance.

Required
1. What will be the face value of the note assuming that:
   a. Interest is paid when the loan is due?
   b. Interest is deducted in advance?
2. Calculate the effective interest rate on the note assuming that:
   a. Interest is paid when the loan is due.
   b. Interest is deducted in advance.
3. Assume that Moton negotiates and signs the one-year note with the bank on July 1, 2008. Also assume that Moton's accounting year ends December 31. Prepare all of the journal entries necessary to record the issuance of the note and the interest on the note assuming that:
   a. Interest is paid when the loan is due.
   b. Interest is deducted in advance.
4. Prepare the appropriate balance sheet presentation for July 1, 2008, immediately after the note has been issued assuming that:
   a. Interest is paid when the loan is due.
   b. Interest is deducted in advance.

LO1,4 **Problem 9-10A** Contingent Liabilities

Several items are listed for which the outcome of events is unknown at year-end.

a. A company has been sued by the federal government for price fixing. The company's legal counsel believes that there will be an unfavorable verdict and has made an estimate of the probable loss.
b. A company is involved in an environmental cleanup lawsuit. The company's legal counsel believes that the outcome may be unfavorable but has not been able to estimate the costs of the possible loss.
c. The company is involved in a trademark infringement suit. The company's legal experts believe that an award of $750,000 in the company's favor will be made.
d. A company offers a three-year warranty on sales of new computers. It believes that 6% of the computers will require repairs.
e. A snack food manufacturer has included a coupon offer in the Sunday newspaper supplements. The manufacturer estimates that 30% of the 40-cent coupons will be redeemed.

Required
1. Identify which of the items (a) through (e) should be recorded at year-end.
2. Identify which of the items (a) through (e) should not be recorded but should be disclosed in the year-end financial statements.

LO6,7 **Problem 9-11A** Time Value of Money Concepts

The following situations involve the application of the time value of money concept.

1. Jan Cain deposited $19,500 in the bank on January 1, 1991, at an interest rate of 11% compounded annually. How much has accumulated in the account by January 1, 2008?

2. Mark Schultz deposited $43,200 in the bank on January 1, 1998. On January 2, 2008, this deposit has accumulated to $84,974. Interest is compounded annually on the account. What rate of interest did Mark earn on the deposit?
3. Les Hinckle made a deposit in the bank on January 1, 2001. The bank pays interest at the rate of 8% compounded annually. On January 1, 2008, the deposit has accumulated to $30,000. How much money did Les originally deposit on January 1, 2001?
4. Val Hooper deposited $11,600 in the bank on January 1 a few years ago. The bank pays an interest rate of 10% compounded annually, and the deposit is now worth $30,052. For how many years has the deposit been invested?

LO6,7

Problem 9-12A Comparison of Alternatives

Darlene Page's grandparents want to give her some money when she graduates from high school. They have offered Darlene three choices:

a. Receive $16,000 immediately. Assume that interest is compounded annually.
b. Receive $2,400 at the end of each six months for four years. Darlene will receive the first check in six months.
c. Receive $4,640 at the end of each year for four years. Assume that interest is compounded annually.

Required
Darlene wants to have money for a new car when she graduates from college in four years. Assuming an interest rate of 8%, what option should she choose to have the most money in four years?

DECISION CASES

READING AND INTERPRETING FINANCIAL STATEMENTS

LO1,2

Decision Case 9-1 General Mills's and Kellogg's Current Liabilities

Refer to **General Mills**'s and **Kellogg's** annual reports reprinted at the back of the book. Using the companies' balance sheets and accompanying notes, write a response to the following questions.

Required
1. Determine General Mills's current ratio for fiscal years 2006 and 2005. What do the ratios indicate about the liquidity of the company?
2. How do the current liabilities of Kellogg's and General Mills compare?
3. Refer to the companies' notes. Do the companies have any contingent liabilities for lawsuits or litigation? If so, how were these contingent liabilities treated on the financial statements?

LO4

Decision Case 9-2 Caribou Coffee's Cash Flow Statement

Following is the current asset and current liability portion of the balance sheet for **Caribou Coffee** as of December 31, 2006 and January 1, 2006:

	December 31, 2006	January 1, 2006
Current assets:		
Cash and cash equivalents	$14,752,269	$33,846,111
Accounts receivable (net of allowance for doubtful accounts of approximately $12,693 and $237,595 at December 31, 2006 and January 1, 2006)	1,663,139	1,137,120
Other receivables	1,769,256	2,260,254
Income tax receivable	—	135,750
Inventories	10,294,493	11,182,512
Prepaid expenses and other current assets	1,339,596	1,251,555
Total current assets	$29,818,753	$49,813,302
Current liabilities:		
Accounts payable	$ 9,681,879	$14,553,743
Accrued compensation	5,676,449	5,462,657
Accrued expenses	7,860,487	8,504,552
Deferred revenue	9,002,588	8,165,260
Total current liabilities	$32,221,403	$36,686,212

HOMEWORK

Required

1. Determine the company's current ratio for each fiscal year. What do the ratios indicate about the liquidity of the company? What were the major causes for any changes in liquidity?
2. Explain why deferred revenue is considered a current liability on the company's balance sheet.

LO3,4 **Decision Case 9-3** Darden Restaurants' Contingent Liabilities

The following excerpts are from the footnotes of **Darden Restaurants**' financial statements of May 29, 2005:

> In March 2003 and March 2002, two purported class action lawsuits were brought against us in the Superior Court of Orange County, California by three current and former hourly restaurant employees alleging violations of California labor laws with respect to providing meal and rest breaks. Although we continue to believe we provided the required meal and rest breaks to our employees, to avoid potentially costly and protracted litigation, we agreed during the second quarter of fiscal 2005 to settle both lawsuits and a similar case filed in Sacramento County, for approximately $9,500. Terms of the settlement, which do not include any admission of liability by us, have received preliminary judicial approval, but completion of the settlement may not occur for several months. We recorded settlement expenses associated with these lawsuits of approximately $4,500 during fiscal 2005 and $5,000 during fiscal 2004, which are included in selling, general and administrative expenses. The settlement amounts of these lawsuits are included in other current liabilities at May 29, 2005.
>
> In August 2003, three former employees in Washington filed a similar purported class action in Washington State Superior Court in Spokane County alleging violations of Washington labor laws with respect to providing rest breaks. The Court stayed the action and ordered the plaintiffs into our mandatory arbitration program; the plaintiffs' motion for reconsideration was not granted, and their appeal of the denial of reconsideration was also not granted. We believe we provided the required meal and rest breaks to our employees, and we intend to vigorously defend our position in this case.

Required

1. Regarding the first paragraph of the contingency note, why did the company accrue an amount in its current liability category? At what point should accrual occur? How does an accrual affect the company's financial statements?
2. Regarding the second paragraph of the contingency note, is disclosure of the legal dispute in the notes to the financial statements all that is required of Darden Restaurants, or is accrual required? Why is there a difference in the actions taken by the company as discussed in the first and second paragraphs?

LO4 **Decision Case 9-4** Hewlett-Packard's Contingent Liability

Following is an excerpt from **Hewlett-Packard**'s notes that accompanied its financial statements for the year ended October 31, 2006:

> HP is party to, or otherwise involved in, proceedings brought by United States or state environmental agencies under the Comprehensive Environmental Response, Compensation and Liability Act ("CERCLA"), known as "Superfund," or state laws similar to CERCLA. HP is also conducting environmental investigations or remediations at several current or former operating sites pursuant to administrative orders or consent agreements with state environmental agencies. It is our policy to apply strict standards for environmental protection to sites inside and outside the United States, even if not subject to regulations imposed by local governments.
>
> The liability for environmental remediation and other environmental costs is accrued when it is considered probable and the costs can be reasonably estimated. We have accrued amounts in conjunction with the foregoing environmental issues that we believe was adequate as of October 31, 2006. These accruals were not material to our operations or financial position, and we do not currently anticipate material capital expenditures for environmental control facilities.

Required

1. Based on the excerpt, how did the company treat the contingency on its financial statements for the year ended December 31, 2006? What critieria were likely used to lead to that treatment?
2. What was the effect on the financial statements of the company's treatment of the contingency?

MAKING FINANCIAL DECISIONS

LO1,2

Decision Case 9-5 Current Ratio Loan Provision

Assume that you are the controller of a small, growing sporting goods company. The prospects for your firm in the future are quite good; but like many other firms, it has been experiencing some cash flow difficulties because all available funds have been used to purchase inventory and to finance start-up costs associated with a new business. At the beginning of the current year, your local bank advanced a loan to your company. Included in the loan is the following provision:

> The company is obligated to pay interest payments each month for the next five years. Principal is due and must be paid at the end of Year 5. The company is further obligated to maintain a current assets to current liabilities ratio of 2 to 1 as indicate on quarterly statements to be submitted to the bank. If the company fails to meet any loan provisions, all amounts of interest and principal are due immediately upon notification by the bank.

You, as controller, have just gathered the following information as of the end of the first month of the current quarter:

Current liabilities:	
Accounts payable	$400,000
Taxes payable	100,000
Accrued expenses	50,000
Total current liabilities	$550,000

You are concerned about the loan provision that requires a 2 to 1 ratio of current assets to current liabilities.

Required

1. Indicate what actions could be taken during the next two months to meet the loan provision. Which of the available actions should be recommended?
2. Could management take short-term actions to make the company's liquidity appear to be better? What are the long-run implications of such actions?

LO7

Decision Case 9-6 Alternative Payment Options

Kathy Clark owns a small company that makes ice machines for restaurants and food-service facilities. Kathy knows a great deal about producing ice machines but is less familiar with the best terms to extend to her customers. One customer is opening a new business and has asked Kathy to consider one of the following options that he can use to pay for his new $20,000 ice machine.

a. Term 1: 10% down, the remainder paid at the end of the year plus 8% simple interest
b. Term 2: 10% down, the remainder paid at the end of the year plus 8% interest, compounded quarterly
c. Term 3: $0 down, but $21,600 due at the end of the year

Required

Make a recommendation to Kathy. She believes that 8% is a fair return on her money at this time. Should she accept (a), (b), or (c) or take the $20,000 cash at the time of the sale? Justify your recommendation with calculations. What factors other than the actual amount of cash received from the sale should you consider?

ETHICAL DECISION MAKING

LO4

Decision Case 9-7 Warranty Cost Estimate

John Walton is an accountant for ABC Auto Dealers, a large auto dealership in a metropolitan area. ABC sells both new and used cars. New cars are sold with a five-year warranty, the cost of which is carried by the manufacturer. For several years, however, ABC has offered a two-year warranty on used cars. The cost of the warranty is an expense to ABC; and John has been asked by his boss, Mr. Sawyer, to review warranty costs and recommend the amount to accrue on the year-end financial statements.

For the past several years, ABC has recorded as warranty expense 5% of used car sales. John analyzed past repair records and found that repairs, although fluctuating somewhat from year to year, have averaged near the 5% level. John is convinced, however, that 5% is inadequate for the coming year. He bases his judgment on industry reports of increased repair costs and on the fact that several cars that were recently sold on warranty have experienced very high repair costs. John believes that the current year repair accrual will be at least 10%. He discussed the higher expense amount with Mr. Sawyer, who is the controller of ABC.

Mr. Sawyer was not happy with John's decision concerning warranty expense. He reminded John of the need to control expenses during the recent sales downturn. He also reminded John that ABC was seeking a large loan from the bank and that its loan officers might not be happy with recent operating results, especially if ABC began to accrue larger amounts for future estimated amounts such as warranties. Finally, Mr. Sawyer reminded John that most of the employees of ABC, including Mr. Sawyer, were members of the company's profit-sharing plan and would not be happy with the reduced share of profits. Mr. Sawyer thanked John for his judgment concerning warranty cost but told him that the accrual for the current year would remain at 5%.

John left the meeting with Mr. Sawyer feeling somewhat frustrated. He was convinced that his judgment concerning the warranty costs was correct. He knew that the owner of ABC would be visiting the office next week and wondered whether he should discuss the matter with him at that time. John also had met one of the loan officers from the bank several times and considered calling her to discuss his concern about the warranty expense amount on the year-end statements.

Required

Discuss the courses of action available to John. What should John do concerning his judgment of warranty costs?

LO4 Decision Case 9-8 Retainer Fees As Sales

Bunch o' Balloons markets balloon arrangements to companies who want to thank clients and employees. Bunch o' Balloons has a unique style that has put it in high demand. Consequently, Bunch o' Balloons has asked clients to establish an account. Clients are asked to pay a retainer fee equal to about three months of purchases. The fee will be used to cover the cost of arrangements delivered and will be reevaluated at the end of each month. At the end of the current month, Bunch o' Balloons has $43,900 of retainer fees in its possession. The controller is eager to show this amount as sales because "it represents certain sales for the company."

Required

Do you agree with the controller? When should the sales be reported? Why would the controller be eager to report the cash receipts as sales?

SOLUTIONS TO KEY TERMS QUIZ

1	Current liability	14	Time value of money
3	Accounts payable	10	Simple interest
8	Notes payable	13	Compound interest
4	Discount on Notes Payable	15	Future value of a single amount
6	Current Maturities of Long-Term Debt	17	Present value of a single amount
7	Accrued liability	5	Annuity
9	Contingent liability	16	Future value of an annuity
11	Estimated liability	2	Present value of an annuity
12	Contingent asset		

ANSWERS TO POD REVIEW

LO1	1. b	2. b
LO2	1. d	2. b
LO3	1. b	2. a
LO4	1. d	2. a
LO5	1. b	2. c
LO6	1. a	2. b
LO7	1. c	2. b

CHAPTER

10

Long-Term Liabilities

Learning Outcomes

After studying this chapter, you should be able to:

LO1 Identify the components of the long-term liability category of the balance sheet.

LO2 Define the important characteristics of bonds payable.

LO3 Determine the issue price of a bond using compound interest techniques.

LO4 Show that you understand the effect on the balance sheet of the issuance of bonds.

LO5 Find the amortization of premium or discount using the effective interest method.

LO6 Find the gain or loss on retirement of bonds.

LO7 Determine whether a lease agreement must be reported as a liability on the balance sheet.

LO8 Explain how investors use ratios to evaluate long-term liabilities.

LO9 Explain the effects that transactions involving long-term liabilities have on the statement of cash flows.

LO10 Explain deferred taxes and calculate the deferred tax liability. (Appendix)

Study Links...

A Look at Previous Chapters
Chapter 9 was concerned with current liabilities and short-term liquidity. It also introduced the concept of the time value of money.

A Look at This Chapter
This chapter examines the use of long-term liabilities as an important source of financing a company's needs. Chapter 10 will utilize the time value of money concept because it is the basis for the valuation of all long-term liabilities.

A Look at Upcoming Chapters
Chapter 11 examines the presentation of stockholders' equity, the other major category on the right-hand side of the balance sheet.

Coca-Cola

MAKING BUSINESS DECISIONS

Coca-Cola® is one of the world's foremost brands with worldwide sales of nearly $22 billion in 2006. The company is truly a global corporation with nearly 300 brands in almost 200 countries. While it began many years ago in the United States, now more than 70% of Coca-Cola Company's income comes from business outside the United States. Recently, the growth in company sales has slowed to 4% or less per year and the company has faced new challenges in the beverage industry. Despite continued turbulence in worldwide markets and challenges from competitors, the firm maintains its focus on growth.

To meet long-term growth objectives, Coca-Cola must make significant investments to support its products. The process also involves investment to develop new global brands and to acquire local or global brands when appropriate. In addition, the company makes significant marketing investments to encourage consumer loyalty. Coca-Cola has developed relationships with many sports organizations, including the **NBA** and **NASCAR**, to enhance consumer awareness and promote sales of its products. Outside the United States, there is a strong push to sell in many other markets, including India and Brazil.

To expand profitably, Coca-Cola requires more money than it generates in profits. Therefore, it uses a common financing tool: *long-term debt*. In fact, the balance sheet of December 31, 2006, indicates the company has over $4 billion of long-term debt, other liabilities, and deferred income taxes. The company monitors interest rate conditions carefully and in 2006 retired nearly $2 billion in long-term debt and in some cases replaced it with other debt. Because it is a global company, Coca-Cola has access to key financial markets around the world, which allows it to borrow at the lowest possible rates. While most of its loans are in U.S. dollars, management continually adjusts the composition of the debt to accommodate shifting interest rates and currency exchange rates to minimize the overall cost.

© Christian Veron/Reuters/Landov

The accompanying balance sheet presents the liabilities and shareowner's equity portion of the balance sheet for The Coca-Cola Company and its subsidiaries. This chapter answers the following questions:

- What are the components of the long-term liability of the balance sheet? (See pp. 480–481.)
- What is the proper accounting and reporting of bonds payable. (See pp. 482–484.)
- What is the importance of financial arrangements such as leases as a means of financing a company? (See pp. 495–499.)

Other issues related to long-term liabilities are also found in this text. This information can help you evaluate the Long-Term Liabilities section of the balance sheet of The Coca-Cola Company.

(*continued*)

Coca-Cola's 2006 Annual Report

Consolidated Balance Sheets

December 31,	2006	2005
LIABILITIES AND SHAREOWNERS' EQUITY		
CURRENT LIABILITIES		
Accounts payable and accrued expenses	$ 5,055	$ 4,493
Loans and notes payable	3,235	4,518
Current maturities of long-term debt	33	28
Accrued income taxes	567	797
TOTAL CURRENT LIABILITIES	**8,890**	**9,836**
LONG-TERM DEBT	1,314	1,154
OTHER LIABILITIES	2,231	1,730
DEFERRED INCOME TAXES	608	352
SHAREOWNERS' EQUITY		
Common stock, $0.25 par value; Authorized - 5,600 shares;		
Issued - 3,511 and 3,507 shares, respectively	878	877
Capital surplus	5,983	5,492
Reinvested earnings	33,468	31,299
Accumulated other comprehensive income (loss)	(1,291)	(1,669)
Treasury stock, at cost - 1,193 and 1,138 shares, respectively)	(22,118)	(19,644)
TOTAL SHAREOWNERS' EQUITY	**16,920**	**16,355**
TOTAL LIABILITIES AND SHAREOWNERS' EQUITY	**$ 29,963**	**$ 29,427**

Balance Sheet Presentation

LO1 Identify the components of the long-term liability category of the balance sheet.

In general, **long-term liabilities** are obligations that will not be satisfied within one year. Essentially, all liabilities that are not classified as current liabilities are classified as long-term. We will concentrate on the long-term liabilities of bonds or notes, leases, and deferred taxes. On the balance sheet, the items are listed after current liabilities. For example, the Noncurrent Liabilities section of **PepsiCo, Inc.**'s balance sheet is highlighted in Exhibit 10-1. PepsiCo has acquired financing through a combination of long-term debt, stock issuance, and internal growth or retained earnings. Exhibit 10-1 indicates that long-term debt is one portion of the long-term liability category of the balance sheet. But the balance sheet also reveals two other items that must be considered part of the long-term liability category: deferred income taxes and other liabilities. We begin by looking at a particular type of long-term debt: bonds payable. We will concentrate on these long-term liabilities:

Long-term liability
An obligation that will not be satisfied within one year or the current operating cycle.

- Bonds or notes
- Leases
- Deferred taxes

EXHIBIT 10-1 **PepsiCo's Balance Sheet**

Consolidated Partial Balance Sheet

PepsiCo, Inc. and Subsidiaries

December 30, 2006 and December 31, 2005

(In millions except per share amounts)	**2006**	**2005**
LIABILITIES AND SHAREHOLDERS' EQUITY		
Current Liabilities		
Short-term obligations	$ 274	$ 2,889
Accounts payable and other current liabilities	6,496	5,971
Income taxes payable	90	546
Total Current Liabilities	6,860	9,406
Long-Term Debt Obligations	2,550	2,313
Other Liabilities	4,624	4,323
Deferred Income Taxes	528	1,434
Total Liabilities	14,562	17,476
Commitments and Contingencies		
Preferred Stock, no par value	41	41
Repurchased Preferred Stock	(120)	(110)
Common Shareholders' Equity		
Common stock, par value 12/3 per share (issued 1,782 shares)	30	30
Capital in excess of par value	584	614
Retained earnings	24,837	21,116
Accumulated other comprehensive loss	(2,246)	(1,053)
	23,205	20,707
Less: repurchased common stock, at cost (144 and 126 shares, respectively)	(7,758)	(6,387)
Total Common Shareholders' Equity	**$15,447**	**$14,320**

© Christian Veron/Reuters/Landov

Hot Topics

Coca-Cola versus Pepsi

Can Coca-Cola take the PepsiCo challenge? The two companies are among the most aggressive competitors in the world. Over the past few years, sales of carbonated soft drinks have been declining for both companies. So they have introduced several noncarbonated products to appeal to health-conscious consumers. PepsiCo introduced a low-calorie Gatorade and developed a bottled water product with caffeine. Coca-Cola countered by making changes to its POWERade product and by teaming with Caribou Coffee to offer a new line of ready-to-drink iced coffees.

But new product lines require money. So both companies are constantly searching for additional long-term funds to finance the large investments necessary to develop and market new products. They borrow from all over the world to get the best rates on their financings. It's part of trying to beat out the competition.

POD REVIEW 10.1

LO1 *Identify the components of the long-term liability category of the balance sheet.*

- Generally, long-term liabilities are obligations of a company that will not be satisfied within one year. On the balance sheet, they are listed after current liabilities.

QUESTIONS

1. *Which of the following is likely to appear in the long-term liability category of the balance sheet?*
   a. accounts payable
   b. bonds payable
   c. unearned revenue
   d. warranty liability

2. *The account Discount on Bonds Payable should be considered what type of account?*
   a. current liability
   b. asset
   c. deferred revenue
   d. contra-liability

Bonds Payable

LO2 Define the important characteristics of bonds payable.

CHARACTERISTICS OF BONDS

A bond is a security or financial instrument that allows firms to borrow money and repay the loan over a long period of time. The bonds are sold, or *issued,* to investors who have amounts to invest and want a return on their investment. The *borrower* (issuing firm) promises to pay interest on specified dates, usually annually or semiannually. The borrower also promises to repay the principal on a specified date, the *due date* or maturity date.

A bond certificate, illustrated in Exhibit 10-2, is issued at the time of purchase and indicates the terms of the bond. Generally, bonds are issued in denominations of $1,000. The denomination of the bond is usually referred to as the **face value** or par value. This is the amount that the firm must pay at the maturity date of the bond.

Face value
The principal amount of the bond as stated on the bond certificate. ***Alternate term:*** *Par value.*

Firms issue bonds in very large amounts, often in millions in a single issue. After bonds are issued, they may be traded on a bond exchange in the same way that stocks are sold on the stock exchanges. Therefore, bonds are not always held until maturity by the initial investor, but may change hands several times before their eventual due date. Because bond maturities are as long as 30 years, the "secondary" market in bonds—the market for bonds already issued—is a critical factor in a company's ability to raise money. Investors in bonds may want to sell them if interest rates paid by competing investments become more attractive or if the issuer becomes less creditworthy. Buyers of these bonds may be betting that interest rates will reverse course or that the company will get back on its feet. Trading in the secondary market does not affect the financial statements of the issuing company.

We have described the general nature of bonds, but all bonds do not have the same terms and features. Following are some important features that often appear in the bond certificate.

Collateral The bond certificate should indicate the *collateral* of the loan. Collateral represents the assets that back the bonds in case the issuer cannot make the interest and principal payments and must default on the loan. **Debenture bonds** are not backed by specific collateral of the issuing company. Rather, the investor must examine the general creditworthiness of the issuer. If a bond is a *secured bond,* the certificate indicates specific assets that serve as collateral in case of default.

Debenture bonds
Bonds that are not backed by specific collateral.

EXHIBIT 10-2 Bond Certificate

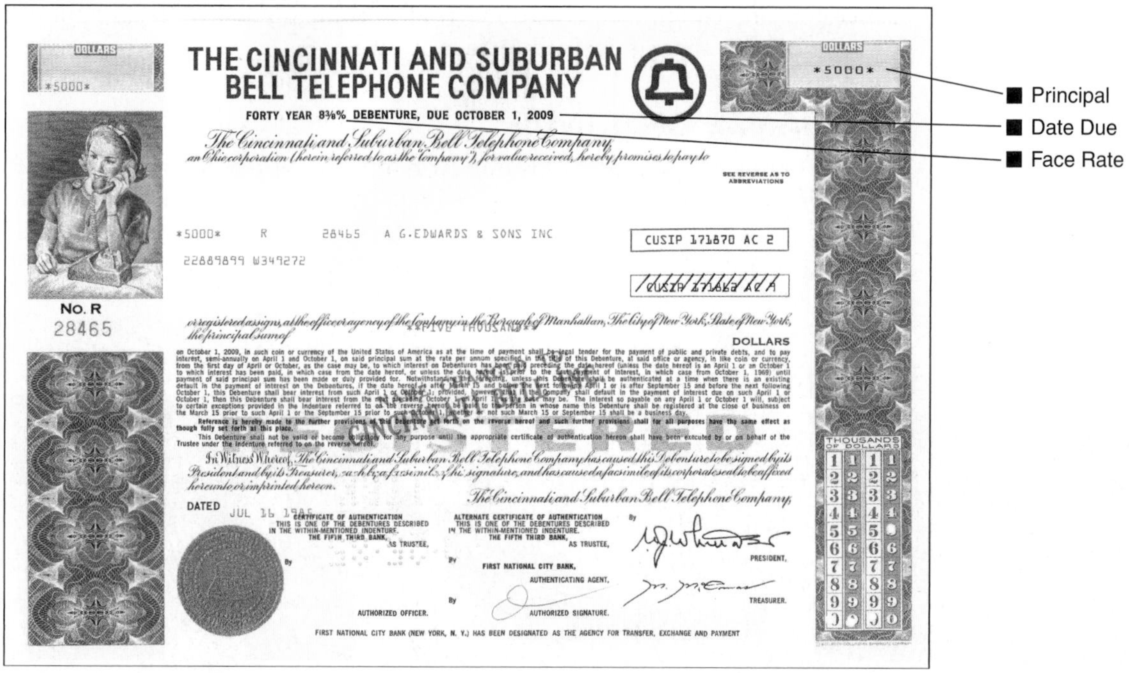

Debenture bonds, like this one from Cincinnati Bell, Inc. (now named Broadwing, Inc.), are backed by the general creditworthiness of the issuing company, not by its assets as collateral. Buyers of such bonds should check the issuer's credit rating, should know how to read the firm's financial statements, and should learn as much as possible about its operations.

Due Date The bond certificate specifies the date that the bond principal must be repaid. Normally, bonds are *term bonds,* meaning that the entire principal amount is due on a single date. Alternatively, bonds may be issued as **serial bonds**, meaning that not all of the principal is due on the same date. For example, a firm may issue serial bonds that have a portion of the principal due each year for the next ten years. Issuing firms may prefer serial bonds because a firm does not need to accumulate the entire amount for principal repayment at one time.

Serial bonds
Bonds that do not all have the same due date; a portion of the bonds comes due each time period.

Other Features Some bonds are issued as convertible or callable bonds. *Convertible bonds* can be converted into common stock at a future time. This feature allows the investor to buy a security that pays a fixed interest rate but that can be converted at a future date into an equity security (stock) if the issuing firm is growing and profitable. The conversion feature is also advantageous to the issuing firm because convertible bonds normally carry a lower rate of interest.

Callable bonds may be retired before their specified due date. *Callable* generally refers to the issuer's right to retire the bonds. If the buyer or investor has the right to retire the bonds, they are referred to as *redeemable bonds.* Usually, callable bonds stipulate the price to be paid at redemption; this price is referred to as the *redemption price* or the *reacquisition price.* The callable feature is like an insurance policy for the company. Assume that a bond pays 10%, but interest rates plummet to 6%. Rather than continuing to pay 10%, the company is willing to offer a slight premium over face value for the right to retire those 10% bonds so that it can borrow at 6%. Of course, the investor is invariably disappointed when the company invokes its call privilege.

Callable bonds
Bonds that may be redeemed or retired before their specified due date.

As you can see, bonds have various terms and features. Each firm seeks to structure the bond agreement in the manner that best meets the firm's financial needs and will attract investors at the most favorable rates.

Bonds are a popular source of financing because of their tax advantages when compared with the issuance of stock. Interest paid on bonds is deductible for tax purposes, but dividends paid on stock are not. This may explain why the amount of debt on many firms' balance sheets has increased in recent years. Debt became popular in the 1980s to finance mergers and again in recent years when interest rates reached 20-year lows. Still, investors and creditors tend to downgrade a company when the amount of debt it has on the balance sheet is deemed to be excessive.

ISSUANCE OF BONDS

When bonds are issued, the issuing firm must recognize the incurrence of a liability in exchange for cash. When bonds are issued at their face amount, the accounting entry is straightforward. For example, assume that on April 1, a firm issues bonds with a face amount of $10,000 and receives $10,000. In this case, the asset Cash and the liability Bonds Payable are both increased by $10,000.

POD REVIEW 10.2

LO2 *Define the important characteristics of bonds payable.*

- Bonds payable result from borrowing funds and are generally issued in denominations of $1,000.
- Important characteristics of bonds payable include par value, due date, interest rate, an indication of whether the bonds are convertible or callable, and any property collateralizing the bonds.

QUESTIONS

1. *Bonds usually pay interest*
   a. only at the due date of the bond.
   b. monthly.
   c. either annually or semiannually.
   d. at the time of issuance.

2. *When serial bonds are issued*
   a. the bonds all come due on the same date.
   b. not all of the bonds come due on the same date.
   c. the interest is paid as a series of monthly payments.
   d. the lender is not required to repay the bond principal.

LO3 Determine the issue price of a bond using compound interest techniques.

FACTORS AFFECTING BOND PRICE

With bonds payable, two interest rates are always involved. The **face rate of interest** (also called the *stated rate, nominal rate, contract rate,* or *coupon rate*) is the rate specified on the bond certificate. It is the amount of interest that will be paid each interest period. For example, if $10,000 worth of bonds was issued with an 8% annual face rate of interest, interest of $800 ($10,000 × 8% × 1 year) would be paid at the end of each annual period. Alternatively, bonds often require the payment of interest semiannually. If the bonds in the example required the 8% annual face rate to be paid semiannually (at 4%), interest of $400 ($10,000 × 8% × 1/2 year) would be paid each semiannual period.

Face rate of interest The rate of interest on the bond certificate. ***Alternate terms:*** *Stated rate, normal rate, contract rate, coupon rate.*

Market rate of interest The rate that investors could obtain by investing in other bonds that are similar to the issuing firm's bonds. ***Alternate terms:*** *Effective rate, bond yield.*

The second important interest rate is the **market rate of interest** (also called the *effective rate* or *bond yield*). The market rate of interest is the rate that bondholders could obtain by investing in other bonds that are similar to the issuing firm's bonds. The issuing firm does not set the market rate of interest. That rate is determined by the bond market on the basis of many transactions for similar bonds. The market rate incorporates all of the "market's" knowledge about economic conditions and all of its expectations about future conditions. Normally, issuing firms try to set a face rate that is equal to the market rate. However, because the market rate changes daily, small differences usually occur between the face rate and the market rate at the time bonds are issued.

In addition to the number of interest payments and the maturity length of the bond, both the face rate and the market rate of interest must be known to calculate the issue price of a bond. The **bond issue price** equals the *present value* of the cash flows that the bond will produce. Bonds produce two types of cash flows for the investor: interest receipts and repayment of principal (face value). The interest receipts constitute an annuity of payments each interest period over the life of the bonds. The repayment of principal (face value) is a one-time receipt that occurs at the end of the term of the bonds. We must calculate the present value of the interest receipts (using Table 9-4 on page 451) and the present value of the principal amount (using Table 9-2 on page 449). The total of the two present-value calculations represents the issue price of the bond.

Study Tip

Calculating the issue price of a bond always involves a calculation of the present value of the cash flows.

Bond issue price
The present value of the annuity of interest payments plus the present value of the principal.

An Example Suppose that on January 1, 2008, Discount Firm wants to issue bonds with a face value of $10,000. The face, or coupon, rate of interest has been set at 8%. The bonds will pay interest annually, and the principal amount is due in four years. Also suppose that the market rate of interest for other similar bonds is currently 10%. Because the market rate of interest exceeds the coupon rate, investors will not be willing to pay $10,000, but something less. We want to calculate the amount that will be obtained from the issuance of Discount Firm's bonds.

Discount's bond will produce two sets of cash flows for the investor: an annual interest payment of $800 ($10,000 × 8%) per year for four years and repayment of the principal of $10,000 at the end of the fourth year. To calculate the issue price, we must calculate the present value of the two sets of cash flows. A time diagram portrays the cash flows as follows:

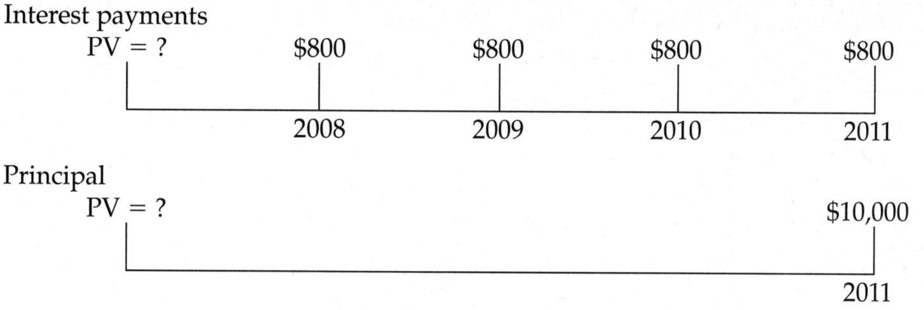

We can calculate the issue price by using the compound-interest tables found in Chapter 9, as follows:

$800 × 3.170 (factor from Table 9-4 for 4 periods, 10%)	$2,536
$10,000 × 0.683 (factor from Table 9-2 for 4 periods, 10%)	6,830
Issue price	$9,366

The factors used to calculate the present value represent four periods and 10% interest. This is a key point. The issue price of a bond is always calculated using the market rate of interest. The face rate of interest determines the amount of the interest payments, but the market rate determines the present value of the payments and the present value of the principal (and therefore the issue price).

The example of Discount Firm reveals that the bonds with a $10,000 face value amount would be issued for $9,366. The bond markets and the financial press often state the issue price as a percentage of the face amount. The percentage for Discount's bonds can be calculated as ($9,366/$10,000) × 100, or 93.66%.

Exhibit 10-3 illustrates how bonds are actually listed in the reporting of the bond markets. The exhibit lists two types of **IBM** bonds that were traded on a particular day. The portion immediately after the company name (e.g., $6\frac{3}{8}$ 09) indicates that the face rate of

Real World Practice

10-1 Reading Coca-Cola's Balance Sheet

Coca-Cola lists three items as long-term liabilities on its 2006 balance sheet. What are those items? Did they increase or decrease?

EXHIBIT 10-3 Listing of Bonds on the Bond Market

Bonds	Cur Yld	Vol	Close	Net Chg
IBM $6\frac{3}{8}$09	6.5	280	$98\frac{3}{4}$	$-\frac{1}{4}$
IBM $7\frac{1}{4}$10	7.1	68	$101\frac{1}{2}$	$+\frac{1}{4}$

interest is $6\frac{3}{8}\%$ and the due date of the bonds is the year 2009. The next column, (e.g., 6.5) indicates that the bond investor who purchased the bonds on that day will receive a yield of 6.5%. The column labeled "Vol" indicates the number of bonds, in thousands, that were bought and sold during the day. The column labeled "Close" indicates the market price of the bonds at the end of the day. For example, the first issue of IBM bonds closed at $98\frac{3}{4}$, which means that the price was $98\frac{3}{4}\%$ of the face value of the bonds. These bonds are trading at a discount because the face rate ($6\frac{3}{8}\%$) is less than the market rate of 6.5%. The bonds in the second issue ($7\frac{1}{4}\%$) have a face rate of $7\frac{1}{4}\%$; will become due in the year 2010; and closed at $101\frac{1}{2}$, or at a premium. The net change column indicates the change in the bond price that occurred for the day's trading.

POD REVIEW 10.3

LO3 *Determine the issue price of a bond using compound interest techniques.*

- Bonds are issued at a price that reflects the market rate of interest on the day the bond is purchased. The actual issue price of a bond represents the present value of all future cash flows related to the bond.

QUESTIONS

1. *On January 1, 2008, Omega Corporation issued a three-year, $1,000 bond with a nominal interest rate of 9%. At the time, the market rate of interest was 9%. The company's issue price for the bond would be*
   a. $1,000.
   b. $1,300.
   c. $1,025.
   d. $700.

2. *If the market rate had been 8% at the time of issuance,*
   a. the bonds would have been issued at a premium.
   b. the bonds would have been issued at a discount.
   c. the bonds would have been issued at face value.
   d. there would have been 1% accrued interest at the time of issuance.

3. *If the market rate had been 10% at the time of issuance,*
   a. the bonds would have been issued at a premium.
   b. the bonds would have been issued at a discount.
   c. the bonds would have been issued at face value.
   d. there would have been 1% accrued interest at the time of issuance.

LO4 Show that you understand the effect on the balance sheet of the issuance of bonds.

Premium
The excess of the issue price over the face value of the bonds.

Discount
The excess of the face value of bonds over the issue price.

PREMIUM OR DISCOUNT ON BONDS

Premium or **discount** represents the difference between the face value and the issue price of a bond. The relationship is stated as follows:

Premium = Issue Price − Face Value
Discount = Face Value − Issue Price

In other words, when issue price exceeds face value, the bonds have sold at a premium and when the face value exceeds the issue price, the bonds have sold at a discount.

We will continue with the Discount Firm example to illustrate the accounting for bonds sold at a discount. Discount Firm's bonds sold at a discount calculated as follows:

Discount = $10,000 − $9,366
= $634

Discount Firm would record both the discount and the issuance of the bonds in the following journal entry:

Jan. 1	Cash	9,366	
	Discount on Bonds Payable	634	
	Bonds Payable		10,000
	To record the issuance of bonds payable.		

Balance Sheet							Income Statement
ASSETS		=	LIABILITIES		+ STOCKHOLDERS' EQUITY	+	REVENUES − EXPENSES
Cash	9,366		Bonds Payable	10,000			
			Discount on Bonds Payable	(634)			

The Discount on Bonds Payable account is shown as a contra liability on the balance sheet in conjunction with the Bonds Payable account and is a deduction from that account. If Discount Firm prepared a balance sheet immediately after the bond issuance, the following would appear in the Long-Term Liabilities category of the balance sheet:

Long-term liabilities:	
Bonds payable	$10,000
Less: Discount on bonds payable	634
	$ 9,366

The Discount Firm example has illustrated a situation in which the market rate of a bond issue is higher than the face rate. Now we will examine the opposite situation, when the face rate exceeds the market rate. Again, we are interested in calculating the issue price of the bonds.

Issuing at a Premium Suppose that on January 1, 2008, Premium Firm wants to issue the same bonds as in the previous example: $10,000 face value bonds with an 8% face rate of interest and with interest paid annually each year for four years. Assume, however, that the market rate of interest is 6% for similar bonds. The issue price is calculated as the present value of the annuity of interest payments plus the present value of the principal at the market rate of interest. The calculations are as follows:

$800 × 3.465 (factor from Table 9-4 for 4 periods, 6%)	$ 2,772
$10,000 × 0.792 (factor from Table 9-2 for 4 periods, 6%)	7,920
Issue price	$10,692

We have calculated that the bonds would be issued for $10,692. Because the bonds would be issued at an amount that is higher than the face value amount, they would be issued at a premium. The amount of the premium is calculated as follows:

Premium = $10,692 − $10,000
= $692

The premium is recorded at the time of bond issuance in the following entry:

Jan. 1	Cash	10,692	
	Bonds Payable		10,000
	Premium on Bonds Payable		692
	To record the issuance of bonds payable.		

Balance Sheet							Income Statement
ASSETS		=	LIABILITIES		+ STOCKHOLDERS' EQUITY	+	REVENUES − EXPENSES
Cash	10,692		Bonds Payable	10,000			
			Premium on Bonds Payable	692			

Study Tip

When interest rates increase, present values decrease. This is called an inverse relationship.

The account Premium on Bonds Payable is an addition to the Bonds Payable account. If Premium Firm presented a balance sheet immediately after the bond issuance, the Long-Term Liabilities category of the balance sheet would appear as follows:

Long-term liabilities:	
Bonds payable	$10,000
Plus: Premium on bonds payable	692
	$10,692

You should learn two important points from the Discount Firm and Premium Firm examples:

- **You should be able to determine whether a bond will sell at a premium or a discount by the relationship that exists between the face rate and the market rate of interest.** *Premium* and *discount* do not mean "good" and "bad," respectively. Premium or discount arises solely because of the difference that exists between the face rate and the market rate of interest for a bond issue. The same relationship always exists, so the following statements hold true:

  If Market Rate = Face Rate, THEN bonds are issued at face value amount.
  If Market Rate > Face Rate, THEN bonds are issued at a discount.
  If Market Rate < Face Rate, THEN bonds are issued at a premium.

- **The relationship between interest rates and bond prices is always inverse.** To understand the term *inverse relationship,* refer to the Discount Firm and Premium Firm examples. The bonds of the two firms are identical in all respects except for the market rate of interest. When the market rate was 10%, the bond issue price was $9,366 (the Discount Firm example). When the market rate was 6%, the bond issue price increased to $10,692 (the Premium Firm example). The examples illustrate that as interest rates decrease, prices on the bond markets increase and that as interest rates increase, bond prices decrease.

Many investors in the stock market perceive that they are taking a great deal of risk with their capital. In truth, bond investors are taking substantial risks too. The most obvious risk is that the company will fail and not be able to pay its debts. But another risk is that interest rates on comparable investments will rise. Interest rate risk can have a devastating impact on the current market value of bonds. One way to minimize interest rate risk is to hold the bond to maturity, at which point the company must pay the face amount.

POD REVIEW 10.4

LO4 ***Show that you understand the effect on the balance sheet of the issuance of bonds.***

- Bonds are recorded on the balance sheet at an amount that takes into account the premium or discount associated with bonds on the date they are issued.
  - Bond premiums represent amounts paid in excess of par, and bond discounts represent amounts paid below par.

QUESTIONS

1. *The excess of the issue price over the face value of the bond is referred to as*

   a. a discount.
   b. a premium.
   c. accrued interest.
   d. prepaid interest.

2. *If the market rate of the bond at the time of issuance is greater than the face rate,*

   a. the bonds will be issued at a premium.
   b. the bonds will be issued at a discount.
   c. a gain will occur.
   d. a loss will occur.

BOND AMORTIZATION

LO5 Find the amortization of premium or discount using the effective interest method.

Purpose of Amortization The amount of interest expense that should be reflected on a firm's income statement for bonds payable is the true, or effective, interest. The effective interest should reflect the face rate of interest as well as interest that results from issuing the bond at a premium or discount. To reflect that interest component, the amount initially recorded in the Premium on Bonds Payable or the Discount on Bonds Payable account must be amortized, or spread over the life of the bond.

Amortization refers to the process of transferring an amount from the discount or premium account to interest expense each time period to adjust interest expense. One commonly used method of amortization is the effective interest method. This section will illustrate how to amortize a discount amount and then how to amortize a premium amount.

To illustrate amortization of a discount, we need to return to the Discount Firm example introduced earlier. We have seen that the issue price of the bond could be calculated as $9,366, resulting in a contra-liability balance of $634 in the Discount on Bonds Payable account. (See the accounting transaction on page 487). But what does the initial balance of the Discount account really represent? The discount should be thought of as additional interest that Discount Firm must pay over and above the 8% face rate. Remember that Discount received only $9,366 but must repay the full principal of $10,000 at the bond due date. For that reason, the $634 discount is an additional interest cost that must be reflected as interest expense. It is reflected as interest expense by the process of amortization. In other words, interest expense is made up of two components: cash interest and amortization. We will now consider how to amortize premium or discount.

Effective Interest Method: Impact on Expense The **effective interest method of amortization** amortizes discount or premium in a manner that produces a constant effective interest rate from period to period. The dollar amount of interest expense will vary from period to period, but the rate of interest will be constant. This interest rate is referred to as the *effective interest rate* and is equal to the market rate of interest at the time the bonds are issued.

Effective interest method of amortization
The process of transferring a portion of the premium or discount to interest expense; this method results in a constant effective interest rate.
Alternate term: *Interest method.*

Carrying value
The face value of a bond plus the amount of unamortized premium or minus the amount of unamortized discount.
Alternate term: *Book value.*

To illustrate this point, we introduce two new terms. The **carrying value** of bonds is represented by the following:

Carrying Value = Face Value − Unamortized Discount

For example, the carrying value of the bonds for the Discount Firm example as of the date of issuance of January 1, 2008, could be calculated as follows:

$10,000 − $634 = $9,366

In those situations in which there is a premium instead of a discount, carrying value is represented by the following:

Carrying Value = Face Value + Unamortized Premium

For example, the carrying value of the bonds for the Premium Firm example as of the date of issuance of January 1, 2008, could be calculated as follows:

$10,000 + $692 = $10,692

The second term was suggested earlier. The *effective rate of interest* is represented by the following:

Effective Rate = Annual Interest Expense/Carrying Value

Effective Interest Method: An Example The amortization table in Exhibit 10-4 illustrates effective interest amortization of the bond discount for the Discount Firm example.

EXHIBIT 10-4 Discount Amortization: Effective Interest Method of Amortization

Date	Column 1 Cash Interest	Column 2 Interest Expense	Column 3 Discount Amortized	Column 4 Carrying Value
	8%	10%	Col. 2 − Col. 1	
1/1/2008	—	—	—	$ 9,366
12/31/2008	$800	$937	$137	9,503
12/31/2009	800	950	150	9,653
12/31/2010	800	965	165	9,818
12/31/2011	800	982	182	10,000

As illustrated in Exhibit 10-4, the effective interest method of amortization is based on several important concepts. The relationships can be stated in equation form as follows:

Cash Interest (in Column 1) = Bond Face Value × Face Rate
Interest Expense (in Column 2) = Carrying Value × Effective Rate
Discount Amortized (in Column 3) = Interest Expense − Cash Interest

The first column of the exhibit indicates that the cash interest to be paid is $800 ($10,000 × 8%). The second column indicates the annual interest expense at the effective rate of interest (market rate at the time of issuance). This is a constant rate of interest (10% in the example) and is calculated by multiplying the carrying value as of the beginning of the period by the market rate of interest. In 2008, the interest expense is $937 ($9,366 × 10%). Note that the amount of interest expense changes each year because the carrying value changes as discount is amortized. The amount of discount amortized each year in Column 3 is the difference between the cash interest in Column 1 and the interest expense in Column 2. Again, note that the amount of discount amortized changes in each of the four years. Finally, the carrying value in Column 4 is the previous year's carrying value plus the discount amortized in Column 3. When bonds are issued at a discount, the carrying value starts at an amount less than face value and increases each period until it reaches the face value amount.

Exhibit 10-4 is the basis for determining the effect of amortization on the firm's financial statements. The firm would record an entry as follows:

Dec. 31	Interest Expense	937	
	Cash		800
	Discount on Bonds Payable		137
	To record annual interest payment and to amortize annual portion of discount on bonds payable.		

Balance Sheet					Income Statement
ASSETS	=	**LIABILITIES**	+	**STOCKHOLDERS' EQUITY** +	**REVENUES − EXPENSES**
Cash (800)		Discount on Bonds Payable 137			Interest Expense (937)

The balance of the Discount on Bonds Payable account as of December 31, 2008, would be calculated as follows:

Beginning balance, January 1, 2008	$634
Less: Amount amortized	137
Ending balance, December 31, 2008	$497

The December 31, 2008, balance represents the amount *unamortized*, or the amount that will be amortized in future time periods. On the balance sheet presented as of December 31, 2008, the unamortized portion of the discount appears as the balance of the Discount on Bonds Payable account as follows:

Long-term liabilities	
Bonds payable	$10,000
Less: Discount on bonds payable	497
	$ 9,503

The process of amortization would continue for four years, until the balance of the Discount on Bonds Payable account has been reduced to zero. By the end of 2011, all of the balance of the Discount on Bonds Payable account will have been transferred to the Interest Expense account and represents an increase in interest expense each period.

The amortization of a premium has an impact opposite that of the amortization of a discount. We will use our Premium Firm example to illustrate. Recall that on January 1, 2008, Premium Firm issued $10,000 face value bonds with a face rate of interest of 8%. At the time the bonds were issued, the market rate was 6%, resulting in an issue price of $10,692 and a credit balance in the Premium on Bonds Payable account of $692.

The amortization table in Exhibit 10-5 illustrates effective interest amortization of the bond premium for Premium Firm. As the exhibit illustrates, effective interest amortization of a premium is based on the same concepts as amortization of a discount. The following relationships still hold true:

Cash Interest (in Column 1) = Bond Face Value × Face Rate
Interest Expense (in Column 2) = Carrying Value × Effective Rate

The first column of the exhibit indicates that the cash interest to be paid is $800 ($10,000 × 8%). The second column indicates the annual interest expense at the effective rate. In 2008, the interest expense is $642 ($10,692 × 6%). Note, however, two differences between Exhibit 10-4 and Exhibit 10-5. In the amortization of a premium, the cash interest in Column 1 exceeds the interest expense in Column 2. Therefore, the premium amortized is defined as follows:

Premium Amortized (in Column 3) = Cash Interest − Interest Expense

Also note that the carrying value in Column 4 starts at an amount higher than the face value of $10,000 ($10,692) and is amortized downward until it reaches face value. Therefore, the carrying value at the end of each year is the carrying value at the beginning of the period minus the premium amortized for that year. For example, the carrying value in Exhibit 10-5 at the end of 2008 ($10,534) was calculated by subtracting the premium amortized for 2008 ($158 in Column 3) from the carrying value at the beginning of 2008 ($10,692).

Study Tip

Amortization of a discount increases interest expense. Amortization of a premium reduces interest expense.

EXHIBIT 10-5 Premium Amortization: Effective Interest Method of Amortization

Date	Column 1 Cash Interest	Column 2 Interest Expense	Column 3 Premium Amortized	Column 4 Carrying Value
	8%	6%	Col. 1 − Col. 2	
1/1/2008	—	—	—	$10,692
12/31/2008	$800	$642	$158	10,534
12/31/2009	800	632	168	10,366
12/31/2010	800	622	178	10,188
12/31/2011	800	612	188	10,000

Exhibit 10-5 is the basis for determining the effect of amortization of a premium on the firm's financial statements. The firm should record an entry as follows:

Dec. 31	Interest Expense	642	
	Premium on Bonds Payable	158	
	Cash		800
	To record annual interest payment and to amortize annual portion of premium on bonds payable.		

Balance Sheet								Income Statement	
ASSETS		=	LIABILITIES		+	STOCKHOLDERS' EQUITY	+	REVENUES − EXPENSES	
Cash	(800)		Premium on Bonds Payable	(158)				Interest Expense	(642)

The balance of the Premium on Bonds Payable account as of December 31, 2008, would be calculated as follows:

Beginning balance, January 1, 2007	$692
Less: Amount amortized	158
Ending balance, December 31, 2007	$534

The December 31, 2008, balance represents the amount *unamortized*, or the amount that will be amortized in future time periods. On the balance sheet presented as of December 31, 2008, the unamortized portion of the premium appears as the balance of the Premium on Bonds Payable account as follows:

Long-term liabilities:	
Bonds payable	$10,000
Plus: Premium on bonds payable	534
	$10,534

The process of amortization would continue for four years, until the balance of the Premium on Bonds Payable account has been reduced to zero. By the end of 2011, all of the balance of the Premium on Bonds Payable account will have been transferred to the Interest Expense account and represents a reduction of interest expense each period.

POD REVIEW 10.5

LO5 *Find the amortization of premium or discount using the effective interest method.*

- The premium or discount on bonds must be amortized over the life of the bond to accurately reflect the interest expense.
- The effective interest method amortizes discounts or premiums in a way that produces a constant interest rate from one period to the next.

QUESTIONS

1. *When a bond is issued at a premium, the interest expense each year*
   a. is greater than the cash payment for interest.
   b. is less than the cash payment for interest.
   c. equals the cash payment for interest.
   d. cannot be determined without details of the bond issue.

2. *When a bond is issued at a discount, the interest expense each year*
   a. is greater than the cash payment for interest.
   b. is less than the cash payment for interest.
   c. equals the cash payment for interest.
   d. cannot be determined without details of the bond issue.

REDEMPTION OF BONDS

LO6 Find the gain or loss on retirement of bonds.

Redemption at Maturity The term *redemption* refers to retirement of bonds by repayment of the principal. When bonds are retired on their due date, the accounting entry is not difficult. Refer again to the Discount Firm example. If Discount Firm retires its bonds on the due date of December 31, 2011, it must repay the principal of $10,000 and Cash is reduced by $10,000. Notice that no gain or loss is incurred because the carrying value of the bond at that point is $10,000.

Retired Early at a Gain A firm may want to retire bonds before their due date for several reasons. A firm may simply have excess cash and determine that the best use of those funds is to repay outstanding bond obligations. Bonds also may be retired early because of changing interest rate conditions. If interest rates in the economy decline, firms may find it advantageous to retire bonds that have been issued at higher rates. Of course, what is advantageous to the issuer is not necessarily so for the investor. Early retirement of callable bonds is always a possibility that must be anticipated. Large institutional investors expect such a development and merely reinvest the money elsewhere. Many individual investors are more seriously inconvenienced when a bond issue is called.

Bond terms generally specify that if bonds are retired before their due date, they are not retired at the face value amount, but at a call price or redemption price indicated on the bond certificate. Also, the amount of unamortized premium or discount on the bonds must be considered when bonds are retired early. The retirement results in a **gain or loss on redemption** that must be calculated as follows:

Gain or loss on redemption The difference between the carrying value and the redemption price at the time bonds are redeemed.

Gain = Carrying Value − Redemption Price
Loss = Redemption Price − Carrying Value

In other words, the issuing firm must calculate the carrying value of the bonds at the time of redemption and compare it with the total redemption price. If the carrying value is higher than the redemption price, the issuing firm must record a gain. If the carrying value is lower than the redemption price, the issuing firm must record a loss.

We will use the Premium Firm example to illustrate the calculation of gain or loss. Assume that on December 31, 2008, Premium Firm wants to retire its bonds due in 2011. Assume, as in the previous section, that the bonds were issued at a premium of $692 at the beginning of 2008. Premium Firm has used the effective interest method of amortization and has recorded the interest and amortization entries for the year. (See page 492.) This has resulted in a balance of $534 in the Premium on Bonds Payable account as of December 31, 2008. Also assume that Premium Firm's bond certificates indicate that the bonds may be retired early at a call price of 102 (meaning 102% of face value). Thus, the redemption price is 102% of $10,000, or $10,200.

Premium Firm's retirement of bonds would result in a gain. The gain can be calculated using two steps:

1. **Calculate the carrying value of the bonds as of the date they are retired.** The carrying value of Premium Firm's bonds at that date is calculated as follows:

   Carrying Value = Face Value + Unamortized Premium
   = $10,000 + $534
   = $10,534

   Note that the carrying value calculated is the same amount indicated for December 31, 2008, in Column 4 of the effective interest amortization table of Exhibit 10-5.

2. **Calculate the gain:**

   Gain = Carrying Value − Redemption Price
   = $10,534 − ($10,000 × 1.02)
   = $10,534 − $10,200
   = $334

   When bonds are retired, the balance of the Bonds Payable account and the remaining balance of the Premium on Bonds Payable account must be eliminated from the balance sheet.

Retired Early at a Loss To illustrate retirement of bonds at a loss, assume that Premium Firm retires bonds at December 31, 2008, as in the previous section. However, assume that the call price for the bonds is 107 (or 107% of face value).

Again, the calculations can be performed in two steps:

1. **Calculate the carrying value:**

Carrying Value = Face Value + Unamortized Premium
= $10,000 + $534
= $10,534

2. **Compare the carrying value with the redemption price to calculate the amount of the loss:**

Loss = Redemption Price − Carrying Value
= ($10,000 × 1.07) − $10,534
= $10,700 − $10,534
= $166

In this case, a loss of $166 has resulted from the retirement of Premium Firm bonds. A loss means that the company paid more to retire the bonds than the amount at which the bonds were recorded on the balance sheet.

Financial Statement Presentation of Gain or Loss The accounts Gain on Bond Redemption and Loss on Bond Redemption are income statement accounts. A gain on bond redemption increases Premium Firm's income; a loss decreases its income. In most cases, a gain or loss should not be considered "unusual" or "infrequent" and, therefore, should not be placed in the section of the income statement where extraordinary items are presented. While gains and losses should be treated as part of the company's operating income, some statement users may consider them as "one-time" events and choose to exclude them when predicting a company's future income. For that reason, it would be very helpful if companies would present their gains and losses separately on the income statement so that readers could determine whether such amounts will affect future periods.

POD REVIEW 10.6

LO6 *Find the gain or loss on retirement of bonds.*

- Bonds are retired for various reasons; and if they are retired before their due date, the amount is different from the face value. Unamortized bond premiums or discounts may result in a gain or loss.
  - When the redemption price is less than the carrying value, a gain results. When the redemption price is greater than the carrying value, a loss results.

QUESTIONS

1. *When bonds are retired or repaid at their due date, there generally will be*
   a. a gain.
   b. a loss.
   c. accrued interest.
   d. no gain or loss.

2. *What does a gain on redemption of bonds indicate?*
   a. The carrying value of the bond was larger than the redemption price.
   b. The carrying value of the bond was less than the redemption price.
   c. The carrying value of the bond was equal to the redemption price.
   d. The bondholders were not paid the full face value at time of redemption.

Liability for Leases

LO7 Determine whether a lease agreement must be reported as a liability on the balance sheet.

Long-term bonds and notes payable are important sources of financing for many large corporations and are quite prominent in the long-term liability category of the balance sheet for many firms. But other important elements of that category of the balance sheet also represent long-term obligations. This section introduces you to leases because they are a major source of financing for many companies. Another liability, deferred taxes, is introduced in the appendix at the end of this chapter. In some cases, these liabilities are required to be reported on the financial statements and are important components of the Long-Term Liabilities section of the balance sheet. In other cases, the items are not required to be presented in the financial statements and can be discerned only by a careful reading of the notes to the financial statements.

LEASES

A *lease,* a contractual arrangement between two parties, allows one party, the *lessee,* the right to use an asset in exchange for making payments to its owner, the *lessor.* A common example of a lease arrangement is the rental of an apartment. The tenant is the lessee, and the landlord is the lessor.

Lease agreements are a form of financing. In some cases, it is more advantageous to lease an asset than to borrow money to purchase it. The lessee can conserve cash because a lease does not require a large initial cash outlay. A wide variety of lease arrangements exists, ranging from simple agreements to complex ones that span a long time period. Lease arrangements are popular because of their flexibility. The terms of a lease can be structured in many ways to meet the needs of the lessee and lessor. This results in difficult accounting questions:

1. **Should the right to use property be reported as an asset by the lessee?**
2. **Should the obligation to make payments be reported as a liability by the lessee?**
3. **Should all leases be accounted for in the same manner regardless of the terms of the lease agreement?**

The answers are that some leases should be reported as an asset and a liability by the lessee and some should not. The accountant must examine the terms of the lease agreement and compare those terms with an established set of criteria.

Lease Criteria From the viewpoint of the lessee, there are two types of lease agreements: operating and capital. In an **operating lease**, the lessee acquires the right to use an asset for a limited period of time. The lessee is *not* required to record the right to use the property as an asset or to record the obligation for payments as a liability. Therefore, the lessee is able to attain a form of *off-balance-sheet financing*. That is, the lessee has attained the right to use property but has not recorded that right, or the accompanying obligation, on the balance sheet. By escaping the balance sheet, the lease does not add to debt or impair the debt-to-equity ratio that investors usually calculate. Management has a responsibility to make sure that such off-balance-sheet financing is not, in fact, a long-term obligation. The company's auditors are supposed to analyze the terms of the lease carefully to make sure that management has exercised its responsibility.

Operating lease
A lease that does not meet any of the four criteria and is not recorded as an asset by the lessee.

The second type of lease agreement is a **capital lease**. In this type of lease, the lessee has acquired sufficient rights of ownership and control of the property to be considered its owner. The lease is called a *capital lease* because it is capitalized (recorded) on the balance sheet by the lessee.

Capital lease
A lease that is recorded as an asset by the lessee.

A lease should be considered a capital lease by the lessee when one or more of the following criteria are met:[1]

1. **The lease transfers ownership of the property to the lessee at the end of the lease term.**
2. **The lease contains a bargain-purchase option to purchase the asset at an amount lower than its fair market value.**

1 *Statement of Financial Accounting Standards No. 13,* "Accounting for Leases" (Stamford, Conn.: FASB, 1976).

3. **The lease term is 75% or more of the property's economic life.**
4. **The present value of the minimum lease payments is 90% or more of the fair market value of the property at the inception of the lease.**

If none of the criteria are met, the lease agreement is accounted for as an operating lease. This is an area in which it is important for the accountant to exercise professional judgment. In some cases, firms may take elaborate measures to evade or manipulate the criteria that would require lease capitalization. The accountant should determine what is full and fair disclosure based on an unbiased evaluation of the substance of the transaction.

Operating Leases You have already accounted for operating leases in previous chapters when recording rent expense and prepaid rent. A rental agreement for a limited time period is also a lease agreement.

Suppose, for example, that Lessee Firm wants to lease a car for a new salesperson. A lease agreement is signed with Lessor Dealer on January 1, 2008, to lease a car for the year for $4,000, payable on December 31, 2008. Typically, a car lease does not transfer title at the end of the term, does not include a bargain-purchase price, and does not last for more than 75% of the car's life. In addition, the present value of the lease payments is not 90% of the car's value. Because the lease does not meet any of the specified criteria, it should be presented as an operating lease. Lessee Firm would simply record lease expense (or rent expense) of $4,000 for the year.

Although operating leases are not recorded on the balance sheet by the lessee, they are mentioned in financial statement notes. The FASB requires note disclosure of the amount of future lease obligations for leases that are considered operating leases. Exhibit 10-6 provides a portion of the note from **Tommy Hilfiger Corporation**'s 2006 annual report. The note reveals that Tommy Hilfiger has used operating leases as an important source of financing and has significant off-balance-sheet commitments in future periods as a result. An investor might want to add this off-balance-sheet item to the debt on the balance sheet to get a conservative view of the company's obligations.

EXHIBIT 10-6 Tommy Hilfiger Corporation's 2006 Note Disclosure of Leases

Operating leases can be used as an important source of financing.

Commitments and Contingencies

Leases (in millions)

The Company leases office, warehouse and showroom space, retail stores and office equipment under operating leases, which expire not later than 2022. The Company records fixed escalations in rental expense under its operating leases on a straight-line basis over the initial lease term, including rent holidays. Minimum annual rentals under non-cancelable operating leases, excluding operating cost escalations and contingent rental amounts based upon retail sales, are payable as follows:

Fiscal Year Ended March 31,	Lease Commitments	Sub Lease Income	Net Commitments
2006	$ 61,106	$(1,384)	$ 59,722
2007	57,814	(1,797)	56,017
2008	48,014	(1,121)	46,893
2009	44,209	(497)	43,712
2010	39,084	(497)	38,587
Thereafter	201,808	(2,525)	199,283
Total	$452,035	$(7,821)	$444,214

Rent expense, including operating cost escalations and contingent rental amounts based upon retail sales, was $52,833, $44,486 and $42,878 for the years ended March 31, 2005, 2004 and 2003, respectively.

Capital Leases Capital leases are presented as assets and liabilities by the lessee because they meet one or more of the lease criteria. Suppose that Lessee Firm in the previous example wanted to lease a car for a longer period of time. Assume that on January 1, 2008, Lessee signs a lease agreement with Lessor Dealer to lease a car. The terms of the agreement specify that Lessee will make annual lease payments of $4,000 per year for five years, payable each December 31. Also assume that the lease specifies that at the end of the lease agreement, the title to the car is transferred to Lessee Firm. Lessee must decide how to account for the lease agreement.

The contractual arrangement between Lessee Firm and Lessor Dealer is called a lease agreement, but clearly the agreement is much different from a year-to-year lease arrangement. Essentially, Lessee Firm has acquired the right to use the asset for its entire life and does not need to return it to Lessor Dealer. You may call this agreement a lease, but it actually represents a purchase of the asset by Lessee with payments made over time.

Study Tip

It is called a *capital lease* because the lease is *capitalized*, or put on the books of the lessee as an asset.

The lease should be treated as a capital lease by Lessee because it meets at least one of the four criteria. (It meets the first criteria concerning transfer of title.) A capital lease must be recorded at its present value by Lessee as an asset and as an obligation. As of January 1, 2008, we must calculate the present value of the annual payments. If we assume an interest rate of 8%, the present value of the payments is $15,972 ($4,000 × an annuity factor of 3.993 from Table 9-4 on page 451).

The first entry is made on the basis of the present value as follows:

Jan. 1	Leased Asset	15,972	
	Lease Obligation		15,972
	To record a capital lease agreement.		

Balance Sheet								Income Statement	
ASSETS		=	LIABILITIES		+	STOCKHOLDERS' EQUITY	+	REVENUES − EXPENSES	
Leased Asset	15,972		Lease Obligation	15,972					

The Leased Asset account is a long-term asset similar to plant and equipment and represents the fact that Lessee has acquired the right to use and retain the asset. Because the leased asset represents depreciable property, depreciation must be reported for each of the five years of asset use as follows. On December 31, 2008, Lessee records depreciation of $3,194 ($15,972/5 years), assuming that the straight-line method is adopted.

Dec. 31	Depreciation Expense	3,194	
	Accumulated Depreciation—Leased Assets		3,194
	To record depreciation of leased assets.		

Balance Sheet								Income Statement	
ASSETS		=	LIABILITIES		+	STOCKHOLDERS' EQUITY	+	REVENUES − EXPENSES	
Accumulated Depreciation—Leased Assets	(3,194)							Depreciation Expense	(3,194)

Some firms refer to depreciation of leased assets as *amortization*.

On December 31, Lessee Firm also must make a payment of $4,000 to Lessor Dealer. A portion of each payment represents interest on the obligation (loan), and the remainder represents a reduction of the principal amount. Each payment must be separated into its principal and interest components. Generally, the effective interest method is used for that purpose. An effective interest table can be established using the same concepts used to amortize a premium or discount on bonds payable.

Exhibit 10-7 illustrates the effective interest method applied to the Lessee Firm example. Note that the table begins with an obligation amount equal to the present value of

EXHIBIT 10-7 Lease Amortization: Effective Interest Method of Amortization

Date	Column 1 Lease Payment	Column 2 Interest Expense	Column 3 Reduction of Obligation	Column 4 Lease Obligation
		8%	Col. 1 − Col. 2	
1/1/2008	—	—	—	$15,972
12/31/2008	$4,000	$1,278	$2,722	13,250
12/31/2009	4,000	1,060	2,940	10,310
12/31/2010	4,000	825	3,175	7,135
12/31/2011	4,000	571	3,429	3,706
12/31/2012	4,000	294	3,706	–0–

the payments of $15,972. Each payment is separated into principal and interest amounts so that the amount of the loan obligation at the end of the lease agreement equals zero. The amortization table is the basis for the amounts that are reflected on the financial statement. Exhibit 10-7 indicates that the $4,000 payment in 2008 should be considered as interest of $1,278 (8% of $15,972) and reduction of principal of $2,722. On December 31, 2008, Lessee Firm records the following entry for the annual payment:

Dec. 31	Interest Expense	1,278	
	Lease Obligation	2,722	
	Cash		4,000
	To record annual lease payment.		

Balance Sheet							Income Statement	
ASSETS		=	LIABILITIES		+ STOCKHOLDERS' EQUITY	+	REVENUES − EXPENSES	
Cash	(4,000)		Lease Obligation	(2,722)			Interest Expense	(1,278)

Therefore, for a capital lease, Lessee Firm must record both an asset and a liability. The asset is reduced by the process of depreciation. The liability is reduced by reductions of principal using the effective interest method. According to Exhibit 10-7, the total lease obligation as of December 31, 2008, is $13,250. This amount must be separated into current and long-term categories. The portion of the liability that will be paid within one year of the balance sheet should be considered a current liability. Reference to Exhibit 10-7 indicates that the liability will be reduced by $2,940 in 2009, and that amount should be considered a current liability. The remaining amount of the liability, $10,310 ($13,250 − $2,940), should be considered long-term. On the balance sheet as of December 31, 2008, Lessee Firm reports the following balances related to the lease obligation:

Assets:		
Leased assets	$15,972	
Less: Accumulated depreciation	3,194	
		$12,778
Current liabilities:		
Lease obligation		$ 2,940
Long-term liabilities:		
Lease obligation		$10,310

Notice that the depreciated asset does not equal the present value of the lease obligation. This is not unusual. For example, an automobile may be completely depreciated but still have payments due on it.

The criteria used to determine whether a lease is an operating or a capital lease have provided a standard accounting treatment for all leases. The accounting for leases in foreign countries generally follows guidelines similar to those used in the United States. The criteria used in foreign countries to determine whether a lease is a capital lease are usually less detailed and less specific, however. As a result, capitalization of leases occurs less frequently in foreign countries than in the United States because of the increased use of judgment necessary in applying the accounting rules.

POD REVIEW 10.7

LO7 *Determine whether a lease agreement must be reported as a liability on the balance sheet.*

- Leases can be classified as two types: operating leases and capital leases. Capital leases imply more rights of ownership. The accounting for these two types of leases is as follows:
  - Under an operating lease, the lessee does not record the right to use the leased asset or any related obligation to make lease payments on the balance sheet.
  - Under a capital lease, the lessee records the right to use the property and the lease payments that are obligated to be paid on the balance sheet.

QUESTIONS

1. *When a lease is classified as an operating lease,*
   a. the lease liability should be presented on the balance sheet of the lessee.
   b. the lease liability should be presented on the balance sheet of the lessor.
   c. title to the leased asset passes to the lessee at the end of the lease.
   d. the leased liability should not be presented on the balance sheet of the lessor.

2. *When a lease is classified as a capital lease,*
   a. the lease liability should be presented on the balance sheet of the lessee.
   b. the lease liability should be presented on the balance sheet of the lessor.
   c. title to the leased asset may not pass to the lessee at the end of the lease.
   d. the leased asset liability should be presented on the balance sheet of the lessor.

Analyzing Debt to Assess a Firm's Ability to Pay Its Liabilities

LO8 Explain how investors use ratios to evaluate long-term liabilities.

Long-term liabilities are a component of the "capital structure" of the company and are included in the calculation of the debt-to-equity ratio:

$$\text{Debt-to-Equity Ratio} = \frac{\text{Total Liabilities}}{\text{Total Stockholders' Equity}}$$

Most investors would prefer to see equity rather than debt on the balance sheet. Debt, and its interest charges, make up a fixed obligation that must be repaid in a finite period of time. In contrast, equity never has to be repaid and the dividends that are declared on it are optional. Stock investors view debt as a claim against the company that must be satisfied before they get a return on their money.

Other ratios used to measure the degree of debt obligation include the times interest earned ratio and the debt service coverage ratio:

$$\text{Times Interest Earned Ratio} = \frac{\text{Income Before Interest and Tax}}{\text{Interest Expense}}$$

$$\text{Debt Service Coverage Ratio} = \frac{\text{Cash Flow from Operations Before Interest and Tax}}{\text{Interest and Principal Payments}}$$

Lenders want to be sure that borrowers can pay the interest and repay the principal on a loan. Both of the preceding ratios reflect the degree to which a company can make its debt payment out of current cash flow.

For more on these ratios for **PepsiCo, Inc.**, and how they are used, see the following Ratio Decision Model.

USING THE RATIO DECISION MODEL: ANALYZING THE DEBT-TO-EQUITY AND TIMES INTEREST EARNED RATIOS

Use the following Ratio Decision Model to evaluate the debt for PepsiCo or any other public company.

1. Formulate the Question

Long-term debt is an important element of the financing of a company. Most companies use a combination of debt and equity (stock) to finance their operations, achieve a profit, and provide a return to their investors. Investors and creditors must carefully review the financial statements to determine whether a company will be able to meet its obligations. The use of debt is a good management strategy, but sometimes a company may have too much debt. The important question to ask is:

What is the amount of debt in relation to the total equity of the company?

A second important question to ask is:

Will the company be able to meet its obligations related to the debt? That is, when an interest payment comes due, will the company have the ability to make the payment?

2. Gather the Information Needed

For those questions to be addressed, information from the balance sheet and the income statement needs to be collected and analyzed.

- Total debt and total equity: From the balance sheet
- Income before interest and tax: From the income statement (Go online to get this statement from PepsiCo.)
- Interest expense: From the income statement

3. Calculate the Ratio

$$\text{Debt-to-Equity Ratio} = \frac{\text{Total Liabilities}}{\text{Total Stockholders' Equity}}$$

PepsiCo, Inc. and Subsidiaries
Partial Consolidated Balance Sheet
December 30, 2006 and December 31, 2005

(In millions except per share amounts)	2006	2005
LIABILITIES AND SHAREHOLDERS' EQUITY		
Total Liabilities	14,562	17,476
...		
Total Common Shareholders' Equity	15,447	14,320

$$\text{Debt-to-Equity Ratio} = \frac{\$14{,}562}{\$15{,}447} = 0.94$$

$$\text{Times Interest Earned Ratio} = \frac{\text{Income Before Interest and Tax}}{\text{Interest Expense}}$$

Partial Consolidated Statement of Income
PepsiCo, Inc. and Subsidiaries
Fiscal years ended December 30, 2006, and December 31, 2005,

(In millions except per share amounts)	2006	2005
Net Revenue	$35,137	$32,562
Cost of sales	15,762	14,176
Selling, general and administrative expenses	12,774	12,314
Amortization of intangible assets	162	150
Operating Profit	6,439	5,922
Bottling equity income	616	557
Interest expense	(239)	(256)
Interest income	173	159
Income from Continuing Operations Before Income Taxes	6,989	6,382

Since the ratio concerns income *before* interest and income tax, you must add the amount of interest, $239, to $6,989 to get $7,228.

$$\textbf{Times Interest Earned Ratio} = \frac{\$7{,}228}{\$239} = 30.24$$

4. Compare the Ratio with Others

PepsiCo's debt-to-equity ratio and times interest earned ratio should be compared to those of prior years and to those of companies in the same industry.

	PepsiCo		Coca-Cola	
	2006	2005	2006	2005
Debt-to-equity ratio	0.94	1.22	0.77	0.80
Times interest earned ratio	30.42	25.92	30.90	28.88

5. Interpret the Results

PepsiCo and Coca-Cola are strong companies with a very safe balance of debt to equity. PepsiCo has slightly more debt than stockholders' equity in both 2006 and 2005, while Coca-Cola has slightly less debt than stockholders' equity. Both companies have a small amount of interest obligations compared to their income available to meet those obligations. PepsiCo has 30.42 times more income than its interest expense for 2006, while Coca-Cola has 30.90. These ratios indicate that the creditors for both companies are confident that each company will be able to meet its interest obligations on its long-term debt.

POD REVIEW 10.8

LO8 *Explain how investors use ratios to evaluate long-term liabilities.*

- Investors use the debt-to-equity ratio and the times interest earned ratio as measures of a company's abilities to meet its long-term obligations.

QUESTIONS

1. *When an investor views the debt-to-equity ratio of a company,*
   a. it is a measure of the company's liquidity.
   b. a high value is generally viewed favorably.
   c. a low value is generally viewed favorably.
   d. it is a measure of the company's ability to generate cash.

2. *When an investor views the times interest earned ratio of a company,*
   a. it is a measure of the company's liquidity.
   b. a high value is generally viewed favorably.
   c. a low value is generally viewed favorably.
   d. it is a measure of the company's ability to generate cash.

How Long-Term Liabilities Affect the Statement of Cash Flows

LO9 Explain the effects that transactions involving long-term liabilities have on the statement of cash flows.

Exhibit 10-8 indicates the impact that long-term liabilities have on a company's cash flow and their placement on the cash flow statement.

Most long-term liabilities are related to a firm's financing activities. Therefore, the change in the balance of each long-term liability account should be reflected in the Financing Activities category of the statement of cash flows. The decrease in a long-term liability account indicates that cash has been used to pay the liability. Therefore, in the statement of cash flows, a decrease in a long-term liability account should appear as a subtraction, or reduction. The increase in a long-term liability account indicates that the firm has obtained additional cash via a long-term obligation. Therefore, an increase in a long-term liability account should appear in the statement of cash flows as an addition.

The statement of cash flows of Coca-Cola Company is presented in Exhibit 10-9. Note that the Financing Activities category contains two items related to long-term liabilities. In 2006, long-term debt was issued for $617 million and is an addition to cash. This indicates that Coca-Cola increased its cash position by borrowings. Second, the payment of debt is listed as a deduction of $2,021 million. This indicates that Coca-Cola paid long-term liabilities, resulting in a reduction of cash.

Although most long-term liabilities are reflected in the Financing Activities category of the statement of cash flows, there are exceptions. The most notable exception involves the Deferred Tax account (discussed in the appendix at the end of this chapter). The change in this account is reflected in the Operating Activities category of the statement of cash flows. This presentation is necessary because the Deferred Tax account is related to an operating item, income tax expense. For example, in Exhibit 10-9, **Coca-Cola** listed a deduction of $35 million in the Operating Activities category of the 2006 statement of cash flows. This indicates that $35 million less was recorded as expense than was paid out in cash. Therefore, the amount is a negative amount in, or an addition to, the Operating Activities category.

POD REVIEW 10.9

LO9 *Explain the effects that transactions involving long-term liabilities have on the statement of cash flows.*

- Cash flows related to long-term liabilities are generally related to a firm's financing activities.

QUESTIONS

1. *If a long-term liability account increases, how should it be presented?*
   a. as an increase in cash in the Operating Activities category
   b. as an increase in cash in the Financing category
   c. as a decrease in cash in the Financing category
   d. as an increase in cash in the Investing category

2. *If a long-term liability account decreases, how should it be presented?*
   a. as an increase in cash in the Operating Activities category
   b. as an increase in cash in the Financing category
   c. as a decrease in cash in the Financing category
   d. as an increase in cash in the Investing category

EXHIBIT 10-8 Long-Term Liabilities on the Statement of Cash Flows

Item	Statement of Cash Flows	
	Operating Activities	
	Net income	xxx
Increase in current liability →		+
Decrease in current liability →		−
	Investing Activities	
	Financing Activities	
Increase in long-term liability →		+
Decrease in long-term liability →		−

EXHIBIT 10-9 The Coca-Cola Company and Subsidiaries' 2006 Consolidated Statements of Cash Flows

CONSOLIDATED STATEMENTS OF CASH FLOWS

Year Ended December 31,	2006	2005	2004
(In millions)			
OPERATING ACTIVITIES			
Net income	$ 5,080	$ 4,872	$ 4,847
Depreciation and amortization	938	932	893
Stock-based compensation expense	324	324	345
Deferred income taxes	(35)	(88)	162
Equity income or loss, net of dividends	124	(446)	(476)
Foreign currency adjustments	52	47	(59)
Gains on issuances of stock by equity investees	—	(23)	(24)
Gains on sales of assets, including bottling interests	(303)	(9)	(20)
Other operating charges	159	85	480
Other items	233	299	437
Net change in operating assets and liabilities	(615)	430	(617)
Net cash provided by operating activities	5,957	6,423	5,968
INVESTING ACTIVITIES			
Acquisitions and investments, principally trademarks and bottling companies	(901)	(637)	(267)
Purchases of other investments	(82)	(53)	(46)
Proceeds from disposals of other investments	640	33	161
Purchases of property, plant, and equipment	(1,407)	(899)	(755)
Proceeds from disposals of property, plant, and equipment	112	88	341
Other investing activities	(62)	(28)	63
Net cash used in investing activities	(1,700)	(1,496)	(503)
FINANCING ACTIVITIES			
Issuances of debt	617	178	3,030
Payments of debt	(2,021)	(2,460)	(1,316)
Issuances of stock	148	230	193
Purchases of stock for treasury	(2,416)	(2,055)	(1,739)
Dividends	(2,911)	(2,678)	(2,429)
Net cash used in financing activities	(6,583)	(6,785)	(2,261)
EFFECT OF EXCHANGE RATE CHANGES ON CASH AND CASH EQUIVALENTS	**65**	**(148)**	**141**
CASH AND CASH EQUIVALENTS			
Net (decrease) increase during the year	(2,261)	(2,006)	3,345
Balance at beginning of year	4,701	6,707	3,362
Balance at end of year	$ 2,440	$ 4,701	$ 6,707

Changes in long-term debt generally affect the financing activities category.

Accounting Tools: Other Liabilities

APPENDIX

This appendix will discuss another item found in the long-term liabilities category of many companies: deferred taxes. The purpose here is to make you aware of its existence when you are reading financial statements.

LO10 Explain deferred taxes and calculate the deferred tax liability.

DEFERRED TAX

The financial statements of most major firms include an item titled Deferred Income Taxes or Deferred Tax. (See PepsiCo's deferred taxes in Exhibit 10-1 and Coca-Cola's in the chapter opening.) In most cases, the account appears in the Long-Term Liabilities section of the balance sheet, and the dollar amount might be large enough to catch the user's attention. In fact, deferred income taxes represent one of the most misunderstood aspects of financial statements. This section addresses some of the questions concerning deferred taxes.

Deferred tax
The account used to reconcile the difference between the amount recorded as income tax expense and the amount that is payable as income tax.

Deferred tax is an amount that reconciles the differences between the accounting done for purposes of financial reporting to stockholders ("book" purposes) and the accounting done for tax purposes. It may surprise you that U.S. firms are allowed to use accounting methods for financial reporting that differ from those used for tax calculations. The reason is that the IRS defines income and expense differently than does the FASB. As a result, companies tend to use accounting methods that minimize income for tax purposes but maximize income in the annual report to stockholders. This is not true in some foreign countries where financial accounting and tax accounting are more closely aligned. Firms in those countries do not report deferred tax because the difference between methods is not significant.

Permanent difference
A difference that affects the tax records but not the accounting records, or vice versa.

When differences between financial and tax reporting do occur, the differences can be classified into two types: permanent and temporary. **Permanent differences** occur when an item is included in the tax calculation and is never included for book purposes—or vice versa, when an item is included for book purposes but not for tax purposes.

For example, the tax laws allow taxpayers to exclude interest on certain investments, usually state and municipal bonds, from their income. These are generally called *tax-exempt bonds.* When a corporation buys tax-exempt bonds, it does not have to declare the interest as income for tax purposes. When the corporation develops its income statement for stockholders (book purposes), however, the interest is included and appears in the Interest Income account. Therefore, tax-exempt interest represents a permanent difference between tax and book calculations.

Temporary difference
A difference that affects both book and tax records but not in the same time period. ***Alternate term:*** *Timing difference.*

Temporary differences occur when an item affects both book and tax calculations but not in the same time period. A difference caused by depreciation methods is the most common type of temporary difference. In previous chapters, you learned that depreciation may be calculated using a straight-line method or an accelerated method such as the double-declining-balance method. Most firms do not use the same depreciation method for book and tax purposes, however. Generally, straight-line depreciation is used for book purposes and an accelerated method is used for tax purposes because accelerated depreciation lowers taxable income—at least in early years—and therefore reduces the tax due. The IRS refers to this accelerated method as the *Modified Accelerated Cost Recovery System (MACRS).* It is similar to other accelerated depreciation methods in that it allows the firm to take larger depreciation deductions for tax purposes in the early years of the asset and smaller deductions in the later years. Over the life of the depreciable asset, the total depreciation using straight-line is equal to that using MACRS. Therefore, this difference is an example of a temporary difference between book and tax reporting.

The Deferred Tax account is used to reconcile the differences between the accounting for book purposes and for tax purposes. It is important to distinguish between permanent and temporary differences because the FASB has ruled that not all differences should affect the Deferred Tax account. The Deferred Tax account should reflect temporary differences but not items that are permanent differences between book accounting and tax reporting.[2]

Example of Deferred Tax Assume that Startup Firm begins business on January 1, 2008. During 2008, the firm has sales of $6,000 and has no expenses other than depreciation and income tax at the rate of 40%. Startup has depreciation on only one asset. That asset was purchased on January 1, 2008, for $10,000 and has a four-year life. Startup has decided to use the straight-line depreciation method for financial reporting purposes. Startup's accountants have chosen to use MACRS for tax purposes, however, resulting in $4,000 depreciation in 2008 and a decline of $1,000 per year thereafter.

The depreciation amounts for each of the four years for Startup's asset are as follows:

Year	Tax Depreciation	Book Depreciation	Difference
2008	$ 4,000	$ 2,500	$1,500
2009	3,000	2,500	500
2010	2,000	2,500	(500)
2011	1,000	2,500	(1,500)
Totals	$10,000	$10,000	$ 0

Startup's tax calculation for 2008 is based on the accelerated depreciation of $4,000, as follows:

Sales	$6,000
Depreciation Expense	4,000
Taxable Income	$2,000
× Tax Rate	40%
Tax Payable to IRS	$ 800

For 2008, Startup owes $800 of tax to the IRS. This amount is ordinarily recorded as tax payable until the time it is remitted.

Startup also wants to develop an income statement to send to the stockholders. What amount should be shown as tax expense on the income statement? You may guess that the Tax Expense account on the income statement should reflect $800 because that is the amount to be paid to the IRS. That guess is not correct in this case, however. Remember that the tax payable amount was calculated using the depreciation method that Startup chose for tax purposes. The income statement must be calculated using the straight-line method, which Startup uses for book purposes. Therefore, Startup's income statement for 2008 appears as follows:

Sales	$6,000
Depreciation Expense	2,500
Income before Tax	$3,500
Tax Expense (40%)	1,400
Net Income	$2,100

Startup must make the following accounting entry to record the amount of tax expense and tax payable for 2008:

Dec. 31	Tax Expense	1,400	
	Tax Payable		800
	Deferred Tax		600
	To record income tax for the year 2008.		

2 *Statement of Financial Accounting Standards No. 109*, "Accounting for Income Taxes" (Stamford, Conn.: FASB, 1992).

Balance Sheet							Income Statement	
ASSETS	=	LIABILITIES		+	STOCKHOLDERS' EQUITY	+	REVENUES − EXPENSES	
		Tax Payable	800				Tax Expense	(1,400)
		Deferred Tax	600					

The Deferred Tax account is a balance sheet account. A balance in it reflects the fact that Startup has received a tax benefit by recording accelerated depreciation, in effect delaying the ultimate obligation to the IRS. To be sure, the amount of deferred tax still represents a liability of Startup. The Deferred Tax account balance of $600 represents the amount of the 2008 temporary difference of $1,500 times the tax rate of 40% ($1,500 × 40% = $600).

What can you learn from the Startup example? First, when you see a firm's income statement, the amount listed as tax expense does not represent the amount of cash paid to the government for taxes. Accrual accounting procedures require that the tax expense amount be calculated using the accounting methods chosen for book purposes.

Second, when you see a firm's balance sheet, the amount in the Deferred Tax account reflects all of the temporary differences between the accounting methods chosen for tax and book purposes. The accounting and financial communities are severely divided on whether the Deferred Tax account represents a "true" liability. For one thing, many investment analysts do not view it as a real liability because they have noticed that it continues to grow year after year. Others look at it as a bookkeeping item that is there simply to balance the books. The FASB has taken the stance that deferred tax is an amount that results in a future obligation and meets the definition of a liability. The controversy concerning deferred taxes is likely to continue for many years.

POD REVIEW 10.10

LO10 *Explain deferred taxes and calculate the deferred tax liability.*

- Differences arise between the tax treatment of revenue and expense items for financial accounting (book) and tax accounting methods. Deferred taxes are those amounts that reconcile these differences.
  - Permanent differences occur when an item is included for tax purposes but not book, or vice versa.
  - Temporary differences occur when there are differences between the time an item is recognized for tax purposes and the time it is recognized for book purposes.

QUESTIONS

1. *When a company uses the straight-line depreciation method for financial reporting purposes and an accelerated depreciation method for tax purposes, what is the result?*
   a. a deferred tax asset
   b. a deferred tax liability
   c. no deferred taxes
   d. a violation of GAAP

2. *Items that are considered permanent differences*
   a. should be reflected as deferred tax assets on the balance sheet.
   b. should be reflected as deferred tax liabilities on the balance sheet.
   c. are items that have been excluded from both tax and financial statement calculation.
   d. should not be reflected in the Deferred Tax account.

RATIO REVIEW

$$\text{Debt-to-Equity Ratio} = \frac{\text{Total Liabilities}}{\text{Total Stockholders' Equity}}$$

$$\text{Times Interest Earned Ratio} = \frac{\text{Income Before Interest and Tax}}{\text{Interest Expense}}$$

ACCOUNTS HIGHLIGHTED

Account Title	Where It Appears	In What Section	Page Number
Bonds Payable	Balance Sheet	Long-Term Liabilities	482
Premium on Bonds Payable	Balance Sheet	Long-Term Liabilities	486
Discount on Bonds Payable	Balance Sheet	Long-Term Liabilities as a contra account	486
Gain on Bond Redemption	Income Statement	Other Income/Expense	493
Loss on Bond Redemption	Income Statement	Other Income/Expense	493
Leased Asset	Balance Sheet	Property, Plant, and Equipment	497
Lease Obligation	Balance Sheet	Long-Term Liabilities	497
Deferred Income Tax	Balance Sheet	May be Asset or Liability	504

KEY TERMS QUIZ

Read each definition below and write the number of the definition in the blank beside the appropriate term. The quiz solutions appear at the end of the chapter.

______ **Long-term liability**

______ **Face value**

______ **Debenture bonds**

______ **Serial bonds**

______ **Callable bonds**

______ **Face rate of interest**

______ **Market rate of interest**

______ **Bond issue price**

______ **Premium**

______ **Discount**

______ **Effective interest method of amortization**

______ **Carrying value**

______ **Gain or loss on redemption**

______ **Operating lease**

______ **Capital lease**

______ **Deferred tax (Appendix)**

______ **Permanent difference (Appendix)**

______ **Temporary difference (Appendix)**

1. The principal amount of the bond as stated on the bond certificate.
2. Bonds that do not all have the same due date. A portion of the bonds comes due each time period.
3. The interest rate stated on the bond certificate. It is also called the *nominal* or *coupon rate.*
4. The total of the present value of the cash flows produced by a bond. It is calculated as the present value of the annuity of interest payments plus the present value of the principal.
5. An obligation that will not be satisfied within one year.
6. The excess of the issue price over the face value of bonds. It occurs when the face rate on the bonds exceeds the market rate.
7. Bonds that are backed by the general creditworthiness of the issuer and are not backed by specific collateral.
8. The excess of the face value of bonds over the issue price. It occurs when the market rate on the bonds exceeds the face rate.
9. Bonds that may be redeemed or retired before their specified due date.
10. The process of transferring a portion of premium or discount to interest expense. This method transfers an amount resulting in a constant effective interest rate.
11. The face value of a bond plus the amount of unamortized premium or minus the amount of unamortized discount.

12. The interest rate that bondholders could obtain by investing in other bonds that are similar to the issuing firm's bonds.
13. The difference between the carrying value and the redemption price at the time bonds are redeemed. This amount is presented as an income statement account.
14. A lease that does not meet any of four criteria and is not recorded by the lessee.
15. A lease that meets one or more of four criteria and is recorded as an asset by the lessee.
16. A difference between the accounting for tax purposes and the accounting for financial reporting purposes. This type of difference affects both book and tax calculations but not in the same time period.
17. The account used to reconcile the difference between the amount recorded as income tax expense and the amount that is payable as income tax.
18. A difference between the accounting for tax purposes and the accounting for financial reporting purposes. This type of difference occurs when an item affects one set of calculations but not the other set.

ALTERNATE TERMS

Bond Face Value Bond par value

Bonds Payable Notes payable

Bond Retirement Extinguishment of bonds

Carrying Value of Bond Book value of bond

Effective Interest Amortization Interest method of amortization

Face Rate of Interest Stated rate, nominal rate, contract rate, or coupon rate of interest

Long-Term Liabilities Noncurrent liabilities

Market Rate of Interest Yield or effective rate of interest

Redemption Price Reacquisition price

Temporary Difference Timing difference

WARMUP EXERCISES & SOLUTIONS

Warmup Exercise 10-1

A bond due in ten years with face value of $1,000 and face rate of interest of 8% is issued when the market rate of interest is 6%.

Required

1. What is the issue price of the bond?
2. What is the amount of premium or discount on the bond at the time of issuance?
3. What amount of interest expense will be shown on the income statement for the first year of the bond?
4. What amount of the premium or discount will be amortized during the first year of the bond?

Warmup Exercise 10-2

You have signed an agreement to lease a car for four years and will make annual payments of $4,000 at the end of each year. (Assume that the lease meets the criteria for a capital lease.)

Required

1. Calculate the present value of the lease payments assuming an 8% interest rate.
2. Record the journal entry for the signing of the lease.
3. When the first lease payment is made, what portion of the payment will be considered interest?

SOLUTIONS TO WARMUP EXERCISES

Warmup Exercise 10-1

1. The issue price of the bond would be calculated at the present value:

$80(7.360) =	$ 588.80	using Table 9-4, where $i = 6\%$ and $n = 10$
$1,000(0.558) =	558.00	using Table 9-2, where $i = 6\%$ and $n = 10$
Issue price	$1,146.80	

REVIEW

2. The amount of the premium is the difference between the issue price and the face value:

$$\text{Premium} = \$1{,}146.80 - \$1{,}000 = \$146.80$$

3. The amount of interest expense can be calculated as follows:

$$\text{Interest Expense} = \$1{,}146.80 \times 0.06 = \$68.81$$

4. The amount that will be amortized can be calculated as follows:

$$\begin{aligned}\text{Amortized} &= \text{Cash Interest} - \text{Interest Expense}\\ &= (\$1{,}000 \times 0.08) - (\$1{,}146.80 \times 0.06)\\ &= \$80.00 - \$68.81\\ &= \$11.19\end{aligned}$$

Warmup Exercise 10-2

1. The present value of the lease payments can be calculated as follows:

$$\begin{aligned}\text{Present Value} &= \$4{,}000(3.312) \text{ using Table 9-4, where } i = 8\%, n = 4\\ &= \$13{,}248\end{aligned}$$

2. The journal entry to record the lease agreement:

Leased Asset	13,248	
Lease Obligation		13,248

Balance Sheet								Income Statement
ASSETS		=	LIABILITIES		+	STOCKHOLDERS' EQUITY	+	REVENUES − EXPENSES
Leased Asset	13,248		Lease Obligation	13,248				

3. The amount of interest can be calculated as follows:

$$\text{Interest} = \$13{,}248 \times 0.08 = \$1{,}059.84$$

REVIEW PROBLEM & SOLUTION

The following items pertain to the liabilities of Brent Foods. You may assume that Brent Foods began business on January 1, 2008; therefore, the beginning balance of all accounts was zero.

a. On January 1, 2008, Brent Foods issued bonds with a face value of $50,000. The bonds are due in five years and have a face interest rate of 10%. The market rate on January 1 for similar bonds was 12%. The bonds pay interest annually each December 31. Brent has chosen to use the effective interest method of amortization for any premium or discount on the bonds.
b. On December 31, 2008, Brent Foods signed a lease agreement with Cordova Leasing. The agreement requires Brent to make annual lease payments of $3,000 per year for four years, with the first payment due on January 1, 2010. The agreement stipulates that ownership of the property is transferred to Brent at the end of the four-year lease. Assume that an 8% interest rate is used for the leasing transaction.
c. On January 1, 2009, Brent redeems its bonds payable at the specified redemption price of 101. Because this item occurs in 2009, it does not affect the balance sheet prepared for year-end 2008.

Required
1. Determine the effect on the accounting equation of the December 31, 2008, interest adjustment in (a) and the signing of the lease in (b).
2. Develop the Long-Term Liabilities section of Brent Foods' balance sheet as of December 31, 2008, based on (a) and (b). You do not need to consider the notes that accompany the balance sheet.
3. Would the company prefer to treat the lease in (b) as an operating lease? Why or why not?
4. Calculate the gain or loss on the bond redemption for (c).

SOLUTION TO REVIEW PROBLEM

1. a. The issue price of the bonds on January 1 must be calculated at the present value of the interest payments and the present value of the principal, as follows:

$5,000 × 3.605	$18,025
$50,000 × 0.567	28,350
Issue price	$46,375

The amount of the discount is calculated as follows:

$50,000 − $46,375 = $3,625

The following is the entry on December 31, 2008, to record interest and to amortize discount:

Dec. 31	Interest Expense	5,565	
	Cash		5,000
	Discount on Bonds Payable		565
	To record interest and amortize discount.		

Balance Sheet							Income Statement	
ASSETS		=	LIABILITIES		+	STOCKHOLDERS' EQUITY	+	REVENUES − EXPENSES	
Cash	(5,000)		Discount on Bonds Payable	565			Interest Expense	(5,565)

The interest expense is calculated using the effective interest method by multiplying the carrying value of the bonds times the market rate of interest ($46,375 × 12%).

Brent must show two accounts in the Long-Term Liabilities section of the balance sheet: Bonds Payable of $50,000 and Discount on Bonds Payable of $3,060 ($3,625 less $565 amortized).

b. The lease meets the criteria to be a capital lease. Brent must report the lease as an asset and report the obligation for lease payments as a liability. The transaction should be reported at the present value of the lease payments, $9,936 (computed by multiplying $3,000 by the annuity factor of 3.312). The accounting entry should be as follows:

Dec. 31	Leased Asset	9,936	
	Lease Obligation		9,936
	To record lease as a capital lease.		

Balance Sheet							Income Statement	
ASSETS		=	LIABILITIES		+	STOCKHOLDERS' EQUITY	+	REVENUES − EXPENSES
Leased Asset	9,936		Lease Obligation	9,936				

Because the lease agreement was signed on December 31, 2008, it is not necessary to amortize the Lease Obligation account in 2008. The account should be stated in the Long-Term Liabilities section of Brent's balance sheet at $9,936.

2. The Long-Term Liabilities section of Brent's balance sheet for December 31, 2008, on the basis of (a) and (b) is as follows:

Brent Foods
Partial Balance Sheet
As of December 31, 2008

Long-term liabilities:		
Bonds payable	$50,000	
Less: Unamortized discount on bonds payable	3,060	$46,940
Lease obligation		9,936
Total long-term liabilities		$56,876

3. The company would prefer that the lease be an operating lease because it would not have to report the asset or liability on the balance sheet. This off-balance-sheet financing may give a more favorable impression of the company.
4. Brent must calculate the loss on the bond redemption as the difference between the carrying value of the bonds ($46,940) and the redemption price ($50,000 × 1.01). The amount of the loss is calculated as follows:

$50,500 − $46,940 = $3,560 loss on redemption

QUESTIONS

1. Which interest rate, the face rate or the market rate, should be used when calculating the issue price of a bond? Why?
2. What is the tax advantage that companies experience when bonds are issued instead of stock?
3. Does the issuance of bonds at a premium indicate that the face rate is higher or lower than the market rate of interest?
4. How does the effective interest method of amortization result in a constant rate of interest?
5. What is the meaning of the following sentence: Amortization affects the amount of interest expense? How does amortization of premium affect the amount of interest expense? How does amortization of discount affect the amount of interest expense?
6. Does amortization of a premium increase or decrease the bond carrying value? Does amortization of a discount increase or decrease the bond carrying value?
7. Is there always a gain or loss when bonds are redeemed? How is the gain or loss calculated?
8. What are the reasons that not all leases are accounted for in the same manner? Do you think it would be possible to develop a new accounting rule that would treat all leases in the same manner? Explain.
9. What is the meaning of the term *off-balance-sheet financing?* Why do some firms want to engage in off-balance-sheet transactions?
10. What are the effects on the financial statements when a lease is considered an operating lease rather than a capital lease?
11. Should depreciation be reported on leased assets? If so, over what period of time should depreciation occur?
12. Why do firms have a Deferred Tax account? Where should that account be shown on the financial statements? (Appendix)
13. How can you determine whether an item should reflect a permanent or a temporary difference when calculating the deferred tax amount? (Appendix)
14. Does the amount of income tax expense presented on the income statement represent the amount of tax actually paid? Why or why not? (Appendix)
15. Do you agree with this statement: All liabilities could be legally enforced in a court of law?

BRIEF EXERCISES

LO1

Brief Exercise 10-1 Classification of Long-Term Liabilities

Which of the following would normally be included in the long-term liability category of the balance sheet?

Accounts payable
Bonds payable
Accrued expenses
Current maturities of long-term debt
Accrued income taxes

LO2

Brief Exercise 10-2 Bond Features

Define the following terms related to bonds payable.

Debenture bonds
Secured bonds
Convertible bonds
Callable bonds
Face value of the bonds
Face rate of interest
Issue price

LO3

Brief Exercise 10-3 Bond Issue Price

A bond payable is dated January 1, 2008, and is issued on that date. The face value of the bond is $100,000, and the face rate of interest is 8%. The bond pays interest semiannually. The bond will mature in five years.

Required

1. What will be the issue price of the bond if the market rate of interest is 6% at the time of issuance?
2. What will be the issue price of the bond if the market rate of interest is 8% at the time of issuance?
3. What will be the issue price of the bond if the market rate of interest is 10% at the time of issuance?

LO4

Brief Exercise 10-4 Effect of Bond Issuance

A bond with a face value of $10,000 is issued at a discount of $800 on January 1, 2008. The face rate of interest on the bond is 7%.

Required

1. Was the market rate at the time of issuance greater than 7% or less than 7%?
2. If a balance sheet is presented on January 1, 2008, how will the bonds appear on the balance sheet?
3. If a balance sheet is presented on December 31, 2008, will the amount for the bonds be higher or lower than on January 1, 2008?

LO5

Brief Exercise 10-5 Amortization of Premium or Discount

Bonds payable are dated January 1, 2008, and are issued on that date. The face value of the bonds is $100,000, and the face rate of interest is 8%. The bonds pay interest semiannually. The bonds will mature in five years. The market rate of interest at the time of issuance was 6%.

Required

1. Using the effective interest amortization method, what amount should be amortized for the first six-month period? What amount of interest expense should be reported for the first six-month period?
2. Using the effective interest amortization method, what amount should be amortized for the period from July 1 to December 31, 2008? What amount of interest expense should be reported for the period from July 1 to December 31, 2008?

LO6

Brief Exercise 10-6 Gain or Loss on Bonds

Refer to Brief Exercise 10-5. Assume that the bonds are redeemed on December 31, 2008, at 102.

Required

1. Calculate the gain or loss on bond redemption.
2. What journal entry should be recorded at the time of bond redemption?

LO7

Brief Exercise 10-7 Lease Classification

Dianne Company signed a ten-year lease agreement on January 1, 2008. The lease requires payments of $5,000 per year every December 31. Dianne estimates that the leased property has a life of 12 years. The interest rate that applies to the lease is 8%.

Required

1. Should Dianne Company treat the lease as an operating lease or a capital lease?
2. If a balance sheet is presented on January 1, 2008, what amounts related to the lease will appear on the balance sheet?
3. Assume that the leased asset is depreciated using the straight-line method. Assume that the lease is amortized using the effective interest method. What amounts should appear on the balance sheet of December 31, 2008?

LO8

Brief Exercise 10-8 Debt-to-Equity Ratio

Will Able Corporation's balance sheet showed the following amounts: Current Liabilities, $10,000; Bonds Payable, $3,000; Lease Obligations, $4,000; and Notes Payable, $600. Total stockholders' equity was $12,000. The debt-to-equity ratio is:

a. 0.63.
b. 0.83.
c. 1.42.
d. 1.47.

LO9

Brief Exercise 10-9 Long-Term Liabilities and Cash Flow

In what category of the statement of cash flows should the following items be shown? Should they appear as a positive or negative amount on the statement of cash flows?

Increases in long-term liabilities
Decreases in long-term liabilities
Interest expense
Depreciation expense on leased assets
Increase in deferred tax

LO10 **Brief Exercise 10-10** Deferred Tax (Appendix)

On January 1, 2008, Deng Company purchased an asset for $100,000. For financial accounting purposes, the asset will be depreciated on a straight-line basis over five years with no residual value at the end of that time. For tax purposes, the asset will be depreciated as follows: 2008, $40,000; 2009, $30,000; 2010, $20,000; 2011, $10,000; and 2012, $0. Assume that the company is subject to a 40% tax rate.

Required

1. What is the amount of deferred tax at December 31, 2008?
2. Does the deferred tax represent an asset or a liability?
3. What is the amount of deferred tax at December 31, 2012?

EXERCISES

LO2 **Exercise 10-1** Relationships

The following components are computed annually when a bond is issued for other than its face value:

- Cash interest payment
- Interest expense
- Amortization of discount/premium
- Carrying value of bond

Required

State whether each component will increase (I), decrease (D), or remain constant (C) as the bond approaches maturity given the following situations:

1. Issued at a discount
2. Issued at a premium

LO3 **Exercise 10-2** Issue Price

Youngblood Inc. plans to issue $500,000 face value bonds with a stated interest rate of 8%. They will mature in ten years. Interest will be paid semiannually. At the date of issuance, assume that the market rate is (a) 8%, (b) 6%, and (c) 10%.

Required

For each market interest rate, answer the following questions:

1. What is the amount due at maturity?
2. How much cash interest will be paid every six months?
3. At what price will the bond be issued?

LO3 **Exercise 10-3** Issue Price

The following terms relate to independent bond issues:

a. 500 bonds; $1,000 face value; 8% stated rate; 5 years; annual interest payments
b. 500 bonds; $1,000 face value; 8% stated rate; 5 years; semiannual interest payments
c. 800 bonds; $1,000 face value; 8% stated rate; 10 years; semiannual interest payments
d. 2,000 bonds; $500 face value; 12% stated rate; 15 years; semiannual interest payments

Required

Assuming the market rate of interest is 10%, calculate the selling price for each bond issue.

LO4 **Exercise 10-4** Impact of Two Bond Alternatives

Yung Chong Company wants to issue 100 bonds, $1,000 face value, in January. The bonds will have a ten-year life and pay interest annually. The market rate of interest on January 1 will be 9%. Yung Chong is considering two alternative bond issues: (a) bonds with a face rate of 8% and (b) bonds with a face rate of 10%.

Required

1. Could the company save money by issuing bonds with an 8% face rate? If it chooses alternative (a), what would be the interest cost as a percentage?
2. Could the company benefit by issuing bonds with a 10% face rate? If it chooses alternative (b), what would be the interest cost as a percentage?

LO6

Exercise 10-5 Redemption of Bonds

Reynolds Corporation issued $75,000 face value bonds at a discount of $2,500. The bonds contain a call price of 103. Reynolds decides to redeem the bonds early when the unamortized discount is $1,750.

Required

1. Calculate Reynolds Corporation's gain or loss on the early redemption of the bonds.
2. Describe how the gain or loss would be reported on the income statement and in the notes to the financial statements.

LO6

Exercise 10-6 Redemption of a Bond at Maturity

On March 31, 2008, Sammonds Inc. issued $250,000 face value bonds at a discount of $7,000. The bonds were retired at their maturity date, March 31, 2018.

Required

Assuming that the last interest payment and the amortization of the discount have already been recorded, calculate the gain or loss on the redemption of the bonds on March 31, 2018. Indicate the effect on the accounting equation of the redemption of the bonds.

LO7

Exercise 10-7 Leased Asset

Hopper Corporation signed a ten-year capital lease on January 1, 2008. The lease requires annual payments of $8,000 every December 31.

Required

1. Assuming an interest rate of 9%, calculate the present value of the minimum lease payments.
2. Explain why the value of the leased asset and the accompanying lease obligation are not reported on the balance sheet initially at $80,000.

LO7

Exercise 10-8 Financial Statement Impact of a Lease

Benjamin's Warehouse signed a six-year capital lease on January 1, 2008, with payments due every December 31. Interest is calculated annually at 10%, and the present value of the minimum lease payments is $13,065.

Required

1. Calculate the amount of the annual payment that Benjamin's must make every December 31.
2. Calculate the amount of the lease obligation that would be presented on the December 31, 2009, balance sheet (after two lease payments have been made).

LO7

Exercise 10-9 Leased Assets

Koffman and Sons signed a four-year lease for a forklift on January 1, 2008. Annual lease payments of $1,510, based on an interest rate of 8%, are to be made every December 31, beginning with December 31, 2008.

Required

1. Assume that the lease is treated as an operating lease.
   a. Will the value of the forklift appear on Koffman's balance sheet?
   b. What account will indicate that lease payments have been made?
2. Assume that the lease is treated as a capital lease.
   a. Prepare any journal entries needed when the lease is signed. Explain why the value of the leased asset is not recorded at $6,040 ($1,510 × 4).
   b. Prepare the journal entry to record the first lease payment on December 31, 2008.
   c. Calculate the amount of depreciation expense on December 31, 2007.
   d. At what amount would the lease obligation be presented on the balance sheet as of December 31, 2008?

LO9

Exercise 10-10 Impact of Transactions Involving Bonds on Statement of Cash Flows

In the following list, identify each item as operating (O), investing (I), financing (F), or not separately reported on the statement of cash flows (N).

_______ Proceeds from issuance of bonds payable
_______ Interest expense
_______ Redemption of bonds payable at maturity

LO9

Exercise 10-11 Impact of Transactions Involving Capital Leases on Statement of Cash Flows

Assume that Garnett Corporation signs a lease agreement with Duncan Company to lease a piece of equipment and determines that the lease should be treated as a capital lease. Garnett records a leased asset in the amount of $53,400 and a lease obligation in the same amount on its balance sheet.

Required

1. Indicate how this transaction would be reported on Garnett's statement of cash flows.
2. In the following list of transactions relating to this lease, identify each item as operating (O), investing (I), financing (F), or not separately reported on the statement of cash flows (N).

_______ Reduction of lease obligation (principal portion of lease payment)
_______ Interest expense
_______ Depreciation expense—leased assets

LO9

Exercise 10-12 Impact of Transactions Involving Tax Liabilities on Statement of Cash Flows

In the following list, identify each item as operating (O), investing (I), financing (F), or not separately reported on the statement of cash flows (N). For items identified as operating, indicate whether the related amount would be added to or deducted from net income in determining the cash flows from operating activities.

_______ Decrease in taxes payable
_______ Increase in deferred taxes

LO10

Exercise 10-13 Temporary and Permanent Differences (Appendix)

Madden Corporation wants to determine the amount of deferred tax that should be reported on its 2008 financial statements. It has compiled a list of differences between the accounting conducted for tax purposes and the accounting used for financial reporting (book) purposes.

Required

For each of the following items, indicate whether the difference should be classified as a permanent or a temporary difference.

1. During 2008, Madden received interest on state bonds purchased as an investment. The interest can be treated as tax-exempt interest for tax purposes.
2. During 2008, Madden paid for a life insurance premium on two key executives. Madden's accountant has indicated that the amount of the premium cannot be deducted for income tax purposes.
3. During December 2008, Madden received money for renting a building to a tenant. Madden must report the rent as income on its 2008 tax form. For book purposes, however, the rent will be considered income on the 2009 income statement.
4. Madden owns several pieces of equipment that it depreciates using the straight-line method for book purposes. An accelerated method of depreciation is used for tax purposes, however.
5. Madden offers a warranty on the product it sells. The corporation records the expense of the warranty repair costs in the year the product is sold (the accrual method) for book purposes. For tax purposes, however, Madden is not allowed to deduct the expense until the period the product is repaired.
6. During 2008, Madden was assessed a large fine by the federal government for polluting the environment. Madden's accountant has indicated that the fine cannot be deducted as an expense for income tax purposes.

LO10

Exercise 10-14 Deferred Tax (Appendix)

On January 1, 2008, Kunkel Corporation purchased an asset for $32,000. Assume that this is the only asset owned by the corporation. Kunkel has decided to use the straight-line method to depreciate it. For tax purposes, it will be depreciated over three years. It will be depreciated over five years, however, for the financial statements provided to stockholders. Assume that Kunkel Corporation is subject to a 40% tax rate.

Required

Calculate the balance to be reflected in the Deferred Tax account for Kunkel Corporation for each year 2008 through 2012.

MULTICONCEPT EXERCISES

LO4,5

Exercise 10-15 Issuance of a Bond at Face Value

On January 1, 2008, Whitefeather Industries issued 300, $1,000 face value bonds. The bonds have a five-year life and pay interest at the rate of 10%. Interest is paid semiannually on July 1 and January 1. The market rate of interest on January 1 was 10%.

Required

1. Calculate the issue price of the bonds and record the issuance of the bonds on January 1, 2008.
2. Explain how the issue price would have been affected if the market rate of interest had been higher than 10%.
3. Prepare the journal entry to record the payment of interest on July 1, 2008.
4. Calculate the amount of interest accrued on December 31, 2008.

LO4,5

Exercise 10-16 Impact of a Discount

Berol Corporation sold 20-year bonds on January 1, 2008. The face value of the bonds was $100,000; and they carry a 9% stated rate of interest, which is paid on December 31 of every year. Berol received $91,526 in return for the issuance of the bonds when the market rate was 10%. Any premium or discount is amortized using the effective interest method.

Required

1. Prepare the journal entry to record the sale of the bonds on January 1, 2008, and the proper balance sheet presentation on this date.
2. Prepare the journal entry to record interest expense on December 31, 2008, and the proper balance sheet presentation on this date.
3. Explain why it was necessary for Berol to issue the bonds for only $91,526 rather than $100,000.

LO4,5

Exercise 10-17 Impact of a Premium

Assume the same set of facts for Berol Corporation as in Exercise 10-16 except that it received $109,862 in return for the issuance of the bonds when the market rate was 8%.

Required

1. Prepare the journal entry to record the sale of the bonds on January 1, 2008, and the proper balance sheet presentation on this date.
2. Prepare the journal entry to record interest expense on December 31, 2008, and the proper balance sheet presentation on this date.
3. Explain why the company was able to issue the bonds for $109,862 rather than for the face amount.

PROBLEMS

LO3

Problem 10-1 Factors That Affect the Bond Issue Price

Becca Company is considering the issue of $100,000 face value, ten-year term bonds. The bonds will pay 6% interest each December 31. The current market rate is 6%; therefore, the bonds will be issued at face value.

Required

1. For each of the following situations, indicate whether you believe the company will receive a premium on the bonds or will issue them at a discount or at face value. Without using numbers, explain your position.
   a. Interest is paid semiannually instead of annually.
   b. Assume instead that the market rate of interest is 7%; the nominal rate is still 6%.
2. For each situation in (1), prove your statement by determining the issue price of the bonds given the changes in (a) and (b).

LO5

Problem 10-2 Amortization of Discount

Stacy Company issued five-year, 10% bonds with a face value of $10,000 on January 1, 2008. Interest is paid annually on December 31. The market rate of interest on this date is 12%, and Stacy Company receives proceeds of $9,275 on the bond issuance.

Required

1. Prepare a five-year table (similar to Exhibit 10-4) to amortize the discount using the effective interest method.
2. What is the total interest expense over the life of the bonds? cash interest payment? discount amortization?
3. Prepare the journal entry for the payment of interest and the amortization of discount on December 31, 2010 (the third year), and determine the balance sheet presentation of the bonds on that date.

LO5

Problem 10-3 Amortization of Premium

Assume the same set of facts for Stacy Company as in Problem 10-2 except that the market rate of interest of January 1, 2008, is 8% and the proceeds from the bond issuance equal $10,803.

Required

1. Prepare a five-year table (similar to Exhibit 10-5) to amortize the premium using the effective interest method.
2. What is the total interest expense over the life of the bonds? cash interest payment? premium amortization?
3. Prepare the journal entry for the payment of interest and the amortization of premium on December 31, 2010 (the third year), and determine the balance sheet presentation of the bonds on that date.

LO6

Problem 10-4 Redemption of Bonds

McGee Company issued $200,000 face value bonds at a premium of $4,500. The bonds contain a call provision of 101. McGee decides to redeem the bonds due to a significant decline in interest rates. On that date, McGee had amortized only $1,000 of the premium.

Required

1. Calculate the gain or loss on the early redemption of the bonds.
2. Calculate the gain or loss on the redemption assuming that the call provision is 103 instead of 101.
3. Indicate where the gain or loss should be presented on the financial statements.
4. Why do you suppose the call price is normally higher than 100?

LO7

Problem 10-5 Financial Statement Impact of a Lease

On January 1, 2008, Muske Trucking Company leased a semitractor and trailer for five years. Annual payments of $28,300 are to be made every December 31 beginning December 31, 2008. Interest expense is based on a rate of 8%. The present value of the minimum lease payments is $113,000 and has been determined to be greater than 90% of the fair market value of the asset on January 1, 2008. Muske uses straight-line depreciation on all assets.

Required

1. Prepare a table similar to Exhibit 10-7 to show the five-year amortization of the lease obligation.
2. Prepare the journal entry for the lease transaction on January 1, 2008.
3. Prepare all necessary journal entries on December 31, 2009 (the second year of the lease).
4. Prepare the balance sheet presentation as of December 31, 2009, for the leased asset and the lease obligation.

LO10

Problem 10-6 Deferred Tax (Appendix)

Erinn Corporation has compiled its 2008 financial statements. Included in the Long-Term Liabilities category of the balance sheet are the following amounts:

	2008	2007
Deferred tax	$180	$100

Included in the income statement are the following amounts related to income taxes:

	2008	2007
Income before tax	$500	$400
Tax expense	200	160
Net income	$300	$240

In the notes that accompany the 2008 statement are the following amounts:

	2008
Current provision for tax	$120
Deferred portion	80

Required

1. Prepare the journal entry in 2008 for income tax expense, deferred tax, and income tax payable.
2. Assume that a stockholder has inquired about the meaning of the numbers recorded and disclosed about deferred tax. Explain why the Deferred Tax liability account exists. Also, what do the terms *current provision* and *deferred portion* mean? Why is the deferred amount in the note $80 when the deferred amount on the 2008 balance sheet is $180?

LO10

Problem 10-7 Deferred Tax Calculations (Appendix)

Wyhowski Inc. reported income from operations, before taxes, for 2006–2008 as follows:

2006	$210,000
2007	240,000
2008	280,000

When calculating income, Wyhowski deducted depreciation on plant equipment. The equipment was purchased January 1, 2006, at a cost of $88,000. The equipment is expected to last three years and have an $8,000 salvage value. Wyhowski uses straight-line depreciation for book purposes. For tax purposes, depreciation on the equipment is $50,000 in 2006, $20,000 in 2007, and $10,000 in 2008. Wyhowski's tax rate is 35%.

Required

1. How much did Wyhowski pay in income tax each year?
2. How much income tax expense did Wyhowski record each year?
3. What is the balance in the Deferred Income Tax account at the end of 2006, 2007, and 2008?

MULTICONCEPT PROBLEMS

LO4,5

Problem 10-8 Bond Transactions

Brand Company issued $1,000,000 face value, eight-year, 12% bonds on April 1, 2008, when the market rate of interest was 12%. Interest payments are due every October 1 and April 1. Brand uses a calendar year-end.

Required

1. Prepare the journal entry to record the issuance of the bonds on April 1, 2008.
2. Prepare the journal entry to record the interest payment on October 1, 2008.
3. Explain why additional interest must be recorded on December 31, 2008. What impact does this have on the amounts paid on April 1, 2009?
4. Determine the total cash inflows and outflows that occurred on the bonds over the eight-year life.

LO1,8,10

Problem 10-9 Partial Classified Balance Sheet for Walgreens

The following items, listed alphabetically, appear on **Walgreens**' consolidated balance sheet at August 31, 2006 (in millions):

Accrued expenses and other liabilities	$1,713.3
Deferred income tax (long-term)	141.1
Income taxes payable	2.8
Other noncurrent liabilities	1,118.9
Trade accounts payable	4,039.2

Required

1. Prepare the Current Liabilities and Long-Term Liabilities sections of Walgreens' classified balance sheet at August 31, 2006.
2. Walgreens had total liabilities of $2,334.8 and total shareholders' equity of $8,889.7 at August 31, 2005. Total shareholders' equity at August 31, 2006, amounted to $10,115.8. (All amounts are in millions.) Compute Walgreens' debt-to-equity ratio at August 31, 2006 and 2005. As an investor, how would you react to the changes in this ratio?
3. What other related ratios would the company's lenders use to assess the company? What do these ratios measure?

ALTERNATE PROBLEMS

LO3

Problem 10-1A Factors That Affect The Bond Issue Price

Rivera Inc. is considering the issuance of $500,000 face value, ten-year term bonds. The bonds will pay 5% interest each December 31. The current market rate is 5%; therefore, the bonds will be issued at face value.

Required

1. For each of the following situations, indicate whether you believe the company will receive a premium on the bonds or will issue them at a discount or at face value. Without using numbers, explain your position.
   a. Interest is paid semiannually instead of annually.
   b. Assume instead that the market rate of interest is 4%; the nominal rate is still 5%.
2. For each situation in (1), prove your statement by determining the issue price of the bonds given the changes in (a) and (b).

LO5

Problem 10-2A Amortization of Discount

Ortega Company issued five-year, 5% bonds with a face value of $50,000 on January 1, 2008. Interest is paid annually on December 31. The market rate of interest on this date is 8%, and Ortega Company receives proceeds of $44,011 on the bond issuance.

Required

1. Prepare a five-year table (similar to Exhibit 10-4) to amortize the discount using the effective interest method.
2. What is the total interest expense over the life of the bonds? cash interest payment? discount amortization?
3. Prepare the journal entry for the payment of interest on December 31, 2010 (the third year), and the balance sheet presentation of the bonds on that date.

LO5

Problem 10-3A Amortization of Premium

Assume the same set of facts for Ortega Company as in Problem 10-2A except that the market rate of interest of January 1, 2008, is 4% and the proceeds from the bond issuance equal $52,230.

Required

1. Prepare a five-year table (similar to Exhibit 10-5) to amortize the premium using the effective interest method.
2. What is the total interest expense over the life of the bonds? cash interest payment? premium amortization?
3. Prepare the journal entry for the payment of interest on December 31, 2010 (the third year), and the balance sheet presentation of the bonds on that date.

LO6

Problem 10-4A Redemption of Bonds

Elliot Company issued $100,000 face value bonds at a premium of $5,500. The bonds contain a call provision of 101. Elliot decides to redeem the bonds due to a significant decline in interest rates. On that date, Elliot had amortized only $2,000 of the premium.

Required

1. Calculate the gain or loss on the early redemption of the bonds.
2. Calculate the gain or loss on the redemption assuming that the call provision is 104 instead of 101.
3. Indicate how the gain or loss would be reported on the income statement and in the notes to the financial statements.
4. Why do you suppose the call price is normally higher than 100?

LO7

Problem 10-5A Financial Statement Impact of a Lease

On January 1, 2008, Kiger Manufacturing Company leased a factory machine for six years. Annual payments of $21,980 are to be made every December 31 beginning December 31, 2008. Interest expense is based on a rate of 9%. The present value of the minimum lease payments is $98,600 and has been determined to be greater than 90% of the fair market value of the machine on January 1, 2008. Kiger uses straight-line depreciation on all assets.

Required

1. Prepare a table similar to Exhibit 10-7 to show the six-year amortization of the lease obligation.
2. Prepare the journal entry for the lease transaction on January 1, 2008.
3. Prepare all necessary journal entries on December 31, 2009 (the second year of the lease).
4. Prepare the balance sheet presentation as of December 31, 2009, for the leased asset and the lease obligation.

LO10

Problem 10-6A Deferred Tax (Appendix)

Thad Corporation has compiled its 2008 financial statements. Included in the Long-Term Liabilities category of the balance sheet are the following amounts:

	2008	2007
Deferred tax	$180	$200

Included in the income statement are the following amounts related to income taxes:

	2008	2007
Income before tax	$500	$400
Tax expense	100	150
Net income	$400	$250

Required

1. Determine the effect on the accounting equation in 2008 for income tax expense, deferred tax, and income tax payable.
2. Assume that a stockholder has inquired about the meaning of the numbers recorded. Explain why the Deferred Tax liability account exists.

LO10

Problem 10-7A Deferred Tax Calculations (Appendix)

Clemente Inc. has reported income for book purposes as follows for the past three years:

(In thousands)	Year 1	Year 2	Year 3
Income before taxes	$120	$120	$120

Clemente has identified two items that are treated differently in the financial records and in the tax records. The first one is interest income on municipal bonds, which is recognized on the financial reports to the extent of $5,000 each year but does not show up as a revenue item on the company's tax return. The other item, equipment, is depreciated using the straight-line method at the rate of $20,000 each year for financial accounting but is depreciated for tax purposes at the rate of $30,000 in Year 1, $20,000 in Year 2, and $10,000 in Year 3.

Required

1. Determine the amount of cash paid for income taxes each year by Clemente. Assume that a 40% tax rate applies to all three years.
2. Calculate the balance in the Deferred Tax account at the end of Years 1, 2, and 3. How does this account appear on the balance sheet?

ALTERNATE MULTICONCEPT PROBLEMS

LO4,6

Problem 10-8A Financial Statement Impact of a Bond

Worthington Company issued $1,000,000 face value, six-year, 10% bonds on July 1, 2008, when the market rate of interest was 12%. Interest payments are due every July 1 and January 1. Worthington uses a calendar year-end.

Required

1. Prepare the journal entry to record the issuance of the bonds on July 1, 2008.
2. Prepare the adjusting journal entry on December 31, 2008, to accrue interest expense.
3. Prepare the journal entry to record the interest payment on January 1, 2009.
4. Calculate the amount of cash that will be paid for the retirement of the bonds on the maturity date.

LO1,8, 10 **Problem 10-9A** Partial Classified Balance Sheet for Boeing

The following items appear on the consolidated balance sheet of **Boeing Inc.** at December 31, 2006 (in millions). The information in parentheses was added to aid in your understanding.

Accounts payable and other liabilities	$16,201
Accrued retiree healthcare	7,671
Advances in excess of related costs	11,449
Short-term debt and current portion of long-term debt	1,381
Income tax payable	670
Long-term debt	8,157
Other long-term liabilities	391
Accrued pension liability (long-term)	1,135

Required

1. Prepare the Current Liabilities and Long-Term Liabilities sections of Boeing's classified balance sheet at December 31, 2006.
2. Boeing had total liabilities of $48,937 and total shareholders' equity of $11,059 at December 31, 2005. Total shareholders' equity amounted to $4,739 at December 31, 2006. (All amounts are in millions.) Compute Boeing's debt-to-equity ratio at December 31, 2006 and 2005. As an investor, how would you react to the changes in this ratio?
3. What other related ratios would the company's lenders use to assess the company? What do these ratios measure?

DECISION CASES

READING AND INTERPRETING FINANCIAL STATEMENTS

LO1,8 **Decision Case 10-1** Evaluating the Liabilities of General Mills

Refer to the **General Mills** financial statements at the end of the text and answer the following questions:

1. What are the items listed as long-term liabilities by General Mills? How did those liabilities change from 2005 to 2006?
2. Calculate the debt-to-equity ratio and the times interest earned ratio of the company for 2005 and 2006. What do those ratios reveal about the company and its ability to meet its obligations on its long-term liabilities?

LO9,10 **Decision Case 10-2** Comparing Two Companies: General Mills and Kellogg's

Refer to **General Mills**'s balance sheet and statement of cash flows at May 29, 2005, and **Kellogg's** balance sheet and statement of cash flows at December 30, 2006. Answer the following questions.

1. Calculate the debt-to-equity ratio for the two companies. How do the ratios compare? What does that tell you about the two companies?
2. Did the long-term liabilities of each company increase or decrease during the year? What were the most important changes? What impact do the changes have on the companies' cash flows?
3. What were the most important sources and uses of cash disclosed in the financing activities portion of the statement of cash flows for each company? Kellogg's had a large cash inflow from the issuance of notes payable during the year. Why does the long-term liability portion of the balance sheet indicate a decrease rather than an increase?

LO9,10 **Decision Case 10-3** Reading PepsiCo's Statement of Cash Flows

A portion of the Financing Activities section of **PepsiCo**'s statement of cash flows for the year ended December 31, 2006, follows (in millions):

Financing Activities:	
Proceeds from the issuance of long-term debt	$ 51
Payment of long-term debt	(157)
Short-term borrowings by original maturity:	
More than three months—proceeds	185
More than three months—payments	(358)
Three months or less, net	(2,168)

Required

1. Explain why proceeds from debt is shown as a positive amount and payment of debt is shown as a negative amount.
2. During 2006, interest rates remained at low levels. Explain why the company might have paid off debt during such conditions.
3. PepsiCo has a Deferred Income Tax account listed in the asset category of its balance sheet. Would an increase in that account result in an addition or a subtraction on the statement of cash flows? in which category?

MAKING FINANCIAL DECISIONS

LO1,7

Decision Case 10-4 Making a Loan Decision

Assume that you are a loan officer in charge of reviewing loan applications from potential new clients at a major bank. You are considering an application from Molitor Corporation, which is a fairly new company with a limited credit history. It has provided a balance sheet for its most recent fiscal year as follows:

Molitor Corporation
Balance Sheet
December 31, 2008

Assets		**Liabilities**	
Cash	$ 10,000	Accounts payable	$100,000
Receivables	50,000	Notes payable	200,000
Inventory	100,000		
Equipment	500,000	**Stockholders' Equity**	
		Common stock	80,000
		Retained earnings	280,000
Total assets	$660,000	Total liabilities and stockholders' equity	$660,000

Your bank has established certain guidelines that must be met before it will make a favorable loan recommendation. These include minimum levels for several financial ratios. You are particularly concerned about the bank's policy that loan applicants must have a total-assets-to-debt ratio of at least 2 to 1 to be acceptable. Your initial analysis of Molitor's balance sheet indicates that the firm has met the minimum total-assets-to-debt ratio requirement. On reading the notes that accompany the financial statements, however, you discover the following statement:

> Molitor has engaged in a variety of innovative financial techniques resulting in the acquisition of $200,000 of assets at very favorable rates. The company is obligated to make a series of payments over the next five years to fulfill its commitments in conjunction with these financial instruments. Current GAAP do not require the assets acquired or the related obligations to be reflected on the financial statements.

Required

1. How should this note affect your evaluation of Molitor's loan application? Calculate a revised total-assets-to-debt ratio for Molitor.
2. Do you believe that the bank's policy concerning a minimum total-assets-to-debt ratio can be modified to consider financing techniques that are not reflected on the financial statements? Write a statement that expresses your position on this issue.

LO6

Decision Case 10-5 Bond Redemption Decision

Armstrong Areo Ace, a flight training school, issued $100,000 of 20-year bonds at face value when the market rate was 10%. The bonds have been outstanding for ten years. The company pays annual interest on January 1. The current rate for similar bonds is 4%. On January 1, the controller would like to purchase the bonds on the open market, retire the bonds, then issue $100,000 of ten-year bonds to pay 4% annual interest.

Required

Draft a memo to the controller advising him to retire the outstanding bonds and issue new debt. Ignore taxes. (*Hint:* Find the selling price of bonds that pay 10% when the market rate is 4%.)

ACCOUNTING AND ETHICS: WHAT WOULD YOU DO?

LO7

Decision Case 10-6 Determination of Asset Life

Jen Latke is an accountant for Hale's Manufacturing Company. Hale's has entered into an agreement to lease a piece of equipment from EZ Leasing. Jen must decide how to report the lease agreement on Hale's financial statements.

Jen has reviewed the lease contract carefully. She also has reviewed the four lease criteria specified in the accounting rules. She has been able to determine that the lease does not meet three of the criteria. However, she is concerned about the criterion that indicates that if the term of the lease is 75% or more of the life of the property, the lease should be classified as a capital lease. Jen is fully aware that Hale's does not want to record the lease agreement as a capital lease, but prefers to show it as a type of off-balance-sheet financing.

Jen's reading of the lease contract indicates that the asset has been leased for seven years. She is unsure of the life of such assets, however, and has consulted two sources to determine it. One of them states that equipment similar to that owned by Hale's is depreciated over nine years. The other, a trade publication of the equipment industry, indicates that equipment of this type will usually last for 12 years.

Required

1. How should Jen report the lease agreement in the financial statements?
2. If Jen decides to present the lease as an off-balance-sheet arrangement, has she acted ethically? Explain.

SOLUTIONS TO KEY TERMS QUIZ

5	Long-term liability	8	Discount
1	Face value	10	Effective interest method of amortization
7	Debenture bonds	11	Carrying value
2	Serial bonds	13	Gain or loss on redemption
9	Callable bonds	14	Operating lease
3	Face rate of interest	15	Capital lease
12	Market rate of interest	17	Deferred tax
4	Bond issue price	18	Permanent difference
6	Premium	16	Temporary difference

ANSWERS TO POD REVIEW

LO1	1. b	2. d
LO2	1. c	2. b
LO3	1. a	2. a
LO4	1. b	2. b
LO5	1. b	2. a
LO6	1. d	2. a
LO7	1. b	2. a
LO8	1. c	2. b
LO9	1. b	2. c
LO10	1. b	2. d

CHAPTER 11

Stockholders' Equity

Learning Outcomes

After studying this chapter, you should be able to:

LO1 Understand the concept of stockholders' equity and identify the components of the Stockholders' Equity category of the balance sheet and the accounts found in each component.

LO2 Show that you understand the characteristics of common and preferred stock and the differences between the classes of stock.

LO3 Determine the financial statement impact when stock is issued for cash or for other consideration.

LO4 Describe the financial statement impact of stock treated as treasury stock.

LO5 Compute the amount of cash dividends when a firm has issued both preferred and common stock.

LO6 Show that you understand the difference between cash and stock dividends and the effect of stock dividends.

LO7 Determine the difference between stock dividends and stock splits.

LO8 Show that you understand the statement of stockholders' equity and comprehensive income.

LO9 Understand how investors use ratios to evaluate stockholders' equity.

LO10 Explain the effects that transactions involving stockholders' equity have on the statement of cash flows.

LO11 Describe the important differences between the sole proprietorship and partnership forms of organization versus the corporate form (Appendix).

Study Links...

A Look at Previous Chapters
The previous chapter indicated how companies use long-term debt as a means of financing the company.

A Look at This Chapter
This chapter concentrates on the issues concerned with the stockholders' equity section of the balance sheet. The use of equity is an important source of financing for all corporations. The chapter also considers the various types of dividends paid to stockholders.

A Look at the Upcoming Chapter
Chapter 12 includes an expanded discussion of the preparation and use of the statement of cash flows.

Southwest Airlines

MAKING BUSINESS DECISIONS

The airline industry is very volatile and has certainly experienced difficulties over the past few years. With reduced revenues, weak demand, high fixed costs, high fuel costs, and increasing expenses for security and insurance, the results for many of the airline companies have been grim. United Airlines declared bankruptcy in order to restructure, and several other airlines also were near bankruptcy. But throughout all of the bad times, **Southwest Airlines** has performed fairly well and has become the model for the future of the industry. The other airlines know that they must cut costs and become more efficient in order to compete with Southwest.

How does Southwest do it? Southwest Airlines Company provides short-haul, high-frequency, point-to-point, low-fare air transportation services. Southwest's 375 aircraft provide service between more than 60 cities in 30 states throughout the United States. In addition, Southwest serves many conveniently located satellite and downtown airports, such as Dallas Love Field, Houston Hobby, and Chicago Midway. The company's operating strategy also permits Southwest to achieve high-asset utilization. Aircraft are scheduled to minimize the amount of time they sit at the gate, pegged at approximately 25 minutes, consequently reducing the number of aircraft and gate facilities that would otherwise be required.

Southwest Airlines has consistently been an innovator in the industry. In January 1995, Southwest introduced a ticketless travel option, eliminating the need to print and then process a paper ticket. The company provides air travel at a low cost while being firmly committed to customer service. Southwest employees are trained to be friendly and efficient and are rewarded for their efforts.

All of the company's efforts are consistent with its financial strategy to build shareholder value, which contributes to the stockholders' equity portion of the balance sheet shown here. Since the company has been consistently profitable for many years, the stockholders have benefited and shareholder value will likely continue to grow. This chapter will consider the following questions:

- What are the components of the Stockholders' Equity section of the balance sheet? (See pp. 528–530.)
- What is the meaning and importance of treasury stock? (See pp. 533–535.)
- What are the types of dividends that a company might pay? (See pp. 536–542.)
- Why is comprehensive income different from net income? (See pp. 543–544.)

Answers to those questions and other issues related to stockholders' equity are found in this text. They can help you evaluate the Stockholders' Equity section of the balance sheet of Southwest Airlines and other companies.

(*continued*)

Southwest Airlines Co.
Consolidated Balance Sheet
(in millions, except share data)

	December 31, 2006	December 31, 2005
Stockholders' equity:		
Common stock, $1.00 par value: 2,000,000,000 shares authorized; 807,611,634 and 801,641,645 shares issued in 2006 and 2005, respectively	$ 808	$ 802
Capital in excess of par value	1,142	963
Retained earnings	4,307	4,018
Accumulated other comprehensive income	582	892
Treasury stock, at cost: 24,302,215 shares in 2006	(390)	—
Total stockholders' equity	$6,449	$6,675

An Overview of Stockholders' Equity

LO1 Understand the concept of stockholders' equity and identify the components of the Stockholders' Equity category of the balance sheet and the accounts found in each component.

EQUITY AS A SOURCE OF FINANCING

Whenever a company needs to raise money, it must choose from the alternative financing sources available. Financing can be divided into two general categories: debt (borrowing from banks or other creditors) and equity (issuing stock). The company's management must consider the advantages and disadvantages of each alternative. Exhibit 11-1 indicates a few of the factors that must be considered.

Issuing stock is a popular method of financing because of its flexibility. It provides advantages for the issuing company and the investors (stockholders). Investors are primarily concerned with the return on their investment. With stock, the return might be in the form of dividends paid to the investors but might also be the price appreciation of the stock. Stock is popular because it generally provides a higher rate of return (but also a higher degree of risk) than can be obtained by creditors who receive interest from lending money. Stock is popular with issuing companies because dividends on stock can be adjusted according to the company's profitability: higher dividends can be paid when the firm is profitable; lower dividends, when it is not. Interest on debt financing, on the other hand, is generally fixed and is a legal liability that cannot be adjusted when a company experiences lower profitability.

There are several disadvantages in issuing stock. Stock usually has voting rights, and issuing stock allows new investors to vote. Existing investors may not want to share the control of the company with new stockholders. From the issuing company's viewpoint, there is also a serious tax disadvantage to stock versus debt. As indicated in Chapter 10, interest on debt is tax-deductible and results in lower taxes. Dividends on stock, on the other hand, are not tax-deductible and do not result in tax savings to the issuing company. Finally, issuing stock has an impact on the company's financial statements. Issuing stock decreases several important financial ratios, such as earnings per share. Issuing debt does not have a similar effect on the earnings per share ratio.

Management must consider many other factors in deciding between debt and equity financing. The company's goal should be financing the company in a manner that results in the lowest overall cost of capital to the firm. Usually, companies attain that goal by having a reasonable balance of both debt and equity financing.

EXHIBIT 11-1 Advantages and Disadvantages of Stock versus Debt Financing

Advantages of Financing with Stock

1. Flexibility → Dividends on stock can be increased in profitable years and reduced when the company is less profitable. Debt interest is fixed. (An advantage for issuing company)
2. Exchanges facilitate trading → Large companies have ready markets for stock through the stock exchanges. (An advantage for issuing company and investors) Sometimes debt is not as widely traded.
3. Return on investment → Stock generally provides a higher return in dividends and in growth than interest on debt. (An advantage for investors)

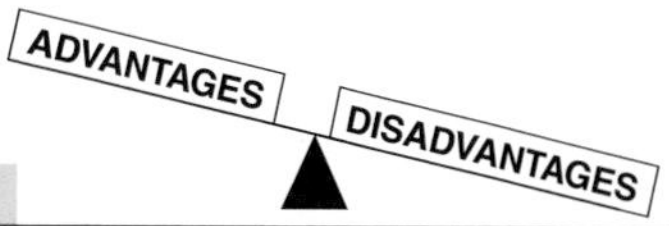

Disadvantages of Financing with Stock

1. Control → Issuing stock involves giving voting rights to new investors, resulting in less control of the company for existing stockholders. (A disadvantage for issuing company)
2. Tax consequences → Interest on debt is tax deductible for the issuing company; dividends on stock are not. (A disadvantage for issuing company)
3. Impact on ratios → Issuing stock decreases several important financial ratios, including earnings per share. (A disadvantage for issuing company)

STOCKHOLDERS' EQUITY ON THE BALANCE SHEET

The basic accounting equation is often stated as follows:

Assets = Liabilities + Owners' Equity

Owners' equity is viewed as a residual amount. That is, the owners of a corporation have a claim to all assets after the claims represented by liabilities to creditors have been satisfied.

This text concentrates on the corporate form of organization and refers to the owners' equity as *stockholders' equity*. To review, the basic accounting equation for a corporation is as follows:

Assets = Liabilities + Stockholders' Equity

The stockholders are the owners of a corporation. They have a residual interest in its assets after the claims of all creditors have been satisfied.

The Stockholders' Equity category of all corporations has two major components or subcategories:

Total Stockholders' Equity = Contributed Capital + Retained Earnings

Contributed capital represents the amount the corporation has received from the sale of stock to stockholders. Retained earnings is the amount of net income the corporation has earned but not paid as dividends. Instead, the corporation retains and reinvests the income.

Real World Practice

11-1 Reading Southwest Airlines' Annual Report

Refer to the Retained Earnings account of Southwest Airlines. Did the account increase or decrease from 2005 to 2006? What factors may cause the account to change?

EXHIBIT 11-2 Retained Earnings Connects the Income Statement and the Balance Sheet

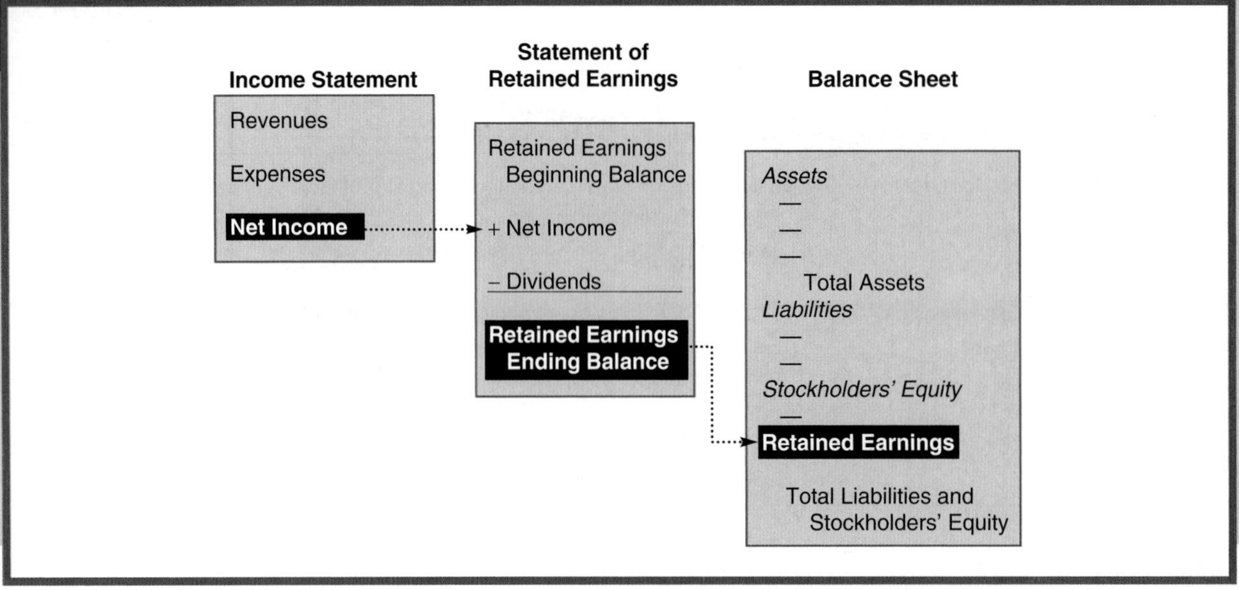

Although all corporations maintain the two primary categories of contributed capital and retained earnings, within these categories, they use a variety of accounts that have several different titles. The next section examines two important items: income and dividends and their impact on the Retained Earnings account.

HOW INCOME AND DIVIDENDS AFFECT RETAINED EARNINGS

The Retained Earnings account plays an important role because it serves as a link between the income statement and the balance sheet. The term *articulated statements* refers to the fact that the information on the income statement is related to the information on the balance sheet. The bridge (or link) between the two statements is the Retained Earnings account. Exhibit 11-2 presents this relationship graphically. As the exhibit indicates, the income statement is used to calculate a company's net income for a given period of time. The amount of the net income is transferred to the statement of retained earnings and is added to the beginning balance of retained earnings (with dividends deducted) to calculate the ending balance of retained earnings. The ending balance of retained earnings is the amount that is portrayed on the balance sheet in the Stockholders' Equity category. That is why you must prepare the income statement before you prepare the balance sheet, as you discovered when developing financial statements in previous chapters of the text.

IDENTIFYING THE COMPONENTS OF THE STOCKHOLDERS' EQUITY SECTION OF THE BALANCE SHEET

The liabilities and stockholders' equity portion of the balance sheet of Southwest Airlines was presented in the chapter opener. We will focus on the Stockholders' (Shareholders') Equity category of the balance sheet. All corporations begin the Stockholders' Equity category with a list of the firm's contributed capital. In some cases, there are two categories of stock: common stock and preferred stock. (The latter is discussed later in this chapter.) Common stock normally carries voting rights. The common stockholders elect the officers of the corporation and establish its bylaws and governing rules. It is not unusual for corporations to have more than one type of common stock, each with different rights or terms.

Authorized shares
The maximum number of shares a corporation may issue as indicated in the corporate charter.

Number of Shares It is important to determine the number of shares of stock for each stock account. Corporate balance sheets report the number of shares in three categories: **authorized**, **issued**, and **outstanding shares**.

To become incorporated, a business must develop articles of incorporation and apply to the proper state authorities for a corporate charter. The corporation must specify the maximum number of shares that it will be allowed to issue. This maximum number of shares is called the *authorized stock.* A corporation applies for authorization to issue many more shares than it will issue immediately to allow for future growth and other events that may occur over its long life. For example, Southwest Airlines indicates that it has 2,000,000,000 shares of common stock authorized but that only 807,611,634 shares had been issued as of December 31, 2006.

Issued shares
The number of shares sold or distributed to stockholders.

Outstanding shares
The number of shares issued less the number of shares held as treasury stock.

The number of shares *issued* indicates the number of shares that have been sold or transferred to stockholders. The number of shares issued does not necessarily mean, however, that those shares are currently outstanding. The term *outstanding* indicates shares actually in the hands of the stockholders. Shares that have been issued by the corporation and then repurchased are counted as shares issued but not as shares outstanding. Quite often corporations repurchase their own stock as treasury stock (explained in more detail later in this chapter). Treasury stock reduces the number of shares outstanding. The number of Southwest Airlines' shares of common stock outstanding at December 31, 2006, could be calculated as follows:

Number of shares issued	807,611,634
Less: Treasury stock	24,302,215
Number of shares outstanding	783,309,419

Study Tip

Treasury stock is included in the number of shares issued. It is not part of the number of shares outstanding.

Par Value: The Firm's "Legal Capital" The Stockholders' Equity category of many balance sheets refers to an amount as the *par value* of the stock. For example, Southwest Airlines' common stock has a par value of $1 per share. **Par value** is an arbitrary amount stated on the face of the stock certificate and represents the legal capital of the corporation. Most corporations set the par value of the stock at very low amounts because there are legal difficulties if stock is sold at less than par. Therefore, par value does not indicate the stock's value or the amount that is obtained when the stock is sold on the stock exchange; it is simply an arbitrary amount that exists to fulfill legal requirements. A company's legal requirement depends on its state of incorporation. Some states do not require corporations to indicate a par value; other states require corporations to designate the *stated value* of the stock. A stated value is accounted for in the same manner as a par value and appears in the Stockholders' Equity category in the same manner as a par value.

Par value
An arbitrary amount that represents the legal capital of the firm.

The amount of the par value is the amount that is presented in the stock account. That is, the dollar amount in a firm's stock account can be calculated as its par value per share times number of shares issued. For Southwest Airlines, the dollar amount appearing in the common stock account can be calculated as follows:

$1 Par Value per Share × 807,611,634 Shares Issued = $807,611,634 million
(rounded to $808 million on the balance sheet) Balance in the Common Stock Account

Additional Paid-in Capital The dollar amounts of the stock accounts in the Stockholders' Equity category do not indicate the amount that was received when the stock was sold to stockholders. The Common Stock and Preferred Stock accounts indicate only the par value of the stock. When stock is issued for an amount higher than the par value, the excess is reported as **additional paid-in capital**. Several different titles are used for this account, including Capital in Excess of Par Value, Capital Surplus (an old term that should no longer be used), and Premium on Stock. Regardless of the title, the account represents the amount received in excess of par when stock was issued.

Additional paid-in capital
The amount received for the issuance of stock in excess of the par value of the stock.
Alternate term: *Paid-in capital in excess of par.*

Southwest Airlines' balance sheet indicates paid-in capital of $1,142 million at December 31, 2006. The company, like many other corporations, presents only one amount for additional paid-in capital for all stock transactions. Therefore, we are unable to determine whether the amount resulted from the issuance of common stock or other stock transactions. As a result, it is often impossible to determine the issue price of each category of stock even with a careful analysis of the balance sheet and the accompanying notes.

Real World Practice

11-2 Reading Kellogg's Annual Report

Refer to the Kellogg's balance sheet for 2006 reproduced at the end of this book. Determine the number of shares of common stock authorized, issued, and outstanding at the balance sheet date.

Retained Earnings: The Amount Not Paid as Dividends **Retained earnings** represents net income that the firm has earned but has *not* paid as dividends. Remember that retained earnings is an amount that is accumulated over the entire life of the corporation and does not represent the income or dividends for a specific year.

Retained earnings Net income that has been made by the corporation but not paid out as dividends. ***Alternate term:*** *Retained income.*

A balance in retained earnings does not indicate that the company had a net income of this amount in the current year; it simply means that over the life of the corporation, the company has retained more net income than it paid out as dividends to stockholders.

It is also important to remember that the balance of the Retained Earnings account does not mean that liquid assets of that amount are available to the stockholders. Corporations decide to retain income because they have needs other than paying dividends to stockholders. The needs may include the purchase of assets, the retirement of debt, or other financial needs. Money spent for those needs usually benefits the stockholders in the long run, but liquid assets equal to the balance of the Retained Earnings account are not necessarily available to stockholders. In theory, income should be retained whenever the company can reinvest the money and get a better return within the business than the shareholders can get on their own. In summary, retained earnings is a Stockholders' Equity account. Although the company's assets have increased, retained earnings does not represent a pool of liquid assets.

POD REVIEW 11.1

LO1 *Understand the concept of stockholders' equity and identify the components of the Stockholders' Equity category of the balance sheet and the accounts found in each component.*

- Stockholders' equity consists of contributed capital from stockholders and retained earnings from the current and prior periods of operation that have not been paid as dividends.
  - Disclosure for stocks must include the number of shares authorized, issued, and outstanding, along with the par value.

QUESTIONS

1. *A company has 10,000 shares of stock authorized at January 1. During the year, 6,000 shares are issued to the stockholders and the company purchases 500 shares as treasury stock. At December 31, the number of shares outstanding is*
   a. 10,000.
   b. 9,500.
   c. 6,000.
   d. 5,500.

2. *Over the lifetime of the corporation, ABC Company has paid out more in dividends than it has had in net income. The balances in the Stockholders' Equity section of the balance sheet would most likely reveal a*
   a. debit balance in the Common Stock account.
   b. credit balance in the Common Stock account.
   c. debit balance in the Retained Earnings account.
   d. credit balance in the Retained Earnings account.

What Is Preferred Stock?

LO2 Show that you understand the characteristics of common and preferred stock and the differences between the classes of stock.

Many companies have a class of stock called *preferred stock.* One of the advantages of preferred stock is the flexibility it provides because its terms and provisions can be tailored to meet the firm's needs. These terms and provisions are detailed in the stock certificate. Generally, preferred stock offers holders a preference to dividends declared by the corporation. That is, if dividends are declared, the preferred stockholders must receive dividends first, before the holders of common stock.

The dividend rate on preferred stock may be stated two ways:

1. **it may be stated as a percentage of the stock's par value. For example, if a stock is presented on the balance sheet as $100 par, 7% preferred stock, its dividend rate is $7 per share ($100 times 7%).**
2. **the dividend may be stated as a per-share amount. For example, a stock may appear on the balance sheet as $100 par, $7 preferred stock, meaning that the dividend rate is $7 per share.**

Investors in common stock should note the dividend requirements of the preferred shareholder. The greater the obligation to the preferred shareholder, the less desirable the common stock becomes.

In the event that a corporation is liquidated, or dissolved, preferred stockholders have a right to the company's assets before the common stockholders. Following are additional terms and features that may be associated with preferred stock:

- *Convertible* Preferred stock may allow stockholders the right to convert the stock into common stock.
- *Redeemable* Preferred stock may allow stockholders to redeem their stock at a specified price.
- *Callable* Preferred stock may be callable at the option of the company. In this case, the company can choose to pay a specified amount to the stockholders in order to redeem or retire the stock.
- *Cumulative* The dividend on preferred stock may be cumulative. When this is the case, dividends that are not paid are considered to be *in arrears*. Before a dividend on common stock can be declared in a subsequent period, the dividends in arrears as well as the current year's dividend must be paid to the preferred stockholders.
- *Participating* When preferred stock carries a participating feature, it allows the preferred stockholders to receive a dividend in excess of the regular rate when the firm has been particularly profitable and declares an abnormally large dividend.

Preferred stock is attractive to many investors because it offers a return in the form of a dividend at a level of risk that is lower than that of most common stocks. Usually, the

Cumulative feature
The right to dividends in arrears before the current-year dividend is distributed.

Participating feature
Allows preferred stockholders to share on a percentage basis in the distribution of an abnormally large dividend.

Convertible feature
Allows preferred stock to be exchanged for common stock.

Callable feature
Allows the firm to eliminate a class of stock by paying the stockholders a specified amount. ***Alternate term:*** *Redeemable.*

POD REVIEW 11.2

LO2 *Show that you understand the characteristics of common and preferred stock and the differences between the classes of stock.*

- The types of stock issued by a firm are common stock and preferred stock.
  - Preferred stock receives first preference for dividends and generally provides a more stable dividend stream to stockholders than does common stock.
  - Common stockholders have a claim to the residual interest in a company after all debtors' and preferred stockholders' claims are satisfied. Generally, only common stockholders are allowed voting rights.

QUESTIONS

1. *A company has issued both common and preferred stock. When a company pays a cash dividend to stockholders,*
   a. the preferred stockholders receive a dividend before an amount is paid to the common stockholders.
   b. the common stockholders receive a dividend before an amount is paid to the preferred stockholders.
   c. both common and preferred stockholders share equally in any dividend that is paid.
   d. the company is legally obligated to pay a dividend to preferred and common stockholders each year.

2. *What does it mean when preferred stock has a cumulative feature?*
   a. A dividend must be paid to the preferred stockholders each year.
   b. A dividend cannot be paid to the common stockholders.
   c. When dividends are not paid in one period, those dividends must be paid in a subsequent period before common stockholders receive a dividend.
   d. The preferred stockholders can sue the company if a dividend is not paid.

dividend available on preferred stock is more stable from year to year; as a result, the market price of the stock is also more stable. In fact, when preferred stock carries certain provisions, the stock is very similar to bonds and notes payable. Management must evaluate whether such securities represent debt and should be presented in the Liability category of the balance sheet or whether they represent equity and should be presented in the Equity category. Such a decision involves the concept of *substance over form*. That is, a company must look not only at the legal form but also at the economic substance of the security to decide whether it is debt or equity.

Issuance of Stock

LO3 Determine the financial statement impact when stock is issued for cash or for other consideration.

STOCK ISSUED FOR CASH

Stock may be issued in several different ways. It may be issued for cash or for noncash assets. When stock is issued for cash, the amount of its par value should be reported in the stock account and the amount in excess of par should be reported in an additional paid-in capital account. For example, assume that on July 1, a firm issued 1,000 shares of $10 par common stock for $15 per share. The transaction is recorded as follows:

July 1	Cash	15,000	
	Common Stock		10,000
	Additional Paid-In Capital—Common		5,000
	To record the issuance of 1,000 shares of $10 common stock at $15 per share.		

Balance Sheet								Income Statement
ASSETS		=	LIABILITIES	+	STOCKHOLDERS' EQUITY		+	REVENUES − EXPENSES
Cash	15,000				Common Stock	10,000		
					Additional Paid-in Capital—Common	5,000		

As noted earlier, the Common Stock account and the Additional Paid-in Capital account are both presented in the Stockholders' Equity category of the balance sheet and represent the contributed capital component of the corporation.

If no-par stock is issued, the corporation does not distinguish between common stock and additional paid-in capital. If the firm in the previous example had issued no-par stock on July 1 for $15 per share, the entire amount of $15,000 would have been presented in the Common Stock account.

STOCK ISSUED FOR NONCASH CONSIDERATION

Occasionally, stock is issued in return for something other than cash. For example, a corporation may issue stock to obtain land or buildings. When such a transaction occurs, the company faces the difficult task of deciding what value to place on the transaction. This is especially difficult when the market values of the elements of the transaction are not known with complete certainty. According to the general guideline, the transaction should be reported at fair market value. Market value may be indicated by the value of the consideration given (stock) or the value of the consideration received (property), whichever can be most readily determined.

Assume that on July 1, a firm issued 500 shares of $10 par preferred stock to acquire a building. The stock is not widely traded, and the current market value of the stock is not evident. The building has recently been appraised by an independent firm as having a market value of $12,000. In this case, the issuance of the stock should be recorded as follows:

July 1	Building	12,000	
	Preferred Stock		5,000
	Additional Paid-In Capital—Preferred		7,000
	To record the issuance of preferred stock for building.		

Balance Sheet								Income Statement
ASSETS		=	LIABILITIES	+	STOCKHOLDERS' EQUITY		+	REVENUES – EXPENSES
Building	12,000				Preferred Stock	5,000		
					Additional Paid-in Capital—Preferred	7,000		

In other situations, the market value of the stock might be more readily determined and should be used as the best measure of the value of the transaction. Market value may be represented by the current stock market quotation or by a recent cash sale of the stock. The company should attempt to develop the best estimate of the market value of the noncash transaction and should neither intentionally overstate nor intentionally understate the assets received by the issuance of stock.

POD REVIEW 11.3

LO3 *Determine the financial statement impact when stock is issued for cash or for other consideration.*

- When stock is issued for cash or other consideration, the number of outstanding shares is increased and the par value of stock is recorded along with any amount in excess of par being recorded to the Additional Paid-in Capital account.
  - When stock is sold for cash, the asset Cash is increased. When issued for noncash consideration, other asset accounts are increased.

QUESTIONS

1. *When a company has common stock with a $10 per share par value and the stock is issued for $15 per share,*
   a. the $5 per share should be considered a gain on the stock and the amount should be shown on the income statement.
   b. the company should show $15 per share in the Common Stock account in the Stockholders' Equity section of the balance sheet.
   c. the company should show $5 per share as a debit balance in the Additional Paid-in Capital portion of stockholders' equity.
   d. the company should show $5 per share as a credit balance in the Additional Paid-in Capital portion of stockholders' equity.

2. *A company has issued 1,000 shares of $10 par common stock in exchange for a machine. The company believes the machine has a fair market value of $12,000. The following amount should be recorded:*
   a. The company should record the machine at $12,000 if the fair market value of the stock cannot be determined.
   b. The company should record the machine at $10,000.
   c. The company should record a credit to the Common Stock account for $12,000.
   d. The company should record a debit to Additional Paid-in Capital for $2,000.

What Is Treasury Stock?

LO4 Describe the financial statement impact of stock treated as treasury stock.

The Stockholders' Equity category of Southwest Airlines' balance sheet in the chapter opener includes **treasury stock** in the amount of $390 million. The Treasury Stock account is created when a corporation buys its own stock sometime after issuing it. For an amount to be treated as treasury stock:

1. **It must be the corporation's own stock.**
2. **It must have been issued to the stockholders at some point.**

Treasury stock
Stock issued by the firm and then repurchased but not retired.

3. **It must have been repurchased from the stockholders.**
4. **It must not be retired, but must be held for some purpose. Treasury stock is not considered outstanding stock and does not have voting rights.**

A corporation might repurchase stock as treasury stock for several reasons. The most common reason is to have stock available to distribute to employees for bonuses or to make available as part of an employee benefit plan. Firms also might buy treasury stock to maintain a favorable market price for the stock or to improve the appearance of the firm's financial ratios. More recently, firms have purchased their stock to maintain control of the ownership and to prevent unwanted takeover or buyout attempts. Of course, the lower the stock price, the more likely a company is to buy back its own stock and wait for the shares to rise in value before reissuing them.

The two methods to account for treasury stock transactions are the cost method and the par value method. We will present the more commonly used cost method. Assume that the Stockholders' Equity section of Rezin Company's balance sheet on December 31, 2008, appears as follows:

Common stock, $10 par value, 1,000 shares issued and outstanding	$10,000
Additional paid-in capital—Common	12,000
Retained earnings	15,000
Total stockholders' equity	$37,000

Assume that on February 1, 2009, Rezin buys 100 of its shares as treasury stock at $25 per share. Rezin records the following transaction at that time:

Feb. 1	Treasury Stock	2,500	
	Cash		2,500
	To record the purchase of 100 shares of treasury stock.		

Balance Sheet								
ASSETS		=	LIABILITIES	+	STOCKHOLDERS' EQUITY		+	Income Statement: REVENUES − EXPENSES
Cash	(2,500)				Treasury Stock	(2,500)		

The purchase of treasury stock does not directly affect the Common Stock account. The Treasury Stock account is considered a contra account and is subtracted from the total of contributed capital and retained earnings in the Stockholders' Equity section. Treasury Stock is *not* an asset account. When a company buys its own stock, it is contracting its size and reducing the equity of stockholders. Therefore, Treasury Stock is a contra-equity account, not an asset.

The Stockholders' Equity section of Rezin's balance sheet on February 1, 2009, after the purchase of the treasury stock, appears as follows:

Common stock, $10 par value, 1,000 shares issued, 900 outstanding	$10,000
Additional paid-in capital—Common	12,000
Retained earnings	15,000
Total contributed capital and retained earnings	$37,000
Less: Treasury stock, 100 shares at cost	2,500
Total stockholders' equity	$34,500

Corporations may choose to reissue stock to investors after it has been held as treasury stock. When treasury stock is resold for more than it cost, the difference between the sales price and the cost appears in the Additional Paid-in Capital—Treasury Stock account. For example, if Rezin resold 100 shares of treasury stock on May 1, 2009, for $30 per share, the Treasury Stock account would be reduced by $2,500 (100 shares times $25 per share) and the Additional Paid-in Capital—Treasury Stock account would be increased by $500 (100 shares times the difference between the purchase price of $25 and the reissue price of $30).

When treasury stock is resold for an amount less than its cost, the difference between the sales price and the cost is deducted from the Additional Paid-in Capital—Treasury Stock account. If that account does not exist, the difference should be deducted from the Retained Earnings account. For example, assume that Rezin Company had resold 100 shares of treasury stock on May 1, 2009, for $20 per share instead of $30 as in the previous example. In this example, Rezin has had no other treasury stock transactions; therefore, no balance existed in the Additional Paid-in Capital—Treasury Stock account. Rezin would then reduce the Treasury Stock account by $2,500 (100 shares times $25 per share) and would reduce Retained Earnings by $500 (100 shares times the difference between the purchase price of $25 and the reissue price of $20 per share). Thus, the Additional Paid-in Capital—Treasury Stock account may have a positive balance, but entries that result in a negative balance in the account should not be made.

Note that **income statement accounts are never involved in treasury stock transactions.** Regardless of whether treasury stock is reissued for more or less than its cost, the effect is reflected in the Stockholders' Equity accounts. It is simply not possible for a firm to engage in transactions involving its own stock and have the result affect the performance of the firm as reflected on the income statement.

POD REVIEW 11.4

LO4 *Describe the financial statement impact of stock treated as treasury stock.*

- Treasury stock results when a corporation buys back its own stock.
  - Treasury stock is accounted for as a contra-equity account and is a reduction of stockholders' equity.

QUESTIONS

1. *The Treasury Stock account should be considered*
   a. an asset account.
   b. an income statement account.
   c. a credit balance account in the Stockholders' Equity portion of the balance sheet.
   d. a debit balance account in the Stockholders' Equity portion of the balance sheet.

2. *A company issued 5,000 shares of $5 par common stock for $20 per share. The company purchased 2,000 shares as treasury stock at $22 per share. Later the company reissued 500 shares of the treasury stock at $23 per share. Which of the following is true?*
   a. The company has a gain of $500 that should appear on the income statement.
   b. The company has a gain of $1,500 that should appear on the income statement.
   c. The Treasury Stock account should have a balance of $33,000.
   d. The Treasury Stock account should have a balance of $32,500.

RETIREMENT OF STOCK

Retirement of stock
When the stock is repurchased with no intention of re-issuing at a later date.

Retirement of stock occurs when a corporation buys back stock after it has been issued to investors and does not intend to reissue the stock. Retirement often occurs because the corporation wants to eliminate a particular class of stock or a particular group of stockholders. When stock is repurchased and retired, the balances of the Stock account and the Paid-in Capital account that were created when the stock was issued must be eliminated. When the original issue price is higher than the repurchase price of the stock, the difference is reflected in the Paid-in Capital from Stock Retirement account. When the repurchase price of the stock is more than the original issue price, the difference reduces the Retained Earnings account. The general principle for retirement of stock is the same as for treasury stock transactions. No income statement accounts are affected by the retirement. The effect is reflected in the Cash account and the Stockholders' Equity accounts.

© AP Photo/Mark Lennihan

Hot Topics

Southwest Airlines' Creation of Stockholders' Value

In July 2007, Southwest Airlines declared a quarterly dividend of $.0045 per share on all shares then issued and outstanding. As the 124th consecutive dividend for the company, it indicates a long history of profitability and growth. Southwest's low-cost/low-fare strategy has been effective for many years. While other airlines have struggled, Southwest has continued to grow, expand, and profit.

But can the company continue the trend? Southwest's annual report listed many potential problems, including increased labor costs, higher fuel charges, continued security concerns about terrorist activities, higher taxes, and more competition from other airlines that have adopted Southwest's operating model. Will Southwest Airlines continue to produce a good return for its stockholders? Only time will tell, but Southwest's management believes it will be the best airline in the industry.

Dividends: Distribution of Income to Shareholders

LO5 Compute the amount of cash dividends when a firm has issued both preferred and common stock.

CASH DIVIDENDS

Corporations may declare and issue several different types of dividends, the most common of which is a cash dividend to stockholders. Cash dividends may be declared quarterly or annually or at other intervals. Normally, cash dividends are declared on one date, referred to as the *date of declaration*, and are paid out on a later date, referred to as the *payment date*. The dividend is paid to the stockholders who own the stock as of a particular date, the *date of record*.

Generally, two requirements must be met before the board of directors can declare a cash dividend. First, sufficient cash must be available by the payment date to pay to the stockholders. Second, the Retained Earnings account must have a sufficient positive balance. Dividends reduce the balance of the account; therefore, Retained Earnings must have a balance before the dividend declaration. Most firms have an established policy concerning the portion of income that will be declared as dividends. The **dividend payout ratio** is calculated as the annual dividend amount divided by the annual net income. The dividend payout ratio for many firms is 50% or 60% and seldom exceeds 70%. Typically, utilities pay a high proportion of their earnings as dividends. In contrast, fast-growing companies in technology often pay

Dividend payout ratio
The annual dividend amount divided by the annual net income.

nothing to stockholders. Some investors want and need the current income of a high-dividend payout, but others would rather not receive dividend income and prefer to gamble that the stock price will appreciate.

Cash dividends become a liability on the date they are declared. An accounting entry should be recorded on that date to acknowledge the liability and reduce the balance of the Retained Earnings account. For example, assume that on July 1, the board of directors of Grant Company declared a cash dividend of $7,000 to be paid on September 1. Grant reflects the declaration as a reduction of Retained Earnings and an increase in Cash Dividend Payable as follows:

July 1	Retained Earnings	7,000	
	Cash Dividend Payable		7,000
	To record the declaration of a cash dividend.		

Study Tip

A dividend is not an expense on the income statement. It is a reduction of retained earnings and appears on the retained earnings statement. If it is a cash dividend, it also reduces the cash balance when paid.

Balance Sheet								Income Statement
ASSETS	=	LIABILITIES		+	STOCKHOLDERS' EQUITY		+	REVENUES − EXPENSES
		Cash Dividend Payable	7,000		Retained Earnings	(7,000)		

The Cash Dividend Payable account is a liability and is normally shown in the Current Liabilities section of the balance sheet.

The important point to remember is that dividends reduce the amount of retained earnings *when declared.* When dividends are paid, the company reduces the liability to stockholders reflected in the Cash Dividend Payable account.

CASH DIVIDENDS FOR PREFERRED AND COMMON STOCK

When cash dividends involving more than one class of stock are declared, the corporation must determine the proper amount to allocate to each class of stock. As indicated earlier, the amount of dividends to which preferred stockholders have rights depends on the terms and provisions of the preferred stock. The proper allocation of cash dividends is illustrated with an example of a firm that has two classes of stock: preferred and common.

Assume that on December 31, 2008, Stricker Company has outstanding 10,000 shares of $10 par, 8% preferred stock and 40,000 shares of $5 par common stock. Stricker was unable to declare a dividend in 2006 or 2007 but wants to declare a $70,000 dividend for 2008. The dividend is to be allocated to preferred and common stockholders in accordance with the terms of the stock agreements.

Noncumulative Preferred Stock If the terms of the stock agreement indicate that the preferred stock is not cumulative, the preferred stockholders do not have a right to dividends in arrears. The dividends that were not declared in 2006 and 2007 are simply lost and do not affect the distribution of the dividend in 2008. Therefore, the cash dividend declared in 2008 is allocated between preferred and common stockholders as follows:

	To Preferred	To Common
Step 1: Distribute current-year dividend to preferred (10,000 shares × $10 par × 8% × 1 year)	$8,000	
Step 2: Distribute remaining dividend to common ($70,000 − $8,000)		$62,000
Total allocated	$8,000	$62,000
Dividend per share		
Preferred: $8,000/10,000 shares	$0.80	
Common: $62,000/40,000 shares		$1.55

Cumulative Preferred Stock If the terms of the stock agreement indicate that the preferred stock is cumulative, the preferred stockholders have a right to dividends in arrears before the current year's dividend is distributed. Therefore, Stricker performs the following steps:

	To Preferred	To Common
Step 1: Distribute dividends in arrears to preferred (10,000 shares × $10 par × 8% × 2 years)	$16,000	
Step 2: Distribute current-year dividend to preferred (10,000 shares × $10 par × 8% × 1 year)	8,000	
Step 3: Distribute remainder to common ($70,000 − $24,000)		$46,000
Total allocated	$24,000	$46,000
Dividend per share		
Preferred: $24,000/10,000 shares	$2.40	
Common: $46,000/40,000 shares		$1.15

POD REVIEW 11.5

LO5 *Compute the amount of cash dividends when a firm has issued both preferred and common stock.*

- The amount of a preferred stock dividend depends on the terms of the stock agreement: cumulative, noncumulative, or cumulative and participating.

QUESTIONS

1. *When are cash dividends a reduction from the Retained Earnings account?*
   a. at the time the dividend is declared
   b. at the time the dividend is paid
   c. only if they are dividends on common stock
   d. only if they are dividends on preferred stock

2. *At December 31, 2008, Rhodes Company has 10,000 shares of $10 par, 6% cumulative preferred stock outstanding and 4,000 shares of $5 par common stock outstanding. The company did not pay a dividend in 2006 or 2007. If the company pays a dividend in 2008, how much must be paid for the common stockholders to receive a dividend?*
   a. $6,000
   b. $12,000
   c. $18,000
   d. $24,000

LO6 Show that you understand the difference between cash and stock dividends and the effect of stock dividends.

Stock dividend
The issuance of additional shares of stock to existing stockholders.

STOCK DIVIDENDS

Cash dividends are the most popular and widely used form of dividend; but at times, corporations may use stock dividends instead of or in addition to cash dividends. A **stock dividend** occurs when a corporation declares and issues additional shares of its own stock to existing stockholders. Firms use stock dividends for several reasons. First, a corporation may not have sufficient cash available to declare a cash dividend. Stock dividends do not require the use of the corporation's resources and allow cash to be retained for other purposes. Second, stock dividends result in additional shares of stock outstanding and may decrease the market price per share of stock if the dividend is large. (Small stock dividends tend to have little effect on market price.) The lower price may make the stock more attractive to a wider range of investors and allow enhanced financing opportunities. Finally, stock dividends normally do not represent taxable income to the recipients and may be attractive to some wealthy stockholders.

Similar to cash dividends, stock dividends are normally declared by the board of directors on a specific date and the stock is distributed to the stockholders at a later date. The corporation recognizes the stock dividend on the date of declaration. Assume that Shah Company's Stockholders' Equity category of the balance sheet appears as follows as of January 1, 2008:

Common stock, $10 par,	
5,000 shares issued and outstanding	$ 50,000
Additional paid-in capital—Common	30,000
Retained earnings	70,000
Total stockholders' equity	$150,000

Assume that on January 2, 2008, Shah declares a 10% stock dividend to common stockholders to be distributed on April 1, 2008. Small stock dividends (usually those of 20% to 25% or less) normally are recorded at the *market value* of the stock as of the date of declaration. Assume that Shah's common stock is selling at $40 per share on that date. Therefore, the total market value of the stock dividend is $20,000 (10% of 5,000 shares outstanding, or 500 shares, times $40 per share). Shah records the transaction on the date of declaration as follows, with the par value per share recorded in the Common Stock Dividend Distributable account:

Jan. 2	Retained Earnings	20,000	
	Additional Paid-in Capital—Common		15,000
	Common Stock Dividend Distributable		5,000
	To record the declaration of a stock dividend.		

Balance Sheet						Income Statement
ASSETS	=	**LIABILITIES**	+	**STOCKHOLDERS' EQUITY**	+	**REVENUES − EXPENSES**
				Retained Earnings (20,000)		
				Common Stock Dividend Distributable 5,000		
				Additional Paid-in Capital—Common 15,000		

The Common Stock Dividend Distributable account represents shares of stock to be issued; it is not a liability account because no cash or assets are to be distributed to the stockholders. Thus, it should be treated as an account in the Stockholders' Equity section of the balance sheet and is a part of the contributed capital component of equity.

Note that the declaration of a stock dividend does not affect the total stockholders' equity of the corporation, although the retained earnings are reduced. That is, the Stockholders' Equity section of Shah's balance sheet on January 2, 2008, is as follows after the declaration of the dividend:

Common stock, $10 par,	
5,000 shares issued and outstanding	$ 50,000
Common stock dividend distributable, 500 shares	5,000
Additional paid-in capital—Common	45,000
Retained earnings	50,000
Total stockholders' equity	$150,000

The account balances are different, but total stockholders' equity is $150,000 both before and after the declaration of the stock dividend. In effect, retained earnings has been capitalized (transferred permanently to the contributed capital accounts). When a corporation actually issues a stock dividend, an amount from the Stock Dividend Distributable account must be transferred to the appropriate stock account.

The stock dividend example has illustrated the general rule that stock dividends should be reported at fair market value. That is, in the transaction to reflect the stock dividend, retained earnings is decreased in the amount of the fair market value per share of the stock times the number of shares to be distributed. When a large stock dividend is declared, however, accountants do not follow the general rule we have illustrated. A large stock dividend is a stock dividend of more than 20% to 25% of the number of shares of stock outstanding. In that case, the stock dividend is reported at *par value* rather than at fair market value. That is, Retained Earnings is decreased in the amount of the par value per share times the number of shares to be distributed.

Refer again to the Shah Company example. Assume that instead of a 10% dividend, on January 2, 2008, Shah declares a 100% stock dividend to be distributed on April 1, 2008. The stock dividend results in 5,000 additional shares being issued and certainly meets the definition of a large stock dividend. Shah records the following transaction on January 2, the date of declaration:

Jan. 2	Retained Earnings	50,000	
	Common Stock Dividend Distributable		50,000
	To record the declaration of a large stock dividend.		

Balance Sheet						Income Statement
ASSETS	=	**LIABILITIES**	+	**STOCKHOLDERS' EQUITY**	+	**REVENUES − EXPENSES**
				Retained Earnings (50,000)		
				Common Stock Dividend Distributable 50,000		

The accounting transaction to be recorded when the stock is actually distributed is as follows:

Apr. 1	Common Stock Dividend Distributable	50,000	
	Common Stock		50,000
	To record the distribution of a stock dividend.		

Balance Sheet						Income Statement
ASSETS	=	**LIABILITIES**	+	**STOCKHOLDERS' EQUITY**	+	**REVENUES − EXPENSES**
				Common Stock Dividend Distributable (50,000)		
				Common Stock 50,000		

The Stockholders' Equity category of Shah's balance sheet as of April 1 after the stock dividend is as follows:

Common stock, $10 par, 10,000 shares issued and outstanding	$100,000
Additional paid-in capital—Common	30,000
Retained earnings	20,000
Total stockholders' equity	$150,000

Again, note that the stock dividend has not affected total stockholders' equity. Shah has $150,000 of stockholders' equity both before and after the stock dividend. The difference between large and small stock dividends is the amount transferred from retained earnings to the contributed capital portion of equity.

POD REVIEW 11.6

LO6 ***Show that you understand the difference between cash and stock dividends and the effect of stock dividends.***

- Stock dividends are given in lieu of cash dividends. Stockholders receive shares of stock, which do not require a current use of cash resources by the corporation.
  - Stock dividends do not affect total stockholders' equity. They reduce retained earnings and increase the amount of common stock and additional paid-in capital.

QUESTIONS

1. *What is the effect on the financial statements when a dividend in the form of stock is declared and issued?*
   a. Retained earnings is not affected.
   b. Retained earnings is decreased, and total stockholders' equity is decreased.
   c. Retained earnings is decreased, and total stockholders' equity is not affected.
   d. Retained earnings is not decreased, but total stockholders' equity does decrease.

2. *What is the effect of a stock dividend declared and issued versus a cash dividend declared and paid?*
   a. A stock dividend does not decrease the company's total assets.
   b. A cash dividend does not decrease the company's total assets.
   c. A stock dividend does not affect retained earnings.
   d. A cash dividend does not affect retained earnings.

STOCK SPLITS

LO7 Determine the difference between stock dividends and stock splits.

A **stock split** is similar to a stock dividend in that it results in additional shares of stock outstanding and is nontaxable. In fact, firms may use a stock split for nearly the same reasons as a stock dividend: to increase the number of shares, reduce the market price per share, and make the stock more accessible to a wider range of investors. There is an important legal difference, however. Stock dividends do not affect the par value per share of the stock, whereas stock splits reduce the par value per share. There also is an important accounting difference. An accounting transaction is *not recorded* when a corporation declares and executes a stock split. None of the Stockholders' Equity accounts are affected by the split. Rather, the note information accompanying the balance sheet must disclose the additional shares and the reduction of the par value per share.

Stock split
The creation of additional shares of stock with a reduction of the par value of the stock.

Return to the Shah Company example. Assume that on January 2, 2008, Shah issued a 2-for-1 stock split instead of a stock dividend. The split results in an additional 5,000 shares of stock outstanding but is not recorded in a formal accounting transaction. Therefore, the Stockholders' Equity section of Shah Company immediately after the stock split on January 2, 2008, is as follows:

Common stock, $5 par,	
10,000 shares issued and outstanding	$ 50,000
Additional paid-in capital—Common	30,000
Retained earnings	70,000
Total stockholders' equity	$150,000

Note that the par value per share has been reduced from $10 to $5 per share of stock as a result of the split. Like a stock dividend, the split does not affect total stockholders' equity because no assets have been transferred. Therefore, the split simply results in more shares of stock with claims to the same net assets of the firm.

EXHIBIT 11-3 Nordstrom's Partial Stockholders' Equity Section

Condensed Consolidated Partial Balance Sheets
(amounts in thousands)

	April 30, 2005	January 29, 2005	May 1, 2004
Shareholders' Equity:			
Common stock, no par:			
500,000 shares authorized;			
136,632, 135,665, and 139,816			
shares issued and outstanding	619,640	552,655	466,573
Unearned stock compensation	(593)	(299)	(522)
Retained earnings	1,266,337	1,227,303	1,254,566
Accumulated other comprehensive earnings	7,568	9,335	11,013
Total shareholders' equity	1,892,952	1,788,994	1,731,630

Shares outstanding before stock split → 136,632

Exhibit 11-3 presents the Stockholders' Equity category of **Nordstrom, Inc.**'s balance sheets as of April 30, 2005. At that time, the company had 136,632 shares of common stock outstanding. After the balance sheet date, the company declared a 2-for-1 stock split. That means that every stockholder that was holding one share of stock before the stock split had two shares after the split. The effect of the split was to double the number of shares of stock. Thus, the number of shares of stock after the split was 136,632 × 2, or 273,264. However, each stockholder still had the same *proportional* ownership of the company. When a company has a stock split, it also restates the number of shares for all previous years. Although a stock split does not increase the wealth of the shareholder, it is usually a good sign. Companies with rising stock prices declare a stock split to make the stock more marketable to the small investor, who would be more likely to buy a stock at $50 per share than at $100.

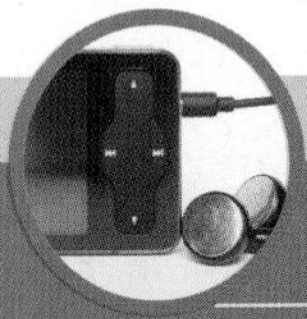

POD REVIEW 11.7

LO7 *Determine the difference between stock dividends and stock splits.*

- Both stock splits and stock dividends increase the number of shares of stock outstanding although they are fundamentally different transactions.
    - Stock splits do not require an accounting transaction to be recorded, do not reduce the par value of the stock, and have no effect on retained earnings or additional paid-in capital.

QUESTIONS

1. *What is the effect of a stock dividend declared and issued versus a stock split issued?*
    a. A stock split does not affect the number of shares of stock outstanding.
    b. A stock dividend does not affect the number of shares of stock outstanding.
    c. A stock dividend does not affect retained earnings.
    d. A stock split does not affect retained earnings.

2. *When a stock split is issued to the stockholders,*
    a. it is likely that the market price per share of the stock will decline.
    b. it is likely that the market price per share of the stock will not decline.
    c. the company's total stockholders' equity will decrease.
    d. the company's total stockholders' equity will increase.

Statement of Stockholders' Equity

LO8 Show that you understand the statement of stockholders' equity and comprehensive income.

In addition to a balance sheet, an income statement, and a cash flow statement, many annual reports contain a **statement of stockholders' equity**. The purpose of this statement is to explain all of the reasons for the difference between the beginning and the ending balance of each of the accounts in the Stockholders' Equity category of the balance sheet. Of course, if the only changes are the result of income and dividends, a statement of retained earnings is sufficient. When other changes have occurred in Stockholders' Equity accounts, this more complete statement is necessary.

Statement of stockholders' equity Reflects the differences between beginning and ending balances for all accounts in the Stockholders' Equity category of the balance sheet.

The statement of stockholders' equity of Fun Fitness, Inc., is presented in Exhibit 11-4 for the year 2008. The statement starts with the beginning balances of each of the accounts as of December 31, 2008. Fun Fitness's stockholders' equity is presented in four categories (the columns on the statement) as of December 31, 2008, as follows (in millions):

Number of shares	1,000,000
Common stock	$50.0
Paid-in capital	$350.0
Retained earnings	$400.0

The statement of stockholders' equity indicates the items or events that affected stockholders' equity during 2008. The items or events were as follows:

Item or Event	Effect on Stockholders' Equity
Net earnings →	Increased retained earnings by $64.0 million
Dividends →	Decreased retained earnings by $25.0 million
Shares issued →	Increased common stock by $5.0 million and Increased paid-in capital by $39.0 million

The last line of the statement of stockholders' equity indicates the ending balances of the Stockholders' Equity accounts as of the balance sheet date, December 31, 2008. Note that each of the Stockholders' Equity accounts increased during 2008. The statement of Stockholders' Equity is useful in explaining the reasons for the changes that occurred.

WHAT IS COMPREHENSIVE INCOME?

There has always been some question about which items or transactions should be shown on the income statement and included in the calculation of net income. Generally, the accounting rule-making bodies have held that the income statement should reflect an *all-inclusive* approach. That is, all events and transactions that affect

EXHIBIT 11-4 Fun Fitness's Statement of Stockholders' Equity, 2008

Fun Fitness, Inc.
Statement of Stockholders' Equity
For the Year Ended December 31, 2008

(dollar amounts in millions)

	Common Stock		Paid-In	Retained
Stockholders' Equity	**Shares**	**Amount**	**Capital**	**Earnings**
Balance, December 31, 2007	1,000,000	$50.0	$350.0	$400.0
Net earnings				64.0
Cash dividend declared				(25.0)
Issuance of stock	100,000	5.0	39.0	
Balance, December 31, 2008	1,100,000	$55.0	$389.0	$439.0

income should be shown on the income statement. This approach prevents manipulation of the income figure by those who would like to show "good news" on the income statement and "bad news" directly on the retained earnings statement or the statement of stockholders' equity. The result of the all-inclusive approach is that the income statement includes items that are not necessarily under management's control, such as losses from natural disasters, meaning that the income statement may not be a true reflection of a company's future potential.

The FASB has accepted certain exceptions to the all-inclusive approach and has allowed items to be recorded directly to the Stockholders' Equity category. This text discussed one such item: unrealized gains and losses on investment securities. Exhibit 11-5 presents several additional items that are beyond the scope of this text. Items such as these have been excluded from the income statement for various reasons. Quite often the justification is a concern for the volatility of the net income number. The items cited in this text are often large dollar amounts; if included in the income statement, they would cause income to fluctuate widely from period to period. Therefore, the income statement is deemed to be more useful when the items are excluded.

Comprehensive income The total change in net assets from all sources except investments by or distributions to the owners.

A new term has been coined to incorporate the "income-type" items that escape the income statement. **Comprehensive income** is the net assets increase resulting from all transactions during a time period (except for investments by owners and distributions to owners). Exhibit 11-5 presents the statement of comprehensive income and its relationship to the traditional income statement. It illustrates that comprehensive income encompasses all of the revenues and expenses that are presented on the income statement to calculate net income and includes items that are not presented on the income statement but that affect total stockholders' equity.[1] The comprehensive income measure is truly all-inclusive because it includes such transactions as unrealized gains and prior-period adjustments that affect stockholders' equity. Firms are required to disclose comprehensive income because it provides a more complete measure of performance.

EXHIBIT 11-5 The Relationship of the Income Statement and the Statement of Comprehensive Income

Income Statement
For Year Ended December 31, 20XX

Revenues	XXX
Expenses	XXX
Other gains and losses	XXX
Income before tax	XXX
Income tax expense	XXX
Net income	XXX

All-Inclusive Earnings
These items, *excluded* from the income statement, are included on a statement of comprehensive income.

Statement of Comprehensive Income
For Year Ended December 31, 20XX

Net income	XXX
Foreign currency translation adjustment	XXX
Unrealized holding gains/losses	XXX
Delayed recognition pension items	XXX
Comprehensive income	XXX

1 The format of Exhibit 11-5 is suggested by the FASB. The FASB also allows other possible formats of the statement of comprehensive income.

POD REVIEW 11.8

LO8 ***Show that you understand the statement of stockholders' equity and comprehensive income.***

- The statement of stockholders' equity shows how all of the equity accounts changed for a particular accounting period or specific periods.
- Comprehensive income is based on the notion that the income statement be inclusive of all items affecting the wealth of an entity. The calculation of comprehensive income takes into account the increase in net assets during a time period.

QUESTIONS

1. *Which of the following would be considered part of other comprehensive income?*
   a. foreign currency translation adjustment items
   b. unrealized holding gains/losses on certain types of securities
   c. delayed recognition pension items
   d. all of the above

2. *Which of the following would be included as an element of other comprehensive income?*
   a. foreign currency translation adjustment items
   b. amounts resulting from treasury stock transactions
   c. issuance of stock for more than par value
   d. issuance of stock dividends or stock splits

What Analyzing Stockholders' Equity Reveals About a Firm's Value

LO9 Understand how investors use ratios to evaluate stockholders' equity.

BOOK VALUE PER SHARE

Users of financial statements are often interested in computing the value of a corporation's stock. This is a difficult task because *value* is not a well-defined term and means different things to different users. One measure of value is the book value of the stock. **Book value per share** of common stock represents the rights that each share of common stock has to the net assets of the corporation. The term *net assets* refers to the total assets of the firm minus total liabilities. In other words, net assets equal the total stockholders' equity of the corporation. Therefore, when only common stock is present, book value per share is measured as follows:

Book value per share Total stockholders' equity divided by the number of shares of common stock outstanding.

$$\text{Book Value per Share} = \frac{\text{Total Stockholders' Equity}}{\text{Number of Shares of Stock Outstanding}}$$

The book value per share is the amount per share of net assets to which the company's common stockholders have the rights. It does not indicate the market value of the common stock. That is, book value per share does not indicate the price that should be paid by those who want to buy or sell the stock on the stock exchange. Book value also is an incomplete measure of value because the corporation's net assets are normally measured on the balance sheet at the original cost, not at the current value of the assets.

For more information on how investors use book value per share and what this measure means, see the Ratio Decision Model that follows.

USING THE RATIO DECISION MODEL: ANALYZING BOOK VALUE PER SHARE

Use the following Ratio Decision Model to evaluate the book value per common share of Kellogg's or any other public company.

1. Formulate the Question

Investors realize that several measures of the value of a company impact the stock price of a company. Investors in common stock also realize that they have a right to the company's assets only after the rights of creditors and preferred stockholders have been satisfied. Investors can determine their rights by calculating the book value per share of the stock. Normally, a company will not be liquidated, but investors still need to understand how the book value per share relates to the actual stock price for the company. The important questions are:

What price per share does an investor want to pay for a company's stock?
Should that price be above or below book value per share?

2. Gather the Information from the Financial Statements

- Total stockholders' equity: From the statement of stockholders' equity
- Number of shares of stock outstanding: From the statement of stockholders' equity

3. Calculate the Ratio

$$\text{Book Value per Share} = \frac{\text{Total Stockholders' Equity}}{\text{Number of Shares of Stock Outstanding}}$$

Kellogg's, Inc.
CONSOLIDATED BALANCE SHEETS
(in millions, except share data)

	2006	2005
Shareholders equity		
Common stock, $.25 par value, 1,000,000,000 shares authorized Issued: 418,515,339 shares in 2006 and 418,451,198 shares in 2005	104.6	104.6
Capital in excess of par value	292.3	58.9
Retained earnings	3,630.4	3,266.1
Treasury stock at cost: 20,817,930 shares in 2006 and 13,121,446 shares in 2005	(912.1)	(569.8)
Accumulated other comprehensive income (loss)	(1,046.2)	(576.1)
TOTAL SHAREHOLDERS EQUITY	$ 2,069.0	$ 2,283.7

$$\text{Book Value per Share} = \frac{\$2{,}069{,}000{,}000}{397{,}697{,}409} = \$5.20$$

Note: Shares outstanding is 418,515,339 issued less 20,817,930 treasury stock.

4. Compare the Ratio with Others

Kellogg's book value per share of common stock may be compared to prior years and to companies in the same industry.

	Kellogg's		General Mills	
	December 31, 2006	December 31, 2005	May 28, 2006	May 29, 2005
Book value per share	$5.20	$5.63	$16.21	$15.38

5. Interpret the Results

For 2006, Kellogg's common stockholders have the right to $5.20 per share of net assets in the corporation. That has decreased from the $5.63 per share in 2005.

The book value per share indicates the recorded minimum value per share of the stock, but it is not a very accurate measure of the price that an investor would be willing to pay for a share of stock. The book value of a stock is often thought to be the "floor" of a stock price. When a company has a stock price that is less than its book value, it may be an indication that the stockholders would be better off if the company were liquidated rather than continue in business.

CALCULATING BOOK VALUE WHEN PREFERRED STOCK IS PRESENT

The focus of the computation of book value per share is always on the value per share of the *common* stock. Therefore, the computation must be adjusted for corporations that have both preferred and common stock. The numerator of the fraction, total stockholders' equity, should be reduced by the rights that preferred stockholders have to the corporation's net assets. Normally, this can be accomplished by deducting the redemption value or liquidation value of the preferred stock along with any dividends in arrears on cumulative preferred stock. The denominator should not include the number of shares of preferred stock.

To illustrate the computation of book value per share when both common and preferred stock are present, we refer to the Stockholders' Equity category of Workout Wonders, presented in Exhibit 11-6. When calculating book value per share, we want to consider only the *common* stockholders' equity. Exhibit 11-6 indicates that the company had total stockholders' equity in 2008 of $13,972 million but also that preferred stockholders had a right to $500 million in the event of liquidation. Therefore, $500 million must be deducted to calculate the rights of the common stockholders:

$13,972 − $500 = $13,472 million common stockholders' equity

The number of shares of common stock *outstanding* for the company is 1,782 million issued less 103 million of treasury stock. Therefore, the computation of book value per share is as follows:

$13,472/1,679 = $8.02 Book Value per Share

This indicates that if the company was liquidated and the assets sold at their recorded values, the common stockholders would receive $8.02 per share. Of course, if the company went bankrupt and had to liquidate assets at distressed values, stockholders would receive something less than book value.

EXHIBIT 11-6 **Workout Wonders' Stockholders' Equity Section**

Stockholders' Equity Section of Balance Sheet

December 31, 2008, and December 31, 2007

(in millions)	2008	2007
Preferred stock, no par value (liquidation value, $500)	400	400
Common stock, par value 1 2/3 per share (issued 1,782 shares)	30	30
Capital in excess of par value	618	548
Retained earnings	18,730	15,961
Accumulated other comprehensive loss	(886)	(1,267)
Less: Repurchased common stock, at cost (103 and 77 shares, respectively)	(4,920)	(3,376)
Total shareholders' equity	13,972	12,296

MARKET VALUE PER SHARE

Market value per share
The selling price of the stock as indicated by the most recent transactions.

The market value of the stock is a more meaningful measure of the value of the stock to those financial statement users interested in buying or selling shares of stock. The **market value per share** is the price at which stock is currently selling. When stock is sold on a stock exchange, the price can be determined by its most recent selling price. For example, the listing for **General Motors** stock on the Internet may indicate the following:

52-Week			Daily			
High	**Low**	**Sym**	**High**	**Low**	**Last**	**Change**
68.17	39.17	GM	43.3	42.01	42.93	+0.48 (1.13%)

The two left-hand columns indicate the stock price for the last 52-week period. General Motors sold as high as $68.17 and as low as $39.17 during that time period. The right-hand portion indicates the high and low for the previous day's trading and the closing price. General Motors sold as high as $43.30 per share and as low as $42.01 per share and closed at $42.93. For the day, the stock increased by 1.13%, or $0.48 per share.

The market value of the stock depends on many factors. Stockholders must evaluate a corporation's earnings and liquidity as indicated in the financial statements. They also must consider a variety of economic factors and project all of the factors into the future to determine the proper market value per share of the stock. Many investors use sophisticated investment techniques, including large databases, to identify factors that affect a company's stock price.

POD REVIEW 11.9

LO9 ***Understand how investors use ratios to evaluate stockholders' equity.***

- Ratios used to analyze stockholders' equity are designed to measure some aspect of the value of the firm held by stockholders. Some common measures include:
  - Book value per share—a measure based on balance sheet accounting amounts recorded.
  - Market value per share—a measure aimed at assessing fair market value based on the current price of stock.

QUESTIONS

1. *The ratio of book value per share*
   a. is an indication of the market value of the stock on the stock exchange.
   b. has total assets as the denominator.
   c. has total assets as the numerator.
   d. is an indication of the rights of the common stockholders to the company's assets.

2. *If a company has both common and preferred stock and wants to calculate book value per share,*
   a. the rights of the preferred stockholders to the company's assets should be deducted before book value per share is calculated.
   b. the rights of the common stockholders to the company's assets should be deducted before book value per share is calculated.
   c. the amount of stock outstanding in the numerator of the fraction should represent only the preferred stock.
   d. the amount of stock outstanding in the numerator of the fraction should represent the total of the common and preferred stock.

How Changes in Stockholders' Equity Affect the Statement of Cash Flows

LO10 Explain the effects that transactions involving stockholders' equity have on the statement of cash flows.

It is important to determine the effect that the issuance of stock, the repurchase of stock, and the payment of dividends have on the statement of cash flows. The impact that each of these business activities has on cash must be reflected on the statement. Exhibit 11-7 indicates how these stockholders' equity transactions affect cash flow and where the items should be placed on the statement of cash flows.

The issuance of stock is a method to finance business. Therefore, the cash *inflow* from the sale of stock to stockholders should be reflected as an inflow in the Financing Activities section of the statement of cash flows. Generally, companies do not disclose separately the amount received for the par value of the stock and the amount received in excess of par. Rather, one amount is listed to indicate the total inflow of cash.

The repurchase or retirement of stock also represents a financing activity. Therefore, the cash *outflow* should be reflected as a reduction of cash in the Financing Activities section of the statement of cash flows. Again, companies do not distinguish between the amount paid for the par of the stock and the amount paid in excess of par. One amount is generally listed to indicate the total cash outflow to retire stock.

Dividends paid to stockholders represent a cost of financing the business with stock. Therefore, dividends paid should be reflected as a cash *outflow* in the Financing Activities section of the statement of cash flows. It is important to distinguish between the declaration of dividends and the payment of dividends. The cash outflow occurs at the time the dividend is paid and should be reflected on the statement of cash flows in that period.

The 2006 partial statement of cash flows for **Continental Airlines, Inc.**, is shown in Exhibit 11-8. During 2006, the company had considerable cash outflows associated with its long-term debt of $948 million. The company had a cash inflow of $574 million when long-term debt was issued and $82 million when common stock was issued. No dividends were paid in 2006, 2005, or 2004.

Study Tip

Transactions affecting the Stockholders' Equity category of the balance sheet will appear in the Financing Activities category of the cash flow statement. Dividends are included in the cash flow statement when they are paid rather than when they are declared.

EXHIBIT 11-7 The Effect of Stockholders' Equity Items on the Statement of Cash Flows

Item	Statement of Cash Flows	
	Operating Activities	
	Net income	xxx
	Investing Activities	
	Financing Activities	
Issuance of stock	→	+
Retirement or repurchase of stock	→	−
Payment of dividends	→	−

EXHIBIT 11-8 Continental Airlines, Inc.'s Partial Statement of Cash Flows

Continental Airlines, Inc.
Consolidated Statements of Cash Flows

(in millions)	Year Ended December 31, 2006	2005	2004
Cash Flows from Financing Activities:			
Proceeds from issuance of long-term debt	574	436	67
Payments on long-term debt and capital lease obligations	(948)	(662)	(447)
Proceeds from issuance of common stock	82	227	5
Other	—	36	11
Net cash (used in) provided by financing activities	(292)	37	(364)

Changes in stockholders' equity are shown in the Financing Activities category.

POD REVIEW 11.10

LO10 *Explain the effects that transactions involving stockholders' equity have on the statement of cash flows.*

- Transactions involving stockholders' equity accounts are classified as financing activities. Issuing stock produces cash inflows. Dividends and the retirement or repurchase of stock produce cash outflows.

QUESTIONS

1. *On the statement of cash flows, where should the effect of the company's stock transactions be reflected?*
   a. in the Operating Activities category
   b. in the Investing Activities category
   c. in the Financing Activities category
   d. none of the above

2. *When treasury stock is purchased by the company, how should it appear?*
   a. as a cash inflow in the Financing Activities category
   b. as a cash outflow in the Financing Activities category
   c. as a cash inflow in the Investing Activities category
   d. as a cash outflow in the Investing Activities category

APPENDIX

Accounting Tools: Unincorporated Businesses

The focus of Chapter 11, as with the rest of the text, has been on the corporate form of organization. Most of the large, influential companies in the United States are organized as corporations. They have a legal and economic existence that is separate from that of the owners of the business, the stockholders. Yet many other companies in the economy are organized as sole proprietorships or partnerships. The purpose of this appendix is to show briefly how the characteristics of such organizations affect the accounting, particularly the accounting for the Owners' Equity category of the balance sheet.

LO11 Describe the important differences between the sole proprietorship and partnership forms of organization versus the corporate form.

SOLE PROPRIETORSHIPS

A sole proprietorship is a business owned by one person. Most sole proprietorships are small in size, with the owner serving as the operator or manager of the company. The primary advantage of the sole proprietorship form of organization is its simplicity. The Owner's Equity category of the balance sheet consists of one account, the owner's capital account. The owner answers to no one but himself or herself. A disadvantage of the sole proprietorship is that all responsibility for the success or failure of the venture attaches to the owner, who often has limited resources.

Sole proprietorship A business with a single owner.

There are three important points to remember about this form of organization:

1. **A sole proprietorship is not a separate entity for legal purposes. This means that the law does not distinguish between the assets of the business and those of its owner. If an owner loses a lawsuit, for example, the law does not limit an owner's liability to the amount of assets of the business, but extends liability to the owner's personal assets. Thus, the owner is said to have *unlimited liability.***
2. **Accountants adhere to the *entity principle* and maintain a distinction between the owner's personal assets and the assets of the sole proprietorship. The balance sheet of a sole proprietorship should reflect only the "business" assets and liabilities, with the difference reflected as owner's capital.**
3. **A sole proprietorship is not treated as a separate entity for federal income tax purposes. That is, the sole proprietorship does not pay tax on its income. Rather, the business income must be declared as income on the owner's personal tax return, and income tax is assessed at the personal tax rate rather than the rate that applies to companies organized as corporations. This may or may not be advantageous depending on the amount of income involved and the owner's tax situation.**

Typical Transactions When the owners of a corporation, the stockholders, invest in the corporation, they normally do so by purchasing stock. When investing in a sole proprietorship, the owner simply contributes cash or other assets into the business.

For example, assume that on January 1, 2008, Peter Tom began a new business by investing $10,000 cash. Peter Tom Company records the transaction as follows:

Jan. 1	Cash	10,000	
	Peter Tom, Capital		10,000
	To record the investment of cash in the business.		

Balance Sheet							Income Statement
ASSETS		=	**LIABILITIES**	+	**OWNER'S EQUITY**		+	**REVENUES – EXPENSES**
Cash	10,000				Peter Tom, Capital	10,000		

The Peter Tom, Capital account is an owner's equity account and reflects the rights of the owner to the business assets.

An owner's withdrawal of assets from the business is recorded as a reduction of owner's equity. Assume that on July 1, 2008, Peter Tom took an auto valued at $6,000 from the business to use as his personal auto. The transaction is recorded as follows:

July 1	Peter Tom, Drawing	6,000	
	Equipment		6,000
	To record the withdrawal of an auto from the business.		

Balance Sheet								Income Statement
ASSETS		=	**LIABILITIES**	+	**OWNER'S EQUITY**		+	**REVENUES – EXPENSES**
Equipment	(6,000)				Peter Tom, Drawing	(6,000)		

The Peter Tom, Drawing account is a contra-equity account. Sometimes a drawing account is referred to as a *withdrawals account,* as in Peter Tom, Withdrawals. An increase in the account reduces the owner's equity. At the end of the fiscal year, the drawing account should be closed to the capital account as follows:

Dec. 31	Peter Tom, Capital	6,000	
	Peter Tom, Drawing		6,000
	To close the drawing account to capital.		

Balance Sheet								Income Statement
ASSETS		=	**LIABILITIES**	+	**OWNER'S EQUITY**		+	**REVENUES – EXPENSES**
					Peter Tom, Capital	(6,000)		
					Peter Tom, Drawing	6,000		

The amount of the net income of the business also should be reflected in the capital account. Assume that all revenue and expense accounts of Peter Tom Company have been closed to the Income Summary account, resulting in a balance of $4,000, the net income for the year. The Income Summary account is closed to capital as follows:

Dec. 31	Income Summary	4,000	
	Peter Tom, Capital		4,000
	To close income summary to the capital account.		

Balance Sheet								Income Statement
ASSETS		=	**LIABILITIES**	+	**OWNER'S EQUITY**		+	**REVENUES – EXPENSES**
					Income Summary	(4,000)		
					Peter Tom, Capital	4,000		

The Owner's Equity section of the balance sheet for Peter Tom Company consists of one account, the capital account, calculated as follows:

Beginning balance, Jan. 1, 2008	$ 0
Plus: Investments	10,000
Net income	4,000
Less: Withdrawals	(6,000)
Ending balance, Dec. 31, 2008	$ 8,000

PARTNERSHIPS

A **partnership** is a company owned by two or more people. Like sole proprietorships, most partnerships are fairly small businesses formed when individuals combine their capital and managerial talents for a common business purpose. Other partnerships are large, national organizations. For example, the major public accounting firms are very large, national companies but are organized in most states as partnerships.

Partnership
A business owned by two or more individuals that has the characteristic of unlimited liability.

Partnerships have characteristics similar to those of sole proprietorships. The following are the most important characteristics of partnerships:

1. ***Unlimited liability.*** **Legally, the assets of the business are not separate from the partners' personal assets. Each partner is personally liable for the debts of the partnership. Creditors have a legal claim first to the assets of the partnership and then to the assets of the individual partners.**
2. ***Limited life.*** **Corporations have a separate legal existence and an unlimited life; partnerships do not. The life of a partnership is limited; it exists as long as the contract between the partners is valid. The partnership ends when a partner withdraws or a new partner is added. A new partnership must be created for the business to continue.**
3. ***Not taxed as a separate entity.*** **Partnerships are subject to the same tax features as sole proprietorships. The partnership itself does not pay federal income tax. Rather, the income of the partnership is treated as personal income on each of the partners' individual tax returns and is taxed as personal income. All partnership income is subject to federal income tax on the individual partners' returns even if it is not distributed to the partners. A variety of other factors affects the tax consequences of partnerships versus the corporate form of organization. Those aspects are quite complex and beyond the scope of this text.**

A partnership is based on a **partnership agreement**. It is very important that the partners agree in writing about all aspects of the partnership. The agreement should detail items such as how much capital each partner is to invest, how much time each partner is expected to devote to the business, what the salary of each partner is, and how income of the partnership is to be divided. If a partnership agreement is not present, the courts may be forced to settle disputes among partners. Therefore, the partners should develop a partnership agreement when the firm is first established and review the agreement periodically to determine if changes are necessary.

Partnership agreement
Specifies how much the owners will invest, what their salaries will be, and how profits will be shared.

Investments and Withdrawals In a partnership, it is important to account separately for the capital of each partner. A capital account should be established in the Owners' Equity section of the balance sheet for each partner of the company. Investments into the company should be credited to the partner making the investment. For example, assume that on January 1, 2008, Paige Thoms and Amy Rebec begin a partnership named AP Company. Paige contributes $10,000 cash, and Amy contributes equipment valued at $5,000. The accounting transaction recorded by AP Company is as follows:

Jan. 1	Cash	10,000	
	Equipment	5,000	
	Paige Thoms, Capital		10,000
	Amy Rebec, Capital		5,000
	To record the contribution of assets to the business.		

Balance Sheet							Income Statement
ASSETS		= LIABILITIES	+	OWNERS' EQUITY		+	REVENUES − EXPENSES
Cash	10,000			Paige Thoms, Capital	10,000		
Equipment	5,000			Amy Rebec, Capital	5,000		

A drawing account also should be established for each owner of the company to account for withdrawals of assets. Assume that on April 1, 2008, each owner withdraws $2,000 of cash from AP Company. The accounting entry is recorded as follows:

Apr. 1	Paige Thoms, Drawing	2,000	
	Amy Rebec, Drawing	2,000	
	Cash		4,000
	To record the withdrawal of assets from the business.		

Balance Sheet							Income Statement
ASSETS		=	**LIABILITIES**	+	**OWNERS' EQUITY**	+	**REVENUES – EXPENSES**
Cash	(4,000)				Paige Thoms, Drawing (2,000)		
					Amy Rebec, Drawing (2,000)		

Distribution of Income The partnership agreement governs the manner in which income should be allocated to partners. The distribution may recognize the partners' relative investment in the business, their time and effort, their expertise and talents, or other factors. Three methods of income allocation will be illustrated, but be aware that partnerships use many other allocation methods. Although these allocation methods are straightforward, partnerships often dissolve because one or more of the partners believes that the allocation is unfair. It is very difficult to devise a method that will make all partners happy.

One way to allocate income is to divide it evenly between or among the partners. In fact, when a partnership agreement is not present, the courts specify that an equal allocation must be applied regardless of the relative contributions or efforts of the partners. For example, assume that AP Company has $30,000 of net income for the period and has established an agreement that income should be allocated evenly between the two partners, Paige and Amy. Each capital account would be increased by $15,000. The accounting entry that AP Company records during the closing entry process is as follows:

Dec. 31	Income Summary	30,000	
	Paige Thoms, Capital		15,000
	Amy Rebec, Capital		15,000
	To record the allocation of income between partners.		

Balance Sheet							Income Statement
ASSETS		=	**LIABILITIES**	+	**OWNERS' EQUITY**	+	**REVENUES – EXPENSES**
					Income Summary (30,000)		
					Paige Thoms, Capital 15,000		
					Amy Rebec, Capital 15,000		

An equal distribution of income to all partners is easy to apply but is not fair to those partners who have contributed more in money or time to the partnership.

Another way to allocate income is to specify in the partnership agreement that income be allocated according to a *stated ratio*. For example, Paige and Amy may specify that all income of AP Company should be allocated in a 2-to-1 ratio, with Paige receiving the larger portion. If that allocation method is applied to the preceding example, Paige Thoms, Capital would be increased by $20,000 and Amy Rebec, Capital would be increased by $10,000. If that allocation method is applied to the preceding example, AP Company records the following transaction at year-end:

Dec. 31	Income Summary	30,000	
	Paige Thoms, Capital		20,000
	Amy Rebec, Capital		10,000
	To record the allocation of income between partners.		

Balance Sheet							Income Statement
ASSETS		=	**LIABILITIES**	+	**OWNERS' EQUITY**	+	**REVENUES – EXPENSES**
					Income Summary (30,000)		
					Paige Thoms, Capital 20,000		
					Amy Rebec, Capital 10,000		

Finally, an allocation method that more accurately reflects the partners' input is illustrated. It is based on salaries, interest on invested capital, and a stated ratio. Assume that the partnership agreement of AP Company specifies that Paige and Amy be allowed a salary of $6,000 and $4,000, respectively; that each partner receive 10% on her capital balance; and that any remaining income be allocated equally. Assume that AP Company has been in operation for several years and that the capital balances of the owners at the end of 2008, before the income distribution, are as follows:

Paige Thoms, Capital	$40,000
Amy Rebec, Capital	50,000

If AP Company calculated that its 2008 net income (before partner salaries) was $30,000, income would be allocated between the partners as follows:

	Paige	Amy
Distributed for salaries:	$ 6,000	$ 4,000
Distributed for interest:		
Paige: ($40,000 × 10%)	4,000	
Amy: ($50,000 × 10%)		5,000
Remainder = $30,000 − $10,000 − $9,000 = $11,000		
Remainder distributed equally:		
Paige: ($11,000/2)	5,500	
Amy: ($11,000/2)		5,500
Total distributed	$15,500	$14,500

Paige Thoms, Capital would be increased by $15,500; and Amy Rebec, Capital, by $14,500. The accounting transaction to transfer the income to the capital accounts is as follows:

Dec. 31	Income Summary	30,000	
	Paige Thoms, Capital		15,500
	Amy Rebec, Capital		14,500
	To record the allocation of income to partners.		

Balance Sheet							Income Statement
ASSETS	=	**LIABILITIES**	+	**OWNERS' EQUITY**		+	**REVENUES − EXPENSES**
				Income Summary	(30,000)		
				Paige Thoms, Capital	15,500		
				Amy Rebec, Capital	14,500		

This indicates that the amounts of $15,500 and $14,500 were allocated to Paige and Amy, respectively. It does not indicate the amount actually paid to (or withdrawn by) the partners. However, for tax purposes, the income of the partnership is treated as personal income on the partners' individual tax returns regardless of whether the income is actually paid in cash to the partners. This aspect often encourages partners to withdraw income from the business and makes it difficult to retain sufficient capital for the business to operate profitably.

POD REVIEW 11.11

LO11 *Describe the important differences between the sole proprietorship and partnership forms of organization versus the corporate form.*

- Sole proprietorships are businesses that are not incorporated and are owned by one individual. The business entity and individual are not distinguished from one another for legal and tax purposes.
- Partnerships are also unincorporated entities but are owned by two or more individuals. The partners and their respective shares of the business are not distinguished from one another for legal purposes. The partnership itself is not taxed on earnings but individual partners are taxed for their share.
- Corporations, unlike partnerships, have some of the following distinguishing characteristics: they are generally taxable entities and have an unlimited life. The corporate form has been adopted by most larger businesses and is therefore emphasized in this text.

QUESTIONS

1. *When a company is organized as a sole proprietorship,*
   a. the assets and liabilities of the company should not be separate from the owner's assets and liabilities.
   b. the assets and liabilities of the company should be kept separate from the owner's assets and liabilities.
   c. the company must pay income tax on its income.
   d. the owner of the company is considered to have a limited liability for the actions of the company.

2. *When a company is organized as a partnership,*
   a. the partners share equally in the income of the company.
   b. all partners must contribute the same amount of money to establish the partnership.
   c. the partnership must pay tax on its income.
   d. each partner is personally liable for the actions of the company.

RATIO REVIEW

$$\textbf{Book Value per Share} = \frac{\textbf{Total Stockholders' Equity*}}{\textbf{Number of Shares of Common Stock Outstanding}}$$

**When preferred stock is outstanding, the redemption value or liquidation value (disclosed on the preferred stock line or in the notes) of the preferred stock must be subtracted from total stockholders' equity.*

ACCOUNTS HIGHLIGHTED

Account Title	Where It Appears	In What Section	Page Number
Common Stock	Balance Sheet	Contributed Capital	538
Preferred Stock	Balance Sheet	Contributed Capital	528
Additional Paid-in Capital	Balance Sheet	Contributed Capital	529
Retained Earnings	Balance Sheet	Retained Earnings	529
Treasury Stock	Balance Sheet	(bottom portion of stockholders' equity as a contra account)	533
Cash Dividend Payable	Balance Sheet	Current Liabilities	536
Stock Dividend Distributable	Balance Sheet	Contributed Capital	538

KEY TERMS QUIZ

Read each definition below and write the number of the definition in the blank beside the appropriate term. The quiz solutions appear at the end of the chapter.

_______ **Authorized shares**
_______ **Issued shares**
_______ **Outstanding shares**
_______ **Par value**
_______ **Additional paid-in capital**
_______ **Retained earnings**
_______ **Cumulative feature**
_______ **Participating feature**
_______ **Convertible feature**
_______ **Callable feature**
_______ **Treasury stock**
_______ **Retirement of stock**
_______ **Dividend payout ratio**
_______ **Stock dividend**
_______ **Stock split**
_______ **Statement of stockholders' equity**
_______ **Comprehensive income**
_______ **Book value per share**
_______ **Market value per share**
_______ **Sole proprietorship (Appendix)**
_______ **Partnership (Appendix)**
_______ **Partnership agreement (Appendix)**

1. The number of shares sold or distributed to stockholders.
2. An arbitrary amount that is stated on the face of the stock certificate and that represents the legal capital of the firm.
3. Net income that has been made by the corporation but not paid out as dividends.
4. The right to dividends in arrears before the current-year dividend is distributed.
5. Allows preferred stock to be returned to the corporation in exchange for common stock.
6. Stock issued by the firm and then repurchased but not retired.
7. The annual dividend amount divided by the annual net income.
8. A statement that reflects the differences between beginning and ending balances for all accounts in the Stockholders' Equity category.
9. Creation of additional shares of stock and reduction of the par value of the stock.
10. Total stockholders' equity divided by the number of shares of common stock outstanding.
11. The total change in net assets from all sources except investments by or distributions to the owners.
12. The selling price of the stock as indicated by the most recent stock transactions on, for example, the stock exchange.
13. The maximum number of shares a corporation may issue as indicated in the corporate charter.
14. The number of shares issued less the number of shares held as treasury stock.
15. The amount received for the issuance of stock in excess of the par value of the stock.
16. A provision allowing the preferred stockholders to share, on a percentage basis, in the distribution of an abnormally large dividend.
17. Allows the issuing firm to eliminate a class of stock by paying the stockholders a fixed amount.
18. When the stock of a corporation is repurchased with no intention of reissuing at a later date.
19. A corporation's declaration and issuance of additional shares of its own stock to existing stockholders.
20. A business owned by two or more individuals that has the characteristic of unlimited liability.
21. A document that specifies how much each owner should invest, what the salary of each owner is, and how profits are to be shared.
22. A business with a single owner.

ALTERNATE TERMS

Additional paid-in capital Paid-in capital in excess of par value

Additional paid-in capital—treasury stock Paid-in capital from treasury stock transactions

Callable Redeemable

Capital account Owners' equity account

Contributed capital Paid-in capital

Retained earnings Retained income

Small stock dividend Stock dividend less than 20%

Stockholders' equity Owners' equity

WARMUP EXERCISES & SOLUTIONS

Warmup Exercise 11-1

A company has a Retained Earnings account with a January 1 balance of $500,000. The accountant has reviewed the following information for the current year:

Increase in cash balance	$50,000
Net income	80,000
Dividends declared	30,000
Dividends paid	20,000
Decrease in accounts receivable balance	10,000

Required

Calculate the ending balance of the Retained Earnings account.

Key to the Solution Cash and accounts receivable do not affect retained earnings. Also note that dividends are deducted from retained earnings at the time they are declared rather than when they are paid.

Warmup Exercise 11-2

A company begins business on January 1 and issues 100,000 shares of common stock. On July 1, the company declares and issues a 2-for-1 stock split. On October 15, the company purchases 20,000 shares of stock as treasury stock and reissues 5,000 shares by the end of the month.

Required

Calculate the number of shares issued and the number of shares outstanding as of the end of the first year of operations.

Warmup Exercise 11-3

A. Company A has total stockholders' equity at year-end of $500,000 and has 10,000 shares of stock.
B. Company B has total stockholders' equity at year-end of $500,000 and has 10,000 shares of stock. The company also has 50,000 shares of preferred stock, which has a $1 par value and a liquidation value of $3 per share.

Required

Calculate the book value per share for Company A and Company B.

Key to the Solution Book value per share is calculated for the common stockholder. If preferred stock is present, an amount must be deducted that represents the amount the preferred stockholder would receive at liquidation.

SOLUTION TO WARMUP EXERCISES

Warmup Exercise 11-1

The ending balance of the Retained Earnings account should be calculated as follows:

Beginning balance	$500,000
Plus: Net income	80,000
Less: Dividends declared	(30,000)
Ending balance	$550,000

REVIEW

Warmup Exercise 11-2

The number of shares of stock issued is 200,000, or 100,000 times 2 because of the stock split. The number of shares outstanding is 185,000, calculated as follows:

Number of shares after split	100,000 × 2 =	200,000
Less purchase of treasury stock		(20,000)
Plus stock reissued		5,000
Total outstanding		185,000 shares

Warmup Exercise 11-3

A. Book value per share is $50, or $500,000/10,000.
B. Book value per share is $35, or ($500,000 − $150,000)/10,000.

REVIEW PROBLEM & SOLUTION

Andrew Company was incorporated on January 1, 2008, under a corporate charter that authorized the issuance of 50,000 shares of $5 par common stock and 20,000 shares of $100 par, 8% preferred stock. The following events occurred during 2008. Andrew wants to record the events and develop financial statements on December 31, 2008.

a. Issued for cash 10,000 shares of common stock at $25 per share and 1,000 shares of preferred stock at $110 per share on January 15, 2008.
b. Acquired a patent on April 1 in exchange for 2,000 shares of common stock. At the time of the exchange, the common stock was selling on the local stock exchange for $30 per share.
c. Repurchased 500 shares of common stock on May 1 at $20 per share. The corporation is holding the stock to be used for an employee bonus plan.
d. Declared a cash dividend of $1 per share to common stockholders and an 8% dividend to preferred stockholders on July 1. The preferred stock is noncumulative, nonparticipating. The dividend will be distributed on August 1.
e. Distributed the cash dividend on August 1.
f. Declared and distributed to preferred stockholders a 10% stock dividend on September 1. At the time of the dividend declaration, preferred stock was valued at $130 per share.
g. On December 31, calculated the annual net income for the year to be $200,000.

Required

1. Record the accounting entries for items (a) through (f).
2. Develop the Stockholders' Equity section of Andrew Company's balance sheet at December 31, 2008. You do not need to consider the notes that accompany the balance sheet.
3. Determine the book value per share of the common stock. Assume that the preferred stock can be redeemed at par.

SOLUTION TO REVIEW PROBLEM

1. The following entries should be recorded:
   a. The entry to record the issuance of stock:

Jan. 15	Cash	360,000	
	Common Stock		50,000
	Additional Paid-In Capital—Common		200,000
	Preferred Stock		100,000
	Additional Paid-In Capital—Preferred		10,000
	To record the issuance of stock for cash.		

Balance Sheet								Income Statement
ASSETS		=	**LIABILITIES**	+	**STOCKHOLDERS' EQUITY**		+	**REVENUES − EXPENSES**
Cash	360,000				Common Stock	50,000		
					Additional Paid-in Capital—Common	200,000		
					Preferred Stock	100,000		
					Additional Paid-in Capital—Preferred	10,000		

b. The patent received for stock should be recorded at the value of the stock:

Apr. 1	Patent	60,000	
	Common Stock		10,000
	Additional Paid-In Capital—Common		50,000
	To record the issuance of stock for patent.		

Balance Sheet								Income Statement
ASSETS		=	LIABILITIES		+	STOCKHOLDERS' EQUITY		+ REVENUES – EXPENSES
Patent	60,000					Common Stock	10,000	
						Additional Paid-in Capital—Common	50,000	

c. Stock reacquired constitutes treasury stock and should be recorded as follows:

May 1	Treasury Stock	10,000	
	Cash		10,000
	To record the purchase of treasury stock.		

Balance Sheet								Income Statement
ASSETS		=	LIABILITIES		+	STOCKHOLDERS' EQUITY		+ REVENUES – EXPENSES
Cash	(10,000)					Treasury Stock	(10,000)	

d. A cash dividend should be declared on the number of shares of stock outstanding as of July 1. The dividend is recorded as follows:

July 1	Retained Earnings	19,500	
	Dividends Payable—Common		11,500
	Dividends Payable—Preferred		8,000
	To record the declaration of a cash dividend.		

Balance Sheet								Income Statement
ASSETS		=	LIABILITIES		+	STOCKHOLDERS' EQUITY		+ REVENUES – EXPENSES
			Dividends Payable—Common	11,500		Retained Earnings	(19,500)	
			Dividends Payable—Preferred	8,000				

The number of common shares outstanding should be calculated as the number of shares issued (12,000) less the number of shares of treasury stock (500). The preferred stock dividend should be calculated as 1,000 shares times $100 par times 8%.

e. The entry to record the distribution of a cash dividend is as follows:

Aug. 1	Dividends Payable—Common	11,500	
	Dividends Payable—Preferred	8,000	
	Cash		19,500
	To record the payment of cash dividend.		

Balance Sheet								Income Statement
ASSETS		=	LIABILITIES		+	STOCKHOLDERS' EQUITY		+ REVENUES – EXPENSES
Cash	(19,500)		Dividends Payable—Common	(11,500)				
			Dividends Payable—Preferred	(8,000)				

REVIEW

f. A stock dividend should be based on the number of shares of stock outstanding and should be declared and recorded at the market value of the stock. The entry is as follows:

Sept. 1	Retained Earnings	13,000	
	Preferred Stock		10,000
	Additional Paid-In Capital—Preferred		3,000
	To record the declaration of a stock dividend.		

Balance Sheet							Income Statement
ASSETS	=	LIABILITIES	+	STOCKHOLDERS' EQUITY		+	REVENUES − EXPENSES
				Retained Earnings	(13,000)		
				Preferred Stock	10,000		
				Additional Paid-in Capital—Preferred	3,000		

2. The Stockholders' Equity for Andrew Company after completing these transactions appears as follows:

Preferred stock, $100 par, 8%, 20,000 shares authorized, 1,100 issued	$110,000
Common stock, $5 par, 50,000 shares authorized, 12,000 issued	60,000
Additional paid-in capital—Preferred	13,000
Additional paid-in capital—Common	250,000
Retained earnings	167,500*
Total contributed capital and retained earnings	$600,500
Less: Treasury stock, 500 shares, common	(10,000)
Total stockholders' equity	$590,500

***$200,000 − $19,500 − $13,000 = $167,500**

3. The book value per share of the common stock is calculated as follows:

($590,500 − $110,000)/11,500 shares = $41.78

QUESTIONS

1. What are the two major components of stockholders' equity? Which accounts generally appear in each component?
2. Corporations disclose the number of shares authorized, issued, and outstanding. What is the meaning of each of those terms? What causes a difference between the number of shares issued and the number outstanding?
3. Why do firms designate an amount as the par value of stock? Does par value indicate the selling price or market value of the stock?
4. If a firm has a net income for the year, will the balance in the Retained Earnings account equal the net income? What is the meaning of the balance of the account?
5. What is the meaning of the statement that preferred stock has a preference to dividends declared by the corporation? Do preferred stockholders have the right to dividends in arrears on preferred stock?
6. Why might some stockholders be inclined to buy preferred stock rather than common stock? What are the advantages of investing in preferred stock?
7. Why are common shareholders sometimes called *residual owners* when a company has both common and preferred stock outstanding?
8. When stock is issued in exchange for an asset, at what amount should the asset be reported? How could the fair market value be determined?
9. What is treasury stock? Why do firms use it? Where does it appear on a corporation's financial statements?
10. When treasury stock is bought and sold, the transactions do not result in gains or losses reported on the income statement. What account or accounts are used instead? Why are no income statement amounts recorded?
11. Many firms operate at a dividend payout ratio of less than 50%. Why do firms not pay a larger percentage of income as dividends?
12. What is a stock dividend? How should it be recorded?
13. Would you rather receive a cash dividend or a stock dividend from a company? Explain.

14. What is the difference between stock dividends and stock splits? How should stock splits be recorded?
15. How is the book value per share calculated? Does the amount calculated as book value per share mean that stockholders will receive a dividend equal to the book value?
16. Can the market value per share of stock be determined by the information on the income statement?
17. What is the difference between a statement of stockholders' equity and a retained earnings statement?
18. What is an advantage of organizing a company as a corporation rather than a partnership? Why don't all companies incorporate? (Appendix)
19. What are some ways that partnerships could share income among the partners? (Appendix)

BRIEF EXERCISES

LO1

Brief Exercise 11-1 Components of Stockholders' Equity

Nash Company has the following accounts among the items on its balance sheet at December 31, 2008:

Common Stock, $10 par, 10,000 shares authorized, 9,000 issued, 8,000 outstanding	
Preferred Stock, $100 par, 8%, cumulative, 1,000 shares authorized, issued and outstanding	
Cash Dividend Payable	$ 50,000
Retained Earnings	100,000
Additional Paid-in Capital	200,000
Investment in Common Stock of Horton Company	60,000
Treasury Stock, 1,000 shares, common stock	20,000
Accumulated Other Comprehensive Income—Unrealized Gain on Investment Security	5,000

Required

Develop the Stockholders' Equity section of the balance sheet for Nash Company at December 31, 2008.

LO2

Brief Exercise 11-2 Common and Preferred Stock

Fielder Company has the following accounts in the Stockholders' Equity category of the balance sheet:

Common Stock, $10 no par, 10,000 shares authorized, 9,000 issued, 8,000 outstanding

Preferred Stock, $100 par, 8%, cumulative, participating, 1,000 shares authorized, issued and outstanding

Required

1. Explain how the issuance of stock affects the financial statements when the stock has no par value.
2. Why would preferred stockholders want to have a cumulative feature in preferred stock?
3. When a participating feature is present in preferred stock, how does it affect the amount of dividends that preferred stockholders can expect to receive?

LO3

Brief Exercise 11-3 Stock Issuance

Morris had the following transactions during 2008:

1. Issued 2,000 shares of $10 par common stock for cash at $17 per share.
2. Issued 1,000 shares of preferred stock to acquire land. The preferred stock has a par value of $5 per share. The land has been appraised at $7,000.
3. Issued 5,000 shares of $10 par common stock as payment to a company that provided advertising for the company. The stock was selling on the stock exchange at $12 per share at the time of issuance.

Required

Record a journal entry for each transaction.

LO4 **Brief Exercise 11-4** Treasury Stock

Indicate whether the following transactions increase, decrease, or have no effect on (a) total assets and on (b) total stockholders' equity.

_______ Issue 1,000 shares of common stock at $10 per share
_______ Purchase 500 shares of common stock as treasury stock at $15 per share
_______ Reissue 400 shares of treasury stock at $18 per share
_______ Reissue 100 shares of treasury stock at $12 per share

LO5 **Brief Exercise 11-5** Cash Dividends

At December 31, 2008, Black Company has the following:

Common Stock, $10 par, 10,000 shares authorized, 9,000 issued, 8,000 outstanding

Preferred Stock, $100 par, 8%, cumulative, 1,000 shares authorized, issued and outstanding

The company did not pay any dividend during 2007 or 2006.

Required
Compute the amount of dividend to be received by the common and preferred stockholders in 2008 if the company declared a dividend of (a) $16,000, (b) $24,000, and (c) $60,000.

LO6 **Brief Exercise 11-6** Cash and Stock Dividends

At December 31, 2008, White Company has the following:

Common Stock, $10 par, 10,000 shares authorized, 9,000 issued, 8,000 outstanding

Required
Indicate whether the following would increase, decrease, or have no effect on (a) assets, (b) retained earnings, and (c) total stockholders' equity.

_______ A company declares and pays a cash dividend of $25,000.
_______ A company declares and issues a 10% stock dividend.

LO7 **Brief Exercise 11-7** Stock Dividends and Stock Splits

At December 31, 2008, Green Company and Blue Company have identical amounts of common stock and retained earnings as follows:

Common Stock, $10 par, 50,000 shares authorized, 9,000 issued, 8,000 outstanding

Retained Earnings, $500,000

At December 31, 2009, Green Company declares and issues a 100% stock dividend, while Blue Company declares and issues a 2-for-1 stock split.

Required
Determine for each company the following amounts as of January 1, 2009:

_______ Number of shares of common stock outstanding
_______ Par value per share of the common stock
_______ Total amount reported in Common Stock account
_______ Retained earnings

LO8 **Brief Exercise 11-8** Develop Stockholders' Equity

Nash Company has the following accounts among the items on the balance sheet at January 1, 2008:

Common Stock, $10 par, 10,000 shares authorized, 9,000 issued, 8,000 outstanding	
Preferred Stock, $100 par, 8%, cumulative, 1,000 shares authorized, issued and outstanding	
Retained Earnings	$100,000
Additional Paid-in Capital	200,000
Treasury Stock, 1,000 shares, common stock	20,000

During 2008, the company issued 500 shares of common stock at $14 per share and reissued 400 shares of treasury stock at $20 per share. The company reported a net income of $60,000 for 2008.

Required
Develop the Statement of Stockholders' Equity section for Nash Company at December 31, 2008.

HOMEWORK

LO9

Brief Exercise 11-9 Book Value per Share

Deer Company has the following amounts in the Stockholders' Equity category of the balance sheet at December 31, 2008:

Preferred Stock, $100 par, 8%, noncumulative (liquidation value of $110 per share)	$100,000
Paid in Capital—Preferred	50,000
Common Stock, $5 par	400,000
Paid in Capital—Common	40,000
Retained Earnings	200,000

Required
Determine the book value per share of the Deer Company stock.

LO10

Brief Exercise 11-10 Cash Flow Effects

For each of the following items, indicate (a) in what category of the statement of cash flows the item will be reported and (b) whether it will appear as a cash inflow or cash outflow or neither.

Issuance of common stock for cash

Purchase of treasury stock

Issuance of a stock dividend

Reissuance of treasury stock

Issuance of common stock to acquire land

LO11

Brief Exercise 11-11 Sole Proprietorship (Appendix)

Furyk Company opened business as a sole proprietorship on January 1, 2008. The owner contributed $500,000 cash on that date. During the year, the company had a net income of $10,000. The company purchased equipment of $100,000 during the year. The owner also withdrew $60,000 to pay for personal expenses during 2008.

Required
Determine the company's owner's equity at December 31, 2008.

EXERCISES

LO1

Exercise 11-1 Stockholders' Equity Accounts

MJ Company has identified the following items. Indicate whether each item is included in an account in the Stockholders' Equity category of the balance sheet and identify the account title. Also indicate whether the item would increase or decrease stockholders' equity.

1. Preferred stock issued by MJ
2. Amount received by MJ in excess of par value when preferred stock was issued
3. Dividends in arrears on MJ preferred stock
4. Cash dividend declared but unpaid on MJ stock
5. Stock dividend declared but unissued by MJ
6. Treasury stock
7. Amount received in excess of cost when treasury stock is reissued by MJ
8. Retained earnings

LO1

Exercise 11-2 Solve for Unknowns

The Stockholders' Equity category of Zache Company's balance sheet appears below.

Common stock, $10 par, 10,000 shares issued, 9,200 outstanding	$??
Additional paid-in capital	??
Total contributed capital	$350,000
Retained earnings	100,000
Treasury stock, ?? shares at cost	10,000
Total stockholders' equity	$??

HOMEWORK

Required
1. Determine the missing values indicated by question marks.
2. What was the cost per share of the treasury stock?

LO3

Exercise 11-3 Stock Issuance

Horace Company had the following transactions during 2008, its first year of business.

a. Issued 5,000 shares of $5 par common stock for cash at $15 per share.
b. Issued 7,000 shares of common stock on May 1 to acquire a factory building from Barkley Company. Barkley had acquired the building in 2004 at a price of $150,000. Horace estimated that the building was worth $175,000 on May 1, 2008.
c. Issued 2,000 shares of stock on June 1 to acquire a patent. The accountant has been unable to estimate the value of the patent but has determined that Horace's common stock was selling at $25 per share on June 1.

Required
1. Record an entry for each transaction.
2. Determine the balance sheet amounts for common stock and additional paid-in capital.

LO3

Exercise 11-4 Stock Issuances

The following transactions are for Weber Corporation in 2008:

a. On March 1, the corporation was organized and received authorization to issue 5,000 shares of 8%, $100 par value preferred stock and 2,000,000 shares of $10 par value common stock.
b. On March 10, Weber issued 5,000 shares of common stock at $35 per share.
c. On March 18, Weber issued 100 shares of preferred stock at $120 per share.
d. On April 12, Weber issued another 10,000 shares of common stock at $45 per share.

Required
1. Prepare the appropriate journal entries.
2. Prepare the Stockholders' Equity section of the balance sheet as of December 31, 2008.
3. Does the balance sheet indicate the market value of the stock at year-end? Explain.

LO5

Exercise 11-5 Treasury Stock

The Stockholders' Equity category of Bradford Company's balance sheet on January 1, 2008, appeared as follows:

Common stock, $10 par, 10,000 shares issued and outstanding	$100,000
Additional paid-in capital	50,000
Retained earnings	80,000
Total stockholders' equity	$230,000

The following transactions occurred during 2008:

a. Reacquired 2,000 shares of common stock at $20 per share on July 1.
b. Reacquired 400 shares of common stock at $18 per share on August 1.

Required
1. Record the entries in journal form.
2. Assume that the company resold the shares of treasury stock at $28 per share on October 1. Did the company benefit from the treasury stock transaction? If so, where is the "gain" presented on the balance sheet?

LO4

Exercise 11-6 Treasury Stock Transactions

The Stockholders' Equity category of Little Joe's balance sheet on January 1, 2008, appeared as follows:

Common stock, $5 par, 40,000 shares issued and outstanding	$200,000
Additional paid-in capital	90,000
Retained earnings	100,000
Total stockholders' equity	$390,000

The following transactions occurred during 2008:

a. Reacquired 5,000 shares of common stock at $20 per share on February 1.
b. Reacquired 1,200 shares of common stock at $13 per share on March 1.

Required

1. Record the entries in journal form.
2. Assume that the treasury stock was reissued on October 1 at $12 per share. Did the company benefit from the treasury stock reissuance? Where is the "gain" or "loss" presented on the financial statements?
3. What effect did the two transactions to purchase treasury stock and the later reissuance of that stock have on the Stockholders' Equity section of the balance sheet?

LO5

Exercise 11-7 Cash Dividends

Kerry Company has 1,000 shares of $100 par value, 9% preferred stock and 10,000 shares of $10 par value common stock outstanding. The preferred stock is cumulative and nonparticipating. Dividends were paid in 2004. Since 2004, Kerry has declared and paid dividends as follows:

2005	$ 0
2006	10,000
2007	20,000
2008	25,000

Required

1. Determine the amount of the dividends to be allocated to preferred and common stockholders for each year, 2006 to 2008.
2. If the preferred stock had been noncumulative, how much would have been allocated to the preferred and common stockholders each year?

LO5

Exercise 11-8 Cash Dividends

The Stockholders' Equity category of Jackson Company's balance sheet as of January 1, 2008, appeared as follows:

Preferred stock, $100 par, 8%,	
2,000 shares issued and outstanding	$200,000
Common stock, $10 par,	
5,000 shares issued and outstanding	50,000
Additional paid-in capital	300,000
Total contributed capital	$550,000
Retained earnings	400,000
Total stockholders' equity	$950,000

The notes that accompany the financial statements indicate that Jackson has not paid dividends for the two years prior to 2008. On July 1, 2008, Jackson declares a dividend of $100,000 to be paid to preferred and common stockholders on August 1.

Required

1. Determine the amounts of the dividends to be allocated to preferred and common stockholders assuming that the preferred stock is noncumulative, nonparticipating stock.
2. Record the appropriate journal entries on July 1 and August 1, 2008.
3. Determine the amounts of the dividends to be allocated to preferred and common stockholders assuming instead that the preferred stock is cumulative, nonparticipating stock.

LO6

Exercise 11-9 Stock Dividends

The Stockholders' Equity category of Worthy Company's balance sheet as of January 1, 2008, appeared as follows:

Common stock, $10 par,	
40,000 shares issued and outstanding	$400,000
Additional paid-in capital	100,000
Retained earnings	400,000
Total stockholders' equity	$900,000

The following transactions occurred during 2008:

a. Declared a 10% stock dividend to common stockholders on January 15. At the time of the dividend, the common stock was selling for $30 per share. The stock dividend was to be issued to stockholders on January 30, 2008.
b. Distributed the stock dividend to the stockholders on January 30, 2008.

Required
1. Record the 2008 events in journal form.
2. Develop the Stockholders' Equity category of Worthy Company's balance sheet as of January 31, 2008, after the stock dividend was issued. What effect did those transactions have on total stockholders' equity?

LO7

Exercise 11-10 Stock Dividends versus Stock Splits

Campbell Company wants to increase the number of shares of its common stock outstanding and is considering a stock dividend versus a stock split. The Stockholders' Equity section of the firm's most recent balance sheet appeared as follows:

Common stock, $10 par,	
50,000 shares issued and outstanding	$ 500,000
Additional paid-in capital	750,000
Retained earnings	880,000
Total stockholders' equity	$2,130,000

If a stock dividend is chosen, the firm wants to declare a 100% stock dividend. Because the stock dividend qualifies as a "large stock dividend," it must be recorded at par value. If a stock split is chosen, Campbell will declare a 2-for-1 split.

Required
1. Compare the effects of the stock dividends and stock splits on the accounting equation.
2. Develop the Stockholders' Equity category of Campbell's balance sheet (a) after the stock dividend and (b) after the stock split.

LO7

Exercise 11-11 Stock Dividends and Stock Splits

Whitacre Company's Stockholders' Equity section of the balance sheet on December 31, 2007, was as follows:

Common stock, $10 par value,	
60,000 shares issued and outstanding	$ 600,000
Additional paid-in capital	480,000
Retained earnings	1,240,000
Total stockholders' equity	$2,320,000

On May 1, 2008, Whitacre declared and issued a 15% stock dividend, when the stock was selling for $20 per share. Then on November 1, it declared and issued a 2-for-1 stock split.

Required
1. How many shares of stock are outstanding at year-end?
2. What is the par value per share of these shares?
3. Develop the Stockholders' Equity category of Whitacre's balance sheet as of December 31, 2008.

LO8

Exercise 11-12 Reporting Changes in Stockholders' Equity Items

On May 1, 2007, Ryde Inc. had common stock of $345,000, additional paid-in capital of $1,298,000, and retained earnings of $3,013,000. Ryde did not purchase or sell any common stock during the year. The company reported net income of $556,000 and declared dividends in the amount of $78,000 during the year ended April 30, 2008.

Required
Prepare a financial statement that explains all of the reasons for the differences between the beginning and ending balances for the accounts in the Stockholders' Equity category of the balance sheet.

LO8

Exercise 11-13 Comprehensive Income

Assume that you are the accountant for Ellis Corporation, which has issued its 2008 annual report. You have received an inquiry from a stockholder who has questions about several items in the annual report, including why Ellis has not shown certain transactions on the income statement. In particular, Ellis's 2008 balance sheet revealed two accounts in Stockholders' Equity (Unrealized Gain/Loss—Available-for-Sale Securities and Loss on Foreign Currency Translation Adjustments) for which the dollar amounts involved were not reported on the income statement.

Required

Draft a written response to the stockholder's inquiry that explains the nature of the two accounts and the reason the amounts involved were not recorded on the 2008 income statement. Do you think that the concept of comprehensive income would be useful to explain the impact of all events for Ellis Corporation? Why or why not?

LO9

Exercise 11-14 Payout Ratio and Book Value per Share

Divac Company has developed a statement of stockholders' equity for the year 2008 as follows:

	Preferred Stock	Paid-In Capital—Preferred	Common Stock	Paid-In Capital—Common	Retained Earnings
Balance, Jan. 1	$100,000	$50,000	$400,000	$40,000	$200,000
Stock issued			100,000	10,000	
Net income					80,000
Cash dividend					−45,000
Stock dividend	10,000	5,000			−15,000
Balance, Dec. 31	$110,000	$55,000	$500,000	$50,000	$220,000

Divac's preferred stock is $100 par, 8% stock. If the stock is liquidated or redeemed, stockholders are entitled to $120 per share. There are no dividends in arrears on the stock. The common stock has a par value of $5 per share.

Required

1. Determine the dividend payout ratio for the common stock.
2. Determine the book value per share of Divac's common stock.

LO10

Exercise 11-15 Impact of Transactions Involving Issuance of Stock on Statement of Cash Flows

From the following list, identify each item as operating (O), investing (I), financing (F), or not separately reported on the statement of cash flows (N).

_______ Issuance of common stock for cash
_______ Issuance of preferred stock for cash
_______ Issuance of common stock for equipment
_______ Issuance of preferred stock for land and building
_______ Conversion of preferred stock into common stock

LO10

Exercise 11-16 Impact of Transactions Involving Treasury Stock on Statement of Cash Flows

From the following list, identify each item as operating (O), investing (I), financing (F), or not separately reported on the statement of cash flows (N).

_______ Repurchase of common stock as treasury stock
_______ Reissuance of common stock (held as treasury stock)
_______ Retirement of treasury stock

LO10

Exercise 11-17 Impact of Transactions Involving Dividends on Statement of Cash Flows

From the following list, identify each item as operating (O), investing (I), financing (F), or not separately reported on the statement of cash flows (N).

_______ Payment of cash dividend on common stock
_______ Payment of cash dividend on preferred stock
_______ Distribution of stock dividend
_______ Declaration of stock split

LO10 **Exercise 11-18** Determining Dividends Paid on Statement of Cash Flows

Clifford Company's comparative balance sheet included dividends payable of $80,000 at December 31, 2007, and $100,000 at December 31, 2008. Dividends declared by Clifford during 2008 amounted to $400,000.

Required

1. Calculate the amount of dividends actually paid to stockholders during 2008.
2. How will Clifford report the dividend payments on its 2008 statement of cash flows?

LO11 **Exercise 11-19** Sole Proprietorship (Appendix)

Terry Woods opened Par Golf as a sole proprietor by investing $50,000 cash on January 1, 2008. Because the business was new, it operated at a net loss of $10,000 for 2008. During the year, Terry withdrew $20,000 from the business for living expenses. Terry also had $4,000 of interest income from sources unrelated to the business.

Required

Present the Owner's Equity category of Par Golf's balance sheet as of December 31, 2008.

LO11 **Exercise 11-20** Partnerships (Appendix)

Sports Central is a sporting goods store owned by Lewis, Jamal, and Lapin in partnership. On January 1, 2008, their capital balances were as follows:

Lewis, Capital	$20,000
Jamal, Capital	50,000
Lapin, Capital	30,000

During 2008, Lewis withdrew $5,000; Jamal, $12,000; and Lapin, $9,000. Income for the partnership for 2008 was $50,000.

Required

If the partners agreed to allocate income equally, what was the ending balance in each of their capital accounts on December 31, 2008?

PROBLEMS

LO1 **Problem 11-1** Stockholders' Equity Category

Peeler Company was incorporated as a new business on January 1, 2008. The corporate charter approved on that date authorized the issuance of 1,000 shares of $100 par, 7% cumulative, nonparticipating preferred stock and 10,000 shares of $5 par common stock. On January 10, Peeler issued for cash 500 shares of preferred stock at $120 per share and 4,000 shares of common stock at $80 per share. On January 20, it issued 1,000 shares of common stock to acquire a building site at a time when the stock was selling for $70 per share.

During 2008, Peeler established an employee benefit plan and acquired 500 shares of common stock at $60 per share as treasury stock for that purpose. Later in 2008, it resold 100 shares of the stock at $65 per share.

On December 31, 2008, Peeler determined its net income for the year to be $40,000. The firm declared the annual cash dividend to preferred stockholders and a cash dividend of $5 per share to the common stockholders. The dividends will be paid in 2009.

Required

Develop the Stockholders' Equity category of Peeler's balance sheet as of December 31, 2008. Indicate on the statement the number of shares authorized, issued, and outstanding for both preferred and common stock.

LO2 **Problem 11-2** Evaluating Alternative Investments

Ellen Hays received a windfall from one of her investments. She would like to invest $100,000 of the money in Linwood Inc., which is offering common stock, preferred stock, and bonds on the open market. The common stock has paid $8 per share in dividends for the past three years, and the company expects to be able to perform as well in the current year. The current market price of the common stock is $100 per share. The preferred stock has an 8% dividend rate, cumulative and nonparticipating. The bonds are selling at par with an 8% stated rate.

1. What are the advantages and disadvantages of each type of investment?
2. Recommend one type of investment over the others to Ellen and justify your reason.

LO5

Problem 11-3 Dividends for Preferred and Common Stock

The Stockholders' Equity category of Greenbaum Company's balance sheet as of December 31, 2008, appeared as follows:

Preferred stock, $100 par, 8%, 1,000 shares issued and outstanding	$ 100,000
Common stock, $10 par, 20,000 shares issued and outstanding	200,000
Additional paid-in capital	250,000
Total contributed capital	$ 550,000
Retained earnings	450,000
Total stockholders' equity	$1,000,000

The notes to the financial statements indicate that dividends were not declared or paid for 2006 or 2007. Greenbaum wants to declare a dividend of $59,000 for 2008.

Required

Determine the total and the per-share amounts that should be declared to the preferred and common stockholders under the following assumptions:

1. The preferred stock is noncumulative, nonparticipating.
2. The preferred stock is cumulative, nonparticipating.

LO6

Problem 11-4 Effect of Stock Dividend

Favre Company has a history of paying cash dividends on its common stock. However, the firm did not have a particularly profitable year in 2008. At the end of the year, Favre found itself without the necessary cash for a dividend and therefore declared a stock dividend to its common stockholders. A 50% stock dividend was declared to stockholders on December 31, 2008. The board of directors is unclear about a stock dividend's effect on Favre's balance sheet and has requested your assistance.

Required

1. Write a statement to indicate the effect the stock dividend has on the financial statements of Favre Company.
2. A group of common stockholders has contacted the firm to express its concern about the effect of the stock dividend and to question the effect the stock dividend may have on the market price of the stock. Write a statement to address the stockholders' concerns.

LO7

Problem 11-5 Dividends and Stock Splits

On January 1, 2008, Frederiksen Inc.'s Stockholders' Equity category appeared as follows:

Preferred stock, $80 par value, 7%, 3,000 shares issued and outstanding	$ 240,000
Common stock, $10 par value, 15,000 shares issued and outstanding	150,000
Additional paid-in capital—Preferred	60,000
Additional paid-in capital—Common	225,000
Total contributed capital	$ 675,000
Retained earnings	2,100,000
Total stockholders' equity	$2,775,000

The preferred stock is noncumulative and nonparticipating. During 2008, the following transactions occurred:

a. On March 1, declared a cash dividend of $16,800 on preferred stock. Paid the dividend on April 1.
b. On June 1, declared a 5% stock dividend on common stock. The current market price of the common stock was $18. The stock was issued on July 1.

c. On September 1, declared a cash dividend of $0.50 per share on the common stock; paid the dividend on October 1.
d. On December 1, issued a 2-for-1 stock split of common stock when the stock was selling for $50 per share.

Required
1. Explain each transaction's effect on the Stockholders' Equity accounts and the total stockholders' equity.
2. Develop the Stockholders' Equity category of the December 31, 2007, balance sheet. Assume that the net income for the year was $650,000.
3. Write a paragraph that explains the difference between a stock dividend and a stock split.

LO8

Problem 11-6 Statement of Stockholders' Equity

Refer to all of the facts in Problem 11-1.

Required
Develop a statement of stockholders' equity for Peeler Company for 2008. The statement should start with the beginning balance of each Stockholders' Equity account and explain the changes that occurred in each account to arrive at the 2008 ending balances.

LO8

Problem 11-7 Wal-Mart's Comprehensive Income

Following is the consolidated statement of shareholders' equity of **Wal-Mart Stores, Inc.**, for the year ended January 31, 2007:

Consolidated Statement of Shareholders' Equity

(Amounts in millions except per share data)	Number of Shares	Common Stock	Capital in Excess of Par Value	Accumulated Other Comprehensive Income	Retained Earnings	Total
Balance January 31, 2006	4,165	417	2,596	1,053	49,105	53,171
Comprehensive income:						
Net income from continuing operations					11,284	11,284
Other comprehensive income:						
Foreign currency translation				1,584		1,584
Net changes in fair values of derivatives				6		6
Minimum pension liability				(15)		(15)
Total comprehensive income						12,859
Adjustment for initial application of SFAS 158, net of tax				(120)		(120)
Cash dividends ($0.67 per share)					(2,802)	(2,802)
Purchase of Company stock	(39)	(4)	(52)		(1,769)	(1,825)
Stock options exercised and other	5		290			290
Balance, January 31, 2007	4,131	$413	$2,834	$2,508	$55,818	$61,573

Required
1. Which items were included in comprehensive income? If these items had been included on the income statement as part of net income, what would have been the effect?
2. Do you think that the concept of comprehensive income would be useful to explain to the stockholders of Wal-Mart the impact of all events that took place during 2006. Why or why not?

LO10

Problem 11-8 Effects of Stockholders' Equity Transactions on Statement of Cash Flows

Refer to all of the facts in Problem 11-1.

Required
Indicate how each transaction affects the cash flow of Peeler Company by preparing the Financing Activities section of the 2008 statement of cash flows. Provide an explanation for the exclusion of any of these transactions from the Financing Activities section of the statement.

LO11

Problem 11-9 Income Distribution of a Partnership (Appendix)

Louise Abbott and Buddie Costello are partners in a comedy club business. The partnership agreement specifies the manner in which income of the business is to be distributed. Louise is to receive a salary of $20,000 for managing the club. Buddie is to receive interest at the rate of 10% on her capital balance of $300,000. Remaining income is to be distributed at a 2-to-1 ratio.

Required
Determine the amount that should be distributed to each partner assuming the following business net incomes:

1. $15,000
2. $50,000
3. $80,000

LO11

Problem 11-10 Sole Proprietorships (Appendix)

On May 1, Chong Yu deposited $120,000 of his own savings in a separate bank account to start a printing business. He purchased copy machines for $42,000. Expenses for the year, including depreciation on the copy machines, were $84,000. Sales for the year, all in cash, were $108,000. Chong withdrew $12,000 during the year.

Required
1. What is the balance in Chong's capital account at the end of the year?
2. Explain why the balance in Chong's capital account is different from the amount of cash on hand.

LO11

Problem 11-11 Partnerships (Appendix)

Kirin Nerise and Milt O'Brien agreed to form a partnership to operate a sandwich shop. Kirin contributed $25,000 cash and will manage the store. Milt contributed computer equipment worth $8,000 and $92,000 cash. Milt will keep the financial records. During the year, sales were $90,000 and expenses (including a salary to Kirin) were $76,000. Kirin withdrew $500 per month. Milt withdrew $4,000 (total). Their partnership agreement specified that Kirin would receive a salary of $7,200 for the year. Milt would receive 6% interest on his initial capital investment. All remaining income or loss would be equally divided.

Required
Calculate the ending balance in each partner's equity account.

MULTICONCEPT PROBLEMS

LO1,4

Problem 11-12 Analysis of Stockholders' Equity

The Stockholders' Equity section of the December 31, 2008, balance sheet of Eldon Company appeared as follows:

Preferred stock, $30 par value,	
5,000 shares authorized, ? shares issued	$120,000
Common stock, ? par,	
10,000 shares authorized, 7,000 shares issued	70,000
Additional paid-in capital—Preferred	6,000
Additional paid-in capital—Common	560,000
Additional paid-in capital—Treasury stock	1,000
Total contributed capital	$757,000
Retained earnings	40,000
Less: Treasury stock, preferred, 100 shares	(3,200)
Total stockholders' equity	$??

Required
Determine the following items based on Eldon's balance sheet.

1. The number of shares of preferred stock issued
2. The number of shares of preferred stock outstanding
3. The average per-share sales price of the preferred stock when issued
4. The par value of the common stock
5. The average per-share sales price of the common stock when issued
6. The cost of the treasury stock per share
7. The total stockholders' equity
8. The per-share book value of the common stock assuming that there are no dividends in arrears and that the preferred stock can be redeemed at its par value

LO3,4,7 **Problem 11-13** Effects of Stockholders' Equity Transactions on the Balance Sheet

The following transactions occurred at Horton Inc. during its first year of operation:

a. Issued 100,000 shares of common stock at $5 each; 1,000,000 shares are authorized at $1 par value.
b. Issued 10,000 shares of common stock for a building and land. The building was appraised for $20,000, but the value of the land is undeterminable. The stock is selling for $10 on the open market.
c. Purchased 1,000 shares of its own common stock on the open market for $16 per share.
d. Declared a dividend of $0.10 per share on outstanding common stock. The dividend is to be paid after the end of the first year of operations. Market value of the stock is $26.
e. Declared a 2-for-1 stock split. The market value of the stock was $37 before the stock split.
f. Reported $180,000 of income for the year.

Required
1. Indicate each transaction's effect on the assets, liabilities, and stockholders' equity of Horton Inc.
2. Prepare the Stockholders' Equity section of the balance sheet.
3. Write a paragraph that explains the number of shares of stock issued and outstanding at the end of the year.

LO1,4 **Problem 11-14** Stockholders' Equity Section of the Balance Sheet

The newly hired accountant at Ives Inc. prepared the following balance sheet:

Assets	
Cash	$ 3,500
Accounts receivable	5,000
Treasury stock	500
Plant, property, and equipment	108,000
Retained earnings	1,000
Total assets	$118,000
Liabilities	
Accounts payable	$ 5,500
Dividends payable	1,500
Stockholders' Equity	
Common stock, $1 par, 100,000 shares issued	100,000
Additional paid-in capital	11,000
Total liabilities and stockholders' equity	$118,000

Required
1. Prepare a corrected balance sheet. Write a short explanation for each correction.
2. Why does the Retained Earnings account have a negative balance?

ALTERNATE PROBLEMS

LO1 **Problem 11-1A** Stockholders' Equity Category

Kebler Company was incorporated as a new business on January 1, 2008. The corporate charter approved on that date authorized the issuance of 2,000 shares of $100 par, 7% cumulative, nonparticipating preferred stock and 20,000 shares of $5 par common stock. On January 10, Kebler issued for cash 1,000 shares of preferred stock at $120 per share and 8,000 shares of common stock at $80 per share. On January 20, it issued 2,000 shares of common stock to acquire a building site at a time when the stock was selling for $70 per share.

During 2008, Kebler established an employee benefit plan and acquired 1,000 shares of common stock at $60 per share as treasury stock for that purpose. Later in 2008, it resold 100 shares of the stock at $65 per share.

On December 31, 2008, Kebler determined its net income for the year to be $80,000. The firm declared the annual cash dividend to preferred stockholders and a cash dividend of $5 per share to the common stockholders. The dividend will be paid in 2009.

Required
Develop the Stockholders' Equity category of Kebler's balance sheet as of December 31, 2008. Indicate on the statement the number of shares authorized, issued, and outstanding for both preferred and common stock.

LO2

Problem 11-2A Evaluating Alternative Investments

Rob Lowe would like to invest $100,000 in Franklin Inc., which is offering common stock, preferred stock, and bonds on the open market. The common stock has paid $1 per share in dividends for the past three years, and the company expects to be able to double the dividend in the current year. The current market price of the common stock is $10 per share. The preferred stock has an 8% dividend rate. The bonds are selling at par with a 5% stated rate.

Required
1. Explain Franklin's obligation to pay dividends or interest on each instrument.
2. Recommend one type of investment over the others to Rob and justify your reason.

LO5

Problem 11-3A Dividends for Preferred and Common Stock

The Stockholders' Equity category of Rausch Company's balance sheet as of December 31, 2008, appeared as follows:

Preferred stock, $100 par, 8%, 2,000 shares issued and outstanding	$ 200,000
Common stock, $10 par, 40,000 shares issued and outstanding	400,000
Additional paid-in capital	500,000
Total contributed capital	$1,100,000
Retained earnings	900,000
Total stockholders' equity	$2,000,000

The notes to the financial statements indicate that dividends were not declared or paid for 2006 or 2007. Rausch wants to declare a dividend of $118,000 for 2008.

Required
Determine the total and the per-share amounts that should be declared to the preferred and common stockholders under the following assumptions:

1. The preferred stock is noncumulative, nonparticipating.
2. The preferred stock is cumulative, nonparticipating.

LO6

Problem 11-4A Effect of Stock Dividend

Travanti Company has a history of paying cash dividends on its common stock. Although the firm has been profitable this year, the board of directors is planning construction of a second manufacturing plant. To reduce the amount that they must borrow to finance the expansion, the directors are contemplating replacing their usual cash dividend with a 40% stock dividend. The board is unsure about a stock dividend's effect on the company's balance sheet and has requested your assistance.

Required
1. Write a statement to indicate the effect the stock dividend has on the financial statements of Travanti Company.
2. A group of common stockholders has contacted the firm to express its concern about the effect of the stock dividend and to question the effect the stock dividend may have on the market price of the stock. Write a statement to address the stockholders' concerns.

LO7

Problem 11-5A Dividends and Stock Splits

On January 1, 2008, Svenberg Inc.'s Stockholders' Equity category appeared as follows:

Preferred stock, $80 par value, 8%, 1,000 shares issued and outstanding	$ 80,000
Common stock, $10 par value, 10,000 shares issued and outstanding	100,000
Additional paid-in capital—Preferred	60,000
Additional paid-in capital—Common	225,000
Total contributed capital	$ 465,000
Retained earnings	1,980,000
Total stockholders' equity	$2,445,000

The preferred stock is noncumulative and nonparticipating. During 2008, the following transactions occurred:

a. On March 1, declared a cash dividend of $6,400 on preferred stock. Paid the dividend on April 1.
b. On June 1, declared an 8% stock dividend on common stock. The current market price of the common stock was $26. The stock was issued on July 1.
c. On September 1, declared a cash dividend of $0.70 per share on the common stock; paid the dividend on October 1.
d. On December 1, issued a 3-for-1 stock split of common stock, when the stock was selling for $30 per share.

Required

1. Explain each transaction's effect on the stockholders' equity accounts and the total stockholders' equity.
2. Develop the Stockholders' Equity category of the balance sheet. Assume that the net income for the year was $720,000.
3. Write a paragraph that explains the difference between a stock dividend and a stock split.

LO8

Problem 11-6A Statement of Stockholders' Equity

Refer to all of the facts in Problem 11-1A.

Required

Develop a statement of Stockholders' Equity for Kebler Company for 2008. The statement should start with the beginning balance of each Stockholders' Equity account and explain the changes that occurred in each account to arrive at the 2008 ending balances.

LO8

Problem 11-7A Costco's Comprehensive Income

Following is the consolidated statement of stockholders' equity of **Costco Wholesale Corporation** for the year ended September 3, 2006:

CONSOLIDATED STATEMENTS OF STOCKHOLDERS' EQUITY AND COMPREHENSIVE INCOME
For the period ended September 3, 2006 (in thousands)

	Common Stock		Additional Paid-In Capital	Other Accumulated Comprehensive Income/(Loss)	Retained Earnings	Total
	Shares	Amount				
Adjusted balance at August 28, 2005	472,480	2,362	$2,244,191	$158,039	$6,484,673	$8,889,265
Comprehensive Income:						
Net Income	—	—	—	—	1,103,215	1,103,215
Foreign currency translation adjustment and other	—	—	—	119,224	—	119,224
Total comprehensive income	—	—	—	119,224	1,103,215	1,222,439
Stock options exercised, including income tax benefits and other	11,712	59	427,291	—	—	427,350
Conversion of convertible notes	6,505	33	188,902	—	—	188,935
Stock repurchase	(28,418)	(142)	(145,129)	—	(1,316,465)	(1,461,736)
Stock-based compensation	—	—	107,397	—	—	107,397
Cash dividends	—	—	—	—	(230,211)	(230,211)
Balance at September 3, 2006	462,279	$2,312	$2,822,652	$277,263	$6,041,212	$9,143,439

Required

1. Costco has an item in the statement of stockholders' equity that is Other Accumulated Comprehensive Income. What are the possible sources of other comprehensive income as discussed in your text?
2. Besides Net Income and Other Accumulated Comprehensive Income, what other items affected stockholders' equity during the period?
3. How do cash dividends affect stockholders' equity? How would a stock dividend affect stockholders' equity?

Problem 11-8A Effects of Stockholders' Equity Transactions on the Statement of Cash Flows

Refer to all of the facts in Problem 11-1A.

Required

Indicate how each transaction affects the cash flow of Kebler Company by preparing the Financing Activities section of the 2008 statement of cash flows. Provide an explanation for the exclusion of any of these transactions from the Financing Activities section of the statement.

Problem 11-9A Income Distribution of a Partnership (Appendix)

Kay Katz and Doris Kan are partners in a dry-cleaning business. The partnership agreement specifies the manner in which income of the business is to be distributed. Kay is to receive a salary of $40,000 for managing the business. Doris is to receive interest at the rate of 10% on her capital balance of $600,000. Remaining income is to be distributed at a 2-to-1 ratio.

Required

Determine the amount that should be distributed to each partner assuming the following business net incomes:

1. $30,000
2. $100,000
3. $160,000

Problem 11-10A Sole Proprietorships (Appendix)

On May 1, Chen Chien Lao deposited $150,000 of her own savings in a separate bank account to start a printing business. She purchased copy machines for $52,500. Expenses for the year, including depreciation on the copy machines, were $105,000. Sales for the year, all in cash, were $135,000. Chen withdrew $15,000 during the year.

Required

1. What is the balance in Chen's capital account at the end of the year?
2. Explain why the balance in Chen's capital account is different from the amount of cash on hand.

Problem 11-11A Partnerships (Appendix)

Karen Locke and Gina Keyes agreed to form a partnership to operate a sandwich shop. Karen contributed $35,000 cash and will manage the store. Gina contributed computer equipment worth $11,200 and $128,800 cash. Gina will keep the financial records. During the year, sales were $126,000 and expenses (including a salary for Karen) were $106,400. Karen withdrew $700 per month. Gina withdrew $5,600 (total). Their partnership agreement specified that Karen would receive a salary of $10,800 for the year. Gina would receive 6% interest on her initial capital investment. All remaining income or loss would be equally divided.

Required

Calculate the ending balance in each partner's equity account.

ALTERNATE MULTICONCEPT PROBLEMS

LO1,4

Problem 11-12A Analysis of Stockholders' Equity

The Stockholders' Equity section of the December 31, 2008, balance sheet of Carter Company appeared as follows:

Preferred stock, $50 par value, 10,000 shares authorized, ? shares issued	$ 400,000
Common stock, ? par value, 20,000 shares authorized, 14,000 shares issued	280,000
Additional paid-in capital—Preferred	12,000
Additional paid-in capital—Common	980,000
Additional paid-in capital—Treasury stock	2,000
Total contributed capital	$1,674,000
Retained earnings	80,000
Less: Treasury stock, preferred, 200 shares	(12,800)
Total stockholders' equity	$??

Required
Determine the following items based on Carter's balance sheet.

1. The number of shares of preferred stock issued
2. The number of shares of preferred stock outstanding
3. The average per-share sales price of the preferred stock when issued
4. The par value of the common stock
5. The average per-share sales price of the common stock when issued
6. The cost of the treasury stock per share
7. The total stockholders' equity
8. The per-share book value of the common stock assuming that there are no dividends in arrears and that the preferred stock can be redeemed at its par value

LO3,4,7 **Problem 11-13A** Effects of Stockholders' Equity Transactions on Balance Sheet

The following transactions occurred at Hilton Inc. during its first year of operation:

a. Issued 10,000 shares of common stock at $10 each; 100,000 shares are authorized at $1 par value.
b. Issued 10,000 shares of common stock for a patent, which is expected to be effective for the next 15 years. The value of the patent is undeterminable. The stock is selling for $10 on the open market.
c. Purchased 1,000 shares of its own common stock on the open market for $10 per share.
d. Declared a dividend of $0.50 per share of outstanding common stock. The dividend is to be paid after the end of the first year of operations. Market value of the stock is $10.
e. Reported $340,000 of income for the year.

Required
1. Indicate each transaction's effect on the assets, liabilities, and stockholders' equity of Hilton Inc.
2. Hilton's president has asked you to explain the difference between contributed capital and retained earnings. Discuss the terms as they relate to Hilton.
3. Determine the book value per share of the stock at the end of the year.

Problem 11-14A Stockholders' Equity Section of the Balance Sheet

The newly hired accountant at Grainfield Inc. is considering the following list of accounts as he prepares the balance sheet. All of the accounts have positive balances. The company is authorized to issue 1,000,000 shares of common stock and 10,000 shares of preferred stock. The treasury stock was purchased at $5 per share.

Treasury stock (common)	$ 15,000
Retained earnings	54,900
Dividends payable	1,500
Common stock, $1 par	100,000
Additional paid-in capital	68,400
Preferred stock, $10 par, 5%	50,000

Required
1. Prepare the Stockholders' Equity section of the balance sheet for Grainfield.
2. Explain why some of the listed accounts are not shown in the Stockholders' Equity section.

DECISION CASES

READING AND INTERPRETING FINANCIAL STATEMENTS

LO1,8 **Decision Case 11-1** Comparing Two Companies in the Same Industry: Kellogg's and General Mills

Refer to the Stockholders' Equity section of the balance sheets of **Kellogg's** as of December 31, 2006, and **General Mills** as of May 28, 2006.

Required
1. For each company, what are the numbers of shares of common stock authorized, issued, and outstanding as of the balance sheet date?

2. Did the balance of the Retained Earnings account of each company increase or decrease during the year? What factors can affect the Retained Earnings balance?
3. How does the total stockholders' equity of each company compare to that of the other company? Does the difference mean that one company's stock is more valuable than the other's? Explain your answer.

LO10

Decision Case 11-2 Reading General Mills's Statement of Cash Flows

Refer to **General Mills's** statement of cash flows for the year ending May 28, 2006.

Required:
1. What sources of cash are revealed in the Financing Activities category of the statement of cash flows?
2. What was the amount of dividends paid to stockholders during the period?
3. The Financing Activities section indicates a large negative amount for the purchase of treasury stock. When treasury stock is purchased, what is the effect on the accounts of the balance sheet?

MAKING FINANCIAL DECISIONS

LO1,2

Decision Case 11-3 Debt versus Preferred Stock

Assume that you are an analyst attempting to compare the financial structures of two companies. In particular, you must analyze the debt and equity categories of the two firms and calculate a debt-to-equity ratio for each firm. The Liability and Equity categories of First Company at year-end appeared as follows:

Liabilities	
Accounts payable	$ 500,000
Loan payable	800,000
Stockholders' Equity	
Common stock	300,000
Retained earnings	600,000
Total liabilities and equity	$2,200,000

First Company's loan payable bears interest at 8%, which is paid annually. The principal is due in five years.

The Liability and Equity categories of Second Company at year-end appeared as follows:

Liabilities	
Accounts payable	$ 500,000
Stockholders' Equity	
Common stock	300,000
Preferred stock	800,000
Retained earnings	600,000
Total liabilities and equity	$2,200,000

Second Company's preferred stock is 8%, cumulative. A provision of the stock agreement specifies that the stock must be redeemed at face value in five years.

Required
1. It appears that the loan payable of First Company and the preferred stock of Second Company are very similar. What are the differences between the two securities?
2. When calculating the debt-to-equity ratio, do you believe that the Second Company preferred stock should be treated as debt or as stockholders' equity? Write a statement expressing your position on the issue.

LO2

Decision Case 11-4 Preferred versus Common Stock

Rohnan Inc. needs to raise $500,000. It is considering two options:

a. Issue preferred stock, $100 par, 8%, cumulative, nonparticipating, callable at $110. The stock could be issued at par.
b. Issue common stock, $1 par, market $10. Currently, the company has 400,000 shares outstanding distributed equally in the hands of five owners. The company has never paid a dividend.

Required
Rohnan has asked you to consider both options and make a recommendation. It is equally concerned with cash flow and company control. Write your recommendations.

ETHICAL DECISION MAKING

LO9

Decision Case 11-5 Inside Information

Jim Brock was an accountant with Hubbard Inc., a large corporation with stock that was publicly traded on the New York Stock Exchange. One of Jim's duties was to manage the corporate reporting department, which was responsible for developing and issuing Hubbard's annual report. At the end of 2008, Hubbard closed its accounting records and initial calculations indicated a very profitable year. In fact, the net income exceeded the amount that had been projected during the year by the financial analysts who followed Hubbard's stock.

Jim was pleased with the company's financial performance. In January 2009, he suggested that his father buy Hubbard's stock because he was sure the stock price would increase when the company announced its 2008 results. Jim's father followed that advice and bought a block of stock at $25 per share.

On February 15, 2009, Hubbard announced its 2008 results and issued the annual report. The company received favorable press coverage about its performance, and the stock price on the stock exchange increased to $32 per share.

Required
What was Jim's professional responsibility to Hubbard Inc. concerning the issuance of the 2008 annual report? Did Jim act ethically in this situation?

LO5

Decision Case 11-6 Dividend Policy

Hancock Inc. is owned by nearly 100 shareholders. Judith Stitch owns 48% of the stock. She needs cash to fulfill her commitment to donate the funds to construct a new art gallery. Some of her friends have agreed to vote for Hancock to pay a larger-than-normal dividend to shareholders. Judith has asked you to vote for the large dividend because she knows that you also support the arts. When informed that the dividend may create a working capital hardship on Hancock, Judith responded: "There is plenty of money in Retained Earnings. The dividend will not affect the cash of the company." Respond to her comment. What ethical questions do you and Judith face? How would you vote?

SOLUTIONS TO KEY TERMS QUIZ

13	**Authorized shares**	18	**Retirement of stock**
1	**Issued shares**	7	**Dividend payout ratio**
14	**Outstanding shares**	19	**Stock dividend**
2	**Par value**	9	**Stock split**
15	**Additional paid-in capital**	8	**Statement of stockholders' equity**
3	**Retained earnings**	11	**Comprehensive income**
4	**Cumulative feature**	10	**Book value per share**
16	**Participating feature**	12	**Market value per share**
5	**Convertible feature**	22	**Sole proprietorship**
17	**Callable feature**	20	**Partnership**
6	**Treasury stock**	21	**Partnership agreement**

INTEGRATIVE PROBLEM

Evaluating financing options for asset acquisition and their impact on financial statements

Following are the financial statements for Griffin Inc. for the year 2008:

Griffin Inc.
Balance Sheet
December 31, 2008
(in millions)

Assets		**Liabilities**	
Cash	$ 1.6	Current portion of lease obligation	$ 1.0
Other current assets	6.4	Other current liabilities	3.0
Leased assets (net of accumulated depreciation)	7.0	Lease obligation—Long-term	6.0
Other long-term assets	45.0	Other long-term liabilities	6.0
		Total liabilities	$16.0
		Stockholders' Equity	
		Preferred stock	$ 1.0
		Additional paid-in capital—Preferred	2.0
		Common stock	4.0
		Additional paid-in capital—Common	16.0
		Retained earnings	21.0
		Total stockholders' equity	$44.0
Total assets	$60.0	Total liabilities and stockholders' equity	$60.0

Griffin Inc.
Income Statement
For the Year Ended December 31, 2008
(in millions)

Revenues		$ 50.0
Expenses:		
Depreciation of leased asset	$ 1.0	
Depreciation—Other assets	3.2	
Interest on leased asset	0.5	
Other expenses	27.4	
Income tax (30% rate)	5.4	
Total expenses		(37.5)
Income before extraordinary loss		$ 12.5
Extraordinary loss (net of $0.9 taxes)		(2.1)
Net income		$ 10.4
EPS before extraordinary loss		$ 3.10
EPS extraordinary loss		(0.53)
EPS—Net income		$ 2.57

Additional information:

Griffin Inc. has authorized 500,000 shares of 10%, $10 par value, cumulative preferred stock. There were 100,000 shares issued and outstanding at all times during 2008. The firm also has authorized 5 million shares of $1 par common stock, with 4 million shares issued and outstanding.

On January 1, 2008, Griffin Inc. acquired an asset, a piece of specialized heavy equipment, for $8 million with a capital lease. The lease contract indicates that the term of the lease is eight years. Payments of $1.5 million are to be made each December 31. The first lease payment was made December 31, 2008, and consisted of $1 million principal and $0.5 million of interest expense. The capital lease is depreciated using the straight-line method over eight years with zero salvage value.

Required

1. Assuming that the equipment was acquired using a capital lease, indicate the entries for the acquisition, depreciation, and lease payment.

2. The management of Griffin Inc. is considering the financial statement impact of methods of financing, other than the capital lease, that could have been used to acquire the equipment. For each alternative (a), (b), and (c), provide all necessary entries, indicate the effect on the accounting equation, and prepare revised 2008 financial statements. Calculate, as revised, the following amounts or ratios:

   Current ratio
   Debt-to-equity ratio
   Net income
   EPS—Net income

Assume that the following alternative actions would have taken place on January 1, 2008:

a. Instead of acquiring the equipment with a capital lease, the company negotiated an operating lease to use the asset. The lease requires annual year-end payments of $1.5 million and results in "off-balance-sheet" financing. (*Hint:* The $1.5 million should be treated as rental expense.)
b. Instead of acquiring the equipment with a capital lease, Griffin Inc. issued bonds for $8 million and purchased the equipment with the proceeds of the bond issue. Assume that the bond interest of $0.5 million was accrued and paid on December 31, 2008. A portion of the principal also is paid each year for eight years. On December 31, 2008, the company paid $1 million of principal and anticipated another $1 million of principal to be paid in 2009. Assume that the equipment would have an eight-year life and would be depreciated on a straight-line basis with zero salvage value.
c. Instead of acquiring the equipment with a capital lease, Griffin Inc. issued 200,000 additional shares of 10% preferred stock to raise $8 million and purchased the equipment for $8 million with the proceeds from the stock issue. Dividends on the stock are declared and paid annually. Assume that a dividend payment was made on December 31, 2008. Assume that the equipment would have an eight-year life and would be depreciated on a straight-line basis with zero salvage value.

ANSWERS TO POD REVIEW

LO1	1. d	2. c
LO2	1. a	2. c
LO3	1. d	2. a
LO4	1. d	2. c
LO5	1. a	2. c
LO6	1. c	2. a
LO7	1. d	2. a
LO8	1. d	2. a
LO9	1. d	2. a
LO10	1. c	2. b
LO11	1. b	2. d

CHAPTER

12

The Statement of Cash Flows

Learning Outcomes

After studying this chapter, you should be able to:

LO1 Understand the concept of cash flows and accrual accounting, and explain the purpose of a statement of cash flows.

LO2 Explain what cash equivalents are and how they are treated on the statement of cash flows.

LO3 Describe operating, investing, and financing activities and give examples of each.

LO4 Describe the difference between the direct and the indirect method of computing cash flow from operating activities.

LO5 Use T accounts to prepare a statement of cash flows using the direct method to determine cash flow from operating activities.

LO6 Use T accounts to prepare a statement of cash flows using the indirect method to determine cash flow from operating activities.

LO7 Use cash flow information to help analyze a company.

LO8 Use a work sheet to prepare a statement of cash flows using the indirect method to determine cash flow from operating activities (Appendix).

Study Links...

A Look at Previous Chapters

Previous chapters showed that assets and liabilities involve important cash flows to a business at one time or another. Chapter 2 introduced the statement of cash flows along with the other financial statements.

Chapter 11 completed examination of the accounting and reporting issues for a company's various assets, liabilities, and equities. Specifically, that chapter considered how companies account for stockholders' equity.

A Look at This Chapter

Now that we have a fuller appreciation of how to account for the various assets and liabilities of a business, we turn our attention in this chapter to an in-depth examination of the statement of cash flows.

A Look at the Upcoming Chapter

Stockholders, creditors, and other groups use financial statements, including the statement of cash flows, to analyze a company. Earlier chapters called attention to various ratios often used to aid in these analyses. The final chapter discusses the use of ratios and other types of analysis to ensure a better understanding of the financial strength and health of companies.

Best Buy MAKING BUSINESS DECISIONS

"Cash is king" is an expression you have undoubtedly heard. After learning the basics of accounting in this course, you now have a good idea of the meaning of that expression. Cash is the one universally recognized medium of exchange in today's world. Currencies vary—from the dollar in this country to the peso in Mexico to the euro in the European community of countries—but regardless, cash is what bankers and other creditors expect when it comes time to settle outstanding obligations. And it's what stockholders expect if dividends are going to be paid.

Best Buy, North America's leading specialty retailer for a wide variety of consumer electronics, computers, and appliances, understands the supremacy of cash as well as any company does. A glance at the company's statement of cash flows on the next page shows a business that not only achieved record earnings that reached nearly \$1.4 billion in fiscal 2007 but also increased its cash and cash equivalents by over 60% to a year-end balance of more than \$1.2 billion.

What a company does with its cash is central to its long-term success. And a statement of cash flows provides a clear picture of what the company has done historically with this most liquid of all assets. When you examine Best Buy's statement, one of the first items to get your attention is that as impressive as its net earnings of \$1,377 million are, the cash provided by its operations was even higher.

So what did the company do with nearly \$1.8 billion of cash that its operations generated during the year? The remaining two sections of the statement provide the answers. First, as any successful company does, Best Buy invested in its future by adding to its property and equipment, which for a merchandiser means expansion of its retail stores. The statement shows that the company used \$780 million of cash from operations in its various investing activities. It then used another \$513 million of cash in its financing activities. Those activities included paying \$599 million to buy back some of its common stock, repaying \$84 million of debt, and returning \$174 million to its stockholders in the form of dividends.

This chapter will take a close look at the relationship between earnings on a company's income statement and

© AP Photo/The Vindicator. Jean Niece

its cash activities as reported on a statement of cash flows. Management of a company, creditors, and stockholders are interested not only in what a company's bottom line is but also in where the company's cash comes from and where it goes. This chapter answers these key questions for Best Buy and for all companies:

- Why are net earnings not the same as cash provided by operating activities? (See pp. 585–587.)
- How do accountants reconcile the difference between these two amounts? (See pp. 594–596.)
- What are the various sources and uses of cash in a company's investing and financing activities? (See pp. 591–592.)
- How can information about a company's cash flows be used to analyze its performance? (See pp. 618–621.)

(*continued*)

Best Buy
Consolidated Statements of Cash Flows
$ in millions

Fiscal Years Ended	March 3, 2007	February 25, 2006	February 26, 2005
Operating Activities			
Net earnings	$ 1,377	$ 1,140	$ 984
Gain from disposal of discontinued operations, net of tax	—	—	(50)
Earnings from continuing operations	1,377	1,140	934
Adjustments to reconcile earnings from continuing operations to total cash provided by operating activities from continuing operations:			
Depreciation	509	456	459
Asset impairment charges	32	4	22
Stock-based compensation	121	132	(1)
Deferred income taxes	82	(151)	(28)
Excess tax benefits from stock-based compensation	(50)	(55)	—
Other, net	(11)	(3)	24
Changes in operating assets and liabilities, net of acquired assets and liabilities:			
Receivables	(70)	(43)	(30)
Merchandise inventories	(550)	(457)	(240)
Other assets	(47)	(11)	(50)
Accounts payable	320	385	347
Other liabilities	185	165	243
Accrued income taxes	(136)	178	301
Total cash provided by operating activities from continuing operations	1,762	1,740	1,981
Investing Activities			
Additions to property and equipment, net of $75 and $117 non-cash capital expenditures in fiscal 2006 and 2005, respectively	(733)	(648)	(502)
Purchases of available-for-sale securities	(4,541)	(4,319)	(8,517)
Sales of available-for-sale securities	4,886	4,187	7,730
Acquisitions of businesses, net of cash acquired	(421)	—	—
Proceeds from disposition of investments	24	—	—
Change in restricted assets	—	(20)	(140)
Other, net	5	46	7
Total cash used in investing activities from continuing operations	(780)	(754)	(1,422)
Financing Activities			
Repurchase of common stock	(599)	(772)	(200)
Issuance of common stock under employee stock purchase plan and for the exercise of stock options	217	292	256
Dividends paid	(174)	(151)	(137)
Repayments of debt	(84)	(69)	(371)
Proceeds from issuance of debt	96	36	—
Excess tax benefits from stock-based compensation	50	55	—
Other, net	(19)	(10)	(7)
Total cash used in financing activities from continuing operations	(513)	(619)	(459)
Effect of Exchange Rate Changes on Cash	(12)	27	9
Increase in Cash and Cash Equivalents	457	394	109
Cash and Cash Equivalents at Beginning of Year	748	354	245
Cash and Cash Equivalents at End of Year	$ 1,205	$ 748	$ 354
Supplemental Disclosure of Cash Flow Information			
Income taxes paid	$ 804	$ 547	$ 241
Interest paid	14	16	35

See Notes to Consolidated Financial Statements.

Record earnings of almost $1.4 billion

Cash from operations more than net earnings

Includes cost to open new stores

Nearly half of cash generated from operations used to invest

Another $.5 billion used in financing activities

Balance increased by over 60%

Cash Flows and Accrual Accounting

LO1 Understand the concept of cash flows and accrual accounting, and explain the purpose of a statement of cash flows.

All external parties have an interest in a company's cash flows.

- Stockholders need some assurance that enough cash is being generated from operations to pay dividends and to invest in the company's future.
- Creditors want to know if cash from operations is sufficient to repay their loans along with interest.

This chapter will show you how to read, understand, and prepare the statement of cash flows, which is perhaps the key financial statement for the survival of every business.

The *bottom line* is a term used many different ways in today's society. "I wish politicians would cut out all of the rhetoric and get to the bottom line." "The bottom line is that the manager was fired because the team wasn't winning." "Our company's bottom line is twice what it was last year." This last use of the term, in reference to a company's net income, is probably the way in which *bottom line* was first used. In recent years, managers, stockholders, creditors, analysts, and other users of financial statements have become more wary of focusing on any one number as an indicator of a company's overall performance. Most experts now agree that there has been a tendency to rely far too heavily on net income and its companion, earnings per share, and in many cases to ignore a company's cash flows. As you know by now from your study of accounting, you can't pay bills with net income; you need cash!

To understand the difference between a company's bottom line and its cash flow, consider the case of **Best Buy** in its 2007 fiscal year. Best Buy reported net earnings (income) of $1,377 million. However, as shown in the chapter opener, during this same time period, its cash increased by only $457 million. How is this possible? First, net income is computed on an accrual basis, not a cash basis. Second, the income statement primarily reflects events related to the operating activities of a business, that is, selling products or providing services.

A company's cash position can increase or decrease over a period, and it can report a net profit or a net loss. If you think about it, one of four combinations is possible:

1. **A company can report an increase in cash and a net profit.**
2. **A company can report a decrease in cash and a net profit.**
3. **A company can report an increase in cash and a net loss.**
4. **A company can report a decrease in cash and a net loss.**

Exhibit 12-1 illustrates this point by showing the performance of four well-known companies, including Best Buy. Best Buy is the only one of the four companies that improved its cash position *and* reported a net profit. **Gateway** reported a net profit but saw its cash decline in 2006. **Northwest Airlines** reported a net loss in 2006 but improved its cash position. Finally, **Circuit City** experienced a net loss *and* saw its cash decline. To summarize, **a company with a profitable year does not necessarily increase its cash position, nor does a company with an unprofitable year always experience a decrease in cash.**

EXHIBIT 12-1 **Cash Flows and Net Income for Four Companies (all amounts in millions of dollars—years ending December 31, 2006, unless otherwise noted)**

Company	Beginning Balance in Cash	Ending Balance in Cash	Increase (Decrease) in Cash	Net Income (Loss)
Best Buy (fiscal year ended March 3, 2007)	$ 748	$ 1,205	$ 457	$ 1,377
Geteway	422.5	345.7	(76.8)	9.6
Northwest Airlines	684	1,461	777	(2,835)
Circuit City (fiscal year ended February 28, 2007)	316.0	141.1	(174.9)	(8.3)

PURPOSE OF THE STATEMENT OF CASH FLOWS

Statement of cash flows The financial statement that summarizes an entity's cash receipts and cash payments during the period from operating, investing, and financing activities.

The **statement of cash flows** is an important complement to the other major financial statements. It summarizes the operating, investing, and financing activities of a business over a period of time. The balance sheet summarizes the cash on hand and the balances in other assets, liabilities, and owners' equity accounts, providing a snapshot at a specific point in time. **The statement of cash flows reports the changes in cash over a period of time and, most importantly, *explains those changes*.**

The income statement summarizes performance on an accrual basis. Income on this basis is considered a better indicator of *future* cash inflows and outflows than is a statement limited to current cash flows. The statement of cash flows complements the accrual-based income statement by allowing users to assess a company's performance on a cash basis. As you will see in the following simple example, however, it also goes beyond presenting data related to operating performance and looks at other activities that affect a company's cash position.

AN EXAMPLE

Consider the following discussion between the owner of Fox River Realty and the company accountant. After a successful first year in business in 2007 in which the company earned a profit of $100,000, the owner reviews the income statement for the second year, as presented in Exhibit 12-2.

The owner is pleased with the results and asks to see the balance sheet. Comparative balance sheets for the first two years are presented in Exhibit 12-3.

Where Did the Cash Go? At first glance, the owner is surprised to see the significant decline in the Cash account. She immediately presses the accountant for answers. With such a profitable year, where has the cash gone? Specifically, why has cash decreased from $150,000 to $50,000 even though income rose from $100,000 in the first year to $250,000 in the second year?

The accountant begins his explanation to the owner by pointing out that income on a cash basis is even higher than the reported $250,000. Because depreciation expense is an expense that does not use cash (cash is used when the plant and equipment are purchased, not when they are depreciated), cash provided from operating activities is calculated as follows:

Net income	$250,000
Add back: Depreciation expense	50,000
Cash provided by operating activities	$300,000

Further, the accountant reminds the owner of the additional $50,000 that she invested in the business during the year. Now the owner is even more bewildered: with

EXHIBIT 12-2 Income Statement for Fox River Realty

Fox River Realty
Income Statement
For the Year Ended December 31, 2008

Revenues	$400,000
Depreciation expense	$ 50,000
All other expenses	100,000
Total expenses	$150,000
Net income	$250,000

EXHIBIT 12-3 Comparative Balance Sheets for Fox River Realty

Fox River Realty
Comparative Balance Sheets
December 31

	2008	2007
Cash	$ 50,000	$150,000
Plant and equipment	600,000	350,000
Accumulated depreciation	(150,000)	(100,000)
Total assets	$500,000	$400,000
Notes payable	$100,000	$150,000
Common stock	250,000	200,000
Retained earnings	150,000	50,000
Total equities	$500,000	$400,000

cash from operations of $300,000 and her own infusion of $50,000, why did cash *decrease* by $100,000? The accountant refreshes the owner's memory about three major outflows of cash during the year. First, even though the business earned $250,000, she withdrew $150,000 in dividends during the year. Second, the comparative balance sheets indicate that notes payable with the bank were reduced from $150,000 to $100,000, requiring the use of $50,000 in cash. Finally, the comparative balance sheets show an increase in plant and equipment for the year from $350,000 to $600,000—a sizable investment of $250,000 in new long-term assets.

Statement of Cash Flows To summarize what happened to the cash, the accountant prepares a statement of cash flows, shown in Exhibit 12-4. Although the owner is not particularly happy with the decrease in cash for the year, she is satisfied with the statement as an explanation of where the cash came from and how it was used. The statement summarizes the important cash activities for the year and fills a void created with the presentation of just an income statement and a balance sheet.

EXHIBIT 12-4 Statement of Cash Flows for Fox River Realty

Fox River Realty
Statement of Cash Flows
For the Year Ended December 31, 2008

Cash provided (used) by operating activities:	
Net income	$ 250,000
Add back: Depreciation expense	50,000
Net cash provided (used) by operating activities	$ 300,000
Cash provided (used) by investing activities:	
Purchase of new plant and equipment	$(250,000)
Cash provided (used) by financing activities:	
Additional investment by owner	$ 50,000
Cash dividends paid to owner	(150,000)
Repayment of notes payable to bank	(50,000)
Net cash provided (used) by financing activities	$(150,000)
Net increase (decrease) in cash	$(100,000)
Cash balance at beginning of year	150,000
Cash balance at end of year	$ 50,000

REPORTING REQUIREMENTS FOR A STATEMENT OF CASH FLOWS

Accounting standards specify both the basis for preparing the statement of cash flows and the classification of items on the statement.[1] First, the statement must be prepared on a cash basis. Second, the cash flows must be classified into three categories:

- Operating activities
- Investing activities
- Financing activities

We now take a closer look at each of these important requirements in preparing a statement of cash flows.

POD REVIEW 12.1

LO1 *Understand the concept of cash flows and accrual accounting, and explain the purpose of a statement of cash flows.*

- The statement of cash flows helps investors understand cash inflows and outflows of an entity based on its operating, investing, and financing activities. It provides complementary information to the accrual-based income statement.

QUESTIONS

1. *Which of the following is a correct statement about the relationship between net income and cash flow?*
   a. Cash will increase during a year in which a company reports net income.
   b. Cash will decrease during a year in which a company reports a net loss.
   c. Cash can increase or decrease during a year in which a company reports net income.
   d. None of the above.

2. *What are the three categories into which cash flows are classified?*
   a. operating, investing, and producing
   b. operating, investing, and financing
   c. operating, nonoperating, and financing
   d. none of the above

The Definition of Cash: Cash and Cash Equivalents

LO2 Explain what cash equivalents are and how they are treated on the statement of cash flows.

The purpose of the statement of cash flows is to provide information about a company's cash inflows and outflows. Thus, it is essential to have a clear understanding of what the definition of *cash* includes. According to accounting standards, certain items are recognized as being equivalent to cash and are combined with cash on the balance sheet and the statement of cash flows.

1 *Statement of Financial Accounting Standards No. 95*, "Statement of Cash Flows" (Stamford, Conn.: Financial Accounting Standards Board, November 1987).

Commercial paper (short-term notes issued by corporations), money market funds, and Treasury bills are examples of cash equivalents. To be classified as a **cash equivalent**, an item must be readily convertible to a known amount of cash and have a maturity *to the investor* of three months or less. For example, a three-year Treasury note purchased two months before its maturity is classified as a cash equivalent. However, the same note purchased two years before maturity would be classified as an investment.

Cash equivalent
An item readily convertible to a known amount of cash with a maturity to the investor of three months or less.

To understand why cash equivalents are combined with cash when a statement of cash flows is prepared, assume that a company has a cash balance of $10,000 and no assets that qualify as cash equivalents. Further assume that the $10,000 is used to purchase 90-day Treasury bills and is recorded using the following entry:

Investment in Treasury Bills	10,000	
Cash		10,000
To record the purchase of 90-day Treasury bills.		

Balance Sheet								Income Statement
ASSETS		=	LIABILITIES	+	STOCKHOLDERS' EQUITY	+		REVENUES – EXPENSES
Investment in Treasury Bills	10,000							
Cash	(10,000)							

For record-keeping purposes, it is important to recognize this transaction as a transfer between cash in the bank and an investment in a government security. In the strictest sense, the investment represents an outflow of cash. The purchase of a security with such a short maturity does not, however, involve any significant degree of risk in terms of price changes and thus is not reported on the statement of cash flows as an outflow. Instead, for purposes of classification on the balance sheet and the statement of cash flows, this is merely a transfer *within* the cash and cash equivalents category. The point is that before the purchase of the Treasury bills the company had $10,000 in cash and cash equivalents; and after the purchase, it still had $10,000 in cash and cash equivalents. *Because nothing changed, the transaction is not reported on the statement of cash flows.*

Consider a different transaction involving the $10,000 and the following entry:

Investment in GM Common Stock	10,000	
Cash		10,000
To record the purchase of GM common stock.		

Balance Sheet								Income Statement
ASSETS		=	LIABILITIES	+	STOCKHOLDERS' EQUITY	+		REVENUES – EXPENSES
Investment in GM Common Stock	10,000							
Cash	(10,000)							

This purchase involves a certain amount of risk for the company making the investment. The GM stock is not convertible to a known amount of cash because its market value is subject to change. Thus, for balance sheet purposes, the investment is not considered a cash equivalent; therefore, it is not combined with cash but is classified as either a short-term or long-term investment depending on the company's intent in holding the stock. In the preparation of a statement of cash flows, the **investment in stock of another company is considered a significant activity and thus is reported on the statement of cash flows.**

POD REVIEW 12.2

LO2 *Explain what cash equivalents are and how they are treated on the statement of cash flows.*

- Cash equivalents are assets that are readily convertible to a determinable amount of cash, having a maturity date of three months or less.
- The term *cash* in the statement of cash flows includes cash and cash equivalents.

QUESTIONS

1. *Where are cash equivalents reported?*
   a. in the Operating Activities section of the statement of cash flows
   b. in the Financing Activities section of the statement of cash flows
   c. on neither the balance sheet nor the statement of cash flows
   d. none of the above

2. *Which of the following is a cash equivalent?*
   a. an investment in the common stock of another company
   b. an investment in the bonds of another company
   c. a money market account
   d. none of the above

Classification of Cash Flows

LO3 Describe operating, investing, and financing activities and give examples of each.

For the statement of cash flows, companies are required to classify activities into three categories: operating, investing, or financing. These categories represent the major functions of an entity, and classifying activities in this way allows users to look at important relationships. For example, one important financing activity for many businesses is borrowing money. Grouping the cash inflows from borrowing money during the period with the cash outflows from repayments of loans during the period makes it easier for analysts and other users of the statements to evaluate the company.

Each of the three types of activities can result in both cash inflows and cash outflows to the company. Thus, the general format for the statement is as shown in Exhibit 12-5.

EXHIBIT 12-5 Format for the Statement of Cash Flows

The Smith Corporation
Statement of Cash Flows
For the Year Ended December 31, 2008

Cash flows from operating activities:		
Inflows	$ xxx	
Outflows	(xxx)	
Net cash provided (used) by operating activities		$xxx
Cash flows from investing activities:		
Inflows	$ xxx	
Outflows	(xxx)	
Net cash provided (used) by investing activities		xxx
Cash flows from financing activities:		
Inflows	$ xxx	
Outflows	(xxx)	
Net cash provided (used) by financing activities		xxx
Net increase (decrease) in cash and cash equivalents		$xxx
Cash and cash equivalents at beginning of year		xxx
Cash and cash equivalents at end of year		$xxx

Note the direct tie between the bottom portion of this statement and the balance sheet. The beginning and ending balances in cash and cash equivalents, shown as the last two lines on the statement of cash flows, are taken directly from the comparative balance sheets. Some companies end their statement of cash flows with the figure for the net increase or decrease in cash and cash equivalents and do not report the beginning and ending balances in cash and cash equivalents directly on the statement of cash flows. Instead, the reader must turn to the balance sheet for those amounts.

Operating Activities **Operating activities** involve acquiring and selling products and services. The specific activities of a business depend on its type. For example, the purchase of raw materials is an important operating activity for a manufacturer. For a retailer, the purchase of inventory from a distributor constitutes an operating activity. For a realty company, the payment of a commission to a salesperson is an operating activity. All three types of businesses sell either products or services, and their sales are important operating activities.

Operating activities
Activities concerned with the acquisition and sale of products and services.

A statement of cash flows reflects the cash effects, either inflows or outflows, associated with each of these activities. For example, the manufacturer's payment for purchases of raw materials results in a cash outflow. The receipt of cash from collecting an account receivable results in a cash inflow. The income statement reports operating activities on an accrual basis. The statement of cash flows reflects a company's operating activities on a cash basis.

Investing Activities **Investing activities** involve acquiring and disposing of long-term assets. Replacing worn-out plant and equipment and expanding the existing base of long-term assets are essential to all businesses. Cash is paid for these acquisitions, often called *capital expenditures*. The following excerpt from **Best Buy**'s 2007 statement of cash flows (also shown in the chapter opener) indicates that the company spent $733 million for ❶ additions to property and equipment during fiscal 2007. (All amounts are in millions of dollars.)

Investing activities
Activities concerned with the acquisition and disposal of long-term assets.

	Investing Activities	
❶	Additions to property and equipment, net of $75 and $117 noncash capital expenditures in fiscal 2006 and 2005, respectively	(733)
❷	Purchases of available-for-sale securities	(4,541)
❸	Sales of available-for-sale securities	4,886
❹	Acquisitions of businesses, net of cash acquired	(421)
	Proceeds from disposition of investments	24
	Change in restricted assets	—
	Other, net	5
	Total cash used in investing activities from continuing operations	(780)

Sales of long-term assets, such as plant and equipment, are not generally a significant source of cash. These assets are acquired to be used in producing goods and services or to support this function, rather than to be resold, as is true for inventory. Occasionally, however, plant and equipment may wear out or no longer be needed and are offered for sale. Best Buy does not separately report any sales of property and equipment during 2007.

Chapter 7 explained why companies sometimes invest in the stocks and bonds of other companies. During 2007, Best Buy spent $4,541 million to ❷ buy the securities of other companies and generated $4,886 million from ❸ selling those investments. Finally, the acquisition of one company by another is an important investing activity, and Best Buy ❹ spent $421 million for that purpose.

Financing Activities All businesses rely on internal financing, external financing, or a combination of the two in meeting their needs for cash. Initially, a new business must have a certain amount of investment by the owners to begin operations. After this, many companies use notes, bonds, and other forms of debt to provide financing. Issuing stock and various forms of debt results in cash inflows that appear as **financing activities** on the statement of cash flows. On the other side, the repurchase of a company's own stock and the repayment of borrowings are important cash outflows to be reported in the Financing Activities section of the statement. Another important activity often listed in the Financing Activities section of the statement is the payment of cash dividends.

Financing activities
Activities concerned with the raising and repaying of funds in the form of debt and equity.

© AP Photo/The Vindicator, Jean Niece

Hot Topics

Spending Money to Make Money

Best Buy's 2007 statement of cash flows shows that it spent $733, or nearly three-quarters of a billion dollars, on additions to property and equipment. Capital expenditures are the lifeblood of all businesses and a necessity for a company such as Best Buy that depends on a large network of retail stores to sell the latest in electronics, appliances, and other products. So it is not surprising that Best Buy continually spends money not only to open new stores but also to remodel and relocate existing stores. In October 2007, Best Buy announced the opening of 15 new stores, complete with ribbon-cutting ceremonies and $10,000 check presentations to local nonprofit organizations. After the opening of 96 new stores in the prior fiscal year, the October openings brought the total count to 904 Best Buy stores in the United States. Obviously, the company sees a direct connection between spending money on new stores and adding to its bottom line.

Source: Best Buy news release, October 19, 2007; http//www.bestbuy.com

Best Buy's 2007 statement of cash flows lists many of the common cash inflows and outflows from financing activities (amounts in millions of dollars):

Financing Activities	
❺ Repurchase of common stock	(599)
❹ Issuance of common stock under employee stock purchase plan and for the exercise of stock options	217
❸ Dividends paid	(174)
❷ Repayments of debt	(84)
❶ Proceeds from issuance of debt	96
Excess tax benefits from stock based compensation	50
Other, net	(19)
Total cash used in financing activities from continuing operations	(513)

In 2007, Best Buy generated $96 million from ❶ issuing new debt and paid $84 million to ❷ retire existing debt. Another $174 million was paid in ❸ dividends to stockholders. Also, during the year, the company raised $217 million by ❹ issuing common stock and paid $599 million to ❺ buy back some of its stock.

Study Tip

Later in the chapter you will learn a technique to use in preparing the statement of cash flows. Recall then the observations made here regarding what types of accounts affect each of the three activities.

Summary of the Three Types of Activities To summarize the categorization of the activities of a business as operating, investing, and financing, refer to Exhibit 12-6. The exhibit lists examples of each of the three activities along with the related balance sheet accounts and the account classifications on the balance sheet.

In the exhibit, operating activities center on the acquisition and sale of products and services and related costs, such as wages and taxes. Two important observations can be made about the cash flow effects from the operating activities of a business:

1. The cash flows from these activities are the cash effects of transactions that enter into the determination of net income. For example, the sale of a product enters into the calculation of net income. The cash effect of this transaction—that is, the collection of the account receivable—results in a cash inflow from operating activities.
2. Cash flows from operating activities usually relate to an increase or decrease in a current asset or in a current liability. For example, the payment of taxes to the government results in a decrease in taxes payable, which is a current liability on the balance sheet.

Note that investing activities normally relate to long-term assets on the balance sheet. For example, the purchase of new plant and equipment increases long-term assets, and the sale of those same assets reduces long-term assets on the balance sheet.

EXHIBIT 12-6 Classification of Items on the Statement of Cash Flows

Activity	Examples	Effect on Cash	Related Balance Sheet Account	Classification on Balance Sheet
Operating	Collection of customer accounts	Inflow	Accounts receivable	Current asset
	Payment to suppliers for inventory	Outflow	Accounts payable	Current liability
			Inventory	Current asset
	Payment of wages	Outflow	Wages payable	Current liability
	Payment of taxes	Outflow	Taxes payable	Current liability
Investing	Capital expenditures	Outflow	Plant and equipment	Long-term asset
	Purchase of another company	Outflow	Long-term investment	Long-term asset
	Sale of plant and equipment	Inflow	Plant and equipment	Long-term asset
	Sale of another company	Inflow	Long-term investment	Long-term asset
Financing	Issuance of capital stock	Inflow	Capital stock	Stockholders' equity
	Issuance of bonds	Inflow	Bonds payable	Long-term liability
	Issuance of bank note	Inflow	Notes payable	Long-term liability
	Repurchase of stock	Outflow	Treasury stock	Stockholders' equity
	Retirement of bonds	Outflow	Bonds payable	Long-term liability
	Repayment of notes	Outflow	Notes payable	Long-term liability
	Payment of dividends	Outflow	Retained earnings	Stockholders' equity

Finally, **note that financing activities usually relate to either Long-Term Liabilities or Stockholders' Equity accounts.** There are exceptions to these observations about the type of balance sheet account involved with each of the three types of activities, but these rules of thumb are useful as you begin to analyze transactions and attempt to determine their classification on the statement of cash flows.

POD REVIEW 12.3

LO3 *Describe operating, investing, and financing activities and give examples of each.*

- Activities that generate or consume cash are classified into three categories for the statement of cash flows.
  - Operating activities usually involve cash flows related to the production of goods or services for customers.
  - Investing activities relate to acquiring and disposing of long-term assets.
  - Financing activities relate to raising funds through debt and equity securities and making payments related to those securities.

QUESTIONS

1. *Which of the following should be classified as an investing activity on the statement of cash flows?*
   a. issuance of capital stock
   b. payment of dividends
   c. payment to suppliers for inventory
   d. none of the above

2. *How should the repurchase of a company's own stock be reported on the statement of cash flows?*
   a. as an operating activity
   b. as an investing activity
   c. as a financing activity
   d. Repurchase of a company's own stock is not reported on the statement of cash flows.

Two Methods of Reporting Cash Flow From Operating Activities

LO4 Describe the difference between the direct and the indirect method of computing cash flow from operating activities.

Direct method
For preparing the Operating Activities section of the statement of cash flows, the approach in which cash receipts and cash payments are reported.

Indirect method
For preparing the Operating Activities section of the statement of cash flows, the approach in which net income is reconciled to net cash flow from operations.

Companies use one of two methods to report the amount of cash flow from operating activities. The first approach, called the **direct method**, involves reporting major classes of gross cash receipts and cash payments. For example, cash collected from customers is reported separately from any interest and dividends received. Each of the major types of cash payments related to the company's operations follows, such as cash paid for inventory, for salaries and wages, for interest, and for taxes. An acceptable alternative to this approach is the **indirect method**. Under the indirect method, net cash flow from operating activities is computed by adjusting net income to remove the effect of all deferrals of past operating cash receipts and payments and all accruals of future operating cash receipts and payments.

Although the direct method is preferred by the FASB, in practice, it is used much less frequently than the indirect method. To compare and contrast the two methods, assume that Boulder Company begins operations as a corporation on January 1, 2008, with the owners' investment of $10,000 in cash. An income statement for 2008 and a balance sheet as of December 31, 2008, are presented in Exhibits 12-7 and 12-8, respectively.

Direct Method To report cash flow from operating activities under the direct method, we look at each of the items on the income statement and determine how much cash each of those activities generated or used. For example, revenues for the period were $80,000. Since the balance sheet at the end of the period shows a balance in Accounts Receivable of $13,000, however, Boulder collected only $80,000 − $13,000, or $67,000, from its sales of the period. Thus, the first line on the statement of cash flows in Exhibit 12-9 reports $67,000 in cash collected from customers. Remember that the *net increase* in Accounts Receivable must be deducted from sales to find cash collected. For a new company, this is the same as the ending balance because the company starts the year without a balance in Accounts Receivable.

EXHIBIT 12-7 Boulder Company's Income Statement

Boulder Company
Income Statement
For the Year Ended December 31, 2008

Revenues	$80,000
Operating expenses	(64,000)
Income before tax	$16,000
Income tax expense	(4,000)
Net income	$12,000

EXHIBIT 12-8 Boulder Company's Balance Sheet

Boulder Company
Balance Sheet
As of December 31, 2008

Assets		Liabilities and Stockholders' Equity	
Cash	$15,000	Accounts payable	$ 6,000
Accounts receivable	13,000	Capital stock	10,000
		Retained earnings	12,000
Total	$28,000	Total	$28,000

EXHIBIT 12-9 **Statement of Cash Flows Using the Direct Method**

Boulder Company
Statement of Cash Flows
For the Year Ended December 31, 2008

Cash flows from operating activities	
Cash collected from customers	$ 67,000
Cash payments for operating purposes	(58,000)
Cash payments for taxes	(4,000)
Net cash inflow from operating activities	$ 5,000
Cash flows from financing activities	
Issuance of capital stock	$ 10,000
Net increase in cash	$ 15,000
Cash balance, beginning of period	–0–
Cash balance, end of period	$ 15,000

The same logic can be applied to determine the amount of cash expended for operating purposes. Operating expenses on the income statement are reported at $64,000. According to the balance sheet, however, $6,000 of the expense is unpaid at the end of the period as evidenced by the balance in Accounts Payable. Thus, the amount of cash expended for operating purposes as reported on the statement of cash flows in Exhibit 12-9 is $64,000 − $6,000, or $58,000. The other cash payment in the Operating Activities section of the statement is $4,000 for income taxes. Because no liability for income taxes is reported on the balance sheet, we know that $4,000 represents both the income tax expense of the period and the amount paid to the government. The only other item on the statement of cash flows in Exhibit 12-9 is the cash inflow from financing activities for the amount of cash invested by the owner in return for capital stock.

Indirect Method When the indirect method is used, the first line in the Operating Activities section of the statement of cash flows as shown in Exhibit 12-10 is the net income of the period. Net income is then adjusted to reconcile it to the amount of cash provided by operating activities. As reported on the income statement, this net income

EXHIBIT 12-10 **Statement of Cash Flows Using the Indirect Method**

Boulder Company
Statement of Cash Flows
For the Year Ended December 31, 2008

Cash flows from operating activities	
Net income	$ 12,000
Adjustments to reconcile net income to net cash from operating activities:	
Increase in accounts receivable	(13,000)
Increase in accounts payable	6,000
Net cash inflow from operating activities	$ 5,000
Cash flows from financing activities	
Issuance of capital stock	$ 10,000
Net increase in cash	$ 15,000
Cash balance, beginning of period	–0–
Cash balance, end of period	$ 15,000

Real World Practice

12-1 Reading Kellogg's Statement of Cash Flows

Does Kellogg's use the direct or the indirect method in the Operating Activities section of its statement of cash flows? How can you tell?

figure includes sales of $80,000 for the period. As we know, however, the amount of cash collected was $13,000 less than this because not all customers paid Boulder the amount due. **The increase in Accounts Receivable for the period is deducted from net income on the statement because the increase indicates that the company sold more during the period than it collected in cash.**

The logic for the addition of the increase in Accounts Payable is similar, although the effect is the opposite. The amount of operating expenses deducted on the income statement was $64,000. We know, however, that the amount of cash paid was $6,000 less than this, as the balance in Accounts Payable indicates. **The increase in Accounts Payable for the period is added back to net income on the statement because the increase indicates that the company paid less during the period than it recognized in expense on the income statement.** One observation can be noted about this example. Because this is the first year of operations for Boulder, we wouldn't be too concerned that accounts receivable is increasing faster than accounts payable. If this becomes a trend, however, we would try to improve the accounts receivable collections process.

Two important observations should be made in comparing the two methods illustrated in Exhibits 12-9 and 12-10:

1. The amount of cash provided by operating activities is the same under the two methods: $5,000; the two methods are simply different computational approaches used to arrive at the cash generated from operations.
2. The remainder of the statement of cash flows is the same regardless of which method is used.

The only difference between the two methods is in the Operating Activities section of the statement.

NONCASH INVESTING AND FINANCING ACTIVITIES

Occasionally, companies engage in important investing and financing activities that do not affect cash. For example, assume that at the end of the year, Wolk Corp. issues capital stock to an inventor in return for the exclusive rights to a patent. Although the patent has no ready market value, the stock could have been sold on the open market for $25,000. Thus, the following entry is made on Wolk's books:

Patent	25,000	
Capital Stock		25,000
To record issuance of stock in exchange for patent.		

Balance Sheet								Income Statement
ASSETS		=	LIABILITIES	+	STOCKHOLDERS' EQUITY		+	REVENUES − EXPENSES
Patent	25,000				Capital Stock	25,000		

This transaction does not involve cash and therefore is not reported on the statement of cash flows. However, what if the scenario was changed slightly? Assume that Wolk wants the patent but the inventor is not willing to accept stock in return for it. So, instead, Wolk sells stock on the open market for $25,000 and then pays this amount in cash to the inventor for the rights to the patent. Now Wolk records two journal entries. The first is as follows:

Cash	25,000	
Capital Stock		25,000
To record issuance of capital stock for cash.		

Balance Sheet								Income Statement
ASSETS		=	LIABILITIES	+	STOCKHOLDERS' EQUITY		+	REVENUES − EXPENSES
Cash	25,000				Capital Stock	25,000		

It next records this entry:

Patent	25,000	
Cash		25,000
To record acquisition of patent for cash.		

		Balance Sheet				Income Statement
ASSETS	=	LIABILITIES	+	STOCKHOLDERS' EQUITY	+	REVENUES – EXPENSES
Patent 25,000						
Cash (25,000)						

How would those two transactions be reported on a statement of cash flows? The first transaction appears as a cash inflow in the Financing Activities section of the statement; the second is reported as a cash outflow in the Investing Activities section. The point is that even though the *form* of this arrangement (with stock sold for cash and then the cash paid to the inventor) differs from the form of the first arrangement (with stock exchanged directly for the patent), the *substance* of the two arrangements is the same. That is, both involve a significant financing activity, the issuance of stock, and an important investing activity, the acquisition of a patent. Because the substance is what matters, accounting standards require that any significant noncash transactions be reported in a separate schedule or in a note to the financial statements. For the transaction in which stock was issued directly to the inventor, presentation in a schedule is as follows:

Supplemental schedule of noncash investing and financing activities	
Acquisition of patent in exchange for capital stock	$25,000

To this point, we have concentrated on the purpose of a statement of cash flows and the major reporting requirements related to it. We turn next to a methodology used in preparing the statement.

POD REVIEW 12.4

LO4 *Describe the difference between the direct and the indirect method of computing cash flow from operating activities.*

- The indirect method derives cash flows from operating activities by starting with net income and then making adjustments for the effects of accruals and deferrals resulting from accrual-based accounting.
- The direct method reports cash receipts and cash disbursements related to operations.

QUESTIONS

1. *The first line on a company's statement of cash flows is net income. Which method does the company use to prepare its statement?*
   a. direct
   b. indirect
   c. operating
   d. not possible to tell from the information provided

2. *Oak began the year with a balance of $5,000 in Accounts Receivable and ended the year with $8,000 in the account. Revenues for the period amounted to $37,000. Under the direct method of preparing the statement of cash flows, Oak will report cash collected from customers of*
   a. $34,000.
   b. $37,000.
   c. $40,000.
   d. $42,000.

How the Statement of Cash Flows Is Put Together

LO5 Use T accounts to prepare a statement of cash flows using the direct method to determine cash flow from operating activities.

Two interesting observations can be made about the statement of cash flows. First, the "answer" to a statement of cash flows is known before it is prepared. That is, the change in cash for the period is known by comparing two successive balance sheets. Thus, it is not the change in cash that is emphasized on the statement of cash flows but the *explanations* for the change in cash. That is, each item on a statement of cash flows helps to explain why cash changed by the amount it did during the period. The second important observation about the statement of cash flows relates even more specifically to how it is prepared. An income statement and a balance sheet are prepared by taking the balances in each of the various accounts in the general ledger and putting them in the right place on the right statement. That is not true for the statement of cash flows. Instead, it is necessary to analyze the transactions during the period and attempt to (1) determine which of them affected cash and (2) classify each of the cash effects into one of the three categories.

In the simple examples presented so far in the chapter, the statement of cash flows was prepared without the use of any special tools. In more complex situations, however, some type of methodology is needed. We will review the basic accounting equation and then illustrate a T-account approach for preparing the statement. The chapter appendix presents a work-sheet approach to the preparation of the statement of cash flows.

THE ACCOUNTING EQUATION AND THE STATEMENT OF CASH FLOWS

The basic accounting equation is as follows:

Assets = Liabilities + Stockholders' Equity

Next, consider this refinement of the equation:

Assets	=	**Liabilities + Stockholders' Equity**
Cash + Noncash current assets + Long-term assets	=	Current liabilities + Long-term liabilities + Capital stock + Retained earnings

The equation can be rearranged so that only cash is on the left side and all other items are on the right side:

Cash	=	Current liabilities + Long-term liabilities + Capital stock + Retained earnings − **Noncash current assets** − **Long-term assets**

Therefore, any changes in cash must be accompanied by a corresponding change in the right side of the equation. For example, an increase or inflow of cash could result from an increase in long-term liabilities in the form of issuing bonds payable, an important financing activity for many companies. Or an increase in cash could come from a decrease in long-term assets in the form of a sale of fixed assets. The various possibilities for inflows (+) and outflows (−) of cash can be summarized by activity as follows:

Activity	Left Side	Right Side	Example
Operating			
	+ Cash	− Noncash current assets	Collect accounts receivable
	− Cash	+ Noncash current assets	Prepay insurance
	+ Cash	+ Current liabilities	Collect customer's deposit
	− Cash	− Current liabilities	Pay suppliers
	+ Cash	+ Retained earnings	Make a cash sale
Investing			
	+ Cash	− Long-term assets	Sell equipment
	− Cash	+ Long-term assets	Buy equipment
Financing			
	+ Cash	+ Long-term liabilities	Issue bonds
	− Cash	− Long-term liabilities	Retire bonds
	+ Cash	+ Capital stock	Issue capital stock
	− Cash	− Capital stock	Buy capital stock
	− Cash	− Retained earnings	Pay dividends

Those examples show that inflows and outflows of cash relate to increases and decreases in the various balance sheet accounts. We now turn to analyzing these accounts as a way to assemble a statement of cash flows.

A MASTER T-ACCOUNT APPROACH TO PREPARING THE STATEMENT OF CASH FLOWS: DIRECT METHOD

The following steps can be used to prepare a statement of cash flows:

1. **Set up three master T accounts with the following headings:**
   a. Cash Flows from Operating Activities
   b. Cash Flows from Investing Activities
   c. Cash Flows from Financing Activities

   These master T accounts take the place of the Cash account. As we analyze the transactions that affect each of the noncash balance sheet accounts, any cash effects are entered on the appropriate master account. When completed, the three master accounts contain all of the information needed to prepare a statement of cash flows.
2. **Determine the cash flows from operating activities.** Generally, this requires analyzing each item on the *income statement* and in the *Current Asset* and *Current Liability* accounts. Draft journal entries for each transaction using a lettering system for identification purposes and post them to the appropriate balance sheet accounts. In many instances, these will be summary entries for the entire period. For example, one entry is made for all credit sales for the period and one entry is made for all collections on account. Enter any increases in cash on the left side of the Cash Flow from Operating Activities master T account and any decreases on the right side.
3. **Determine the cash flows from investing activities.** Generally, this requires analyzing the *Long-Term Asset* accounts and any additional information provided. Draft journal entries for each transaction and post them to the appropriate balance sheet accounts. Enter any increases in cash on the left side of the Cash Flow from Investing Activities master T account and any decreases on the right side. Enter any significant noncash activities on a supplemental schedule.

EXHIBIT 12-11 Julian Corp.'s Income Statement

Julian Corp.
Income Statement
For the Year Ended December 31, 2008

Revenues and gains:		
Sales revenue	$670,000	
Interest revenue	15,000	
Gain on sale of machine	5,000	
Total revenues and gains		$690,000
Expenses and losses:		
Cost of goods sold	$390,000	
Salaries and wages	60,000	
Depreciation	40,000	
Insurance	12,000	
Interest	15,000	
Income taxes	50,000	
Loss on retirement of bonds	3,000	
Total expenses and losses		570,000
Net income		$120,000

4. **Determine the cash flows from financing activities.** Generally, this requires analyzing the *Long-Term Liability* and *Stockholders' Equity* accounts and any additional information provided. Draft journal entries for each transaction. Enter any increases in cash on the left side of the Cash Flow from Financing Activities master T account and any decreases on the right side of the T account. Enter any significant noncash activities on a supplemental schedule.

Remember that these are general rules that the cash effects of changes in current accounts are reported in the Operating section; those relating to long-term asset accounts, in the Investing section; and those relating to long-term liabilities and stockholders' equity, in the Financing section. The general rules for classification of activities have a few exceptions, but they will not be covered here.

To illustrate this approach, we will refer to the income statement in Exhibit 12-11 and to the comparative balance sheets and the additional information provided for Julian Corp. in Exhibit 12-12.

Determine the Cash Flows from Operating Activities To do this, you need to consider each of the items on the income statement and any related current assets or liabilities from the balance sheet.

Sales Revenue and Accounts Receivable Sales as reported on the income statement in Exhibit 12-11 amounted to $670,000. The journal entry was as follows:

(a)	Accounts Receivable	670,000	
	Sales Revenue		670,000
	To record sales on account.		

Balance Sheet							Income Statement	
ASSETS		=	LIABILITIES	+	STOCKHOLDERS' EQUITY	+	REVENUES − EXPENSES	
Accounts Receivable	670,000						Sales Revenue	670,000

Based on the beginning and ending balances in Exhibit 12-12, a T account for Accounts Receivable appears as follows after the debit for the sales of the period is posted:

Accounts Receivable

Bal., Jan. 1	57,000		
(a) Sales on account	670,000	?	Cash collections (b)
Bal., Dec. 31	63,000		

EXHIBIT 12-12 Julian Corp.'s Comparative Balance Sheets

Julian Corp.
Comparative Balance Sheets

	December 31	
	2008	**2007**
Cash	$ 35,000	$ 46,000
Accounts receivable	63,000	57,000
Inventory	84,000	92,000
Prepaid insurance	12,000	18,000
Total current assets	$194,000	$213,000
Long-term investments	$120,000	$ 90,000
Land	150,000	100,000
Property and equipment	320,000	280,000
Accumulated depreciation	(100,000)	(75,000)
Total long-term assets	$490,000	$395,000
Total assets	$684,000	$608,000
Accounts payable	$ 38,000	$ 31,000
Salaries and wages payable	7,000	9,000
Income taxes payable	8,000	5,000
Total current liabilities	$ 53,000	$ 45,000
Notes payable	$ 85,000	$ 35,000
Bonds payable	200,000	260,000
Total long-term liabilities	$285,000	$295,000
Capital stock	$100,000	$ 75,000
Retained earnings	246,000	193,000
Total stockholders' equity	$346,000	$268,000
Total liabilities and stockholders' equity	$684,000	$608,000

Additional Information

1. Long-term investments were purchased for $30,000. The securities are classified as available for sale.
2. Land was purchased by issuing a $50,000 note payable.
3. Equipment was purchased for $75,000.
4. A machine with an original cost of $35,000 and a book value of $20,000 was sold for $25,000.
5. Bonds with a face value of $60,000 were retired by paying $63,000 in cash.
6. Capital stock was issued in exchange for $25,000 in cash.

Accounts Receivable increased by $6,000 for the period. *This indicates that Julian had $6,000 more in sales to its customers than it collected in cash from them* (assuming that all sales are on credit). Thus, cash collections must have been $670,000 − $6,000, or $664,000. Another way to look at this is as follows:

Beginning accounts receivable	$ 57,000
+ Sales revenue	670,000
− Cash collections	(*X*)
= Ending accounts receivable	$ 63,000

Solving for *X*, we can find cash collections:

$$57{,}000 + 670{,}000 - X = 63{,}000$$
$$X = 664{,}000$$

The journal entry to record cash collections was as follows:

(b)	Cash	664,000	
	Accounts Receivable		664,000
	To record cash collected on account.		

Balance Sheet						Income Statement
ASSETS	=	LIABILITIES	+	STOCKHOLDERS' EQUITY	+	REVENUES − EXPENSES
Cash 664,000						
Accounts Receivable (664,000)						

At this point, note the debit to Cash for $664,000 as shown in the master T account Cash Flows from Operating Activities in Exhibit 12-13.

Interest Revenue Julian reported interest revenue on the income statement of $15,000. Did the company actually receive that amount of cash, or was it merely an accrual of revenue earned but not yet received? The answer can be found by examining the Current Assets section of the balance sheet. *Because there is no Interest Receivable account, the amount of interest earned was the amount of cash received:*

(c)	Cash	15,000	
	Interest Revenue		15,000
	To record interest earned and received.		

Balance Sheet						Income Statement
ASSETS	=	LIABILITIES	+	STOCKHOLDERS' EQUITY	+	REVENUES − EXPENSES
Cash 15,000						Interest Revenue 15,000

The debit should be entered in the master T account Cash Flows from Operating Activities, as shown in Exhibit 12-13.

Gain on Sale of Machine A gain on the sale of machine of $5,000 is reported as the next line on the income statement. Any cash received from the sale of a long-term asset is reported in the Investing Activities section of the statement of cash flows. Thus, we ignore the gain when reporting cash flows from operating activities under the direct method.

Cost of Goods Sold, Inventory, and Accounts Payable Cost of goods sold, as reported on the income statement, amounts to $390,000 and was recorded with this entry:

(d)	Cost of Goods Sold	390,000	
	Inventory		390,000
	To record cost of goods sold.		

Balance Sheet						Income Statement
ASSETS	=	LIABILITIES	+	STOCKHOLDERS' EQUITY	+	REVENUES − EXPENSES
Inventory (390,000)						Cost of Goods Sold (390,000)

EXHIBIT 12-13 Master T Account for Cash Flows from Operating Activities

Cash Flows from Operating Activities

Cash receipts from:		Cash payments for:	
(b) Sales on account	664,000	(f) Inventory purchases	375,000
(c) Interest	15,000	(h) Salaries and wages	62,000
		(k) Insurance	6,000
		(l) Interest	15,000
		(n) Taxes	47,000

We see that $390,000 is not the amount of cash expended to pay suppliers of inventory. First, cost of goods sold represents the cost of the inventory sold during the period, not the amount purchased. Thus, we must analyze the Inventory account to determine the purchases of the period. Second, the amount of purchases is not the same as the cash paid to suppliers because purchases are normally on account. Thus, we must analyze the Accounts Payable account to determine the cash payments.

Based on the beginning and ending balances in Exhibit 12-12, a T account for Inventory appears as follows after the reduction in the account for cost of goods sold is posted:

Inventory

Bal., Jan. 1	92,000		
(e) Purchases on account	?	390,000	Cost of goods sold (d)
Bal., Dec. 31	84,000		

Note the $8,000 net decrease in Inventory. *This means that the cost of inventory sold was $8,000 more than the purchases of the period.* Thus, purchases must have been $390,000 − $8,000, or $382,000. Another way to look at this is as follows:

Beginning inventory	$ 92,000
+ Purchases	*X*
− Cost of goods sold	(390,000)
= Ending inventory	$ 84,000

Solving for *X*, we can find purchases:

$$92{,}000 + X - 390{,}000 = 84{,}000$$
$$X = 382{,}000$$

The journal entry to record purchases was as follows:

(e)	Inventory	382,000	
	Accounts Payable		382,000
	To record purchases on account.		

Balance Sheet						Income Statement
ASSETS	=	**LIABILITIES**	+	**STOCKHOLDERS' EQUITY**	+	**REVENUES − EXPENSES**
Inventory 382,000		Accounts Payable 382,000				

From Exhibit 12-12, a T account for Accounts Payable appears as follows after the credit for purchases of the period is posted:

Accounts Payable

		31,000	Bal., Jan. 1
(f) Cash payments	?	382,000	Purchases (e)
		38,000	Bal., Dec. 31

Note the $7,000 net increase in Accounts Payable. *This means that Julian's purchases were $7,000 more during the period than its cash payments.* Thus, cash payments must have been $382,000 − $7,000, or $375,000. Another way to look at this is as follows:

Beginning accounts payable	$ 31,000
+ Purchases	382,000
− Cash payments	(*X*)
= Ending accounts payable	$ 38,000

Solving for *X*, we can find cash payments:

$$31{,}000 + 382{,}000 - X = 38{,}000$$
$$X = 375{,}000$$

The journal entry to record payments on account was as follows:

(f)	Accounts Payable	375,000	
	Cash		375,000
	To record cash payments on account.		

Balance Sheet						Income Statement
ASSETS	=	LIABILITIES	+	STOCKHOLDERS' EQUITY	+	REVENUES − EXPENSES
Cash (375,000)		Accounts Payable (375,000)				

At this point, the credit to cash should be entered in the master T account Cash Flows from Operating Activities, as shown in Exhibit 12-13.

Salaries and Wages Expense and Salaries and Wages Payable The entry to record salaries and wages expense was as follows:

(g)	Salaries and Wages Expense	60,000	
	Salaries and Wages Payable		60,000
	To record salaries and wages.		

Balance Sheet						Income Statement
ASSETS	=	LIABILITIES	+	STOCKHOLDERS' EQUITY	+	REVENUES − EXPENSES
		Salaries and Wages Payable 60,000				Salaries and Wages Expense (60,000)

After this entry is posted to Salaries and Wages Payable, note the $2,000 net decrease in the account for the period:

Salaries and Wages Payable

		9,000	Bal., Jan. 1
(h) Cash payments	?	60,000	Expense (g)
		7,000	Bal., Dec. 31

This means that the amount of cash paid to employees was $2,000 more than the amount of expense accrued. Another way to look at the cash payments of $60,000 + $2,000, or $62,000, is as follows:

Beginning salaries and wages payable	$ 9,000
+ Salaries and wages expense	60,000
− Cash payments to employees	(*X*)
= Ending salaries and wages payable	$ 7,000

Solving for *X*, we can find cash payments:

$$9{,}000 + 60{,}000 - X = 7{,}000$$
$$X = \underline{\underline{62{,}000}}$$

The journal entry to record the cash paid was as follows:

(h)	Salaries and Wages Payable	62,000	
	Cash		62,000
	To record cash paid to employees.		

Balance Sheet						Income Statement
ASSETS	=	LIABILITIES	+	STOCKHOLDERS' EQUITY	+	REVENUES − EXPENSES
Cash (62,000)		Salaries and Wages Payable (62,000)				

As you can see in Exhibit 12-13, the credit of $62,000 in this entry appears in the T account for Cash Flows from Operating Activities.

Depreciation Expense The next item on the income statement is depreciation of $40,000. The entry to record depreciation was as follows:

(i)	Depreciation Expense	40,000	
	Accumulated Depreciation		40,000
	To record depreciation.		

Balance Sheet							Income Statement
ASSETS	=	LIABILITIES	+	STOCKHOLDERS' EQUITY	+		REVENUES – EXPENSES
Accumulated Depreciation (40,000)							Depreciation Expense (40,000)

Depreciation of tangible long-term assets, amortization of intangible assets, and depletion of natural resources are different from most other expenses in that they have no effect on cash flow. The only related cash flows are from the purchase and sale of these long-term assets, and these are reported in the Investing Activities section of the statement of cash flows.

Insurance Expense and Prepaid Insurance According to the income statement in Exhibit 12-11, Julian recorded Insurance Expense of $12,000 during 2008. This amount is not the cash payments for insurance, however, because Julian has a Prepaid Insurance account on the balance sheet. The entry to record expense involves a reduction in the Prepaid Insurance account as follows:

(j)	Insurance Expense	12,000	
	Prepaid Insurance		12,000
	To record expiration of insurance.		

Balance Sheet							Income Statement
ASSETS	=	LIABILITIES	+	STOCKHOLDERS' EQUITY	+		REVENUES – EXPENSES
Prepaid Insurance (12,000)							Insurance Expense (12,000)

When the credit to Prepaid Insurance is posted, note the $6,000 net decrease in the account for the period:

Prepaid Insurance			
Bal., Jan. 1	18,000		
(k) Cash payments	?	12,000	Expense (j)
Bal., Dec. 31	12,000		

This means that the amount of cash paid for insurance was $6,000 less than the amount of expense recognized. Thus, the cash payments must have been $12,000 – $6,000, or $6,000. Another way to look at the cash payments is as follows:

Beginning prepaid insurance	$18,000
+ Cash payments for insurance	X
– Insurance expense	(12,000)
= Ending prepaid insurance	$12,000

Solving for X, we can find the amount of cash paid:

$$18{,}000 + X - 12{,}000 = 12{,}000$$
$$X = 6{,}000$$

The journal entry to record the cash paid was as follows:

(k)	Prepaid Insurance	6,000	
	Cash		6,000
	To record cash paid for insurance.		

Balance Sheet							Income Statement
ASSETS		=	LIABILITIES	+	STOCKHOLDERS' EQUITY	+	REVENUES – EXPENSES
Prepaid Insurance	6,000						
Cash	(6,000)						

Note that the credit to Cash is entered in Exhibit 12-13 in the T account for Cash Flows from Operating Activities.

Interest Expense The amount of interest expense reported on the income statement is $15,000. Because the balance sheet does not report an accrual of interest owed but not yet paid (an Interest Payable account), we know that $15,000 is also the amount of cash paid:

(l)	Interest Expense	15,000	
	Cash		15,000
	To record interest expense.		

Balance Sheet							Income Statement
ASSETS		=	LIABILITIES	+	STOCKHOLDERS' EQUITY	+	REVENUES – EXPENSES
Cash	(15,000)						Interest Expense (15,000)

The entry is recorded as a cash outflow in Exhibit 12-13. Whether interest paid is properly classified as an operating activity is subject to considerable debate. The FASB decided in favor of classification of interest as an operating activity because, unlike dividends, it appears on the income statement. This, it was argued, provides a direct link between the statement of cash flows and the income statement. Many argue, however, that it is inconsistent to classify dividends paid as a financing activity but interest paid as an operating activity. After all, both represent returns paid to providers of capital: interest to creditors and dividends to stockholders.

Income Tax Expense and Income Taxes Payable The entry to record Income Tax Expense was as follows:

(m)	Income Taxes Expense	50,000	
	Income Taxes Payable		50,000
	To record income taxes.		

Balance Sheet						Income Statement
ASSETS	=	LIABILITIES	+	STOCKHOLDERS' EQUITY	+	REVENUES – EXPENSES
		Income Taxes Payable 50,000				Income Taxes Expense (50,000)

When the credit to Income Taxes Payable is posted, note the $3,000 net increase in the account for the period:

Income Taxes Payable

		5,000	Bal., Jan. 1
(n) Cash payments	?	50,000	Expense (m)
		8,000	Bal., Dec. 31

This means that the amount of cash paid to the government in taxes was $3,000 less than the amount of expense accrued. Another way to look at the cash payments of $50,000 − $3,000, or $47,000, is as follows:

Beginning income taxes payable	$ 5,000
+ Income tax expense	50,000
− Cash payments for taxes	(*X*)
= Ending income taxes payable	$ 8,000

Solving for *X*, we can find the amount of cash paid:

$$5{,}000 + 50{,}000 - X = 8{,}000$$
$$X = 47{,}000$$

The journal entry to record cash paid was as follows:

(n)	Income Taxes Payable	47,000	
	Cash		47,000
	To record cash paid in taxes.		

Balance Sheet							Income Statement
ASSETS		=	LIABILITIES		+	STOCKHOLDERS' EQUITY +	REVENUES − EXPENSES
Cash	(47,000)		Income Taxes Payable	(47,000)			

As you can see by examining Exhibit 12-13, the cash payments for taxes is the last item in the T account for Cash Flows from Operating Activities.

Loss on Retirement of Bonds A $3,000 loss on the retirement of bonds is reported as the last item under expenses and losses on the income statement in Exhibit 12-11. Any cash paid to retire a long-term liability is reported in the Financing Activities section of the statement of cash flows. Thus, we ignore the loss when reporting cash flows from operating activities under the direct method.

COMPARE NET INCOME WITH NET CASH FLOW FROM OPERATING ACTIVITIES

At this point, all of the items on the income statement have been analyzed, as have all of the current asset and current liability accounts. All of the information needed to prepare the Operating Activities section of the statement of cash flows has been gathered.

To summarize, preparation of the Operating Activities section of the statement of cash flows requires the conversion of each item on the income statement to a cash basis. The Current Asset and Current Liability accounts are analyzed to discover the cash effects of each item on the income statement. Exhibit 12-14 summarizes this conversion process.

Note in the exhibit the various adjustments made to put each income statement item on a cash basis. For example, the $6,000 increase in accounts receivable for the period is deducted from sales revenue of $670,000 to arrive at cash collected from customers. Similar adjustments are made to each of the other income statement items with the exception of depreciation, the gain, and the loss. Depreciation is ignored because it does not have an effect on cash flow. The gain relates to the sale of a long-term asset, and any cash effect is reflected in the Investing Activities section of the statement of cash flows. Similarly, the loss resulted from the retirement of bonds and any cash flow effect is reported in the Financing Activities section. The bottom of the exhibit highlights an important point: Julian reported net income of $120,000, but generated $174,000 in cash from operations.

Determine the Cash Flows from Investing Activities At this point, we turn our attention to the Long-Term Asset accounts and any additional information available about these accounts. Julian has three long-term assets on its balance sheet: Long-Term Investments, Land, and Property and Equipment.

EXHIBIT 12-14 Conversion of Income Statement Items to Cash Basis

Income Statement	Amount	Adjustments	Cash Flows
Sales revenue	$670,000		$670,000
		+ Decreases in accounts receivable	–0–
		− Increases in accounts receivable	(6,000)
		Cash collected from customers	$664,000
Interest revenue	15,000		$ 15,000
		+ Decreases in interest receivable	–0–
		− Increases in interest receivable	–0–
		Cash collected in interest	$ 15,000
Gain on sale of machine	5,000	*Not an operating activity*	$ –0–
Cost of goods sold	390,000		$390,000
		+ Increases in inventory	–0–
		− Decreases in inventory	(8,000)
		+ Decreases in accounts payable	–0–
		− Increases in accounts payable	(7,000)
		Cash paid to suppliers	$375,000
Salaries and wages	60,000		$ 60,000
		+ Decreases in salaries/wages payable	2,000
		− Increases in salaries/wages payable	–0–
		Cash paid to employees	$ 62,000
Depreciation	40,000	*No cash flow effect*	$ –0–
Insurance	12,000		$ 12,000
		+ Increases in prepaid insurance	–0–
		− Decreases in prepaid insurance	(6,000)
		Cash paid for insurance	$ 6,000
Interest	15,000		$ 15,000
		+ Decreases in interest payable	–0–
		− Increases in interest payable	–0–
		Cash paid for interest	$ 15,000
Income taxes	50,000		$ 50,000
		+ Decreases in income taxes payable	–0–
		− Increases in income taxes payable	(3,000)
		Cash paid for taxes	$ 47,000
Loss on retirement of bonds	3,000	*Not an operating activity*	$ –0–
Net income	$120,000	Net cash flow from operating activities	$174,000

Long-Term Investments Item 1 in the additional information in Exhibit 12-12 indicates that Julian purchased $30,000 of investments during the year. The $30,000 net increase in the Long-Term Investments account confirms this. (No mention is made of the sale of any investments during 2008.)

Long-Term Investments

Bal., Jan. 1	90,000	
(o) Purchases	?	
Bal., Dec. 31	120,000	

EXHIBIT 12-15 **Master T Account for Cash Flows from Investing Activities**

Cash Flows from Investing Activities

Cash inflows from:		Cash outflows for:	
(r) Sale of machine	25,000	(o) Purchase of investments	30,000
		(q) Purchase of property and equipment	75,000

The entry to record the purchase was as follows:

(o)	Long-Term Investments	30,000	
	Cash		30,000
	To record purchase of investments.		

Balance Sheet: ASSETS	=	LIABILITIES	+	STOCKHOLDERS' EQUITY	+	Income Statement: REVENUES – EXPENSES
Long-Term Investments 30,000						
Cash (30,000)						

The credit in this entry is the first cash outflow in the master T account Cash Flows from Investing Activities, as shown in Exhibit 12-15.

Land Note the $50,000 net increase in land:

Land

Bal., Jan. 1	100,000	
(p) Acquisitions	?	
Bal., Dec. 31	150,000	

Item 2 in the additional information indicates that Julian purchased land by issuing a $50,000 note payable. The entry to record the purchase was as follows:

(p)	Land	50,000	
	Notes Payable		50,000
	To record acquisition of land in exchange for note.		

Balance Sheet: ASSETS	=	LIABILITIES	+	STOCKHOLDERS' EQUITY	+	Income Statement: REVENUES – EXPENSES
Land 50,000		Notes Payable 50,000				

This entry obviously does not involve cash. The transaction has an important financing element and an investing component, however. The issuance of the note is a financing activity, and the acquisition of land is an investing activity. Because no cash was involved, the transaction is reported in a separate schedule instead of directly on the statement of cash flows:

Supplemental schedule of noncash investing and financing activities	
Acquisition of land in exchange for note payable	$50,000

Property and Equipment Property and equipment increased by $40,000 during 2007. However, Julian acquired equipment and sold a machine (item 3 and item 4, respectively, in the additional information). The acquisition of the equipment for $75,000 resulted in this journal entry:

(q)	Property and Equipment	75,000	
	Cash		75,000
	To record acquisition of equipment for cash.		

Balance Sheet								Income Statement
ASSETS		=	LIABILITIES	+	STOCKHOLDERS' EQUITY	+		REVENUES − EXPENSES
Property and Equipment	75,000							
Cash	(75,000)							

As was discussed earlier in the chapter, acquisitions of new plant and equipment are important investing activities for most businesses. Thus, the credit to Cash appears in the master T account Cash Flows from Investing Activities in Exhibit 12-15.

After this entry is posted to the Property and Equipment account, it appears as follows:

Property and Equipment

Bal., Jan. 1	280,000		
(q) Acquisitions	75,000	?	Disposals (r)
Bal., Dec. 31	320,000		

Julian obviously disposed of fixed assets during the period. In fact, item 4 in the additional information in Exhibit 12-12 reports the sale of a machine with an original cost of $35,000. An analysis of the Property and Equipment account confirms this amount:

Beginning property and equipment	$280,000
+ Acquisitions	75,000
− Disposals	(*X*)
= Ending property and equipment	$320,000

Solving for X, we can find the *cost* of the fixed assets sold during the year:

$$280{,}000 + 75{,}000 - X = 320{,}000$$
$$X = \$35{,}000$$

A T account for Accumulated Depreciation appears as follows after Depreciation Expense is posted in entry (i):

Accumulated Depreciation

		75,000	Bal., Jan. 1
(r) Disposals	?	40,000	Depreciation expense (i)
		100,000	Bal., Dec. 31

The additional information also indicates that the book value of the machine sold was $20,000. This means that if the original cost was $35,000 and the book value was $20,000, the Accumulated Depreciation on the machine sold must have been $35,000 − $20,000, or $15,000. An analysis similar to the one we just looked at for Property and Equipment confirms this amount:

Beginning accumulated depreciation	$ 75,000
+ Depreciation expense (entry i)	40,000
− Accumulated depreciation on assets sold	(*X*)
= Ending accumulated depreciation	$100,000

Solving for X, we can find the accumulated depreciation on the assets disposed of during the year:

$$75{,}000 + 40{,}000 - X = 100{,}000$$
$$X = \underline{\underline{\$15{,}000}}$$

Finally, we are told in the additional information that the machine was sold for $25,000. *If the selling price was $25,000 and the book value was $20,000, Julian reports a gain on sale of $5,000, an amount that is confirmed on the income statement in Exhibit 12-11.* The journal entry to record the sale of the machine was as follows:

(r)	Cash	25,000	
	Accumulated Depreciation	15,000	
	Property and Equipment		35,000
	Gain on Sale of Machine		5,000
	To record sale of machine.		

Balance Sheet: ASSETS		= LIABILITIES	+ STOCKHOLDERS' EQUITY	+ Income Statement: REVENUES − EXPENSES	
Cash	25,000			Gain on Sale of Machine	5,000
Accumulated Depreciation	15,000				
Property and Equipment	(35,000)				

To summarize, the machine was sold for $25,000, an amount that exceeded its book value of $20,000, thus generating a gain of $5,000. The debit to Cash is entered in the master T account for Cash Flows from Investing Activities in Exhibit 12-15.

Determine the Cash Flows from Financing Activities These activities generally involve long-term liabilities and stockholders' equity. First, we consider Julian's two long-term liabilities: Notes Payable and Bonds Payable; then, the two stockholders' equity accounts: Capital Stock and Retained Earnings.

Notes Payable Recall that item 2 in the additional information reported that Julian purchased land in exchange for a $50,000 note payable. The T account for Notes Payable confirms this amount:

Notes Payable

Debit	Credit	
	35,000	Bal., Jan. 1
	?	Additional issuances (p)
	85,000	Bal., Dec. 31

In the discussion of investing activities, we recorded entry (p) to account for this exchange and entered the transaction on a supplemental schedule of noncash activities because it was a significant financing activity but did not involve cash.

Bonds Payable A T account for Bonds Payable appears as follows:

Bonds Payable

	Debit	Credit	
		260,000	Bal., Jan. 1
(s) Retirement	?		
		200,000	Bal., Dec. 31

Item 5 in the additional information in Exhibit 12-12 indicates that bonds with a face value of $60,000 were retired by paying $63,000 in cash. The book value of the bonds retired is the same as the face value of $60,000 because there is no unamortized discount or premium on the records. *When a company has to pay more in cash ($63,000) to settle a debt than the book value of the debt ($60,000), it reports a loss.* Recall the $3,000 loss reported on the income statement in Exhibit 12-11. The entry to record the retirement of the bonds was as follows:

(s)	Loss on Retirement of Bonds	3,000	
	Bonds Payable	60,000	
	Cash		63,000
	To record retirement of bonds.		

Balance Sheet								Income Statement
ASSETS		=	LIABILITIES		+	STOCKHOLDERS' EQUITY	+	REVENUES – EXPENSES
Cash	(63,000)		Bonds Payable	(60,000)				Loss on Retirement of Bonds (3,000)

The credit to Cash in this entry is presented in the master T account Cash Flows from Financing Activities shown in Exhibit 12-16.

Capital Stock The Capital Stock account indicates a $25,000 net increase during 2008:

Capital Stock

	75,000	Bal., Jan. 1
	?	Stock issued (t)
	100,000	Bal., Dec. 31

According to item 6 in the additional information in Exhibit 12-12, Julian issued capital stock in exchange for $25,000 in cash. Some companies issue additional stock after the initial formation of the corporation to raise needed capital. The entry was as follows:

(t)	Cash	25,000	
	Capital Stock		25,000
	To record issuance of stock in exchange for cash.		

Balance Sheet								Income Statement
ASSETS		=	LIABILITIES	+	STOCKHOLDERS' EQUITY		+	REVENUES – EXPENSES
Cash	25,000				Capital Stock	25,000		

The debit to Cash in this entry is presented as a cash inflow in the master T account Cash Flows from Financing Activities shown in Exhibit 12-16.

EXHIBIT 12-16 Master T Account for Cash Flows from Financing Activities

Cash Flows from Financing Activities

Cash inflows from:		Cash outflows for:	
(t) Issuance of stock	25,000	(s) Retirement of bonds	63,000
		(u) Payment of cash dividends	67,000

Retained Earnings An analysis of the Retained Earnings account indicates the following:

Retained Earnings			
		193,000	Bal., Jan. 1
(u) Cash dividends	?	120,000	Net income for 2008
		246,000	Bal., Dec. 31

We can determine the amount of cash dividends for 2008 in the following manner:

Beginning retained earnings	$193,000
+ Net income	120,000
− Cash dividends	(X)
= Ending retained earnings	$246,000

Solving for X, we can find the amount of cash dividends paid during the year.[2]

$$193{,}000 + 120{,}000 - X = 246{,}000$$
$$X = \$67{,}000$$

Item 7 in the additional information confirms that this was in fact the amount of dividends paid during the year. The final entry was as follows:

(u)	Retained Earnings	67,000	
	Cash		67,000
	To record cash dividends paid.		

Balance Sheet								Income Statement
ASSETS		=	LIABILITIES	+	STOCKHOLDERS' EQUITY		+	REVENUES − EXPENSES
Cash	(67,000)				Retained Earnings	(67,000)		

The credit to Cash in this entry appears in the master T account Cash Flows from Financing Activities presented in Exhibit 12-16.

Using the Master T Accounts to Prepare a Statement of Cash Flows All of the information needed to prepare a statement of cash flows is now available in the three master T accounts, along with the supplemental schedule prepared earlier. From the information gathered in Exhibits 12-13, 12-15, and 12-16, a completed statement of cash flows appears in Exhibit 12-17.

What does Julian's statement of cash flows tell us? Cash flow from operations totaled $174,000. Cash used to acquire investments and equipment amounted to $80,000 after $25,000 was received from the sale of a machine. A net amount of $105,000 was used for financing activities. Thus, Julian used more cash than it generated, which is why the cash balance declined. That's okay for a year or two; but if this continues, the company won't be able to pay its bills.

2 Any decrease in Retained Earnings represents the dividends *declared* during the period rather than the amount paid. If there had been a Dividends Payable account, we would have analyzed it to find the amount of dividends paid. The lack of a balance in such an account at the beginning or end of the period tells us that Julian paid the same amount of dividends that it declared during the period.

POD REVIEW 12.5

LO5 *Use T accounts to prepare a statement of cash flows using the direct method to determine cash flow from operating activities.*

- Using T accounts, it is possible to determine the cash flow from the major operating activities, such as sales, purchases, salaries and wages, and operating expenses, and from investing and financing activities.

QUESTIONS

1. *Baxter began the year with a balance of $15,000 in Salaries and Wages Payable and ended the year with $10,000 in the account. Salaries and Wages Expense for the period amounted to $98,000. Under the direct method of preparing the statement of cash flows, Baxter will report cash payments for salaries and wages of*
   a. $93,000.
   b. $98,000.
   c. $103,000.
   d. $108,000.

2. *How is depreciation expense treated under the direct method of preparing the statement of cash flows?*
   a. as an outflow in the Operating Activities section of the statement
   b. as an outflow in the Investing Activities section of the statement
   c. as an addition to net income in the Operating Activities section of the statement
   d. Depreciation expense does not appear on the statement of cash flows when the direct method is used.

A Master T-Account Approach to Preparing the Statement of Cash Flows: Indirect Method

LO6 Use T accounts to prepare a statement of cash flows using the indirect method to determine cash flow from operating activities.

The purpose of the Operating Activities section of the statement changes when the indirect method is used. Instead of reporting cash receipts and cash payments, **the objective is to reconcile net income to net cash flow from operating activities.** The other two sections of the completed statement in Exhibit 12-17, the Investing and Financing sections, are unchanged. The use of the indirect or direct method for presenting cash flow from operating activities does not affect those two sections.

A T-account methodology similar to that used for the direct method can be used to prepare the Operating Activities section of the statement of cash flows under the indirect method.

Net Income Recall that the first line in the Operating Activities section of the statement under the indirect method is net income. That is, we start with the assumptions that all revenues and gains reported on the income statement increase cash flow and that all expenses and losses decrease cash flow. Julian's net income of $120,000, as reported on its income statement in Exhibit 12-11, is reported as the first item in the Operating Activities section of the statement of cash flows shown in Exhibit 12-18.

Accounts Receivable The net increase in Accounts Receivable, as shown in T-account form, indicates that Julian recorded more sales than cash collections during the period:

Accounts Receivable

Bal., Jan. 1	57,000	
Net increase	6,000	
Bal., Dec. 31	63,000	

Because net income includes sales (as opposed to cash collections), the $6,000 *net increase* must be *deducted* to adjust net income to cash from operations. To help you remember to deduct the net increase in accounts receivable in the Operating

Real World Practice

12-2 Reading Best Buy's Statement of Cash Flows

Did Best Buy's Receivables increase or decrease during the most recent year? Why is the change in this account deducted on the statement of cash flows?

EXHIBIT 12-17 **Completed Statement of Cash Flows for Julian Corp.**

Julian Corp.
Statement of Cash Flows
For the Year Ended December 31, 2008

Cash flows from operating activities	
Cash receipts from:	
Sales on account	$ 664,000
Interest	15,000
Total cash receipts	$ 679,000
Cash payments for:	
Inventory purchases	$(375,000)
Salaries and wages	(62,000)
Insurance	(6,000)
Interest	(15,000)
Taxes	(47,000)
Total cash payments	$(505,000)
Net cash provided by operating activities	$ 174,000
Cash flows from investing activities	
Purchase of investments	$ (30,000)
Purchase of property and equipment	(75,000)
Sale of machine	25,000
Net cash used by investing activities	$ (80,000)
Cash flows from financing activities	
Retirement of bonds	$ (63,000)
Issuance of stock	25,000
Payment of cash dividends	(67,000)
Net cash used by financing activities	$(105,000)
Net decrease in cash	$ (11,000)
Cash balance, December 31, 2007	46,000
Cash balance, December 31, 2008	$ 35,000
Supplemental schedule of noncash investing and financing activities	
Acquisition of land in exchange for note payable	$ 50,000

Activities section of the statement, consider the following. The $6,000 net increase appears in the preceding T account as a *debit*. Think of the deduction on the statement of cash flows as the equivalent of a *credit*. That is, the debit is to Accounts Receivable, and the credit is recorded as a bracketed amount (i.e., as a deduction) on the statement of cash flows.

Gain on Sale of Machine The gain itself did not generate any cash, but the sale of the machine did. And as we found earlier, the cash generated by selling the machine was reported in the Investing Activities section of the statement. The cash proceeds included the gain. Because the gain is included in the net income figure, it must be *deducted* to determine cash from operations. Also note that the gain is included twice in cash inflows if it is not deducted from the net income figure in the Operating Activities section. Note the deduction of $5,000 in Exhibit 12-18.

Inventory As the $8,000 net decrease in the Inventory account indicates, Julian liquidated a portion of its stock of inventory during the year:

Inventory

Bal., Jan. 1	92,000		
		8,000	Net decrease
Bal., Dec. 31	84,000		

EXHIBIT 12-18 Indirect Method for Reporting Cash Flows from Operating Activities

Julian Corp.
Partial Statement of Cash Flows
For the Year Ended December 31, 2008

Net cash flows from operating activities	
Net income	$120,000
Adjustments to reconcile net income to net cash provided by operating activities:	
Increase in accounts receivable	(6,000)
Gain on sale of machine	(5,000)
Decrease in inventory	8,000
Increase in accounts payable	7,000
Decrease in salaries and wages payable	(2,000)
Depreciation expense	40,000
Decrease in prepaid insurance	6,000
Increase in income taxes payable	3,000
Loss on retirement of bonds	3,000
Net cash provided by operating activities	$174,000

A net decrease in this account indicates that the company sold more products than it purchased during the year. As shown in Exhibit 12-18, the *net decrease* of $8,000 is *added back* to net income. As discussed for Accounts Receivable, note the debit and credit logic for this adjustment. Because Inventory is credited in the T account for the decrease, the statement of cash flows shows an increase, which is equivalent to a debit to Cash.

Accounts Payable Julian owed suppliers $31,000 at the start of the year. By the end of the year, the balance had grown to $38,000. A T account for Accounts Payable follows:

Accounts Payable

		31,000	Bal., Jan. 1
		7,000	Net increase
		38,000	Bal., Dec. 31

Effectively, the company saved cash by delaying the payment of some of its outstanding accounts payable. The *net increase* of $7,000 in this account is *added back* to net income, as shown in Exhibit 12-18.

Salaries and Wages Payable A T account for Salaries and Wages Payable indicates a net decrease of $2,000:

Salaries and Wages Payable

		9,000	Bal., Jan. 1
Net decrease	2,000		
		7,000	Bal., Dec. 31

The rationale for *deducting* the $2,000 *net decrease* in this liability in Exhibit 12-18 follows from what was just said about an increase in Accounts Payable. The payment to employees of $2,000 more than the amount included in expense on the income statement requires an additional deduction under the indirect method.

Depreciation Expense Depreciation is a noncash expense. Because it was deducted to arrive at net income, we must *add back* $40,000, the amount of depreciation, to find cash from operations. The same holds true for amortization of intangible assets and depletion of natural resources.

Prepaid Insurance This account decreased by $6,000, according to the T account:

Prepaid Insurance

Bal., Jan. 1	18,000		
		6,000	Net decrease
Bal., Dec. 31	12,000		

A decrease in this account indicates that Julian deducted more on the income statement for the insurance expense of the period than it paid in cash for new policies. That is, the cash outlay for insurance protection was not as large as the amount of expense reported on the income statement. Thus, the *net decrease* in the account is *added back* to net income in Exhibit 12-18.

Income Taxes Payable A T account for Income Taxes Payable indicates a net increase of $3,000:

Income Taxes Payable		
	5,000	Bal., Jan. 1
	3,000	Net increase
	8,000	Bal., Dec. 31

The *net increase* of $3,000 in this liability is *added back* to net income in Exhibit 12-18 because the payments to the government were $3,000 less than the amount included on the income statement.

Loss on Retirement of Bonds The $3,000 loss from retiring bonds was reported on the income statement as a deduction. There are two parts to the explanation for adding back the loss to net income to eliminate its effect in the Operating Activities section of the statement. First, any cash outflow from retiring bonds is properly classified as a financing activity, not an operating activity. The entire cash outflow should be reported in one classification rather than being allocated between two classifications. Second, the amount of the cash outflow is $63,000, not $3,000. To summarize, to convert net income to a cash basis, the loss is added back in the Operating Activities section to eliminate its effect. The actual use of cash to retire the bonds is shown in the Financing section of the statement.

Summary of Adjustments to Net Income under the Indirect Method Following is a list of the most common adjustments to net income when the indirect method is used to prepare the Operating Activities section of the statement of cash flows:

Additions to Net Income	Deductions from Net Income
Decrease in accounts receivable	Increase in accounts receivable
Decrease in inventory	Increase in inventory
Decrease in prepayments	Increase in prepayments
Increase in accounts payable	Decrease in accounts payable
Increase in accrued liabilities	Decrease in accrued liabilities
Losses on sales of long-term assets	Gains on sales of long-term assets
Losses on retirements of bonds	Gains on retirements of bonds
Depreciation, amortization, and depletion	

COMPARISON OF THE INDIRECT AND DIRECT METHODS

The amount of cash provided by operating activities is the same under the direct and indirect methods. The relative merits of the two methods, however, have stirred considerable debate in the accounting profession. The FASB has expressed a strong preference for the direct method but allows companies to use the indirect method.

If a company uses the indirect method, it must separately disclose two important cash payments: income taxes paid and interest paid. Thus, if Julian uses the indirect method, it reports the following at the bottom of the statement of cash flows or in a note to the financial statements:

Income taxes paid	$47,000
Interest paid	$15,000

Advocates of the direct method believe that the information provided with this approach is valuable in evaluating a company's operating efficiency. For example, use of the direct method allows the analyst to follow any trends in cash receipts from customers and compare them with cash payments to suppliers. The information presented in the Operating Activities section of the statement under the direct method is certainly user-friendly. Someone without a technical background in accounting can easily tell where cash came from and where it went during the period.

Study Tip

Notice in this list how changes in current assets and current liabilities are treated on the statement. For example, because accounts receivable and accounts payable are on opposite sides of the balance sheet, increases in each of them are handled in opposite ways. But an increase in one and a decrease in the other are treated in the same way.

Real World Practice

12-3 Reading Best Buy's Statement of Cash Flows

According to the supplemental disclosure at the bottom of Best Buy's statement of cash flows, what amount did the company pay in income taxes in the most recent year? Would this necessarily be the same amount that the company reported as income tax expense on its income statement? Explain your answer.

Advocates of the indirect method argue two major points. Many companies believe that the use of the direct method reveals too much about their business by telling readers the amount of cash receipts and cash payments from operations. Whether the use of the direct method tells the competition too much about a company is subject to debate. The other argument made for the indirect method is that it focuses attention on the differences between income on an accrual basis and a cash basis. In fact, this reconciliation of net income and cash provided by operating activities is considered to be important enough that **if a company uses the direct method, it must present a separate schedule to reconcile net income to net cash from operating activities.** This schedule, in effect, is the same as the Operating Activities section for the indirect method.

POD REVIEW 12.6

LO6 *Use T accounts to prepare a statement of cash flows using the indirect method to determine cash flow from operating activities.*

- Using T accounts, this approach uses the changes in current asset and liability accounts related to accruals and deferrals to adjust net income to cash flows from operating activities.

QUESTIONS

1. *Which of the following is an addition to net income when the indirect method is used to prepare the statement of cash flows?*
   a. increase in inventory
   b. decrease in accounts payable
   c. loss on sale of equipment
   d. None of the above are an addition to net income under the indirect method.

2. *How is depreciation expense treated under the indirect method of preparing the statement of cash flows?*
   a. as an outflow in the Operating Activities section of the statement
   b. as an outflow in the Investing Activities section of the statement
   c. as an addition to net income in the Operating Activities section of the statement
   d. Depreciation expense does not appear on the statement of cash flows when the indirect method is used.

The Use of Cash Flow Information

LO7 Use cash flow information to help analyze a company.

The statement of cash flows is a critical disclosure to a company's investors and creditors. Many investors focus on cash flow from operations rather than net income as their key statistic. Similarly, many bankers are as concerned with cash flow from operations as they are with net income because they care about a company's ability to pay its bills. There is the concern that accrual accounting can mask cash flow problems. For example, a company with smooth earnings could be building up accounts receivable and inventory. This may not become evident until the company is in deep trouble.

The statement of cash flows provides investors, analysts, bankers, and other users with a valuable starting point as they attempt to evaluate a company's financial health. From this point, these groups must decide how to use the information presented on the statement. They pay particular attention to the relationships among various items on the statement, as well as to other financial statement items. In fact, many large banks have their own cash flow models, which typically involve a rearrangement of the items on the statement of cash flows to suit their needs. We now consider two examples of how various groups use cash flow information.

CREDITORS AND CASH FLOW ADEQUACY

Bankers and other creditors are especially concerned with a company's ability to meet its principal and interest obligations. *Cash flow adequacy* is a measure intended to help in this regard.[3] It gauges the cash that a company has available to meet future debt obligations after paying taxes and interest costs and making capital expenditures. Because capital expenditures on new plant and equipment are a necessity for most companies, analysts are concerned with the cash available to repay debt *after* the company has replaced and updated its existing base of long-term assets.

Cash flow adequacy can be computed as follows:

$$\text{Cash Flow Adequacy} = \frac{\text{Cash Flow from Operating Activities} - \text{Capital Expenditures}}{\text{Average Amount of Debt Maturing over Next Five Years}}$$

How could you use the information in an annual report to measure a company's cash flow adequacy? First, whether a company uses the direct or indirect method to report cash flow from operating activities, this number represents cash flow after interest and taxes are paid. The numerator of the ratio is determined by deducting capital expenditures, as they appear in the Investing Activities section of the statement, from cash flow from operating activities. A disclosure required by the SEC provides the information needed to calculate the denominator of the ratio. This regulatory body requires companies to report the annual amount of long-term debt maturing over each of the next five years. For more on the cash flow adequacy of **Best Buy**, see the Ratio Decision Process that follows.

Best Buy's Cash Flow Adequacy As an example of the calculation of this ratio, consider the following amounts from Best Buy's statement of cash flows for the year ended March 3, 2007 (amounts in millions of dollars):

Total cash provided by operating activities from continuing operations	$1,762
Additions to property and equipment	$ 733

Note 5 in Best Buy's 2007 annual report provides the following information:

At March 3, 2007, the future maturities of long-term debt, including capitalized leases, consisted of the following:

Fiscal Year	
2008	$ 19
2009	18
2010	27
2011	18
2012(1)	420
Thereafter	107
	$609[4]

(1) Holders of our debentures due in 2022 may require us to purchase all or a portion of their debentures on January 15, 2012. The table assumes that all holders of our debentures exercise their redemption options.

3 An article appearing in the January 10, 1994, edition of *The Wall Street Journal* reported that **Fitch Investors Service Inc.** has published a rating system to compare the cash flow adequacy of companies that it rates single-A in its credit ratings. The rating system is intended to help corporate bond investors assess the ability of these companies to meet their maturing debt obligations. Lee Berton, "Investors Have a New Tool for Judging Issuers' Health: 'Cash-Flow Adequacy,'" p. C1.

4 Best Buy 2007 Annual Report, p. 76.

USING THE RATIO DECISION MODEL: ANALYZING CASH FLOW ADEQUACY

Use the following Ratio Decision Model to evaluate the cash flow adequacy of Best Buy or any other public company.

1. Formulate the Question

Managers, investors, and creditors are all interested in a company's cash flows. They must be able to answer the following question:

Did the company generate enough cash this year from its operations to pay for its capital expenditures and meet its maturing debt obligations?

2. Gather the Information from the Financial Statements

- Total cash from operating activities: From the statement of cash flows
- Necessary capital expenditures: From the statement of cash flows
- Average debt maturing over next five years: From the note disclosures.

3. Calculate the Ratio

$$\text{Cash Flow Adequacy} = \frac{\text{Cash Flow from Operating Activities} - \text{Capital Expenditures}}{\text{Average Amount of Debt Maturing over Next Five Years}}$$

Best Buy
Consolidated Statements of Cash Flows (Partial)
$ in millions

Fiscal Years Ended	March 3, 2007	February 25, 2006	February 26, 2005
Operating Activities			
Total cash provided by operating activities from continuing operations	$1,762	$1,740	$1,981
Investing Activities			
Additions to property and equipment	(733)	(648)	(502)

Best Buy
Notes to Consolidated Financial Statements

4. Debt

. . . the future maturities of long-term debt, including capitalized leases, consisted of the following:

Fiscal Year	
2008	$ 19
2009	18
2010	27
2011	18
2012[(1)]	420
Thereafter	107
	$609

Average amount of debt maturing in next five years = [($19 + $18 + $27 + $18 + $420)/5 = $100.4]

(1) Holders of our debentures due in 2022 may require us to purchase all or a portion of their debentures on January 15, 2012. The table assumes that all holders of our debentures exercise their redemption options.

$$\text{Cash Flow Adequacy} = \frac{\$1,762 - \$733}{\$100.4} = 10.2$$

4. Compare the Ratio with Others

Best Buy's cash flow adequacy may be compared to that of prior years and to that of companies of similar size in the same industry.

	Best Buy		Circuit City	
	Year Ended March 3, 2007	Year Ended February 25, 2006	Year Ended February 28, 2007	Year Ended February 28, 2006
Cash Flow Adequacy	10.2	11.1	7.0	20.5

5. Interpret the Results

Best Buy's ratio of 10.2 is slightly lower than the prior year's ratio; however, the ratio in both years indicates that the company's cash flow was more than sufficient to repay its average annual debt over the next five years. Circuit City's ratio was higher in the prior year than it was in the current year.

STOCKHOLDERS AND CASH FLOW PER SHARE

One measure of the relative worth of an investment in a company is the ratio of the stock's market price per share to the company's earnings per share (that is, the price/earnings ratio). But many stockholders and Wall Street analysts are even more interested in the price of the stock in relation to the company's cash flow per share. Cash flow for purposes of this ratio is normally limited to cash flow from operating activities. These groups have used this ratio to evaluate investments—even though the accounting profession has expressly forbidden the reporting of cash flow per share information in the financial statements. The accounting profession's belief is that this type of information is not an acceptable alternative to earnings per share as an indicator of company performance.

POD REVIEW 12.7

LO7 *Use cash flow information to help analyze a company.*

- Cash flow per share and cash flow adequacy are two measures that investors and creditors can use to evaluate the financial health of an entity.

QUESTIONS

1. *Where would a person find the information needed to compute the cash flow adequacy ratio?*
   a. the statement of cash flows only
   b. the income statement only
   c. the statement of cash flows and the notes to the statements
   d. the balance sheet only

2. *Cash flow per share is*
   a. the same as earnings per share.
   b. computed by dividing cash on the balance sheet by the number of shares outstanding.
   c. an acceptable alternative to earnings per share according to the accounting profession.
   d. not an acceptable alternative to earnings per share according to the accounting profession.

Accounting Tools: A Work-Sheet Approach to the Statement of Cash Flows

APPENDIX

LO8 Use a work sheet to prepare a statement of cash flows using the indirect method to determine cash flow from operating activities.

The chapter illustrated the use of T accounts to aid in the preparation of a statement of cash flows. We pointed out that T accounts are simply tools to help in analyzing the transactions of the period. We now consider the use of a work sheet as an alternative tool to organize the information needed to prepare the statement. We will use the information given in the chapter for Julian Corp. (Refer to Exhibit 12-11 and Exhibit 12-12 for the income statements and comparative balance sheets, respectively.) Although it is possible to use a work sheet to prepare the statement when the Operating Activities section is prepared under the direct method, we illustrate the use of a work sheet using the more popular indirect method.

A work sheet for Julian Corp. is presented in Exhibit 12-19. The following steps were taken to prepare the work sheet:

Step 1: The balances in each account at the end and the beginning of the period are entered in the first two columns of the work sheet. For Julian, these balances can be found in its comparative balance sheets in Exhibit 12-12. Note that credit balances are shown in parentheses on the work sheet. Because the work sheet lists all balance sheet accounts, the total of the debit balances must equal the total of the credit balances; thus, the totals at the bottom for these first two columns equal $0.

Step 2: The additional information listed at the bottom of Exhibit 12-12 is used to record the various investing and financing activities on the work sheet. (The item numbers that follow correspond to the superscript numbers on the work sheet in Exhibit 12-19):

1. Long-term investments were purchased for $30,000. Because this transaction required the use of cash, it is entered in parentheses in the Investing column and in the Changes column as an addition to the Long-Term Investments account.
2. Land was acquired by issuing a $50,000 note payable. This transaction is entered on two lines on the work sheet. First, $50,000 is added to the Changes column for Land and as a corresponding deduction in the Noncash column (the last column on the work sheet). Likewise, $50,000 is added to the Changes column for Notes Payable and to the Noncash column.
3. Item 3 in the additional information indicates the acquisition of equipment for $75,000. This amount appears on the work sheet as an addition to Property and Equipment in the Changes column and as a deduction (cash outflow) in the Investing column.
4. A machine with an original cost of $35,000 and a book value of $20,000 was sold for $25,000, resulting in four entries on the work sheet. First, the amount of cash received, $25,000, is entered as an addition in the Investing column on the line for property and equipment. On the same line, the cost of the machine, $35,000, is entered as a deduction in the Changes column. The difference between the cost of the machine, $35,000, and its book value, $20,000, is its accumulated depreciation of $15,000. This amount is shown as a deduction from this account in the Changes column. Because the gain of $5,000 is included in net income, it is deducted in the Operating column (on the Retained Earnings line).
5. Bonds with a face value of $60,000 were retired by paying $63,000 in cash, resulting in the entry of three amounts on the work sheet. The face value of the bonds, $60,000, is entered as a reduction of Bonds Payable in the Changes column. The amount paid

EXHIBIT 12-19 **Julian Corp. Statement of Cash Flows Work Sheet**

Julian Corp.
Statement of Cash Flows Work Sheet (Indirect Method)
(all amounts in thousands of dollars)

	Balances			Cash Inflows (Outflows)			
Accounts	**12/31/07**	**12/31/06**	**Changes**	**Operating**	**Investing**	**Financing**	**Noncash Activities**
Cash	35	46	(11)[16]				
Accounts Receivable	63	57	6[10]	(6)[10]			
Inventory	84	92	(8)[11]	8[11]			
Prepaid Insurance	12	18	(6)[12]	6[12]			
Long-Term Investments	120	90	30[1]		(30)[1]		
Land	150	100	50[2]				(50)[2]
Property and Equipment	320	280	75[3]		(75)[3]		
			(35)[4]		25[4]		
Accumulated Depreciation	(100)	(75)	15[4]				
			(40)[9]	40[9]			
Accounts Payable	(38)	(31)	(7)[13]	7[13]			
Salaries and Wages Payable	(7)	(9)	2[14]	(2)[14]			
Income Taxes Payable	(8)	(5)	(3)[15]	3[15]			
Notes Payable	(85)	(35)	(50)[2]				50[2]
Bonds Payable	(200)	(260)	60[5]			(63)[5]	
Capital Stock	(100)	(75)	(25)[6]			25[6]	
Retained Earnings	(246)	(193)	67[7]	(5)[4]		(67)[7]	
				3[5]			
			(120)[8]	120[8]			
Totals	–0–	–0–	–0–	174	(80)	(105)	–0–
Net decrease in cash				(11)[16]			

Source: The authors are grateful to Jeannie Folk for the development of this work sheet.

to retire the bonds, $63,000, is entered on the same line in the Financing column. The loss of $3,000 is added in the Operating column because it was a deduction to arrive at net income.

6. Capital stock was issued for $25,000. This amount is entered on the Capital Stock line under the Changes column (as an increase in the account) and under the Financing column as an inflow.
7. Dividends of $67,000 were paid. This amount is entered as a reduction in Retained Earnings in the Changes column and as a cash outflow in the Financing Activities column.

Step 3: Because the indirect method is being used, net income of $120,000 for the period is entered as an addition to Retained Earnings in the Operating column of the work sheet (entry 8). The amount is also entered as an increase (in parentheses) in the Changes column.

Step 4: Any noncash revenues or expenses are entered on the work sheet on the appropriate lines. For Julian, depreciation expense of $40,000 is added (in parentheses) to Accumulated Depreciation in the Changes column and in the Operating column. This entry is identified on the work sheet as entry 9.

Step 5: Each of the changes in the noncash current asset and current liability accounts is entered in the Changes column and in the Operating column. These entries are identified on the work sheet as entries 10 through 15.

Step 6: Totals are determined for the Operating, Investing, and Financing columns and entered at the bottom of the work sheet. The total for the final column, Noncash Activities, of $0, is also entered.

Step 7: The net cash inflow (outflow) for the period is determined by adding the totals of the Operating, Investing, and Financing columns. For Julian, the net cash *outflow* is $11,000, shown as entry 16 at the bottom of the statement. This same amount is then transferred to the line for Cash in the Changes column. Finally, the total of the Changes column at this point should net to $0.

POD REVIEW 12.8

LO8 *Use a work sheet to prepare a statement of cash flows using the indirect method to determine cash flow from operating activities.*

- A work sheet is an alternative to T accounts to help in the preparation of a statement of cash flows.

QUESTIONS

1. *On the worksheet illustrated in this appendix, what should be the total of the Changes column?*
   a. zero
   b. the same number as total assets
   c. the same number as net income
   d. A changes column does not appear on the worksheet.

2. *What if the Changes column on the type of worksheet illustrated in this chapter shows a negative $50,000 for bonds payable. What will the worksheet also show?*
   a. $50,000 inflow in the Operating Activities column
   b. $50,000 inflow in the Investing Activities column
   c. $50,000 inflow in the Financing Activities column
   d. $50,000 outflow in the Financing Activities column

RATIO REVIEW

$$\text{Cash Flow Adequacy} = \frac{\text{Cash Flow from Operating Activities} - \text{Capital Expenditures (Statement of Cash Flows)}}{\text{Average Amount of Debt Maturing over Next Five Years (Notes to the Financial Statements)}}$$

KEY TERMS QUIZ

Read each definition below and write the number of the definition in the blank beside the appropriate term. The quiz solutions appear at the end of the chapter.

______	**Statement of cash flows**	______	**Financing activities**
______	**Cash equivalent**	______	**Direct method**
______	**Operating activities**	______	**Indirect method**
______	**Investing activities**		

1. Activities concerned with the acquisition and sale of products and services.
2. For preparing the Operating Activities section of the statement of cash flows, the approach in which net income is reconciled to net cash flow from operations.
3. The financial statement that summarizes an entity's cash receipts and cash payments during the period from operating, investing, and financing activities.
4. An item readily convertible to a known amount of cash with a maturity to the investor of three months or less.
5. Activities concerned with the acquisition and disposal of long-term assets.
6. For preparing the Operating Activities section of the statement of cash flows, the approach in which cash receipts and cash payments are reported.
7. Activities concerned with the raising and repaying of funds in the form of debt and equity.

ALTERNATE TERMS

Bottom line Net income

Cash flow from operating activities Cash flow from operations

Statement of cash flows Cash flows statement

WARMUP EXERCISES & SOLUTIONS

LO1

Warmup Exercise 12-1 Purpose of the Statement of Cash Flows

Most companies begin the statement of cash flows by indicating the amount of net income and ending it with the beginning and ending cash balances. Why is the statement necessary if net income already appears on the income statement and the cash balances can be found on the balance sheet?

Key to the Solution Recall the purpose of the statement of cash flows as described in the beginning of the chapter.

LO3

Warmup Exercise 12-2 Classification of Activities

For each of the following activities, indicate whether it should appear on the statement of cash flows as an operating (O), investing (I), or financing (F) activity. Assume that the company uses the direct method of reporting in the Operating Activities section.

______ 1. New equipment is acquired for cash.
______ 2. Thirty-year bonds are issued.
______ 3. Cash receipts from the cash register are recorded.
______ 4. The biweekly payroll is paid.
______ 5. Common stock is issued for cash.
______ 6. Land that was being held for future expansion is sold at book value.

Key to the Solution Recall the general rules for each of the categories: operating activities involve acquiring and selling products and services, investing activities deal with acquiring and disposing of long-term assets, and financing activities are concerned with the raising and repaying of funds in the form of debt and equity.

LO6

Warmup Exercise 12-3 Adjustments to Net Income with the Indirect Method

Assume that a company uses the indirect method to prepare the Operating Activities section of the statement of cash flows. For each of the following items, indicate whether it would be added to net income (A), be deducted from net income (D), or not be reported in this section of the statement under the indirect method (NR).

______ 1. Decrease in accounts payable
______ 2. Increase in accounts receivable
______ 3. Decrease in prepaid insurance
______ 4. Purchase of new factory equipment
______ 5. Depreciation expense
______ 6. Gain on retirement of bonds

Key to the Solution Refer to the summary of adjustments to net income under the indirect method on page 617.

SOLUTIONS TO WARMUP EXERCISES

Warmup Exercise 12-1

The statement of cash flows is a complement to the other statements in that it summarizes the operating, investing, and financing activities over a period of time. Even though the net income and cash balances are available on other statements, the statement of cash flows explains to the reader why net income is different from cash flow from operations and why cash changed by the amount it did during the period.

Warmup Exercise 12-2

1. I 2. F 3. O 4. O 5. F 6. I

Warmup Exercise 12-3

1. D 2. D 3. A 4. NR 5. A 6. D

REVIEW PROBLEM & SOLUTION

An income statement and comparative balance sheets for Dexter Company follow.

Dexter Company Income Statement
For the Year Ended December 31, 2008

Sales revenue	$89,000
Cost of goods sold	57,000
Gross profit	$32,000
Depreciation expense	$ 6,500
Advertising expense	3,200
Salaries expense	12,000
Total operating expenses	$21,700
Operating income	$10,300
Loss on sale of land	2,500
Income before tax	$ 7,800
Income tax expense	2,600
Net income	$ 5,200

Dexter Company
Comparative Balance Sheets

	December 31	
	2008	**2007**
Cash	$ 12,000	$ 9,500
Accounts receivable	22,000	18,400
Inventory	25,400	20,500
Prepaid advertising	10,000	8,600
Total current assets	$ 69,400	$ 57,000
Land	$120,000	$ 80,000
Equipment	190,000	130,000
Accumulated depreciation	(70,000)	(63,500)
Total long-term assets	$240,000	$146,500
Total assets	$309,400	$203,500
Accounts payable	$ 15,300	$ 12,100
Salaries payable	14,000	16,400
Income taxes payable	1,200	700
Total current liabilities	$ 30,500	$ 29,200
Capital stock	$200,000	$100,000
Retained earnings	78,900	74,300
Total stockholders' equity	$278,900	$174,300
Total liabilities and stockholders' equity	$309,400	$203,500

Additional Information

1. Land was acquired during the year for $70,000.
2. An unimproved parcel of land was sold during the year for $27,500. Its original cost to Dexter was $30,000.
3. A specialized piece of equipment was acquired in exchange for capital stock in the company. The value of the capital stock was $60,000.
4. In addition to the capital stock issued in (3), stock was sold for $40,000.
5. Dividends of $600 were paid.

Required

Prepare a statement of cash flows for 2008 using the direct method in the Operating Activities section of the statement. Include supplemental schedules to report any noncash investing and financing activities and to reconcile net income to net cash provided by operating activities.

SOLUTION TO REVIEW PROBLEM

Dexter Company
Statement of Cash Flows
For the Year Ended December 31, 2008

Cash flows from operating activities	
Cash collections from customers	$ 85,400
Cash payments:	
To suppliers	$(58,700)
For advertising	(4,600)
To employees	(14,400)
For income taxes	(2,100)
Total cash payments	$(79,800)
Net cash provided by operating activities	$ 5,600
Cash flows from investing activities	
Purchase of land	$(70,000)
Sale of land	27,500
Net cash used by investing activities	$(42,500)
Cash flows from financing activities	
Issuance of capital stock	$ 40,000
Payment of cash dividends	(600)
Net cash provided by financing activities	$ 39,400
Net increase in cash	$ 2,500
Cash balance, December 31, 2007	9,500
Cash balance, December 31, 2008	$ 12,000
Supplemental schedule of noncash investing and financing activities	
Acquisition of specialized equipment in exchange for capital stock	$ 60,000
Reconciliation of net income to net cash provided by operating activities	
Net income	$ 5,200
Adjustments to reconcile net income to net cash provided by operating activities:	
Increase in accounts receivable	(3,600)
Increase in inventory	(4,900)
Increase in prepaid advertising	(1,400)
Increase in accounts payable	3,200
Decrease in salaries payable	(2,400)
Increase in income taxes payable	500
Depreciation expense	6,500
Loss on sale of land	2,500
Net cash provided by operating activities	$ 5,600

QUESTIONS

1. What is the purpose of the statement of cash flows? As a flows statement, explain how it differs from the income statement.
2. What is a cash equivalent? Why is it included with cash for purposes of preparing a statement of cash flows?
3. Preston Corp. acquires a piece of land by signing a $60,000 promissory note and making a down payment of $20,000. How should this transaction be reported on the statement of cash flows?
4. Hansen Inc. made two purchases during December. One was a $10,000 Treasury bill that matures in 60 days from the date of purchase. The other was a $20,000 investment in Motorola common stock that will be held indefinitely. How should each purchase be treated for purposes of preparing a statement of cash flows?
5. Companies are required to classify cash flows as operating, investing, or financing. Which of these three categories do you think will most likely have a net cash *outflow* over a number of years? Explain your answer.
6. A fellow student says to you: "The statement of cash flows is the easiest of the basic financial statements to prepare because you know the answer before you start. You compare the beginning and ending balances in cash on the balance sheet and compute the net inflow or outflow of cash. What could be easier?" Do you agree? Explain your answer.
7. What is your evaluation of the following statement? Depreciation is responsible for providing some of the highest amounts of cash for capital-intensive businesses. This is obvious by examining the Operating Activities section of the statement of cash flows. Other than the net income of the period, depreciation is often the largest amount reported in this section of the statement.
8. Which method for preparing the Operating Activities section of the statement of cash flows, the direct or the indirect method, do you believe provides more information to users of the statement? Explain your answer.
9. Assume that a company uses the indirect method to prepare the Operating Activities section of the statement of cash flows. Why would a decrease in accounts receivable during the period be added back to net income?
10. Why is it necessary to analyze both inventory and accounts payable in trying to determine cash payments to suppliers when the direct method is used?
11. A company has a very profitable year. What explanations might there be for a decrease in cash?
12. A company reports a net loss for the year. Is it possible that cash could increase during the year? Explain your answer.
13. What effect does a decrease in income taxes payable for the period have on cash generated from operating activities? Does it matter whether the direct or the indirect method is used?
14. Why do accounting standards require a company to separately disclose income taxes paid and interest paid if it uses the indirect method?
15. Is it logical that interest paid is classified as a cash outflow in the Operating Activities section of the statement of cash flows but that dividends paid are included in the Financing Activities section? Explain your answer.
16. Jackson Company prepays the rent on various office facilities. The beginning balance in Prepaid Rent was $9,600, and the ending balance was $7,300. The income statement reports Rent Expense of $45,900. Under the direct method, what amount would appear for cash paid in rent in the Operating Activities section of the statement of cash flows?
17. Baxter Inc. buys as treasury stock 2,000 shares of its own common stock at $20 per share. How is this transaction reported on the statement of cash flows?
18. Duke Corp. sold a delivery truck for $9,000. Its original cost was $25,000, and the book value at the time of the sale was $11,000. How does the transaction to record the sale appear on a statement of cash flows prepared under the indirect method?
19. Billings Company has a patent on its books with a balance at the beginning of the year of $24,000. The ending balance for the asset was $20,000. The company did not buy or sell any patents during the year, nor does it use an Accumulated Amortization account. Assuming that the company uses the indirect method in preparing a statement of cash flows, how is the decrease in the Patents account reported on the statement?
20. Ace Inc. declared and distributed a 10% stock dividend during the year. Explain how, if at all, you think this transaction should be reported on a statement of cash flows.
21. Explain where to find the information needed to determine a company's cash flow adequacy.

BRIEF EXERCISES

LO1 **Brief Exercise 12-1** Purpose of the Statement of Cash Flows

You have been studying accounting for nearly a semester now and have become convinced of the value of determining a company's net income on an accrual basis. Why do you think the accounting profession requires companies also to prepare a statement of cash flows, especially since you can look at two successive balance sheets to see the change in cash?

LO2 **Brief Exercise 12-2** Cash Equivalents

A friend in your class is confused and asks for your help in understanding cash equivalents: "Say a company invests $50,000 in a 60-day certificate of deposit. Since the company obviously used cash to buy the CD, why is this not classified as an investing activity on the statement of cash flows?" How would you respond to your friend's question?

LO3

Brief Exercise 12-3 Three Types of Activities

For each of the following transactions on the statement of cash flows, indicate whether it would appear in the Operating Activities section (O), in the Investing Activities section (I), or in the Financing Activities section (F). Assume the use of the direct method in the Operating Activities section.

_____ 1. Repayment of long-term debt
_____ 2. Purchase of equipment
_____ 3. Collection of customer's account
_____ 4. Issuance of common stock
_____ 5. Purchase of another company
_____ 6. Payment of dividends
_____ 7. Payment of income taxes
_____ 8. Sale of equipment

LO4

Brief Exercise 12-4 Direct versus Indirect Method

For each of the following items, indicate whether it would appear on a statement of cash flows prepared using the direct method (D) or the indirect method (I).

_____ 1. Net income
_____ 2. Increase in accounts receivable
_____ 3. Collections on accounts receivable
_____ 4. Payments on accounts payable
_____ 5. Decrease in accounts payable
_____ 6. Depreciation expense
_____ 7. Gain on early retirement of bonds
_____ 8. Cash sales

LO5

Brief Exercise 12-5 Direct Method

Fill in the blank for each of the following situations.

Balance Sheet	Beginning	Ending	Income Statement	Cash Inflow (Outflow)
1. Accounts receivable	$2,000	$5,000	Sales on account $15,000	$ _____
2. Prepaid insurance	$4,000	$3,000	Insurance expense $7,000	$ _____
3. Income taxes payable	$6,000	$9,000	Income tax expense $20,000	$ _____
4. Wages payable	$5,000	$3,000	Wages expense $25,000	$ _____

LO6

Brief Exercise 12-6 Indirect Method

For each of the following items, indicate whether it would be added to (A) or deducted from (D) net income to arrive at net cash flow provided by operating activities under the indirect method.

_____ 1. Increase in accounts receivable
_____ 2. Decrease in prepaid rent
_____ 3. Decrease in inventory
_____ 4. Decrease in accounts payable
_____ 5. Increase in income taxes payable
_____ 6. Depreciation expense
_____ 7. Gain on sale of equipment
_____ 8. Loss on early retirement of bonds

LO7

Brief Exercise 12-7 Cash Flow Adequacy

A company generated $1,500,000 from its operating activities and spent $900,000 on additions to its plant and equipment during the year. The total amount of debt that matures in the next five years is $750,000. Compute the company's cash flow adequacy ratio for the year.

LO8

Brief Exercise 12-8 Worksheet

Assume that a company uses a worksheet as illustrated in Exhibit 12-19 to prepare its statement of cash flows and that it uses the indirect method in the Operating Activities section of the statement. For each of the following changes in balance sheet accounts, indicate in one of the three columns whether it is an addition (A) or a deduction (D). Assume that the change in (2) and (6) includes a corresponding change in cash.

	Type of Activity		
Balance Sheet Change	**Operating**	**Investing**	**Financing**
1. Accounts receivable increased	______	______	______
2. Land increased	______	______	______
3. Inventory decreased	______	______	______
4. Accounts payable decreased	______	______	______
5. Income taxes payable increased	______	______	______
6. Capital stock increased	______	______	______

EXERCISES

LO2

Exercise 12-1 Cash Equivalents

Metropolis Industries invested its excess cash in the following instruments during December 2008:

Certificate of deposit, due January 31, 2009	$ 35,000
Certificate of deposit, due June 30, 2009	95,000
Investment in City of Elgin bonds, due May 1, 2010	15,000
Investment in Quantum Data stock	66,000
Money Market Fund	105,000
90-day Treasury bills	75,000
Treasury note, due December 1, 2009	200,000

Required

Determine the amount of cash equivalents that should be combined with cash on the company's balance sheet at December 31, 2008, and for purposes of preparing a statement of cash flows for the year ended December 31, 2008.

LO3

Exercise 12-2 Classification of Activities

For each of the following transactions reported on a statement of cash flows, indicate whether it would appear in the Operating Activities section (O), in the Investing Activities section (I), or in the Financing Activities section (F). Put an *S* in the blank if the transaction does not affect cash but is reported in a supplemental schedule of noncash activities. Assume that the company uses the direct method in the Operating Activities section.

______ 1. A company purchases its own common stock in the open market and immediately retires it.

______ 2. A company issues preferred stock in exchange for land.

______ 3. A six-month bank loan is obtained.

______ 4. Twenty-year bonds are issued.

______ 5. A customer's open account is collected.

______ 6. Income taxes are paid.

______ 7. Cash sales for the day are recorded.

______ 8. Cash dividends are declared and paid.

______ 9. A creditor is given shares of common stock in the company in return for cancellation of a long-term loan.

______ 10. A new piece of machinery is acquired for cash.

______ 11. Stock of another company is acquired as an investment.

______ 12. Interest is paid on a bank loan.

______ 13. Factory workers are paid.

HOMEWORK

LO3 **Exercise 12-3** Retirement of Bonds Payable on the Statement of Cash Flows—Indirect Method

Redstone Inc. has the following debt outstanding on December 31, 2008:

10% bonds payable, due 12/31/12	$500,000	
Discount on bonds payable	(40,000)	$460,000

On this date, Redstone retired the entire bond issue by paying cash of $510,000.

Required

1. Prepare the journal entry to record the bond retirement.
2. Describe how the bond retirement would be reported on the statement of cash flows assuming that Redstone uses the indirect method.

LO5 **Exercise 12-4** Cash Collections—Direct Method

Stanley Company's comparative balance sheets included accounts receivable of $80,800 at December 31, 2007, and $101,100 at December 31, 2008. Sales reported by Stanley on its 2008 income statement amounted to $1,450,000. What is the amount of cash collections that Stanley will report in the Operating Activities section of its 2008 statement of cash flows assuming that the direct method is used?

LO5 **Exercise 12-5** Cash Payments—Direct Method

Lester Enterprises' comparative balance sheets included inventory of $90,200 at December 31, 2007, and $70,600 at December 31, 2008. Lester's comparative balance sheets also included accounts payable of $57,700 at December 31, 2007, and $39,200 at December 31, 2008. Lester's accounts payable balances are composed solely of amounts due to suppliers for purchases of inventory on account. Cost of goods sold, as reported by Lester on its 2008 income statement, amounted to $770,900. What is the amount of cash payments for inventory that Lester will report in the Operating Activities section of its 2008 statement of cash flows assuming that the direct method is used?

LO5 **Exercise 12-6** Operating Activities Section—Direct Method

The following account balances for the noncash current assets and current liabilities of Labrador Company are available:

	December 31	
	2008	**2007**
Accounts receivable	$ 4,000	$ 6,000
Inventory	32,000	25,000
Office supplies	7,000	10,000
Accounts payable	7,500	4,500
Salaries and wages payable	1,500	2,500
Interest payable	500	1,000
Income taxes payable	4,500	3,000

In addition, the income statement for 2008 is as follows:

	2008
Sales revenue	$100,000
Cost of goods sold	75,000
Gross profit	$ 25,000
General and administrative expense	$ 8,000
Depreciation expense	3,000
Total operating expenses	$ 11,000
Income before interest and taxes	$ 14,000
Interest expense	3,000
Income before tax	$ 11,000
Income tax expense	5,000
Net income	$ 6,000

Required

1. Prepare the Operating Activities section of the statement of cash flows using the direct method.
2. What does the use of the direct method reveal about a company that the indirect method does not?

LO5

Exercise 12-7 Determination of Missing Amounts—Cash Flow from Operating Activities

The computation of cash provided by operating activities requires analysis of the noncash current asset and current liability accounts. Using T accounts, determine the missing amounts for each of the following independent cases:

Case 1	
Accounts receivable, beginning of year	$150,000
Accounts receivable, end of year	100,000
Credit sales for the year	175,000
Cash sales for the year	60,000
Write-offs of uncollectible accounts	35,000
Total cash collections for the year (from cash sales and collections on account)	?
Case 2	
Inventory, beginning of year	$ 80,000
Inventory, end of year	55,000
Accounts payable, beginning of year	25,000
Accounts payable, end of year	15,000
Cost of goods sold	175,000
Cash payments for inventory (assume all purchases of inventory are on account)	?
Case 3	
Prepaid insurance, beginning of year	$ 17,000
Prepaid insurance, end of year	20,000
Insurance expense	15,000
Cash paid for new insurance policies	?
Case 4	
Income taxes payable, beginning of year	$ 95,000
Income taxes payable, end of year	115,000
Income tax expense	300,000
Cash payments for taxes	?

LO5

Exercise 12-8 Dividends on the Statement of Cash Flows

The following selected account balances are available from the records of Lewistown Company:

	December 31	
	2008	**2007**
Dividends payable	$ 30,000	$ 20,000
Retained earnings	375,000	250,000

Other information available for 2008 is as follows:

a. Lewistown reported $285,000 net income for the year.
b. It declared and distributed a stock dividend of $50,000 during the year.
c. It declared cash dividends at the end of each quarter and paid them within the next 30 days of the following quarter.

Required

1. With the use of T accounts, determine the amount of cash dividends *paid* during the year for presentation in the Financing Activities section of the statement of cash flows.
2. Should the stock dividend described in (b) appear on a statement of cash flows? Explain your answer.

LO6

Exercise 12-9 Adjustments to Net Income with the Indirect Method

Assume that a company uses the indirect method to prepare the Operating Activities section of the statement of cash flows. For each of the following items, indicate whether it would be added to net income (A), deducted from net income (D), or not reported in this section of the statement under the indirect method (NR).

_______ 1. Depreciation expense
_______ 2. Gain on sale of used delivery truck
_______ 3. Bad debts expense
_______ 4. Increase in accounts payable
_______ 5. Purchase of new delivery truck
_______ 6. Loss on retirement of bonds
_______ 7. Increase in prepaid rent
_______ 8. Decrease in inventory
_______ 9. Issuance of note payable due in three years
_______ 10. Amortization of patents

LO6

Exercise 12-10 Operating Activities Section—Indirect Method

The following account balances for the noncash current assets and current liabilities of Suffolk Company are available:

	December 31	
	2008	**2007**
Accounts receivable	$43,000	$35,000
Inventory	30,000	40,000
Prepaid rent	17,000	15,000
Totals	$90,000	$90,000
Accounts payable	$26,000	$19,000
Income taxes payable	6,000	10,000
Interest payable	15,000	12,000
Totals	$47,000	$41,000

Net income for 2008 is $40,000. Depreciation expense is $20,000. Assume that all sales and all purchases are on account.

Required

1. Prepare the Operating Activities section of the statement of cash flows using the indirect method.
2. Provide a brief explanation as to why cash flow from operating activities is more or less than the net income of the period.

LO7

Exercise 12-11 Cash Flow Adequacy

On its most recent statement of cash flows, a company reported net cash provided by operating activities of $12,000,000. Its capital expenditures for the same year were $2,000,000. A note to the financial statements indicated that the total amount of debt that would mature over the next five years was $20,000,000.

Required

1. Compute the company's cash flow adequacy ratio.
2. If you were a banker considering loaning money to this company, why would you be interested in knowing its cash flow adequacy ratio? Would you feel comfortable making a loan based on the ratio you computed in (1)? Explain your answer.

MULTICONCEPT EXERCISES

LO2,3

Exercise 12-12 Classification of Activities

Use the following legend to indicate how each transaction would be reported on the statement of cash flows. (Assume that the stocks and bonds of other companies are classified as long-term investments.)

II = Inflow from investing activities
OI = Outflow from investing activities
IF = Inflow from financing activities
OF = Outflow from financing activities
CE = Classified as a cash equivalent and included with cash for purposes of preparing the statement of cash flows

_______ 1. Purchased a six-month certificate of deposit
_______ 2. Purchased a 60-day Treasury bill
_______ 3. Issued 1,000 shares of common stock
_______ 4. Purchased 1,000 shares of stock in another company
_______ 5. Purchased 1,000 shares of its own stock to be held in the treasury
_______ 6. Invested $1,000 in a money market fund
_______ 7. Sold 500 shares of stock of another company
_______ 8. Purchased 20-year bonds of another company
_______ 9. Issued 30-year bonds
_______ 10. Repaid a six-month bank loan

LO3,5

Exercise 12-13 Classification of Activities

Use the following legend to indicate how each transaction would be reported on the statement of cash flows. (Assume that the company uses the direct method in the Operating Activities section.)

IO = Inflow from operating activities
OO = Outflow from operating activities
II = Inflow from investing activities
OI = Outflow from investing activities
IF = Inflow from financing activities
OF = Outflow from financing activities
NR = Not reported in the body of the statement of cash flows but included in a supplemental schedule

_______ 1. Collected $10,000 in cash from customers' open accounts for the period
_______ 2. Paid one of the company's inventory suppliers $500 in settlement of an open account
_______ 3. Purchased a new copier for $6,000; signed a 90-day note payable
_______ 4. Issued bonds at face value of $100,000
_______ 5. Made $23,200 in cash sales for the week
_______ 6. Purchased an empty lot adjacent to the factory for $50,000. The seller of the land agrees to accept a five-year promissory note as consideration
_______ 7. Renewed the property insurance policy for another six months; cash of $1,000 is paid for the renewal
_______ 8. Purchased a machine for $10,000
_______ 9. Paid cash dividends of $2,500
_______ 10. Reclassified as short-term a long-term note payable of $5,000 that is due within the next year
_______ 11. Purchased 500 shares of the company's own stock on the open market for $4,000
_______ 12. Sold 500 shares of Nike stock for book value of $10,000 (they had been classified as long-term investments)

LO3,6 **Exercise 12-14** Long-Term Assets on the Statement of Cash Flows—Indirect Method

The following account balances are taken from the records of Martin Corp. for the past two years. (Credit balances are shown in parentheses.)

	December 31	
	2008	**2007**
Plant and equipment	$ 750,000	$ 500,000
Accumulated depreciation	(160,000)	(200,000)
Patents	92,000	80,000
Retained earnings	(825,000)	(675,000)

Other information available for 2008 is as follows:

a. Net income for the year was $200,000.
b. Depreciation expense on plant and equipment was $50,000.
c. Plant and equipment with an original cost of $150,000 were sold for $64,000. (You will need to determine the book value of the assets sold.)
d. Amortization expense on patents was $8,000.
e. Both new plant and equipment and patents were purchased for cash during the year.

Required
Indicate, with amounts, how all items related to these long-term assets would be reported in the 2008 statement of cash flows, including any adjustments in the Operating Activities section of the statement. Assume that Martin uses the indirect method.

LO1,5 **Exercise 12-15** Income Statement, Statement of Cash Flows (Direct Method), and Balance Sheet

The following events occurred at Handsome Hounds Grooming Company during its first year of business:

a. To establish the company, the two owners contributed a total of $50,000 in exchange for common stock.
b. Grooming service revenue for the first year amounted to $150,000, of which $40,000 was on account.
c. Customers owe $10,000 at the end of the year from the services provided on account.
d. At the beginning of the year, a storage building was rented. The company was required to sign a three-year lease for $12,000 per year and make a $2,000 refundable security deposit. The first year's lease payment and the security deposit were paid at the beginning of the year.
e. At the beginning of the year, the company purchased a patent at a cost of $100,000 for a revolutionary system to be used for dog grooming. The patent is expected to be useful for ten years. The company paid 20% down in cash and signed a four-year note at the bank for the remainder.
f. Operating expenses, including amortization of the patent and rent on the storage building, totaled $80,000 for the first year. No expenses were accrued or unpaid at the end of the year.
g. The company declared and paid a $20,000 cash dividend at the end of the first year.

Required
1. Prepare an income statement for the first year.
2. Prepare a statement of cash flows for the first year using the direct method in the Operating Activities section.
3. Did the company generate more or less cash flow from operations than it earned in net income? Explain why there is a difference.
4. Prepare a balance sheet as of the end of the first year.

PROBLEMS

LO6

Problem 12-1 Statement of Cash Flows—Indirect Method

The following balances are available for Chrisman Company:

	December 31 2008	December 31 2007
Cash	$ 8,000	$ 10,000
Accounts receivable	20,000	15,000
Inventory	15,000	25,000
Prepaid rent	9,000	6,000
Land	75,000	75,000
Plant and equipment	400,000	300,000
Accumulated depreciation	(65,000)	(30,000)
Totals	$462,000	$401,000
Accounts payable	$ 12,000	$ 10,000
Income taxes payable	3,000	5,000
Short-term notes payable	35,000	25,000
Bonds payable	75,000	100,000
Common stock	200,000	150,000
Retained earnings	137,000	111,000
Totals	$462,000	$401,000

Bonds were retired during 2008 at face value, plant and equipment were acquired for cash, and common stock was issued for cash. Depreciation expense for the year was $35,000. Net income was reported at $26,000.

Required

1. Prepare a statement of cash flows for 2008 using the indirect method in the Operating Activities section.
2. Did Chrisman generate sufficient cash from operations to pay for its investing activities? How did it generate cash other than from operations? Explain your answers.

LO8

Problem 12-2 Statement of Cash Flows Using a Work Sheet—Indirect Method (Appendix)

Refer to all of the facts in Problem 12-1.

Required

1. Using the format in the chapter's appendix, prepare a statement of cash flows work sheet.
2. Prepare a statement of cash flows for 2008 using the indirect method in the Operating Activities section.
3. Did Chrisman generate sufficient cash from operations to pay for its investing activities? How did it generate cash other than from operations? Explain your answers.

LO5

Problem 12-3 Statement of Cash Flows—Direct Method

Peoria Corp. just completed another successful year, as indicated by the following income statement:

	For the Year Ended December 31, 2008
Sales revenue	$1,250,000
Cost of goods sold	700,000
Gross profit	$ 550,000
Operating expenses	150,000
Income before interest and taxes	$ 400,000
Interest expense	25,000
Income before taxes	$ 375,000
Income tax expense	150,000
Net income	$ 225,000

Presented here are comparative balance sheets:

	December 31	
	2008	2007
Cash	$ 52,000	$ 90,000
Accounts receivable	180,000	130,000
Inventory	230,000	200,000
Prepayments	15,000	25,000
Total current assets	$ 477,000	$ 445,000
Land	$ 750,000	$ 600,000
Plant and equipment	700,000	500,000
Accumulated depreciation	(250,000)	(200,000)
Total long-term assets	$1,200,000	$ 900,000
Total assets	$1,677,000	$1,345,000
Accounts payable	$ 130,000	$ 148,000
Other accrued liabilities	68,000	63,000
Income taxes payable	90,000	110,000
Total current liabilities	$ 288,000	$ 321,000
Long-term bank loan payable	$ 350,000	$ 300,000
Common stock	$ 550,000	$ 400,000
Retained earnings	489,000	324,000
Total stockholders' equity	$1,039,000	$ 724,000
Total liabilities and stockholders' equity	$1,677,000	$1,345,000

Other information is as follows:

a. Dividends of $60,000 were declared and paid during the year.
b. Operating expenses include $50,000 of depreciation.
c. Land and plant and equipment were acquired for cash, and additional stock was issued for cash. Cash also was received from additional bank loans.

The president has asked you some questions about the year's results. She is very impressed with the profit margin of 18% (net income divided by sales revenue). She is bothered, however, by the decline in the company's cash balance during the year. One of the conditions of the existing bank loan is that the company maintain a minimum cash balance of $50,000.

Required

1. Prepare a statement of cash flows for 2008 using the direct method in the Operating Activities section.
2. On the basis of your statement in (1), draft a brief memo to the president to explain why cash decreased during such a profitable year. Include in your explanation any recommendations for improving the company's cash flow in future years.

LO6

Problem 12-4 Statement of Cash Flows—Indirect Method

Refer to all of the facts in Problem 12-3.

Required

1. Prepare a statement of cash flows for 2008 using the indirect method in the Operating Activities section.
2. On the basis of your statement in (1), draft a brief memo to the president to explain why cash decreased during such a profitable year. Include in your explanation any recommendations for improving the company's cash flow in future years.

LO8

Problem 12-5 Statement of Cash Flows Using a Work Sheet—Indirect Method (Appendix)

Refer to all of the facts in Problem 12-3.

Required

1. Using the format in the chapter's appendix, prepare a statement of cash flows work sheet.
2. Prepare a statement of cash flows for 2008 using the indirect method in the Operating Activities section.
3. On the basis of your statement in (2), draft a brief memo to the president to explain why cash decreased during such a profitable year. Include in your explanation any recommendations for improving the company's cash flow in future years.

LO5

Problem 12-6 Statement of Cash Flows—Direct Method

The income statement for Astro Inc. for 2008 is as follows:

	For the Year Ended December 31, 2008
Sales revenue	$ 500,000
Cost of goods sold	400,000
Gross profit	$ 100,000
Operating expenses	180,000
Loss before interest and taxes	$ (80,000)
Interest expense	20,000
Net loss	$(100,000)

Presented here are comparative balance sheets:

	December 31	
	2008	2007
Cash	$ 95,000	$ 80,000
Accounts receivable	50,000	75,000
Inventory	100,000	150,000
Prepayments	55,000	45,000
Total current assets	$300,000	$350,000

	December 31	
	2008	2007
Land	$ 475,000	$ 400,000
Plant and equipment	870,000	800,000
Accumulated depreciation	(370,000)	(300,000)
Total long-term assets	$ 975,000	$ 900,000
Total assets	$1,275,000	$1,250,000
Accounts payable	$ 125,000	$ 100,000
Other accrued liabilities	35,000	45,000
Interest payable	15,000	10,000
Total current liabilities	$ 175,000	$ 155,000
Long-term bank loan payable	$ 340,000	$ 250,000
Common stock	$ 450,000	$ 400,000
Retained earnings	310,000	445,000
Total stockholders' equity	$ 760,000	$ 845,000
Total liabilities and stockholders' equity	$1,275,000	$1,250,000

Other information is as follows:

a. Dividends of $35,000 were declared and paid during the year.
b. Operating expenses include $70,000 of depreciation.
c. Land and plant and equipment were acquired for cash, and additional stock was issued for cash. Cash also was received from additional bank loans.

The president has asked you some questions about the year's results. He is disturbed with the $100,000 net loss for the year. He notes, however, that the cash position at the end of the year is improved. He is confused about what appear to be conflicting signals: "How could we have possibly added to our bank accounts during such a terrible year of operations?"

Required

1. Prepare a statement of cash flows for 2008 using the direct method in the Operating Activities section.
2. On the basis of your statement in (1), draft a brief memo to the president to explain why cash increased during such an unprofitable year. Include in your memo your recommendations for improving the company's bottom line.

LO6 **Problem 12-7** Statement of Cash Flows—Indirect Method

Refer to all of the facts in Problem 12-6.

Required

1. Prepare a statement of cash flows for 2008 using the indirect method in the Operating Activities section.
2. On the basis of your statement in (1), draft a brief memo to the president to explain why cash increased during such an unprofitable year. Include in your memo your recommendations for improving the company's bottom line.

LO8 **Problem 12-8** Statement of Cash Flows Using a Work Sheet—Indirect Method (Appendix)

Refer to all of the facts in Problem 12-6.

Required

1. Using the format in the chapter's appendix, prepare a statement of cash flows work sheet.
2. Prepare a statement of cash flows for 2008 using the indirect method in the Operating Activities section.
3. On the basis of your statement in (2), draft a brief memo to the president to explain why cash increased during such an unprofitable year. Include in your memo your recommendations for improving the company's bottom line.

LO6 **Problem 12-9** Year-End Balance Sheet and Statement of Cash Flows—Indirect Method

The balance sheet of Terrier Company at the end of 2007 is presented here, along with certain other information for 2008:

	December 31, 2007
Cash	$ 140,000
Accounts receivable	155,000
Total current assets	$ 295,000
Land	$ 300,000
Plant and equipment	500,000
Accumulated depreciation	(150,000)
Investments	100,000
Total long-term assets	$ 750,000
Total assets	$1,045,000
Current liabilities	$ 205,000
Bonds payable	$ 300,000
Common stock	$ 400,000
Retained earnings	140,000
Total stockholders' equity	$ 540,000
Total liabilities and stockholders' equity	$1,045,000

Other information is as follows:

a. Net income for 2008 was $70,000.
b. Included in operating expenses was $20,000 in depreciation.
c. Cash dividends of $25,000 were declared and paid.
d. An additional $150,000 of bonds was issued for cash.
e. Common stock of $50,000 was purchased for cash and retired.
f. Cash purchases of plant and equipment during the year were $200,000.
g. An additional $100,000 of bonds was issued in exchange for land.
h. During the year, sales exceeded cash collections on account by $10,000. All sales are on account.
i. The amount of current liabilities remained unchanged during the year.

Required

1. Prepare a statement of cash flows for 2008 using the indirect method in the Operating Activities section. Include a supplemental schedule for noncash activities.
2. Prepare a balance sheet at December 31, 2008.
3. Provide a possible explanation as to why Terrier decided to issue additional bonds for cash during 2008.

LO8 **Problem 12-10** Statement of Cash Flows Using a Work Sheet—Indirect Method (Appendix)

Refer to all of the facts in Problem 12-9.

Required

1. Prepare a balance sheet at December 31, 2008.
2. Using the format in the chapter's appendix, prepare a statement of cash flows work sheet.
3. Prepare a statement of cash flows for 2008 using the indirect method in the Operating Activities section.
4. Provide a possible explanation as to why Terrier decided to issue additional bonds for cash during 2008.

MULTICONCEPT PROBLEMS

LO4,5 **Problem 12-11** Statement of Cash Flows—Direct Method

Glendive Corp. is in the process of preparing its statement of cash flows for the year ended June 30, 2008. An income statement for the year and comparative balance sheets are as follows:

	For the Year Ended June 30, 2008
Sales revenue	$550,000
Cost of goods sold	350,000
Gross profit	$200,000
General and administrative expenses	$ 55,000
Depreciation expense	75,000
Loss on sale of plant assets	5,000
Total expenses and losses	$135,000
Income before interest and taxes	$ 65,000
Interest expense	15,000
Income before taxes	$ 50,000
Income tax expense	17,000
Net income	$ 33,000

	June 30	
	2008	**2007**
Cash	$ 31,000	$ 40,000
Accounts receivable	90,000	75,000
Inventory	80,000	95,000
Prepaid rent	12,000	16,000
Total current assets	$213,000	$226,000
Land	$250,000	$170,000
Plant and equipment	750,000	600,000
Accumulated depreciation	(310,000)	(250,000)
Total long-term assets	$690,000	$520,000
Total assets	$903,000	$746,000
Accounts payable	$155,000	$148,000
Other accrued liabilities	32,000	26,000
Income taxes payable	8,000	10,000
Total current liabilities	$195,000	$184,000
Long-term bank loan payable	$100,000	$130,000
Common stock	$350,000	$200,000
Retained earnings	258,000	232,000
Total stockholders' equity	$608,000	$432,000
Total liabilities and stockholders' equity	$903,000	$746,000

Dividends of $7,000 were declared and paid during the year. New plant assets were purchased during the year for $195,000 in cash. Also, land was purchased for cash. Plant assets were sold during the year for $25,000 in cash. The original cost of the assets sold was $45,000, and their book value was $30,000. Additional stock was issued for cash, and a portion of the bank loan was repaid.

Required

1. Prepare a statement of cash flows for 2008 using the direct method in the Operating Activities section.
2. Evaluate the following statement: Whether a company uses the direct or indirect method to report cash flows from operations is irrelevant because the amount of cash flow from operating activities is the same regardless of which method is used.

LO4,6

Problem 12-12 Statement of Cash Flows—Indirect Method

Refer to all of the facts in Problem 12-11.

Required

1. Prepare a statement of cash flows for 2008 using the indirect method in the Operating Activities section.
2. Evaluate the following statement: Whether a company uses the direct or indirect method to report cash flows from operations is irrelevant because the amount of cash flow from operating activities is the same regardless of which method is used.

LO2,5

Problem 12-13 Statement of Cash Flows—Direct Method

Lang Company has not yet prepared a formal statement of cash flows for 2008. Following are comparative balance sheets as of December 31, 2008 and 2007, and a statement of income and retained earnings for the year ended December 31, 2008:

Lang Company
Balance Sheet
December 31

(thousands omitted)

Assets	**2008**	**2007**
Current assets:		
Cash	$ 60	$ 100
U.S. Treasury bills (six-month)	–0–	50
Accounts receivable	610	500
Inventory	720	600
Total current assets	$1,390	$1,250
Long-term assets:		
Land	$ 80	$ 70
Buildings and equipment	710	600
Accumulated depreciation	(180)	(120)
Patents (less amortization)	105	130
Total long-term assets	$ 715	$ 680
Total assets	$2,105	$1,930

Liabilities and Owners' Equity	**2008**	**2007**
Current liabilities:		
Accounts payable	$ 360	$ 300
Taxes payable	25	20
Notes payable	400	400
Total current liabilities	$ 785	$ 720
Term notes payable—due 2012	200	200
Total liabilities	$ 985	$ 920
Owners' equity:		
Common stock outstanding	$ 830	$ 700
Retained earnings	290	310
Total owners' equity	$1,120	$1,010
Total liabilities and owners' equity	$2,105	$1,930

(continued)

Lang Company
Statement of Income and Retained Earnings
For the Year Ended December 31, 2008

(thousands omitted)

Sales		$2,408
Less expenses and interest:		
Cost of goods sold	$1,100	
Salaries and benefits	850	
Heat, light, and power	75	
Depreciation	60	
Property taxes	18	
Patent amortization	25	
Miscellaneous expense	10	
Interest	55	2,193
Net income before income taxes		$ 215
Income taxes		105
Net income		$ 110
Retained earnings—January 1, 2008		310
		$ 420
Stock dividend distributed		130
Retained earnings—December 31, 2008		$ 290

Required

1. For purposes of a statement of cash flows, are the U.S. Treasury bills cash equivalents? If not, how should they be classified? Explain your answers.
2. Prepare a statement of cash flows for 2008 using the direct method in the Operating Activities section. (CMA adapted)

ALTERNATE PROBLEMS

LO6

Problem 12-1A Statement of Cash Flows—Indirect Method

The following balances are available for Madison Company:

	December 31	
	2008	2007
Cash	$ 12,000	$ 10,000
Accounts receivable	10,000	12,000
Inventory	8,000	7,000
Prepaid rent	1,200	1,000
Land	75,000	75,000
Plant and equipment	200,000	150,000
Accumulated depreciation	(75,000)	(25,000)
Totals	$231,200	$230,000
Accounts payable	$ 15,000	$ 15,000
Income taxes payable	2,500	2,000
Short-term notes payable	20,000	22,500
Bonds payable	75,000	50,000
Common stock	100,000	100,000
Retained earnings	18,700	40,500
Totals	$231,200	$230,000

Bonds were issued during 2008 at face value, and plant and equipment were acquired for cash. Depreciation expense for the year was $50,000. A net loss of $21,800 was reported.

Required

1. Prepare a statement of cash flows for 2008 using the indirect method in the Operating Activities section.
2. Briefly explain how Madison was able to increase its cash balance during a year in which it incurred a net loss.

LO8

Problem 12-2A Statement of Cash Flows Using a Work Sheet—Indirect Method (Appendix)

Refer to all of the facts in Problem 12-1A.

Required

1. Using the format in the chapter's appendix, prepare a statement of cash flows work sheet.
2. Prepare a statement of cash flows for 2008 using the indirect method in the Operating Activities section.
3. Briefly explain how Madison was able to increase its cash balance during a year in which it incurred a net loss.

LO5

Problem 12-3A Statement of Cash Flows—Direct Method

Wabash Corp. just completed another successful year, as indicated by the following income statement:

	For the Year Ended December 31, 2008
Sales revenue	$2,460,000
Cost of goods sold	1,400,000
Gross profit	$1,060,000
Operating expenses	460,000
Income before interest and taxes	$ 600,000
Interest expense	100,000
Income before taxes	$ 500,000
Income tax expense	150,000
Net income	$ 350,000

Presented here are comparative balance sheets:

	December 31	
	2008	2007
Cash	$ 140,000	$ 210,000
Accounts receivable	60,000	145,000
Inventory	200,000	180,000
Prepayments	15,000	25,000
Total current assets	$ 415,000	$ 560,000
Land	$ 600,000	$ 700,000
Plant and equipment	850,000	600,000
Accumulated depreciation	(225,000)	(200,000)
Total long-term assets	$1,225,000	$1,100,000
Total assets	$1,640,000	$1,660,000
Accounts payable	$ 140,000	$ 120,000
Other accrued liabilities	50,000	55,000
Income taxes payable	80,000	115,000
Total current liabilities	$ 270,000	$ 290,000
Long-term bank loan payable	$ 200,000	$ 250,000
Common stock	$ 450,000	$ 400,000
Retained earnings	720,000	720,000
Total stockholders' equity	$1,170,000	$1,120,000
Total liabilities and stockholders' equity	$1,640,000	$1,660,000

Other information is as follows:

a. Dividends of $350,000 were declared and paid during the year.
b. Operating expenses include $25,000 of depreciation.
c. Land was sold for its book value, and new plant and equipment was acquired for cash.
d. Part of the bank loan was repaid, and additional common stock was issued for cash.

The president has asked you some questions about the year's results. She is very impressed with the profit margin of 14% (net income divided by sales revenue). She is bothered, however, by the decline in the company's cash balance during the year. One of the conditions of the existing bank loan is that the company maintain a minimum cash balance of $100,000.

Required

1. Prepare a statement of cash flows for 2008 using the direct method in the Operating Activities section.
2. On the basis of your statement in (1), draft a brief memo to the president to explain why cash decreased during such a profitable year. Include in your explanation any recommendations for improving the company's cash flow in future years.

LO6

Problem 12-4A Statement of Cash Flows—Indirect Method

Refer to all of the facts in Problem 12-3A.

Required

1. Prepare a statement of cash flows for 2008 using the indirect method in the Operating Activities section.
2. On the basis of your statement in (1), draft a brief memo to the president to explain why cash decreased during such a profitable year. Include in your explanation any recommendations for improving the company's cash flow in future years.

LO8

Problem 12-5A Statement of Cash Flows Using a Work Sheet—Indirect Method (Appendix)

Refer to all of the facts in Problem 12-3A.

Required

1. Using the format in the chapter's appendix, prepare a statement of cash flows work sheet.
2. Prepare a statement of cash flows for 2008 using the indirect method in the Operating Activities section.
3. On the basis of your statement in (2), draft a brief memo to the president to explain why cash decreased during such a profitable year. Include in your explanation any recommendations for improving the company's cash flow in future years.

LO5

Problem 12-6A Statement of Cash Flows—Direct Method

The income statement for Pluto Inc. for 2008 is as follows:

	For the Year Ended December 31, 2008
Sales revenue	$350,000
Cost of goods sold	150,000
Gross profit	$200,000
Operating expenses	250,000
Loss before interest and taxes	$(50,000)
Interest expense	10,000
Net loss	$(60,000)

Presented here are comparative balance sheets:

	December 31	
	2008	2007
Cash	$ 25,000	$ 10,000
Accounts receivable	30,000	80,000
Inventory	100,000	100,000
Prepayments	36,000	35,000
Total current assets	$191,000	$225,000
Land	$300,000	$200,000
Plant and equipment	500,000	250,000
Accumulated depreciation	(90,000)	(50,000)
Total long-term assets	$710,000	$400,000
Total assets	$901,000	$625,000
Accounts payable	$ 50,000	$ 10,000
Other accrued liabilities	40,000	20,000
Interest payable	22,000	12,000
Total current liabilities	$112,000	$ 42,000
Long-term bank loan payable	$450,000	$100,000
Common stock	$300,000	$300,000
Retained earnings	39,000	183,000
Total stockholders' equity	$339,000	$483,000
Total liabilities and stockholders' equity	$901,000	$625,000

Other information is as follows:

a. Dividends of $84,000 were declared and paid during the year.
b. Operating expenses include $40,000 of depreciation.
c. Land and plant and equipment were acquired for cash. Cash was received from additional bank loans.

The president has asked you some questions about the year's results. He is disturbed with the net loss of $60,000 for the year. He notes, however, that the cash position at the end of the year is improved. He is confused about what appear to be conflicting signals: "How could we have possibly added to our bank accounts during such a terrible year of operations?"

Required

1. Prepare a statement of cash flows for 2008 using the direct method in the Operating Activities section.
2. On the basis of your statement in (1), draft a brief memo to the president to explain why cash increased during such an unprofitable year. Include in your memo your recommendations for improving the company's bottom line.

LO6

Problem 12-7A Statement of Cash Flows—Indirect Method

Refer to all of the facts in Problem 12-6A.

Required

1. Prepare a statement of cash flows for 2008 using the indirect method in the Operating Activities section.
2. On the basis of your statement in (1), draft a brief memo to the president to explain why cash increased during such an unprofitable year. Include in your memo your recommendations for improving the company's bottom line.

LO8

Problem 12-8A Statement of Cash Flows Using a Work Sheet—Indirect Method (Appendix)

Refer to all of the facts in Problem 12-6A.

Required

1. Using the format in the chapter's appendix, prepare a statement of cash flows work sheet.
2. Prepare a statement of cash flows for 2008 using the indirect method in the Operating Activities section.
3. On the basis of your statement in (2), draft a brief memo to the president to explain why cash increased during such an unprofitable year. Include in your memo your recommendations for improving the company's bottom line.

LO6

Problem 12-9A Year-End Balance Sheet and Statement of Cash Flows—Indirect Method

The balance sheet of Poodle Company at the end of 2007 is presented here, along with certain other information for 2008:

	December 31, 2007
Cash	$ 155,000
Accounts receivable	140,000
Total current assets	$ 295,000
Land	$ 100,000
Plant and equipment	700,000
Accumulated depreciation	(175,000)
Investments	125,000
Total long-term assets	$ 750,000
Total assets	$1,045,000
Current liabilities	$ 325,000
Bonds payable	$ 100,000
Common stock	$ 500,000
Retained earnings	120,000
Total stockholders' equity	$ 620,000
Total liabilities and stockholders' equity	$1,045,000

Other information is as follows:

a. Net income for 2008 was $50,000.
b. Included in operating expenses was $25,000 in depreciation.
c. Cash dividends of $40,000 were declared and paid.
d. An additional $50,000 of common stock was issued for cash.
e. Bonds payable of $100,000 were purchased for cash and retired at no gain or loss.
f. Cash purchases of plant and equipment during the year were $60,000.
g. An additional $200,000 of land was acquired in exchange for a long-term note payable.
h. During the year, sales exceeded cash collections on account by $15,000. All sales are on account.
i. The amount of current liabilities decreased by $20,000 during the year.

Required

1. Prepare a statement of cash flows for 2008 using the indirect method in the Operating Activities section. Include a supplemental schedule for noncash activities.
2. Prepare a balance sheet at December 31, 2008.
3. What primary uses did Poodle make of the cash it generated from operating activities?

LO8

Problem 12-10A Statement of Cash Flows Using a Work Sheet—Indirect Method (Appendix)

Refer to all of the facts in Problem 12-9A.

Required

1. Prepare a balance sheet at December 31, 2008.
2. Using the format in the chapter's appendix, prepare a statement of cash flows work sheet.
3. Prepare a statement of cash flows for 2008 using the indirect method in the Operating Activities section.
4. Provide a possible explanation as to why Poodle decided to purchase and retire bonds during 2008.

ALTERNATE MULTICONCEPT PROBLEMS

LO4,5

Problem 12-11A Statement of Cash Flows—Direct Method

Bannack Corp. is in the process of preparing its statement of cash flows for the year ended June 30, 2008. An income statement for the year and comparative balance sheets are as follows:

	For the Year Ended June 30, 2008
Sales revenue	$400,000
Cost of goods sold	240,000
Gross profit	$160,000
General and administrative expenses	$ 40,000
Depreciation expense	80,000
Loss on sale of plant assets	10,000
Total expenses and losses	$130,000
Income before interest and taxes	$ 30,000
Interest expense	15,000
Income before taxes	$ 15,000
Income tax expense	5,000
Net income	$ 10,000

	June 30	
	2008	2007
Cash	$ 25,000	$ 40,000
Accounts receivable	80,000	69,000
Inventory	75,000	50,000
Prepaid rent	2,000	18,000
Total current assets	$182,000	$177,000

(continued)

Land	$ 60,000	$150,000
Plant and equipment	575,000	500,000
Accumulated depreciation	(310,000)	(250,000)
Total long-term assets	$325,000	$400,000
Total assets	$507,000	$577,000
Accounts payable	$145,000	$140,000
Other accrued liabilities	50,000	45,000
Income taxes payable	5,000	15,000
Total current liabilities	$200,000	$200,000
Long-term bank loan payable	$ 75,000	$150,000
Common stock	$100,000	$100,000
Retained earnings	132,000	127,000
Total stockholders' equity	$232,000	$227,000
Total liabilities and stockholders' equity	$507,000	$577,000

Dividends of $5,000 were declared and paid during the year. New plant assets were purchased during the year for $125,000 in cash. Also, land was sold for cash at its book value. Plant assets were sold during the year for $20,000 in cash. The original cost of the assets sold was $50,000, and their book value was $30,000. A portion of the bank loan was repaid.

Required

1. Prepare a statement of cash flows for 2008 using the direct method in the Operating Activities section.
2. Evaluate the following statement: Whether a company uses the direct or indirect method to report cash flows from operations is irrelevant because the amount of cash flow from operating activities is the same regardless of which method is used.

LO4,6

Problem 12-12A Statement of Cash Flows—Indirect Method

Refer to all of the facts in Problem 12-11A.

Required

1. Prepare a statement of cash flows for 2008 using the indirect method in the Operating Activities section.
2. Evaluate the following statement: Whether a company uses the direct or indirect method to report cash flows from operations is irrelevant because the amount of cash flow from operating activities is the same regardless of which method is used.

LO2,5

Problem 12-13A Statement of Cash Flows—Direct Method

Shepard Company has not yet prepared a formal statement of cash flows for 2008. Following are comparative balance sheets as of December 31, 2008 and 2007, and a statement of income and retained earnings for the year ended December 31, 2008:

Shepard Company
Balance Sheet
December 31

(thousands omitted)

Assets	2008	2007
Current assets:		
Cash	$ 50	$ 75
U.S. Treasury bills (six-month)	25	0
Accounts receivable	125	200
Inventory	525	500
Total current assets	$ 725	$ 775
Long-term assets:		
Land	$ 100	$ 80
Buildings and equipment	510	450
Accumulated depreciation	(190)	(150)
Patents (less amortization)	90	110
Total long-term assets	$ 510	$ 490
Total assets	$1,235	$1,265

(continued)

Shepard Company
Balance Sheet
December 31

(thousands omitted)

Liabilities and Owners' Equity	2008	2007
Current liabilities:		
Accounts payable	$ 370	$ 330
Taxes payable	10	20
Notes payable	300	400
Total current liabilities	$ 680	$ 750
Term notes payable—due 2012	200	200
Total liabilities	$ 880	$ 950
Owners' equity:		
Common stock outstanding	$ 220	$ 200
Retained earnings	135	115
Total owners' equity	$ 355	$ 315
Total liabilities and owners' equity	$1,235	$1,265

Shepard Company
Statement of Income and Retained Earnings
for the Year Ended December 31, 2008

(thousands omitted)

Sales		$1,416
Less expenses and interest:		
Cost of goods sold	$990	
Salaries and benefits	195	
Heat, light, and power	70	
Depreciation	40	
Property taxes	2	
Patent amortization	20	
Miscellaneous expense	2	
Interest	45	1,364
Net income before income taxes		$ 52
Income taxes		12
Net income		$ 40
Retained earnings—January 1, 2008		115
		$ 155
Stock dividend distributed		20
Retained earnings—December 31, 2008		$ 135

Required

1. For purposes of a statement of cash flows, are the U.S. Treasury bills cash equivalents? If not, how should they be classified? Explain your answers.
2. Prepare a statement of cash flows for 2008, using the direct method in the Operating Activities section. (CMA adapted)

DECISION CASES

LO3,4

Decision Case 12-1 Comparing Two Companies in the Same Industry: Kellogg's and General Mills

Refer to the statement of cash flows for both **Kellogg's** and **General Mills** for the most recent year and any other pertinent information reprinted at the back of this book.

Required

1. Which method, direct or indirect, does each company use in preparing the Operating Activities section of their statements of cash flows? Explain.

2. By what amount did net cash provided by operating activities increase or decrease from the prior year for each company? What is the largest adjustment to reconcile net income to net cash provided by operating activities for each company?
3. What amount did each company spend during the most recent year to acquire property and equipment? How does this amount compare with the amount that each company spent in the prior year?
4. What is the primary source of financing for each of the two companies? Did either or both companies buy back some of their own shares during the most recent year? If so, what might be some reasons for doing this?

LO7

Decision Case 12-2 Comparing Two Companies in the Same Industry: Kellogg's and General Mills Cash Flow Adequacy

Refer to the statement of cash flows for both Kellogg's and General Mills for the most recent year and any other pertinent information reprinted at the back of this book.

Required

1. Compute each company's cash flow adequacy ratio for the most recent year.
2. What do the ratios computed in (1) tell you about each company's cash flow adequacy? Which company's ratio is higher?

LO2,3

Decision Case 12-3 Reading and Interpreting Best Buy's Statement of Cash Flows

Refer to Best Buy's statement of cash flows shown in the chapter opener and answer the following questions for the most recent year.

Required

1. Which method, direct or indirect, does Best Buy use in preparing the Operating Activities section of its statement of cash flows? Explain how you know which method is being used.
2. By what amount does net cash provided by operating activities from continuing operations differ from net earnings? What are the two largest adjustments to reconcile the two numbers? Explain the nature of these adjustments. Why is one added and the other deducted?
3. What is the largest source of cash in the Investing Activities section of the statement? What is the largest use in this section? Explain how these two items are related.
4. What is the largest use of cash in the Financing Activities section of the statement? Explain the nature of this outflow. Why might the company engage in this type of activity?

MAKING FINANCIAL DECISIONS

LO1,5

Decision Case 12-4 Dividend Decision and the Statement of Cash Flows—Direct Method

Bailey Corp. just completed the most profitable year in its 25-year history. Reported earnings of \$1,020,000 on sales of \$8,000,000 resulted in a very healthy profit margin of 12.75%. Each year before releasing the financial statements, the board of directors meets to decide on the amount of dividends to declare for the year. For each of the past nine years, the company has declared a dividend of \$1 per share of common stock, which has been paid on January 15 of the following year.

Presented here are the income statement for the year and the comparative balance sheets as of the end of the last two years.

	For the Year Ended December 31, 2008
Sales revenue	\$8,000,000
Cost of goods sold	4,500,000
Gross profit	\$3,500,000
Operating expenses	1,450,000
Income before interest and taxes	\$2,050,000
Interest expense	350,000
Income before taxes	\$1,700,000
Income tax expense (40%)	680,000
Net income	\$1,020,000

(continued)

HOMEWORK

	December 31	
	2008	2007
Cash	$ 480,000	$ 450,000
Accounts receivable	250,000	200,000
Inventory	750,000	600,000
Prepayments	60,000	75,000
Total current assets	$1,540,000	$1,325,000
Land	$3,255,000	$2,200,000
Plant and equipment	4,200,000	2,500,000
Accumulated depreciation	(1,250,000)	(1,000,000)
Long-term investments	500,000	900,000
Patents	650,000	750,000
Total long-term assets	$7,355,000	$5,350,000
Total assets	$8,895,000	$6,675,000
Accounts payable	$ 350,000	$ 280,000
Other accrued liabilities	285,000	225,000
Income taxes payable	170,000	100,000
Dividends payable	0	200,000
Notes payable due within next year	200,000	0
Total current liabilities	$1,005,000	$ 805,000
Long-term notes payable	$ 300,000	$ 500,000
Bonds payable	2,200,000	1,500,000
Total long-term liabilities	$2,500,000	$2,000,000
Common stock, $10 par	$2,500,000	$2,000,000
Retained earnings	2,890,000	1,870,000
Total stockholders' equity	$5,390,000	$3,870,000
Total liabilities and stockholders' equity	$8,895,000	$6,675,000

Additional information follows:

a. All sales are on account, as are all purchases.
b. Land was purchased through the issuance of bonds. Additional land (beyond the amount purchased through the issuance of bonds) was purchased for cash.
c. New plant and equipment were acquired during the year for cash. No plant assets were retired during the year. Depreciation expense is included in operating expenses.
d. Long-term investments were sold for cash during the year.
e. No new patents were acquired, and none were disposed of during the year. Amortization expense is included in operating expenses.
f. Notes payable due within the next year represents the amount reclassified from long-term to short-term.
g. Fifty thousand shares of common stock were issued during the year at par value.

As Bailey's controller, you have been asked to recommend to the board whether to declare a dividend this year and, if so, whether the precedent of paying a $1 per share dividend can be maintained. The president is eager to keep the dividend at $1 in view of the successful year just completed. He is also concerned, however, about the effect of a dividend on the company's cash position. He is particularly concerned about the large amount of notes payable that comes due next year. He further notes the aggressive growth pattern in recent years, as evidenced this year by large increases in land and plant and equipment.

Required

1. Using the format in Exhibit 12-14, convert the income statement from an accrual basis to a cash basis.
2. Prepare a statement of cash flows using the direct method in the Operating Activities section.
3. What do you recommend to the board of directors concerning the declaration of a cash dividend? Should the $1 per share dividend be declared? Should a smaller amount be declared? Should no dividend be declared? Support your answer with any necessary computations. From a cash flow perspective, include in your response your concerns about the following year.

LO1,6

Decision Case 12-5 Equipment Replacement Decision and Cash Flows from Operations

Conrad Company has been in operation for four years. The company is pleased with the continued improvement in net income but is concerned about a lack of cash available to replace existing equipment. Land, buildings, and equipment were purchased at the beginning of Year 1. No subsequent fixed asset purchases have been made, but the president believes that equipment will need to be replaced in the near future. The following information is available. (All amounts are in millions of dollars.)

	Year of Operation			
	Year 1	Year 2	Year 3	Year 4
Net income (loss)	$(10)	$(2)	$15	$20
Depreciation expense	30	25	15	14
Increase (decrease) in:				
Accounts receivable	32	5	12	20
Inventories	26	8	5	9
Prepayments	0	0	10	5
Accounts payable	15	3	(5)	(4)

Required

1. Compute the cash flow from operations for each of Conrad's first four years of operation.
2. Write a memo to the president explaining why the company is not generating sufficient cash from operations to pay for the replacement of equipment.

ETHICAL DECISION MAKING

LO1,6 **Decision Case 12-6** Loan Decision and the Statement of Cash Flows—Indirect Method

Mega Enterprises is in the process of negotiating an extension of its existing loan agreements with a major bank. The bank is particularly concerned with Mega's ability to generate sufficient cash flow from operating activities to meet the periodic principal and interest payments. In conjunction with the negotiations, the controller prepared the following statement of cash flows to present to the bank:

Mega Enterprises
Statement of Cash Flows
For the Year Ended December 31, 2008
(all amounts in millions of dollars)

Cash flows from operating activities	
Net income	$ 65
Adjustments to reconcile net income to net cash provided by operating activities:	
Depreciation and amortization	56
Increase in accounts receivable	(19)
Decrease in inventory	27
Decrease in accounts payable	(42)
Increase in other accrued liabilities	18
Net cash provided by operating activities	$ 105
Cash flows from investing activities	
Acquisitions of other businesses	$(234)
Acquisitions of plant and equipment	(125)
Sale of other businesses	300
Net cash used by investing activities	$ (59)
Cash flows from financing activities	
Additional borrowings	$ 150
Repayments of borrowings	(180)
Cash dividends paid	(50)
Net cash used by financing activities	$ (80)
Net decrease in cash	$ (34)
Cash balance, January 1, 2008	42
Cash balance, December 31, 2008	$ 8

During 2008, Mega sold one of its businesses in California. A gain of $150 million was included in 2008 income as the difference between the proceeds from the sale of $450 million and the book

HOMEWORK

value of the business of $300 million. The entry to record the sale is as follows (in millions of dollars):

Cash	450	
California Properties		300
Gain on Sale		150
To record sale of business.		

Balance Sheet							Income Statement	
ASSETS		=	LIABILITIES	+	STOCKHOLDERS' EQUITY	+	REVENUES − EXPENSES	
Cash	450						Gain on Sale	150
California Properties	(300)							

Required

1. Comment on the presentation of the sale of the California business on the statement of cash flows. Does the way in which the sale was reported violate GAAP? Regardless of whether it violates GAAP, does the way in which the transaction was reported on the statement result in a misstatement of the net decrease in cash for the period? Explain your answers.
2. Prepare a revised statement of cash flows for 2008 with the proper presentation of the sale of the California business.
3. Has the controller acted in an unethical manner in the way the sale was reported on the statement of cash flows? Explain your answer.

LO2,3

Decision Case 12-7 Cash Equivalents and the Statement of Cash Flows

In December 2008, Rangers Inc. invested $100,000 of idle cash in U.S. Treasury notes. The notes mature on October 1, 2009, at which time Rangers expects to redeem them at face value of $100,000. The treasurer believes that the notes should be classified as cash equivalents because of the plans to hold them to maturity and receive face value. He also wants to avoid presentation of the purchase as an investing activity because the company made sizable capital expenditures during the year. The treasurer realizes that the decision about classification of the Treasury notes rests with you as controller.

Required

1. According to GAAP, how should the investment in U.S. Treasury notes be classified for purposes of preparing a statement of cash flows for the year ended December 31, 2008? Explain your answer.
2. If the notes are classified as an operating rather than investing activity, is the information provided to outside readers free from bias? Explain.
3. As controller for Rangers, what would you do in this situation? What would you tell the treasurer?

SOLUTIONS TO KEY TERMS QUIZ

3	Statement of cash flows	7	Financing activities
4	Cash equivalent	6	Direct method
1	Operating activities	2	Indirect method
5	Investing activities		

ANSWERS TO POD REVIEW

LO1	1. c	2. b
LO2	1. d	2. c
LO3	1. d	2. c
LO4	1. b	2. a
LO5	1. c	2. d
LO6	1. c	2. c
LO7	1. c	2. d
LO8	1. a	2. c

CHAPTER

13

Financial Statement Analysis

Learning Outcomes

After studying this chapter, you should be able to:

LO1 Explain the various limitations and considerations in financial statement analysis.

LO2 Use comparative financial statements to analyze a company over time (horizontal analysis).

LO3 Use common-size financial statements to compare various financial statement items (vertical analysis).

LO4 Compute and use various ratios to assess liquidity.

LO5 Compute and use various ratios to assess solvency.

LO6 Compute and use various ratios to assess profitability.

LO7 Explain how to report on and analyze other income statement items (Appendix).

Study Links...

A Look at Previous Chapters
Chapter 2 introduced a few key financial ratios and explained how investors and creditors use them to better understand a company's financial statements. Many of the subsequent chapters introduced ratios relevant to the particular topic being discussed.

A Look at This Chapter
Ratio analysis is one important type of *analysis used to interpret financial statements*. This chapter expands the discussion of ratio analysis and introduces other valuable techniques used by investors, creditors, and analysts in making informed decisions. The chapter shows that ratios and other forms of analyses can provide additional insight beyond that available from merely reading the financial statements.

Wm. Wrigley Jr. Company

MAKING BUSINESS DECISIONS

Turn to the outside to grow the business. That was the decision the world's largest manufacturer of chewing and bubble gum made in 2005. Two of **Wrigley**'s brand names, Juicy Fruit® and Spearmint®, are among the most recognizable in the world and have heritages that go back more than 110 years. Wrigley did not stray too far from its core business in adding certain confectionary assets of **Kraft Foods** to its list of top performers. With the acquisition, Wrigley picked up brand names such as Altoids® and Life Savers®. One need look no further than the purchase price of $1.46 billion to know that Wrigley is serious about expanding its reach and capturing more of the world's market for confectionary products.

Undoubtedly, investors closely scrutinized Wrigley's financial statements after this major acquisition. Has the company founded in 1891 improved its already impressive track record? Sales and earnings have grown steadily, with both reaching record levels in 2006. Most companies (and their stockholders) would be envious of this solid performance indicated by Wrigley's Financial Highlights reproduced here. A quick calculation shows a profit margin of around 11% in 2006, the first full year after the acquisition of the new brands. Over one-half of those profits were returned to stockholders in the form of dividends. Few companies are able to report a return on equity of the 23% that Wrigley achieved in 2006.

What are the tools that investors use to measure the success of Wrigley and other companies that they follow? Earlier chapters looked at various ratios; this last chapter examines additional tools available to judge the financial health of a company. This chapter answers these questions:

© Gary Gardiner/Bloomberg

- What tools can be used to assess the performance of a company over time? (See pp. 658–664.)
- How can common-size financial statements be used to assess a company's performance in any one period? (See pp. 664–666.)
- What ratios are available to judge a company's liquidity, solvency, and profitability? (See pp. 668–681.)

(continued)

Wm. Wrigley Jr. Company
Financial Highlights

Over one-half of earnings paid out in dividends

Profit margin over 11%

	2006	2005
Net Earnings	$ 529,377	$ 517,252
Diluted EPS	$ 1.90	$ 1.83
Sales	$4,686,011	$4,159,306
Dividends Paid	$ 276,021	$ 241,669
Additions to Property, Plant, and Equipment	$ 327,758	$ 281,769
Stockholders' Equity	$2,388,092	$2,214,422
Return on Average Equity	23.0%	23.5%
Stockholders of Record	40,986	41,105
Dilutive Shares Outstanding	278,399	282,284

In thousands of dollars and shares, except per share amounts and stockholders of record
For additional historical financial data see page 32.

Sources: Wm. Wrigley Jr. Co. Web site and 2006 annual report.

Precautions in Statement Analysis

LO1 Explain the various limitations and considerations in financial statement analysis.

Various groups have different purposes for analyzing a company's financial statements. For example, a banker is interested primarily in the likelihood that a loan will be repaid. Certain ratios indicate the ability to repay principal and interest. A stockholder, on the other hand, is concerned with a fair return on the amount invested in the company. Again, certain ratios are helpful in assessing the return to the stockholder. The managers of a business also are interested in the tools of financial statement analysis because various outside groups judge managers by using certain key ratios. Fortunately, most financial statements provide information about financial performance. Publicly held corporations are required to include in their annual reports a section that reviews the past year, with management's comments on its performance as measured by selected ratios and other forms of analysis.

Before turning to various techniques commonly used in the financial analysis of a company, it is important that you understand some of the limitations and other considerations in statement analysis.

WATCH FOR ALTERNATIVE ACCOUNTING PRINCIPLES

Every set of financial statements is based on various assumptions. For example, a cost-flow method must be assumed in valuing inventory and recognizing cost of goods sold. The accountant chooses FIFO, LIFO, or one of the other acceptable methods. The analyst or other user finds this type of information in the notes to the financial statements. The selection of a particular inventory valuation method has a significant effect on certain key ratios. Recognition of the acceptable alternatives is especially important in comparing two or more companies. Changes in accounting methods, such as a change in the depreciation method, also make comparing results for a given company over time more difficult. Again, the reader must turn to the notes for information regarding these changes.

TAKE CARE WHEN MAKING COMPARISONS

Users of financial statements often place too much emphasis on summary indicators and key ratios such as the current ratio and the earnings per share amount. No single ratio is capable of telling the user everything there is to know about a particular company. The calculation of various ratios for a company is only a starting point. One technique discussed is the comparison of ratios for different periods of time. Has the ratio gone up or down from last year? What is the percentage of increase or decrease in the ratio over the last five years? Recognizing trends in ratios is important when analyzing any company.

The potential investor also must recognize the need to compare one company with others in the same industry. For example, a particular measure of performance may cause an investor to conclude that the company is not operating efficiently. Comparison with an industry standard, however, might indicate that the ratio is normal for companies in that industry. Various organizations publish summaries of selected ratios for a sample of companies in the United States. The ratios are usually organized by industry.

Although industry comparisons are useful, caution is necessary in interpreting the results of such analyses. Few companies in today's economy operate in a single industry. Exceptions exist, but most companies cross the boundaries of a single industry. *Conglomerates,* companies operating in more than one industry, present a special challenge to the analyst. Also keep in mind the point made earlier about alternative accounting methods. It is not unusual to find companies in the same industry using different inventory valuation techniques or depreciation methods.

Finally, many corporate income statements contain nonoperating items such as extraordinary items and gains and losses from discontinued operations. When these items exist, the reader must exercise extra caution in making comparisons. To assess the future prospects of a group of companies, you may want to compare income statements *before* taking into account the effects these items have on income.

UNDERSTAND THE POSSIBLE EFFECTS OF INFLATION

Inflation, or an increase in the level of prices, is another important consideration in analyzing financial statements. The statements, to be used by outsiders, are based on historical costs and are not adjusted for the effects of increasing prices. For example, consider the following trend in a company's sales for the past three years:

	2008	2007	2006
Net sales	$121,000	$110,000	$100,000

As measured by the actual dollars of sales, sales have increased by 10% each year. Caution is necessary in concluding that the company is better off in each succeeding year because of the increase in sales *dollars.* Assume, for example, that 2006 sales of $100,000 are the result of selling 100,000 units at $1 each. Are 2007 sales of $110,000 the result of selling 110,000 units at $1 each or of selling 100,000 units at $1.10 each? Although, on the surface, knowing which result accounts for the sales increase may seem unimportant, the answer can have significant ramifications. If the company found it necessary to increase selling price to $1.10 in the face of increasing costs, it may be no better off than it was in 2006 in terms of gross profit. On the other hand, if the company is able to increase sales revenue by 10% based primarily on growth in unit sales, its performance would be considered stronger than if the increase were due merely to a price increase. The point to be made is one of caution: published financial statements are stated in historical costs and therefore have not been adjusted for the effects of inflation.

Fortunately, inflation has been relatively subdued in the past several years. During the late 1970s, the FASB actually required a separate note in the financial statements to calculate the effects of inflation. The requirement was abandoned in the mid-1980s when inflation had subsided and the profession decided that the cost of providing inflation-adjusted information exceeded the benefits to the users.

POD REVIEW 13.1

LO1 *Explain the various limitations and considerations in financial statement analysis.*

- Financial statement analysis can be a powerful and useful tool in assessing various characteristics of a firm's operations, but the following factors should be considered when conducting this analysis:
  - Alternative accounting principles may sometimes be used.
  - Comparisons must consider inflation, trends over time, and industry norms, among many other variables that influence a business.
  - Ratios from financial statements tell only part of the story about a firm's performance.

QUESTIONS

1. *Which of the following should be taken into account when a company's performance is analyzed?*
   a. the effects of inflation
   b. trends over time
   c. industry norms
   d. all of the above should be considered

2. *Two companies in the same industry use different methods to value inventory; one uses FIFO and the other uses LIFO. Using different methods to value inventory*
   a. makes comparisons easier.
   b. makes it impossible to compare two companies.
   c. makes comparisons more difficult but not impossible.
   d. will never happen because all companies in a particular industry must use the same method.

Analysis of Comparative and Common-Size Statements

LO2 Use comparative financial statements to analyze a company over time (horizontal analysis).

We are now ready to analyze a set of financial statements. We will begin by looking at the comparative statements of a company for a two-year period. The analysis of the statements over a series of years is often called **horizontal analysis**. We will then see how the statements can be recast in what are referred to as *common-size statements*. The analysis of common-size statements is called **vertical analysis**. Finally, we will consider the use of a variety of ratios to analyze a company.

Horizontal analysis
A comparison of financial statement items over a period of time.

HORIZONTAL ANALYSIS

Comparative balance sheets for a hypothetical entity, Henderson Company, are presented in Exhibit 13-1. The increase or decrease in each of the major accounts on the balance sheet is shown in absolute dollars and as a percentage. The base year for

EXHIBIT 13-1 **Comparative Balance Sheets—Horizontal Analysis**

Read from earlier year to later year. Usually, this is from right to left.

Henderson Company
Comparative Balance Sheets
December 31, 2008 and 2007
(all amounts In thousands of dollars)

	December 31		Increase (Decrease)	
	2008	2007	Dollars	Percent
Cash	**$ 320**	**$ 1,350**	**$ (1,030)**	❶ **(76)%**
Accounts receivable	5,500	4,500	1,000	22
Inventory	**4,750**	**2,750**	**2,000**	❷ **73**
Prepaid insurance	150	200	(50)	(25)
Total current assets	$10,720	$ 8,800	$ 1,920	22
Land	$ 2,000	$ 2,000	$ –0–	–0–
Buildings and equipment	6,000	4,500	1,500	33
Accumulated depreciation	(1,850)	(1,500)	(350)	(23)
Total long-term assets	$ 6,150	$ 5,000	$ 1,150	23
Total assets	$16,870	$13,800	$ 3,070	22
Accounts payable	**$ 4,250**	**$ 2,500**	**$ 1,750**	❸ **70**
Taxes payable	2,300	2,100	200	10
Notes payable	600	800	(200)	(25)
Current portion of bonds	100	100	–0–	–0–
Total current liabilities	$ 7,250	$ 5,500	$ 1,750	32
Bonds payable	700	800	(100)	(13)
Total liabilities	$ 7,950	$ 6,300	$ 1,650	26
Preferred stock, $5 par	$ 500	$ 500	$ –0–	–0–
Common stock, $1 par	1,000	1,000	–0–	–0–
Retained earnings	7,420	6,000	1,420	24
Total stockholders' equity	$ 8,920	$ 7,500	$ 1,420	19
Total liabilities and stockholders' equity	$16,870	$13,800	$ 3,070	22

NOTE: Referenced amounts are boldfaced for convenience.

The base year is normally on the right.

Dollar change from year to year.

Percentage change from one year to the next year.

In **horizontal analysis**, read right to left to compare one year's results with the next as a dollar amount of change and as a percentage of change from year to year.

computing the percentage increase or decrease in each account is the first year, 2007, and is normally shown on the right side. By reading across from right to left (thus the term *horizontal analysis*), the analyst can quickly spot any unusual changes in accounts from the previous year. Three accounts stand out: ❶ Cash decreased by 76%, ❷ Inventory increased by 73%, and ❸ Accounts Payable increased by 70%. (These lines are also boldfaced for convenience.) Individually, each of these large changes is a red flag. Taken together these changes send the financial statement user the warning that the business may be deteriorating. Each of these large changes should be investigated further.

Vertical analysis
A comparison of various financial statement items within a single period with the use of common-size statements.

Exhibit 13-2 shows comparative statements of income and retained earnings for Henderson for 2008 and 2007. At first glance, ❶ the 20% increase in sales to $24 million appears promising; but management was not able to limit the increase in ❷ cost of goods sold or ❸ selling, general, and administrative expense to 20%. The analysis indicates that cost of goods sold increased by 29% and selling, general, and administrative expense increased by 50%. The increases in these two expenses more than offset the increase in sales and resulted in a ❹ decrease in operating income of 25%.

EXHIBIT 13-2 Comparative Statements of Income and Retained Earnings—Horizontal Analysis

Henderson Company
Comparative Statements of Income and Retained Earnings
For the Years Ended December 31, 2008 and 2007
(all amounts in thousands of dollars)

	December 31		Increase (Decrease)	
	2008	2007	Dollars	Percent
Net sales	**$24,000**	**$20,000**	**$ 4,000**	❶ **20%**
Cost of goods sold	**18,000**	**14,000**	**4,000**	❷ **29**
Gross profit	$ 6,000	$ 6,000	$ –0–	–0–
Selling, general, and administrative expense	**3,000**	**2,000**	**1,000**	❸ **50**
Operating income	**$ 3,000**	**$ 4,000**	**$(1,000)**	❹ **(25)**
Interest expense	140	160	(20)	(13)
Income before tax	$ 2,860	$ 3,840	$ (980)	(26)
Income tax expense	1,140	1,540	(400)	(26)
Net income	$ 1,720	$ 2,300	$ (580)	(25)
Preferred dividends	50	50		
Income available to common	$ 1,670	$ 2,250		
Common dividends	250	250		
To retained earnings	$ 1,420	$ 2,000		
Retained earnings, 1/1	6,000	4,000		
Retained earnings, 12/31	$ 7,420	$ 6,000		

These three increases in revenue and expenses resulted in an operating income *decrease* of 25%.

NOTE: Referenced amounts are boldfaced for convenience.

Companies that experience sales growth often become lax about controlling expenses. Their managements sometimes forget that the bottom line is what counts, not the top line. Perhaps the salespeople are given incentives to increase sales without considering the costs of the sales. Maybe management is spending too much on overhead, including its own salaries. The owners of the business will have to address these concerns if they want to get a reasonable return on their investment.

Horizontal analysis can be extended to include more than two years of results. At a minimum, publicly held companies are required to include income statements and statements of cash flows for the three most recent years and balance sheets as of the end of the two most recent years. Many annual reports include, as supplementary information, financial summaries of operations for extended periods of time. As illustrated in Exhibit 13-3, for example, **Wrigley** includes an 11-year summary of selected financial data, such as net sales, dividends paid, return on average equity, and total assets. Note the increase in net sales in every year over the 11-year period. Also note, however, that Wrigley does not include in the summary the gross profit ratio (gross profit divided by net sales), although it can easily be found by dividing the second line on the exhibit by the first line. A comparison of the trend in this ratio would help to determine whether the company has effectively controlled the cost to manufacture its products. The summary does show that Wrigley also reported an increase in net earnings every year, an enviable record for any company.

Tracking items over a series of years, a practice called *trend analysis*, can be a very powerful tool for the analyst. Advanced statistical techniques are available for analyzing trends in financial data and, most importantly, for projecting those trends to future periods. Some of the techniques, such as time series analysis, have been used extensively in forecasting sales trends.

Historically, attention has focused on the balance sheet and income statement in analyzing a company's position and results of operation. Only recently have analysts and other users begun to appreciate the value in incorporating the statement of cash flows into their analyses.

Comparative statements of cash flows for Henderson appear in Exhibit 13-4. Henderson's financing activities remained constant over the two-year period, as indicated in that section of the statements. Each year the company paid $200,000 on notes, another $100,000 to retire bonds, and $300,000 to stockholders in dividends. Cash outflow from investing activities slowed down somewhat in 2008 with the purchase of $1,500,000 in new buildings compared with $2,000,000 the year before.

The most noticeable difference between Henderson's statements of cash flows for the two years is in the Operating Activities section. Operations ❶ generated almost $2 million less in cash in 2008 than in 2007 ($1.07 million in 2008 versus $2.95 million in 2007). The decrease in ❷ net income was partially responsible for this reduction in cash from operations. However, the increases in ❸ accounts receivable and ❹ inventories in 2008 had a significant impact on the decrease in cash generated from operating activities.

POD REVIEW 13.2

LO2 ***Use comparative financial statements to analyze a company over time (horizontal analysis).***

- Amounts appearing on comparative financial statements may be used to perform what is known as horizontal analysis.

QUESTIONS

1. *A comparison of financial statement items for a single company over a period of time is called*
   a. horizontal analysis.
   b. vertical analysis.
   c. operational analysis.
   d. none of the above.

2. *What is the minimum number of years for which publicly traded companies must include the following statements in their annual report filed with the SEC?*
   a. two years for income statements and statements of cash flows and three years for balance sheets
   b. three years for income statements and statements of cash flows and two years for balance sheets
   c. three years for income statements, statements of cash flows, and balance sheets
   d. one year for income statements, statements of cash flows, and balance sheets

EXHIBIT 13-3 **Wrigley Financial Summary**

Selected Financial Data

In thousands of dollars and shares, except per share amounts, stockholders of record and employees

	2006	2005	2004	2003
OPERATING DATA				
Net sales	$4,686,011	4,159,306	3,648,592	3,069,088
Gross profit (1)	2,429,822	2,255,904	2,033,375	1,746,672
Income taxes	239,670	237,408	227,542	205,647
Net earnings (2)	529,377	517,252	492,954	445,894
Per share of Common Stock (diluted)	1.90	1.83	1.75	1.58
Dividends paid	276,021	241,669	207,803	194,633
Per share of Common Stock	.992	.860	.740	.692
As a percent of net earnings	52%	47%	42%	44%
Dividends declared per share of Common Stock	1.024	.896	.752	.704
Average shares outstanding	277,556	280,964	280,796	281,203
OTHER FINANCIAL DATA	**2006**	**2005**	**2004**	**2003**
Net property, plant, and equipment	$1,422,516	1,282,412	1,142,620	956,180
Total assets	4,661,598	4,394,353	3,166,703	2,527,371
Working capital (3)	454,098	325,283	787,940	825,797
Debt (4)	1,065,000	1,100,000	90,000	—
Stockholders' equity	2,388,092	2,214,422	2,178,684	1,820,821
Return on average equity	23.0%	23.5%	24.7%	26.7%
Stockholders of record at close of year	40,986	41,105	41,376	40,954
Employees at close of year	15,800	14,800	14,800	12,000
Market price of stock				
High	54.54	58.20	55.78	47.12
Low	43.16	50.81	44.18	40.84

Both net sales and net earnings have increased each year for ten consecutive years.

(1) 2006 and 2005 include restructuring charges related to the North American production network of $45,074 and $40,223, respectively.

(2) 2006 includes restructuring charges, net of tax, related to the North American production of $31,011 or $0.11 per share and stock option expense, net of tax, of $23,825 or $0.09 per share; 2005 includes restructuring charges, net of tax, related to the North American production network of $27,553 or $0.10 per share; 1998 includes factory closure gain, net of tax, of $6,763 or $0.02 per share; and 1997 and 1996 include factory closure costs, net of tax, of $2,145 or $0.01 per share and $12,990 or $0.05 per share, respectively.

EXHIBIT 13-3 **Wrigley Financial Summary (continued)**

2002	2001	2000	1999	1998	1997	1996
2,746,318	2,401,419	2,126,114	2,045,227	1,990,286	1,923,963	1,835,987
1,559,633	1,371,290	1,193,312	1,121,596	1,095,298	1,031,212	976,573
181,896	164,380	150,370	136,247	136,378	122,614	128,840
401,525	362,986	328,942	308,183	304,501	271,626	230,272
1.42	1.29	1.16	1.06	1.05	.936	.792
181,232	167,922	159,138	153,812	150,835	135,680	118,308
.644	.596	.561	.531	.520	.585	.408
45%	46%	48%	50%	50%	50%	51%
.656	.608	.561	.592	.524	.468	.408
281,431	281,686	283,796	289,653	289,910	289,910	289,958

2002	2001	2000	1999	1998	1997	1996
836,110	684,379	607,034	599,140	520,090	430,474	388,149
2,108,296	1,777,793	1,574,740	1,547,745	1,520,855	1,343,126	1,233,543
620,205	581,519	540,505	551,921	624,546	571,857	511,272
—	—	—	—	—	—	—
1,522,576	1,276,197	1,132,897	1,138,775	1,157,032	985,379	897,431
28.7%	30.1%	29.0%	26.8%	28.4%	28.9%	27.2%
40,534	38,701	37,781	38,626	38,052	36,587	34,951
11,250	10,800	9,800	9,300	9,200	8,200	7,800
47.12	42.64	38.65	40.25	41.73	32.82	25.15
35.37	34.35	23.95	26.60	28.38	21.82	19.35

(3) Working Capital equals current assets less current liabilities.

(4) 2005 includes issuance of long-term debt and commercial paper used to fund the acquisition of certain confectionery assets from Kraft Foods Global, Inc.; 2004 includes line of credit used to fund the acquisition of certain confectionery businesses of the Joyco Group.

Note: The Company acquired certain confectionery assets from Kraft Foods Global, Inc. on June 26, 2005 and certain confectionery businesses of the Joyco Group on April 1, 2004.

Real World Practice

13-1 Reading Wrigley's Annual Report

Refer to Wrigley's financial highlights in Exhibit 13-3. Compute the company's gross profit ratio for each of the 11 years. Is there a noticeable upward or downward trend in the ratio over this time period?

EXHIBIT 13-4 **Comparative Statements of Cash Flow—Horizontal Analysis**

Henderson Company
Comparative Statements of Cash Flows
For the Years Ended December 31, 2008 and 2007
(all amounts in thousands of dollars)

	2008	2007	Increase (Decrease) Dollars	Increase (Decrease) Percent
Net Cash Flows from Operating Activities				
❷ Net income	**$1,720**	**$2,300**	**$ (580)**	**(25)%**
Adjustments:				
Depreciation expense	350	300		
Changes in:				
❸ Accounts receivable	**(1,000)**	**500**		
❹ Inventory	**(2,000)**	**(300)**		
Prepaid insurance	50	50		
Accounts payable	1,750	(200)		
Taxes payable	200	300		
Net cash provided by operating activities ❶ Unfavorable	**$1,070** ←	**$2,950**	**$(1,880)**	**(64)%**
Net Cash Flows from Investing Activities				
Purchase of buildings	**$(1,500)**	**$(2,000)**	**$ (500)**	**(25)%**
Net Cash Flows from Financing Activities				
Repayment of notes	**$ (200)**	**$ (200)**	–0–	–0–
Retirement of bonds	**(100)**	**(100)**	–0–	–0–
Cash dividends—preferred	**(50)**	**(50)**	–0–	–0–
Cash dividends—common	**(250)**	**(250)**	–0–	–0–
Net cash used by financing activities	$ (600)	$ (600)	–0–	–0–
Net increase (decrease) in cash	$(1,030)	$ 350		
Beginning cash balance	1,350	1,000		
Ending cash balance	$ 320	$ 1,350		
Supplemental Information				
Interest paid	$ 140	$ 160		
Income taxes paid	$ 940	$ 1,440		

NOTE: Referenced amounts are boldfaced for convenience.

LO3 Use common-size financial statements to compare various financial statement items (vertical analysis).

VERTICAL ANALYSIS

Often it is easier to examine comparative financial statements when they have been standardized. *Common-size statements* recast all items on the statement as a percentage of a selected item on the statement. This excludes size as a relevant variable in the analysis. This type of analysis could be used to compare **Wal-Mart** with the smaller **Target** or to compare **IBM** with the much smaller **Apple Computer**. It is also a convenient way to compare the same company from year to year.

Vertical analysis involves looking at the relative size and composition of various items on a particular financial statement. Common-size comparative balance sheets for Henderson Company are presented in Exhibit 13-5. Note that all asset accounts are stated as a percentage of total assets. Similarly, all Liability and Stockholders' Equity accounts are stated as a percentage of total liabilities and stockholders' equity. The combination of the comparative balance sheets for the two years and the common-size feature allows the analyst to spot critical changes in the composition of the assets. We noted in Exhibit 13-1 that cash had decreased by 76% over the two years. The decrease of ❶ cash from 9.8% of total assets to only 1.9% is highlighted in Exhibit 13-5.

EXHIBIT 13-5 Common-Size Comparative Balance Sheets—Vertical Analysis

Henderson Company
Common-Size Comparative Balance Sheets
December 31, 2008 and 2007
(all amounts in thousands of dollars)

	December 31, 2008		December 31, 2007	
	Dollars	**Percent**	**Dollars**	**Percent**
Cash	**$ 320**	**1.9%**	**$ 1,350** ❶	**9.8%**
Accounts receivable	5,500	32.6	4,500	32.6
Inventory	**4,750**	**28.1**	**2,750** ❸	**19.9**
Prepaid insurance	150	0.9	200	1.5
Total current assets	**$ 10,720**	❷ **63.5%**	**$ 8,800**	**63.8%**
Land	$ 2,000	11.9%	$ 2,000	14.5%
Buildings and equipment, net	4,150	24.6	3,000	21.7
Total long-term assets	$ 6,150	36.5%	$ 5,000	36.2%
Total assets	$16,870	100.0%	$13,800	100.0%
Accounts payable	$ 4,250	25.2%	$ 2,500	18.1%
Taxes payable	2,300	13.6	2,100	15.2
Notes payable	600	3.6	800	5.8
Current portion of bonds	100	0.6	100	0.7
Total current liabilities	**$ 7,250**	❹ **43.0%**	**$ 5,500**	**39.8%**
Bonds payable	700	❺ 4.1	800	5.8
Total liabilities	$ 7,950	47.1%	$ 6,300	45.6%
Preferred stock, $5 par	$ 500	3.0%	$ 500	3.6%
Common stock, $1 par	1,000	5.9	1,000	7.3
Retained earnings	7,420	44.0	6,000	43.5
Total stockholders' equity	**$ 8,920**	❻ **52.9%**	**$ 7,500**	**54.4%**
Total liabilities and stockholders' equity	$16,870	100.0%	$13,800	100.0%

NOTE: Referenced amounts are boldfaced for convenience.

Compare percentages across years to spot year-to-year trends.

In **vertical analysis**, compare each line item as a percentage of total (100%) to highlight a company's overall condition.

You can also observe in the exhibit that ❷ total current assets have continued to represent just under two-thirds (63.5%) of total assets. If cash has decreased significantly in terms of the percentage of total assets, what accounts have increased to maintain current assets at two-thirds of total assets? We can quickly determine from the data in Exhibit 13-5 that although ❸ inventory represented 19.9% of total assets at the end of 2007, the percentage is up to 28.1% at the end of 2008. This change in the relative composition of current assets between cash and inventory may have important implications. The change, for instance, may signal that the company is having trouble selling inventory.

Total ❹ current liabilities represent a slightly higher percentage of total liabilities and stockholders' equity at the end of 2008 than at the end of 2007. The increase is balanced by a slight decrease in the relative percentages of ❺ long-term debt (the bonds) and ❻ stockholders' equity. We will return later to further analysis of the composition of both the current and the noncurrent accounts.

Common-size comparative income statements for Henderson are presented in Exhibit 13-6. The *base*, or benchmark, on which all other items in the income statement are compared is ❶ net sales. Again, observations from the comparative statements alone are further confirmed by examining the common-size statements. Although the **gross profit ratio**—gross profit as a percentage of net sales—was 30% in 2007, the same ratio for 2008 is only 25% ❷. Recall the earlier observation that although sales increased by 20% from one year to the next, ❸ cost of goods sold increased by 29%.

Real World Practice

13-2 Reading Kellogg's Income Statement

Refer to Kellogg's three-year comparative income statements reprinted in the back of this book. For each of the three years presented, compute the gross profit and profit margin ratios. Also compute the percentage increase or decrease of each ratio for each of the last two years. What conclusions can you draw from your analysis?

EXHIBIT 13-6 Common-Size Comparative Income Statements—Vertical Analysis

Henderson Company
Common-Size Comparative Income Statements
For the Years Ended December 31, 2008 and 2007
(all amounts in thousands of dollars)

	2008		2007	
	Dollars	Percent	Dollars	Percent
Net sales	**$24,000**	(1) **100.0%**	**$20,000**	**100.0%**
Cost of goods sold	(3) 18,000	75.0	14,000	70.0
Gross profit	**$ 6,000**	(2) **25.0%**	**$ 6,000**	**30.0%**
Selling, general, and administrative expense	3,000	12.5	2,000	10.0
Operating income	$ 3,000	12.5%	$ 4,000	20.0%
Interest expense	140	0.6	160	0.8
Income before tax	**$ 2,860**	**11.9%**	**$ 3,840**	**19.2%**
Income tax expense	1,140	4.8	1,540	7.7
Net income	**$ 1,720**	(4) **7.1%**	**$ 2,300**	**11.5%**

NOTE: Referenced amounts are boldfaced for convenience.

Gross profit as a percentage of sales is the **gross profit ratio.**

The ratio of net income to net sales is the **profit margin ratio.**

Gross profit ratio
Gross profit to net sales.

Profit margin ratio
Net income to net sales.

In addition to the gross profit ratio, an important relationship from Exhibit 13-6 is the ratio of net income to net sales, or **profit margin ratio**. The ratio, an overall indicator of management's ability to control expenses, reflects the amount of income for each dollar of sales. Some analysts prefer to look at income before tax rather than at final net income because taxes are not typically an expense that can be controlled. Further, if the company does not earn a profit before tax, it will incur no tax expense. Note the decrease in Henderson's (4) profit margin: from 11.5% in 2007 to 7.1% in 2008 (or from 19.2% to 11.9% on a before-tax basis).

POD REVIEW 13.3

LO3 *Use common-size financial statements to compare various financial statement items (vertical analysis).*

- Common-size statements recast all items as a percentage of a selected item on the statement, such as sales on the income statement.
- The use of common-size financial statements, also known as vertical analysis, facilitates comparisons between companies in addition to comparisons between different periods for the same company.

QUESTIONS

1. *Assume that you were concerned about whether selling and administrative expenses were reasonable this past year given the level of sales. Which type of analysis would you perform to help address your concern?*
   a. horizontal analysis
   b. trend analysis
   c. vertical analysis
   d. none of the above

2. *On common-size comparative income statements, all line items are stated as a percentage of*
   a. net sales.
   b. net income.
   c. total assets.
   d. none of the above.

Liquidity Analysis and the Management of Working Capital

LO4 Compute and use various ratios to assess liquidity.

Two ratios were discussed in the last section: the *gross profit ratio* and the *profit margin ratio*. A ratio is simply the relationship, normally stated as a percentage, between two financial statement amounts. This section considers a wide range of ratios that management, analysts, and others use for a variety of purposes. The ratios are classified in three main categories according to their use in performing (1) liquidity analysis, (2) solvency analysis, and (3) profitability analysis.

Liquidity The nearness to cash of the assets and liabilities.

Liquidity is a relative measure of the nearness to cash of the assets and liabilities of a company. Nearness to cash deals with the length of time before cash is realized. Various ratios are used to measure liquidity, and they concern basically the company's ability to pay its debts as they come due. Recall the distinction between the current and long-term classifications on the balance sheet. Current assets are assets that will be converted into cash or consumed within one year or within the operating cycle if the cycle is longer than one year. The operating cycle for a manufacturing company is the length of time between the purchase of raw materials and the eventual collection of any outstanding account receivable from the sale of the product. Current liabilities are a company's obligations that require the use of current assets or the creation of other current liabilities to satisfy the obligations.

The nearness to cash of the current assets is indicated by their placement on the balance sheet. Current assets are listed on the balance sheet in descending order of their nearness to cash. Liquidity is, of course, a matter of degree, with cash being the most liquid of all assets. With few exceptions, such as prepaid insurance, most current assets are convertible into cash. However, accounts receivable is closer to being converted into cash than is inventory. An account receivable need only be collected to be converted to cash. An item of inventory must first be sold; then assuming that sales of inventory are on account, the account must be collected before cash is realized.

WORKING CAPITAL

Working capital Current assets minus current liabilities.

Working capital is the excess of current assets over current liabilities at a point in time:

Working Capital = Current Assets − Current Liabilities

Reference to Henderson's comparative balance sheets in Exhibit 13-1 indicates the following:

	December 31	
	2008	**2007**
Current assets	$10,720,000	$8,800,000
Current liabilities	7,250,000	5,500,000
Working capital	$ 3,470,000	$3,300,000

The management of working capital is an extremely important task for any business. A comparison of Henderson's working capital at the end of each of the two years indicates a slight increase in the degree of protection for short-term creditors of the company. Management must strive for the ideal balance of current assets and current liabilities. The amount of working capital is limited in its informational value, however. For example, it reveals nothing about the composition of the current accounts. Also, the dollar amount of working capital may not be useful for comparison with other companies of different sizes in the same industry. Working capital of $3,470,000 may be adequate for Henderson Company, but it might signal impending bankruptcy for a company much larger than Henderson.

CURRENT RATIO

Current ratio
The ratio of current assets to current liabilities.

The **current ratio**, one of the most widely used financial statement ratios, is calculated as follows:

$$\text{Current Ratio} = \frac{\text{Current Assets}}{\text{Current Liabilities}}$$

For Henderson Company, the ratio at each year-end is as follows:

December 31	
2008	**2007**
$\frac{\$10{,}720{,}000}{\$7{,}250{,}000} = 1.48 \text{ to } 1$	$\frac{\$8{,}800{,}000}{\$5{,}500{,}000} = 1.60 \text{ to } 1$

Study Tip

Some of the ratios discussed in this chapter, such as the current ratio, were introduced in earlier chapters. Use the information here as a review of those earlier introductions.

At the end of 2008, Henderson had $1.48 of current assets for every $1 of current liabilities. Is this current ratio adequate? Or is it a sign of impending financial difficulties? There is no definitive answer to either of those questions. Some analysts use a general rule of thumb of 2 to 1 for the current ratio as a sign of short-term financial health. The answer depends first on the industry. Companies in certain industries have historically operated with current ratios much less than 2 to 1.

A second concern in interpreting the current ratio involves the composition of the current assets. Cash is usually the only acceptable means of payment for most liabilities. Therefore, it is important to consider the makeup, or *composition*, of the current assets. Refer to Exhibit 13-5 and Henderson's common-size balance sheets. Not only did the current ratio decline during 2008 but the proportion of the total current assets made up by inventory increased, whereas the proportion made up by accounts receivable remained the same. Recall that accounts receivable is only one step removed from cash, whereas inventory requires both sale and collection of the subsequent account.

ACID-TEST RATIO

Acid-test or quick ratio
A stricter test of liquidity than the current ratio; excludes inventory and prepayments from the numerator.

The **acid-test or quick ratio** is a stricter test of a company's ability to pay its current debts as they are due. Specifically, it is intended to deal with the composition problem because it *excludes* inventories and prepaid assets from the numerator of the fraction:

$$\text{Acid-Test or Quick Ratio} = \frac{\text{Quick Assets}}{\text{Current Liabilities}}$$

where

$$\text{Quick Assets} = \text{Cash} + \text{Marketable Securities} + \text{Current Receivables}$$

Henderson's quick assets consist of only cash and accounts receivable, and its quick ratios are as follows:

December 31	
2008	**2007**
$\frac{\$320{,}000 + \$5{,}500{,}000}{\$7{,}250{,}000} = 0.80 \text{ to } 1$	$\frac{\$1{,}350{,}000 + \$4{,}500{,}000}{\$5{,}500{,}000} = 1.06 \text{ to } 1$

Does the quick ratio of less than 1 to 1 at the end of 2008 mean that Henderson will be unable to pay creditors on time? **For many companies, an acid-test ratio below 1 is not desirable because it may signal the need to liquidate marketable securities to pay bills, regardless of the current trading price of the securities.** (Recall that Henderson has no marketable securities.) Although the quick ratio is a better indication of short-term debt-paying ability than the current ratio, it is still not perfect. For example, we would want to know the normal credit terms that Henderson extends to its customers as well as the credit terms that the company receives from its suppliers.

Assume that Henderson requires its customers to pay their accounts within 30 days and that the normal credit terms extended by Henderson's suppliers allow payment anytime within 60 days. The relatively longer credit terms extended by Henderson's suppliers give the company some cushion in meeting its obligations. The due date of the $2,300,000 in taxes payable also could have a significant effect on the company's ability to remain in business.

CASH FLOW FROM OPERATIONS TO CURRENT LIABILITIES

Two limitations exist with either the current ratio or the quick ratio as a measure of liquidity. First, almost all debts require the payment of cash. Thus, a ratio that focuses on cash is more useful. Second, both ratios focus on liquid assets at a *point in time.* Cash flow from operating activities, as reported on the statement of cash flows, can be used to indicate the flow of cash during the year to cover the debts due.[1] The **cash flow from operations to current liabilities ratio** is computed as follows:

Cash flow from operations to current liabilities ratio
A measure of the ability to pay current debts from operating cash flows.

$$\text{Cash Flow from Operations to Current Liabilities Ratio} = \frac{\text{Net Cash Provided by Operating Activities}}{\text{Average Current Liabilities}}$$

Note the use of *average* current liabilities in the denominator. This results in a denominator that is consistent with the numerator, which reports the cash flow over a period of time. Because we need to calculate the *average* current liabilities for both years, it is necessary to add the ending balance sheet for 2006 for use in the analysis. The balance sheet for Henderson on December 31, 2006, is given in Exhibit 13-7. The ratio for Henderson for each year is as follows:

2008	2007
$\frac{\$1{,}070{,}000}{(\$7{,}250{,}000 + \$5{,}500{,}000)/2} = 16.8\%$	$\frac{\$2{,}950{,}000}{(\$5{,}500{,}000 + \$5{,}600{,}000)/2} = 53.2\%$

Two factors are responsible for the large decrease in this ratio from 2007 to 2008. First, cash generated from operations during 2008 was less than half what it was during 2007 (the numerator). Second, average current liabilities were smaller in 2007 than in 2008 (the denominator). In examining the health of the company in terms of its liquidity, an analyst would concentrate on the reason for these decreases.

ACCOUNTS RECEIVABLE ANALYSIS

The analysis of accounts receivable is an important component in the management of working capital. A company must be willing to extend credit terms that are liberal enough to attract and maintain customers; but at the same time, management must continually monitor the accounts to ensure collection on a timely basis. One measure of the efficiency of the collection process is the **accounts receivable turnover ratio**:

Accounts receivable turnover ratio
A measure of the number of times accounts receivable are collected in a period.

$$\text{Accounts Receivable Turnover Ratio} = \frac{\text{Net Credit Sales}}{\text{Average Accounts Receivable}}$$

Note an important distinction between this ratio and either the current or the quick ratio. Although both of those ratios measure liquidity at a point in time and all numbers come from the balance sheet, a turnover ratio is an *activity* ratio and consists of an activity (sales in this case) divided by a base to which it is naturally related (accounts receivable). Because an activity such as sales is for a period of time (a year in this case), the base should be stated as an average for that same period of time.

1 For a detailed discussion on the use of information contained in the statement of cash flows in performing ratio analysis, see Charles A. Carslaw and John R. Mills, "Developing Ratios for Effective Cash Flow Statement Analysis," *Journal of Accountancy* (November 1991), pp. 63–70.

EXHIBIT 13-7 **Henderson Company's Balance Sheet, End of 2006**

Henderson Company
Balance Sheet
December 31, 2006
(all amounts in thousands of dollars)

Cash	$ 1,000
Accounts receivable	5,000
Inventory	2,450
Prepaid insurance	250
Total current assets	$ 8,700
Land	$ 2,000
Buildings and equipment, net	1,300
Total long-term assets	$ 3,300
Total assets	$12,000
Accounts payable	$ 2,700
Taxes payable	1,800
Notes payable	1,000
Current portion of bonds	100
Total current liabilities	$ 5,600
Bonds payable	900
Total liabilities	$ 6,500
Preferred stock, $5 par	$ 500
Common stock, $1 par	1,000
Retained earnings	4,000
Total stockholders' equity	$ 5,500
Total liabilities and stockholders' equity	$12,000

The accounts receivable turnover ratios for both years can now be calculated. (We assume that all sales are on account.)

2008	2007
$\frac{\$24,000,000}{(\$5,500,000 + \$4,500,000)/2} = 4.8 \text{ times}$	$\frac{\$20,000,000}{(\$4,500,000 + \$5,000,000)/2} = 4.2 \text{ times}$

Accounts turned over, on average, 4.2 times in 2007, compared with 4.8 times in 2008. This means that the average number of times accounts were collected during each year was between four and five. What does this mean about the average length of time that an account was outstanding? Another way to measure efficiency in the collection process is to calculate the **number of days' sales in receivables**:

Number of days' sales in receivables
A measure of the average age of accounts receivable.

$$\text{Number of Days' Sales in Receivables} = \frac{\text{Number of Days in the Period}}{\text{Accounts Receivable Turnover}}$$

For simplicity, we assume 360 days in a year:

2008	2007
$\frac{360 \text{ days}}{4.8 \text{ times}} = 75 \text{ days}$	$\frac{360 \text{ days}}{4.2 \text{ times}} = 86 \text{ days}$

The average number of days an account is outstanding, or the average collection period, is 75 days in 2008, down from 86 days in 2007. Is this acceptable? The answer depends on the company's credit policy. If Henderson's normal credit terms require payment within 60 days, further investigation is needed even though the number of days outstanding has decreased from the previous year.

Management needs to be concerned with both the collectibility of an account as it ages and the cost of funds tied up in receivables. For example, a $1 million average receivable balance that requires an additional month to collect suggests that the company is forgoing $10,000 in lost profits assuming that the money could be reinvested in the business to earn 1% per month, or 12% per year.

INVENTORY ANALYSIS

A similar set of ratios can be calculated to analyze the efficiency in managing inventory. The **inventory turnover ratio** is as follows:

Inventory turnover ratio A measure of the number of times inventory is sold during a period.

$$\text{Inventory Turnover Ratio} = \frac{\text{Cost of Goods Sold}}{\text{Average Inventory}}$$

The ratio for each of the two years is as follows:

2008	2007
$\frac{\$18{,}000{,}000}{(\$4{,}750{,}000 + \$2{,}750{,}000)/2} = 4.8$ times	$\frac{\$14{,}000{,}000}{(\$2{,}750{,}000 + \$2{,}450{,}000)/2} = 5.4$ times

Henderson was slightly more efficient in 2007 in moving its inventory. The number of "turns" each year varies widely for different industries. For example, a wholesaler of perishable fruits and vegetables may turn over inventory at least 50 times per year. An airplane manufacturer, however, may turn over its inventory once or twice a year. What does the number of turns per year reveal about the average length of time it takes to sell an item of inventory? The **number of days' sales in inventory** is an alternative measure of the company's efficiency in managing inventory. It is the number of days between the date an item of inventory is purchased and the date it is sold:

Number of days' sales in inventory A measure of how long it takes to sell inventory.

$$\text{Number of Days' Sales in Inventory} = \frac{\text{Number of Days in the Period}}{\text{Inventory Turnover}}$$

The number of days' sales in inventory for Henderson is as follows:

2008	2007
$\frac{360 \text{ days}}{4.8 \text{ times}} = 75$ days	$\frac{360 \text{ days}}{5.4 \text{ times}} = 67$ days

This measure can reveal a great deal about inventory management. For example, an unusually low turnover (and, of course, a high number of days in inventory) may signal a large amount of obsolete inventory or problems in the sales department. Or it may indicate that the company is pricing its products too high and the market is reacting by reducing demand for the company's products.

CASH OPERATING CYCLE

The **cash-to-cash operating cycle** is the length of time between the purchase of merchandise for sale, assuming a retailer or wholesaler, and the eventual collection of the cash from the sale. One method to approximate the number of days in a company's operating cycle involves combining two measures:

Cash-to-cash operating cycle The length of time from the purchase of inventory to the collection of any receivable from the sale.

$$\text{Cash-to-Cash Operating Cycle} = \text{Number of Days' Sales in Inventory} + \text{Number of Days' Sales in Receivables}$$

Henderson's operating cycles for 2008 and 2007 are as follows:

2008	2007
75 days + 75 days = 150 days	67 days + 86 days = 153 days

The average length of time between the purchase of inventory and the collection of cash from sale of the inventory was 150 days in 2008. Note that although the length of the operating cycle did not change significantly from 2007 to 2008, the composition did change: the increase in the average number of days in inventory was offset by the decrease in the average number of days in receivables.

POD REVIEW 13.4

LO4 Compute and use various ratios to assess liquidity.

- Liquidity is a measure of the relative ease with which assets can be converted to cash. Several ratios may be used to assess different aspects of liquidity, including:
  - Current, acid-test (quick), cash from operations to current liabilities, accounts receivable turnover, and inventory turnover ratios.
  - The cash-to-cash operating cycle measures the average length of time between the purchase of inventory and collection of cash after a sale takes place.

QUESTIONS

1. *Which of the following current assets are excluded from the numerator used to compute the acid-test or quick ratio?*
   a. inventories
   b. accounts receivable
   c. prepaid assets
   d. Both inventories and prepaid assets are excluded.

2. *What numerators are used in the computation of the accounts receivable turnover ratio and the inventory turnover ratio, respectively?*
   a. Net credit sales and Cost of goods sold
   b. Cost of goods sold and Net credit sales
   c. Net credit sales for both
   d. Cost of goods sold for both

Solvency Analysis

LO5 Compute and use various ratios to assess solvency.

Solvency refers to a company's ability to remain in business over the long term. It is related to liquidity but differs in time. Although liquidity relates to the firm's ability to pay next year's debts as they come due, solvency concerns the ability of the firm to stay financially healthy over the period of time that existing debt (short- and long-term) is outstanding.

Solvency
The ability of a company to remain in business over the long term.

DEBT-TO-EQUITY RATIO

Capital structure is the focal point in solvency analysis. This refers to the composition of the right side of the balance sheet and the mix between debt and stockholders' equity. The composition of debt and equity in the capital structure is an important determinant of the cost of capital to a company. We will have more to say later about the effects that the mix of debt and equity has on profitability. For now, consider the **debt-to-equity ratio**:

Debt-to-equity ratio
The ratio of total liabilities to total stockholders' equity.

$$\text{Debt-to-Equity Ratio} = \frac{\text{Total Liabilities}}{\text{Total Stockholders' Equity}}$$

Henderson's debt-to-equity ratio at each year-end is as follows:

December 31	
2008	**2007**
$\frac{\$7,950,000}{\$8,920,000} = 0.89$ to 1	$\frac{\$6,300,000}{\$7,500,000} = 0.84$ to 1

The 2008 ratio indicates that for every $1.00 of capital that stockholders provided, creditors provided $0.89. Variations of the debt-to-equity ratio are sometimes used to assess solvency. For example, an analyst might calculate the ratio of total liabilities to the sum of total liabilities and stockholders' equity. This results in a ratio that differs from the debt-to-equity ratio, but the objective of the measure is the same—to determine the degree to which the company relies on outsiders for funds.

What is an acceptable ratio of debt to equity? As with all ratios, the answer depends on the company, the industry, and many other factors. **You should not assume that a lower debt-to-equity ratio is better.** Certainly, taking on additional debt is risky. Many companies are able to benefit from borrowing money, however, by putting the cash raised to good uses in their businesses. Later in the chapter we discuss the concept of leverage: using borrowed money to benefit the company and its stockholders.

In the 1980s, investors and creditors tolerated a much higher debt-to-equity ratio than is considered prudent today. The savings and loan crisis in the 1980s prompted the federal government to enact regulations requiring financial institutions to have a lower proportion of debt to equity. By the mid-1990s, investors and creditors were demanding that all types of companies display lower debt-to-equity ratios.

Study Tip

The elements in many ratios are intuitive and should not require memorization. For example, it is logical that the debt-to-equity ratio is computed by dividing total liabilities by total stockholders' equity.

TIMES INTEREST EARNED

The debt-to-equity ratio is a measure of the company's overall long-term financial health. Management must also be aware of its ability to meet current interest payments to creditors. The **times interest earned ratio** indicates the company's ability to meet the current year's interest payments out of the current year's earnings:

Times interest earned ratio
An income statement measure of the ability of a company to meet its interest payments.

$$\text{Times Interest Earned Ratio} = \frac{\text{Net Income} + \text{Interest Expense} + \text{Income Tax Expense}}{\text{Interest Expense}}$$

Both interest expense and income tax expense are added back to net income in the numerator because interest is a deduction in arriving at the amount of income subject to tax. Stated slightly differently, if a company had just enough income to cover the payment of interest, tax expense would be zero. As far as lenders are concerned, the greater the interest coverage, the better. Bankers often place more importance on the times interest earned ratio than on earnings per share. The ratio for Henderson for each of the two years indicates a great deal of protection in this regard:

2008	2007
$\frac{\$1{,}720{,}000 + \$140{,}000 + \$1{,}140{,}000}{\$140{,}000}$	$\frac{\$2{,}300{,}000 + \$160{,}000 + \$1{,}540{,}000}{\$160{,}000}$
= 21.4 to 1	= 25 to 1

DEBT SERVICE COVERAGE

Two problems exist with the times interest earned ratio as a measure of the ability to pay creditors. First, the denominator of the fraction considers only *interest*. Management must also be concerned with the *principal* amount of loans maturing in the next year. The second problem deals with the difference between the cash and the accrual bases of accounting. The numerator of the times interest earned ratio is not a measure of the *cash* available to repay loans. Keep in mind the various noncash adjustments, such as depreciation, that enter into the determination of net income. Also recall that the denominator of the times interest earned ratio is a measure of interest expense, not interest payments. The **debt service coverage ratio** is a measure of the amount of cash that is generated from operating activities during the year and that is available to repay interest due and any maturing principal amounts (i.e., the amount available to "service" the debt):

Debt service coverage ratio
A statement of cash flows measure of the ability of a company to meet its interest and principal payments.

$$\text{Debt Service Coverage Ratio} = \frac{\text{Cash Flow from Operations Before Interest and Tax Payments}}{\text{Interest and Principal Payments}}$$

Some analysts use an alternative measure in the numerator of this ratio as well as for other purposes. The alternative is referred to as EBITDA, which stands for earnings before interest, taxes, depreciation, and amortization. Whether EBITDA is a good substitute for cash flow from operations before interest and tax payments depends on whether there were significant changes in current assets and current liabilities during the period. If significant changes in these accounts occurred during the period, cash flow from operations before interest and tax payments is a better measure of a company's ability to cover interest and debt payments.

Cash flow from operations is available on the comparative statement of cash flows in Exhibit 13-4. As was the case with the times interest earned ratio, the net cash provided by operating activities is adjusted to reflect the amount available before paying interest and taxes.

Keep in mind that the income statement in Exhibit 13-2 reflects the *expense* for interest and taxes each year. The amounts of interest and taxes paid each year are shown as supplemental information at the bottom of the statement of cash flows in Exhibit 13-4 and are relevant in computing the debt service coverage ratio.

Any principal payments must be included with interest paid in the denominator of the debt service coverage ratio. According to the Financing Activities section of the statements of cash flows in Exhibit 13-4, Henderson repaid \$200,000 each year on the notes payable and \$100,000 each year on the bonds. The debt service coverage ratios for the two years are calculated as follows:

2008

$$\frac{\$1{,}070{,}000 + \$140{,}000 + \$940{,}000}{\$140{,}000 + \$200{,}000 + \$100{,}000} = 4.89 \text{ times}$$

2007

$$\frac{\$2{,}950{,}000 + \$160{,}000 + \$1{,}440{,}000}{\$160{,}000 + \$200{,}000 + \$100{,}000} = 9.89 \text{ times}$$

Like Henderson's times interest earned ratio, its debt service coverage ratio decreased during 2008. According to the calculations, however, Henderson still generated almost \$5 of cash from operations during 2008 to "cover" every \$1 of required interest and principal payments.

CASH FLOW FROM OPERATIONS TO CAPITAL EXPENDITURES RATIO

Cash flow from operations to capital expenditures ratio
A measure of the ability of a company to finance long-term asset acquisitions with cash from operations.

One final measure is useful in assessing the solvency of a business. The **cash flow from operations to capital expenditures ratio** measures a company's ability to use operations to finance its acquisitions of productive assets. To the extent that a company is able to do this, it should rely less on external financing or additional contributions by the owners to replace and add to the existing capital base. The ratio is computed as follows:

$$\text{Cash Flow from Operations to Capital Expenditures Ratio} = \frac{\text{Cash Flow from Operations} - \text{Total Dividends Paid}}{\text{Cash Paid for Acquisitions}}$$

Note that the numerator of the ratio measures the cash flow *after* all dividend payments are met.[2] The calculation of the ratios for Henderson follows:

2008	2007
$\frac{\$1{,}070{,}000 - \$300{,}000}{\$1{,}500{,}000} = 51.3\%$	$\frac{\$2{,}950{,}000 - \$300{,}000}{\$2{,}000{,}000} = 132.5\%$

Although the amount of capital expenditures was less in 2008 than in 2007, the company generated considerably less cash from operations in 2008 to cover these acquisitions. In fact, the ratio of less than 100% in 2008 indicates that Henderson was not able to finance all of its capital expenditures from operations *and* cover its dividend payments.

2 Dividends paid are reported on the statement of cash flows in the Financing Activities section. The amount *paid* should be used for this calculation rather than the amount declared, which appears on the statement of retained earnings.

POD REVIEW 13.5

LO5 *Compute and use various ratios to assess solvency.*

- Solvency measures a company's ability to maintain its financial health over the long term. Several ratios may be used to assess different aspects of solvency, including:
  - Debt-to-equity, times interest earned, debt service coverage, and cash flow from operations to capital expenditures ratios.

QUESTIONS

1. *Which of the following measures of solvency focuses specifically on the extent to which a company relies on outsiders for funds?*
   a. debt-to-equity ratio
   b. times interest earned ratio
   c. debt service coverage ratio
   d. cash flow from operations to capital expenditures ratio

2. *Solvency is concerned with the ability of a company to*
   a. pay next year's debts as they come due.
   b. remain in business over the long term.
   c. provide a reasonable return to stockholders.
   d. none of the above.

Profitability Analysis

LO6 Compute and use various ratios to assess profitability.

Liquidity analysis and solvency analysis deal with management's ability to repay short- and long-term creditors. Creditors are concerned with a company's profitability because a profitable company is more likely to be able to make principal and interest payments. Of course, stockholders care about a company's profitability because it affects the market price of the stock and the ability of the company to pay dividends. Various measures of **profitability** indicate how well management is using the resources at its disposal to earn a return on the funds invested by various groups. Two frequently used profitability measures, the gross profit ratio and the profit margin ratio, were discussed earlier in the chapter. We now turn to other measures of profitability.

Profitability
How well management is using company resources to earn a return on the funds invested by various groups.

RATE OF RETURN ON ASSETS

Before computing the rate of return, we must answer an important question: *return to whom?* **Every return ratio is a measure of the relationship between the income earned by the company and the investment made in the company by various groups.** The broadest rate of return ratio is the **return on assets ratio** because it considers the investment made by *all* providers of capital, from short-term creditors to bondholders to stockholders. Therefore, the denominator, or base, for the return on assets ratio is average total liabilities and stockholders' equity—which, of course, is the same as average total assets.

Return on assets ratio
A measure of a company's success in earning a return for all providers of capital.

The numerator of a return ratio will be some measure of the company's income for the period. The income selected for the numerator must match the investment or base in the denominator. For example, if average total assets is the base in the denominator, it is necessary to use an income number that is applicable to all providers of capital. Therefore, the income number used in the rate of return on assets is income *after* interest expense is added back. This adjustment considers creditors as one of the groups that has provided funds to the company. In other words, we want the amount of income before creditors or stockholders have been given any distributions (i.e., interest to creditors or dividends to stockholders). Interest expense must be added back on a net-of-tax basis. Because net income is on an after-tax basis, for consistency purposes, interest must also be placed on a net, or after-tax, basis.

The return on assets ratio is as follows:

$$\text{Return on Assets Ratio} = \frac{\text{Net Income + Interest Expense, Net of Tax}}{\text{Average Total Assets}}$$

If we assume a 40% tax rate (which is the actual ratio of income tax expense to income before tax for Henderson), its return on assets ratios will be as follows:

		2008		2007
Net income		$ 1,720,000		$ 2,300,000
Add back:				
Interest expense	$140,000		$160,000	
× (1 − tax rate)	× 0.6	84,000	× 0.6	96,000
Numerator		$ 1,804,000		$ 2,396,000
Assets, beginning of year		$13,800,000		$12,000,000
Assets, end of year		16,870,000		13,800,000
Total		$30,670,000		$25,800,000
Denominator:				
Average total assets (total above divided by 2)		$15,335,000		$12,900,000
		$ 1,804,000 / $15,335,000		$ 2,396,000 / $12,900,000
Return on assets ratio		= 11.76%		= 18.57%

COMPONENTS OF RETURN ON ASSETS

Return on sales ratio
A variation of the profit margin ratio; measures earnings before payments to creditors.

What caused Henderson's return on assets to decrease so dramatically from the previous year? The answer can be found by considering the two components that make up the return on assets ratio. The first of these components is the **return on sales ratio** and is calculated as follows:

$$\text{Return on Sales Ratio} = \frac{\text{Net Income + Interest Expense, Net of Tax}}{\text{Net Sales}}$$

The return on sales ratios for Henderson for the two years are as follows:

2008	2007
$\frac{\$1{,}720{,}000 + \$84{,}000}{\$24{,}000{,}000} = 7.52\%$	$\frac{\$2{,}300{,}000 + \$96{,}000}{\$20{,}000{,}000} = 11.98\%$

The ratio for 2008 indicates that for every $1.00 of sales, the company was able to earn a profit (before the payment of interest) of between $0.07 and $0.08, as compared with a return of almost $0.12 on the dollar in 2007.

Asset turnover ratio
The relationship between net sales and average total assets.

The other component of the rate of return on assets is the **asset turnover ratio**. The ratio is similar to both the inventory turnover and the accounts receivable turnover ratios because it is a measure of the relationship between some activity (net sales in this case) and some investment base (average total assets):

$$\text{Asset Turnover Ratio} = \frac{\text{Net Sales}}{\text{Average Total Assets}}$$

For Henderson, the ratio for each of the two years follows:

2008	2007
$\frac{\$24{,}000{,}000}{\$15{,}335{,}000} = 1.57 \text{ times}$	$\frac{\$20{,}000{,}000}{\$12{,}900{,}000} = 1.55 \text{ times}$

It now becomes evident that the explanation for the decrease in Henderson's return on assets lies in the drop in the return on sales since the asset turnover ratio was almost the same. To summarize, note the relationship among the three ratios:

Return on Assets = Return on Sales × Asset Turnover

For 2008, Henderson's return on assets consists of the following:

$$\frac{\$1,804,000}{\$24,000,000} \times \frac{\$24,000,000}{\$15,335,000} = 7.52\% \times 1.57 = 11.8\%$$

Finally, notice that net sales cancels out of both ratios, leaving the net income adjusted for interest divided by average assets as the return on assets ratio.

RETURN ON COMMON STOCKHOLDERS' EQUITY

Reasoning similar to that used to calculate return on assets can be used to calculate the return on capital provided by the common stockholder. Because we are interested in the return to the common stockholder, our base is no longer average total assets, but average common stockholders' equity. Similarly, the appropriate income figure for the numerator is net income less preferred dividends because we are interested in the return to the common stockholder after all claims have been settled. Income taxes and interest expense have already been deducted in arriving at net income, but preferred dividends have not been because dividends are a distribution of profits, not an expense.

The **return on common stockholders' equity ratio** is computed as follows:

Return on common stockholders' equity ratio
A measure of a company's success in earning a return for the common stockholders.

$$\text{Return on Common Stockholders' Equity Ratio} = \frac{\text{Net Income} - \text{Preferred Dividends}}{\text{Average Common Stockholders' Equity}}$$

The average common stockholders' equity for Henderson is calculated using information from Exhibits 13-1 and 13-7:

	Account Balances at December 31		
	2008	2007	2006
Common stock, $1 par	$1,000,000	$1,000,000	$1,000,000
Retained earnings	7,420,000	6,000,000	4,000,000
Total common equity	$8,420,000	$7,000,000	$5,000,000

Average common equity:
2007: ($7,000,000 + $5,000,000)/2 = $6,000,000
2008: ($8,420,000 + $7,000,000)/2 = $7,710,000

Net income less preferred dividends—or "income available to common" as it is called—can be found by referring to net income on the income statement and to preferred dividends on the statement of retained earnings. The combined statement of income and retained earnings in Exhibit 13-2 gives the relevant amounts for the numerator. Henderson's return on equity for the two years is as follows:

2008	2007
$\frac{\$1,720,000 - \$50,000}{\$7,710,000} = 21.66\%$	$\frac{\$2,300,000 - \$50,000}{\$6,000,000} = 37.50\%$

Even though Henderson's return on stockholders' equity ratio decreased significantly from one year to the next, most stockholders would be very happy to achieve these returns on their money. Very few investments offer more than 10% return unless substantial risk is involved.

RETURN ON ASSETS, RETURN ON EQUITY, AND LEVERAGE

The return on assets for 2008 was 11.8%. But the return to the common stockholders was much higher: 21.7%. How do you explain this phenomenon? Why are the stockholders receiving a higher return on their money than all of the providers of money combined are getting? A partial answer to those questions can be found by reviewing the cost to Henderson of the various sources of capital.

Exhibit 13-1 indicates that notes, bonds, and preferred stock are the primary sources of capital other than common stock. (Accounts payable and taxes payable are *not* included because they represent interest-free loans to the company from suppliers and the government.) These sources and the average amount of each outstanding during 2008 follow:

	Account Balances at December 31		
	2008	**2007**	**Average**
Notes payable	$ 600,000	$ 800,000	$ 700,000
Current portion of bonds	100,000	100,000	100,000
Bonds payable—Long-term	700,000	800,000	750,000
Total liabilities	$1,400,000	$1,700,000	$1,550,000
Preferred stock	$ 500,000	$ 500,000	$ 500,000

What was the cost to Henderson of each of these sources? The cost of the money provided by the preferred stockholders is clearly the amount of dividends of $50,000. The cost as a percentage is $50,000/$500,000, or 10%. The average cost of the borrowed money can be approximated by dividing the 2008 interest expense of $140,000 by the average of the notes payable and bonds payable of $1,550,000. The result is an average cost of these two sources of $140,000/$1,550,000, or approximately 9%.

Leverage
The use of borrowed funds and amounts contributed by preferred stockholders to earn an overall return higher than the cost of these funds.

The concept of **leverage** refers to the practice of using borrowed funds and amounts received from preferred stockholders in an attempt to earn an overall return that is higher than the cost of these funds. Recall the rate of return on assets for 2008: 11.8%. Because this return is on an after-tax basis, it is necessary for comparative purposes to convert the average cost of borrowed funds to an after-tax basis. Although we computed an average cost for borrowed money of 9%, the actual cost of the borrowed money is 5.4% [9% × (100% − 40%)] after taxes. Because dividends are *not* tax-deductible, the cost of the money provided by preferred stockholders is 10%, as calculated earlier.

Has Henderson successfully employed favorable leverage? That is, has it been able to earn an overall rate of return on assets that is higher than the amounts that it must pay creditors and preferred stockholders? Henderson has been successful in using outside money: neither of the sources must be paid a rate in excess of the 11.8% overall rate on assets used. Also keep in mind that Henderson has been able to borrow some amounts on an interest-free basis. As mentioned earlier, the accounts payable and taxes payable represent interest-free loans from suppliers and the government, although the loans are typically for a short period of time, such as 30 days.

In summary, the excess of the 21.7% return on equity over the 11.8% return on assets indicates that Henderson's management has been successful in employing leverage; that is, there is favorable leverage. Is it possible to be unsuccessful in this pursuit; that is, can there be unfavorable leverage? If the company must pay more for the amounts provided by creditors and preferred stockholders than it can earn overall, as indicated by the return on assets, there will, in fact, be unfavorable leverage. This may occur when interest requirements are high and net income is low. A company would likely have a high debt-to-equity ratio as well when there is unfavorable leverage.

EARNINGS PER SHARE

Earnings per share
A company's bottom line stated on a per-share basis.

Earnings per share is one of the most quoted statistics for publicly traded companies. Stockholders and potential investors want to know what their share of profits is, not just the total dollar amount. Presentation of profits on a per-share basis also allows the stockholder to relate earnings to what he or she paid for a share of stock or to the current trading price of a share of stock.

In simple situations such as the Henderson Company example, earnings per share (EPS) is calculated as follows:

$$\text{Earnings per Share} = \frac{\text{Net Income} - \text{Preferred Dividends}}{\text{Weighted Average Number of Common Shares Outstanding}}$$

Because Henderson had 1,000,000 shares of common stock outstanding throughout both 2007 and 2008, its EPS for each of the two years is as follows:

2008	2007
$\frac{\$1{,}720{,}000 - \$50{,}000}{1{,}000{,}000 \text{ shares}} = \$1.67$ per share	$\frac{\$2{,}300{,}000 - \$50{,}000}{1{,}000{,}000 \text{ shares}} = \$2.25$ per share

A number of complications can arise in the computation of EPS, and the calculations can become exceedingly complex for a company with many different types of securities in its capital structure. These complications are beyond the scope of this book and are discussed in more advanced accounting courses.

PRICE/EARNINGS RATIO

Earnings per share is an important ratio for an investor because of its relationship to dividends and market price. Stockholders hope to earn a return by receiving periodic dividends or eventually selling the stock for more than they paid for it or both. Although earnings are related to dividends and market price, the latter two are of primary interest to the stockholder.

Mentioned earlier was the desire of investors to relate the earnings of the company to the market price of the stock. Now that we have stated Henderson's earnings on a per-share basis, we can calculate the **price/earnings (P/E) ratio**. What market price is relevant? Should we use the market price that the investor paid for a share of stock, or should we use the current market price? Because earnings are based on the most recent evaluation of the company for accounting purposes, it seems logical to use current market price, which is based on the stock market's current assessment of the company. Therefore, the ratio is computed as follows:

Price/earnings (P/E) ratio The relationship between a company's performance according to the income statement and its performance in the stock market.

$$\text{Price/Earnings Ratio} = \frac{\text{Current Market Price}}{\text{Earnings per Share}}$$

Assume that the current market price for Henderson's common stock is $15 per share at the end of 2008 and $18 per share at the end of 2007. The price/earnings ratio for each of the two years is as follows:

2008	2007
$\frac{\$15 \text{ per share}}{\$1.67 \text{ per share}} = 9$ to 1	$\frac{\$18 \text{ per share}}{\$2.25 \text{ per share}} = 8$ to 1

What is normal for a P/E ratio? As is the case for all other ratios, it is difficult to generalize as to what is good or bad. The P/E ratio compares the stock market's assessment of a company's performance with the company's success as reflected on the income statement. A relatively high P/E ratio may indicate that a stock is overpriced by the market; a P/E ratio that is relatively low could indicate that a stock is underpriced.

The P/E ratio is often thought to indicate the "quality" of a company's earnings. For example, assume that two companies have identical EPS ratios of $2 per share. Why should investors be willing to pay $20 per share (or 10 times earnings) for the stock of one company but only $14 per share (or 7 times earnings) for the stock of the other company? First, we must realize that many factors in addition to the reported earnings of the company affect market prices. General economic conditions, the outlook for the particular industry, and pending lawsuits are just three examples of the various factors that can affect the trading price of a company's stock. The difference in P/E ratios for the two companies may reflect the market's assessment of the accounting practices of the companies, however. Assume that the company with a market price of $20 per share uses LIFO in valuing inventory and that the company trading at $14 per share uses FIFO. The difference in prices may indicate that investors believe that even though the companies have the same EPS, the LIFO company is "better off" because it will have a lower amount of taxes to pay. (Recall that in a period of inflation, the use of LIFO results in more cost of goods sold, less income, and therefore lower income taxes.) Finally, aside from the way investors view the accounting practices of different companies, they also consider the fact that, to a large extent, earnings reflect the use of historical costs, as opposed to fair market values, in assigning values to assets. Investors must consider the extent to which a company's assets are worth more than what was paid for them.

DIVIDEND RATIOS

Dividend payout ratio The percentage of earnings paid out as dividends.

Dividend yield ratio The relationship between dividends and the market price of a company's stock.

Two ratios are used to evaluate a company's dividend policies: the **dividend payout ratio** and the **dividend yield ratio**. The dividend payout ratio is the ratio of the common dividends per share to the earnings per share:

$$\text{Dividend Payout Ratio} = \frac{\text{Common Dividends per Share}}{\text{Earnings per Share}}$$

Exhibit 13-2 indicates that Henderson paid $250,000 in common dividends each year, or with 1 million shares outstanding, $0.25 per share. The two payout ratios are as follows:

2008	2007
$\frac{\$0.25}{\$1.67} = 15.0\%$	$\frac{\$0.25}{\$2.25} = 11.1\%$

Henderson's management was faced with an important financial policy decision in 2008. Should the company maintain the same dividend of $0.25 per share even though EPS dropped significantly? Many companies prefer to maintain a level dividend pattern, hoping that a drop in earnings is only temporary.

The second dividend ratio of interest to stockholders is the dividend yield ratio:

$$\text{Dividend Yield Ratio} = \frac{\text{Common Dividends per Share}}{\text{Market Price per Share}}$$

The yield to Henderson's stockholders would be calculated as follows:

2008	2007
$\frac{\$0.25}{\$15} = 1.7\%$	$\frac{\$0.25}{\$18} = 1.4\%$

As shown, Henderson common stock does not provide a high yield to its investors. The relationship between the dividends and the market price indicates that investors buy the stock for reasons other than the periodic dividend return.

The dividend yield is very important to investors who depend on dividend checks to pay their living expenses. Utility stocks are popular among retirees because these shares have dividend yields as high as 5%. That is considered a good investment with relatively low risk and some opportunity for gains in the stock price. On the other hand, investors who want to put money into growing companies are willing to forego dividends if it means the potential for greater price appreciation.

SUMMARY OF SELECTED FINANCIAL RATIOS

We have completed our review of the various ratios used to assess a company's liquidity, solvency, and profitability. For ease of reference, Exhibit 13-8 summarizes the ratios discussed in this chapter. Keep in mind that this list is not all-inclusive and that certain ratios used by analysts and others may be specific to a particular industry or type of business.

EXHIBIT 13-8 Summary of Selected Financial Ratios

Liquidity Analysis	
Working capital	Current Assets − Current Liabilities
Current ratio	$\frac{\text{Current Assets}}{\text{Current Liabilities}}$
Acid-test ratio (quick ratio)	$\frac{\text{Cash + Marketable Securities + Current Receivables}}{\text{Current Liabilities}}$
Cash flow from operations to current liabilities ratio	$\frac{\text{Net Cash Provided by Operating Activities}}{\text{Average Current Liabilities}}$
Accounts receivable turnover ratio	$\frac{\text{Net Credit Sales}}{\text{Average Accounts Receivable}}$
Number of days' sales in receivables	$\frac{\text{Number of Days in the Period}}{\text{Accounts Receivable Turnover}}$
Inventory turnover ratio	$\frac{\text{Cost of Goods Sold}}{\text{Average Inventory}}$
Number of days' sales in inventory	$\frac{\text{Number of Days in the Period}}{\text{Inventory Turnover}}$
Cash-to-cash operating cycle	Number of Days' Sales in Inventory + Number of Days' Sales in Receivables
Solvency Analysis	
Debt-to-equity ratio	$\frac{\text{Total Liabilities}}{\text{Total Stockholders' Equity}}$
Times interest earned ratio	$\frac{\text{Net Income + Interest Expense + Income Tax Expense}}{\text{Interest Expense}}$
Debt service coverage ratio	$\frac{\text{Cash Flow from Operations before Interest and Tax Payments}}{\text{Interest and Principal Payments}}$
Cash flow from operations to capital expenditures ratio	$\frac{\text{Cash Flow from Operations − Total Dividends Paid}}{\text{Cash Paid for Acquisitions}}$
Profitability Analysis	
Gross profit ratio	$\frac{\text{Gross Profit}}{\text{Net Sales}}$
Profit margin ratio	$\frac{\text{Net Income}}{\text{Net Sales}}$
Return on assets ratio	$\frac{\text{Net Income + Interest Expense, Net of Tax}}{\text{Average Total Assets}}$
Return on sales ratio	$\frac{\text{Net Income + Interest Expense, Net of Tax}}{\text{Net Sales}}$
Asset turnover ratio	$\frac{\text{Net Sales}}{\text{Average Total Assets}}$
Return on common stockholders' equity ratio	$\frac{\text{Net Income − Preferred Dividends}}{\text{Average Common Stockholders' Equity}}$
Earnings per share	$\frac{\text{Net Income − Preferred Dividends}}{\text{Weighted Average Number of Common Shares Outstanding}}$
Price/earnings ratio	$\frac{\text{Current Market Price}}{\text{Earnings per Share}}$
Dividend payout ratio	$\frac{\text{Common Dividends per Share}}{\text{Earnings per Share}}$
Dividend yield ratio	$\frac{\text{Common Dividends per Share}}{\text{Market Price per Share}}$

POD REVIEW 13.6

LO6 *Compute and use various ratios to assess profitability.*

- Profitability concerns the ability of management to use a company's resources to earn a return on funds invested. Measures of profitability include:
    - Return on assets, return on common stockholders' equity, earnings per share, price/earnings, dividend payout, and dividend yield ratios.

QUESTIONS

1. *The multiplication of which two ratios yields the return on assets ratio?*
    a. return on sales and asset turnover
    b. profit margin and return on sales
    c. profit margin and asset turnover
    d. return on common stockholders' equity and asset turnover

2. *Which of the following is an indication that a company has successfully employed leverage?*
    a. The return on assets exceeds the return on common stockholders' equity.
    b. The return on common stockholders' equity exceeds the return on assets.
    c. The return on common stockholders' equity exceeds the price/earnings ratio.
    d. None of the above.

APPENDIX

Accounting Tools: Reporting and Analyzing Other Income Statement Items

LO7 Explain how to report on and analyze other income statement items.

Not all companies have income statements that are as easy to understand and interpret as **Wrigley**'s statement. Some companies report either or both discontinued operations and extraordinary items on their income statements. Although the nature of these two items is very distinct, the two do share some common characteristics. First, they are all reported near the end of the income statement, after income from continuing operations. Second, they are reported separately on the income statement to call the reader's attention to their unique nature and to the fact that any additions to or deductions from income they give rise to may not necessarily reoccur in future periods. Finally, each of these items is shown net of their tax effects. This means that any additional taxes due because of them or any tax benefits from them are deducted from the items themselves. Following is a brief description of each item.

DISCONTINUED OPERATIONS

When a company decides to sell or otherwise dispose of one of its operations, it must report separately on that division or segment of the business on its income statement. This includes any gain or loss from the disposal of the business as well as any net income or loss from operating the business until the date of disposal. Because the discontinued segment of the business will not be part of the company's operations in the future, **discontinued operations** are disclosed separately on the income statement. Analysts and other users would normally consider only income from continuing operations in making their decisions.

Discontinued operations
A line item on the income statement to reflect any gains or losses from the disposal of a segment of the business as well as any net income or loss from operating that segment.

EXTRAORDINARY ITEMS

According to accounting standards, certain events that give rise to gains or losses are deemed to be extraordinary and are thus disclosed separately on the income statement. To qualify for extraordinary treatment, the gain or loss must be due to an event that is both unusual in nature and infrequent in occurrence.[3] Under current accounting standards, an **extraordinary item** is relatively rare; for example, when a natural catastrophe such as a tornado destroys a plant in an area not known for tornadoes. As is the case for discontinued operations, analysts and others often ignore the amount of such gains and losses in reaching their decisions since they are aware that these items are not likely to reoccur in the future.

Extraordinary item
A line item on the income statement to reflect any gains or losses that arise from an event that is both unusual in nature and infrequent in occurrence.

POD REVIEW 13.7

LO7 *Explain how to report on and analyze other income statement items.*

- Two components of the income statement are reported after income from operations or are reported separately because of their unique nature. These items include:
  - Discontinued operations and extraordinary items.

QUESTIONS

1. *Which of the following items are reported on the income statement net of their tax effects?*
   a. discontinued operations
   b. extraordinary items
   c. Neither of the above are reported net of their tax effects.
   d. Both (a) and (b) are reported net of their tax effects.

2. *What conditions are necessary for a gain or loss to qualify for extraordinary treatment on the income statement?*
   a. It must be unusual in nature and never have occurred before.
   b. It must be unusual in nature and infrequent in occurrence.
   c. It must be nonoperating in nature and infrequent in occurrence.
   d. Extraordinary gains and losses are not reported on the income statement.

3 *APB Opinion No. 30,* "Reporting the Results of Operations," Accounting Principles Board, 1973.

© Gary Gardiner/Bloomberg

Hot Topics

Wrigley Sweetens Its Business in Another Part of the World

Over its 100-plus years in business, Wrigley has shown its ability to find new opportunities without straying too far from its chewing gum roots. A good example is its January 2007 acquisition of a large stake in a Russian premium chocolate maker. Wrigley paid approximately $294 million for an 80% interest in A. Korkunov, a privately held company that two Russian entrepreneurs started in 1999. Although this venture is not Wrigley's first foray into Russia, it does give the company an inroad into the premium chocolate segment of the confectionary business. The purchase price represents approximately 3 times the Russian company's 2006 sales and was funded with cash on hand and by issuing short-term debt.

Source: Wrigley press release, January 23, 2007; http://www.wrigley.com

KEY TERMS QUIZ

Because of the number of terms introduced in this chapter, there are two quizzes on key terms. For each quiz, read each definition below and write the number of that definition in the blank beside the appropriate term. The quiz solutions appear at the end of the chapter.

Quiz 1:

_______ **Horizontal analysis**
_______ **Vertical analysis**
_______ **Gross profit ratio**
_______ **Profit margin ratio**
_______ **Liquidity**
_______ **Working capital**
_______ **Current ratio**
_______ **Acid-test or quick ratio**
_______ **Cash flow from operations to current liabilities ratio**
_______ **Accounts receivable turnover ratio**
_______ **Number of days' sales in receivables**
_______ **Inventory turnover ratio**
_______ **Number of days' sales in inventory**
_______ **Cash-to-cash operating cycle**

1. A stricter test of liquidity than the current ratio; excludes inventory and prepayments from the numerator.
2. Current assets minus current liabilities.
3. The ratio of current assets to current liabilities.
4. A measure of the average age of accounts receivable.
5. A measure of the ability to pay current debts from operating cash flows.
6. A measure of the number of times accounts receivable are collected in a period.
7. A measure of how long it takes to sell inventory.
8. The length of time from the purchase of inventory to the collection of any receivable from the sale.
9. A measure of the number of times inventory is sold during a period.
10. Gross profit to net sales.
11. A comparison of various financial statement items within a single period with the use of common-size statements.
12. Net income to net sales.
13. The nearness to cash of the assets and liabilities.
14. A comparison of financial statement items over a period of time.

Quiz 2:

_______ **Solvency**

_______ **Debt-to-equity ratio**

_______ **Times interest earned ratio**

_______ **Debt service coverage ratio**

_______ **Cash flow from operations to capital expenditures ratio**

_______ **Profitability**

_______ **Return on assets ratio**

_______ **Return on sales ratio**

_______ **Asset turnover ratio**

_______ **Return on common stockholders' equity ratio**

_______ **Leverage**

_______ **Earnings per share**

_______ **Price/earnings (P/E) ratio**

_______ **Dividend payout ratio**

_______ **Dividend yield ratio**

_______ **Discontinued operations (Appendix)**

_______ **Extraordinary item (Appendix)**

1. A measure of a company's success in earning a return for the common stockholders.
2. The relationship between a company's performance according to the income statement and its performance in the stock market.
3. The ability of a company to remain in business over the long term.
4. A variation of the profit margin ratio; measures earnings before payments to creditors.
5. A company's bottom line stated on a per-share basis.
6. The percentage of earnings paid out as dividends.
7. The ratio of total liabilities to total stockholders' equity.
8. A measure of the ability of a company to finance long-term asset acquisitions with cash from operations.
9. A measure of a company's success in earning a return for all providers of capital.
10. The relationship between net sales and average total assets.
11. The relationship between dividends and the market price of a company's stock.
12. The use of borrowed funds and amounts contributed by preferred stockholders to earn an overall return higher than the cost of these funds.
13. An income statement measure of the ability of a company to meet its interest payments.
14. A statement of cash flows measure of the ability of a company to meet its interest and principal payments.
15. How well management is using company resources to earn a return on the funds invested by various groups.
16. A line item on the income statement to reflect any gains or losses that arise from an event that is both unusual in nature and infrequent in occurrence.
17. A line item on the income statement to reflect any gains or losses from the disposal of a segment of the business as well as any net income or loss from operating that segment.

ALTERNATE TERMS

Acid-test ratio Quick ratio

Horizontal analysis Trend analysis

Number of days' sales in receivables Average collection period

Price/earnings ratio P/E ratio

WARMUP EXERCISES & SOLUTIONS

LO4,5,6

Warmup Exercise 13-1 Types of Ratios

Fill in the blanks to indicate whether each of the following ratios is concerned with a company's liquidity (L), its solvency (S), or its profitability (P).

_______ 1. Return on assets ratio
_______ 2. Current ratio
_______ 3. Debt-to-equity ratio
_______ 4. Earnings per share
_______ 5. Inventory turnover ratio
_______ 6. Gross profit ratio

Key to the Solution Review the summary of selected ratios in Exhibit 13-8.

LO4

Warmup Exercise 13-2 Accounts Receivable Turnover

Company A reported sales during the year of $1,000,000. Its average accounts receivable balance during the year was $250,000. Company B reported sales during the same year of $400,000 and had an average accounts receivable balance of $40,000.

Required

1. Compute the accounts receivable turnover for both companies.
2. What is the average length of time each company takes to collect its receivables?

Key to the Solution Review the summary of selected ratios in Exhibit 13-8.

LO6

Warmup Exercise 13-3 Earnings per Share

A company reported net income during the year of $90,000 and paid dividends of $15,000 to its common stockholders and $10,000 to its preferred stockholders. During the year, 20,000 shares of common stock were outstanding and 10,000 shares of preferred stock were outstanding.

Required

Compute earnings per share for the year.

Key to the Solution Recall that earnings per share has relevance only to the common stockholders; therefore, it is a measure of the earnings per common share outstanding, after taking into account any claims of preferred stockholders.

SOLUTIONS TO WARMUP EXERCISES

Warmup Exercise 13-1

1. P 2. L 3. S 4. P 5. L 6. P

Warmup Exercise 13-2

1. On average, Company A turns over its accounts receivable four times during the year ($1,000,000/$250,000); Company B, ten times during the year ($400,000/$40,000).
2. Assuming 360 days in a year, Company A takes, on average, 90 days to collect its accounts receivable; Company B takes, on average, 36 days.

Warmup Exercise 13-3

Earnings per share: ($90,000 − $10,000)/20,000 shares = $4 per share

REVIEW PROBLEM & SOLUTION

On pages 687–689 are three comparative financial statements for **Wm. Wrigley Jr. Company**, the chewing gum manufacturer, as shown in its 2006 annual report.

Required

1. Compute the following ratios for the two years 2006 and 2005 for each year or as of the end of each of the years, as appropriate. Beginning balances for 2005 are not available; that is, you do not have a balance sheet as of the end of 2004. Therefore, to be consistent, use year-end balances for both years where you would normally use average amounts for the year. To compute the return on assets ratio, you need to find the tax rate. Use the relationship between income taxes and earnings before taxes to find the rate for each year.
   a. Current ratio
   b. Quick ratio
   c. Cash flow from operations to current liabilities ratio
   d. Number of days' sales in receivables
   e. Number of days' sales in inventory
   f. Debt-to-equity ratio
   g. Debt service coverage ratio
   h. Cash flow from operations to capital expenditures ratio
   i. Return on assets ratio
   j. Return on common stockholders' equity ratio
2. Comment on Wrigley's liquidity. Has it improved or declined over the two-year period?
3. Does Wrigley appear to be solvent to you? Does there appear to be anything unusual about its capital structure? Explain.
4. Comment on Wrigley's profitability. Would you buy stock in the company? Why or why not?

Wm. Wrigley Jr. Company
Consolidated Statement of Earnings
In thousands of dollars except per share amounts

	2006	2005	2004
Net sales	$4,686,011	$4,159,306	$3,648,592
Cost of sales	2,211,115	1,863,179	1,615,217
Restructuring charges	45,074	40,223	—
Gross profit	2,429,822	2,255,904	2,033,375
Selling, general and administrative expense	1,608,349	1,479,568	1,313,156
Operating income	821,473	776,336	720,219
Interest expense	(61,820)	(31,648)	(3,879)
Investment income	8,029	15,713	11,872
Other income (expense), net	1,365	(5,741)	(7,716)
Earnings before income taxes	769,047	754,660	720,496
Income taxes	239,670	237,408	227,542
Net earnings	$ 529,377	$ 517,252	$ 492,954
PER SHARE AMOUNTS			
Net earnings per share of Common Stock:			
Basic	$ 1.91	$ 1.84	$ 1.76
Diluted	$ 1.90	$ 1.83	$ 1.75
Dividends paid per share of Common Stock	$ .992	$ .860	$ .740

See accompanying Notes to Consolidated Financial Statements.

Wm. Wrigley Jr. Company
Consolidated Statement of Cash Flows
In thousands of dollars

	2006	2005	2004
OPERATING ACTIVITIES			
Net earnings	$ 529,377	$ 517,252	$ 492,954
Adjustments to reconcile net earnings to net cash provided by operating activities:			
Depreciation and amortization	200,113	175,285	141,851
Net loss on retirements of property, plant, and equipment	6,182	11,714	12,417
Noncash share-based compensation	49,269	26,685	21,278
(Increase) decrease in:			
Accounts receivable	(22,984)	(80,686)	25,706
Inventories	(75,579)	(67,676)	(3,213)
Other current assets	(31,757)	(30,791)	8,937
Deferred charges and other assets	111,656	10,514	(48,911)
Increase (decrease) in:			
Accounts payable	1,684	106,044	43,013
Accrued expenses	(26,869)	85,584	27,285
Income and other taxes payable	78,490	3,363	(6,070)
Other noncurrent liabilities	(23,084)	(23,328)	16,274
Deferred income taxes	(74,062)	6,344	(7,014)
Net cash provided by operating activities	722,436	740,304	724,507
INVESTING ACTIVITIES			
Additions to property, plant, and equipment	(327,758)	(281,769)	(220,322)
Proceeds from retirements of property, plant, and equipment	13,990	10,127	2,468
Acquisitions, net of cash acquired	—	(1,437,428)	(264,477)
Purchases of short-term investments	—	(7,484)	(40,464)
Maturities of short-term investments	—	29,148	40,453
Net cash used in investing activities	(313,768)	(1,687,406)	(482,342)
FINANCING ACTIVITIES			
Dividends paid	(276,021)	(241,669)	(207,803)
Common stock purchased	(143,454)	(214,656)	(84,985)
Common stock issued	26,381	66,102	56,576
Debt issuance costs	—	(16,375)	—
Borrowings (repayments) under the line of credit	—	(90,000)	90,000
Issuances (redemptions) of commercial paper, net	(35,000)	100,000	—
Borrowings of long-term debt	—	1,000,000	—
Net cash provided by (used in) financing activities	(428,094)	603,402	(146,212)
Effect of exchange rate changes on cash and cash equivalents	15,388	(27,149)	27,383
Net increase (decrease) in cash and cash equivalents	(4,038)	(370,849)	123,336
Cash and cash equivalents at beginning of year	257,704	628,553	505,217
Cash and cash equivalents at end of year	$ 253,666	$ 257,704	$ 628,553
SUPPLEMENTAL CASH FLOW INFORMATION			
Income taxes paid	$ 219,873	$ 249,824	$ 234,800
Interest paid	$ 57,621	$ 8,752	$ 3,541
Interest and dividends received	$ 8,031	$ 15,711	$ 11,871

See accompanying Notes to Consolidated Financial Statements.

Wm. Wrigley Jr. Company
Consolidated Balance Sheet
In thousands of dollars and shares

	2006	2005
ASSETS		
Current assets:		
Cash and cash equivalents	$ 253,666	$ 257,704
Short-term investments, at amortized cost	1,100	1,100
Accounts receivable (less allowance for doubtful accounts: 2006-$6,431; 2005-$8,013)	463,231	412,931
Inventories:		
Finished goods	241,897	213,915
Raw materials, work in process and supplies	351,088	287,810
Total inventories	592,985	501,725
Other current assets	170,245	131,617
Total current assets	1,481,227	1,305,077
Deferred charges and other assets	194,382	301,540
Goodwill	1,147,603	1,094,219
Other intangible assets	415,870	411,105
Property, plant, and equipment, at cost:		
Land	78,625	55,882
Buildings and building equipment	717,374	647,479
Machinery and equipment	1,886,018	1,629,231
Total property, plant, and equipment	2,682,017	2,332,592
Less accumulated depreciation	1,259,501	1,050,180
Net property, plant, and equipment	1,422,516	1,282,412
TOTAL ASSETS	$4,661,598	$4,394,353

	2006	2005
LIABILITIES AND STOCKHOLDERS' EQUITY		
Current liabilities:		
Commercial paper	$ 65,000	$ 100,000
Accounts payable	327,671	312,954
Accrued expenses	413,942	432,674
Dividends payable	71,106	62,459
Income and other taxes payable	149,410	71,707
Total current liabilities	1,027,129	979,794
Other noncurrent liabilities	246,377	200,137
Long-term debt	1,000,000	1,000,000
Total liabilities	2,273,506	2,179,931
Stockholders' equity:		
Preferred Stock—no par value Authorized: 20,000 shares Issued: None		
Common Stock—no par value		
Common Stock Authorized: 1,000,000 shares Issued: 2006-228,945 shares; 2005-199,230 shares	14,018	13,274
Class B Common Stock—convertible Authorized: 300,000 shares Issued: 2006-61,606 shares; 2005-91,321 shares	1,478	2,222
Additional paid-in capital	93,602	37,760
Retained earnings	2,949,705	2,702,947
Common Stock and Class B Common Stock in treasury, at cost 2006-13,644 shares; 2005-12,039 shares	(606,045)	(513,763)
Accumulated other comprehensive loss	(64,666)	(28,018)
Total stockholders' equity	2,388,092	2,214,422
TOTAL LIABILITIES AND STOCKHOLDERS' EQUITY	$4,661,598	$4,394,353

See accompanying Notes to Consolidated Financial Statements.

SOLUTION TO REVIEW PROBLEM

1. Ratios:
   a. 2006: $1,481,227/$1,027,129 = 1.44
      2005: $1,305,077/$979,794 = 1.33
   b. 2006: ($253,666 + $1,100 + $463,231)/$1,027,129 = 0.70
      2005: ($257,704 + $1,100 + $412,931)/$979,794 = 0.69
   c. 2006: $722,436/$1,027,129 = 0.70
      2005: $740,304/$979,794 = 0.76
   d. 2006: 360 days/[($4,686,011/$463,231)] = 360/10.12 = 36 days
      2005: 360 days/[($4,159,306/$412,931)] = 360/10.07 = 36 days

e. 2006: 360 days/[($2,211,115/$592,985)] = 360/3.73 = 97 days

2005: 360 days/[($1,863,179/$501,725)] = 360/3.71 = 97 days

f. 2006: $2,273,506/$2,388,092 = 0.95

2005: $2,179,931/$2,214,422 = 0.98

g. 2006: ($722,436 + $219,873 + $57,621)/($57,621 + $35,000[a]) = 10.80

2005: ($740,304 + $249,824 + $8,752)/($8,752 + $90,000[b]) = 10.12

h. 2006: ($722,436 − $276,021)/$327,758 = 1.36

2005: ($740,304 − $241,669)/$281,769 = 1.77

i. 2006: $529,377 + [$61,820(1 − 0.31[c])]/$4,661,598 = 12.3%

2005: $517,252 + [$31,648(1 − 0.31[c])]/$4,394,353 = 12.3%

j. 2006: $529,377/$2,388,092[d] = 22.2%

2005: $517,252/$2,214,420[d] = 23.4%

2. Both the current ratio and the quick ratio improved during 2006. Cash flow from operations to current liabilities declined, although not to a significant extent. Wrigley appears to be liquid and able to meet its short-term obligations.
3. Prior to 2005, Wrigley did not rely in any significant way on long-term debt to finance its business. That changed to a certain extent in 2005 when the company borrowed $1 billion by issuing long-term notes. (See the balance sheet and the Financing Activities section of the statement of cash flows.) Even with this new infusion of debt, the company's debt to equity ratio remained under 1 to 1 at the end of the two most recent years. Also, the debt service coverage ratios at the end of each year are over 10 to 1, indicating that Wrigley had ample funds available to repay interest and principal on its outstanding debt.
4. The return on assets for 2006 is 12.3%, and the return on common stockholders' equity is 22.2%. Although the return on equity ratio is down slightly from the prior year, it indicates a very profitable company. It should be noted that the company paid over half of its 2006 earnings in dividends. Wrigley appears to be a very sound investment; but many other factors, including information on the current market price of the stock, should be considered before making a decision.

[a]Redemptions of commercial paper on the statement of cash flows.
[b]Repayments under line of credit on the statement of cash flows.
[c]Tax rate for each of the two years:
2006: $239,670/$769,047 = 0.31
2005: $237,408/$754,660 = 0.31

[d]In addition to its common stock, Wrigley has outstanding Class B common stock. Because this is a second class of stock (similar in many respects to preferred stock), the contributed capital attributable to it should be deducted from total stockholders' equity in the denominator. Similarly, any dividends paid on the Class B common stock should be deducted from net income in the numerator to find the return to the regular common stockholders. We have ignored the difficulties involved in determining these adjustments in our calculations of return on equity.

HOMEWORK

QUESTIONS

1. Two companies are in the same industry. Company A uses the LIFO method of inventory valuation, and Company B uses FIFO. What difficulties does this present when comparing the two companies?

2. You are told to compare the company's results for the year, as measured by various ratios, with one of the published surveys that arranges information by industry classification. What are some of the difficulties you may encounter when making comparisons using industry standards?

3. What types of problems does inflation cause when financial statements are analyzed?

4. Distinguish between horizontal and vertical analysis. Why is the analysis of common-size statements called *vertical* analysis? Why is horizontal analysis sometimes called *trend* analysis?

5. A company experiences a 15% increase in sales over the previous year. However, gross profit actually decreased by 5% from the previous year. What are some of the possible causes for an increase in sales but a decline in gross profit?

6. A company's total current assets have increased by 5% over the prior year. Management is concerned, however, about the composition of the current assets. Why is the composition of current assets important?

7. Ratios were categorized in the chapter according to their use in performing three different types of analysis. What are the three types of ratios?

8. Describe the operating cycle for a manufacturing company. How would the cycle differ for a retailer?

9. What accounts for the order in which current assets are presented on a balance sheet?

10. A company has a current ratio of 1.25 but an acid-test (or quick) ratio of only 0.65. How can this difference in the two ratios be explained? What concerns might you have about this company?

11. Explain the basic concept underlying all turnover ratios. Why is it advisable in computing a turnover ratio to use an average in the denominator (for example, average inventory)?

12. Sanders Company's accounts receivable turned over nine times during the year. The credit department extends terms of 2/10, net 30. Does the turnover ratio indicate any problems that management should investigate? Explain.

13. The turnover of inventory for Ace Company has slowed from 6.0 times per year to 4.5. What are some possible explanations for this decrease?

14. How does the operating cycle for a manufacturer differ from the operating cycle for a service company (e.g., an airline?)

15. What is the difference between liquidity analysis and solvency analysis?

16. Why is the debt service coverage ratio a better measure of solvency than the times interest earned ratio?

17. A friend tells you that the best way to assess solvency is by comparing total debt to total assets. Another friend says that solvency is measured by comparing total debt to total stockholders' equity. Which friend is correct?

18. A company is in the process of negotiating with a bank for an additional loan. Why will the bank be interested in the company's debt service coverage ratio?

19. What is the rationale for deducting dividends when computing the ratio of cash flow from operations to capital expenditures?

20. The rate of return on assets ratio is computed by dividing net income and interest expense, net of tax, by average total assets. Why is the numerator net income and interest expense, net of tax, rather than just net income?

21. A company has a return on assets of 14% and a return on common stockholders' equity of 11%. The president of the company has asked you to explain the reason for this difference. What causes the difference? How is the concept of financial leverage involved?

22. What is meant by the "quality" of a company's earnings? Explain why the price/earnings ratio for a company may indicate the quality of earnings.

23. Some ratios are more useful for management, whereas others are better suited to the needs of outsiders, such as stockholders and bankers. What is an example of a ratio that is primarily suited to management use? What ratio is more suited to use by outsiders?

24. The needs of service-oriented companies in analyzing financial statements differ from those of product-oriented companies. Why is this true? Give an example of a ratio that is meaningless to a service business.

25. What is the reason for reporting discontinued operations and extraordinary items in a separate section of an income statement? (Appendix)

BRIEF EXERCISES

LO1

Brief Exercise 13-1 Limitations in Ratio Analysis

A supplier is thinking of extending credit to a company but decides not to because the company's current ratio is only 0.50. Do you agree with the supplier's decision? What other factors need to be considered in drawing any conclusions about a company's liquidity?

LO2

Brief Exercise 13-2 Horizontal Analysis

Fill in the blanks for each of the following statements.
A comparison of financial statement items within a single period is called ________ analysis.
A comparison of financial statement items over a period of time is called ________ analysis.

LO3

Brief Exercise 13-3 Vertical Analysis

Assume that your boss has asked you to prepare common-size financial statements. All accounts on the balance sheet should be stated as a percentage of which number? All accounts on the income statement should be stated as a percentage of which number?

LO4

Brief Exercise 13-4 Liquidity Analysis

For each of the following ratios, fill in the missing numerator.

Ratio

Ratio	Numerator / Denominator
Current:	________ / Current Liabilities
Acid-Test:	________ / Current Liabilities
Accounts Receivable Turnover:	________ / Average Accounts Receivable
Inventory Turnover:	________ / Average Inventory

LO5

Brief Exercise 13-5 Solvency Analysis

Fill in the blank with the name of the ratio that would be used for each of the following situations.

Ratio	Measures the ability of the company to
________	Meet its interest and principal payments
________	Finance long-term asset acquisitions with cash from operations
________	Meet its interest payments

LO6

Brief Exercise 13-6 Profitability Analysis

For each of the following ratios, indicate what adjustment must be made to net income in the numerator and whether the adjustment is an addition to (A) or a deduction from (D) net income.

Ratio	Adjustment to Net Income in Numerator (A) or (D)
Return on assets	________
Return on common stockholders' equity	________
Earnings per share	________
Return on sales	________

LO7

Brief Exercise 13-7 Other Income Statement Items

Fill in the blank to indicate the line item that would appear on the income statement for each of the following events.

Item on Income Statement	Event
________	Disposed of a segment of the business
________	Incurred a loss from an event that was unusual and infrequently occurring

EXERCISES

LO4

Exercise 13-1 Accounts Receivable Analysis

The following account balances are taken from the records of the Faraway Travel Agency:

	December 31		
	2008	**2007**	**2006**
Accounts receivable	$150,000	$100,000	$80,000
	2008	**2007**	
Net credit sales	$600,000	$540,000	

Faraway extends credit terms requiring full payment in 60 days, with no discount for early payment.

Required
1. Compute Faraway's accounts receivable turnover ratio for 2008 and 2007.
2. Compute the number of days' sales in receivables for 2008 and 2007. Assume 360 days in a year.
3. Comment on the efficiency of Faraway's collection efforts over the two-year period.

LO4

Exercise 13-2 Inventory Analysis

The following account balances are taken from the records of Lewis Inc., a wholesaler of fresh fruits and vegetables:

	December 31		
	2008	2007	2006
Merchandise inventory	$ 200,000	$ 150,000	$120,000
	2008	2007	
Cost of goods sold	$7,100,000	$8,100,000	

Required
1. Compute Lewis's inventory turnover ratio for 2008 and 2007.
2. Compute the number of days' sales in inventory for 2008 and 2007. Assume 360 days in a year.
3. Comment on your answers in (1) and (2) relative to the company's management of inventory over the two years. What problems do you see in its inventory management?

LO4

Exercise 13-3 Accounts Receivable and Inventory Analyses for Coca-Cola and PepsiCo

The following information was obtained from the 2006 and 2005 financial statements of **Coca-Cola Company and Subsidiaries** and **PepsiCo Inc. and Subsidiaries.** (Year-ends for PepsiCo are December 30, 2006 and December 31, 2005.)

(in millions)		Coca-Cola	PepsiCo
Accounts and notes receivable, net[a]	12/31/06	$ 2,587	$ 3,725
	12/31/05	2,281	3,261
Inventories	12/31/06	1,641	1,926
	12/31/05	1,379	1,693
Net revenue[b]	2006	24,088	35,137
	2005	23,104	32,562
Cost of goods sold[c]	2006	8,164	15,762
	2005	8,195	14,176

[a]Described as "trade accounts receivable, less allowances" by Coca-Cola.
[b]Described as "net operating revenues" by Coca-Cola.
[c]Described as "cost of sales" by PepsiCo.

Required
1. Using the information provided, compute the following for each company for 2006:
   a. Accounts receivable turnover ratio
   b. Number of days' sales in receivables
   c. Inventory turnover ratio
   d. Number of days' sales in inventory
   e. Cash-to-cash operating cycle
2. Comment briefly on the liquidity of each of these two companies.

LO4

Exercise 13-4 Liquidity Analyses for Coca-Cola and PepsiCo

The following information was summarized from the balance sheets of the **Coca-Cola Company and Subsidiaries** at December 31, 2006, and **PepsiCo Inc. and Subsidiaries** at December 30, 2006:

(in millions)	Coca-Cola	PepsiCo
Cash and cash equivalents	$2,440	$1,651
Short-term investments/marketable securities	150	1,171
Accounts and notes receivables, net*	2,587	3,725
Inventories	1,641	1,926
Prepaid expenses and other current assets	1,623	657
Total current assets	$8,441	$9,130
Current liabilities	$8,890	$6,860

**Described as "trade accounts receivable, less allowances" by Coca-Cola.*

Required

1. Using the information provided, compute the following for each company at the end of 2006:
   a. Current ratio
   b. Quick ratio
2. Comment briefly on the liquidity of each of these two companies. Which appears to be more liquid?
3. What other ratios would help you more fully assess the liquidity of these companies?

LO4

Exercise 13-5 Liquidity Analyses for McDonald's and Wendy's

The following information was summarized from the balance sheets of **McDonald's Corporation** and **Wendy's International Inc.** at December 31, 2006.

	McDonald's (in millions)	Wendy's (in thousands)
Current Assets:		
Cash and cash equivalents	$ 2,136.4	$ 457,614
Accounts receivable, net*	904.2	84,841
Deferred income taxes	0	29,651
Inventories**	149.0	30,252
Other current assets	435.7	54,374
Total current assets	$ 3,625.3	$ 656,732
Current liabilities	$ 3,008.1	$ 394,666
Noncurrent liabilities	$10,557.4	$ 654,004
Shareholders' equity	$15,458.3	$1,011,677

**McDonald's combines accounts and notes receivable.*
***Inventories and other for Wendy's.*

Required

1. Using the information provided, compute the following for each company at year end:
   a. Working capital
   b. Current ratio
   c. Quick ratio
2. Comment briefly on the liquidity of each of these two companies. Which appears to be more liquid?
3. McDonald's reported cash flows from operations of $4,341.5 million during 2006. Wendy's reported cash flows from operations of $271,379 thousand. Current liabilities reported by McDonald's at December 31, 2005, and Wendy's at January 1, 2006, were $4,107.7 million and $583,352 thousand, respectively. Calculate the cash flow from operations to current liabilities ratio for each company. Does the information provided by this ratio change your opinion as to the relative liquidity of each of these two companies?

LO5

Exercise 13-6 Solvency Analyses for IBM

The following information was obtained from the comparative financial statements included in **IBM**'s 2006 annual report. (All amounts are in millions of dollars.)

	December 31, 2006	December 31, 2005
Total liabilities	$74,728	$72,650
Total stockholders' equity	28,506	33,098

	For the Years Ended December 31	
	2006	2005
Interest expense	$ 278	$ 220
Provision for income taxes	3,901	4,232
Net income	9,492	7,934
Net cash provided by operating activities from continuing operations	15,019	14,914
Cash dividends paid	1,683	1,250
Payments for plant, rental machines and other property	4,362	3,842
Payments to settle debt	3,400	3,522

Required

1. Using the information provided, compute the following for 2006 and 2005:
   a. Debt-to-equity ratio (at each year-end)
   b. Times interest earned ratio
   c. Debt service coverage ratio
   d. Cash flow from operations to capital expenditures ratio
2. Comment briefly on the company's solvency.

LO5

Exercise 13-7 Solvency Analysis

The following information is available from the balance sheets at the ends of the two most recent years and the income statement for the most recent year of Impact Company:

	December 31	
	2008	2007
Accounts payable	$ 65,000	$ 50,000
Accrued liabilities	25,000	35,000
Taxes payable	60,000	45,000
Short-term notes payable	0	75,000
Bonds payable due within next year	200,000	200,000
Total current liabilities	$ 350,000	$ 405,000
Bonds payable	$ 600,000	$ 800,000
Common stock, $10 par	$1,000,000	$1,000,000
Retained earnings	650,000	500,000
Total stockholders' equity	$1,650,000	$1,500,000
Total liabilities and stockholders' equity	$2,600,000	$2,705,000

	2008
Sales revenue	$1,600,000
Cost of goods sold	950,000
Gross profit	$ 650,000
Selling and administrative expense	300,000
Operating income	$ 350,000
Interest expense	89,000
Income before tax	$ 261,000
Income tax expense	111,000
Net income	$ 150,000

Other Information

a. Short-term notes payable represents a 12-month loan that matured in November 2008. Interest of 12% was paid at maturity.
b. One million dollars of serial bonds had been issued ten years earlier. The first series of $200,000 matured at the end of 2008, with interest of 8% payable annually.
c. Cash flow from operations was $185,000 in 2008. The amounts of interest and taxes paid during 2008 were $89,000 and $96,000, respectively.

Required

1. Compute the following for Impact Company:
   a. The debt-to-equity ratio at December 31, 2008, and December 31, 2007
   b. The times interest earned ratio for 2008
   c. The debt service coverage ratio for 2008
2. Comment on Impact's solvency at the end of 2008. Do the times interest earned ratio and the debt service coverage ratio differ in their indication of Impact's ability to pay its debts? Explain.

LO6

Exercise 13-8 Return Ratios and Leverage

The following selected data are taken from the financial statements of Evergreen Company:

Sales revenue	$ 650,000
Cost of goods sold	400,000
Gross profit	$ 250,000
Selling and administrative expense	100,000
Operating income	$ 150,000
Interest expense	50,000
Income before tax	$ 100,000
Income tax expense (40%)	40,000
Net income	$ 60,000
Accounts payable	$ 45,000
Accrued liabilities	70,000
Income taxes payable	10,000
Interest payable	25,000
Short-term loans payable	150,000
Total current liabilities	$ 300,000
Long-term bonds payable	$ 500,000
Preferred stock, 10%, $100 par	$ 250,000
Common stock, no par	600,000
Retained earnings	350,000
Total stockholders' equity	$1,200,000
Total liabilities and stockholders' equity	$2,000,000

Required

1. Compute the following ratios for Evergreen Company:
   a. Return on sales
   b. Asset turnover (Assume that total assets at the beginning of the year were $1,600,000.)
   c. Return on assets
   d. Return on common stockholders' equity (Assume that the only changes in stockholders' equity during the year were from the net income for the year and dividends on the preferred stock.)
2. Comment on Evergreen's use of leverage. Has it successfully employed leverage? Explain.

LO6

Exercise 13-9 Relationships among Return on Assets, Return on Sales, and Asset Turnover

A company's return on assets is a function of its ability to turn over its investment (asset turnover) and earn a profit on each dollar of sales (return on sales). For each of the following independent cases, determine the missing amounts. (*Note:* Assume in each case that the company has no interest expense; that is, net income is used as the definition of income in all calculations.)

Case 1	
Net income	$10,000
Net sales	$80,000
Average total assets	$60,000
Return on assets	?
Case 2	
Net income	$25,000
Average total assets	$250,000
Return on sales	2%
Net sales	?
Case 3	
Average total assets	$80,000
Asset turnover	1.5 times
Return on sales	6%
Return on assets	?
Case 4	
Return on assets	10%
Net sales	$50,000
Asset turnover	1.25 times
Net income	?

Case 5	
Return on assets	15%
Net income	$20,000
Return on sales	5%
Average total assets	?

LO6 **Exercise 13-10** EPS, P/E Ratio, and Dividend Ratios

The stockholders' equity section of the balance sheet for Cooperstown Corp. at the end of 2008 appears as follows:

8%, $100 par, cumulative preferred stock, 200,000 shares authorized, 50,000 shares issued and outstanding	$ 5,000,000
Additional paid-in capital on preferred	2,500,000
Common stock, $5 par, 500,000 shares authorized, 400,000 shares issued and outstanding	2,000,000
Additional paid-in capital on common	18,000,000
Retained earnings	37,500,000
Total stockholders' equity	$65,000,000

Net income for the year was $1,300,000. Dividends were declared and paid on the preferred shares during the year, and a quarterly dividend of $0.40 per share was declared and paid each quarter on the common shares. The closing market price for the common shares on December 31, 2008, was $24.75 per share.

Required

1. Compute the following ratios for the common stock:
   a. Earnings per share
   b. Price/earnings ratio
   c. Dividend payout ratio
   d. Dividend yield ratio
2. Assume that you are an investment adviser. What other information would you want to have before advising a client regarding the purchase of Cooperstown stock?

MULTICONCEPT EXERCISES

LO6,7 **Exercise 13-11** Earnings per Share and Extraordinary Items

The stockholders' equity section of the balance sheet for Lahey Construction Company at the end of 2008 is as follows:

9%, $10 par, cumulative preferred stock, 500,000 shares authorized, 200,000 shares issued and outstanding	$ 2,000,000
Additional paid-in capital on preferred	7,500,000
Common stock, $1 par, 2,500,000 shares authorized, 1,500,000 shares issued and outstanding	1,500,000
Additional paid-in capital on common	21,000,000
Retained earnings	25,500,000
Total stockholders' equity	$57,500,000

The lower portion of the 2008 income statement indicates the following:

Net income before tax		$ 9,750,000
Income tax expense (40%)		(3,900,000)
Income before extraordinary items		$ 5,850,000
Extraordinary loss from flood	$(6,200,000)	
Less related tax effect (40%)	2,480,000	(3,720,000)
Net income		$ 2,130,000

Assume that the number of shares outstanding did not change during the year.

Required

1. Compute earnings per share *before* extraordinary items.
2. Compute earnings per share *after* the extraordinary loss.
3. Which of the two EPS ratios is more useful to management? Explain your answer. Would your answer be different if the ratios were to be used by an outsider (e.g., by a potential stockholder)? Why or why not?

LO2,3

Exercise 13-12 Common-Size Balance Sheets and Horizontal Analysis

Comparative balance sheets for Farinet Company for the past two years are as follows:

	December 31	
	2008	2007
Cash	$ 16,000	$ 20,000
Accounts receivable	40,000	30,000
Inventory	30,000	50,000
Prepaid rent	18,000	12,000
Total current assets	$104,000	$112,000
Land	$150,000	$150,000
Plant and equipment	800,000	600,000
Accumulated depreciation	(130,000)	(60,000)
Total long-term assets	$820,000	$690,000
Total assets	$924,000	$802,000
Accounts payable	$ 24,000	$ 20,000
Income taxes payable	6,000	10,000
Short-term notes payable	70,000	50,000
Total current liabilities	$100,000	$ 80,000
Bonds payable	$150,000	$200,000
Common stock	$400,000	$300,000
Retained earnings	274,000	222,000
Total stockholders' equity	$674,000	$522,000
Total liabilities and stockholders' equity	$924,000	$802,000

Required

1. Using the format in Exhibit 13-5, prepare common-size comparative balance sheets for the two years for Farinet Company.
2. What observations can you make about changes in the relative composition of Farinet's accounts from the common-size balance sheets? List at least five observations.
3. Using the format in Exhibit 13-1, prepare comparative balance sheets for Farinet Company, including columns for the dollars and for the percentage increase or decrease in each item on the statement.
4. Identify the five items on the balance sheet that experienced the largest change from one year to the next. For each of these items, explain where you would look to find additional information about the change.

LO2,3

Exercise 13-13 Common-Size Income Statements and Horizontal Analysis

Income statements for Mariners Corp. for the past two years are as follows:

	(amounts in thousands of dollars)	
	2008	2007
Sales revenue	$60,000	$50,000
Cost of goods sold	42,000	30,000
Gross profit	$18,000	$20,000
Selling and administrative expense	9,000	5,000
Operating income	$ 9,000	$15,000
Interest expense	2,000	2,000
Income before tax	$ 7,000	$13,000
Income tax expense	2,000	4,000
Net income	$ 5,000	$ 9,000

Required

1. Using the format in Exhibit 13-6, prepare common-size comparative income statements for the two years for Mariners Corp.
2. What observations can you make about the common-size statements? List at least four observations.
3. Using the format in Exhibit 13-2, prepare comparative income statements for Mariners Corp., including columns for the dollars and for the percentage increase or decrease in each item on the statement.
4. Identify the two items on the income statement that experienced the largest change from one year to the next. For each of these items, explain where you would look to find additional information about the change.

PROBLEMS

LO4

Problem 13-1 Effect of Transactions on Working Capital, Current Ratio, and Quick Ratio

(*Note:* Consider completing Problem 13-2 after this problem to ensure that you obtain a clear understanding of the effect of various transactions on these measures of liquidity.)
The following account balances are taken from the records of Liquiform Inc.:

Cash	$ 70,000
Short-term investments	60,000
Accounts receivable	80,000
Inventory	100,000
Prepaid insurance	10,000
Accounts payable	75,000
Taxes payable	25,000
Salaries and wages payable	40,000
Short-term loans payable	60,000

Required

1. Use the information provided to compute the amount of working capital and Liquiform's current and quick ratios (round to three decimal points).
2. Determine the effect that each of the following transactions will have on Liquiform's working capital, current ratio, and quick ratio by recalculating each and then indicating whether the measure is increased, decreased, or not affected by the transaction. (For the ratios, round to three decimal points.) Consider each transaction independently; that is, assume that it is the *only* transaction that takes place.

	Effect of Transaction on		
Transaction	**Working Capital**	**Current Ratio**	**Quick Ratio**
a. Purchased inventory on account for $20,000			
b. Purchased inventory for cash, $15,000			
c. Paid suppliers on account, $30,000			
d. Received cash on account, $40,000			
e. Paid insurance for next year, $20,000			
f. Made sales on account, $60,000			
g. Repaid short-term loans at bank, $25,000			
h. Borrowed $40,000 at bank for 90 days			
i. Declared and paid $45,000 cash dividend			
j. Purchased $20,000 of short-term investments			
k. Paid $30,000 in salaries			
l. Accrued additional $15,000 in taxes			

LO4

Problem 13-2 Effect of Transactions on Working Capital, Current Ratio, and Quick Ratio

(*Note:* Consider completing this problem after Problem 13-1 to ensure that you obtain a clear understanding of the effect of various transactions on these measures of liquidity.)
The following account balances are taken from the records of Veriform Inc.:

Cash	$ 70,000
Short-term investments	60,000
Accounts receivable	80,000
Inventory	100,000
Prepaid insurance	10,000
Accounts payable	75,000
Taxes payable	25,000
Salaries and wages payable	40,000
Short-term loans payable	210,000

Required

1. Use the information provided to compute the amount of working capital and Veriform's current and quick ratios (round to three decimal points).
2. Determine the effect that each of the following transactions will have on Veriform's working capital, current ratio, and quick ratio by recalculating each and then indicating whether the measure is increased, decreased, or not affected by the transaction. (For the ratios, round to three decimal points.) Consider each transaction independently; that is, assume that it is the *only* transaction that takes place.

	Effect of Transaction on		
Transaction	**Working Capital**	**Current Ratio**	**Quick Ratio**
a. Purchased inventory on account for $20,000			
b. Purchased inventory for cash, $15,000			
c. Paid suppliers on account, $30,000			
d. Received cash on account, $40,000			
e. Paid insurance for next year, $20,000			
f. Made sales on account, $60,000			
g. Repaid short-term loans at bank, $25,000			
h. Borrowed $40,000 at bank for 90 days			
i. Declared and paid $45,000 cash dividend			
j. Purchased $20,000 of short-term investments			
k. Paid $30,000 in salaries			
l. Accrued additional $15,000 in taxes			

LO6

Problem 13-3 Goals for Sales and Return on Assets

The president of Blue Skies Corp. is reviewing with his vice presidents the operating results of the year just completed. Sales increased by 15% from the previous year to $60,000,000. Average total assets for the year were $40,000,000. Net income, after adding back interest expense, net of tax, was $5,000,000.

The president is happy with the performance over the past year but is never satisfied with the status quo. He has set two specific goals for next year: (1) a 20% growth in sales and (2) a return on assets of 15%.

To achieve the second goal, the president has stated his intention to increase the total asset base by 12.5% over the base for the year just completed.

Required

1. For the year just completed, compute the following ratios:
   a. Return on sales
   b. Asset turnover
   c. Return on assets

HOMEWORK

2. Compute the necessary asset turnover for next year to achieve the president's goal of a 20% increase in sales.
3. Calculate the income needed next year to achieve the goal of a 15% return on total assets. (*Note:* Assume that *income* is defined as net income plus interest, net of tax.)
4. Based on your answers to (2) and (3), comment on the reasonableness of the president's goals. On what must the company focus to attain these goals?

LO6

Problem 13-4 Goals for Sales and Income Growth

Sunrise Corp. is a major regional retailer. The chief executive officer (CEO) is concerned with the slow growth both of sales and of net income and the subsequent effect on the trading price of the common stock. Selected financial data for the past three years follow.

Sunrise Corp.
(in millions)

	2008	2007	2006
1. Sales	$200.0	$192.5	$187.0
2. Net income	6.0	5.8	5.6
3. Dividends declared and paid	2.5	2.5	2.5
December 31 balances:			
4. Owners' equity	70.0	66.5	63.2
5. Debt	30.0	29.8	30.3
Selected year-end financial ratios			
Net income to sales	3.0%	3.0%	3.0%
Asset turnover	2 times	2 times	2 times
6. Return on owners' equity*	8.6%	8.7%	8.9%
7. Debt to total assets	30.0%	30.9%	32.4%

**Based on year-end balances in owners' equity.*

The CEO believes that the price of the stock has been adversely affected by the downward trend of the return on equity, the relatively low dividend payout ratio, and the lack of dividend increases. To improve the price of the stock, she wants to improve the return on equity and dividends.

She believes that the company should be able to meet these objectives by (1) increasing sales and net income at an annual rate of 10% a year and (2) establishing a new dividend policy that calls for a dividend payout of 50% of earnings or $3,000,000, whichever is larger.

The 10% annual sales increase will be accomplished through a new promotional program. The president believes that the present net income to sales ratio of 3% will be unchanged by the cost of this new program and any interest paid on new debt. She expects that the company can accomplish this sales and income growth while maintaining the current relationship of total assets to sales. Any capital that is needed to maintain this relationship and that is not generated internally would be acquired through long-term debt financing. The CEO hopes that debt would not exceed 35% of total liabilities and owners' equity.

Required

1. Using the CEO's program, prepare a schedule that shows the appropriate data for the years 2009, 2010, and 2011 for the items numbered 1 through 7 on the preceding schedule.
2. Can the CEO meet all of her requirements if a 10% per-year growth in income and sales is achieved? Explain your answer.
3. What alternative actions should the CEO consider to improve the return on equity and to support increased dividend payments?
4. Explain the reasons that the CEO might have for wanting to limit debt to 35% of total liabilities and owners' equity.

(CMA adapted)

MULTICONCEPT PROBLEMS

LO4,5,6

Problem 13-5 Basic Financial Ratios

The accounting staff of CCB Enterprises has completed the financial statements for the 2008 calendar year. The statement of income for the current year and the comparative statements of financial position for 2008 and 2007 follow.

CCB Enterprises
Statement of Income
For the Year Ended December 31, 2008
(thousands omitted)

Revenue:	
Net sales	$800,000
Other	60,000
Total revenue	$860,000
Expenses:	
Cost of goods sold	$540,000
Research and development	25,000
Selling and administrative	155,000
Interest	20,000
Total expenses	$740,000
Income before income taxes	$120,000
Income taxes	48,000
Net income	$ 72,000

CCB Enterprises
Comparative Statements of Financial Position
December 31, 2008 and 2007
(thousands omitted)

	2008	2007
Assets		
Current assets:		
Cash and short-term investments	$ 26,000	$ 21,000
Receivables, less allowance for doubtful accounts ($1,100 in 2008 and $1,400 in 2007)	48,000	50,000
Inventories, at lower of FIFO cost or market	65,000	62,000
Prepaid items and other current assets	5,000	3,000
Total current assets	$144,000	$136,000
Other assets:		
Investments, at cost	$106,000	$106,000
Deposits	10,000	8,000
Total other assets	$116,000	$114,000
Property, plant, and equipment:		
Land	$ 12,000	$ 12,000
Buildings and equipment, less accumulated depreciation ($126,000 in 2008 and $122,000 in 2007)	268,000	248,000
Total property, plant, and equipment	$280,000	$260,000
Total assets	$540,000	$510,000
Liabilities and Owners' Equity		
Current liabilities:		
Short-term loans	$ 22,000	$ 24,000
Accounts payable	72,000	71,000
Salaries, wages, and other	26,000	27,000
Total current liabilities	$120,000	$122,000
Long-term debt	$160,000	$171,000
Total liabilities	$280,000	$293,000
Owners' equity:		
Common stock, at par	$ 44,000	$ 42,000
Paid-in capital in excess of par	64,000	61,000
Total paid-in capital	$108,000	$103,000
Retained earnings	152,000	114,000
Total owners' equity	$260,000	$217,000
Total liabilities and owners' equity	$540,000	$510,000

Required:

1. Calculate the following financial ratios for 2008 for CCB Enterprises:
   a. Times interest earned
   b. Return on total assets
   c. Return on common stockholders' equity
   d. Debt-equity ratio (at December 31, 2008)
   e. Current ratio (at December 31, 2008)
   f. Quick (acid-test) ratio (at December 31, 2008)
   g. Accounts receivable turnover ratio (Assume that all sales are on credit.)
   h. Number of days' sales in receivables
   i. Inventory turnover ratio (Assume that all purchases are on credit.)
   j. Number of days' sales in inventory
   k. Number of days in cash operating cycle
2. Prepare a few brief comments on the overall financial health of CCB Enterprises. For each comment, indicate any information that is not provided in the problem and that you would need to fully evaluate the company's financial health.

(CMA adapted)

LO5,6

Problem 13-6 Projected Results to Meet Corporate Objectives

Tablon Inc. is a wholly owned subsidiary of Marbel Co. The philosophy of Marbel's management is to allow the subsidiaries to operate as independent units. Corporate control is exercised through the establishment of minimum objectives for each subsidiary, accompanied by substantial rewards for success and penalties for failure. The time period for performance review is long enough for competent managers to display their abilities.

Each quarter the subsidiary is required to submit financial statements. The statements are accompanied by a letter from the subsidiary president explaining the results to date, a forecast for the remainder of the year, and the actions to be taken to achieve the objectives if the forecast indicates that the objectives will not be met.

Marbel management, in conjunction with Tablon management, had set the objectives listed below for the year ending May 31, 2009. These objectives are similar to those set in previous years.

- Sales growth of 20%
- Return on stockholders' equity of 15%
- A long-term debt-to-equity ratio of not more than 1.0
- Payment of a cash dividend of 50% of net income, with a minimum payment of at least $400,000

Tablon's controller has just completed the financial statements for the six months ended November 30, 2008, and the forecast for the year ending May 31, 2009. The statements follow.

After a cursory glance at the financial statements, Tablon's president concluded that not all objectives would be met. At a staff meeting of the Tablon management, the president asked the controller to review the projected results and recommend possible actions that could be taken during the remainder of the year so that Tablon would be more likely to meet the objectives.

Tablon Inc.
Income Statement
(thousands omitted)

	Year Ended May 31, 2008	Six Months Ended November 30, 2008	Forecast for Year Ending May 31, 2009
Sales	$25,000	$15,000	$30,000
Cost of goods sold	$13,000	$ 8,000	$16,000
Selling expenses	5,000	3,500	7,000
Administrative expenses and interest	4,000	2,500	5,000
Income taxes (40%)	1,200	400	800
Total expenses and taxes	$23,200	$14,400	$28,800
Net income	$ 1,800	$ 600	$ 1,200
Dividends declared and paid	600	0	600
Income retained	$ 1,200	$ 600	$ 600

Tablon Inc.
Statement of Financial Position
(thousands omitted)

	May 31, 2008	November 30, 2008	Forecast for May 31, 2009
Assets			
Cash	$ 400	$ 500	$ 500
Accounts receivable (net)	4,100	6,500	7,100
Inventory	7,000	8,500	8,600
Plant and equipment (net)	6,500	7,000	7,300
Total assets	$18,000	$22,500	$23,500
Liabilities and Equities			
Accounts payable	$ 3,000	$ 4,000	$ 4,000
Accrued taxes	300	200	200
Long-term borrowing	6,000	9,000	10,000
Common stock	5,000	5,000	5,000
Retained earnings	3,700	4,300	4,300
Total liabilities and equities	$18,000	$22,500	$23,500

Required

1. Calculate the projected results for each of the four objectives established for Tablon Inc. State which results will not meet the objectives by year-end.
2. From the data presented, identify the factors that seem to contribute to the failure of Tablon Inc. to meet all of its objectives.
3. Explain the possible actions that the controller could recommend in response to the president's request.

(CMA adapted)

LO4,5,6

Problem 13-7 Comparison with Industry Averages

Heartland Inc. is a medium-size company that has been in business for 20 years. The industry has become very competitive in the last few years, and Heartland has decided that it must grow if it is going to survive. It has approached the bank for a sizable five-year loan, and the bank has requested Heartland's most recent financial statements as part of the loan package.

The industry in which Heartland operates consists of approximately 20 companies relatively equal in size. The trade association to which all of the competitors belong publishes an annual survey of the industry, including industry averages for selected ratios for the competitors. All companies voluntarily submit their statements to the association for this purpose.

Heartland's controller is aware that the bank has access to this survey and is very concerned about how the company fared this past year compared with the rest of the industry. The ratios included in the publication and the averages for the past year are as follows:

Ratio	Industry Average
Current ratio	1.23
Acid-test (quick) ratio	0.75
Accounts receivable turnover	33 times
Inventory turnover	29 times
Debt-to-equity ratio	0.53
Times interest earned	8.65 times
Return on sales	6.57%
Asset turnover	1.95 times
Return on assets	12.81%
Return on common stockholders' equity	17.67%

The financial statements to be submitted to the bank in connection with the loan follow.

Heartland Inc.
Statement of Income and Retained Earnings
For the Year Ended December 31, 2008
(thousands omitted)

Sales revenue	$542,750
Cost of goods sold	(435,650)
Gross profit	$107,100
Selling, general, and administrative expenses	$(65,780)
Loss on sales of securities	(220)
Income before interest and taxes	$ 41,100
Interest expense	(9,275)
Income before taxes	$ 31,825
Income tax expense	(12,730)
Net income	$ 19,095
Retained earnings, January 1, 2008	58,485
	$ 77,580
Dividends paid on common stock	(12,000)
Retained earnings, December 31, 2008	$ 65,580

Heartland Inc.
Comparative Statements of Financial Position
(thousands omitted)

	December 31, 2008	December 31, 2007
Assets		
Current assets:		
Cash	$ 1,135	$ 750
Marketable securities	1,250	2,250
Accounts receivable, net of allowances	15,650	12,380
Inventories	12,680	15,870
Prepaid items	385	420
Total current assets	$ 31,100	$ 31,670
Long-term investments	$ 425	$ 425
Property, plant, and equipment:		
Land	$ 32,000	$ 32,000
Buildings and equipment, net of accumulated depreciation	216,000	206,000
Total property, plant, and equipment	$248,000	$238,000
Total assets	$279,525	$270,095
Liabilities and Stockholders' Equity		
Current liabilities:		
Short-term notes	$ 8,750	$ 12,750
Accounts payable	20,090	14,380
Salaries and wages payable	1,975	2,430
Income taxes payable	3,130	2,050
Total current liabilities	$ 33,945	$ 31,610
Long-term bonds payable	$ 80,000	$ 80,000
Stockholders' equity:		
Common stock, no par	$100,000	$100,000
Retained earnings	65,580	58,485
Total stockholders' equity	$165,580	$158,485
Total liabilities and stockholders' equity	$279,525	$270,095

Required

1. Prepare a columnar report for the controller of Heartland Inc. comparing the industry averages for the ratios published by the trade association with the comparable ratios for Heartland. For Heartland, compute the ratios as of December 31, 2008, or for the year ending December 31, 2008, whichever is appropriate.
2. Briefly evaluate Heartland's ratios relative to the industry averages.
3. Do you think that the bank will approve the loan? Explain your answer.

ALTERNATE PROBLEMS

LO5

Problem 13-1A Effect of Transactions on Debt-to-Equity Ratio

(*Note:* Consider completing Problem 13-2A after this problem to ensure that you obtain a clear understanding of the effect of various transactions on this measure of solvency.)
The following account balances are taken from the records of Monet's Garden Inc.:

Current liabilities	$150,000
Long-term liabilities	375,000
Stockholders' equity	400,000

Required
1. Use the information provided to compute Monet's debt-to-equity ratio (round to three decimal points).
2. Determine the effect that each of the following transactions will have on Monet's debt-to-equity ratio by recalculating the ratio and then indicating whether the ratio is increased, decreased, or not affected by the transaction. (Round to three decimal points.) Consider each transaction independently; that is, assume that it is the *only* transaction that takes place.

Transaction	Effect of Transaction on Debt-to-Equity Ratio
a. Purchased inventory on account for $20,000	
b. Purchased inventory for cash, $15,000	
c. Paid suppliers on account, $30,000	
d. Received cash on account, $40,000	
e. Paid insurance for next year, $20,000	
f. Made sales on account, $60,000	
g. Repaid short-term loans at bank, $25,000	
h. Borrowed $40,000 at bank for 90 days	
i. Declared and paid $45,000 cash dividend	
j. Purchased $20,000 of short-term investments	
k. Paid $30,000 in salaries	
l. Accrued additional $15,000 in taxes	

LO5

Problem 13-2A Effect of Transactions on Debt-to-Equity Ratio

(*Note:* Consider completing this problem after Problem 13-1A to ensure that you obtain a clear understanding of the effect of various transactions on this measure of solvency.)
The following account balances are taken from the records of Degas Inc.:

Current liabilities	$ 25,000
Long-term liabilities	125,000
Stockholders' equity	400,000

Required
1. Use the information provided to compute Degas' debt-to-equity ratio (round to three decimal points).
2. Determine the effect that each of the following transactions will have on Degas' debt-to-equity ratio by recalculating the ratio and then indicating whether the ratio is increased, decreased, or not affected by the transaction. (Round to three decimal points.) Consider each transaction independently; that is, assume that it is the *only* transaction that takes place.

Transaction	Effect of Transaction on Debt-to-Equity Ratio
a. Purchased inventory on account for $20,000	
b. Purchased inventory for cash, $15,000	
c. Paid suppliers on account, $30,000	
d. Received cash on account, $40,000	
e. Paid insurance for next year, $20,000	
f. Made sales on account, $60,000	
g. Repaid short-term loans at bank, $25,000	

h. Borrowed $40,000 at bank for 90 days
i. Declared and paid $45,000 cash dividend
j. Purchased $20,000 of short-term investments
k. Paid $30,000 in salaries
l. Accrued additional $15,000 in taxes

LO6

Problem 13-3A Goals for Sales and Return on Assets

The president of Blue Moon Corp. is reviewing with her department managers the operating results of the year just completed. Sales increased by 12% from the previous year to $750,000. Average total assets for the year were $400,000. Net income, after adding back interest expense, net of tax, was $60,000.

The president is happy with the performance over the past year but is never satisfied with the status quo. She has set two specific goals for next year: (1) a 15% growth in sales and (2) a return on assets of 20%.

To achieve the second goal, the president has stated her intention to increase the total asset base by 10% over the base for the year just completed.

Required

1. For the year just completed, compute the following ratios:
   a. Return on sales
   b. Asset turnover
   c. Return on assets
2. Compute the necessary asset turnover for next year to achieve the president's goal of a 15% increase in sales.
3. Calculate the income needed next year to achieve the goal of a 20% return on total assets. (*Note:* Assume that *income* is defined as net income plus interest, net of tax.)
4. Based on your answers to (2) and (3), comment on the reasonableness of the president's goals. On what must the company focus to attain these goals?

LO6

Problem 13-4A Goals for Sales and Income Growth

Sunset Corp. is a major regional retailer. The chief executive officer (CEO) is concerned with the slow growth both of sales and of net income and the subsequent effect on the trading price of the common stock. Selected financial data for the past three years follow.

Sunset Corp.
(in millions)

	2008	2007	2006
1. Sales	$100.0	$96.7	$93.3
2. Net income	3.0	2.9	2.8
3. Dividends declared and paid	1.2	1.2	1.2
December 31 balances:			
4. Stockholders' equity	40.0	38.2	36.5
5. Debt	10.0	10.2	10.2
Selected year-end financial ratios			
Net income to sales	3.0%	3.0%	3.0%
Asset turnover	2 times	2 times	2 times
6. Return on stockholders' equity*	7.5%	7.6%	7.7%
7. Debt to total assets	20.0%	21.1%	21.8%

**Based on year-end balances in stockholders' equity.*

The CEO believes that the price of the stock has been adversely affected by the downward trend of the return on equity, the relatively low dividend payout ratio, and the lack of dividend increases. To improve the price of the stock, he wants to improve the return on equity and dividends.

He believes that the company should be able to meet these objectives by (1) increasing sales and net income at an annual rate of 10% a year and (2) establishing a new dividend policy that calls for a dividend payout of 60% of earnings or $2,000,000, whichever is larger.

The 10% annual sales increase will be accomplished through a product enhancement program. The president believes that the present net income to sales ratio of 3% will be unchanged by the cost of this new program and any interest paid on new debt. He expects that the company can accomplish this sales and income growth while maintaining the current relationship of total assets to sales. Any capital that is needed to maintain this relationship and that is not generated internally would be acquired through long-term debt financing. The CEO hopes that debt would not exceed 25% of total liabilities and stockholders' equity.

Required

1. Using the CEO's program, prepare a schedule that shows the appropriate data for the years 2009, 2010, and 2011 for the items numbered 1 through 7 on the preceding schedule.
2. Can the CEO meet all of his requirements if a 10% per-year growth in income and sales is achieved? Explain your answers.
3. What alternative actions should the CEO consider to improve the return on equity and to support increased dividend payments?

(CMA adapted)

ALTERNATE MULTICONCEPT PROBLEMS

LO4,5,6

Problem 13-5A Basic Financial Ratios

The accounting staff of SST Enterprises has completed the financial statements for the 2008 calendar year. The statement of income for the current year and the comparative statements of financial position for 2008 and 2007 follow.

SST Enterprises
Statement of Income
Year Ended December 31, 2008
(thousands omitted)

Revenue:	
Net sales	$600,000
Other	45,000
Total revenue	$645,000
Expenses:	
Cost of goods sold	$405,000
Research and development	18,000
Selling and administrative	120,000
Interest	15,000
Total expenses	$558,000
Income before income taxes	$ 87,000
Income taxes	27,000
Net income	$ 60,000

SST Enterprises
Comparative Statements of Financial Position
December 31, 2008 and 2007
(thousands omitted)

	2008	2007
Assets		
Current assets:		
Cash and short-term investments	$ 27,000	$ 20,000
Receivables, less allowance for doubtful accounts ($1,100 in 2008 and $1,400 in 2007)	36,000	37,000
Inventories, at lower of FIFO cost or market	35,000	42,000
Prepaid items and other current assets	2,000	1,000
Total current assets	$100,000	$100,000
Property, plant, and equipment:		
Land	$ 9,000	$ 9,000
Buildings and equipment, less accumulated depreciation ($74,000 in 2008 and $62,000 in 2007)	191,000	186,000
Total property, plant, and equipment	$200,000	$195,000
Total assets	$300,000	$295,000

	2008	2007
Liabilities and Stockholders' Equity		
Current liabilities:		
Short-term loans	$ 20,000	$ 15,000
Accounts payable	80,000	68,000
Salaries, wages, and other	5,000	7,000
Total current liabilities	$105,000	$ 90,000
Long-term debt	15,000	40,000
Total liabilities	$120,000	$130,000
Stockholders' equity:		
Common stock, at par	$ 50,000	$ 50,000
Paid-in capital in excess of par	25,000	25,000
Total paid-in capital	$ 75,000	$ 75,000
Retained earnings	105,000	90,000
Total stockholders' equity	$180,000	$165,000
Total liabilities and stockholders' equity	$300,000	$295,000

Required

1. Calculate the following financial ratios for 2008 for SST Enterprises:
   a. Times interest earned
   b. Return on total assets
   c. Return on common stockholders' equity
   d. Debt-equity ratio (at December 31, 2008)
   e. Current ratio (at December 31, 2008)
   f. Quick (acid-test) ratio (at December 31, 2008)
   g. Accounts receivable turnover ratio (Assume that all sales are on credit.)
   h. Number of days' sales in receivables
   i. Inventory turnover ratio (Assume that all purchases are on credit.)
   j. Number of days' sales in inventory
   k. Number of days in cash operating cycle
2. Prepare a few brief comments on the overall financial health of SST Enterprises. For each comment, indicate any information that is not provided in the problem and that you would need to fully evaluate the company's financial health.

(CMA adapted)

LO5,6 **Problem 13-6A** Projected Results to Meet Corporate Objectives

Grout Inc. is a wholly owned subsidiary of Slait Co. The philosophy of Slait's management is to allow the subsidiaries to operate as independent units. Corporate control is exercised through the establishment of minimum objectives for each subsidiary, accompanied by substantial rewards for success and penalties for failure. The time period for performance review is long enough for competent managers to display their abilities.

Each quarter the subsidiary is required to submit financial statements. The statements are accompanied by a letter from the subsidiary president explaining the results to date, a forecast for the remainder of the year, and the actions to be taken to achieve the objectives if the forecast indicates that the objectives will not be met.

Slait management, in conjunction with Grout management, had set the objectives listed below for the year ending September 30, 2009. These objectives are similar to those set in previous years.

- Sales growth of 10%
- Return on stockholders' equity of 20%
- A long-term debt-to-equity ratio of not more than 1.0
- Payment of a cash dividend of 50% of net income, with a minimum payment of at least $500,000

Grout's controller has just completed preparing the financial statements for the six months ended March 31, 2009, and the forecast for the year ending September 30, 2009. The statements are presented on the following page.

After a cursory glance at the financial statements, Grout's president concluded that not all objectives would be met. At a staff meeting of the Grout management, the president asked the controller to review the projected results and recommend possible actions that could be taken during the remainder of the year so that Grout would be more likely to meet the objectives.

Grout Inc.
Income Statement
(thousands omitted)

	Year Ended September 30, 2008	Six Months Ended March 31, 2009	Forecast for Year Ending September 30, 2009
Sales	$10,000	$6,000	$12,000
Cost of goods sold	$ 6,000	$4,000	$ 8,000
Selling expenses	1,500	900	1,800
Administrative expenses and interest	1,000	600	1,200
Income taxes	500	300	600
Total expenses and taxes	$ 9,000	$5,800	$11,600
Net income	$ 1,000	$ 200	$ 400
Dividends declared and paid	500	0	400
Income retained	$ 500	$ 200	$ 0

Grout Inc.
Statement of Financial Position
(thousands omitted)

	September 30, 2008	March 31, 2009	Forecast for September 30, 2009
Assets			
Cash	$ 400	$ 500	$ 500
Accounts receivable (net)	2,100	3,400	2,600
Inventory	7,000	8,500	8,400
Plant and equipment (net)	2,800	2,500	3,200
Total assets	$12,300	$14,900	$14,700
Liabilities and Equities			
Accounts payable	$ 3,000	$ 4,000	$ 4,000
Accrued taxes	300	200	200
Long-term borrowing	4,000	5,500	5,500
Common stock	4,000	4,000	4,000
Retained earnings	1,000	1,200	1,000
Total liabilities and equities	$12,300	$14,900	$14,700

Required

1. Calculate the projected results for each of the four objectives established for Grout Inc. State which results will not meet the objectives by year-end.
2. From the data presented, identify the factors that seem to contribute to the failure of Grout Inc. to meet all of its objectives.
3. Explain the possible actions that the controller could recommend in response to the president's request.

(CMA adapted)

LO4,5,6

Problem 13-7A Comparison with Industry Averages

Midwest Inc. is a medium-size company that has been in business for 20 years. The industry has become very competitive in the last few years, and Midwest has decided that it must grow if it is going to survive. It has approached the bank for a sizable five-year loan, and the bank has requested Midwest's most recent financial statements as part of the loan package.

The industry in which Midwest operates consists of approximately 20 companies relatively equal in size. The trade association to which all of the competitors belong publishes an annual survey of the industry, including industry averages for selected ratios for the competitors. All companies voluntarily submit their statements to the association for this purpose.

Midwest's controller is aware that the bank has access to this survey and is very concerned about how the company fared this past year compared with the rest of the industry. The ratios included in the publication and the averages for the past year are as follows:

Ratio	Industry Average
Current ratio	1.20
Acid-test (quick) ratio	0.50
Inventory turnover	35 times
Debt-to-equity ratio	0.50
Times interest earned	25 times
Return on sales	3%
Asset turnover	3.5 times
Return on common stockholders' equity	20%

The financial statements to be submitted to the bank in connection with the loan follow.

Midwest Inc.
Statement of Income and Retained Earnings
For the Year Ended December 31, 2008
(thousands omitted)

Sales revenue	$420,500
Cost of goods sold	(300,000)
Gross profit	$120,500
Selling, general, and administrative expenses	(85,000)
Income before interest and taxes	$ 35,500
Interest expense	(8,600)
Income before taxes	$ 26,900
Income tax expense	(12,000)
Net income	$ 14,900
Retained earnings, January 1, 2008	12,400
	$ 27,300
Dividends paid on common stock	(11,200)
Retained earnings, December 31, 2008	$ 16,100

Midwest Inc.
Comparative Statements of Financial Position
(thousands omitted)

	December 31, 2008	December 31, 2007
Assets		
Current assets:		
Cash	$ 1,790	$ 2,600
Marketable securities	1,200	1,700
Accounts receivable, net of allowances	400	600
Inventories	8,700	7,400
Prepaid items	350	400
Total current assets	$ 12,440	$ 12,700
Long-term investments	$ 560	$ 400
Property, plant, and equipment:		
Land	$ 12,000	$ 12,000
Buildings and equipment, net of accumulated depreciation	87,000	82,900
Total property, plant, and equipment	$ 99,000	$ 94,900
Total assets	$112,000	$108,000
Liabilities and Stockholders' Equity		
Current liabilities:		
Short-term notes	$ 800	$ 600
Accounts payable	6,040	6,775
Salaries and wages payable	1,500	1,200
Income taxes payable	1,560	1,025
Total current liabilities	$ 9,900	$ 9,600
Long-term bonds payable	$ 36,000	$ 36,000
Stockholders' equity:		
Common stock, no par	$ 50,000	$ 50,000
Retained earnings	16,100	12,400
Total stockholders' equity	$ 66,100	$ 62,400
Total liabilities and stockholders' equity	$112,000	$108,000

Required

1. Prepare a columnar report for the controller of Midwest Inc. comparing the industry averages for the ratios published by the trade association with the comparable ratios for Midwest. For Midwest, compute the ratios as of December 31, 2008, or for the year ending December 31, 2008, whichever is appropriate.
2. Briefly evaluate Midwest's ratios relative to the industry averages.
3. Do you think that the bank will approve the loan? Explain your answer.

DECISION CASES

READING AND INTERPRETING FINANCIAL STATEMENTS

LO2

Decision Case 13-1 Horizontal Analysis for Kellogg's

Refer to the financial statement information of **Kellogg's** reprinted at the back of the book.

Required

1. Prepare a work sheet with the following headings:

	Increase (Decrease) from			
	2005 to 2006		2004 to 2005	
Income Statement Accounts	Dollars	Percent	Dollars	Percent

2. Complete the work sheet using each of the account titles on Kellogg's income statement. Round all percentages to the nearest one-tenth of a percent.
3. What observations can you make from this horizontal analysis? What is your overall analysis of operations? Have the company's operations improved over the three-year period?

LO3

Decision Case 13-2 Vertical Analysis for Kellogg's

Refer to the financial statement information of **Kellogg's** reprinted at the back of the book.

Required

1. Using the format in Exhibit 13-6, prepare common-size comparative income statements for 2006 and 2005. Use as the base "Net sales." Round all percentages to the nearest one-tenth of a percent.
2. What changes do you detect in the income statement relationships from 2005 to 2006?
3. Using the format in Exhibit 13-5, prepare common-size comparative balance sheets at the end of 2004 and 2005. Round all percentages to the nearest one-tenth of a percent.
4. What observations can you make about the relative composition of Kellogg's assets from the common-size statements? What observations can be made about the changes in the relative composition of liabilities and stockholders' equity accounts?

LO3

Decision Case 13-3 Comparing Two Companies in the Same Industry: Kellogg's and General Mills

This case should be completed after responding to the requirements in Case 13-2. Refer to the financial statement information of **Kellogg's** and **General Mills** reprinted at the back of the book.

Required:

1. Using the format in Exhibit 13-6, prepare common-size comparative income statements for the years ending May 28, 2006, and May 29, 2005, for General Mills. Round all percentages to the nearest one-tenth of a percent.
2. The common-size comparative income statements indicate the relative importance of items on the statement. Compare the common-size income statements of General Mills and Kellogg's. What are the most important differences between the two companies' income statements?
3. Using the format in Exhibit 13-5, prepare common-size comparative balance sheets on May 28, 2006, and May 29, 2005, for General Mills. Round all percentages to the nearest one-tenth of a percent.
4. The common-size comparative balance sheets indicate the relative importance of items on the statement. Compare the common-size balance sheets of General Mills and Kellogg's. What are the most important differences between the two companies' balance sheets?

HOMEWORK

LO4,5,6 **Decision Case 13-4** Ratio Analysis for General Mills

Refer to the financial statement information of **General Mills** reprinted at the back of the book.

Required

1. Compute the following ratios and other amounts for each of the two years, ending May 28, 2006 and May 29, 2005. Because only two years of data are given on the balance sheets, to be consistent, you should use year-end balances for each year in lieu of average balances. Assume 360 days to a year. State any other necessary assumptions in making the calculations. Round all ratios to the nearest one-tenth of a percent.
   a. Working capital
   b. Current ratio
   c. Acid-test ratio
   d. Cash flow from operations to current liabilities
   e. Debt-to-equity ratio
   f. Cash flow from operations to capital expenditures
   g. Asset turnover
   h. Return on sales
   i. Return on assets
   j. Return on common stockholders' equity
2. What is your overall analysis of the financial health of General Mills?

MAKING FINANCIAL DECISIONS

LO4,5, 6,7 **Decision Case 13-5** Acquisition Decision

Diversified Industries is a large conglomerate that is continually in the market for new acquisitions. The company has grown rapidly over the last ten years through buyouts of medium-size companies. Diversified does not limit itself to companies in any one industry, but looks for firms with a sound financial base and the ability to stand on their own financially.

The president of Diversified recently told a meeting of the company's officers: "I want to impress two points on all of you. First, we are not in the business of looking for bargains. Diversified has achieved success in the past by acquiring companies with the ability to be a permanent member of the corporate family. We don't want companies that may appear to be a bargain on paper but can't survive in the long run. Second, a new member of our family must be able to come in and make it on its own—the parent is not organized to be a funding agency for struggling subsidiaries."

Ron Dixon is the vice president of acquisitions for Diversified, a position he has held for five years. He is responsible for making recommendations to the board of directors on potential acquisitions. Because you are one of his assistants, he recently brought you a set of financials for a manufacturer, Heavy Duty Tractors. Dixon believes that Heavy Duty is a "can't-miss" opportunity for Diversified and asks you to confirm his hunch by performing basic financial statement analysis on the company. The most recent comparative balance sheets and income statement for the company follow.

Heavy Duty Tractors Inc.
Comparative Statements of Financial Position
(thousands omitted)

	December 31, 2008	December 31, 2007
Assets		
Current assets:		
Cash	$ 48,500	$ 24,980
Marketable securities	3,750	0
Accounts receivable, net of allowances	128,420	84,120
Inventories	135,850	96,780
Prepaid items	7,600	9,300
Total current assets	$324,120	$215,180
Long-term investments	$ 55,890	$ 55,890
Property, plant, and equipment:		
Land	$ 45,000	$ 45,000
Buildings and equipment, less accumulated depreciation of $385,000 in 2008 and $325,000 in 2007	545,000	605,000
Total property, plant, and equipment	$590,000	$650,000
Total assets	$970,010	$921,070

(continued)

HOMEWORK

	December 31, 2008	December 31, 2007
Liabilities and Stockholders' Equity		
Current liabilities:		
Short-term notes	$ 80,000	$ 60,000
Accounts payable	65,350	48,760
Salaries and wages payable	14,360	13,840
Income taxes payable	2,590	3,650
Total current liabilities	$162,300	$126,250
Long-term bonds payable, due 2015	$275,000	$275,000
Stockholders' equity:		
Common stock, no par	$350,000	$350,000
Retained earnings	182,710	169,820
Total stockholders' equity	$532,710	$519,820
Total liabilities and stockholders' equity	$970,010	$921,070

Heavy Duty Tractors Inc.
Statement of Income and Retained Earnings
For the Year Ended December 31, 2008
(thousands omitted)

Sales Revenue	$875,250
Cost of goods sold	542,750
Gross profit	$332,500
Selling, general, and administrative expenses	264,360
Operating income	$ 68,140
Interest expense	45,000
Net income before taxes and extraordinary items	$ 23,140
Income tax expense	9,250
Income before extraordinary items	$ 13,890
Extraordinary gain, less taxes of $6,000	9,000
Net income	$ 22,890
Retained earnings, January 1, 2008	169,820
	$192,710
Dividends paid on common stock	10,000
Retained earnings, December 31, 2008	$182,710

Required

1. How liquid is Heavy Duty Tractors? Support your answer with any ratios that you believe are necessary to justify your conclusion. Also indicate any other information that you would want to have in making a final determination on its liquidity.
2. In light of the president's comments, should you be concerned about the solvency of Heavy Duty Tractors? Support your answer with the necessary ratios. How does the maturity date of the outstanding debt affect your answer?
3. Has Heavy Duty demonstrated the ability to be a profitable member of the Diversified family? Support your answer with the necessary ratios.
4. What will you tell your boss? Should he recommend to the board of directors that Diversified put in a bid for Heavy Duty Tractors?

LO3

Decision Case 13-6 Pricing Decision

BPO's management believes the company has been successful at increasing sales because it has not increased the selling price of its products even though its competition has increased prices and costs have increased. Price and cost relationships in Year 1 were established because they represented industry averages. The following income statements are available for BPO's first three years of operation:

	Year 3	Year 2	Year 1
Sales	$125,000	$110,000	$100,000
Cost of goods sold	62,000	49,000	40,000
Gross profit	$ 63,000	$ 61,000	$ 60,000
Operating expenses	53,000	49,000	45,000
Net income	$ 10,000	$ 12,000	$ 15,000

Required

1. Using the format in Exhibit 13-6, prepare common-size comparative income statements for the three years.
2. Explain why net income has decreased while sales have increased.
3. Prepare an income statement for Year 4. Sales volume in units is expected to increase by 10%, and costs are expected to increase by 8%.
4. Do you think BPO should raise its prices or maintain the same selling prices? Explain your answer.

ETHICAL DECISION MAKING

LO4,5

Decision Case 13-7 Provisions in a Loan Agreement

As controller of Midwest Construction Company, you are reviewing with your assistant, Dave Jackson, the financial statements for the year just ended. During the review, Jackson reminds you of an existing loan agreement with Southern National Bank. Midwest has agreed to the following conditions:

- The current ratio will be maintained at a minimum level of 1.5 to 1.0 at all times.
- The debt-to-equity ratio will not exceed 0.5 to 1.0 at any time.

Jackson has drawn up the following preliminary condensed balance sheet for the year just ended:

Midwest Construction Company
Balance Sheet
December 31
(in millions of dollars)

Current assets	$16	Current liabilities	$10
Long-term assets	64	Long-term debt	15
		Stockholders' equity	55
Total	$80	Total	$80

Jackson wants to discuss two items with you. First, long-term debt currently includes a $5 million note payable to Eastern State Bank that is due in six months. The plan is to go to Eastern before the note is due and ask it to extend the maturity date of the note for five years. Jackson doesn't believe that Midwest needs to include the $5 million in current liabilities because the plan is to roll over the note.

Second, in December of this year, Midwest received a $2 million deposit from the state for a major road project. The contract calls for the work to be performed over the next 18 months. Jackson recorded the $2 million as revenue this year because the contract is with the state; there shouldn't be any question about being able to collect.

Required

1. Based on the balance sheet that Jackson prepared, is Midwest in compliance with its loan agreement with Southern? Support your answer with any necessary computations.
2. What would you do with the two items in question? Do you see anything wrong with the way Jackson has handled each of them? Explain your answer.
3. Prepare a revised balance sheet based on your answer to (2). Also compute a revised current ratio and debt-to-equity ratio. Based on the revised ratios, is Midwest in compliance with its loan agreement?

LO4

Decision Case 13-8 Inventory Turnover

Garden Fresh Inc. is a wholesaler of fresh fruits and vegetables. Each year it submits a set of financial ratios to a trade association. Even though the association doesn't publish the individual ratios for each company, the president of Garden Fresh thinks it is important for public relations that his company look as good as possible. Due to the nature of the fresh fruits and vegetables business, one of the major ratios tracked by the association is inventory turnover. Garden Fresh's inventory stated at FIFO cost was as follows:

	Year Ending December 31	
	2008	**2007**
Fruits	$10,000	$ 9,000
Vegetables	30,000	33,000
Totals	$40,000	$42,000

Sales revenue for the year ending December 31, 2008, is $3,690,000. The company's gross profit ratio is normally 40%.

Based on these data, the president thinks the company should report an inventory turnover ratio of 90 times per year.

Required

1. Using the necessary calculations, explain how the president came up with an inventory turnover ratio of 90 times.
2. Do you think the company should report a turnover ratio of 90 times? If not, explain why you disagree and explain, with calculations, what you think the ratio should be.
3. Assume that you are the controller for Garden Fresh. What will you tell the president?

SOLUTIONS TO KEY TERMS QUIZ

Quiz 1:

Answer	Term
14	**Horizontal analysis**
11	**Vertical analysis**
10	**Gross profit ratio**
12	**Profit margin ratio**
13	**Liquidity**
2	**Working capital**
3	**Current ratio**
1	**Acid-test or quick ratio**
5	**Cash flow from operations to current liabilities ratio**
6	**Accounts receivable turnover ratio**
4	**Number of days' sales in receivables**
9	**Inventory turnover ratio**
7	**Number of days' sales in inventory**
8	**Cash-to-cash operating cycle**

Quiz 2:

Answer	Term
3	**Solvency**
7	**Debt-to-equity ratio**
13	**Times interest earned ratio**
14	**Debt service coverage ratio**
8	**Cash flow from operations to capital expenditures ratio**
15	**Profitability**
9	**Return on assets ratio**
4	**Return on sales ratio**
10	**Asset turnover ratio**
1	**Return on common stockholders' equity ratio**
12	**Leverage**
5	**Earnings per share**
2	**Price/earnings (P/E) ratio**
6	**Dividend payout ratio**
11	**Dividend yield ratio**
17	**Discontinued operations**
16	**Extraordinary item**

INTEGRATIVE PROBLEM

Presented here are a statement of income and retained earnings and comparative balance sheets for Gallagher, Inc., which operates a national chain of sporting goods stores.

Gallagher, Inc.
Statement of Income and Retained Earnings
For the Year Ended December 31, 2008
(all amounts in thousands of dollars)

Net sales	$48,000
Cost of goods sold	36,000
Gross profit	$12,000
Selling, general, and administrative expense	6,000
Operating income	$ 6,000
Interest expense	280
Income before tax	$ 5,720
Income tax expense	2,280
Net income	$ 3,440
Preferred dividends	100
Income available to common	$ 3,340
Common dividends	500
To retained earnings	$ 2,840
Retained earnings, 1/1	12,000
Retained earnings, 12/31	$14,840

Gallagher, Inc.
Comparative Balance Sheets
December 31, 2008 and 2007
(all amounts in thousands of dollars)

	December 31	
	2008	**2007**
Cash	$ 840	$ 2,700
Accounts receivable	12,500	9,000
Inventory	8,000	5,500
Prepaid insurance	100	400
Total current assets	$21,440	$17,600
Land	$ 4,000	$ 4,000
Buildings and equipment	12,000	9,000
Accumulated depreciation	(3,700)	(3,000)
Total long-term assets	$12,300	$10,000
Total assets	$33,740	$27,600
Accounts payable	$ 7,300	$ 5,000
Taxes payable	4,600	4,200
Notes payable	2,400	1,600
Current portion of bonds	200	200
Total current liabilities	$14,500	$11,000
Bonds payable	1,400	1,600
Total liabilities	$15,900	$12,600
Preferred stock, $5 par	$ 1,000	$ 1,000
Common stock, $1 par	2,000	2,000
Retained earnings	14,840	12,000
Total stockholders' equity	$17,840	$15,000
Total liabilities and stockholders' equity	$33,740	$27,600

Required

1. Prepare a statement of cash flows for Gallagher, Inc., for the year ended December 31, 2008, using the *indirect* method in the Operating Activities section of the statement.
2. Gallagher's management is concerned with its short-term liquidity and its solvency over the long run. To help management evaluate these, compute the following ratios, rounding all answers to the nearest one-tenth of a percent:
   a. Current ratio
   b. Acid-test ratio
   c. Cash flow from operations to current liabilities ratio
   d. Accounts receivable turnover ratio
   e. Number of days' sales in receivables
   f. Inventory turnover ratio
   g. Number of days' sales in inventory
   h. Debt-to-equity ratio
   i. Debt service coverage ratio
   j. Cash flow from operations to capital expenditures ratio
3. Comment on Gallagher's liquidity and its solvency. What additional information do you need to fully evaluate the company?

ANSWERS TO POD REVIEW

LO1	1. d	2. c
LO2	1. a	2. b
LO3	1. c	2. a
LO4	1. d	2. a
LO5	1. a	2. b
LO6	1. a	2. b
LO7	1. d	2. b

These excerpts consist of Item 8, which are the financial statements and supplementary data for each company. For full annual reports for these companies, please see the links at the company Web sites or go to http://www.academic.cengage.com/accounting/porter and select this text.

APPENDIX A

The Accounting Profession

Accountants play many different roles in society. Understanding the various roles will help you to appreciate more fully the importance of accounting in organizations.

EMPLOYMENT BY PRIVATE BUSINESS

Many accountants work for business entities. Regardless of the types of activities companies engage in, accountants perform a number of important functions for them. A partial organization chart for a corporation is shown in Exhibit A-1. The chart indicates that three individuals report directly to the chief financial officer: the controller, the treasurer, and the director of internal auditing.

The **controller** is the chief accounting officer for a company and typically has responsibility for the overall operation of the accounting system. Accountants working for the controller record the company's activities and prepare periodic financial statements. In this organization, the payroll function is assigned to the controller's office, as well as responsibility for the preparation of budgets.

Controller
The chief accounting officer for a company.

The **treasurer** of an organization is typically responsible for both the safeguarding and efficient use of the company's liquid resources, such as cash. Note that the director of the tax department in this corporation reports to the treasurer. Accountants in the tax department are responsible for both preparing the company's tax returns and planning transactions in such a way that the company pays the least amount of taxes possible within the laws of the Internal Revenue Code.

Treasurer
The officer responsible in an organization for the safeguarding and efficient use of a company's liquid assets.

EXHIBIT A-1 **Partial Organization Chart**

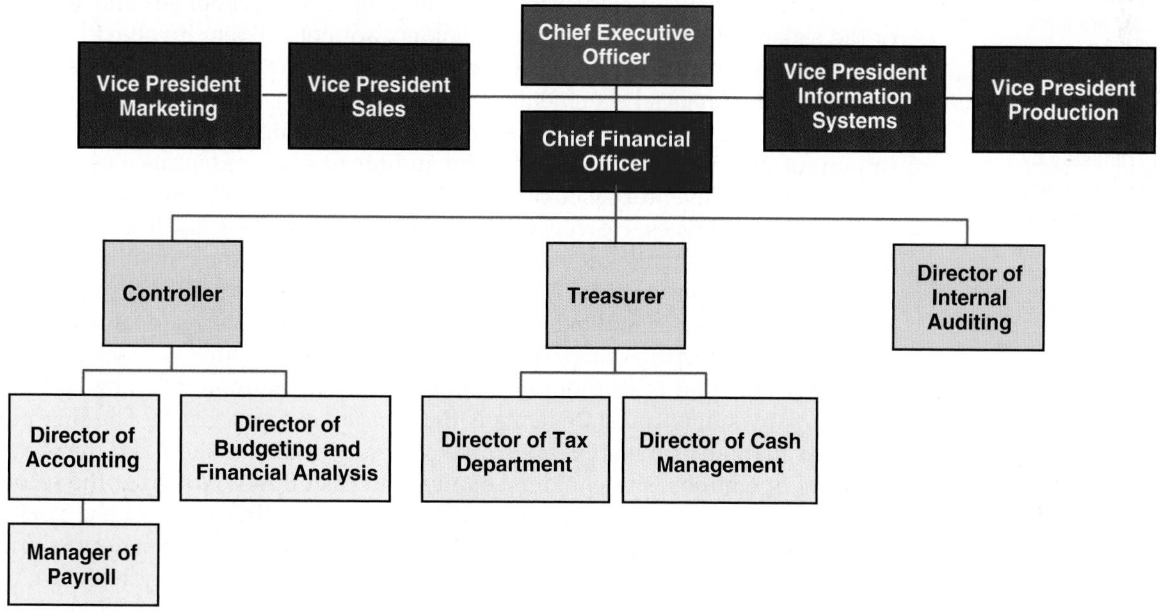

This partial organization chart does not show details of the other departments in the company—such as marketing, sales, production, and so on. That does not mean they are unimportant to the flow of accounting information. In fact, accounting information for internal decision making forms a complex system of reporting, responsibility, and control collectively known as management accounting.

Internal auditing
The department responsible in a company for the review and appraisal of its accounting and administrative controls.

Internal auditing is the department responsible in a company for the review and appraisal of accounting and administrative controls. The department must determine whether the company's assets are properly accounted for and protected from losses. Recommendations are made periodically to management for improvements in the various controls.

EMPLOYMENT BY NONBUSINESS ENTITIES

Nonbusiness organizations, such as hospitals, universities, and various branches of the government, have as much need for accountants as do companies organized to earn a profit. Although the profit motive is not paramount to nonbusiness entities, all organizations must have financial information to operate efficiently. A county government needs detailed cost information in determining the taxes to levy on its constituents. A university must pay close attention to its various operating costs in setting the annual tuition rates. Accountants working for nonbusiness entities perform most of the same tasks as their counterparts in the business sector. In fact, many of the job titles in business entities, such as controller and treasurer, are also used by nonbusiness entities.

EMPLOYMENT IN PUBLIC ACCOUNTING

Public accounting firms provide valuable services in much the same way as do law firms or architectural firms. They provide a professional service for their clients in return for a fee. The usual services provided by public accounting firms include auditing and tax and management consulting services.

Auditing Services The auditing services rendered by public accountants are similar in certain respects to the work performed by internal auditors. However, there are key differences between the two types of auditing. Internal auditors are more concerned with the efficient operation of the various segments of the business, and therefore, the work they do is often called *operational auditing*. On the other hand, the primary objective of the external auditor, or public accountant, is to assure stockholders and other users that the statements are fairly presented. In this respect, **auditing** is the process of examining the financial statements and the underlying records of a company in order to render an opinion as to whether the statements are fairly presented.

Auditing
The process of examining the financial statements and the underlying records of a company in order to render an opinion as to whether the statements are fairly presented.

The financial statements are prepared by the company's accountants. The external auditor performs various tests and procedures to be able to render his or her opinion. The public accountant has a responsibility to the company's stockholders and any other users of the statements. Because most stockholders are not actively involved in the daily affairs of the business, they must rely on the auditors to ensure that management is fairly presenting the financial statements of the business.

Auditors' report
The opinion rendered by a public accounting firm concerning the fairness of the presentation of the financial statements.
Alternate term: *Report of independent accountants.*

Note that the **auditors' report** is an *opinion*, not a statement of fact. For example, one important procedure performed by the auditor to obtain assurance as to the validity of a company's inventory is to observe the year-end physical count of inventory by the company's employees. However, this is done on a sample basis. It would be too costly for the auditors to make an independent count of every single item of inventory.

The auditors' report on the financial statements for General Mills's is shown in Exhibit A-2. The company is audited by **KPMG LLP**, a large international accounting firm. Public accounting firms range in size from those with a single owner to others, such as KPMG LLP, that have thousands of partners. The opinion given by KPMG LLP on the company's financial statements is the *standard auditors' report*. The first paragraph indicates that the firm has examined the company's balance sheet and the related statements of operations, shareholders' equity, and cash flows. Note that the second paragraph of the report indicates that evidence supporting the amounts and disclosures in the statements was examined on a *test* basis. The third paragraph states the firm's *opinion* that the financial statements are fairly presented in conformity with GAAP.

Tax Services In addition to auditing, public accounting firms provide a variety of tax services. Firms often prepare the tax returns for the companies they audit. They also usually work throughout the year with management to plan acquisitions and other transactions to take full advantage of the tax laws. For example, if tax rates are scheduled to decline next year, a public accounting firm would advise its client to accelerate certain expenditures this year as much as possible to receive a higher tax deduction than would be possible by waiting until next year.

EXHIBIT A-2 General Mills's Auditors' Report

REPORT OF INDEPENDENT REGISTERED PUBLIC ACCOUNTING FIRM ON THE CONSOLIDATED FINANCIAL STATEMENTS AND RELATED FINANCIAL STATEMENT SCHEDULE

The Board of Directors and Stockholders General Mills, Inc.:

We have audited the accompanying consolidated balance sheets of General Mills, Inc. and subsidiaries as of May 28, 2006 and May 29, 2005, and the related consolidated statements of earnings, stockholders' equity and comprehensive income, and cash flows for each of the fiscal years in the three-year period ended May 28, 2006. In connection with our audits of the consolidated financial statements we also have audited the accompanying financial statement schedule. These consolidated financial statements and financial statement schedule are the responsibility of the Company's management. Our responsibility is to express an opinion on these consolidated financial statements and financial statement schedule based on our audits.

We conducted our audits in accordance with the standards of the Public Company Accounting Oversight Board (United States). Those standards require that we plan and perform the audit to obtain reasonable assurance about whether the financial statements are free of material misstatement. An audit includes examining, on a test basis, evidence supporting the amounts and disclosures in the financial statements. An audit also includes assessing the accounting principles used and significant estimates made by management, as well as evaluating the overall financial statement presentation. We believe that our audits provide a reasonable basis for our opinion.

In our opinion, the consolidated financial statements referred to above present fairly,in all material respects, the financial position of General Mills, Inc. and subsidiaries as of May 28, 2006 and May 29, 2005, and the results of their operations and their cash flows for each of the fiscal years in the three-year period ended May 28, 2006 in conformity with U.S. generally accepted accounting principles. Also, in our opinion, the accompanying financial statement schedule,when considered in relation to the basic consolidated financial statements taken as a whole, presents fairly, in all material respects, the information set forth therein.

We also have audited, in accordance with the standards of the Public Company Accounting Oversight Board (United States), the effectiveness of General Mills' internal control over financial reporting as of May 28, 2006, based on criteria established in Internal Control—Integrated Framework issued by the Committee of Sponsoring Organizations of the Treadway Commission (COSO), and our report dated July 27, 2006 expressed an unqualified opinion on management's assessment of, and the effective operation of, internal control over financial reporting.

KPMG LLP

Minneapolis, Minnesota
July 27, 2006

Standard Auditor's Report

First Paragraph says that the auditor has examined the statements.

Second Paragraph indicates that evidence was gathered on a test basis.

Third Paragraph states the auditor's opinion.

Management Consulting Services By working closely with management to provide auditing and tax services, a public accounting firm becomes very familiar with various aspects of a company's business. This vantage point allows the firm to provide expert advice to the company to improve its operations. In the past, management consulting services rendered by public accounting firms to their clients took a variety of forms. For example, the firm might advise the company on the design and installation of a computer system to fill its needs. However, as we will see later in this section, serious doubts have been raised about an auditor's ability to remain independent while providing these other services. These doubts have caused the federal government to place restrictions on the nonaudit services the auditor can provide.

ACCOUNTANTS IN EDUCATION

Some accountants choose a career in education. As the demand for accountants in business entities, nonbusiness organizations, and public accounting has increased, so has the need for qualified professors to teach this discipline. Accounting programs range from two years of study at community colleges to doctoral programs at some universities. All these programs require the services of knowledgeable instructors. In addition to their teaching duties, many accounting educators are actively involved in research. The **American Accounting Association** is a professional organization of accounting educators and others interested in the future of the profession. The group advances its ideas through its many committees and the publication of a number of journals.

American Accounting Association
The professional organization for accounting educators.

ACCOUNTING AS A CAREER

As you can see, a number of different career paths in accounting are possible. The stereotypical view of the accountant as a "numbers person and not a people person" is a seriously outdated notion. Various specialties are now emerging, including tax accounting, environmental accounting, forensic accounting, software development, and accounting in the entertainment and telecommunications industries. Some of these opportunities exist in both the business and the nonbusiness sectors. For example, forensic accounting has become an exciting career field as both corporations and various agencies of the federal government, such as the FBI, concern themselves with fraud and white-collar crime.

As in any profession, salaries in accounting vary considerably depending on numerous factors, including educational background and other credentials, number of years of experience, and size of the employer. For example, most employers pay a premium for candidates with a master's degree and professional certification, such as the CPA. Exhibit A-3 indicates salaries for various positions within the accounting field.[1]

EXHIBIT A-3 Salaries in the Accounting Profession

Position	Salary Range	
Public Accounting		
→ Staff Auditors (1–3 years' experience)	$33,750–$51,250	$
Managers/Directors	$63,750–$119,000	$$
Partners	$150,000+	$$$
Industry		
→ Staff Accountants (1–3 years' experience)	$33,250–$49,250	$
Corporate Controllers	$61,250–$145,750	$$–$$$
Chief Financial Officers and Treasurers	$84,250–$346,750	$$–$$$$
→ Government (entry-level)		
Federal	$34,990 average	$
State/Local	$35,255 average	$

Accounting graduates start here.

1 The information in this section regarding career opportunities and salaries was drawn primarily from the AICPA's Web site (http://www.aicpa.org).

APPENDIX B

Excerpts from Kellogg's Form 10-K for 2006

UNITED STATES SECURITIES AND EXCHANGE COMMISSION
Washington, D.C. 20549

Form 10-K

ANNUAL REPORT PURSUANT TO SECTION 13 OR 15(d) OF THE SECURITIES EXCHANGE ACT of 1934
For the Fiscal Year Ended December 30, 2006
Commission file number 1-4171

Kellogg Company

(Exact Name of Registrant as Specified in its Charter)

Delaware	**38-0710690**
(State of Incorporation)	(I.R.S. Employer Identification No.)

One Kellogg Square
Battle Creek, Michigan 49016-3599
(Address of Principal Executive Offices)

Registrant's telephone number: (269) 961-2000

Securities registered pursuant to Section 12(b) of the Securities Act:

Title of each class:	Name of each exchange on which registered:
Common Stock, $.25 par value per share	**New York Stock Exchange**

Securities registered pursuant to Section 12(g) of the Securities Act: None

Indicate by a check mark if the registrant is a well-known seasoned issuer, as defined in Rule 405 of the Securities Act. Yes ☑ No ☐

Indicate by check mark if the registrant is not required to file reports pursuant to Section 13 or Section 15 (d) of the Securities Exchange Act of 1934. Yes ☐ No ☑

Indicate by check mark whether the registrant: (1) has filed all reports required to be filed by Section 13 or 15(d) of the Securities Exchange Act of 1934 during the preceding 12 months (or for such shorter period that the registrant was required to file such reports), and (2) has been subject to such filing requirements for the past 90 days. Yes ☑ No ☐

Indicate by check mark if disclosure of delinquent filers pursuant to Item 405 of Regulation S-K is not contained herein, and will not be contained, to the best of the registrant's knowledge in definitive proxy or information statements incorporated by reference in Part III of this Form 10-K or any amendment to this Form 10-K. ☐

Indicate by check mark whether the registrant is a large accelerated filer, an accelerated filer or a non-accelerated filer. See definition of "accelerated filer" and "large accelerated filer" in Rule 12b-2 of the Securities Exchange Act of 1934. (Check one)

Large accelerated filer ☑ Accelerated filer ☐ Non-accelerated filer ☐

Indicate by check mark whether the registrant is a shell company (as defined in Rule 12b-2 of the Securities Exchange Act of 1934). Yes ☐ No ☑

The aggregate market value of the common stock held by non-affiliates of the registrant (assuming only for purposes of this computation that the W.K. Kellogg Foundation Trust, directors and executive officers may be affiliates) was approximately $14.5 billion, as determined by the June 30, 2006, closing price of $48.43 for one share of common stock, as reported for the New York Stock Exchange — Composite Transactions.

As of January 26, 2007, 397,969,170 shares of the common stock of the registrant were issued and outstanding.

Parts of the registrant's Proxy Statement for the Annual Meeting of Shareowners to be held on April 27, 2007 are incorporated by reference into Part III of this Report.

Item 8. ***Financial Statements and Supplementary Data***

Kellogg Company and Subsidiaries

Consolidated Statement of Earnings

(millions, except per share data)	**2006**	2005	2004
Net sales	**$10,906.7**	$10,177.2	$9,613.9
Cost of goods sold	**6,081.5**	5,611.6	5,298.7
Selling, general, and administrative expense	**3,059.4**	2,815.3	2,634.1
Operating profit	**$ 1,765.8**	$ 1,750.3	$1,681.1
Interest expense	**307.4**	300.3	308.6
Other income (expense), net	**13.2**	(24.9)	(6.6)
Earnings before income taxes	**1,471.6**	1,425.1	1,365.9
Income taxes	**466.5**	444.7	475.3
Earnings (loss) from joint venture	**(1.0)**	—	—
Net earnings	**$ 1,004.1**	$ 980.4	$ 890.6
Per share amounts:			
Basic	**$ 2.53**	$ 2.38	$ 2.16
Diluted	**2.51**	2.36	2.14

Refer to Notes to Consolidated Financial Statements.

Kellogg Company and Subsidiaries

Consolidated Statement of Shareholders' Equity

(millions)	Common stock shares	Common stock amount	Capital in excess of par value	Retained earnings	Treasury stock shares	Treasury stock amount	Accumulated other comprehensive income	Total shareholders' equity	Total comprehensive income
Balance, December 27, 2003	415.5	$103.8	$ 24.5	$2,247.7	5.8	$(203.6)	$ (729.2)	$1,443.2	$ 911.3
Common stock repurchases					7.3	(297.5)		(297.5)	
Net earnings				890.6				890.6	890.6
Dividends				(417.6)				(417.6)	
Other comprehensive income							289.3	289.3	289.3
Stock options exercised and other			(24.5)	(19.4)	(10.7)	393.1		349.2	
Balance, January 1, 2005	415.5	$103.8	$ —	$2,701.3	2.4	$(108.0)	$ (439.9)	$2,257.2	$1,179.9
Common stock repurchases					15.4	(664.2)		(664.2)	
Net earnings				980.4				980.4	980.4
Dividends				(435.2)				(435.2)	
Other comprehensive income							(136.2)	(136.2)	(136.2)
Stock options exercised and other	3.0	.8	58.9	19.6	(4.7)	202.4		281.7	
Balance, December 31, 2005	418.5	$104.6	$ 58.9	$3,266.1	13.1	$(569.8)	$ (576.1)	$2,283.7	$ 844.2
Revision (a)			101.4	(101.4)				—	
Common stock repurchases					14.9	(649.8)		(649.8)	
Net earnings				1,004.1				1,004.1	1,004.1
Dividends				(449.9)				(449.9)	
Other comprehensive income							121.8	121.8	121.8
Stock compensation			85.7					85.7	
Stock options exercised and other			46.3	(88.5)	(7.2)	307.5		265.3	
Impact of adoption of SFAS No. 158 (a)							(591.9)	(591.9)	
Balance, December 30, 2006	**418.5**	**$104.6**	**$292.3**	**$3,630.4**	**20.8**	**$(912.1)**	**$(1,046.2)**	**$2,069.0**	**$1,125.9**

Refer to Notes to Consolidated Financial Statements.

(a) Refer to Note 5 for further information on these items.

Kellogg Company and Subsidiaries

Consolidated Balance Sheet

(millions, except share data)	2006	2005
Current assets		
Cash and cash equivalents	$ 410.6	$ 219.1
Accounts receivable, net	944.8	879.1
Inventories	823.9	717.0
Other current assets	247.7	381.3
Total current assets	$ 2,427.0	$ 2,196.5
Property, net	2,815.6	2,648.4
Other assets	5,471.4	5,729.6
Total assets	$10,714.0	$10,574.5
Current liabilities		
Current maturities of long-term debt	$ 723.3	$ 83.6
Notes payable	1,268.0	1,111.1
Accounts payable	910.4	883.3
Other current liabilities	1,118.5	1,084.8
Total current liabilities	$ 4,020.2	$ 3,162.8
Long-term debt	3,053.0	3,702.6
Other liabilities	1,571.8	1,425.4
Shareholders' equity		
Common stock, $.25 par value, 1,000,000,000 shares authorized		
Issued: 418,515,339 shares in 2006 and 418,451,198 shares in 2005	104.6	104.6
Capital in excess of par value	292.3	58.9
Retained earnings	3,630.4	3,266.1
Treasury stock at cost:		
20,817,930 shares in 2006 and 13,121,446 shares in 2005	(912.1)	(569.8)
Accumulated other comprehensive income (loss)	(1,046.2)	(576.1)
Total shareholders' equity	$ 2,069.0	$ 2,283.7
Total liabilities and shareholders' equity	$10,714.0	$10,574.5

Refer to Notes to Consolidated Financial Statements. In particular, refer to Note 15 for supplemental information on various balance sheet captions and Note 1 for details on the impact of adopting SFAS No. 158 "Employers' Accounting for Defined Benefit Pension and Other Postretirement Plans."

Kellogg Company and Subsidiaries

Consolidated Statement of Cash Flows

(millions)	**2006**	2005	2004
Operating activities			
Net earnings	**$1,004.1**	$ 980.4	$ 890.6
Adjustments to reconcile net earnings to operating cash flows:			
Depreciation and amortization	**352.7**	391.8	410.0
Deferred income taxes	**(43.7)**	(59.2)	57.7
Other (a)	**235.2**	199.3	104.5
Pension and other postretirement benefit plan contributions	**(99.3)**	(397.3)	(204.0)
Changes in operating assets and liabilities	**(38.5)**	28.3	(29.8)
Net cash provided by operating activities	**$1,410.5**	$ 1,143.3	$1,229.0
Investing activities			
Additions to properties	**$ (453.1)**	$ (374.2)	$ (278.6)
Acquisitions of businesses	**—**	(50.4)	—
Property disposals	**9.4**	9.8	7.9
Investment in joint venture and other	**(1.7)**	(.2)	.3
Net cash used in investing activities	**$ (445.4)**	$ (415.0)	$ (270.4)
Financing activities			
Net increase (reduction) of notes payable, with maturities less than or equal to 90 days	**$ (344.2)**	$ 360.2	$ 388.3
Issuances of notes payable, with maturities greater than 90 days	**1,065.4**	42.6	142.3
Reductions of notes payable, with maturities greater than 90 days	**(565.2)**	(42.3)	(141.7)
Issuances of long-term debt	**—**	647.3	7.0
Reductions of long-term debt	**(84.7)**	(1,041.3)	(682.2)
Issuances of common stock	**217.5**	221.7	291.8
Common stock repurchases	**(649.8)**	(664.2)	(297.5)
Cash dividends	**(449.9)**	(435.2)	(417.6)
Other	**21.9**	5.9	(6.7)
Net cash used in financing activities	**$ (789.0)**	$ (905.3)	$ (716.3)
Effect of exchange rate changes on cash	**15.4**	(21.3)	33.9
Increase (decrease) in cash and cash equivalents	**$ 191.5**	$ (198.3)	$ 276.2
Cash and cash equivalents at beginning of year	**219.1**	417.4	141.2
Cash and cash equivalents at end of year	**$ 410.6**	$ 219.1	$ 417.4

Refer to Notes to Consolidated Financial Statements.

(a) Consists principally of non-cash expense accruals for employee compensation and benefit obligations.

Note 1 Accounting policies

Basis of presentation

The consolidated financial statements include the accounts of Kellogg Company and its majority-owned subsidiaries. Intercompany balances and transactions are eliminated.

The Company's fiscal year normally ends on the Saturday closest to December 31 and as a result, a 53rd week is added approximately every sixth year. The Company's 2006 and 2005 fiscal years ended on December 30 and December 31, respectively. The Company's 2004 fiscal year ended on January 1, 2005, and included a 53rd week.

Cash and cash equivalents

Highly liquid temporary investments with original maturities of less than three months are considered to be cash equivalents. The carrying amount approximates fair value.

Accounts receivable

Accounts receivable consist principally of trade receivables, which are recorded at the invoiced amount, net of allowances for doubtful accounts and prompt payment discounts. Trade receivables generally do not bear interest. Terms and collection patterns vary around the world and by channel. In the United States, the Company generally has required payment for goods sold eleven or sixteen days subsequent to the date of invoice as 2% 10/net 11 or 1% 15/net 16, and days sales outstanding (DSO) has averaged approximately 19 days during the periods presented. The allowance for doubtful accounts represents management's estimate of the amount of probable credit losses in existing accounts receivable, as determined from a review of past due balances and other specific account data. Account balances are written off against the allowance when management determines the receivable is uncollectible. The Company does not have any off-balance sheet credit exposure related to its customers. Refer to Note 15 for an analysis of the Company's accounts receivable and allowance for doubtful account balances during the periods presented.

Inventories

Inventories are valued at the lower of cost (principally average) or market.

In November 2004, the Financial Accounting Standards Board (FASB) issued Statement of Financial Accounting Standard (SFAS) No. 151 "Inventory Costs" to converge U.S. GAAP principles with International Accounting Standards on inventory valuation. SFAS No. 151 clarifies that abnormal amounts of idle facility expense, freight, handling costs, and spoilage should be recognized as period charges, rather than as inventory value. This standard also provides that fixed production overheads should be allocated to units of production based on the normal capacity of production facilities, with excess overheads being recognized as period charges. The provisions of this standard are effective for inventory costs incurred during fiscal years beginning after June 15, 2005, with earlier application permitted. The Company adopted this standard at the beginning of its 2006 fiscal year. The Company's pre-existing accounting policy for inventory valuation was generally consistent with this guidance. Accordingly, the adoption of SFAS No. 151 did not have a significant impact on the Company's 2006 financial results.

Property

The Company's property consists mainly of plant and equipment used for manufacturing activities. These assets are recorded at cost and depreciated over estimated useful lives using straight-line methods for financial reporting and accelerated methods, where permitted, for tax reporting. Major property categories are depreciated over various periods as follows (in years): manufacturing machinery and equipment 5-20; computer and other office equipment 3-5; building components 15-30; building structures 50. Cost includes an amount of interest associated with significant capital projects. Plant and equipment are reviewed for impairment when conditions indicate that the carrying value may not be recoverable. Such conditions include an extended period of idleness or a plan of disposal. Assets to be abandoned at a future date are depreciated over the remaining period of use. Assets to be sold are written down to realizable value at the time the assets are being actively marketed for sale and the disposal is expected to occur within one year. As of year-end 2005 and 2006, the carrying value of assets held for sale was insignificant.

Goodwill and other intangible assets

The Company's intangible assets consist primarily of goodwill and major trademarks arising from the 2001 acquisition of Keebler Foods Company ("Keebler"). Management expects the Keebler trademarks, collectively, to contribute indefinitely to the cash flows of the Company. Accordingly, this asset has been classified as an "indefinite-lived" intangible pursuant to SFAS No. 142 "Goodwill and Other Intangible Assets." Under this standard, goodwill and indefinite-lived intangibles are not amortized, but are tested at least annually for impairment. Goodwill impairment testing first requires a comparison between the carrying value and fair value of a "reporting unit," which for the Company is generally equivalent to a North American product group or International country market. If carrying value exceeds fair value, goodwill is considered impaired and is reduced to the implied fair value. Impairment testing for non-amortized intangibles requires a comparison between the fair value and carrying value of the intangible asset. If carrying value exceeds fair value, the intangible is considered impaired and is reduced to fair value. The Company uses various market valuation techniques to determine the fair value of intangible assets and periodically engages third-party valuation consultants for this purpose. Refer to Note 2 for further information on goodwill and other intangible assets.

Revenue recognition and measurement

The Company recognizes sales upon delivery of its products to customers net of applicable provisions for discounts, returns, allowances, and various government withholding taxes. Methodologies for determining these provisions are dependent on local customer pricing and promotional practices, which range from contractually fixed percentage price reductions to reimbursement based on actual occurrence or performance. Where applicable, future reimbursements are estimated based on a combination of historical patterns and future expectations regarding specific in-market product performance. The Company classifies promotional payments to its customers, the cost of consumer coupons, and other cash redemption offers in net sales. The cost of promotional package inserts are recorded in cost of goods sold. Other types of consumer promotional expenditures are normally recorded in selling, general, and administrative (SGA) expense.

Advertising

The costs of advertising are generally expensed as incurred and are classified within SGA expense.

Research and development

The costs of research and development (R&D) are generally expensed as incurred and are classified within SGA expense. R&D includes expenditures for new product and process innovation, as well as significant technological improvements to existing products and processes. Total annual expenditures for R&D are disclosed in Note 15 and are principally comprised of internal salaries, wages, consulting, and supplies attributable to time spent on R&D activities. Other costs include depreciation and maintenance of research facilities and equipment, including assets at manufacturing locations that are temporarily engaged in pilot plant activities.

Stock compensation

The Company uses various equity-based compensation programs to provide long-term performance incentives for its global workforce. Refer to Note 8 for further information on these programs and the amount of compensation expense recognized during the periods presented.

In December 2004, the FASB issued SFAS No. 123(R) "Share-Based Payment," which generally requires public companies to measure the cost of employee services received in exchange for an award of equity instruments based on the grant-date fair value and to recognize this cost over the requisite service period. The Company adopted SFAS No. 123(R) as of the beginning of its 2006 fiscal year, using the modified prospective method. Accordingly, prior years were not restated, but 2006 results include compensation expense associated with unvested equity-based awards, which were granted prior to 2006.

Prior to adoption of SFAS No. 123(R), the Company used the intrinsic value method prescribed by Accounting Principles Board Opinion (APB) No. 25 "Accounting for Stock Issued to Employees" to account for its employee stock options and other stock-based compensation. Under this method, because the exercise price of stock options granted to employees and directors equaled the market price of the underlying stock on the date of the grant, no compensation expense was recognized. Expense attributable to other types of stock-based awards was generally recognized in the Company's reported results under APB No. 25.

Certain of the Company's equity-based compensation plans contain provisions that accelerate vesting of awards upon retirement, disability, or death of eligible employees and directors. Prior to adoption of SFAS No. 123(R), the Company generally recognized stock compensation expense over the stated vesting period of the award, with any unamortized expense recognized immediately if an acceleration event occurred. SFAS No. 123(R) specifies that a stock-based award is considered vested for expense attribution purposes when the employee's retention of the award is no longer contingent on providing subsequent service. Accordingly, beginning in 2006, the Company has prospectively revised its expense attribution method so that the related compensation cost is recognized immediately for awards granted to retirement-eligible individuals or over the period from the grant date to the date retirement eligibility is achieved, if less than the stated vesting period.

The Company classifies pre-tax stock compensation expense principally in SGA expense within its corporate operations. Expense attributable to awards of equity instruments is accrued in capital in excess of par value within the Consolidated Balance Sheet.

SFAS No. 123(R) also provides that any corporate income tax benefit realized upon exercise or vesting of an award in excess of that previously recognized in earnings (referred to as a "windfall tax benefit") will be presented in the Consolidated Statement of Cash Flows as a financing (rather than an operating) cash flow. Realized windfall tax benefits are credited to capital in excess of par value in the Consolidated Balance Sheet. Realized shortfall tax benefits (amounts which are less than that previously recognized in earnings) are first offset against the cumulative balance of windfall tax benefits, if any, and then charged directly to income tax expense. Under the transition rules for adopting SFAS No. 123(R) using the modified prospective method, the Company was permitted to calculate a cumulative memo balance of windfall tax benefits from post-1995 years for the purpose of accounting for future shortfall tax benefits. The Company completed such study prior to the first period of adoption and currently has sufficient cumulative memo windfall tax benefits to absorb arising shortfalls, such that earnings were not affected in 2006. Correspondingly, the Company includes the impact of pro forma deferred tax assets (i.e., the "as if" windfall or shortfall) for purposes of determining assumed proceeds in the treasury stock calculation of diluted earnings per share under SFAS No. 128 "Earnings Per Share."

Employee postretirement and postemployment benefits

The Company sponsors a number of U.S. and foreign plans to provide pension, health care, and other welfare benefits to retired employees, as well as salary continuance, severance, and long-term disability to former or inactive employees. Refer to Notes 9 and 10 for further information on these benefits and the amount of expense recognized during the periods presented.

In order to improve the reporting of pension and other postretirement benefit plans in the financial statements, in September 2006, the FASB issued SFAS No. 158 "Employers' Accounting for Defined Benefit Pension and Other Postretirement Plans," which is effective at the end of fiscal years ending after December 15, 2006. Prior periods are not restated. The standard generally requires company plan sponsors to measure the net over- or under-funded position of a defined postretirement benefit plan as of the sponsor's fiscal year end and to display that position as an asset or liability on the balance sheet. Any unrecognized prior service cost, experience gains/losses, or transition obligation are reported as a component of other comprehensive income, net of tax, in shareholders' equity. In contrast, under pre-existing guidance, these unrecognized amounts were generally disclosed only in financial statement footnotes, often resulting in a disparity between plan balance sheet positions and the funded status. Furthermore, plan measurement dates could occur up to three months prior to year end.

The Company adopted SFAS No. 158 as of the end of its 2006 fiscal year. The Company had previously applied postretirement accounting concepts for purposes of recognizing its postemployment benefit obligations; accordingly, the adoption of SFAS No. 158 as of December 30, 2006, affected the balance sheet display of both the Company's postretirement and postemployment benefit obligations, as follows:

(millions)	Before application of SFAS No. 158 (a)	Adjustments	After application of SFAS No. 158
Other assets:			
Other intangibles — pension	$ 9.5	$ (9.5)	$ —
Pension	855.5	(502.9)	352.6
	$865.0	**$(512.4)**	**$ 352.6**
Total assets	**$865.0**	**$(512.4)**	**$ 352.6**
Other current liabilities:			
Pension, postretirement, and postemployment benefits	53.0	(34.2)	18.8
	$ 53.0	**$ (34.2)**	**$ 18.8**
Other liabilities:			
Pension, postretirement, and postemployment benefits (a)	287.2	412.6	699.8
Deferred income taxes (b)	(6.8)	(298.9)	(305.7)
	$280.4	**$ 113.7**	**$ 394.1**
Total liabilities	**$333.4**	**$ 79.5**	**$ 412.9**
Accumulated other comprehensive income (loss) (a)	**$ (12.2)**	**$(591.9)**	**$(604.1)**

(a) Includes additional minimum pension liability adjustment under pre-existing guidance of $28.5, which reduced accumulated other comprehensive income by $12.2 on an after-tax basis.

(b) Represents an asset component of deferred tax liabilities, which are presented on a net basis at the jurisdiction level.

The Company's net earnings, cash flow, liquidity, debt covenants, and plan funding requirements were not affected by this change in accounting principle. The Company has historically used its fiscal year end as the measurement date for its company-sponsored defined benefit plans.

Recently issued pronouncements

Uncertain tax positions

In July 2006, the FASB issued Interpretation No. 48 "Accounting for Uncertainty in Income Taxes" (FIN No. 48) to clarify what criteria must be met prior to recognition of the financial statement benefit, in accordance with FASB Statement No. 109, "Accounting for Income Taxes," of a position taken in a tax return. The provisions of the final interpretation apply broadly to all tax positions taken by an enterprise, including the decision not to report income in a tax return or the decision to classify a transaction as tax exempt. The prescribed approach is based on a two-step benefit recognition model. The first step is to evaluate the tax position for recognition by determining if the weight of available evidence indicates it is more likely than not, based on the technical merits and without consideration of detection risk, that the position will be sustained on audit, including resolution of related appeals or litigation processes, if any. The second step is to measure the appropriate amount of the benefit to recognize. The amount of benefit to recognize is measured as the largest amount of tax benefit that is greater than 50 percent likely of being ultimately realized upon settlement. The tax position must be derecognized when it is no longer more likely than not of being sustained. The interpretation also provides guidance on recognition and classification of related penalties and interest, classification of liabilities, and disclosures of unrecognized tax benefits. The change in net assets, if any, as a result of applying the provisions of this interpretation is considered a change in accounting principle with the cumulative effect of the change treated as an offsetting adjustment to the opening balance of retained earnings in the period of transition. The final interpretation is effective for the first annual period beginning after December 15, 2006, with earlier application encouraged.

The Company adopted FIN No. 48 as of the beginning of its 2007 fiscal year. Prior to adoption, the Company's pre-existing policy was to establish reserves for uncertain tax positions that reflected the probable outcome of known tax contingencies. As compared to the Company's historical approach, the application of FIN No. 48 resulted in a net decrease to accrued income tax and related interest liabilities of approximately $2 million, with an offsetting increase to retained earnings.

Interest recognized in accordance with FIN No. 48 may be classified in the financial statements as either income taxes or interest expense, based on the accounting policy election of the enterprise. Similarly, penalties may be classified as income taxes or another expense. The Company has historically classified income tax-related interest and penalties as interest expense and SGA expense, respectively, and will continue to do so under FIN No. 48.

Fair value

In September 2006, the FASB issued SFAS No. 157 "Fair Value Measurements" to provide enhanced guidance for using fair value to measure assets and liabilities. The standard also expands disclosure requirements for assets and liabilities measured at fair value, how fair value is determined, and the effect of fair value measurements on earnings. The standard applies whenever other authoritative literature requires (or permits) certain assets or liabilities to be measured at fair value, but does not expand the use of fair value. SFAS No. 157 is effective for financial statements issued for fiscal years beginning after November 15, 2007, and interim periods within those years. Early adoption is permitted. The Company plans to adopt SFAS No. 157 in the first quarter of its 2008 fiscal year. For the Company, balance sheet items carried at fair value consist primarily of derivatives and other financial instruments, assets held for sale, exit liabilities, and the trust asset component of net benefit plan obligations. Additionally, the Company uses fair value concepts to test various long-lived assets for impairment and to initially measure assets and liabilities acquired in a business combination. Management is currently evaluating the impact of adoption on how these assets and liabilities are currently measured.

Use of estimates

The preparation of financial statements in conformity with generally accepted accounting principles requires management to make estimates and assumptions that affect the reported amounts of assets and liabilities and disclosure of contingent assets and liabilities at the date of the financial statements and the reported amounts of revenues and expenses during the reporting period. Actual results could differ from those estimates.

Note 2 Acquisitions, other investments, and intangibles

Acquisitions

In order to support the continued growth of its North American fruit snacks business, the Company completed two separate business acquisitions during 2005 for a total of approximately $50 million in cash, including related transaction costs. In June 2005, the Company acquired a fruit snacks manufacturing facility and related assets from Kraft Foods Inc. The facility is located in Chicago, Illinois and employs approximately 400 active hourly and salaried employees. In November 2005, the Company acquired substantially all of the assets and certain liabilities of a Washington State-based manufacturer of natural and organic fruit snacks. Assets, liabilities, and results of the acquired businesses have been included in the Company's consolidated financial statements since the respective dates of acquisition. The combined purchase price for both transactions was allocated to property ($22 million); goodwill and other indefinite-lived intangibles ($16 million); and inventory and other working capital ($12 million).

Joint venture arrangement

In early 2006, a subsidiary of the Company formed a joint venture with a third-party company domiciled in Turkey, for the purpose of selling co-branded products in the surrounding region. As of December 30, 2006, the Company had contributed approximately $3.5 million in cash for a 50% equity interest in this arrangement. The Turkish joint venture is reflected in the consolidated financial statements on the equity basis of accounting. Accordingly, the Company records its share of the earnings or loss from this arrangement as well as other direct transactions with or on behalf of the joint venture entity such as product sales and certain administrative expenses. Summary financial information for one hundred percent of the joint venture is as follows:

(millions)	2006
Net sales	$ 6.0
Gross profit	1.9
Net earnings (loss)	(1.9)
Current assets	5.9
Noncurrent assets	—
Current liabilities	1.3
Noncurrent liabilities	—

Goodwill and other intangible assets

For 2004, the Company recorded in selling, general, and administrative expense impairment losses of $10.4 million to write off the remaining carrying value of a $7.9 million contract-based intangible asset in North America and $2.5 million of goodwill in Latin America.

For the periods presented, the Company's intangible assets consisted of the following:

Intangible assets subject to amortization

(millions)	Gross carrying amount		Accumulated amortization	
	2006	2005	**2006**	2005
Trademarks	**$29.5**	$29.5	**$21.6**	$20.5
Other	**29.1**	29.1	**27.5**	27.1
Total	**$58.6**	$58.6	**$49.1**	$47.6

	2006	2005
Amortization expense (a)	**$1.5**	$1.5

(a) The currently estimated aggregate amortization expense for each of the four succeeding fiscal years is approximately $1.5 per year and $1.1 for the fifth succeeding fiscal year.

Intangible assets not subject to amortization

(millions)	Total carrying amount	
	2006	2005
Trademarks	**$1,410.2**	$1,410.2
Pension (a)	**—**	17.0
Total	**$1,410.2**	$1,427.2

(a) The Company adopted SFAS No. 158 "Employers' Accounting for Defined Benefit Pension and Other Postretirement Plans" as of the end of its 2006 fiscal year. The standard generally requires company plan sponsors to reflect the net over- or under-funded position of a defined postretirement benefit plan as an asset or liability on the balance sheet. Accordingly, the pension-related intangible included in the preceding table for 2005 was eliminated by the adoption of this standard. Refer to Note 1 for further information.

Changes in the carrying amount of goodwill

(millions)	United States	Europe	Latin America	Asia Pacific (a)	Consoli-dated
January 1, 2005	$3,443.3	—	—	$2.2	$3,445.5
Acquisitions	10.2	—	—	—	10.2
Other	(.3)	—	—	(.1)	(.4)
December 31, 2005	$3,453.2	—	—	$2.1	$3,455.3
Purchase accounting adjustments (b)	**(7.0)**	**—**	**—**	**—**	**(7.0)**
Other	**(.1)**	**—**	**—**	**.1**	**—**
December 30, 2006	**$3,446.1**	**—**	**—**	**$2.2**	**$3,448.3**

(a) Includes Australia and Asia.

(b) Relates principally to the recognition of an acquired tax benefit arising from the purchase of Keebler Foods Company in 2001.

Note 3 Cost-reduction initiatives

The Company views its continued spending on cost-reduction initiatives as part of its ongoing operating principles to reinvest earnings so as to provide greater reliability in meeting long-term growth targets. Initiatives undertaken must meet certain pay-back and internal rate of return (IRR) targets. Each cost-reduction initiative is normally one to three years in duration. Upon completion (or as each major stage is completed in the case of multi-year programs), the project begins to deliver cash savings and/or reduced depreciation, which is then used to fund new initiatives. To implement these programs, the Company has incurred various up-front costs, including asset write-offs, exit charges, and other project expenditures.

Cost summary

For 2006, the Company recorded total program-related charges of approximately $82 million, comprised of $20 million of asset write-offs, $30 million for severance and other exit costs, $9 million for other cash expenditures, $4 million for a multiemployer pension plan withdrawal liability, and $19 million for pension and other postretirement plan curtailment losses and special termination benefits. Approximately $74 million of the total 2006 charges were recorded in cost of goods sold within operating segment results, with approximately $8 million recorded in selling, general, and administrative (SGA) expense within corporate results. The Company's operating segments were impacted as follows (in millions): North America–$46; Europe–$28.

For 2005, the Company recorded total program-related charges of approximately $90 million, comprised of $16 million for a multiemployer pension plan withdrawal liability, $44 million of asset write-offs, $21 million for severance and other exit costs, and $9 million for other cash expenditures. All of the 2005 charges were recorded in cost of goods sold within the Company's North America operating segment.

For 2004, the Company recorded total program-related charges of approximately $109 million, comprised of $41 million in asset write-offs, $1 million for special pension termination benefits, $15 million in severance and other exit costs, and $52 million in other cash expenditures such as relocation and consulting. Approximately $46 million of the total 2004 charges were recorded in cost of goods sold, with approximately $63 million recorded in SGA expense. The 2004 charges impacted the Company's operating segments as follows (in millions): North America–$44; Europe–$65.

Exit cost reserves were approximately $14 million at December 30, 2006, consisting principally of severance obligations associated with projects commenced in 2006, which are expected to be paid out in 2007. At December 31, 2005, exit cost reserves were approximately $13 million, primarily representing severance costs that were substantially paid out in 2006.

Specific initiatives

In September 2006, the Company approved a multi-year European manufacturing optimization plan to improve utilization of its facility in Manchester, England and to better align production in Europe. Based on forecasted foreign exchange rates, the Company currently expects to incur approximately $60 million in total up-front costs (including those already incurred in 2006), comprised of approximately 80% cash and 20% non-cash asset write-offs, to complete this initiative. The cash portion of the total up-front costs results principally from management's plan to eliminate approximately 220 hourly and salaried positions from the Manchester facility by the end of 2008 through voluntary early retirement and severance programs. The pension trust funding requirements of these early retirements are expected to exceed the recognized benefit expense impact by approximately $10 million; most of this incremental funding occurred in 2006. During this period, certain manufacturing equipment will also be removed from service. For 2006, the Company incurred approximately $28 million of total up-front costs, including $9 million of pension plan curtailment losses and special termination benefits.

During 2006, the Company commenced several initiatives to enhance the productivity and efficiency of its U.S. cereal manufacturing network, primarily through technological and sourcing improvements in warehousing and packaging operations. In conjunction with these initiatives, the Company offered voluntary separation incentives, which resulted in the retirement of approximately 80 hourly employees by early 2007. During the fourth quarter of 2006, the Company incurred approximately $15 million of total up-front costs, comprised of approximately 20% asset write-offs and 80% cash costs, including $10 million of pension and other postretirement plan curtailment losses.

Also during 2006, the Company undertook an initiative to improve customer focus and selling efficiency within a particular Latin American market, leading to a shift from a third-party distributor to a direct sales force model. As a result of this initiative, the Company paid $8 million in cash during the fourth quarter of 2006 to exit the existing distribution arrangement.

To improve operational efficiency and better position its North American snacks business for future growth, during 2005, the Company undertook an initiative to consolidate U.S. bakery capacity, which was completed by the end of 2006. The project resulted in the closure and sale of the Company's Des Plaines, Illinois facility in late 2005 and closure of its Macon, Georgia facility in April 2006, with sale occurring in September 2006. These closures resulted in the elimination of over 700 hourly and salaried employee positions, through the combination of involuntary severance and attrition. Related to this initiative, the Company incurred up-front costs of approximately $80 million in 2005, comprised of approximately one-half asset write-offs and one-half cash costs, including $16 million for the present value of a projected multiemployer pension plan withdrawal liability associated with closure of the Macon facility. The Company incurred approximately $31 million in up-front costs for 2006, comprised of approximately one-third asset write-offs and two-thirds cash costs, including a $4 million increase in the Company's estimated pension plan withdrawal liability to $20 million. This increase was principally attributable to investment loss experienced during 2005 in conjunction with increased benefit levels for all participating employers. The final calculation of this liability is pending full-year 2007 employee hours attributable to the Company's remaining participation in this plan, and is therefore subject to adjustment in early 2008. The associated cash obligation is payable to the pension fund over a 20-year maximum period; management has not currently determined the actual period over which the payments will be made. Except for this pension plan withdrawal liability, the Company's cash obligations attributable to this initiative were substantially paid out by year end 2006.

During 2004, the Company commenced an operational improvement initiative which resulted in the consolidation of veggie foods manufacturing at its Zanesville, Ohio facility and the closure and sale of its Worthington, Ohio facility by mid 2005. As a result of this closing, approximately 280 employee positions were eliminated through separation and attrition. Related to this initiative, the Company recognized approximately $20 million of up-front costs in 2004 and $10 million in 2005. For both years, the total amounts were comprised of approximately two-thirds asset write-offs and one-third cash costs such as severance and removal, which were entirely paid out by the end of 2005.

During 2004, the Company's global rollout of its SAP information technology system resulted in accelerated depreciation of legacy software assets to be abandoned in 2005, as well as related consulting and other implementation expenses. Total incremental costs for 2004 were approximately $30 million. In close association with this SAP rollout, management undertook a major initiative to improve the organizational design and effectiveness of pan-European operations. Specific benefits of this initiative were expected to include improved marketing and promotional coordination across Europe, supply chain network savings, overhead cost reductions, and tax savings. To achieve these benefits, management implemented, at the beginning of 2005, a new European legal and operating structure headquartered in Ireland, with strengthened pan-European management authority and coordination. During 2004, the Company incurred various up-front costs, including relocation, severance, and consulting, of approximately $30 million. Additional relocation and other costs to complete this business transformation after 2004 have been insignificant.

In order to integrate it with the rest of our U.S. operations, during 2004, the Company completed the relocation of its U.S. snacks business unit from Elmhurst, Illinois (the former headquarters of Keebler Foods Company) to Battle Creek, Michigan. About one-third of the approximately 300 employees affected by this initiative accepted relocation or reassignment offers. The recruiting effort to fill the remaining open positions was substantially completed by year-end 2004. Attributable to this initiative, the Company incurred approximately $15 million in relocation, recruiting, and severance costs during 2004. Subject to achieving certain employment levels and other regulatory requirements, management expects to defray a significant portion of these up-front costs through various multi-year tax incentives, which began in 2005. The Elmhurst office building was sold in late 2004, and the net sales proceeds approximated carrying value.

Note 4 Other income (expense), net

Other income (expense), net includes non-operating items such as interest income, charitable donations, and foreign exchange gains and losses. Net foreign exchange transaction losses for the periods presented were approximately (in millions): 2006–$2; 2005–$2; 2004–$15.

Other expense includes charges for contributions to the Kellogg's Corporate Citizenship Fund, a private trust established for charitable giving, as follows (in millions): 2006–$3; 2005–$16; 2004–$9. Other expense for 2005 also includes a charge of approximately $7 million to reduce the carrying value of a corporate commercial facility to estimated selling value. This facility was sold in August 2006.

Note 5 Equity

During the year ended December 30, 2006, the Company revised the classification of $101.4 million of prior net losses realized upon reissuance of treasury shares from capital in excess of par value to retained earnings on the Consolidated Balance Sheet. Such reissuances occurred in connection with employee and director stock option exercises and other share-based settlements. The revision did not have an effect on the Company's results of operations, total shareholders' equity, or cash flows.

Earnings per share

Basic net earnings per share is determined by dividing net earnings by the weighted-average number of common shares outstanding during the period. Diluted net earnings per share is similarly determined, except that the denominator is increased to include the number of additional common shares that would have been outstanding if all dilutive potential common shares had been issued. Dilutive potential common shares are comprised principally of employee stock options issued by the Company. Basic net earnings per share is reconciled to diluted net earnings per share in the following table. The total number of anti-dilutive potential common shares excluded from the reconciliation for each period was (in millions): 2006–.7; 2005–1.5; 2004–4.3.

(millions, except per share data)	Earnings	Average shares outstanding	Per share
2006			
Basic	**$1,004.1**	**397.0**	**$2.53**
Dilutive potential common shares	**—**	**3.4**	**(.02)**
Diluted	**$1,004.1**	**400.4**	**$2.51**
2005			
Basic	$ 980.4	412.0	$2.38
Dilutive potential common shares	—	3.6	(.02)
Diluted	$ 980.4	415.6	$2.36
2004			
Basic	$ 890.6	412.0	$2.16
Dilutive potential common shares	—	4.4	(.02)
Diluted	$ 890.6	416.4	$2.14

Stock transactions

The Company issues shares to employees and directors under various equity-based compensation and stock purchase programs, as further discussed in Note 8. The number of shares issued during the periods presented was (in millions): 2006–7.2; 2005–7.7; 2004–10.7. Additionally, during 2006, the Company established *Kellogg Direct*™, a direct stock purchase and dividend reinvestment plan for U.S. shareholders and issued less than .1 million shares for that purpose in 2006.

To offset these issuances and for general corporate purposes, the Company's Board of Directors has authorized management to repurchase specified amounts of the Company's common stock in each of the periods presented. In 2006, the Company spent $650 million to repurchase approximately 14.9 million shares. This activity consisted principally of a February 2006 private transaction with the W.K. Kellogg Foundation Trust to repurchase approximately 12.8 million shares for $550 million. In 2005, the Company spent $664 million to repurchase approximately 15.4 million shares. This activity consisted principally of a November 2005 private transaction with the W.K. Kellogg Foundation Trust to repurchase approximately 9.4 million shares for $400 million. In 2004, the Company spent $298 million to repurchase approximately 7.3 million shares.

On December 8, 2006, the Company's Board of Directors authorized a stock repurchase program of up to $650 million for 2007.

Comprehensive income

Comprehensive income includes net earnings and all other changes in equity during a period except those resulting from investments by or distributions to shareholders. Other comprehensive income for the periods presented consists of foreign currency translation adjustments pursuant to SFAS No. 52 "Foreign Currency Translation," unrealized gains and losses on cash flow hedges pursuant to SFAS No. 133 "Accounting for Derivative Instruments and Hedging Activities," and minimum pension liability adjustments pursuant to SFAS No. 87 "Employers' Accounting for Pensions." Additionally, accumulated other comprehensive income at December 30, 2006, reflects the adoption of SFAS No. 158 "Employers' Accounting for Defined Benefit Pension and Other Postretirement Plans" as of the

Company's 2006 fiscal year end. Refer to Note 1 for further information.

(millions)	Pretax amount	Tax (expense) benefit	After-tax amount
2006			
Net earnings			**$1,004.1**
Other comprehensive income:			
Foreign currency translation adjustments	**$ 10.0**	**$ —**	**10.0**
Cash flow hedges:			
Unrealized loss on cash flow hedges	**(12.6)**	**4.6**	**(8.0)**
Reclassification to net earnings	**11.9**	**(4.3)**	**7.6**
Minimum pension liability adjustments	**172.3**	**(60.1)**	**112.2**
	$ 181.6	**$ (59.8)**	**121.8**
Total comprehensive income			**$1,125.9**
2005			
Net earnings			$ 980.4
Other comprehensive income:			
Foreign currency translation adjustments	$ (85.2)	$ —	(85.2)
Cash flow hedges:			
Unrealized loss on cash flow hedges	(3.7)	1.6	(2.1)
Reclassification to net earnings	26.4	(9.9)	16.5
Minimum pension liability adjustments	(102.7)	37.3	(65.4)
	$(165.2)	$ 29.0	(136.2)
Total comprehensive income			$ 844.2
2004			
Net earnings			$ 890.6
Other comprehensive income:			
Foreign currency translation adjustments	$ 71.7	$ —	71.7
Cash flow hedges:			
Unrealized loss on cash flow hedges	(10.2)	3.1	(7.1)
Reclassification to net earnings	19.3	(6.9)	12.4
Minimum pension liability adjustments	308.9	(96.6)	212.3
	$ 389.7	$(100.4)	289.3
Total comprehensive income			$1,179.9

Accumulated other comprehensive income (loss) at year end consisted of the following:

(millions)	**2006**	2005
Foreign currency translation adjustments	**$ (409.5)**	$(419.5)
Cash flow hedges — unrealized net loss	**(32.6)**	(32.2)
Minimum pension liability adjustments	**—**	(124.4)
Postretirement and postemployment benefits:		
Net experience loss	**(540.5)**	—
Prior service cost	**(63.6)**	—
Total accumulated other comprehensive income (loss)	**$(1,046.2)**	$(576.1)

Note 6 Leases and other commitments

The Company's leases are generally for equipment and warehouse space. Rent expense on all operating leases was (in millions): 2006–$122.8; 2005–$115.1; 2004–$107.4. Additionally, the Company is subject to a residual value guarantee on one operating lease of approximately $13 million which expires in July 2007. At December 30, 2006, the Company had not recorded any liability related to this residual value guarantee. During 2006 and 2005, the Company entered into approximately $2 million and $3 million, respectively, in capital lease agreements to finance the purchase of equipment. Similar transactions in 2004 were insignificant.

At December 30, 2006, future minimum annual lease commitments under noncancelable operating and capital leases were as follows:

(millions)	Operating leases	Capital leases
2007	$119.7	$ 2.1
2008	103.4	1.4
2009	85.9	1.3
2010	67.7	1.0
2011	49.8	.6
2012 and beyond	148.6	3.0
Total minimum payments	$575.1	$ 9.4
Amount representing interest		(1.6)
Obligations under capital leases		7.8
Obligations due within one year		(2.1)
Long-term obligations under capital leases		$ 5.7

One of the Company's subsidiaries is guarantor on loans to independent contractors for the purchase of DSD route franchises. At year-end 2006, there were total loans outstanding of $16.0 million to 517 franchisees. All loans are variable rate with a term of 10 years. Related to this arrangement, the Company has established with a financial institution a one-year renewable loan facility up to $17.0 million with a five-year term-out and servicing arrangement. The Company has the right to revoke and resell the route franchises in the event of default or any other breach of contract by franchisees. Revocations are infrequent. The Company's maximum potential future payments under these guarantees are limited to the outstanding loan principal balance plus unpaid interest. The estimated fair value of these guarantees is recorded in the Consolidated Balance Sheet and was insignificant for the periods presented.

The Company has provided various standard indemnifications in agreements to sell business assets and lease facilities over the past several years, related primarily to pre-existing tax, environmental, and employee benefit obligations. Certain of these indemnifications are limited by agreement in either amount and/or term and others are unlimited. The Company has also provided various "hold harmless" provisions within certain service type agreements. Because the Company is not currently aware of any actual exposures associated with these indemnifications, management is unable to estimate the maximum potential future payments to be made. At December 30, 2006, the Company had not recorded any liability related to these indemnifications.

Note 7 Debt

Notes payable at year end consisted of commercial paper borrowings in the United States and Canada, and to a lesser extent, bank loans of foreign subsidiaries at competitive market rates, as follows:

(dollars in millions)	**2006**		2005	
	Principal amount	**Effective interest rate**	Principal amount	Effective interest rate
U.S. commercial paper	**$1,140.7**	**5.3%**	$ 797.3	4.4%
Canadian commercial paper	**87.5**	**4.4%**	260.4	3.4%
Other	**39.8**		53.4	
	$1,268.0		$1,111.1	

Long-term debt at year end consisted primarily of issuances of fixed rate U.S. Dollar and floating rate Euro Notes, as follows:

(millions)	**2006**	2005
(a) 6.6% U.S. Dollar Notes due 2011	**$1,496.2**	$1,495.4
(a) 7.45% U.S. Dollar Debentures due 2031	**1,087.8**	1,087.3
(b) 4.49% U.S. Dollar Notes due 2006	**—**	75.0
(c) 2.875% U.S. Dollar Notes due 2008	**464.6**	464.6
(d) Guaranteed Floating Rate Euro Notes due 2007	**722.1**	650.6
Other	**5.6**	13.3
	3,776.3	3,786.2
Less current maturities	**(723.3)**	(83.6)
Balance at year end	**$3,053.0**	$3,702.6

(a) In March 2001, the Company issued $4.6 billion of long-term debt instruments, primarily to finance the acquisition of Keebler Foods Company. The preceding table reflects the remaining principal amounts outstanding as of year-end 2006 and 2005. The effective interest rates on these Notes, reflecting issuance discount and swap settlement, were as follows: due 2011 – 7.08%; due 2031 – 7.62%. Initially, these instruments were privately placed, or sold outside the United States, in reliance on exemptions from registration under the Securities Act of 1933, as amended (the "1933 Act"). The Company then exchanged new debt securities for these initial debt instruments, with the new debt securities being substantially identical in all respects to the initial debt instruments, except for being registered under the 1933 Act. These debt securities contain standard events of default and covenants. The Notes due 2011 and the Debentures due 2031 may be redeemed in whole or in part by the Company at any time at prices determined under a formula (but not less than 100% of the principal amount plus unpaid interest to the redemption date).

(b) In November 2001, a subsidiary of the Company issued $375 million of five-year 4.49% fixed rate U.S. Dollar Notes to replace other maturing debt. These Notes were guaranteed by the Company and matured $75 million per year over the five-year term, with the final principal payment made in November 2006. These Notes, which were privately placed, contained standard warranties, events of default, and covenants. They also required the maintenance of a specified consolidated interest expense coverage ratio, and limited capital lease obligations and subsidiary debt. In conjunction with this issuance, the subsidiary of the Company entered into a $375 million notional US$/Pound Sterling currency swap, which effectively converted this debt into a 5.302% fixed rate Pound Sterling obligation for the duration of the five-year term.

(c) In June 2003, the Company issued $500 million of five-year 2.875% fixed rate U.S. Dollar Notes, using the proceeds from these Notes to replace maturing long-term debt. These Notes were issued under an existing shelf registration statement. The effective interest rate on these Notes, reflecting issuance discount and swap settlement, is 3.35%. The Notes contain customary covenants that limit the ability of the Company and its restricted subsidiaries (as defined) to incur certain liens or enter into certain sale and lease-back transactions. In December 2005, the Company redeemed $35.4 million of these Notes.

(d) In November 2005, a subsidiary of the Company (the "Borrower") issued Euro 550 million of Guaranteed Floating Rate Notes (the "Euro Notes") due May 2007. The Euro Notes were issued and sold in transactions outside the United States in reliance on exemptions from registration under the 1933 Act. The Euro Notes are guaranteed by the Company and bear interest at a rate of 0.12% per annum above three-month EURIBOR for each quarterly interest period. The Euro Notes contain customary covenants that limit the ability of the Company and its restricted subsidiaries (as defined) to incur certain liens or enter into certain sale and lease-back transactions. The Euro Notes were redeemable in whole or in part at par on interest payment dates or upon the occurrence of certain events in 2006 and 2007. In accordance with these terms, on January 31, 2007, the Borrower announced that it had exercised its right to call for early redemption all of the outstanding Euro Notes effective February 28, 2007, at a redemption price equal to the principal amount, plus accrued and unpaid interest through the redemption date.

At December 30, 2006, the Company had $2.2 billion of short-term lines of credit, virtually all of which were unused and available for borrowing on an unsecured basis. These lines were comprised principally of an unsecured Five-Year Credit Agreement, which the Company entered into during November 2006 to replace an existing facility, which would have expired in 2009. The agreement allows the Company to borrow, on a revolving credit basis, up to $2.0 billion, to obtain letters of credit in an aggregate amount up to $75 million, and to provide a procedure for lenders to bid on short-term debt of the Company. The agreement contains customary covenants and warranties, including specified restrictions on indebtedness, liens, sale and leaseback transactions, and a specified interest coverage ratio. If an event of default occurs, then, to the extent permitted, the administrative agent may terminate the commitments under the credit facility, accelerate any outstanding loans, and demand the deposit of cash collateral equal to the lender's letter of credit exposure plus interest. The facility is available for general corporate purposes, including commercial paper back-up, although the Company does not currently anticipate any usage under the facility.

Scheduled principal repayments on long-term debt are (in millions): 2007–$723.3; 2008–$466.1; 2009–$1.2; 2010–$1.1; 2011–$1,500.5; 2012 and beyond–$1,100.2.

Interest paid was (in millions): 2006–$299; 2005–$295; 2004–$333. Interest expense capitalized as part of the construction cost of fixed assets was (in millions): 2006–$2.7; 2005–$1.2; 2004–$.9.

Subsequent events

As discussed in preceding subnote (d), on January 31, 2007, a subsidiary of the Company announced an early redemption, effective February 28, 2007, of Euro 550 million of Guaranteed Floating Rate Notes otherwise due May 2007. To partially refinance this redemption, the Company and two of its subsidiaries (the "Issuers") established a program under which the Issuers may issue euro-commercial paper notes up to a maximum aggregate amount outstanding at any time of $750 million or its equivalent in alternative currencies. The notes may have maturities ranging up to 364 days and will be senior unsecured obligations of the applicable Issuer. Notes issued by subsidiary Issuers will be guaranteed by the Company. The notes may be issued at a discount or may bear fixed or floating rate interest or a coupon calculated by reference to an index or formula.

In connection with these financing activities, the Company increased its short-term lines of credit from $2.2 billion at December 30, 2006 to approximately $2.6 billion, via a $400 million unsecured 364-Day Credit Agreement effective January 31, 2007. The 364-Day Agreement contains customary covenants, warranties, and restrictions similar to those described herein for the Five-Year Credit Agreement. The facility is available for general corporate purposes, including commercial paper back-up, although the Company does not currently anticipate any usage under the facility.

Note 8 Stock compensation

The Company uses various equity-based compensation programs to provide long-term performance incentives for its global workforce. Currently, these incentives consist principally of stock options, and to a lesser extent, executive performance shares and restricted stock grants. The Company also sponsors a discounted stock purchase plan in the United States and matching-grant programs in several international locations. Additionally, the Company awards stock options and restricted stock to its outside directors. These awards are administered through several plans, as described within this Note.

The 2003 Long-Term Incentive Plan ("2003 Plan"), approved by shareholders in 2003, permits benefits to be awarded to employees and officers in the form of incentive and non-qualified stock options, performance units, restricted stock or restricted stock units, and stock appreciation rights. The 2003 Plan authorizes the issuance of a total of (a) 25 million shares plus (b) shares not issued under the 2001 Long-Term Incentive Plan, with no more than 5 million shares to be issued in satisfaction of performance units, performance-based restricted shares and other awards (excluding stock options and stock appreciation rights), and with additional annual limitations on awards or payments to individual participants. At December 30, 2006, there were 15.0 million remaining authorized, but unissued, shares under the 2003 Plan. During the periods presented, specific awards and terms of those awards granted under the 2003 Plan are described in the following sections of this Note.

The Non-Employee Director Stock Plan ("Director Plan") was approved by shareholders in 2000 and allows each eligible non-employee director to receive 1,700 shares of the Company's common stock annually and annual grants of options to purchase 5,000 shares of the Company's common stock. At December 30, 2006, there were

.4 million remaining authorized, but unissued, shares under this plan. Shares other than options are placed in the Kellogg Company Grantor Trust for Non-Employee Directors (the "Grantor Trust"). Under the terms of the Grantor Trust, shares are available to a director only upon termination of service on the Board. Under this plan, awards were as follows: 2006–50,000 options and 17,000 shares; 2005–55,000 options and 17,000 shares; 2004–55,000 options and 18,700 shares. Options granted to directors under this plan are included in the option activity tables within this Note.

The 2002 Employee Stock Purchase Plan was approved by shareholders in 2002 and permits eligible employees to purchase Company stock at a discounted price. This plan allows for a maximum of 2.5 million shares of Company stock to be issued at a purchase price equal to the lesser of 85% of the fair market value of the stock on the first or last day of the quarterly purchase period. Total purchases through this plan for any employee are limited to a fair market value of $25,000 during any calendar year. At December 30, 2006, there were 1.5 million remaining authorized, but unissued, shares under this plan. Shares were purchased by employees under this plan as follows (approximate number of shares): 2006–237,000; 2005–218,000; 2004–214,000. Options granted to employees to repurchase discounted stock under this plan are included in the option activity tables within this Note.

Additionally, during 2002, a foreign subsidiary of the Company established a stock purchase plan for its employees. Subject to limitations, employee contributions to this plan are matched 1:1 by the Company. Under this plan, shares were granted by the Company to match an approximately equal number of shares purchased by employees as follows (approximate number of shares): 2006–80,000; 2005–80,000; 2004–82,000.

The Executive Stock Purchase Plan was established in 2002 to encourage and enable certain eligible employees of the Company to acquire Company stock, and to align more closely the interests of those individuals and the Company's shareholders. This plan allows for a maximum of 500,000 shares of Company stock to be issued. At December 30, 2006, there were .5 million remaining authorized, but unissued, shares under this plan. Under this plan, shares were granted by the Company to executives in lieu of cash bonuses as follows (approximate number of shares): 2006–4,000; 2005–2,000; 2004–8,000.

For 2006, the Company used the fair value method prescribed by SFAS No. 123(R) "Share-Based Payment" to account for its equity-based compensation programs. Prior to 2006, the Company used the intrinsic value method prescribed by Accounting Principles Board Opinion (APB) No. 25 "Accounting for Stock Issued to Employees." Refer to Note 1 for further information on the Company's accounting policy for stock compensation.

For the year ended December 30, 2006, compensation expense for all types of equity-based programs and the related income tax benefit recognized was $95.7 million and $34.0 million, respectively. As a result of adopting SFAS No. 123(R) in 2006, the Company's reported pre-tax stock-based compensation expense for the year was $65.4 million higher (with net earnings and net earnings per share (basic and diluted) correspondingly lower by $42.4 million and $.11, respectively) than if it had continued to account for its equity-based programs under APB No. 25. Amounts for the prior years are presented in the following table in accordance with SFAS No. 123 "Accounting for Stock-Based Compensation" and related interpretations. Reported amounts consist principally of expense recognized for executive performance share and restricted stock awards; pro forma amounts are attributable primarily to stock option grants.

(millions, except per share data)	2005	2004
Stock-based compensation expense, pre-tax:		
As reported	$ 18.5	$ 17.5
Pro forma	$ 76.4	$ 64.1
Associated income tax benefit recognized:		
As reported	$ 6.7	$ 6.1
Pro forma	$ 27.7	$ 22.3
Stock-based compensation expense, net of tax:		
As reported	$ 11.8	$ 11.4
Pro forma	$ 48.7	$ 41.8
Net earnings:		
As reported	$980.4	$890.6
Pro forma	$943.5	$860.2
Basic net earnings per share:		
As reported	$ 2.38	$ 2.16
Pro forma	$ 2.29	$ 2.09
Diluted net earnings per share:		
As reported	$ 2.36	$ 2.14
Pro forma	$ 2.27	$ 2.07

As of December 30, 2006, total stock-based compensation cost related to nonvested awards not yet recognized was approximately $36 million and the weighted-average period over which this amount is expected to be recognized was approximately 1.4 years.

Cash flows realized upon exercise or vesting of stock-based awards in the periods presented are included in the following table. Within this table, the 2006 windfall tax benefit (amount realized in excess of that previously recognized in earnings) of $21.5 million represents the operating cash flow reduction (and financing cash flow increase) related to the Company's adoption of SFAS No. 123(R) in 2006. (Refer to Note 1 for further information on the Company's accounting policies regarding tax benefit windfalls and shortfalls.) Cash used by the Company to settle equity instruments granted under stock-based awards was insignificant.

(millions)	2006	2005	2004
Total cash received from option exercises and similar instruments	**$217.5**	$221.7	$291.8
Tax benefits realized upon exercise or vesting of stock-based awards:			
Windfall benefits classified as financing cash flow	**$ 21.5**	n/a	n/a
Other amounts classified as operating cash flow	**23.4**	40.3	38.6
Total	**$ 44.9**	$ 40.3	$ 38.6

Shares used to satisfy stock-based awards are normally issued out of treasury stock, although management is authorized to issue new shares to the extent permitted by respective plan provisions. Refer to Note 5 for information on shares issued during the periods presented to employees and directors under various long-term incentive plans and share repurchases under the Company's stock repurchase authorizations. The Company does not currently have a policy of repurchasing a specified number of shares issued under employee benefit programs during any particular time period.

Stock Options

During the periods presented, non-qualified stock options were granted to eligible employees under the 2003 Plan with exercise prices equal to the fair market value of the Company's stock on the grant date, a contractual term of ten years, and a two-year graded vesting period. Grants to outside directors under the Non-Employee Director Stock Plan included similar terms, but vested immediately. Additionally, "reload" options were awarded to eligible employees and directors to replace previously-owned Company stock used by those individuals to pay the exercise price, including related employment taxes, of vested pre-2004 option awards containing this accelerated ownership feature. These reload options are immediately vested, with an expiration date which is the same as the original option grant.

Management estimates the fair value of each annual stock option award on the date of grant using a lattice-based option valuation model. Due to the already-vested status and short expected term of reload options, management uses a Black-Scholes model to value such awards. Composite assumptions, which are not materially different for each of the two models, are presented in the following table. Weighted-average values are disclosed for certain inputs which incorporate a range of assumptions. Expected volatilities are based principally on historical volatility of the Company's stock, and to a lesser extent, on implied volatilities from traded options on the Company's stock. For the lattice-based model, historical volatility corresponds to the contractual term of the options granted; whereas, for the Black-Scholes model, historical volatility corresponds to the expected term. The Company generally uses historical data to estimate option exercise and employee termination within the valuation models; separate groups of employees that have similar historical exercise behavior are considered separately for valuation purposes. The expected term of options granted (which is an input to the Black-Scholes model and an output from the lattice-based model) represents the period of time that options granted are expected to be outstanding; the weighted-average expected term for all employee groups is presented in the following table. The risk-free rate for periods within the contractual life of the options is based on the U.S. Treasury yield curve in effect at the time of grant.

Stock option valuation model assumptions for grants within the year ended:	2006	2005	2004
Weighted-average expected volatility	**17.94%**	22.00%	23.00%
Weighted-average expected term (years)	**3.21**	3.42	3.69
Weighted-average risk-free interest rate	**4.65%**	3.81%	2.73%
Dividend yield	**2.40%**	2.40%	2.60%
Weighed-average fair value of options granted	**$ 6.67**	$ 7.35	$ 6.39

A summary of option activity for the year ended December 30, 2006, is presented in the following table:

Employee and director stock options	Shares (millions)	Weighted-average exercise price	Weighted-average remaining contractual term (yrs.)	Aggregate intrinsic value (millions)
Outstanding, beginning of year	28.8	$38		
Granted	9.6	46		
Exercised	(10.9)	37		
Forfeitures	(.3)	43		
Expirations	(.2)	43		
Outstanding, end of year	27.0	$41	6.1	$243.0
Exercisable, end of year	19.9	$40	5.1	$199.0

Additionally, option activity for comparable prior-year periods is presented in the following table:

(millions, except per share data)	2005	2004
Outstanding, beginning of year	32.5	37.0
Granted	8.3	9.7
Exercised	(10.9)	(12.9)
Forfeitures and expirations	(1.1)	(1.3)
Outstanding, end of year	28.8	32.5
Exercisable, end of year	21.3	22.8
Weighted-average exercise price:		
Outstanding, beginning of year	$ 35	$ 33
Granted	44	40
Exercised	34	32
Forfeitures and expirations	41	41
Outstanding, end of year	$ 38	$ 35
Exercisable, end of year	$ 37	$ 35

The total intrinsic value of options exercised during the periods presented was (in millions): 2006–$114; 2005–$116; 2004–$119.

Other stock-based awards

During the periods presented, other stock-based awards consisted principally of executive performance shares and restricted stock granted under the 2003 Plan.

In 2005 and 2006, the Company granted performance shares to a limited number of senior executive-level employees, which entitled these employees to receive a specified number of shares of the Company's common stock on the vesting date, provided cumulative three-year net sales growth targets were achieved. Subsequent to the adoption of SFAS No. 123(R), management has estimated the fair value of performance share awards based on the market price of the underlying stock on the date of grant, reduced by the present value of estimated dividends foregone during the performance period. The 2005 and 2006 target grants (as revised for non-vested forfeitures and other adjustments) currently correspond to approximately 275,000 and 260,000 shares, respectively; each with a grant-date fair value of approximately $41 per share. The actual number of shares issued on the vesting date could range from zero to 200% of target, depending on actual performance achieved. Based on the market price of the Company's common stock at year-end 2006, the maximum future value that could be awarded on the vesting date is (in millions): 2005 award–$27.5; 2006 award–$25.8. In addition to these performance share plans, a 2003 performance unit plan (payable in stock or cash under certain conditions) was settled at 74% of target in February 2006 for a total dollar equivalent of $2.9 million.

The Company also periodically grants restricted stock and restricted stock units to eligible employees under the 2003 Plan. Restrictions with respect to sale or transferability generally lapse after three years and the grantee is normally entitled to receive shareholder dividends during the vesting period. Management estimates the fair value of restricted stock grants based on the market price of the underlying stock on the date of grant. A summary of restricted stock activity for the year ended December 30, 2006, is presented in the following table:

Employee restricted stock and restricted stock units	Shares (thousands)	Weighted-average grant-date fair value
Non-vested, beginning of year	447	$39
Granted	190	47
Vested	(176)	34
Forfeited	(27)	43
Non-vested, end of year	434	$45

Grants of restricted stock and restricted stock units for comparable prior-year periods were: 2005–141,000; 2004–140,000.

The total fair value of restricted stock and restricted stock units vesting in the periods presented was (in millions): 2006–$8; 2005–$4; 2004–$4.

Note 9 Pension benefits

The Company sponsors a number of U.S. and foreign pension plans to provide retirement benefits for its employees. The majority of these plans are funded or unfunded defined benefit plans, although the Company does participate in a few multiemployer or other defined contribution plans for certain employee groups. Defined benefits for salaried employees are generally based on salary and years of service, while union employee benefits are generally a negotiated amount for each year of service. The Company uses its fiscal year end as the measurement date for its defined benefit plans.

Obligations and funded status

The aggregate change in projected benefit obligation, plan assets, and funded status is presented in the following tables. The Company adopted SFAS No. 158 "Employers' Accounting for Defined Benefit Pension and Other Postretirement Plans" as of the end of its 2006 fiscal year. The impact of the adoption is discussed in Note 1. The standard generally requires company plan sponsors to reflect the net over- or under-funded position of a defined postretirement benefit plan as an asset or liability on the balance sheet.

(millions)	2006	2005
Change in projected benefit obligation		
Beginning of year	**$3,145.1**	$2,972.9
Service cost	**94.2**	80.2
Interest cost	**172.0**	160.1
Plan participants' contributions	**1.7**	2.5
Amendments	**24.2**	42.2
Actuarial loss (gain)	**(96.7)**	114.3
Benefits paid	**(160.4)**	(144.0)
Curtailment and special termination benefits	**15.3**	1.3
Foreign currency adjustments and other	**113.9**	(84.4)
End of year	**$3,309.3**	$3,145.1
Change in plan assets		
Fair value beginning of year	**$2,922.6**	$2,685.9
Actual return on plan assets	**448.4**	277.9
Employer contributions	**85.7**	156.4
Plan participants' contributions	**1.7**	2.5
Benefits paid	**(149.6)**	(132.3)
Foreign currency adjustments and other	**117.7**	(67.8)
Fair value end of year	**$3,426.5**	$2,922.6
Funded status at year end	**$ 117.2**	$ (222.5)
Unrecognized net loss	**—**	826.3
Unrecognized transition amount	**—**	1.9
Unrecognized prior service cost	**—**	100.1
Net balance sheet position	**$ 117.2**	$ 705.8
Amounts recognized in the Consolidated Balance Sheet consist of		
Prepaid benefit cost		$ 683.3
Accrued benefit liability		(185.8)
Intangible asset		17.0
Other comprehensive income — minimum pension liability		191.3
Noncurrent assets	**$ 352.6**	
Current liabilities	**(9.6)**	
Noncurrent liabilities	**(225.8)**	
Net amount recognized	**$ 117.2**	$ 705.8
Amounts recognized in accumulated other comprehensive income consist of		
Net experience loss	**$ 502.7**	
Prior service cost	**115.5**	
Net amount recognized	**$ 618.2**	$ 191.3

The accumulated benefit obligation for all defined benefit pension plans was $2.99 billion and $2.87 billion at December 30, 2006 and December 31, 2005, respectively. Information for pension plans with accumulated benefit obligations in excess of plan assets were:

(millions)	2006	2005
Projected benefit obligation	**$253.4**	$1,621.4
Accumulated benefit obligation	**202.5**	1,473.7
Fair value of plan assets	**55.5**	1,289.1

The significant decrease in accumulated benefit obligations in excess of plan assets for 2006 is due primarily to favorable asset returns in a major U.S. pension plan.

Expense

The components of pension expense are presented in the following table. Pension expense for defined contribution plans relates principally to multiemployer plans in which the Company participates on behalf of certain unionized workforces in the United States. The amounts for 2006 and 2005 include charges of approximately $4 million and $16 million, respectively, for the Company's current estimate of a multiemployer plan withdrawal liability, which is further described in Note 3.

(millions)	2006	2005	2004
Service cost	**$ 94.2**	$ 80.2	$ 76.0
Interest cost	**172.0**	160.1	157.3
Expected return on plan assets	**(256.7)**	(229.0)	(238.1)
Amortization of unrecognized transition obligation	**—**	.3	.2
Amortization of unrecognized prior service cost	**12.4**	10.0	8.2
Recognized net loss	**79.8**	64.5	54.1
Curtailment and special termination benefits — net loss	**16.7**	1.6	12.2
Pension expense:			
Defined benefit plans	**118.4**	87.7	69.9
Defined contribution plans	**18.7**	31.9	14.4
Total	**$ 137.1**	$ 119.6	$ 84.3

Any arising obligation-related experience gain or loss is amortized using a straight-line method over the average remaining service period of active plan participants. Any asset-related experience gain or loss is recognized as described on page 46. The estimated net experience loss and prior service cost for defined benefit pension plans that will be amortized from accumulated other comprehensive income into pension expense over the next fiscal year are approximately $61 million and $13 million, respectively.

Net losses from curtailment and special termination benefits recognized in 2006 are related primarily to plant workforce reductions in the United States and England, as further described in Note 3. Net losses from curtailment and special termination benefits recognized in 2004 are related primarily to special termination benefits granted to the Company's former CEO and other former executive officers pursuant to separation agreements, and to a lesser extent, liquidation of the Company's pension fund in South Africa and plant workforce reductions in Great Britain.

Certain of the Company's subsidiaries sponsor 401(k) or similar savings plans for active employees. Expense related to these plans was (in millions): 2006–$33; 2005–$30; 2004–$26. Company contributions to these savings plans approximate annual expense. Company contributions to multiemployer and other defined contribution pension plans approximate the amount of annual expense presented in the preceding table.

Assumptions

The worldwide weighted-average actuarial assumptions used to determine benefit obligations were:

	2006	2005	2004
Discount rate	**5.7%**	5.4%	5.7%
Long-term rate of compensation increase	**4.4%**	4.4%	4.3%

The worldwide weighted-average actuarial assumptions used to determine annual net periodic benefit cost were:

	2006	2005	2004
Discount rate	**5.4%**	5.7%	5.9%
Long-term rate of compensation increase	**4.4%**	4.3%	4.3%
Long-term rate of return on plan assets	**8.9%**	8.9%	9.3%

To determine the overall expected long-term rate of return on plan assets, the Company works with third party financial consultants to model expected returns over a 20-year investment horizon with respect to the specific investment mix of its major plans. The return assumptions used reflect a combination of rigorous historical performance analysis and forward-looking views of the financial markets including consideration of current yields on long-term bonds, price-earnings ratios of the major stock market indices, and long-term inflation. The U.S. model, which corresponds to approximately 70% of consolidated pension and other postretirement benefit plan assets, incorporates a long-term inflation assumption of 2.8% and an active management premium of 1% (net of fees) validated by historical analysis. Similar methods are used for various foreign plans with invested assets, reflecting local economic conditions. Although management reviews the Company's expected long-term rates of return annually, the benefit trust investment performance for one particular year does not, by itself, significantly influence this evaluation. The expected rates of return are generally not revised, provided these rates continue to fall within a "more likely than not" corridor of between the 25th and 75th percentile of expected long-term returns, as determined by the Company's modeling process. The expected rate of return for 2006 of 8.9% equated to approximately the 50th percentile expectation. Any future variance between the expected and actual rates of return on plan assets is recognized in the calculated value of plan assets over a five-year period and once recognized, experience gains and losses are amortized using a declining-balance method over the average remaining service period of active plan participants.

Plan assets

The Company's year-end pension plan weighted-average asset allocations by asset category were:

	2006	2005
Equity securities	**76%**	73%
Debt securities	**21%**	24%
Other	**3%**	3%
Total	**100%**	100%

The Company's investment strategy for its major defined benefit plans is to maintain a diversified portfolio of asset classes with the primary goal of meeting long-term cash requirements as they become due. Assets are invested in a prudent manner to maintain the security of funds while maximizing returns within the Company's guidelines. The current weighted-average target asset allocation reflected by this strategy is: equity securities—74%; debt securities—24%; other—2%. Investment in Company common stock represented 1.5% of consolidated plan assets at December 30, 2006 and December 31, 2005. Plan funding strategies are influenced by tax regulations. The Company currently expects to contribute approximately $39 million to its defined benefit pension plans during 2007.

Benefit payments

The following benefit payments, which reflect expected future service, as appropriate, are expected to be paid (in millions): 2007—$169; 2008—$174; 2009—$184; 2010—$189; 2011—$191; 2012 to 2016—$1,075.

Note 10 Nonpension postretirement and postemployment benefits

Postretirement

The Company sponsors a number of plans to provide health care and other welfare benefits to retired employees in the United States and Canada, who have met certain age and service requirements. The majority of these plans are funded or unfunded defined benefit plans, although the Company does participate in a few multiemployer or other defined contribution plans for certain employee groups. The Company contributes to voluntary employee benefit association (VEBA) trusts to fund certain U.S. retiree health and welfare benefit obligations. The Company uses its fiscal year end as the measurement date for these plans.

Obligations and funded status

The aggregate change in accumulated postretirement benefit obligation, plan assets, and funded status is presented in the following tables. The Company adopted SFAS No. 158 "Employers' Accounting for Defined Benefit Pension and Other Postretirement Plans" as of the end of its 2006 fiscal year. The impact of the adoption is discussed in Note 1. The standard generally requires company plan sponsors to reflect the net over- or under-funded position of a defined postretirement benefit plan as an asset or liability on the balance sheet.

(millions)	2006	2005
Change in accumulated benefit obligation		
Beginning of year	**$1,224.9**	$1,046.7
Service cost	**17.4**	14.5
Interest cost	**65.8**	58.3
Actuarial loss (gain)	**(54.4)**	164.6
Amendments	**3.6**	—
Benefits paid	**(56.0)**	(60.4)
Curtailment and special termination benefits	**6.2**	—
Foreign currency adjustments	**.1**	1.2
End of year	**$1,207.6**	$1,224.9
Change in plan assets		
Fair value beginning of year	**$ 682.7**	$ 468.4
Actual return on plan assets	**123.6**	32.5
Employer contributions	**13.6**	240.9
Benefits paid	**(56.0)**	(59.1)
Fair value end of year	**$ 763.9**	$ 682.7
Funded status	**$ (443.7)**	$ (542.2)
Unrecognized net loss	**—**	446.0
Unrecognized prior service credit	**—**	(26.3)
Accrued postretirement benefit cost	**$ (443.7)**	$ (122.5)
Amounts recognized in the Consolidated Balance Sheet consist of		
Current liabilities	**$ (1.4)**	
Noncurrent liabilities	**(442.3)**	
Total liabilities	**$ (443.7)**	$ (122.5)
Amounts recognized in accumulated other comprehensive income consist of		
Net experience loss	**$ 294.8**	$ —
Prior service credit	**(19.2)**	—
Net amount recognized	**$ 275.6**	$ —

Expense

Components of postretirement benefit expense were:

(millions)	2006	2005	2004
Service cost	**$ 17.4**	$ 14.5	$ 12.1
Interest cost	**65.8**	58.3	55.6
Expected return on plan assets	**(58.2)**	(42.1)	(39.8)
Amortization of unrecognized prior service credit	**(2.6)**	(2.9)	(2.9)
Recognized net loss	**30.6**	19.8	14.8
Curtailment and special termination benefits — net loss	**6.2**	—	—
Postretirement benefit expense:			
Defined benefit plans	**59.2**	47.6	39.8
Defined contribution plans	**1.9**	1.3	1.8
Total	**$ 61.1**	$ 48.9	$ 41.6

Any arising health care claims cost-related experience gain or loss is recognized in the calculated amount of claims experience over a four-year period and once recognized, is amortized using a straight-line method over 15 years, resulting in at least the minimum amortization prescribed by SFAS No. 106. Any asset-related experience gain or loss is recognized as described for pension plans on page 46. The estimated net experience loss for defined benefit plans that will be amortized from accumulated other comprehensive income into nonpension postretirement benefit expense over the next fiscal year is approximately $24 million, partially offset by amortization of prior service credit of $3 million.

Net losses from curtailment and special termination benefits recognized in 2006 are related primarily to plant workforce reductions in the United States as further described in Note 3.

Assumptions

The weighted-average actuarial assumptions used to determine benefit obligations were:

	2006	2005	2004
Discount rate	**5.9%**	5.5%	5.8%

The weighted-average actuarial assumptions used to determine annual net periodic benefit cost were:

	2006	2005	2004
Discount rate	**5.5%**	5.8%	6.0%
Long-term rate of return on plan assets	**8.9%**	8.9%	9.3%

The Company determines the overall expected long-term rate of return on VEBA trust assets in the same manner as that described for pension trusts in Note 9.

The assumed health care cost trend rate is 9.5% for 2007, decreasing gradually to 4.75% by the year 2012 and remaining at that level thereafter. These trend rates reflect the Company's recent historical experience and management's expectations regarding future trends. A one percentage point change in assumed health care cost trend rates would have the following effects:

(millions)	One percentage point increase	One percentage point decrease
Effect on total of service and interest cost components	$ 9.2	$ (10.5)
Effect on postretirement benefit obligation	$127.8	$(125.4)

Plan assets

The Company's year-end VEBA trust weighted-average asset allocations by asset category were:

	2006	2005
Equity securities	**77%**	78%
Debt securities	**22%**	22%
Other	**1%**	—
Total	**100%**	100%

The Company's asset investment strategy for its VEBA trusts is consistent with that described for its pension trusts in Note 9. The current target asset allocation is 75% equity securities and 25% debt securities. The Company currently expects to contribute approximately $15 million to its VEBA trusts during 2007.

Postemployment

Under certain conditions, the Company provides benefits to former or inactive employees in the United States and several foreign locations, including salary continuance, severance, and long-term disability. The Company recognizes an obligation for any of these benefits that vest or accumulate with service. Postemployment benefits that do not vest or accumulate with service (such as severance based solely on annual pay rather than years of service) or costs arising from actions that offer benefits to employees in excess of those specified in the respective plans are charged to expense when incurred. The Company's postemployment benefit plans are unfunded. Actuarial assumptions used are generally consistent with those presented for pension benefits on page 46. The Company previously applied postretirement accounting concepts for purposes of recognizing its postemployment benefit obligations. Accordingly, the Company's adoption of SFAS No. 158 "Employers' Accounting for Defined Benefit Pension and Other Postretirement Plans" as of the end of its 2006 fiscal year impacted its presentation of postemployment benefits as discussed in Note 1. The aggregate change in accumulated postemployment benefit obligation and the net amount recognized were:

(millions)	**2006**	2005
Change in accumulated benefit obligation		
Beginning of year	**$ 42.2**	$ 37.9
Service cost	**4.3**	4.5
Interest cost	**2.0**	2.0
Actuarial loss (gain)	**(.8)**	7.4
Benefits paid	**(8.6)**	(9.0)
Foreign currency adjustments	**.4**	(.6)
End of year	**$ 39.5**	$ 42.2
Funded status	**$(39.5)**	$(42.2)
Unrecognized net loss	**—**	19.1
Accrued postemployment benefit cost	**$(39.5)**	$(23.1)
Amounts recognized in the Consolidated Balance Sheet consist of		
Current liabilities	**$ (7.8)**	
Noncurrent liabilities	**(31.7)**	
Total liabilities	**$(39.5)**	$(23.1)
Amounts recognized in accumulated other comprehensive income consist of		
Net experience loss	**$ 16.0**	$ —
Net amount recognized	**$ 16.0**	$ —

Components of postemployment benefit expense were:

(millions)	**2006**	2005	2004
Service cost	**$4.3**	$ 4.5	$3.5
Interest cost	**2.0**	2.0	1.9
Recognized net loss	**2.4**	3.5	4.5
Postemployment benefit expense	**$8.7**	$10.0	$9.9

All gains and losses are recognized over the average remaining service period of active plan participants. The estimated net experience loss that will be amortized from accumulated other comprehensive income into postemployment benefit expense over the next fiscal year is approximately $2 million.

Benefit payments

The following benefit payments, which reflect expected future service, as appropriate, are expected to be paid:

(millions)	Postretirement	Postemployment
2007	$ 64.0	$ 8.0
2008	67.7	7.3
2009	71.2	7.0
2010	73.9	7.3
2011	76.5	7.7
2012-2016	397.5	44.4

Note 11 Income taxes

Earnings before income taxes and the provision for U.S. federal, state, and foreign taxes on these earnings were:

(millions)	**2006**	2005	2004
Earnings before income taxes			
United States	**$1,048.3**	$ 971.4	$ 952.0
Foreign	**423.3**	453.7	413.9
	$1,471.6	$1,425.1	$1,365.9
Income taxes			
Currently payable			
Federal	**$ 342.0**	$ 376.8	$ 249.8
State	**34.1**	26.4	30.0
Foreign	**134.1**	100.7	137.8
	510.2	503.9	417.6
Deferred			
Federal	**(9.6)**	(69.6)	51.5
State	**(4.4)**	.6	5.3
Foreign	**(29.7)**	9.8	.9
	(43.7)	(59.2)	57.7
Total income taxes	**$ 466.5**	$ 444.7	$ 475.3

The difference between the U.S. federal statutory tax rate and the Company's effective income tax rate was:

	2006	2005	2004
U.S. statutory income tax rate	**35.0%**	35.0%	35.0%
Foreign rates varying from 35%	**−3.5**	−3.8	−.5
State income taxes, net of federal benefit	**1.3**	1.2	1.7
Foreign earnings repatriation	**1.2**	—	2.1
Tax audit settlements	**−1.7**	—	—
Net change in valuation allowances	**.5**	−.2	−1.5
Statutory rate changes, deferred tax impact	**—**	—	.1
Other	**−1.1**	−1.0	−2.1
Effective income tax rate	**31.7%**	31.2%	34.8%

As presented in the preceding table, the Company's 2006 consolidated provision for income taxes included two significant, but partially-offsetting, discrete adjustments. First, during the second quarter, the Company revised its repatriation plan for certain foreign earnings, giving rise to an incremental net tax cost of $18 million. Also in the second quarter, the Company reduced its reserves for uncertain tax positions by $25 million, related principally to closure of several domestic tax audits.

The consolidated effective income tax rate for 2004 of nearly 35% was higher than the rates for 2006 and 2005 primarily because this period preceded the final reorganization of the Company's European operations which favorably affected the country-weighting impact on the rate. (Refer to Note 3 for further information on this initiative.) Additionally, the 2004 consolidated effective income tax rate included a provision of approximately $40 million, partially offset by related foreign tax credits of approximately $12 million, for approximately $1.1 billion of dividends from foreign subsidiaries which the Company elected to repatriate in 2005 under the American Jobs Creation Act. Finally, 2005 was the first year in which the Company was permitted to claim a phased-in deduction from U.S. taxable income equal to a stipulated percentage of qualified production income ("QPI").

Generally, the changes in valuation allowances on deferred tax assets and corresponding impacts on the effective income tax rate result from management's assessment of the Company's ability to utilize certain operating loss and tax credit carryforwards prior to expiration. For 2004, the 1.5 percent rate reduction presented in the preceding table primarily reflects reversal of a valuation allowance against U.S. foreign tax credits, which were utilized in conjunction with the aforementioned 2005 foreign earnings repatriation. Total tax benefits of carryforwards at year-end 2006 and 2005 were approximately $29 million and $23 million, respectively. Of the total carryforwards at year-end 2006, less than $2 million expire in 2007 with the remainder principally expiring after five years. After valuation allowance, the carrying value of carryforward tax benefits at year-end 2006 was only $1 million.

The deferred tax assets and liabilities included in the balance sheet at year end are presented in a table on page 50. The Company adopted SFAS No. 158 "Employers' Accounting for Defined Benefit Pension and Other Postretirement Plans" as of the end of its 2006 fiscal year. The standard generally requires company plan sponsors to reflect the net over- or under-funded position of a defined postretirement benefit plan as an asset or liability on the balance sheet. Any unrecognized prior service cost, experience gains/losses, or transition obligation are reported as a component of other comprehensive income, net of tax, in shareholders' equity. As a result of adopting this standard, the employee benefits component of the Company's deferred tax assets increased (or liabilities decreased) by a total of $298.9 million at December 30, 2006. Refer to Note 1 for further information.

	Deferred tax assets		Deferred tax liabilities	
(millions)	**2006**	2005	**2006**	2005
Current:				
U.S. state income taxes	**$ 7.6**	$ 12.1	**$ —**	$ —
Advertising and promotion-related	**19.7**	19.4	**11.0**	8.8
Wages and payroll taxes	**26.3**	28.8	**—**	—
Inventory valuation	**22.5**	25.5	**4.6**	6.3
Employee benefits	**18.0**	32.0	**—**	—
Operating loss and credit carryforwards	**13.9**	7.0	**—**	—
Hedging transactions	**19.2**	17.5	**.8**	.1
Depreciation and asset disposals	**.1**	.1	**—**	—
Deferred intercompany revenue	**6.1**	76.3	**—**	—
Other	**26.4**	22.6	**15.2**	22.8
	159.8	241.3	**31.6**	38.0
Less valuation allowance	**(15.2)**	(3.2)	**—**	—
	$144.6	$238.1	**$ 31.6**	$ 38.0
Noncurrent:				
U.S. state income taxes	**$ —**	$ —	**$ 47.0**	$ 54.4
Employee benefits	**217.4**	20.4	**53.2**	129.7
Operating loss and credit carryforwards	**15.2**	15.5	**—**	—
Hedging transactions	**2.0**	1.7	**—**	—
Depreciation and asset disposals	**15.1**	12.7	**306.5**	340.8
Capitalized interest	**5.3**	5.1	**11.9**	12.7
Trademarks and other intangibles	**.1**	.1	**473.9**	472.4
Deferred compensation	**40.6**	34.9	**—**	—
Stock options	**22.4**	—	**—**	—
Other	**12.0**	15.3	**6.3**	2.1
	330.1	105.7	**898.8**	1,012.1
Less valuation allowance	**(13.0)**	(16.2)	**—**	—
	317.1	89.5	**898.8**	1,012.1
Total deferred taxes	**$461.7**	$327.6	**$930.4**	$1,050.1

The change in valuation allowance against deferred tax assets was:

(millions)	**2006**	2005	2004
Balance at beginning of year	**$19.4**	$22.3	$ 36.8
Additions charged to income tax expense	**11.4**	.2	13.3
Reductions credited to income tax expense	**(3.6)**	(3.2)	(28.9)
Currency translation adjustments	**1.0**	.1	1.1
Balance at end of year	**$28.2**	$19.4	$ 22.3

At December 30, 2006, accumulated foreign subsidiary earnings of approximately $1.1 billion were considered permanently invested in those businesses. Accordingly, U.S. income taxes have not been provided on these earnings.

Cash paid for income taxes was (in millions): 2006–$428; 2005–$425; 2004–$421. Income tax benefits realized from stock option exercises and deductibility of other equity-based awards are presented in Note 8.

Note 12 Financial instruments and credit risk concentration

The fair values of the Company's financial instruments are based on carrying value in the case of short-term items, quoted market prices for derivatives and investments, and in the case of long-term debt, incremental borrowing rates currently available on loans with similar terms and maturities. The carrying amounts of the Company's cash, cash equivalents, receivables, and notes payable approximate fair value. The fair value of the Company's long-term debt at December 30, 2006, exceeded its carrying value by approximately $275 million.

The Company is exposed to certain market risks which exist as a part of its ongoing business operations. Management uses derivative financial and commodity instruments, where appropriate, to manage these risks. In general, instruments used as hedges must be effective at reducing the risk associated with the exposure being hedged and must be designated as a hedge at the inception of the contract. In accordance with SFAS No. 133, the Company designates derivatives as either cash flow hedges, fair value hedges, net investment hedges, or other contracts used to reduce volatility in the translation of foreign currency earnings to U.S. Dollars. The fair values of all hedges are recorded in accounts receivable or other current liabilities. Gains and losses representing either hedge ineffectiveness, hedge components excluded from the assessment of effectiveness, or hedges of translational exposure are recorded in other income (expense), net. Within the Consolidated Statement of Cash Flows, settlements of cash flow and fair value hedges are classified as an operating activity; settlements of all other derivatives are classified as a financing activity.

Cash flow hedges

Qualifying derivatives are accounted for as cash flow hedges when the hedged item is a forecasted transaction. Gains and losses on these instruments are recorded in other comprehensive income until the underlying transaction is recorded in earnings. When the hedged item is realized, gains or losses are reclassified from accumulated other comprehensive income to the Consolidated Statement of Earnings on the same line item as the underlying transaction. For all cash flow hedges, gains and losses representing either hedge ineffectiveness or hedge components excluded from the assessment of effectiveness were insignificant during the periods presented.

The total net loss attributable to cash flow hedges recorded in accumulated other comprehensive income at December 30, 2006, was $32.6 million, related primarily to forward interest rate contracts settled during 2001 and 2003 in conjunction with fixed rate long-term debt issuances and to a lesser extent, to 10-year natural gas price swaps entered into in 2006. The interest rate contract losses will be reclassified into interest expense over the next 25 years. The natural gas swap losses will be reclassified to cost of goods sold over 10 years. Other insignificant amounts related to foreign currency and commodity price cash flow hedges will be reclassified into earnings during the next 18 months.

Fair value hedges

Qualifying derivatives are accounted for as fair value hedges when the hedged item is a recognized asset, liability, or firm commitment. Gains and losses on these instruments are recorded in earnings, offsetting gains and losses on the hedged item. For all fair value hedges, gains and losses representing either hedge ineffectiveness or hedge components excluded from the assessment of effectiveness were insignificant during the periods presented.

Net investment hedges

Qualifying derivative and nonderivative financial instruments are accounted for as net investment hedges when the hedged item is a nonfunctional currency investment in a subsidiary. Gains and losses on these instruments are recorded as a foreign currency translation adjustment in other comprehensive income.

Other contracts

The Company also periodically enters into foreign currency forward contracts and options to reduce volatility in the translation of foreign currency earnings to U.S. Dollars. Gains and losses on these instruments are recorded in other income (expense), net, generally reducing the exposure to translation volatility during a full-year period.

Foreign exchange risk

The Company is exposed to fluctuations in foreign currency cash flows related primarily to third-party purchases, intercompany transactions, and nonfunctional currency denominated third-party debt. The Company is also exposed to fluctuations in the value of foreign currency investments in subsidiaries and cash flows related to repatriation of these investments. Additionally, the Company is exposed to volatility in the translation of foreign currency earnings to U.S. Dollars. Management assesses foreign currency risk based on transactional cash flows and translational volatility and enters into forward contracts, options, and currency swaps to reduce fluctuations in net long or short currency positions. Forward contracts and options are generally less than 18 months duration. Currency swap agreements are established in conjunction with the term of underlying debt issues.

For foreign currency cash flow and fair value hedges, the assessment of effectiveness is generally based on changes in spot rates. Changes in time value are reported in other income (expense), net.

Interest rate risk

The Company is exposed to interest rate volatility with regard to future issuances of fixed rate debt and existing issuances of variable rate debt. The Company periodically uses interest rate swaps, including forward-starting swaps, to reduce interest rate volatility and funding costs associated with certain debt issues, and to achieve a desired proportion of variable versus fixed rate debt, based on current and projected market conditions.

Variable-to-fixed interest rate swaps are accounted for as cash flow hedges and the assessment of effectiveness is based on changes in the present value of interest payments on the underlying debt. Fixed-to-variable interest rate swaps are accounted for as fair value hedges and the assessment of effectiveness is based on changes in the fair value of the underlying debt, using incremental borrowing rates currently available on loans with similar terms and maturities.

Price risk

The Company is exposed to price fluctuations primarily as a result of anticipated purchases of raw and packaging materials, fuel, and energy. The Company has historically used the combination of long-term contracts with suppliers, and exchange-traded futures and option contracts to reduce price fluctuations in a desired percentage of forecasted raw material purchases over a duration of generally less than 18 months. During 2006, the Company entered into two separate 10-year over-the-counter commodity swap transactions to reduce fluctuations in the price of natural gas used principally in its manufacturing processes.

Commodity contracts are accounted for as cash flow hedges. The assessment of effectiveness for exchange-traded instruments is based on changes in futures prices. The assessment of effectiveness for over-the-counter transactions is based on changes in designated indexes.

Credit risk concentration

The Company is exposed to credit loss in the event of nonperformance by counterparties on derivative financial and commodity contracts. This credit loss is limited to the cost of replacing these contracts at current market rates. Management believes the probability of such loss is remote.

Financial instruments, which potentially subject the Company to concentrations of credit risk are primarily cash, cash equivalents, and accounts receivable. The Company places its investments in highly rated financial institutions and investment-grade short-term debt instruments, and limits the amount of credit exposure to any one entity. Management believes concentrations of credit risk with respect to accounts receivable is limited due to the generally high credit quality of the Company's major customers, as well as the large number and geographic dispersion of smaller customers. However, the Company conducts a disproportionate amount of business with a small number of large multinational grocery retailers, with the five largest accounts comprising approximately 27% of consolidated accounts receivable at December 30, 2006.

Note 13 Quarterly financial data (unaudited)

	Net sales		Gross profit	
(millions, except per share data)	**2006**	2005	**2006**	2005
First	**$ 2,726.5**	$ 2,572.3	**$1,196.7**	$1,135.9
Second	**2,773.9**	2,587.2	**1,235.5**	1,198.6
Third	**2,822.4**	2,623.4	**1,273.3**	1,186.0
Fourth	**2,583.9**	2,394.3	**1,119.7**	1,045.1
	$10,906.7	$10,177.2	**$4,825.2**	$4,565.6

	Net earnings		Net earnings per share			
	2006	2005	**2006**		2005	
			Basic	**Diluted**	Basic	Diluted
First	**$ 274.1**	$254.7	**$.69**	**$.68**	$.62	$.61
Second	**266.5**	259.0	**.68**	**.67**	.63	.62
Third	**281.1**	274.3	**.71**	**.70**	.66	.66
Fourth	**182.4**	192.4	**.46**	**.45**	.47	.47
	$1,004.1	$980.4				

The principal market for trading Kellogg shares is the New York Stock Exchange (NYSE). The shares are also traded on the Boston, Chicago, Cincinnati, Pacific, and Philadelphia Stock Exchanges. At year-end 2006, the closing price (on the NYSE) was $50.06 and there were 41,450 shareholders of record.

Dividends paid per share and the quarterly price ranges on the NYSE during the last two years were:

	Dividend per share	Stock price High	Stock price Low
2006 — Quarter			
First	**$ .2775**	**$45.78**	**$42.41**
Second	**.2775**	**48.50**	**43.06**
Third	**.2910**	**50.87**	**47.31**
Fourth	**.2910**	**50.95**	**47.71**
	$1.1370		
2005 — Quarter			
First	$ .2525	$45.59	$42.41
Second	.2525	46.89	42.35
Third	.2775	46.99	43.42
Fourth	.2775	46.70	43.22
	$1.0600		

Note 14 Operating segments

Kellogg Company is the world's leading producer of cereal and a leading producer of convenience foods, including cookies, crackers, toaster pastries, cereal bars, fruit snacks, frozen waffles, and veggie foods. Kellogg products are manufactured and marketed globally. Principal markets for these products include the United States and United Kingdom. The Company currently manages its operations in four geographic operating segments, comprised of North America and the three International operating segments of Europe, Latin America, and Asia Pacific. For the periods presented, the Asia Pacific operating segment included Australia and Asian markets. Beginning in 2007, this segment will also include South Africa, which was formerly a part of Europe.

The measurement of operating segment results is generally consistent with the presentation of the Consolidated Statement of Earnings and Balance Sheet. Intercompany transactions between operating segments were insignificant in all periods presented.

(millions)	**2006**	2005	2004
Net sales			
North America	**$ 7,348.8**	$ 6,807.8	$6,369.3
Europe	**2,143.8**	2,013.6	2,007.3
Latin America	**890.8**	822.2	718.0
Asia Pacific (a)	**523.3**	533.6	519.3
Consolidated	**$10,906.7**	$10,177.2	$9,613.9
Segment operating profit			
North America	**$ 1,340.5**	$ 1,251.5	$1,240.4
Europe	**334.1**	330.7	292.3
Latin America	**220.1**	202.8	185.4
Asia Pacific (a)	**76.9**	86.0	79.5
Corporate	**(205.8)**	(120.7)	(116.5)
Consolidated	**$ 1,765.8**	$ 1,750.3	$1,681.1

(a) Includes Australia and Asia.

(millions)	2006	2005	2004
Depreciation and amortization			
North America	**$ 241.8**	272.3	$ 261.4
Europe	**66.4**	61.2	95.7
Latin America	**21.9**	20.0	15.4
Asia Pacific (a)	**17.2**	20.9	20.9
Corporate	**5.4**	17.4	16.6
Consolidated	**$ 352.7**	391.8	$ 410.0
Interest expense			
North America	**$ 8.7**	$ 1.4	$ 1.7
Europe	**27.0**	12.4	15.6
Latin America	**.1**	.2	.2
Asia Pacific (a)	**.4**	.3	.2
Corporate	**271.2**	286.0	290.9
Consolidated	**$ 307.4**	$ 300.3	$ 308.6
Income taxes			
North America	**$ 396.2**	$ 372.7	$ 371.5
Europe	**9.8**	30.2	64.5
Latin America	**31.8**	21.5	39.8
Asia Pacific (a)	**14.4**	12.4	(.8)
Corporate	**14.3**	7.9	.3
Consolidated	**$ 466.5**	$ 444.7	$ 475.3
Total assets (b)			
North America	**$ 7,996.2**	$ 7,944.6	$ 7,641.5
Europe	**2,380.7**	2,356.7	2,324.2
Latin America	**661.4**	450.6	411.1
Asia Pacific (a)	**328.8**	294.7	347.4
Corporate	**4,934.0**	5,336.4	5,619.0
Elimination entries	**(5,587.1)**	(5,808.5)	(5,781.3)
Consolidated	**$10,714.0**	$10,574.5	$10,561.9
Additions to long-lived assets (c)			
North America	**$ 316.0**	$ 317.0	$ 167.4
Europe	**62.6**	42.3	59.7
Latin America	**52.8**	38.1	37.2
Asia Pacific (a)	**18.9**	14.4	9.9
Corporate	**2.8**	.4	4.4
Consolidated	**$ 453.1**	$ 412.2	$ 278.6

(a) Includes Australia and Asia.

(b) The Company adopted SFAS No. 158 "Employers' Accounting for Defined Benefit Pension and Other Postretirement Plans" as of the end of its 2006 fiscal year. The standard generally requires company plan sponsors to reflect the net over- or under-funded position of a defined postretirement benefit plan as an asset or liability on the balance sheet. Accordingly, the Company's consolidated and corporate total assets for 2006 were reduced by $512.4 and $152.4 respectively. Operating segment total assets were reduced as follows: North America–$71.8; Europe–$284.3; Latin America–$2.9; Asia Pacific–$1.0. Refer to Note 1 for further information.

(c) Includes plant, property, equipment, and purchased intangibles.

The Company's largest customer, Wal-Mart Stores, Inc. and its affiliates, accounted for approximately 18% of consolidated net sales during 2006, 17% in 2005, and 14% in 2004, comprised principally of sales within the United States.

Supplemental geographic information is provided below for net sales to external customers and long-lived assets:

(millions)	2006	2005	2004
Net sales			
United States	**$ 6,842.8**	$ 6,351.6	$5,968.0
United Kingdom	**893.9**	836.9	859.6
Other foreign countries	**3,170.0**	2,988.7	2,786.3
Consolidated	**$10,906.7**	$10,177.2	$9,613.9
Long-lived assets (a)			
United States	**$ 6,629.5**	$ 6,576.8	$6,539.2
United Kingdom	**369.2**	323.8	432.5
Other foreign countries	**684.9**	641.3	631.1
Consolidated	**$ 7,683.6**	$ 7,541.9	$7,602.8

(a) Includes plant, property, equipment, and purchased intangibles.

Supplemental product information is provided below for net sales to external customers:

(millions)	2006	2005	2004
North America			
Retail channel cereal	**$ 2,667.0**	$ 2,587.7	$2,404.5
Retail channel snacks	**3,318.4**	2,976.6	2,801.4
Frozen and specialty channels	**1,363.4**	1,243.5	1,163.4
International			
Cereal	**3,010.3**	2,932.8	2,829.2
Convenience foods	**547.6**	436.6	415.4
Consolidated	**$10,906.7**	$10,177.2	$9,613.9

Note 15 Supplemental financial statement data

(millions)

Consolidated Statement of Earnings	2006	2005	2004
Research and development expense	**$190.6**	$181.0	$148.9
Advertising expense	**$915.9**	$857.7	$806.2

Consolidated Statement of Cash Flows	2006	2005	2004
Trade receivables	**$ (57.7)**	$ (86.2)	$ 13.8
Other receivables	**(21.0)**	(25.4)	(39.5)
Inventories	**(107.0)**	(24.8)	(31.2)
Other current assets	**(10.8)**	(15.3)	(17.8)
Accounts payable	**27.5**	156.4	63.4
Accrued income taxes	**65.6**	74.7	(13.5)
Accrued interest expense	**4.3**	(6.3)	(38.4)
Other current liabilities	**60.6**	(44.8)	33.4
Changes in operating assets and liabilities	**$ (38.5)**	$ 28.3	$(29.8)

(millions)

Consolidated Balance Sheet	2006	2005
Trade receivables	**$ 839.4**	$ 782.7
Allowance for doubtful accounts	**(5.9)**	(6.9)
Other receivables	**111.3**	103.3
Accounts receivable, net	**$ 944.8**	$ 879.1
Raw materials and supplies	**$ 200.7**	$ 188.6
Finished goods and materials in process	**623.2**	528.4
Inventories	**$ 823.9**	$ 717.0

(millions)

Consolidated Balance Sheet	**2006**	2005
Deferred income taxes	**$ 115.9**	$ 207.6
Other prepaid assets	**131.8**	173.7
Other current assets	**$ 247.7**	$ 381.3
Land	**$ 77.5**	$ 75.5
Buildings	**1,521.3**	1,458.8
Machinery and equipment (a)	**4,992.0**	4,692.4
Construction in progress	**326.8**	237.3
Accumulated depreciation	**(4,102.0)**	(3,815.6)
Property, net	**$ 2,815.6**	$ 2,648.4
Goodwill	**$ 3,448.3**	$ 3,455.3
Other intangibles (b)	**1,468.8**	1,485.8
—Accumulated amortization	**(49.1)**	(47.6)
Pension (b)	**352.6**	629.8
Other	**250.8**	206.3
Other assets	**$ 5,471.4**	$ 5,729.6
Accrued income taxes	**$ 151.7**	$ 148.3
Accrued salaries and wages	**311.1**	276.5
Accrued advertising and promotion	**338.0**	320.9
Other (b)	**317.7**	339.1
Other current liabilities	**$ 1,118.5**	$ 1,084.8
Nonpension postretirement benefits (b)	**$ 442.3**	$ 74.5
Deferred income taxes (b)	**619.3**	945.8
Other (b)	**510.2**	405.1
Other liabilities	**$ 1,571.8**	$ 1,425.4

(a) Includes an insignificant amount of capitalized internal-use software.

(b) The Company adopted SFAS No. 158 "Employers' Accounting for Defined Benefit Pension and Other Postretirement Plans" as of the end of its 2006 fiscal year. The standard generally requires company plan sponsors to reflect the net over- or under-funded position of a defined postretirement benefit plan as an asset or liability on the balance sheet. Accordingly, the 2006 balances associated with the identified captions within the preceding table were materially affected by the adoption of this standard. Refer to Note 1 for further information.

(millions)

Allowance for doubtful accounts	**2006**	2005	2004
Balance at beginning of year	**$ 6.9**	$13.0	$15.1
Additions charged to expense	**1.6**	—	2.1
Doubtful accounts charged to reserve	**(2.8)**	(7.4)	(4.3)
Currency translation adjustments	**.2**	1.3	.1
Balance at end of year	**$ 5.9**	$ 6.9	$13.0

Management's Responsibility for Financial Statements

Management is responsible for the preparation of the Company's consolidated financial statements and related notes. We believe that the consolidated financial statements present the Company's financial position and results of operations in conformity with accounting principles that are generally accepted in the United States, using our best estimates and judgments as required.

The independent registered public accounting firm audits the Company's consolidated financial statements in accordance with the standards of the Public Company Accounting Oversight Board and provides an objective, independent review of the fairness of reported operating results and financial position.

The Board of Directors of the Company has an Audit Committee composed of three non-management Directors. The Committee meets regularly with management, internal auditors, and the independent registered public accounting firm to review accounting, internal control, auditing and financial reporting matters.

Formal policies and procedures, including an active Ethics and Business Conduct program, support the internal controls and are designed to ensure employees adhere to the highest standards of personal and professional integrity. We have a vigorous internal audit program that independently evaluates the adequacy and effectiveness of these internal controls.

Management's Report on Internal Control over Financial Reporting

Our management is responsible for establishing and maintaining adequate internal control over financial reporting, as such term is defined in Exchange Act Rules 13a-15(f). Under the supervision and with the participation of management, we conducted an evaluation of the effectiveness of our internal control over financial reporting based on the framework in *Internal Control — Integrated Framework* issued by the Committee of Sponsoring Organizations of the Treadway Commission.

Because of its inherent limitations, internal control over financial reporting may not prevent or detect misstatements. Also, projections of any evaluation of effectiveness to future periods are subject to risk that controls may become inadequate because of changes in conditions, or that the degree of compliance with the policies or procedures may deteriorate.

Based on our evaluation under the framework in *Internal Control — Integrated Framework,* management concluded that our internal control over financial reporting was effective as of December 30, 2006. Our management's assessment of the effectiveness of our internal control over financial reporting as of December 30, 2006 has been audited by PricewaterhouseCoopers LLP, an independent registered public accounting firm, as stated in their report which follows on page 56.

A.D. David Mackay
President and Chief Executive Officer

John A. Bryant
Executive Vice President,
Chief Financial Officer, Kellogg Company
and President, Kellogg International

REPORT OF INDEPENDENT REGISTERED PUBLIC ACCOUNTING FIRM

To the Shareholders and Board of Directors of Kellogg Company:

We have completed integrated audits of Kellogg Company's consolidated financial statements and of its internal control over financial reporting as of December 30, 2006, in accordance with the standards of the Public Company Accounting Oversight Board (United States). Our opinions, based on our audits, are presented below.

Consolidated financial statements

In our opinion, the consolidated financial statements listed in the index appearing under Item 15(a)1 present fairly, in all material respects, the financial position of Kellogg Company and its subsidiaries at December 30, 2006 and December 31, 2005, and the results of their operations and their cash flows for each of the three years in the period ended December 30, 2006 in conformity with accounting principles generally accepted in the United States of America. These financial statements are the responsibility of the Company's management. Our responsibility is to express an opinion on these financial statements based on our audits. We conducted our audits of these statements in accordance with the standards of the Public Company Accounting Oversight Board (United States). Those standards require that we plan and perform the audit to obtain reasonable assurance about whether the financial statements are free of material misstatement. An audit of financial statements includes examining, on a test basis, evidence supporting the amounts and disclosures in the financial statements, assessing the accounting principles used and significant estimates made by management, and evaluating the overall financial statement presentation. We believe that our audits provide a reasonable basis for our opinion.

As discussed in Note 1 to the consolidated financial statements, the Company changed the manner in which it accounted for share-based compensation and defined benefit pension, other postretirement, and postemployment plans in 2006.

Internal control over financial reporting

Also, in our opinion, management's assessment, included in Management's Report on Internal Control over Financial Reporting, appearing under Item 8, that the Company maintained effective internal control over financial reporting as of December 30, 2006 based on criteria established in *Internal Control — Integrated Framework* issued by the Committee of Sponsoring Organizations of the Treadway Commission (COSO), is fairly stated, in all material respects, based on those criteria. Furthermore, in our opinion, the Company maintained, in all material respects, effective internal control over financial reporting as of December 30, 2006, based on criteria established in *Internal Control — Integrated Framework* issued by the COSO. The Company's management is responsible for maintaining effective internal control over financial reporting and for its assessment of the effectiveness of internal control over financial reporting. Our responsibility is to express opinions on management's assessment and on the effectiveness of the Company's internal control over financial reporting based on our audit. We conducted our audit of internal control over financial reporting in accordance with the standards of the Public Company Accounting Oversight Board (United States). Those standards require that we plan and perform the audit to obtain reasonable assurance about whether effective internal control over financial reporting was maintained in all material respects. An audit of internal control over financial reporting includes obtaining an understanding of internal control over financial reporting, evaluating management's assessment, testing and evaluating the design and operating effectiveness of internal control, and performing such other procedures as we consider necessary in the circumstances. We believe that our audit provides a reasonable basis for our opinions.

A company's internal control over financial reporting is a process designed to provide reasonable assurance regarding the reliability of financial reporting and the preparation of financial statements for external purposes in accordance with generally accepted accounting principles. A company's internal control over financial reporting includes those policies and procedures that (i) pertain to the maintenance of records that, in reasonable detail, accurately and fairly reflect the transactions and dispositions of the assets of the company; (ii) provide reasonable assurance that transactions are recorded as necessary to permit preparation of financial statements in accordance with generally accepted accounting principles, and that receipts and expenditures of the company are being made only in accordance with authorizations of management and directors of the company; and (iii) provide reasonable assurance regarding prevention or timely detection of unauthorized acquisition, use, or disposition of the company's assets that could have a material effect on the financial statements.

Because of its inherent limitations, internal control over financial reporting may not prevent or detect misstatements. Also, projections of any evaluation of effectiveness to future periods are subject to the risk that controls may become inadequate because of changes in conditions, or that the degree of compliance with the policies or procedures may deteriorate.

PricewaterhouseCoopers LLP

Battle Creek, Michigan
February 23, 2007

Excerpts from General Mills's Form 10-K for 2006

UNITED STATES
SECURITIES AND EXCHANGE COMMISSION
Washington, D.C. 20549

FORM 10-K

ANNUAL REPORT PURSUANT TO SECTION 13 OR 15(d) OF THE SECURITIES EXCHANGE ACT OF 1934
FOR THE FISCAL YEAR ENDED MAY 28, 2006

Commission File Number 1-1185

GENERAL MILLS, INC.

(Exact name of registrant as specified in its charter)

Delaware	**41-0274440**
(State or other jurisdiction of incorporation or organization)	(IRS Employer Identification No.)
Number One General Mills Boulevard **Minneapolis, Minnesota** **(Mail: P.O. Box 1113)**	**55426** **(Mail: 55440)**
(Address of principal executive offices)	(Zip Code)

(763) 764-7600
(Registrant's telephone number, including area code)

Securities registered pursuant to Section 12(b) of the Act:

Title of each class	Name of each exchange on which registered
Common Stock, $.10 par value	New York Stock Exchange

Securities registered pursuant to Section 12(g) of the Act: None

Indicate by check mark if the registrant is a well-known seasoned issuer, as defined in Rule 405 of the Securities Act. Yes ☒ No ☐

Indicate by check mark if the registrant is not required to file reports pursuant to Section 13 or Section 15(d) of the Act. Yes ☐ No ☒

Indicate by check mark whether the registrant (1) has filed all reports required to be filed by Section 13 or 15(d) of the Securities Exchange Act of 1934 during the preceding 12 months (or for such shorter period that the registrant was required to file such reports), and (2) has been subject to such filing requirements for the past 90 days. Yes ☒ No ☐

Indicate by check mark if disclosure of delinquent filers pursuant to Item 405 of Regulation S-K is not contained herein, and will not be contained, to the best of registrant's knowledge, in definitive proxy or information statements incorporated by reference in Part III of this Form 10-K or any amendment to this Form 10-K. ☐

Indicate by check mark whether the registrant is a large accelerated filer, an accelerated filer or a non-accelerated filer. See definition of "accelerated filer and large accelerated filer" in Rule 12b-2 of the Act. (Check one)

Large accelerated filer ☒ Accelerated filer ☐ Non-accelerated filer ☐

Indicate by check mark whether the registrant is a shell company (as defined in Rule 12b-2 of the Exchange Act). Yes ☐ No ☒

Aggregate market value of Common Stock held by non-affiliates of the registrant, based on the closing price of $48.10 per share as reported on the New York Stock Exchange on November 25, 2005 (the last business day of the registrant's most recently completed second fiscal quarter): $17,078 million.

Number of shares of Common Stock outstanding as of July 14, 2006: 352,811,767 (excluding 149,494,897 shares held in the treasury).

DOCUMENTS INCORPORATED BY REFERENCE

Portions of the registrant's Proxy Statement for its 2006 Annual Meeting of Stockholders are incorporated by reference into Part III.

ITEM 8 FINANCIAL STATEMENTS AND SUPPLEMENTARY DATA

MANAGEMENT'S REPORT ON INTERNAL CONTROL OVER FINANCIAL REPORTING

The management of General Mills, Inc. is responsible for establishing and maintaining adequate internal control over financial reporting, as such term is defined in Rule 13a-15(f) under the Securities Exchange Act of 1934. The Company's internal control system was designed to provide reasonable assurance to our management and the Board of Directors regarding the preparation and fair presentation of published financial statements. Under the supervision and with the participation of management, including our Chief Executive Officer and Chief Financial Officer, we conducted an assessment of the effectiveness of our internal control over financial reporting as of May 28, 2006. In making this assessment, management used the criteria set forth by the Committee of Sponsoring Organizations of the Treadway Commission (COSO) in Internal Control—Integrated Framework.

Based on our assessment using the criteria set forth by COSO in Internal Control—Integrated Framework, management concluded that our internal control over financial reporting was effective as of May 28, 2006.

KPMG LLP, an independent registered public accounting firm, has issued an audit report on management's assessment of the Company's internal control over financial reporting.

S. W. Sanger
Chairman of the Board
and
Chief Executive Officer

J. A. Lawrence
Vice Chairman and
Chief Financial Officer

July 27, 2006

REPORT OF INDEPENDENT REGISTERED PUBLIC ACCOUNTING FIRM REGARDING INTERNAL CONTROL OVER FINANCIAL REPORTING

The Board of Directors and Stockholders
General Mills, Inc.:

We have audited management's assessment, included in the accompanying Management's Report on Internal Control over Financial Reporting, that General Mills, Inc. and subsidiaries maintained effective internal control over financial reporting as of May 28, 2006, based on criteria established in Internal Control—Integrated Framework issued by the Committee of Sponsoring Organizations of the Treadway Commission (COSO). General Mills' management is responsible for maintaining effective internal control over financial reporting and for its assessment of the effectiveness of internal control over financial reporting. Our responsibility is to express an opinion on management's assessment and an opinion on the effectiveness of the Company's internal control over financial reporting based on our audit.

We conducted our audit in accordance with the standards of the Public Company Accounting Oversight Board (United States). Those standards require that we plan and perform the audit to obtain reasonable assurance about whether effective internal control over financial reporting was maintained in all material respects. Our audit included obtaining an understanding of internal control over financial reporting, evaluating management's assessment, testing and evaluating the design and operating effectiveness of internal control, and performing such other procedures as we considered necessary in the circumstances. We believe that our audit provides a reasonable basis for our opinion.

A company's internal control over financial reporting is a process designed to provide reasonable assurance regarding the reliability of financial reporting and the preparation of financial statements for external purposes in accordance with generally accepted accounting principles. A company's internal control over financial reporting includes those policies and procedures that (1) pertain to the maintenance of records that, in reasonable detail, accurately and fairly reflect the transactions and dispositions of the assets of the company; (2) provide reasonable assurance that transactions are recorded as necessary to permit preparation of financial statements in accordance with generally accepted accounting principles, and that receipts and expenditures of the company are being made only in accordance with authorizations of management and directors of the company; and (3) provide reasonable assurance regarding prevention or timely detection of unauthorized acquisition, use, or disposition of the company's assets that could have a material effect on the financial statements.

Because of its inherent limitations, internal control over financial reporting may not prevent or detect misstatements. Also, projections of any evaluation of effectiveness to future periods are subject to the risk that controls may become inadequate because of changes in conditions, or that the degree of compliance with the policies or procedures may deteriorate.

In our opinion, management's assessment that General Mills maintained effective internal control over financial reporting as of May 28, 2006, is fairly stated, in all material respects, based on criteria established in Internal Control—Integrated Framework issued by COSO. Also, in our opinion, General Mills maintained, in all material respects, effective internal control over financial reporting as of May 28, 2006, based on criteria established in Internal Control—Integrated Framework issued by COSO.

We also have audited, in accordance with the standards of the Public Company Accounting Oversight Board (United States), the consolidated balance sheets of General Mills, Inc. and subsidiaries as of May 28, 2006 and May 29, 2005, and the related consolidated statements of earnings, stockholders' equity and comprehensive income, and cash flows, for each of the fiscal years in the three-year period ended May 28, 2006, and our report dated July 27, 2006 expressed an unqualified opinion on those consolidated financial statements.

KPMG LLP

Minneapolis, Minnesota
July 27, 2006

REPORT OF MANAGEMENT RESPONSIBILITIES

The management of General Mills, Inc. is responsible for the fairness and accuracy of the consolidated financial statements. The statements have been prepared in accordance with accounting principles that are generally accepted in the United States, using management's best estimates and judgments where appropriate. The financial information throughout this Annual Report on Form 10-K is consistent with our consolidated financial statements.

Management has established a system of internal controls that provides reasonable assurance that assets are adequately safeguarded and transactions are recorded accurately in all material respects, in accordance with management's authorization. We maintain a strong audit program that independently evaluates the adequacy and effectiveness of internal controls. Our internal controls provide for appropriate separation of duties and responsibilities, and there are documented policies regarding use of our assets and proper financial reporting. These formally stated and regularly communicated policies demand highly ethical conduct from all employees.

The Audit Committee of the Board of Directors meets regularly with management, internal auditors and our independent auditors to review internal control, auditing and financial reporting matters. The independent auditors, internal auditors and employees have full and free access to the Audit Committee at any time.

The Audit Committee reviewed and approved the Company's annual financial statements and recommended to the full Board of Directors that they be included in the Annual Report. The Audit Committee also recommended to the Board of Directors that the independent auditors be reappointed for fiscal 2007, subject to ratification by the stockholders at the annual meeting.

S. W. Sanger
Chairman of the Board
and
Chief Executive Officer

J. A. Lawrence
Vice Chairman and
Chief Financial Officer

July 27, 2006

REPORT OF INDEPENDENT REGISTERED PUBLIC ACCOUNTING FIRM ON THE CONSOLIDATED FINANCIAL STATEMENTS AND RELATED FINANCIAL STATEMENT SCHEDULE

The Board of Directors and Stockholders
General Mills, Inc.:

We have audited the accompanying consolidated balance sheets of General Mills, Inc. and subsidiaries as of May 28, 2006 and May 29, 2005, and the related consolidated statements of earnings, stockholders' equity and comprehensive income, and cash flows for each of the fiscal years in the three-year period ended May 28, 2006. In connection with our audits of the consolidated financial statements we also have audited the accompanying financial statement schedule. These consolidated financial statements and financial statement schedule are the responsibility of the Company's management. Our responsibility is to express an opinion on these consolidated financial statements and financial statement schedule based on our audits.

We conducted our audits in accordance with the standards of the Public Company Accounting Oversight Board (United States). Those standards require that we plan and perform the audit to obtain reasonable assurance about whether the financial statements are free of material misstatement. An audit includes examining, on a test basis, evidence supporting the amounts and disclosures in the financial statements. An audit also includes assessing the accounting principles used and significant estimates made by management, as well as evaluating the overall financial statement presentation. We believe that our audits provide a reasonable basis for our opinion.

In our opinion, the consolidated financial statements referred to above present fairly, in all material respects, the financial position of General Mills, Inc. and subsidiaries as of May 28, 2006 and May 29, 2005, and the results of their operations and their cash flows for each of the fiscal years in the three-year period ended May 28, 2006 in conformity with U.S. generally accepted accounting principles. Also, in our opinion, the accompanying financial statement schedule, when considered in relation to the basic consolidated financial statements taken as a whole, presents fairly, in all material respects, the information set forth therein.

We also have audited, in accordance with the standards of the Public Company Accounting Oversight Board (United States), the effectiveness of General Mills' internal control over financial reporting as of May 28, 2006, based on criteria established in Internal Control—Integrated Framework issued by the Committee of Sponsoring Organizations of the Treadway Commission (COSO), and our report dated July 27, 2006 expressed an unqualified opinion on management's assessment of, and the effective operation of, internal control over financial reporting.

KPMG LLP

Minneapolis, Minnesota
July 27, 2006

GENERAL MILLS, INC. AND SUBSIDIARIES
CONSOLIDATED STATEMENTS OF EARNINGS

In Millions, Except per Share Data Fiscal Year Ended	May 28, 2006	May 29, 2005	May 30, 2004
Net Sales	$11,640	$11,244	$11,070
Costs and Expenses:			
Cost of sales	6,966	6,834	6,584
Selling, general and administrative	2,678	2,418	2,443
Interest, net	399	455	508
Restructuring and other exit costs	30	84	26
Divestitures (gain)	–	(499)	–
Debt repurchase costs	–	137	–
Total Costs and Expenses	10,073	9,429	9,561
Earnings before Income Taxes and After-tax Earnings from Joint Ventures	1,567	1,815	1,509
Income Taxes	541	664	528
After-tax Earnings from Joint Ventures	64	89	74
Net Earnings	$ 1,090	$ 1,240	$ 1,055
Earnings per Share – Basic	$ 3.05	$ 3.34	$ 2.82
Earnings per Share – Diluted	$ 2.90	$ 3.08	$ 2.60
Dividends per Share	$ 1.34	$ 1.24	$ 1.10

See accompanying notes to consolidated financial statements.

GENERAL MILLS, INC. AND SUBSIDIARIES
CONSOLIDATED BALANCE SHEETS

In Millions	May 28, 2006	May 29, 2005
ASSETS		
Current Assets:		
Cash and cash equivalents	$ 647	$ 573
Receivables	1,076	1,034
Inventories	1,055	1,037
Prepaid expenses and other current assets	216	203
Deferred income taxes	182	208
Total Current Assets	3,176	3,055
Land, Buildings and Equipment	2,997	3,111
Goodwill	6,652	6,684
Other Intangible Assets	3,607	3,532
Other Assets	1,775	1,684
Total Assets	$18,207	$18,066
LIABILITIES AND EQUITY		
Current Liabilities:		
Accounts payable	$ 1,151	$ 1,136
Current portion of long-term debt	2,131	1,638
Notes payable	1,503	299
Other current liabilities	1,353	1,111
Total Current Liabilities	6,138	4,184
Long-term Debt	2,415	4,255
Deferred Income Taxes	1,822	1,851
Other Liabilities	924	967
Total Liabilities	11,299	11,257
Minority Interests	1,136	1,133
Stockholders' Equity:		
Cumulative preference stock, none issued	–	–
Common stock, 502 shares issued	50	50
Additional paid-in capital	5,737	5,691
Retained earnings	5,107	4,501
Common stock in treasury, at cost, shares of 146 in 2006 and 133 in 2005	(5,163)	(4,460)
Unearned compensation	(84)	(114)
Accumulated other comprehensive income	125	8
Total Stockholders' Equity	5,772	5,676
Total Liabilities and Equity	$18,207	$18,066

See accompanying notes to consolidated financial statements.

GENERAL MILLS, INC. AND SUBSIDIARIES CONSOLIDATED STATEMENTS OF STOCKHOLDERS' EQUITY AND COMPREHENSIVE INCOME

	$.10 Par Value Common Stock (One Billion Shares Authorized)							
	Issued		Treasury					
In Millions, Except per Share Data	Shares	Amount	Shares	Amount	Retained Earnings	Unearned Compensation	Accumulated Other Comprehensive Income (Loss)	Total
Balance at May 25, 2003	502	$5,684	(132)	$(4,203)	$3,079	$ (43)	$(342)	$4,175
Comprehensive Income:								
Net earnings					1,055			1,055
Other comprehensive income, net of tax:								
Net change on hedge derivatives							101	101
Net change on securities							(10)	(10)
Foreign currency translation							75	75
Minimum pension liability adjustment							32	32
Other comprehensive income							198	198
Total comprehensive income								1,253
Cash dividends declared ($1.10 per share)					(412)			(412)
Stock compensation plans (includes income tax benefits of $5)	–	(4)	10	306				302
Shares purchased			(1)	(24)				(24)
Unearned compensation related to restricted stock awards						(77)		(77)
Earned compensation and other						31		31
Balance at May 30, 2004	502	$5,680	(123)	$(3,921)	$3,722	$ (89)	$(144)	$5,248
Comprehensive Income:								
Net earnings					1,240			1,240
Other comprehensive income, net of tax:								
Net change on hedge derivatives							99	99
Foreign currency translation							75	75
Minimum pension liability adjustment							(22)	(22)
Other comprehensive income							152	152
Total comprehensive income								1,392
Cash dividends declared ($1.24 per share)					(461)			(461)
Stock compensation plans (includes income tax benefits of $62)	–	104	7	232				336
Shares purchased			(17)	(771)				(771)
Forward purchase contract fees	–	(43)						(43)
Unearned compensation related to restricted stock awards						(66)		(66)
Earned compensation and other						41		41
Balance at May 29, 2005	502	$5,741	(133)	$(4,460)	$4,501	$(114)	$ 8	$5,676
Comprehensive Income:								
Net earnings					1,090			1,090
Other comprehensive income, net of tax:								
Net change on hedge derivatives							20	20
Foreign currency translation							73	73
Minimum pension liability adjustment							24	24
Other comprehensive income							117	117
Total comprehensive income								1,207
Cash dividends declared ($1.34 per share)					(484)			(484)
Stock compensation plans (includes income tax benefits of $41)	–	46	6	189				235
Shares purchased			(19)	(892)				(892)
Unearned compensation related to restricted stock awards						(17)		(17)
Earned compensation and other						47		47
Balance at May 28, 2006	502	$5,787	(146)	$(5,163)	$5,107	$ (84)	$ 125	$5,772

See accompanying notes to consolidated financial statements.

GENERAL MILLS, INC. AND SUBSIDIARIES
CONSOLIDATED STATEMENTS OF CASH FLOWS

In Millions Fiscal Year Ended	May 28, 2006	May 29, 2005	May 30, 2004
Cash Flows – Operating Activities			
Net earnings	$ 1,090	$ 1,240	$ 1,055
Adjustments to reconcile net earnings to net cash provided by operating activities:			
Depreciation and amortization	424	443	399
Deferred income taxes	26	9	109
Changes in current assets and liabilities	184	258	(186)
Tax benefit on exercised options	41	62	63
Pension and other postretirement costs	(74)	(70)	(21)
Restructuring and other exit costs	30	84	26
Divestitures (gain)	–	(499)	–
Debt repurchase costs	–	137	–
Other, net	50	47	16
Net Cash Provided by Operating Activities	1,771	1,711	1,461
Cash Flows – Investing Activities			
Purchases of land, buildings and equipment	(360)	(434)	(653)
Investments in businesses	(26)	–	(10)
Investments in affiliates, net of investment returns and dividends	78	84	32
Purchases of marketable securities	–	(1)	(7)
Proceeds from sale of marketable securities	1	33	129
Proceeds from disposal of land, buildings and equipment	11	24	36
Proceeds from disposition of businesses	–	799	–
Other, net	4	(9)	2
Net Cash Provided (Used) by Investing Activities	(292)	496	(470)
Cash Flows – Financing Activities			
Change in notes payable	1,197	(1,057)	(1,023)
Issuance of long-term debt	–	2	576
Payment of long-term debt	(1,386)	(1,115)	(248)
Proceeds from issuance of preferred membership interests of subsidiary	–	835	–
Common stock issued	157	195	192
Purchases of common stock for treasury	(885)	(771)	(24)
Dividends paid	(485)	(461)	(413)
Other, net	(3)	(13)	(3)
Net Cash Used by Financing Activities	(1,405)	(2,385)	(943)
Increase (Decrease) in Cash and Cash Equivalents	74	(178)	48
Cash and Cash Equivalents – Beginning of Year	573	751	703
Cash and Cash Equivalents – End of Year	$ 647	$ 573	$ 751
Cash Flow from Changes in Current Assets and Liabilities:			
Receivables	$ (18)	$ (9)	$ (22)
Inventories	(6)	30	24
Prepaid expenses and other current assets	(7)	9	(15)
Accounts payable	14	(19)	(161)
Other current liabilities	201	247	(12)
Changes in Current Assets and Liabilities	$ 184	$ 258	$ (186)

See accompanying notes to consolidated financial statements.

GENERAL MILLS, INC. AND SUBSIDIARIES
NOTES TO CONSOLIDATED FINANCIAL STATEMENTS

1. Summary of Significant Accounting Policies

Basis of Presentation Our consolidated financial statements include the accounts of General Mills, Inc. and all subsidiaries in which it has a controlling financial interest. Intercompany transactions and accounts are eliminated in consolidation. Certain prior years' amounts have been reclassified to conform to the current year presentation.

Our fiscal year ends on the last Sunday in May. Fiscal years 2006 and 2005 each consisted of 52 weeks, and fiscal 2004 consisted of 53 weeks. Our International segment, with the exception of Canada and our export operations, is reported for the 12 calendar months ended April 30.

Cash and Cash Equivalents We consider all investments purchased with an original maturity of three months or less to be cash equivalents.

Inventories Most U.S. inventories are valued at the lower of cost, using the last-in, first-out (LIFO) method, or market. Grain inventories are valued at market. The balance of the U.S. inventories and inventories of consolidated operations outside of the U.S. are valued at the lower of cost, using the first-in, first-out (FIFO) method, or market.

Shipping costs associated with the distribution of finished product to our customers are recorded as selling, general and administrative expense and are recognized when the related finished product is shipped to the customer.

Land, Buildings, Equipment and Depreciation Land is recorded at historical cost. Buildings and equipment are recorded at historical cost and depreciated over estimated useful lives, primarily using the straight-line method. Ordinary maintenance and repairs are charged to operating costs. Buildings are usually depreciated over 40 to 50 years, and equipment is usually depreciated over three to 15 years. Accelerated depreciation methods generally are used for income tax purposes. When an item is sold or retired, the accounts are relieved of its cost and related accumulated depreciation; the resulting gains and losses, if any, are recognized in earnings.

Long-lived assets are reviewed for impairment whenever events or changes in circumstances indicate that their carrying amount may not be recoverable. An impairment loss would be recognized when estimated undiscounted future cash flows from the operation and disposition of the asset group are less than the carrying amount of the asset group. Asset groups are identifiable and largely independent of other asset groups. Measurement of an impairment loss would be based on the excess of the carrying amount of the asset group over its fair value. Fair value is measured using discounted cash flows or independent appraisals as appropriate.

Goodwill and Other Intangible Assets Goodwill represents the difference between the purchase prices of acquired companies and the related fair values of net assets acquired. Goodwill is not subject to amortization and is tested for impairment annually for each of our reporting units and whenever events or changes in circumstances indicate that an impairment may have occurred. Impairment testing compares the carrying amount of goodwill for a reporting unit with its fair value. Fair value is estimated based on discounted cash flows. When the carrying amount of goodwill exceeds its fair value, an impairment has occurred. We have completed our annual impairment testing and determined none of our goodwill is impaired.

The costs of patents, copyrights and other intangible assets with finite lives are amortized over their estimated useful lives. Intangibles with indefinite lives, principally brands, are carried at cost. Finite and indefinite-lived intangible assets are also tested for impairment annually and whenever events or changes in circumstances indicate that their carrying value may not be recoverable. An impairment loss would be recognized when estimated undiscounted future cash flows are less than the carrying amount of the intangible. Measurement of an impairment loss would be based on the excess of the carrying amount of the intangible over its fair value. We have completed our annual impairment testing and determined none of our other intangible assets are impaired.

Investments in Joint Ventures Our investments in companies over which we have the ability to exercise significant influence are stated at cost plus our share of undistributed earnings or losses. We also receive royalty income from certain joint ventures, incur various expenses (primarily research and development) and record the tax impact of certain joint venture operations that are structured as partnerships.

Variable Interest Entities At May 28, 2006, we had invested in four variable interest entities (VIEs). We are the primary beneficiary (PB) of General Mills Capital, Inc. (GM Capital), a subsidiary that we consolidate as set forth in Note Eight. We also have an interest in a contract manufacturer at our former facility in Geneva, Illinois. Even though we are the PB, we have not consolidated this entity because it is not material to our results of operations, financial condition, or liquidity at May 28, 2006. This entity had property and equipment of $50 million and long-term debt of $50 million at May 28, 2006. We are not the PB of the remaining two VIEs. Our maximum exposure to loss from these VIEs is limited to the $150 million minority interest in GM Capital, the contract manufacturer's debt and our $6 million equity investments in the remaining two VIEs.

Revenue Recognition We recognize sales revenue upon acceptance of the shipment by our customers. Sales are reported net of consumer coupon, trade promotion and other costs, including estimated returns. Coupons are expensed when distributed based on estimated redemptions. Trade promotions are expensed based on estimated participation and performance levels for offered programs. We generally do not allow a right of return. However, on a limited case-by-case basis with prior approval, we may allow customers to return product in saleable condition for redistribution to other customers or outlets. Returns are expensed as reductions of net sales.

Advertising Production Costs We expense the production costs of advertising the first time that the advertising takes place.

Research and Development All expenditures for research and development are charged against earnings in the year incurred.

Foreign Currency Translation Results of foreign operations are translated into U.S. dollars using the average exchange rates each month. Assets and liabilities of these operations are translated at the period-end exchange rates, and the differences from historical exchange rates are reflected within Accumulated Other Comprehensive Income in Stockholders' Equity as cumulative translation adjustments.

Derivative Instruments We use derivatives primarily to hedge our exposure to changes in foreign exchange rates, interest rates and commodity prices. All derivatives are recognized on the Consolidated Balance Sheets at fair value based on quoted market prices or management's estimate of their fair value and are recorded in either current or noncurrent assets or liabilities based on their maturity. Changes in the fair values of derivatives are recorded in earnings or other comprehensive income, based on whether the instrument is designated as a hedge transaction and, if so, the type of hedge transaction. Gains or losses on derivative instruments reported in other comprehensive income are reclassified to earnings in the period the hedged item affects earnings. If the underlying hedged transaction ceases to exist, any associated amounts reported in other comprehensive income are reclassified to earnings at that time. Any ineffectiveness is recognized in earnings in the current period.

Stock-based Compensation We use the intrinsic value method for measuring the cost of compensation paid in our common stock. This method defines our cost as the excess of the stock's market value at the time of the grant over the amount that the employee is required to pay. Our stock option plans require that the employee's payment (i.e., exercise price) be at least the market value as of the grant date.

Restricted share awards, including restricted stock and restricted stock units, are measured at the fair market value of our stock on the date of the award, and are initially recorded in Stockholders' Equity as unearned compensation, net of estimated forfeitures. Unearned compensation is amortized to compensation expense on a straight-line basis over the requisite service period.

The following table illustrates the pro forma effect on net earnings and earnings per share if we had applied the fair value recognition provisions of Statement of Financial Accounting Standard (SFAS) No. 123, (SFAS 123) "Accounting for Stock-Based Compensation," to all employee stock-based compensation, net of estimated forfeitures.

In Millions, Except per Share Data, Fiscal Year Ended	May 28, 2006	May 29, 2005	May 30, 2004
Net earnings, as reported	$1,090	$1,240	$1,055
Add: After-tax stock-based employee compensation expense included in reported net earnings	28	24	17
Deduct: After-tax stock-based employee compensation expense determined under fair value requirements of SFAS 123	(48)	(62)	(67)
Pro forma net earnings	$1,070	$1,202	$1,005
Earnings per share:			
Basic – as reported	$ 3.05	$ 3.34	$ 2.82
Basic – pro forma	$ 2.99	$ 3.24	$ 2.68
Diluted – as reported	$ 2.90	$ 3.08	$ 2.60
Diluted – pro forma	$ 2.84	$ 2.99	$ 2.49

The weighted-average grant date fair values of the employee stock options granted were estimated as $8.04 in fiscal 2006, $8.32 in fiscal 2005, and $8.54 in fiscal 2004 using the Black-Scholes option-pricing model with the following assumptions:

Fiscal Year	2006	2005	2004
Risk-free interest rate	4.3%	4.0%	3.9%
Expected life	7 years	7 years	7 years
Expected volatility	20.0%	21.0%	21.0%
Expected dividend growth rate	10.2%	9.8%	10.0%

In December 2004, the Financial Accounting Standards Board (FASB) issued SFAS No. 123(Revised) "Share-Based Payment" (SFAS 123R), which generally requires public companies to measure the cost of employee services received in exchange for an award of equity instruments based on the grant-date fair value and to recognize this cost over the period during which the employee is required to provide service in exchange for the award. The standard is effective for public companies for annual periods beginning after June 15, 2005, with several transition options regarding prospective versus retrospective application. We will adopt SFAS 123R in the first quarter of fiscal 2007, using the modified prospective method. Accordingly, prior year results will not be restated, but fiscal 2007 results will be presented as if we had applied the fair value method of accounting for stock-based compensation from the beginning of fiscal 1997. SFAS 123R also requires the benefits of tax deductions in excess of recognized compensation cost to be reported as a financing cash flow, rather than as an operating cash flow as currently required, thereby reducing net operating cash flows and increasing net financing cash flows in periods following adoption. While those amounts cannot be estimated for future periods, the amount of operating cash flows generated in prior periods for such excess tax deductions was $41 million for fiscal 2006, $62 million for fiscal 2005 and $63 million for fiscal 2004.

Certain equity-based compensation plans contain provisions that accelerate vesting of awards upon retirement, disability or death of eligible employees and directors. For the periods presented, we generally recognized stock compensation expense over the stated vesting period of the award, with any unamortized expense recognized immediately if an acceleration event occurred. SFAS No. 123R specifies that a stock-based award is vested when the employee's retention of the award is no longer contingent on providing subsequent service. Accordingly, beginning in fiscal 2007, we will prospectively revise our expense attribution method so that the related compensation cost is recognized immediately for awards granted to retirement-eligible individuals or over the period from the grant date to the date retirement eligibility is achieved, if less than the stated vesting period.

Use of Estimates Preparing our consolidated financial statements in conformity with accounting principles generally accepted in the United States requires us to make estimates and assumptions that affect reported amounts of assets and liabilities, disclosures of contingent assets and liabilities at the date of the financial statements, and the reported amounts of revenues and expenses during the reporting period. Actual results could differ from our estimates.

New Accounting Standards The FASB ratified in October 2004, Emerging Issues Task Force Issue No. 04-8, "The Effect of Contingently Convertible Debt on Diluted Earnings per Share" (EITF 04-8). EITF 04-8 was effective for us in the third quarter of fiscal 2005. The adoption of EITF 04-8 increased diluted shares outstanding to give effect to shares that were contingently issuable related to our zero coupon convertible debentures issued in October 2002. Also, net earnings used for earnings per share calculations were adjusted, using the if-converted method. See Note Eleven.

In the second quarter of fiscal 2006, we adopted SFAS No. 153, "Exchanges of Nonmonetary Assets – An Amendment of APB Opinion No. 29." SFAS 153 eliminates the exception from fair value measurement for nonmonetary exchanges of similar productive assets and replaces it with an exception for exchanges that do not have commercial substance. The adoption of SFAS 153 did not have any impact on our results of operations or financial condition.

In March 2005, the FASB issued FASB Interpretation No. 47, "Accounting for Conditional Asset Retirement Obligations" (FIN 47). FIN 47 requires that liabilities be recognized for the fair value of a legal obligation to perform asset retirement activities that are conditional on a future event if the amount can be reasonably estimated. We adopted FIN 47 in the fourth quarter of fiscal 2006 and it did not have a material impact on our results of operations or financial condition.

2. Acquisitions and Divestitures

On March 3, 2006, we acquired Elysées Consult S.A., the franchise operator of a *Häagen-Dazs* shop in France. On November 21, 2005, we acquired Croissant King, a producer of frozen pastry products in Australia. On October 31, 2005, we acquired a controlling financial interest in Pinedale Holdings Pte. Limited, an operator of *Häagen-Dazs* cafes in Singapore and Malaysia. The aggregate purchase price of our fiscal 2006 acquisitions was $26 million. The pro forma effect of these acquisitions was not material.

On February 28, 2005, Snack Ventures Europe (SVE), our snacks joint venture with PepsiCo, Inc., was terminated and our 40.5 percent interest was redeemed. On April 4, 2005, we sold our Lloyd's barbecue business to Hormel Foods Corporation. We received $799 million in cash proceeds from these dispositions and recorded $499 million in gains in fiscal 2005.

3. Restructuring and Other Exit Costs

In fiscal 2006, we recorded restructuring and other exit costs of $30 million pursuant to approved plans consisting of: $13 million related to the closure of our Swedesboro, New Jersey plant; $6 million related to the closure of a production line at our Montreal, Quebec plant; $4 million related to restructuring actions at our Allentown, Pennsylvania plant; $3 million of asset impairment charges for one of our plants; and $4 million related primarily to fiscal 2005 initiatives. The fiscal 2006 restructuring charges included $17 million to write down assets to fair value, $7 million of severance costs for 425 employees being terminated, and $6 million of other exit costs. The carrying value of the assets written down was $18 million.The fair values of the assets written down were determined using discounted cash flows.

The fiscal 2006 initiatives were undertaken to increase asset utilization and reduce manufacturing costs. The actions included decisions to: close our leased frozen dough foodservice plant in Swedesboro, New Jersey, affecting 101 employees; shut down a portion of our frozen dough foodservice plant in Montreal, Quebec, affecting 77 employees; realign and modify product and manufacturing capabilities at our frozen waffle plant in Allentown, Pennsylvania, affecting 72 employees; and complete the fiscal 2005 initiative to relocate our frozen baked goods line from our plant in Chelsea, Massachusetts, to another facility, affecting 175 employees.

In fiscal 2005, we recorded restructuring and other exit costs of $84 million pursuant to approved plans, consisting of: $74 million of charges associated with fiscal 2005 supply chain initiatives; $3 million of charges associated with Bakeries and Foodservice severance charges resulting from fiscal 2004 decisions; and $7 million of charges associated with restructuring actions prior to fiscal 2005. The charges from the fiscal 2005 initiatives included severance and pension and postretirement curtailment costs of $14 million for 551 employees being terminated, $20 million to write off assets, $30 million for the write-down of assets to their net realizable value and $10 million of other exit costs. The carrying value of the assets written down was $36 million. Net realizable value was determined by independent market analysis.

The fiscal 2005 initiatives were undertaken to further increase asset utilization and reduce manufacturing and sourcing costs, resulting in decisions regarding plant closures and production realignment. The actions included decisions to: close our flour milling plant in Vallejo, California, affecting 43 employees; close our par-baked bread plant in Medley, Florida, affecting 42 employees; relocate bread production from our Swedesboro, New Jersey plant, affecting 110 employees; relocate a portion of our cereal production from Cincinnati, Ohio, affecting 45 employees; close our snacks foods plant in Iowa City, Iowa, affecting 83 employees; close our dry mix production at Trenton, Ontario, affecting 53 employees; and relocate our frozen baked goods line from our plant in Chelsea, Massachusetts to another facility.

These fiscal 2005 supply chain actions also resulted in certain associated expenses in fiscal 2005, primarily resulting from adjustments to the depreciable life of the assets necessary to reflect the shortened asset lives which coincided with the final production dates at the Cincinnati and Iowa City plants. These associated expenses were recorded as cost of sales and totaled $18 million.

In fiscal 2004, we recorded restructuring and other exit costs of $26 million pursuant to approved plans. These costs included: a severance charge for 142 employees being terminated as a result of a plant closure in the Netherlands; costs related to a plant closure in Brazil, including a severance charge for 201 employees; costs for the closure of our tomato canning facility in Atwater, California, including severance costs for 47 employees; adjustments of costs associated with previously announced closures of manufacturing facilities; and a severance charge for 132 employees, related primarily to actions in our Bakeries and Foodservice organization. The carrying value of the assets written down was $3 million.

The analysis of our restructuring and other exit costs is as follows:

In Millions	Severance	Asset Write-down	Pension and Postretirement Curtailment Cost	Other	Total
Reserve balance at May 25, 2003	$ 10	$ 16	$ –	$ 11	$ 37
2004 Charges	16	4	–	6	26
Utilized in 2004	(13)	(18)	–	(9)	(40)
Reserve balance at May 30, 2004	13	2	–	8	23
2005 Charges	12	51	4	17	84
Utilized in 2005	(16)	(53)	(4)	(16)	(89)
Reserve Balance at May 29, 2005	9	–	–	9	18
2006 Charges	7	17	–	6	30
Utilized in 2006	(8)	(17)	–	(8)	(33)
Reserve Balance at May 28, 2006	$ 8	$ –	$ –	$ 7	$ 15

4. Investments in Joint Ventures

We have a 50 percent equity interest in Cereal Partners Worldwide (CPW), a joint venture with Nestlé S.A. that manufactures and markets cereal products outside the United States and Canada. We have guaranteed a portion of CPW's debt. See Note Fifteen. We have a 50 percent equity interest in 8th Continent, LLC, a domestic joint venture with DuPont to develop and market soy-based products. We have 50 percent equity interests in the following joint ventures for the manufacture, distribution and marketing of *Häagen-Dazs* frozen ice cream products and novelties: Häagen-Dazs Japan K.K.; Häagen-Dazs Korea Company Limited; and Häagen-Dazs Marketing & Distribution (Philippines) Inc. We have a 49 percent equity interest in Häagen-Dazs Distributors (Thailand) Company Limited. We also have a 50 percent equity interest in Seretram, a joint venture with Co-op de Pau for the production of *Green Giant* canned corn in France. In May 2006, we acquired a controlling financial interest in our Häagen-Dazs joint venture in the Philippines for less than $1 million.

Fiscal 2005 and fiscal 2004 results of operations include our share of the after-tax earnings of SVE through the date of its termination on February 28, 2005.

On July 14, 2006, CPW acquired the Uncle Tobys cereal business in Australia for approximately $385 million. This business had revenues of approximately $100 million for the fiscal year ended June 30, 2006. We funded our 50 percent share of the purchase price by making an additional equity contribution in CPW from cash generated from our international operations, including our international joint ventures.

In February 2006, CPW announced a restructuring of its manufacturing plants in the United Kingdom. Our after-tax earnings from joint ventures were reduced by $8 million for our share of the restructuring costs, primarily accelerated depreciation and severance, incurred in fiscal 2006.

Our cumulative investment in these joint ventures was $186 million at the end of fiscal 2006 and $211 million at the end of fiscal 2005. We made aggregate investments in the joint ventures of $7 million in fiscal 2006, $15 million in fiscal 2005 and $31 million in fiscal 2004. We received aggregate dividends from the joint ventures of $77 million in fiscal 2006, $83 million in fiscal 2005 and $60 million in fiscal 2004.

Results from our CPW joint venture are reported as of and for the twelve months ended March 31. The Häagen-Dazs and Seretram joint venture results are reported as of and for the twelve months ended April 30. 8th Continent's results are presented on the same basis as our fiscal year.

Summary combined financial information for the joint ventures (including SVE through the date of its termination on February 28, 2005) on a 100 percent basis follows:

In Millions, Fiscal Year Ended	2006	2005	2004
Net Sales	$1,796	$2,652	$2,625
Gross Margin	770	1,184	1,180
Earnings before Income Taxes	157	231	205
Earnings after Income Taxes	120	184	153

Gross margin is defined as net sales less cost of sales.

In Millions, At End of Fiscal Year	2006	2005
Current Assets	$634	$604
Noncurrent Assets	578	612
Current Liabilities	756	695
Noncurrent Liabilities	6	7

5. Goodwill and Intangible Assets

The components of goodwill and other intangible assets are as follows:

In Millions	May 28, 2006	May 29, 2005
Goodwill	$ 6,652	$ 6,684
Other Intangible Assets:		
Intangible assets not subject to amortization:		
Brands	3,595	3,516
Pension intangible	–	3
Total intangible assets not subject to amortization	3,595	3,519
Intangible assets subject to amortization:		
Patents, trademarks and other finite-lived intangibles	19	19
Less accumulated amortization	(7)	(6)
Total intangible assets subject to amortization	12	13
Total Other Intangible Assets	3,607	3,532
Total Goodwill and Other Intangible Assets	$10,259	$10,216

Brand intangibles increased by $79 million, as a result of foreign currency translation.

The changes in the carrying amount of goodwill for fiscal 2004, 2005 and 2006 are as follows:

In Millions	U.S. Retail	International	Bakeries and Foodservice	Total
Balance at May 25, 2003	$5,024	$421	$1,205	$6,650
Goodwill acquired	–	14	–	14
Other activity, including translation	–	20	–	20
Balance at May 30, 2004	5,024	455	1,205	6,684
Goodwill acquired	–	1	–	1
Other activity, including translation	(22)	25	(4)	(1)
Balance at May 29, 2005	5,002	481	1,201	6,684
Goodwill acquired	–	15	–	15
Deferred tax adjustment related to Pillsbury acquisition	(42)	–	–	(42)
Other activity, including translation	–	(5)	–	(5)
Balance at May 28, 2006	$4,960	$491	$1,201	$6,652

Future purchase price adjustments to goodwill may occur upon the resolution of certain income tax accounting matters. See Note Fourteen.

6. Financial Instruments and Risk Management Activities

Financial Instruments The carrying values of cash and cash equivalents, receivables, accounts payable, other current liabilities and notes payable approximate fair value. Marketable securities are carried at fair value. As of May 28, 2006, a comparison of cost and market values of our marketable debt and equity securities is as follows:

In Millions	Cost	Market Value	Gross Gains	Gross Losses
Held to maturity:				
Equity securities	$ 2	$ 2	$ –	$ –
Total	$ 2	$ 2	$ –	$ –
Available for sale:				
Debt securities	$20	$20	$ –	$ –
Equity securities	4	8	4	–
Total	$24	$28	$ 4	$ –

Earnings include realized gains from sales of available-for-sale marketable securities of less than $1 million in fiscal 2006, $2 million in fiscal 2005 and $20 million in fiscal 2004. Gains and losses are determined by specific identification. The aggregate unrealized gains and losses on available-for-sale securities, net of tax effects, are classified in Accumulated Other Comprehensive Income within Stockholders' Equity. At May 28, 2006, we owned twenty marketable securities with a fair market value less than cost. The fair market value of these securities was $0.3 million below their cost.

Scheduled maturities of our marketable securities are as follows:

	Held to Maturity		Available for Sale	
In Millions	Cost	Market Value	Cost	Market Value
Under one year (current)	$ –	$ –	$ 5	$ 5
From 1 to 3 years	–	–	5	5
From 4 to 7 years	–	–	2	2
Over 7 years	–	–	8	8
Equity securities	2	2	4	8
Total	$ 2	$ 2	$24	$28

Cash, cash equivalents and marketable securities totaling $48 million as of May 28, 2006, and $63 million as of May 29, 2005, were pledged as collateral. These assets are primarily pledged as collateral for certain derivative contracts.

The fair values and carrying amounts of long-term debt, including the current portion, were $4,566 million and $4,546 million at May 28, 2006, and $6,074 million and $5,893 million at May 29, 2005. The fair value of long-term debt was estimated using discounted cash flows based on our current incremental borrowing rates for similar types of instruments.

Risk Management Activities As a part of our ongoing business operations, we are exposed to market risks such as changes in interest rates, foreign currency exchange rates and commodity prices. To manage these risks, we may enter into various derivative transactions (e.g., futures, options and swaps) pursuant to our established policies.

Interest Rate Risk We are exposed to interest rate volatility with regard to existing variable-rate debt and planned future issuances of fixed-rate debt. We use a combination of interest rate swaps and forward-starting swaps to reduce interest rate volatility and to achieve a desired proportion of variable versus fixed-rate debt, based on current and projected market conditions.

Variable Interest Rate Exposures – Except as discussed below, variable-to-fixed interest rate swaps are accounted for as cash flow hedges, as are all hedges of forecasted issuances of debt. Effectiveness is assessed based on either the perfectly effective hypothetical derivative method or changes in the present value of interest payments on the underlying debt. Amounts deferred to Accumulated Other Comprehensive Income are reclassified into earnings over the life of the associated debt. The amount of hedge ineffectiveness was less than $1 million in fiscal 2006, 2005 and 2004.

Fixed Interest Rate Exposures – Fixed-to-variable interest rate swaps are accounted for as fair value hedges with effectiveness assessed based on changes in the fair value of the underlying debt, using incremental borrowing rates currently available on loans with similar terms and maturities. Effective gains and losses on these derivatives and the underlying hedged items are recorded as interest expense. The amount of hedge ineffectiveness was less than $1 million in fiscal 2006, 2005 and 2004.

In anticipation of the Pillsbury acquisition and other financing needs, we entered into pay-fixed interest rate swap contracts during fiscal 2001 and fiscal 2002 totaling $7.1 billion to lock in our interest payments on the associated debt. During fiscal 2004, $750 million of these swaps matured. In fiscal 2005, $2 billion of these swaps matured. At May 28, 2006, we still owned $3.15 billion of Pillsbury-related pay-fixed swaps that were previously neutralized with offsetting pay-floating swaps in fiscal 2002. At May 28, 2006, $500 million of our pay-floating interest rate swaps were designated as a fair value hedge of our 2.625 percent notes due October 2006.

In May 2006, we entered into a $100 million pay-fixed, forward-starting interest rate swap with a fixed rate of 5.7 percent in anticipation of fixed-rate debt refinancing probable of occurring in fiscal 2007. Subsequent to May 28, 2006, we entered into an additional $600 million of pay-fixed, forward-starting interest rate swaps with an average fixed rate of 5.7 percent.

The following table summarizes the notional amounts and weighted average interest rates of our interest rate swaps. As discussed above, we have neutralized all of our pay-fixed swaps with pay-floating swaps; however, we cannot present them on a net basis in the following table because the offsetting occurred with different counterparties. Average variable rates are based on rates as of the end of the reporting period.

In Millions	May 28, 2006	May 29, 2005
Pay-floating swaps – notional amount	$3,770	$3,795
Average receive rate	4.8%	4.8%
Average pay rate	5.1%	3.1%
Pay-fixed swaps – notional amount	$3,250	$3,150
Average receive rate	5.1%	3.1%
Average pay rate	6.8%	6.9%

The swap contracts mature at various dates from 2007 to 2015, as follows:

In Millions Fiscal Year Maturity Date	Pay Floating	Pay Fixed
2007	$1,923	$1,400
2008	22	–
2009	20	–
2010	20	–
2011	18	–
Beyond 2011	1,767	1,850
Total	$3,770	$3,250

Foreign Exchange Transaction Risk We are exposed to fluctuations in foreign currency cash flows related primarily to third-party purchases, intercompany product shipments and intercompany loans. Our primary U.S. dollar exchange rate exposures are with the Canadian dollar, the euro, the Australian dollar, the Mexican peso and the British pound. Forward contracts of generally less than 12 months duration are used to hedge some of these risks. Hedge effectiveness is assessed based on changes in forward rates. The amount of hedge ineffectiveness was $1 million or less in fiscal 2006, 2005 and 2004.

Commodity Price Risk We are exposed to price fluctuations primarily as a result of anticipated purchases of ingredient and packaging materials. The principal raw materials that we use are cereal grains, sugar, dairy products, vegetables, fruits, meats, vegetable oils, and other agricultural products as well as paper and plastic packaging materials, operating supplies and energy. We use a combination of long cash positions with suppliers, exchange-traded futures and option contracts and over-the-counter hedging mechanisms to reduce price fluctuations in a desired percentage of forecasted purchases over a period of less than two years. Except as discussed below, commodity derivatives are accounted for as cash flow hedges, with effectiveness assessed based on changes in futures prices. The amount of hedge ineffectiveness was a gain of $3 million in fiscal 2006, and were losses of $1 million or less in fiscal 2005 and 2004.

Other Risk Management Activities We enter into certain derivative contracts in accordance with our risk management strategy that do not meet the criteria for hedge accounting, including those in our grain merchandising operation, certain foreign currency derivatives and offsetting interest rate swaps as discussed above. Even though they may not qualify as hedges, these derivatives have the economic impact of largely mitigating the associated risks. These derivatives were not acquired for trading purposes and are recorded at fair value with changes in fair value recognized in earnings each period.

Our grain merchandising operation provides us efficient access to and more informed knowledge of various commodities markets. This operation uses futures and options to hedge its net inventory position to minimize market exposure. As of May 28, 2006, our grain merchandising operation had futures and options contracts that essentially hedged its net inventory position. None of the contracts extended beyond May 2007. All futures contracts and options are exchange-based instruments with ready liquidity and determinable market values. Neither the results of operations nor the year-end positions of our grain merchandising operation were material.

Unrealized losses from cash flow hedges recorded in Accumulated Other Comprehensive Income as of May 28, 2006, totaled $92 million, primarily related to interest rate swaps we entered into in contemplation of future borrowings and other financing requirements (primarily related to the Pillsbury acquisition), which are being reclassified into interest expense over the lives of the hedged forecasted transactions. The majority of the remaining gains and losses from cash flow hedges recorded in Accumulated Other Comprehensive Income as of May 28, 2006, were related to foreign currency contracts. The net amount of the gains and losses in Accumulated Other Comprehensive Income as of May 28, 2006, that is expected to be reclassified into earnings within the next twelve months is $39 million in expense. See Note Seven for the impact of these reclassifications on interest expense.

Concentrations of Credit Risk We enter into interest rate, foreign exchange, and certain commodity and equity derivatives primarily with a diversified group of highly rated counterparties. We continually monitor our positions and the credit ratings of the counterparties involved and, by policy, limit the amount of credit exposure to any one party. These transactions may expose us to potential losses due to the credit risk of nonperformance by these counterparties; however, we have not incurred a material loss nor are losses anticipated. We also enter into commodity futures transactions through various regulated exchanges.

Our top five customers in the U.S. Retail segment account for 47 percent of the segment's net sales. Payment terms vary depending on product categories and markets. We establish and monitor credit limits to manage our credit risk. We have not incurred a material loss nor are any such losses anticipated.

7. Debt

Notes Payable The components of notes payable and their respective weighted average interest rates at the end of the periods were as follows:

Dollars In Millions	May 28, 2006 Notes Payable	May 28, 2006 Weighted Average Interest Rate	May 29, 2005 Notes Payable	May 29, 2005 Weighted Average Interest Rate
U.S. commercial paper	$ 713	5.1%	$125	3.1%
Euro commercial paper	462	5.1	–	–
Financial institutions	328	5.7	174	7.2
Total Notes Payable	$1,503	5.2%	$299	5.5%

To ensure availability of funds, we maintain bank credit lines sufficient to cover our outstanding short-term borrowings. As of May 28, 2006, we had $2.95 billion in committed lines and $335 million in uncommitted lines. Our committed lines consist of a $750 million five-year credit facility expiring in January 2009, a $1.1 billion 364-day credit facility expiring in October 2006 and a new $1.1 billion five-year credit facility expiring in October 2010.

Long-term Debt On October 28, 2005, we repurchased a significant portion of our zero coupon convertible debentures pursuant to the put rights of the holders for an aggregate purchase price of $1.33 billion, including $77 million of accreted original issue discount classified within financing cash flows in the Consolidated Statement of Cash Flows. These debentures had an aggregate principal amount at maturity of $1.86 billion. We incurred no gain or loss from this repurchase. As of May 28, 2006, there were $371 million in aggregate principal amount at maturity of the debentures outstanding, or $268 million of accreted value. We used proceeds from the issuance of commercial paper to fund our repurchase of the debentures. We have also reclassified the remaining zero coupon convertible debentures to long-term debt based on the put rights of the holders.

Our credit facilities, certain of our long-term debt agreements and our minority interests contain restrictive debt covenants. At May 28, 2006, we were in compliance with all of these covenants.

On March 23, 2005, we commenced a cash tender offer for our outstanding 6 percent notes due in 2012. The tender offer resulted in the purchase of $500 million principal amount of the notes. Subsequent to the expiration of the tender offer, we purchased an additional $260 million principal amount of the notes in the open market. The aggregate purchases resulted in debt repurchase costs of $137 million, consisting of $73 million of noncash interest rate swap losses reclassified from Accumulated Other Comprehensive Income, $59 million of purchase premium and $5 million of noncash unamortized cost of issuance expense.

As of May 28, 2006, the $86 million recorded in Accumulated Other Comprehensive Income associated with our previously designated interest rate swaps will be reclassified to interest expense over the remaining lives of the hedged forecasted transaction. The amount expected to be reclassified from Accumulated Other Comprehensive Income to interest expense in fiscal 2007 is $33 million. The amount reclassified from Accumulated Other Comprehensive Income in fiscal 2006 was $33 million.

A summary of our long-term debt is as follows:

In Millions	May 28, 2006	May 29, 2005
5 1/8% notes due February 15, 2007	$ 1,500	$ 1,500
6% notes due February 15, 2012	1,240	1,240
2.625% notes due October 24, 2006	500	500
Medium-term notes, 4.8% to 9.1%, due 2006 to 2078[(a)]	362	413
3 7/8% notes due November 30, 2007	350	350
Zero coupon convertible debentures yield 2.0%, $371 due October 28, 2022	268	1,579
3.901% notes due November 30, 2007	135	135
Zero coupon notes, yield 11.1%, $261 due August 15, 2013	121	108
Other, primarily due July 11, 2008	66	62
8.2% ESOP loan guaranty, due through June 30, 2007	4	6
	4,546	5,893
Less amounts due within one year	(2,131)	(1,638)
Total Long-term Debt	$ 2,415	$ 4,255

(a) Medium-term notes of $131 million may mature in fiscal 2007 based on the put rights of these note holders.

See Note Six for a description of related interest-rate derivative instruments.

We have guaranteed the debt of our Employee Stock Ownership Plan; therefore, the loan is reflected on our consolidated balance sheets as long-term debt with a related offset in Unearned Compensation in Stockholders' Equity.

Principal payments due on long-term debt in the next five years based on stated contractual maturities or put rights of certain note holders are (in millions) $2,131 in fiscal 2007, $854 in fiscal 2008, $117 in fiscal 2009, $55 in fiscal 2010 and $0 in fiscal 2011.

8. Minority Interests

In April 2002, we and certain of our wholly owned subsidiaries contributed assets with an aggregate fair market value of approximately $4 billion to another wholly owned subsidiary, General Mills Cereals, LLC (GMC), a limited liability company. GMC is a separate and distinct legal entity from the Company and its subsidiaries, and has separate assets, liabilities, businesses and operations. The contributed assets consist primarily of manufacturing assets and intellectual property associated with the production and retail sale of Big G ready-to-eat cereals, *Progresso* soups and *Old El Paso* products. In exchange for the contribution of these assets, GMC issued the managing membership interest and preferred membership interests to our wholly owned subsidiaries. The managing member directs the business activities and operations of GMC and has fiduciary responsibilities to GMC and its members. Other than rights to vote on certain matters, holders of the preferred membership interests have no right to direct the management of GMC.

In May 2002, one of our wholly owned subsidiaries sold 150,000 Class A preferred membership interests in GMC to an unrelated third-party investor in exchange for $150 million. On October 8, 2004, another of our wholly owned subsidiaries sold 835,000 Series B-1 preferred membership interests in GMC in exchange for $835 million. In connection with the sale of the Series B-1 interests, GMC and its existing members entered into a Third Amended and Restated Limited Liability Company Agreement of GMC (the LLC Agreement), setting forth, among other things, the terms of the Series B-1 and Class A interests held by the third-party investors and the rights of those investors. Currently, all interests in GMC, other than the 150,000 Class A interests and 835,000 Series B-1 interests, but including all managing member interests, are held by our wholly owned subsidiaries.

The Class A interests receive quarterly preferred distributions at a floating rate equal to (i) the sum of three-month LIBOR plus 90 basis points, divided by (ii) 0.965. The LLC Agreement requires that the rate of the distributions on the Class A interests be adjusted by agreement between the third-party investor holding the Class A interests and GMC every five years, beginning in June 2007. If GMC and the investor fail to mutually agree on a new rate of preferred distributions, GMC must remarket the Class A interests to set a new distribution rate. Upon a failed remarketing, the rate over LIBOR will be increased by 75 basis points until the next scheduled remarketing date. GMC, through its managing member, may elect to repurchase all of the Class A interests at any time for an amount equal to the holder's capital account, plus any applicable make-whole amount. Under certain circumstances, GMC also may be required to be dissolved and liquidated, including, without limitation, the bankruptcy of GMC or its subsidiaries, failure to deliver the preferred distributions, failure to comply with portfolio requirements, breaches of certain covenants, lowering of our senior debt rating below either Baa3 by Moody's or BBB by Standard & Poor's, and a failed attempt to remarket the Class A interests as a result of a breach of GMC's obligations to assist in such remarketing. In the event of a liquidation of GMC, each member of GMC would receive the amount of its then capital account balance. The managing member may avoid liquidation in most circumstances by exercising an option to purchase the Class A interests. An election to purchase the preferred membership interests could impact our liquidity by requiring us to refinance the purchase price.

The Series B-1 interests are entitled to receive quarterly preferred distributions at a fixed rate of 4.5 percent per year, which is scheduled to be reset to a new fixed rate through a remarketing in October 2007. Beginning in October 2007, the managing member of GMC may elect to repurchase the Series B-1 interests for an amount equal to the holder's then current capital account balance plus any applicable make-whole amount. GMC is not required to purchase the Series B-1 interests nor may these investors put these interests to us.

Upon the occurrence of certain exchange events (as described below), the Series B-1 interests will be exchanged for shares of our perpetual preferred stock. An exchange will occur upon our senior unsecured debt rating falling below either Ba3 as rated by Moody's Investors Service, Inc. or BB- as rated by Standard & Poor's or Fitch, Inc., our bankruptcy or liquidation, a default on any of our senior indebtedness resulting in an acceleration of indebtedness having an outstanding principal balance in excess of $50 million, failing to pay a dividend on our common stock in any fiscal quarter, or certain liquidating events as set forth in the LLC Agreement.

If GMC fails to make a required distribution to the holders of Series B-1 interests when due, we will be restricted from paying any dividend (other than dividends in the form of shares of common stock) or other distributions on shares of our common or preferred stock, and may not repurchase or redeem shares of our common or preferred stock, until all such accrued and undistributed distributions are paid to the holders of the Series B-1 interests. If the required distributions on the Series B-1 interests remain undistributed for six quarterly distribution periods, the managing member will form a nine-member board of directors to manage GMC. Under these circumstances, the holder of the Series B-1 interests will have the right to appoint one director. Upon the payment of the required distributions, the GMC board of directors will be dissolved. At May 28, 2006, we have made all required distributions to the Series B-1 interests. Upon the occurrence of certain events the Series B-1 interests will be included in our computation of diluted earnings per share as a participating security.

For financial reporting purposes, the assets, liabilities, results of operations and cash flows of GMC are included in our consolidated financial statements. The third-party investors' Class A and Series B-1 interests in GMC are reflected as minority interests on our Consolidated Balance Sheets, and the return to the third party investors is reflected as interest expense, net, in the Consolidated Statements of Earnings.

In fiscal 2003, General Mills Capital, Inc. (GM Capital), a subsidiary, sold $150 million of its Series A preferred stock to an unrelated third-party investor. GM Capital regularly purchases our receivables. These receivables are included in the Consolidated Balance Sheets and the $150 million purchase price for the Series A preferred stock is reflected as minority interest on the Consolidated Balance Sheets. The proceeds from the issuance of the preferred stock were used to reduce short-term debt. The return to the third-party investor is reflected as interest expense, net, in the Consolidated Statements of Earnings.

At May 28, 2006, our cash and cash equivalents included $11 million in GMC and $21 million in GM Capital that are restricted from use for our general corporate purposes pursuant to the terms of our agreements with third-party minority interest investors.

9. Stockholders' Equity

Cumulative preference stock of 5 million shares, without par value, is authorized but unissued.

We had a stockholder rights plan that expired on February 1, 2006.

The Board of Directors has authorized the repurchase, from time to time, of common stock for our treasury, provided that the number of treasury shares shall not exceed 170 million.

In October 2004, we purchased 17 million shares of our common stock from Diageo plc (Diageo) for $750 million, or $45.20 per share. This share repurchase was made in conjunction with Diageo's sale of 33 million additional shares of our common stock in an underwritten public offering.

Concurrently in October 2004, Lehman Brothers Holdings Inc. issued $750 million of notes, which are mandatorily exchangeable for shares of our common stock. In connection with the issuance of those notes, an affiliate of Lehman Brothers entered into a forward purchase contract with us, under which we are obligated to deliver to such affiliate between 14 million and 17 million shares of our common stock, subject to adjustment under certain circumstances. These shares will generally be deliverable by us in October 2007, in exchange for $750 million in cash or, in certain circumstances, securities of an affiliate of Lehman Brothers. We recorded a $43 million fee for this forward purchase contract as an adjustment to Stockholders' Equity.

The following table provides details of Other Comprehensive Income:

In Millions	Pretax Change	Tax (Expense) Benefit	Other Comprehensive Income
Fiscal 2004			
Foreign currency translation	$ 75	$ –	$ 75
Minimum pension liability	51	(19)	32
Other fair value changes:			
Securities	5	(2)	3
Hedge derivatives	24	(9)	15
Reclassifications to earnings:			
Securities	(20)	7	(13)
Hedge derivatives	136	(50)	86
Other Comprehensive Income	$271	$(73)	$198
Fiscal 2005			
Foreign currency translation	$ 75	$ –	$ 75
Minimum pension liability	(35)	13	(22)
Other fair value changes:			
Securities	2	(1)	1
Hedge derivatives	(30)	11	(19)
Reclassifications to earnings:			
Securities	(2)	1	(1)
Hedge derivatives	187	(69)	118
Other Comprehensive Income	$197	$(45)	$152
Fiscal 2006			
Foreign currency translation	$ 73	$ –	$ 73
Minimum pension liability	38	(14)	24
Other fair value changes:			
Securities	2	(1)	1
Hedge derivatives	(13)	5	(8)
Reclassifications to earnings:			
Hedge derivatives	44	(17)	27
Other Comprehensive Income	$144	$(27)	$117

Except for reclassifications to earnings, changes in Other Comprehensive Income are primarily noncash items.

Accumulated Other Comprehensive Income balances, net of tax effects, were as follows:

In Millions	May 28, 2006	May 29, 2005
Foreign currency translation adjustments	$208	$135
Unrealized gain (loss) from:		
Securities	2	1
Hedge derivatives	(57)	(76)
Minimum pension liability	(28)	(52)
Accumulated Other Comprehensive Income	$125	$ 8

10. Stock Plans

We use broad-based stock plans to help ensure management's alignment with our stockholders' interests. As of May 28, 2006, a total of 15,021,864 shares were available for grant in the form of stock options, restricted shares, restricted stock units and shares of common stock under the 2005 Stock Compensation Plan (2005 Plan) through December 31, 2007, and the 2001 Compensation Plan for Nonemployee Directors (2001 Director Plan) through September 30, 2006. Restricted shares and restricted stock units may also be granted under the Executive Incentive Plan (EIP) through September 25, 2010. Stock-based awards now outstanding include some granted under the 1990, 1993, 1995, 1996, 1998 (senior management), 1998 (employee) and 2003 stock plans, under which no further awards may be granted. The stock plans provide for full vesting of options, restricted shares and restricted stock units upon completion of specified service periods or in the event of a change of control. On May 28, 2006, a total of 3,606,659 restricted shares and restricted stock units were outstanding under all plans.

Stock Options Options may be priced at 100 percent or more of the fair market value on the date of grant, and generally vest four years after the date of grant. Options generally expire within 10 years and one month after the date of grant. The 2001 Director Plan allows each nonemployee director to receive upon election and re-election to the Board of Directors options to purchase 10,000 shares of common stock that generally vest one year, and expire within 10 years, after the date of grant.

Information on stock option activity follows:

	Options Exercisable (Thousands)	Weighted Average Exercise Price per Share	Options Outstanding (Thousands)	Weighted Average Exercise Price per Share
Balance at May 25, 2003	37,743	$31.61	74,360	$37.07
Granted			5,180	46.12
Exercised			(9,316)	27.27
Expired			(1,111)	43.06
Balance at May 30, 2004	37,191	$33.73	69,113	$38.97
Granted			4,544	46.94
Exercised			(8,334)	29.27
Expired			(1,064)	45.78
Balance at May 29, 2005	36,506	$36.08	64,259	$40.68
Granted[(a)]			136	46.56
Exercised			(5,572)	32.99
Expired			(620)	45.67
Balance at May 28, 2006	42,071	$39.93	58,203	$41.45

(a) In fiscal 2005 we changed the timing of our annual stock option grant from December to June. As a result, we did not make an annual stock option grant during fiscal 2006. On June 26, 2006, we granted (in thousands) 5,175 stock options at an exercise price of $51.26 per share.

Range of Exercise Price per Share	Options Exercisable (Thousands)	Weighted Average Exercise Price per Share	Options Outstanding (Thousands)	Weighted Average Exercise Price per Share	Weighted Average Remaining Contractual Life (In Years)
Under $30	233	$26.85	233	$26.85	0.16
$30 — $35	13,915	33.45	13,915	33.45	2.77
$35 — $40	6,625	37.42	6,625	37.42	2.26
$40 — $45	10,730	41.33	17,520	42.31	5.19
Over $45	10,569	48.91	19,910	47.79	6.85
	42,071	$39.93	58,203	$41.45	4.83

Restricted Stock Awards Stock and units settled in stock subject to a restricted period and a purchase price, if any (as determined by the Compensation Committee of the Board of Directors), may be granted to key employees under the 2005 Plan. Restricted shares and restricted stock units, up to 50 percent of the value of an individual's cash incentive award, may also be granted through the EIP. Certain restricted share and restricted stock unit awards require the employee to deposit personally owned shares (on a one-for-one basis) with us during the restricted period. Restricted shares and restricted stock units generally vest and become unrestricted four years after the date of grant. Participants are entitled to cash dividends on such awarded shares and units, but the sale or transfer of these shares and units is restricted during the vesting period. Participants holding restricted shares, but not restricted stock units, are also entitled to vote on matters submitted to holders of common stock for a vote. The 2001 Director Plan allows each nonemployee director to receive upon election and re-election to the Board 1,000 restricted stock units that generally vest one year after the date of grant.

Information on restricted stock activity follows:

Fiscal Year	2006	2005	2004
Number of shares awarded[(a)]	629,919	1,497,480	1,738,581
Weighted average price per share	$ 49.75	$ 46.73	$ 46.35

(a) In fiscal 2005 we changed the timing of our annual restricted stock unit grant from December to June. As a result, we did not make an annual restricted stock unit grant during fiscal 2006. On June 26, 2006, we granted 1,614,338 restricted stock units at a price per share of $51.26.

Stock-based compensation expense related to restricted stock awards was $45 million for fiscal 2006, $38 million for fiscal 2005 and $27 million for fiscal 2004.

11. Earnings Per Share

Basic and diluted earnings per share were calculated using the following:

In Millions, Except per Share Data, Fiscal Year	2006	2005	2004
Net earnings – as reported	$1,090	$1,240	$1,055
Interest on contingently convertible debentures, after tax[(a)]	9	20	20
Net Earnings for Diluted Earnings per Share Calculation	$1,099	$1,260	$1,075
Average number of common shares – basic earnings per share	358	371	375
Incremental share effect from:			
Stock options[(b)]	6	8	8
Restricted stock, restricted stock units and other[(b)]	2	1	1
Contingently convertible debentures[(a)]	13	29	29
Average Number of Common Shares – Diluted Earnings per Share	379	409	413
Earnings per Share – Basic	$ 3.05	$ 3.34	$ 2.82
Earnings per Share – Diluted	$ 2.90	$ 3.08	$ 2.60

(a) Shares from contingently convertible debentures are reflected using the if-converted method. On December 12, 2005, we completed a consent solicitation and entered into a supplemental indenture related to our zero coupon convertible debentures. We also made an irrevocable election: (i) to satisfy all future obligations to repurchase debentures solely in cash and (ii) to satisfy all future conversions of debentures (a) solely in cash up to an amount equal to the accreted value of the debentures and (b) at our discretion, in cash, stock or a combination of cash and stock to the extent the conversion value of the debentures exceeds the accreted value. As a result of these actions, no shares of common stock underlying the debentures were considered outstanding after December 12, 2005, for purposes of calculating our diluted earnings per share.

(b) Incremental shares from stock options, restricted stock and restricted stock units are computed by the treasury stock method.

The diluted EPS calculation does not include stock options for 8 million shares in fiscal 2006, 9 million shares in fiscal 2005 and 12 million shares in fiscal 2004 that were considered anti-dilutive because their exercise price was greater than the average market price of our stock during the period.

12. Interest, Net

The components of interest, including distributions to minority interest holders, net are as follows:

In Millions, Fiscal Year	2006	2005	2004
Interest expense	$367	$449	$529
Distributions paid on preferred stock and interests in subsidiaries	60	39	8
Capitalized interest	(1)	(3)	(8)
Interest income	(27)	(30)	(21)
Interest, Net	$399	$455	$508

We made cash interest payments of $378 million in fiscal 2006, $450 million in fiscal 2005 and $497 million in fiscal 2004.

13. Retirement Benefits

Pension Plans We have defined-benefit retirement plans covering most U.S., Canadian and United Kingdom employees. Benefits for salaried employees are based on length of service and final average compensation. The hourly plans include various monthly amounts for each year of credited service. Our funding policy is consistent with the requirements of applicable laws. Our principal domestic retirement plan covering salaried employees has a provision that any excess pension assets would vest in plan participants if the plan is terminated within five years of a change in control.

Other Postretirement Benefit Plans We sponsor plans that provide health-care benefits to the majority of our U.S. and Canadian retirees. The salaried health care benefit plan is contributory, with retiree contributions based on years of service. We fund related trusts for certain employees and retirees on an annual basis and made $95 million of voluntary contributions to these plans in fiscal 2006. Assumed health care cost trend rates are as follows:

Fiscal Year	2006	2005
Health care cost trend rate for next year [(a)]	10.0% and 11.0%	9.0%
Rate to which the cost trend rate is assumed to decline (ultimate rate)	5.2%	5.2%
Year that the rate reaches the ultimate trend rate	2013/2014	2010

(a) In fiscal 2006, we raised our health care cost trend rate for plan participants greater than 65 years of age to 10 percent and for those less than 65 years of age to 11 percent. The year the ultimate trend rate is reached is 2013 for plan participants greater than 65 years of age and 2014 for plan participants less than 65 years of age.

We use our fiscal year-end as a measurement date for all our pension and postretirement benefit plans.

Summarized financial information about pension and other postretirement benefit plans is presented below. For fiscal 2006, the impact of plan amendments on the projected benefit obligation is primarily related to incremental benefits under agreements with the unions representing the hourly workers at certain of our U.S. cereal, dough and foodservice plants covering the four-year period ending April 25, 2010.

	Pension Plans		Other Postretirement Benefit Plans	
In Millions, Fiscal Year End	2006	2005	2006	2005
Change in Plan Assets:				
Fair value at beginning of year	$3,237	$2,850	$ 242	$ 219
Actual return on assets	502	486	38	39
Employer contributions	8	46	95	20
Plan participant contributions	1	1	9	8
Benefit payments	(154)	(146)	(55)	(44)
Fair Value at End of Year	$3,594	$3,237	$ 329	$ 242
Change in Projected Benefit Obligation:				
Benefit obligation at beginning of year	$3,082	$2,578	$ 971	$ 826
Service cost	76	62	18	15
Interest cost	167	167	50	53
Plan amendment	31	1	(4)	–
Curtailment/Other	–	2	1	2
Plan participant contributions	1	1	9	8
Actuarial loss (gain)	(315)	417	(43)	116
Benefits payments from plans	(154)	(146)	(52)	(49)
Projected Benefit Obligation at End of Year	$2,888	$3,082	$ 950	$ 971
Funded Status:				
Plan assets in excess of (less than) benefit obligation	$ 706	$ 155	$(621)	$(729)
Unrecognized net actuarial loss	464	993	317	393
Unrecognized prior service costs (credits)	69	43	(14)	(11)
Net Amount Recognized	$1,239	$1,191	$(318)	$(347)
Amounts Recognized in Consolidated Balance Sheets:				
Prepaid benefit cost	$1,320	$1,239	$ –	$ –
Accrued benefit cost	(131)	(134)	(318)	(347)
Intangible asset	–	3	–	–
Other comprehensive loss - minimum pension liability	50	83	–	–
Net Amount Recognized	$1,239	$1,191	$(318)	$(347)

The accumulated benefit obligation for all defined-benefit plans was $2,689 million at May 28, 2006, and $2,868 million at May 29, 2005.

Plans with accumulated benefit obligations in excess of plan assets are as follows:

	Pension Plans		Other Postretirement Benefit Plans	
In Millions, Fiscal Year End	2006	2005	2006	2005
Projected benefit obligation	$173	$293	N/A	N/A
Accumulated benefit obligation	147	279	$ 950	$ 971
Plan assets at fair value	15	144	329	242

Components of net periodic benefit (income) costs are as follows:

	Pension Plans			Other Postretirement Benefit Plans		
In Millions, Fiscal Year	2006	2005	2004	2006	2005	2004
Service cost	$ 76	$ 62	$ 70	$ 18	$ 15	$ 16
Interest cost	167	167	160	50	53	47
Expected return on plan assets	(323)	(301)	(300)	(24)	(22)	(22)
Amortization of losses	37	10	18	19	14	13
Amortization of prior service costs (credits)	5	6	5	(2)	(2)	(2)
Settlement or curtailment losses	–	2	–	2	2	–
Net periodic benefit (income) costs	$ (38)	$ (54)	$ (47)	$ 63	$ 60	$ 52

Assumptions Weighted-average assumptions used to determine benefit obligations are as follows:

	Pension Plans		Other Postretirement Benefit Plans	
Fiscal Year End	2006	2005	2006	2005
Discount rate	6.55%	5.55%	6.50%	5.50%
Rate of salary increases	4.4	4.4	–	–

Weighted-average assumptions used to determine net periodic benefit (income) costs are as follows:

	Pension Plans			Other Postretirement Benefit Plans		
Fiscal Year	2006	2005	2004	2006	2005	2004
Discount rate	5.55%	6.65%	6.00%	5.50%	6.65%	6.00%
Rate of salary increases	4.4	4.4	4.4	–	–	–
Expected long-term rate of return on plan assets	9.6	9.6	9.6	9.6	9.6	9.6

Our expected rate of return on plan assets is determined by our asset allocation, our historical long-term investment performance, our estimate of future long-term returns by asset class (using input from our actuaries, investment services and investment managers), and long-term inflation assumptions.

Weighted-average asset allocations for the past two fiscal years for our pension and other postretirement benefit plans are as follows:

	Pension Plans		Other Postretirement Benefit Plans	
Fiscal Year	2006	2005	2006	2005
Asset Category:				
U.S. equities	34%	37%	24%	40%
International equities	20	18	16	17
Private equities	10	7	7	5
Fixed income	22	26	43	28
Real assets	14	12	10	10
Total	100%	100%	100%	100%

The investment objective for the U.S. pension and other postretirement benefit plans is to secure the benefit obligations to participants at a reasonable cost to us. The goal is to optimize the long-term return on plan assets at a moderate level of risk. The pension and postretirement portfolios are broadly diversified across asset classes. Within asset classes, the portfolios are further diversified across investment styles and investment organizations. For the pension and other postretirement plans, the long-term investment policy allocations are: 30 percent to U.S. equities, 20 percent to international equities, 10 percent to private equities, 30 percent to fixed income and 10 percent to real assets (real estate, energy and timber). The actual allocations to these asset classes may vary tactically around the long-term policy allocations based on relative market valuations.

Contributions and Future Benefit Payments We expect to contribute $15 million to our pension plans and other postretirement benefit plans in fiscal 2007. Estimated benefit payments, which reflect expected future service, as appropriate, are expected to be paid as follows:

In Millions, Fiscal Year	Pension Plans	Other Postretirement Benefit Plans Gross	Medicare Subsidy Receipts
2007	$ 157	$ 54	$ 6
2008	161	56	7
2009	165	59	7
2010	171	62	8
2011	177	66	8
2012 – 2016	1,011	367	49

Certain international operations have defined-benefit pension plans that are not presented in the tables above. These international operations had prepaid pension assets of less than $1 million at the end of fiscal 2006 and 2005, and they had accrued pension plan liabilities of $4 million at the end of fiscal 2006 and $7 million at the end of fiscal 2005. Pension expense associated with these plans was $3 million for fiscal 2006, $6 million for fiscal 2005 and $3 million for fiscal 2004.

Defined Contribution Plans The General Mills Savings Plan is a defined contribution plan that covers salaried and nonunion employees. It had net assets of $2,031 million as of May 28, 2006, and $1,797 million as of May 29, 2005. This plan is a 401(k) savings plan that includes a number of investment funds and an Employee Stock Ownership Plan (ESOP). Our total expense related to defined-contribution plans recognized was $46 million in fiscal 2006, $17 million in fiscal 2005 and $20 million in fiscal 2004.

The ESOP's only assets are our common stock and temporary cash balances. The ESOP's share of the total defined contribution expense was $38 million in fiscal 2006, $11 million in fiscal 2005 and $15 million in fiscal 2004. The ESOP's expense is calculated by the "shares allocated" method.

The ESOP uses our common stock to convey benefits to employees and, through increased stock ownership, to further align employee interests with those of stockholders. We match a percentage of employee contributions to the General Mills Savings Plan with a base match plus a variable year-end match that depends on annual results. Employees receive our match in the form of common stock.

The ESOP originally purchased our common stock principally with funds borrowed from third parties and guaranteed by us. The ESOP shares are included in net shares outstanding for the purposes of calculating earnings per share. The ESOP's third-party debt is described in Note Seven.

We treat cash dividends paid to the ESOP the same as other dividends. Dividends received on leveraged shares (i.e., all shares originally purchased with the debt proceeds) are used for debt service, while dividends received on unleveraged shares are passed through to participants.

Our cash contribution to the ESOP is calculated so as to pay off enough debt to release sufficient shares to make our match. The ESOP uses our cash contributions to the plan, plus the dividends received on the ESOP's leveraged shares, to make principal and interest payments on the ESOP's debt. As loan payments are made, shares become unencumbered by debt and are committed to be allocated. The ESOP allocates shares to individual employee accounts on the basis of the match of employee payroll savings (contributions), plus reinvested dividends received on previously allocated shares. The ESOP incurred interest expense of less than $1 million in fiscal 2006, 2005 and 2004. The ESOP used dividends of $4 million in fiscal 2006, $4 million in fiscal 2005 and $5 million in fiscal 2004, along with our contributions of less than $1 million in fiscal 2006, 2005 and 2004 to make interest and principal payments.

The number of shares of our common stock in the ESOP is summarized as follows:

Number of Shares, in Thousands, Fiscal Year Ended	May 28, 2006	May 29, 2005
Unreleased shares	150	280
Allocated to participants	5,187	5,334
Total Shares	5,337	5,614

Executive Incentive Plan Our Executive Incentive Plan provides incentives to key employees who have the greatest potential to contribute to current earnings and successful future operations. All employees at the level of vice president and above participate in the plan. These awards are approved by the Compensation Committee of the Board of Directors, which consists solely of independent, outside directors. Awards are based on performance against pre-established goals approved by the Committee. Profit-sharing expense was $23 million, $17 million and $16 million in fiscal 2006, 2005 and 2004, respectively.

14. Income Taxes

The components of Earnings before Income Taxes and After-tax Earnings from Joint Ventures and the corresponding income taxes thereon are as follows:

In Millions, Fiscal Year	2006	2005	2004
Earnings before Income Taxes and After-tax Earnings from Joint Ventures:			
U.S.	$1,380	$1,723	$1,408
Foreign	187	92	101
Total Earnings before Income Taxes and After-tax Earnings from Joint Ventures	$1,567	$1,815	$1,509
Income taxes:			
Currently payable:			
Federal	$ 395	$ 557	$ 366
State and local	56	60	31
Foreign	64	38	22
Total Current	515	655	419
Deferred:			
Federal	38	14	85
State and local	(4)	(3)	7
Foreign	(8)	(2)	17
Total Deferred	26	9	109
Total Income Taxes	$ 541	$ 664	$ 528

We paid income taxes of $321 million in fiscal 2006, $227 million in fiscal 2005 and $225 million in fiscal 2004.

The following table reconciles the U.S. statutory income tax rate with our effective income tax rate:

Fiscal Year	2006	2005	2004
U.S. statutory rate	35.0%	35.0%	35.0%
State and local income taxes, net of federal tax benefits	2.6	2.0	1.6
Divestitures, net	–	1.8	–
Other, net	(3.1)	(2.2)	(1.6)
Effective Income Tax Rate	34.5%	36.6%	35.0%

The tax effects of temporary differences that give rise to deferred tax assets and liabilities are as follows:

In Millions	May 28, 2006	May 29, 2005
Accrued liabilities	$ 189	$ 180
Restructuring and other exit charges	8	7
Compensation and employee benefits	318	316
Unrealized hedge losses	45	72
Unrealized losses	850	855
Tax credit carry forwards	51	76
Other	19	14
Gross deferred tax assets	1,480	1,520
Valuation allowance	858	855
Net deferred tax assets	622	665
Brands	1,292	1,322
Depreciation	257	263
Prepaid pension asset	482	450
Intangible assets	75	58
Tax lease transactions	61	64
Zero coupon convertible debentures	18	73
Other	77	78
Gross deferred tax liabilities	2,262	2,308
Net Deferred Tax Liability	$1,640	$1,643

Of the total valuation allowance of $858 million, $768 million relates to a deferred tax asset for losses recorded as part of the Pillsbury acquisition. In the future, when tax benefits related to these losses are finalized, the reduction in the valuation allowance will be allocated to reduce goodwill. Of the remaining valuation allowance, $66 million relates to state and foreign operating loss carry forwards. In the future, if tax benefits are realized related to the operating losses, the reduction in the valuation allowance will reduce tax expense. At May 28, 2006, we believe it is more likely than not that the remainder of our deferred tax asset is realizable.

The carry forward period on the net tax benefited amounts of our foreign loss carry forwards are as follows: $20 million do not expire; $5 million will expire in 2007 and 2008; $21 million will expire between 2009 and 2014; and $16 million will expire in 2018.

We have not recognized a deferred tax liability for unremitted earnings of $1.03 billion from our foreign operations because we do not expect those earnings to become taxable to us in the foreseeable future.

15. Leases and Other Commitments

An analysis of rent expense by property leased follows:

In Millions, Fiscal Year	2006	2005	2004
Warehouse space	$ 44	$ 41	$42
Equipment	27	30	20
Other	35	37	34
Total Rent Expense	$106	$108	$96

Some leases require payment of property taxes, insurance and maintenance costs in addition to the rent payments. Contingent and escalation rent in excess of minimum rent payments and sublease income netted in rent expense were insignificant.

Noncancelable future lease commitments (in millions) are: $92 in fiscal 2007; $75 in fiscal 2008; $67 in fiscal 2009; $52 in fiscal 2010; $37 in fiscal 2011; and $85 after fiscal 2011, with a cumulative total of $408. These future lease commitments will be partially offset by estimated future sublease receipts of $55 million.

We are contingently liable under guarantees and comfort letters for $171 million. The guarantees and comfort letters are principally issued to support borrowing arrangements, primarily for our joint ventures.

We are involved in various claims, including environmental matters, arising in the ordinary course of business. In the opinion of management, the ultimate disposition of these matters, either individually or in aggregate, will not have a material adverse effect on our financial position or results of operations.

16. Business Segment and Geographic Information

We operate exclusively in the consumer foods industry, with multiple operating segments organized generally by product categories. We aggregate our operating segments into three reportable segments by type of customer and geographic region as follows: U.S. Retail, 69 percent of our fiscal 2006 consolidated net sales; International, 16 percent of our fiscal 2006 consolidated net sales; and Bakeries and Foodservice, 15 percent of our fiscal 2006 consolidated net sales.

U.S. Retail reflects business with a wide variety of grocery stores, mass merchandisers, club stores, specialty stores and drug, dollar and discount chains operating throughout the United States. Our major product categories in this business segment are ready-to-eat cereals, meals, refrigerated and frozen dough products, baking products, snacks, yogurt and organic foods. Our International segment is made up of retail businesses outside of the United States, including a retail business in Canada that largely mirrors our U.S. Retail product mix, and foodservice businesses outside of the United States and Canada. Our Bakeries and Foodservice segment consists of products marketed throughout the United States and Canada to retail and wholesale bakeries, commercial and noncommercial foodservice distributors and operators, restaurants, and convenience stores.

During fiscal 2006, one customer, Wal-Mart Stores, Inc. (Wal-Mart), accounted for approximately 18 percent of our consolidated net sales and 24 percent of our sales in the U.S. Retail segment. No other customer accounted for 10 percent or more of our consolidated net sales. At May 28,

2006, Wal-Mart accounted for 17 percent of our trade receivables invoiced in the U.S. Retail segment. The top five customers in our U.S. Retail segment accounted for approximately 47 percent of its fiscal 2006 net sales, and the top five customers in our Bakeries and Foodservice segment accounted for approximately 36 percent of its fiscal 2006 net sales.

Our management reviews operating results to evaluate segment performance. Operating profit for the reportable segments excludes unallocated corporate items (including a foreign currency transaction gain of $2 million in fiscal 2006 and foreign currency transaction losses of $6 million and $2 million in fiscal 2005 and 2004, respectively); net interest; restructuring and other exit costs; gain on divestitures; debt repurchase costs; income taxes; and after-tax earnings from joint ventures, as these items are centrally managed at the corporate level and are excluded from the measure of segment profitability reviewed by management. Under our supply chain organization, our manufacturing, warehouse and distribution activities are substantially integrated across our operations in order to maximize efficiency and productivity. As a result, fixed assets, capital expenditures for long-lived assets, and depreciation and amortization expenses are neither maintained nor available by operating segment. Transactions between reportable segments were not material in the periods presented.

In Millions, Fiscal Year	2006	2005	2004
Net Sales:			
U.S. Retail	$ 8,024	$ 7,779	$ 7,763
International	1,837	1,725	1,550
Bakeries and Foodservice	1,779	1,740	1,757
Total	$11,640	$11,244	$11,070
Segment Operating Profit:			
U.S. Retail	$ 1,779	$ 1,719	$ 1,809
International	201	171	119
Bakeries and Foodservice	139	134	132
Total	2,119	2,024	2,060
Unallocated corporate items	(123)	(32)	(17)
Interest, net	(399)	(455)	(508)
Restructuring and other exit costs	(30)	(84)	(26)
Divestitures – gain	–	499	–
Debt repurchase costs	–	(137)	–
Earnings before income taxes and after-tax earnings from joint ventures	1,567	1,815	1,509
Income taxes	(541)	(664)	(528)
After-tax earnings from joint ventures	64	89	74
Net Earnings	$ 1,090	$ 1,240	$ 1,055

The following table provides net sales information for our reportable segments:

In Millions, Fiscal Year	2006	2005	2004
U.S. Retail:			
Big G Cereals	$ 1,854	$ 1,874	$ 1,990
Meals	1,794	1,676	1,658
Pillsbury USA	1,538	1,546	1,518
Yoplait	1,096	962	893
Snacks	956	913	909
Baking Products	643	609	586
Other	143	199	209
Total U.S. Retail	8,024	7,779	7,763
International:			
Europe	629	622	557
Canada	566	514	470
Asia/Pacific	403	370	324
Latin America/Other	239	219	199
Total International	1,837	1,725	1,550
Bakeries and Foodservice	1,779	1,740	1,757
Total	$11,640	$11,244	$11,070

The following table provides financial information identified by geographic area:

In Millions, Fiscal Year	2006	2005	2004
Net sales:			
U.S.	$ 9,739	$ 9,447	$ 9,441
Non-U.S.	1,901	1,797	1,629
Total	$11,640	$11,244	$11,070

In Millions	May 28, 2006	May 29, 2005
Long-lived assets:		
U.S.	$2,584	$2,722
Non-U.S.	413	389
Total	$2,997	$3,111

17. Supplemental Information

The components of certain balance sheet accounts are as follows:

In Millions	May 28, 2006	May 29, 2005
Receivables:		
From customers	$ 931	$ 910
Other	163	143
Less allowance for doubtful accounts	(18)	(19)
Total	$1,076	$1,034

In Millions	May 28, 2006	May 29, 2005
Inventories:		
At the lower of cost, determined on the FIFO or weighted average cost methods, or market:		
Raw materials and packaging	$ 226	$ 214
Finished goods	813	795
Grain	78	73
Excess of FIFO or weighted-average cost over LIFO cost	(62)	(45)
Total	$1,055	$1,037

Inventories of $739 million at May 28, 2006, and $758 million at May 29, 2005, were valued at LIFO.

In Millions	May 28, 2006	May 29, 2005
Land, Buildings and Equipment:		
Land	$ 54	$ 54
Buildings	1,430	1,396
Equipment	3,859	3,722
Capitalized software	211	196
Construction in progress	252	302
Total land, buildings and equipment	5,806	5,670
Less accumulated depreciation	(2,809)	(2,559)
Total	$ 2,997	$ 3,111
Other Assets:		
Prepaid pension	$ 1,320	$ 1,239
Marketable securities, at market	25	24
Investments in and advances to joint ventures	186	211
Miscellaneous	244	210
Total	$ 1,775	$ 1,684

In Millions	May 28, 2006	May 29, 2005
Other Current Liabilities:		
Accrued payroll	$ 308	$ 240
Accrued interest	152	134
Accrued taxes	743	588
Miscellaneous	150	149
Total	$1,353	$1,111
Other Noncurrent Liabilities:		
Interest rate swaps	$ 196	$ 221
Accrued compensation and benefits	638	658
Miscellaneous	90	88
Total	$ 924	$ 967

Certain statement of earnings amounts are as follows:

In Millions, Fiscal Year	2006	2005	2004
Depreciation, including depreciation of capitalized software	$424	$443	$399
Shipping costs associated with the distribution of finished product to our customers (recorded in selling, general and administrative expense)	474	388	352
Research and development	173	168	158
Advertising (including production and communication costs)	515	477	512

18. Quarterly Data (Unaudited)

Summarized quarterly data for fiscal 2006 and 2005 follows:

In Millions, Except per Share and Market Price Amounts	First Quarter		Second Quarter		Third Quarter		Fourth Quarter	
	2006	2005	2006	2005	2006	2005	2006	2005
Net sales	$2,662	$2,585	$3,273	$3,168	$2,860	$2,772	$2,845	$2,719
Gross margin	1,105	1,004	1,345	1,279	1,114	1,077	1,110	1,050
Net earnings	252	183	370	367	246	230	222	460[(a)]
Net earnings per share:								
Basic	.69	.48	1.04	.99	.69	.63	.62	1.25
Diluted	.64	.45	.97	.92	.68	.58	.61	1.14
Dividends per share	.33	.31	.33	.31	.34	.34	.34	.31
Market price of common stock:								
High	51.45	48.15	49.38	47.63	50.49	53.89	52.16	52.86
Low	45.49	44.72	44.67	43.01	47.05	44.96	48.51	48.05

(a) Net earnings in the fourth quarter of fiscal 2005 include a pretax $499 million gain from the dispositions of our 40.5 percent interest in SVE and the Lloyd's barbecue business, and $137 million of pretax debt repurchase expenses. See Notes Two and Seven.

Gross margin is defined as net sales less cost of sales.

GLOSSARY

A

Accelerated depreciation A higher amount of depreciation is recorded in the early years and a lower amount in the later years. (p. 384)
Account Record used to accumulate amounts for each individual asset, liability, revenue, expense, and component of owners' equity. (p. 113)
Account receivable A receivable arising from the sale of goods or services with a verbal promise to pay. (p. 336)
Accounting The process of identifying, measuring, and communicating economic information to various users. (p. 11)
Accounting controls Procedures concerned with safeguarding the assets or the reliability of the financial statements. (p. 311)
Accounting cycle A series of steps performed each period and culminating with the preparation of a set of financial statements. (p. 177)
Accounting system Methods and records used to accurately report an entity's transactions and to maintain accountability for its assets and liabilities. (p. 310)
Accounts payable Amounts owed for inventory, goods, or services acquired in the normal course of business. (p. 427)
Accounts receivable turnover ratio A measure of the number of times accounts receivable are collected in a period. (p. 669)
Accrual Cash has not yet been paid or received, but expense has been incurred or revenue earned. (p. 171)
Accrual basis A system of accounting in which revenues are recognized when earned and expenses when incurred. (p. 156)
Accrued asset An asset resulting from the recognition of a revenue before the receipt of cash. (p. 171)
Accrued liability A liability resulting from the recognition of an expense before the payment of cash. (pp. 171, 431)
Acid-test or quick ratio A stricter test of liquidity than the current ratio; excludes inventory and prepayments from the numerator. (p. 668)
Acquisition cost The amount that includes all of the cost normally necessary to acquire an asset and prepare it for its intended use. (p. 379)
Additional paid-in capital The amount received for the issuance of stock in excess of the par value of the stock. (p. 529)
Adjusting entries Journal entries made at the end of a period by a company using the accrual basis of accounting. (p. 162)
Administrative controls Procedures concerned with efficient operation of the business and adherence to managerial policies. (p. 311)
Aging schedule A form used to categorize the various individual accounts receivable according to the length of time each has been outstanding. (p. 341)
Allowance for doubtful accounts A contra-asset account used to reduce accounts receivable to its net realizable value. (p. 339)
Allowance method A method of estimating bad debts on the basis of either the net credit sales of the period or the accounts receivable at the end of the period. (p. 339)
American Accounting Association The professional organization for accounting educators. (p. A-4)
American Institute of Certified Public Accountants (AICPA) The professional organization for certified public accountants. (p. 25)
Annuity A series of payments of equal amounts. (p. 443)
Asset A future economic benefit. (p. 9)
Asset turnover ratio The relationship between net sales and average total assets. (p. 676)
Audit committee Board of directors subset that acts as a direct contact between stockholders and the independent accounting firm. (p. 308)
Auditing The process of examining the financial statements and the underlying records of a company in order to render an opinion as to whether the statements are fairly represented. (pp. 25, A-2)
Auditors' report The opinion rendered by a public accounting firm concerning the fairness of the presentation of the financial statements. (pp. 83, A-2)
Authorized shares The maximum number of shares a corporation may issue as indicated in the corporate charter. (p. 528)

B

Balance sheet The financial statement that summarizes the assets, liabilities, and owners' equity at a specific point in time. (p. 15)
Bank reconciliation A form used by the accountant to reconcile the balance shown on the bank statement for a particular account with the balance shown in the accounting records. (p. 300)
Bank statement A detailed list, provided by the bank, of all the activity for a particular account during the month. (p. 299)
Blind receiving report Form used by the receiving department to account for the quantity and condition of merchandise received from a supplier. (p. 319)
Board of directors Group composed of key officers of a corporation and outside members responsible for general oversight of the affairs of the entity. (p. 308)
Bond A certificate that represents a corporation's promise to repay a certain amount of money and interest in the future. (p. 7)
Bond issue price The present value of the annuity of interest payments plus the present value of the principal. (p. 485)
Book value The original cost of an asset minus the amount of accumulated depreciation. (p. 383)
Book value per share Total stockholders equity divided by the number of shares of common stock outstanding. (p. 545)
Business All the activities necessary to provide the members of an economic system with goods and services. (p. 4)
Business entity An organization operated to earn a profit. (p. 6)

C

Callable bonds Bonds that may be redeemed or retired before their specified due date. (p. 483)
Callable feature Allows the firm to eliminate a class of stock by paying the stockholders a specified amount. (p. 531)
Capital expenditure A cost that improves the asset and is added to the asset account. (p. 389)

Capital lease A lease that is recorded as an asset by the lessee. (p. 495)
Capital stock Indicates the owners' contributions to a corporation. (p. 8)
Capitalization of interest Interest on constructed assets is added to the asset account. (p. 382)
Carrying value The face value of a bond plus the amount of unamortized premium or minus the amount of unamortized discount. (p. 489)
Cash basis A system of accounting in which revenues are recognized when cash is received and expenses when cash is paid. (p. 156)
Cash equivalent An investment that is readily convertible to a known amount of cash and a maturity to the investor of three months or less. (pp. 297, 589)
Cash flow from operations to capital expenditures ratio A measure of the ability of a company to finance long-term asset acquisitions with cash from operations. (p. 674)
Cash flow from operations to current liabilities ratio A measure of the ability to pay current debts from operating cash flows. (p. 669)
Cash to cash operating cycle The length of time from the purchase of inventory to the collection of any receivable from the sale. (p. 671)
Certified Public Accountant (CPA) The designation for an individual who has passed a uniform exam administered by the AICPA and met other requirements as determined by individual states. (p. 25)
Change in estimate A change in the life of the asset or in its residual value. (p. 387)
Chart of accounts A numerical list of all the accounts used by a company. (p. 114)
Closing entries Journal entries made at the end of the period to return the balance in all nominal accounts to zero and transfer the net income or loss and the dividends to Retained Earnings. (p. 178)
Comparability For accounting information, the quality that allows a user to analyze two or more companies and look for similarities and differences. (p. 58)
Compound interest Interest calculated on the principal plus previous amounts of interest. (p. 440)
Comprehensive income The total change in net assets from all sources except investments by or distributions to the owners. (p. 544)
Conservatism The practice of using the least optimistic estimate when two estimates of amounts are about equally likely. (p. 59)
Consistency For accounting information, the quality that allows a user to compare two or more accounting periods for a single company. (p. 58)
Contingent assets An existing condition for which the outcome is not known but by which the company stands to gain. (p. 437)
Contingent liability An existing condition for which the outcome is not known but depends on some future event. (p. 434)
Contra account An account with a balance that is opposite that of a related account. (p. 164)
Control account The general ledger account that is supported by a subsidiary ledger. (p. 337)
Controller The chief accounting officer for a company. (p. A-1)
Convertible feature Allows preferred stock to be exchanged for common stock. (p. 531)
Corporation A form of entity organized under the laws of a particular state; ownership evidenced by shares of stock. (p. 7)
Cost of goods available for sale Beginning inventory plus cost of goods purchased. (p. 226)
Cost of goods sold Cost of goods available for sale minus ending inventory. (p. 227)
Cost principle Assets recorded at the cost to acquire them. (p. 22)
Credit An entry on the right side of an account. (p. 116)
Credit card draft A multiple-copy document used by a company that accepts a credit card for a sale. (p. 349)
Credit memoranda Additions on a bank statement for such items as interest paid on the account and notes collected by the bank for the customer. (p. 301)
Creditor Someone to whom a company or person has a debt. (p. 9)
Cumulative feature The right to dividends in arrears before the current-year dividend is distributed. (p. 531)
Current asset An asset that is expected to be realized in cash or sold or consumed during the operating cycle or within one year if the cycle is shorter than one year. (p. 62)
Current liability An obligation that will be satisfied within the next operating cycle or within one year if the cycle is shorter than one year. (pp. 64, 426)
Current maturities of long-term debt The portion of a long-term liability that will be paid within one year. (p. 429)
Current ratio Current assets divided by current liabilities. (pp. 68, 668)
Current value The amount of cash, or its equivalent, that could be received by selling an asset currently. (p. 153)

D

Debenture bonds Bonds that are not backed by specific collateral. (p. 482)
Debit An entry on the left side of an account. (p. 116)
Debit memoranda Deductions on a bank statement for such items as NSF checks and various service charges. (p. 301)
Debt securities Bonds issued by corporations and governmental bodies as a form of borrowing. (p. 351)
Debt service coverage ratio A statement of cash flow measure of the ability of a company to meet its interest and principal payments. (p. 673)
Debt-to-equity ratio The ratio of total liabilities to total stockholders' equity. (p. 672)
Deferral Cash has either been paid or received, but expense or revenue has not yet been recognized. (p. 170)
Deferred expense An asset resulting from the payment of cash before the incurrence of expense. (p. 170)
Deferred revenue A liability resulting from the receipt of cash before the recognition of revenue. (p. 171)
Deferred tax The account used to reconcile the difference between the amount recorded as income tax expense and the amount that is payable as income tax. (p. 504)
Deposit in transit A deposit recorded on the books but not yet reflected on the bank statement. (p. 299)
Depreciation The process of allocating the cost of a long-term tangible asset over its useful life. (pp. 58, 383)
Direct method For preparing the Operating Activities section of the statement of cash flows, the approach in which cash receipts and cash payments are reported. (p. 594)
Direct write-off method The recognition of bad debts expense at the point an account is written off as uncollectible. (p. 338)
Discontinued operations A line item on the income statement to reflect any gains or losses from the disposal of a segment of the business as well as any net income or loss from operating that segment. (p. 683)
Discount The excess of the face value of bonds over the issue price. (p. 486)
Discount on notes payable A contra liability that represents interest deducted from a loan in advance. (p. 428)
Discounting The process of selling a promissory note. (p. 350)
Dividend payout ratio The annual dividend amount divided by the annual net income. (pp. 536, 680)
Dividend yield ratio The relationship between dividends and the market price of a company's stock. (p. 680)
Dividends A distribution of the net income of a business to its owners. (p. 17)
Double-declining-balance method Depreciation is recorded at twice the straight-line rate, but the balance is reduced each period. (p. 384)

Double-entry system A system of accounting in which every transaction is recorded with equal debits and credits and the accounting equation is kept in balance. (p. 118)

E

Earnings per share A company's bottom line stated on a per-share basis. (p. 678)
Economic entity concept The assumption that a single, identifiable unit must be accounted for in all situations. (p. 6)
Effective interest method of amortization The process of transferring a portion of the premium or discount to interest expense; this method results in a constant effective interest rate. (p. 489)
Equity securities Securities issued by corporations as a form of ownership in the business. (p. 351)
Estimated liability A contingent liability that is accrued and reflected on the balance sheet. (p. 435)
Event A happening of consequence to an entity. (p. 106)
Expenses Outflows of assets or incurrences of liabilities resulting from delivering goods, rendering services, or carrying out other activities. (pp. 9, 161)
External event An event involving interaction between an entity and its environment. (p. 106)
Extraordinary item A line item on the income statement to reflect any gains or losses that arise from an event that is both unusual in nature and infrequent in occurrence. (p. 683)

F

Face rate of interest The rate of interest on the bond certificate. (p. 484)
Face value The principal amount of the bond as stated on the bond certificate. (p. 482)
FIFO method An inventory costing method that assigns the most recent costs to ending inventory. (p. 239)
Financial accounting The branch of accounting concerned with the preparation of financial statements for outsider use. (p. 11)
Financial Accounting Standards Board (FASB) The group in the private sector with authority to set accounting standards. (p. 25)
Financing activities Activities concerned with the raising and repayment of funds in the form of debt and equity. (p. 591)
Finished goods A manufacturer's inventory that is complete and ready for sale. (p. 221)
FOB destination point Terms that require the seller to pay for the cost of shipping the merchandise to the buyer. (p. 231)
FOB shipping point Terms that require the buyer to pay for the shipping costs. (p. 231)
Future value of a single amount Amount accumulated at a future time from a single payment or investment. (p. 441)
Future value of an annuity Amount accumulated in the future when a series of payments is invested and accrues interest. (p. 444)

G

Gain on Sale of Asset The excess of the selling price over the asset's book value. (p. 392)
Gain or loss on redemption The difference between the carrying value and the redemption price at the time bonds are redeemed. (p. 493)
General journal The journal used in place of a specialized journal. (p. 122)
General ledger A book, file, hard drive, or other device containing all the accounts. (p. 114)
Generally accepted accounting principles (GAAP) The various methods, rules, practices, and other procedures that have evolved over time in response to the need to regulate the preparation of financial statements. (p. 23)
Going concern The assumption that an entity is not in the process of liquidation and that it will continue indefinitely. (p. 23)
Goodwill The excess of the purchase price of a business over the total market value of identifiable assets. (p. 394)
Gross profit Sales less cost of goods sold. (pp. 70, 223)
Gross profit method A technique used to establish an estimate of the cost of inventory stolen, destroyed, or otherwise damaged or of the amount of inventory on hand at an interim date. (p. 252)
Gross profit ratio Gross profit to net sales. (pp. 233, 666)

H

Historical cost The amount paid for an asset and used as a basis for recognizing it on the balance sheet and carrying it on later balance sheets. (p. 153)
Horizontal analysis A comparison of financial statement items over a period of time. (p. 658)

I

Income statement A statement that summarizes revenues and expenses. (p. 16)
Indirect method For preparing the Operating Activities section of the statement of cash flows, the approach in which net income is reconciled to net cash flow from operations. (p. 594)
Intangible assets Assets with no physical properties. (p. 393)
Interest The difference between the principal amount of the note and its maturity value. (p. 347)
Interim statements Financial statements prepared monthly, quarterly, or at other intervals less than a year in duration. (p. 180)
Internal audit staff Department responsible for monitoring and evaluating the internal control system. (p. 312)
Internal auditing The department responsible in a company for the review and appraisal of its accounting and administrative controls. (p. A-2)
Internal control report A report, required by Section 404 of Sarbanes-Oxley Act, to be included in a company's annual report, in which management assesses the effectiveness of the internal control structure. (p. 307)
Internal control system Policies and procedures necessary to ensure the safeguarding of an entity's assets, the reliability of its accounting records, and the accomplishment of overall company objectives. (p. 307)
Internal event An event occurring entirely within an entity. (p. 106)
International Accounting Standards Board (IASB) The organization formed to develop worldwide accounting standards. (p. 25)
Inventory profit The portion of the gross profit that results from holding inventory during a period of rising prices. (p. 244)
Inventory turnover ratio A measure of the number of times inventory is sold during a period. (pp. 254, 671)
Investing activities Activities concerned with the acquisition and disposal of long-term assets. (p. 591)
Invoice Form sent by the seller to the buyer as evidence of a sale. (p. 318)
Invoice approval form Form the accounting department uses before making payment to document the accuracy of all the information about a purchase. (p. 319)
Issued shares The number of shares sold or distributed to stockholders. (p. 529)

J

Journal A chronological record of transactions, also known as the book of original entry. (p. 121)
Journalizing The act of recording journal entries. (p. 122)

L

Land improvements Costs that are related to land but that have a limited life. (p. 382)

Leverage The use of borrowed funds and amounts contributed by preferred stockholders to earn an overall return higher than the cost of these funds. (p. 678)

Liability An obligation of a business. (p. 8)

LIFO conformity rule The IRS requirement that if LIFO is used on the tax return, it must also be used in reporting income to stockholders. (p. 242)

LIFO liquidation The result of selling more units than are purchased during the period, which can have negative tax consequences if a company is using LIFO. (p. 242)

LIFO method An inventory method that assigns the most recent costs to cost of goods sold. (p. 239)

LIFO reserve The excess of the value of a company's inventory stated at FIFO over the value stated at LIFO. (p. 243)

Liquidity The nearness to cash of the assets and liabilities. (pp. 67, 667)

Long-term liability An obligation that will be settled within one year or the current operating cycle. (p. 480)

Loss on Sale of Asset The amount by which selling price is less than book value. (p. 393)

Lower-of-cost-or-market (LCM) rule A conservative inventory valuation approach that is an attempt to anticipate declines in the value of inventory before its actual sale. (p. 248)

M

Maker The party that agrees to repay the money for a promissory note at some future date. (p. 346)

Management accounting The branch of accounting concerned with providing management with information to facilitate planning and control. (p. 11)

Market rate of interest The rate that investors could obtain by investing in other bonds that are similar to the issuing firm's bonds. (p. 484)

Market value per share The selling price of the stock as indicated by the most recent transactions. (p. 548)

Matching principle The association of revenue of a period with all of the costs necessary to generate that revenue. (p. 160)

Materiality The magnitude of an accounting information omission or misstatement that will affect the judgment of someone relying on the information. (p. 59)

Maturity date The date that the promissory note is due. (p. 347)

Maturity value The amount of cash the maker is to pay the payee on the maturity date of the note. (p. 347)

Merchandise Inventory The account wholesalers and retailers use to report inventory held for resale. (p. 221)

Monetary unit The yardstick used to measure amounts in financial statements; the dollar in the United States. (p. 23)

Moving average The name given to an average cost method when it is used with a perpetual inventory system. (p. 261)

Multiple-step income statement An income statement that shows classifications of revenues and expenses as well as important subtotals. (p. 70)

N

Net income The excess of revenues over expenses. (p. 17)

Net sales Sales revenue less sales returns and allowances and sales discounts. (p. 223)

Nominal accounts The name given to revenue, expense, and dividend accounts because they are temporary and are closed at the end of the period. (p. 178)

Nonbusiness entity Organization operated for some purpose other than to earn a profit. (p. 7)

Note receivable An asset resulting from the acceptance of a promissory note from another company. (p. 346)

Note payable A liability resulting from the signing of a promissory note. (pp. 346, 428)

Number of days' sales in inventory A measure of how long it takes to sell inventory. (pp. 256, 671)

Number of days' sales in receivables A measure of the average age of accounts receivable. (p. 670)

O

Operating activities Activities concerned with the acquisition and sale of products and services. (p. 591)

Operating cycle The period of time between the purchase of inventory and collection of any receivable from the sale of the inventory. (p. 61)

Operating lease A lease that does not meet any of the four criteria and is not recorded as an asset by the lessee. (p. 495)

Outstanding check A check written by a company but not yet presented to the bank for payment. (p. 299)

Outstanding shares The number of shares issued less the number of shares held as treasury stock. (p. 529)

Owners' equity The owners' claim on the assets of an entity. (p. 15)

P

Par value An arbitrary amount that represents the legal capital of the firm. (p. 529)

Participating feature Allows preferred stockholders to share on a percentage basis in the distribution of an abnormally large dividend. (p. 531)

Partnership A business owned by two or more individuals and with the characteristic of unlimited liability. (pp. 6, 553)

Partnership agreement Specifies how much the owners will invest, their salaries, and how profits will be shared. (p. 553)

Payee The party that will receive the money from a promissory note at some future date. (p. 346)

Periodic system System in which the Inventory account is updated only at the end of the period. (p. 227)

Permanent difference A difference that affects the tax records but not the accounting records, or vice versa. (p. 504)

Perpetual system System in which the inventory account is increased at the time of each purchase and decreased at the time of each sale. (p. 227)

Petty cash fund Money kept on hand for making minor disbursements in coin and currency rather than by writing checks. (p. 304)

Posting The process of transferring amounts from a journal to the ledger accounts. (p. 121)

Premium The excess of the issue price over the face value of the bonds. (p. 486)

Present value of a single amount Amount at a present time that is equivalent to a payment or investment at a future time. (p. 442)

Present value of an annuity The amount at a present time that is equivalent to a series of payments and interest in the future. (p. 445)

Price/earnings (P/E) ratio The relationship between a company's performance according to the income statement and its performance in the stock market. (p. 679)

Principal The amount of cash received, or the fair value of the products or services received, by the maker when a promissory note is issued. (p. 347)

Profit margin Net income divided by sales. (p. 72)

Profit margin ratio Net income to net sales. (p. 666)

Profitability How well management is using company resources to earn a return on the funds invested by various groups. (p. 675)

Promissory note A written promise to repay a definite sum of money on demand or at a fixed or determinable date in the future. (p. 346)

Public Company Accounting Oversight Board (PCAOB) A five-member body created by an act of Congress in 2002 that was given the authority to set auditing standards in the United States. (pp. 25, 307)
Purchase Discounts Contra-purchases account used to record reductions in purchase price for early payment to a supplier. (p. 230)
Purchase order Form sent by the purchasing department to the supplier. (p. 317)
Purchase requisition form Form a department uses to initiate a request to order merchandise. (p. 315)
Purchase Returns and Allowances Contra-purchases account used in a periodic inventory system when a refund is received from a supplier or a reduction given in the balance owed to a supplier. (p. 229)
Purchases Account used in a periodic inventory system to record acquisitions of merchandise. (p. 229)

R

Raw materials The inventory of a manufacturer before the addition of any direct labor or manufacturing overhead. (p. 221)
Real accounts The name given to balance sheet accounts because they are permanent and are not closed at the end of the period. (p. 178)
Recognition The process of recording an item in the financial statements as an asset, liability, revenue, expense, or the like. (p. 152)
Relevance The capacity of information to make a difference in a decision. (p. 57)
Reliability The quality that makes accounting information dependable in representing the events that it purports to represent. (p. 58)
Replacement cost The current cost of a unit of inventory. (p. 243)
Research and development costs Costs incurred in the discovery of new knowledge. (p. 395)
Retail inventory method A technique used by retailers to convert the retail value of inventory to a cost basis. (p. 253)
Retained earnings The part of owners' equity that represents the income earned less dividends paid over the life of an entity. (pp. 15, 530)
Retirement of stock When the stock is repurchased with no intention to reissue at a later date. (p. 536)
Return on assets ratio A measure of a company's success in earning a return for all providers of capital. (p. 675)
Return on common stockholders' equity ratio A measure of a company's success in earning a return for the common stockholders. (p. 677)
Return on sales ratio A variation of the profit margin ratio; measures earnings before payments to creditors. (p. 676)
Revenue expenditure A cost that keeps an asset in its normal operating condition and is treated as an expense. (p. 389)
Revenue recognition principle Revenues are recognized in the income statement when they are realized, or realizable, and earned. (p. 159)
Revenues Inflows of assets or settlements of liabilities from delivering or producing goods, rendering services, or conducting other activities. (pp. 9, 159)

S

Sales Discounts Contra-revenue account used to record discounts given customers for early payment of their accounts. (p. 224)
Sales Returns and Allowances Contra-revenue account used to record both refunds to customers and reductions of their accounts. (p. 224)
Sales revenue A representation of the inflow of assets. (p. 223)
Sarbanes-Oxley Act An act of Congress in 2002 intended to bring reform to corporate accountability and stewardship in the wake of a number of major corporate scandals. (pp. 30, 307)
Securities and Exchange Commission (SEC) The federal agency with ultimate authority to determine the rules in preparing statements for companies whose stock is sold to the public. (p. 24)
Serial bonds Bonds that do not all have the same due date; a portion of the bonds comes due each time period. (p. 483)
Share of stock A certificate that acts as ownership in a corporation. (p. 7)
Simple interest Interest is calculated on the principal amount only. (p. 439)
Single-step income statement An income statement in which all expenses are added together and subtracted from all revenues. (p. 70)
Sole proprietorship A business with a single owner. (pp. 6, 551)
Solvency The ability of a company to remain in business over the long term. (p. 672)
Source document A piece of paper that is used as evidence to record a transaction. (p. 107)
Specific identification method An inventory costing method that relies on matching unit costs with the actual units sold. (p. 237)
Statement of cash flows The financial statement that summarizes an entity's cash receipts and cash payments during the period from operating, investing, and financing activities. (pp. 18, 586)
Statement of retained earnings The statement that summarizes the income earned and dividends paid over the life of a business. (p. 17)
Statement of stockholders' equity Reflects the differences between beginning and ending balances for all accounts in the Stockholders' Equity category of the balance sheet. (p. 543)
Stock dividend The issuance of additional shares of stock to existing stockholders. (p. 538)
Stock split The creation of additional shares of stock with a reduction of the par value of the stock. (p. 541)
Stockholder One of the owners of a corporation. Also called a shareholder. (p. 9)
Stockholders' equity The owners' equity in a corporation. (p. 15)
Straight-line method A method by which the same dollar amount of depreciation is recorded in each year of asset use. (pp. 164, 383)
Subsidiary ledger The detail for a number of individual items that collectively make up a single general ledger account. (p. 337)

T

Temporary difference A difference that affects both book and tax records but not in the same time period. (p. 504)
Term The length of time a note is outstanding; that is, the period of time between the date it is issued and the date it matures. (p. 347)
Time period Artificial segment on the calendar, used as the basis for preparing financial statements. (p. 23)
Time value of money An immediate amount should be preferred over an amount in the future. (p. 438)
Times interest earned ratio An income statement measure of the ability of a company to meet its interest payments. (p. 673)
Transaction Any event that is recognized in a set of financial statements. (p. 107)
Transportation-in Adjunct account used to record freight costs paid by the buyer. (p. 229)
Treasurer The officer responsible in an organization for the safeguarding and efficient use of a company's liquid assets. (p. A-1)
Treasury stock Stock issued by the firm and then repurchased but not retired. (p. 534)
Trial balance A list of each account and its balance; used to prove equality of debits and credits. (p. 124)

U

Understandability The quality of accounting information that makes it comprehensible to those willing to spend the necessary time. (p. 57)

Units-of-production method Depreciation is determined as a function of the number of units the asset produces. (p. 383)

V

Vertical analysis A comparison of various financial statement items within a single period with the use of common-size statements. (p. 659)

W

Weighted average cost method An inventory costing method that assigns the same unit cost to all units available for sale during the period. (p. 238)

Work in process The cost of unfinished products in a manufacturing company. (p. 221)

Work sheet A device used at the end of the period to gather the information needed to prepare financial statements without actually recording and posting adjusting entries. (p. 178)

Working capital Current assets minus current liabilities. (pp. 67, 667)

INDEX

A

D

E

F

G

T

U

V